This book has proved an invaluable resource for research projects during my PGCE course and currently for my MA in Education. It provides detailed coverage on methodology and is a comprehensive and accessible guide to conducting ethical research. In my opinion, it is an excellent resource for the novice as well as the more experienced; a 'mu

Ma *ashire and Secondary*
ersity of Cumbria, UK

Cohen et al will re *ill the* key text for *all*
education students *mproved the text. The*
book not only cove

mpton University, UK

This seventh editi *written and illustrated*
key text for anyor *resource for both the*
novice and profes *ced methods research,*
visual media and i

nstitute of Leadership,
geons Ireland, Ireland

This is a must-rea *explanations, easy-to-*
follow examples, *s how useful this book*
is for teaching intr *lly grounded in educa-*
tional research.

Institute of Education,
University, Singapore

This 7th edition *overage is comprehen-*
sive and authorita *al examples and lively*
illustrations of co *debates about different*
paradigms and m *voking. It represents a*
landmark in publ *lend it to students and*
instructors alike.

, Program Coordinator
, Faculty of Education,
Queensland, Australia

This text is truly a superb introduction to ALL paradigms of educational research. I recommend it without reservation to professors of research in the US and elsewhere. It does what few other texts of a similar nature do by providing a balanced and rigorous treatment of both qualitative and quantitative methodologies. Important emphases on critical educational research, ethics, virtual worlds, cross-cultural research, and many other essential and innovative areas also make the book stand out. I will certainly use it, and I strongly urge others to do so.
David F. Hemphill, Associate Dean and Professor, College of Education, San Francisco State University, USA

Research Methods in Education

This rewritten, expanded and updated seventh edition of the long-running bestseller *Research Methods in Education* encompasses the whole range of methods currently employed by educational research at all stages. It offers plentiful and rich practical advice, underpinned by clear theoretical foundations, research evidence and up-to-date references.

Chapters new to this edition cover:

- causation, critical educational research, evaluation and the politics of research, including material on cross-cultural research, mixed methods and participatory research
- choosing and planning a research project, including material on sampling, research questions, literature reviews and ethical issues
- meta-analysis, research syntheses and systematic reviews
- virtual worlds and internet research
- using and analysing visual media and data in educational research
- organizing and presenting qualitative data, content analysis, coding and computer analysis, themes, narratives, conversations and discourses and grounded theory
- understanding and choosing statistical tests, descriptive and inferential statistics, multi-dimensional measurement and factor analysis.

Research Methods in Education is essential reading for both the professional researcher and students of education at undergraduate and postgraduate level, who need to understand how to plan, conduct, analyse and use research.

Louis Cohen is Emeritus Professor of Education at Loughborough University, UK.

Lawrence Manion was former Principal Lecturer at Didsbury School of Education, Manchester Metropolitan University, UK.

Keith Morrison is Professor and Registrar at Macau University of Science and Technology, formerly at Durham University, UK.

Research Methods in Education

Seventh edition

Louis Cohen, Lawrence Manion and
Keith Morrison

With contributions from
Richard Bell, Stewart Martin,
Gary McCulloch and Carmel O'Sullivan

Routledge
Taylor & Francis Group

LONDON AND NEW YORK

This seventh edition published 2011
by Routledge
2 Park Square, Milton Park, Abingdon, Oxon OX14 4RN

Simultaneously published in the USA and Canada
by Routledge
711 Third Avenue, New York, NY 10017

*Routledge is an imprint of the Taylor & Francis Group, an
informa business*

British Library Cataloguing in Publication Data
A catalogue record for this book is available from the British
Library

Library of Congress Cataloging-in-Publication Data
Cohen, Louis, 1928–
    Research methods in education / Louis Cohen, Lawrence
    Manion, and Keith Morrison. – 7th ed.
    p. cm.
    Includes bibliographical references and index.
    1. Education–Research. 2. Education–Research–Great Britain.
    I. Manion, Lawrence. II. Morrison, Keith (Keith R. B.) III.
    Title.
    LB1028.C572 2011
    370.7′2–dc22
                                                    2010032342

ISBN13: 978-0-415-58335-0 (hbk)
ISBN13: 978-0-415-58336-7 (pbk)

Typeset in Times Roman by Wearset Ltd, Boldon, Tyne and Wear
Printed and bound in Great Britain by Ashford Colour Press Ltd,
Gosport, Hampshire

Contents

Figures

Tables

Boxes

Contributors

Richard Bell is Associate Professor at Psychological Sciences, University of Melbourne, Australia.

Stewart Martin is Principal Lecturer at the School of Social Science and Law, Teesside University, UK.

Gary McCulloch is Brian Simon Professor of the History of Education at the Institute of Education, University of London, UK.

Carmel O'Sullivan is Deputy Head of School and Director of Postgraduate Teaching and Learning at the School of Education, Trinity College Dublin, Ireland.

Preface to the seventh edition

It is four years since the sixth edition of *Research Methods in Education* was published and we are indebted to Routledge for the opportunity to produce a seventh edition. The book continues to be received very favourably worldwide and is the standard text for many courses in research methods.

The seventh edition contains much new material, including entirely new chapters on:

- The search for causation
- Choosing a research project
- Critical educational research
- Evaluation and the politics of educational research
- Meta-analysis, research syntheses and systematic reviews
- Virtual worlds in educational research
- Visual media in educational research
- Organizing and presenting qualitative data
- Content analysis, coding and computer analysis
- Themes, narratives, conversations and discourses
- Grounded theory
- Analysing visual media as data
- The background to statistical tests
- Descriptive statistics
- Inferential statistics
- Multidimensional measurement and factor analysis.

Whilst retaining the best features of the former edition, the reshaping, updating and new additions undertaken for this new volume now mean that the book covers a greater spread of issues than the previous editions, and in greater depth. In addition to updating the book throughout, new material has been added as follows:

Part 1:

- ontology and epistemology in educational research
- complexity theory and research
- cross-cultural research
- mixed methods research
- participatory research.

Part 2:

- choosing a research project
- planning educational research
- modelling the planning process
- research questions
- conducting, searching and reporting a literature review
- ethics, managing ethical dilemmas, ethics committees and pro-formas
- ownership of data
- quality in educational research
- sampling, particularly non-probability sampling
- sampling in mixed methods research

- cross-cultural validity
- validity in mixed methods research.

Part 3:
- historical and documentary research
- autoethnography
- internet ethnographies
- generalizability in qualitative research
- internet surveys
- internet sources and online resources
- surveys and online surveys
- sampling in surveys and experiments
- interview and telephone surveys
- longitudinal studies
- case studies and their data
- databases and data sources for *ex post facto* research
- experiments and design experiments
- randomization in experiments
- research syntheses, systematic reviews and meta-analysis: 'what works'
- action research and participatory action research
- reporting action research
- qualitative research and short-duration qualitative research
- social networking
- virtual worlds in educational research.

Part 4:
- conducting research with children
- personal constructs
- planning and conducting questionnaires
- internet questionnaires
- software for questionnaire preparation
- role-playing
- telephone interviewing
- interview control questions
- interviewing minority and marginalized people
- network analysis
- timing and causality for observational data
- software for test preparation
- video recording in educational research
- ethical issues in video research
- visual media in educational research: artefacts, still and moving images.

Part 5:
- computer analysis in qualitative data
- thick descriptions and their interpretation
- discourse analysis
- analysing narratives, biographies and autobiographies
- analysing and interpreting visual data: artefacts, still and moving images
- coding and grounded theory
- further statistics and how to calculate, use and report them in data analysis
- curves of distribution, range and standardized scores
- further analysis with the chi-square statistic

- partial correlations and controls
- structural equation modelling and multilevel modelling
- signs and symbols in statistical analysis.

Additionally there are copious website references in nearly every chapter, most of which provide free online materials. A signal feature of this edition is the inclusion of very many extensively worked examples and more figures, diagrams and graphics to illustrate and summarize key points clearly. Several of the tables in Part 5 include SPSS (Statistical Package for the Social Sciences software) output, so that readers can check their own SPSS analysis against the examples provided.

We have introduced a numbering system in each chapter, for ease of referencing and locating material.

To accompany this volume, a companion website provides a comprehensive range of materials to cover all aspects of research (including a full course on research methods on PowerPoint slides), exercises and examples, explanatory material and further notes, SPSS data files and SPSS manual for novice researchers, QSR (Qualitative Solutions and Research) data files and manual for qualitative data treatment, together with further statistics and statistical tables. These are indicated in the book. A wealth of supporting materials is available on the website www.routledge.com/textbooks/cohen7e.

This book stands out for its practical advice that is securely rooted in theory and up-to-date discussion from a range of sources. We hope that it will continue to constitute the first 'port of call' for educational researchers and continue to be the definitive text in its field.

Acknowledgements

Our thanks are due to the following publishers and authors for permission to include materials in the text:

Beamish Museum Limited, UK, for photograph No. 29474.

British Medical Journal Publishing Group Ltd., for material from D. Curr (1994) Role play, *British Medical Journal*, January 1.

Continuum Books, for material from Walford, G. (2001) *Doing Qualitative Educational Research*, pp. 30, 31, 36, 137.

Deakin University Press, Deakin, Australia, for words from Kemmis, S. and McTaggart, R. (1981) *The Action Research Planner*, and Kemmis, S. and McTaggart, R. (1992): 8 and 21–8 *The Action Research Planner* (third edition).

Elsevier, for material reprinted from: *International Journal of Educational Research*, vol. 19 (3), Edwards, D. Concepts, memory and the organisation of pedagogic discourse, pp. 205–25, copyright 1993, with permission from Elsevier; *Social Method and Social Life*, M. Brenner (ed.), article by J. Brown and J. Sime: A methodology of accounts, p. 163, copyright 1981, with permission from Elsevier.

HarperCollins Publishers Ltd., for materials from: L. Cohen (1977) *Educational Research in Classrooms and Schools: A Manual of Materials and Methods*; L. Cohen and M. Holliday (1979) *Statistics for Education and Physical Education*.

Mosaic Books and *PRIA: Society for Participatory Research in Asia*, for material from R. Tandon (ed.) (2005) *Participatory Research: Revisiting the Roots*, pp. 17–19, 23, 30, 183.

National Foundation for Education Research, for material from R. McAleese and D. Hamilton (eds) (1978) *Understanding Classroom Life*.

Organizational Systems Research Association, for material from p. 48 of J. E. II Bartlett, J. W. Kotrlik and C. C. Higgins (2001) Organizational research: deter-mining appropriate sample size in survey research. *Information Technology, Learning and Performance Journal*, 19(1), 43–50.

Penguin Group UK, for material from E. Goffman (1968) *Asylums: Essays on the Social Situation of Mental Patients and Other Inmates* (Penguin Books 1968). Copyright © Erving Goffman, 1961.

Perseus Books Group, for material from C. Geertz (1977) *The Interpretation of Cultures*. Copyright © 1977 Clifford Geertz. Reprinted by permission of Basic Books, a member of the Perseus Books Group.

Prentice-Hall, for material from Garfinkel, H. (1967) *Studies in Ethnomethodology*; Smith, H. W. (1978) *Strategies in Social Research*. Reproduced by permission of Pearson Education Inc.

Princeton University Press, for material from Swenson, David; *Concluding Unscientific Postscript* by Sören Kierkegaard, © 1941 Princeton University Press, 1969 renewed. Reprinted by permission of Princeton University Press, p. 178.

Sage Publications Inc., for material from M. Q. Patton (1980) *Qualitative Evaluation Methods*, p. 206.

Springer, for Hycner, R. H. (1985) Some guidelines for the phenomenological analysis of interview data, *Human Studies*, 8, pp. 279–303, with kind permission of Springer Science and Business Media.

Taylor and Francis, for Brenner, M. and Marsh, P. (eds) (1978) *The Social Contexts of Method*; Burgess, R. G. (ed.) (1993) *Educational Research for Policy and Practice*, pp. 119 and 135; Burgess R. (ed.) (1985) *Issues in Educational Research*, pp. 116–26 and 244–7; Burgess, R. (ed.) (1989) *The Ethics of Educational Research*, p. 194; Cuff, E. G. and Payne G. C. F. (1979) *Perspectives in Sociology*, p. 4; Ezzy, D. (2002) *Qualitative Analysis: Practice and Innovation*, pp. 83, 94; Hammersley, M. and Atkinson, P. (1983) *Ethnography: Principles in Practice*, pp. 18, 19, 76; Hitchcock, G. and Hughes, D. (1989) *Research and the*

Teacher; Hitchcock, G. and Hughes, D. (1995) *Research and the Teacher* (second edition), pp. 20–2, 41; Kincheloe, J. L. (2003) *Teachers as Researchers: Qualitative Inquiry as a Path to Empowerment* (second edition), pp. 138–9; McCormick, J. and Solman, R. (1992) Teachers' attributions of responsibility for occupational stress and satisfaction: an organisational perspective, *Educational Studies*, 18 (92), pp. 201–22; McNiff, J. (2002) *Action Research: Principles and Practice (second edition)*, pp. 85–91; Medawar, P. B. (1972) *The Hope of Progress*; Oldroyd, D. (1986) *The Arch of Knowledge: An Introductory Study of the History of the Philosophy and Methodology of Science*; Morrison, K. R. B. (2009) *Causation in Educational Research*, pp. 65, 143–4, 181; Plummer, K. (1983) *Documents of Life: An Introduction to the Problems and Literature of a Humanistic Method*; Rex, J. (ed.) (1974) *Approaches to Sociology*; Simons, H. and Usher, R. (eds) (2000) *Situated Ethics in Educational Research*, pp. 1–2; Walford, G. (ed.) (1994) *Researching the Powerful in Education*; Zuber-Skerritt, O. (1996) *New Directions in Action Research*, p. 99; Winter, R. (1982) Dilemma analysis: a contribution to methodology for action research, *Cambridge Journal of Education*, 12 (3), pp. 161–74.

Tripp, D. H. for material from D. Tripp (2003) Action inquiry. *Action Research e-Reports*. No. 17, available online at www.fhs.usyd.edu.au/arow/arer/017.htm#Distinguishing%20action%20research.

University of Chicago Press, for brief quotations from Whyte, W. F. (1993) *Street Corner Society*, pp. 292, 301, 358–9, 366–7; Merton, R. K. and Kendall, P. L. (1946) The focused interview. *American Journal of Sociology*, vol. 51, pp. 541–57.

Wiley-Blackwell, for material from: Dyer, C. (1995) *Beginning Research in Psychology*; Robson, C. (1993) *Real World Research*; Robson, C. (2002) *Real World Research* (second edition).

Disclaimer: The publishers have made every effort to contact authors/copyright holders of works reprinted in the 7th edition of *Research Methods in Education*. This has not been possible in every case, however, and we would welcome correspondence from those individuals/companies whom we have been unable to trace.

Part 1
The context of educational research

This part commences by introducing positivist and scientific contexts of research and some strengths and weaknesses of these for educational research. As an alternative paradigm, the cluster of approaches that can loosely be termed interpretive, naturalistic, phenomenological, interactionist and ethnographic are brought together, and their strengths and weaknesses for educational research are examined. The paradigm of mixed methods research is then introduced, and its strengths, weaknesses and contribution to educational research are discussed.

Critical theory as a paradigm of educational research is discussed, and its implications for the research undertaking indicated in several ways, resonating with curriculum research, participatory research and feminist research. These are concerned not only with understanding a situation or phenomenon but with *changing* it, often with an explicit political agenda. Critical theory links the conduct of educational research with politics and policy making, and this is reflected in the discussions here of research and evaluation, noting how some educational research has become evaluative in nature. A more recent perspective discussed here is that of complexity theory, originally from the natural sciences, but moving into social sciences. In all, this part introduces readers to different research traditions, with the advice that 'fitness for purpose' must be the guiding principle: different research paradigms for different research purposes.

A major message stressed in Part 1 is that the nature and foundations of educational research have witnessed a proliferation of paradigms over time. From the earlier days of either quantitative or qualitative research have arisen the several approaches introduced in this part. We present normative and interpretive perspectives in a complementary light and try to lessen the tension that sometimes exists between them.

The chapters in this part are deliberately of unequal size. Chapter 1, a sizeable chapter, provides a solid theoretical foundation to many of the subsequent approaches to educational research discussed in the book. It pays special attention to the underpinnings of qualitative, quantitative and mixed methods research.

The term *research* itself has many meanings. We restrict its usages here to those activities and undertakings aimed at developing a science of behaviour, the word *science* itself implying both normative and interpretive perspectives. Accordingly, when we speak of social research, we have in mind the systematic and scholarly application of the principles of a science of behaviour to the problems of people within their social contexts, and when we use the term educational research, we likewise have in mind the application of these same principles to the problems of teaching and learning within education and to the clarification of issues having direct or indirect bearing on these concepts.

CHAPTER 1

The nature of enquiry

Setting the field

This large chapter explores the context of educational research. It sets out several foundations on which different kinds of empirical research are constructed:

- scientific and positivistic methodologies
- naturalistic and interpretive methodologies
- mixed methods and methodologies
- introducing post-positivism, post-structuralism and postmodernism

Given the emphasis placed in educational research on quantitative and qualitative approaches, this chapter sets out the basis on which these two main approaches are founded. Then it indicates how both are combined in mixed methods research. It introduces post-positivism, post-structuralism and postmodernism not only in their own right but as having affinities with interpretive approaches and also as bridges into complexity theory.

1.1 Introduction

Our analysis takes an important notion from Hitchcock and Hughes (1995: 21) who suggest that ontological assumptions (assumptions about the nature of reality and the nature of things) give rise to epistemological assumptions (ways of researching and enquiring into the nature of reality and the nature of things); these, in turn, give rise to methodological considerations; and these, in turn, give rise to issues of instrumentation and data collection. Indeed, added to ontology and epistemology is axiology (the values and beliefs that we hold). This view moves us beyond regarding research methods as simply a technical exercise and as concerned with understanding the world; this is informed by how we view our world(s), what we take understanding to be and what we see as the purposes of understanding, and what is deemed valuable. The chapter also acknowledges that educational research, politics and decision making are inextricably intertwined, and it draws attention to the politics of educational research and the implications that this has for undertaking research (e.g. the move towards applied

and evaluative research and away from 'pure' research). Finally, we add a note about methodology.

1.2 The search for truth

People have long been concerned to come to grips with their environment and to understand the nature of the phenomena it presents to their senses. The means by which they set out to achieve these ends may be classified into three broad categories: *experience*, *reasoning* and *research* (Mouly, 1978). Far from being independent and mutually exclusive, however, these categories must be seen as complementary and overlapping, features most readily in evidence where solutions to complex problems are sought.

In our endeavours to come to terms with the problems of day-to-day living, we are heavily dependent upon experience and authority. However, as tools for uncovering ultimate truth they have decided limitations. The limitations of personal experience in the form of *common-sense knowing*, for instance, can quickly be exposed when compared with features of the scientific approach to problem-solving. Consider, for example, the striking differences in the way in which theories are used. Laypeople base them on haphazard events and use them in a loose and uncritical manner. When they are required to test them, they do so in a selective fashion, often choosing only that evidence that is consistent with their hunches and ignoring that which is counter to them. Scientists, by contrast, construct their theories carefully and systematically. Whatever hypotheses they formulate have to be tested empirically so that their explanations have a firm basis in fact. And there is the concept of *control* distinguishing the layperson's and the scientist's attitude to experience. Laypeople may make little or no attempt to control any extraneous sources of influence when trying to explain an occurrence. Scientists, on the other hand, only too conscious of the multiplicity of causes for a given occurrence, resort to definite techniques and procedures to isolate and test the effect of one or more of the alleged causes. Finally, there is the difference of attitude to the relationships among phenomena. Laypeople's concerns with such relationships may be loose, unsystematic and uncontrolled. The chance occurrence of two events in close proximity is sufficient reason to predicate a causal link between them. Scientists, however, display a much more serious professional concern with relationships and only as a result of rigorous experimentation and testing will they postulate a relationship between two phenomena.

People attempt to comprehend the world around them, by using three types of reasoning: *deductive reasoning*, *inductive reasoning* and the *combined inductive-deductive* approach. Deductive reasoning is based on the syllogism which was Aristotle's great contribution to formal logic. In its simplest form the syllogism consists of a major premise based on an *a priori* or self-evident proposition, a minor premise providing a particular instance, and a conclusion. Thus:

All planets orbit the sun;
The earth is a planet;
Therefore the earth orbits the sun.

The assumption underlying the syllogism is that through a sequence of formal steps of logic, from the general to the particular, a valid conclusion can be deduced from a valid premise. Its chief limitation is that it can handle only certain kinds of statement. The syllogism formed the basis of systematic reasoning from the time of its inception until the Renaissance. Thereafter its effectiveness was diminished because it was no longer related to observation and experience and became merely a mental exercise. One of the consequences of this was that empirical evidence as the basis of proof was superseded by authority and the more authorities one could quote, the stronger one's position became. Naturally, with such abuse of its principal tool, science became sterile.

The history of reasoning was to undergo a dramatic change in the 1600s when Francis Bacon began to lay increasing stress on the observational basis of science. Being critical of the model of deductive reasoning on the grounds that its major premises were often preconceived notions which inevitably bias the conclusions, he proposed in its place the method of inductive reasoning by means of which the study of a number of individual cases would lead to a hypothesis and eventually to a generalization. Mouly (1978) explains it by suggesting that Bacon's basic premise was that, with sufficient data, even if one does not have a preconceived idea of their significance or meaning, nevertheless important relationships and laws would be discovered by the alert observer. Bacon's major contribution to science was thus that he was able to rescue it from the stranglehold of the deductive method whose abuse had brought scientific progress to a standstill. He thus directed the attention of scientists to nature for solutions to people's problems, demanding empirical evidence for verification. Logic and authority in themselves were no longer regarded as conclusive means of proof and instead became sources of hypotheses about the world and its phenomena.

Bacon's inductive method was eventually followed by the inductive-deductive approach which combines Aristotelian deduction with Baconian induction. Here the researcher is involved in a back-and-forth process of induction (from observation to hypothesis, from the specific to the general) and deduction (from hypothesis to implications) (Mouly, 1978). Hypotheses are tested rigorously and, if necessary, revised.

Although both deduction and induction have their weaknesses, their contributions to the development of science are enormous, for example: (1) the suggestion of hypotheses; (2) the logical development of these hypotheses; and (3) the clarification and interpretation of scientific findings and their synthesis into a conceptual framework.

A further means by which we set out to discover truth is *research*. This has been defined by Kerlinger (1970) as the systematic, controlled, empirical and critical investigation of hypothetical propositions about the presumed relations among natural phenomena. Research has three characteristics in particular which distinguish it from the first means of problem-solving identified earlier, namely, experience. First, whereas experience deals with events occurring in a haphazard manner, research is systematic and controlled, basing its operations on the inductive-deductive model outlined above. Second, research is empirical. The scientist turns to experience for validation. As Kerlinger puts it, subjective, personal belief has to have a reality check against objective, empirical facts and tests. And third, research is self-correcting. Not only does the scientific method have built-in mechanisms to protect scientists from error as far as is humanly possible, but also their procedures and results are open to public scrutiny by fellow professionals. Incorrect results in time will be found and either revised or discarded (Mouly, 1978). Research is a combination of both experience and reasoning and must be regarded as the most successful approach to the discovery of truth, particularly as far as the natural sciences are concerned (Borg, 1963).[1]

Educational research has absorbed several competing views of the social sciences – the established, traditional view and an interpretive view, and several others that we explore in this chapter, including critical theory, feminist theory and complexity theory. The established, traditional view holds that the social sciences are essentially the same as the natural sciences and are therefore concerned with discovering natural and universal laws regulating and determining individual and social behaviour; the interpretive view, however, while sharing the rigour of the natural sciences and the same concern of traditional social science to describe and explain human behaviour, emphasizes how people differ from inanimate natural phenomena and, indeed, from each other. These contending views – and also their corresponding reflections in educational research – stem in the first instance from different conceptions of social reality and of individual and social behaviour. It will help our understanding of the issues to be developed subsequently if we examine these in a little more detail.

Since the ground-breaking work of Kuhn (1962), approaches to methodology in research have been seen to reside in 'paradigms' and communities of scholars. A paradigm is a way of looking at or researching phenomena, a world view, a view of what counts as accepted or correct scientific knowledge or way of working, an 'accepted model or pattern' (Kuhn, 1962: 23), a shared belief system or set of principles, the identity of a research community, a way of pursuing knowledge, consensus on what problems are to be investigated and how to investigate them, typical solutions to problems, and an understanding that is more acceptable than its rivals. A notable example of this is the old paradigm that placed the earth at the centre of the universe, only to be replaced by the Copernican heliocentric model as evidence and explanation became more persuasive of the new paradigm. Importantly, one has to note that the old orthodoxy retained its value for generations because it was supported by respected and powerful scientists and, indeed, others (witness the attempts made by the Catholic Church to silence Galileo in his advocacy of the heliocentric model of the universe). More recently the Newtonian view of the mechanical universe has been replaced by the Einsteinian view of a relativistic, evolving universe. More recently still, the idea of a value-free, neutral, objective, positivist science has been replaced by a post-positivist, critical realist view of science with its hallmarks in conjecture (Popper, 1980), the (subjective) value systems of researchers, phenomenology, subjectivity, the need for reflexivity in research (discussed later in this book), the value of qualitative approaches to research, and the contribution of critical theory and feminist approaches to research methodologies and principles.

Post-positivists argue that facts and observations are theory-laden and value-laden (Popper, 1980; Feyerabend, 1975; Reichardt and Rallis, 1994), that facts and theories are fallible, that different theories may support specific observations/facts, and that social facts, even ways of thinking and observing, are social constructions rather than objectively and universally true (Nisbett, 2005).

At issue here is the significance of regarding approaches to research as underpinned by different paradigms, an important characteristic of which is their incommensurability with each other (i.e. one cannot hold two distinct paradigms simultaneously as there is no common asset of principles, standards or measures). That said, the later part of this chapter sets out a new 'paradigm' of mixed methods research, and this might be seen to challenge, if only in part, the incommensurability argument.

As more knowledge is acquired to challenge an existing paradigm, such that the original paradigm cannot explain a phenomenon as well as the new paradigm, there comes about a 'scientific revolution', a paradigm shift, in which the new paradigm replaces the old as the orthodoxy – the 'normal science' – of the day. Kuhn's (1962) notions of paradigms and paradigm shifts link here objects of study and communities of scholars, where the field of knowledge or paradigm is seen to be only as good as the evidence and the respect in which it is held by 'authorities'.

This chapter sets out several paradigms of educational research.

1.3 Two conceptions of social reality

The views of social science that we have mentioned represent strikingly different ways of looking at social reality and are constructed on correspondingly different ways of interpreting it. We can perhaps most profitably approach these conceptions of the social world by examining the explicit and implicit assumptions underpinning them. Our analysis is based on the work of Burrell and Morgan (1979) who identified four sets of such assumptions.

First, there are assumptions of an ontological kind – assumptions which concern the very nature or essence of the social phenomena being investigated. Thus, the authors ask, is social reality external to individuals – imposing itself on their consciousness from without – or is it the product of individual consciousness? Is reality of an objective nature, or the result of individual cognition? Is it a given 'out there' in the world, or is it created by one's own mind? These questions spring directly from what philosophy terms the nominalist-realist debate. The former view holds that objects of thought are merely words and that there is no independently accessible thing constituting the meaning of a word. The realist position, however, contends that objects have an independent existence and are not dependent for it on the knower.

The second set of assumptions identified by Burrell and Morgan (1979) are of an epistemological kind. These concern the very bases of knowledge – its nature and forms, how it can be acquired, and how communicated to other human beings. How one aligns oneself in this particular debate profoundly affects how one will go about uncovering knowledge of social behaviour. The view that knowledge is hard, objective and tangible will demand of researchers an observer role, together with an allegiance to the methods of natural science; to see knowledge as personal, subjective and unique, however, imposes on researchers an involvement with their subjects and a rejection of the ways of the natural scientist. To subscribe to the former is to be positivist; to the latter, anti-positivist or post-positivist.

The third set of assumptions concern human nature and, in particular, the relationship between human beings and their environment. Since the human being is both its subject and object of study, the consequences for social science of assumptions of this kind are indeed far-reaching. Two images of human beings emerge from such assumptions – the one portrays them as responding mechanically and deterministically to their environment, i.e. as products of the environment, controlled like puppets; the other, as initiators of their own actions with free will and creativity, producing their own environments. The difference is between *determinism* and *voluntarism* respectively (Burrell and Morgan, 1979).

It would follow from what we have said so far that the three sets of assumptions identified above have direct implications for the methodological concerns of researchers, since the contrasting ontologies, epistemologies and models of human beings will in turn demand different research methods. Investigators adopting an objectivist (or positivist) approach to the social world and who treat it like the world of natural phenomena as being real and external to the individual will choose from a range of traditional options – surveys, experiments and the like. Others favouring the more subjectivist (or anti-positivist) approach and who view the social world as being of a much more personal and humanly created kind will select from a comparable range of recent and emerging techniques – accounts, participant observation and personal constructs, for example.

Where one subscribes to the view which treats the social world like the natural world – as if it were an external and objective reality – then scientific investigation will be directed at analysing the relationships and regularities between selected factors in that world. It will be predominantly quantitative and will be concerned with identifying and defining elements and discovering ways in which their relationships can be expressed. Hence, they argue, methodological issues, of fundamental importance, are thus the concepts themselves, their measurement and the identification of underlying themes in a search for universal laws which explain and govern that which is being observed (Burrell and Morgan, 1979). An approach characterized by procedures and methods designed to discover general laws may be referred to as *nomothetic*.

However, if one favours the alternative view of social reality which stresses the importance of the subjective experience of individuals in the creation of the social world, then the search for understanding focuses upon different issues and approaches them in different ways. The principal concern is with an understanding of the way in which individuals create, modify and interpret the world in which they find themselves. The approach now takes on a qualitative as well as quantitative aspect. As Burrell and Morgan (1979) and Kirk and Miller (1986: 14) observe, emphasis here is placed on explanation and understanding of the unique and the particular individual case rather than the general and the universal; the interest is in a subjective, relativistic social world rather than an absolutist, external reality. In its emphasis on the particular and individual this approach to understanding individual behaviour may be termed *idiographic*.

In this review of Burrell and Morgan's analysis of the ontological, epistemological, human and methodological assumptions underlying two ways of conceiving social reality, we have laid the foundations for a more extended study of the two contrasting perspectives evident in the practices of researchers investigating human behaviour and, by adoption, educational problems. Figure 1.1 summarizes these assumptions along a subjective/objective dimension. It identifies the four sets of assumptions by using terms we have adopted in the text and by which they are known in the literature of social philosophy.

Each of the two perspectives on the study of human behaviour outlined above has profound implications for research in classrooms and schools. The choice of problem, the formulation of questions to be answered, the characterization of pupils and teachers, methodological concerns, the kinds of data sought and their mode of treatment, all are influenced by the viewpoint held. Some idea of the considerable practical implications of the contrasting views can be gained by examining Table 1.1 which compares them with respect to a number of critical issues within a broadly societal and organizational framework. Implications of the two perspectives for research into classrooms and schools will unfold in the course of the text.

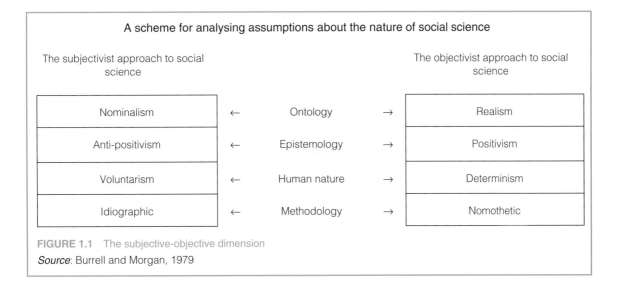

A scheme for analysing assumptions about the nature of social science

The subjectivist approach to social science				The objectivist approach to social science
Nominalism	←	Ontology	→	Realism
Anti-positivism	←	Epistemology	→	Positivism
Voluntarism	←	Human nature	→	Determinism
Idiographic	←	Methodology	→	Nomothetic

FIGURE 1.1 The subjective-objective dimension

Source: Burrell and Morgan, 1979

Because of its significance for the epistemological basis of social science and its consequences for educational research, we devote much discussion in this chapter to the debate on positivism and anti-positivist/post-positivism, and on alternative paradigms and rationales for understanding educational research.

1.4 Positivism

Although positivism has been a recurrent theme in the history of western thought from the Ancient Greeks to the present day, it is historically associated with the nineteenth-century French philosopher, Auguste Comte, who was the first thinker to use the word for a philosophical position (Beck, 1979) and who gave rise to sociology as a distinct discipline. His positivism turns to observation and reason as means of understanding behaviour; explanation proceeds by way of scientific description. In his study of the history of the philosophy and methodology of science, Oldroyd (1986) says that, in this view, social phenomena could be researched in ways similar to natural, physical phenomena, i.e. generating laws and theories that could be investigated empirically.

Comte's position was to lead to a general doctrine of positivism which held that all genuine knowledge is based on sense experience and can only be advanced by means of observation and experiment. Following in the empiricist tradition, it limited enquiry and belief to what can be firmly established, and in thus abandoning metaphysical and speculative attempts to gain knowledge by reason alone, the movement developed a rigorous orientation to social

facts and natural phenomena to be investigated empirically (Beck, 1979).

Though the term positivism is used by philosophers and social scientists, a residual meaning is always present and this derives from an acceptance of natural science as the paradigm of human knowledge (Duncan, 1968). This includes the following connected suppositions, identified by Giddens (1975). First, the methodological procedures of natural science may be directly applied to the social sciences. Positivism here implies a particular stance concerning the social scientist as an observer of social reality. Second, the end-product of investigations by social scientists can be formulated in terms parallel to those of natural science. This means that their analyses must be expressed in laws or law-like generalizations of the same kind that have been established in relation to natural phenomena. Positivism here involves a definite view of social scientists as analysts or interpreters of their subject matter. Positivism claims that science provides us with the clearest possible ideal of knowledge.

Where positivism is less successful, however, is in its application to the study of human behaviour where the immense complexity of human nature and the elusive and intangible quality of social phenomena contrast strikingly with the order and regularity of the natural world. This point is nowhere more apparent than in the contexts of classroom and school where the problems of teaching, learning and human interaction present the positivistic researcher with a mammoth challenge.

We now look more closely at some of the features of the scientific method that is underpinned by positivism.

TABLE 1.1   ALTERNATIVE BASES FOR INTERPRETING SOCIAL REALITY

	Conceptions of social reality	
Dimensions of comparison	Objectivist	Subjectivist
Philosophical basis	Realism: the world exists and is knowable as it really is. Organizations are real entities with a life of their own.	Idealism: the world exists but different people construe it in very different ways. Organizations are invented social reality.
The role of social science	Discovering the universal laws of society and human conduct within it.	Discovering how different people interpret the world in which they live.
Basic units of social reality	The collectivity: society or organizations.	Individuals acting singly or together.
Methods of understanding	Identifying conditions or relationships which permit the collectivity to exist. Conceiving what these conditions and relationships are.	Interpretation of the subjective meanings which individuals place upon their action. Discovering the subjective rules for such action.
Theory	A rational edifice built by scientists to explain human behaviour.	Sets of meanings which people use to make sense of their world and behaviour within it.
Research	Experimental or quasi-experimental validation of theory.	The search for meaningful relationships and the discovery of their consequences for action.
Methodology	Abstraction of reality, especially through mathematical models and quantitative analysis.	The representation of reality for purposes of comparison. Analysis of language and meaning.
Society	Ordered. Governed by a uniform set of values and made possible only by those values.	Conflicted. Governed by the values of people with access to power.
Organizations	Goal oriented. Independent of people. Instruments of order in society serving both society and the individual.	Dependent upon people and their goals. Instruments of power which some people control and can use to attain ends which seem good to them.
Organizational pathologies	Organizations get out of kilter with social values and individual needs.	Given diverse human ends, there is always conflict among people acting to pursue them.
Prescription for change	Change the structure of the organization to meet social values and individual needs.	Find out what values are embodied in organizational action and whose they are. Change the people or change their values if you can.

Source: Adapted from Barr Greenfield, 1975.

1.5 The assumptions and nature of science

We begin with an examination of the tenets of scientific faith: the kinds of assumptions held by scientists, often implicitly, as they go about their daily work. First, there is the assumption of *determinism*. This means simply that events have causes, that events are determined by other circumstances; and science proceeds on the belief that these causal links can eventually be uncovered and understood, that the events are explicable in terms of their antecedents. Moreover, not only are events in the natural world determined by other circumstances, but there is regularity about the way in which they are determined: the universe does not behave capriciously. It is the ultimate aim of scientists to formulate laws to account for the happenings in the world, thus giving them a firm basis for prediction and control.

The second assumption is that of *empiricism*. We have already touched upon this viewpoint, which holds that certain kinds of reliable knowledge can only derive from experience. In practice, this means scientifically that the tenability of a theory or hypothesis depends on the nature of the empirical evidence for its support. Empirical here means that which is verifiable by observation and direct experience (Barratt, 1971); and evidence, data yielding proof or strong confirmation, in probability terms, of a theory or hypothesis in a research setting.

Mouly (1978) identifies five steps in the process of empirical science:

1 *experience* – the starting point of scientific endeavour at the most elementary level
2 *classification* – the formal systematization of otherwise incomprehensible masses of data
3 *quantification* – a more sophisticated stage where precision of measurement allows more adequate analysis of phenomena by mathematical means
4 *discovery of relationships* – the identification and classification of functional relationships among phenomena
5 *approximation to the truth* – science proceeds by gradual approximation to the truth.

The third assumption underlying the work of the scientist is the principle of *parsimony*. The basic idea is that phenomena should be explained in the most economical way possible, as Einstein was known to remark – one should make matters as simple as possible, but no simpler! The first historical statement of the principle was by William of Occam when he said that explanatory principles (entities) should not be needlessly multiplied ('Occam's razor'). It may, of course, be interpreted in various ways: that it is preferable to account for a phenomenon by two concepts rather than three; that a simple theory is to be preferred to a complex one.

The final assumption, that of *generality*, played an important part in both the deductive and inductive methods of reasoning. Indeed, historically speaking, it was the problematic relationship between the concrete particular and the abstract general that was to result in two competing theories of knowledge – the rational and the empirical. Beginning with observations of the particular, scientists set out to generalize their findings to the world at large. This is so because they are concerned ultimately with explanation. Of course, the concept of generality presents much less of a problem to natural scientists working chiefly with inanimate matter than to human scientists who, of necessity having to deal with samples of larger human populations, have to exercise great caution when generalizing their findings to the particular parent populations.

We come now to the core question: What is science? Kerlinger (1970) points out that in the scientific world itself two broad views of science may be found: the *static* and the *dynamic*. The *static* view, which has particular appeal for laypeople, is that science is an activity that contributes systematized information to the world. The work of the scientist is to uncover new facts and add them to the existing corpus of knowledge. Science is thus seen as an accumulated body of findings, the emphasis being chiefly on the present state of knowledge and adding to it.[2] The *dynamic* view, by contrast, conceives science more as an activity, as something that scientists *do*. According to this conception it is important to have an accumulated body of knowledge of course, but what really matter most are the discoveries that scientists make. The emphasis here, then, is more on the heuristic nature of science.

Contrasting views exist on the functions of science. We give a composite summary of these in Box 1.1. For the professional scientists however, science is seen as a way of comprehending the world; as a means of explanation and understanding, of prediction and control. For them the ultimate aim of science is theory.

Theory has been defined by Kerlinger as 'a set of interrelated constructs [concepts], definitions, and propositions that presents a systematic view of phenomena by specifying relations among variables, with the purpose of explaining and predicting the phenomena' (Kerlinger, 1970: 9). In a sense, theory gathers together all the isolated bits of empirical data into a coherent conceptual framework of wider applicability. More than this, however, theory is itself a potential source of further information and discoveries. It is in this way a source of new hypotheses and hitherto unasked questions; it identifies critical areas for further investigation; it discloses gaps in our knowledge; and enables a researcher to postulate the existence of previously unknown phenomena.

Clearly there are several different types of theory, and each type of theory defines its own kinds of 'proof'. For example, Morrison (1995a) identifies *empirical theories*, 'grand' theories and 'critical' theory. Empirical theories and critical theories are discussed below. 'Grand theory' is a metanarrative, defining an area of study, being speculative, clarifying conceptual structures and frameworks, and creatively enlarging the way we consider behaviour and organizations (Layder, 1994). It uses fundamental ontological

---

BOX 1.1   THE FUNCTIONS OF SCIENCE

1 Its problem-seeking, question-asking, hunch-encouraging, hypotheses-producing function.
2 Its testing, checking, certifying function; its trying out and testing of hypotheses; its repetition and checking of experiments; its piling up of facts.
3 Its organizing, theorizing, structuring, function; its search for larger and larger generalizations.
4 Its history-collecting, scholarly function.
5 Its technological side; instruments, methods, techniques.
6 Its administrative, executive and organizational side.
7 Its publicizing and educational functions.
8 Its applications to human use.
9 Its appreciation, enjoyment, celebration and glorification.

Source: Maslow, 1954

---

and epistemological postulates which serve to define a field of enquiry (Hughes, 1976). Here empirical material tends to be used by way of illustration rather than 'proof'. This is the stuff of some sociological theories, for example Marxism, consensus theory and functionalism. Whilst sociologists may be excited by the totalizing and all-encompassing nature of such theories, they have been subject to considerable undermining. For example, Merton (1949), Coser and Rosenberg (1969), Doll (1993) and Layder (1994) contend that whilst they might possess the attraction of large philosophical systems of considerable – Byzantine – architectonic splendour and logical consistency, nevertheless they are scientifically sterile, irrelevant and out of touch with a world that is characterized by openness, fluidity, change, heterogeneity and fragmentation. This book does not endeavour to refer to this type of theory.

The status of theory varies quite considerably according to the discipline or area of knowledge in question. Some theories, as in the natural sciences, are characterized by a high degree of elegance and sophistication; others, perhaps like educational theory, are only at the early stages of formulation and are thus characterized by great unevenness. Popper (1968), Lakatos (1970),[3] Mouly (1978), Laudan (1990) and Rasmussen (1990) identify the following characteristics of an effective empirical theory:

1 A theoretical system must permit deductions and generate laws that can be tested empirically; that is, it must provide the means for its confirmation or rejection. One can test the validity of a theory only through the validity of the propositions (hypotheses) that can be derived from it. If repeated attempts to disconfirm its various hypotheses fail, then greater confidence can be placed in its validity. This can go on indefinitely, until possibly some hypothesis proves untenable. This would constitute indirect evidence of the inadequacy of the theory and could lead to its rejection (or more commonly to its replacement by a more adequate theory that can incorporate the exception).

2 Theory must be compatible with both observation and previously validated theories. It must be grounded in empirical data that have been verified and must rest on sound postulates and hypotheses. The better the theory, the more adequately it can explain the phenomena under consideration, and the more facts it can incorporate into a meaningful structure of ever-greater generalizability. There should be internal consistency between these facts. It should clarify the precise terms in which it seeks to explain, predict and generalize about empirical phenomena.

3 Theories must be stated in simple terms; theory is best that explains the most in the simplest way. This is the law of parsimony. A theory must explain the data adequately and yet must not be so comprehensive as to be unwieldy. On the other hand, it must not overlook variables simply because they are difficult to explain.

4 A theory should have considerable explanatory and predictive potential.

5 A theory should be able to respond to observed anomalies.

6 A theory should spawn a research enterprise (echoing Siegel's (1987) comment that one of the characteristics of an effective theory is its fertility).

7 A theory should demonstrate precision and universality, and set the grounds for its own falsification and verification, identifying the nature and operation of a 'severe test' (Popper, 1968). An effective empirical theory is tested in contexts which are different from those that gave rise to the theory, i.e. they should move beyond simply corroboration and

induction and towards 'testing' (Laudan, 1990). It should identify the type of evidence which is required to confirm or refute the theory.

8 A theory must be operationalizable precisely.
9 A test of the theory must be replicable.

Sometimes the word *model* is used instead of, or interchangeably with, *theory*. Both may be seen as explanatory devices or schemes having a broadly conceptual framework, though models are often characterized by the use of analogies to give a more graphic or visual representation of a particular phenomenon. Providing they are accurate and do not misrepresent the facts, models can be of great help in achieving clarity and focusing on key issues in the nature of phenomena.

Hitchcock and Hughes draw together the strands of the discussion so far when they describe a theory thus:

Theory is seen as being concerned with the development of systematic construction of knowledge of the social world. In doing this theory employs the use of concepts, systems, models, structures, beliefs and ideas, hypotheses (theories) in order to make statements about particular types of actions, events or activities, so as to make analyses of their causes, consequences and process. That is, to explain events in ways which are consistent with a particular philosophical rationale or, for example, a particular sociological or psychological perspective. Theories therefore aim to both propose and analyse sets of relations existing between a number of variables when certain regularities and continuities can be demonstrated via empirical enquiry.

(Hitchcock and Hughes, 1995: 20–1)

Scientific theories must, by their very nature, be provisional. A theory can never be complete in the sense that it encompasses all that can be known or understood about the given phenomenon. As Mouly (1978) argues, one scientific theory is replaced by a superior, more sophisticated theory, as new knowledge is acquired; this rehearses the matter of paradigms and paradigm shifts introduced earlier.

In referring to theory and models, we have begun to touch upon the tools used by scientists in their work. We look now in more detail at two such tools which play a crucial role in science – the concept and the hypothesis.

1.6 The tools of science

Concepts express generalizations from particulars – anger, achievement, alienation, velocity, intelligence,

democracy. Examining these examples more closely, we see that each is a word representing an idea: more accurately, a concept is the relationship between the word (or symbol) and an idea or conception. Whoever we are and whatever we do, we all make use of concepts. Naturally, some are shared and used by all groups of people within the same culture – child, love, justice, for example; others, however, have a restricted currency and are used only by certain groups, specialists or members of professions – idioglossia, retroactive inhibition, anticipatory socialization.

Concepts enable us to impose some sort of meaning on the world; through them reality is given sense, order and coherence. They are the means by which we are able to come to terms with our experience. How we perceive the world, then, is highly dependent on the repertoire of concepts we can command. The more we have, the more sense data we can pick up and the surer will be our perceptual (and cognitive) grasp of whatever is 'out there'. If our perceptions of the world are determined by the concepts available to us, it follows that people with differing sets of concepts will tend to view the 'same' objective reality differently – a doctor diagnosing an illness will draw upon a vastly different range of concepts from, say, the restricted and perhaps simplistic notions of the layperson in that context.

So, you may ask, where is all this leading? Simply to this: that social scientists have likewise developed, or appropriated by giving precise meaning to, a set of concepts which enable them to shape their perceptions of the world in a particular way, to represent that slice of reality which is their special study. And collectively, these concepts form part of their wider meaning system which permits them to give accounts of that reality, accounts which are rooted and validated in the direct experience of everyday life. These points may be exemplified by the concept of social class. Hughes says that it offers 'a rule, a grid, even though vague at times, to use in talking about certain sorts of experience that have to do with economic position, life-style, life-chances, and so on' (Hughes, 1976: 34).

There are two important points to stress when considering scientific concepts. The first is that they do not exist independently of us: they are indeed our inventions, enabling us to acquire some understanding of nature. The second is that they are limited in number and in this way contrast with the infinite number of phenomena they are required to explain.

A second tool of great importance to the scientist is the *hypothesis*. It is from this that much research proceeds, especially where cause-and-effect or concomitant relationships are being investigated. The hypothesis has been defined by Kerlinger (1970) as a conjectural statement of the relations between two or more variables, or 'an educated guess', though it is unlike an educated guess in that it is often the result of considerable study, reflective thinking and observation. Medawar writes of the hypothesis and its function thus:

> All advances of scientific understanding, at every level, begin with a speculative adventure, an imaginative preconception *of what might be true* – a preconception which always, and necessarily, goes a little way (sometimes a long way) beyond anything which we have logical or factual authority to believe in. It is the invention of a possible world, or of a tiny fraction of that world. The conjecture is then exposed to criticism to find out whether or not that imagined world is anything like the real one. Scientific reasoning is therefore at all levels an interaction between two episodes of thought – a dialogue between two voices, the one imaginative and the other critical; a dialogue, if you like, between the possible and the actual, between proposal and disposal, conjecture and criticism, between what might be true and what is in fact the case.
>
> (Medawar, 1972: 22)

Kerlinger (1970) has identified two criteria for 'good' hypotheses. The first is that hypotheses are statements about the relations between variables; and second, that hypotheses carry clear implications for testing the stated relations. To these he adds two ancillary criteria: that hypotheses disclose compatibility with current knowledge; and that they are expressed as economically as possible. Thus if we conjecture that social class background determines academic achievement, we have a relationship between one variable, social class, and another, academic achievement. And since both can be measured, the primary criteria specified by Kerlinger can be met. Neither do they violate the ancillary criteria proposed by Kerlinger (see also Box 1.2).

He further identifies four reasons for the importance of hypotheses as tools of research. First, they organize the efforts of researchers. The relationship expressed in the hypothesis indicates what they should do. Hypotheses enable researchers to understand the problem with greater clarity and provide them with a framework for collecting, analysing and interpreting their data. Second, they are, in Kerlinger's words, the working instruments of theory. They can be deduced from theory or from other hypotheses. Third, they can be tested, empirically or experimentally, thus resulting in confirmation or rejection. And there is always the possibility that a hypothesis, once supported and established, may become a law. And fourth, hypotheses are powerful tools for the advancement of knowledge because, as Kerlinger explains, they enable us to get outside ourselves. Hypotheses and concepts play a crucial part in the scientific method and it is to this that we now turn our attention.

1.7 The scientific method

If the most distinctive feature of science is its empirical nature, the next most important characteristic is its set of procedures which show not only how findings have been arrived at, but are sufficiently clear for fellow-scientists to repeat them, i.e. to check them out with the same or other materials and thereby test the results. As Cuff and Payne say: 'A scientific approach necessarily involves standards and procedures for demonstrating the "empirical warrant" of its findings, showing the match or fit between its statements and what is happening or has happened in the world' (Cuff and Payne, 1979: 4). These standards and procedures we will call for convenience 'the scientific method', though this can be somewhat misleading, as the combination of the definite article, adjective and singular noun conjures up in the minds of some people a single invariant approach to problem-solving, an approach frequently involving

---

BOX 1.2   THE HYPOTHESIS

Once one has a hypothesis to work on, the scientist can move forward; the hypothesis will guide the researcher on the selection of some observations rather than others and will suggest experiments. Scientists soon learn by experience the characteristics of a good hypothesis. A hypothesis that is so loose as to accommodate *any* phenomenon tells us precisely nothing; the more phenomena it prohibits, the more informative it is.

A good hypothesis must also have *logical immediacy*, i.e. it must provide an explanation of whatever it is that needs to be explained and not an explanation of other phenomena. Logical immediacy in a hypothesis means that it can be tested by comparatively direct and practicable means. A large part of the *art of the soluble* is the art of devising hypotheses that can be tested by practicable experiments.

Source: Adapted from Medawar, 1981

atoms or rats, and taking place within the confines of a laboratory. Yet there is much more to it than this. The term in fact cloaks a number of methods which vary in their degree of sophistication depending on their function and the particular stage of development a science has reached.

Box 1.3 sets out the sequence of stages through which a science normally passes in its development or, perhaps more realistically, that are constantly present in its progress and on which scientists may draw depending on the kind of information they seek or the kind of problem confronting them. Of particular interest in our efforts to elucidate the term 'scientific method' are stages 2, 3 and 4. Stage 2 is a relatively uncomplicated point at which the researcher is content to observe and record facts and possibly arrive at some system of classification. Much research in the field of education, especially at classroom and school level, is conducted in this way, e.g. surveys and case studies. Stage 3 introduces a note of added sophistication as attempts are made to establish relationships between variables within a loose framework of inchoate theory. Stage 4 is the most sophisticated stage and often the one that many people equate exclusively with the scientific method. In order to arrive at causality, as distinct from mere measures of association, researchers here design experimental situations in which variables are manipulated to test their chosen hypotheses. This process moves from early, inchoate ideas, to more rigorous hypotheses, to empirical testing of those hypotheses, thence to confirmation or modification of the hypotheses (Kerlinger, 1970).

With stages 3 and 4 of Box 1.3 in mind, we may say that the scientific method begins consciously and deliberately by selecting from the total number of elements in a given situation.

Hitchcock and Hughes (1995: 23) suggest an eight-stage model of the scientific method that echoes Kerlinger. This is represented in Box 1.4.

The elements the researchers fasten on to will naturally be suitable for scientific formulation; this means simply that they will possess quantitative aspects. Their principal working tool will be the hypothesis which, as we have seen, is a statement indicating a relationship (or its absence) between two or more of the chosen elements and stated in such a way as to carry clear implications for testing. Researchers then choose the most appropriate method and put their hypotheses to the test.

BOX 1.3   STAGES IN THE DEVELOPMENT OF A SCIENCE

1 Definition of the science and identification of the phenomena that are to be subsumed under it.
2 Observational stage at which the relevant factors, variables or items are identified and labelled; and at which categories and taxonomies are developed.
3 Correlational research in which variables and parameters are related to one another and information is systematically integrated as theories begin to develop.
4 The systematic and controlled manipulation of variables to see if experiments will produce expected results, thus moving from correlation to causality.
5 The firm establishment of a body of theory as the outcomes of the earlier stages are accumulated. Depending on the nature of the phenomena under scrutiny, laws may be formulated and systematized.
6 The use of the established body of theory in the resolution of problems or as a source of further hypotheses.

BOX 1.4   AN EIGHT-STAGE MODEL OF THE SCIENTIFIC METHOD

Stage 1: Hypotheses, hunches and guesses
Stage 2: Experiment designed; samples taken; variables isolated
Stage 3: Correlations observed; patterns identified
Stage 4: Hypotheses formed to explain regularities
Stage 5: Explanations and predictions tested; falsifiability
Stage 6: Laws developed or disconfirmation (hypothesis rejected)
Stage 7: Generalizations made
Stage 8: New theories

1.8 Criticisms of positivism and the scientific method

In spite of the scientific enterprise's proven success using positivism – especially in the field of natural science – its ontological and epistemological bases have been the focus of sustained and sometimes vehement criticism from some quarters. Beginning in the second half of the nineteenth century, the revolt against positivism occurred on a broad front, attracting some of the best intellectuals in Europe – philosophers, scientists, social critics and creative artists. Essentially, it has been a reaction against the world picture projected by science which, it is contended, undermines life and mind. The precise target of the anti-positivists' attack has been science's mechanistic and reductionist view of nature which, by definition, defines life in measurable terms rather than inner experience, and excludes notions of choice, freedom, individuality and moral responsibility, regarding the universe as a living organism rather than as a machine (e.g. Nesfield-Cookson, 1987).

Another challenge to the claims of positivism came from Søren Kierkegaard, the Danish philosopher, one of the originators of existentialism. Kierkegaard was concerned with individuals and their need to fulfil themselves to the highest level of development. This realization of a person's potential was for him the meaning of existence which he saw as 'concrete and individual, unique and irreducible, not amenable to conceptualization' (Beck, 1979). Characteristic features of the age in which we live – democracy's apparent mutation into crowd mentality, the ascendancy of reason, scientific and technological progress – all militate against the achievement of this end and contribute to the dehumanization of the individual. In his desire to free people from their illusions, the illusion Kierkegaard was most concerned about was that of objectivity. By this he meant the imposition of rules of behaviour and thought, and the making of a person into an observer set on discovering general laws governing human behaviour. The capacity for subjectivity, he argued, should be regained and retained. This he regarded as the ability to consider one's own relationship to whatever constitutes the focus of enquiry. The contrast he made between objectivity and subjectivity is brought out in the following passage:

> When the question of truth is raised in an objective manner, reflection is directed objectively to the truth as an object to which the knower is related. Reflection is not focused on the relationship, however, but upon the question of whether it is the truth to which the knower is related. If only the object to which he is related is the truth, the subject is accounted to be in the truth. When the question of truth is raised subjectively, reflection is directed subjectively to the nature of the individual's relationship; if only the mode of this relationship is in the truth, the individual is in the truth, even if he should happen to be thus related to what is not true.
>
> (Kierkegaard, 1974: 178)

For Kierkegaard, 'subjectivity and concreteness of truth are together the light. Anyone who is committed to science, or to rule-governed morality, is benighted, and needs to be rescued from his state of darkness' (Warnock, 1970).

Also concerned with the dehumanizing effects of the social sciences is Ions (1977). While acknowledging that they can take much credit for throwing light in dark corners, he expresses serious concern at the way in which quantification and computation, assisted by statistical theory and method, are used. He argues that quantification is a form of collectivism, but that this runs the risk of depersonalization. His objection is not directed at quantification per se, but at quantification when it becomes an end in itself – 'a branch of mathematics rather than a humane study seeking to explore and elucidate the gritty circumstances of the human condition' (Ions, 1977). This echoes Horkheimer's (1972) powerful critique of positivism as the mathematization of concepts about nature and of scientism – science's belief in itself as the only way of conducting research and explaining phenomena.

Another forceful critic of the objective consciousness has been Roszak (1970, 1972), who argues that science, in its pursuit of objectivity, is a form of alienation from our true selves and from nature. The justification for any intellectual activity lies in the effect it has on increasing our awareness and degree of consciousness. This increase, some claim, has been retarded in our time by the excessive influence that the positivist paradigm has exerted on areas of our intellectual life. Holbrook (1977), for example, affording consciousness a central position in human existence and deeply concerned with what happens to it, condemns positivism and empiricism for their bankruptcy of the inner world, morality and subjectivity.

Hampden-Turner (1970) concludes that the social science view of human beings is biased in that it is conservative and ignores important qualities. This restricted image of humans, he contends, comes about because social scientists concentrate on the repetitive, predictable and invariant aspects of the person, on 'visible externalities' to the exclusion of the subjective world and on the parts of the person in their endeavours to understand the whole.

Habermas (1972), in keeping with the Frankfurt School of critical theory (critical theory is discussed below) provides a corrosive critique of positivism, arguing that the scientific mentality has been elevated to an almost unassailable position – almost to the level of a religion (scientism) – as being the only epistemology of the west. In this view all knowledge becomes equated with scientific knowledge. This neglects hermeneutic, aesthetic, critical, moral, creative and other forms of knowledge. It reduces behaviour to technicism.

Positivism's concern for control and, thereby, its appeal to the passivity of behaviourism and for instrumental reason is a serious danger to the more open-ended, creative, humanitarian aspects of social behaviour. Habermas (1972, 1974) and Horkheimer (1972) argue that scientism silences an important debate about values, informed opinion, moral judgements and beliefs. Scientific explanation seems to be the only means of explaining behaviour, and, for them, this seriously diminishes the very characteristics that make humans human. It makes for a society without conscience. Positivism is unable to answer many interesting or important areas of life (Habermas, 1972: 300). Indeed this is an echo of Wittgenstein's (1974) famous comment that when all possible scientific questions have been addressed they have left untouched the main problems of life.

Other criticisms are commonly levelled at positivistic social science from within its own ranks. One is that it fails to take account of our unique ability to interpret our experiences and represent them to ourselves. We can, and do, construct theories about ourselves and our world; moreover, we act on these theories. In failing to recognize this, positivistic social science is said to ignore the profound differences between itself and the natural sciences. Social science, unlike natural science, stands in a subject-subject rather than a subject-object relation to its field of study, and works in a pre-interpreted world in the sense that the meanings that subjects hold are part of their construction of the world (Giddens, 1976).

The difficulty in which positivism finds itself is that it regards human behaviour as passive, essentially determined and controlled, thereby ignoring intention, individualism and freedom. This approach suffers from the same difficulties that inhere in behaviourism, which has scarcely recovered from Chomsky's (1959) withering criticism where he writes that a singular problem of behaviourism is its inability to infer causes from behaviour, to identify the stimulus that has brought about

the response – the weakness of Skinner's stimulus-response theory. This problem with positivism also rehearses the familiar problem in social theory, namely, the tension between agency and structure (Layder, 1994): humans exercise agency – individual choice and intention – not necessarily in circumstances of their own choosing, but nevertheless they do not behave simply or deterministically like puppets.

Finally, the findings of positivistic social science are often said to be so banal and trivial that they are of little consequence to those for whom they are intended, namely, teachers, social workers, counsellors, managers, and the like. The more effort, it seems, that researchers put into their scientific experimentation in the laboratory by restricting, simplifying and controlling variables, the more likely they are to end up with a 'pruned, synthetic version of the whole, a constructed play of puppets in a restricted environment'.[4]

These are formidable criticisms; but what alternatives are proposed by the detractors of positivistic social science?

1.9 Alternatives to positivistic social science – naturalistic approaches

Although the opponents of positivism within social science itself subscribe to a variety of schools of thought each with its own subtly different epistemological viewpoint, they are united by their common rejection of the belief that human behaviour is governed by general, universal laws and characterized by underlying regularities. Moreover, they would agree that the social world can only be understood from the standpoint of the individuals who are part of the ongoing action being investigated and that their model of a person is an autonomous one, not the plastic version favoured by positivist researchers. In rejecting the viewpoint of the detached, objective observer – a mandatory feature of traditional research – anti-positivists and post-positivists would argue that individuals' behaviour can only be understood by the researcher sharing their frame of reference: understanding of individuals' interpretations of the world around them has to come from the inside, not the outside. Social science is thus seen as a subjective rather than an objective undertaking, as a means of dealing with the direct experience of people in specific contexts, and where social scientists understand, explain and demystify social reality through the eyes of different participants; the participants themselves define the social reality (Beck, 1979).

The anti-positivist/post-positivist movement has influenced those constituent areas of social science of most concern to us, namely, psychology, social psychology and sociology. In the case of psychology, for instance, a school of humanistic psychology has emerged alongside the coexisting behaviouristic and psychoanalytic schools. Arising as a response to the challenge to combat the growing feelings of dehumanization which characterize many social and cultural milieux, it sets out to study and understand the person as a *whole* (Buhler and Allen, 1972). Humanistic psychologists present a model of people that is positive, active and purposive, and at the same time stresses their own involvement with the life experience itself. They do not stand apart, introspective, hypothesizing. Their interest is directed at the intentional and creative aspects of the human being. The perspective adopted by humanistic psychologists is naturally reflected in their methodology. They are dedicated to studying the individual in preference to the group, and consequently prefer idiographic approaches to nomothetic ones. The implications of the movement's philosophy for the education of the human being have been drawn by Carl Rogers (1942, 1945, 1969).[5]

Comparable developments within social psychology may be perceived in the 'science of persons' movement. It is argued here that we must use ourselves as a key to our understanding of others and, conversely, our understanding of others as a way of finding out about ourselves, an anthropomorphic model of people. Since anthropomorphism means, literally, the attribution of human form and personality, the implied criticism is that social psychology as traditionally conceived has singularly failed, so far, to model people as they really are. As some wry commentators have pleaded, 'For scientific purposes, treat people as if they were human beings' (Harré and Secord, 1972), which entails treating them as capable of monitoring and arranging their own actions, exercising their agency.

Social psychology's task is to understand people in the light of this anthropomorphic model. Proponents of this 'science of persons' approach place great store on the systematic and painstaking analysis of social episodes, i.e. behaviour in context. In Box 1.5 we give an example of such an episode taken from a classroom study. Note how the particular incident would appear on an interaction analysis coding sheet of a researcher employing a positivistic approach. Note, too, how this slice of classroom life can only be understood by knowledge of the specific organizational background and context in which it is embedded.

BOX 1.5 A CLASSROOM EPISODE

Walker and Adelman describe an incident in the following manner:

> In one lesson the teacher was listening to the boys read through short essays that they had written for homework on the subject of 'Prisons'. After one boy, Wilson, had finished reading out his rather obviously skimped piece of work the teacher sighed and said, rather crossly:

> T: Wilson, we'll have to put you away if you don't change your ways, and do your homework. Is that all you've done?
> P: Strawberries, strawberries. (Laughter)

Now at first glance this is meaningless. An observer coding with Flanders Interaction Analysis Categories (FIAC) would write down:

'7' (teacher criticizes) followed by a,
'4' (teacher asks question) followed by a,
'9' (pupil irritation) and finally a,
'10' (silence or confusion) to describe the laughter.

Such a string of codings, however reliable and valid, would not help anyone to *understand* why such an interruption was funny. Human curiosity makes us want to know *why* everyone laughs – and so, I would argue, the social scientist needs to know too. Walker and Adelman asked subsequently why 'strawberries' was a stimulus to laughter and were told that the teacher frequently said the pupils' work was 'like strawberries – good as far as it goes, but it doesn't last nearly long enough'. Here a casual comment made in the past has become an integral part of the shared meaning system of the class. It can only be comprehended by seeing the relationship as developing over time.

Source: Adapted from Delamont, 1976

The approach to analysing social episodes in terms of the 'actors' themselves is known as the 'ethogenic method'.[6] Unlike positivistic social psychology which ignores or presumes its subjects' interpretations of situations, ethogenic social psychology concentrates upon the ways in which persons construe their social world. By probing at their accounts of their actions, it endeavours to come up with an understanding of what those persons were doing in the particular episode.

As an alternative to positivist approaches, naturalistic, qualitative, interpretive approaches of various hues possess particular distinguishing features:

- people are deliberate and creative in their actions, they act intentionally and make meanings in and through their activities (Blumer, 1969);
- people actively construct their social world – they are not the 'cultural dopes' or passive dolls of positivism (Becker, 1970; Garfinkel, 1967);
- situations are fluid and changing rather than fixed and static; events and behaviour evolve over time and are richly affected by context – they are 'situated activities';
- events and individuals are unique and largely non-generalizable;
- a view that the social world should be studied in its natural state, without the intervention of, or manipulation by, the researcher (Hammersley and Atkinson, 1983);
- fidelity to the phenomena being studied is fundamental;
- people interpret events, contexts and situations, and act on the bases of those events (echoing Thomas's (1928) famous dictum that if people define their situations as real then they are real in their consequences – if I believe there is a mouse under the table, I will act as though there is a mouse under the table, whether there is or not (Morrison, 1998));
- there are multiple interpretations of, and perspectives on, single events and situations;
- reality is multilayered and complex;
- many events are not reducible to simplistic interpretation, hence 'thick descriptions' (Geertz, 1973) are essential rather than reductionism, that is to say thick descriptions representing the complexity of situations are preferable to simplistic ones;
- we need to examine situations through the eyes of participants rather than the researcher.

The anti-positivist/post-positivist movement in sociology is represented by three schools of thought – phenomenology, ethnomethodology and symbolic interactionism. A common thread running through the three schools is a concern with phenomena, that is, the things we directly apprehend through our senses as we go about our daily lives, together with a consequent emphasis on qualitative as opposed to quantitative methodology. The differences between them and the significant roles each phenomenon plays in research in classrooms and schools are such as to warrant a more extended consideration of them in the discussion below.

1.10 A question of terminology: the normative and interpretive paradigms

So far we have introduced and used a variety of terms to describe the numerous branches and schools of thought embraced by the positivist and anti-positivist viewpoints. As a matter of convenience and as an aid to communication, we clarify at this point two generic terms conventionally used to describe these two perspectives and the categories subsumed under each, particularly as they refer to social psychology and sociology. The terms in question are 'normative' and 'interpretive'. The normative paradigm (or model) contains two major orienting ideas (Douglas, 1973): first, that human behaviour is essentially rule-governed; and second, that it should be investigated by the methods of natural science. The interpretive paradigm, in contrast to its normative counterpart, is characterized by a concern for the individual. Whereas normative studies are positivist, all theories constructed within the context of the interpretive paradigm tend to be anti-positivist. As we have seen, the central endeavour in the context of the interpretive paradigm is to understand the subjective world of human experience. To retain the integrity of the phenomena being investigated, efforts are made to get inside the person and to understand from within. The imposition of external form and structure is resisted, since this reflects the viewpoint of the observer as opposed to that of the actor directly involved.

Two further differences between the two paradigms may be identified at this stage: the first concerns the concepts of 'behaviour' and 'action'; the second, the different conceptions of 'theory'. A key concept within the normative paradigm, behaviour refers to responses either to external environmental stimuli (another person, or the demands of society, for instance) or to internal stimuli (hunger, or the need to achieve, for example). In either case, the cause of the behaviour lies in the past. Interpretive approaches, on the other hand, focus on action. This may be thought of as behaviour-with-meaning; it is intentional behaviour and as such, future-oriented. Actions are only meaningful to us in so far as we are able to ascertain the intentions of actors to share their experiences. A large number of our every-day interactions with one another rely on such shared experiences.

As regards theory, normative researchers try to devise general theories of human behaviour and to vali-date them through the use of increasingly complex research methodologies which, some believe, push them further and further from the experience and under-standing of the everyday world and into a world of abstraction. For them, the basic reality is the collectiv-ity; it is external to the actor and manifest in society, its institutions and its organizations. The role of theory is to say how reality hangs together in these forms or how it might be changed so as to be more effective. The researcher's ultimate aim is to establish a comprehen-sive 'rational edifice', a universal theory, to account for human and social behaviour.

But what of the interpretive researchers? They begin with individuals and set out to understand their inter-pretations of the world around them. Theory is emer-gent and must arise from particular situations; it should be 'grounded' in data generated by the research act (Glaser and Strauss, 1967). Theory should not precede research but follow it. Investigators work directly with experience and understanding to build their theory on them. The data thus yielded will include the meanings and purposes of those people who are their source. Further, the theory so generated must make sense to those to whom it applies. The aim of scientific investi-gation for the interpretive researcher is to understand how this glossing of reality goes on at one time and in one place and compare it with what goes on in different times and places. Thus theory becomes sets of mean-ings which yield insight and understanding of people's behaviour. These theories are likely to be as diverse as the sets of human meanings and understandings that they are to explain. From an interpretive perspective the hope of a universal theory which characterizes the normative outlook gives way to multifaceted images of human behaviour as varied as the situations and con-texts supporting them.

1.11 Phenomenology, ethnomethodology and symbolic interactionism

There are many variants of qualitative, naturalistic approaches (Jacob, 1987; Hitchcock and Hughes, 1995). Here we focus on three significant 'traditions' in this style of research – phenomenology, ethnomethod-ology and symbolic interactionism. In its broadest meaning, phenomenology is a theoretical point of view

that advocates the study of direct experience taken at face value; and one which sees behaviour as determined by the phenomena of experience rather than by exter-nal, objective and physically described reality (English and English, 1958). Although phenomenologists differ among themselves on particular issues, there is fairly general agreement on the following points identified by Curtis (1978) which can be taken as distinguishing fea-tures of their philosophical viewpoint:

1 a belief in the importance, and in a sense the primacy, of subjective consciousness;
2 an understanding of consciousness as active, as meaning bestowing; and
3 a claim that there are certain essential structures to consciousness of which we gain direct knowledge by a certain kind of reflection. Exactly what these structures are is a point about which phenomenolo-gists have differed.

Various strands of development may be traced in the phenomenological movement: we shall briefly examine two of them – the transcendental phenomenology of Husserl; and existential phenomenology, of which Schutz is perhaps the most characteristic representative.

Husserl, regarded by many as the founder of phenomenology, was concerned with investigating the source of the foundation of science and with question-ing the common-sense, 'taken-for-granted' assumptions of everyday life (see Burrell and Morgan, 1979). To do this, he set about opening up a new direction in the analysis of consciousness. His catchphrase was 'back to the things!' which for him meant finding out how things appear directly to us rather than through the media of cultural and symbolic structures. In other words, we are asked to look beyond the details of everyday life to the essences underlying them. To do this, Husserl exhorts us to 'put the world in brackets' or free ourselves from our usual ways of perceiving the world. What is left over from this reduction is our con-sciousness of which there are three elements – the 'I' who thinks, the mental acts of this thinking subject, and the intentional objects of these mental acts. The aim, then, of this method of *epoché*, as Husserl called it, is the dismembering of the constitution of objects in such a way as to free us from all preconceptions about the world (see Warnock, 1970).

Schutz was concerned with relating Husserl's ideas to the issues of sociology and to the scientific study of social behaviour. Of central concern to him was the problem of understanding the meaning structure of the world of everyday life. The origins of meaning he thus sought in the 'stream of consciousness' – basically an unbroken stream of lived experiences which have no meaning in themselves. One can only impute meaning to them retrospectively, by the process of turning back on oneself and looking at what has been going on. In other words, meaning can be accounted for in this way by the concept of reflexivity. For Schutz, the attribution of meaning reflexively is dependent on the people identifying the purpose or goal they seek (see Burrell and Morgan, 1979).

According to Schutz, the way we understand the behaviour of others is dependent on a process of typification by means of which the observer makes use of concepts resembling 'ideal types' to make sense of what people do. These concepts are derived from our experience of everyday life and it is through them, claims Schutz, that we classify and organize our everyday world. As Burrell and Morgan (1979) observe, we learn these typifications through our biographical locations and social contexts. Our knowledges of the everyday world inheres in social order and this world is socially ordered.

The fund of everyday knowledge by means of which we are able to typify other people's behaviour and come to terms with social reality varies from situation to situation. We thus live in a world of multiple realities, and social actors move within and between these with ease (Burrell and Morgan, 1979), abiding by the rules of the game for each of these worlds.

Like phenomenology, ethnomethodology is concerned with the world of everyday life. In the words of its proponent, Harold Garfinkel, it sets out 'to treat practical activities, practical circumstances, and practical sociological reasonings as topics of empirical study, and by paying to the most commonplace activities of daily life the attention usually accorded extraordinary events, seeks to learn about them as phenomena in their own right' (Garfinkel, 1967: vii). He maintains that students of the social world must doubt the reality of that world; and that in failing to view human behaviour more sceptically, sociologists have created an ordered social reality that bears little relationship to the real thing. He thereby challenges the basic sociological concept of order.

Ethnomethodology, then, is concerned with how people make sense of their everyday world. More especially, it is directed at the mechanisms by which participants achieve and sustain interaction in a social encounter – the assumptions they make, the conventions they utilize and the practices they adopt. Ethnomethodology thus seeks to understand social accomplishments in their own terms; it is concerned to understand them from within (see Burrell and Morgan, 1979).

In identifying the 'taken-for-granted' assumptions characterizing any social situation and the ways in which the people involved make their activities rationally accountable, ethnomethodologists use notions like 'indexicality' and 'reflexivity'. Indexicality refers to the ways in which actions and statements are related to the social contexts producing them; and to the way their meanings are shared by the participants but not necessarily stated explicitly. Indexical expressions are thus the designations imputed to a particular social occasion by the participants in order to locate the event in the sphere of reality. Reflexivity, on the other hand, refers to the way in which all accounts of social settings – descriptions, analyses, criticisms, etc. – and the social settings occasioning them are mutually interdependent.

It is convenient to distinguish between two types of ethnomethodologists: linguistic and situational. The linguistic ethnomethodologists focus upon the use of language and the ways in which conversations in everyday life are structured. Their analyses make much use of the unstated 'taken-for-granted' meanings, the use of indexical expressions and the way in which conversations convey much more than is actually said. The situational ethnomethodologists cast their view over a wider range of social activity and seek to understand the ways in which people negotiate the social contexts in which they find themselves. They are concerned to understand how people make sense of and order their environment. As part of their empirical method, ethnomethodologists may consciously and deliberately disrupt or question the ordered 'taken-for-granted' elements in everyday situations in order to reveal the underlying processes at work.

The substance of ethnomethodology thus largely comprises a set of specific techniques and approaches to be used in studying what Garfinkel has described as the 'awesome indexicality' of everyday life. It is geared to empirical study, and the stress which its practitioners place upon the uniqueness of the situation encountered, projects its essentially relativist standpoint. A commitment to the development of methodology and fieldwork has occupied first place in the interests of its adherents, so that related issues of ontology, epistemology and the nature of human beings have received less attention than perhaps they deserve.

Essentially, the notion of symbolic interactionism derives from the work of Mead (1934). Although subsequently to be associated with such noted researchers as Blumer, Hughes, Becker and Goffman, the term does not represent a unified perspective in that it does not embrace a common set of assumptions and concepts accepted by all who subscribe to the approach. For our purposes, however, it is possible to identify three basic postulates. These have been set out by Woods (1979) as follows. First, human beings act towards things on the basis of the meanings they have for them. Humans inhabit two different worlds: the 'natural' world wherein they are organisms of drives and instincts and where the external world exists independently of them, and the social world where the existence of symbols, like language, enables them to give meaning to objects. This attribution of meanings, this interpreting, is what makes them distinctively human and social. Interactionists therefore focus on the world of subjective meanings and the symbols by which they are produced and represented. This means not making any prior assumptions about what is going on in an institution, and taking seriously, indeed giving priority to, inmates' own accounts. Thus, if pupils appear preoccupied for too much of the time – 'being bored', 'mucking about', 'having a laugh', etc. – the interactionist is keen to explore the properties and dimensions of these processes.

Second, this attribution of meaning to objects through symbols is a continuous process. Action is not simply a consequence of psychological attributes such as drives, attitudes or personalities, or determined by external social facts such as social structure or roles, but results from a continuous process of meaning attribution which is always emerging in a state of flux and subject to change. The individual constructs, modifies, pieces together, weighs up the pros and cons and bargains.

Third, this process takes place in a social context. Individuals align their actions to those of others. They do this by 'taking the role of the other', by making indications to 'themselves' about others' likely responses. They construct how others wish or might act in certain circumstances, and how they themselves might act. They might try to 'manage' the impressions others have of them, put on a 'performance', try to influence others' 'definition of the situation'.

Instead of focusing on the individual, then, and his or her personality characteristics, or on how the social structure or social situation causes individual behaviour, symbolic interactionists direct their attention at the nature of interaction, the dynamic activities taking place between people. In focusing on the interaction itself as a unit of study, the symbolic interactionist creates a more active image of the human being and rejects the image of the passive, determined organism. Individuals interact; societies are made up of interacting individuals. People are constantly undergoing change in interaction and society is changing through interaction. Interaction implies human beings acting in relation to each other, taking each other into account,

acting, perceiving, interpreting, acting again. Hence, a more dynamic and active human being emerges rather than an actor merely responding to others. Woods (1983: 15–16) summarizes key emphases of symbolic interaction thus:

- individuals as constructors of their own actions;
- the various components of the self and how they interact; the indications made to self, meanings attributed, interpretive mechanisms, definitions of the situation; in short, the world of subjective meanings, and the symbols by which they are produced and represented;
- the process of negotiation, by which meanings are continually being constructed;
- the social context in which they occur and whence they derive;
- by taking the 'role of the other' – a dynamic concept involving the construction of how others wish to or might act in a certain circumstance, and how individuals themselves might act – individuals align their actions to those of others.

A characteristic common to the phenomenological, ethnomethodological and symbolic interactionist perspectives, which makes them singularly attractive to the would-be educational researcher, is the way they fit naturally to the kind of concentrated action found in classrooms and schools. Yet another shared characteristic is the manner in which they are able to preserve the integrity of the situation where they are employed. Here the influence of the researcher in structuring, analysing and interpreting the situation is present to a much smaller degree than would be the case with a more traditionally oriented research approach.

1.12 Criticisms of the naturalistic and interpretive approaches

Critics have wasted little time in pointing out what they regard as weaknesses in these newer qualitative perspectives. They argue that while it is undeniable that our understanding of the actions of our fellow-beings necessarily requires knowledge of their intentions, this, surely, cannot be said to comprise *the* purpose of a social science. As Rex has observed:

Whilst patterns of social reactions and institutions may be the product of the actors' definitions of the situations there is also the possibility that those actors might be falsely conscious and that sociologists have an obligation to seek an objective perspective which is not necessarily that of any of the participating actors at all.... We need not be confined purely and simply to that ... social reality which is made available to us by participant actors themselves.

(Rex, 1974)

While these more recent perspectives have presented models of people that are more in keeping with common experience, some argue that anti-positivists/post-positivists have gone too far in abandoning scientific procedures of verification and in giving up hope of discovering useful generalizations about behaviour. Are there not dangers in rejecting the approach of physics in favour of methods more akin to literature, biography and journalism? Some specific criticisms of the methodologies are well directed, for example Argyle (1978) questions whether, if carefully controlled interviews such as those used in social surveys are inaccurate, then the less controlled interviews carry even greater risks of inaccuracy. Indeed Bernstein (1974) suggests that subjective reports may be incomplete and misleading. As Morrison (2009) suggests, I may believe that the teacher does not like me, and, therefore, act as though the teacher does not like me (a self-fulfilling prophecy), but, in fact, all the time the teacher actually does like me; my perception is wrong.

Bernstein's criticism is directed at the overriding concern of phenomenologists and ethnomethodologists with the meanings of situations and the ways in which these meanings are negotiated by the actors involved. What is overlooked about such negotiated meanings, observes Bernstein, is that the very process whereby one interprets and defines a situation is itself a product of the circumstances in which one is placed. One important factor in such circumstances that must be considered is the power of others to impose their own definitions of situations upon participants. Doctors' consulting rooms and headteachers' studies are locations in which inequalities in power are regularly imposed upon unequal participants. The ability of certain individuals, groups, classes and authorities to persuade others to accept their definitions of situations demonstrates that while – as ethnomethodologists insist – social structure is a consequence of the ways in which we perceive social relations, it is clearly more than this.

Conceiving of social structure as external to ourselves helps us take its self-evident effects upon our daily lives into our understanding of the social behaviour going on about us. Here is rehearsed the tension between agency and structure of social theorists (Layder, 1994); the danger of interactionist and interpretive approaches is their relative neglect of the power of external – structural – forces to shape behaviour and

events. There is a risk in interpretive approaches that they become hermetically sealed from the world outside the participants' theatre of activity – they put artificial boundaries around subjects' behaviour. Just as positivistic theories can be criticized for their macro-sociological persuasion, so interpretive and qualitative models can be criticized for their narrowly micro-sociological perspectives.

1.13 Mixed methods research: a new paradigm?

The 'paradigm wars' (Gage, 1989), in which one stood by one's allegiances to quantitative or qualitative methodologies, and which sanctioned the rise of qualitative methods and the partial eclipse of solely numerical methods (Denzin, 2008: 316), have given way to mixed methods research (Gorard and Taylor, 2004; Gorard and Smith, 2006; Teddlie and Tashakkori, 2009). This recognizes that 'qualitative or quantitative represents only one, perhaps not very useful, way of classifying methods' (Gorard and Smith, 2006: 61), that there is a need for less confrontational approaches to be adopted between different research paradigms (Denzin, 2008: 322), greater convergence between the two (Brannen, 2005), and a greater dialogue to be engaged between them and their proponents. Mixed methods research is 'a research paradigm whose time has come' (Johnson and Onwuegbuzie, 2004).

Ercikan and Roth (2006) argue against the polarization of research into either quantitative or qualitative approaches, and their associated objectivity and subjectivity respectively, as this is neither meaningful nor productive and because, in fact, there is compatibility between the two (see also Denscombe, 2008: 273). Schwandt (2000: 210), for example, argues that 'all research is interpretive' whilst, by contrast, Miles and Huberman (1994: 40) report Kerlinger's comment that there is no such thing as qualitative data, and that 'everything is either 1 or 0'. However, Onwuegbuzie and Leech (2005a: 377) argue that not all quantitative approaches are positivist and not all qualitative approaches are hermeneutic. They suggest that the terms 'quantitative' and 'qualitative' would be better replaced by 'confirmatory and exploratory research' (p. 382). They argue that methodological puritanism should give way to methodological pragmatism in addressing research questions. Indeed Caracelli and Greene (1993), Greene (2008) and Creswell (2009) suggest that mixed methods research established an early presence in evaluation research (discussed later in this chapter).

Far from assuming the incommensurability of paradigms (Denzin, 2008; Trifonas, 2009: 297; Creswell,

2009: 102), mixed methods research follows from the demise of such polarities and argues for their compatibility. These same authors (see also Howe, 1988) suggest the power of integrating different approaches, ways of viewing a problem, and types of data in conducting both confirmatory and exploratory research, induction and deduction, in answering research questions, in strengthening the inferences (both in terms of processes of analysis and outcomes of analysis) that can be made from research and data, and in generating theory. Indeed Reams and Twale (2008: 133) argue that mixed methods are 'necessary to uncover information and perspective, increase corroboration of the data, and render less biased and more accurate conclusions'.

Denscombe (2008: 272) suggests that mixed methods research can: (a) increase the accuracy of data; (b) provide a more complete picture of the phenomenon under study than would be yielded by a single approach, thereby overcoming the weaknesses and biases of single approaches; (c) enable the researcher to develop the analysis and build on the original data; and (d) aid sampling (he gives the example of where a questionnaire might be used to screen potential participants who might be approached for interview purposes).

The rise of mixed methods research is a signal feature of research debate in recent years, meteoric to the extent that it has been called the 'third methodological movement' (Teddlie and Tashakkori, 2009; Johnson et al., 2007), the 'third research paradigm' (Johnson and Onwuegbuzie, 2004; Johnson et al., 2007: 112; Denscombe, 2008), and the 'third path' (Gorard and Taylor, 2004). The rise of this approach is evidenced in the number of recent papers and 'special issues' of journals (e.g. *Evaluation and Research in Education*, 19(2), 2006), an entirely new *Journal of Mixed Methods Research*, the online journal *International Journal of Multiple Research Approaches*, the *Handbook of Mixed Methods Research* (Tashakkori and Teddlie, 2003) and its subsequent *Foundations of Mixed Methods Research* (Teddlie and Tashakkori, 2009). Mixed methods research recognizes, and works with, the fact that the world is not exclusively quantitative or qualitative; it is not an either/or world, but a mixed world, even though the researcher may find that the research has a predominant disposition to, or requirement for, numbers or qualitative data. Leech and Onwuegbuzie (2009: 265) suggest that conducting mixed methods research involves 'collecting, analyzing, and interpreting quantitative and qualitative data in a single study or in a series of studies that investigate the same underlying phenomenon'.

As a comparatively young discipline, mixed methods research has a range of different definitions (Tashakkori and Teddlie, 2003). Johnson et al. (2007: 119–21) give nineteen different definitions that vary according to what is being mixed, where and when the mixing takes place, the breadth and scope of the mixing, the reasons for the mixing, and the orientation of the research. Greene (2008: 20) suggests that a mixed method way of thinking recognizes that there are many legitimate approaches to social research and that, as a corollary, a single approach on its own will only yield a partial understanding of the phenomenon being investigated. Johnson et al. (2007) also present nine types of legitimation (validity) in mixed methods (p. 126): 'inside-outside, sample integration, weakness minimization, sequential, conversion, paradigmatic mixing, commensurability, multiple validities, and political validity'.

Tashakkori and Teddlie (2003) indicate that varieties of meanings of mixed methods research lie in six major domains: (1) basic definitions; (2) utility of mixed methods research; (3) paradigmatic foundations of mixed methods research; (4) design issues; (5) drawing inferences; and (6) logistical issues on conducting mixed methods research. Teddlie and Tashakkori (2006) set out seven dimensions in organizing different views of mixed methods research:

1 the number of methodological approaches used;
2 the number of strands or phases in the research;
3 the type of implementation process in the research;
4 the stage(s) at which the integration of approaches occur(s);
5 the priority given to one or more methodological approaches (e.g. quantitative over qualitative or vice versa, or of equal emphasis);
6 the purpose and function of the research study;
7 the theoretical perspective(s) in the research.

In a later paper (Creswell and Tashakkori, 2007) they set out four different realms of mixed methods research: (1) methods (quantitative and qualitative methods for the research and data types); (2) methodologies (mixed methods as a distinct methodology that integrates world views, research questions, methods, inferences and conclusions); (3) paradigms (philosophical foundations and world views of, and underpinning, mixed methods research); and (4) practice (mixed methods procedures in research designs). The significance of these different views is that mixed methods operate at all stages and levels of the research.

Greene (2008: 8–10) organized mixed methods research into four domains:

1   philosophical assumptions and stances (assumptions about ontology – the nature of the world; and epistemology – how we understand and research the world; and the warrants we use);
2   enquiry logics (e.g. purposes and research questions, designs, methodologies of research, sampling, data collection and analysis, reporting and writing);
3   guidelines for practice (how to mix methods in empirical research and in the study of phenomena);
4   sociopolitical commitment (what and whose interests, purposes and political stances are being served).

This sees a mixed methods approach as being implicit in all the stages of research: philosophical foundations and paradigms; approaches to the conduct of research and the realities it is researching; methodology, research questions and design; instrumentation, sampling, validity and reliability, data collection; data analysis and interpretation; reporting; and outcomes and uses of the research (cf. Creswell and Tashakkori, 2007). This echoes Yin (2006: 42), who sees mixed methods as entering the stages of: research questions; units of analysis; samples; instrumentation and data collection; and analytic strategies. He argues that the stronger is the mix of methods and their integration at all stages, the stronger is the benefit of mixed methods approaches (p. 46).

Mixed methods approaches work beyond quantitative and qualitative exclusivity or affiliation, and in a 'pragmatist paradigm' (Onwuegbuzie and Leech, 2005a; Johnson et al., 2007: 113; Teddlie and Tashakkori, 2009: 4) which draws on, and integrates, both numeric and narrative approaches and data, quantitative and qualitative methods as necessary and relevant, to meet the needs of the research rather than the allegiances or preferences of the researcher, and in order to answer research questions fully (Johnson et al., 2007). Whereas positivist approaches are premised on scientific, objectivist ontologies and epistemologies, and whereas interpretive approaches are premised on humanistic and existential ontologies and epistemologies, by contrast, mixed methods approaches are premised on pragmatism ontologies and epistemologies.

Pragmatism is essentially practical rather than idealistic; it is 'practice-driven' (Denscombe, 2008: 280). It argues that there may be both singular and multiple versions of the truth and reality, sometimes subjective and sometimes objective, sometimes scientific and sometimes humanistic. It is a matter-of-fact approach to life, oriented to the solution of practical problems in the practical world. It prefers utility, practical consequences and outcomes, and heurism over the singular

pursuit of the most accurate representation of 'reality'. Rather than engaging in the self-absorbed debate over qualitative or quantitative affiliations, it gets straight down to the business of judging research by whether it has enabled the researcher to find out what he or she wants to know, regardless of whether the data and methodologies are quantitative or qualitative (Feilzer, 2010: 14).

Pragmatism adopts a methodologically eclectic, pluralist approach to research, drawing on positivism and interpretive epistemologies based on the criteria of fitness for purpose and applicability, and regarding 'reality' as both objective and socially constructed (Johnson and Onwuegbuzie, 2004). No longer is one a slave to methodological loyalty and a particular academic community or social context (Oakley, 1999), though, in Kuhnian terms, Denscombe (2008) argues for the mixed methods paradigm to be defined in terms of a new 'community of practice' of those like-minded researchers who adopt the principles of mixed methods research, and that regarding the mixed methods approach in terms of a 'community of practice' respects the pragmatic underpinning of this approach.

Pragmatism suggests that 'what works' to answer the research questions is the most useful approach to the investigation, be it a combination of experiments, case studies, surveys or whatever, as such combinations enhance the quality of the research (e.g. Suter, 2005). Indeed Chatterji (2004) argues that mixed methods are unavoidable if one wishes to discover 'what works', in particular Extended-Term Mixed-Methods designs. Pragmatism is not an 'anything goes', sloppy, unprincipled approach; it has its own standards of rigour, and these are that the research must answer the research questions and 'deliver' useful answers to questions put by the research (Denscombe, 2008).

Methodological pluralism rather than affinity to a single paradigm is the order of the day (Johnson et al., 2007: 116) as this enables errors in single approaches to be identified and rectified. It also enables meanings in data to be probed, corroboration and triangulation to be practised, rich(er) data to be gathered, and new modes of thinking to emerge where paradoxes between two individual data sources are found (Johnson et al., 2007: 115; Sechrest and Sidana, 1995).

The consequences of this are that the research is driven by the research questions (which are often more than one in number and which require both quantitative and qualitative data to answer them) rather than the methodological preferences of the researcher. Greene (2008: 13) comments on the wide agreement in the mixed methods research community that methodology 'follows from' the purposes and questions in the research rather than vice versa, and that different kinds of mixed methods research designs follow from different kinds of research purposes (e.g. hypothesis testing, understanding, explanation, democratization (see the discussion of critical theory in Chapter 2)). Such purposes can adopt probability and non-probability samples (discussed in Chapter 8), multiple instruments for data collection and a range of data analysis methods, both numerical and qualitative.

Bryman (2007a: 8) indicates a signal feature of mixed methods research, that distinguishes it from the simple usage of quantitative and qualitative research separately within a single piece of research, where he suggests that mixed methods researchers must write up their research in 'such a way that the quantitative and qualitative components are mutually illuminating'. This criterion of 'mutually illuminating' not only argues for the fully integrated mixed design but it also argues for research purposes and questions to *require* such integration is being addressed, i.e. that the research question cannot be answered sufficiently by drawing only on one or the other of quantitative or qualitative methods, but that it requires both types of data.

Indeed Tashakkori and Creswell (2007: 207) write that 'a strong mixed methods study starts with a strong mixed methods research question', and they suggest that such a question could ask 'what and how' or 'what and why' (p. 207), i.e. the research question, rather than requiring *only* numerical or qualitative data, is a 'hybrid' (p. 208). The research question, in fact, might be broken down into separate subquestions, each of which could be either quantitative or qualitative, as in 'parallel' or concurrent mixed methods designs (see below) or in 'sequential mixed designs' (see below), but which must converge into a combined, integrated answer to the research question. Bryman (2007a: 13) goes further, to suggest not only that qualitative and quantitative data must be mutually informing, but that the research design itself has to be set up in a way that ensures that integration will take place, i.e. so that it is not biased to, say, a numerical survey.

Such a research question could be, for example: 'What are the problems of staff turnover in inner city schools, and why do they occur?' Here qualitative data might provide an indication of what the problems are and a range of reasons for these, whilst numerical data might provide an indication of the extent of the problems. Here qualitative data subsequently might be 'quantitized' into the numbers of responses expressing given reasons, or the quantitative data subsequently might be 'qualitized' in a narrative case study.

Day and Sammons (2008) indicate how a mixed method approach can provide more nuanced and authentic accounts than single methods approaches of the complexities of phenomena under investigation. Greene (2005: 207) argues for a mixed methods approach that welcomes multiple methodological traditions, as these catch diversity and difference and are 'anchored in values of tolerance, acceptance, respect' and democracy (p. 208). She argues (Greene, 2008) that mixed methods research calls for equity and social justice. Indeed this is taken further by Mertens (2007), who argues that mixed methods, in seeking social justice, operates in a 'transformative paradigm', which is discussed in Chapter 2 (on critical theory).

Further, mixed methods approaches enable a more comprehensive understanding of phenomena to be obtained than single methods approaches, combining particularity with generality, 'patterned regularity' with 'contextual complexity', 'inside *and* outside perspectives, and the whole *and* its constituent parts' (p. 208), and the causes of effects (discussed in Chapter 4).

Onwuegbuzie and Leech (2005a: 376) argue that using mixed methods recognizes similarities between different philosophies and epistemologies (in quantitative and qualitative traditions), rather than the differences that keep them apart, and that there are far more similarities than differences between the two approaches, as both use observational data, both describe data and construct explanations and speculations about the reasons why observed outcomes are as they are (p. 379). Both concern corroboration, elaboration, both complement each other and identify important conflicts, where they arise, between findings from the two kinds of data (Brannen, 2005: 176).

Mixed methods research can combine data types (numerical and qualitative) in answering research questions and also convert data (Bazeley, 2006: 66). Caracelli and Greene (1993) suggest four strategies for integrating data in mixed methods research:

1 data transformation (discussed below);
2 typology development (where classifications from one set or type of data are applied to the other set or type of data);
3 extreme case analysis (where outliers that are found in one set of data are explored using different data and methods);
4 data consolidation/merging (where new variables are created by merging data).

'Data conversion' ('transformation') (Teddlie and Tashakkori, 2009: 27), is where qualitative data are 'quantitized' (converted into numbers, typically nominal or ordinal (see Chapter 34)) (e.g. Miles and Huberman, 1994), for example by giving frequency counts of certain responses, codes, data or themes in order to establish regularities or peculiarities (Sandelowski *et al.*, 2009: 210), or rating scales of intensity of those responses, data, codes or themes (Teddlie and Tashakkori, 2009: 269). Bazeley (2006: 68) reports software which can assist the researcher (e.g. QDAS), for example in frequency counts. 'Data conversion' can also take place where numerical data are 'qualitized' (converted into narratives and then analysed using qualitative data analysis processes).

Mixed methods research addresses both the 'what' (numerical and qualitative data) and 'how or why' (qualitative) types of research questions. This is particularly important if the intention of the researcher is really to understand the different explanations of outcomes. For example, let us say that the researcher has found that a hundred people decide that schools are like prisons. This might be an interesting finding in itself, but it might be that forty of the respondents thought they were like prisons because they restricted students' freedom and had very harsh, controlling discipline. Twenty respondents might say that schools were like prisons because they were overcrowded; fifteen might say that schools were like prisons because the food was awful; ten might say that schools were like prisons because there was a lot of violence and bullying; ten might say schools were like prisons because they taught people how to steal and become involved in criminality; and another five might say that schools were like prisons because students had an easy life as long as they obeyed the rules. Here the reasons given for the simple statistic are very different from each other, and it is here that qualitative data can shed a lot of useful light on a simple statistic (cf. Feilzer's (2010: 12) study of the reasons given for the limited effects of prison sentences on reducing recidivism).

Teddlie and Tashakkori (2009) suggest that mixed methods research can adopt different designs:

a   'parallel mixed designs' (p. 26) (also termed 'concurrent designs' (Teddlie and Tashakkori, 2006)), in which both qualitative and quantitative approaches run simultaneously but independently in addressing research questions (akin to the familiar notion of triangulation of method, theory, methodologies, investigators, perspectives and data, discussed later in this book);

b   'sequential mixed designs' (p. 26), in which one or other of quantitative and qualitative approaches run one after the other, as the research requires, and in which one strand of the research or research approach determines the subsequent strand or

approach and in which the major findings from all strands are subsequently synthesized;

c   'quasi-mixed designs' (p. 142), in which both quantitative and qualitative data are gathered but which are not integrated in answering a particular research question, i.e. quantitative data might answer one research question and qualitative data another research question, even though both research questions are included in the same piece of research;

d   'conversion mixed designs' (p. 151), in which data are transformed (qualitative to quantitative and vice versa (in a parallel mixed design));

e   'multilevel mixed designs' (in parallel of sequential research designs) (p. 151) (also termed 'hierarchical' research designs), where different types of data (both quantitative and qualitative) are integrated and/or used at different levels of the research (e.g. student, class, school, district, region), for instance numerical data may be used at one level (students) and qualitative data used at another level (school);

f   'fully integrated mixed designs' (p. 151), in which mixed methods are used at each and all stages (perhaps iteratively: where one stage influences the next) and levels of the research.

Mixed methods research has to attend to several important decisions (Ivankova *et al.*, 2006: 9–11; Greene, 2008: 14–17):

a   priority (whether quantitative or qualitative approaches dominate, or are given equal weight at the stages of data collection and analysis);

b   implementation/timing (whether and where quantitative or qualitative data collection and analysis occur concurrently or *seriatim*/one after the other);

c   integration (where – at which stages – the integration of quantitative and qualitative methods occurs);

d   issues (around what issues the mixed methods occur, e.g. at the levels of constructs, variables, research questions, purposes of the research);

e   independence/interaction (the extent to which different methods are conceptualized, designed and 'implemented independently or interactively' (Greene, 2008: 14);

f   transformative intention (whether the research has an explicitly political agenda);

g   scope (whether the mixing of methods occurs within a single study or across more than one study in a set of coordinated studies within a single programme of research);

h   strands (the 'number of different strands that are mixed in a study' (Greene, 2008: 14));

i   methods characteristics (the nature and extent to

which there are 'offsetting differences' (Greene, 2008: 14), for example in perspectives and stances, in the methods that are being mixed in the study).

1.14 Is mixed methods research a new paradigm?

Whilst it is perhaps too early to judge whether mixed methods research really constitutes a new paradigm, as was claimed at the start of the previous section, or whether it is just another out of a growing number of paradigms, with equal status to them, is an open question. It is a young paradigm, and it is dangerous to predict what an adult will be like on the basis of his or her characteristics when a baby.

On the one hand, the advocates of mixed methods research hail it as an important approach that is driven by pragmatism, that yields real answers to real questions, that is useful in the real world, that avoids mistaken allegiance to either quantitative or qualitative approaches on their own, that enables rich data to be gathered which afford the triangulation that has been advocated in research for many years, that respects the mixed, messy real world, and that increases validity and reliability; in short, that 'delivers'. It possesses the flexibility in usage that reflects the changing and integrated nature of the world and the phenomenon under study. Further, it has its own ways of working and methodologies of enquiry, ontology, epistemology and values. It is a way of thinking, in which researchers have to see the world as integrated and in which they have to approach research from a standpoint of integrated purposes and research questions. Mixed methods research, its advocates suggest, enters into all stages of the research process: (a) philosophical foundations, ontologies, world views and epistemologies; (b) research purposes and research questions; (c) research design, methodology, sampling, instrumentation and data collection; (d) data analysis; (e) data interpretation; (f) conclusions and reporting results.

On the other hand mixed methods research has been taking place for years, before it was given the cachet of a new paradigm; it is not unusual for different methods to be used at different stages of a piece of research or even at the same stage, or with different samples within a single piece of research. It does not really have the novelty that seems to be claimed for it. Maybe it is a neat piece of marketing by researchers anxious to catch the real world by real-world research, which necessarily is mixed! Further, underneath mixed methods research are still, to some extent, the existing paradigms of quantitative and qualitative research, and they are different in ontology and epistemology, so to mix

them is to dilute and adulterate them, trying to mix oil and water, though, of course, the way in which they are used together is a very important step forward. Indeed Giddings (2006) sees a suppressed, or covert, support for positivism residing within mixed methods research, though this is questionable. Can one call a paradigm new simply because it blends two previous paradigms and makes a powerful case for thinking in a mixed methods way? Perhaps the jury is still out, though this book underlines the importance of combining methods wherever necessary and relevant in planning and doing research, and we return to mixed methods research throughout the book, as an indication of its importance.

Denzin (2008: 317) argues that the impact of 'the third methodological movement' (Teddlie and Tashakkori, 2003: 9) has had two distinct outcomes: first, it has spawned the mixed methods paradigm, and second, it has endorsed a proliferation of paradigms, not least of which are complexity theory and 'critical interpretive social science traditions' (p. 317). This chapter introduces some features of complexity theory in educational research, whilst the next chapter turns to critical theory (for examples of mixed methods empirical studies see Notes 1 and 7). Before we move to complexity theory, it is worth pausing momentarily to link the preceding discussion to complexity theory, by way of introducing post-positivism, post-structuralism and postmodernism in educational research.

1.15 A note on post-positivism, postmodernism and post-structuralism

Whilst it is not the intention of this chapter to pursue these terms in detail, it is fitting here to note their presence in the educational research arena. The positivist, modernist view of the world is of an ordered, controllable, predictable, standardized, mechanistic, deterministic, stable, objective, rational, impersonal, largely inflexible, closed system whose study yields immutable, universal laws and patterns of behaviour (a 'grand narrative', a 'metanarrative') and which can be studied straightforwardly through the empirical means of the scientific method. It suggests that there is a single grand design to the world, that there are straightforward laws of cause and effect of a linear nature (a specific cause produces a predictable effect, a small cause (stimulus) produces a small effect (response) and a large cause produces a large effect) which can be understood typically through the application of the scientific method as set out earlier in this chapter. Like a piece of clockwork, there is a place for everything and everything is in its place. It argues for an external and largely singular view of an objective reality (i.e. external to, and independent of, the researcher) that is susceptible to comparatively straightforward scientific discovery and laws.

By contrast, post-positivists challenge such a view of the world. Rather, following Popper (1968), our knowledge of the world is conjectural, falsifiable, challengeable, changing. Secure, once-and-for-all foundational knowledge and grand narratives of a singular objective reality are replaced by tentative speculation in which multiple perspectives and multiple warrants are brought forward by the researcher; the world is multilayered, able to tolerate multiple interpretations, and in which – depending on the particular view of post-positivism that is being embraced – there exist multiple external realities or knowledge is regarded as subjective rather than objective. Here the separation of fact and value in positivism is unsustainable: our values, perspectives, paradigms, even research communities determine what we focus on, how we research, what we deem to be important, what counts as knowledge, what research 'shows' and how we interpret research findings, and what constitutes 'good' research.

On the one hand, post-positivism argues for the continuing existence of an objective reality, but adopts a pluralist view of multiple, coexisting realities rather than a single reality. On the other hand, post-positivism has an affinity with the phenomenological, interpretive approaches to research, arguing for the centrality of the subjective and multiple interpretations of the phenomenon made by the researcher and other parties involved in the research (e.g. participants, researchers, audiences of the research).

It is not only post-positivists who challenge the modernist, positivist conception of the world. Whilst it is perhaps invidious to try to characterize postmodernists (as they would argue against any singular or all-embracing definitions), in a seminal text Jameson (1991) argues that postmodernism does have several distinguishing hallmarks, including, for example:

■ the absence of 'grand narratives' (metanarratives) and grand designs, laws and patterns of behaviour;
■ the valorization of discontinuity, difference, diversity, variety, uniqueness, subjectivity, distinctiveness and individuality;
■ the importance of the local, the individual and the particular;
■ the 'utter forgetfulness of the past' and the 'autoreferentiality' of the present (Jameson, 1991: 42);
■ the importance of temporality and context in understanding phenomena: meanings are rooted in time,

space, cultures, societies and are not universal across these;
■ the celebration of depthlessness, multiple realities (and, as Jameson argues, multiple superficialities) and the rectitude of individual interpretations and meanings;
■ relativism rather than absolutism in deciding what constitutes worthwhile knowledge, research and their findings;
■ the view of knowledge as a human, social construct;
■ multiple, sometimes contradictory, yet coexistent interpretations of the world, in which the researcher's interpretation is only one out of several possible interpretations, i.e. the equal value of different interpretations and the reduction in the authority of the researcher, yet, simultaneously, the privileging of some interpretations of the world to the neglect of others (i.e. the nexus between knowledge and power, a feature of critical theory, discussed in Chapter 2);
■ the recognition that researchers are part of the world that they are researching;
■ the emancipatory potential of according value to individual views, values, perspectives and interpretations (see Chapter 2).

This interpretation of postmodernism has deliberately not discussed its role in understanding culture and cultural studies, nor has it addressed postmodernism as 'the cultural logic of late capitalism' (Jameson, 1991). Rather, it has expressed those features which impact on the conduct and meaning of educational research. In one sense postmodernism supports the interpretive paradigm set out earlier in this chapter. In another sense it supports complexity theory as discussed below, and in a third sense it supports critical theory as set out in Chapter 2. Postmodernism has a chameleon-like nature in this respect.

Post-structuralism, like postmodernism, has many different interpretations (we will not discuss here the interpretation that relates to semiology). Here we take a necessarily selective interpretation, to focus on those features that are relevant to the foundations and conduct of educational research. In this sense, post-structuralism can be regarded as a counter to those structural-functionalists who adopt a systems view of society (e.g. Marxism, or functionalist anthropologists such as Levi-Strauss) or behaviour, as a set of interrelated parts which, in law-like fashion, pattern themselves and fit together neatly into a fixed view of the world and its operations and in which individual behaviour is largely determined by given, structural features of society (e.g. social class, position in society, role in society). In post-structuralist approaches, data (e.g. conversations, observations), even artefacts (Burman and Parker, 1993) can be regarded as texts, as discourses that are constructed and performed through discourses (see Chapters 31 and 32), open to different meaning and interpretations (Francis, 2010: 327).

Post-structuralists (e.g. Foucault, Derrida) argue individual agency has prominence; individuals are not simply puppets of a given system, people are diverse and different, indeed they may carry contradictions and tensions within themselves (e.g. in terms of class, ethnicity, sex, employment, social group, family membership and tasks, and so on), they are not simply the decentred bearers of given roles. Individuals have views of themselves, and one task of the researcher is to locate research findings within the views of the self that the participants hold, and to identify the meanings which the participants accord to phenomena. Hence not only do the multiple perspectives of the participants have to be discerned, but also those of the researchers, the audiences of the research and the readers of research. The task of the research is to 'deconstruct', e.g. to expose, the different meanings, layers of meanings and privileging of meanings inherent in a phenomenon or piece of research. There is no single, 'essential' meaning, but many, and one task of research is to understand how meanings and knowledge are produced, legitimized and used. (This links post-structuralism to critical theory, perhaps, though some critical theorists, e.g. Habermas (1987), argue against critical theory's affinity to postmodernism or post-structuralism.)

One can detect affinities between post-positivism, postmodernism and post-structuralism, in underpinning interpretive and qualitative approaches to educational research, complexity theory and critical theory, and the significance given to individual and subjective accounts in the research process, along with reflexivity on the part of the researcher. (That said, many post-positivists, postmodernists and post-structuralists would reject such a simple affinity, or even the links between their views and, for example, phenomenology and interpretivism. We do not explore this here.) One can suggest that post-positivism, postmodernism and post-structuralism argue for multiple interpretations of a phenomenon to be provided, to accord legitimacy to individual voices in research, and to abandon the search for deterministic, simple cause-and-effect laws of behaviour and action.

1.16 The paradigm of complexity theory

An emerging paradigm in educational research is that of complexity theory (Medd, 2002; Radford, 2006,

2007, 2008; Kuhn, 2007; Morrison, 2002a, 2008), as schools can be regarded as 'complex adaptive systems' (Kauffman, 1995). Complexity theory looks at the world in ways which break with simple cause-and-effect models, simple determinism and linear predictability (Gomm and Hammersley, 2001), and a dissection/atomistic approach to understanding phenomena (Byrne, 1997; Radford, 2007, 2008), replacing them with organic, non-linear and holistic approaches (Santonus, 1998: 3). Relations within interconnected, dynamic and changing networks are the order of the day (Youngblood, 1997: 27; Wheatley, 1999: 10), and there is a 'multiplicity of simultaneously interacting variables' (Radford, 2008: 510). Here key terms are feedback, recursion, emergence, connectedness and self-organization. Out go the simplistic views of linear causality (Radford, 2007; Morrison, 2009), the ability to predict, control and manipulate, to apply reductive techniques to research; and in come uncertainty, networks and connection, holism, self-organization, emergence over time through feedback and the relationships of the internal and external environments, and survival and development through adaptation and change.

In complexity theory, a self-organizing system is autocatalytic and possesses its own unique characteristics and identity (Kelly and Allison, 1999: 28) which enable it to perpetuate and renew itself over time – it creates the conditions for its own survival. This takes place through engagement with others in a system (Wheatley, 1999: 20). The system is aware of its own identity and core properties, and is self-regenerating (able to sustain that identity even though aspects of the system may change, e.g. staff turnover in a school).

Through feedback, recursion, perturbance, autocatalysis, connectedness and self-organization, higher levels of complexity and differentiated, new forms of life, behaviour and systems arise from lower levels of complexity and existing forms. These complex forms derive from often comparatively simple sets of rules – local rules and behaviours generating emergent complex global order and diversity (Waldrop, 1992: 16–17; Lewin, 1993: 38). General laws of emergent order can govern adaptive, dynamical processes (Waldrop, 1992: 86; Kauffman, 1995: 27).

The interaction of individuals feeds into the wider environment, which, in turn, influences the individual units of the network; they co-evolve, shaping each other (Stewart, 2001), and co-evolution requires connection, cooperation and competition: competition to force development and cooperation for mutual survival. The behaviour of a complex system as a whole, formed from its several elements, is greater than the sum of the parts (Bar-Yam, 1997; Goodwin, 2000).

Feedback must occur between the interacting elements of the system. Negative feedback is regulatory (Marion, 1999: 75), for example learning that one has failed in a test. Positive feedback brings increasing returns and uses information to change, grow and develop (Wheatley, 1999: 78); it amplifies small changes (Stacey, 1992: 53; Youngblood, 1997: 54). Once a child has begun to read she is gripped by reading, she reads more and learns at an exponential rate.

Connectedness, a key feature of complexity theory, exists everywhere. In a rainforest ants eat leaves, birds eat ants and leave droppings, which fertilize the soil for growing trees and leaves for the ants (Lewin, 1993: 86). In schools, children are linked to families, teachers, peers, societies and groups; teachers are linked to other teachers, support agencies (e.g. psychological and social services), policy-making bodies, funding bodies, the legislature, and so on. The child (indeed the school) is not an island, but is connected externally and internally in several ways. Disturb one element and the species or system must adapt or die; the message is ruthless.

Emergence is the partner of *self-organization*. Systems possess the ability for self-organization, which is not according to an a priori grand design – a cosmological argument – nor a teleological argument; complexity is neither. Further, self-organization emerges, it is internally generated; it is the opposite of external control. As Kauffman (1995) suggests, order comes for free and replaces control. Order is not imposed; it emerges; in this way it differs from control. Self-organized order emerges of itself as the result of the interaction between the organism and its environment, and new structures emerge that could not have been predicted; that emerged system is, itself, complex and cannot be reduced to those parts that gave rise to the system. As Davis and Sumara (2005: 313) write: 'phenomena have to be studied at their level of emergence, i.e. not in terms of their lower level activities but at their new – emerged – level'.

Stacey (2000: 395) suggests that a system can only evolve, and evolve spontaneously, where there is diversity and deviance (p. 399) – a salutary message for command-and-control teachers who exact compliance from their pupils. The future is largely unpredictable. At the point of 'self-organized criticality' (Bak, 1996), a tipping point, the effects of a single event are likely to be very large, breaking the linearity of Newtonian reasoning wherein small causes produce small effects; the straw that breaks the camel's back.

Chaos and complexity theories argue against the linear, deterministic, patterned, universalizable, stable, atomized, modernistic, objective, mechanist, controlled, closed systems of law-like behaviour which may be operating in the laboratory but which do not operate in the social world of education. These features of chaos and complexity theories seriously undermine the value of experiments and positivist research in education (e.g. Gleick, 1987; Waldrop, 1992; Lewin, 1993).

Complexity theory replaces these with an emphasis on networks, linkages, holism, feedback, relationships and interactivity in context (Cohen and Stewart, 1995), emergence, dynamical systems, self-organization and an open system (rather than the closed world of the experimental laboratory). Even if one could conduct an experiment, its applicability to ongoing, emerging, interactive, relational, open situations, in practice, is limited (Morrison, 2001). It is misconceived to hold variables constant in a dynamical, evolving, fluid, open situation. What is measured is history.

Complexity theory challenges randomized controlled trials – the 'gold standard' of research. Classical experimental methods, abiding by the need for replicability and predictability, may not be particularly fruitful since, in complex phenomena, results are never clearly replicable or predictable: As Heraclitus noted, we never jump into the same river twice. Complexity theory suggests that educational research should concern itself with: (a) how multivalency and non-linearity enter into education; (b) how voluntarism and determinism, intentionality, agency and structure, lifeworld and system, divergence and convergence interact in learning (Morrison, 2002a, 2005); (c) how to both use, but transcend, simple causality in understanding the processes of education; (d) how viewing a system holistically, as having its own ecology of multiple interacting elements, is more powerful than an atomized approach. To atomize phenomena into measurable variables and then to focus only on certain of these is to miss synergy and the significance of the whole. Measurement, however acute, may tell us little of value about a phenomenon; one can measure every observable variable of a person to an infinitesimal degree, but his/her nature, what makes him/her who he or she is, eludes atomization and measurement.

Complexity theory suggests that phenomena must be looked at holistically; to atomize phenomena into a restricted number of variables and then to focus only on certain factors is to miss the necessary dynamic interaction of several parts (Morrison, 2008). More fundamentally, complexity theory suggests that the conventional units of analysis in educational research (as in other fields) should move away from, for example, individuals, institutions, communities and systems (cf. Lemke, 2001). These should merge, so that the unit of analysis becomes a web or ecosystem (Capra, 1996: 301), focused on, and arising from, a specific topic or centre of interest (a 'strange attractor'). Individuals, families, students, classes, schools, communities and societies exist in symbiosis; complexity theory tells us that their relationships are necessary, not contingent, and analytic, not synthetic. This is a challenging prospect for educational research, and complexity theory, a comparatively new perspective in educational research (Radford, 2006; Morrison, 2008), offers considerable leverage into understanding societal, community, individual and institutional change; it provides the nexus between macro and micro-research in understanding and promoting change.

In addressing holism, complexity theory suggests the need for case study methodology, narratives, action research and participatory forms of research, premised in many ways on interactionist, qualitative accounts, i.e. looking at situations through the eyes of as many participants or stakeholders as possible. This enables multiple causality, multiple perspectives and multiple effects to be charted. Self-organization, a key feature of complexity theory, argues for participatory, collaborative and multi-perspectival approaches to educational research. This is not to deny 'outsider' research; it is to suggest that, if it is conducted, outsider research has to take in as many perspectives as possible.

In educational research terms, complexity theory stands against simple linear methodologies based on linear views of causality, arguing for multiple causality and multi-directional causes and effects, as organisms (however defined: individuals, groups, communities) are networked and relate at a host of different levels and in a range of diverse ways. No longer can one be certain that a simple cause brings a simple or single effect, or that a single effect is the result of a single cause, or that the location of causes will be in single fields only, or that the location of effects will be in a limited number of fields (Morrison, 2009).

Complexity theory not only questions the values of positivist research and experimentation, but it also underlines the importance of educational research to catch the deliberate, intentional, agentic actions of participants and to adopt interactionist and constructivist perspectives. Kuhn (2007: 172–3) sets out a series of axioms for complexity-based research: (a) reality is dynamic, emergent and self-organizing, and requires multiple perspectives to be addressed (see also Medd, 2002); (b) the relationship between the knower and the known is, itself, dynamic, emergent and self-organizing; (c) hypotheses for research must relate to time and context (see also Medd, 2002; Radford, 2006); (d) it is impossible to distinguish cause from effect, as entities are mutually shaping and influencing (co-evolution); (e) enquiry is not value-free.

Addressing complexity theory's argument for self-organization, the call is for the teacher-as-researcher movement to be celebrated, and complexity theory suggests that research in education could concern itself with the symbiosis of internal and external researchers and research partnerships. Just as complexity theory suggests that there are multiple views of reality, so this accords not only with the need for several perspectives on a situation (using multi-methods), but resonates with those tenets of critical research that argue for different voices and views to be heard. Heterogeneity is the watchword. Complexity theory provides not only a powerful challenge to conventional approaches to educational research, but it suggests both a substantive agenda and also a set of methodologies, arguing for methodological, paradigmatic and theoretical pluralism. In addressing holism, complexity theory suggests the need for case study methodology, qualitative research and participatory, multi-perspectival and collaborative (self-organized), partnership-based forms of research, premised on interactionist, qualitative and interpretive accounts (e.g. Lewin and Regine, 2000). It provides an emerging new paradigm for research.

 ## Companion Website

The companion website to the book includes PowerPoint slides for this chapter, which list the structure of the chapter and then provide a summary of the key points in each of its sections. In addition there is further information on complexity theory. These resources can be found online at **www.routledge.com/textbooks/cohen7e**.

CHAPTER 2

Critical educational research

This chapter sets out key features of critical theory as they apply to educational research, and then it links these to:

- curriculum research
- participatory action research
- feminist theory

It recognizes that other approaches can be included under the umbrella of critical theory (e.g. post-colonial theory, queer theory), and, whilst the chapter includes a note on these, it does not develop them here. Indeed critical theory embraces a range of other theories, e.g. critical race theory, critical pedagogy, critical disability theory.

2.1 Critical theory and critical educational research

Positivist and interpretive paradigms are essentially concerned with understanding phenomena through two different lenses. Positivism strives for objectivity, measurability, predictability, controllability, patterning, the construction of laws and rules of behaviour, and the ascription of causality; the interpretive paradigms strive to understand and interpret the world in terms of its actors. In the former, observed phenomena are important; in the latter, meanings and interpretations are paramount. Habermas (1984: 109–10), echoing Giddens (1976), describes this latter as a 'double hermeneutic', where people strive to interpret and operate in an already interpreted world; researchers have their own values, views and interpretations, and these affect their research, and, indeed that which they are researching is a world in which other people act on their own interpretations and views.

It was suggested earlier that mixed methods research has an affinity with equity, social justice and a 'transformative paradigm' (Mertens, 2007), and it is to this that we turn now. An emerging approach to educational research is the paradigm of *critical educational research*. This regards the two previous paradigms of positivism and interpretivism as presenting incomplete accounts of social behaviour by their neglect of the political and ideological contexts of much educational research. Positivistic and interpretive paradigms are seen as preoccupied with technical and hermeneutic knowledge respectively (Gage, 1989). The paradigm of critical educational research is heavily influenced by the early work of Habermas and, to a lesser extent, his predecessors in the Frankfurt School, most notably Adorno, Marcuse, Horkheimer and Fromm. Here the expressed intention is deliberately political – the emancipation of individuals and groups in an egalitarian society.

Critical theory is explicitly prescriptive and normative, entailing a view of what behaviour in a social democracy *should* entail (Fay, 1987; Morrison, 1995a). Its intention is not merely to give an account of society and behaviour but to realize a society that is based on equality and democracy for all its members. Its purpose is not merely to understand situations and phenomena but to change them. In particular it seeks to emancipate the disempowered, to redress inequality and to promote individual freedoms within a democratic society.

In this enterprise critical theory identifies the 'false' or 'fragmented' consciousness (Eagleton, 1991) that has brought an individual or social group to relative powerlessness or, indeed, to power, and it questions the legitimacy of this. It holds up to the lights of legitimacy and equality issues of repression, voice, ideology, power, participation, representation, inclusion and interests. It argues that much behaviour (including research behaviour) is the outcome of particular illegitimate, dominatory and repressive factors; illegitimate in the sense that they do not operate in the general interest – one person's or group's freedom and power is bought at the price of another's freedom and power. Hence critical theory seeks to uncover the *interests* at work in particular situations and to interrogate the legitimacy of those interests, identifying the extent to which they are legitimate in their service of equality and democracy. Its intention is *transformative*: to change society and individuals to social democracy. In this respect the purpose of critical educational research is intensely practical and political, to bring about a more just, egalitarian society in which individual and collective freedoms are practised, and to eradicate the exercise and effects of illegitimate power. The pedigree of critical theory in Marxism, thus, is not difficult to discern. For critical theorists, researchers can no longer claim neutrality and ideological or political innocence.

Critical theory and critical educational research, then, have their substantive agenda – for example by examining and interrogating the relationships between school and society: how schools perpetuate or reduce inequality; the social construction of knowledge and curricula – who defines worthwhile knowledge, what ideological interests this serves, and how this reproduces inequality in society; how power is produced and reproduced through education; whose interests are served by education and how legitimate these are (e.g. rich, white, middle-class males rather than poor, non-white, females).

The significance of critical theory for research is immense, for it suggests that much social research is comparatively trivial in that it *accepts* rather than *questions* given agendas for research, compounded by the funding for research, which underlines the political dimension of research sponsorship (discussed later) (Norris, 1990). Critical theorists would argue that the positivist and interpretive paradigms are essentially technicist, seeking to understand and render more efficient an existing situation, rather than to question or transform it.

Habermas's early work (1972) offers a useful tripartite conceptualization of interests that catches three of the paradigms of research in this chapter. He suggests that knowledge – and hence research knowledge – serves different interests. Interests, he argues, are socially constructed, and are 'knowledge-constitutive', because they shape and determine what counts as the objects and types of knowledge. Interests have an ideological function (Morrison, 1995a), for example, a 'technical interest' (discussed below) can have the effect of keeping the empowered in their empowered position and the disempowered in their powerlessness – i.e. reinforcing and perpetuating the status quo. An 'emancipatory interest' (discussed below) threatens the status quo. In this view knowledge – and research knowledge – is not neutral (see also Mannheim, 1936). What counts as worthwhile knowledge is determined by the social and positional power of the advocates of that knowledge. The link here between objects of study and communities of scholars echoes Kuhn's (1962) notions of paradigms and paradigm shifts, discussed earlier. Knowledge and definitions of knowledge reflect the interests of the community of scholars who operate in particular paradigms. Habermas (1972) constructs

the definition of worthwhile knowledge and modes of understanding around three cognitive interests:

i   prediction and control;
ii understanding and interpretation;
iii emancipation and freedom.

He names these the '*technical*', '*practical*' and '*emancipatory*' interests respectively. The technical interest characterizes the scientific, positivist method outlined earlier, with its emphasis on laws, rules, prediction and control of behaviour, with passive research objects – instrumental knowledge. The practical interest, an attenuation of the positivism of the scientific method, is exemplified in the hermeneutic, interpretive methodologies outlined in the qualitative approaches earlier (e.g. symbolic interactionism). Here research methodologies seek to clarify, understand and interpret the communications of 'speaking and acting subjects' (Habermas, 1974: 8).

Hermeneutics focuses on interaction and language; it seeks to understand situations through the eyes of the participants, echoing the *verstehen* approaches of Weber (Ringer, 1997) and premised on the view that reality is socially constructed (Berger and Luckmann, 1967). Indeed Habermas (1988: 12) suggests that sociology must understand social facts in their cultural significance and as socially determined. Hermeneutics involves recapturing the *meanings* of interacting others, recovering and reconstructing the *intentions* of the other actors in a situation. Such an enterprise involves the analysis of *meaning in a social context* (Held, 1980). Gadamer (1975: 273) argues that the hermeneutic sciences (e.g. qualitative approaches) involve the *fusion of horizons* between participants. Meanings rather than phenomena take on significance here.

The emancipatory interest subsumes the previous two paradigms; it requires them but goes beyond them (Habermas, 1972: 211). It is concerned with *praxis* – action that is informed by reflection with the aim to emancipate (Kincheloe, 1991: 177). The twin intentions of this interest are to expose the operation of power and to bring about social justice as domination and repression act to prevent the full existential realization of individual and social freedoms (Habermas, 1979: 14). The task of this knowledge-constitutive interest, indeed of critical theory itself, is to restore to consciousness those suppressed, repressed and submerged determinants of unfree behaviour with a view to their dissolution (Habermas, 1984: 194–5). This is a transformative agenda, concerned to move from oppression and inequality in society to the bringing about of social justice, equity and equality. These concern fairness in the egalitarian distribution of opportunities for, uptake of, processes in, participation in and outcomes of education and its impact on society, together with distributive justice, social justice and equality.

Mertens (2007: 213) argues that a transformative paradigm enters into every stage of the research process, because it concerns an interrogation of power. A transformative paradigm, she avers (pp. 216 and 224) has several 'basic beliefs':

Ontology (the nature of reality or of a phenomenon): politics and interests shape multiple beliefs and values, as these beliefs and values are socially constructed, privileging some views of reality and under-representing others.

Epistemology (how we come to know these multiple realities): influenced by communities of practice who define what counts as acceptable ways of knowing, and affecting the relationships between the researcher and the communities who are being researched, such that partnerships are formed that are based on equality of power and esteem.

Methodology (how we research complex, multiple realities): influenced by communities of practice who define what counts as acceptable ways of researching, and in which mixed methods have a significant role to play, as they enable a qualitative dialogue to be established between the participants in the research.

Axiology (principles and meanings in conducting research, and the ethics that govern these): beneficence, respect and the promotion of social justice (see Chapter 5).

Mertens argues (2007: 220) for mixed methods in a transformative paradigm, as they reduce the privileging of only powerful voices in society, and she suggests that participatory action research is a necessary, if not sufficient, element of a transformative paradigm, as it involves people as equals. This is introduced later in the chapter.

In Habermas's early work we attempt to conceptualize three research styles: the scientific, positivist style; the interpretive style; and the emancipatory, ideology critical style. Not only does critical theory have its own research agenda, but it also has its own research methodologies, in particular ideology critique and action research. The three methodologies, then, aligned to Habermas's knowledge-constitutive interests, are shown in Table 2.1.

With regard to ideology critique, a particular reading of ideology is being adopted here: the *suppression of generalizable interests* (Habermas, 1976: 113), where systems, groups and individuals operate in rationally indefensible ways because their power to act relies on the disempowering of other groups, i.e. that their principles of behaviour cannot be generalized.

Ideology – the values and practices emanating from particular dominant groups – is the means by which powerful groups promote and legitimate their particular – sectoral – interests at the expense of disempowered groups. Ideology critique exposes the operation of ideology in many spheres of education, the working out of vested interests under the mantle of the general good. The task of ideology critique is to uncover the vested interests at work which may be occurring consciously or subliminally, revealing to participants how they may be acting to perpetuate a system which keeps them either empowered or disempowered (Geuss, 1981), i.e. which suppresses a generalizable interest. Explanations for situations might be other than those

---

TABLE 2.1   HABERMAS'S KNOWLEDGE-CONSTITUTIVE INTERESTS AND THE NATURE OF RESEARCH

Interest	Methodology	Characteristics
Technical interest	Scientific testing and proof	Scientific methodology; positivist (e.g. surveys, experiments); hypothesis testing; quantitative.
Practical interest	Hermeneutic; interpretive, understanding	Interactionist; phenomenological; humanistic; ethnographic; existential; anthropological; naturalistic; narratives; qualitative.
Emancipatory interest	Ideology critique	Political agenda, interrogation of power, transformative potential: people gaining control over their own lives; concern for social justice and freedom from oppression and from the suppression of generalizable interests; research to change society and to promote democracy.

'natural', taken-for-granted, explanations that the participants might offer or accept. Situations are not natural but problematic (Carr and Kemmis, 1986). They are the outcomes or processes wherein interests and powers are protected and suppressed, and one task of ideology critique is to expose this (Grundy, 1987). The interests at work are uncovered by ideology critique, which, itself, is premised on reflective practice (Morrison, 1995a, 1995b, 1996a). Habermas (1972: 230) suggests that ideology critique through reflective practice can be addressed in four stages:

Stage 1: a description and interpretation of the existing situation – a hermeneutic exercise that identifies and attempts to make sense of the current situation (echoing the *verstehen* approaches of the interpretive paradigm).

Stage 2: a presentation of the reasons that brought the existing situation to the form that it takes – the causes and purposes of a situation and an evaluation of their legitimacy, involving an analysis of interests and ideologies at work in a situation, their power and legitimacy (both in micro- and macro-sociological terms). Habermas's early work (1972) likens this to psychoanalysis as a means for bringing into the consciousness of 'patients' those repressed, distorted and oppressive conditions, experiences and factors that have prevented them from a full, complete and accurate understanding of their conditions, situations and behaviour, and that, on such exposure and examination, will be liberatory and emancipatory. Critique here reveals to individuals and groups how their views and practices might be ideological distortions that, in their effects, perpetuate a social order or situation that works against their democratic freedoms, interests and empowerment (see also Carr and Kemmis, 1986: 138–9).

Stage 3: an agenda for altering the situation – in order for moves to an egalitarian society to be furthered (the 'transformative paradigm' mentioned earlier).

Stage 4: an evaluation of the achievement of the situation in practice.

In the world of education Habermas's stages are paralleled by Smyth (1989) who, too, denotes a four-stage process: *description* (what am I doing?); *information* (what does it mean?); *confrontation* (how did I come to be like this?); and *reconstruction* (how might I do things differently?). It can be seen that ideology critique here has both a reflective, theoretical and a practical side to it; without reflection it is hollow and without practice it is empty.

As ideology is not mere theory but impacts directly on practice (Eagleton, 1991) there is a strongly prac-

tical methodology implied by critical theory, which articulates with action research (Callawaert, 1999). Action research (discussed in Chapter 18), as its name suggests, is about research that impacts on, and focuses on, practice. In its espousal of practitioner research, for example teachers in schools, participant observers and curriculum developers, action research recognizes the significance of *contexts* for practice – locational, ideological, historical, managerial, social. Furthermore it accords power to those who are operating in those contexts, for they are both the engines of research and of practice. In that sense the claim is made that action research is strongly empowering and emancipatory in that it gives practitioners a 'voice' (Carr and Kemmis, 1986; Grundy, 1987), participation in decision making, and control over their environment and professional lives. Whether the strength of the claims for empowerment are as strong as their proponents would hold is another matter, for action research might be relatively powerless in the face of mandated changes in education. Here action research might be more concerned with intervening in existing practice to ensure that mandated change is addressed efficiently and effectively.

2.2 Criticisms of approaches from critical theory

Morrison (1995a) suggests that critical theory, because it has a practical intent to transform and empower, can – and should – be examined and perhaps tested empirically. For example, critical theory claims to be empowering; that is a testable proposition. Indeed, in a departure from some of his earlier writing, Habermas (1990) acknowledges this; he argues for the need to find 'counter examples' (p. 6), to 'critical testing' (p. 7) and empirical verification (p. 117). He acknowledges that his views have only 'hypothetical status' (p. 32) that need to be checked against specific cases (p. 9). One could suggest, for instance, that the effectiveness of his critical theory can be examined by charting the extent to which equality, freedom, democracy, emancipation, empowerment have been realized by dint of his theory; the extent to which transformative practices have been addressed or occurred as a result of his theory; the extent to which subscribers to his theory have been able to assert their agency; the extent to which his theories have broken down the barriers of instrumental rationality. The operationalization and testing (or empirical investigation) of his theories clearly is a major undertaking, and one which Habermas has not done. In this respect critical theory, a theory that strives to improve practical living, runs the risk of becoming merely contemplative.

There are several criticisms that have been voiced against critical approaches. Morrison (1995a) suggests that there is an artificial separation between Habermas's three interests – they are drawn far more sharply (Hesse, 1982; Bernstein, 1983: 33). For example, one has to bring hermeneutic knowledge to bear on positivist science and vice versa in order to make meaning of each other and in order to judge their own status. Further, the link between ideology critique and emancipation is neither clear nor proven, nor a logical necessity (Morrison, 1995a: 67) – whether a person or society can become emancipated simply by the exercise of ideology critique or action research is an empirical rather than a logical matter (Morrison, 1995a; Wardekker and Miedama, 1997). Indeed one can become emancipated by means other than ideology critique; emancipated societies do not necessarily demonstrate or require an awareness of ideology critique. Moreover it could be argued that the rationalistic appeal of ideology critique actually obstructs action designed to bring about emancipation. Roderick (1986: 65), for example, questions whether the espousal of ideology critique is itself as ideological as the approaches that it proscribes. Habermas, in his allegiance to the view of the social construction of knowledge through 'interests', is inviting the charge of relativism.

Whilst the claim to there being three forms of knowledge has the epistemological attraction of simplicity, one has to question this very simplicity (e.g. Keat, 1981: 67); there are a multitude of interests and ways of understanding the world and it is simply artificial to reduce these to three. Indeed it is unclear whether Habermas, in his three knowledge-constitutive interests, is dealing with a conceptual model, a political analysis, a set of generalities, a set of transhistorical principles, a set of temporally specific observations or a set of loosely defined slogans (Morrison, 1995a: 71) that survive only by dint of their ambiguity (Kolakowsi, 1978). Lakomski (1999) questions the acceptability of the consensus theory of truth on which Habermas's work is premised (pp. 179–82); she argues that Habermas's work is silent on social change, and is little more than speculation, a view echoed by Fendler's (1999) criticism of critical theory as inadequately problematizing subjectivity and ahistoricity.

More fundamental to a critique of this approach is the view that critical theory has a deliberate political agenda, and that the task of the researcher is not to be an ideologue or to have an agenda, but to be dispassionate, disinterested and objective (Morrison, 1995a). Of course, critical theorists would argue that the call for researchers to be ideologically neutral is itself ideologically saturated with laissez-faire values which allow the status quo to be reproduced, i.e. that the call for researchers to be neutral and disinterested is just as value-laden as is the call for them to intrude their own perspectives. The rights of the researcher to move beyond disinterestedness are clearly contentious, though the safeguard here is that the researcher's is only one voice in the community of scholars (Kemmis, 1982). Critical theorists as researchers have been hoisted by their own petard, for if they are to become more than merely negative Jeremiahs and sceptics, berating a particular social order that is dominated by scientism and instrumental rationality (Eagleton, 1991; Wardekker and Miedama, 1997), then they have to generate a positive agenda, but in so doing they are violating the traditional objectivity of researchers. Because their focus is on an ideological agenda, they themselves cannot avoid acting ideologically (Morrison, 1995a).

Claims have been made for the power of action research to empower participants as researchers (e.g. Carr and Kemmis, 1986; Grundy, 1987). This might be over-optimistic in a world in which power is often through statute; the reality of political power seldom extends to teachers. That teachers might be able to exercise some power in schools but that this has little effect on the workings of society at large was caught in Bernstein's (1970) famous comment that 'education cannot compensate for society'. Giving action researchers a small degree of power (to research their own situations) has little effect on the *real* locus of power and decision making, which often lies outside the control of action researchers. Is action research genuinely and full-bloodedly empowering and emancipatory? Where is the evidence?

2.3 Critical theory and curriculum research

For research methods, the tenets of critical theory suggest their own substantive fields of enquiry and their own methods (e.g. ideology critique and action research). Beyond that the contribution to this text on empirical research methods is perhaps limited by the fact that the agenda of critical theory is highly particularistic, prescriptive and, as has been seen, problematical. Though it is an influential paradigm, it is influential in certain fields rather than in others. For example its impact on curriculum research has been far-reaching.

It has been argued for many years that the most satisfactory account of the curriculum is given by a modernist, positivist reading of the development of education and society. This has its curricular expression in Tyler's (1949) famous and influential rationale for the curriculum in terms of four questions:

1 What educational purposes should the school seek to attain?
2 What educational experiences can be provided that are likely to attain these purposes?
3 How can these educational experiences be effectively organized?
4 How can we determine whether these purposes are being attained?

Underlying this rationale is a view that the curriculum is controlled (and controllable), ordered, predetermined, uniform, predictable and largely behaviourist in outcome – all elements of the positivist mentality that critical theory eschews. Tyler's rationale resonates sympathetically with a modernist, scientific, managerialist mentality of society and education that regards ideology and power as unproblematic, indeed it claims the putative political neutrality and objectivity of positivism (Doll, 1993); it ignores the advances in psychology and psychopedagogy made by constructivism.

However, this view has been criticized for precisely these sympathies. Doll (1993) argues that it represents a *closed* system of planning and practice that sits uncomfortably with the notion of education as an *opening* process and with the view of postmodern society as open and diverse, multidimensional, fluid and with power less monolithic and more problematical. This view takes seriously the impact of chaos and complexity theory and derives from them some important features for contemporary curricula. These are incorporated into a view of curricula as being *rich*, *relational*, *recursive* and *rigorous* (Doll, 1993) with an emphasis on *emergence*, *process epistemology* and *constructivist psychology*.

Not all knowledge can be included in the curriculum; the curriculum is a selection of what is deemed to be worthwhile knowledge. The justification for that selection reveals the ideologies and power in decision making in society and through the curriculum. Curriculum is an ideological selection from a range of possible knowledge. This resonates with Habermas's (1972) view that knowledge and its selection is neither neutral nor innocent.

Ideologies can be treated unpejoratively as sets of beliefs or, more sharply, as sets of beliefs emanating from powerful groups in society, designed to protect the interests of the dominant. If curricula are value-based then why is it that some values hold more sway than others? The link between values and power is strong. This theme asks not only *what* knowledge is

important but *whose* knowledge is important in curricula, *what and whose interests* such knowledge serves, and *how* the curriculum and pedagogy serve (or do not serve) differing interests. Knowledge is not neutral (as was the tacit view in modernist curricula). The curriculum is ideologically contestable terrain.

The study of the sociology of knowledge indicates how the powerful might retain their power through curricula and how knowledge and power are legitimated in curricula. The study of the sociology of knowledge suggests that the curriculum should be both subject to ideology critique and itself promote ideology critique in students. A research agenda for critical theorists, then, is how the curriculum perpetuates the societal status quo and how can it (and should it) promote equality in society.

The notion of ideology critique engages the early writings of Habermas (1972), in particular his theory of three knowledge-constitutive interests. His *technical interest* (in control and predictability) resonates with Tyler's model of the curriculum and reveals itself in technicist, instrumentalist and scientist views of curricula that are to be 'delivered' to passive recipients – the curriculum is simply another commodity in a consumer society in which differential cultural capital is inevitable. Habermas's *hermeneutic interest* (in understanding others' perspectives and views) resonates with a *process* view of the curriculum. His *emancipatory interest* (in promoting social emancipation, equality, democracy, freedoms and individual and collective empowerment) requires an exposure of the ideological interests at work in curricula in order that teachers and students can take control of their own lives for the collective, egalitarian good. Habermas's emancipatory interest denotes an inescapably political reading of the curriculum and the purposes of education – the movement away from authoritarianism and elitism and towards social democracy.

Habermas's work underpins and informs much curriculum theory (e.g. Grundy, 1987; Apple, 1990; UNESCO, 1996) and is a useful heuristic device for understanding the motives behind the heavy prescription of curriculum content in, for example, the UK, New Zealand, Hong Kong and France. For instance, one can argue that the National Curriculum of England and Wales is heavy on the technical and hermeneutic interests but very light on the emancipatory interest (Morrison, 1995a), and that this (either deliberately or in its effects) supports – if not contributes to – the reproduction of social inequality. As Bernstein (1971: 47) argues: 'how a society selects, classifies, distributes, transmits and evaluates the educational knowledge it considers to be public, reflects both the distribution of power and the principles of social control'.

Several writers on curriculum theory (e.g. McLaren, 1995; Leistyna *et al.*, 1996) argue that power is a central, defining concept in matters of the curriculum. Here considerable importance is accorded to the political agenda of the curriculum, and the empowerment of individuals and societies is an inescapable consideration in the curriculum. One means of developing student and societal empowerment finds its expression in Habermas's (1972) emancipatory interest and critical pedagogy.

In the field of critical pedagogy the argument is advanced that educators must work with, and on, the lived experience that students bring to the pedagogical encounter rather than imposing a dominatory curriculum that reproduces social inequality. In this enterprise teachers are to transform the experience of domination in students and empower them to become 'emancipated' in a full democracy. Students' everyday experiences of oppression, of being 'silenced', of having their cultures and 'voices' excluded from curricula and decision making are to be examined for the ideological messages that are contained in such acts. Raising awareness of such inequalities is an important step to overcoming them. Teachers and students together move forward in the progress towards 'individual autonomy within a just society' (Masschelein, 1991: 97). In place of centrally prescribed and culturally biased curricula that students simply receive, critical pedagogy regards the curriculum as a form of cultural politics in which *participants in* (rather than *recipients of*) curricula question the cultural and dominatory messages contained in curricula and replace them with a 'language of possibility' and empowering, often community-related curricula. In this way curricula serve the 'socially critical' rather than the culturally and ideologically passive school.

One can discern a utopian and generalized tenor in some of this work, and applying critical theory to education can be criticized for its limited comments on practice. Indeed Miedama and Wardekker (1999: 68) go so far as to suggest that critical pedagogy has had its day, that it was a stillborn child and that critical theory is a philosophy of science without a science (p. 75)! Nevertheless it is an important field for it recognizes and makes much of the fact that curricula and pedagogy are problematical and political.

2.4 Participatory research and critical theory

The call to action in research, particularly in terms of participatory action, and particularly in respect of oppressed, disempowered, underprivileged and exploited groups finds its research voice in terms of participatory research (PR) (e.g. Freire, 1972; Giroux, 1989). Here the groups (e.g. community groups) themselves establish and implement interventions to bring about change, development and improvement to their lives, acting collectively rather than individually.

Participatory research, an instance of critical theory in research, breaks with conventional ways of construing research, as it concerns doing research *with* people and communities rather than doing research *to* or *for* people and communities. It is premised on the view that research can be conducted by everyday people rather than an elite group of researchers; that ordinary people are entirely capable of reflective and critical analysis of their situation (Pinto, 2000: 7). It is profoundly democratic, with all participants as equals; it strives for a participatory rather than a representative democracy (Giroux, 1983, 1989). PR regards power as shared and equalized, rather than as the property of an elite, and the researcher shares his or her humanity with the participants (Tandon, 2005a: 23). In PR, the emphasis is on research for change and development of communities rather than for its own sake, i.e. emphasis is placed on knowledge that is useful in improving lives rather than for the interests and under the control of the academic or the researcher. It is research with a practical intent, for the transformation of lives and communities; it makes the practical more political and the political more practical (cf. Giroux, 1983). As Tandon (2005a: 23) writes: 'the very act of inquiry tends to have some impact on the social system under study'.

Campbell (2002: 20) suggests that participatory research arose in the 1970s, as a reaction to those western researchers and developers who adopted a 'top-down' approach to working with local communities, neglecting and relegating their local knowledge and neglecting their empowerment and improvement. Rather, PR is emancipatory (p. 20), eclectic and, like mixed methods research, adopts whatever research methodology will deliver the results that will enable action and local development to follow. As with mixed methods research and action research, it is pragmatic, and, if necessary, sacrifices 'rigorous control, for the sake of "pragmatic utility"' (Brown, 2005a: 92). PR challenges the conventional distance between researchers and participants; together they work for local development. It has as its focus micro-development rather than macro-development, using knowledge to pursue well-being rather than truth (Tandon, 2005b: ix; Brown, 2005a: 98).

Participatory research respects the indigenous, popular knowledge that resides in members of communities, rather than the relatively antiseptic world and knowledge of the expert researcher. Indeed it is, like Freire's work, itself educative. Local community knowledge is legitimized and re-legitimized in PR (Pinto, 2000: 21), and participants are active and powerful in the research rather than passive subjects. Local people can transform their lives through knowledge and their use of that knowledge; knowledge is power, with local members of the community collectively being active and in control. Researchers are facilitators, catalysts and change agents rather than assuming dominatory or controlling positions (Pinto, 2000: 13). The agenda of PR is empowerment of all and liberation from oppression, exploitation and poverty. Research here promotes both understanding and also change. As one of its proponents, Lewin (1946: 34) wrote: 'if you want truly to understand something, try to change it'. PR blends knowledge and action (Tandon, 2005c: 49).

Participatory research recognizes the centrality of power in research and everyday life, and has an explicit agenda of wresting power from those elites who hold it, and returning it to the grassroots, the communities, the mainstream citizenry. As Pinto (2000: 13) remarks, a core feature that runs right through all stages of PR is the nagging question of 'who controls?'.

Participatory research has as its object the better-ment of communities, societies and groups, often the disempowered, oppressed, impoverished and exploited communities, groups and societies, the poor, the 'have-nots' (Hall, 2005: 10; Tandon, 2005c:50). Its principles concern improvement, group decision-making, the need for research to have a practical outcome that benefits communities and in which participants are agents of their own decisions (Hall, 2005: 10; INCITE, 2010). It starts with problems as experienced in the local communities or workplace, and brings together into an ongoing working relationship both researchers and participants. As Bryceson *et al.* (2005: 183) remark, PR is a 'three-pronged activity: an approach to social investigation with the full and active participation of the community in the entire research process; a means of taking action for development; and an educational process of mobilization for development, all of which are closely interwoven with each other'.

The essence of participatory research, as its name suggests, is participation, the equal control of the research by both participants and researchers and the movement towards change through empowerment. These features enter all stages of the research, from identification of problems to the design of the research, the implementation of the research, the data analysis,

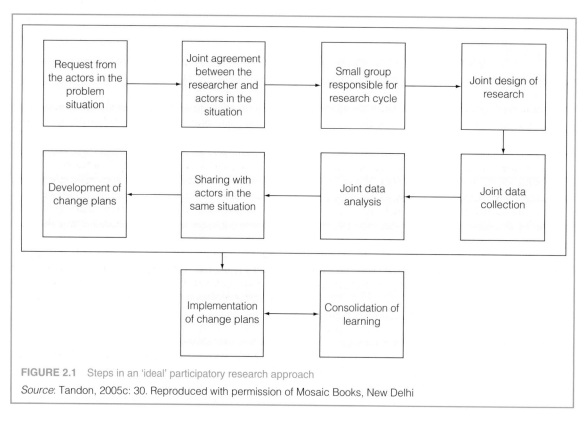

FIGURE 2.1   Steps in an 'ideal' participatory research approach

Source: Tandon, 2005c: 30. Reproduced with permission of Mosaic Books, New Delhi

the reporting, and catalysed changes and developments in the community. Empowerment and development are both the medium and the outcome of the research. Tandon (2005c: 30) sets out a sequence for PR as shown in Figure 2.1.

Whilst conventional approaches to data collection may have their value (e.g. surveys, interviews), too often these are instruments that regard people solely as sources of information rather than as participants in their own community development (Hall, 2005: 13). Indeed Tandon (2005d: 106) reports that, in many cases, surveys are entirely irrelevant to the communities involved in the research, and alternative forms of collecting data have to be used (e.g. dialogue (Tandon, 2005e); enumeration such as census data (though, clearly these are used in conventional research) (Batliwala and Patel, 2005); and popular theatre for consciousness-raising (Khot, 2005)). Hall cites the example of the UNESCO evaluation of the Experimental World Literacy Programme, in which local expertise was neglected, which oversimplified the phenomena under investigation, and disempowered the very communities under review. Such research is alienating rather than empowering. Rather, Hall avers, each should respect, and take seriously, resident knowledge (he gives the example of adult learning).

Hall (2005: 17–19) sets out several principles for participatory research:

1 A research project – both process and results – can be of immediate and direct benefit to a community (as opposed to serving merely as the basis of an academic paper of obscure policy analysis).
2 A research project should involve the community in the entire research project, from the formulation of the problem and the interpretation of the findings to planning corrective action based upon them.
3 The research process should be seen as part of a total educational experience which serves to determine community needs, and to increase awareness of problems and commitment to solutions within the community.
4 Research should be viewed as a dialectic process, a dialogue over time, and not a static picture of reality at one point in time.
5 The object of research, like the object of education, should be the liberation of human creative potential and the mobilization of human resources for the solution of social problems.
6 Research has ideological implications.... First is the re-affirmation of the political nature of all we do.... Research that allows for popular involvement and

increased capacities of analysis will also make conflictual action possible, or necessary.

(Hall, 2005: 17–19)

In participatory research the problem to be investigated originates in, and is defined by, the community or workplace. The members of that community or workplace are involved in the research and have control over it, and the research leads to development and improvement of their lives and communities (Brown and Tandon, 2005: 55). Brown and Tandon (p. 60) recognize the challenge (and likely resistance) that these principles might pose for the powerful, specific dominant interest groups, but they argue that this is unavoidable, as the researcher typically mobilizes community groups to action (p. 61). Hence PR has to consider the likely responses of the researchers, the participants and their possible opponents (p. 62); as Giroux (1983) avers, knowledge is not only powerful, but dangerous, and participants may run substantial risks (Brown and Tandon, 2005: 65) in conducting this type of research, for it upsets existing power structures in society and the workplace.

As can be seen, participatory research has some affinity to action research (INCITE, 2010), though it is intensely more political than action research. It is not without its critics. For example Brown (2005b) argues that participatory action research is ambiguous about:

a its research objectives (e.g. social change, raising awareness, development work, challenging conventional research paradigms);
b the relationships between the researcher and participants (e.g. overemphasizing similarities and neglecting differences between them);
c the methods and technologies that it uses (e.g. being overcritical of conventional approaches which might serve the interests of participatory research, and the lack of a clear method for data collection); and
d the outcomes of participatory research (e.g. what these are, when these are decided, and who decides).

These notwithstanding, however, PR has much to commend it in the everyday sphere of education, and it is a clear instance of the tenets of critical theory, transformative action and empowerment put into practice.

2.5 Feminist research

It is perhaps no mere coincidence that feminist research should surface as a serious issue at the same time as ideology-critical paradigms for research; they are closely connected. Usher (1996), although criticizing

Habermas (p. 124) for his faith in family life as a haven from a heartless, exploitative world, nevertheless sets out several principles of feminist research that resonate with the ideology critique of the Frankfurt School:

1 The acknowledgement of the pervasive influence of gender as a category of analysis and organization.
2 The deconstruction of traditional commitments to truth, objectivity and neutrality.
3 The adoption of an approach to knowledge creation which recognizes that all theories are perspectival.
4 The utilization of a multiplicity of research methods.
5 The interdisciplinary nature of feminist research.
6 Involvement of the researcher and the people being researched.
7 The deconstruction of the theory/practice relationship.

Her suggestions build on earlier recognition of the significance of addressing the 'power issue' in research ('whose research', 'research for whom', 'research in whose interests') and the need to address the emancipatory element of educational research – that research should be empowering to all participants. The paradigm of critical theory questioned the putative objective, neutral, value-free, positivist, 'scientific' paradigm for the splitting of theory and practice and for its reproduction of asymmetries of power (reproducing power differentials in the research community and for treating participants/respondents instrumentally – as objects).

Robson (1993: 64) suggests seven sources of sexism in research:

androcentricity: seeing the world through male eyes and applying male research paradigms to females;
overgeneralization: when a study generalizes from males to females;
gender insensitivity: ignoring sex as a possible variable;
double standards: using male criteria, measures and standards to judge the behaviour of women and vice versa (e.g. in terms of social status);
sex appropriateness: e.g. that child-rearing is women's responsibility;
familism: treating the family, rather than the individual, as the unit of analysis;
sexual dichotomism: treating the sexes as distinct social groups when, in fact, they may share characteristics.

Feminist research, too, challenges the legitimacy of research that does not empower oppressed and otherwise invisible groups – women. Ezzy (2002: 20) writes of the need to replace a traditional masculine picture of science with an emancipatory commitment to knowledge that stems from a feminist perspective, since, 'if women's experience is analyzed using only theories and observations from the standpoint of men, the resulting theories oppress women' (p. 23). Gender, as Ezzy writes (p. 43), is 'a category of experience'.

Positivist research served a given set of power relations, typically empowering the white, male-dominated research community at the expense of other groups whose voices were silenced. Feminist research seeks to demolish and replace this with a different substantive agenda – of empowerment, voice, emancipation, equality and representation for oppressed groups. In doing so, it recognizes the necessity for foregrounding issues of power, silencing and voicing, ideology critique and a questioning of the legitimacy of research that does not emancipate hitherto disempowered groups. In feminist research, women's consciousness of oppression, exploitation and disempowerment becomes a focus for research – the paradigm of ideology critique.

Far from treating educational research as objective and value-free, feminists argue that this is merely a smokescreen that serves the existing, disempowering status quo, and that the subject and value-laden nature of research must be surfaced, exposed and engaged (Haig, 1999: 223). Supposedly value-free, neutral research perpetuates power differentials. Indeed Jayaratne and Stewart (1991) question the traditional, exploitative nature of much research in which the researchers receive all the rewards whilst the participants remain in their – typically powerless – situation, i.e. in which the status quo of oppression, underprivilege and inequality remain undisturbed. As Scott (1985: 80) writes: 'we may simply use other women's experiences to further our own aims and careers'. Creswell (1998: 83), too, suggests that feminist research strives to establish collaborative and non-exploitative relationships. Indeed Scott (1985) questions how ethical it is for a woman researcher to interview those who are less privileged and more exploited than she herself is.

Changing this situation entails taking seriously issues of reflexivity, the effects of the research on the researched and the researchers, the breakdown of the positivist paradigm, and the raising of consciousness of the purposes and effects of the research. Ezzy (2002: 153) writes that 'the personal experience of the researcher is an integral part of the research process', and reinforces the point that objectivity is a false claim by researchers.

Ribbens and Edwards (1997) suggest that it is important to ask how researchers can produce work with reference to theoretical perspectives and formal traditions and requirements of public, academic knowledge whilst still remaining faithful to the experiences and accounts of research participants. Denzin (1989), Mies (1993), Haig (1999) and De Laine (2000) argue for several principles in feminist research:

- the asymmetry of gender relations and representation must be studied reflexively as constituting a fundamental aspect of social life (which includes educational research);
- women's issues, their history, biography and biology, feature as a substantive agenda/focus in research – moving beyond mere perspectival/methodological issues to setting a research agenda;
- the raising of consciousness of oppression, exploitation, empowerment, equality, voice and representation is a methodological tool;
- the acceptability and notion of objectivity and objective research must be challenged;
- the substantive, value-laden dimensions and purposes of feminist research must be paramount;
- research must empower women;
- research need not only be undertaken by academic experts;
- collective research is necessary – women need to collectivize their own individual histories if they are to appropriate these histories for emancipation;
- there is a commitment to revealing core processes and recurring features of women's oppression
- an insistence on the inseparability of theory and practice;
- an insistence on the connections between the private and the public, between the domestic and the political;
- a concern with the construction and reproduction of gender and sexual difference;
- a rejection of narrow disciplinary boundaries;
- a rejection of the artificial subject/researcher dualism;
- a rejection of positivism and objectivity as male mythology;
- the increased use of qualitative, introspective biographical research techniques;
- a recognition of the gendered nature of social research and the development of anti-sexist research strategies;
- a review of the research process as consciousness- and awareness-raising and as fundamentally participatory;
- the primacy of women's personal subjective experience;
- the rejection of hierarchies in social research;
- the vertical, hierarchical relationships of researchers/research community and research objects, in

which the research itself can become an instrument of domination and the reproduction and legitimation of power elites has to be replaced by research that promotes the interests of dominated, oppressed, exploited groups;

- the recognition of equal status and reciprocal relationships between subjects and researchers;
- there is a need to change the status quo, not merely to understand or interpret it;
- the research must be a process of conscientization, not research solely by experts for experts, but to empower oppressed participants.

Indeed Webb *et al.* (2004) set out six principles for a feminist pedagogy in the teaching of research methodology:

1 Reformulation of the professor–student relationship (from hierarchy to equality and sharing).
2 Empowerment (for a participatory democracy).
3 Building community (through collaborative learning).
4 Privileging the individual voice (not only the lecturer's).
5 Respect for diversity of personal experience (rooted, for example, in gender, race, ethnicity, class, sexual preference).
6 Challenging traditional views (e.g. the sociology of knowledge).

Gender shapes research agendas, the choice of topics and foci, the choice of data collection techniques and the relationships between researchers and researched. Several methodological principles flow from a 'rationale' for feminist research (Denzin, 1989; Mies, 1993; Haig, 1997; 1999; De Laine, 2000):

- the replacement of quantitative, positivist, objective research with qualitative, interpretive, ethnographic reflexive research, as objectivity in quantitative research is a smokescreen for masculine interests and agendas;
- collaborative, collectivist research undertaken by collectives – often of women – combining researchers and researched in order to break subject/object and hierarchical, non-reciprocal relationships;
- the appeal to alleged value-free, neutral, indifferent and impartial research has to be replaced by conscious, deliberate partiality – through researchers identifying with participants;
- the use of ideology-critical approaches and paradigms for research;
- the spectator theory or contemplative theory of

knowledge in which researchers research from ivory towers has to be replaced by a participatory approach – perhaps action research – in which all participants (including researchers) engage in the struggle for women's emancipation – a liberatory methodology;

- the need to change the status quo is the starting point for social research – if we want to know something we change it. (Mies (1993) cites the Chinese saying that if you want to know a pear then you must chew it!);
- the extended use of triangulation and multiple methods (including visual techniques such as video, photograph and film);
- the use of linguistic techniques such as conversational analysis;
- the use of textual analysis such as deconstruction of documents and texts about women;
- the use of meta-analysis to synthesize findings from individual studies (see Chapter 17);
- a move away from numerical surveys and a critical evaluation of them, including a critique of question wording.

Edwards and Mauthner (2002: 15, 27) characterize feminist research as that which concerns a critique of dominatory and value-free research, the surfacing and rejection of exploitative power hierarchies between the researcher and the participants, and the espousal of close – even intimate – relationships between the researcher and the researched. Positivist research is rejected as per se oppressive (Gillies and Alldred, 2002: 34) and inherently unable to abide by its own principle of objectivity; it is a flawed epistemology. Research, and its underpinning epistemologies, are rooted in, and inseparable from, interests (Habermas, 1972).

The move is towards 'participatory action research' in which empowerment and emancipation are promoted and which is an involved and collaborative process (e.g. De Laine, 2000: 109ff.). Participation recognizes 'power imbalances and the need to engage oppressed people as agents of their own change' (Ezzy, 2002: 44), whilst action research recognizes the value of 'using research findings to inform intervention decisions' (p. 44). As De Laine (2000: 16) writes: the call is 'for more participation and less observation, of *being with* and *for* the other, not *looking at*', with relations of reciprocity and equality rather than impersonality, exploitation and power/status differentials between researcher and participants.

The relationship between the researcher and participant, De Laine (2000) argues, must break a conventional patriarchy. The emphasis is on partnerships between researchers and participants (p. 107), to the extent that researchers are, themselves participants rather than outsiders and the participants shape the research process as co-researchers (p. 107), defining the problem, the methods, the data collection and analysis, interpretation and dissemination. The relationship between researchers and participants is one of equality, and outsider, objective, distant, positivist research relations are off the agenda; researchers are inextricably bound up in the lives of those they research. That this may bring difficulties in participant and researcher reactivity is a matter to be engaged in rather than built out of the research.

Thapar-Björkert and Henry (2004) argue that the conventional, one-sided and unidirectional view of the researcher as powerful and the research participants as less powerful, with the researcher exploiting and manipulating the researched, could be a construction by western white researchers. They report research that indicates that power is exercised by the researched as well as the researchers, and is a much more fluid, shifting and negotiated matter than conventionally suggested, being dispersed through both the researcher and the researched. Indeed they show how the research participants can, and do, exercise considerable power over the researchers, both before, during and after the research process. They provide a fascinating example of interviewing women in their homes in India, where, far from the home being a location of oppression, was a site of their power and control.

With regard to methods of data collection, Oakley (1981) suggests that 'interviewing women' in the standardized, impersonal style which expects a response to a prescribed agenda and set of questions may be a 'contradiction in terms', as it implies an exploitative relationship. Rather, the subject/object relationship should be replaced by a guided dialogue. She criticizes the conventional notion of 'rapport' in conducting interviews (p. 35), arguing that they are instrumental, non-reciprocal and hierarchical, all of which are masculine traits. Rapport in this sense, she argues, is not genuine in that the researcher is using it for scientific rather than human ends (p. 55). Here researchers are 'faking friendship' for their own ends (Duncombe and Jessop, 2002: 108), equating 'doing rapport' with trust, and, thereby, operating a very 'detached' form of friendship (p. 110). Similarly Thapar-Björkert and Henry (2004) suggest that attempts at friendship between researchers and participants are disingenuous, with 'purported solidarity' being a fraud perpetrated by well-intentioned feminists.

Duncombe and Jessop (2002: 111) ask a very searching question when they query whether, if interviewees are persuaded to take part in an interview by virtue of the researcher's demonstration of empathy and 'rapport', this is really given informed consent. They suggest that informed consent, particularly in exploratory interviews, has to be continually renegotiated and care has to be taken by the interviewer not to be too intrusive. Personal testimonies, oral narratives and long interviews also figure highly in feminist approaches (De Laine, 2000: 110; Thapar-Björkert and Henry, 2004), not least in those that touch on sensitive issues. These, it is argued (Ezzy, 2002: 45), enable women's voices to be heard, to be close to lived experiences and avoid unwarranted assumptions about people's experiences.

The drive towards collective, egalitarian and emancipatory qualitative research is seen as necessary if women are to avoid colluding in their own oppression by undertaking positivist, uninvolved, dispassionate, objective research. Mies (1993: 67) argues that for women to undertake this latter form of research puts them into a schizophrenic position of having to adopt methods which contribute to their own subjugation and repression by ignoring their experience (however vicarious) of oppression and by forcing them to abide by the 'rules of the game' of the competitive, male-dominated academic world. In this view, argue Roman and Apple (1990: 59), it is not enough for women simply to embrace ethnographic forms of research, as this does not necessarily challenge the existing and constituting forces of oppression or asymmetries of power. Ethnographic research, they argue, has to be accompanied by ideology critique, indeed they argue that the transformative, empowering, emancipatory potential of research is a critical standard for evaluating that piece of research.

This latter point resonates with the call by Lather (1991) for researchers to be concerned with the political consequences of their research (e.g. consequential validity), not only the conduct of the research and data analysis itself. Research must lead to change and improvement, particularly, in this context, for women (Gillies and Alldred, 2002: 32). Research is a political activity with a political agenda (Gillies and Alldred, 2002: 33; see also Lather, 1991). Research and action – praxis – must combine: 'knowledge *for*' as well as 'knowledge *what*' (Ezzy, 2002: 47). As Marx reminds us in his *Theses on Feuerbach*: 'the philosophers have only interpreted the world, in various ways; the point, however, is to change it'. Gillies and Alldred (2002: 45), however, point out that 'many feminists have agonized over whether politicizing participants is necessarily helpful', as it raises awareness of constraints on their actions without being able to offer solutions or to challenge their structural causes. Research, thus politicized but unable to change conditions, may actually be disempowering and, indeed, patronizing in its simplistic call for enlightenment and emancipation. It could render women more vulnerable than before. Emancipation is a struggle.

Several of these views of feminist research and methodology are contested by other feminist researchers. For example Jayaratne (1993: 109) argues for 'fitness for purpose', suggesting that exclusive focus on qualitative methodologies might not be appropriate either for the research purposes or, indeed, for advancing the feminist agenda (see also Scott, 1985: 82–3). Jayaratne refutes the argument that quantitative methods are unsuitable for feminists because they neglect the emotions of the people under study. Indeed she argues for beating quantitative research on its own grounds (p. 121), suggesting the need for feminist quantitative data and methodologies in order to counter sexist quantitative data in the social sciences. She suggests that feminist researchers can accomplish this without 'selling out' to the positivist, male-dominated academic research community. Indeed Oakley (1998) suggests that the separation of women from quantitative methodology may have the unintended effect of perpetuating women as the 'other', and, thereby, discriminating against them, and Finch (2004) argues that, whilst qualitative research might have helped to establish the early feminist movement, it is important to recognize the place of both quantitative and qualitative methods to be the stuff of feminist research.

De Laine (2000: 112) argues that shifting from quantitative to qualitative techniques may not solve many ethical problems in research, as these are endemic in any form of fieldwork. She argues that some feminist researchers may not wish to seek either less participation or more detachment, and that more detachment and less participation are not solutions to ethical dilemmas and 'morally responsible fieldwork' as these, too, bring their own ethical dilemmas, e.g. the risk of threat. She reports work (p. 113) that suggests that close relationships between researchers and participants may be construed as just as exploitative, if more disguised, as conventional researcher roles, and that they may bring considerable problems if data that were revealed in an intimate account between friends (researcher and participant) are then used in public research. The researcher is caught in a dilemma: if she is a true friend then this imposes constraints on the researcher, and yet if she is only pretending to be a friend, or limiting that friendship, then this provokes questions of honesty and personal integrity. Are research friendships real, ephemeral or impression management used to gather data?

De Laine (2000: 115) suggests that it may be misguided to privilege qualitative research for its claim to non-exploitative relationships. Whilst she acknowledges that quantitative approaches may perpetuate power differentials and exploitation, there is no guarantee that qualitative research will not do the same, only in a more disguised way. Qualitative approaches too, she suggests, can create and perpetuate unequal relations, not least simply because the researcher is in the field qua researcher rather than a friend; if it were not for the research then the researcher would not be present. Stacey (1988) suggests that the intimacy advocated for feminist ethnography may render exploitative relationships *more* rather than *less* likely. We refer readers to Chapter 9 on sensitive educational research for a further discussion of these issues.

Gillies and Alldred (2002: 43–6) suggest that action research, an area strongly supported in some quarters of feminist researchers, is, itself, problematic. It risks being an intervention in people's lives (i.e. a potential abuse of power), and the researcher typically plays a significant, if not central, role in initiating, facilitating, crystallizing and developing the meanings involved in, or stemming from, the research, i.e. the researcher is the one exercising power and influence.

Ezzy (2002: 44) reports that, just as there is no single feminist methodology, both quantitative and qualitative methods are entirely legitimate. Indeed, Kelly (1978) argues that a feminist commitment should enter research at the stages of formulating the research topic and interpreting the results, but it should be left out during the stages of data collection and conduct of the research.

Thapar-Björkert and Henry (2004) indicate that the researcher being an outsider might bring more advantages than if she were an insider. For example, being a white female researching non-white females may not be a handicap, as many non-white women might disclose information to white women that they would not disclose to a non-white person. Similarly, having interviewers and interviewees of the same racial and ethnic background does not mean that non-hierarchical relationships will still not be present. They also report that the categories of 'insider' and 'outsider' were much more fuzzy than exclusive. Researchers are both 'subject' and 'object', and those being researched are both 'observed' and 'observers'.

De Laine (2000: 110) suggests that there is a division amongst feminists between those who advocate closeness in relationships between researchers and subjects – a human researching fellow humans – and those who advocate 'respectful distance' between researchers and those being studied. Close relationships may turn into quasi-therapeutic situations rather than research (Duncombe and Jessop, 2002: 111), yet it may be important to establish closeness in reaching deeper issues. Further, one has to question how far close relationships lead to reciprocal and mutual disclosure (Duncombe and Jessop, 2002: 120). The debate is open: should the researcher share, be close and be prepared for more intimate social relations – a 'feminist ethic of care' (p. 111) – or keep those cool, outsider relations which might objectify those being researched? It is a moral as well as a methodological matter.

The issue runs deep: the suggestion is that emotions and feelings are integral to the research, rather than to be built out of the research in the interests of objectivity (Edwards and Mauthner, 2002: 19). Emotions should not be seen as disruptive of research or as irrelevant (De Laine, 2000: 151–2), but central to it, just as they are central to human life. Indeed emotional responses are essential in establishing the veracity of enquiries and data, and the 'feminist communitarian model' which De Laine (2002: 212–13) outlines values connectedness at several levels: emotions, emotionality and personal expressiveness, empathy. The egalitarian feminism that De Laine (2000) and others advocate suggests a community of insiders in the same culture, in which empathy, reciprocity and egalitarianism are hallmarks (p. 108).

Swantz (1996: 134) argues that there may be some self-deception by the researcher in adopting a dual role as a researcher and one who shares the situation and interests of the participants. She questions the extent to which the researcher may be able to be genuinely involved with the participants in other that a peripheral way and whether, simply because the researcher may have 'superior knowledge', a covert power differential may exist. De Laine (2000: 114) suggests that such superior knowledge may stem from the researcher's own background in anthropology or ethnography, or simply more education. The primary purpose of the researcher is research, and that is different from the primary purpose of the participants.

Further, the researcher's desire for identification and solidarity with her research subjects may be pious but unrealistic optimism, not least because she may not share the same race, ethnicity, background, life chances, experiences or colour as those being researched. Indeed Gillies and Alldred (2002: 39–40) raise the question of how far researchers can, or should, try to represent groups to which they themselves do not belong, not least those groups without power or voice, as this, itself, is a form of colonization and oppression.

Affinity, they argue (p. 40), is no authoritative basis for representative research. Even the notion of affinity becomes suspect when it overlooks, or underplays, the significance of difference, thereby homogenizing groups and their particular experiences. In response to this, some feminist researchers (p. 40) suggest that researchers only have the warrant to confine themselves to their own immediate communities, though this is a contentious issue. There is value in speaking for others, not least for those who are silenced and marginalized, and in not speaking for others for fear of oppression and colonization. One has to question the acceptability and appropriateness of, and fidelity to, the feminist ethic, if one represents and uses others' stories (p. 41).

An example of a feminist approach to research is the Girls Into Science and Technology (GIST) action research project. This took place over three years, involving 2,000 students and their teachers in ten co-educational, comprehensive schools in one area of the UK, eight schools serving as the bases of the 'action', the remaining two acting as 'controls'. Several publications have documented the methodologies and findings of the GIST study (Whyte, 1986; Kelly, 1986, 1989a, 1989b; Kelly and Smail, 1986), described by its co-director as 'simultaneous-integrated action research' (Kelly, 1987) (i.e. integrating action and research). Kelly is open about the feminist orientation of the GIST project team, seeking deliberately to change girls' option choices and career aspirations, because the researchers saw that girls were disadvantaged by traditional sex-stereotypes. The researchers' actions, she suggests, were a small attempt to ameliorate women's subordinate social position (Kelly, 1987).

2.6 A note on post-colonial theory and queer theory

Under the umbrella of critical theory also fall post-colonial theory, queer theory and critical race theory. Whilst this chapter does not unpack these, it notes them as avenues which educational researchers may wish to explore. For example, post-colonial theory, as its name suggests, with an affinity to postmodernism, addresses the experiences (often through film, literature, cultural studies, political and social sciences) of post-colonial

societies and the cultural legacies of colonialism. It examines the after-effects, or continuation, of ideologies and discourses of imperialism, domination and repression, value systems (e.g. the domination of western values and the delegitimization of non-western values), their effects on the daily lived experiences of participants, i.e. their materiality, and the regard in which peoples in post-colonial societies are held (e.g. Said's (1978) ground-breaking work on orientalism and the casting down of non-western groups as the 'other'). It also discusses the valorization of multiple voices and heterogeneity in post-colonial societies, the resistance to marginalization of groups within them (Babha, 1994: 113) and the construction of identities in a post-colonial world.

Queer theory builds on, but moves beyond, feminist theory and gay/lesbian studies to explore the social construction and privileging or denial of identities, sexual behaviour, deviant behaviour and the categorizations and ideologies involved in such constructions. As Halperin (1997: 62) writes, queer theory 'acquires its meaning from its oppositional relation to the norm. Queer is by definition whatever is at odds with the normal, the legitimate, the dominant. There is nothing in particular to which it necessarily refers. It is an identity without an essence. "Queer" then, demarcates not a positivity but a positionality vis-à-vis the normative.' The task of queer theory, then, is to explore, problematize and interrogate gender, sexuality and also their mediation by other characteristics or forms of oppression, e.g. social class, ethnicity, colour, disability. It rejects simplistic categorization of individuals, and argues for the respect of their individuality and uniqueness.

2.7 A summary of three major paradigms

The two chapters have discussed very different approaches to educational research, that rest on quantitative, qualitative and critical theoretical foundation, or a combination of these. Table 2.2 summarizes some of the broad differences between the three approaches that we have considered so far.

We present the paradigms and their affiliates in Figure 2.2.

TABLE 2.2   DIFFERING APPROACHES TO THE STUDY OF BEHAVIOUR

Normative	Interpretive	Complexity theoretical	Critical
Society and the social system	The individual	Wholes, groups, systems and the individuals within them	Societies, groups and individuals
Medium/large-scale research	Small-scale research	Micro- and macro-scale research	Small-scale research
Impersonal, anonymous forces regulating behaviour	Human actions continuously recreating social life	Individuals and their environments constantly and dynamically interact to produce new, emergent systems and behaviours through self-organization, connectedness and feedback	Political, ideological factors, power and interests shaping behaviour
Model of natural sciences	Non-statistical	Action research, case study and narrative research	Ideology critique, action research and critical ethnography
Quantitative, objective	Qualitative, subjective	Quantitative, qualitative, objective and subjective, algorithmic	Ideology critique, participatory, objective and subjective
Positivist and scientific	Hermeneutic and interpretive	Systems-driven, social network driven	Ideology critical
Linear causality	Multiple directions of causality	Multiple directions of causality	Main trends of causality
Reductionist and atomistic	Phenomenologists, symbolic interactionists, ethnomethodologists	Holistic understanding of emergent conditions and systems	Change and emancipation
Research conducted 'from the outside'	Insider and outsider research	Non-reductionist	Interpretive, macro- and micro-concepts: political and ideological interests, operations of power
Outsider research	Personal involvement of the researcher	Objective analysis of systems	Critical theorists, action researchers, practitioner researchers
Generalizing from the specific	Interpreting the specific	Understanding wholes	Collectivity
Explaining behaviour/seeking causes	Understanding actions/meanings rather than causes	Understanding causal interactions	Participant researchers, researchers and facilitators
Assuming the taken-for-granted	Investigating the taken-for-granted	Investigating emergent systems	Critiquing the specific
Macro-concepts: society, institutions, norms, positions, roles, expectations	Micro-concepts: individual perspective, personal constructs, negotiated meanings, definitions of situations	Micro- and macro-level analysis informing each other	Understanding, interrogating, critiquing, transforming actions and interests
Structuralists	Hermeneutic	Explaining and observing, iterative	Interrogating, critiquing and changing the taken-for-granted
Prediction and control	Understanding and explanation	Understanding emergence of complex adaptive systems	Transformation and praxis
Technical interest	Practical interest	Technical and practical interest	Emancipatory interest

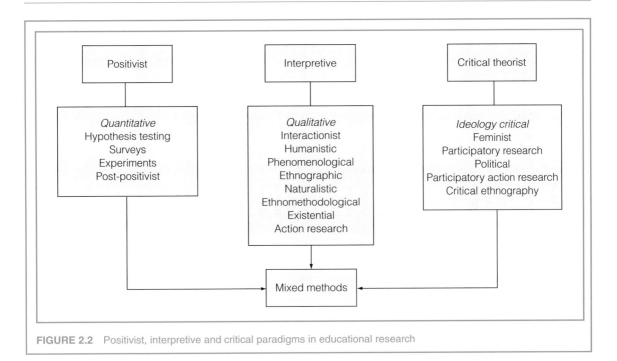

FIGURE 2.2 Positivist, interpretive and critical paradigms in educational research

 Companion Website

The companion website to the book includes PowerPoint slides for this chapter, which list the structure of the chapter and then provide a summary of the key points in each of its sections. This resource can be found online at **www.routledge.com/textbooks/cohen7e**.

CHAPTER 3

Evaluation and the politics of educational research

This brief chapter confines itself to indicating some of the key similarities and differences between research and evaluation. The chapter sets out:

■ similarities between research and evaluation
■ differences between research and evaluation
■ connections between evaluation, politics and policy making

The chapter is deliberately of an introductory nature only, providing an overview rather than the extended analysis of the opening chapter. This is because many of the points concerning research and evaluation overlap, e.g. their methodologies, ethical issues, sampling, reliability and validity, instrumentation, data analysis.

3.1 Research and evaluation

The chapter introduces only the conceptual and political similarities and differences between research and evaluation, as many of their operational procedures are similar.

Key differences lie in their audiences (evaluations are often commissioned and they become the property of the sponsors and not for the public domain), scope (evaluations often have a more limited scope), purposes (e.g. to judge), setting of the agenda (the evaluator works within a given brief), uses to which the results are put (e.g. the evaluation might be used to increase or withhold resources), ownership of the data (the evaluator often cedes ownership to the sponsor, upon completion), policy orientation, control of the project (e.g. the sponsor can sponsor but not control the independence of the evaluator), power (the evaluator may have the power to control the operation of the project but not the brief), and the politics of the situation (e.g. the evaluator may be unable to stand outside the politics of the purposes and uses of, or participants in, an evaluation).

As mentioned in the previous chapter, research and politics are inextricably bound together. This can be taken further, as researchers in education will be advised to pay serious consideration to the politics of their research enterprise and the ways in which politics can steer research. For example one can detect a trend in educational research towards more evaluative research, where, for instance, a researcher's task is to evaluate the effectiveness (often of the implementation) of given policies and projects. This is particularly true in the case of 'categorically funded' and commissioned research – research which is funded by policy makers (e.g. governments, fund-awarding bodies) under any number of different headings that those policy makers devise (Burgess, 1993). On the one hand this is laudable, for it targets research directly towards policy; on the other hand it is dangerous in that it enables others to set the research agenda. Research ceases to become open-ended, pure research, and, instead, becomes the evaluation of *given* initiatives. Less politically charged, much research is evaluative, and indeed there are many similarities between research and evaluation. The two overlap but possess important differences.

The problem of trying to identify differences between evaluation and research is compounded because not only do they share several of the same methodological characteristics but one branch of research is called *evaluative research* or *applied research*.[1] This is often kept separate from 'blue skies' research in that the latter is open-ended, exploratory, contributes something original to the substantive field and extends the frontiers of knowledge and theory whereas in the former the theory is *given* rather than *interrogated* or *tested*. As Plewis and Mason (2005: 192) suggest, evaluation research is, at heart, applied research that uses the tools of research in the social sciences to provide answers to the effectiveness and effects of programmes. One can detect many similarities between the two in that they both use methodologies and methods of social science research generally, covering, for example:

■ the need to clarify the *purposes* of the investigation;
■ the need to *operationalize* purposes and areas of investigation;
■ the need to address principles of *research* design that include:

a formulating *operational questions*;
b deciding appropriate *methodologies*;
c deciding which *instruments* to use for data collection;
d deciding on the *sample* for the investigation;
e addressing *reliability* and *validity* in the investigation and instrumentation;
f addressing *ethical* issues in conducting the investigation;
g deciding on *data analysis* techniques;
h deciding on *reporting* and *interpreting* results.

Indeed Norris (1990: 97) argues that evaluation applies research methods to shed light on a problem of action; he suggests that evaluation can be viewed as an extension of research, because it shares its methodologies and methods, and because evaluators and researchers possess similar skills in conducting investigations. In many senses the eight features outlined above embrace many elements of the *scientific method*, which Smith and Glass (1987) set out thus:

Step 1: a *theory* about the phenomenon exists;
Step 2: a *research problem* within the theory is detected and a *research question* is devised;
Step 3: a *research hypothesis* is deduced (often about the relationship between constructs);
Step 4: a *research design* is developed, *operationalizing* the research question and stating the *null hypothesis*;
Step 5: the research is conducted;
Step 6: the null hypothesis is tested based on the data gathered;
Step 7: the original theory is revised or supported based on the results of the hypothesis testing.

Indeed, if steps 1 and 7 were removed then there would be nothing to distinguish between research and evaluation. Both researchers and evaluators pose questions and hypotheses, select samples, manipulate and measure variables, compute statistics and data, and state conclusions. Nevertheless there are important differences between evaluation and research that are not always obvious simply by looking at publications. Publications do not always make clear the background events that gave rise to the investigation, nor do they always make clear the uses of the material that they report, nor do they always make clear what the dissemination rights (Sanday, 1993) are and who holds them. Several commentators set out some of the differences between evaluation and research. For example Smith and Glass (1987) offer eight main differences:

1 *The intents and purposes of the investigation* – the researcher wants to advance the frontiers of knowledge of phenomena, to contribute to theory and to be able to make generalizations; the evaluator is less interested in contributing to theory or general body of knowledge. Evaluation is more parochial than universal (pp. 33–4).
2 *The scope of the investigation* – evaluation studies tend to be more comprehensive than research in the number and variety of aspects of a programme that are being studied (p. 34).
3 *Values in the investigation* – research aspires to value neutrality, evaluations must represent multiple sets of values and include data on these values.
4 *The origins of the study* – research has its origins and motivation in the researcher's curiosity and desire to know (p. 34). The researcher is answerable to colleagues and scientists (i.e. the research community) whereas the evaluator is answerable to the 'client'. The researcher is autonomous whereas the evaluator is answerable to clients and stakeholders. The researcher is motivated by a search for knowledge, the evaluator is motivated by the need to solve problems, allocate resources and make decisions. Research studies are public, evaluations are for a restricted audience.
5 *The uses of the study* – the research is used to further knowledge, evaluations are used to inform decisions.
6 *The timeliness of the study* – evaluations must be timely, research need not be. Evaluators' timescales are given, researchers' timescales need not be given.
7 *Criteria for judging the study* – evaluations are judged by the criteria of utility and credibility, research is judged methodologically and by the contribution that it makes to the field (i.e. internal and external validity).
8 *The agendas of the study* – an evaluator's agenda is given, a researcher's agenda is her own.

Norris (1990) reports an earlier piece of work by Glass and Worthen in which they identified eleven main differences between evaluation and research:

1 *The motivation of the enquirer* – research is pursued largely to satisfy curiosity, evaluation is undertaken to contribute to the solution of a problem.
2 *The objectives of the search* – research and evaluation seek different ends. Research seeks conclusions, evaluation leads to decisions.
3 *Laws versus description* – research is the quest for laws (nomothetic), evaluation merely seeks to describe a particular thing (idiographic).

4 *The role of explanation* – proper and useful evaluation can be conducted without producing an explanation of why the product or project is good or bad or of how it operates to produce its effects.

5 *The autonomy of the enquiry* – evaluation is undertaken at the behest of a client, while researchers set their own problems.

6 *Properties of the phenomena that are assessed* – evaluation seeks to assess social utility directly, research may yield evidence of social utility but often only indirectly.

7 *Universality of the phenomena studied* – researchers work with constructs having a currency and scope of application that make the objects of evaluation seem parochial by comparison.

8 *Salience of the value question* – in evaluation value questions are central and usually determine what information is sought.

9 *Investigative techniques* – while there may be legitimate differences between research and evaluation methods, there are far more similarities than differences with regard to techniques and procedures for judging validity.

10 *Criteria for assessing the activity* – the two most important criteria for judging the adequacy of research are internal and external validity, for evaluation they are utility and credibility.

11 *Disciplinary base* – the researcher can afford to pursue enquiry within one discipline and the evaluator cannot.

A clue to some of the differences between evaluation and research can be seen in the definition of evaluation. Most definitions of evaluation include reference to several key features: (1) answering specific, given questions; (2) gathering information; (3) making judgements; (4) taking decisions; (5) addressing the politics of a situation (Morrison, 1993: 2). Morrison provides one definition of evaluation as: *the provision of information about specified issues upon which judgements are based and from which decisions for action are taken* (1993: 2). This view echoes MacDonald in his comments that the evaluator:

is faced with competing interest groups, with divergent definitions of the situation and conflicting informational needs.... He has to decide which decision makers he will serve, what information will be of most use, when it is needed and how it can be obtained.... The resolution of these issues commits the evaluator to a political stance, an attitude to the government of education. No such commitment is required of the researcher. He stands outside the

political process, and values his detachment from it. For him the production of new knowledge and its social use are separated. The evaluator is embroiled in the action, built into a political process which concerns the distribution of power, i.e. the allocation of resources and the determination of goals, roles and tasks.... When evaluation data influences power relationships the evaluator is compelled to weight carefully the consequences of his task specification.... The researcher is free to select his questions, and to seek answers to them. The evaluator, on the other hand, must never fall into the error of answering questions which no one but he is asking

(MacDonald, 1987: 42)

MacDonald argues that evaluation is an inherently political enterprise. His much-used threefold typology of evaluations as autocratic, bureaucratic and democratic is premised on a political reading of evaluation (see also Chelinsky and Mulhauser (1993) who refer to 'the inescapability of politics' (p. 54) in the world of evaluation). MacDonald (1987), noting that 'educational research is becoming more evaluative in character' (p. 101), argues for research to be kept out of politics and for evaluation to square up to the political issues at stake:

The danger therefore of conceptualizing evaluation as a branch of research is that evaluators become trapped in the restrictive tentacles of research respectability. Purity may be substituted for utility, trivial proofs for clumsy attempts to grasp complex significance. How much more productive it would be to define research as a branch of evaluation, a branch whose task it is to solve the technological problems encountered by the evaluator.

(MacDonald, 1987: 43)

However, the truth of the matter is far more blurred than these distinctions suggest. Two principle causes of this blurring lie in the *funding* and the *politics* of both evaluation and research. For example, the view of research as uncontaminated by everyday life is naive and simplistic; Norris (1990: 99) argues that such an antiseptic view of research ignores the social context of educational research, some of which is located in the hierarchies of universities and research communities and the funding support provided for some research projects but not all is by governments. His point has a pedigree that reaches back to Kuhn (1962), and is commenting on the politics of research funding and research utilization. For over two decades one can detect a huge rise in 'categorical' funding of projects, i.e. defined, *given* projects (often by government or research sponsors) for which bids have to be placed. This may seem unsurprising if one is discussing research grants by government bodies, which are deliberately policy-oriented, though one can also detect in projects that have been granted by non-governmental organizations (e.g. the Economic and Social Research Council in the UK) a move towards sponsoring policy-oriented projects rather than the 'blue skies' research mentioned earlier. Indeed Burgess (1993: 1) argues that 'researchers are little more than contract workers ... research in education must become policy relevant ... research must come closer to the requirement of practitioners'.

This view is reinforced by several articles in the collection edited by Anderson and Biddle (1991) which show that research and politics go together uncomfortably because researchers have different agendas and longer timescales than politicians and try to address the complexity of situations, whereas politicians, anxious for short-term survival want telescoped timescales, simple remedies and research that will be consonant with their political agendas. Indeed James (1993) argues that

> the power of research-based evaluation to provide evidence on which rational decisions can be expected to be made is quite limited. Policy-makers will always find reasons to ignore, or be highly selective of, evaluation findings if the information does not support the particular political agenda operating at the time when decisions have to be made.
>
> (James, 1993: 135)

The politicization of research has resulted in funding bodies awarding research grants for categorical research that specify timescales and the terms of reference. Burgess's view also points to the constraints under which research is undertaken; if it is not concerned with policy issues then research tends not to be funded. One could support Burgess's view that research must have some impact on policy making.

Not only is *research* becoming a political issue, but this extends to the use being made of *evaluation* studies. It was argued above that evaluations are designed to provide useful data to inform decision making. However, as evaluation has become more politicized so its uses (or non-uses) have become more politicized. Indeed Norris (1990) shows how politics frequently overrides evaluation or research evidence. He writes (p. 135) that the announcement of the decision to extend the Technical and Vocational Education Initiation (TVEI) project in the UK was made without any evaluation reports having been received

from evaluation teams in Leeds or the National Foundation for Educational Research. This echoes James (1993) where she writes:

> The classic definition of the role of evaluation as providing information for decision makers ... is a fiction if this is taken to mean that policy-makers who commission evaluations are expected to make rational decisions based on the best (valid and reliable) information available to them.
>
> (James, 1993: 119)

Where evaluations are commissioned and have heavily political implications, Stronach and Morris (1994) argue that the response to this is that evaluations become more 'conformative', possessing several characteristics:

1 Short-term, taking project goals as given, and supporting their realization.
2 Ignoring the evaluation of longer-term learning outcomes, or anticipated economic/social consequences of the programme.
3 Giving undue weight to the perceptions of programme participants who are responsible for the successful development and implementation of the programme; as a result, tending to 'over-report' change.
4 Neglecting and 'under-reporting' the views of classroom practitioners, and programme critics.
5 Adopting an atheoretical approach, and generally regarding the aggregation of opinion as the determination of overall significance.
6 Involving a tight contractual relationship with the programme sponsors that either disbars public reporting, or encourages self-censorship in order to protect future funding prospects.
7 Undertaking various forms of implicit advocacy for the programme in its reporting style.
8 Creating and reinforcing a professional schizophrenia in the research and evaluation community, whereby individuals come to hold divergent public and private opinions, or offer criticisms in general rather than in particular, or quietly develop 'academic' critiques which are at variance with their contractual evaluation activities, alternating between 'critical' and 'conformative' selves.

The argument so far has been confined to large-scale projects that are influenced by and may or may not influence political decision making. However the argument need not remain there. Morrison (1993), for example, indicates how evaluations might influence the 'micro-politics of the school'. Hoyle (1986), for example, asks whether evaluation data are used to bring resources into, or take resources out of, a department or faculty. In this respect the evaluator may have to choose carefully his or her affinities and allegiances (Barton, 2002), as the outcomes and consequences of the evaluation may call these into question. He writes that, although the evaluator may wish to remain passive and apolitical, in reality this view is not shared by those who commission the evaluation or the reality of the situation, not least when the evaluation data are used in ways that distort the data or use them selectively to justify different options (p. 377).

The issue does not relate only to evaluations, for school-based research, far from the emancipatory claims for it made by action researchers (e.g. Carr and Kemmis, 1986; Grundy, 1987), is often concerned more with finding out the most successful ways of organization, planning, teaching and assessment of a *given agenda* rather *than setting agendas* and following one's own research agendas. This is *problem-solving* rather than *problem-setting*. That evaluation and research are being drawn together by politics at both a macro- and micro-level is evidence of a growing interventionism by politics into education, thus reinforcing the hegemony of the government in power. Several points have been made here:

- there is considerable overlap between evaluation and research;
- there are some conceptual differences between evaluation and research, though, in practice, there is considerable blurring of the edges of the differences between the two;
- the funding and control of research and research agendas reflect the persuasions of political decision makers;
- evaluative research has increased in response to categorical funding of research projects;
- the attention being given to, and utilization of, evaluation varies according to the consonance between the findings and their political attractiveness to political decision makers.

In this sense the views expressed earlier by MacDonald (1987) are now little more than a historical relic; there is very considerable blurring of the edges between evaluation and research because of the political intrusion into, and use of, these two types of study. One response to this can be seen in Burgess's (1993) view that a researcher needs to be able to meet the sponsor's requirements for evaluation whilst also generating research data (engaging the issues of the need to nego-

tiate ownership of the data and intellectual property rights).

3.2 Research, politics and policy making

The preceding discussion has suggested that there is an inescapable political dimension to educational research, both in the macro- and micro-political senses. In the macro-political sense this manifests itself in funding arrangements, where awards are made provided that the research is 'policy-related' (Burgess, 1993) – guiding policy decisions, improving quality in areas of concern identified by policy makers, facilitating the implementation of policy decisions, evaluating the effects of the implementation of policy. Burgess notes a shift here from a situation where the researcher specifies the topic of research and towards the sponsor specifying the focus of research. The issue of sponsoring research reaches beyond simply commissioning research towards the dissemination (or not) of research – who will receive or have access to the findings and how the findings will be used and reported. This, in turn, raises the fundamental issue of who owns and controls data, and who controls the release of research findings. Unfavourable reports might be withheld for a time, suppressed or selectively released. Research can be brought into the service of wider educational purposes – the politics of a local education authority, or indeed the politics of government agencies.

Though research and politics intertwine, the relationships between educational research, politics and policy making are complex because research designs strive to address a complex social reality (Anderson and Biddle, 1991); a piece of research does not feed simplistically or directly into a specific piece of policy making. Rather, research generates a range of different types of knowledge – concepts, propositions, explanations, theories, strategies, evidence, methodologies (Caplan, 1991). These feed subtly and often indirectly into the decision-making process, providing, for example, direct inputs, general guidance, a scientific gloss, orienting perspectives, generalizations and new insights. Basic and applied research have significant parts to play in this process.

The degree of influence exerted by research depends on careful dissemination: too little and its message is ignored; too much and data overload confounds decision makers and makes them cynical – the syndrome of the boy who cried wolf (Knott and Wildavsky, 1991). Hence researchers must give care to utilization by policy makers (Weiss, 1991a), reduce jargon, provide summaries and improve links between the two cultures of researchers and policy makers (Cook, 1991) and, further, to the educational community. Researchers must cultivate ways of influencing policy, particularly when policy makers can simply ignore research findings, commission their own research (Cohen and Garet, 1991) or underfund research into social problems (Coleman, 1991; Thomas, 1991). Researchers must recognize their links with the power groups who decide policy. Research utilization takes many forms depending on its location in the process of policy making, e.g. in research and development, problem-solving, interactive and tactical models (Weiss, 1991b). Researchers will have to judge the most appropriate forms of utilization of their research (Alkin *et al.*, 1991).

The impact of research on policy making depends on its degree of consonance with the political agendas of governments (Thomas, 1991) and policy makers anxious for their own political survival (Cook, 1991) and the promotion of their social programmes. Research is used if it is politically acceptable. That the impact of research on policy is intensely and inescapably political is a truism (Selleck, 1991; Kamin, 1991; Horowitz and Katz, 1991; Wineburg, 1991). Research too easily becomes simply an 'affirmatory text' which 'exonerates the system' (Wineburg, 1991) and is used by those who seek to hear in it only echoes of their own voices and wishes (Kogan and Atkin, 1991).

There is a significant tension between researchers and policy makers. The two parties have different, and often conflicting, interests, agendas, audiences, timescales, terminology and concern for topicality (Levin, 1991). These have huge implications for research styles. Policy makers anxious for the quick fix of superficial facts, unequivocal data, short-term solutions and simple, clear remedies for complex and generalized social problems (Cartwright, 1991; Cook, 1991; Radford, 2008: 506) – the Simple Impact model (Biddle and Anderson, 1991; Weiss, 1991a, 1991b) – find positivist methodologies attractive, often debasing the data through illegitimate summary. Moreover policy makers find much research too uncertain in its effects (Kerlinger, 1991; Cohen and Garet, 1991), dealing in a *Weltanschauung* rather than specifics, and being too complex in its designs and of limited applicability (Finn, 1991). This, reply the researchers, misrepresents the nature of their work (Shavelson and Berliner, 1991) and belies the complex reality which they are trying to investigate (Blalock, 1991). Capturing social complexity and serving political utility can run counter to each other. As Radford (2008: 506) remarks, the work of researchers is driven by objectivity, and independence from, or disinterestedness in, ideology, whereas policy makers are driven by interests, ideologies and values.

The issue of the connection between research and politics – power and decision making – is complex. On another dimension, the notion that research is inherently a political act because it is part of the political processes of society has not been lost on researchers. Usher and Scott (1996: 176) argue that positivist research has allowed a traditional conception of society to be preserved relatively unchallenged – the white, male, middle-class researcher – to the relative exclusion of 'others' as legitimate knowers. That this reaches into epistemological debate is evidenced in the issues of who defines the 'traditions of knowledge' and the disciplines of knowledge; the social construction of knowledge has to take into account the differential power of groups to define what is worthwhile research knowledge, what constitutes acceptable foci and methodologies of research and how the findings will be used.

 Companion Website

The companion website to the book includes PowerPoint slides for this chapter, which list the structure of the chapter and then provide a summary of the key points in each of its sections. This resource can be found online at **www.routledge.com/textbooks/cohen7e**.

The search for causation ◀ CHAPTER 4

This chapter introduces key issues in understanding causation in educational research. These include:

- causes and conditions
- causal inference and probabilistic causation
- causation, explanation, prediction and correlation
- causal over-determination
- the timing and scope of the cause and the effect
- causal direction, directness and indirectness
- establishing causation
- the role of action narratives in causation
- researching causes and effects
- researching the effects of causes
- researching the causes of effects

Educationists and social scientists are concerned not only for 'what works' but 'why', 'how', 'for whom' and 'under what conditions and circumstances'. They want to predict what will happen if such-and-such an intervention is introduced, and how and why it will produce a particular effect. This points us to an important feature of educational research, which is to look for causation: what are the effects of causes and what are the causes of effects? This is not a straightforward enterprise, not least because causation is not often observable but can only be inferred, and it is highly unlikely that indisputable causality is ever completely discoverable in the social sciences. At best probabilistic causation offers a more fitting characterization of causation in educational research. Causation is often considered to be the 'holy grail' of educational research, and this chapter introduces some key considerations in investigating causation.

4.1 Causes and conditions

Novice researchers are faced with many decisions concerning causation in their research, for example:

- Whether the research is seeking to establish causation, and if so, why.
- Deciding when causation is demonstrated, recognizing that causation is never 100 per cent certain.

- Deciding what constitutes a cause and what constitutes an effect.
- Deciding what constitutes evidence of the cause and evidence of the effect.
- Deciding the kind of research and the methodology of research that is necessary if causation is to be investigated.
- Deciding whether the research is investigating the cause of an effect, the effect of a cause, or both.

To infer simple, deterministic or regular causation may be to misread many situations excepting, perhaps, those where massive single causation is clear. It may be more useful for the researcher to consider causal processes than single events (Salmon, 1998), not least because there is often more than a single cause at work in any effect and there may be more than one effect from a single cause. Indeed, the researcher has to distinguish between causes, reasons, motives, determination and entailment, and whilst these might all exert causal force in some circumstances or enable us to make causal explanations or predictions, in other circumstances they do not.

What then makes a cause a cause, and an effect an effect? How do we know? Though we can say that causation takes places in a temporal sequence – the cause precedes the effect, and with temporal succession (Hume's criterion of 'priority' (Hume, 1955; Norton and Norton, 2000)), this does not help the researcher very much.

One distinguishing indication that causation is taking place or has taken place is the presence of counterfactuals (Mackie, 1993), i.e. the determination that the absence of X (the supposed cause) would have led to the absence of Y (the effect). If we are seeking to establish that such-and-such is a contributing cause (X) of an effect (Y) we ask ourselves whether, if that supposed cause had not been present, then would the effect have occurred or been what it actually was; if the answer is 'no' then we can suppose that X is a true cause. For example, if there had been no ice on a path then I would not have fallen over and broken my arm. So the presence of ice must have been a contributing cause of the effect – one of many causes (e.g. my poor sense of balance, my poor eyesight in not seeing the ice, the ambient darkness, wearing slippery soled shoes, my brittle bones because of my age, etc.).

The counterfactual argument is persuasive, but problematical: how do we know, for example, what the outcome would have been if there had been no patch of ice on the path where I was walking? Can we predict with sufficient certainty to attribute the counterfactual causality here? How can we prove that the effect would *not* have happened if a particular cause had not been present? How do we know that I would or would not have slipped and fallen if the ice had not been present? In true experiments this is addressed by having a control group: the control group is supposed to indicate what would have happened if the intervention had not occurred. The problem is that much research is not experimental.

If it were only the presence of ice that caused me to fall and break my arm, then this would be a very simple indication of causality; the problem is that the presence of ice in this instance is perhaps not a sufficient cause – had my balance been good, my eyesight good, the ambient light good, my shoes had good grips on their soles and my bones been less brittle then I would not have fallen and broken my arm.

The difficulty here is to establish the relative strength of the causes in a multi-causal situation, i.e. the several conditions that, themselves, contribute to the accident. The presence of those included causes affects their relative strengths in a specific context, and the absence of some of these causes in the same context may raise or lower the relative strengths of others.

The example of falling on the ice also indicates an important feature of causation: causes cannot be taken in isolation, they may need to be taken together (compound causes, i.e. they only exert causative force when acting in concert), and there may be interaction effects between them. On its own, the patch of ice might not have caused my fall and broken arm; it was perhaps neither sufficient nor necessary, as I could have fallen and broken my arm anyway because of my slippery shoes and poor balance. On its own, my poor balance did not cause me to fall and break my arm. On its own, the darkness did not cause me to fall and break my arm. On their own, my slippery soles did not cause me to fall and break my arm. On their own, my brittle bones did not cause me to fall and break my arm. But put all these together and we have sufficient conditions to cause the accident. For the researcher, looking for individual causes in a contextualized situation may be futile.

In understanding the causes of effects one has to understand the circumstances and conditions in which the two independent factors – the cause and the effect –

are located and linked (the link is contingent rather than analytic). Discovering the circumstances – conditions – in which one variable causes an effect on another is vital in understanding causation, for it is the specific combination of necessary and/or sufficient conditions that may produce an effect. Causes of effects work in specific circumstances and situations, and account has to be taken of these circumstances and conditions.

For the researcher, the difficulty in unravelling the effects of causes and the causes of effects is heightened by the fact that causes may be indirect rather than direct (cause A causes effect B, and effect B causes effect C) or that they may only become a cause in the presence of other factors (I may fall over on ice and not break my arm if I am young and land well, but as an older person with more brittle bones I may land awkwardly and break my arm – the fall is not a sufficient condition or cause of my broken arm).

4.2 Causal inference and probabilistic causation

Identifying and understanding causation may be problematic for researchers, as effects may not be direct, linear functions of causes, and because there may be few, many, increasing, reducing, unpredictable, i.e. non-linear effects of causes. A small cause can bring about a large or irregular effect; a large cause may bring about a small or irregular effect. Causation is often an inductive and empirical, rather than a logical, deductive matter, and, indeed, it is often unclear what constitutes a cause and what constitutes an effect as these are often umbrella terms, under which are sub-causes and sub-effects, causal processes and causal links bringing several factors together both at a particular point in time (the moment of falling, in the example above) and in a temporal sequence (e.g. taking and passing a public examination).

Further, there is an asymmetry at work in causation effect: a cause can produce an effect but not vice versa: being young, good looking and female may help me to pass my driving test if I am in the presence of a leering male examiner, but passing my driving test does not cause me to be young, good looking and female.

It is often dangerous to say that such-and-such is *definitely* the cause of something, or that such-and-such is *definitely* the effect of something. Causation in the human sciences is much more tentative, and may be probabilistic rather than deterministic. Hume's (2000) own rules for causation are:

- *contiguity* (of space and time) (the cause is contiguous with the effect);

- *priority/succession* (the cause precedes the effect);
- *constant conjunction* (the coupling of one event and its successor are found to recur repeatedly);
- *necessary connection* (which is learned from experience, habit and custom rather than from deductive, logical, necessary proof).

One can detect correlation in Hume's ideas rather than actual causation. He argues that causation is inferred, inductively, by humans rather than being an objective matter.

The inferential, conjectural and probabilistic nature of much causation in educational research (rather than being absolute, deductive and deterministic), coupled with the fact that causation is frequently unobserved or unobservable, renders the study of causation problematic for educational researchers. Indeed there is a danger in isolating and focusing on singular causes separately from other contributing causes, contexts and conditions, and it is perhaps more fitting to regard causes as processes over time rather than single events. Further, in an interconnected world of multiple causes and causal nets, conditions and interactions may provide better accounts of causation than linear determinism.

In unravelling causes and effects, the researcher is faced with the task of identifying what actually constitutes a cause and what constitutes an effect. The contexts and conditions of an event are as important as the trigger of an effect, and may be contributing causes. In the example earlier, my falling and breaking my arm was precipitated – triggered – by the ice on the path, but, without the presence of other contributing factors I might not have fallen and I might not have broken my arm. The trigger of the effect may not be its sole cause but only the last cause in a causal chain, sequence of events, series or network of conditions before the effect occurs, even though causes often raise the likelihood of their effects rather than guaranteeing them (Mellor, 1995: 69–70). Indeed, whilst probability often concerns identifying *likelihood*, the strongest probability is not always the same as the strongest causation. I might think that putting pressure on a child to succeed has the strongest possibility of causing her success, but the actual cause might lie elsewhere, e.g. the teacher might be very effective, the students might be highly motivated or the examination might be very easy.

4.3 Causation, explanation, prediction and correlation

The demonstration of causation is difficult. Causation is neither the same as explanation (Clogg and Haritou,

1997: 106; Salmon, 1998: 5–8) (e.g. an explanation may be wrong, or it may be giving the meaning of something, or it may be indicating how to do something), nor is causation the same as giving a reason. For example, I might take a day off work, giving the reason that I am sick, but the real reason may be simply that I am lazy or want to go shopping instead.

Nor is causation the same as prediction. Just because I observe something happening once does not mean I can predict that it will happen again (the problem of induction), as the conditions could be different, or indeed, even if the conditions were very similar (as chaos theory tells us).

I might be able to predict something even though my prediction is based on the wrong identification of causes – I can predict that there will be a storm because I have observed the barometric reading falling, but the fall in the barometric reading does not cause the storm. Formally put, the two variables – the barometric reading and the storm – are 'screened off', separated and kept apart from each other (Reichenbach, 1956; Salmon, 1998). They have correlational but no causal relationships to each other, and are both caused by a third factor – the drop in air pressure, see Figure 4.1.

I might predict that a person's hands might be large if she has large feet, but having large hands does not cause her to have large feet – the cause might lie in a genetic predisposition to both. It is one thing to say that a change in one variable (A) is associated with a change in another variable (B); it is an entirely different thing to say that a change in one variable (A) *brings about* a change in another variable (B); and it is an entirely different thing again to say that a change in one variable (B) is brought about by a change in another variable (A), i.e. that it *is caused* by that change in variable A.

In attributing genuine causation, it is useful to 'screen off' unrelated dependent variables from the variables that are directly relevant to the situation being researched, in order to ensure that the effect of one variable is removed from the equation, e.g. to

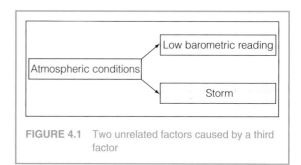

FIGURE 4.1 Two unrelated factors caused by a third factor

discount that variable or to control for the effects of other variables, such as the presence of a third variable or several variables, by partial correlations and structural equation modelling. It is also important in screening off to ensure that one variable is not deemed to have an influence on another when, in fact, this is not the case. This presumes that it is actually possible to identify which factors to screen off from which (Pearl (2009: 423–7) indicates how this can be approached), and, in the case of multiple causality (or in the cases of over-determination, discussed below), this may not be possible.

Screening off requires the ability to separate out causes, and this may be difficult to the point of impossibility. However, in seeking to establish genuine causation, the researcher must consider controlling for the effects of additional variables, be they prior/exogenous variables or intervening/endogenous variables, as these will exert a non-causal influence on the dependent variables.

In conducting research that seeks to attribute causation, it is important to control for the effects of variables, i.e. to hold them constant (matched) so that fair attribution of causality and the weight of causal variables can be assessed (though relative weights of causes are, strictly speaking, superfluous in discussing causation, they are questionable indicators of causation). Further, identifying the relative strengths of causes depends on the presence or absence of other causes. For example, in looking at examination success (the effect), if my research confines itself to looking at the relative strength of causes A (hours of study), B (IQ) and C (motivation) in producing the effect, I might find that C (motivation) is the strongest of the three causes. However, if I were to add a new variable (D) (an outstanding teacher helping the student), then it may be that D is the overriding cause and that A, B and C are of equally low strength, or that A becomes the second strongest factor.

Statistical tools such as crosstabulations, correlation and partial correlation, regression and multiple regression, and structural equation models (see Chapters 34–36) can be used to assist here in the analysis of causation, though it is often difficult to control direct, indirect, antecedent, intervening and combined influences of variables on outcomes (though statistical tools and graphical methods can assist here (Pearl, 2009: 423–7)).

In considering the control of variables, let us examine, for example, the subject choices of secondary school male and female students (Table 4.1). Here we can see overwhelmingly that males choose physics far more than females, and females choose biology far more than males. The researcher wishes to know if the allocation of certain teachers to teach the secondary school science subjects affects the students' choice (i.e. whether it is the subject of the teacher, or some combination of these) that is causing the students to choose the subjects that they choose. The researcher introduces the third variable of the 'teacher' as a control variable, with two values: Teacher A and Teacher B, and then partitions the data for males and females according to either Teacher A or Teacher B, see Table 4.2.

When the data are partitioned by teacher (Teacher A and Teacher B) the researcher notes that the percentages in each of the partial tables (one part of the table for Teacher A and the other part of the table for Teacher B) in Table 4.2 are very similar to the original percentages of the root table (Table 4.1). She concludes that whether Teacher A or Teacher B is teaching the class makes no appreciable difference to the choices made by the students. The percentages in the new table (4.2) replicate very closely those in the original table (4.1). The researcher concludes that the teacher involved is exerting no causal influence on the choice of subjects by the secondary school males and females.

However, let us imagine that the partial tables had yielded different data (Table 4.3). This time the results of the choices made by males and females who are with Teacher A and Teacher B are very different. The percentages in the new table (4.3) are very different from those in the original table (4.1). This suggests to the researcher that, in this instance, the teacher of the class in question is making a causal difference to the choices of science subject made by the students.

TABLE 4.1   SCIENCE CHOICES OF SECONDARY SCHOOL MALES AND FEMALES

	Male	Female	Total
Preference for physics	175 (55.1%)	87 (27.9%)	262 (41.6% of total)
Preference for biology	143 (44.9%)	225 (72.1%)	368 (58.4% of total)
Column total	318 (100%)	312 (100%)	630
Percentage of total	50.5%	49.5%	100%

TABLE 4.2   SCIENCE CHOICES OF MALE AND FEMALE SECONDARY STUDENTS WITH TEACHER A OR B

	Males with Teacher A	Females with Teacher A	Males with Teacher B	Females with Teacher B	Total
Preference for physics	86 (55.8%)	44 (28.4%)	89 (54.3%)	43 (27.4%)	262 (62.5% of total)
Preference for biology	68 (44.2%)	111 (71.6%)	75 (45.7%)	114 (72.6%)	368 (37.5% of total)
Column total	154 (100%)	155 (100%)	164 (100%)	157 (100%)	630
Percentage of total	24.4%	24.6%	26.1%	24.9%	100%

TABLE 4.3   FURTHER SCIENCE CHOICES OF MALE AND FEMALE SECONDARY STUDENTS WITH TEACHER A OR B

	Males with Teacher A	Females with Teacher A	Males with Teacher B	Females with Teacher B	Total
Preference for physics	133 (56.8%)	55 (23.5%)	39 (46.4%)	35 (44.8%)	262 (62.5% of total)
Preference for biology	101 (43.2%)	179 (76.5%)	45 (53.6%)	43 (55.1%)	368 (37.5% of total)
Column total	234 (100%)	234 (100%)	84 (100%)	78 (100%)	630
Percentage of total	37.1%	37.1%	13.3%	12.5%	100%

However, this only tells us the 'what' of causation, or, to be more precise, it only gives us an indication of association and possible causation: it appears that the teacher makes no difference in Table 4.2 but *does* make a difference in Table 4.3. How this becomes a *causal* matter is another question altogether: how does the teacher *actually* affect the males' or females' choices of which science subject to follow. For example is it that: (a) Teacher A is male and Teacher B is female, and students tend to prefer to be with teachers of their own sex; (b) Teacher A has a better reputation than Teacher B for helping students to pass public examinations with high grades, and students are anxious to do well; (c) Teacher A is more sympathetic than Teacher B, so that students can relate more easily to Teacher A, and so they choose Teacher A; (d) Teacher A has a better sense of humour than Teacher B, and students prefer a good humoured teacher; (e) Teacher A explains matters more clearly than Teacher B, and students prefer clear explanations, and so on. The point here is that, though one can deduce certain points from contingency tables and partial tables, they may not actually indicate causality. The same principle for holding variables constant, this time in correlational research, is discussed in Chapter 35.

In establishing causation, it is important to separate covariance and correlation between two unrelated and non-interacting dependent variables due to a common cause from the interaction of dependent variables due to the presence of a common cause (as in the examples of the barometer and the storm earlier).

4.4 Causal over-determination

It is rare to find a single cause of a single effect. It is more often the case that there are several causes at work in a single situation and that these produce a multiplicity of effects. For example, why are so many young children well behaved at school, when nobody has explicitly taught them the hidden curriculum (Jackson, 1968) of rules, regulations, taking turns, sharing, being quiet, knowing that the teacher is in charge and has all the power, putting up with delay, denial and only being one out of many children who has to gain the teacher's attention? The answer is over-determination: many events, both separately and in combination, lead to the same outcome: the young child must do as she is told and that having a nice time at school depends on how effectively she learns these rules and abides by them. Many causes; same effect: good behaviour.

Causal over-determination is 'where a particular effect is the outcome of more than one cause, each of which, in itself, would have been sufficient to have produced the effect' (Morrison, 2009: 51). A familiar example is the issue of which bullet can be said to have killed a man, which causes his death (Horwich, 1993), if two bullets simultaneously strike a man's head. Either one bullet *or* the other caused the death (cf. Mellor, 1995: 102). 'The man would have died, even if one or the other of the bullets was not fired, and if bullet A did not cause the death, it would be causally true to say that the man would have died' (Morrison, 2009: 51). Let us say that, in a study of homework and its effect on mathematics performance, a rise in homework might produce a rise in students' mathematics performance. However, this is not all: there may have been tremendous parental pressure on the child to do well in mathematics, or the student might have been promised a vast sum of money if her mathematics performance increased, or the school might have exerted huge pressure on the student to succeed, or the offer of a university place was contingent on a high mathematics score. The rise in mathematics performance may not have required all of the factors to have been present in order to bring about the effect; any one of them could have produced the effect. The effect is 'over-determined'. One effect may have one or several causes. Whilst this is commonplace, it is important to note this in order to refute the claims frequently made by protagonists of such-and-such an intervention in education that it alone improves performance; if only it were that simple!

4.5 The timing and scope of the cause and the effect

Turn back to the earlier example of my falling on the ice and breaking my arm. Maybe I had a weakness in my arm from an injury many years before, and maybe when I injured my arm years before, I could not have predicted that, many years later, I would fall on ice and break my arm. The issue is not idle for researchers, for it requires them to consider, in terms of temporality, what are relevant causes and what to include and exclude from studies of causation, how far back in time to go in establishing causes and how far forward in time to go in establishing effects.

Just as the timing of causes may be unclear, so the timing of the effects of a cause may be unclear. Effects may be short term only, delayed, instantaneous, immediate, cumulative and long term; indeed the full effects of a cause may not be revealed in a single instance, as an effect may be a covering term for many effects that emerge over time (e.g. the onset and presenting of cancer has several stages; cancer is not a single event at one point in time). Temporality and causation are intimately connected but separate.

The examples above also indicate that terms such as 'cause' and 'effect' are, in many cases, a shorthand for many sub-causes, sub-processes and sub-effects. Further, causes and effects may only reveal themselves over time, and, indeed, it may be difficult to indicate when a cause begins (which cigarette brought about the onset of cancer, or when did smoking first bring about the onset of the cancer) or ends, and when an effect begins (e.g. I may continue smoking even after the early onset of lung cancer). I might hate studying mathematics at school but find it very attractive twenty years later; had my interest in mathematics been post-tested immediately I left school, the result would have been lower than if I had been tested twenty years later.

Where a cause begins and ends, where an effect begins and ends, when and how causes and effects should be measured, evaluated, ascertained and assessed, are often open questions, requiring educational researchers to clarify and justify their decisions on timings in isolating and investigating causes and effects. Quantitative data may be useful for identifying the 'what' of causation – what causes an effect – but qualitative data are pre-eminently useful for identifying the 'how' of causation – how causation actually works, the causal processes at work.

Consider, too, the reason for the ice patch being present on the path in the earlier example, and my being on the ice on the day in question. Maybe the local government services had not properly cleared the path of ice on that day, or maybe, as an ailing pensioner, I would normally be accompanied by a carer or with an assistant whenever I went out, but on that day the service provider failed to turn up, so I was forced to go out on my own. Again, the issue is not idle for researchers, for it requires them to consider how widely or narrowly to cast their net in terms of looking for causes (how far out and how far in). In determining what are relevant causes the researcher has to decide what to include and exclude from studies of causation, e.g. from the psychological to the social, from the micro to the macro, and to decide the direction and combination of such causes.

The determination of a cause involves decisions on how far to go back in a temporal causal chain or network of events, and how wide or narrow to go in the causal space (how many conditions and circumstances contribute to the causation at work in a given situation). It may be difficult, if not impossible, to identify and include all the causal antecedents in a piece of research.

Here the concept of *necessary* and *sufficient* conditions is raised, as is the importance of identifying the causal trigger in a situation (the last cause in a causal chain or a linkage of several conditions). The striking of a match might cause it to flare, but that is not the only factor to be taken into account. Whether it flares depends on the abrasiveness of the striking surface, the dryness of the materials, the strength of the strike, the duration of the strike, the presence of sufficient oxygen in the atmosphere, and so on.

There may be an infinite number of causes and effects, depending on how far back one goes in time and how wide one goes in terms of contexts. This presents a problem of where to establish the 'cut off' point in identifying causes of an effect. Whilst this may be addressed through the identification of necessary and sufficient conditions (Mackie, 1993), in fact this does little to attenuate the problem in social sciences, as not only is it problematic to identify what qualify as necessary or sufficient conditions, but these will vary from context to context, and even though there may be regularities of cause and effect from context to context, there are also differences from context to context.

The issue to be faced by researchers here is one of 'boundary conditions' and 'circumscription' (Pearl, 2009: 420) – which factors we include or exclude can affect our judgements of causality. If, in a study of student performance, I only look at teacher behaviour and its influence on student performance then I might be led to believe that teacher behaviour is the cause of student performance, whereas if I only look at student motivation and its influence on student performance then I might be led to believe that student motivation is the cause of student performance. Researchers rarely, if ever, include the universe of conditions, only a selection from that universe, and this might distort the judgements made about causation or where to look for causation. Whilst it may not be possible to identify the universe of conditions, the researcher has to be aware of the dangers of circularity, i.e. I am only interested in effect Y, so I only look at possible causes X, and then I find, wonder upon wonders, that X is the cause of Y, simply because I have not considered alternatives. It is important to identify and justify the inclusion and exclusion of variables in researching causation, that is to select the field of focus sufficiently widely and to consider possible alternative explanations of cause and effect.

4.6 Causal direction, directness and indirectness

The problem of identifying causes and effects is further compounded by consideration of direct and indirect causes and effects. It is also useful to describe causation in terms of recursive (single lines of direction) rather than non-recursive (mutual lines of direction) models, as causation can take more than one direction at a time. This justifies the use of non-recursive models of causation and of causal nets: clusters of causes that act together in multiple directions. In a recursive model the causality is unidirectional (which may oversimplify the direction of causation), whereas in a non-recursive model causation is in one or more directions. Many structural equation models are non-recursive.

Whilst the research may wish to identify a cause A that brings about the direct effect B, in practice this is seldom the case, as between A and B might be a huge number of intervening variables and processes operating, both exogenous and endogenous:

An *exogenous variable* is one whose values are determined outside the model (e.g. a structural equation model or a causal model) in which that variable is being used, or which is considered not to be caused by another variable in the model, or which is extraneous to the model.

An *endogenous variable* is one whose values or variations are explained by other variables within the model, or which is caused by one or more variables within the model. It is important to identify which causes mediate, and are mediated by, other causes. How the researcher does this takes many forms, from theoretical modelling and testing of the model with data, to eliciting from participants what are the causes.

Whilst causation is not straightforward to demonstrate, this is not to suggest that establishing causation should not be attempted. There are regularities, there are likelihoods based on experience, there are similarities between situations and people, indeed the similarities may be stronger than the differences. This suggests that establishing probabilistic causation or inferring causation, whilst complex and daunting, may be possible for the researcher.

The problem for the researcher is to decide which variables to include, as the identification and inclusion/exclusion of relevant variables in determining causation is a major difficulty in research. Causes, like effects, might often be better regarded in conjunction with other causes, circumstances and conditions rather than in isolation. Contextuality – the conditions in which the cause and effect take place – and the careful identification and inclusion of all relevant causes are key factors in identifying causation.

4.7 Establishing causation

It is not an easy task to establish causation. For example, causation may be present but unobserved and indeed unobservable, particularly in the presence of stronger causes or impeding factors. I might take medication for a headache but the headache becomes worse; this is not to say that the medication has not worked, as the headache might have become even stronger without the medication. The effects of some causes may be masked by the presence of others, but nonetheless causation may be occurring.

Morrison (2009: 45) gives an example where,

in the case of the causal relationship between smoking (A), heart disease (B) and exercise (C), smoking (A) is highly correlated with exercise (C): smokers exercise much more than non-smokers. Though smoking causes heart disease, exercise actually is an even stronger preventative measure that one can take against heart disease. The corollary of this is that smoking prevents heart disease.

(Hitchcock, 2002: 9)

The way in which the cause operates may also be unclear. There are many examples one can give, Morrison (2009: 45), for instance, gives the example of small class teaching. In one class operating with small class teaching, the teacher in that class uses highly didactic, formal teaching with marked social distance between the teacher and the student (Factor A), and this is deemed to be an inhibitor of the beneficial effects of small class teaching on students' attainment in mathematics: didactic teaching reduces mathematics performance. However the same highly didactic, formal class teaching (Factor A) significantly raises the amount of pressure placed on the students to achieve highly (Factor B), and this (Factor B) is known to be the *overriding* cause of any rise in students' performance in mathematics, e.g. in small classes the teacher can monitor very closely the work of each child: high pressure raises mathematics performance. Now, it could be argued that Factor A – an ostensibly *inhibiting* factor for the benefits of small class teaching – actually causes *improvements* in mathematics performance in the small class teaching situation.

Another example is where greater examination pressure on students (A) increases their lack of self-confidence (C), but it also increases the student's hard work (B), and hard work reduces the student's lack of self-confidence (C). In other words, the likelihood of the effect of A on C may be lower than the effect of B on C, given A. Let us say that A increases the likeli-

hood of C by 20 per cent, and A increases the likelihood of B by 35 per cent, whilst B reduces the likelihood of C by 75 per cent. In this instance increasing the examination pressure increases the student's self-confidence rather than reduces it (see Figure 4.2).

The point here that a cause might raise the likelihood of an effect, but it may also lower that likelihood, and the presence of other conditions or causes affects the likelihood of an effect of a cause. A diagrammatic representation of these examples is in Figure 4.2 (note that the length of the lines indicates the relative strength of the influence). A cause might lower the likelihood of an effect rather than increase it.

Many cause-and-effect models are premised on linear relationships between cause and effect (i.e. a regular relationship, e.g. a small cause has a regular small effect and a large cause has a regular large effect, or a small cause has a regular large effect and a large cause has a regular small effect). However, seeking linear relations between cause and effect might be misguided, as the effects of causes might be non-linear (e.g. a small or large cause may produce a large, small, irregular or no effect), and it might be to deal with singular or a few causes and singular or a few effects, overlooking the interrelatedness and interactions of multiple causes with each other, with multiple effects and indeed with the multiple interactions of multiple effects. Relationships and their analysis may be probabilistic, conditional and subjunctive rather than linear. Indeed nets and conditions of causation might be more fitting descriptions of causation than causal lines or chains of events or factors.

One way of focusing a causal explanation is to examine regularities and then to consider rival explanations of causes and rival hypotheses of these regularities. The observation of regularities, however, is not essential to an understanding of causation, as all cases may be different but no less causative. Further, the best

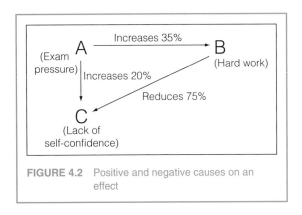

FIGURE 4.2 Positive and negative causes on an effect

causal explanation is that which is founded on, and draws from, the most comprehensive theory (e.g. that theory which embraces intentionality, agency, inter-action as well as structure, i.e. micro- and macro-factors), that explain all the elements of the phenomenon, that fit the *explanandum* (that which must be explained) and data more fully than rival theories, and which are tested in contexts and with data other than those that have given rise to the theory and causal explanation.

Given the complexity of probabilistic causation, it would be invidious to suppose that a particular inter-vention will necessarily bring about the intended effect. Any cause or intervention is embedded in a web of other causes, contexts, conditions, circumstances and effects, and these can exert a mediating and altering influence between the cause and its effect.

4.8 The role of action narratives in causation

Statistics, both inferential and descriptive, can indicate powerful relationships. However, these do not neces-sarily establish unequivocal, direct causation; they may establish the 'what' of causation but not the 'how'. I might assume that A and B cause C, and that C causes D; it is a causal model, and I might measure the effects of A and B on C and the effect of C on D. However, here causation lies in the assumptions behind the model rather than in the statistical tests of the model, and the causal assumptions that lie behind the model may derive from theory rather than the model itself. Statistics alone do not prove causation. To believe that they do is to engage in circular thinking. Rather, causation is embodied in the theoretical underpinnings and assumptions that support the model, and the role of statistics is to confirm, chal-lenge, extend and refine these underpinnings and assumptions. Behind statistics that may illuminate causa-tion lie theories and models, and it is in the construct validity of these that causation lies. It is the *mechanisms* of causation that should concern researchers rather than solely numbers and statistical explanations.

Many statistics rely on correlational analysis or on assumptions that pre-exist the statistics, i.e. the statist-ics might only reinforce existing assumptions and models rather than identify actual causation. Even more sophisticated statistics such as structural equation mod-elling, multiple regression and multivariate analysis succumb to the charge of being no more powerful than the assumptions of causation underpinning them, and, indeed, they often grossly simplify the number or range of causes in a situation, in the pursuit of a simple, clear and easily identifiable model.

How is it that X causes Y; what is happening in X to cause Y? In short, what are the processes of causation? In order to understand this involves regarding causation as dynamic rather than static, as a process rather than a single event, and as involving motives, volitions, reasons, understandings, perceptions, individuality, conditions and context, and the dynamic and emerging interplay of factors, more often than not over time. It is here that qualitative data come into their own, for they 'get inside the head' of the actors in a situation.

A neat example of this is what has come to be known as the 'Rashomon effect' in social sciences (e.g. Roth and Mehta, 2002). It is over 60 years since Kurosawa's film *Rashomon* stunned audiences at the Venice film festival. It provides four discrepant witness accounts of the same event – an encounter between a samurai, his wife and a bandit, that led to the effect of the samurai's death – in which the causes could have been murder or suicide, consensual sex or rape, fidelity or infidelity. The causal accounts are given by a woodcutter, the bandit, the wife and the spirit of the dead samurai speaking through a medium. Each self-serving account protects the honour of the teller and tries to exonerate each. At the end, there is no clear statement of whose version is correct; truth flounders in the quagmire of epistemology, perception and motives.

Anthropologists, lawyers and social scientists (Roth and Mehta, 2002) seized on the film as an example of the multilayered, contested truth of any situation or its interpretation, coining the term the 'Rashomon effect' to describe an event or truth which is reported or explained in contradictory terms, that gives differing and incompatible causal accounts of an effect: a death. There is more than one causal explanation at work in a situation, and it is the task of the researcher to uncover these, and to examine the causation through the eyes of those imputing the causation.

Action narratives and agency are important in accounting for causation and effects, and, because of a multiplicity of action narratives and individual motiva-tions in a situation, there are multiple pathways of cau-sation rather than simple input–output models. In understanding the processes of causation, the power of qualitative data is immense and, indeed, argues for mixed methods in establishing causation: numerical data to identify the variables at work, and qualitative data to indicate how they are working in specific situations.

Causal explanations that dwell at the level of aggregate variables are incomplete, as behind them, and feeding into them, lie individuals' motives, values, goals and circumstances, and it is these that could be exerting the causal influence; hence a theory of individual motives might be required in understanding and explaining the causation here.

For example, it is commonplace for a survey to ask respondents to indicate their sex, but it is an entirely different matter – even if different responses are given by males and females to rating scales in a survey – to say that sex *causes* the differences in response. How, actually, is sex a causal factor?

Further, between aggregate independent and dependent variables of cause and effect respectively lie a whole range of causal processes, and these could be influencing the effect and, therefore, have to be taken into account in any causal explanation. The argument supports micro- to macro-analysis and explanation rather than macro- to micro-analysis and explanation. How macro-structural features from society actually enter into individuals' actions and interactions, and how individuals' actions and interactions determine social structures – the causal processes involved – need cautious elucidation, their current status often being opaque processes in a black box, input–output model of causation.

4.9 Researching causes and effects

The researcher investigating the effects of a cause or the causes of an effect has many questions to answer, for example:

- What is the causal connection between the cause and the effect (how does the cause bring about the effect and how has the effect been brought about by the cause)?
- What are the causal processes at work in the situation being investigated?
- What constitutes the evidence of the causal connection?
- On what basis will the inference of causality be made?
- What constitutes the evidence that a cause is a cause and that an effect is an effect?
- What constitutes the evidence that a cause is *the* cause (and that there is not another cause) and that an effect is *the* effect (and that there is not another effect)?
- Is the research investigating the effects of a cause (an interventionist strategy) or the cause of an effect (a *post hoc* investigation)?
- How will the research separate out a range of possible causes and effects, and how will decisions be made to include and/or exclude possible causes and effects?

- What methodology will be chosen to examine the effects of causes?
- What methodology will be chosen to examine the causes of effects?
- What kind of data will establish probabilistic causation?
- When will the data be collected from which causation will be inferred?

As mentioned earlier, the timing of data collection is a critical feature in establishing causation and the effects of causes. Here the greater the need to establish causal processes, the closer and more frequent should be the data collection points. Moreover, qualitative data could hold pre-eminence over quantitative methods in establishing causation and causal processes. Indeed longitudinal studies might yield accounts of causation that are more robust than cross-sectional studies.

It is not enough to say *that* such-and-such a cause brings about such-and-such an effect, for, whilst it might establish the likelihood *that* the cause brings about an effect or that an effect has been brought about by a cause, this does not tell the researcher *how* the cause brings about the effect or how the effect has been brought about by the cause, i.e. what are the causal processes at work in connecting the cause with the effect and vice versa. If the research really wishes to investigate the processes of causation then this requires detailed, in-depth analysis of the connections between causes and effects.

For example, it is not enough to say that smoking can cause cancer; what is required is to know *how* smoking can cause cancer – what happens between the inhalation of smoke and the presentation of cancer cells. I might say that turning on a light switch causes the light bulb to shine, but this is inaccurate, as turning on the switch completes a circuit of electricity and the electricity causes a filament to heat up such that, when white hot, it emits light.

In education, it is not enough to say that increasing the time spent on reading causes students' reading to improve; that is naive. What might be required is to know how and why the increase in time devoted to reading improves reading. This opens up many possible causes: motivation; concentration levels and spans; interest level of the materials; empathy between the reader and the material; level of difficulty of the text; purposes of the reading (e.g. for pleasure, for information, for learning, for a test); reading abilities and skills in the reader; subject matter of the text; ambient noise; where, when and for how long the reading is done; prior discussion of, and preparation for, the reading material; follow-up to the reading; choice of reading materials; whether the reading is done individually or in groups; teacher help and support in the reading time; relatedness of the reading to other activities; the nature, contents and timing of the pre-test and post-test; the evidence of improvement (and improvement in which aspects of reading); and so on.

It can be seen immediately in this example of reading that the simple input variable – increasing time for reading – may bring about an improvement in reading, but that may only be one of several causes of the improvement, or an umbrella term, or may liberate a range of other causes to come into play, both direct and indirect causes. Identifying the true cause(s) of an effect is extremely difficult to pin down.

Take for example the introduction of total quality management into schools. Here several interventions are introduced into a school for school improvement, and, at the next school inspection, the school is found to have improved. The problem is trying to decide which intervention(s) has/have brought about the improvement, or which combinations of interventions have worked, or which interventions were counterproductive, and so on. It is akin to one going to the doctor about a digestion problem, where the doctor prescribes six medicines and the digestion problem goes but the patient then contracts a stomach ulcer. Which medicine(s) were responsible for the cure and the ulcer, and in what combinations, or is it actually the medicines that have brought about the cure and/or the ulcer; were there other factors that brought about the cure or the ulcer, or would the digestion problem have been cured naturally?

The researcher has to identify which cause (A) or combination of causes have brought about which effect (B), both intended and unintended, or whether the supposed cause (A) brought about another effect (C), which in turn became the cause of the effect (B) in question, and whether the effect (B) is really the consequence of the supposed cause(s) (A), and not the consequence of something else. What looks like being a simple cause-and-effect actually explodes into a multiplicity of causes and effects (Figure 4.3) (cf. Morrison, 2009: 124).

How, then, can the researcher proceed in trying to uncover causes and effects? A main principle underpinning how some researchers operate here is through *control*, isolating and controlling all the variables deemed to be at work in the situation. By such isolation and control, one can then manipulate one or more variables and see the difference that they make to the effect. If all the variables in a situation are controlled, and one of these is manipulated, and that changes the effect, then the researcher concludes that the effect is

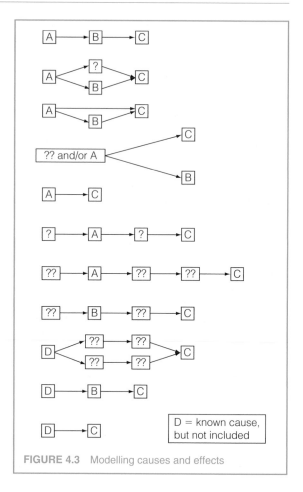

FIGURE 4.3 Modelling causes and effects

caused by the variable that has been manipulated. Moreover, if the research (e.g. an experiment) can be repeated, or if further data (e.g. survey data) are added, and the same findings are discovered, then this might give added weight to the inferred cause-and-effect connection (though regularity – Hume's (2000) 'constant conjunction' – is no requirement for causation to be demonstrated). This assumes that one has identified, isolated and controlled all the relevant variables, but, as the earlier part of this chapter has suggested, this may be an impossibility.

One way in which the problem of isolation and control of variables is addressed is through randomization – a key feature of the 'true' experiment (see Chapter 16). For example, random allocation of individuals to a control group or an experimental group is one widely used means of allowing for the many uncontrolled variables that are part of the make-up of the groups in question (Schneider *et al.*, 2007). It adopts the *ceteris paribus* condition (all other things being equal) that assumes that the distribution of these many other variables is evenly distributed across the groups, such that there is no need to control for them. This is a bold and perhaps dangerous assumption to make, not least as chaos and complexity theory tell us that small changes and differences can bring about major differences in outcome.

Whilst control is one prime means of trying to establish causation, it does raise several problems of the possibility, acceptability or manageability of isolating and controlling variables, of disturbing and distorting the real work of the participants, and of operating an undesirable – even unethical – control and manipulation of people. This is the world in which the researcher is king or queen and the participants are subjects – subjected to control and manipulation. On the one hand the claim is made that the research is 'objective', 'clean' (i.e. not affected by the particular factors within each participant), laboratory based and not prone to bias; on the other hand it is a manipulative and perhaps unrealistic attempt to control a world that cannot in truth be controlled. Are there alternatives?

A major alternative is one that keeps the 'real' world of participants as undisturbed as possible, avoids the researcher controlling the situation and uses qualitative data to investigate causation. Here observational, interview and ethnographic methods come to the fore, and these are very powerful in addressing the *processes* of causation and in establishing the causes of an effect as recounted by the participants or the observers themselves. These methods deliberately 'get inside the heads' of individuals and groups, as well as including the researcher's own views, identifying and reporting causation in their terms. They yield considerable authenticity to the causal accounts given or which compile a sufficiently detailed account of a situation for the researcher to make informed comments on the workings of causation in the situation under investigation. Further, it is often the participants themselves who identify what are the causes of effects in the situations being investigated (though the researcher would need to be assured that these are genuine, as participants may have reasons for not disclosing the real causes or motives in a situation or, indeed, may be mistaken).

These two approaches are not mutually exclusive in a piece of research, and, as Chapter 1 has indicated, there is an advantage in adopting a mixed methods approach, or, indeed, in a mixed methodology approach, in which positivist and experimental approaches might yield accounts of the 'what' of causation – which variables are operating to produce an effect; whilst an interpretive approach might be used to yield data on the 'how' of causation – how the causal processes are actually working.

Researchers examining causes and effects have to decide whether they are researching the effects of causes (e.g. in which they introduce an intervention and see what happens as a consequence) or the causes of effects (e.g. backtracking from an observed situation to try to discover its causes). These are discussed below.

4.10 Researching the effects of causes

In trying to investigate the effects of one or more causes, the researcher can commence with a theory of causality operating in a situation (e.g. bringing pressure to bear on students causes them to work harder, or dropping out of school reduces income at age 50 by a factor of five, or improving self-esteem improves creativity), operationalize it, and then test it, eliminate rival theories and explanations using data other than those that gave rise to the explanation, and then proceed to the drawing and delimiting of conclusions. The use of continuous rather than categorical variables might be more effective in establishing the nature and extent of causation.

On the other hand, the researcher can proceed along an entirely different track, using qualitative research to really understand the causal processes at work in a situation and in the minds of the participants in that situation – the 'how' of causation.

Determining the effects of causes is often undertaken using an interventionist strategy in educational research, installing an intervention either to test a hypothesized causal influence or a causal model, or because it is already known that it may exert a causal influence on effects, i.e. manipulating variables in order to produce effects. (Of course, a non-intervention may also be a cause, for example, I may cause a plant to die by not watering it, i.e. by doing nothing.)

Manipulation takes many forms, including:

- action research (discussed in Chapter 18), but which has the problems of rigour brought about by a lack of controls and a lack of external checks such that the attribution of causation may be misplaced;
- a range of experimental approaches (discussed in Chapter 16), which assume, perhaps correctly or incorrectly, acceptably or unacceptably, that variables and people can be isolated, controlled and manipulated; and
- participant observation in qualitative research.

In addressing these approaches, however, serious attention has to be paid to a range of factors:

- the context of the intervention and the power of the situation could affect the outcomes and behaviours of participants (the Hawthorne effect or the Lucifer effect (Zimbardo, 2007a));
- the same causes do not always produce the same effects;
- inappropriate timing of the pre-test and post-test measurements of effects could undermine the reliability of the statement of the effects of the cause;
- there is a problem of accuracy, as groups and individuals cannot both be in a group that is and is not receiving an intervention (Holland's (1986: 947) 'fundamental problem of causal inference', which may not be sufficiently attenuated by randomization) (see Chapter 16);
- process variables and factors, and not only input variables, as these feature in understanding causation;
- the characteristics, personae and specific individual features of participants and their agency, as these influence interventions and their effects.

Experimental techniques, particularly randomized controlled trials (RCT), have considerable potency in establishing causation, and it is here that the identification, isolation and control of independent variables is undertaken, manipulating one independent variable to see if it makes a difference to the outcome. The other variables are held constant and, if a change of outcome is found by manipulating the one independent variable, then the change can be attributed to that independent variable (it becomes the cause), as the other variables have been held constant, i.e. their influence has been ruled out.

In experimental approaches, randomization is an important element in determining causation in order to overcome the myriad range of variables present in, and operating in, participants (the *ceteris paribus* condition discussed earlier). RCTs and experiments (see Chapter 16) are an example of strongly interventionist approaches that seek to establish the effects of causes by introducing one or more interventions into a situation and observing the outcomes of these under controlled conditions.

However, RCTs are often not possible in education and, indeed, are not immune to criticism. For example, the assumptions on which they are founded may be suspect (e.g. oversimplifying the variables at work in a situation, and overriding the influence of mediating or process variables). They frequently do not establish the causal processes or causal chains that obtain in the situation. They neglect participants' motives and motivations. They neglect the context in which the action is located, and they might neglect the moral agency of participants and the ethics of researchers. Indeed context can exert a more powerful causal force than the initial causal intervention, as evidenced in the examples of the Stanford Prison Experiment and the Milgram experiments on obedience (see Chapter 26).

Caution must be exercised in supposing that RCTs, the epitome of causal manipulation and the 'gold standard' in the determination of the effects of causes, will yield sufficient evidence of causation, as these overlook the significance of context and conditions, of processes, of human intentionality, motives and agency, in short of the contiguous causal connections between the intervention and its putative effects. Indeed, even the issue of when and whether an effect is an effect (short-term to long-term, immediate or delayed) is problematic, and attention has to be given to effects that have been caused by the intervention other than those in which the researcher might be initially interested. For example, a researcher might find that pressuring students to learn improves their mathematics scores but leads to an enduring dislike of mathematics. In the contest of moves towards judging 'what works', deciding 'what works' is also as much a matter of values and judgement as it is of empirical outcomes of causation. Success is a value judgement, not simply a measure or a matter of performance. Judging 'what works' in terms of cause and effect is an incomplete analysis of the situation under investigation. A more fitting question should be 'what works for whom, under what conditions, according to what criteria, with what ethical justifiability, and with what consequences for participants?'.

A range of issues in judging the reliability and validity of experimental approaches in establishing causation include the acceptability of laboratory experiments that are divorced from the 'real world' of multiple human behaviours and actions. Here field experiments and natural experiments (see Chapter 16) may attenuate the difficulties posed by laboratory experiments, though these, too, may also create their own problems of reliability and validity.

As an alternative to action research and experimental methods in determining effects from causes, observational approaches can be used, employing both participant and non-participant approaches (see Chapter 23). Whilst these can catch human intentionality, agency and perceptions of causality and events more fully than experimental methods, nevertheless they encounter the same difficulty as action research and experiments, as they, too, have to provide accounts of causal processes and causal chains. Further, in addressing intentionality and agency in causal processes and chains, it is also possible that whilst perceptions might be correct, they might also be fallacious, partial, incomplete, selective, blind and misinformed. I might think that there is a mouse in the room (a cause), and act on the basis of this (an effect), but, in fact, there may be no mouse in the room.

Interventionist approaches, and the determination of the effects of causes, risk mixing perception with fact, and, regardless of evidence, human inclinations may be to judge data and situations on the basis of personal perceptions and opinions that may fly in the face of evidence (the 'base rate fallacy' (Morrison, 2009: 170–1)). This is only one source of unreliability, and it is important to consider carefully what actually are the effects of causes, rather than jumping to statements of causation based on premature evidence of connections.

4.11 Researching the causes of effects

In determining the causes of effects, the enterprise is even more provisional, tentative and inferential than determining the effects of causes, as data are incomplete and backtracking along causal chains and/or searching within causal nets is difficult, as it requires the searching for clues and testing rival hypotheses about causation. It is possible to generate a huge number of potential causes of observed effects, and the problem is in deciding which one(s) is/are correct. Morrison (2009) suggests that approaches that can be adopted in tracing causes from effects include: (a) variants of *ex post facto* research (see Chapter 15); and (b) a seven-stage sequence of steps (see below).

In different forms of *ex post facto* research – quasi-experiments – difficulties arise in their sometimes inability to control and manipulate independent variables or to establish randomization in the sample.

A seven-stage process of tracing causes from effect can be set out thus:

Stage 1: Establish exactly what has to be explained.
Stage 2: Set out possible theoretical foundations for the investigation.
Stage 3: Examine, evaluate and eliminate rival theoretical foundations, selecting the most fitting.
Stage 4: Hypothesize a causal explanation on the basis of the best theoretical foundation.
Stage 5: Set out the assumptions underlying the causal explanation.
Stage 6: Test the causal hypotheses empirically.
Stage 7: Draw conclusions based on the test.

As this poses several concerns for researchers, a worked example is provided here, from Goldthorpe (2007). Goldthorpe seeks to explain the causes of 'persistent differentials in educational attainment' despite increased educational expansion, provision and uptake across the class structure (p. 21), i.e. in the context of increased educational opportunity and its putative weakening influence on class-based determination of life chances.

He proceeds in the seven stages indicated above. Only after that test does he provide a causal explanation for his observed effects.

Stage 1: Establish what it is that has to be explained

First, Goldthorpe observes some 'regularities' (effects) (p. 45):

a In all economically advanced societies over the previous 50 years there has been an expansion of education provision and in the numbers of children staying on in full-time education beyond the minimum schooling age (e.g. going into higher education).
b At the same time, class differentials in educational attainment have remained stubbornly stable and resistant to change, i.e. though children from all classes have participated in expanded education, class origins and their relationship to the likelihood of children staying on in education or entering higher education has only reduced slightly, if at all, and this applies to most societies.

He is establishing social regularities that any causal and theoretical account should seek to explain: the creation, persistence and continued existence of class stratification in modern societies, and the continuing class-relatedness of educational inequality and life chances (p. 24).

Stage 2: Set out possible theoretical foundations for the investigation

Goldthorpe's work is premised on the view that theories are necessary to provide explanatory foundations for how established regularities came to be as they are (p. 21). He initially suggests four theoretical foundations: Marxist theory, liberal theory, cultural theory and rational choice theory.

Stage 3: Examine, evaluate and eliminate rival theoretical foundations

For several reasons which he gives (pp. 22–34), he rejects the first three of these and argues that rational choice theory provides a fitting theoretical foundation for his investigation of the causes of the effects observed (pp. 34–41). True to rational action theory, Goldthorpe (2007: 31) places emphasis on aspirations, in particular noting their relative rather than their absolute status, that is to say, aspirations are relative to class position, as working-class aspirations may not be the same as those of other classes. Different social classes have different levels and kinds of aspiration, influenced – as rational action theory suggests – by the constraints under which they operate, and the perceived costs and benefits that obtain when making decisions (p. 32). Taking *relative* rather than absolute views of aspiration enable accounts to be given that include the fact of increased provision of, and participation in, education by students from all classes, i.e. class differentials have not widened as education provision and participation have widened.

Goldthorpe (2007: 32) suggests that cultural theory may account for what Boudon (1973) terms 'primary effects', that is initial levels of achievement and ability in the early stages of schooling. However Goldthorpe is more concerned with Boudon's 'secondary effects', that is those effects that come into play when children reach branching points (transition points, e.g. from primary to secondary schooling, from secondary education to university) (p. 32) and which have increasingly powerful effects as one progresses through schooling. 'Secondary effects' take account of the aspirations and values that children and their parents hold for education, success and life options, i.e. the intentionality and agency of rational action theory in a way that 'primary effects' do not. Goldthorpe notes that at each successive 'branching point', children from more advantaged backgrounds remain in the educational system and those from less advantaged backgrounds either leave school or choose courses that lead to lower qualifications (hence reducing their opportunities for yet further education).

Goldthorpe (2007: 33) argues that more ambitious options may be regarded less favourably by those from less advantaged class backgrounds as they involve: (a) greater risk of failure; (b) greater cost; and (c) relatively less benefit. In other words, the level of aspiration may vary according to class and the associated levels of assessed cost and risk by members of different classes, and children from less advantaged backgrounds have to be more ambitious than those from more advantaged backgrounds if they are to meet the aspirations and success levels of those from more advantaged backgrounds. Class origins influence risk assessment, cost assessment and benefit assessment – all aspects that are embraced in rational action theory. These determine the choices made by children and their parents.

Stage 4: Hypothesize a causal explanation on the basis of the best theoretical foundation

Goldthorpe (2007: 34) argues that class differentials in educational attainment have persisted because even though there has been expansion and reform of education, and even though the overall costs and benefits that are associated with having more ambitious options have encouraged their take-up, in practice, there has been little concurrent change in the 'relativities between *class-specific* balances': different classes view the costs, risks and benefits differently (p. 34). This is his working hypothesis in trying to establish cause from effect.

Stage 5: Set out the assumptions underlying the causal explanation

Goldthorpe tests his theory initially by drawing attention to the ongoing income differentials between classes; indeed he argues that they have widened (p. 35), with manual labourers more prone to unemployment than professional or managerial workers, i.e. the costs of education are still a factor for less advantaged families, particularly at the end of the period of compulsory schooling. At the time when their children come to the end of compulsory schooling, the income of manual workers will already have peaked (e.g. when they are in their forties), whereas for professional and managerial workers it will still be rising, that is costs are more of a problem for manual workers than for professional and managerial workers, i.e. the costs of higher education relative to income, and the consequent effects on family lifestyle if families are having to finance higher education, are much higher for manual workers. This increased proportion of family income to be spent on education for less advantaged families is coupled with the fact that if children from these families are to succeed, then they need even more ambition than their professional and managerial class counterparts, that is they are at a potential double disadvantage, i.e. relative advantage and disadvantage are not disturbed, a feature on which liberal theory is silent (p. 36).

Goldthorpe makes the point that class position conditions educational decisions made by members of different classes. These different class positions influence different evaluations of the costs and benefits of education, and these are socially reproductive, i.e. the social class position is undisturbed.

Another element of his argument concerns risk aversion. His view is that a major concern of members of different classes is to minimize their risk of downward class mobility, and to maximize their chances for upward class mobility or, at least, maintenance of their existing class location (p. 37). This exerts greater pressure on the already-advantaged classes (e.g. the salariat) to have their children complete higher education (in order to preserve intergenerational class stability) than it does on the children from less advantaged classes (e.g. the waged). It costs more for the children of the advantaged classes to preserve their class position than it does for children of the less advantaged classes to preserve theirs.

With regard to families in the less advantaged classes, Goldthorpe (2007: 38) suggests that they regard higher education in a much more guarded light. Not only does it cost less for them to maintain their class position, but it costs relatively more to achieve upward class mobility; their best options might be for vocational education, as it is cheaper and gives a strong guarantee of *not* moving downwards in class situation (e.g. to be unemployed or unskilled).

Further, for children in this class, the costs (and likelihood) of failure in higher education could be proportionately greater than those for children from more advantaged families. For example in terms of: the relative costs of the higher education; lost earning time; lost opportunity to follow a vocational route in which they have greater likelihood of being successful (p. 38); loss of social solidarity if working-class children pursue higher education, the consequences of which may be to remove them from their class origin and community (pp. 38–9). These factors combine to suggest that children and families from less advantaged backgrounds will require a greater assurance, or expectation, of success in higher education before committing themselves to it, than is the case for children and families from more advantaged backgrounds (p. 68).

Goldthorpe then offers his causal explanation of the effects observed: the persistence of class differentials in educational attainment despite expansion of educational provision and participation (p. 39):

1 Class differentials in the uptake of more ambitious educational options remain because the conditions also remain in which the perceived costs and benefits of these options operate, and these lead to children from less advantaged families generally requiring a greater assurance of success than children from more advantaged families before they (the former) pursue more ambitious educational options.
2 There is a rational explanation for the persistence of these different considerations of ambitious options by class over time, which is rooted in class-based conditions.

These are the two main hypotheses that he seeks to test.

Stage 6: Test the hypotheses empirically

Goldthorpe then proceeds to test his two hypotheses (pp. 39–44, 53–6, and his chapters 3 and 4), adducing evidence concerning several factors, e.g.

- the greater sensitivity of working-class families to the chances of success and failure in comparison to middle-class families (p. 40);
- different levels of ambition in working-class and middle-class families (p. 40);
- relative (class-based) risk aversion in decision making, e.g. the risk of failure and/or of closing options (pp. 55–6);
- the loss of foregone earnings (pp. 53–5);
- expectations of success (pp. 55–6);
- evaluation of the potential benefits, value and utility of higher education (pp. 38–9);
- influences on choices and decision making in different classes (his chapter 3);
- actual choices made by members of different classes;
- fear of downward social mobility (pp. 53–4);
- the need to preserve, or improve on, intergenerational mobility (pp. 53–4);
- financial costs (p. 56).

Goldthorpe indicates that students from lower socio-economic groups either cannot afford, or cannot afford to take risks in, higher education, and he identifies three clusters of possible explanations of persistence of class differentials in educational attainment, including (but not limited to):

Cluster 1: Differences in aspirations and decisions are caused by perceptions of costs: (a) loss of earnings during study time (a bigger drawback for families and students from low-income households than for those from privileged backgrounds); (b) students from low-income households have to work harder than privileged students in order to compete with them; (c) students from low-income households must have greater ambition than privileged students in order to be successful in a higher social class; (d) the financial costs of higher education (HE), proportional to income, are higher for less advantaged students than for more advantaged students and families.

Cluster 2: Differences in aspiration and decisions are caused by relative risk aversion: (a) the risk of failure in HE is greater for students from disadvantaged classes; (b) the risk of loss of further educational opportunities if failure ensues or incorrect options are followed is greater for students from disadvantaged classes than for students from more privileged classes; (c) the risk of loss of social solidarity is greater for students from working-class groups than for students from more privileged classes; (d) less advantaged students must have greater ambition than privileged students in order to be successful in higher social classes.

Cluster 3: Differences in aspiration and decisions are caused by perceptions of relative benefit: (a) the opportunity for upward social mobility through HE is an attraction for students from lower class backgrounds; (b) HE is differentially necessary for preferred or likely employment for those from privileged and less privileged groups.

Stage 7: Draw conclusions based on the test

Goldthorpe indicates that class differentials have, indeed, continued to affect the take-up of educational options. He finds that class differentials in terms of the take-up of more ambitious educational options have been maintained because so too have the conditions in which the perceived costs and benefits of these options lead to children from less advantaged families requiring, on average, a greater assurance of success than their more advantaged counterparts before they decide to pursue such options. There are class differences in terms of relative ambition, risk aversion, perceived costs and benefits, amounts of effort required, assurances of success (and the significance of this), fear of downward social mobility, income, occupational choices and the need for qualifications.

He concludes that the results of empirical tests support his explanation of the factors of relative risk aversion and fear of downward social mobility exerting causal power on educational decision making which, in turn, lead to class differentials in educational attainment being maintained (p. 99).

Goldthorpe argues that this hypothesis is better supported than alternative hypotheses (e.g. educational choices being predetermined by culture, class identity and the class structure).

This example here offers a robust account of how to track backwards from an effect to a cause and how to evaluate the likelihood that the putative cause of the effect actually is the cause of that effect. In summary, for researchers seeking to establish the causes of effects, the task has several aspects:

- Indicate what needs to be done to test the theory and to falsify it.

- Identify the kinds of data required for the theory to be tested.
- Identify the actual data required to test the theory.
- Identify the test conditions and criteria.
- Construct the empirical test.
- Consider the use of primary and secondary data.
- Consider using existing published evidence as part of the empirical test.
- Ensure that action narratives and intentionality are included in causal accounts.

The fundamental problem in determining causes from effects is the uncertainty that surrounds the status of the putative cause; it can only ever be the best to date, and the researcher does not know if it is the best in absolute terms. One effect stems from many causes, and to try to unravel and support hypotheses about these may present immense difficulties for the researcher. Morrison (2009: 204) suggests that there are several ways in which causes may be inferred from effects:

- recognizing that a high level of detail may be required in order to establish causation: high granularity;
- identifying several causal chains, mechanisms and processes in a situation;
- combining micro- and macro-levels of analysis;
- addressing both agency and structure;
- underpinning the data analysis and causal explanation with theory;
- using different kinds of *ex post facto* analysis;
- using correlational and causal-comparative, criterion group analysis;
- ensuring matching of groups in samples and that similar causes apply to both groups;
- adopting the seven-stage process set out above, of generating, testing and elimination of hypotheses and rival hypotheses;
- ensuring clarity on the direction of causation;
- using empirical data to test the causal explanation;
- identification of which is cause and which is effect, and/or which effect then, subsequently, becomes a cause;
- avoiding the problem of over-selective data;
- ensuring that the data fairly represent the phenomenon under investigation;
- recognizing that cause and effect may be blurred;
- accepting that effects may become causes in a cyclical sequence of causation;
- seeking out and recognizing over-determination at work in causal accounts;
- keeping separate the *explanans* (the explanation) from the *explanandum* (that which is to be explained);

- ensuring that alternative theories and causal explanations are explored and tested;
- drawing conclusions based on the evidence, and the evidence alone.

In seeking to establish the causes of effects, there is a need to review and test rival causal theories and to retain those with the greatest explanatory potential and which fit the evidence most comprehensively and securely. Testing of rival hypotheses must be done with data that are different from those that gave rise to the hypotheses, in order to avoid circularity.

The determination of causes from effects does not have the luxury afforded to causal manipulation available in determining effects from causes. Whilst this renders the determination of causes from effects more intractable, nevertheless this is not to say that it cannot be attempted or achieved, only that it is difficult.

Morrison (2009) argues that, in seeking to identify the causes of effects, there is a need for a theoretical foundation to inform causal explanation. Possible causal explanations should be evaluated against rival theories and rival explanations, being operationalized in considerable detail (high granularity), and tested against data that are different from those that gave rise to the causal explanation. Causal explanations should link micro- and macro-factors, include agency and intentionality as well as structural constraints, and contain a level of detail that is sufficiently high in granularity to explain the phenomenon to be explained without concealing or swamping the main points with detail overload, that is the researcher must be able to distinguish the wood from the trees.

4.12 Conclusion

In approaching causal research, then, the researcher is faced with a range of challenges, including for example (Morrison, 2009: 213–14):

- focusing more on causal processes than input/output/results models of causation;
- establishing causation other than through reduction and recombination of atomistic, individual items and elements;
- regarding causation as the understanding of the emergent history of a phenomenon or a whole;
- investigating multiple and simultaneous causes and their multiple and simultaneous effects in a multiply-connected and networked world;
- separating causation from predictability, and drawing the boundaries of predictability for an understanding of the frequent uniqueness of a causal

sequence, that may not be repeatable, i.e. living with uncertainty and with unpredictability;
- learning to work with causation in a situation in which randomness often 'trumps' causation (Gorard, 2001a: 21);
- indicating the utility of an understanding of causation if it has little subsequent predictive strength;
- understanding how to investigate causation in holistic webs of connections, i.e. how it is possible to discover or demonstrate causation when looking at events holistically;
- understanding causation and causal processes in a multi-causal, multi-effect, non-linear and multiply-connected world;
- identifying the causal processes at work in determining social and macro-structures from the actions and interaction of individuals (the micro-worlds) and, conversely, in determining the actions and interactions of individuals from the structures of society and its institutions (the macro-worlds), their ontologies and epistemologies.

The researcher has to decide whether the research is investigating the cause of an effect, the effect of a cause, or both, and when causation is demonstrated, given that absolute certainty is illusory. If one is investigating the effects of causes then the methodologies and approaches to be used might include experiments, action research, survey analysis, observational approaches, or a combination of these (and others). If one is investigating the causes of effects then, in the context of the likelihood of greater uncertainty than in establishing the effects of causes, one can employ numerical and qualitative data in backtracking from effects to causes and in testing hypothesized causes of effects. In all these approaches this chapter has suggested that probabilistic rather than deterministic causation is a more fitting description of the nature of the conclusions reached. It has suggested that, even if it sounds simplistic at first, nevertheless it is both important yet difficult to establish what actually constitutes a cause and an effect. The chapter has suggested that causal processes, with high granularity, are often closer to identifying the operations of causes and effects and the links between them, and that here qualitative data might hold pre-eminence in educational research. However, the chapter has also suggested that there is an important role for numerical approaches, for examining the 'regularities' that might be evidenced in survey approaches, and in the isolation and control of variables in experimental approaches. In short, the chapter is arguing for the power of mixed methodologies and mixed methods in investigating and establishing causation.

Companion Website

The companion website to the book includes PowerPoint slides for this chapter, which list the structure of the chapter and then provide a summary of the key points in each of its sections. This resource can be found online at **www.routledge.com/textbooks/cohen7e**.

Part 2
Planning educational research

The planning of educational research is not an arbitrary matter; the research itself is an inescapably ethical enterprise. We place ethical issues at a very early point in the book to signal this. The research community and those using the findings have a right to expect that research is conducted rigorously, scrupulously and in an ethically defensible manner. All this necessitates careful planning, and this part introduces some key planning issues. Part 2 contains an entirely new chapter on how to choose a research project and a full set of considerations in the planning of educational research. In designing research, we need to consider the issues of how to choose a research project, how to plan it, how to conduct a literature search and review, and how to ensure that the project is practicable. This chapter suggests several ways in which researchers can approach the choice of a research project, and comments on the need for the project to be significant, to consider its purposes and intended outcomes, feasibility, research questions, literature review and overall design.

Further, this part amplifies earlier editions that addressed sampling, including here sampling in mixed methods research, particularly non-probability samples. Further, sampling, reliability and validity are key matters in research – without due attention to these the research could turn out to be worthless. Hence this part addresses these issues in detail. These are complex matters, and we take readers through them systematically. The chapter on sensitive educational research is included here, to underline the point that not only is the very decision to conduct research a sensitive matter, but that often access itself is difficult and sensitive, and this could be the major issue to be faced in planning research. This part sets out a range of planning possibilities so that the eventual selection of sampling procedures, together with decisions on reliability and validity, are made on the basis of *fitness for purpose*, and so that sensitivities in research are anticipated and addressed.

The ethics of educational and social research

In this chapter we review seriatim several issues in the ethical field. These constitute a set of initial considerations that researchers should address in planning research:

- informed consent
- gaining access to and acceptance in the research setting
- the nature of ethics in social research generally
- sources of tension in the ethical debate, including non-maleficence, beneficence and human dignity, absolutist and relativist ethics
- problems and dilemmas confronting the researcher, including matters of privacy, anonymity, confidentiality, internet ethics, betrayal and deception
- ethical problems endemic in particular research methods
- ethics and evaluative research
- regulatory ethical frameworks, guidelines, codes of practice for research and university ethics committees
- personal codes of practice
- sponsored research
- responsibilities to the research community

These provide a useful overview of key considerations planning educational research, and are intended to guide the reader through a maze of ethical concerns in educational research, and the foundations on which they are built. The chapter provides practical examples of checklists of ethics considerations.

5.1 Introduction

The awareness of ethical concerns in research is reflected in the growth of relevant literature and in the appearance of regulatory codes of research practice formulated by various agencies and professional bodies.[1] A major ethical dilemma is that which requires researchers to strike a balance between the demands placed on them as professional scientists in pursuit of truth, and their subjects' rights and values potentially threatened by the research. This is known as the 'costs/benefits ratio', the essence of which is outlined by Frankfort-Nachmias and Nachmias (1992) in Box 5.1, and is a concept we return to later in the chapter. Ethical problems for researchers can multiply surprisingly when they move from the general to the particular, and from the abstract to the concrete.

BOX 5.1   THE COSTS/BENEFITS RATIO

The *costs/benefits ratio* is a fundamental concept expressing the primary ethical dilemma in social research. In planning their proposed research, social scientists have to consider the likely social benefits of their endeavours against the personal costs to the individuals taking part. Possible benefits accruing from the research may take the form of crucial findings leading to significant advances in theoretical and applied knowledge. Failure to do the research may cost society the advantages of the research findings and ultimately the opportunity to improve the human condition. The costs to participants may include affronts to dignity, embarrassment, loss of trust in social relations, loss of autonomy and self-determination and lowered self-esteem. On the other hand, the benefits to participants could take the form of satisfaction in having made a contribution to science and a greater personal understanding of the research area under scrutiny. The process of balancing benefits against possible costs is chiefly a subjective one and not at all easy. There are few or no absolutes and researchers have to make decisions about research content and procedures in accordance with professional and personal values. This costs/benefits *ratio* is the basic dilemma residual in a great deal of social research.

Source: Adapted from Frankfort-Nachmias and Nachmias, 1992

Ethical issues may stem from the kinds of problems investigated by social scientists and the methods they use to obtain valid and reliable data. This means that each stage in the research sequence raises ethical issues. They may arise from the nature of the research project itself (ethnic differences in school achievement, for example); the context for the research (a home for young offenders); the procedures to be adopted (producing high levels of anxiety); methods of data collection (covert observation); the nature of the participants (emotionally challenged adolescents); the type of data collected (highly personal and sensitive information); and what is to be done with the data (publishing in a manner that may cause participants embarrassment or harm); reporting the data (e.g. in a way that the participants will understand) (Oliver, 2003: 17).

In this chapter we present a conspectus of the main issues that may confront researchers. Each research undertaking is an event *sui generis*, and the conduct of researchers cannot be, indeed should not be, forced into a Procrustean system of ethics. When it comes to the resolution of a specific moral problem, each situation frequently offers a spectrum of possibilities. Ethics are 'situated', i.e. they have to be interpreted in specific, local situations (Simons and Usher, 2000).

Whilst many of the issues addressed in this chapter concern procedural ethics, we have to recall that ethics concern right and wrong, good and bad, and so procedural ethics are not enough; one has to consider how the research purposes, contents, methods, reporting and outcomes abide by ethical principles and practices.

For example, a *deontological* view of ethics concerns what one has a duty or obligation to undertake. It involves treating people as ends in themselves rather than as means (Howe and Moses, 1999: 22). By contrast, a *consequentialist* view of ethics concerns the outcomes of actions, for example the utilitarian view that ethical behaviour is that which produces the greatest good for the greatest number. In this view a costs/benefits analysis is considered, but this is problematical, as (a) it is unclear which costs and which benefits should be factored into the analysis, and (b) it assumes that all costs and all benefits are of the same strength (Howe and Moses, 1999: 23).

A third view is a *virtue ethics* basis, in which one pursues what is good simply because it is good and right. These may not sit comfortably together; for example a utilitarian view might argue that a person who has a healthy body and healthy organs should be killed, and his organs used to save five or six lives of those who would otherwise die, whereas a virtue ethics viewpoint (Hammersley, 2009: 213) would argue that this is murder and cannot be justified.

A further example of values clashing is where a deontological view might argue that a failing school should be closed, whereas a utilitarian view would argue against its closure because those 2,000 students would go to an even worse school. An argument from the standpoint of *situational ethics* (e.g. Simons and Usher, 2000; Oliver, 2003), i.e. that what we should do or what is right to do depends on the situation in question, could be challenged on the grounds that it sanctions relativist ethics over absolutist principles (e.g. in debates on euthanasia or abortion).

Seedhouse (1998a) suggests that there are four layers of ethical decisions which, together, constitute an 'epistemological device' (Stutchbury and Fox, 2009: 492) for considering ethical issues in research:

- external (e.g. codes of practice, laws);
- consequential (consequences for individuals, groups, society);
- deontological (what is one's duty to do, largely regardless of consequences, and how decisions about this are reached, rather than the consequences of these actions);
- individual (the core rationale of respect for individual freedom and autonomy).

These can be presented in an ethical grid, a three-dimensional pyramid (Figure 5.1) (one has to imagine that one is looking down on a pyramid) (see also Stutchbury and Fox, 2009: 492).

Ethical decisions have to work in all four layers of the pyramid simultaneously, and this may give rise to points of conflict within and between the different layers of the pyramid, for example, individual and external layers might conflict (e.g. if I find that my friend, who is a school principal, is putting school funds to questionable use, should I report it and lose a friend, or keep silent and, thereby, collude to prevent the public from hearing what it needs to hear). Stutchbury and Fox (2009) provide a clear analysis of Seedhouse's pyramidal grid and indicate important questions to be raised at each level of the grid.

Ethical decisions are built on ethical principles, but different ethical principles may conflict (Hammersley, 2009), and we explore this in the chapter.

This chapter exposes the problematic nature of many key ethical issues in educational research, and, in a sense, though we devote a particular section of the chapter to ethical dilemmas, the whole of the chapter suggests that ethics in educational research is fraught with dilemmas. We start with one of the fundamental concepts in research: informed consent.

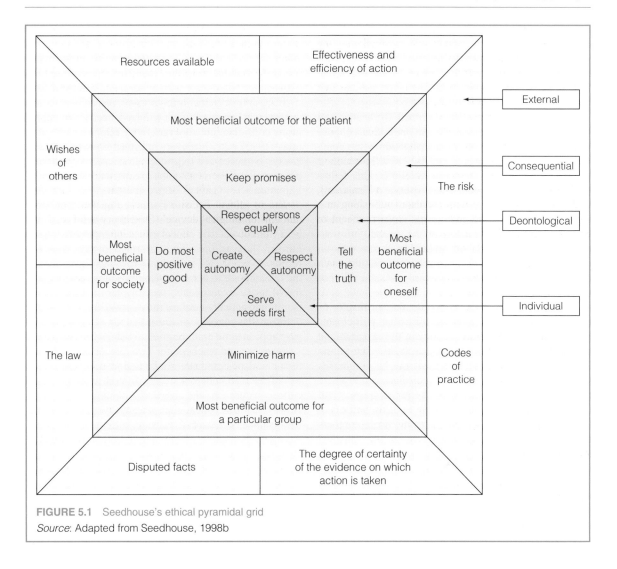

FIGURE 5.1 Seedhouse's ethical pyramidal grid
Source: Adapted from Seedhouse, 1998b

5.2 Informed consent

Much social research necessitates obtaining the consent and cooperation of subjects who are to assist in investigations and of significant others in the institutions or organizations providing the research facilities. Whilst some cultures may not be stringent about informed consent, in others there are strict protocols for informed consent. Frankfort-Nachmias and Nachmias (1992) suggest that informed consent is particularly important if participants are going to be exposed to any stress, pain, invasion of privacy, or if they are going to lose control over what happens (e.g. in drug research); such informed consent requires full information about the possible consequences and dangers. Informed consent,

aver Howe and Moses (1999), is a cornerstone of ethical behaviour, as it respects the right of individuals to exert control over their lives and to take decisions for themselves.

The principle of informed consent arises from the subject's right to freedom and self-determination. Being free is a condition of living in a democracy, and when restrictions and limitations are placed on that freedom they must be justified and consented to, as in research. Consent thus protects and respects the right of self-determination and places some of the responsibility on the participant should anything go wrong in the research. Self-determination requires participants to have the right to weigh up the risks and benefits of being involved in a piece of research, and deciding for themselves whether to take part (Howe and Moses, 1999: 24). As part of the right to self-determination, the subject has the right to refuse to take part, or to withdraw once the research has begun (see Frankfort-Nachmias and Nachmias, 1992). Thus informed consent implies informed refusal.

Informed consent has been defined by Diener and Crandall as 'the procedures in which individuals choose whether to participate in an investigation after being informed of facts that would be likely to influence their decisions' (Diener and Crandall, 1978: 57). This definition involves four elements: competence, voluntarism, full information and comprehension. 'Competence' implies that responsible, mature individuals will make correct decisions if they are given the relevant information. It is incumbent on researchers to ensure they do not engage individuals incapable of making such decisions either because of immaturity or some form of psychological impairment.

'Voluntarism' entails applying the principle of informed consent and thus ensuring that participants freely choose to take part (or not) in the research and guarantees that exposure to risks is undertaken knowingly and voluntarily. This element can be problematical, especially in the field of medical research where unknowing patients are used as guinea pigs. 'Full information' implies that consent is fully informed, though in practice it is often impossible for researchers to inform subjects on everything, e.g. on the statistical treatment of data; and, as we shall see below, on those occasions when the researchers themselves do not know everything about the investigation. In such circumstances, the strategy of reasonably informed consent has to be applied. Box 5.2 illustrates a set of guidelines used in the USA that are based on the idea of *reasonably informed consent*.[2] 'Comprehension' refers to the fact that participants fully understand the nature of the research project, even when procedures are complicated and entail risks. Suggestions have been made to ensure that subjects fully comprehend the situation they are putting themselves into, e.g. by using highly educated subjects, by engaging a consultant to explain difficulties, or by building into the research scheme a time lag between the request for participation and decision time.

If these four elements are present, researchers can be assured that subjects' rights will have been given appropriate consideration. As Frankfort-Nachmias and Nachmias (1992) note, however, informed consent may not always be necessary (e.g. deception may be justified), but that, as a general rule, the greater the risk, the more important it is to gain informed consent.

Ruane (2005: 21) also raises the question of 'how much information is enough'; she argues that this may be an unknown, not necessarily deliberately withheld. Further, just as providing information may bias the results (i.e. it is important for the integrity of the research *not* to disclose its purposes or contents, e.g. the Milgram experiments, see Chapter 26), she argues that it may actually confuse the respondents.

From the remarks on informed consent so far, we may appear to be assuming relationships between peers – researcher and teachers, for example, or research professor and postgraduate students and this assumption would seem to underpin many of the discussions of an ethical nature in the research literature generally. However, much educational research involves children who cannot be regarded as being on equal terms with the researcher and it is important to keep this in mind at all stages in the research process including the point where informed consent is sought. In this connection we refer to the important work of Fine and Sandstrom (1988), whose ethnographic and participant observational studies of children and young people focus, among other issues, on this asymmetry with respect to the problems of obtaining informed consent from their young subjects and explaining the research in a comprehensible fashion. As a guiding principle, they advise that, while it is desirable to lessen the power differential

---

BOX 5.2 GUIDELINES FOR REASONABLY INFORMED CONSENT

1 A fair explanation of the procedures to be followed and their purposes.
2 A description of the attendant discomforts and risks reasonably to be expected.
3 A description of the benefits reasonably to be expected.
4 A disclosure of appropriate alternative procedures that might be advantageous to the participants.
5 An offer to answer any enquiries concerning the procedures.
6 An instruction that the person is free to withdraw consent and to discontinue participation in the project at any time without prejudice to the participant.

Source: US Department of Health, Education and Welfare, *Institutional Guide to DHEW Policy*, 1971

between children and adult researchers, the difference will remain and its elimination may be ethically inadvisable.

There are other aspects of the problem of informed consent (or refusal) in relation to young, or very young, children (Greig and Taylor, 1999: 143–55), not the least of which is to abide by the requirements of legislation on working with children and on child protection. Greig and Taylor argue (1999: 150) that non-therapeutic research should only be conducted with children where there is negligible risk and where the informed consent of gatekeepers (e.g. guardians and parents) has been obtained in advance, including how data will be stored (e.g. ICT-related issues), destroyed (e.g. of confidential data or audio/visual recordings) upon completion of the research and, indeed, how recording data may be switched off during an interview, and how data will be used. For a fuller guide on ethical issues in conducting research on early childhood education see Mukherji and Albon (2010).

Gatekeepers are in a very responsible position and they should not be overlooked. Oliver (2003: 39) comments that they have much more at stake – to lose – than researchers, since, whereas researchers can move on from one participant or research field to another, gatekeepers live with the daily consequences of the research and its effects on participants. Researchers, therefore, have an ethical obligation to seek informed consent of gatekeepers.

Seeking informed consent with regard to minors involves two stages. First, researchers consult and seek permission from those adults responsible for the prospective subjects and second, they approach the young people themselves. The adults in question will be, for example, parents, teachers, tutors or psychiatrists, youth leaders or team coaches, depending on the research context. The point of the research will be explained, questions invited and permission to proceed to the next stage sought. Objections, for whatever reason, will be duly respected. Obtaining approval from relevant adults may be more difficult than in the case of the children, but, being sensitive to children's welfare, it is vital that researchers secure such approval. It may be useful if, in seeking the consent of children, researchers bear in mind the provisory comments below.

While seeking children's permission and cooperation is an automatic part of quantitative research (a child cannot unknowingly complete a simple questionnaire), the importance of informed consent in qualitative research is not always recognized. Speaking of participant observation, for example, Fine and Sandstrom (1988) say that researchers must provide a credible and meaningful explanation of their research intentions, especially in situations where they have little authority, and that children must be given a real and legitimate opportunity to say that they do not want to take part. The authors advise that where subjects do refuse, they should not be questioned, their actions should not be recorded and they should not be included in any book or article (even under a pseudonym). Where they form part of a group, they may be included as part of a collectivity. Fine and Sandstrom consider that such rejections are sometimes a result of mistrust of the researcher. They suggest that at a later date, when the researcher has been able to establish greater rapport with the group, those who refused initially may be approached again, perhaps in private.

Two particular groups of children require special mention: very young children, and those not capable of making a decision. Researchers intending to work with pre-school or nursery children may dismiss the idea of seeking informed consent from their would-be subjects because of their age, but Fine and Sandstrom (1988) would recommend otherwise. Even though such children would not understand what research was, the authors advise that the children be given some explanation. For example, one to the effect that an adult will be watching and playing with them might be sufficient to provide a measure of informed consent consistent with the children's understanding. As Fine and Sandstrom (1988) comment, 'children should be told as much as possible, even if some of them cannot understand the full explanation. Their age should not diminish their rights, although their level of understanding must be taken into account in the explanations that are shared with them.'

The second group consists of those children who are to be used in a research project and who may not meet Diener and Crandall's (1978) criterion of 'competence' (a group of psychologically impaired children, for example – the issue of 'advocacy' applies here). In such circumstances there may be institutional or local authority guidelines to follow. In the absence of these, the requirements of informed consent would be met by obtaining the permission of headteachers acting *in loco parentis* or who have had delegated to them the responsibility for providing informed consent by the parents.

Two cautions: first, where an extreme form of research is planned, parents would have to be fully informed in advance and their consent obtained; and second, whatever the nature of the research and whoever is involved, should a child show signs of discomfort or stress, the research should be terminated immediately. For further discussion on the care that needs to be exercised in working with children we refer readers to Greig and Taylor (1999); Holmes (1998) and Graue and Walsh (1998).

Informed consent not only applies to children, but to a range of vulnerable groups (adults, the disabled, those who cannot speak, see or hear, those in hospital, those in care, those suffering from autism (cf. Waltz, 2007), even children undergoing neuroimaging research (Coch, 2007)). Oliver (2003: 35–6) defines vulnerable groups as 'those individuals or categories of people who may not have the required degree of understanding (for whatever reason) to give their informed consent to participation in research'. In many cases ethics committees will require a full indication of how the ethics of the research will be addressed, and this requires researchers to 'think hard' about ethical issues (Crow *et al.*, 2006: 86).

Informed consent requires an explanation and description of several factors, including, for example:

- the purposes, contents, procedures, reporting and dissemination of the research;
- any foreseeable risks and negative outcomes, discomfort or consequences and how they will be handled;
- benefits that might derive from the research;
- incentives to participate and rewards from participating;
- right to voluntary non-participation, withdrawal and re-joining the project;
- rights and obligations to confidentiality and nondisclosure of the research, participants and outcomes;
- disclosure of any alternative procedures that may be advantageous;
- opportunities for participants to ask questions about any aspect of the research;
- signed contracts for participation.

Researchers who seek informed consent must ensure – check – that participants really do understand the implications of the research, not mindlessly sign a consent form. There are many more issues, and researchers will need to decide what to include in informed consent. Not least amongst these is the issue of volunteering. Participants may feel coerced or pressurized to volunteer (e.g. by a school principal), or may not wish to offend a researcher by refusing to participate, or may succumb to peer pressure to volunteer (or not to volunteer), or may wish to volunteer for reasons other than the researcher's (e.g. to malign a school principal or senior colleagues, to gain resources for his or her department, or to gain approval from colleagues). Indeed it is important to ensure that participants are not 'railroaded' into participating, e.g. by a school principal

who makes the decision for the staff, or where staff are not given sufficient time to come to a decision on whether or not to participate, or where staff do not wish to appear unhelpful to researchers (who, indeed, may be friends or acquaintances of the researcher), even though they actually would rather not take part in the research (Oliver, 2003: 27). The choice on whether or not to participate must be genuinely free, with no negative repercussions for not taking part, and no feelings of researchers having taken advantage of powerless participants.

The issue is also raised here of whether participants should be given inducements to participate, such as payment, gifts or the opportunity to enter a 'lucky draw'. On the one hand the argument runs that any kind of material inducement distorts a genuine relationship between the researcher and the participants, such that participants may say something only because they will be paid for it, or may give perfunctory information just to be able to obtain the reward, and whose commitment is actually very small. On the other hand participants are giving their time and effort to the research, so they should be paid for it, just as in other kinds of work (cf. Oliver, 2003: 23 and 59). Researchers have to ensure that volunteers have real freedom of choice if informed consent is to be fulfilled.

Arguments against informed consent

It must also be remembered that there are some research methods where it is impossible to seek informed consent. Covert observation, for example, as used in Patrick's study of a Glasgow gang (Chapter 11), or experimental techniques involving deception, as in Milgram's Obedience-to-authority experiments (Chapter 26) would, by their very nature, rule out the option. And, of course, there may be occasions when problems arise even though consent has been obtained. Burgess (1989), for example, cites his own research in which teachers had been informed that research was taking place but in which it was not possible to specify exactly what data would be collected or how they would be used. It could be said, in this particular case, that individuals were not fully informed, that consent had not been obtained and that privacy had been violated.

Some researchers advocate informed consent on the grounds that it yields better data because it is a consequence of establishing rapport and trust between researchers and participants (e.g. Crow *et al.*, 2006: 76). Indeed it might bring better participation rates in research, as participants might be more likely to agree to being involved if they are given the 'full picture' of the research or if assurances of confidentiality are given.

On the other hand, informed consent is seen less positively, as it renders some research (e.g. necessarily covert research) unresearchable, as it provides poorer participation rates where some participants may be reluctant to sign a consent form or may regard the research as too bureaucratic (Crow *et al.*, 2006: 88), antagonistic, coercive and alienating. Indeed it might be seen as bringing a level of formality into what some cultures and communities would prefer to keep on an informal footing (Crow *et al.*, 2006: 88–9), be they lower social groups or powerful persons (and the latter might find several ways of concealing their true views). Indeed Howe and Moses (1999: 33–4) argue that informed consent does not only mean that of the individual but of the community; they write: 'it is not up to the individual community members to give informed consent to have social researchers peering into the social life of the community, for it is not always *theirs* to give'.

Informing people of the research might provoke the Hawthorne effect (discussed in Chapter 10) or might disturb the natural behaviour of participants (Oliver, 2003: 53) as they will be conscious of being watched.

Seeking formal informed consent might lead to a narrow range of data and a neglect of the richest, most authentic data, as participants might become more guarded in what they disclose (e.g. about relationships). Indeed in some cultures, Oliver (2003: 103) writes, participants may find it an unusual experience to be asked to complete a questionnaire, and they may regard it as a 'test'. Howe and Moses (1999: 89) ask how realistic it is to obtain informed consent from both parents, to interview their child, if the parents are separated. The effects of all of these difficulties might lead to research only concerning itself with 'safe', easily researchable topics and to the neglect of research into vulnerable and excluded groups. As Humphreys (1975), the author of the celebrated study *Tearoom Trade* (1970), a study of homosexual meeting arrangements, wrote in his 1975 postscript on ethics: 'the greatest harm a social scientist could do to this man would be to ignore him' (p. 169).

Informed consent may not be possible in covert research, or research in which important yet sensitive issues or groups are being investigated (see Chapter 9), as it is only through covert research and perhaps deception that one can gain access to such sensitive groups or practices. It might be important to research such groups (see Mitchell's (1993) defence of secrecy in research for the public good).

Wax (1982: 44) holds a powerful position against informed consent, arguing that it offers both 'too much and too little': 'too much' in the sense that it is 'over-

scrupulous and disruptive', particularly in emergent situations and qualitative research where casual conversations figure highly as field notes, and 'too little' in the sense that field researchers often require much more than informed consent, for example they seek trust, 'active assistance' from participants and 'colleague-ship'. Indeed he suggests that informed consent reinforces asymmetries of power between researchers and participants, rather than equalizing them. Wax makes a telling point (p. 42) that informed consent in many kinds of research is not a 'one-shot, once-and-for-all' affair (as befits experimental research rather than qualitative or ethnographic research), but has to be continuously negotiated in qualitative, emergent research.

As a general rule, however, informed consent is an important principle. It is this principle that will form the basis of an implicit contractual relationship between the researcher and the researched and will serve as a foundation on which subsequent ethical considerations can be structured.

5.3 Access and acceptance

The relevance of the principle of informed consent becomes apparent at the initial stage of the research project – that of access to the institution or organization where the research is to be conducted, and acceptance by those whose permission one needs before embarking on the task. We highlight this stage of access and acceptance in particular at this point because it offers the best opportunity for researchers to present their credentials as serious investigators and establish their own ethical position with respect to their proposed research.

Investigators cannot expect access to a nursery, school, college or university as a matter of right. They have to demonstrate that they are worthy, as researchers and human beings, of being accorded the facilities needed to carry out their investigations. The advice of Bell (1991: 37) is to gain permission early on, with fully informed consent gained, and indicating to participants the possible benefits of the research.

The first stage thus involves the gaining of official permission to undertake one's research in the target community. This will mean contacting, in person or in writing, an appropriate official and/or the chairperson of the governors if one is to work in a school, along with the headteacher or principal. At a later point, significant figures who will be responsible for, or assist in, the organization and administration of the research will also need to be contacted – the deputy head or senior teacher, for instance, and most certainly the classteacher if children are to be used in the research. Since the researcher's potential for intrusion and perhaps disruption is considerable, amicable relations with the classteacher in particular should be fostered as expeditiously as possible. If the investigation involves teachers as participants, propositions may have to be put to the stakeholders and conditions negotiated. Where the research is to take place in another kind of institution, the approach will be similar, although the organizational structure will be different.

Achieving goodwill and cooperation is especially important where the proposed research extends over a period of time: days, perhaps, in the case of an ethnographic study; months (or perhaps years) where longitudinal research is involved. Access does not present quite such a problem when, for example, a one-off survey requires respondents to give up half-an-hour of their time or when a researcher is normally a member of the organization where the research is taking place (an insider), though in the case of the latter, it is generally unwise to take cooperation for granted. Where research procedures are extensive and complicated, however, or where the design is developmental or longitudinal, or where researchers are not normally based in the target community, the problems of access are more involved and require greater preparation. Box 5.3 gives a flavour of the kinds of accessibility problems that can be experienced (Foster, 1989).

Having identified the official and significant figures whose permission must be sought, and before actually meeting them, researchers will need to clarify in their own minds the precise nature and scope of their research. It is desirable that they have a total picture of what it all entails, even if the overall scheme is a provisional one (though we have to bear in mind that this may cause difficulties later). In this respect researchers could, for instance, identify the aims of the research; its practical applications, if any, the design, methods and procedures to be used, the nature and size of samples or groups, what tests are to be administered and how, what

activities are to be observed, which subjects are to be interviewed, observational needs, the time involved, the degree of disruption envisaged, arrangements to guarantee confidentiality with respect to data (if this is necessary), the role of feedback and how findings can best be disseminated, the overall timetable within which the research is to be encompassed, and finally, whether assistance will be required in the organization and administration of the research.

By such planning and foresight, both researchers and institutions will have a good idea of the demands likely to be made on both subjects (be they children or teachers) and organizations. It is also a good opportunity to anticipate and resolve likely problems, especially those of a practical kind. A long, complicated questionnaire, for example, may place undue demands on the comprehension skills and attention spans of a particular class of 13-year-olds or a relatively inexperienced teacher could feel threatened by sustained research scrutiny. Once this kind of information has been sorted out and clarified, researchers will be in a stronger position to discuss their proposed plans in an informed, open and frank manner (though not necessarily too open, as we shall see) and may thereby more readily gain permission, acceptance, and support. It must be remembered that hosts will have perceptions of researchers and their intentions and that these need to be positive. Researchers can best influence such perceptions by presenting themselves as competent, trustworthy and accommodating.

Once this preliminary information has been collected, researchers are duly prepared for the next stage: making actual contact in person, perhaps after an introductory letter, with appropriate people in the organization with a view to negotiating access. If the research is university-based, they will have the support of their university and supervisor. Festinger and Katz (1966) consider that there is real economy in going to the very top of the organization or system in question to obtain assent and coopera-

---

BOX 5.3   CLOSE ENCOUNTERS OF A RESEARCHER KIND

My first entry into a staffroom at the college was the occasion of some shuffling and shifting of books and chairs so that I could be given a comfortable seat whilst the tutor talked to me from a standing position. As time progressed my presence was almost taken for granted and later, when events threatened the security of the tutors, I was ignored. No one enquired as to whether they could assist me and my own enquiries were met with cursory answers and confused looks, followed by the immediate disappearance of the individuals concerned, bearing a pile of papers. I learned not to make too many enquiries. Unfortunately, when individuals feel insecure, when their world is threatened with change that is beyond their control, they are likely to respond in an unpredictable manner to persons within their midst whose role is unclear, and the role of the researcher is rarely understood by those not engaged in research.

Source: Foster, 1989: 194

tion. This is particularly so where the structure is clearly hierarchical and where lower levels are always dependent on their superiors. They consider it likely that the nature of the research will be referred to the top of the organization sooner or later, and that there is a much better chance for a favourable decision if leaders are consulted at the outset. It may also be the case that heads will be more open-minded than those lower down, who because of their insecurity may be less cooperative.

The authors also warn against using the easiest entrances into the organization when seeking permission. Researchers may perhaps seek to come in as allies of individuals or groups who have a special interest to exploit and who see research as a means to their ends, rather than entering the situation in the common interests of all parties, with findings equally available to all groups and persons (Festinger and Katz, 1966). Investigators should thus seek as broad a basis for their support as possible. Other potential problems may be circumvented by making use of accepted channels of communication in the institution or organization. Festinger and Katz caution (1966) that if information is limited to a single channel then the study risks becoming identified with the interests that are associated with that channel.

Following contact, there will be a negotiation process. At this point researchers will give as much information about the aims, nature and procedures of the research as is appropriate. This is very important: information that may prejudice the results of the investigation may have to be withheld. Aronson and Carlsmith (1969), for instance, note that one cannot imagine researchers who are studying the effects of group pressure on conformity announcing their intentions in advance. On the other hand, researchers may find themselves on dangerous ground if they go to the extreme of maintaining a 'conspiracy of silence', because, as Festinger and Katz (1966) note, such a stance is hard to keep up if the research is extensive and lasts over several days or weeks, and trying to preserve secrecy might lead to an increase in the spread and wildness of rumours. If researchers do not want their potential hosts and/or subjects to know too much about specific hypotheses and objectives, then a simple way out is to present an explicit statement at a fairly general level with one or two examples of items that are not crucial to the study as a whole. As most research entails some risks, especially where field studies are concerned, and as the presence of an observer scrutinizing various aspects of community or school life may not be relished by all in the group, investigators must at all times manifest a sensitive appreciation of their hosts' and subjects' position and reassure anyone who feels threatened by the work. Such reassurance could take the form of a statement of conditions and guarantees given by researchers at this negotiation stage. By way of illustration, Box 5.4 contains conditions laid down for the Open University students' school-based research project.

Ethical considerations pervade the whole process of research; these will be no more so than at the stage of access and acceptance, where appropriateness of topic, design, methods, guarantees of confidentiality, analysis and dissemination of findings must be negotiated with relative openness, sensitivity, honesty, accuracy and scientific impartiality. There can be no rigid rules in this context. It will be a case of formulating and abiding by one's own situated ethics. These will determine what is acceptable and what is not acceptable. As Hitchcock and Hughes say in this regard:

Individual circumstances must be the final arbiter. As far as possible it is better if the teacher can discuss the research with all parties involved. On other occasions it may be better for the teacher to develop a pilot study and uncover some of the problems in advance of the research proper. If it appears that the research is going to come into conflict with aspects of school policy, management styles, or individual personalities, it is better to confront the issues

---

BOX 5.4 CONDITIONS AND GUARANTEES PROFFERED FOR A SCHOOL-BASED RESEARCH PROJECT

1 All participants must be given the chance to remain anonymous.
2 All data must be given strict confidentiality.
3 Interviewees should have the chance to verify statements at the stage of drafting the report (respondent validation).
4 Participants should be given a copy of the final report.
5 Permission for publication must be gained from the participants.
6 If possible, the research report should be of benefit to the school and participants.

Source: Adapted from Bell, 1991

head on, consult relevant parties, and make rearrangements in the research design where possible or necessary.

(Hitchcock and Hughes, l995: 41)

A pilot study can be useful to judge the effects of a piece of research on participants (Oliver, 2003: 37). Where a pilot study is not feasible it may be possible to arrange one or two scouting forays to assess possible problems and risks. By way of summary, we refer the reader to Box 5.5.

5.4 The field of ethics

Whatever the specific nature of their work, social researchers must take into account the effects of the research on participants, and act in such a way as to preserve their dignity as human beings: this is their responsibility to participants. Such is ethical behaviour. Indeed, ethics has been defined as 'a matter of principled sensitivity to the rights of others', and that 'while truth is good, respect for human dignity is better' (Cavan, 1977: 810).

Kimmel (1988) has pointed out that it is important we recognize that the distinction between ethical and unethical behaviour is not dichotomous, even though the normative code of prescribed ('ought') and proscribed ('ought not') behaviours, as represented by the ethical standards of a profession, seem to imply that it is. Judgements about whether behaviour conflicts with professional values lie on a *continuum* that ranges from the clearly ethical to the clearly unethical. The point here is that ethical principles are not absolute, generally speaking, though some maintain that they are as we shall see shortly, but must be interpreted in the light of the research context and of other values at stake.

BOX 5.5 NEGOTIATING ACCESS CHECKLIST

1 **Clear official channels by formally requesting permission to carry out your investigation as soon as you have an agreed project outline.**
   Some local education authorities (LEAs) insist that requests to carry out research are channelled through the LEA office. Check what is required in your area.
2 **Speak to the people who will be asked to cooperate.**
   Getting the LEA or head's permission is one thing, but you need to have the support of the people who will be asked to give interviews or complete questionnaires.
3 **Submit the project outline to the head, if you are carrying out a study in your or another educational institution.**
   List people you would like to interview or to whom you wish to send questionnaires and state conditions under which the study will be conducted.
4 **Decide what you mean by anonymity and confidentiality.**
   Remember that if you are writing about 'the head of English' and there is only one head of English in the school, the person concerned is immediately recognizable.
5 **Decide whether participants will receive a copy of the report and/or see drafts or interview transcripts.**
   There are cost and time implications. Think carefully before you make promises.
6 **Inform participants what is to be done with the information they provide.**
   For your eyes and those of the examiner only? Shown to the head, the LEA, etc.?
7 **Prepare an outline of intentions and conditions under which the study will be carried out to hand to the participants.**
   Even if you explain the purpose of the study the conditions and the guarantees, participants may forget.
8 **Be honest about the purpose of the study and about the conditions of the research.**
   If you say an interview will last ten minutes, you will break faith if it lasts an hour. If you are conducting the investigation as part of a degree or diploma course, say so.
9 **Remember that people who agree to help are doing you a favour.**
   Make sure you return papers and books in good order and on time. Letters of thanks should be sent, no matter how busy you are.
10 **Never assume 'it will be all right'. Negotiating access is an important stage in your investigation.**
   If you are an inside researcher, you will have to live with your mistakes, so take care.

Source: Adapted from Bell, 1991

Of course, a considerable amount of research does not cause pain or indignity to the participants, self-esteem is not necessarily undermined nor confidences betrayed, and the social scientist may only infrequently be confronted with an unresolvable ethical dilemma. Where research is ethically sensitive, however, many factors may need to be taken into account and these may vary from situation to situation, for example: the age of those being researched; whether the subject matter of the research is a sensitive area; whether the aims of the research are in any way subversive (vis-à-vis subjects, teachers or institution); the extent to which the researcher and researched can participate and collaborate in planning the research; how the data are to be processed, interpreted and used.

Ethics also features in discussions of ownership of the data, and when the ownership passes from the participants to the researcher, and with what constraints, requirements, conditions and powers over the use and dissemination of the findings placed upon the data by the participants (cf. Howe and Moses, 1999: 43). Researchers need to be clear whether they own the data, once the data have been given, or whether the participants have control over what is released, and to whom; this should be agreed, where possible, before the research commences. Oliver (2003: 63), for example, argues that the raw data are still the property of the participants, but once the data have been analysed and interpreted, they become the property of the researcher. This is unclear, however, as it does not cover, for example, observational data, field notes and suchlike, which are written by the researcher though often about other people. Negotiating ownership rights, rights to release or withdraw data, rights to control access to data, rights to verify and validate data, rights to vet data or see interim or incomplete or uncompleted reports, rights to select data and decide on their representativeness, rights to own or change the final report, rights to retain data after the research (e.g. for other purposes, as in the ongoing compilation of a longitudinal or comparative study), move the conduct of research beyond being a mechanical exercise to being an ethical exercise (cf. Oliver, 2003: 63–5).

5.5 Sources of tension

Non-maleficence, beneficence and human dignity

The first tension, as expressed by Aronson and Carlsmith (1969), is that which exists between two sets of related values held by society: a belief in the value of free scientific enquiry in pursuit of truth and knowledge; and a belief in the dignity of individuals and their right to those considerations that follow from it. It is this polarity that we referred to earlier as the costs/benefits ratio and by which 'greater consideration must be given to the risks to physical, psychological, humane, proprietary and cultural values than to the potential contribution of research to knowledge' (Social Sciences and Humanities Research Council of Canada, 1981), i.e. the issue of 'non-maleficence' (where no harm is wished upon subjects or occurs).

Non-maleficence (do no harm) is enshrined in the Hippocratic oath, in which the principle of *primum non nocere* (first of all, do no harm) is held as a guiding precept. So also with research. The research should not damage the participants at all, physically, psychologically, emotionally, professionally, personally and so on (e.g. participants may find it very distressing to relive the experience of being bullied by students or other staff and this must either be avoided, pointed out in advance in terms of informed consent, or participants should be given the opportunity not to take part in that area of the research) (cf. Oliver, 2003: 32). It requires researchers and the participants to consider carefully the possible consequences of the research on both participants and the researchers (e.g. the negative effects on the participants and the researchers in Scheper-Hughes's (1979) study of a village in Ireland, or the possible effects of 'whistle-blowing'). Indeed Oliver (2003: 89) raises the question of whether private organizations, such as those with trade secrets, should be permitted to keep those secrets private.

This moves beyond the costs/benefits analysis of utilitarianism, as it considers the need to avoid doing moral harm to participants. At first sight this seems uncontentious; of course we do not wish to bring harm to our research subjects, and it is a golden rule that the research must ensure that participants are no worse off at the end of the research than they were at the start of the research. However, what constitutes 'harm' is unclear, one person's harm is a society's benefit, and whether a little harm for a few is tolerable in the interests of a major benefit for all, or even for the person concerned, throws into relief the tension involved here. The question is whether the end justifies the means. As a general principle we would advocate the application of *primum non nocere*, and, indeed, ethics regulatory boards, for example in universities perusing research proposals (discussed later), are guided heavily by this principle. However, there could be tensions here. What do you do if you discover that the headteacher has a serious alcohol problem or is having an affair with a parent? What do you do if your research shows teachers in the school with very serious weaknesses, such that their contracts should be terminated in the interests of the students?

When researchers are confronted with dilemmas such as these (though they are likely to occur much less in education than in social psychology or medicine), it is generally considered that they resolve them in a manner that avoids the extremes of, on the one hand, giving up the idea of research and, on the other, ignoring the rights of the subjects. At all times the welfare of subjects should be kept in mind (cf. British Educational Research Association, 2004), even if it involves compromising the impact of the research. Researchers should never lose sight of the obligations they owe to those who are helping, and should constantly be alert to alternative techniques should the ones they are employing at the time prove controversial. Sikes (2006: 112) quotes the words of Lather (1986) in describing 'rape research' as 'research in which the researcher gets what they want and then clears off, giving little or nothing in return and maybe even causing damage'. This is unethical.

Laing (1967: 53) offers a cautionary view of data where he writes that they are 'not so much given as *taken* out of a constantly elusive matrix of happenings. We should speak of *capta* rather than data', or as 'vanity ethnography' (to boost the researcher's self-image) (Maynard, 1993: 329, cited in Sikes, 2006: 114), 'narrative catharsis' (Tierney, 2002: 393, cited in Sikes, 2006: 114) or 'narcissism' (Reed-Danahay, 2002: 424, cited in Sikes, 2006: 114).

The relationship between the research and the researched is reflected in the principles of the American Psychological Association which, as Zechmeister and Shaughnessy (1992) show, attempt to strike a balance between the rights of investigators to seek an understanding of human behaviour, and the rights and welfare of individuals who participate in the research. In the final reckoning, the decision to go ahead with a research project rests on a subjective evaluation of the costs both to the individual and society.

The corollary of non-maleficence is beneficence: what benefits will the research bring, and to whom? Many would-be participants could be persuaded to take part in research if it is made clear that it will, or may, bring personal, educational and social benefits. For example, it may lead to the improvement of learning, increased funding and resources for a particular curriculum area, improved approaches to the teaching of a subject, increased self-esteem for students, or additional teachers in a school, increased self-awareness in the participants (Oliver, 2003: 35) and so on. Whilst it is sometimes worth including a statement of potential benefit when contacting schools and individuals, it may

also be an actual requirement for ethics regulatory boards or sponsors.

The recipients of the benefit also have to be factored into the discussion here. A researcher may gain promotion, publications, a degree, research sponsorship and celebrity from a piece of research. However, the research might still leave the participants untouched, underprivileged, living and working in squalid and under-resourced conditions, under-supported, and with no material, educational or other improvements brought to the quality of their lives and work. As one of Whyte's contacts remarked ruefully in his celebrated study of an Italian slum in *Street Corner Society* (1955), the locals had helped many researchers to become famous and get their doctorates, though leaving the locals' quality of life with no improvement.

On the one hand it could be argued that research that did not lead to such benefits is unethical; on the other hand it could be that the research helps to place the issue on the agenda of decision makers and that, in the long run, it could contribute to a groundswell of opinion that, itself, brings change. Whilst it may be fanciful to believe that a single piece of research will automatically lead to improvement, the ethical question raised here – who benefits? – suggests that a selfish approach to the benefits of the research by the researcher is unethical.

This latter point requires researchers to do more than pay lip service to the notion of treating research participants as subjects rather than as objects to be used instrumentally – research fodder, so to speak – imbuing them with self-esteem and respect. One can treat people with respect but still the research may make no material difference to their lives. Whilst it is surely impossible to argue against treating people with dignity and respect, it raises the issue of the obligations and commitments of the researcher. Let us say that the researcher has been working closely in a school for one or two years; surely that researcher has an obligation to improve the lives of those being researched, rather than simply gathering data instrumentally? To do the latter would be inhumane and deeply disrespectful. The issue is tension-ridden: is the research *for* people and issues or *about* people and issues? We have to be clear about our answer to the question 'what will this research do for the participants and the wider community, not just for the researcher?'.

Bailey (1994: 457) suggests that there are several approaches that can be used to avoid harming research subjects, including:

- using computer simulations;
- finding a situation in which the negative effects of harm already exist, i.e. where the research does not

have the responsibility for having produced these conditions;

- applying only a very low level of potential harm, or for only a short period of time, so that any effects are minimal;
- informed consent (providing details of the potential negative effects and securing participants' consent);
- justifying the research on the grounds that the small amount of harm caused is much less than the harm caused by the existing situation (which the research is trying to improve);
- using samples rather than complete populations, so that fewer people are exposed to the harm;
- maintaining the privacy of participants through the use of aggregated or anonymized data.

Whilst some of these are uncontentious, others in this list are debatable, and researchers will need to be able to justify the decision they reach.

With regard to respecting dignity, there is the need to treat participants as equals, not as objects or as subordinate to the researcher. This may mean to avoid treating them as 'subjects' rather than as equals (Oliver, 2003).[3] It also means avoiding stigmatizing groups (e.g. the unemployed, the homeless, religious groups, ethnic groups, those considered deviant by virtue of their sexual orientation, dress, beliefs). On a larger scale, the researcher has to ensure that the research does not raise issues and difficulties where none might exist (e.g. raising an issue of ethnic conflicts in a community in which ethnic conflicts do not exist and where harmonious relations obtain between the ethnic groups in the community).

Absolutist and relativist ethics

The second source of tension in this context is that generated by the competing absolutist and relativist positions. The absolutist view holds that clear, set principles should guide the researchers in their work and that these should determine what ought and what ought not to be done (see Box 5.6). To have taken a wholly absolutist

stance, for example, in the case of the Stanford Prison Experiment (see Chapter 26) where the researchers studied interpersonal dynamics in a simulated prison, would have meant that the experiment should not have taken place at all or that it should have been terminated well before the sixth day. Zimbardo (1984) has stated that the absolutist ethical position, in which it is unjustified to induce any human suffering, would bring about the end of much psychological or medical research, regardless of its possible benefits to society. By this absolute principle, the Stanford Prison Experiment must be regarded as unethical because the participants suffered considerably.

In absolutist principles – 'duty ethics of principles' (Edwards and Mauthner, 2002: 20), a deontological model – research is governed by universal precepts such as justice, honesty and respect (amongst others). In the 'utilitarian ethics of consequences' (*ibid.*), ethical research is judged in terms of its consequences, e.g. increased knowledge, benefit for many.

Those who hold a relativist position would argue that there can be no absolute guidelines and that ethical considerations will arise from the very nature of the particular research being pursued at the time: situation determines behaviour. Indeed they would argue that it is essential to respect the context in which the research takes place, culturally, ethnically, socio-economically, and that these should be judged in their own terms (Oliver, 2003: 53). This underlines the significance of 'situated ethics' (Simons and Usher, 2000), where overall guidelines may offer little help when confronted with a very specific situation.

There are some contexts, however, where neither the absolutist nor the relativist position is clear-cut. Writing of the application of the principle of informed consent with respect to life history studies, Plummer says:

> Both sides have a weakness. If, for instance, as the absolutists usually insist, there should be informed consent, it may leave relatively privileged groups

---

BOX 5.6 ABSOLUTE ETHICAL PRINCIPLES IN SOCIAL RESEARCH

Ethics embody individual and communal codes of conduct based upon a set of explicit or implicit principles and which may be abstract and impersonal or concrete and personal. Ethics can be 'absolute' and 'relative'. When behaviour is guided by absolute ethical standards, a higher-order moral principle is invoked which does not vary with regard to the situation in hand. Such absolutist ethics permit no degree of freedom for ends to justify means or for any beneficial or positive outcomes to justify occasions where the principle is suspended, altered or diluted, i.e. there are no special or extenuating circumstances which can be considered as justifying a departure from, or modification to, the ethical standard.

Source: Adapted from Zimbardo, 1984

---

under-researched (since they will say 'no') and underprivileged groups over-researched (they have nothing to lose and say 'yes' in hope). If the individual conscience is the guide, as the relativists insist, the door is wide open for the unscrupulous – even immoral – researcher.

(Plummer, 1983)

He suggests that broad guidelines laid down by professional bodies which offer the researcher room for personal ethical choice are a way out of the problem. We consider these later in this chapter.

5.6 Voices of experience

Whatever the ethical stance one assumes and no matter what forethought one brings to bear on one's work, there will always be unknown, unforeseen problems and difficulties lying in wait (Kimmel, 1988). Baumrind (1964), for example, warns of the possible failure on the researchers' part to perceive a positive indebtedness to their subjects for their services, perhaps, she suggests, because the detachment which investigators bring to their task prevents appreciation of subjects as individuals. This kind of omission can be averted if the experimenters are prepared to spend a few minutes with subjects afterwards in order to thank them for their participation, answer their questions, reassure them that they did well and generally talk to them for a time. If the research involves subjects in a failure experience, isolation or loss of self-esteem, for example, researchers must ensure that the subjects do not leave the situation more humiliated, insecure and alienated than when they arrived. From the subject's point of view, procedures which involve loss of dignity, injury to self-esteem or affect trust in rational authority are probably most harmful in the long run and may require the most carefully organized ways of recompensing the subject in some way if the researcher chooses to carry on with those methods.

With particularly sensitive areas, participants need to be fully informed of the dangers of serious after-effects. There is reason to believe that at least some of the obedient subjects in Milgram's (1963) experiments (see Chapter 26) came away from the experience with a lower self-esteem, having to live with the realization that they were willing to yield to destructive authority to the point of inflicting extreme pain on a fellow human being (Kelman, 1967). It follows that researchers need to reflect attitudes of compassion, respect, gratitude and common sense without being too effusive. Subjects clearly have a right to expect that the researchers with whom they are interacting have some concern for the welfare of participants.

Further, the subject's sensibilities need also to be taken into account when the researcher comes to write up the research. It is unacceptable for researchers to show scant regard for subjects' feelings at the report stage. A related and not insignificant issue concerns the formal recognition of those who have assisted in the investigation, if such be the case. This means that whatever form the written account takes, be it a report, article, chapter or thesis, and no matter the readership for which it is intended, its authors must acknowledge and thank all who helped in the research, even to the extent of identifying by name those whose contribution was significant. This can be done in a foreword, introduction or footnote. All this is really a question of common-sensical ethics.

Ethical problems in educational research can often result from thoughtlessness, oversight or taking matters for granted. Again, researchers engaged in sponsored research may feel they do not have to deal with ethical issues, believing their sponsors to have them in hand. Likewise, each researcher in a collaborative venture may take it for granted, wrongly, that colleagues have the relevant ethical questions in mind, consequently appropriate precautions go by default. A student whose research is part of a course requirement and who is motivated wholly by self-interest, or academic researchers with professional advancement in mind, may overlook the 'oughts' and 'ought nots'.

A related issue here is that it is unethical for the researcher to be incompetent in the area of research. Competence may require training (Ticehurst and Veal, 2000: 55). Indeed an ethical piece of research must demonstrate rigour in the design, conduct, analysis and reporting of the research (Morrison, 1996b).

An ethical dilemma that is frequently discussed is in the experiment. Gorard (2001b: 146) summarizes the issue as being that the design is discriminatory, in that the control group is being denied access to a potentially better treatment (e.g. curriculum, teaching style). Of course, the response to this is that, in a genuine experiment, we do not know which treatment is better, and that, indeed, this is the point of the experiment.

5.7 Ethical dilemmas

Robson (1993: 33) raises ten questionable practices in social research:

- Involving people without their knowledge or consent.
- Coercing them to participate.
- Withholding information about the true nature of the research.

- Otherwise deceiving participants.
- Inducing them to commit acts diminishing their self-esteem.
- Violating rights of self-determination (e.g. in studies seeking to promote individual change).
- Exposing participants to physical or mental stress.
- Invading their privacy.
- Withholding benefits from some participants (e.g. in comparison groups).
- Not treating participants fairly, or with consideration, or with respect.

Interestingly, he calls these 'questionable practices' rather than areas to be proscribed, indicating that they are not black and white, right or wrong matters. They constitute the problem of ethical dilemmas.

At the beginning of this chapter, we spoke of the costs/benefits ratio. Frankfort-Nachmias and Nachmias (1992) express this as a conflict between two rights: the rights to conduct research in order to gain knowledge versus the rights of participants to self-determination, privacy and dignity. This constitutes the fundamental ethical dilemma of the social scientist for whom there are no absolute right or wrong answers. Which proposition is favoured or how a balance between the two is struck will depend very much on the background, experience and personal values of the individual researcher. We examine here other dilemmas that may confront investigators once they have come to some accommodation with this fundamental dilemma and decided to proceed with their research.

Sikes (2006) argues that ethical issues not only rear their head at every turn in educational research, but that they are problematic. She cites examples that touch the researcher – his or her career prospects, motives, promotion opportunities, even sexuality, that may be affected by the research, particularly if it is 'insider research' in which a researcher researches her/his own institution, which might affect professional relationships, as issues of power (and knowledge from research may give power) may be present (p. 110), and that ethics touch 'researchers and their research choices, research topics, methodologies and methods, and writing styles' (p. 106).

Newcomers to the field need to be aware of those kinds of research which, by their nature, lead from one problem to another. Indeed, the researcher will frequently find that methodological and ethical issues are inextricably interwoven in much of the research we have designated as qualitative or interpretive. As Hitchcock and Hughes note:

Doing participant observation or interviewing one's peers raises ethical problems that are directly related to the nature of the research technique employed. The degree of openness or closure of the nature of the research and its aims is one that directly faces the teacher researcher.

(Hitchcock and Hughes, 1989)

They go on to pose the kinds of question that may arise in such a situation. 'Where for the researcher does formal observation end and informal observation begin?' 'Is it justifiable to be open with some teachers and closed with others?' 'How much can the researcher tell the pupils about a particular piece of research?' 'When is a casual conversation part of the research data and when is it not?' 'Is gossip legitimate data and can the researcher ethically use material that has been passed on in confidence?' As Hitchcock and Hughes conclude, the list of questions is endless yet they can be related to the nature of both the research technique involved and the social organization of the setting being investigated. The key to the successful resolution of such questions lies in establishing good relations. This will involve the development of a sense of rapport between researchers and their subjects that will lead to feelings of trust and confidence.

Fine and Sandstrom (1988) discuss in some detail the ethical and practical aspects of doing fieldwork with children. In particular they show how the ethical implications of participant observation research differ with the age of the children. Another feature of qualitative methods in this connection has been identified by Finch (1985: 116–17) who comments on the possible acute political and ethical dilemmas arising from how data are used, both by the researcher and others, and that the researcher has a duty of trust placed in him/her by the participants to use privileged data appropriately, not least for improvement of the condition of the participants.

Kelly (1989a) suggests that the area in qualitative research where one's ethical antennae need to be especially sensitive is that of action research, and it is here that researchers, be they teachers or outsiders, must show particular awareness of the traps that lie in wait. These difficulties have been summed up by Hopkins (1985: 135) when he suggests that, as the researcher's actions are deeply embedded in the organization, it is important to work within these, and this throws into relief issues of confidentiality and personal respect.

Box 5.7 presents a set of principles specially formulated for action researchers by Kemmis and McTaggart (1981) and quoted by Hopkins (1985).

BOX 5.7 ETHICAL PRINCIPLES FOR THE GUIDANCE OF ACTION RESEARCHERS

Observe protocol: Take care to ensure that the relevant persons, committees, and authorities have been consulted, informed and that the necessary permission and approval have been obtained.

Involve participants: Encourage others who have a stake in the improvement you envisage to shape and form the work.

Negotiate with those affected: Not everyone will want to be directly involved; your work should take account of the responsibilities and wishes of others.

Report progress: Keep the work visible and remain open to suggestions so that unforeseen and unseen ramifications can be taken account of; colleagues must have the opportunity to lodge a protest to you.

Obtain explicit authorizations: This applies where you wish to observe your professional colleagues; and where you wish to examine documentation.

Negotiate descriptions of people's work: Always allow those described to challenge your accounts on the grounds of fairness, relevance and accuracy.

Negotiate accounts of others' points of view (e.g. in accounts of communication): Always allow those involved in interviews, meetings and written exchanges to require amendments which enhance fairness, relevance and accuracy.

Obtain explicit authorization before using quotations: Verbatim transcripts, attributed observations, excerpts of audio and video recordings, judgements, conclusions or recommendations in reports (written or to meetings).

Negotiate reports for various levels of release: Remember that different audiences require different kinds of reports; what is appropriate for an informal verbal report to a faculty meeting may not be appropriate for a staff meeting, a report to council, a journal article, a newspaper, a newsletter to parents; be conservative if you cannot control distribution.

Accept responsibility for maintaining confidentiality.

Retain the right to report your work: Provided that those involved are satisfied with the fairness, accuracy and relevance of accounts which pertain to them, and that the accounts do not unnecessarily expose or embarrass those involved, then accounts should not be subject to veto or be sheltered by prohibitions of confidentiality.

Make your principles of procedure binding and known: All the people involved in your action research project must agree to the principles before the work begins; others must be aware of their rights in the process.

Source: Adapted from Kemmis and McTaggart, 1981, and quoted in Hopkins, 1985: 134–6

5.8 Privacy

For the most part, individual 'right to privacy' is usually contrasted with public 'right to know' (Pring, 1984) and this has been defined in the *Ethical Guidelines for the Institutional Review Committee for Research with Human Subjects* as that which:

> extends to all information relating to a person's physical and mental condition, personal circumstances and social relationships which is not already in the public domain. It gives to the individual or collectivity the freedom to decide for themselves when and where, in what circumstances and to what extent their personal attitudes, opinions, habits, eccentricities, doubts and fears are to be communicated to or withheld from others.
>
> (Social Sciences and Humanities Research Council of Canada, 1981)

In the context of research, therefore, 'right to privacy' may easily be violated during the course of an investigation or denied after it has been completed. At either point the participant is vulnerable.

Privacy is a primordial value, a 'basic human need' (Caplan, 1982: 320), which, like the right to self-determination, 'trumps' utilitarian calculations (Howe and Moses, 1999: 24). Its corollaries are anonymity, confidentiality and informed consent. It has been considered from three different perspectives by Diener and Crandall (1978). These are: the sensitivity of the information being given, the setting being observed and dissemination of information. Sensitivity of information refers to how personal or potentially threatening the information is that is being collected by the researcher. Certain kinds of information are more personal than others and may be more threatening. According to a report by the American Psychological Association, for example, 'Religious preferences, sexual practices, income, racial prejudices, and other personal attributes such as intelligence, honesty, and courage are more sensitive items than "name, rank and serial number"' (American Psychological Association, 1973). Thus, the greater the sensitivity of the information, the more safeguards are called for to protect the privacy of the participants.

The setting being observed may vary from very private to completely public. The home, for example, is considered one of the most private settings and intrusions into people's homes without their consent are forbidden by law. Dissemination of information concerns the ability to match personal information with the identity of the research participants. Indeed, personal data are defined at law as those data which uniquely identify the individual providing them. When such information is publicized with names through the media, for example, privacy is seriously violated. The more people there are who can learn about the information, the more concern there must be about privacy (see Diener and Crandall, 1978).

As is the case with most rights, privacy can be voluntarily relinquished. Research participants may choose to give up their right to privacy by either allowing a researcher access to sensitive topics or settings or by agreeing that the research report may identify them by name. The latter case at least would be an occasion where informed consent would need to be sought.

Generally speaking, if researchers intend to probe into the private aspects or affairs of individuals, their intentions should be made clear and explicit and informed consent should be sought from those who are to be observed or scrutinized in private contexts. Other methods to protect participants are anonymity and confidentiality and our examination of these follows.

Privacy is more than simple confidentiality (discussed below). The right to privacy means that a person has the right not to take part in the research, not to answer questions, not to be interviewed, not to have their home intruded into, not to answer telephones or emails, and to engage in private behaviour in their own private place without fear of being observed. It is *freedom from* as well as *freedom for*. This is frequently an issue with intrusive journalism. Hence researchers may have an obligation to inform participants of their rights to refuse to take part in any or all of the research, to obtain permission to conduct the research, to limit the time needed for participation and to limit the observation to public behaviour.

5.9 Anonymity

Frankfort-Nachmias and Nachmias (1992) underline the need for confidentiality of participants' identities, and that any violations of this should be made with the agreement of the participants. The essence of anonymity is that information provided by participants should in no way reveal their identity. The obverse of this is, as we saw earlier, personal data that uniquely identify their supplier. A participant or subject is therefore considered anonymous when the researcher or another person cannot identify the participant or subject from the information provided. For example, a questionnaire might only contain a number instead of a person's name. Where this situation holds, a participant's privacy is guaranteed, no matter how personal or sensitive the information is. Thus a respondent completing a questionnaire that bears absolutely no identifying marks – names, addresses, occupational details or coding symbols – is ensured complete and total anonymity. A subject agreeing to a face-to-face interview, on the other hand, can in no way expect anonymity. At most, the interviewer can promise confidentiality. Non-traceability is an important matter, and this extends to aggregating data in some cases, so that an individual's response is unknowable.

The principal means of ensuring anonymity, then, is not using the names of the participants or any other personal means of identification. Further ways of achieving anonymity have been listed by Frankfort-Nachmias and Nachmias (1992), such as the use of aliases, the use of codes for identifying people (to keep the information on individuals separate from access to them) and the use of password-protected files.

These may work satisfactorily in most situations, but as Raffe *et al.* (1989) have shown, there is sometimes the difficulty of maintaining an assurance of anonymity when, for example, combining data may uniquely identify an individual or institution or when there is access to incoming returns by support staff. Plummer (1983), likewise, refers to life studies in which names have been changed, places shifted, and fictional events added to prevent acquaintances of subjects discovering their identity. Although one can go a long way down this path, there is no absolute guarantee of total anonymity as far as life studies are concerned. In experimental research the experimenter is interested in 'human' behaviour rather than in the behaviour of specific individuals (Aronson and Carlsmith, 1969). Consequently the researcher has absolutely no interest in linking the person as a unique, named individual to actual behaviour, and the research data can be transferred to coded, unnamed data sheets. As they comment, 'the very impersonality of the process is a great advantage ethically because it eliminates some of the negative consequences of the invasion of privacy' (Aronson and Carlsmith, 1969).

5.10 Confidentiality

The second way of protecting a participant's right to privacy is through the promise of confidentiality: not disclosing information from a participant in any way that might identify that individual or that might enable the individual to be traced. It can also mean not discussing an individual with anybody else. This means that although researchers know who has provided the information or are able to identify participants from the information given, they will in no way make the connection known publicly; the boundaries surrounding the shared secret will be protected. The essence of the matter is the extent to which investigators keep faith with those who have helped them. It is generally at the access stage or at the point where researchers collect their data that they make their position clear to the hosts and/or subjects. They will thus be quite explicit in explaining to subjects what the meaning and limits of confidentiality are in relation to the particular research project. On the whole, the more sensitive, intimate or discrediting the information, the greater is the obligation on the researcher's part to make sure that guarantees of confidentiality are carried out in spirit and letter. Promises must be kept.

Kimmel (1988) notes that some potential respondents in research on sensitive topics will refuse to cooperate when an assurance of confidentiality is weak, vague, not understood or thought likely to be breached. He concludes that the usefulness of data in sensitive research areas may be seriously affected by the researcher's inability to provide a credible promise of confidentiality. Assurances do not appear to affect cooperation rates in innocuous studies perhaps because, as Kimmel suggests, there is expectation on the part of most potential respondents that confidentiality will be protected.

A number of techniques have been developed to allow public access to data and information without confidentiality being betrayed. These have been listed by Frankfort-Nachmias and Nachmias (1992) as follows:

- deletion of identifiers (for example, deleting the names, addresses or other means of identification from the data released on individuals);
- crude report categories (for example, releasing the year of birth rather than the specific date, profession but not the speciality within that profession, general information rather than specific);
- microaggregation (that is, the construction of 'average persons' from data on individuals and the release of these data, rather than data on individuals);

- error inoculation (deliberately introducing errors into individual records while leaving the aggregate data unchanged).

Cooper and Schindler (2001: 117) suggest that confidentiality can be protected by obtaining signed statements indicating nondisclosure of the research, restricting access to data which identify respondents, seeking the approval of the respondents before any disclosure about respondents takes place, nondisclosure of data (e.g. subsets that may be able to be combined to identify an individual).

5.11 Against privacy, confidentiality and anonymity

Whilst a deontological and 'virtue ethics' approach to the ethics of educational research might demand that rights to privacy be respected, on the other hand a utilitarian, consequentialist approach might argue that privacy could be violated if it is in the public good. Lincoln (1990) suggests that privacy protects the powerful and reproduces inequalities of power, whilst Howe and Moses (1999: 43) give examples where privacy should not be able to cloak wrongdoing (e.g. 'an abusive teacher ... a sexist curriculum').

Wiles *et al.* (2008: 419) indicate some of the complexities of the ethical issues of confidentiality in their discussion of whether confidentiality should be broken in the interests of public or private safety, issues of actual or predicted criminal activity, if a person is at risk (e.g. a child who reports being abused), and with vulnerable groups such as children, those with special needs, the recently bereaved, children whose parents have separated or who come from violent families. In many cases the researcher makes it clear before any interview commences that any information of a legal nature may be disclosed if the interviewer thinks the interviewee is at risk or if there is a legal matter at stake, but it is not always as simple as this, as an interviewee may reveal some information that had not been anticipated. In other cases the researcher may want to give advice to a participant about seeking counselling or therapy. Oliver (2003: 71) however cautions that the researcher is not herself/himself a counsellor or therapist.

Further, in the case of covert research, there are no guarantees of confidentiality given in the first place. At issue here is where the duty of the researcher lies – to the research, to the individual, to the public or to whom, and the possible tensions between illegality, morality and the need to bring a matter to the public awareness or knowledge. For example, if one is deliberately researching criminal activity it may be necessary to ensure confidentiality or else the research will not take place at all. What does the researcher do if a court order is issued that requires the release of the data?

If researchers decide to opt for confidentiality then this can place them in a difficult situation where the research is emotionally draining, because, as Wiles *et al.* (2008: 421) remark, it means that researchers cannot 'offload' their difficulties onto any other person.

Walford (2005: 84–5) suggests that, whilst confidentiality, anonymity and non-traceability may be accepted or desirable norms or educational research, in some cases these norms may not apply or be achievable. For example, some participants or institutions may wish, or have a right, to be identified, as it might advance their cause or institution. Schools and headteachers might welcome publicity (Oliver, 2003: 77). As Wiles *et al.* (2008: 426) remark, in an age of increasing individualization, some individuals will insist on being identified. Further, the researcher is placed in a difficult situation with regard to confidentiality if a participant comments about another person who is not in the research and/or from whom no informed consent has been sought or obtained (Crow *et al.*, 2006: 92): does the investigator use the data? Is it fair to exclude or include data about a third party because that third party has not been approached for informed consent?

Anonymity is also a double-edged sword. Whilst it might protect people, that may not be the main question; rather the question should be 'protect them from what?', as anonymity might become a cloak behind which participants can hide whilst making a range of negative, unsupported, even slanderous or libellous comments (cf. Oliver, 2003: 81). Maybe confidentiality and anonymity are only confined to certain forms of research.

However, more problematic is the question of what confidentiality actually means if the data are to be used for the research; if data are to be confidential and cannot be used or passed on, then what is the point of collecting or having the data? In this case it is perhaps anonymity that should be addressed rather than confidentiality, or that the *scope* of confidentiality (its boundaries) should be clarified rather than a guarantee be given of absolute confidentiality (e.g. Oliver, 2003: 15).

However, it is often simply impossible to guarantee the anonymity of a person or an institution, as people can reassemble or combine data to identify an individual or an institution can be identified by the 'locals' or indeed it can be identified by entering a few simple key words from the research into an internet search (Walford, 2005). Oliver (2003: 80) writes that 'there are no absolute guarantees of anonymity, particularly in the case of people who hold named posts'.

Here the commonly used advocacy of pseudonyms is no guarantee of anonymity. Walford (2005: 88) argues that promises of anonymity are often used by the researcher in order to gain access, though anonymity cannot actually be guaranteed, and, hence, it is ethically questionable whether anonymity should be promised. Whilst anonymity may bring data that are richer, keener and more acute or poignant than more anodyne research data given where there are no promises of anonymity, this is not necessarily a justification for making promises of anonymity that cannot be kept.

Many devices can be used in the protection of anonymity, to 'put people off the scent', for example, using pseudonyms, reporting a different geographical location from the one in which the research is actually carried out, providing misinformation (deliberately giving incorrect details of ages or sex), concealing identifying details (cf. Howe and Moses, 1999: 45), i.e. moving from 'disguise' to 'distortion' (Wiles *et al.*, 2008: 422), in short, removing context and, further, not always indicating that this has been done.

However, this is problematic, as not only does it smack of telling lies and dishonesty, but it actually removes some of the very contextual data that are important for the research (Walford, 2005: 90), particularly for ethnographic research. To omit such necessary contextual details for a researcher to understand the situation gives a spurious generalizability to the research. As Walford writes, each school and its development 'can only be understood in the context of its history and socio-political location' (2005: 90). He suggests that it may be important to identify institutions and individuals, but that they should be given the right to reply in the research report, though this, in turn, is problematic. Who has the right to reply? (all the participants?); what if very different replies are given? How are transparency, frankness and trust addressed in the relations between researchers and participants? These are knotty problems.

Howe and Moses (1999: 44–5) make a cogent case against privacy and confidentiality, arguing that the 'thick descriptions' of interpretive research require a level of detail that cannot be obtained if privacy, confidentiality and anonymity are required. They argue that as descriptions move towards becoming more 'objective' they become more anodyne and lose the very richness that they are intended to demonstrate, i.e. they become 'thin'. For example, consider the contrast between stating that 'the secondary school girls alternated between being bored, intimidated and silent in English discussion sessions' and 'the girls participated less than boys in the English discussion sessions' (cf. Howe and Moses, 1999: 45). Where the former provides a rich description, the latter, being sanitized, is thin.

5.12 Ethics in electronic research

Privacy and anonymity are linked in the burgeoning field of online research. James and Busher (2007) argue that online research poses difficult issues of confirming the authenticity of respondents and responses, and of the protection of vulnerable groups' privacy, confidentiality and anonymity, particularly if emails are being used, as these are susceptible to others' viewing them either deliberately or accidentally (e.g. if mails are forwarded or shared). There is a need for researchers to establish not only their own bona fide status but that of their correspondents.

Further, there is a possibility that online correspondents may or may not distort their stated views, or, indeed withhold them (James and Busher, 2007: 107), in ways that may not be so likely in face-to-face research.

Hudson and Bruckman (2005: 298) suggest that 'people in public, online environments often act as if these environments were private', and that, furthermore, they feel that their privacy has been violated if data from public chatrooms are used for research purposes and, indeed, the public remove them from their chatrooms, even though the data cannot not be traced back to anonymous chatroom participants.

Lewis (2006) indicted that, as a researcher, he took time (five months) to establish a relation of trust with online contacts. In that way he developed a relationship of trust with his participants as a member of an online community before he approached them to participate in his research.

The Association of Internet Researchers (Ess and the Association of Internet Researchers, 2002) has established some ethical guidelines for researchers using the internet for data collection and research, including, for example:

- Do not assume that emails are secure.
- Ensure that nobody is harmed by the research.
- Enable participants to correspond in private if they wish.
- Indicate the steps taken to ensure privacy.
- Check where the communication comes from.
- Determine the most suitable online method of requesting and receiving informed consent.
- The greater is the acknowledged publicity of the venue, the less obligation there may be to protect

individual privacy, confidentiality and rights to informed consent.
- The greater is the vulnerability of the researcher to the participant, the greater is the obligation of the researcher to protect the participant.
- Indicate clearly how material will be used and whether or how it will be attributed, and whether data will be used verbatim, aggregated or summarized.
- Work within the framework of legal obligations of protection (e.g. data protection and privacy laws).
- Indicate who has access to the communication, and whether it is private.
- Consider the possible outcomes to individuals if private data are made public.

Similarly, in telephone interviewing, Gwartney (2007) argues for professional ethics to be respected, and she indicates a range of websites that can provide guidance to researchers on this (p. 53), including codes of conduct, informed consent, confidentiality, privacy, avoidance of harassment, email solicitation, active agent technology (e.g. behind-the-scenes data mining), installing software and setting cookies or hard-to-uninstall software, codes and standards for minimal disclosure, unsolicited telephone calls and setting up 'Do Not Call' lists, professional responsibilities in working with people, how to handle people who break down in a telephone interview, and the need for training for telephone interviewers. Such organizations include:

American Association for Public Opinion Research: www.aapor.org and www.aapor.org/AM/Template.cfm?Section=AAPOR_Code&Template=/CM/ContentDisplay.cfm&ContentID=1806
Council of American Survey Research Organizations: www.casro.org and www.casro.org/codeofstandards.cfm
American Evaluation Association: www.eval.org and www.eval.org/Publications/GuidingPrinciplesPrintable.asp
American Statistical Association, Survey Methods Section: http://amstat.org and www.amstat.org/about/ethicalguidelines.cfm.

Gwartney (2007) reproduces some of these ethical guidelines (pp. 57–69).

5.13 Betrayal

The term 'betrayal' is usually applied to those occasions where data disclosed in confidence are revealed publicly in such a way as to cause embarrassment, anxiety or perhaps suffering to the subject or participant disclosing the information. It is a breach of trust, in contrast to confidentiality, and is often a consequence of selfish motives of either a personal or professional nature. As Plummer comments, 'in sociology, there is something slightly awry when a sociologist can enter a group and a person's life for a lengthy period, learn their most closely guarded secrets, and then expose all in a critical light to the public' (Plummer, 1983).

One of the research methods that is perhaps most vulnerable to betrayal is action research. As Kelly (1989a) notes, this can produce several ethical problems. She says that if we treat teachers as collaborators in our day-to-day interactions, it may seem like betrayal of trust if these interactions are recorded and used as evidence. This is particularly the case where the evidence is negative. One way out, Kelly suggests, could be to submit reports and evaluations of teachers' reactions to the teachers involved for comment; to get them to assess their own changing attitudes. She warns, however, that this might work well with teachers who have become converts, but is more problematic where teachers remain indifferent or hostile to the aims of the research project. How does one write an honest but critical report of teachers' attitudes, she asks, if one hopes to continue to work with those involved?

Similarly Morrison (2006) considers the case of a school that is underperforming, poorly managed or badly led. Does not the consumer, indeed the state, have a right or a duty respectively to know or address this, such action typically involving the exposure to the public of a school's shortcomings, and will this not damage individuals working in the school, the principal and the teachers? What 'fiduciary trust' (Mitchell, 1993) not to harm individuals (the ethical issue of 'non-maleficence') does the researcher have to the school or to the public, and how can these two potentially contradictory demands be reconciled? Should the researcher expose the school's weaknesses, which almost certainly could damage individuals but which may be in the public interest, or, in the interests of *primum non nocere*, remain silent? The issue hinges on trust: the pursuit of truth and the pursuit of trust may run counter to each other (Kelly, 1985: 147); indeed Kelly herself writes that 'I do not think we have yet found a satisfactory way of resolving this dilemma.'

Finch (1985: 117) raises ethical issues in the consequences of reporting. In her research she worried that her reporting 'could well mean that I was further reinforcing those assumptions deeply embedded in our culture and political life that working class women (especially the urban poor) are inadequate mothers and

too incompetent to be able to organize facilities that most normal women could manage'. Indeed she uses the word 'betrayal' (p. 118) in her concern that she might be betraying the trust of the women with whom she had worked for three years, not least because they were in a far worse economic and personal state than she herself was.

Sikes (2006: 111) argues that, whilst some researchers may place an embargo on having their research made available to the public (e.g. for five years), this calls into question the values, purposes and ethical justifiability of research that cannot be disseminated and hence 'cannot contribute to the cumulativeness of knowledge' (p. 111).

5.14 Deception

The use of deception in social psychological and sociological research has attracted a certain amount of adverse publicity. Deception may occur in not telling people that they are being researched (in some people's eyes this is tantamount to spying), not telling the truth, telling lies or compromising the truth. It may also occur in using people in a degrading or dehumanizing way (e.g. as a rat in an experiment). In social psychological research, the term is applied to that kind of experimental situation where the researcher knowingly conceals the true purpose and conditions of the research, or else positively misinforms the subjects, or exposes them to unduly painful, stressful or embarrassing experiences, without the subjects having knowledge of what is going on. The deception occurs in not telling the whole truth. Bailey (1994: 463) gives a clear example here, where respondents may be asked to complete a postal questionnaire, and believe that they are being asked for information about length and type of postage, whereas, in fact, the study is designed to compare different kinds of questionnaire. He reports that 88 per cent of studies from a sample of 457 studies used deception.

Advocates of the method feel that if a deception experiment is the only way to discover something of real importance, the truth so discovered is worth the lies told in the process, so long as no harm comes to the subject (see Aronson *et al.*, 1990). Deception may be justified on the grounds that the research serves the public good, and that the deception prevents any bias from entering the research, and also that it may protect the confidentiality of a third party (for example, a sponsor). The problem from the researcher's point of view is: 'What is the proper balance between the interests of science and the thoughtful, humane treatment of people who, innocently, provide the data?' In other words, the problem again hinges on the costs/benefits ratio.

The pervasiveness of the issue of deception becomes even more apparent when we remember that it is even built into many of our measurement devices, since it is important to keep the respondent ignorant of the personality and attitude dimensions that we wish to investigate. There are many problems that cannot be investigated without deception and, although there is some evidence that most subjects accept without resentment the fact of having been duped once they understand the necessity for it (e.g. the Milgram Obedience-to-authority experiment; see Chapter 26), it is important to keep in the forefront of one's mind the question of whether the amount and type of deception is justified by the significance of the study and the unavailability of alternative procedures.

The use of deception resulting in particularly harmful consequences is another occasion where ethical considerations need to be given priority. An example here is the study by Campbell *et al.* (1964) which created extremely stressful conditions by using drugs to induce temporary interruption of breathing (see Box 5.8).

Kelman (1967) has suggested three ways of dealing with the problem of deception. First, it is important that we increase our active awareness that it exists as a problem. It is crucial that we always ask ourselves the question whether deception is necessary and justified. We must be wary of the tendency to dismiss the question as irrelevant and to accept deception as a matter of course. Active awareness is thus in itself part of the solution, for it makes the use of deception a focus for discussion, deliberation, investigation and choice.

The second way of approaching the problem concerns counteracting and minimizing the negative effects of deception. For example, subjects must be selected in a way that will exclude individuals who are especially vulnerable; any potentially harmful manipulation must be kept to a moderate level of intensity; researchers must be sensitive to danger signals in the reactions of subjects and be prepared to deal with crises when they arise; and at the conclusion of the research, researchers must take time not only to reassure subjects, but also help them work through their feelings about the experience to whatever degree may be required. The principle that subjects ought not to leave the research situation with greater anxiety or lower levels of self-esteem than they came with is a good one to follow (the issue of non-maleficence again). Desirably, subjects should be enriched by the experience and should leave it with the feeling that they have learned something.

The primary way of counteracting negative effects of research employing deception is to ensure that adequate feedback is provided at the end of the research or research session. Feedback must be kept inviolable and in no circumstances should subjects be given false feedback or be misled into thinking they are receiving feedback when the researcher is in fact introducing another experimental manipulation. Debriefing may include (Cooper and Schindler, 2001: 116):

- explaining any deception and the reasons for it;
- description of the purposes, hypotheses, objectives and methods of the research;
- sharing of the results after the research;
- follow-up psychological or medical attention after the research.

Even here, however, there are dangers. As Aronson and Carlsmith say:

debriefing a subject is not simply a matter of exposing him to the truth. There is nothing magically curative about the truth; indeed ... if harshly presented, the truth can be more harmful than no explanation at all. There are vast differences in how this is accomplished, and it is precisely these differences that are of crucial importance in determining whether or not

---

BOX 5.8   AN EXTREME CASE OF DECEPTION

In an experiment designed to study the establishment of a conditioned response in a situation that is traumatic but not painful, Campbell, Sanderson and Laverty induced – through the use of a drug – a temporary interruption of respiration in their subjects. The subjects' reports confirmed that this was a 'horrific' experience for them. All the subjects thought they were dying. The subjects, male alcoholic patients who had volunteered for the experiment when they were told that it was connected with a possible therapy for alcoholism, were not warned in advance about the effect of the drug, since this information would have reduced the traumatic impact of the experience.

Source: Adapted from Kelman, 1967

a subject is uncomfortable when he leaves the experimental room.

(Aronson and Carlsmith, 1969: 31)

They consider that the one essential aspect of the debriefing process is that researchers communicate their own sincerity as scientists seeking the truth and their own discomfort about the fact that they found it necessary to resort to deception in order to uncover the truth. As they say, 'No amount of postexperimental gentleness is as effective in relieving a subject's discomfort as an honest accounting of the experimenter's *own* discomfort in the situation' (Aronson and Carlsmith, 1969).

The third way of dealing with the problem of deception is to ensure that new procedures and novel techniques are developed. It is a question of tapping one's own creativity in the quest for alternative methods. It has been suggested that role-playing, or 'as-if' experiments, could prove a worthwhile avenue to explore – the 'role-playing versus deception' debate we raise in Chapter 26. By this method, as we shall see, the subject is asked to behave as if he/she were a particular person in a particular situation. Whatever form they take, however, new approaches will involve a radically different set of assumptions about the role of the subject in this type of research. They require us to *use* subjects' motivations rather than bypassing them. They may even call for increasing the sophistication of potential subjects, rather than maintaining their naivety.

Plummer (1983) informs us that even in an unlikely area like life history, deceptions of a lesser nature occur. Thus, for example, the general description given of research may leave out some key issues; indeed, to tell the subject what it is you are looking for may bias the outcome quite substantially. Further, different accounts of the research may have to be presented to different groups. He quotes an instance from his own research, a study of sexual minorities, which required various levels of release – for the subjects, for colleagues, for general enquiries and for outside friends. None of these accounts actually lied, they merely emphasized a different aspect of the research.

In the social sciences, the dilemma of deception has played an important part in experimental social psychology where subjects are not told the true nature of the experiment. Another area where it is used is that of sociology, where researchers conceal their identities and 'con' their way into alien groups – the overt/covert debate (Mitchell, 1993). Covert or secret participation, then, refers to that kind of research where researchers spend an extended period of time in particular research settings, concealing the fact that they are researchers and pretending to play some other role.

Bulmer (1982) notes that there are no simple and universally agreed answers to the ethical issues that covert research produces. Erikson (1967), for example, suggests that sociologists have responsibilities to their subjects and that secret research can injure other people in ways that cannot be anticipated or compensated for afterwards; and that sociologists have responsibilities towards fellow-sociologists. Hornsby-Smith (1993: 65) argues that covert research violates informed consent, invades personal privacy, deceives people, risks harming participants when the research is published (e.g. Scheper-Hughes, 1979), and impairs the likelihood of other researchers researching the issue in the future, not least when overt research might have been used instead.

Douglas (1976), by contrast, argues that covert observation is necessary, useful and revealing. Bulmer (1982), too, concludes that the most compelling argument in favour of covert research is that it has produced good social science which would not have been possible without the method. It would be churlish, he adds, not to recognize that the use of covert methods has advanced our understanding of society.

Kimmel (1988) claims that few researchers feel that they can do without deception entirely, since the adoption of an overtly conservative approach could render the study of important research hardly worth the effort. A study of racial prejudice, for example, accurately labelled as such, would certainly affect the behaviour of the subjects taking part. Deception studies, he considers, differ so greatly that even the harshest critics would be hard-pressed to state unequivocally that all deception has potentially harmful effects on participants or is wrong. Indeed whilst the American Educational Research Association's standards on ethics (discussed below) discourages deception in research, it also recognizes that, in some cases, it may be necessary and useful, but that this requires careful justification.

Covert research may be justified, for example, if the important data gathered could not have been gathered in any other way, or if it is necessary in order to gain access to organizations which would deny access (Mitchell, 1993), or to uncover questionable practices that, otherwise, would not come to light (e.g. sexist employment practices) (cf. Oliver, 2003: 6). The consequentialist argument for covert research is powerful.

5.15 Ethics and evaluative research

Strike (1990), discussing the ethics of educational evaluation, offers two broad principles which may form the basis of further considerations in the field of evaluation. These are the principle of benefit maximization and the principle of equal respect. The principle of benefit maximization holds that the best decision is the one that results in the greatest benefit for most people. It is pragmatic in the sense that it judges the rightness of our actions by their consequences or, as Strike says, the best action is the one with the best results. The principle of utilitarianism requires us to identify the particular benefits we wish to maximize, to identify a suitable population for maximization, specify what is to count as maximization and fully understand the consequences of our actions. The second principle, that of equal respect, demands that we respect the equal worth of all people. This requires us to treat people as ends rather than means, to regard them as free and rational, and to accept that they are entitled to the same basic rights as others.

Strike lists the following ethical principles which he regards as particularly important to evaluative research and which may be seen in the light of the two broad principles outlined above:

- *Due process* Evaluative procedures must ensure that judgements are reasonable: that known and accepted standards are consistently applied from case to case, that evidence is reasonable and that there are systematic and reasonable procedures for collecting and testing evidence.
- *Privacy* This involves a right to control information about oneself, and protects people from unwarranted interference in their affairs. In evaluation, it requires that procedures are not overtly intrusive and that such evaluation pertains only to those aspects of a teacher's activity which are job related. It also protects the confidentiality of evaluation information.
- *Equality* In the context of evaluation, this can best be understood as a prohibition against making decisions on irrelevant grounds, such as race, religion, gender, ethnicity or sexual orientation.
- *Public perspicuity* This principle requires openness to the public concerning evaluative procedures, their purposes and their results.
- *Humaneness* This principle requires that consideration is shown to the feelings and sensitivities of those in evaluative contexts.
- *Client benefit* This principle requires that evaluative decisions are made in a way that respects the interests of students, parents and the public, in preference to those of educational institutions and their staff. This extends to treating participants as subjects rather than as 'research fodder'.
- *Academic freedom* This requires that an atmosphere of intellectual openness is maintained in the classroom

for both teachers and students. Evaluation should not be conducted in a way that chills this environment.
- *Respect for autonomy* Teachers are entitled to reasonable discretion in, and to exercise reasonable judgement about, their work. Evaluations should not be conducted so as to unreasonably restrict discretion and judgement.

Strike (1990) develops these principles in a more extended and systematic form in his article.

5.16 Research and regulation: ethical codes and review boards

Ethical regulation exists at several levels: legislation, ethics review committees to oversee research in universities and other institutions (these can constitute a major hurdle for those planning to undertake research), ethical codes of the professional bodies and associations as well as the personal ethics of individual researchers are all important regulatory mechanisms. All investigators, from undergraduates pursuing a course-based research project to professional researchers striving at the frontiers of knowledge, must take cognizance of the ethical codes and regulations governing their practice. Failure to meet these responsibilities on the part of researchers is perceived as undermining the whole scientific process and may lead to legal and financial penalties and liabilities for individuals and institutions.

Professional societies and associations have formulated codes of practice which express the consensus of values within a particular group and which help individual researchers in indicating what is desirable and what is to be avoided. Of course, this does not solve all problems, for there are few absolutes and in consequence ethical principles may be open to a wide range of interpretations. The establishment of comprehensive regulatory mechanisms is well founded in the UK, but it is perhaps in the field of information and data – how they are stored and the uses to which they are put, for example – that educational researchers are likely to find growing interest. This category would include, for instance, statistical data, data used as the basis for evaluation, curricular records, written records, transcripts, data sheets, personal documents, research data, computer files, and audio and video recordings.

As information technology establishes itself in a centre-stage position and as society has become increasingly dependent on information, the concept of information is important not only for what it is, but for what it can do. Numerous writers have pointed out the connection between information and power (e.g. Harris *et al.* (1992) comment on the power over individuals through the control of personal information and its relationship to power of professionalism in which submission to expert knowledge is required). Data misuse, therefore, or disclosure at the wrong time or to the wrong client or organ, can result in the most unfortunate consequences for an individual, group or institution. And matters are greatly exacerbated if it is the wrong information, or incomplete, or deliberately misleading.

In an increasingly information-rich world, it is essential that safeguards be established to protect data from misuse or abuse. The UK's Data Protection Acts of 1984 and 1998 are designed to achieve such an end. These cover the principles of data protection, the responsibilities of data users and the rights of data subjects. Data held for 'historical and research' purposes are exempted from the principle which gives individuals the right of access to personal data about themselves, provided the data are not made available in a form which identifies individuals. Research data also have partial exemption from two further principles, with the effect that such data may be held indefinitely and the use of the data for research purposes need not be disclosed at the time of data collection.

Of the two most important principles which do concern research data, one states that personal data (i.e. data that uniquely identify the person supplying them) shall be held only for specified and lawful purposes. The second principle states that appropriate security measures shall be taken against unauthorized access to, or alteration, disclosure or destruction of personal data and against accidental loss or destruction of personal data.

Most institutions of higher education have their own ethics committees, and these usually have their own codes of ethics against which they evaluate research proposals. In addition, some important codes of practice and guidelines are published by research associations, for example the British Educational Research Association (www.bera.ac.uk), the British Psychological Society (www.bps.org.uk), the British Sociological Association (www.britsoc.co.uk), the Social Research Association (www.the-sra.org.uk), the American Educational Research Association (www.aera.net), the American Psychological Association (www.apa.org), and the American Sociological Association (www.asanet.org). We advise readers to consult these in detail.

The British Psychological Society's *Code of Conduct, Ethical Principles and Guidelines* (2005) includes, amongst many others, sections on competence, obtaining consent, confidentiality and personal conduct. Its section on 'Ethical Principles for Conducting Research with Human Participants' first discusses

deception, debriefing, risk and implementation (pp. 6–7) and then moves to eleven main sections: introduction; general principles (including the guiding precept that 'the essential principle is that the investigation should be considered from the standpoint of all the participants; foreseeable threats to their psychological well-being, health, values or dignity should be eliminated' (p. 8)); consent; deception; debriefing; withdrawal from the investigation; confidentiality; protection of participants; observational research; giving advice; and colleagues. Interestingly it does not insist on informed consent, rather expressing it as 'wherever possible, the investigator should inform all participants of the objectives of the investigation' (para. 3.1). Similarly it does not proscribe deception, indicating that 'it may be impossible to study some psychological processes without withholding information about the true object of the study or deliberately misleading the participants' (para. 4.3). However, it says that these need to be rigorously justified, and alternatives must have been explored and found to be unavailable.

The American Psychological Association's *Ethical Principles and Code of Conduct* (2002) states five general principles: beneficence and non-maleficence, fidelity and responsibility, integrity, justice, and respect for people's rights and dignity. These principles then become the basis for ten sections of 'ethical standards': resolving ethical issues; competence; human relations (including 'avoiding harm', 'exploitative relationships' and 'informed consent'); privacy and confidentiality; advertising and other public statements; record keeping and fees; education and training; research and publication; assessment; and therapy.

The American Sociological Association's *Code of Ethics and Policies and Procedures of the ASA Committee on Professional Ethics* (1999) has five general principles: professional competence; integrity; professional and scientific responsibility; respect for people's rights, dignity and diversity; and social responsibility. These are then devolved onto 20 *ethical standards*, including non-exploitation, confidentiality, informed consent, deception, offering inducements and many others.

The British Sociological Association's *Statement of Ethical Practice for the British Sociological Association* (2002) (Appendix update 2004) includes sections on: professional integrity; relations with and responsibilities towards research participants; relationships with research participants; covert research; anonymity, privacy and confidentiality; relations with and responsibilities towards sponsors and/or funders; carrying obligations, roles and rights; pre-empting outcomes and negotiations about research; and obligations to sponsors and/or funders during the research process.

The Social Research Association's *Ethical Guidelines* (2003) draws on European law (www.respect-project.org) and indicates four levels of obligations: (1) to society; (2) to funders and employer; (3) to colleagues; and (4) to subjects (including avoiding undue intrusion, obtaining informed consent, modifications to informed consent, protecting the interests of subjects, enabling participation, maintaining confidentiality of records and preventing disclosure of identities).

The British Educational Research Association's (2004) *Revised Ethical Guidelines* are devolved onto: responsibilities to the research profession; responsibility to the participants (including working with children, informed consent, rights to withdrawal); responsibility to the public; relationships with funding agencies; publication; intellectual ownership; relationship with host institutions. Similarly, the American Educational Research Association's (2000) *Ethical Standards of the American Educational Research Association* includes: (a) responsibilities to the field; (b) research populations, educational institutions and the public (including working with children, informed consent, confidentiality, honesty ('deception is discouraged' and 'should be used only when clearly necessary', after which the reasons for the deception should be explained (para. B3)), rights of withdrawal, exploitation for personal gain, sensitivity to local circumstances (e.g. culture, religion, gender), avoidance of negative consequences, dissemination, anonymity); (c) intellectual ownership; (d) editing, reviewing and appraising research; (e) sponsors, policy makers and other users of research; and (f) students and student researchers.

The UK's Economic and Social Research Council's *Research Ethics Framework* (2009) includes sections on: minimum requirements; identifying risk in social research; governance, ethics and ethical principles; context for the research ethics framework; illustrative case studies; a research ethics review checklist; and a flowchart of the review process.

Websites of these research associations' and organizations' ethical principles and guidelines can be found either on the homepage of each association or as follows:

American Sociological Association:
  www.asanet.org/about/ethics.cfm
American Psychological Association:
  www.apa.org/ethics/code/index.aspx
British Educational Research Association:
  www.bera.ac.uk/files/guidelines/ethical.pdf

www.bera.ac.uk/ethics-and-educational-research/literature-on-ethical-regulation/
British Sociological Association:
  www.britsoc.co.uk/equality/Statement+Ethical+Practice.htm
British Psychological Society:
  www.bps.org.uk/document-download-area/document-download$.cfm?file_uuid=E6917759–9799–434A-F313–9C35698E1864&ext=pdf
Economic and Social Research Council:
  www.esrc.ac.uk/ESRCInfoCentre/Images/ESRC_Re_Ethics_Frame_tcm6–11291.pdf
Social Research Association:
  www.the-sra.org.uk/ethical.htm
American Educational Research Association:
  www.aera.net/aboutaera/?id=222

Against ethical codes and regulation

Ethical regulation of research is often conducted by university ethical committees. Whilst the intentions here might be honourable in protecting individuals and institutions, they may not fulfil these high ideals in practice. In a blistering paper against ethical regulation by ethical committees, Hammersley (2009: 212–19) argues that research ethics committees:

a   are incapable of making sound or 'superior' ethical decisions, such that their work will not improve the ethical quality of research. This is because: (i) ethical issues are contentious and there is a lack of consensus amongst social scientists on ethical matters, principles, priorities of principles and practices, or consequences (discussed early on in this chapter); (ii) ethical issues and practical research are complex (e.g. secrecy and deception in research); (iii) ethical answers cannot simply be cranked out, mechanistically or algorithmically, but are framed in specific contexts (which may be unknown to ethical committees); (iv) the remit of ethical committees is unclear (e.g. whether to approve, prevent, control methodology or topics); (v) ethical committees only need to be persuaded that the researcher has the ethical capability to conduct the research but this confuses ethical audit with ethical decision making and confuses substance and procedures of ethical review;

b   have no legitimacy to control researchers, and that this is inherent in ethical principles themselves: (i) researchers should have their autonomy respected; (ii) it is the researchers themselves – and not ethics committees – who have the responsibility for the ethical conduct of research and such responsibility cannot and should not be passed to a committee; (iii) ethics committees must apply the principle of 'informed consent' to researchers, and not just to those being researched; (iv) ethics committees operate prospectively, not only retrospectively, and this kind of prospective regulation is highly unusual in most areas of life; (v) there is almost no evidence that researchers operate unethically apart from some illegal cases, and so the processes of ethics committees is unnecessary, i.e. there is no problem that needs to be fixed;

c lead to undesirable consequences in research: (i) the bureaucratization of research; (ii) the time and effort required to meet bureaucratic requirements will deter many researchers from proceeding; (iii) researchers will avoid sensitive, difficult or contested yet important areas and marginalized or powerful groups, i.e. where informed consent may not be possible, and we may not discover important data; (iv) researchers will avoid important research areas because they may consider it difficult to obtain the consent of the ethics committee.

Hammerlsey argues that if ethics committees – as seems likely – are here to stay, then their roles should be clipped to providing advice, providing a forum for discussion on ethical matters and initiating such discussions. This echoes the comment from Howe and Moses (1999: 46–5) that research ethics committees have no special expertise to judge many educational research issues about such-and-such a project, and that they are bureaucratic and tend to discharge their duties in a perfunctory manner. They may provide advice and guidance, but not prospective judgements about specific research projects (Howe and Moses, 1999: 53).

The difficulty with and yet strength of ethical codes is that they cannot and do not provide specific advice for what to do in specific situations. And the difficulty for ethics committees is that their operations are seen as impractical and, ultimately, anti-ethical, anti-research and anti-researchers. Ultimately, it is researchers themselves, their integrity, conscience, informed by an acute awareness of ethical issues, underpinned by guideline codes and regulated practice, which should decide what to do in a specific situation, and this should be justified, justifiable, thought through and defensible.

There is a certain degree of homogeneity between the codes and guidelines cited above. Whilst they are helpful in providing guidance, they cannot tell the researcher what to do in every unique circumstance. The issue here is that ethics are 'situated', to quote Simons and Usher (2000); indeed, they state at the outset that

while ethics has traditionally been seen as a set of general principles invariantly and validly applied to all situations,... on the contrary, ethical principles are mediated within different research practices and thus take on different significances in relation to those practices.

(Simons and Usher, 2000: 1)

The authors state that this implies that situated ethics are 'immune to universalization', because

researchers cannot avoid weighing up conflicting considerations and dilemmas which are located in the specificities of the research situation and where there is a need to make ethical decisions but where those decisions cannot be reached by appeal to unambiguous and univalent principles or codes.

(Simons and Usher, 2000: 2)

As was observed earlier, many ethical codes and guidelines themselves avoid univalency and unambiguity, arguing, for example, that deception, covert research and the lack of informed consent may be justified. The need for polyvalency (multiple interpretations of what is worthwhile, acceptable and valuable) and situated ethics, Simons and Usher (2000: 11) argue, arises from the practicality of conducting research, the need for sensitivity to socio-political contexts and to be fair to disadvantaged groups, and to take account of the diversity and uniqueness of different research practices. What this suggests, then, is that whilst codes and guidelines may be useful in raising issues and orienting researchers, they cannot decide what should and should not be done in a specific situation; that is for individual researchers and their informed conscience to decide.

5.17 Sponsored research

Sponsored research does not absolve the researcher from ethical behaviour. For example, it may be considered unethical for the sponsor to tell the researcher:

- how to conduct the research;
- what results he/she should look for and what findings should be suppressed;
- what should and should not be reported;
- to conceal who the sponsor is;
- what are the purposes of the research.

On the other hand sponsors do have the right to remain confidential; they may have the right to nondisclosure of who they are, and the purposes and findings of the research.

Whilst sponsored research is usually contractual between the researcher and the sponsor, and between the researcher and the participants, and whilst the research may be for the sponsor alone and not for the public, this does not privilege the sponsor in dictating how the research should be conducted and what it should find; in short, 'fixing' the study.

Of course the researcher's responsibilities may lie only in conducting the study and providing the sponsor with a report; what happens to the report after that (e.g. whether it is released completely, selectively or not at all to the public or other parties within the sponsor's organization) is a matter for the sponsor. However, this does not absolve the researcher from decisions about the conduct of the study, and the researcher must retain the right to conduct the study as she or he thinks fit, informed by, but not decided by, the sponsor. The researcher's integrity must be absolute. It is often the case that researchers will negotiate publication rights with the sponsor in advance of the research and what confidentiality the researcher must respect.

The sponsor has a right to expect high-quality, rigorous and useable research. The researcher should not succumb to pressure to:

- betray the confidentiality of the respondents;
- tamper with data, their analysis or presentation to meet a particular objective;
- present selective and unrepresentative data and conclusions;
- make recommendations that do not arise from the data themselves;
- use the data for non-negotiated personal interests, agendas, purposes and advancement;
- conduct a study in which personal research objectives influence the nature, contents and conduct of the research.

The researcher has obligations to the sponsor, but not to doctor or compromise the research.

5.18 Responsibilities to the research community

The researcher has responsibilities to the research community, for example not to jeopardize the reputation of the research community (e.g. the university) or spoil the opportunities for further research. Thus, a novice researcher working for a higher degree may approach a school directly, using a clumsy approach, with inadequate data collection instruments and a poor research design, and then proceed to publicize the results as though they are valid and reliable. It is questionable

whether he or she deserves the degree! At the very least the novice should have sought and gained advice from the supervisor, modified the research as necessary, gained approval for the research, made suitably sensitive overtures to the school and agreed rights of disclosure. Not to do so puts the researcher's institution at risk of being denied further access, of damaging the reputation of the institution, and, if word spreads, of being publicly vilified and denied the opportunity for further research to be conducted. In this case the novice researcher has behaved unethically.

Further, what responsibility to the research community does the researcher have? If a negative research report is released will schools retrench, preventing future research in schools from being undertaken? Negative research data, such as reported evidence on deliberate grade inflation by schools in order to preserve reputation (Morrison and Tang, 2002) may not endear researchers to schools.

The researcher has a responsibility to colleagues to:

- protect their safety (e.g. in conducting sensitive research or research in dangerous locations);
- protect their well-being;
- protect their reputation;
- enable further research to be conducted;
- expect them to behave ethically;
- ensure that they adhere to correct and agreed procedures;
- protect the anonymity and confidentiality of sponsors if so agreed.

The researcher is a member of a research community, and this brings ethical responsibilities.

5.19 Conclusion

In this chapter we have attempted to acquaint readers with some of the ethical difficulties they are likely to experience in the conduct of such research. It is not possible to identify all potential ethical questions or adjudicate on what is correct researcher behaviour.[4] It is hoped that these pages will have induced in readers a certain disposition that will enable them to approach their own projects with a greater awareness and fuller understanding of the ethical dilemmas and moral issues lurking in the interstices of the research process. However inexperienced in these matters researchers are, they bring to social research a sense of rightness (Huizinga, 1949) on which they can construct a set of rational principles appropriate to their own circumstances and based on personal, professional and societal values (we stress the word 'rational' since reason is a prime ingredient of ethical thinking and it is the combination of reason and a sense of rightness that researchers must keep faith with if they are to bring a rich ethical quality to their work).

Although no code of practice can anticipate or resolve all problems, there is a six-fold advantage in fashioning a personal code of ethical practice. First, such a code establishes one as a member of the wider scientific community having a shared interest in its values and concerns. Second, a code of ethical practice makes researchers aware of their obligations to their subjects and also to those problem areas where there is a general consensus about what is acceptable and what is not. In this sense it has a clarificatory value. Third, when one's professional behaviour is guided by a principled code of ethics, then it is possible to consider that there may be alternative ways of doing the same thing, ways that are more ethical or less unethical should one be confronted by a moral challenge. Fourth, a balanced code can be an important organizing factor in researchers' perceptions of the research situation, and as such may assist them in their need to anticipate and prepare. Fifth, a code of practice validated by their own sense of rightness will help researchers to develop an intuitive sensitivity that will be particularly helpful to them in dealing with the unknown and the unexpected, especially where the more fluidic methods such as ethnography and participant observation are concerned. And sixth, a code of practice will bring discipline to researchers' awareness. Box 5.10 gives a short ethical code, by way of example. It must be stressed, however, that bespoke items, i.e. those designed to meet the needs of a specific project, are preferable to standard ones. The items in Box 5.9 are illustrative, and in no way exhaustive.

BOX 5.9 AN ETHICAL CODE – AN ILLUSTRATION

1 It is important for the researcher to reveal fully his or her identity and background.
2 The purpose and procedures of the research should be fully explained to the subjects at the outset.
3 The research and its ethical consequences should be seen from the subjects' and institution's point of view.
4 Possible controversial findings need to be anticipated and where they ensue, handled with great sensitivity.
5 The research should be as objective as possible. This will require careful thought being given to the design, conduct and reporting of research.
6 Informed consent should be sought from all participants. All agreements reached at this stage should be honoured.
7 Sometimes it is desirable to obtain informed consent in writing.
8 Subjects should have the option to refuse to take part and know this; and the right to terminate their involvement at any time and know this also.
9 Arrangements should be made during initial contacts to provide feedback for participants who request it. This may take the form of a written résumé of findings.
10 The dignity, privacy and interests of the participants should be respected and protected at all times.
11 Deceit should only be used when absolutely necessary.
12 When ethical dilemmas arise, the researcher may need to consult other researchers or teachers.

Source: Adapted from Reynolds, 1979

BOX 5.10 ETHICAL PRINCIPLES FOR EDUCATIONAL RESEARCH (TO BE AGREED BEFORE THE RESEARCH COMMENCES)

Responsibility to research
- The researcher should be competent and aware of what is involved in conducting research.
- The research must be conducted rigorously and with the correct procedures – avoid misuse of procedures at all stages.
- Report procedures accurately and publicly (rigour).
- Don't jeopardize future research(ers).
- Report clearly and make data available for checking.
- Tell the truth (do not tell lies or falsify data, avoid being unfairly selective, e.g. to support a case, do not misrepresent data).

continued

- Maintain the integrity and autonomy of the research, e.g. avoid censorship of, or interference with, the research by sponsors/those who give permission for the research to be undertaken.

Responsibility to participants and audience(s)
- Gain fully informed consent where appropriate (usually in writing), in order to respect self-determination and autonomy; provide information on all aspects of the research and its possible consequences.
- Decide whether, and how, overt or covert research is required/justified.
- Decide whether, and how, deception is required/justified; be honest or justify dishonesty.
- Ensure non-maleficence (no harm, hurt or suffering to be caused to participants and those who might be affected by the research); be humane.
- Ensure beneficence (the research will bring benefit to the participants or will contribute to the welfare of participants).
- Ensure that participants do not leave the research worse off than when they started it.
- Respect people's rights and dignity and interests, and be respectful – research participants are subjects, not objects to be exploited. Treat people as subjects, not objects.
- Agree individual's rights to privacy.
- Ensure participants have the right to withdraw at any time.
- Inform participants who will have access to the data/report, i.e. the audiences of the research, how public it will be, when it will become public and how it will be disseminated; negotiate levels of release (i.e. who see which parts of the research).
- Ensure anonymity/confidentiality/non-traceability; if these are not possible then tell participants in advance.
- Indicate how anonymity will be addressed (e.g. by confidentiality, aggregation of data).
- Inform participants how data will be collected and how files/questionnaires/audio data/video data/computer files will be stored during the research and destroyed after use.
- Ensure sensitivity to people (e.g. age, ethnicity, gender, culture, religion, language, socio-economic status, etc.).
- Gain permission from all relevant parties (e.g. parents/guardians, school, principals, etc.) for access.
- Respect vulnerability (e.g. in interviewing children/those without power).
- Agree respondent validation.
- Agree ownership of the data (and when ownership passes from participants to researcher).
- Allow time for review.
- Avoid causing unnecessary offence. Thank the participants.
- Ensure that participants and sponsors have the right to dissent/distance themselves from the research.
- Demonstrate social responsibility and obligations.
- Consider indemnification, liabilities and disclaimers.
- Don't abuse your position/power as a researcher.

In more detail, one can suggest that the considerations outlined in Box 5.10 have to be borne in mind in planning, conducting and reporting research. Box 5.10 raises issues and suggestions, not solutions or decisions. These will have to be decided by each researcher in respect of the particular situation he or she faces. For a summary of ethical principles for social research see the accompanying website.

 Companion Website

The companion website to the book includes PowerPoint slides for this chapter, which list the structure of the chapter and then provide a summary of the key points in each of its sections. In addition there is further information on ethical principles for social research. These resources can be found online at **www.routledge.com/textbooks/cohen7e**.

CHAPTER 6

Choosing a research project

This chapter provides a set of key decision points of reference on which researchers can reflect and plan. It addresses:

- how to choose a research project
- the importance of the research
- the purposes of the research
- ensuring that the research can be conducted
- research questions
- the scope of the literature review
- summary of key issues in choosing a research topic or project

This is the first of two chapters that concern the planning of research. This chapter concerns the selection of the research and the initial, practical matters that researchers will find it helpful to address, whilst Chapter 7 unpacks several of these in greater detail. The reader is advised to take these two chapters together.

6.1 Introduction

This chapter sets out a range of very practical issues that researchers have to face when choosing and deciding the project on which they will be working. It is drawn not only from relevant literature but from our own experiences of supervising several hundred research students. Research is a practical activity, and the advice that we give here is practical. This is not a simplistic recipe or low-level 'tips for researchers'; rather it is distillation of key features of practicable research that, together, deliver relevant and useful findings.

Choosing a research project is normally the decisive feature of successful research. Many novice students and researchers start with an overambitious project. The task of a mentor or supervisor is to help the novice student or researcher to narrow and hone down the research field in order to render the research practicable, useful and workable. Indeed part of the discipline of choosing and conducting a piece of research is fining it down to manageable/researchable proportions (cf. Hopkins, 1985: 47), to enable rigour (e.g. fitness for purposes and methodological soundness) to be inserted into the research. Rigour in planning and doing research lies in choosing a project that is tightly framed. A research topic is only one small aspect of the field of the subject, and careful boundaries must be drawn around the topic: what it will and will not do.

For novice researchers, a piece of educational research often starts by wanting to be their life story or the opportunity to give their personal opinions some grounding in literature and empirical study that will support their opinions or prejudices. This is not the task of research. The task of research is to find out, to investigate, to develop, to test out (e.g. a theory), to address questions that ask, for example: 'what if', 'how', 'why', 'how well', 'what' and 'where'.

6.2 What gives rise to the research project?

Several points can give rise to a research topic. For example, for many teachers it may be a problem that they encounter in their day-to-day work: they may want to find out the causes of the problem and how to solve it; they may want to plan an intervention to see how well it addresses or solves the problem. Examples of these might be: 'how can teachers improve students' learning of algebra in lower secondary schools?'; 'how to maximize the learning of students with Asperger's syndrome in mainstream schooling?'; 'how to conduct a music lesson with many musical instruments, without the lesson descending into chaos and noise?'; 'how to teach speaking of a foreign language in large, mixed-ability classes?'.

Some research projects may begin with an area of interest or personal experience that researchers may have been wanting to investigate, for example: 'why do boys appear to underachieve in secondary school music?'; 'what is the long-term effect on employment of early school dropout?'; 'how effective is early identification of behaviour disorders on educational provision for such students?'; 'how can teachers improve students' motivation to learn a second language?'; 'why do young teachers leave teaching and older teachers stay?'.

Some research topics may begin with a recognized area of importance or topical concern in the field, for example: 'how to maximize primary students' learning using ICT'; 'what is the effect of frequent testing on students' stress?'; 'do screening tests of attainment actually measure attainment?'; 'how can developments in brain research and cognitive neuroscience impact on pedagogy?'; 'what is the predictive validity of personality tests or learning style inventories on success of first-time employees' applications for employment?'; 'do interactive teaching methods produce higher test scores in university students than lecture-based teaching?'. Such importance may arise from coverage of the topic in the press, articles, conference papers and journals.

Some research is conducted as part of a sponsored research project, in which the field and purposes of the research have to be spelled out very clearly in order for the sponsorship to be obtained (for example in the UK the Economic and Social Research Council (www.esrc.ac.uk/ESRCInfoCentre/index.aspx), and the Leverhulme Trust (www.leverhulme.org.uk/) require detailed applications to be completed, and in the USA the United States National Research Council (http://sites.nationalacademies.org/NRC/index.htm) and the Social Science Research Council (www.ssrc.org) require similarly high levels of detail). Such funding might also need to fit into categories of research areas set out by the funding agencies.

A decision on what to research can arise from several wellsprings:

- a problem encountered in researchers' everyday work or outside their everyday work (e.g. conceptual, theoretical, substantive, practical, methodological);
- an issue that the researcher has read about in a journal, book or other media;
- a problem that has arisen in the locality, perhaps in response to government policy or practices or to local developments;
- an area of the researcher's own interest;
- an area of the researcher's own experience;
- a perceived area of importance;
- an interesting question;
- a testable guess or hunch;
- a topical matter;
- disquiet with a particular research finding that one has met in the literature or a piece of policy (e.g. from the school, from a government), and a wish to explore it further;
- an awareness that a particular issue or area has been covered only partially or selectively in the literature, and a wish to plug the gap;
- a wish to apply a piece of conceptual research to actual practice, or to test a theory in practice;

- a wish to rework the conceptual or theoretical frameworks that are often used in a specific area;
- a wish to revise or replace the methodologies that are often used in researching a specific area;
- a desire to improve practice in a particular area;
- a desire to involve participants in research and development;
- a desire to test out a particular methodology in research;
- an interest in seeing if reported practice (e.g. in the literature) holds true for the researcher's own context (e.g. a comparative study);
- an interest in investigating the causes of a phenomenon or the effects of a particular intervention in the area of the phenomenon;
- a wish to address an issue or topic that has been under-researched in the literature;
- a priority identified by funding agencies;
- an issue identified by the researcher's supervisor or a project team of which the researcher is a member;
- a wish to explore further or to apply an issue or topic that one has encountered, e.g. in the literature.

Moreover, a salutary point for researchers to observe is that the study on which they might embark will probably take weeks, months and maybe years. Sustaining interest and momentum in the researcher(s) are important considerations. Researchers should ask themselves whether they really have the interest in studying the issue in question or in conducting the research for a long period of time. If the answer is 'no' then, if they have the luxury of not having to do this particular piece of research, they may wish to consider an alternative area of research that will enable them to sustain interest in, and motivation for, the research. A piece of research that is conducted by an unwilling or bored researcher could easily turn out to be unimpressive.

6.3 The importance of the research

Whatever research area or topic is identified, it is important for the research to be original, significant, non-trivial, relevant, topical, interesting to a wider audience and to advance the field. For example, I may want to investigate the use of such-and-such a textbook in Business Studies with 16-year-olds in Madagascar, but, really, is this actually a useful, formal research topic – will it actually help or benefit other teachers or educationists, even though it yields original data?

Or I might conduct research that finds that older primary children in a deprived area of Aberdeen, Scotland, prefer to have their lunch between 12 noon and 1.00 p.m. rather than between 1.00 p.m. and 2.00 p.m., but, really, does anybody actually care? The topic is original and, indeed, the data are original, but both are insignificant and maybe not worth knowing.

In both these examples the research brings about original data, but that is all. Research needs to go beyond this, to choose a significant topic that will actually make an important contribution to our understanding and to practice. Originality alone is not enough. Rather, the research should be able to move forward the field, perhaps in only a small-scale, piecemeal, incremental way, but nevertheless to advance it such that, without the research, the field would be poorer. Hence it is important to consider how the research takes the field forwards not only in terms of data, but also conceptually, theoretically, substantively, methodologically. At issue here is not only the contribution to knowledge that the research makes, but the *impact* of that knowledge, indeed funding agencies typically require an indication of the impact that the research will make on the research community and more widely, and how that impact will be assessed and known. What will be the impact, uptake and effects of the research, and on whom?

Further, it is useful for the researcher to identify what benefit the research will bring, and to whom, as this will help to focus the research and its audience. Fundamentally, the questions are: 'What is the use of this research?' 'What is the point of doing this research?' 'Is this research worth doing?' If the answers to the last question is 'no', then maybe the researcher should abandon it, otherwise it ceases to be useful research and becomes an indulgence of the dilettante.

Many novice researchers may not know whether the research is original, significant, important, complex, difficult, topical and so on. Here it is important for such a novice to read around the topic, to conduct a literature search, to conduct an online search, to attend conferences on the topic, to read newspaper reports on the topic, in short, to review the state of the field before coming to a firm decision on whether to pursue research in that field. In this respect, if the researcher is a student, it is vital to discuss the proposed topic with a possible supervisor, to receive expert feedback on the possible topic.

The University of California at Santa Cruz (2010: 1) (http://library.ucsc.edu/help/howto/choose-a-research-topic) notes that, before a researcher takes a final decision on whether to pursue a particular piece of research, it is useful to consider selecting a topic that interests the researcher, read through background materials and information and compile a list of keywords, clarify the main concepts and write the topic as a statement (or a hypothesis). Whilst this is perhaps incomplete, nevertheless it provides a useful starting point for novice researchers contemplating what to research.

6.4 The purposes of the research

Implicit in the previous section is the question 'why do the research?'. This is ambiguous, as 'why' can refer to reasons/causes and purposes, though the two may overlap. Whereas the previous section concerned reasons, this section concerns purposes: what we want the research to achieve.

It is vital that the researcher will know what she or he wants the research to 'deliver', i.e. to answer the question 'what are the "deliverables" in the research?'. In other words, what do we want to know as a result of the research that we did not know before the research commenced? What do we want the research to do? What do we want the research to find out (which is not the same as what we want the results to be: we cannot predict the outcome, as this would be to 'fix' the research; rather we state the kind of information or answers we want the research to provide)?

In this respect it is important for the researcher to be very clear on what the purposes of the research are, for example:

- to try to demonstrate that such-and-such works under a specified set of conditions or in a particular context (experiment; action research);
- to increase understanding and knowledge of learning theories (literature-based research);
- to identify common features of successful schools (research synthesis; descriptive research);
- to examine the effects of early musical tuition on general intelligence (meta-analysis; multilevel research);
- to develop and evaluate community education in rural and dispersed communities (participatory research; evaluative research; action research);
- to collect opinions on a particular educational proposal (survey);
- to examine teacher–student interactions in a language programme (ethnography; observational research);
- to investigate the organizational culture of the science faculty in a university (ethnography; survey);
- to identify the relative strengths of a range of specified factors on secondary school student motivations for learning (survey; observational study; multiple regression analysis; structural equation modelling);
- to see which of two approaches to teaching music

results in the most effective learning (comparative study; experiment; causal research);

■ to see what happens if a particular intervention in setting homework is introduced (experiment; action research; causal research);

■ to investigate trends in social networking in foreign language teacher communities (network analysis);

■ to identify the main ways in which teachers in a large secondary school view the leadership of the senior staff of the school (personal constructs; accounts; survey);

■ to interrogate government policy on promotion criteria in schools (ideology critique; feminist critique);

■ to see the effects of assigning each student to a mentor in a university (survey; case study; causal research);

■ to examine the long-term effects of early student dropout from school (survey; causal or correlational research);

■ to see if repeating a year at school improves student performance (survey; generalization; causal or correlational research);

■ to chart the effects of counselling disruptive students in a secondary class (case study; causal or correlational research);

■ to see which catches richer survey data on student drug usage: questionnaires or face-to-face interviews (testing instrumentation; methodology-related research);

■ to examine the cues that teachers give to students in question-and-answer classroom episodes (discourse analysis);

■ to investigate vandalism in schools (covert research; informer-based research);

■ to investigate whether case studies or surveys are more effective in investigating truancy in primary school (comparative methodology);

■ to run a role-play exercise on communication between a school principal and senior teachers (role play);

■ to examine the effects of resource allocations to underperforming schools (ideology critique; case study; survey; causal research);

■ to understand the dynamics of power in primary classrooms (ethnography; interpretive research);

■ to investigate the demise of the private school system in such-and-such a town at the end of the nineteenth century (historical research);

■ to understand the nature of trauma and its treatment, on primary aged children living in violent households (case study; action research; grounded theory; ex post facto research);

■ to generate a theory of effective use of textbooks in

secondary school physics teaching (grounded theory);

■ to clarify the concept of 'the stereotype activation effect' for investigating the effect of sex stereotyping on reading in young teenagers (survey; case study; experiment; causal research);

■ to test the hypothesis/theory that increasing rewards lose their effect on students over time (experiment; survey; longitudinal research; causal or correlational research).

As can be seen in these examples, different purposes suggest different approaches, so 'fitness for purpose' takes on importance in planning research (discussed in the following chapter). One can also see that there is a range of purposes and types of research in education. The researcher cannot simply say that he or she likes questionnaires, or is afraid of numbers, or prefers to conduct interviews, or feels that it is wrong to undertake covert research so no covert research will be done. That is to have the tail wagging the dog. Rather, the research purposes determine what follow in respect of the kind of research, the research questions, the instruments for data collection, the sampling, whether the research is overt or covert (the ethics of research), the scope of the research and so on.

6.5 Ensuring that the research can be conducted

Many novice researchers, with the innocence and optimism of ignorance, may believe that whatever they want to do can actually be done. This is very far from the case. There is often a significant gulf between what researchers want to do and what actually turns out to be what they can do.

A formidable issue to be faced here is one of *access*. Many new researchers fondly imagine that they will be granted access to schools, teachers, students, parents, difficult children, students receiving therapy, truants, dropouts, high performers, star teachers and so on. This is usually NOT the case: gaining access to people and institutions is one of the most difficult tasks for any empirical researcher, particularly if the research is in any way sensitive. Access problems can prevent the research from starting at all, or they can distort or change the original plans for the research.

It is difficult to overstate the importance of researchers doing their homework before planning the research in any detail, to see if it is actually feasible to gain access to the research sites or people that they want. If the answer is 'no' then the research plan either stops or has to be modified. This means that it is not uncommon for the researcher to approach some organizations (schools, colleges, universities, government departments) with some initial, outline plans of the research, to see if there is a possibility, likelihood or little or no chance of doing the research.

Nor is it enough to be clear on access; supplementary to this is 'access to what?'. It is of little use to be given access to a school by the school principal if the teachers have not been consulted about this, or if they are entirely uncooperative (this relates to the issue of informed consent, discussed in Chapter 5). One of the authors recalls an example of a Master's student who wanted to study truancy; the student had the permission of the school principal, turned up on the day to commence the research with the school truants, only to find that they had truanted, and were not present! The same is true for sensitive research. For example, let us suppose that one wished to research child abuse in primary school students; the last people to consent, or even to be identified and found, might be the child abusers or those children who have been abused; even if they *were* identified and found, why should they agree to being interviewed by a stranger who is conducting research? Or, let us suppose that one wished to investigate the effects on teachers in hospitals of working with HIV-positive children in hospital; those teachers might be so traumatized or emotionally exhausted at the end of a day's work that the last thing they want to do is to talk about it further with an outside researcher whom they have never met before; they simply want to go home and 'switch off'. These are real issues, and we authors have experienced them with our research students. The researcher has to check out the situation before embarking on a fully worked-out plan, because the plan might come to nothing if useful access is not possible.

It is not only the people with whom the researcher is working that have to be considered; it is the researcher herself/himself. For example, does the researcher have the right personality, dispositions, sympathies, interpersonal skills, empathy, emotional intelligence, perseverance and so on to conduct the research? For instance, it would be a likely disaster if a researcher were to be conducting a piece of research on student depression if the researcher tacitly believed that students were just lazy or work-shy and that they used 'feeling down' (as she put it) as an excuse, i.e. who refused to recognize the seriousness of depression as a clinical condition or as a pathological disorder. Equally, it would be an unwise researcher who would choose to conduct a study if she had limited perseverance or if she knew that she was going to move overseas in the near future.

Further, researchers themselves will need to decide whether they have sufficient expertise in the field in which they want to do the research. It could be dangerous to the researcher and to the participants if the researcher were to be comparatively ignorant of the field of the proposed research, as this could mean that direction, relevance, prioritization or even safety might be jeopardized. This is a prime reason for the need for the researcher to conduct a literature review, to demonstrate that she/he is sufficiently versed in the field to know what to do, what to look for, and where, when and how to proceed.

Researchers will also have a personal commitment to the research; it may help to further their specialist interest or expertise; it may help to establish their reputation; it may make for career advancement or professional development. These considerations, though secondary perhaps in choosing a piece of research, nevertheless are important features, given the commitment of time and effort that the research will require.

In addition to access, there are issues of time to be considered. Part of the initial discipline of doing research is to choose a project that is manageable – can actually be done – within the time frames that the researcher has at her/his disposal. So, for example, it would be ridiculous for a researcher to propose to conduct a longitudinal study if that researcher only has maybe six or nine months to plan, conduct and report the entire research project. The time frames may prevent certain types of research from being conducted.

Similarly, the time availability of the researcher has to be considered: many researchers are part-time students who may not have much time to conduct research, and often their research is a lonely, one-person affair rather than a group affair that has a team of full-time researchers. This places a practical boundary around what can and cannot be done in the research. Again, these are real issues. Not only does the issue of availability of the researcher feature in ensuring that the research can be conducted, but this also applies to the participants: are they willing and able to give up their time in participating in the research, for example, not only in being interviewed, but in keeping diaries, conducting follow-up debriefings, participating in focus groups and writing reports of their activities?

Whilst access and time are important factors, so is the issue of resources (e.g. human, material). For example, if one is conducting a postal survey there are costs for printing, distribution, mail-back returns and follow-up reminders. If one is conducting a questionnaire survey on a large, dispersed university campus then one will need the cooperation of academic and administrative staff to arrange for the distribution, collection and return of the questionnaires. If one is conducting an online survey of teachers' views of such-and-such, e.g. government assessment policy, can it be assured that all teachers will have access to the online facilities, at times that are convenient for them, and that poor connectivity, slow speed and instability of the system will not end in them abandoning the survey before it is completed?

If one is conducting an analysis of trends in public education in early twentieth-century Scotland, then one needs to have time to search and retrieve public records (and this may involve payment), maybe to visit geographically dispersed archives, and time to sit down in front of microfiche readers or computers in public record offices and libraries.

A further consideration in weighing up the practicalities of the research is whether, in fact, the research will make any difference. This is particularly true in participatory research. As Hopkins (1985: 47) remarks, researchers may wish to think twice before tackling issues about which they can do nothing or over which they may exert little or no influence, such as changing an education or schooling system, changing the timetabling or the catchment of a school, changing the uses made of textbooks by senior staff, changing a national or school-level assessment system. This is not to say that such research cannot or should not be done; rather it is to ask whether the researcher's own investigation will do this, and, if not, then what the purposes of the research really are or can be.

Many researchers who are contemplating empirical enquiries will be studying for a degree. It is important that they will be able to receive expert, informed supervision for their research topic. Indeed, in many universities a research proposal will be turned down if the university feels that it is unable to supervise the research sufficiently. This will require the student researcher to check out whether his/her topic can be supervised properly by a member of the staff with suitable expertise, and many students find this out before even registering with a particular university. It is a sound principle.

A final feature of practicality is the scope of the research. This returns us to the opening remarks in this chapter, concerning the need to narrow down the field of the study. Principally, we advise a single piece of research to be narrow and limited in scope in order to achieve manageability as well as rigour. As the saying goes 'the best way to eat an elephant is one bite at a time'! Researchers will need to put clear, perceptible, realistic, fair and manageable boundaries round their research. If this cannot be done straightforwardly then maybe the researcher should reconsider whether to proceed with the planned enterprise, as uncontrolled research may wander everywhere and actually arrive

nowhere. Part of the discipline of research is to set its boundaries clearly and unequivocally. In choosing a piece of research, the manageability of setting the boundaries is an important issue; if these cannot be set, then the question is raised of the utility of the proposed endeavour.

For example, if one were to investigate students' motivations for learning, say, biology, this would involve not only identifying a vast range of independent variables, but also handling likely data overload, and ensuring that all the theories of motivation were included in the research. This quickly goes out of control and becomes an impossible task. Rather, one or two theories of motivation might be addressed, within a restricted, given range of specified independent variables (unless, of course, the research was genuinely exploratory), and with students of a particular age range or kind of experience of biology.

Small samples, narrowly focused research, can yield remarkable results. For example Axline's *Dibs in Search of Self* (1964) study of the restorative and therapeutic effects of play therapy focused on one child, and Piaget's (1932) seminal theory of moral development, in his *The Moral Judgement of the Child*, focused on a handful of children. In both these cases the detailed carefully bounded research yielded great benefits for educationists.

Practical issues, such as those mentioned here, often attenuate what can be done in research. They are real issues. The researcher is advised to consider carefully the practicability of the research before embarking on a lost cause in trying to conduct a study that is doomed from the very start because insufficient attention has been paid to practical constraints.

6.6 Considering research questions

In deciding whether to embark on a particular piece of research, it is often useful for the researcher to consider the role of the research questions and the guidance to the investigation that they might provide. Some research – often qualitative (Bryman, 2007b) – may not have research questions. Similarly it is important to recognize that research methods are not always driven by the research questions (Bryman, 2007b: 18), and that one should avoid the 'dictatorship of the research questions' (Bryman, 2007b: 14) in steering the design and conduct of the enquiry. Nevertheless, in many kinds of research the research questions figure significantly, and hence the chapter moves to considering their importance.

Some kinds of research (e.g. ethnography) might not begin with research questions but, in their closing stages, might use open-ended research (e.g. an ethnography, survey or focus groups) to raise research questions for further study in subsequent investigations. Such research, being exploratory in nature, might not wish to steer the enquiry too tightly, and, indeed, one of the features of naturalistic research (see Chapter 11) is that it endeavours not to disturb the everyday, natural setting for the participants. However, for many kinds of research, one of the early considerations that researchers might wish to address in choosing a project is the research questions that the study might generate (or should, as they derive from the overall purposes of the research).

In considering the proposed research, a useful approach is to brainstorm the possible areas of the field, moving from a general set of purposes to a range of specific, concrete issues and areas to be addressed in the research, and, for each, to frame these in terms of one or more research questions (or in terms of a thesis to be defended).

It is the answers to the research questions that might provide some of the 'deliverables' referred to earlier in this chapter. A useful way of deciding whether to pursue a particular study is the clarity and ease in which research questions can be conceived and answered. As mentioned in more detail in the next chapter, research questions turn a general purpose or aim into specific questions to which specific, data-driven, concrete answers can be given. Questions such as 'what is happening?', 'what has happened?', 'what might/will/should happen?' (cf. Newby, 2010: 67–9) open up the field of research questions. Chapter 4 also mentioned causal questions. Here 'what are the effects of such-and-such a cause?' and 'what are the causes of such-and-such an effect?' are two such questions, to which can be added the frequently used questions 'How?' and 'Why?'. These questions ask for explanations as well as reasons.

Research questions can concern, for example:

- Prediction;
- Understanding;
- Exploring;
- Causation;
- Testing;
- 'What?';
- 'What if:';
- 'Who?';
- 'When?';
- 'Where?';
- 'Why?';
- 'How?';
- Explanation;
- Description;

- Relations (e.g. between variables, people, events);
- Comparisons;
- Correlations;
- Processes;
- Factors;
- Evaluation;
- Function or purpose;
- How to achieve certain outcomes;
- Types of something;
- Properties and characteristics;
- Stages of something;
- How to do something;
- How to achieve something;
- Structures of something (cf. University of Berkeley, 2002);
- Alternatives to something;
- How to improve or develop something.

Chapter 1 drew attention to numerical, non-numerical and mixed methods research questions. Some research questions might only need to be answered by gathering numerical data; others by only qualitative data. However, we recommended in that chapter that, for mixed methods research, attention should be paid to the research questions such that they can *only* be answered by mixed – combined – types of data, or by adopting mixed methodologies, or by having a set of purposes that can only be addressed by mixed methods, or by taking mixed samples, or by having more than one researcher on the project (mixed researchers), in short, by building a mixed methods format into the very heart of the research (which goes beyond simple triangulation, as discussed in Chapter 10). So, a research question in this vein might combine 'how' and 'what' into the same research question, or 'why and who' might be combined in the same question, or description and explanation might be combined, or prediction, explanation and causation might be combined, and so on. We provided examples of these in Chapter 1.

It has been suggested (Bryman, 2007b) that in mixed methods research the research question takes on added prominence in guiding the research design and sampling, yet it is often more difficult to frame research questions in mixed methods enquiries than in single paradigm research (e.g. quantitative or qualitative) (Onwuegbuzie and Leech, 2006a: 477). This is because it requires quantitative and qualitative strategies to be addressed within the same research questions. Onwuegbuzie and Leech (2006a: 483–4) provide examples of mixed methods research questions, such as 'What is the relationship between graduate students' levels of reading comprehension and their perceptions of barriers that prevent them from reading empirical research articles?' Here both numerical and qualitative data are required in order to provide a complete answer to the research question (e.g. numerical data on levels of reading comprehension and qualitative data on barriers to reading articles (p. 484)). They provide another example (p. 494) of mixed methods research questions thus: 'What is the difference in perceived classroom atmosphere between male and female graduate students enrolled in a statistics course?' This could involve combining measures with interviews.

Here is not the place to discuss the framing of research questions. Rather, we wish to draw attention to research questions per se – in particular their clarity, ease of answering, comprehensiveness, comprehensibility, specificity, concreteness, complexity, difficulty, contents, focus, purposes, kinds of data required to answer them and utility of the answers provided – to enable researchers to decide whether the particular piece of research is worth pursuing. This will require researchers to pause, generate and reflect on the kinds of research question(s) required, before they decide whether to pursue a particular investigation. This is not to say that a study must require 'plain sailing' in its research questions; it is to argue that researchers may wish to consider whether they really want to embark on an enquiry whose research questions are too difficult or complex to answer within the scope or time frames of the study. Many of the most useful pieces of research stem from complex issues, complex research questions and 'difficult-to-answer' research questions.

Further, researchers may wish to ponder on whether they want to embark on investigations that have no clearly defined research questions or, indeed, any research questions, for example an ethnography, a naturalistic observational study or qualitative research (Bryman, 2007b).

6.7 Considering the scope of the literature review

A literature review is an essential part of many kinds of research, particularly so if the research is part of a thesis or dissertation. It serves many purposes, for example:

- it ensures that the researcher's proposed research will not simply recycle existing material (reinventing the wheel), unless, of course, it is a replication study;
- it gives credibility and legitimacy to the research, showing readers that the researcher has 'done his/ her homework' and knows the up-to-date, key issues, and the theoretical, conceptual, methodological and substantive problems in the field in which the research is being proposed;

- it clarifies the key concepts, issues, terms and the meanings of these for the research;
- it acts as a springboard into the researcher's own study, raising issues, showing where there are gaps in the research field, and providing a partial justification for the research or a need for it to be undertaken;
- it indicates the researcher's own critical judgement on prior research or theoretical matters in the field and, indeed, provides new theoretical, conceptual, methodological and substantive insights and issues for research;
- it sets the context for the research and establishes the key issues to be addressed;
- it makes clear where new ground has to be broken in the field and it shows where, how and why the proposed research will break that new ground and/ or plug any gaps in the current field.

A literature review must be useful, not only to show that the researcher has read some relevant materials, which is a trivial, self-indulgent reason, but that this actually informs the research. A literature review must be formative and lead into, or give rise to, all aspects of the research: the field, the particular topic, the methodology, the data analysis and implications for future research. Amongst other kinds of written or online materials, a sound literature review will include up-to-date information from materials such as: books, articles, reports, research papers, newspaper articles, conference papers, theses, reviews, government documents, material from databases and internet sources, primary and secondary sources and so on.

The researcher who is contemplating conducting a particular piece of research will need to give careful consideration to the necessary size and scope of the literature review, as this has implications for time, manageability, practicability and decision making on whether the project is too large, unfocused, diffuse, general or difficult to have justice done to it in the time and resources available. It is a determinant of whether to opt for a particular piece of research.

6.8 Summary of key issues in choosing a research topic or project

This chapter has set out several practical considerations in choosing a research topic. We advise researchers, both novice and experienced, to approach the selection of, and decision making on, a research topic with caution, going into it 'with their eyes open', aware of its possible pitfalls as well as its benefits and implications. We summarize the points discussed in the chapter in Box 6.1.

BOX 6.1   ISSUES TO BE FACED IN CHOOSING A PIECE OF RESEARCH

1 Make the topic small. Think small rather than big.
2 Limit the scope and scale of the research.
3 Think narrow rather than broad.
4 Keep the focus clear, limited, bounded and narrow.
5 Don't be overambitious.
6 Be realistic on what can be done in the time available, and whether, or how much, this might compromise the viability or worth of the research.
7 Make it clear what has given rise to the research – why choose this topic/project.
8 Choose a topic that might enable you to find your niche or specialism in the research or academic world or which might help to establish your reputation.
9 Decide why the research is important, topical, interesting, timely, significant, original, relevant and positively challenging.
10 Decide what contribution the research will make to the conceptual, practical, substantive, theoretical, methodological fields.
11 Choose a research project that will be useful, and decide how and for whom it will be useful.
12 Decide why your research will be useful and who will/might be interested in it.
13 Decide what might be the impact of your research, and on whom.
14 Choose a topic that is manageable and practicable.
15 Choose a topic that will enable rigour to be exercised.
16 Choose a topic that has clear boundaries or where clear, realistic, fair boundaries can be set.
17 Decide what the research will 'deliver'.
18 What will the research do?
19 What will the research seek to find out?
20 Choose a topic for which there is a literature.
21 Decide whether you will have the required access and access to what/whom in order to be able to conduct the research.
22 Decide what can and cannot be done within the time and timescales available.
23 Decide what can and cannot be done within the personal, people-related, material, effort-related, financial and scope of the research.
24 Consider the likely clarity, scope, practicability, comprehensiveness, ease of answering, framing, focus, kinds of data required, comprehensibility of the research questions and their combination.
25 Consider whether the research will influence, or make a difference to, practice, and, if not, why it might still be important.
26 Consider whether you have the right personality, characteristics, experience and interpersonal behaviour to conduct the proposed piece of research.
27 Consider whether the research will sustain your creativity, imagination, positive attitude and motivation over time.
28 Choose a topic for which you know you will be able to receive expert, informed supervision.
29 Be clear on why you – personally, professionally, career-relatedly – want to do the research, and what you personally want out of it, and whether the research will enable you to achieve this. How will the research benefit you?
30 How will the research benefit the participants?
31 How will the research benefit the world of education?
32 Choose a topic that will sustain your interest over the duration of the research.
33 Consider whether you have sufficient experience, skills and expertise in the field in which you want to conduct the research for you to be able to act in an informed way.
34 Consider whether it is advisable to embark on a piece of research that deliberately does not have research questions.
35 Consider the necessary complexity (where it exists) of the research phenomenon, scope and conduct of the research, and the difficulty of the research issues, foci and conduct.
36 Consider how future research will be able to build on your research, i.e. that the research opens up possibilities rather than closes them down.

Companion Website

The companion website to the book includes PowerPoint slides for this chapter, which list the structure of the chapter and then provide a summary of the key points in each of its sections. This resource can be found online at **www.routledge.com/textbooks/cohen7e**.

Planning educational research

This chapter sets out a range of key issues in planning research, including:

- approaching research planning
- a framework for planning research
- conducting and reporting a literature review
- searching for literature on the internet
- orienting decisions in planning research
- research design and methodology
- how to operationalize research questions
- data analysis
- presenting and reporting the results
- a planning matrix for research
- managing the planning of research
- ensuring quality in the planning of research

It also provides an extended worked example of planning a piece of research.

7.1 Introduction

There is no single blueprint for planning research. Research design is governed by the notion of 'fitness for purpose'. The purposes of the research determine the methodology and design of the research. For example, if the purpose of the research is to map the field, or to make generalizable comments then a survey approach might be desirable, using some form of stratified sample; if the effects of a specific intervention are to be evaluated then an experimental or action research model may be appropriate; if an in-depth study of a particular situation or group is important then an ethnographic model might be suitable.

That said, it is possible, nevertheless, to identify a set of issues that researchers need to address, regardless of the specifics of their research. This chapter addresses this set of issues, to indicate those matters that need to be addressed in practice so that an area of research interest can become practicable and feasible. This chapter indicates how research might be operationalized, i.e. how a general set of research aims and purposes can be translated into a practical, researchable topic.

It is essential to try as far as possible to plan every stage of the research. To change the 'rules of the game' in midstream once the research has commenced is a sure recipe for problems. The terms of the research and the mechanism of its operation must be ironed out in advance if it is to be credible, legitimate and practicable. Once they have been decided upon, the researcher is in a very positive position to undertake the research. The setting up of the research is a balancing act, for it requires the harmonizing of *planned possibilities* with *workable, coherent practice*, i.e. the resolution of the difference between what could be done/what one would like to do and what will actually work/what one can actually do, for, at the end of the day, research has to work. In planning research there are two phases: a divergent phase and a convergent phase. The divergent phase will open up a range of possible options facing the researcher, whilst the convergent phase will sift through these possibilities, see which ones are desirable, which ones are compatible with each other, which ones will actually work in the situation, and move towards an action plan that can realistically operate. This can be approached through the establishment of a framework of planning issues.

7.2 Approaching research planning

What the researcher does depends on what the researcher wants to know and how she or he will go about finding out about the phenomenon in question. The planning of research (the research design) depends on the kind(s) of questions being asked or investigated. This is not a mechanistic exercise, but depends on the researcher's careful consideration of the purpose of the research (discussed in the previous chapter) and the phenomenon being investigated, for example see Table 7.1.

Part 1 set out a range of paradigms which inform and underpin the planning and conduct of research, for example:

- positivist and post-positivist
- quantitative, scientific and hypothesis-testing

TABLE 7.1   PURPOSES AND KINDS OF RESEARCH

Kinds of research purpose	Kinds of research
Does the research want to test a hypothesis or theory?	Experiment, survey, action research, case study
Does the research want to develop a theory?	Ethnography, qualitative research, grounded theory
Does the research need to measure?	Survey, experiment
Does the research want to understand a situation?	Ethnographic and interpretive/qualitative approaches
Does the research want to see what happens if…?	Experiment, participatory research, action research
Does the research want to find out 'what' and 'why'?	Mixed methods research
Does the research want to find out what happened in the past?	Historical research

---

- qualitative
- interpretive and naturalistic
- phenomenological and existential
- interactionist and ethnographic
- experimental
- ideology critical
- participatory
- feminist
- political
- complexity theoretical
- evaluative
- mixed methods.

It was argued that these paradigms rest on different ontologies (e.g. different views of the essential nature or characteristics of the phenomenon in question) and different epistemologies (e.g. theories of the nature of knowledge, its structure, organization and how we investigate knowledge and phenomena: how we know, what constitutes valid knowledge, our cognition of a phenomenon). For example:

- a positivist paradigm rests, in part, on an objectivist ontology and a scientific, empirical, hypothesis-testing epistemology;
- an interpretive paradigm rests, in part, on a subjectivist, interactionist, socially constructed ontology and on an epistemology that recognized multiple realities, agentic behaviours and the importance of understanding a situation through the eyes of the participants;
- a complexity theory paradigm rests, in part, on an ontology of self-organized emergence and change through the unpredictable interactions and outcomes of constituent elements of a whole ecological entity, and on an epistemology that argues for understanding multiple directions of causality and a need to understand phenomena holistically and by examining the processes and outcomes of interactions;

- an ideology critique paradigm rests, in part, on an ontology of phenomena as organized both within, and as outcomes of, power relations and asymmetries of power, inequality and empowerment, and on an epistemology that is explicitly political, critiquing the ideological underpinnings of phenomena that perpetuate inequality and asymmetries of power to the advantage of some and the disadvantage of others, and the need to combine critique with participatory action for change to being about greater social justice;
- a mixed methods paradigm rests on an ontology that recognizes that phenomena are complex to the extent that single methods approaches might result in partial, selective and incomplete understanding, and on an epistemology that requires pragmatic combinations of methods – in sequence, in parallel or in synthesis – in order to fully embrace and comprehend the phenomenon and to do justice to its several facets.

At issue here is the need for researchers not only to consider the nature of the phenomenon under study, but what are or are not the ontological premises that underpin it, the epistemological bases for investigating it and conducting the research into it. These are points of reflection and decision, turning the planning of research from being solely a mechanistic or practical exercise into a reflection on the nature of knowledge and the nature of being.

7.3 A framework for planning research

Planning research depends on the design of the research which, in turn, depends on (a) the kind of questions being asked or investigated; (b) the purposes of the research; (c) the research paradigms and principles in which one is working, and the philosophies, ontologies and epistemologies which underpin them. Planning research is not an arbitrary matter. There will be different designs for different types of research, and we give three examples here.

For example, a piece of quantitative research that seeks to test a hypothesis could proceed thus:

Literature review → generate and formulate the hypothesis/the theory to be tested/the research questions to be addressed → design the research to test the hypothesis/theory (e.g. an experiment a survey) → conduct the research → analyse results → consider alternative explanations for the findings → report whether the hypothesis/theory is supported or not supported, and/or answer the research questions → consider the generalizability of the findings.

A qualitative or ethnographic piece of research could have a different sequence, for example:

Identify the topic/group/phenomenon in which you are interested → literature review → design the research questions and the research and data collection → locate the fields of study and your role in the research and the situation → locate informants, gatekeepers, sources of information → develop working relations with the participants → conduct the research and the data collection simultaneously → conduct the data analysis either simultaneously, on an ongoing basis as the situation emerges and evolves, or conduct the data analysis subsequent to the research → report the results and the grounded theory or answers to the research questions that emerge from the research → generate a hypothesis for further research or testing.

One can see in the examples that, for one method the hypothesis drives the research whilst for another the hypothesis (if, in fact, there is one) emerges from the research, at the end of the study (some qualitative research does not proceed to this hypothesis-raising stage).

A mixed methods research might proceed thus:

Identify the problem or issue that you wish to investigate → identify your research questions → identify the several kinds of data and the methods for collecting them which, together and/or separately will yield answers to the research questions → plan the mixed methods design (e.g. parallel mixed design, fully integrated mixed design, sequential mixed design (see Chapter 1)) → conduct the research →

analyse results → consider alternative explanations for the findings → answer the research questions → report the results.

These three examples proceed in a linear sequence; this is beguilingly deceptive, for rarely is such linearity so clear. The reality is that:

- different areas of the research design influence each other;
- research designs, particularly in qualitative, naturalistic and ethnographic research, change, evolve and emerge over time rather than being a 'once-and-for-all' plan that is decided and finalized at the outset of the research;
- ethnographic and qualitative research starts with a very loose set of purposes and research questions, indeed there may not be any;
- research does not always go to plan, so designs change.

In recognition of this Maxwell (2005: 5–6) develops an interactive (rather than linear) model of research design (for qualitative research), in which key areas are mutually informing and shape each other. His five main areas are:

1 *Goals* (informed by perceived problems, personal goals, participant concerns, funding and funder goals, and ethical standards);
2 *Conceptual framework* (informed by personal experience, existing theory and prior research, exploratory and pilot research, thought experiments, and preliminary data and conclusions);
3 *Research questions* (informed by participant concerns, funding and funder goals, ethical standards, the research paradigm);
4 *Methods* (informed by the research paradigm, researcher skills and preferred style of research, the research setting, ethical standards, funding and funder goals, and participant concerns); and
5 *Validity* (informed by the research paradigm, preliminary data and conclusions, thought experiments, exploratory and pilot research, and existing theory and a priori research).

At the heart of Maxwell's model lie the research questions (3), but these are heavily informed by the four other areas. Further, Maxwell attributes strong connections between goals (1) and conceptual frameworks (2), and between methods (4) and validity (5). The links between conceptual frameworks (2) and validity (5) are less strong, as are the links between goals (1) and methods (4). His model is iterative and recursive over time; the research design emerges from the interplay of these elements and as the research unfolds.

Though, clearly, the set of issues that constitute a framework for planning research will need to be interpreted differently for different styles of research, nevertheless it is useful to indicate what those issues might be, and some of these are included in Box 7.1.

BOX 7.1   THE ELEMENTS OF RESEARCH DESIGN

1 A clear statement of the problem/need that has given rise to the research.
2 A clear grounding in literature for construct and content validity: theoretically, substantively, conceptually, methodologically.
3 Constraints on the research (e.g. access, time, people, politics).
4 The general aims and purposes of the research.
5 The intended outcomes of the research: what the research will do and what are the 'deliverable' outcomes.
6 Reflecting on the nature of the phenomena to be investigated, and how to address their ontological and epistemological natures.
7 How to operationalize research aims and purposes.
8 Generating research questions (where appropriate) (specific, concrete questions to which concrete answers can be given) and hypotheses (if appropriate).
9 The foci of the research.
10 Identifying and setting in order the priorities for the research.
11 Approaching the research design.
12 Focusing the research.
13 Research methodology (approaches and research styles, e.g. survey; experimental; ethnographic/naturalistic; longitudinal; cross-sectional; historical; correlational; *ex post facto*).
14 Ethical issues and ownership of the research (e.g. informed consent; overt and covert research; anonymity; confidentiality; non-traceability; non-maleficence; beneficence; right to refuse/withdraw; respondent validation; research subjects; social responsibility; honesty and deception).
15 Politics of the research: who is the researcher; researching one's own institution; power and interests; advantage; insider and outsider research.
16 Audiences of the research.
17 Instrumentation, e.g. questionnaires; interviews; observation; tests; field notes; accounts; documents; personal constructs; role play.
18 Sampling: size/access/representativeness; type; probability: random, systematic, stratified, cluster, stage, multi-phase; non-probability: convenience, quota, purposive, dimensional, snowball.
19 Piloting: technical matters: clarity, layout and appearance, timing, length, threat, ease/difficulty, intrusiveness; questions: validity, elimination of ambiguities, types of questions (e.g. multiple choice, open-ended, closed), response categories, identifying redundancies; pre-piloting: generating categories, grouping and classification.
20 Time frames and sequence (what will happen, when and with whom).
21 Resources required.
22 Reliability and validity:
   validity: construct; content; concurrent; face; ecological; internal; external;
   reliability: consistency (replicability); equivalence (inter-rater, equivalent forms), predictability; precision; accuracy; honesty; authenticity; richness; dependability; depth; overcoming Hawthorne and halo effects; triangulation: time; space; theoretical; investigator; instruments.
23 Data analysis.
24 Verifying and validating the data.
25 Reporting and writing up the research.

A possible sequence of consideration is:

Preparatory issues		Methodology		Sampling and instrumentation		Piloting		Timing and sequencing
Ontology, epistemology, constraints, purposes, foci, ethics, research question, politics, literature review	→	Approaches Reliability and validity	→	Reliability and validity Pre-piloting	→		→	

Clearly this need not be the actual sequence; for example it may be necessary to consider access to a possible sample at the very outset of the research.

These issues can be arranged into four main areas (Morrison, 1993):

1 orienting decisions;
2 research design and methodology;
3 data analysis;
4 presenting and reporting the results.

These are discussed later in this chapter. Orienting decisions are those decisions which set the boundaries or the constraints on the research. For example, let us say that the overriding feature of the research is that it has to be completed within six months; this will exert an influence on the enterprise. On the one hand it will 'focus the mind', requiring priorities to be settled and data to be provided in a relatively short time. On the other hand this may reduce the variety of possibilities available to the researcher. Hence questions of timescale will affect:

■ the research questions which might be answered feasibly and fairly (for example, some research questions might require a long data collection period);
■ the number of data collection instruments used (for example, there might be only enough time for a few instruments to be used);
■ the sources (people) to whom the researcher might go (for example, there might only be enough time to interview a handful of people);
■ the number of foci which can be covered in the time (for example, for some foci it will take a long time to gather relevant data);
■ the size and nature of the reporting (there might only be time to produce one interim report).

By clarifying the timescale a valuable note of realism is injected into the research, which enables questions of practicability to be answered.

Let us take another example. Suppose the overriding feature of the research is that the costs in terms of time, people and materials for carrying it out are to be negligible. This, too, will exert an effect on the research. On the one hand it will inject a sense of realism into proposals, identifying what is and what is not manageable. On the other hand it will reduce, again, the variety of possibilities which are available to the researcher. Questions of cost will affect:

■ the research questions which might be feasibly and fairly answered (for example, some research questions might require: (a) interviewing which is costly in time both to administer and transcribe; (b) expensive commercially produced data collection instruments, e.g. tests, and costly computer services, which may include purchasing software for example);
■ the number of data collection instruments used (for example, some data collection instruments, e.g. postal questionnaires, are costly for reprographics and postage);
■ the people, to whom the researcher might go (for example, if teachers are to be released from teaching in order to be interviewed then cover for their teaching may need to be found);
■ the number of foci which can be covered in the time (for example, in uncovering relevant data, some foci might be costly in researcher's time);
■ the size and nature of the reporting (for example, the number of written reports produced, the costs of convening meetings).

Certain timescales permit certain types of research, e.g. a short timescale permits answers to short-term issues, whilst long-term or large questions might require a long-term data collection period to cover a range of foci. Costs in terms of time, resources and people might affect the choice of data collection instruments. Time and cost will require the researcher to determine, for example, what will be the minimum representative sample of teachers or students in a school, as interviews are time-consuming and questionnaires are expensive to produce. These are only two examples of the real constraints on the research which must be addressed. Planning the research early on will enable the researcher to identify the boundaries within which the research must operate and what the constraints are on it.

Further, some research may be 'front-loaded' whilst other kinds are 'end-loaded'. 'Front-loaded' research is that which takes a considerable time to set up, for example to develop, pilot and test instruments for data collection, but then the data are quick to process and analyse. Quantitative research is often of this type (e.g. survey approaches) as it involves identifying the items for inclusion on the questionnaire, writing and piloting the questionnaire, and making the final adjustments. By contrast, 'end-loaded' research is that which may not take too long to set up and begin, but then the data collection and analysis may take a much longer time. Qualitative research is often of this type (e.g. ethnographic research), as a researcher may not have specific research questions in mind but may wish to enter a situation, group or community and only then discover – as they emerge over time – the key dynamics, features, characteristics and issues in the group (e.g. Turnbull's (1972) notorious study of the descent into inhumanity of the contemptible Ik tribe in their quest for daily survival as '*The*

Mountain People'). Alternatively a qualitative researcher may have a research question in mind but an answer to this may require a prolonged ethnography of a group (e.g. Willis's (1977) celebrated study of 'how working-class kids get working-class jobs, and others let them'). Between these two types – 'front-loaded' and 'end-loaded' – are many varieties of research that may take different periods of time to set up, conduct, analyse data and report the results. For example, a mixed methods research project may have several stages (Table 7.2).

In Table 7.2, in Example One, in the first two stages of the research, the mixed methods run in sequence (qualitative then quantitative), and are only integrated in the final stage. In Example Two, in the first two stages the quantitative and qualitative stages run in parallel, i.e. they are separate from each other, and they only combine in the final stage of the research. In Example Three the mixed methods are synthesized – combined – from the very start of the research.

The researcher must look at the timescales that are both required and available for planning and conducting the different stages of the research project.

Let us take another important set of questions: is the research feasible? Can it actually be done? Will the researchers have the necessary access to the schools, institutions and people? These issues were explored in

TABLE 7.2   THREE EXAMPLES OF PLANNING FOR TIME FRAMES FOR DATA COLLECTION IN MIXED METHODS RESEARCH

Example One	*Example Two*	*Example Three*
Qualitative data to answer research questions in total or in part, or to develop items for quantitative instruments (e.g. a numerical questionnaire survey)	Quantitative data and qualitative data in parallel to answer research questions in total or in part, or to identify participants for qualitative study	Quantitative and qualitative data together to answer research questions in total or in part and to raise further research questions
↓	↓	↓
Quantitative data to answer research questions in total or in part, or to identify participants for qualitative study (e.g. interviews)	Quantitative and qualitative data in parallel to answer research questions in total or in part	Quantitative and qualitative data to answer research questions in total or in part
↓	↓	↓
Quantitative and qualitative data to answer one or more research questions	Quantitative and qualitative data to answer one or more research questions	Quantitative and qualitative data to answer research questions in total or in part

the previous chapter. This issue becomes a major feature if the research is in any way sensitive (see Chapter 9).

7.4 Conducting and reporting a literature review

Before one can progress very far in planning research it is important to ground the project in validity and reliability. This is achieved, in part, by a thorough literature review of the state of the field and how it has been researched to date. Chapter 6 indicated that it is important for a researcher to conduct and report a literature review. A literature review should establish a theoretical framework for the research, indicating the nature and state of the theoretical and empirical fields and important research that has been conducted and policies that have been issued, defining key terms, constructs and concepts, reporting key methodologies used in other research into the topic. The literature review sets out what the key issues are in the field to be explored, and why they are, in fact, key issues, and it identifies gaps that need to be plugged in the field. As Chapter 6 indicated, all of this contributes not only to the credibility and validity of the research but to its topicality and significance, and it acts as a springboard into the study, defining the field, what needs to be addressed in it, why, and how it relates to – and extends – existing research in the field.

A literature review may report contentious areas in the field and why they are contentious; contemporary problems that researchers are trying to investigate in the field; difficulties that the field is facing from a research angle; new areas that need to be explored in the field.

A literature review synthesizes several different kinds of materials into an ongoing, cumulative argument that leads to a conclusion (e.g. of what needs to be researched in the present research, how and why). It can be like an extended essay that sets out clearly:

- the argument(s) that the literature review will advance;
- points in favour of the argument(s) or thesis to be advanced/supported;
- points against the argument(s) or thesis to be advanced/supported;
- a conclusion based on the points raised and evidence presented in the literature review.

There are several points to consider in researching and writing a literature review (cf. University of North

Carolina, 2007; Heath, 2009; University of Loughborough, 2009). A literature review:

- establishes and justifies the need for the research to be conducted, and establishes its significance and originality;
- establishes and justifies the methodology to be adopted in the research;
- establishes and justifies the focus of the research;
- is not just a descriptive summary, but an organized and developed argument, usually with subtitles, such that, if the materials were presented in a sequence other than that used, the literature review would lose meaning, coherence, cogency, logic and purpose;
- presents, contextualizes, analyses, interprets, critiques and evaluates sources and issues, not just accepting what they say (e.g. it exposes and addresses what the sources overlook, misinterpret, misrepresent, neglect, say something that is contentious, about which they are outdated);
- presents arguments and counter-arguments, evidence and counter-evidence about an issue;
- reveals similarities and differences between authors, about the same issue;
- must state its purposes, methods of working, organization and how it will move to a conclusion, i.e. what it will do, what it will argue, what it will show, what it will conclude, and how this links into or informs the subsequent research project;
- must state its areas of focus, maybe including a statement of the problem or issue that is being investigated, the hypothesis that the research will test, the themes or topics to be addressed, or the thesis that the research will defend;
- is a springboard into, and foundation for, all areas and stages of the research in question: purpose, foci, research questions, methodology, data analysis, discussion and conclusions;
- must be conclusive;
- must be focused yet comprehensive in its coverage of relevant issues;
- must present both sides of an issue or argument;
- should address theories, models (where relevant), empirical research, methodological materials, substantive issues, concepts, content and elements of the field in question;
- must include and draw on many sources and types of written material and kinds of data, for example Box 7.2.

For a fuller treatment of conducting and reporting a literature review we refer readers to Ridley (2008).

BOX 7.2   TYPES OF INFORMATION IN A LITERATURE REVIEW

Books (hard copy and e-books)

Articles in journals: academic and professional (hard copy and online)

Empirical and non-empirical research

Reports: from governments, NGOs, organizations, influential associations

Policy documents: from governments, organizations, 'think-tanks'

Public and private records

Research papers and reports, e.g. from research centres, research organizations

Theses and dissertations

Manuscripts

Databases (searchable collections of records, electronic or otherwise)

Conference papers – local, regional, national, international

Primary sources (original, first-hand, contemporary source materials such as documents, speeches, diaries and personal journals, letters, emails, autobiographies, memoirs, public records and reports, emails and other correspondence, interview and raw research data, minutes and agendas of meetings, memoranda, proceedings of meetings, communiqués, charters, acts of parliament or government, legal documents, pamphlets, witness statements, oral histories, unpublished works, patents, websites, video or film footage, photographs, pictures and other visual materials, audio-recordings, artefacts, clothing or other evidence. These are usually produced directly at the time of, close to, or in connection with, the research in question.)

Online databases

Electronic journals or media

Secondary sources (second-hand, non-original materials, materials written about primary sources, or materials based on sources that were originally elsewhere or which other people have written or gathered, where primary materials have been worked on or with, described, reported, analysed, discussed, interpreted, evaluated, summarized or commented upon, or which are at one remove from the primary sources, or which are written some time after the event, e.g. encyclopedias, dictionaries, newspaper articles, reports, critiques, commentaries, digests, textbooks, research syntheses, meta-analyses, research reviews, histories, summaries, analyses, magazine articles, pamphlets, biographies, monographs, treatises, works of criticism (e.g. literary or political))

Tertiary sources (distillations, collections or compilations of primary and secondary sources, e.g. almanacs, bibliographies, catalogues, dictionaries, encyclopedias, facts books, directories, indexes, abstracts, bibliographies, manuals, guidebooks, handbooks, chronologies).

7.5 Searching for literature on the internet

The storage and retrieval of research data on the internet play an important role not only in keeping researchers abreast of developments across the world, but also in providing access to data which can inform literature searches to establish construct and content validity in their own research. Indeed, some kinds of research are essentially large-scale literature searches (e.g. the research papers published in the journals *Review of Educational Research* and *Review of Research in Education*, and materials from the Evidence and Policy and Practice Information and Co-ordinating Centre (EPPI-Centre) at the University of London (http://eppi.ioe.ac.uk/cms/) and the What Works Clearinghouse in the United States (http://ies.ed.gov/ncee/wwc/)). Online journals, abstracts and titles enable researchers to keep up with the cutting edge of research and to conduct a literature search of relevant material on their chosen topic. Websites and email correspondence enable networks and information to be shared. For example, researchers wishing to gain instantaneous global access to literature and recent developments in research associations can reach Australia, East Asia, the UK and America in a matter of seconds through such websites as:

www.aera.net (the website of the American Educational Research Association);

www.eduref.org/ (The Educators' Reference Desk, the source of ERIC in the USA (publications of the American Educational Research Association));

www.acer.edu.au/index2.html (the website of the Australian Council for Educational Research);

www.bera.ac.uk (the website of the British Educational Research Association);

http://scre.ac.uk (the website of the Scottish Council for Research in Education);

www.scre.ac.uk/is/webjournals.html (the website of the Scottish Council for Research in Education's links to electronic journals);

www.eera.ac.uk/ (the website of the European Educational Research Association);

www.cem.dur.ac.uk (the website of the Curriculum Evaluation and Management Centre, amongst the largest monitoring centres of its kind in the world);

www.nfer.ac.uk (the website of the National Foundation for Educational Research in the UK);

www.fed.cuhk.edu.hk/~hkera (the website of the Hong Kong Educational Research Association);

www.wera-web.org/index.html (the website of the Washington Educational Research Association);

www.msstate.edu/org/msera/msera.html (the website of the mid-South Educational Research Association, a very large regional association in the USA);

www.esrc.ac.uk (the website of the Economic and Social Research Council in the UK).

Researchers wishing to access online journal indices and references for published research results (rather than to specific research associations as in the websites above) have a variety of websites which they can visit, for example:

www.leeds.ac.uk/bei (to gain access to the British Education Index);

http://brs.leeds.ac.uk/~beiwww/beid.html (the website for online searching of the British Educational Research Association's archive);

www.routledge.com:9996/routledge/journal/er.html (the website of an international publisher that provides information on all its research articles);

www.sagepub.co.uk (Sage publications);

www.intute.ac.uk (database that gives access to several other sources of information);

www.tandf.co.uk/journals/ (Taylor and Francis website of journals);

www.tandf.co.uk/era/ (Educational Research Abstracts Online, an alerting service from the publisher Taylor and Francis);

http://bubl.ac.uk (a national information service in the UK, provided for the higher education community);

www.gashe.ac.uk (data for the archives of Scottish Higher Education);

www.sosig.ac.uk (the Social Science Information Gateway, providing access to worldwide resources and information);

http://sosig.ac.uk/social_science_general/social_science_methodology) (the Social Science Information Gateway's sections on research methods, both quantitative and qualitative);

http://wos.mimas.ac.uk (the website of the Web of Science, that, amongst other functions, provides access to the Social Science Citation Index, the Science Citation Index and the Arts and Humanities Citation Index);

www.statistics.gov.uk (the UK's home site for national statistics);

www.dcsf.gov.uk/ (the UK Government's Department for Children, Schools and Families);

www.communities.gov.uk/corporate/ (UK website for Communities and Local Government);

www.hesa.ac.uk/ (the UK's Higher Education Statistics Agency);

www.civilservice.gov.uk/my-civil-service/networks/professional/gsr/index.aspx (the UK Government's Social Research website);

http://surveynet.ac.uk/sqb/ (the Survey Question Bank for the UK's Economic and Social Research Council);

www.esds.ac.uk/ (the UK's Economic and Social Data Service);

www.unesco.org/new/en/unesco/ (UNESCO homepage);

www.oecd.org/education (homepage of the Organization for Economic Cooperation and Development that can direct researchers to the statistics databases);

www.coe.int/T/E/Cultural_Co-operation/education/ (The Council of Europe's education homepage);

www.cessda.org/ (The Council of European Social Science Data Archive);

www.data-archive.ac.uk/ (The UK Data Archive);

http://europa.eu/index_en.htm (the gateway site to the European Union);

http://nces.ed.gov/ (the Unites States National Center for Educational Statistics);

http://worldbank.org (World Bank, that is a gateway to its data and statistics section).

With regard to searching libraries, there are several useful websites:

www.loc.gov (the United States Library of Congress);

www.lcweb.loc.gov/z3950 (gateway to US libraries);

www.libdex.com/ (the Library Index website, linking to 18,000 libraries);

www.copac.ac.uk (this enables researchers to search major UK libraries);

http://catalogue.bl.uk/F/?func=file&file_name=login-bl-list (the British Library integrated catalogue);

www.bl.uk/reshelp/findhelprestype/catblhold/all/allcat.html (all the British Library's online catalogues);

http://vlib.org/ (the Virtual Library, and provides online resources).

For checking what is in print, www.booksinprint.com provides a comprehensive listing of current books in print, whilst www.bibliofind.com is a site of old, out-of-print and rare books. The website www.lights.com links researchers to some 6,000 publishers.

Additional useful websites are:

www.nap.edu (the website of the National Academies Press), and www.nap.edu/topics.php?topic=282 (the National Academies Press, Education Section);

www.educationindex.com/ and www.shawmultimedia.com/links2.html (centres for the provision of free educational materials and related websites);

www.ipl.org/ (this is the website of the merged internet Public Library and the Librarians' Internet Index);

www.ncrel.org/ (the website of the North Central Regional Educational Laboratories, an organization providing a range of educational resources);

www.sedl.org/ (the website of the Southwest Educational Development Laboratory, an organization providing a range of educational resources).

Most journals provide access to abstracts free online, though access to the full article is usually by subscription only. Providers of online journals include, for example (in alphabetical order):

Bath Information and Data Services (BIDS) (www.bids.ac.uk);

EBSCO (www.ebsco.com)

Elsevier (www.elsevier.com)

Emerald (www.emeraldinsight.com)

FirstSearch (www.oclc.org)

Ingenta (www.ingenta.com)

JSTOR (www.jstor.org)

Kluweronline (www.kluweronline.com)

Northern Light (www.northernlight.com)

ProQuest (www.proquest.com and www.bellhowell, infolearning.com.proquest)

ProQuest Digital Dissertations and Theses (www.proquest.com/en-US/catalogs/databases/detail/pqdt.shtml)

Science Direct (www.sciencedirect.com)

Swets (www.swets.com)

Web of Science (now Web of Knowledge) (http://wok.mimas.ac.uk/

For theses, Aslib Index to Theses is useful (www.theses.com) and the Networked Digital Library of Theses and Dissertations can be located at www.theses.org and www.ndltd.org/find. Some major government websites also have a free alerting service (e.g. OFSTED).

Researchers who do not possess website addresses have at their disposal a variety of search engines to locate them. At the time of writing some widely used engines are (in alphabetical order):

AltaVista (www.altavista.com);

AOL Search (www.search.aol.com);

Ask Jeeves (www.askjeeves.com);

Direct Hit (www.directhit.com);

Excite (www.Excite.com);

Fast Search (www.alltheweb.com);

Go To (www.goto.com);

Google (www.google.com);

Google Scholar (http:/scholar.google.com);

HotBot (www.hotbot.com);

Internet Explorer (www.microsoft.com);

Lycos (www.Lycos.com);

Metacrawler (www.metacrawler.com);

MSN Search (www.msn.com);

Netscape Navigator (www.netscape.com);

Northern Light (www.northernlight.com);

Yahoo (www.yahoo.com).

There are very many more. All of these search engines enable researchers to conduct searches by keywords. Some of these are parallel search engines (which will search several single search engines at a time), and file search engines (which will search files across the world).

When searching the internet it is useful to keep in mind several points:

- placing words, phrases or sentences inside inverted commas ("...") will keep those words together and in that order in searching for material; this helps to reduce an overload of returned sites;

- placing an asterisk (*) after a word or part of a word will return sites that start with that term but which have different endings, e.g. teach* will return sites on teach, teaching, teacher;

- placing a tilde mark (~) before a word will identify similar words to that which have been entered, e.g. ~English teaching will return sites on English language as well as English teaching;

- placing the words *and*, *not*, *or* between phrases or

words will return websites where the command indicated in each one of these words is addressed.

Finding research information, where not available from databases and indices on CD-ROMs, is often done through the internet by trial and error and serendipity, identifying the key words singly or in combination (between inverted commas). The system of 'bookmarking' websites enables rapid retrieval of these websites for future reference; this is perhaps essential, as some internet connections are slow, and a vast amount of material on it is, at best, unhelpful!

Evaluating websites

The use of the internet for educational research will require an ability to evaluate websites. The internet is a vast store of disorganized and largely unvetted material, and researchers will need to be able to ascertain quite quickly how far the web-based material is appropriate. There are several criteria for evaluating websites, including the following (e.g. Tweddle *et al.*, 1998; Rodrigues and Rodriques, 2000):

- the *purpose* of the site, as this will enable users to establish its relevance and appropriateness;
- the *authority and authenticity* of the material, which should both be authoritative and declare its sources;
- the *content* of the material – its up-to-dateness, relevance and coverage;
- the *credibility* and *legitimacy* of the material (e.g. is it from a respected source or institution);
- the *correctness, accuracy, completeness* and *fairness* of the material;
- the *objectivity* and *rigour* of the material being presented and/or discussed.

In evaluating educational research materials on the web, researchers and teachers can ask themselves several questions (Hartley *et al.*, 1997):

- Is the author identified?
- Does the author establish her/his expertise in the area, and institutional affiliation?
- Is the organization reputable?
- Is the material referenced; does the author indicate how the material was gathered?
- What is the role that this website is designed to play (e.g. to provide information, to persuade)?
- Is the material up to date?
- Is the material free from biases, personal opinions and offence?
- How do we know that the author is authoritative on this website?

It is important for the researcher to keep full bibliographic data of the website material used, including the date on which it was retrieved and the website address.

With these preliminary comments, let us turn to the four main areas of the framework for planning research.

7.6 Orienting decisions in planning research

Decisions in this field are strategic; they set the general nature of the research, and the questions that researchers may need to consider are:

- Who wants the research?
- Who will receive the research/who is it for?
- Who are the possible/likely audiences of the research?
- What powers do the recipients of the research have?
- What are the general aims and purposes of the research?
- What are the main priorities for and constraints on the research?
- Is access realistic?
- What are the timescales and time frames of the research?
- Who will own the research?
- At what point will the ownership of the research pass from the participants to the researcher and from the researcher to the recipients of the research?
- Who owns the data?
- What ethical issues are to be faced in undertaking the research?
- What resources (e.g. physical, material, temporal, human, administrative) are required for the research?

It can be seen that decisions here establish some key parameters of the research, including some political decisions (for example, on ownership and on the power of the recipients to take action on the basis of the research). At this stage the overall feasibility of the research will be addressed.

7.7 Research design and methodology

If the preceding orienting decisions are strategic then decisions in this field are tactical; they establish the practicalities of the research, assuming that, generally, it is feasible (i.e. that the orienting decisions have been taken). Decisions here include addressing such questions as:

- What are the specific purposes of the research?
- Does the research need research questions?
- How are the general research purposes and aims operationalized into specific research questions?
- What are the specific research questions?
- What needs to be the focus of the research in order to answer the research questions?
- What is the main methodology of the research (e.g. a quantitative survey, qualitative research, an ethnographic study, an experiment, a case study, a piece of action research, etc.)?
- Does the research need mixed methods, and if so, is the mixed methods research a parallel, sequential, combined or hierarchical approach (see Chapter 1)?
- Are mixed methods research questions formulated where appropriate?
- How will validity and reliability be addressed?
- What kinds of data are required?
- From whom will data be acquired (i.e. sampling)?
- Where else will data be available (e.g. documentary sources)?
- How will the data be gathered (i.e. instrumentation)?
- Who will undertake the research?

7.8 How to operationalize research questions

Chapter 6 indicated that there are many different kinds of research questions that derive from different purposes of the research. For example research questions may seek:

- to describe what a phenomenon is and what is, or was, happening in a particular situation (e.g. ethnographies, case studies, complexity theory-based studies, surveys);
- to predict what will happen (e.g. experimentation, causation studies, research syntheses);
- to investigate what should happen (e.g. evaluative research, policy research, ideology critique, participatory research);
- to examine the effects of an intervention (e.g. experimentation, *ex post facto* studies, case studies, action research, causation studies);
- to examine perceptions of what is happening (e.g. ethnography, survey);
- to compare the effects of an intervention in different contexts (experimentation, comparative studies);
- to develop, implement, monitor and review an intervention (e.g. participatory research, action research) (cf. Newby, 2010: 66).

Indeed research questions can ask 'what', 'who', 'why', 'when', where', and 'how' (cf. Newby, 2010: 65–6). In

all these the task of the researcher is to turn the general purposes of the research into actual practice, i.e. to operationalize the research.

The process of *operationalization* is critical for effective research. Operationalization means specifying a set of operations or behaviours that can be measured, addressed or manipulated. What is required here is translating a very general research aim or purpose into specific, concrete questions to which specific, concrete answers can be given. The process moves from the general to the particular, from the abstract to the concrete. Thus the researcher breaks down each general research purpose or general aim into more specific research purposes and constituent elements, continuing the process until specific, concrete questions have been reached to which specific answers can be provided. Two examples of this are provided below.

Let us imagine that the overall research aim is to ascertain the continuity between primary and secondary education (Morrison, 1993: 31–3). This is very general, and needs to be translated into more specific terms. Hence the researcher might deconstruct the term 'continuity' into several components, for example experiences, syllabus content, teaching and learning styles, skills, concepts, organizational arrangements, aims and objectives, ethos, assessment. Given the vast scope of this the decision is taken to focus on continuity of pedagogy. This is then broken down into its component areas:

- the level of continuity of pedagogy;
- the nature of continuity of pedagogy;
- the degree of success of continuity of pedagogy;
- the responsibility for continuity;
- record keeping and documentation of continuity;
- resources available to support continuity.

The researcher might take this further into investigating: the *nature* of the continuity (i.e. the provision of information about continuity); the *degree* of continuity (i.e. a measure against a given criterion); the *level of success of the continuity* (i.e. a judgement). An operationalized set of research questions, then, might be:

- How much continuity of pedagogy is occurring across the transition stages in each curriculum area? What kind of evidence is required to answer this question? On what criteria will the level of continuity be decided?
- What pedagogical styles operate in each curriculum area? What are the most frequent and most preferred? What is the balance of pedagogical styles? How is pedagogy influenced by resources? To what

extent is continuity planned and recorded? On what criteria will the nature of continuity be decided? What kind of evidence is required to answer this question?

■ On what aspects of pedagogy does planning take place? By what criteria will the level of success of continuity be judged? Over how many students/teachers/curriculum areas will the incidence of continuity have to occur for it to be judged successful? What kind of evidence is required to answer this question?

■ Is continuity occurring by accident or design? How will the extent of planned and unplanned continuity be gauged? What kind of evidence is required to answer this question?

■ Who has responsibility for continuity at the transition points? What is being undertaken by these people?

■ How are records kept on continuity in the schools? Who keeps these records? What is recorded? How frequently are the records updated and reviewed? What kind of evidence is required to answer this question?

■ What resources are there to support continuity at the point of transition? How adequate are these resources? What kind of evidence is required to answer this question?

It can be seen that these questions, several in number, have moved the research from simply an expression of interest (or a general aim) into a series of issues that lend themselves to being investigated in concrete terms. This is precisely what we mean by *the process of operationalization*. It is now possible to identify not only the specific questions to be posed, but also the instruments that might be needed to acquire data to answer them (e.g. semi-structured interviews, rating scales on questionnaires or documentary analysis). By this process of operationalization we thus make a general purpose amenable to investigation, e.g. by measurement (Rose and Sullivan, 1993: 6) or some other means. The number of operationalized research questions is large here, and may have to be reduced to maybe four or five at most, in order to render the research manageable.

An alternative way of operationalizing research questions takes the form of hypothesis raising and hypothesis testing. A 'good' hypothesis has several features:

■ It is clear on whether it is directional or non-directional: a directional hypothesis states the kind or direction of difference or relationship between two conditions or two groups of participants (e.g. students' performance increases when they are intrinsically motivated). A non-directional hypothesis simply predicts that there will be a difference or relationship between two conditions or two groups of participants (e.g. there is a *difference* in students' performance according to their level of intrinsic motivation), without stating whether the difference, for example, is an increase or a decrease. (For statistical purposes, a directional hypothesis requires a one-tailed test whereas a non-directional hypothesis uses a two-tailed test, see Part 5.) Directional hypotheses are often used when past research, predictions, or theory suggest that the findings may go in a particular direction, whereas non-directional hypotheses are used when past research or theory is unclear or contradictory or where prediction is not possible, i.e. where the results are more open-ended.

■ It is written in a testable form, i.e. in a way that makes it clear how the researcher will design an experiment or survey to test the hypothesis, e.g. *people perform a mathematics task better when there is silence in the room than when there is not*. The concept of interference by noise has been operationalized in order to produce a testable hypothesis.

■ It is written in a form that can yield measurable results.

For example, in the hypothesis *people work better in quiet rather than noisy conditions* it is important to define the operations for 'work better', 'quiet' and 'noisy'. Here 'perform better' might mean 'obtain a higher score on the mathematics test', 'quiet' might mean 'silence', and 'noisy' might mean 'having music playing'. Hence the fully operationalized hypothesis might be *people obtain a higher score on a mathematics test when tested when there is silence rather than when there is music playing*. One can see here that the score is measurable and that there is zero noise, i.e. a measure of the noise level.

In conducting research using hypotheses one has to be prepared to use several hypotheses (Muijs, 2004: 16) in order to catch the complexity of the phenomenon being researched, and not least because mediating variables have to be included in the research. For example, the degree of 'willing cooperation' (dependent variable) in an organization's staff is influenced by 'professional leadership' (independent variable) and the 'personal leadership qualities of the leader' (mediating variable) which needs to be operationalized more specifically, of course.

There is also the need to consider the null hypothesis and the alternative hypothesis (discussed in Part 5) in research that is cast into a hypothesis testing model. The *null hypothesis* states that, for example, there is *no* relationship between two variables, or that there has been *no* difference in participants' scores on a pre-test and a post-test of history, or that there is *no* difference between males and females in respect of their science examination results. The *alternative hypothesis* states, for example: there *is* a correlation between motivation and performance; there *is* a difference between males' and females' scores on science; there *is* a difference between the pre-test and post-test scores on history. The alternative hypothesis is often supported when the null hypothesis is 'not supported', i.e. if the null hypothesis is not supported then the alternative hypothesis is. The two kinds of hypothesis are usually written thus:

H_0: the null hypothesis
H_1: the alternative hypothesis

We address the hypothesis-testing approach fully in Part 5.

Distinguishing methods from methodologies

In planning research it is important to clarify a distinction that needs to be made between methodology and methods, approaches and instruments, styles of research and ways of collecting data. Several of the later chapters of this book are devoted to specific instruments for collecting data, e.g.

- interviews
- questionnaires
- observation
- tests
- accounts
- biographies and case studies
- role playing
- simulations
- personal constructs.

TABLE 7.3 ELEMENTS OF RESEARCH STYLES

Model	Purposes	Foci	Key terms	Characteristics
Survey	Gathering large-scale data in order to make generalizations Generating statistically manipulable data Gathering context-free data	Opinions Scores Outcomes Conditions Ratings	Measuring Testing Representativeness Generalizability	Describes and explains Represents wide population Gathers numerical data Much use of questionnaires and assessment/test data
Experiment	Comparing under controlled conditions Making generalizations about efficacy Objective measurement of treatment Establishing causality	Initial states, intervention and outcomes Randomized controlled trials	Pre-test and post-test Identification, isolation and control of key variables Generalizations Comparing Causality	Control and experimental groups Treats situations like a laboratory Causes due to experimental intervention Does not judge worth Simplistic
Ethnography	Portrayal of events in subjects' terms Subjective and reporting of multiple perspectives Description, understanding and explanation of a specific situation	Perceptions and views of participants Issues as they emerge over time	Subjectivity Honesty, authenticity Non-generalizable Multiple perspectives Exploration and rich reporting of a specific context Emergent issues	Context specific Formative and emergent Responsive to emerging features Allows room for judgements and multiple perspectives Wide database gathered over a long period of time Time-consuming to process data

Action research	To plan, implement, review and evaluate an intervention designed to improve practice/solve local problem To empower participants through research involvement and ideology critique To develop reflective practice To promote equality democracy To link practice and research To promote collaborative research	Everyday practices Outcomes of interventions Participant empowerment Reflective practice Social democracy and equality Decision making	Action Improvement Reflection Monitoring Evaluation Intervention Problem-solving Empowering Planning Reviewing	Context-specific Participants as researchers Reflection on practice Interventionist – leading to solution of 'real' problems and meeting 'real' needs Empowering for participants Collaborative Promoting praxis and equality Stakeholder research
Case study	To portray, analyse and interpret the uniqueness of real individuals and situations through accessible accounts To catch the complexity and situatedness of behaviour To contribute to action and intervention To present and represent reality – to give a sense of 'being there'	Individuals and local situations Unique instances A single case Bounded phenomena and systems: ■ individual ■ group ■ roles ■ organizations ■ community	Individuality, uniqueness In-depth analysis and portrayal Interpretive and inferential analysis Subjective Descriptive Analytical Understanding specific situations Sincerity Complexity Particularity	In-depth, detailed data from wide data source Participant and non-participant observation Non-interventionist Empathic Holistic treatment of phenomena What can be learned from the particular case
Testing and assessment	To measure achievement and potential To diagnose strengths and weaknesses To assess performance and abilities	Academic and non-academic, cognitive, affective and psychomotor domains – low order to high order Performance, achievement, potential, abilities Personality characteristics	Reliability Validity Criterion-referencing Norm-referencing Domain-referencing Item-response Formative Summative Diagnostic Standardization Moderation	Materials designed to provide scores that can be aggregated Enables individuals and groups to be compared In-depth diagnosis Measures performance

The decision on which instrument (method) to use frequently follows from an important earlier decision on which kind (methodology) of research to undertake, for example:

■ a survey
■ an experiment
■ an in-depth ethnography
■ action research
■ case study research
■ testing and assessment.

Subsequent chapters of this book set out each of these research styles, their principles, rationales and purposes, and the instrumentation and data types that seem suitable for them. For conceptual clarity it is possible to set out some key features of these models (Table 7.3). It is intended that, when decisions have been reached on the stage of research design and methodology, a clear plan of action will have been prepared. To this end, considering models of research might be useful (Morrison, 1993).

7.9 Data analysis

The prepared researcher will need to consider how the data will be analysed. This is very important, as it has a specific bearing on the form of the instrumentation. For example, a researcher will need to plan the layout and structure of a questionnaire survey very carefully in order to assist data entry for computer reading and analysis; an inappropriate layout may obstruct data entry and subsequent analysis by computer. The planning of data analysis will need to consider:

- What needs to be done with the data when they have been collected – how will they be processed and analysed?
- How will the results of the analysis be verified, cross-checked and validated?

Decisions will need to be taken with regard to the statistical tests that will be used in data analysis as this will affect the layout of research items (for example in a questionnaire), and the computer packages that are available for processing quantitative and qualitative data, e.g. SPSS and N-Vivo respectively. For statistical processing the researcher will need to ascertain the level of data being processed – nominal, ordinal, interval or ratio (discussed in Chapter 34). Part 5 addresses issues of data analysis and which statistics to use: the choice is not arbitrary (Siegel, 1956; Cohen and Holliday, 1996; Hopkins *et al.*, 1996). For qualitative data analysis researchers have at their disposal a range of techniques, for example:

- coding and content analysis of field notes (Miles and Huberman, 1984);
- cognitive mapping (Jones, 1987; Morrison, 1993);
- seeking patterning of responses;
- looking for causal pathways and connections (Miles and Huberman, 1984);
- presenting cross-site analysis (Miles and Huberman, 1984);
- case studies;
- personal constructs;
- narrative accounts;

- action research analysis;
- analytic induction (Denzin, 1970);
- constant comparison and grounded theory (Glaser and Strauss, 1967);
- discourse analysis (Stillar, 1998);
- biographies and life histories (Atkinson, 1998).

The criteria for deciding which forms of data analysis to undertake are governed both by fitness for purpose and legitimacy – the form of data analysis must be appropriate for the kinds of data gathered. For example it would be inappropriate to use certain statistics with certain kinds of numerical data (e.g. using means on nominal data), or to use causal pathways on unrelated cross-site analysis.

7.10 Presenting and reporting the results

As with the stage of planning data analysis, the prepared researcher will need to consider the form of the reporting of the research and its results, giving due attention to the needs of different audiences (for example an academic audience may require different contents from a wider professional audience and, *a fortiori*, from a lay audience). Decisions here will need to consider:

- How to write up and report the research.
- When to write up and report the research (e.g. ongoing or summative).
- How to present the results in tabular and/or written-out form.
- How to present the results in non-verbal forms.
- To whom to report (the necessary and possible audiences of the research).
- How frequently to report.

For an example of setting out a research report, see the accompanying website.

7.11 A planning matrix for research

In planning a piece of research, the range of questions to be addressed can be set into a matrix. Table 7.4 provides such a matrix, in the left-hand column of which are the questions which figure in the four main areas set out so far:

1 orienting decisions;
2 research design and methodology;
3 data analysis;
4 presenting and reporting the results.

TABLE 7.4   A MATRIX FOR PLANNING RESEARCH

Orienting decisions

Question	Sub-issues and problems	Decisions
1 Who wants the research?	Is the research going to be useful? Who might wish to use the research? Are the data going to be public? What if different people want different things from the research? Can people refuse to participate?	Find out the controls over the research which can be exercised by respondents. Decide what are the scope and audiences of the research. Determine the reporting mechanisms.
2 Who will receive the research?	Will participants be able to veto the release of parts of the research to specified audiences? Will participants be able to give the research to whomsoever they wish? Will participants be told to whom the research will go?	Determine the proposed internal and external audiences of the research. Determine the controls over the research which can be exercised by the participants. Determine the rights of the participants and the researcher to control the release of the research.
3 What powers do the recipients of the research have?	What use will be made of the research? How might the research be used for or against the participants? What might happen if the data fall into the 'wrong' hands? Will participants know in advance what use will and will not be made of the research?	Determine the rights of recipients to do what they wish with the research. Determine the respondents' rights to protection as a result of the research.
4 What are the timescales of the research?	Is there enough time to do all the research? How to decide what to be done within the timescale?	Determine the timescales and timing of the research.
5 What are the purposes of the research?	What are the formal and hidden agendas here? Whose purposes are being served by the research? Who decides the purposes of the research? How will different purposes be served in the research?	Determine all the possible uses of the research. Determine the powers of the respondents to control the uses made of the research. Decide on the form of reporting and the intended and possible audiences of the research.
6 What are the research questions?	Who decides what the questions will be? Do participants have rights to refuse to answer or take part? Can participants add their own questions?	Determine the participants' rights and powers to participate in the planning, form and conduct of the research. Decide the balance of all interests in the research.
7 What must be the focus in order to answer the research questions?	Is sufficient time available to focus on all the necessary aspects of the research? How will the priority foci be decided? Who decides the foci?	Determine all the aspects of the research, prioritize them and agree on the minimum necessary areas of the research. Determine decision-making powers on the research.
8 What costs are there – human, material, physical, administrative, temporal?	What support is available for the researcher? What materials are necessary?	Cost out the research.

9 Who owns the research?	Who controls the release of the report?	Determine who controls the release of the report.
	What protections can be given to participants?	Decide the rights and powers of the researcher.
	Will participants be identified and identifiable/traceable?	Decide the rights of veto.
	Who has the ultimate decision on what data are included?	Decide how to protect those who may be identified/identifiable in the research.
10 At what point does the ownership pass from the respondent to the researcher and from the researcher to the recipients?	Who decides the ownership of the research?	Determine the ownership of the research at all stages of its progress.
	Can participants refuse to answer certain parts if they wish, or, if they have the option not to take part, must they opt out of everything?	Decide the options available to the participants.
	Can the researcher edit out certain responses?	Decide the rights of different parties in the research, e.g. respondents, researcher, recipients.
11 What are the specific purposes of the research?	How do these purposes derive from the overall aims of the research?	Decide the specific research purposes and write them as concrete questions.
	Will some areas of the broad aims be covered, or will the specific research purposes have to be selective?	
	What priorities are there?	
12 How are the general research purposes and aims operationalized into specific research questions?	Do the specific research questions together cover all the research purposes?	Ensure that each main research purpose is translated into specific, concrete questions that, together, address the scope of the original research questions.
	Are the research questions sufficiently concrete as to suggest the kinds of answers and data required and the appropriate instrumentation and sampling?	Ensure that the questions are sufficiently specific as to suggest the most appropriate data types, kinds of answers required, sampling and instrumentation.
	How to balance adequate coverage of research purposes with the risk of producing an unwieldy list of sub-questions?	Decide how to ensure that any selectivity still represents the main fields of the research questions.
13 What are the specific research questions?	Do the specific research questions demonstrate construct and content validity?	Ensure that the coverage and operationalization of the specific questions addresses content and construct validity respectively.
14 What needs to be the focus of the research in order to answer the research questions?	How many foci are necessary?	Decide the number of foci of the research questions.
	Are the foci clearly identifiable and operationalizable?	Ensure that the foci are clear and can be operationalized.
15 What is the main methodology of the research?	How many methodologies are necessary?	Decide the number, type and purposes of the methodologies to be used.
	Are several methodologies compatible with each other?	Decide whether one or more methodologies is necessary to gain answers to specific research questions.
	Will a single focus/research question require more than one methodology (e.g. for triangulation and concurrent validity)?	Ensure that the most appropriate form of methodology is employed.

16 How will validity and reliability be addressed?	Will there be the opportunity for cross-checking?	Determine the process of respondent validation of the data.
	Will the depth and breadth required for content validity be feasible within the constraints of the research (e.g. time constraints, instrumentation)?	Decide a necessary minimum of topics to be covered.
	In what senses are the research questions valid (e.g. construct validity)?	Subject the plans to scrutiny by critical friends ('jury' validity).
	Are the questions fair?	Pilot the research.
	How does the researcher know if people are telling the truth?	Build in cross-checks on data.
	What kinds of validity and reliability are to be addressed?	Address the appropriate forms of reliability and validity.
	How will the researcher take back the research to respondents for them to check that the interpretations are fair and acceptable?	Decide the questions to be asked and the methods used to ask them.
	How will data be gathered consistently over time?	Determine the balance of open and closed questions.
	How to ensure that each respondent is given the same opportunity to respond?	
17 How will reflexivity be addressed?	How will reflexivity be recognized?	Determine the need to address reflexivity and to make this public.
	Is reflexivity a problem?	Determine how to address reflexivity in the research.
	How can reflexivity be included in the research?	
18 What kinds of data are required?	Does the research need words, numbers or both?	Determine the most appropriate types of data for the foci and research questions.
	Does the research need opinions, facts or both?	Balance objective and subjective data.
	Does the research seek to compare responses and results or simply to illuminate an issue?	Determine the purposes of collecting different types of data and the ways in which they can be processed.
19 From whom will data be acquired (i.e. sampling)?	Will there be adequate time to go to all the relevant parties?	Determine the minimum and maximum sample.
	What kind of sample is required (e.g. probability/ non-probability/random/stratified, etc.)?	Decide on the criteria for sampling.
	How to achieve a representative sample (if required)?	Decide the kind of sample required.
		Decide the degree of representativeness of the sample.
		Decide how to follow up and not to follow up on the data gathered.
20 Where else will data be available?	What documents and other written sources of data can be used?	Determine the necessary/desirable/ possible documentary sources.
	How to access and use confidential material?	Decide access and publication rights and protection of sensitive data.
	What will be the positive or negative effects on individuals of using certain documents?	
21 How will the data be gathered (i.e. instrumentation)?	What methods of data gathering are available and appropriate to yield data to answer the research questions?	Determine the most appropriate data collection instruments to gather data to answer the research questions.
	What methods of data gathering will be used?	Pilot the instruments and refine them subsequently.
	How to construct interview schedules/ questionnaires/tests/observation schedules?	Decide the strengths and weaknesses of different data collection instruments in the short and long term.
	What will be the effects of observing participants?	Decide which methods are most suitable for which issues.
	How many methods should be used (e.g. to ensure reliability and validity)?	Decide which issues will require more than one data collection instrument.
	Is it necessary or desirable to use more than one method of data collection on the same issue?	Decide whether the same data collection methods will be used with all the participants.
	Will many methods yield more reliable data?	
	Will some methods be unsuitable for some people or for some issues?	

22 Who will undertake the research?	Can different people plan and carry out different parts of the research?	Decide who will carry out the data collection, processing and reporting.
23 How will the data be analysed?	Are the data to be processed numerically or verbally? What computer packages are available to assist data processing and analysis? What statistical tests will be needed? How to perform a content analysis of word data? How to summarize and present word data? How to process all the different responses to open-ended questions? Will the data be presented person by person, issue by issue, aggregated to groups, or a combination of these? Does the research seek to make generalizations? Who will process the data?	Clarify the legitimate and illegitimate methods of data processing and analysis of quantitative and qualitative data. Decide which methods of data processing and analysis are most appropriate for which types of data and for which research questions. Check that the data processing and analysis will serve the research purposes. Determine the data protection issues if data are to be processed by 'outsiders' or particular 'insiders'.
24 How to verify and validate the data and their interpretation?	What opportunities will there be for respondents to check the researcher's interpretation? At what stages of the research is validation necessary? What will happen if respondents disagree with the researcher's interpretation?	Determine the process of respondent validation during the research. Decide the reporting of multiple perspectives and interpretations. Decide respondents' rights to have their views expressed or to veto reporting.
25 How to write up and report the research?	Who will write the report and for whom? How detailed must the report be? What must the report contain? What channels of dissemination of the research are to be used?	Ensure that the most appropriate form of reporting is used for the audiences. Keep the report as short, clear and complete as possible. Provide summaries if possible/fair. Ensure that the report enables fair critique and evaluation to be undertaken.
26 When to write up and report the research (e.g. ongoing or summative)?	How many times are appropriate for reporting? For whom are interim reports compiled? Which reports are public?	Decide the most appropriate timing, purposes and audiences of the reporting. Decide the status of the reporting (e.g. formal, informal, public, private).
27 How to present the results in tabular and/or written-out form?	How to ensure that everyone will understand the language or the statistics? How to respect the confidentiality of the participants? How to report multiple perspectives?	Decide the most appropriate form of reporting. Decide whether to provide a glossary of terms. Decide the format(s) of the reports. Decide the number and timing of the reports. Decide the protection of the individual's rights, balancing this with the public's rights to know.
28 How to present the results in non-verbal forms?	Will different parties require different reports? How to respect the confidentiality of the participants? How to report multiple perspectives?	Decide the most appropriate form of reporting. Decide the number and timing of the reports. Ensure that a written record is kept of oral reports. Decide the protection of the individual's rights, balancing this with the public's rights to know.

29 To whom to report (the necessary and possible audiences of the research)?	Do all participants receive a report? What will be the effects of not reporting to stakeholders?	Identify the stakeholders. Determine the least and most material to be made available to the stakeholders.
30 How frequently to report?	Is it necessary to provide interim reports? If interim reports are provided, how might this affect the future reports or the course of the research?	Decide on the timing and frequency of the reporting. Determine the formative and summative nature of the reports.

Questions 1–10 are the orienting decisions, questions 11–22 concern the research design and methodology, questions 23–4 cover data analysis, and questions 25–30 deal with presenting and reporting the results. Within each of the 30 questions there are several sub-questions which research planners may need to address. For example, within question 5 ('What are the purposes of the research?') the researcher would have to differentiate major and minor purposes, explicit and maybe implicit purposes, whose purposes are being served by the research, and whose interests are being served by the research. An example of these sub-issues and problems is contained in the second column.

At this point the planner is still at the divergent phase of the research planning, dealing with *planned possibilities* (Morrison, 1993: 19), opening up the research to all facets and interpretations. In the column headed 'decisions' the research planner is moving towards a convergent phase, where planned possibilities become visible within the terms of constraints available to the researcher. To do this the researcher has to move down the column marked 'decisions' to see how well the decision which is taken in regard to one issue/question fits in with the decisions in regard to other issues/questions. For one decision to fit with another, four factors must be present:

1   all the cells in the 'decisions' column must be coherent – they must not contradict each other;
2   all the cells in the 'decisions' column must be mutually supporting;
3   all the cells in the 'decisions' column must be practicable when taken separately;
4   all the cells in the 'decisions' column must be practicable when taken together.

Not all the planned possibilities might be practicable when these four criteria are applied. It would be of very little use if the methods of data collection listed in the 'decisions' column of question 21 ('How will the data

be gathered?') offered little opportunity to fulfil the needs of acquiring information to answer question 7 ('What must be the focus in order to answer the research questions?'), or if the methods of data collection were impracticable within the timescales available in question 4.

In the matrix of Table 7.4 the cells have been completed in a deliberately content-free way, i.e. the matrix as presented here does not deal with the specific, actual points which might emerge in a particular research proposal. If the matrix were to be used for planning an actual piece of research, then, instead of couching the wording of each cell in generalized terms, it would be more useful if *specific, concrete* responses were given which addressed particular issues and concerns in the research proposal in question.

Many of these questions concern rights, responsibilities and the political uses (and abuses) of the research. This underlines the view that research is an inherently political and moral activity; it is not politically or morally neutral. The researcher has to be concerned with the uses as well as the conduct of the research.

7.12 Managing the planning of research

The preceding discussion has revealed the complexity of planning a piece of research, yet it should not be assumed that research will always go according to plan! For example, the mortality of the sample might be a feature (participants leaving during the research), or a poor response rate to questionnaires might be encountered, rendering subsequent analysis, reporting and generalization problematic; administrative support might not be forthcoming, or there might be serious slippage in the timing. This is not to say that a plan for the research should not be made; rather it is to suggest that it is dangerous to put absolute faith in it! For an example of what to include in a research proposal see the accompanying website.

To manage the complexity in planning outlined above a simple four-stage model can be proposed:

Stage 1: Identify the purposes of the research.
Stage 2: Identify and give priority to the constraints under which the research will take place.
Stage 3: Plan the possibilities for the research within these constraints.

Stage 4: Decide the research design.

Each stage contains several operations. Figure 7.1 clarifies this four-stage model, drawing out the various operations contained in each stage.

It may be useful for research planners to consider which instruments will be used at which stage of the research and with which sectors of the sample popula-

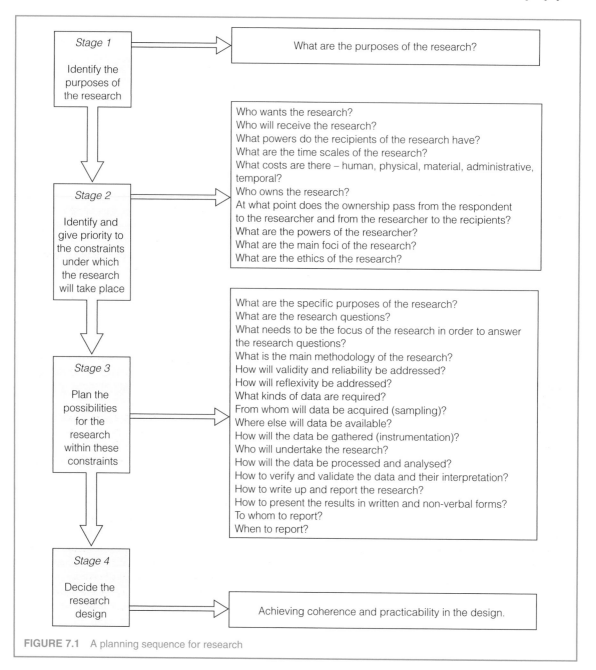

FIGURE 7.1   A planning sequence for research

TABLE 7.5   A PLANNING MATRIX FOR RESEARCH

Time sample	Stage 1 (start)	Stage 2 (3 months)	Stage 3 (6 months)	Stage 4 (9 months)	Stage 5 (12 months)
Principal/ Headteacher	Documents Interview Questionnaire 1	Interview	Documents Questionnaire 2	Interview	Documents Interview Questionnaire 3
Teacher group 1	Questionnaire 1		Questionnaire 2		Questionnaire 3
Teacher group 2	Questionnaire 1		Questionnaire 2		Questionnaire 3
Teacher group 3	Questionnaire 1		Questionnaire 2		Questionnaire 3
Students			Questionnaire 2		Interview
Parents	Questionnaire 1		Questionnaire 2		Questionnaire 3
University teacher educators	Interview Documents				Interview Documents

tion. Table 7.5 sets out a matrix of these for planning (see also Morrison, 1993: 109), for example, a small-scale piece of research.

A matrix approach such as this enables research planners to see at a glance their coverage of the sample and of the instruments used at particular points in time, making omissions clear, and promoting such questions as:

- Why are certain instruments used at certain times and not at others?
- Why are certain instruments used with certain people and not with others?
- Why do certain times in the research use more instruments than other times?
- Why is there such a heavy concentration of instruments at the end of the study?
- Why are certain groups involved in more instruments than other groups?
- Why are some groups apparently neglected (e.g. parents), i.e. is there a political dimension to the research?
- Why are questionnaires the main kinds of instrument to be used?
- Why are some instruments (e.g. observation, testing) not used at all?
- What makes the five stages separate?
- Are documents only held by certain parties (and, if so, might one suspect an 'institutional line' to be revealed in them)?

- Are some parties more difficult to contact than others (e.g. university teacher educators)?
- Are some parties more important to the research than others (e.g. the principals)?
- Why are some parties excluded from the sample (e.g. school governors, policy makers, teachers' associations and unions)?
- What is the difference between the three groups of teachers?

Matrix planning is useful for exposing key features of the planning of research. Further matrices might be constructed to indicate other features of the research, for example:

- the timing of the identification of the sample;
- the timing of the release of interim reports;
- timing of the release of the final report;
- the timing of pre-tests and post-tests (in an experimental style of research);
- the timing of intensive necessary resource support (e.g. reprographics);
- the timing of meetings of interested parties.

These examples cover timings only; other matrices might be developed to cover other combinations, for example: reporting by audiences; research team meetings by reporting; instrumentation by participants, etc. They are useful summary devices.

7.13 A worked example

Let us say that a school is experiencing very low morale and the researcher has been brought in to investigate the school's organizational culture. The researcher has been given open access to the school and has five months from the start of the project to producing the report. (For a fuller version of this see the accompanying website.) She plans the research thus:

1 Purposes

i   to present an overall and in-depth picture of the organizational culture(s) and subcultures, including the prevailing cultures and subcultures, within the school;
ii   to provide an indication of the strength of the organizational culture(s);
iii   to make suggestions and recommendations about the organizational culture of, and its development at, the school.

2 Research questions

i   What are the major and minor elements of organizational culture in the school?
ii   What are the organizational cultures and subcultures in the school?
iii   Which (sub)cultures are the most and least prevalent in the school, and in which parts of the school are these most and least prevalent?
iv   How strong and intense are the (sub)cultures in the school?
v   What are the causes and effects of the (sub)cultures in the school?
vi   How can the (sub)cultures be improved in the school?

3 Focus

Three levels of organizational culture will be examined:

i   underlying values and assumptions
ii   espoused values and enacted behaviours
iii   artefacts.

Organizational culture concerns values, assumptions, beliefs, espoused theories and mental models, observed practices, areas of conflict and consensus, the formal and hidden messages contained in artefacts, messages, documents and language, the 'way we do things', the physical environment, relationships, power, control, communication, customs and rituals, stories, the reward system and motivation, the micropolitics of the school, involvement in decision making, empowerment and exploitation/manipulation, leadership, commitment, and so on.

4 Methodology

Organizational culture is intangible yet its impact on a school's operations is very tangible. This suggests that, whilst quantitative measures may be used, they are likely only to yield comparatively superficial information about the school's culture. In order to probe beneath the surface of the school's culture, to examine the less overt aspects of the school's culture(s) and subcultures, it is important to combine quantitative and qualitative methodologies for data collection. A mixed methodology will be used for the empirical data collection, using numerical and verbal data, in order to gather rounded, reliable data. A survey approach will be used to gain an overall picture, and a more fine-grained analysis will be achieved through individual and group interviews and focus groups (Figure 7.2).

5 Instrumentation

The data gathered will be largely perception based, and will involve gathering employees' views of the (sub) cultures. As the concept of organizational culture is derived in part from ethnography and anthropology, the research will use qualitative and ethnographic methods.

One of the difficulties anticipated is that the less tangible aspects of the school might be the most difficult on which to collect data. Not only will people find it harder to articulate responses and constructs, but they may also be reluctant to reveal these in public. The more the project addresses intangible and unmeasurable elements, and the richer the data that are to be collected, the more there is a need for increased and sensitive interpersonal behaviour, face-to-face data collection methods and qualitative data.

There are several instruments for data collection: questionnaires, semi-structured interviews (individual and group), observational data, documentary data and reports will constitute a necessary minimum, as follows:

i   *questionnaire surveys*, using commercially available instruments, each of which measures different aspects of school's culture, in particular:
■   the organizational culture questionnaire by Harrison and Stokes (1992), which looks at overall cultures and provides a general picture in terms of *role*, *power*, *achievement* and *support* cultures, and examines the differences between existing and preferred cultures;
■   the Organizational Culture Inventory (Cooke and Lafferty, 1989), which provides a comprehensive

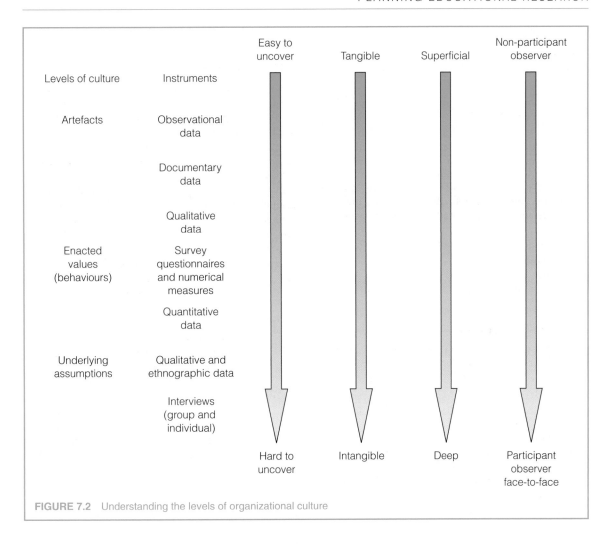

FIGURE 7.2 Understanding the levels of organizational culture

and reliable analysis of the presenting organizational cultures.

Questionnaires, using rating scales, will catch articulated, espoused, enacted, visible aspects of organizational culture, and will measure, for example, the extent of sharedness of culture, congruence between existing and ideal, strength and intensity of culture.

ii *semi-structured qualitative interviews for individuals and groups*, gathering data on the more intangible aspects of the school's culture, e.g. values, assumptions, beliefs, wishes, problems. Interviews will be semi-structured, i.e. with a given agenda and open-ended questions. As face-to-face individual interviews might be intimidating for some groups, group interviews will be used. In all the interviews the important part will be the supplementary question 'why'.

iii *observational data* will comment on the physical environment, and will then be followed up with interview material to discover participants' responses to, perceptions of, messages contained in, attitudes to the physical environment. Artefacts, clothing, shared and private spaces, furniture, notices, regulations, etc. all give messages to participants.

iv *documentary analysis and additional stored data*, reporting the formal matters in the school, examined for what they include and what they exclude.

6 Sampling

i the questionnaire will be given to all employees who are willing to participate;

ii the semi-structured interviews will be conducted on

a 'critical case' basis, i.e. with participants who are in key positions and who are 'knowledgeable people' about the activities and operations of the school.

There will be stratified sampling for the survey instruments, in order to examine how perceptions of the school's organizational culture vary according to the characteristics of the sub-samples. This will enable the levels of congruence or disjunction between the responses of the various subgroups to be charted. Nominal characteristics of the sampling will be included, e.g. age, level in the school, departments, sex, ethnicity, nationality, years of working in the school.

7 Parameters

i   the data will be collected on a 'one-shot' basis rather than longitudinally;
ii a multi-method approach will be used for data collection.

8 Stages in the research

There are five stages in the research:

Stage 1: Development and operationalization, including:
i   a review of literature and commercially produced instruments;
ii clarification of the research questions;
iii clarification of methodology and sampling.

Stage 2: Instrumentation and the piloting of the instruments:
i   questionnaire development and piloting;
ii   semi-structured interview schedules and piloting;
iii gathering of observational data;
iv   analysis of documentary data.

Because of the limited number of senior staff, it will not be possible to conduct pilot interviews with them, as this will preclude them from the final data collection.

Stage 3: Data collection, which will proceed in the following sequence:
Administration of the questionnaire → Analysis of questionnaire data to provide material for the interviews → Interviews will be conducted concurrently.

Stage 4: Data analysis and interpretation:
Numerical data will be analysed using SPSS, which will also enable the responses from subgroups of the

school to be separated for analysis. Qualitative data will be analysed using protocols of content analysis.

Stage 5: Reporting:
A full report on the findings will include conclusions, implications and recommendations.

9 Ethics and ownership

Participation in the project will be on the basis of informed consent, and on a voluntary basis, with rights of withdrawal at any time. Given the size and scope of the cultural survey, it is likely that key people in the school will be able to be identified, even though the report is confidential. This will be made clear to the potential participants. Copies of the report will be available for all the employees. Data, once given to the researcher, are his/hers, and s/he may not use them in any way which will publicly identify the school; the report is the property of the school.

10 Time frames

The project will be completed in five months:

- the first month for a review of the relevant literature;
- the second month to develop the instrumentation and research design;
- the third month to gather the data;
- the fourth month to analyse the data;
- the fifth month to complete the report.

The example indicates a systematic approach to the planning and conduct of the research, that springs from a perceived need in the school. It works within given constraints and makes clear what it will 'deliver'. Though the research does not specify hypotheses to be tested, nevertheless it would not be difficult to convert the research questions into hypotheses if this style of research were preferred.

7.14 Ensuring quality in the planning of research

The notion of 'fitness for purpose' reigns in planning research; the research plan must suit the purposes of the research. If at the end of this chapter the reader is left feeling that the task of research is complex, then that is an important message, for rigour and thoughtful, thorough planning are necessary if the research is to be worthwhile and effective. For a checklist for evaluating research see Box 7.3 and the accompanying website.

BOX 7.3 A CHECKLIST FOR PLANNING RESEARCH

1 How have you taken account of the ontological and epistemological characteristics of the phenomenon to be investigated?
2 Have you clarified the purposes of the research?
3 What do you want the research to do, to 'deliver', to find out?
4 What are the purposes and objectives of the research?
5 Have you identified the constraints on your research? What are they?
6 Is your research feasible within the required time frames?
7 What approaches to the research (methodologies) are most suitable for the research, in terms of the ontology and epistemology of the phenomenon under investigation, and the purposes of the research?
8 What are the methodology(ies) and paradigm(s) on which the research is built? How comfortably do they fit the research purposes and the nature of the phenomena under investigation?
9 Does your research seek to test a theory or hypothesis, to develop a theory, to investigate and explore, to understand, to describe, to develop specific practices, to evaluate, to investigate?
10 Will your research best be accomplished by research that is naturalistic, interpretive, positivist, post-positivist, mixed methods based, participatory, evaluatory, ideology critical, feminist, complexity theory based, either alone or in combination?
11 Will your research use survey, documentary research, quantitative methods, ethnographic or qualitative methods, experiments, historical sources, action research, case studies, *ex post facto* designs, either alone or in combination?
12 Do you need to identify independent and dependent variables?
13 Is your research seeking to establish causation?
14 Are you seeking to generalize from your research?
15 In planning your research, have you indicated how you will address validity and reliability in the conceptualization, planning, methodology, instrumentation, data analysis, discussion, the drawing of conclusions and reporting?
16 Who will gather, enter, process, analyse, interpret and verify your data?
17 Have you identified how you will address reflexivity?
18 Have you identified what you need to focus on in order to answer the research questions and conduct the research?
19 Have you identified whom you need to contact in connection with conducting the research?
20 Have you checked that all the ethical issues in the research have been addressed with all the necessary parties? Have you gained ethical clearance to conduct the research?
21 Is your research overt or covert? If it is covert, or involves intentional deceit, how is this justified?
22 Have you conducted a literature review, and how does the literature review inform your research?
23 Does your research need research questions? If not, why not? If so, what are they and have they been operationalized comprehensively, concretely and fairly?
24 Have you operationalized your research purposes into research questions?
25 What are the timescales for the different stages of your research?
26 Have you identified what kinds of data you need at different stages of the research, and why?
27 Have you identified the instruments that you will need for data collection at the different stages of the research, e.g. interviews, questionnaires, observations, role plays, accounts, personal constructs, tests, case studies, field notes, diaries, documents, etc.?
28 Is your research 'front-loaded' or 'end-loaded' in terms of planning, conduct and analysis?
29 Who are the participants?
30 Do you need a sample or a population? What is the population and what is the sample and the sampling strategy?
31 Have you planned how you will analyse the data, and at what stages of the research?
32 Have you planned how you will validate your data and your interpretation of the data?
33 Have you planned when and how you will report and present the research findings, and to whom?
34 Have you planned how you will disseminate your research findings?
35 Have you identified what controls you will place on the release of your findings, and to whom, why, for how long, and who owns the research and the data?

The intention of the research planning and design is to ensure that rigour, fitness for purpose and high quality are addressed. Furlong and Oancea (2005: 11–15) identify several clear dimensions of quality in educational research. For theoretical and methodological robustness (their 'epistemic dimension' (pp. 11–12)) they identify quality in terms of: (a) the 'trustworthiness' of the research; (b) its 'contribution to knowledge'; (c) its 'explicitness in designing and reporting'; (d) its 'propriety' (conformance to legal and ethical requirements); and (e) the 'paradigm-dependence' (fidelity to the paradigm, ontology and epistemological premises of the research) that the research demonstrates.

For 'value for use' (their 'technological dimension') Furlong and Oancea (2005: 12–13) identify key indicators of quality as: (a) the 'salience/timeliness' of the research; (b) its 'purposivity' (fitness for purpose); (c) its 'specificity and accessibility' (scope, responsiveness to user needs and predicted usage); (d) its 'concern for enabling impact' (dissemination for impact); and (e) its 'flexibility and operationalisability' (development into practical terms and utility for audiences).

For 'capacity building and value for people' (Furlong and Oancea, 2005: 13–14), they identify key indicators of quality as residing in: (a) 'partnership, collaboration and engagement'; (b) 'plausibility' ('from the practitioner's perspective'); (c) 'reflection and criticism' (research that develops reflexivity and self-reflection); (d) 'receptiveness' (research that enhances the receptiveness of practitioners and a wider audience); and (e) 'stimulating personal growth'.

For their 'economic dimension' Furlong and Oancea (2005: 14–15) indicate six elements of quality in research: (a) 'cost-effectiveness'; (b) 'marketability' and 'competitiveness' (e.g. in the research market); (c) 'auditability'; (d) 'feasibility'; (e) 'originality'; and (f) 'value-efficiency'.

The sections of this chapter and the preceding chapter, separately and together, have indicated how these can be addressed in the planning of research.

 Companion Website

The companion website to the book includes PowerPoint slides for this chapter, which list the structure of the chapter and then provide a summary of the key points in each of its sections. In addition there is further information in the form of guidelines for the contents of a research proposal, a worked example of a short research proposal, plus a checklist for evaluating a piece of research. These resources can be found online at **www.routledge.com/textbooks/cohen7e**.

Sampling

Sampling is a crucial element of research, and this chapter introduces key issues in sampling, including:

- sample size
- sampling error
- sample representativeness
- access to the sample
- sampling strategy
- probability samples
- non-probability samples
- sampling in qualitative research
- sampling in mixed methods research
- planning the sampling

8.1 Introduction

The quality of a piece of research not only stands or falls by the appropriateness of methodology and instrumentation but also by the suitability of the sampling strategy that has been adopted. Questions of sampling arise directly out of the issue of defining the population on which the research will focus.

Researchers must take sampling decisions early in the overall planning of a piece of research. Factors such as expense, time and accessibility frequently prevent researchers from gaining information from the whole population. Therefore they often need to be able to obtain data from a smaller group or subset of the total population in such a way that the knowledge gained is representative of the total population (however defined) under study. This smaller group or subset is the *sample*. Experienced researchers start with the total population and work down to the sample. By contrast, less experienced researchers often work from the bottom up, that is, they determine the minimum number of respondents needed to conduct the research (Bailey, 1994). However, unless they identify the total population in advance, it is virtually impossible for them to assess how representative the sample is that they have drawn.

Suppose that a class teacher has been released from her teaching commitments for one month in order to conduct some research into the abilities of 13-year-old students to undertake a set of science experiments; that the research is to draw on three secondary schools which contain 300 such students each, a total of 900 students, and that the method that the teacher has been asked to use for data collection is a semi-structured interview. Because of the time available to the teacher it would be impossible for her to interview all 900 students (the total population being all the cases). Therefore she has to be selective and to interview fewer than all 900 students. How will she decide that selection; how will she select which students to interview?

If she were to interview 200 of the students, would that be too many? If she were to interview just 20 of the students would that be too few? If she were to interview just the males or just the females, would that give her a fair picture? If she were to interview just those students whom the science teachers had decided were 'good at science', would that yield a true picture of the total population of 900 students? Perhaps it would be better for her to interview those students who were experiencing difficulty in science and who did not enjoy science, as well as those who were 'good at science'. Suppose that she turns up on the days of the interviews only to find that those students who do not enjoy science have decided to absent themselves from the science lesson. How can she reach those students?

Decisions and problems such as these face researchers in deciding the sampling strategy to be used. Judgements have to be made about five key factors in sampling:

1 the sample size;
2 the representativeness and parameters of the sample;
3 access to the sample;
4 the sampling strategy to be used;
5 the kind of research that is being undertaken (e.g. quantitative/qualitative/mixed methods).

The decisions here will determine the sampling strategy to be used. This assumes that a sample is actually required; there may be occasions on which the researcher can access the whole population rather than a sample.

8.2 The sample size

A question that often plagues novice researchers is just how large their samples for the research should be. There is no clear-cut answer, for the correct sample size depends on the purpose of the study, the nature of the population under scrutiny, the level of accuracy required, the anticipated response rate, the number of variables that are included in the research, and whether the research is quantitative or qualitative. However, it is possible to give some advice on this matter. Generally speaking, for quantitative research, the larger the sample the better, as this not only gives greater reliability but also enables more sophisticated statistics to be used.

Thus, a sample size of 30 is held by many to be the minimum number of cases if researchers plan to use some form of statistical analysis on their data, though this is a very small number and we would advise very considerably more. Researchers need to think out in advance of any data collection the sorts of relationships that they wish to explore within subgroups of their eventual sample. The number of variables researchers set out to control in their analysis and the types of statistical tests that they wish to make must inform their decisions about sample size prior to the actual research undertaking. Typically an anticipated minimum of 30 cases per variable should be used as a 'rule of thumb', i.e. one must be assured of having a minimum of 30 cases for each variable (of course, the 30 cases for variable one could also be the same 30 as for variable two), though this is a very low estimate indeed. This number rises rapidly if different subgroups of the population are included in the sample (discussed below), which is frequently the case.

Further, depending on the kind of analysis to be performed, some statistical tests will require larger samples. For example, let us imagine that one wished to calculate the chi-square statistic, a commonly used test (discussed in Part 5) with crosstabulated data, for example looking at two subgroups of stakeholders in a primary school containing 60 10 year olds and 20 teachers and their responses to a question on a five-point scale.

Here one can notice that the sample size is 80 cases, an apparently reasonably sized sample. However, six of the ten cells of responses (60 per cent) contain fewer than five cases. The chi-square statistic requires there to be five cases or more in 80 per cent of the cells (i.e. eight out of the ten cells). In this example only 40 per cent of the cells contained more than five cases, so even with a comparatively large sample, the statistical

Variable: 10 year olds should do one hour's homework each weekday evening					
	Strongly disagree	*Disagree*	*Neither agree nor disagree*	*Agree*	*Strongly agree*
10-year-old pupils in the school	25	20	3	8	4
Teachers in the school	6	4	2	4	4

requirements for reliable data with a straightforward statistic such as chi-square have not been met. The message is clear, one needs to anticipate, as far as one is able, some possible distributions of the data and see if these will prevent appropriate statistical analysis; if the distributions look unlikely to enable reliable statistics to be calculated then one should increase the sample size, or exercise great caution in interpreting the data because of problems of reliability, or not use particular statistics, or, indeed, consider abandoning the exercise if the increase in sample size cannot be achieved.

The point here is that each variable may need to be ensured of a reasonably large sample size (a minimum of maybe six to ten cases). Indeed Gorard (2003: 63) suggests that one can start from the minimum number of cases required in each cell, multiply this by the number of cells, and then double the total. In the example above, with six cases in each cell, the minimum sample would be 120 (6 × 10 × 2), though, to be on the safe side, to try to ensure ten cases in each cell, a minimum sample of 200 might be better (10 × 10 × 2), though even this is no guarantee.

The issue arising out of the example here is also that one can observe considerable variation in the responses from the participants in the research. Gorard (2003: 62) suggests that if a phenomenon contains a lot of potential variability then this will increase the sample size. Surveying a variable such as IQ (intelligence quotient) for example, with a potential range from 70 to around 150, may require a larger sample rather than a smaller sample.

As well as the requirement of a minimum number of cases in order to examine relationships between subgroups, researchers must obtain the minimum sample size that will accurately represent the population being targeted. With respect to size, will a large sample guarantee representativeness? Not necessarily! In our first example of the class teacher's research, she could have interviewed a total sample of 450 females and still not have represented the male population. Will a small size guarantee representativeness? Again, not necessarily! The latter could fall into the trap of saying that 50 per cent of those who expressed an opinion said that they enjoyed science, when the 50 per cent was only one student, a researcher having interviewed only two students in all. Furthermore, too large a sample might become unwieldy and too small a sample might be unrepresentative (e.g. in the first example, the researcher might have wished to interview 450 students but this would have been unworkable in practice or the researcher might have interviewed only ten students, which, in all likelihood, would have been unrepresentative of the total population of 900 students).

Where simple random sampling is used, the sample size needed to reflect the population value of a particular variable depends both on the size of the population and the amount of heterogeneity in the population (Bailey, 1994). Generally, for populations of equal heterogeneity, the larger the population, the larger the sample that must be drawn. For populations of equal size, the greater the heterogeneity on a particular variable, the larger the sample that is needed. To the extent that a sample fails to represent accurately the population involved, there is sampling error, discussed below.

Sample size is also determined to some extent by the style of the research. For example, a survey style usually requires a large sample, particularly if inferential statistics are to be calculated. In ethnographic or qualitative research it is more likely that the sample size will be small. Sample size might also be constrained by cost – in terms of time, money, stress, administrative support, the number of researchers and resources. Borg and Gall (1979: 194–5) suggest that correlational research requires a sample size of no fewer than 30 cases, that causal-comparative and experimental methodologies require a sample size of no fewer than 15 cases, and that survey research should have no fewer than 100 cases in each major subgroup and 20 to 50 in each minor subgroup.

They advise (Borg and Gall, 1979: 186) that sample size has to begin with an estimation of the smallest number of cases in the smallest subgroup of the sample, and 'work up' from that, rather than vice versa. So, for example, if 5 per cent of the sample must be teenage boys, and this subsample must be 30 cases (e.g. for correlational research), then the total sample will be 30 ÷ 0.05 = 600; if 15 per cent of the sample must be teenage girls and the subsample must be 45 cases, then the total sample must be 45 ÷ 0.15 = 300 cases.

The size of a probability (random) sample can be determined in two ways, either by the researcher exercising prudence and ensuring that the sample represents the wider features of the population with the minimum number of cases or by using a table which, from a mathematical formula, indicates the appropriate size of a random sample for a given number of the wider population (Morrison, 1993: 117). One such example is provided by Krejcie and Morgan (1970), whose work suggests that if the researcher were devising a sample from a wider population of 30 or fewer (e.g. a class of students or a group of young children in a class) then she/he would be well advised to include the whole of the wider population as the sample.

Krejcie and Morgan (1970) indicate that the smaller the number of cases there are in the wider, whole population, the larger the proportion of that population must be which appears in the sample; the converse of this is true: the larger the number of cases there are in the wider, whole population, the smaller the proportion of that population can be which appears in the sample. They note that as the population increases the proportion of the population required in the sample diminishes and, indeed, remains constant at around 384 cases (p. 610). Hence, for example, a piece of research involving all the children in a small primary or elementary school (up to 100 students in all) might require between 80 per cent and 100 per cent of the school to be included in the sample, whilst a large secondary school of 1,200 students might require a sample of 25 per cent of the school in order to achieve randomness. As a rough guide in a random sample, the larger the sample, the greater is its chance of being representative.

In determining sample size for a probability sample one has to consider not only the population size but also the error margins that one wishes to tolerate. These are expressed in terms of the confidence level and confidence interval, two further pieces of terminology. The confidence level, usually expressed as a percentage (usually 95 per cent or 99 per cent), is an index of how sure we can be (95 per cent of the time or 99 per cent of the time) that the responses lie within a given variation range. The confidence interval is that degree of variation or variation range (e.g. ± 1 per cent, or ± 2 per cent, or ± 3 per cent) that one wishes to ensure. For example the confidence interval in many opinion polls is ± 3 per cent; this means that, if a voting survey indicates that a political party has 52 per cent of the votes then it could be as low as 49 per cent (52 – 3) or as high as 55 per cent (52 + 3). A confidence level of 95 per cent here would indicate that we could be sure of this result within this range (± 3 per cent) for 95 per cent of the time.

If we want to have a very high confidence level (say 99 per cent of the time) then the sample size will be high. On the other hand, if we want a less stringent confidence level (say 90 per cent of the time), then the sample size will be smaller. Usually a compromise is reached, and researchers opt for a 95 per cent confidence level. Similarly, if we want a very small confidence interval (i.e. a limited range of variation, e.g. 3 per cent) then the sample size will be high, and if we are comfortable with a larger degree of variation (e.g. 5 per cent) then the sample size will be lower.

A full table of sample sizes for a probability sample is given in Table 8.1, with three confidence levels (90 per cent, 95 per cent and 99 per cent) and three confidence intervals (5 per cent, 4 per cent and 3 per cent). We can see that the size of the sample reduces at an increasing rate as the population size increases; generally (but, clearly, not always) the larger the population, the smaller the proportion the probability sample can be. Also, the higher the confidence level, the greater the sample, and the lower the confidence interval, the higher the sample. A conventional sampling strategy will be to use a 95 per cent confidence level and a 3 per cent confidence interval.

There are several websites that offer sample size calculation services for random samples. Some free sites at the time of writing are:

www.surveysystem.com/sscalc.htm;
www.macorr.com/ss_calculator.htm;
www.raosoft.com/samplesize.html;
www.researchinfo.com/docs/calculators/samplesize.
  cfm;
www.nss.gov.au/nss/home.nsf/pages/Sample+Size+Cal
  culator+Description?OpenDocument.

Here the researcher inputs the desired confidence level, confidence interval, and the population size, and the sample size is automatically calculated.

A further consideration in the determination of sample size is the nature of the variables included. Bartlett *et al.* (2001) indicate that sample sizes for categorical variables (e.g. sex, education level) will differ from those of continuous data (e.g. marks in a test, money in the bank); they show that typically categorical data require larger samples than continuous data. They provide a summary table (Table 8.2) to indicate the different sample sizes required for categorical and continuous data:

Within the discussion of categorical and continuous variables, Bartlett *et al.* (2001: 45) suggest that, for categorical data a 5 per cent margin of error is commonplace, whilst for continuous data, a 3 per cent margin of error is usual, and these are the intervals that they use in their table (Table 8.2). One can see that, for both categorical and continuous data, the proportion of the population decreases as the sample increases, and that, for continuous data, there is no difference in the sample sizes for populations of 2,000 or more. The researcher should normally opt for the larger sample size (i.e. the sample size required for categorical data) if both categorical and continuous data are being used.

Bartlett *et al.* (2001: 48–9) also suggest that the sample size will vary according to the statistics that will be required to be used. They suggest that if multiple regressions are to be calculated then 'the ratio of observations [cases] to independent variables should not fall below five', though some statisticians suggest a ratio of 10 to 1, particularly for continuous data, as, in continuous data, the sample sizes tend to be smaller than for categorical data. They also suggest that, in multiple regression: (a) for *continuous* data, if the number of independent variables is in the ratio of 5 to 1 then the sample size should be no fewer than 111 and the number of regressors (independent variables) should be no more than 22; (b) for *continuous* data, if the number of independent variables is in the ratio of 10 to 1 then the sample size should be no fewer than 111 and the number of regressors (independent variables) should be no more than 11; (c) for *categorical* data, if the number of independent variables is in the ratio of 5 to 1 then the sample size should be no fewer than 313 and the number of regressors (independent variables) should be no more than 62; (d) for *categorical* data, if the number of independent variables is in the ratio of 10 to 1 then the sample size should be no fewer than 313 and the number of regressors (independent variables) should be no more than 31. Bartlett *et al.* (2001: 49) also suggest that, for factor analysis, a sample size of no fewer than 100 observations (cases) should be the general rule.

If different subgroups or strata (discussed below) are to be used then the requirements placed on the total sample also apply to each subgroup. For example, let us imagine that we are surveying a whole school of 1,000 students in a multi-ethnic school. The formulae above suggest that we need 278 students in our random sample, to ensure representativeness. However, let us imagine that we wished to stratify our groups into, for example, Chinese (100 students), Spanish (50 students), English (800 students) and American (50 students). From tables of random sample sizes we work out a random sample:

TABLE 8.1 SAMPLE SIZE, CONFIDENCE LEVELS AND CONFIDENCE INTERVALS FOR RANDOM SAMPLES

Population size	Confidence level 90%			Confidence level 95%			Confidence level 99%		
	Confidence interval 5%	Confidence interval 4%	Confidence interval 3%	Confidence interval 5%	Confidence interval 4%	Confidence interval 3%	Confidence interval 5%	Confidence interval 4%	Confidence interval 3%
30	27	28	29	28	29	29	29	29	30
50	42	45	47	44	46	48	46	48	49
75	59	64	68	63	67	70	67	70	72
100	73	81	88	79	86	91	87	91	95
120	83	94	104	91	100	108	102	108	113
150	97	111	125	108	120	132	122	131	139
200	115	136	158	132	150	168	154	168	180
250	130	157	188	151	176	203	182	201	220
300	143	176	215	168	200	234	207	233	258
350	153	192	239	183	221	264	229	262	294
400	162	206	262	196	240	291	250	289	329
450	170	219	282	207	257	317	268	314	362
500	176	230	301	217	273	340	285	337	393
600	187	249	335	234	300	384	315	380	453
650	192	257	350	241	312	404	328	400	481
700	196	265	364	248	323	423	341	418	507
800	203	278	389	260	343	457	363	452	558
900	209	289	411	269	360	468	382	482	605
1,000	214	298	431	278	375	516	399	509	648
1,100	218	307	448	285	388	542	414	534	689
1,200	222	314	464	291	400	565	427	556	727
1,300	225	321	478	297	411	586	439	577	762
1,400	228	326	491	301	420	606	450	596	796
1,500	230	331	503	306	429	624	460	613	827
2,000	240	351	549	322	462	696	498	683	959
2,500	246	364	581	333	484	749	524	733	1,061
5,000	258	392	657	357	536	879	586	859	1,347
7,500	263	403	687	365	556	934	610	911	1,480
10,000	265	408	703	370	566	964	622	939	1,556
20,000	269	417	729	377	583	1,013	642	986	1,688
30,000	270	419	738	379	588	1,030	649	1,002	1,737
40,000	270	421	742	381	591	1,039	653	1,011	1,762
50,000	271	422	745	381	593	1,045	655	1,016	1,778
100,000	272	424	751	383	597	1,056	659	1,026	1,810
150,000	272	424	752	383	598	1,060	661	1,030	1,821
200,000	272	424	753	383	598	1,061	661	1,031	1,826
250,000	272	425	754	384	599	1,063	662	1,033	1,830
500,000	272	425	755	384	600	1,065	663	1,035	1,837
1,000,000	272	425	756	384	600	1,066	663	1,036	1,840

TABLE 8.2   SAMPLE SIZES FOR CATEGORICAL AND CONTINUOUS DATA

Population size	Sample size					
	Continuous data (margin of error = 0.3)			Categorical data (margin of error = 0.05)		
	Alpha = 0.10	Alpha = 0.05	Alpha = 0.01	Alpha = 0.10	Alpha = 0.05	Alpha = 0.01
100	46	55	68	74	80	87
200	59	75	102	116	132	154
300	65	85	123	143	169	207
400	69	92	137	162	196	250
500	72	96	147	176	218	286
600	73	100	155	187	235	316
700	75	102	161	196	249	341
800	76	104	166	203	260	363
900	76	105	170	209	270	382
1,000	77	106	173	213	278	399
1,500	79	110	183	230	306	461
2,000	83	112	189	239	323	499
4,000	83	119	198	254	351	570
6,000	83	119	209	259	362	598
8,000	83	119	209	262	367	613
10,000	83	119	209	264	370	623

Source: Bartlett *et al.*, 2001: 48

	Population	Sample
Chinese	100	80
Spanish	50	44
English	800	260
American	50	44
Total	1,000	428

Our original sample size of 278 has now increased, very quickly, to 428. The message is very clear: the greater the number of strata (subgroups), the larger the sample will be. Much educational research concerns itself with strata rather than whole samples, so the issue is significant. One can rapidly generate the need for a very large sample. If subgroups are required then the same rules for calculating overall sample size apply to each of the subgroups.

Further, determining the size of the sample will also have to take account of non-response, attrition and respondent mortality, i.e. some participants will fail to return questionnaires, leave the research, return incomplete or spoiled questionnaires (e.g. missing out items, putting two ticks in a row of choices instead of only one). Hence it is advisable to overestimate (oversample) rather than to underestimate the size of the sample required, to build in redundancy (Gorard, 2003: 60).

Unless one has guarantees of access, response and, perhaps, the researcher's own presence at the time of conducting the research (e.g. presence when questionnaires are being completed), then it might be advisable to estimate up to double the size of the required sample in order to allow for such loss of clean and complete copies of questionnaires/responses.

Further, with very small subgroups of populations, it may be necessary to operate a weighted sample – an oversampling – in order to gain any responses at all as, if a regular sample were to be gathered, there would be so few people included as to risk being unrepresentative of the subgroup in question. A weighted sample, in this instance, is where a higher proportion of the subgroup is sampled, and then the results are subsequently scaled down to be fairer in relation to the whole sample.

In some circumstances, meeting the requirements of sample size can be done on an evolutionary basis. For example, let us imagine that you wish to sample 300 teachers, randomly selected. You succeed in gaining positive responses from 250 teachers to, for example, a telephone survey or a questionnaire survey, but you are 50 short of the required number. The matter can be resolved simply by adding another 50 to the random sample, and, if not all of these are successful, then adding some more until the required number is reached.

Borg and Gall (1979: 195) suggest that, as a general rule, sample sizes should be large where:

■ there are many variables;
■ only small differences or small relationships are expected or predicted;
■ the sample will be broken down into subgroups;
■ the sample is heterogeneous in terms of the variables under study;
■ reliable measures of the dependent variable are unavailable.

Oppenheim (1992: 44) adds to this the view that the nature of the scales to be used also exerts an influence on the sample size. For nominal data the sample sizes may well have to be larger than for interval and ratio data (i.e. a variant of the issue of the number of subgroups to be addressed, the greater the number of subgroups or possible categories, the larger the sample will have to be).

Borg and Gall (1979) set out a formula-driven approach to determining sample size (see also Moser and Kalton, 1977; Ross and Rust, 1997: 427–38), and they also suggest using correlational tables for correlational studies – available in most texts on statistics – as it were 'in reverse' to determine sample size (p. 201), i.e. looking at the significance levels of correlation coefficients and then reading off the sample sizes usually required to demonstrate that level of significance. For example, a correlational significance level of 0.01 would require a sample size of ten if the estimated coefficient of correlation is 0.65, or a sample size of 20 if the estimated correlation coefficient is 0.45, and a sample size of 100 if the estimated correlation co-efficient is 0.20. Again, an inverse proportion can be seen – the larger the sample population, the smaller the estimated correlation co-efficient can be to be deemed significant.

With both qualitative and quantitative data, the essential requirement is that the sample is representative of the population from which it is drawn. In a dissertation concerned with a life history (i.e. n=1), the sample is the population!

In a qualitative study of 30 highly able girls of similar socio-economic background following an A-level Biology course, a sample of five or six may suffice the researcher who is prepared to obtain additional corroborative data by way of validation.

Where there is heterogeneity in the population, then a larger sample must be selected on some basis that respects that heterogeneity. Thus, from a staff of 60 secondary school teachers differentiated by gender, age, subject specialism, management or classroom responsibility, etc., it would be insufficient to construct a sample consisting of ten female classroom teachers of Arts and Humanities subjects.

For quantitative data, a precise sample number can be calculated according to the *level of accuracy* and the *level of probability* that the researcher requires in her work. She can then report in her study the rationale and the basis of her research decision (Blalock, 1979).

By way of example, suppose a teacher/researcher wishes to sample opinions among 1,000 secondary school students. She intends to use a 10-point scale ranging from 1=totally unsatisfactory to 10=absolutely fabulous. She already has data from her own class of 30 students and suspects that the responses of other students will be broadly similar. Her own students rated the activity (an extra-curricular event) as follows: mean score=7.27; standard deviation=1.98. In other words, her students were pretty much 'bunched' about a warm, positive appraisal on the 10-point scale. How many of the 1,000 students does she need to sample in order to gain an accurate (i.e. reliable) assessment of what the whole school (n=1,000) thinks of the extra-curricular event? *It all depends on what degree of accuracy and what level of probability she is willing to accept.*

A simple calculation from a formula by Blalock (1979: 215–18) shows that:

■ if she is happy to be within + or – 0.5 of a scale point and accurate 19 times out of 20, then she requires a sample of 60 out of the 1,000;
■ if she is happy to be within + or – 0.5 of a scale point and accurate 99 times out of 100, then she requires a sample of 104 out of the 1,000;
■ if she is happy to be within + or – 0.5 of a scale point and accurate 999 times out of 1,000, then she requires a sample of 170 out of the 1,000;
■ if she is a perfectionist and wishes to be within + or – 0.25 of a scale point and accurate 999 times out of 1,000, then she requires a sample of 679 out of the 1,000.

It is clear that sample size is a matter of judgement as well as mathematical precision; even formula-driven approaches make it clear that there are elements of prediction, standard error and human judgement involved in determining sample size.

8.3 Sampling error

If many samples are taken from the same population, it is unlikely that they will all have characteristics identical with each other or with the population; their means will be different. In brief, there will be sampling error (see Cohen and Holliday, 1979, 1996). Sampling error is often taken to be the difference between the sample mean and the population mean. Sampling error is not necessarily the result of mistakes made in sampling procedures. Rather, variations may occur due to the chance selection of different individuals. For example, if we take a large number of samples from the population and measure the mean value of each sample, then the sample means will not be identical. Some will be relatively high, some relatively low, and many will cluster around an average or mean value of the samples. We show this diagrammatically in Figure 8.1.

Why should this occur? We can explain the phenomenon by reference to the Central Limit Theorem which is derived from the laws of probability. This states that if random large samples of equal size are repeatedly drawn from any population, then the mean of those samples will be approximately normally distributed. The distribution of sample means approaches the normal distribution as the size of the sample increases, regardless of the shape – normal or otherwise – of the parent population (Hopkins *et al.*, 1996: 159, 388). Moreover, the average or mean of the sample means will be approximately the same as the population mean. Hopkins *et al.* (1996: 159–62) demonstrate this by reporting the use of computer simulation to examine the sampling distribution of means when computed 10,000 times (a method that we discuss in Chapter 10). Rose and Sullivan (1993: 144) remind us that 95 per cent of all sample means fall between plus or minus 1.96 standard errors of the sample and population means, i.e. that we have a 95 per cent chance of having a single sample mean within these limits, that

the sample mean will fall within the limits of the population mean.

By drawing a large number of samples of equal size from a population, we create a sampling distribution. We can calculate the error involved in such sampling. The standard deviation of the theoretical distribution of sample means is a measure of sampling error and is called the standard error of the mean (SE_M). Thus,

$$\text{S.E.} = \frac{SD_s}{\sqrt{N}}$$

where SD_S = the standard deviation of the sample and N = the number in the sample.

Strictly speaking, the formula for the standard error of the mean is:

$$\text{S.E.} = \frac{SD_{pop}}{\sqrt{N}}$$

where SD_{pop} = the standard deviation of the population.

However, as we are usually unable to ascertain the SD of the total population, the standard deviation of the sample is used instead. The standard error of the mean provides the best estimate of the sampling error. Clearly, the sampling error depends on the variability (i.e. the heterogeneity) in the population as measured by SD_{pop} as well as the sample size (N) (Rose and Sullivan, 1993: 143). The smaller the SD_{pop} the smaller the sampling error; the larger the N, the smaller the sampling error. Where the SD_{pop} is very large, then N needs to be very large to counteract it. Where SD_{pop} is very small, then N, too, can be small and still give a reasonably small sampling error. As the sample size increases the sampling error decreases. Hopkins *et al.* (1996: 159) suggest that, unless there are some very unusual distributions, samples of 25 or greater usually yield a normal sampling distribution of the mean. For further analysis of steps that can be taken to cope with the estimation of sampling in surveys we refer the reader to Ross and Wilson (1997).

The standard error of proportions

We said earlier that one answer to 'How big a sample must I obtain?' is 'How accurate do I want my results to be?' This is well illustrated in the following example: a school principal finds that the 25 students she talks to at random are reasonably in favour of a proposed change in the lunch break hours, 66 per cent being in favour and 34 per cent being against. How can she be sure that these proportions are truly representative of the whole school of 1,000 students?

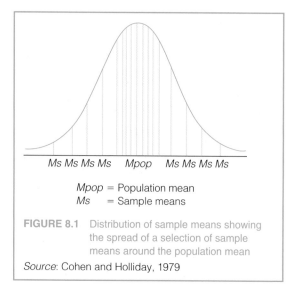

Ms Ms Ms Ms   Mpop   Ms Ms Ms Ms

Mpop = Population mean
Ms   = Sample means

FIGURE 8.1 Distribution of sample means showing the spread of a selection of sample means around the population mean

Source: Cohen and Holliday, 1979

A simple calculation of the standard error of proportions provides the principal with her answer.

$$S.E. = \sqrt{\frac{P \times Q}{N}}$$

where
P = the percentage in favour
Q = 100 per cent – P
N = the sample size.

The formula assumes that each sample is drawn on a simple random basis. A small correction factor called the finite population correction (fpc) is generally applied as follows:

$$S.E. \text{ of proportions} = \sqrt{\frac{(1-f)P \times Q}{N}}$$

where f is the proportion included in the sample.

Where, for example, a sample is 100 out of 1,000, f is 0.1.

$$S.E \text{ of proportions} = \sqrt{\frac{(1-0.1)(66 \times 34)}{100}} = 4.49$$

With a sample of 25, the S.E. = 9.4. In other words, the favourable vote can vary between 56.6 per cent and 75.4 per cent; likewise, the unfavourable vote can vary between 43.4 per cent and 24.6 per cent. Clearly, a voting possibility ranging from 56.6 per cent in favour to 43.4 per cent against is less decisive than 66 per cent as opposed to 34 per cent. Should the school principal enlarge her sample to include 100 students, then the S.E. becomes 4.5 and the variation in the range is reduced to 61.5 per cent – 70.5 per cent in favour and 38.5 per cent – 29.5 per cent against. Sampling the whole school's opinion (n = 1,000) reduces the S.E. to 1.5 and the ranges to 64.5 per cent – 67.5 per cent in favour and 35.5 per cent – 32.5 per cent against. It is easy to see why political opinion surveys are often based upon sample sizes of 1,000 to 1,500 (Gardner, 1978).

What is being suggested here generally is that, in order to overcome problems of sampling error, in order to ensure that one can separate random effects and variation from non-random effects, and in order for the power of a statistic to be felt, one should opt for as large a sample as possible. As Gorard (2003: 62) says: 'power is an estimate of the ability of the test you are using to separate the effect size from random variation',

and a large sample helps the researcher to achieve statistical power. Samples of fewer than 30 are dangerously small, as they allow the possibility of considerable standard error, and, for over around 80 cases, any increases to the sample size have little effect on the standard error.

8.4 The representativeness of the sample

The researcher will need to consider the extent to which it is important that the sample in fact represents the whole population in question (in the example above, the 1,000 students), if it is to be a valid sample. The researcher will need to be clear what it is that is being represented, i.e. to set the parameter characteristics of the wider population – the sampling frame – clearly and correctly. There is a popular example of how poor sampling may be unrepresentative and unhelpful for a researcher. A national newspaper reports that one person in every two suffers from backache; this headline stirs alarm in every doctor's surgery throughout the land. However, the newspaper fails to make clear the parameters of the study which gave rise to the headline. It turns out that the research took place (a) in a damp part of the country where the incidence of backache might be expected to be higher than elsewhere, (b) in a part of the country which contained a disproportionate number of elderly people, again who might be expected to have more backaches than a younger population, (c) in an area of heavy industry where the working population might be expected to have more backache than in an area of lighter industry or service industries, (d) by using two doctors' records only, overlooking the fact that many backache sufferers went to those doctors' surgeries because the two doctors concerned were known to be overly sympathetic to backache sufferers rather than responsibly suspicious.

These four variables – climate, age group, occupation and reported incidence – were seen to exert a disproportionate effect on the study, i.e. if the study were to have been carried out in an area where the climate, age group, occupation and reporting were to have been different, then the results might have been different. The newspaper report sensationally generalized beyond the parameters of the data, thereby overlooking the limited representativeness of the study.

It is important to consider adjusting the weightings of subgroups in the sample once the data have been collected. For example, in a secondary school where half the students are male and half are female, consider the following table of pupils' responses to the question

'How far does your liking of the form teacher affect your attitude to school work?':

Variable: How far does your liking of the form teacher affect your attitude to school work?					
	Very little	A little	Somewhat	Quite a lot	A very great deal
Male	10	20	30	25	15
Female	50	80	30	25	15
Total	60	100	60	50	30

Let us say that we are interested in the attitudes according to the gender of the respondents, as well as overall. In this example one could surmise that generally the results indicate that the liking of the form teacher has only a small to moderate effect on the students' attitude to work. However, we have to observe that twice as many girls as boys are included in the sample, and this is an unfair representation of the population of the school, which comprises 50 per cent girls and 50 per cent boys, i.e. girls are over-represented and boys are under-represented. If one equalizes the two sets of scores by gender to be closer to the school population (either by doubling the number of boys or halving the number of girls) then the results look very different, e.g.:

Variable: How far does your liking of the form teacher affect your attitude to school work?					
	Very little	A little	Somewhat	Quite a lot	A very great deal
Male	20	40	60	50	30
Female	50	80	30	25	15
Total	70	120	90	75	45

In this latter case a much more positive picture is painted, indicating that the students regard their liking of the form teacher as a quite important feature in their attitude to school work. Here equalizing the sample to represent more fairly the population by weighting yields a different picture. Weighting the results is an important consideration.

8.5 The access to the sample

Access is a key issue and is an early factor that must be decided in research. Researchers will need to ensure not only that access is permitted but is, in fact, practica-

ble. For example, if a researcher were to conduct research into truancy and unauthorized absence from school, and she decided to interview a sample of truants, the research might never commence as the truants, by definition, would not be present! Similarly access to sensitive areas might not only be difficult but problematical both legally and administratively, for example, access to child abuse victims, child abusers, disaffected students, drug addicts, school refusers, bullies and victims of bullying. In some sensitive areas access to a sample might be denied by the potential sample participants themselves, for example an AIDS counsellor might be so seriously distressed by her work that she simply cannot face discussing with a researcher the subject matter of her traumatic work; it is distressing enough to do the job without living through it again with a researcher.

Access might also be denied by the potential sample participants themselves for very practical reasons, for example a doctor or a teacher simply might not have the time to spend with the researcher. Further, access might be denied by people who have something to protect, for example a school which has recently received a very poor inspection result or poor results on external examinations, or a person who has made an important discovery or a new invention and who does not wish to disclose the secret of her success; the trade in intellectual property has rendered this a live issue for many researchers. There are very many reasons which might prevent access to the sample, and researchers cannot afford to neglect this potential source of difficulty in planning research.

In many cases access is guarded by 'gatekeepers' – people who can control the researcher's access to those whom she/he really wants to target. For school staff this might be, for example, headteachers, school governors, school secretaries, form teachers; for pupils this might be friends, gang members, parents, social workers and so on. It is critical for researchers not only to consider whether access is possible but how access will be undertaken – to whom does one have to go, both formally and informally, to gain access to the target group.

Not only might access be difficult but its corollary – release of information – might be problematic. For example, a researcher might gain access to a wealth of sensitive information and appropriate people, but there might be a restriction on the release of the data collection; in the field of education in the UK reports have been known to be suppressed, delayed or 'doctored'. It is not always enough to be able to 'get to' the sample, the problem might be to 'get the information out' to the wider public, particularly if it could be critical of powerful people.

8.6 The sampling strategy to be used

There are two main methods of sampling (Cohen and Holliday, 1979, 1982, 1996; Schofield, 1996). The researcher must decide whether to opt for a probability (also known as a random sample) or a non-probability sample (also known as a purposive sample). The difference between them is this: in a probability sample the chances of members of the wider population being selected for the sample are known, whereas in a non-probability sample the chances of members of the wider population being selected for the sample are unknown. In the former (probability sample) every member of the wider population has an equal chance of being included in the sample; inclusion or exclusion from the sample is a matter of chance and nothing else. In the latter (non-probability sample) some members of the wider population definitely will be excluded and others definitely included (i.e. every member of the wider population does not have an equal chance of being included in the sample). In this latter type the researcher has deliberately – purposely – selected a particular section of the wider population to include in or exclude from the sample.

8.7 Probability samples

A probability sample, because it draws randomly from the wider population, will be useful if the researcher wishes to be able to make generalizations, because it seeks representativeness of the wider population. (It also permits two-tailed tests to be administered in statistical analysis of quantitative data.) This is a form of sampling that is popular in randomized controlled trials. On the other hand, a non-probability sample deliberately avoids representing the wider population; it seeks only to represent a particular group, a particular named section of the wider population, e.g. a class of students, a group of students who are taking a particular examination, a group of teachers.

A probability sample will have less risk of bias than a non-probability sample, whereas, by contrast, a non-probability sample, being unrepresentative of the whole population, may demonstrate skewness or bias. (For this type of sample a one-tailed test will be used in processing statistical data.) This is not to say that the former is bias-free; there is still likely to be sampling error in a probability sample (discussed below), a feature that has to be acknowledged; for example opinion polls usually declare their error factors, e.g. ± 3 per cent.

There are several types of probability samples: simple random samples; systematic samples; stratified samples; cluster samples; stage samples; and multiphase samples. They all have a measure of randomness built into them and therefore have a degree of generalizability.

Simple random sampling

In simple random sampling, each member of the population under study has an equal chance of being selected and the probability of a member of the population being selected is unaffected by the selection of other members of the population, i.e. each selection is entirely independent of the next. The method involves selecting at random from a list of the population (a sampling frame) the required number of subjects for the sample. This can be done by drawing names out of a hat until the required number is reached, or by using a table of random numbers set out in matrix form (these are reproduced in many books on quantitative research methods and statistics), and allocating these random numbers to participants or cases (e.g. Hopkins *et al.*, 1996: 148–9). Because of probability and chance, the sample should contain subjects with characteristics similar to the population as a whole; some old, some young, some tall, some short, some fit, some unfit, some rich, some poor, etc. One problem associated with this particular sampling method is that a complete list of the population is needed and this is not always readily available.

Systematic sampling

This method is a modified form of simple random sampling. It involves selecting subjects from a population list in a systematic rather than a random fashion. For example, if from a population of, say, 2,000, a sample of 100 is required, then every twentieth person can be selected. The starting point for the selection is chosen at random.

One can decide how frequently to make systematic sampling by a simple statistic – the total number of the wider population being represented divided by the sample size required:

$$f = \frac{N}{sn}$$

f = frequency interval
N = the total number of the wider population
sn = the required number in the sample.

Let us say that the researcher is working with a school of 1,400 students; by looking at the table of sample size (Table 8.1) required for a random sample of these 1,400 students we see that 301 students are required to be in the sample. Hence the frequency interval (f) is:

$$\frac{1400}{301} = 4.651 \text{ (which rounds up to 5.0)}$$

Hence the researcher would pick out every fifth name on the list of cases.

Such a process, of course, assumes that the names on the list themselves have been listed in a random order. A list of females and males might list all the females first, before listing all the males; if there were 200 females on the list, the researcher might have reached the desired sample size before reaching that stage of the list which contained males, thereby distorting (skewing) the sample. Another example might be where the researcher decides to select every thirtieth person identified from a list of school students, but it happens that: (a) the school has just over 30 students in each class; (b) each class is listed from high ability to low ability students; (c) the school listing identifies the students by class.

In this case, although the sample is drawn from each class, it is not fairly representing the whole school population since it is drawing almost exclusively on the lower ability students. This is the issue of *periodicity* (Calder, 1979). Not only is there the question of the order in which names are listed in systematic sampling, but there is also the issue that this process may violate one of the fundamental premises of probability sampling, namely that every person has an equal chance of being included in the sample. In the example above where every fifth name is selected, this guarantees that names 1–4, 6–9, etc. will be excluded, i.e. everybody does not have an equal chance to be chosen. The ways to minimize this problem are to ensure that the initial listing is selected randomly and that the starting point for systematic sampling is similarly selected randomly.

Random stratified sampling

Random stratified sampling involves dividing the population into homogenous groups, each group containing subjects with similar characteristics. For example, group A might contain males and group B, females. In order to obtain a sample representative of the whole population in terms of sex, a random selection of subjects from group A and group B must be taken. If needed, the exact proportion of males to females in the whole population can be reflected in the sample. The researcher will have to identify those characteristics of the wider population which must be included in the sample, i.e. to identify the parameters of the wider population. This is the essence of establishing the sampling frame.

To organize a stratified random sample is a simple two-stage process. First, identify those characteristics which appear in the wider population which must also appear in the sample, i.e. divide the wider population into homogenous and, if possible, discrete groups (strata), for example males and females. Second, randomly sample within these groups, the size of each group being determined either by the judgement of the researcher or by reference to Tables 8.1 or 8.2.

The decision on which characteristics to include should strive for simplicity as far as possible, as the more factors there are, not only the more complicated the sampling becomes, but often the larger the sample will have to be to include representatives of all strata of the wider population.

A random stratified sample is, therefore, a useful blend of randomization and categorization, thereby enabling both a quantitative and qualitative piece of research to be undertaken. A quantitative piece of research will be able to use analytical and inferential statistics, whilst a qualitative piece of research will be able to target those groups in institutions or clusters of participants who will be able to be approached to participate in the research.

Cluster sampling

When the population is large and widely dispersed, gathering a simple random sample poses administrative problems. Suppose we want to survey students' fitness levels in a particularly large community or across a country. It would be completely impractical to select students randomly and spend an inordinate amount of time travelling about in order to test them. By cluster sampling, the researcher can select a specific number of schools and test all the students in those selected schools, i.e. a geographically close cluster is sampled.

One would have to be careful to ensure that cluster sampling does not build in bias. For example, let us imagine that we take a cluster sample of a city in an area of heavy industry or great poverty; this may not represent all kinds of cities or socio-economic groups, i.e. there may be similarities within the sample that do not catch the variability of the wider population. The issue here is one of representativeness; hence it might be safer to take several clusters and to sample lightly within each cluster, rather to take fewer clusters and sample heavily within each.

Cluster samples are widely used in small-scale research. In a cluster sample the parameters of the wider population are often drawn very sharply; a researcher, therefore, would have to comment on the generalizability of the findings. The researcher may also need to stratify within this cluster sample if useful data, i.e. those which are focused and which demonstrate discriminability, are to be acquired.

Stage sampling

Stage sampling is an extension of cluster sampling. It involves selecting the sample in stages, that is, taking samples from samples. Using the large community example in cluster sampling, one type of stage sampling might be to select a number of schools at random, and from within each of these schools, select a number of classes at random, and from within those classes select a number of students.

Morrison (1993: 121–2) provides an example of how to address stage sampling in practice. Let us say that a researcher wants to administer a questionnaire to all 16 year olds in each of 11 secondary schools in one region. By contacting the 11 schools she finds that there are 2,000 16 year olds on roll. Because of questions of confidentiality she is unable to find out the names of all the students so it is impossible to draw their names out of a hat to achieve randomness (and even if she had the names, it would be a mind-numbing activity to write out 2,000 names to draw out of a hat!). From looking at Table 8.1 she finds that, for a random sample of the 2,000 students, the sample size is 322 students. How can she proceed?

The first stage is to list the 11 schools on a piece of paper and then to put the names of the 11 schools onto a small card and place each card in a hat. She draws out the first name of the school, puts a tally mark by the appropriate school on her list and returns the card to the hat. The process is repeated 321 times, bringing the total to 322. The final totals might appear thus:

School	1	2	3	4	5	6	7	8	9	10	11	Total
Required number of students	22	31	32	24	29	20	35	28	32	38	31	322

For the second stage she then approaches the 11 schools and asks each of them to select randomly the required number of students for each school. Randomness has been maintained in two stages and a large number (2,000) has been rendered manageable. The process at work here is to go from the general to the specific, the wide to the focused, the large to the small. Caution has to be exercised here, as the assumption is that the schools are of the same size and are large; that may not be the case in practice, in which case this strategy may be inadvisable.

Multi-phase sampling

In stage sampling there is a single unifying purpose throughout the sampling. In the previous example the purpose was to reach a particular group of students from a particular region. In a multi-phase sample the purposes change at each phase, for example, at phase one the selection of the sample might be based on the criterion of geography (e.g. students living in a particular region); phase two might be based on an economic criterion (e.g. schools whose budgets are administered in markedly different ways); phase three might be based on a political criterion (e.g. schools whose students are drawn from areas with a tradition of support for a particular political party), and so on. What is evident here is that the sample population will change at each phase of the research.

8.8 Non-probability samples

The selectivity which is built into a non-probability sample derives from the researcher targeting a particular group, in the full knowledge that it does not represent the wider population; it simply represents itself. This is frequently the case in small-scale research, for example, as with one or two schools, two or three groups of students, or a particular group of teachers, where no attempt to generalize is desired; this is frequently the case for some ethnographic research, action research or case study research. Small-scale research often uses non-probability samples because, despite the disadvantages that arise from their non-representativeness, they are far less complicated to set up, are considerably less expensive and can prove perfectly adequate where researchers do not intend to generalize their findings beyond the sample in question, or where they are simply piloting a questionnaire as a prelude to the main study.

Just as there are several types of probability sample, so there are several types of non-probability sample: convenience sampling, quota sampling, purposive sampling, dimensional sampling and snowball sampling. Each type of sample seeks only to represent itself or instances of itself in a similar population, rather than attempting to represent the whole, undifferentiated population.

Convenience sampling

Convenience sampling – or, as it is sometimes called, accidental or opportunity sampling – involves choosing the nearest individuals to serve as respondents and continuing that process until the required sample size has been obtained or those who happen to be available and accessible at the time. Captive audiences such as students or student teachers often serve as respondents based on convenience sampling. The researcher simply chooses the sample from those to whom she has easy access. As it does not represent any group apart from itself, it does not seek to generalize about the wider population; for a convenience sample that is an irrelevance. The researcher, of course, must take pains to report this point – that the parameters of generalizability in this type of sample are negligible. A convenience sample may be the sampling strategy selected for a case study or a series of case studies.

Quota sampling

Quota sampling has been described as the non-probability equivalent of stratified sampling (Bailey, 1994). Like a stratified sample, a quota sample strives to represent significant characteristics (strata) of the wider population; unlike stratified sampling it sets out to represent these in the proportions in which they can be found in the wider population. For example, suppose the wider population (however defined) were composed of 55 per cent females and 45 per cent males, then the sample would have to contain 55 per cent females and 45 per cent males; if the population of a school contained 80 per cent of students up to and including the age of 16 and 20 per cent of students aged 17 and over, then the sample would have to contain 80 per cent of students up to the age of 16 and 20 per cent of students aged 17 and above. A quota sample, then, seeks to give proportional weighting to selected factors (strata) which reflects their weighting in which they can be found in the wider population. The researcher wishing to devise a quota sample can proceed in three stages:

Stage 1: Identify those characteristics (factors) which appear in the wider population which must also appear in the sample, i.e. divide the wider population into homogenous and, if possible, discrete groups (strata), for example, males and females, Asian, Chinese and African-Caribbean.
Stage 2: Identify the proportions in which the selected characteristics appear in the wider population, expressed as a percentage.
Stage 3: Ensure that the percentaged proportions of the characteristics selected from the wider population appear in the sample.

Ensuring correct proportions in the sample may be difficult to achieve if the proportions in the wider community are unknown or if access to the sample is difficult; sometimes a pilot survey might be necessary in order to establish those proportions (and even then

sampling error or a poor response rate might render the pilot data problematical).

It is straightforward to determine the minimum number required in a quota sample. Let us say that the total number of students in a school is 1,700, made up thus:

Performing arts	300 students
Natural sciences	300 students
Humanities	600 students
Business and Social Sciences	500 students

The proportions being 3:3:6:5, a minimum of 17 students might be required $(3+3+6+5)$ for the sample. Of course this would be a minimum only, and it might be desirable to go higher than this. The price of having too many characteristics (strata) in quota sampling is that the minimum number in the sample very rapidly could become very large, hence in quota sampling it is advisable to keep the numbers of strata to a minimum. The larger the number of strata the larger the number in the sample will become, usually at a geometric rather than an arithmetic rate of progression.

Purposive sampling

In purposive sampling, often (but by no means exclusively) a feature of qualitative research, researchers hand-pick the cases to be included in the sample on the basis of their judgement of their typicality or possession of the particular characteristics being sought. In this way, they build up a sample that is satisfactory to their specific needs.

Purposive sampling is undertaken (Teddlie and Yu, 2007) for several kinds of research including: to achieve representativeness, to enable comparisons to be made, to focus on specific, unique issues or cases, to generate theory through the gradual accumulation of data from different sources. Purposive sampling, Teddlie and Yu (2007) aver, involves a trade-off: on the one hand it provides greater depth to the study than does probability sampling; on the other hand it provides lesser breadth to the study than does probability sampling.

As its name suggests, a purposive sample has been chosen for a specific purpose, for example: (a) a group of principals and senior managers of secondary schools is chosen as the research is studying the incidence of stress amongst senior managers; (b) a group of disaffected students has been chosen because they might indicate most distinctly the factors which contribute to students' disaffection (they are *critical cases*, akin to 'critical events' discussed in Chapter 28, or *deviant cases*, those cases which go against the norm (Anderson and Arsenault, 1998: 124)); (c) one class of students has been selected to be tracked throughout a week in order to report on the curricular and pedagogic diet which is offered to them so that other teachers in the school might compare their own teaching to that reported. Whilst it may satisfy the researcher's needs to take this type of sample, it does not pretend to represent the wider population; it is deliberately and unashamedly selective and biased.

In many cases purposive sampling is used in order to access 'knowledgeable people', i.e. those who have in-depth knowledge about particular issues, maybe by virtue of their professional role, power, access to networks, expertise or experience (Ball, 1990). There is little benefit in seeking a random sample when most of the random sample may be largely ignorant of particular issues and unable to comment on matters of interest to the researcher, in which case a purposive sample is vital. Though they may not be representative and their comments may not be generalizable, this is not the primary concern in such sampling; rather the concern is to acquire in-depth information from those who are in a position to give it.

Another variant of purposive sampling is the *boosted* sample. Gorard (2003: 71) comments on the need to use a boosted sample in order to include those who may otherwise be excluded from, or under-represented in, a sample because there are so few of them. For example, one might have a very small number of special needs teachers or pupils in a primary school or nursery, or one might have a very small number of children from certain ethnic minorities in a school, such that they may not feature in a sample. In this case the researcher will deliberately seek to include a sufficient number of them to ensure appropriate statistical analysis or representation in the sample, adjusting any results from them, through weighting, to ensure that they are not over-represented in the final results. This is an endeavour perhaps to reach and meet the demands of social inclusion.

A further variant of purposive sample is *negative case sampling*. Here the researcher deliberately seeks those people who might disconfirm the theories being advanced (the Popperian equivalent of falsifiability), thereby strengthening the theory if it survives such disconfirming cases. A softer version of negative case sampling is *maximum variation sampling*, selecting cases from as diverse a population as possible (Anderson and Arsenault, 1998: 124) in order to ensure strength and richness to the data, their applicability and their interpretation. In this latter case, it is almost inevitable that the sample size will increase or be large.

Teddlie and Yu (2007) and Teddlie and Tashakkori (2009: 174) provide a typology of several kinds of purposive sample, and group these under several main areas. In terms of sampling in order to achieve representativeness or comparability they include six types of purposive sample:

- *Typical case sampling* (in which the sample includes the most typical cases of the group or population under study, i.e. representativeness).
- *Extreme or deviant case sampling* (in which the most extreme cases (at either end of a continuum e.g. success and failure, tolerance and intolerance, most and least stressed) are studied in order to provide the most outstanding examples of a particular issue, to compare with the typical cases (i.e. comparability) or to expose issues that might not otherwise present themselves (e.g. what can happen when a young child is exposed to drug pushers, family violence or repeated failure at school)).
- *Intensity sampling* (a particular group, e.g. highly effective teachers, highly talented children) in which the sample provides clear examples of the issue in question.
- *Maximum variation sampling* (in which samples are chosen that possess or exhibit a very wide range of characteristics or behaviours respectively, in connection with a particular issue).
- *Homogeneous sampling* (in which the samples are chosen for their similarity, which can then be used for contrastive analysis or comparison with maximum variation groups or intensity sampling of other groups).
- *Reputational case sampling* (in which samples are selected by key informants, on the recommendation of others or because the researchers are aware of their characteristics (e.g. a minister of education, a politician) – see below, snowball sampling and respondent-driven sampling).

In terms of sampling of special or unique cases they include four types of purposive sample:

- *Revelatory case sampling* (in which individuals are approached because they are the first members of a particular group and can reveal heretofore unknown insights, e.g. fundamentalist religious schools, schools for refugees or single ethnic minorities).
- *Critical case sampling* (a widely used sampling technique, akin to extreme case sampling, in which a particular individual, group of individuals or cases is studied in order to yield insights that might have wider application, e.g. Tripp's (1993) study of critical incidents in teaching, or Morrison's (2006) study

of sensitive educational research, focusing on small states and territories, and both of which treat the same territory of Macau as a critical case study of issues in the fields in question, which are felt are their strongest, and which can illuminate issues in the topic which are of wider concern for other small states and territories).

■ *Politically important case sampling* (for example Ball's (1990) interviews with senior politicians and Bowe *et al.*'s (1992) interviews with a UK cabinet minister and politicians).

■ *Complete collection sampling* (in which all the members of a particular group are included, e.g. all the high-achieving, musically gifted students in a sixth form).

Teddlie and Tashakkori (2009: 174) also indicate four examples of 'sequential sampling' in their typologies of purposive sampling:

■ *Theoretical sampling* (discussed below, cf. Glaser and Strauss, 1967) (in which cases are selected that will yield greater insight into the theoretical issue(s) under investigation. As Glaser and Strauss (1967: 45) suggest, the data collection is for theory generation, and, as the theory emerges, so will the next step in the data collection suggest itself, i.e. the theory drives the investigation. An example of this might be in order to examine childhood poverty in the UK, in which the researchers might look at those who have always been poor, those who have moved out of – or into – poverty, rural poverty, urban poverty, poverty in small families, poverty in large families, poverty in single-parent families, and so on).

■ *Conforming and disconfirming case sampling* (in which samples are selected from those that do and do not conform to typical trends or patterns, in order to study the causes or reasons for their conformity or disconformity).

■ *Opportunistic sampling* (see also above, convenience sampling) (in which further individuals or groups are sampled as the research develops or changes and which, as validity and reliability dictate, should be included).

■ *Snowball sampling* (discussed below, in which researchers use social networks, informants and contacts to put them in touch with further individuals or groups).

Purposive sampling is a key feature of qualitative research.

Dimensional sampling

One way of reducing the problem of sample size in quota sampling is to opt for dimensional sampling. Dimensional sampling is a further refinement of quota sampling. It involves identifying various factors of interest in a population and obtaining at least one respondent of every combination of those factors. Thus, in a study of race relations, for example, researchers may wish to distinguish first, second and third generation immigrants. Their sampling plan might take the form of a multidimensional table with 'ethnic group' across the top and 'generation' down the side. A second example might be of a researcher who may be interested in studying disaffected students, girls and secondary aged students and who may find a single disaffected secondary female student, i.e. a respondent who is the bearer of all of the sought characteristics.

Snowball sampling

In snowball sampling researchers identify a small number of individuals who have the characteristics in which they are interested. These people are then used as informants to identify, or put the researchers in touch with, others who qualify for inclusion and these, in turn, identify yet others – hence the term snowball sampling (also known as 'chain-referral methods'). This method is useful for sampling a population where access is difficult, maybe because the topic for research (and hence the sample) is sensitive (e.g. teenage solvent abusers; issues of sexuality; criminal gangs) or where participants might be suspicious of researchers, or where contact is difficult (e.g. those without telephones, the homeless (Heckathorn, 2002)). As Faugier and Sargeant (1997), Browne (2005) and Morrison (2006) argue, the more sensitive is the research, the more difficulty there is in sampling and gaining access to a sample.

Hard-to-reach groups include minorities, marginalized or stigmatized groups, 'hidden groups' (those who do not wish to be contacted or reached (e.g. drug pushers, gang members; sex workers; problem drinkers or gamblers; residents of 'safe houses' or women's refuges)), old or young people with disabilities, the very powerful or social elite (Noy, 2008), dispersed communities (e.g. rural farm workers) (Brackertz, 2007).

Snowball sampling is also useful where communication networks are undeveloped (e.g. where a researcher wishes to interview stand-in 'supply' teachers – teachers who are brought in on an ad hoc basis to cover for absent regular members of a school's teaching staff – but finds it difficult to acquire a list of these stand-in teachers), or where an outside researcher has difficulty in gaining access to schools (going through informal networks of friends/acquaintance and their friends and acquaintances and so on rather than through formal channels). The task for the researcher is to establish who are the critical or key informants with whom initial contact must be made.

Snowball sampling is particularly valuable in qualitative research, indeed is often pre-eminent in qualitative research; it is a means in itself, rather than a default, fall-back position (Noy, 2008: 330). It uses participants' social networks and personal contacts for gaining access to people. In snowball sampling, interpersonal relations feature very highly (Browne, 2005), as the researcher is reliant on: (a) friends, friends of friends, friends of friends of friends; (b) acquaintances, acquaintances of acquaintances, acquaintances of acquaintances of acquaintances; (c) contacts (personally known or not personally known), contacts of contacts, contacts of contacts of contacts. 'Snowball sampling is essentially social' (Noy, 2008: 332), as it often relies on strong interpersonal relations, known contacts and friends; it requires social knowledge and an equalization of power relations (Noy, 2008: 329). In this respect it reduces, even dissolves, asymmetrical power relations between researcher and participants, as the contacts might be built on friendships, peer group membership and personal contacts and because participants can act as gatekeepers to other participants, and informants exercise control over whom else to involve and refer. Indeed in respondent-driven sampling (discussed below), a variant of snowball sampling, the respondents not only identify further contacts for the researcher but actively recruit them to be involved in the research (Heckathorn, 1997: 178), i.e. participants who might be initially uncooperative with researchers might be cooperative for their peer group members who approach them (Heckathorn, 1997: 197).

Snowball sampling, then, is 'respondent-driven' (Heckathorn, 1997, 2002). In researching 'hidden populations' typically there are no sampling frames so researchers do not know the population from which the sample can be drawn, and there is often a problem of access as such groups may guard their privacy (e.g. if their behaviour is illegal, or stigmatized) and, even if access is gained, truthful responses may not be forthcoming as participants may deliberately conceal the truth in order to protect themselves (Heckathorn, 1997: 174). Respondent-driven sampling uses snowball sampling, with variants of key informant sampling and targeted sampling (Heckathorn, 1997: 174), where respondents identify others for the researcher to contact.

Snowball sampling may rely on personal, social contacts, but it can also rely on 'reputational contacts' (e.g. Farquharson, 2005), where people may be able to identify to the researcher other known persons in the field. The 'reputational snowball' (Farquharson, 2005: 347) can be a powerful means of identifying significant others in a 'micro-network' (p. 349), particularly if one is researching powerful individuals and policy makers who are not always known to the public. As Farquharson (2005: 346) remarks, 'policy networks' are groups of interconnected institutions and/or people who are influential in the field, perhaps to advance, promote, block, develop or initiate policy. A reputational snowball can be generated by asking individuals – either at interview or by open-ended questions on a questionnaire – to identify others in the field who are particularly influential, important or worth contacting.

On the one hand snowball sampling can reach the hard-to-reach, not least if the researcher is a member of the groups being researched (e.g. Browne's (2005) study of non-heterosexual women, of which she was one and therefore had her own circle of friends and contacts, and in which rapport and trust were easier to establish).

On the other hand it can be prone to biases of the influence of the initial contact and the problem of volunteer-only samples (Heckathorn, 2002: 12). Browne (2005) indicates that, because she was a member of a white, middle-class group of non-heterosexual women, her contacts tended to be from similar backgrounds, and that other non-heterosexual women were not included because they were not in the same 'loop' of social contacts. In other words, snowball sampling is influenced heavily by the researcher's initial points of contact as these drive the subsequent contacts and, indeed, can lead to sampling or over-sampling of cooperative groups or individuals (Heckathorn, 1997: 175). Two methods can be employed to overcome this: (a) key informant sampling asks participants about others' behaviours (but this raises the problem of informed consent and confidentiality of others (Heckathorn, 2002: 13)), whilst targeted sampling tries to ensure a non-biased sample, to include all those who should be included (i.e. to prevent under-sampling) and who represent different facets of the issue or group under study (see Heckathorn (1997, 2007) for a fuller discussion of this matter and for how to address and overcome bias in respondent-driven samples).

Further, if a researcher is to move beyond his or her personal contacts, to try to be more inclusive of otherwise excluded subgroups or individuals, then there is a risk having such small numbers of others as to be simply tokenism at work. Browne (2005: 53) writes that the women who participated in her research were

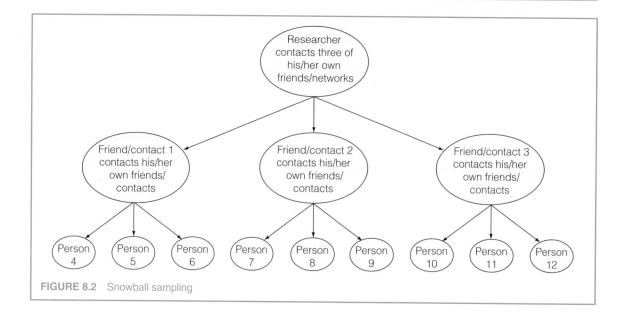

FIGURE 8.2 Snowball sampling

also gatekeepers of contact to other non-heterosexual women who, for a variety of reasons (not least of which was the wish to avoid revealing too much to a friend), may not have wished to be involved. Bias can both include and exclude members of a population and a sample; it 'can create other "hidden populations"' (Browne, 2005: 53) (see Figure 8.2), and the gatekeepers can protect friends by not referring them to the researcher (Heckathorn, 1997: 175).

Figure 8.2 indicates a linear, sequential method of sampling (the arrows are unidirectional). Noy (2008: 333) comments that, as the ordinal succession proceeds, the later members of the sample might have different characteristics or attributes from the earlier members of the sample, i.e. the sample is not necessarily homogeneous. This is important, as it overcomes the problem indicated earlier, where the influence of initial contacts on later contacts is high; having many waves of contacts reduces this influence (Heckathorn, 1997: 197).

Snowball sampling can be used as the main method of gaining access to people or as an auxiliary method of gaining access to people for further, in-depth data collection and exploration of issues.

Volunteer sampling

In cases where access is difficult, the researcher may have to rely on volunteers, for example, personal friends, or friends of friends, or participants who reply to a newspaper advertisement, or those who happen to be interested from a particular school, or those attending courses. Sometimes this is inevitable (Morrison,

2006), as it is the only kind of sampling that is possible, and it is maybe better to have this kind of sampling than no research at all.

In these cases one has to be very cautious in making any claims for generalizability or representativeness, as volunteers may have a range of different motives for volunteering, e.g. wanting to help a friend, interest in the research, wanting to benefit society, an opportunity for revenge on a particular school or headteacher. Volunteers may be well intentioned, but they do not necessarily represent the wider population, and this would have to be made clear.

Theoretical sampling

This is a feature of grounded theory. In grounded theory the sample size is relatively immaterial, as one works with the data that one has. Indeed grounded theory would argue that the sample size could be infinitely large, or, as a fall-back position, large enough to saturate the categories and issues, such that new data will not cause the theory that has been generated to be modified.

Theoretical sampling requires the researcher to have sufficient data to be able to generate and 'ground' the theory in the research context, however defined, i.e. to create theoretical explanation of what is happening in the situation, without having any data that do not fit the theory. Since the researcher will not know in advance how much or what range of data will be required, it is difficult, to the point of either impossibility, exhaustion or time limitations, to know in advance the sample size required. The researcher proceeds in gathering more and more data until the theory remains unchanged or until the boundaries of the context of the study have been reached, until no modifications to the grounded theory are made in light of the constant comparison method. Theoretical saturation (Glaser and Strauss, 1967: 61) occurs when no additional data are found that advance, modify, qualify, extend or add to the theory developed (see also Krueger and Casey, 2000).

Glaser and Strauss (1967: 45) write that theoretical sampling is where, during the data collection process as part of theory generation, the researcher collects data, codes the data and analyses them, and this analysis influences what data to collect next, from whom and where. The two key questions for the grounded theorist using theoretical sampling are: (a) to which groups does one turn next for data? (b) for what theoretical purposes does one seek further data? In response to (a), the authors (p. 49) suggest that the decision is based on theoretical relevance, i.e. those groups that will assist in the generation of as many properties and categories as possible.

Hence the size of the data set may be fixed by the number of participants in the organization, or the number of people to whom one has access, but the researcher has to consider that the door may have to be left open for him/her to seek further data in order to ensure theoretical adequacy and to check what has been found so far with further data (Flick *et al.*, 2004: 170). In this case it is not always possible to predict at the start of the research just how many, and who, the researcher will need for the sampling; it becomes an iterative process.

Non-probability samples also reflect the issue that sampling can be of *people* but it can also be of *issues*. Samples of people might be selected because the researcher is concerned to address specific issues, for example, those students who misbehave, those who are reluctant to go to school, those with a history of drug dealing, those who prefer extra-curricular to curricular activities. Here it is the issue that drives the sampling, and so the question becomes not only 'whom should I sample' but 'what should I sample' (Mason, 2002: 127–32). In turn this suggests that it is not only people who may be sampled, but texts, documents, records, settings, environments, events, objects, organizations, occurrences, activities and so on.

8.9 Sampling in qualitative research

It is often the case in qualitative research that non-probability, purposive samples are taken. However,

whilst much of the discussion of probability samples is more relevant to quantitative research (though not exclusively so), and whilst much of the discussion of non-probability samples is more relevant to qualitative research (though not exclusively so), some qualitative research also raises a fundamental question about sampling. The question is this: if sampling presupposes an identifiable population from which a sample is drawn, then is it actually realistic or relevant to identify a population or its sample?

In much qualitative research the emphasis is placed on the uniqueness, the idiographic and exclusive distinctiveness of the phenomenon, group or individuals in question, i.e. they only represent themselves, and nothing or nobody else. In such cases it is perhaps unwise to talk about a 'sample', and more fitting to talk about a group, or individuals. How far they are representative of a wider population or group is irrelevant, as much qualitative research seeks to explore the particular group under study, not to generalize. If, in the process, other groups find that issues raised apply to them then this is a fortunate bonus rather than a necessity; in this respect it is akin to case study research.

Further, a corollary of the sympathy between qualitative research and non-probability sampling is that there are no clear rules on the size of the sample in qualitative research; size is informed by 'fitness for purpose'. For example a case study might involve only one child (e.g. Axline, 1964), a grounded theory might continue to add samples until theoretical saturation is reached (i.e. where new data no longer add to the theory construction or themes, or their elements), an ethnography takes in the whole of the group under study, sometimes without any intention of representing a wider population (e.g. Patrick, 1973) and at other times seeking to represent some key features of a wider population (e.g. Willis, 1977).

This is not to say that there are no occasions on which, in qualitative research, a sample cannot fairly represent a population. Indeed Onwuegbuzie and Leech (2007: 240) argue that external generalizability and inferences to a whole population can feature in qualitative research, and that, as in quantitative research, this typically requires a large sample to be drawn (p. 242). The authors contrast this with internal generalizability, in which data from a subgroup of a sample seek to be generalizable to the whole sample. That said, they note (p. 249) that, many times, the purpose of the sampling is not to make generalizations, not to make comparisons, but to present unique cases that have their own, intrinsic value.

Onwuegbuzie and Leech (2007: 242) suggest that, in qualitative research, the sample size should be large enough to generate 'thick descriptions' (Geertz, 1973) and rich data, though not so large as to prevent this from happening due to data overload or moves towards generalizability, and not so small as to prevent theoretical saturation (discussed earlier) from being achieved. Onwuegbuzie and Leech (2007: 245) also counsel that subgroups in a sample should not be so small as to prevent data redundancy or data saturation, and, in this respect, they recommend that each subgroup should contain no fewer than three cases. As with quantitative data (discussed earlier), they note that as the number of strata increase, so will the size of the sample.

8.10 Sampling in mixed methods research

Teddlie and Tashakkori (2009: 180–1), drawing on the work of Teddlie and Yu (2007), indicate that it is commonplace for mixed methods research to use more than one kind of sample (probability, non-probability) and to use samples of different sizes, scope and types (cases: people; materials: written, oral observational; other elements in social situations: locations, times, events, etc.) within the same piece of research. This is akin to the work of Spradley (1980) on participant observation, Patton (1990) on qualitative research, and Miles and Huberman (1994) in discussing actors (participants), settings, events and processes. Even though mixed methods may be used in a piece of research, this is not to rule out the fact that, in some research, the numerical approach may predominate – with the sampling implications indicated earlier in this chapter (e.g. probability sampling and sample size calculation) – whilst in other mixed methods approaches qualitative data may predominate, with an emphasis on purposive and non-probability sampling (cf. Teddlie and Yu, 2007: 85).

Teddlie and Tashakkori (2009: 185–91) provide a useful overview of different mixed methods sampling designs (see also Chapter 1). In *parallel mixed methods sampling* both probability and non-probability samples are selected, running side by side simultaneously, but separate from each other, i.e. data from one sample do not influence the collection of data from the other and vice versa. Onwuegbuzie and Leech (2007: 239) add that parallel sampling designs enable comparisons to be made across two or more subgroups of a sample that are within the same level of the sample (e.g. girls and boys).

In *sequential mixed methods sampling* (Teddlie and Tashakkori, 2009: 185–91) one kind of sample (both probability and non-probability) precedes another and influences the proceeding sample; in other words what one gathers from an early sample will influence what

one will do in the next stage with a different sample. This might mean that numerical data set the scene for in-depth interviewing, perhaps identifying extreme or deviant cases, critical cases, variables on which the results are either homogeneous or highly varied; alternatively it might mean that qualitative data (e.g. case studies or focus groups) might identify issues for exploration in a numerical survey.

In *multilevel mixed methods sampling*, different kinds of sample (both probability and non-probability and either separately or together) are used at different levels of units of analysis, for example: individual students, classes, schools, local authorities, regions. Onwuegbuzie and Leech (2007: 240) suggest that multilevel sampling designs enable comparisons to be made between two or more subgroups that are drawn from different levels of the study (e.g. individual students and teachers, or individual students and schools, as there is a perceptible hierarchy operating here). They add that this is facilitated by software (e.g. N-Vivo) that enables such comparative data to be collected and presented by subgroup. They also caution researchers to note that, often, a subsample from one level is not the same size as the subsample from another (p. 249), for instance there may be 30 individual students but only one or two teachers for that group of students (they note, in this context, that it is frequently the case that the levels are related, e.g. students and teachers from the same school, rather than being separate, e.g. students from one school and teachers from another).

Teddlie and Tashakkori (2009: 191) provide a worked example of a multilevel, mixed method sampling design for a school effectiveness study, in which:

- at level one, students were selected by probability (random) and purposive sampling (typical cases and complete collection sampling);
- at level two, teachers and classrooms were selected by probability (random and random stratified) and purposive sampling (intensity and typical case sampling);
- at level three, schools were sampled using purposive samples (extreme and deviant case sampling, intensity sampling and typical case sampling);
- at level four, school districts were sampled using probability sampling (cluster samples) and stratified purposive samples;
- at level five, state school systems were sampled using purposive or convenience sampling.

Teddlie and Tashakkori (2009: 186) suggest that *stratified purposive sampling* is useful. Here the researcher identifies the different strata (e.g. subgroups) within the population under study, and then selects a limited number of cases from within each of those subgroups, ensuring that the selection of these cases is based on purposive sampling strategies (i.e. fitness for purpose), drawing on the range of purposive sampling strategies outlined earlier in this chapter. This, they aver, enables the researcher to make comparisons across groups (strata) as required. In this case the purposive sample is a subset of the probability sample (Teddlie and Yu, 2007: 93).

Teddlie and Tashakkori (2009: 186–7) also commend the use of *purposeful random sampling*, in which the researcher takes a random sample from a small number of cases from the population (a probability sample) that has already been drawn from a purposive sample (where the population has been chosen for a specific purpose).

Onwuegbuzie and Leech (2007: 239) introduce *nested sampling designs*, which enable comparisons to be made between two or more members of the same subgroup and the whole sample. The members of a subgroup represent a subsample of the whole sample (p. 246). They give the example (p. 240) of a comparison between key informants and the whole sample.

Teddlie and Tashakkori (2009: 192–3) also provide useful guidance for sampling in mixed methods research, suggesting that the sampling strategy should:

- derive logically the research questions or hypotheses being investigated/tested;
- be faithful to the assumptions on which the sampling strategies are based (e.g. random allocation, even distributions of characteristics in the population, etc.);
- generate qualitative and quantitative data in order to answer the research questions;
- enable clear inferences to be drawn from both the numerical and qualitative data;
- abide by ethical principles;
- be practicable (able to be done) and efficient;
- enable generalizabilty of the results (and should indicate to whom the results are generalizable);
- be reported in a level of detail that will enable other researchers to understand it and perhaps use it in the future.

8.11 Planning a sampling strategy

There are several stages in planning the sampling strategy:

Stage 1: Decide whether you need a sample, or whether it is possible to have the whole population.

Stage 2: Identify the population, its important features (the sampling frame) and its size.

Stage 3: Identify the kind of sampling strategy you require (e.g. which variant of probability, non-probability or mixed methods sample you require).

Stage 4: Ensure that access to the sample is guaranteed. If not, be prepared to modify the sampling strategy (Stage 2).

Stage 5: For probability sampling, identify the confidence level and confidence intervals that you require. For non-probability sampling, identify the people whom you require in the sample.

Stage 6: Calculate the numbers required in the sample, allowing for non-response, incomplete or spoiled responses, attrition and sample mortality, i.e. build in redundancy by oversampling.

Stage 7: Decide how to gain and manage access and contact (e.g. advertisement, letter, telephone, email, personal visit, personal contacts/friends).

Stage 8: Be prepared to weight (adjust) the data, once collected.

8.12 Conclusion

The message from this chapter is the same as for many of the others, namely that every element of the research should not be arbitrary but planned and deliberate, and that, as before, the criterion of planning must be fitness for purpose. The selection of a sampling strategy must be governed by the criterion of suitability. The choice of which strategy to adopt must be mindful of the purposes of the research, the timescales and constraints on the research, the research design, the methods of data collection and the methodology of the research. The sampling chosen must be appropriate for all these factors if validity is to be served.

To the question 'how large should my sample be?'. the answer is complicated. This chapter has suggested that it all depends on:

- the research purposes, questions and design;
- the population size;
- the confidence level and confidence interval required;
- the likely response rate;
- the accuracy required (the smallest sampling error sought);
- the kinds of variables to be used (categorical, continuous);
- the statistics to be used;
- the number of strata required;
- the number of variables included in the study;
- the variability of the factor under study;

TABLE 8.3 TYPES OF SAMPLE

Probability samples	Non-probability samples	Mixed methods sampling designs
Simple random sampling	Convenience sampling	Parallel mixed methods sampling
Systematic sampling	Quota sampling	Sequential mixed methods sampling
Random stratified sampling	Purposive sampling:	Multilevel mixed methods sampling
Cluster sampling	Boosted sample	Stratified purposive sampling
Stage sampling	Negative case sampling	Purposeful random sampling
Multi-phase sampling	Typical case sampling	Nested sampling designs
	Extreme/deviant case sampling	
	Intensity sampling	
	Maximum variation sampling	
	Homogeneous sampling	
	Reputational case sampling	
	Revelatory case sampling	
	Critical case sampling	
	Politically important case sampling	
	Complete collection sampling	
	Theoretical sampling	
	Confirming and disconfirming case sampling	
	Opportunistic sampling	
	Snowball sampling	
	Dimensional sampling	
	Volunteer sampling	

- the kind(s) of sample (different kinds of sample within probability, non-probability and mixed methods sampling);
- the representativeness of the sample;
- the allowances to be made for attrition and non-response;
- the need to keep proportionality in a proportionate sample;
- the kind of research that is being undertaken (qualitative/quantitative/mixed methods).

That said, this chapter has urged researchers to use large rather than small samples in quantitative research and sufficiently large and small samples to enable thick descriptions to be achieved. Table 8.3 presents a summary of the types of samples that we have introduced in this chapter.

 Companion Website

The companion website to the book includes PowerPoint slides for this chapter, which list the structure of the chapter and then provide a summary of the key points in each of its sections. This resource can be found online at **www.routledge.com/textbooks/cohen7e**.

Sensitive educational research

This chapter addresses several aspects of sensitive research:

- defining sensitive research
- issues of sampling and access
- ethical issues
- researching powerful people
- researching powerless and vulnerable people
- asking questions

It argues that researchers have to be acutely aware of the sensitivities at work in any piece of research that they are undertaking.

9.1 Introduction

All educational research is sensitive; the question is one of degree. The researcher has to be sensitive to the context, the cultures, the participants, the consequences of the research on a range of parties, the powerless, the powerful, people's agendas and suchlike. Being sensitive is as much about ethics and behaving ethically as it is about the research itself. Researchers have to be very careful on a variety of delicate issues.

The chapter sets out different ways in which educational research might be sensitive. It then takes two significant issues in the planning and conduct of sensitive research – sampling and access – and indicates why these twin concerns might be troublesome for researchers, and how they might be addressed. The outline includes a discussion of gatekeepers and their roles. Sensitive research raises a range of difficult, sometimes intractable, ethical issues, and we set out some of these in the chapter. Investigations involving powerful people are taken as an instance of sensitive educational research, and this is used as a vehicle for examining several key problematic matters in this area. The chapter moves to a practical note, proffering advice on how to ask questions in sensitive research. Finally, the chapter sets out a range of key issues to be addressed in the planning, conduct and reporting of sensitive research.

9.2 What is sensitive research?

Sensitive research is that 'which potentially poses a substantial threat to those who are involved or have been involved in it' (Lee, 1993: 4), or when those studied view the research as somehow undesirable (Van Meter, 2000). Sensitivity can derive from many sources, including:

- consequences for the participants (Sieber and Stanley, 1988: 49; Kavanaugh *et al.*, 2006: 245);
- consequences for other people, e.g. family members, associates, social groups and the wider community, research groups and institutions (Lee, 1993: 5);
- contents, e.g. taboo or emotionally charged areas of study (Farberow, 1963), e.g. criminality, deviance, sex, race, bereavement, violence, politics, policing, human rights, drugs, poverty, illness, religion and the sacred, lifestyle, family, finance, physical appearance, power and vested interests (Lee, 1993; Arditti, 2002; Chambers, 2003);
- situational and contextual circumstances (Lee, 1993);
- intrusion into private, intimate spheres and deep personal experience (Lee and Renzetti, 1993: 5), e.g. sexual behaviour, religious practices, death and bereavement, even income and age;
- potential sanction, risk or threat of stigmatization, incrimination, costs or career loss to the researcher, participants or others, e.g. groups and communities (Lee and Renzetti; 1993; Renzetti and Lee, 1993; De Laine, 2000), a particular issue for the researcher who studies human sexuality and who, consequently, suffers from 'stigma contagion', i.e. sharing the same stigma as those being studied (Lee, 1993: 9);
- impingement on political alignments (Lee, 1993);
- penetration of personal defences (Dickson-Swift *et al.*, 2006);
- cultural and cross-cultural factors and inhibitions (Sieber, 1992: 129; Tillman, 2002);
- fear of scrutiny and exposure (Payne *et al.*, 1980);
- threat to the researcher and to the family members

and associates of those studied (Lee, 1993); Lee (1993: 34) suggests that 'chilling' may take place, i.e. where researchers are 'deterred from producing or disseminating research' because they anticipate hostile reactions from colleagues, e.g. on race. 'Guilty knowledge' may bring personal and professional risk from colleagues (De Laine, 2000: 67); it is threatening both to researchers and participants (De Laine, 2000: 84);

■ methodologies and conduct, e.g. when junior researchers conduct research on powerful people, when men interview women, when senior politicians are involved, or where access and disclosure are difficult (Simons, 1989; Ball, 1990, 1994a; Liebling and Shah, 2001).

Sometimes all, or nearly all the issues listed above are present simultaneously. Indeed, in some situations the very activity of actually undertaking educational research per se may be sensitive. This has long been the situation in totalitarian regimes, where permission has typically had to be granted from senior government officers and departments in order to undertake educational research. Closed societies may only permit educational research on approved, typically non-sensitive and comparatively apolitical topics. As Lee (1993: 6) suggests: 'research for some groups … is quite literally an anathema'. The very *act* of doing the educational research, regardless of its purpose, focus, methodology or outcome, is itself a sensitive matter (Morrison, 2006). In this situation the conduct of educational research may hinge on interpersonal relations, local politics and micro-politics. What start as being simply methodological issues can turn out to be ethical and political/micro-political minefields.

Lee (1993: 4) suggests that sensitive research falls into three main areas: (a) intrusive threat (probing into areas which are 'private, stressful or sacred'); (b) studies of deviance and social control, i.e. which could reveal information that could stigmatize or incriminate (threat of sanction); and (c) political alignments, revealing the vested interests of 'powerful persons or institutions, or the exercise of coercion or domination', or extremes of wealth and status (Lee, 1993). As Beynon (1988: 23) says 'the rich and powerful have encouraged hagiography, not critical investigation'. Indeed, Lee (1993: 8) argues that there has been a tendency to 'study down' rather than 'study up', i.e. to direct attention to powerless rather than powerful groups, not least because these are easier and less sensitive to investigate. Sensitive educational research can act as a voice for the weak, the oppressed, those without a voice or who are not listened to; equally it can focus on the powerful and those in high-profile positions.

The three kinds of sensitivities indicated above (a), (b) and (c) may appear separately or in combination. The sensitivity not only concerns the topic itself, but, perhaps more importantly, 'the relationship between that topic and the social context' within which the research is conducted (Lee, 1993: 5). What appears innocent to the researcher may be highly sensitive to the researched or to other parties. Threat is a major source of sensitivity; indeed Lee (1993: 5) suggests that, rather than generating a list of sensitive topics, it is more fruitful to look at the conditions under which 'sensitivity' arises within the research process. Given this issue, the researcher will need to consider how sensitive the educational research will be, not only in terms of the subject matter itself, but also in terms of the several parties that have a stake in it, for example: headteachers and senior staff; parents; students; schools; governors; local politicians and policy makers; the researcher(s) and research community; government officers; the community; social workers and school counsellors; sponsors and members of the public; members of the community being studied; and so on.

Sensitivity inheres both in the educational topic under study, but also, much more significantly, in the social context in which the educational research takes place and on the likely consequences of that research on all parties. Doing research is not only a matter of designing a project and collecting, analysing and reporting data – that is the optimism of idealism or ignorance; it is a matter of interpersonal relations, potentially continual negotiation, delicate forging and sustaining of relationships, setback, modification and compromise. In an ideal world educational researchers would be able to plan and conduct their studies untrammelled; however the ideal world, in the poet Yeats's words, is 'an image of air'. Sensitive educational research exposes this very clearly. Whilst most educational research will incur sensitivities, the attraction of discussing sensitive research per se is that it highlights what these delicate issues might be and how they might be felt at their sharpest. We advise readers to consider most educational research as sensitive, to anticipate what those sensitivities might be, and what trade-offs might be necessary.

9.3 Sampling and access

Walford (2001: 33) argues that gaining access and becoming accepted is a slow process. Hammersley and Atkinson (1983: 54) suggest that gaining access is not only a practical matter but it provides insights into the 'social organisation of the setting'.

Lee (1993: 60) suggests that there are potentially serious difficulties in sampling and access in sensitive research, not least because of the problem of estimating the size of the population from which the sample is to be drawn, as members of particular groups, e.g. deviant or clandestine groups, will not want to disclose their associations. Similarly, like-minded groups may not wish to open themselves to public scrutiny. They may have much to lose by revealing their membership and, indeed, their activities may be illicit, critical of others, unpopular, threatening to their own professional security, deviant and less frequent than activities in other groups, making access to them a major obstacle. What if a researcher is researching truancy, or teenage pregnancy, or bullying, or solvent abuse amongst school students, or alcohol and medication use amongst teachers, or family relationship problems brought about by the stresses of teaching?

Lee (1993: 61) suggests several strategies to be used either separately or in combination, for sampling 'special' populations (e.g. rare or deviant populations):

- *List sampling*: looking through public domain lists, for example, of the recently divorced (though such lists may be more helpful to social researchers than, specifically, educational researchers).
- *Multi-purposing*: using an existing survey to reach populations of interest (though problems of confidentiality may prevent this from being employed).
- *Screening*: targeting a particular location and canvassing within it (which may require much effort for little return).
- *Outcropping*: this involves going to a particular location where known members of the target group congregate or can be found (e.g. Humphreys' celebrated study of homosexual 'tearoom trade' in 1970); in education this may be a particular staffroom (for teachers), or meeting place for students. Outcropping risks bias, as there is no simple check for representativeness of the sample.
- *Servicing*: Lee (1993: 72) suggests that it may be possible to reach research participants by offering them some sort of service in return for their participation. Researchers must be certain that they really are able to provide the services promised. As Walford (2001: 36) writes: 'people don't buy products; they buy benefits', and researchers need to be clear on the benefits offered.
- *Professional informants*: Lee (1993: 73) suggests these could be, for example, police, doctors, priests or other professionals. In education these may include social workers and counsellors. This may be unrealistic optimism, as these very people may be bound by terms of legal or ethical confidentiality or voluntary self-censorship (e.g. an AIDS counsellor, after a har-

rowing day at work, may not wish to continue talking to a stranger about AIDS counselling, or a social worker or counsellor may be constrained by professional confidentiality, or an exhausted teacher may not wish to talk about her teaching difficulties). Further, Lee suggests that, even if such people agree to participate, they may not know the full story. He gives the example of drug users (p. 73), whose contacts with the police may be very different from their contacts with doctors or social workers, or, the corollary of this, the police, doctors and social workers may not see the same group of drug users.

- *Advertising*: though this can potentially reach a wide population, it may be difficult to control the nature of those who respond, in terms of representativeness or suitability.
- *Networking*: this is akin to snowball sampling, wherein one set of contacts puts the researcher in touch with more contacts, who puts the researcher in touch with yet more contacts and so on. This is a widely used technique, though Lee (1993: 66) reports that it is not always easy for contacts to be passed on, as initial informants may be unwilling to divulge members of a close-knit community. On the other hand, Morrison (2006) reports that networking is a popular technique where it is difficult to penetrate a formal organization such as a school, if the gatekeepers (those who can grant or prevent access to others, e.g. the headteacher or senior staff) refuse access. He reports the extensive use of informal networks by researchers, in order to contact friends and professional associates, and, in turn, their friends and professional associates, thereby sidestepping the formal lines of contact through schools.

Walford (2001: 36–47) sets out a four-stage process of gaining access:

Stage 1: Approach (gaining entry, perhaps through a mutual friend or colleague – a link person). In this context Walford cautions that an initial letter should only be used to gain an initial interview or an appointment, or even to arrange to telephone the headteacher in order to arrange an interview, not to conduct the research or to gain access.

Stage 2: Interest (using a telephone call to arrange an initial interview). In this respect Walford notes (p. 43) that headteachers like to talk, and so it is important to let them talk, even on the telephone when arranging an interview to discuss the research.

Stage 3: Desire (which comprises overcoming objections and stressing the benefits of the research). As he wisely comments (p. 44): 'after all, schools have purposes other than to act as research sites'. He makes the telling point that the research may actually benefit the school, but that the school may not realize this until it is pointed out. For example, a headteacher may wish to confide in a researcher, teachers may benefit from discussions with a researcher, students may benefit from being asked about their learning.

Stage 4: Sale (where the participants agree to the research).

Whitty and Edwards (1994: 22) argue that in order to overcome problems of access, ingenuity and even the temptation to use subterfuge could be considered: 'denied co-operation initially by an independent school, we occasionally contacted some parents through their child's primary school and then told the independent schools we already were getting some information about their pupils'. They also add that it is sometimes necessary for researchers to indicate that they are 'on the same side' as those being researched.[1] Indeed they report that 'we were questioned often about our own views, and there were times when to be viewed suspiciously from one side proved helpful in gaining access to the other' (p. 22). This harks back to Becker's (1968) advice to researchers to decide whose side they are on.

The use of snowball sampling builds in 'security' (Lee, 1993), as the contacts are those who are known and trusted by the members of the 'snowball'. That said, this itself can lead to bias, as relationships between participants in the sample may consist of 'reciprocity and transitivity' (Lee, 1993: 67), i.e. participants may have close relationships with one another and may not wish to break these. Thus homogeneity of the sample's attributes may result.

Such snowball sampling may alter the research, for example changing random, stratified or proportionate sampling into convenience sampling, thereby compromising generalizability or generating the need to gain generalizability by synthesizing many case studies. Nevertheless, it often comes to a choice between accepting non-probability strategies or doing nothing.

The issues of access to people in order to conduct sensitive research may require researchers to demonstrate a great deal of ingenuity and forethought in their planning. Investigators have to be adroit in anticipating problems of access, and set up their studies in ways that circumvent such problems, preventing them from arising in the first place, e.g. by exploring their own institutions or personal situations, even if this compromises generalizability. Such anticipatory behaviour can lead to a glut of case studies, action research and accounts of their own institutions, as these are the only kinds of research possible, given the problem of access.

Gatekeepers

Access might be gained through gatekeepers, that is, those who control access. Lee (1993: 123) suggests that 'social access crucially depends on establishing *interpersonal trust*'. Gatekeepers play a significant role in research, particularly in ethnographic research (Miller and Bell, 2002: 53). They control access and re-access (Miller and Bell, 2002: 55). They may provide or block access; they may steer the course of a piece of research, 'shepherding the fieldworker in one direction or another' (Hammersley and Atkinson, 1983: 65), or exercise surveillance over the research.

Gatekeepers may wish to avoid, contain, spread or control risk and therefore may bar access or make access conditional. Making research conditional may require researchers to change the nature of their original plans in terms of methodology, sampling, focus, dissemination, reliability and validity, reporting and control of data (Morrison, 2006). Morrison (2006) found that in conducting sensitive educational research there were problems of:

- gaining access to schools and teachers;
- gaining permission to conduct the research (e.g. from school principals), resentment by principals;
- people vetting which data can be used;
- finding enough willing participants for the sample;
- schools/institutions/people not wishing to divulge information about themselves;
- schools/institutions not wishing to be identifiable, even with protections guaranteed;
- local political factors that impinge on the school/ educational institution;
- teachers'/participants' fear of being identified/traceable, even with protections guaranteed;
- fear of participation by teachers (e.g. if they say critical matters about the school or others they could lose their contracts);
- unwillingness of teachers to be involved because of their workload;
- the principal deciding whether to involve the staff, without consultation with the staff;
- schools' fear of criticism/loss of face or reputation;
- the sensitivity of the research – the issues being investigated;
- the power/position of the researcher (e.g. if the researcher is a junior or senior member of staff or an influential person in education).

Risk reduction may result in participants imposing conditions on research (e.g. on what information investigators may or may not use; to whom the data can be shown; what is 'public'; what is 'off the record' and what should be done with off-the-record remarks). It may also lead to surveillance/'chaperoning' of the researcher whilst the study is being conducted on site (Lee, 1993: 125).

Gatekeepers may want to 'inspect, modify or suppress the published products of the research' (Lee, 1993: 128). They may also wish to use the research for their own ends, i.e. their involvement may not be selfless or disinterested, or they may wish for something in return, e.g. for the researcher to include in the study an area of interest to the gatekeeper, or to report directly – and maybe exclusively – to the gatekeeper. The researcher has to negotiate a potential minefield here, for example, not to be seen as an informer for the headteacher. As Walford (2001: 45) writes: 'headteachers [may] suggest that researchers observe certain teachers whom they want information about'. Researchers may need to reassure participants that their data will not be given to the headteacher.

On the other hand Lee (1993: 127) suggests that the researcher may have to make a few concessions in order to be able to undertake the investigation, i.e. that it is better to do a little of the gatekeeper's bidding rather than not to be able to do the research at all.

In addition to gatekeepers the researcher may find a 'sponsor' in the group being studied. A sponsor may provide access, information and support. A celebrated example of this is in the figure of 'Doc' in Whyte's classic study of 'Street Corner Society' (1993: the original study published in 1943). Here Doc, a leading gang figure in the Chicago street corner society, is quoted as saying:

You tell me what you want me to see, and we'll arrange it. When you want some information, I'll ask for it, and you listen. When you want to find out their philosophy of life, I'll start an argument and get it for you.... You won't have any trouble. You come in as a friend.

(Whyte, 1993: 292)

As Whyte writes:

My relationship with Doc changed rapidly.... At first he was simply a key informant – and also my sponsor. As we spent more time together, I ceased to treat him as a passive informant. I discussed with him quite frankly what I was trying to do, what problems were puzzling me, and so on ... so that Doc became, in a real sense, a collaborator in the research.

(Whyte, 1993: 301)

Whyte comments on how Doc was able to give him advice on how best to behave when meeting people as part of the research:

Go easy on that 'who', 'what', 'why', 'when', 'where' stuff, Bill. You ask those questions and people will clam up on you. If people accept you, you can just hang around, and you'll learn the answers in the long run without even having to ask the questions.

(Whyte, 1993: 303)

BOX 9.1   ISSUES OF SAMPLING AND ACCESS IN SENSITIVE RESEARCH

- How to calculate the population and sample.
- How representative of the population the sample may or may not be.
- What kind of sample is desirable (e.g. random), but what kind may be the only sort that is practicable (e.g. snowball).
- How to use networks for reaching the sample, and what kinds of networks to utilize.
- How to research in a situation of threat to the participants (including the researcher).
- How to protect identities and threatened groups.
- How to contact the hard-to-reach.
- How to secure and sustain access.
- How to find and involve gatekeepers and sponsors.
- What to offer gatekeepers and sponsors.
- On what matters compromise may need to be negotiated.
- On what matters can there be no compromise.
- How to negotiate entry and sustained field relations.
- What services the researcher may provide.
- How to manage initial contacts with potential groups for study.

Indeed Doc played a role in the writing of the research: 'As I wrote, I showed the various parts to Doc and went over them in detail. His criticisms were invaluable in my revision' (p. 341). In his 1993 edition, Whyte reflects on the study with the question as to whether he exploited Doc (p. 362); it is a salutary reminder of the essential reciprocity that might be involved in conducting sensitive research.

In addressing issues of sampling and access, there are several points that arise from the discussion (Box 9.1).

Much research stands or falls on the sampling. These points reinforce our view that, rather than barring the research altogether, compromises may have to be reached in sampling and access. It may be better to compromise rather than to abandon the research altogether.

9.4 Ethical issues in sensitive research

A difficulty arises in sensitive research in that the researcher can be party to 'guilty knowledge' (De Laine, 2000) and have 'dirty hands' (Klockars, 1979) about deviant groups or members of a school who may be harbouring counter-attitudes to those prevailing in the school's declared mission. Pushed further, this means that the researcher will need to decide the limits of tolerance, beyond which he/she will not venture. For example, in Patrick's (1973) study of a Glasgow gang, the researcher is witness to a murder. Should he report the matter to the police and, thereby, 'blow his cover', or remain silent in order to keep contact with the gang, thereby breaking the law which requires a murder to be reported?

In interviewing students they may reveal sensitive matters about themselves, their family, their teachers, and the researcher will need to decide whether and how to act on this kind of information. What should the researcher do, for example, if, during the course of an interview with a teacher about the leadership of the headteacher, the interviewee indicates that the headteacher has had sexual relations with a parent, or has an alcohol problem? Does the researcher, in such cases, do nothing in order to gain research knowledge, or does s/he act? What is in the public interest – the protection of an individual participant's private life, or the interests of the researcher? Indeed Lee (1993: 139) suggests that some participants may even deliberately engineer situations whereby the researcher gains 'guilty knowledge' in order to test the researcher's affinities: 'trust tests'.

Ethical issues are thrown into sharp relief in sensitive educational research. The question of covert research rises to the fore, as the study of deviant or sensitive situations may require the researcher to go undercover in order to obtain data. Access is often a serious problem in educational and social research (Munro et al., 2004: 295), particularly if such access is controlled by powerful people (Morrison, 2006). Powerful gatekeepers who may control other aspects of the participants' lives (Munro et al., 2004: 302) such as promotion, in-service training, work allocations, and it may be necessary to consider covert research or deception. Covert research may overcome 'problems of reactivity' (Lee, 1993: 143) wherein the research influences the behaviour of the participants (Hammersley and Atkinson, 1983: 71). Deception, though questioned in codes of practice for educational research (see Chapter 5), is not ruled out in these same codes, and there may be cases where the violation of informed consent, or telling lies, or not disclosing that one is conducting research, may be considered to be justified in order to obtain data on honest, natural behaviours, views or practices. Let us be frank: if a researcher seeks the informed consent of violent teachers to study their violent behaviour, is there any real likelihood that the research will actually take place, whereas if one asks permission to study the behaviour of the students in their class, and keeps quiet about the real purpose which is to study violent teachers, is it more likely that access will be granted? And yet, surely, it is important in the interests of the students, the school, even the violent teacher themselves, that the problem be exposed and be evidence-based?

Covert research or deliberate deception may also enable the researcher to obtain insiders' true views, for, without the cover of those being researched not knowing that they are being studied, entry could easily be denied, and access to important areas of understanding could be lost. This is particularly so in the case of researching powerful people who may not wish to disclose information and who, therefore, may prevent or deny access. The ethical issue of informed consent, in this case, is violated in the interests of exposing matters that are in the public interest.

To the charge that this is akin to spying, Mitchell (1993: 46) makes it clear that there is a vast difference between covert research and spying:

- 'Spying is ideologically proactive, whereas research is ideologically naïve' (p. 46). Spies, he argues, seek to further a particular value system or ideology; research seeks to understand rather than to persuade.
- Spies have a sense of mission and try to achieve certain instrumental ends, whereas research has no such specific mission.

■ Spies believe that they are morally superior to their subjects, whereas researchers have no such feelings; indeed, with reflexivity being so important, they are sensitive to how their own role in the investigation may distort the research.

■ Spies are supported by institutions which train them to behave in certain ways of subterfuge, whereas researchers have no such training.

■ Spies are paid to do the work, whereas researchers often operate on a not-for-profit or individualistic basis.

On the other hand, not to gain informed consent could lead to participants feeling duped, very angry, used and exploited, when the results of the research are eventually published and they realize that they have been studied without their approval or informed consent.[2] The researcher is seen as a predator (Lee, 1993: 157), using the research 'as a vehicle for status, income or professional advancement which is denied to those studied'. As Lee remarks (p. 157), 'it is not unknown for residents in some ghetto areas of the United States to complain wryly that they have put dozens of students through graduate school'. Further, the researched may: have no easy right of reply; feel misrepresented by the research; feel that they have been denied a voice; have wished not to be identified and their situation put into the public arena; feel that they have been exploited.

The cloak of anonymity is often vital in sensitive research, such that respondents are entirely untraceable. This raises the issue of 'deductive disclosure' (Boruch and Cecil, 1979), wherein it is possible to identify individuals (people, schools, departments, etc.) in question by reconstructing and combining data. Researchers should guard against this possibility. Where the details that are presented could enable identification of a person (e.g. in a study of a school there may be only one male teacher aged 50 who teaches biology, such that putting a name is unnecessary, as he will be identifiable), it may be incumbent on the researcher not to disclose such details, so that readers, even if they wished to reassemble the details in order to identify the respondent, are unable to do so.

The researcher may wish to preserve confidentiality, but may also wish to be able to gather data from individuals on more than one occasion. In this case a 'linked file' system (Lee, 1993: 173) can be employed. Here three files are kept; in the first file the data are held and arbitrary numbers are assigned to each participant; the second file contains the list of respondents; the third file contains the list information necessary to be able to link the arbitrarily assigned numbers from the first file to the names of the respondents in the

second, and this third file is kept by a neutral 'broker', not the researcher. This procedure is akin to double-blind clinical experiments, in which the researcher does not know the names of those who are or are not receiving experimental medication or a placebo. That this may be easier in respect of quantitative rather than qualitative data is acknowledged by Lee (1993: 179).

Clearly, in some cases, it is impossible for individual people, schools and departments not to be identified (e.g. schools may be highly distinctive and, therefore, identifiable (Whitty and Edwards, 1994: 22)). In such cases clearance may need to be obtained for the disclosure of information. This is not as straightforward as it may seem. For example, a general principle of educational research is that no individuals should be harmed (non-maleficence), but what if a matter that is in the legitimate public interest (e.g. a school's failure to keep to proper accounting procedures) is brought to light? Should the researcher follow up the matter privately, publicly or not at all? If it is followed up then certainly harm may come to the school's officers.

Ethical issues in the conduct of research are thrown into sharp relief against a backdrop of personal, institutional and societal politics, and the boundaries between public and private spheres are not only relative but highly ambiguous. The ethical debate is heightened, for example concerning the potential tension between the individual's right to privacy versus the public's right to know and the concern not to damage or harm individuals versus the need to serve the public good. Because public and private spheres may merge, it is difficult, if not impossible, to resolve such tensions straightforwardly (cf. Day, 1985; Lee, 1993). As Walford (2001: 30) writes: 'the potential gain to public interest ... was great. There would be some intrusion into the private lives of those involved, but this could be justified in research on ... an important policy issue.' The end justified the means.

These issues are felt most sharply if the research risks revealing negative findings. To expose practices to research scrutiny may be like taking the plaster off an open wound (Wood, 1980). What responsibility to the research community does the researcher have? If a negative research report is released, will schools retrench, preventing future research in schools from being undertaken (a particular problem if the researcher wishes to return or wishes not to prevent further researchers from gaining access)? Whom is the researcher serving – the public, the schools, the research community? The sympathies of the researcher may be called into question here; politics and ethics may be uncomfortable bedfellows in such circumstances. Research data, such as the negative hidden curriculum of training for conformity in schools (Morrison, 2009) may not endear researchers to schools. This can risk stifling educational research – it is simply not worth the personal or public cost. As Simons (2000: 45) says: 'the price is too high'.

Further, Mitchell (1993: 54) writes that 'timorous social scientists may excuse themselves from the risk of confronting powerful, privileged, and cohesive groups that wish to obscure their actions and interests from public scrutiny' (see also Lee, 1993: 8). Researchers may not wish to take the risk of offending the powerful or of placing themselves in uncomfortable situations. As Simons and Usher (2000: 5) remark: 'politics and ethics are inextricably entwined'.

In private, students and teachers may criticize their own schools, for example in terms of management, leadership, work overload and stress, but they may be reluctant to do so in public, and, indeed, teachers who are on renewable contracts will not bite the hand that feeds them; they may say nothing rather than criticize (Burgess, 1993; Morrison, 2002b).

The field of ethics in sensitive research is different from ethics in everyday research in significance rather than range of focus. The same issues as must be faced in all educational research are addressed here, and we advise readers to review Chapter 5 on ethics. However, sensitive research highlights particular ethical issues very sharply; these are presented in Box 9.2.

These are only introductory issues. We refer the reader to Chapter 5 for further discussion of these and other ethical issues. The difficulty with ethical issues is that they are 'situated' (Simons and Usher, 2000), i.e. contingent on specific local circumstances and situations. They have to be negotiated and worked out in relation to the specifics of the situation; universal guidelines may help but they don't usually solve the practical problems; they have to be interpreted locally.

9.5 Researching powerful people

A branch of sensitive research concerns that which is conducted on, or with, powerful people, those in key positions, or elite institutions. In education, for example, this would include headteachers and senior teachers, politicians, senior civil servants, decision makers, local authority officers and school governors. This is particularly the case in respect of research on policy and leadership issues (Walford, 1994a: 3). Researching the powerful is an example of 'researching up' rather than the more conventional 'researching down' (e.g. researching children, teachers and student teachers).

What makes the research sensitive is that it is often dealing with key issues of policy generation and decision making, or issues about which there is high-profile debate and contestation, as issues of a politically sensitive nature. Policy-related research is sensitive. This can be also one of the reasons why access is frequently refused. The powerful are those who exert control to secure what they want or can achieve, those with great responsibility and whose decisions have significant effects on large numbers of people.

BOX 9.2 ETHICAL ISSUES IN SENSITIVE RESEARCH

- How does the researcher handle 'guilty knowledge' and 'dirty hands'?
- Whose side is the researcher on? Does this need to be disclosed? What if the researcher is not on the side of the researched?
- When are covert research or deception justified?
- When is the lack of informed consent justified?
- Is covert research spying?
- How should the researcher overcome the charge of exploiting the participants (i.e. treating them as objects instead of as subjects of research)?
- How should the researcher address confidentiality and anonymity?
- How should the balance be struck between the individual's right to privacy and the public's right to know?
- What is really in the public interest?
- How to handle the situation where it is unavoidable to identify participants?
- What responsibility does the researcher have to the research community, some of whom may wish to conduct further research in the field?
- How does the researcher handle frightened or threatened groups who may reveal little?
- What protections are in the research, for whom, and from what?
- What obligations does the researcher have?

Academic educational research on the powerful may be unlike other forms of educational research in that confidentiality may not be able to be assured. The participants are identifiable and public figures. This may produce 'problems of censorship and self-censorship' (Walford, 1994c: 229). It also means that information given in confidence and 'off the record' unfortunately may have to remain so. The issue raised in researching the powerful is the disclosure of identities, particularly if it is unclear what has been said 'on the record' and 'off the record' (Fitz and Halpin, 1994: 35–6).

Fitz and Halpin (1994) indicate that the government minister whom they interviewed stated, at the start of the interview, what was to be attributable. They also report that they used semi-structured interviews in their research of powerful people, valuing both the structure and the flexibility of this type of interview, and that they gained permission to record the interviews for later transcription, for the sake of a research record. They also used two interviewers for each session, one to conduct the main part of the interview and the other to take notes and ask supplementary questions; having two interviewers present also enabled a post-interview cross-check to be undertaken. Indeed having two questioners helped to negotiate the way through the interview in which advisers to the interviewee were also present (p. 38) to monitor the proceedings and interject where deemed fitting (p. 44), and to take notes (p. 47).

Fitz and Halpin (1994) comment on the considerable amount of gatekeeping that was present in researching the powerful (p. 40), in terms of access to people (with officers guarding entrances and administrators deciding whether interviews will take place), places ('elite settings'), timing (and scarcity of time with busy respondents), 'conventions that screen off the routines of policy-making from the public and the academic gaze' (p. 48), conditional access and conduct of the research ('boundary maintenance' (p. 49)), monitoring and availability. Gewirtz and Ozga (1994: 192–3) suggest that gatekeeping in researching the powerful can produce difficulties which include 'misrepresentation of the research intention, loss of researcher control, mediation of the research process, compromise and researcher dependence'.

Research with powerful people usually takes place on their territory, under their conditions and agendas (a 'distinctive civil service voice' (Fitz and Halpin, 1994: 42)), working within discourses set by the powerful (and, in part, reproduced by the researchers (p. 40)), and with protocols concerning what may or may not be disclosed (e.g. under a government's Official Secrets Act or privileged information), within a world which may be unfamiliar and, thereby, disconcerting for researchers and with participants who may be overly assertive, and sometimes rendering the researcher as having to pretend to know less than he or she actually knows. As Fitz and Halpin (1994: 40) commented: 'we glimpsed an unfamiliar world that was only ever partially revealed', and one in which they did not always feel comfortable. Similarly, Ball (1994b: 113) suggests that 'we need to recognize ... the interview as an extension of the "play of power" rather than separate from it, merely a commentary upon it', and that, when interviewing powerful people 'the interview is both an ethnographic ... and a political event'. As Walford (1994c: 225) remarks:

> Those in power are well used to their ideas being taken notice of. They are well able to deal with interviewers, to answer and avoid particular questions to suit their own ends, and to present their own role in events in a favourable light. They are aware of what academic research involves, and are familiar with being interviewed and having their words tape-recorded. In sum, their power in the educational world is echoed in the interview situation, and interviews pose little threat to their own positions.
>
> (Walford, 1994c: 225)

McHugh (1994) comments that access to powerful people may take place not only through formal channels but through intermediaries who introduce researchers to them (p. 55). Here his own vocation as a priest helped him to gain access to powerful Christian policy makers and, as he was advised, 'if you say whom you have met, they'll know you are not a way-out person who will distort what they say' (p. 56). Access is a significant concern in researching the powerful, particularly if the issues being researched are controversial or contested. Walford (1994c: 222) suggests that it can be eased through informal and personal 'behind the scenes' contacts: 'the more sponsorship that can be obtained, the better' (p. 223), be it institutional or personal. Access can be eased if the research is seen to be 'harmless' (p. 223); in this respect Walford reports that female researchers may be at an advantage in that they are viewed as more harmless and non-threatening. Walford also makes the point that 'persistence pays' (p. 224); as he writes elsewhere (Walford, 2001: 31), 'access is a process and not a once-only decision'.

McHugh (1994) also reports the need for meticulous preparation for an interview with the powerful person, to understand the full picture and to be as fully informed as the interviewee, in terms of facts, information and terminology, so that it is an exchange between the informed rather than an airing of ignorance, i.e. to do one's homework. He also states the need for the interview questions to be thoroughly planned and prepared, with very careful framing of questions. McHugh suggests (p. 60) that during the interview it is important for the interviewer to be as flexible as possible, to follow the train of thought of the respondent, but also to be persistent (p. 62) if the interviewee does not address the issue. However, he reminds us that 'an interview is of course not a courtroom' (p. 62) and so tact, diplomacy and – importantly – empathy, are essential. Diplomacy in great measure is necessary when tackling powerful people about issues that might reveal their failure or incompetence, and powerful people may wish to exercise control over which questions they answer. Preparation for the conduct as well as the content of the interview is vital.

There are difficulties in reporting sensitive research with the powerful, as charges of bias may be difficult to avoid, not least because research reports and publications are placed in the pubic domain. Walford (2001: 141) indicates the risk of libel actions if public figures are named. He asks (1994b: 84) 'to what extent is it right to allow others to believe that you agree with them?' even if you do not? Should the researcher's own political, ideological or religious views be declared? As Mickelson (1994: 147) states: 'I was not completely candid when I interviewed these powerful people. I am far more genuine and candid when I am interviewing non-powerful people.' Deem (1994: 156) reports that she and her co-researcher encountered 'resistance and access problems in relation to our assumed ideological opposition to Conservative government education

reforms', where access might be blocked 'on the grounds that ours was not a neutral study'.

Mickelson (1994: 147) takes this further in identifying an ethical dilemma when 'at times, the powerful have uttered abhorrent comments in the course of the interview'. Should the researcher say nothing, thereby tacitly condoning the speaker's comments, or speak out, thereby risking closing the interview? She contends that, in retrospect, she wished that she had challenged these views, and had been more assertive (p. 148). Walford (2001: 137) reports the example of an interview with a church minister whose views included ones with which he disagreed: 'AIDS is basically a homosexual disease … and is doing a very effective job of ridding the population of undesirables. In Africa it's basically a non-existent disease in many places.… If you're a woolly woofter, you get what you deserve.… I would never employ a homosexual to teach at my school.'

In researching powerful people Mickelson (1994: 132) observes that they are rarely women, yet researchers are often women. This gender divide might prove problematic. Deem (1994: 157) reports that, as a woman, she encountered greater difficulty in conducting research than did her male colleague, even though, in fact, she held a more senior position than him. On the other hand she reports that males tended to be more open with female than male researchers, as female researchers were regarded as less important. Gewirtz and Ozga (1994: 196) report that 'we felt [as researchers] that we were viewed as women in very stereotypical ways, which included being seen as receptive and supportive, and

---

BOX 9.3   RESEARCHING POWERFUL PEOPLE

- What renders the research sensitive?
- How to gain and sustain access to powerful people.
- How much are the participants likely to disclose or withhold?
- What is on and off the record?
- How to prepare for interviews with powerful people.
- How to probe and challenge powerful people.
- How, and whether to gain informed consent.
- Is the research overt or covert, with or without deceit?
- How to conduct interviews that balance the interviewer's agenda and the interviewee's agenda and frame of reference.
- How to reveal the researcher's own knowledge, preparation and understanding of the key issues.
- The status of the researcher vis-à-vis the participants.
- Who should conduct interviews with powerful people?
- How neutral and accepting the researcher should be with the participant.
- Whether to identify the participants in the reporting.
- How to balance the public's right to know and the individual's right to privacy.
- What is in the public interest?

that we were obliged to collude, to a degree, with that version of ourselves because it was productive of the project'.

In approaching researching powerful people, then, it is wise to consider several issues. These are set out in Box 9.3.

9.6 Researching powerless and vulnerable people

Researching powerless people is also a highly sensitive matter, not least, as Munro *et al.* (2004: 299) point out, it is important not to add to their powerlessness. Similarly for vulnerable people – those who are unable to protect their own interests and who may suffer from negative labelling, stigmatization, exclusion or discrimination. The great claim of participatory research is that it empowers otherwise powerless groups (Healy, 2001; see also Chapter 2). Powerless people are easily negatively stereotyped and stigmatized (Fiske, 1993; Munro *et al.*, 2004): the poor, the unemployed, the homeless, travellers, the disabled, the psychologically disturbed, AIDS patients, people with learning difficulties, minority groups such as non-heterosexuals, females (Skelton *et al.*, 2006), etc.

In conducting research it is important not to add to the disempowerment of already disempowered groups, but it is also important actively to promote their empowerment or to leave then untouched and in the condition in which contact was first made (Munro *et al.*, 2004: 299).

What does the researcher do, for example, if she finds that women are 'talking down' their own achievements, lives, capabilities or career prospects, such that they will not achieve? If she simply notes this and reports it then she could be seen as complicit in the oppression of women; if she decides not to report it then she could be seen as distorting the research; if she decides to challenge it with the women in question then she could be seen as coming out of the role of the neutral researcher and invading the research site, or, indeed to be raising expectations that are not realistic.

Powerless groups may well feel resentful of the well-dressed researcher (Munro *et al.*, 2004), even if the researcher's intentions are honourable, or they may feel unable to disclose their true feelings and opinions for fear of bringing yet further negativity to their own situation. They may feel antagonized if interviews are conducted in well-kept surroundings which are very different from their own. Indeed for many, an interview may be the first occasion in their lives that they have experienced such an activity.

Children may well feel powerless and insecure in the presence of a researcher (Greig and Taylor, 1999)

and may say what they feel the researcher wishes to hear, what is the school's view, what is socially desirable (p. 131). They may be too shy or embarrassed to reveal their true feelings or to say what really happened in a situation (e.g. child abuse). The researcher must be acutely sensitive to this, and must recognize her/his own limitations in conducting such research on sensitive matters with vulnerable participants, if necessary handing over such interviews (and, for example, handling projection or displacement techniques) to trained professionals. The setting for such interviews should be familiar to the children, non-threatening and designed to put them at their ease.

Hart (1992) sets out a 'ladder of participation' in research with children. At the bottom of the ladder is 'manipulation', in which children do what the adults say, without necessarily understanding why. The rungs of the ladder move up from 'decoration' to 'tokenism', to 'assigned but not informed', to 'consultation and information', to 'child initiated: shared decisions with adults', and, at the top of the ladder, 'child initiated and directed'. The researcher should locate her/his research more to the upper rungs of the ladder in order to be inclusive.

Whilst this may be seen as an argument supporting covert research, it need not be: researchers can conduct honest, sympathetic research on the participants' home ground (as did researchers examining poverty in Hong Kong, who conducted structured interviews in the participants' own homes (Sequeira *et al.*, 1996)). Care must be taken by researchers to avoid sounding condescending, patronizing, powerful, domineering or high-handed. This is a matter of non-verbal behaviour, dress and, significantly, choice of language, such that it becomes inclusive rather than exclusive yet without being contrived or artificial. As mentioned in Chapter 5, data are gifts, not entitlements. The researcher has to conduct the research with respect, affording dignity to the participants, whilst not necessarily making promises (e.g. to change their situation) which cannot be kept.

The researcher studying powerless and vulnerable groups has an obligation to be inclusive (i.e. to enable all members of the group in question to participate and on an equal footing, and to feel valued), and to abide by the ethical principles outlined in Chapter 5 (e.g. informed consent, privacy and confidentiality, recognition of participants' time and efforts, consultation, keeping participants informed, maintaining and concluding relationships, addressing the well-being of participants, indicating any possible adverse effects of participation, ensuring the safety and well-being of researchers) (Connolly, 2003). In many senses, powerless participants might feel 'used' in educational research, not only providing data but advancing the careers of the researchers whilst leaving themselves disempowered. The researcher must avoid this.

Box 9.4 summarizes some key issues in researching powerless and vulnerable people.

It can be seen that very many of the issues that were raised in considering researching powerful groups are identical to those raised in researching powerless and vulnerable groups (Boxes 9.3 and 9.4). This is deliberate, as both concern ethical, sensitive behaviour and, though perhaps interpreted differently for the two groups, they apply equally powerfully to both.

The Joseph Rowntree Foundation (www.jrf.org.uk/search/site/Ethics) publishes ethical guidelines for researchers working with vulnerable, marginalized groups, powerless people and children.

9.7 Asking questions

Even though an anonymized questionnaire may give participants the freedom to respond in private, in depth and with honesty, and even though a face-to-face interview may be very threatening in connection with some sensitive issues, such that honest or complete answers may be unlikely, as a general rule, the more sensitive is the research, the more important it is to conduct face-to-

face interviews for data collection. In asking questions in research, Sudman and Bradburn (1982: 50–1) suggest that open questions may be preferable to closed questions and long questions may be preferable to short questions. Both of these enable respondents to answer in their own words, which might be more suitable for sensitive topics. Indeed they suggest that whilst short questions may be useful for gathering information about attitudes, longer questions are more suitable for asking questions about behaviour, and can include examples to which respondents may wish to respond. Longer questions may reduce the under-reporting of the frequency of behaviour addressed in sensitive topics (for example, the use of alcohol or medication by stressed teachers). On the other hand, the researcher has to be cautious to avoid tiring, emotionally exhausting or stressing the participant by a long questionnaire or interview.

Lee (1993: 78) advocates using familiar words in questions as these can reduce a sense of threat in addressing sensitive matters and help the respondent to feel more relaxed. He also suggests the use of 'vignettes' (p. 79) – 'short descriptions of a person or a social situation which contain precise references to what are thought to be the most important factors in the decision-making or judgement making processes of respondents' (Lee, 1993: 79). These can not only encapsulate concretely the issues

---

BOX 9.4 RESEARCHING POWERLESS AND VULNERABLE GROUPS

- What renders the research sensitive?
- How to gain and sustain access to powerless and vulnerable people.
- How much are the participants likely to disclose or withhold?
- What is on and off the record?
- How to prepare for interviews with powerless and vulnerable people.
- Where will the interviews/data collection take place?
- How to probe powerless and vulnerable people.
- How to ensure non-maleficence and beneficence, dignity and respect.
- How to avoid further stigmatization, negative stereotyping, and marginalization of participants.
- How to act in the interests of the participants.
- How, and whether, to gain informed consent.
- Is the research overt or covert, with or without deceit?
- How to conduct interviews that balance the interviewer's agenda and the interviewee's agenda and frame of reference.
- How to reveal the researcher's own knowledge, preparation and understanding of the key issues.
- How to equalize status between the researcher and the participants.
- How to ensure inclusiveness of participants.
- Who should conduct interviews with powerless and vulnerable people?
- Does the researcher have the expertise to conduct interviews with the participants?
- What protections are there for the participants?
- Whether to identify the participants in the reporting.
- How to balance the public's right to know and the individual's right to privacy.
- What is in the public interest?

under study, but can also deflect attention away from personal sensitivities by projecting them onto another external object – the case or vignette – and the respondent can be asked to react to them personally, e.g. 'what would you do in this situation?'.

Researchers investigating sensitive topics have to be acutely percipient of the situation themselves. For example, their non-verbal communication may be critical in interviews. They must, therefore, give no hint of judgement, support or condemnation. They must avoid countertransference (projecting the researchers' own views, values, attitudes, biases, background onto the situation). Interviewer effects are discussed in Chapter 21 in connection with sensitive research; these effects concern:

- The characteristics of the researcher (e.g. sex, race, age, status, clothing, appearance, rapport, background, expertise, institutional affiliation, political affiliation, type of employment or vocation, e.g. a priest). Females may feel more comfortable being interviewed by a female; males may feel uncomfortable being interviewed by a female; powerful people may feel insulted by being interviewed by a lowly, novice research assistant.
- The expectations that the interviewers may have of the interview (Lee, 1993: 99). For example, a researcher may feel apprehensive about, or uncomfortable with, an interview about a sensitive matter. Bradburn and Sudman (1979, in Lee, 1993: 101) report that interviewers who did not anticipate difficulties in the interview achieved a 5–30 per cent higher level of reporting on sensitive topics than those who anticipated difficulties. This suggests the need for interviewer training.

Lee (1993: 102–14) suggests several issues to be addressed in conducting sensitive interviews:

- How to approach the topic (in order to prevent participants' inhibitions and to help them address the issue in their preferred way). Here the advice is to let the topic 'emerge gradually over the course of the interview' (p. 103) and to establish trust and informed consent.
- How to deal with contradictions, complexities and emotions (which may require training and supervision of interviewers); how to adopt an accepting and non-judgemental stance, how to handle respondents who may not be people whom interviewers particularly like or with whom they agree.
- How to handle the operation of power and control in the interview: (a) where differences of power and status operate: where the interviewer has greater or

lesser status than the respondent and where there is equal status between the interviewer and the respondent; (b) how to handle the situation where the interviewer wants information but is in no position to command that this be given and where the respondent may or may not wish to disclose information; (c) how to handle a situation wherein powerful people use the interview as an opportunity for lengthy and perhaps irrelevant self-indulgence; (d) how to handle the situation in which the interviewer, by the end of the session, has information that is sensitive and could give the interviewer power over the respondent and make the respondent feel vulnerable; (e) what the interviewer should do with information that may act against the interests of the people who gave it (e.g. if some groups in society say that they are not clever enough to handle higher or further education); and (f) how to handle the conduct of the interview (e.g. conversational, formal, highly structured, highly directed).

- Handling the conditions under which the exchange takes place, Lee (1993: 112) suggests that interviews on sensitive matters should 'have a one-off character', i.e. the respondent should feel that the interviewer and the interviewee may never meet again. This, can secure trust, and can lead to greater disclosure than in a situation where a closer relationship between interviewer and interviewee exists. On the other hand this does not support the development of a collaborative research relationship (Lee, 1993: 113).

Much educational research is more or less sensitive; it is for the researcher to decide how to approach the issue of sensitivities and how to address their many forms, allegiances, ethics, access, politics and consequences.

9.8 Conclusion

In approaching educational research, our advice is to consider it to be far from a neat, clean, tidy, unproblematic and neutral process, but to regard it as shot through with actual and potential sensitivities. With this in mind we have resisted the temptation to provide a list of sensitive topics, as this could be simplistic and overlook the fundamental issue which is that it is the *social context* of the research that makes the research sensitive. What may appear to the researcher to be a bland and neutral study can raise deep sensitivities in the minds of the participants. We have argued that it is *these* that often render the research sensitive rather than the selection of topics of focus. Researchers have to consider the likely or possible effects of the research project, conduct, outcomes, reporting and dissemination not only on themselves but on the participants, on those connected to the participants and on those affected by, or with a stakeholder interest in the research (i.e. to consider 'consequential validity': the effects of the research). This suggests that it is wise to be cautious and to regard all educational research as potentially sensitive. There are several questions that can be asked by researchers, in their planning, conduct, reporting and dissemination of their studies, and we present these in Box 9.5.

These questions reinforce the importance of regarding ethics as 'situated' (Simons and Usher, 2000), i.e.

contingent on particular situations rather than largely on ethical codes and guidelines. In this respect sensitive educational research is like any other research, but sharper in the criticality of ethical issues. Also, behind many of these questions of sensitivity lurks the nagging issue of power: who has it, who does not, how it circulates around research situations (and with what consequences), and how it should be addressed. Sensitive educational research is often as much a power play as it is substantive. We advise researchers to regard most educational research as involving sensitivities; these need to be identified and addressed.

BOX 9.5   KEY QUESTIONS IN CONSIDERING SENSITIVE EDUCATIONAL RESEARCH

- What renders the research sensitive?
- What are the obligations of the researcher, to whom, and how will these be addressed? How do these obligations manifest themselves?
- What is the likely effect of this research (at all stages) to be on participants (individuals and groups), stakeholders, the researcher, the community? Who will be affected by the research, and how?
- Who is being discussed and addressed in the research?
- What rights of reply and control do participants have in the research?
- What are the ethical issues that are rendered more acute in the research?
- Over what matters in the planning, focus, conduct, sampling, instrumentation, methodology, reliability, analysis, reporting and dissemination might the researcher have to compromise in order to effect the research? On what can there be compromise? On what can there be no compromise?
- What securities, protections (and from what), liabilities and indemnifications are there in the research, and for whom? How can these be addressed?
- Who is the research for? Who are the beneficiaries of the research? Who are the winners and losers in the research (and about what issues)?
- What are the risks and benefits of the research, and for whom? What will the research 'deliver' and do?
- Should the researcher declare his/her own values, and challenge those with which he/she disagrees or considers to be abhorrent?
- What might be the consequences, repercussions and backlash from the research, and for whom?
- What sanctions might there be in connection with the research?
- What has to be secured in a contractual agreement, and what is deliberately left out?
- What guarantees must and should the researcher give to the participants?
- What procedures for monitoring and accountability must there be in the research?
- What must and must not, should and should not, may or may not, could or could not be disclosed in the research?
- Should the research be covert, overt, partially overt, partially covert, honest in its disclosure of intentions?
- Should participants be identifiable and identified? What if identification is unavoidable?
- How will access and sampling be secured and secure respectively?
- How will access be sustained over time?
- Who are the gatekeepers and how reliable are they?

 Companion Website

The companion website to the book includes PowerPoint slides for this chapter, which list the structure of the chapter and then provide a summary of the key points in each of its sections. This resource can be found online at **www.routledge.com/textbooks/cohen7e**.

Validity and reliability

CHAPTER 10

This chapter discusses validity and reliability in quantitative, qualitative, naturalistic and mixed methods research. It suggests that both of these terms can be applied to these different types of research, though how validity and reliability are addressed in different approaches varies. The chapter indicates how validity and reliability are addressed, using different instruments for data collection. The chapter proceeds in several stages:

- defining validity
- validity in quantitative and qualitative research
- types of validity
- triangulation
- validity in mixed methods research
- ensuring validity
- reliability
- reliability in quantitative and qualitative research
- validity and reliability in interviews, experiments, questionnaires, observations, tests and life histories

There are many different types of validity and reliability. Threats to validity and reliability can never be erased completely; rather the effects of these threats can be attenuated by attention to validity and reliability throughout a piece of research.

It is suggested that reliability is a necessary but insufficient condition for validity in research; reliability is a necessary precondition of validity, and validity may be a sufficient but not necessary condition for reliability. Brock-Utne (1996: 612) contends that the widely held view that reliability is the sole preserve of quantitative research has to be exploded, and this chapter demonstrates the significance of her view.

10.1 Defining validity

Validity is an important key to effective research. If a piece of research is invalid then it is worthless. Validity is thus a requirement for both quantitative and qualitative/naturalistic research.

Whilst earlier versions of validity were based on the view that it was essentially a demonstration that a particular instrument in fact measures what it purports to measure, or that an account accurately represents 'those features that it is intended to describe, explain or theorise' (Winter, 2000: 1), more recently validity has taken many forms. For example, in qualitative data validity might be addressed through the honesty, depth, richness and scope of the data achieved, the participants approached, the extent of triangulation and the disinterestedness or objectivity of the researcher (Winter, 2000). In quantitative data validity might be improved through careful sampling, appropriate instrumentation and appropriate statistical treatments of the data. It is impossible for research to be 100 per cent valid; that is the optimism of perfection. Quantitative research possesses a measure of standard error which is inbuilt and which has to be acknowledged. In qualitative data the subjectivity of respondents, their opinions, attitudes and perspectives together contribute to a degree of bias. Validity, then, should be seen as a matter of degree rather than as an absolute state (Gronlund, 1981). Hence at best we strive to minimize invalidity and maximize validity.

There are several different kinds of validity, e.g.

- catalytic validity
- concurrent validity
- consequential validity
- construct validity
- content validity
- criterion-related validity
- convergent and discriminant validity
- cross-cultural validity
- cultural validity
- descriptive validity
- ecological validity
- evaluative validity
- external validity
- face validity
- internal validity
- interpretive validity
- jury validity
- predictive validity
- systemic validity
- theoretical validity.

It is not our intention in this chapter to discuss all these terms in depth. Rather the main types of validity will be addressed. The argument will be made that, whilst some of these terms are more comfortably the preserve of quantitative methodologies, this is not exclusively the case. Indeed, validity is the touchstone of all types of educational research. That said, it is important that validity in different research traditions is faithful to those traditions; it would be absurd to declare a piece of research invalid if it were not striving to meet certain kinds of validity, e.g. generalizability, replicability, controllability. Hence the researcher will need to locate discussions of validity within the research paradigm that is being used. This is not to suggest, however, that research should be paradigm-bound, that is a recipe for stagnation and conservatism. Validity and reliability have different meanings in quantitative and qualitative research, and it is important not only to indicate these clearly, but for the researcher to demonstrate fidelity to the approach in which she or he is working and to abide by the principles of validity and reliability they require. We address this in the chapter here, locating different interpretations of validity and reliability within the different paradigms. Hammersley (1992a: 39) argues that there are only two paradigms – quantitative and qualitative – and that these are more or less mutually exclusive. However, one of the purposes of the opening three chapters of this book was to indicate the multiplicity of paradigms. Our reference to quantitative and qualitative paradigms here is for simple, heuristic purposes.

10.2 Validity in quantitative research

In much quantitative research, validity must be faithful to its premises of positivism and positivist principles, e.g.

- controllability
- replicability
- predictability
- the derivation of laws and universal statements of behaviour (i.e. generalizability)
- context-freedom
- fragmentation and atomization of research
- randomization of samples
- neutrality/objectivity
- observability.

It must also ensure that the types of validity discussed below are satisfactorily addressed. In many cases this involves being faithful to the assumptions underpinning the statistics used, the construct and content validity of

the measures used, the careful sampling, and the avoidance of a range of threats to internal and external validity outlined later in this chapter.

10.3 Validity in qualitative research

Much qualitative research abides by principles of validity that are very different from those of positivism and quantitative methods. Validity in qualitative research has several principles (Lincoln and Guba, 1985; Bogdan and Biklen, 1992):

- the natural setting is the principal source of data;
- context-boundedness and 'thick description';
- data are socially situated, and socially and culturally saturated;
- the researcher is part of the researched world;
- as we live in an already interpreted world, a doubly hermeneutic exercise (Giddens, 1979) is necessary to understand others' understandings of the world; the paradox here is that the most sufficiently complex instrument to understand human life is another human (Lave and Kvale, 1995: 220), but that this risks human error in all its forms;
- holism in the research;
- the researcher – rather than a research tool – is the key instrument of research;
- the data are descriptive;
- there is a concern for processes rather than simply with outcomes;
- data are analysed inductively rather than using a priori categories;
- data are presented in terms of the respondents rather than researchers;
- seeing and reporting the situation through the eyes of participants – from the native's point of view (Geertz, 1974);
- respondent validation is important;
- catching meaning and intention are essential.

Indeed Maxwell (1992) argues that qualitative researchers need to be cautious not to be working within the agenda of the positivists in arguing for the need for research to demonstrate concurrent, predictive, convergent, criterion-related, internal and external validity. The discussion below indicates that this need not be so. He argues, with Guba and Lincoln (1989), for the need to replace positivist notions of validity in qualitative research with the notion of authenticity. Maxwell, echoing Mishler (1990), suggests that 'understanding' is a more suitable term than 'validity' in qualitative research. We, as researchers, are part of the world that we are researching, and we cannot be completely objective about that, hence other people's perspectives are equally as valid as our own, and the task of research is to uncover these. Validity, then, attaches to accounts, not to data or methods (Hammersley and Atkinson, 1983); it is the meaning that subjects give to data and inferences drawn from the data that are important. 'Fidelity' (Blumenfeld-Jones, 1995) requires the researcher to be as honest as possible to the self-reporting of the researched.

The claim is made (Agar, 1993) that in qualitative data collection the intensive personal involvement and in-depth responses of individuals secure a sufficient level of validity and reliability. This claim is contested by Hammersley (1992b: 144) and Silverman (1993: 153), who argue that these are insufficient grounds for validity and reliability, and that the individuals concerned have no privileged position on interpretation. (Of course, neither are actors 'cultural dopes' who need a sociologist or researcher to tell them what is 'really' happening!) Silverman argues that, whilst immediacy and authenticity make for interesting journalism, ethnography must have more rigorous notions of validity and reliability. This involves moving beyond selecting data simply to fit a preconceived or ideal conception of the phenomenon or because they are spectacularly interesting (Fielding and Fielding, 1986). Data selected must be representative of the sample, the whole data set, the field, i.e. they must address content, construct and concurrent validity.

Hammersley (1992a: 50–1) suggests that validity in qualitative research replaces certainty with confidence in our results, and that, as reality is independent of the claims made for it by researchers, our accounts will only be representations of that reality rather than reproductions of it. Lincoln and Guba (1985) suggest that key criteria of validity in qualitative research are: (a) credibility (replacing the quantitative concepts of internal validity); (b) transferability (replacing the quantitative concept of external validity); (c) dependability (replacing the quantitative concept of reliability); and (d) confirmability (replacing the quantitative concept of objectivity).

Lincoln and Guba (1985) argue that, within these criteria of validity, rigour can be achieved by careful audit trails of evidence, member checking/respondent validation (confirmation by participants) when coding or categorizing results, peer debriefing, negative case analysis, 'structural corroboration' (triangulation, discussed below) and 'referential material adequacy' (adequate reference to standard materials in the field). Trustworthiness, they suggest, can be addressed in the credibility, fittingness, auditability and confirmability of the data (see also Morse *et al.*, 2002).

Whereas quantitative data, particularly in the positivist tradition, place great store by both external validity and internal validity, the emphasis in much qualitative research is on internal validity, and, in many cases, external validity is an irrelevance for qualitative research (Winter, 2000: 8) – it does not seek to generalize but only to represent the phenomenon being investigated, fairly and fully. (Of course, some qualitative research, e.g. Miles and Huberman (1994) does move towards generalizability, and, indeed, Chapter 1 indicated that qualitative data could be 'quantitized'. It is possible, but the overwhelming feature of qualitative research is its concern with the phenomenon or situation in question, and not generalizability.) Hence issues such as random sampling, replicability, alpha coefficients of reliability, isolation and control of variables, and predictability simply do not matter in much qualitative research.

Maxwell (1992) argues for five kinds of validity in qualitative methods that explore his notion of 'understanding':

- *descriptive validity* (the factual accuracy of the account, that it is not made up, selective, or distorted (cf. Winter, 2000: 4)); in this respect validity subsumes reliability; it is akin to Blumenfeld-Jones's (1995) notion of 'truth' in research – what actually happened (objectively factual) and to Glaser and Strauss's (1967) term 'credibility';
- *interpretive validity* (the ability of the research to catch the meaning, interpretations, terms, intentions that situations and events, i.e. data, have for the participants/ subjects themselves, in their terms); it is akin to Blumenfeld-Jones's (1995) notion of 'fidelity' – what it means to the researched person or group (subjectively meaningful); interpretive validity has no clear counterpart in experimental/positivist methodologies;
- *theoretical validity* (the theoretical constructions that the researcher brings to the research (including those of the researched)); theory here is regarded as explanation. Theoretical validity is the extent to which the research explains phenomena; in this respect is it akin to construct validity (discussed below); in theoretical validity the constructs are those of all the participants;
- *generalizability* (the view that the theory generated may be useful in understanding other similar situations); generalizing here refers to generalizing *within* specific groups or communities, situations or circumstances (internal validity) and, beyond, to specific *outsider* communities, situations or circumstance (external validity); internal validity has greater significance here than external validity;

■ *evaluative validity* (the application of an evaluative, judgmental stance towards that which is being researched, rather than a descriptive, explanatory or interpretive framework). Clearly this resonates with critical-theoretical perspectives, in that the researcher's own evaluative agenda might intrude.

To this one can add Auerbach and Silverstein's (2003) category of *transparency*, i.e. how far the reader can understand, and is informed of, the processes by which the interpretation made is actually reached.

Validity in qualitative research depends on the purposes of the participants, the actors, and the appropriateness of the data collection methods used to catch those purposes (Winter, 2000: 7).

Differences in the meanings and criteria for validity in quantitative and qualitative are summarized in Table 10.1. Clearly the criteria are not the exclusive preserve of each of the two main types of research here (quantitative and qualitative). The intention of Table 10.1 is heuristic and to indicate emphases only.

Onwuegbuzie and Leech (2006b 239–46) set out many steps that researchers can take in order to ensure validity in qualitative research (several of which derive from Lincoln and Guba, 1985; see also Teddlie and Tashakkori, 2009: 295–7). These include:

■ prolonged engagement in the field (to gather rich and sufficient data);
■ persistent observation (to identify key relevant

issues and to separate these from comparative irrelevancies);
■ triangulation (discussed later in this chapter);
■ leaving an audit trail (documentation and records used in the study that include: raw data; records of analysis and data reduction; reconstructions and syntheses of data; 'process notes' (on how the research and analysis are proceeding); notes on 'intentions and dispositions' of the researcher as the study proceeds; information concerning the development of instruments for data collection);
■ member checking/informant feedback (respondent validation, discussed below);
■ weighting the evidence (ensuring that correct attention is paid to higher quality data (e.g. those data gathered from long engagement, detailed study and trusted participants) and less attention is paid to low quality data);
■ checking for representativeness (ensuring that unsupported generalizability of the findings is avoided);
■ checking for researcher effects/clarifying researcher bias (how far the personal biases, assumptions or values of the researcher, or how far the researcher's personal characteristics (e.g. clothing, appearance, sex, age, ethnicity) affect the research);
■ making contrast/comparisons (e.g. between subgroups, sites, literature);
■ theoretical sampling (following the data and where they lead, rather than leading the data, and ensuring

TABLE 10.1   COMPARING VALIDITY IN QUANTITATIVE AND QUALITATIVE RESEARCH

Bases of validity in quantitative research		Bases of validity in qualitative research
Controllability	⟷	Natural
Isolation, control and manipulation of required variables	⟷	Thick description and high detail on required or important aspects
Replicability	⟷	Uniqueness
Predictability	⟷	Emergence, unpredictability
Generalizability	⟷	Uniqueness
Context-freedom	⟷	Context-boundedness
Fragmentation and atomization of research	⟷	Holism
Randomization of samples	⟷	Purposive sample/no sampling
Neutrality	⟷	Value-ladenness of observations/double hermeneutic
Objectivity	⟷	Confirmability
Observability	⟷	Observability and non-observable meanings and intentions
Inference	⟷	Description, inference and explanation
'Etic' research	⟷	'Emic' research
Internal validity	⟷	Credibility
External validity	⟷	Transferability
Reliability	⟷	Dependability
Observations	⟷	Meanings

that the research addresses all the required aspects of the theory);

- checking the meaning of outliers (rather than ignoring outliers and exceptions, researchers should examine to see what leverage into an understanding of the phenomenon in question is provided by outliers);
- using extreme cases (e.g. to identify what is missing in the majority of cases);
- ruling out spurious relations (avoiding attributing causality or association where none exists);
- replicating a finding (identifying how far the findings might apply to other groups);
- referential adequacy (how well referenced are the findings to benchmark or significant literature);
- following up surprises (avoiding/ignoring surprise results);
- structural relationships (looking for consistency between the findings – with each other and with literature);
- peer debriefing (external evaluation of the research, its conduct and findings);
- rich and thick description (providing detail to support and corroborate findings);
- the modus operandi approach (specifically looking for possible sources of invalidity in the research);
- assessing rival explanations (looking for alternative interpretations and explanations of the data);
- negative case analysis (examining disconfirming cases to see if the hypotheses or findings need to be amended in light of them);
- confirmatory data analysis (conducting qualitative replication studies where possible);
- effect sizes (avoiding simply 'binarizing' matters (e.g. strong/weak; present/absent; positive/negative) and replacing these with indications of size/power or strength of the findings).

This comprehensive list of ways of striving to ensure validity in qualitative research has similarities in some places with those of quantitative research (e.g. replication, researcher bias, external evaluation, representativeness, suitable generalizability, theoretical sampling triangulation, transparency, etc.). This suggests that whilst there may be different canons of validity between quantitative and qualitative research, and whilst there may be different interpretations of the meaning of 'validity' in different kinds of research, nevertheless there is some common ground between them; they are not mutually exclusive.

In the following sections, which describe types of validity, where it is useful to separate the interpretations of that form of validity in quantitative and quali-

tative research, this has been done. In some cases (e.g. catalytic, consequential validity), as the issues remain the same regardless of the types of research, this separation has not been done. The scene is set by considerations of internal and external validity, and then the remaining types of validity are considered in alphabetical order of the titles of each type.

10.4 Types of validity

Internal validity

Both qualitative and quantitative methods can address internal and external validity. Internal validity seeks to demonstrate that the explanation of a particular event, issue or set of data which a piece of research provides can actually be sustained by the data. In some degree this concerns accuracy, which can be applied to quantitative and qualitative research. The findings must describe accurately the phenomena being researched. Onwuegbuzie and Leech (2006b: 234) define internal validity as the 'truth value, applicability, consistency, neutrality, dependability, and/or credibility of interpretations and conclusions within the underlying setting or group'.

Internal validity in quantitative research
The following summaries adapted from Campbell and Stanley (1963), Bracht and Glass (1968) and Lewis-Beck (1993) distinguish between 'internal validity' and 'external validity'. Internal validity is concerned with the question, do the experimental treatments, in fact, make a difference in the specific experiments under scrutiny? External validity, on the other hand, asks the question, given these demonstrable effects, to what populations or settings can they be generalized?

There are several kinds of threat to internal validity in quantitative research, for example (many of these apply strongly, though not exclusively, to experimental research):

- *History* Frequently in educational research, events other than the intervention treatments occur during the time between pre-test and post-test observations (e.g. in a longitudinal survey, experiment, action research). Such events produce effects that can mistakenly be attributed to differences in treatment.
- *Maturation* Between any two observations subjects change in a variety of ways. Such changes can produce differences that are independent of the research. The problem of maturation is more acute in protracted educational studies than in brief laboratory experiments.
- *Statistical regression* Like maturation effects, regression effects increase systematically with the

time interval between pre-tests and post-tests (e.g. in action research, experiments or longitudinal research). Statistical regression occurs in educational (and other) research due to the unreliability of measuring instruments and to extraneous factors unique to each group, e.g. in an experiment. Regression means, simply, that subjects scoring highest on a pre-test are likely to score relatively lower on a post-test; conversely, those scoring lowest on a pre-test are likely to score relatively higher on a post-test. In short, in pre-test/post-test situations, there is regression to the mean. Regression effects can lead the educational researcher mistakenly to attribute post-test gains and losses to low scoring and high scoring respectively.

- *Testing* Pre-tests at the beginning of research (e.g. experiments, action research, observational research) can produce effects other than those due to the research treatments. Such effects can include sensitizing subjects to the true purposes of the research and practice effects which produce higher scores on post-test measures.

- *Instrumentation* Unreliable tests or instruments can introduce serious errors into research (e.g. testing, surveys, experiments). With human observers or judges or changes in instrumentation and calibration, error can result from changes in their skills and levels of concentration over the course of the research.

- *Selection* Bias may be introduced as a result of differences in the selection of subjects for the comparison groups or when intact classes are employed as experimental or control groups. Selection bias, moreover, may interact with other factors (history, maturation, etc.) to cloud even further the effects of the comparative treatments.

- *Experimental mortality* The loss of subjects through dropout often occurs in long-running research (e.g. experiments, longitudinal research, action research) and may result in confounding the effects of the variables, for whereas initially the groups may have been randomly selected, the residue that stays the course is likely to be different from the unbiased sample that began it.

- *Instrument reactivity* The effects that the instruments of the study exert on the people in the study (e.g. observational research, action research, experiments, case studies) (see also Vulliamy *et al.*, 1990).

- *Selection-maturation interaction* Where there is a confusion between the research design effects and the variable's effects.

- *Type I and Type II errors* Failure to find something (e.g. a difference between groups) when it exists, and finding something (e.g. a difference between groups) when nothing exists, respectively.

A Type I error is committed where the researcher rejects the null hypothesis when it is in fact true (akin to convicting an innocent person (Mitchell and Jolley, 1988: 121)); this can be addressed by setting a more rigorous level of significance (e.g. $p < 0.01$ rather than $p < 0.05$). A Type II error is committed where the null hypothesis is accepted when it is in fact not true (akin to finding a guilty person innocent (Mitchell and Jolley, 1988: 121)). Boruch (1997: 211) suggests that a Type II error may occur if: (a) the measurement of a response to the intervention is insufficiently valid; (b) the measurement of the intervention is insufficiently relevant; (c) the statistical power of the experiment is too low; (d) the wrong population was selected for the intervention.

A Type II error can be addressed by reducing the level of significance (e.g. $p < 0.20$ or $p < 0.30$ rather than $p < 0.05$). Of course, the more one reduces the chance of a Type I error the more chance there is of committing a Type II error, and vice versa. In qualitative data a Type I error is committed when a statement is believed when it is, in fact, not true, and a Type II error is committed when a statement is rejected when it is in fact true.

Internal validity in qualitative research

In ethnographic research internal validity can be addressed in several ways (LeCompte and Preissle, 1993: 338):

- using low-inference descriptors;
- using multiple researchers;
- using participant researchers;
- using peer examination of data;
- using mechanical means to record, store and retrieve data.

In ethnographic, qualitative research there are several overriding kinds of internal validity (LeCompte and Preissle, 1993: 323–4):

- confidence in the data;
- the authenticity of the data (the ability of the research to report a situation through the eyes of the participants);
- the cogency of the data;
- the soundness of the research design;
- the credibility of the data;
- the auditability of the data;
- the dependability of the data;
- the confirmability of the data.

The writers provide greater detail on the issue of authenticity, arguing for the following:

- *fairness* (that there should be a complete and balanced representation of the multiple realities in, and constructions of, a situation);
- *ontological authenticity* (the research should provide a fresh and more sophisticated understanding of a situation, e.g. making the familiar strange, a significant feature in reducing 'cultural blindness' in a researcher, a problem which might be encountered in moving from being a participant to being an observer (Brock-Utne, 1996: 610));
- *educative authenticity* (the research should generate a new appreciation of these understandings);
- *catalytic authenticity* (the research gives rise to specific courses of action);
- *tactical authenticity* (the research should bring benefit to all involved – the ethical issue of 'beneficence').

Hammersley (1992b: 71) suggests that internal validity for qualitative data requires attention to:

- plausibility and credibility;
- the kinds and amounts of evidence required (such that the greater the claim that is being made, the more convincing the evidence has to be for that claim);
- clarity on the kinds of claim made from the research (e.g. definitional, descriptive, explanatory, theory generative).

Lincoln and Guba (1985: 219, 301) suggest that credibility in naturalistic enquiry can be addressed by:

- prolonged engagement in the field;
- persistent observation (in order to establish the relevance of the characteristics for the focus);
- triangulation (of methods, sources, investigators and theories);
- peer debriefing (exposing oneself to a disinterested peer in a manner akin to cross-examination, in order to test honesty, working hypotheses and to identify the next steps in the research);
- negative case analysis (in order to establish a theory that fits every case, revising hypotheses retrospectively);
- member checking (respondent validation to assess intentionality, to correct factual errors, to offer respondents the opportunity to add further information or to put information on record; to provide summaries and to check the adequacy of the analysis).

Whereas in positivist research, history and maturation are viewed as threats to the validity of the research, ethnographic research simply assumes that this will happen; ethnographic research allows for change over time – it builds it in. Internal validity in ethnographic research is also addressed by the reduction of observer effects by having the observers sample both widely and staying in the situation for such a long time that their presence is taken for granted. Further, by tracking and storing information clearly, it is possible for the ethnographer to eliminate rival explanations of events and situations.

Onwuegbuzie and Leech (2006b: 235–7) identify twelve kinds of threat to internal validity in qualitative research:

1 *Ironic legitimation* (how far the research recognizes and is able to work with multiple realities and interpretations of the same situation, even if they are simultaneously contradictory).

2 *Paralogical legitimation* (how far the research is able to catch and address paradoxes in the claims to validity).

3 *Rhizomatic legitimation* (how much the research loses data when mapping of data rather than describing takes place).

4 *Voluptuous legitimation* (how far the interpretation placed on the data exceeds the capability of the researcher to support that interpretation from the data).

5 *Descriptive validity* (the accuracy of the account given by the researcher).

6 *Observational bias* (inadequate sampling of words, observations or behaviours in the study).

7 *Researcher bias* (discussed earlier).

8 *Reactivity* (how far the research alters the situation being researched or the participants in the research, e.g. the Hawthorne effect (discussed below) and the novelty effect).

9 *Confirmation bias* (the tendency for a piece of research to confirm existing findings or hypotheses (e.g. a circular argument)).

10 *Illusory confirmation* (the tendency to find relationships (e.g. between people, behaviours or events) when, in fact, they do not exist).

11 *Causal error* (inferring causal relations when none exist or where no evidence has been provided of their existence).

12 *Effect size* (avoiding taking numerical effect sizes and qualitizing them, when such a step would enrich the analysis; failure to take into account effect sizes and the meaningfulness that they could bring to the interpretation of the data).

External validity

External validity refers to the degree to which the results can be generalized to the wider population, cases, settings, times or situations, i.e. to the transferability of the findings. The issue of generalization is problematical. For positivist researchers generalizability is a sine qua non, whilst this is far less the case in naturalistic research. For one school of thought, generalizability through stripping out contextual variables is fundamental, whilst, for another, generalizations that say little about the context have little that is useful to say about human behaviour (Schofield, 1990). For positivists variables have to be isolated, controlled and samples randomized, whilst for ethnographers human behaviour is infinitely complex, irreducible, socially situated and unique.

External validity in quantitative research

External validity in quantitative research concerns generalizability, typically how far we can generalize from a sample to a population.

Bogdan and Biklen (1992: 45) argue that positivist researchers are more concerned to derive universal statements of general social processes rather than to provide accounts of the degree of commonality between various social settings (e.g. schools and classrooms).

Threats to external validity are likely to limit the degree to which generalizations can be made from the particular – often experimental – conditions to other populations or settings. Below, we summarize a number of factors (adapted from Campbell and Stanley, 1963; Bracht and Glass, 1968; Hammersley and Atkinson, 1983; Vulliamy, 1990; Lewis-Beck, 1993; Onwuegbuzie and Johnson, 2006b) that jeopardize external validity.

- *Failure to describe independent variables explicitly* Unless independent variables are adequately described by the researcher, future replications of the research conditions are virtually impossible.
- *Lack of representativeness of available and target populations* Whilst those participating in the research may be representative of an available population, they may not be representative of the population to which the researcher seeks to generalize her findings, i.e. poor sampling and/or randomization.
- *Hawthorne effect* Medical research has long recognized the psychological effects that arise out of mere participation in drug experiments, and placebos and double-blind designs are commonly employed to counteract the biasing effects of participation. Similarly, so-called Hawthorne effects threaten to contaminate research treatments in educational research when subjects realize their role as guinea pigs.

- *Inadequate operationalizing of dependent variables* Dependent variables that the researcher operationalizes must have validity in the non-research setting to which she wishes to generalize her findings. A paper and pencil questionnaire on career choice, for example, may have little validity in respect of the actual employment decisions made by undergraduates on leaving university.
- *Sensitization/reactivity to experimental/research conditions* As with threats to internal validity, pretests may cause changes in the subjects' sensitivity to the intervention variables and thus cloud the true effects of the treatment.
- *Interaction effects of extraneous factors and experimental/research treatments* All the above threats to external validity represent interactions of various clouding factors with treatments. As well as these, interaction effects may also arise as a result of any or all those factors, see threats to internal validity below.
- *Invalidity or unreliability of instruments* The use of instruments which yield data in which confidence cannot be placed (see below on tests).
- *Ecological validity*, and its partner, the extent to which behaviour observed in one context can be generalized to another. Hammersley and Atkinson (1983: 10) comment on the serious problems that surround attempts to relating inferences from responses gained under experimental conditions, or from interviews, to everyday life.
- *Multiple treatment validity* Applying several treatments simultaneously or in sequence may cause interaction effects between these treatments, such that it is difficult, if not impossible, to isolate the effects of particular treatments.

External validity in qualitative research

Generalizability in naturalistic research is interpreted as comparability and transferability (Lincoln and Guba, 1985; Eisenhart and Howe, 1992: 647). These writers suggest that it is possible to assess the typicality of a situation, the participants and settings, to identify possible comparison groups, and to indicate how data might translate into different settings and cultures (see also LeCompte and Preissle, 1993: 348). Schofield (1996: 200) suggests that it is important in qualitative research to provide a clear, detailed and in-depth description so that others can decide the extent to which findings from one piece of research are generalizable to another situation, i.e. to address the twin issues of *comparability* and *translatability*. Indeed, qualitative research can be generalizable, his paper argues (p. 209), by studying the typical (for its applicability to other situations – the issue of *transferability* (LeCompte and Preissle, 1993: 324)) and by performing multi-site studies (e.g. Miles and Huberman, 1984), though it could be argued that this is injecting a degree of positivism into non-positivist research. Lincoln and Guba (1985: 316) caution the naturalistic researcher against this; they argue that it is not the researcher's task to provide an index of transferability; rather, they suggest, researchers should provide sufficiently rich data for the readers and users of research to determine whether transferability is possible. In this respect transferability requires thick description.

Bogdan and Biklen (1992: 45) argue that in qualitative research we are more interested not with the issue of whether the findings are generalizable in the widest sense but with the question of the settings, people and situations to which they might be generalizable.

In naturalistic research threats to external validity include (Lincoln and Guba, 1985: 189, 300):

- selection effects (where constructs selected in fact are only relevant to a certain group);
- setting effects (where the results are largely a function of their context);
- history effects (where the situations have been arrived at by unique circumstances and, therefore, are not comparable);
- construct effects (where the constructs being used are peculiar to a certain group).

Onwuegbuzie and Leech (2006b: 237–8) identify several threats to external validity in qualitative research that lie in the following fields:

1 *Catalytic validity* (how far the research empowers the research community, or the effects of a piece of research).
2 *Action validity* (how much use is made of the research findings by stakeholders and decision makers).
3 *Investigation validity* (the ethical rigour, expertise, quality control and, indeed, personality of the researcher).
4 *Interpretive validity* (how far the research catches the meanings and interpretations of the participants in the study).
5 *Evaluative validity* (how far an evaluative structure (rather than a descriptive, interpretive or explanatory structure) can be applied to the research).
6 *Consensual validity* (how far the 'competent others' agree on the interpretations made by the research).
7 *Population generalizability/ecological generalizability/temporal generalizability* (how successfully

have the researchers kept within the bounds of generalizability/non-generalizability of their findings).
8 *Researcher bias* (as for internal validity in qualitative research).
9 *Reactivity* (as for internal validity in qualitative research).
10 *Order bias* (where the order of the questions posed in an interview/observation/questionnaire affects the dependability of the results).
11 *Effect size* (as for internal validity in qualitative research).

Catalytic validity

Catalytic validity embraces the paradigm of critical theory discussed in Chapter 2. Put neutrally, catalytic validity simply strives to ensure that research leads to action, echoing the paradigm of participatory research in Chapter 2. However, the story does not end there, for discussions of catalytic validity are substantive; like critical theory, catalytic validity suggests an agenda. Lather (1986, 1991) and Kincheloe and McLaren (1994) suggest that the agenda for catalytic validity is to help participants to understand their worlds in order to transform them. The agenda is explicitly political, for catalytic validity suggests the need to expose whose definitions of the situation are operating in the situation. Lincoln and Guba (1986) suggest that the criterion of 'fairness' should be applied to research, meaning that it should (a) augment and improve the participants' experience of the world, and (b) that it should improve the empowerment of the participants. In this respect the research might focus on what *might* be (the leading edge of innovations and future trends) and what *could* be (the ideal, possible futures) (Schofield, 1990: 209).

Catalytic validity – a major feature in feminist research which, Usher (1996) suggests, needs to permeate all research – requires solidarity in the participants, an ability of the research to promote emancipation, autonomy and freedom within a just, egalitarian and democratic society (Masschelein, 1991), to reveal the distortions, ideological deformations and limitations that reside in research, communication and social structures (see also LeCompte and Preissle, 1993). Validity, it is argued (Mishler, 1990; Scheurich, 1996), is no longer an ahistorical given, but contestable, suggesting that the definitions of valid research reside in the academic communities of the powerful. Lather (1986) calls for research to be emancipatory and to empower those who are being researched, suggesting that catalytic validity, akin to Freire's notion of 'conscientization', should empower participants to understand and transform their oppressed situation.

Validity, it is proposed (Sheurich, 1996), is but a mask that in fact polices and sets boundaries to what is considered to be acceptable research by powerful research communities; discourses of validity in reality are discourses of power to define worthwhile knowledge.

How defensible it is to suggest that researchers should have such ideological intents is, perhaps, a moot point, though not to address this area is to perpetuate inequality by omission and neglect. Catalytic validity reasserts the centrality of ethics in the research process, for it requires researchers to interrogate their allegiances, responsibilities and self-interestedness (Burgess, 1989).

Consequential validity

Partially related to catalytic validity is consequential validity, which argues that the ways in which research data are used (the consequences of the research) are in keeping with the capability or intentions of the research, i.e. the consequences of the research do not exceed the capability of the research and the action-related consequences of the research are both legitimate and fulfilled. Clearly, once the research is in the public domain the researcher has little or no control over the way in which it is used. However, and this is often a political matter, research should not be used in ways in which it was not intended to be used, for example by exceeding the capability of the research data to make claims, by acting on the research in ways that the research does not support (e.g. by using the research for illegitimate epistemic support), by making illegitimate claims by using the research in unacceptable ways (e.g. by selection, distortion), and by not acting on the research in ways that were agreed, i.e. errors of omission and commission.

A clear example of consequential validity is formative assessment. This is concerned with the extent to which students improve as a result of feedback given, hence if there is insufficient feedback for students to improve, or if students are unable to improve as a result of – a consequence of – the feedback, then the formative assessment has little consequential validity.

Content validity

To demonstrate this form of validity the instrument must show that it fairly and comprehensively covers the domain or items that it purports to cover (Carmines and Zeller, 1979: 20). It is unlikely that each issue will be able to be addressed in its entirety simply because of the time available or respondents' motivation to complete, for example, a long questionnaire. If this is the case, then the researcher must ensure that the elements of the main issue to be covered in the research are both a fair representation of the wider issue under investigation (and its weighting) and that the elements chosen for the research sample are themselves addressed in depth and breadth. Careful sampling of items is required to ensure their representativeness. For example, if the researcher wished to see how well a group of students could spell 1,000 words in French but decided only to have a sample of 50 words for the spelling test, then that test would have to ensure that it represented the range of spellings in the 1,000 words – maybe by ensuring that the spelling rules had all been included or that possible spelling errors had been covered in the test in the proportions in which they occurred in the 1,000 words.

Construct validity

A construct is an abstract; this separates it from the previous types of validity which dealt in actualities – defined content. In this type of validity agreement is sought on the 'operationalized' forms of a construct, clarifying what we mean when we use this construct. Hence in this form of validity the articulation of the construct is important; is my understanding of this construct similar to that which is generally accepted to be the construct? For example, let us say that I wished to assess a child's intelligence (assuming, for the sake of this example, that it is a unitary quality). I could say that I construed intelligence to be demonstrated in the ability to sharpen a pencil. How acceptable a construction of intelligence is this? Is not intelligence something else (e.g. that which is demonstrated by a high score in an intelligence test)? To establish construct validity I would need to be assured that *my construction* of a particular issue agreed with other constructions or theories of the same underlying issue, e.g. intelligence, creativity, anxiety, motivation.

Construct validity, then, concerns the extent to which a particular measure or instrument for data collection conforms to the theoretical context in which it is located.

Demonstrating construct validity means not only confirming the construction with that given in relevant literature, but requires me to look for counter examples which might falsify my construction. When I have balanced confirming and refuting evidence I am in a position to demonstrate construct validity. I can stipulate what I take this construct to be. In the case of conflicting interpretations of a construct, I might have to acknowledge that conflict and then stipulate the interpretation that I shall use.

Construct validity in quantitative research
Construct validity in quantitative research can be achieved through correlations with other measures of

the issue or by rooting my construction in a wide literature search which teases out the meaning of a particular construct (i.e. a theory of what that construct is) and its constituent elements.

Campbell and Fiske (1959), Brock-Utne (1996) and Cooper and Schindler (2001) suggest that construct validity is addressed by convergent and discriminant techniques. *Convergent techniques* imply that different methods for researching the same construct should give a relatively high inter-correlation, whilst *discriminant techniques* suggest that using similar methods for researching different constructs should yield relatively low inter-correlations, i.e. that the construct in question is different from other potentially similar constructs. Such discriminant validity can also be yielded by factor analysis, which clusters together similar issues and separates them from others.

Construct validity in qualitative research

In qualitative/ethnographic research construct validity must demonstrate that the categories that the researchers are using are meaningful *to the participants themselves* (Eisenhart and Howe, 1992: 648), i.e. that they reflect the way in which the participants actually experience and construe the situations in the research, that they see the situation through the actors' eyes.

Convergent and discriminant validity

Convergent and discriminant validity are two sides of the same coin, and are both facets of construct validity. Convergent validity is demonstrated when two related or similar factors or elements of a particular construct are shown (e.g. by measures or indicators) to be related or similar to each other, i.e. the results converge or are consistent with each other. Convergent validity is demonstrated when factors that *should* be related to each other are found, by indicators, actually to be related. Measures of correlation, regression or factor analysis are often used in quantitative research to demonstrate convergent validity. In qualitative research, where convergent validity is required to be shown, the researcher (e.g. using N-Vivo analysis and 'proximity searches', see Chapter 30) will be able to show, by collating and collecting together data from people, groups, samples and subsamples, whether convergence has been found.

By contrast, discriminant (divergent) validity requires two or more unrelated items, attributes, elements or factors to be shown, e.g. by measurement, to be unrelated to, or different from, each other, i.e. difference is found where it should be found. In quantitative research, statistics such as difference-testing (e.g. t-tests, chi-square tests, analysis of variance, collinearity diagnostics) are calculated. In qualitative research

where discriminant validity is required to be shown, the researcher can examine negative cases, deviant cases and compare data from subgroups of people, samples and subsamples, cases and factors, to determine if, indeed, differences are found to exist in terms of key factors, constructs, sub-elements or issues.

Convergent and discriminant validity can be addressed powerfully by mixed methods research. Here one can examine whether a set of data from one method accords with the data found by another method which focused on the same issues, variables or constructs. For example, the researcher could investigate to see whether the findings on, say, social class uptake of higher education in terms of cost-benefit to working-class students yield similar results from both qualitative and quantitative data. If they do, and if this was either predicted or supported by the literature, then one could suggest that intended convergent validity has been demonstrated. By contrast, let us say that the researcher hypothesized that family income and social class upward mobility aspirations for working-class students were not significantly related (the former being an index of wealth and the latter being an index of culture), and the data found two different, discordant results, then discriminant validity has been shown.

Convergent and discriminant validity draw on triangulation of methods, instruments, samples and theories. These are important features of test construction (we return to them in Chapter 24).

Criterion-related validity

This form of validity endeavours to relate the results of one particular instrument to another external criterion. Within this type of validity there are two principal forms: predictive validity and concurrent validity.

Criterion-related validity in quantitative research

Predictive validity is achieved if the data acquired at the first round of research correlate highly with data acquired at a future date. For example, if the results of examinations taken by 16 year olds correlate highly with the examination results gained by the same students when aged 18, then we might wish to say that the first examination demonstrated strong predictive validity.

A variation on this theme is encountered in the notion of concurrent validity. To demonstrate this form of validity the data gathered from using one instrument must correlate highly with data gathered from using another instrument. For example, suppose I wished to research a student's problem-solving ability. I might observe the student working on a problem, or I might talk to the student about how she is tackling the problem, or I might ask the student to write down how she tackled the problem. Here I have three different data-collecting instruments – observation, interview and documentation respectively. If the results all agreed – concurred – that, according to given criteria for problem-solving ability, the student demonstrated a good ability to solve a problem, then I would be able to say with greater confidence (validity) that the student was good at problem-solving than if I had arrived at that judgement simply from using one instrument.

Concurrent validity is very similar to its partner – predictive validity – in its core concept (i.e. agreement with a second measure); what differentiates concurrent and predictive validity is the absence of a time element in the former; concurrence can be demonstrated simultaneously with another instrument.

An important partner to concurrent validity, which is also a bridge into later discussions of reliability, is triangulation, and this is discussed later in this chapter.

Cross-cultural validity

A considerable body of educational and psychological research seeks to understand the extent to which there are similarities and differences between cultures and their members. Matsumoto and Yoo (2006) identify four main phases of cross-cultural research:

- The first phase consists of making comparatively coarse cross-cultural comparisons of similarities and differences between cultures, though there is no attempt to demonstrate empirically that differences found between groups are the result of cultural factors (pp. 234–5) and what are the elements of the culture that have given rise to the differences.

- The second phase of 'identifying meaningful dimensions of cultural variability' (p. 235) identifies important dimensions of culture, and tests across cultures for the applicability, universality, extent and strength of these, for example Hofstede's (1980) well-known dimensions of individualism-collectivism (see also Triandis, 1994), power-distance, uncertainty avoidance, masculinity-femininity and later long-term to short-term orientation (Hofstede and Bond, 1984). These studies have been criticized (Matsumoto and Yoo, 2006) for the assumption that: (a) countries are the same as cultures; (b) individual behaviour is the same as group behaviour (the ecological fallacy, discussed later); (c) there is a single or main culture in a culture (i.e. overlooking differences within countries as well as between countries); and (d) attributing the causes of differences found between cultures to cultural sources rather than to other factors (e.g. economic factors, psychological factors).

- The third phase involves cultural studies in which theoretical models of culture and their influence on individuals were used to explain differences found between cultures (e.g. Markus and Kitayama (1991) on cognition, emotion and motivation, Nisbett (2005) on thought processes and cognition). This phase has been criticized for the limited empirical testing of 'cultural ingredients' (Matsumoto and Yoo, 2006).

- The fourth phase consists of establishing 'linkages' between empirical research on cultural variables and the models that hypothesize such linkages (p. 236).

It appears, then, that for cross-cultural research to demonstrate validity, it is important to ensure that appropriate models of cross-cultural features and phenomena are developed, that make clear their causal rootedness in cultural variables (rather than, for example psychological, economic or personality variables), that these models are operationalized into specific variables that constitute elements of culture, and that these are then tested empirically.

A major question to be faced by the cross-cultural researcher is the extent to which an instrument which has been developed, tested and validated in one country (e.g. a commercially produced instrument) can be used in another culture or country. Are there sufficient similarities between the cultures or cultural properties (e.g. cultural 'universals') to enable the same instrument to be applied meaningfully in the other culture, given the particularities, uniqueness and sensitivities of each culture (e.g. Hilton and Skrutkowski, 2002; Sumathipala and Murray, 2006). This section addresses this topic, as it raises a prime matter of validity.

In conducting cross-cultural research another fundamental issue to be addressed is in whose terms, constructs and definitions the researcher is working. This rehearses the 'emic'/'etic' discussion in Chapter 11, i.e. does the researcher use his/her own constructs, definitions, variables and elements of culture ('etic' views), or those that arise from the participants themselves ('emic views') (Hammerlsey, 2006: 6). Whose 'definition of the situation' drives the research? Are participants sufficiently aware of their own culture to be able to articulate it or, if the researcher uses/imposes her or his own construction of culture, is this a form of 'symbolic violence' to participants (Hammerlsey, 2006: 6)? In practice these may not be mutually exclusive, for the researcher can conduct pilot research (e.g. ethnographic research) to establish the categories, items and variables that are relevant, important and meaningful to participants, and then convert these into measurement scales for further investigation. 'Emic' research may be essential in cross-cultural research, as it is the locals who know more about their environment than an outside researcher (cf. Brock-Utne, 1996: 607) and who may know which are the important questions to ask in any environment (indeed Brock-Utne (1996: 610) argues for the researcher being a local rather than an outsider, as a local researcher will have more experience of, and hence more insight into, the local culture, though, of course, this should not blind the local researcher to the situation). Brock-Utne gives a fascinating example of the interpretation of riddles in an African society; the outsider expatriate interprets them as entertainment and amusement, whereas the locals saw them as essential teaching and educational tools and promoters of cognitive development (pp. 610–12).

Items that are present in one culture may not be present in another, or may have different relevance, meanings or importance (Banville *et al.*, 2000: 374). Banville *et al.* (2000) suggest the use of a team of experts in both cultures to work in parallel in order to establish the 'etic' constructs, and then they formulate questions for study that are subsequently operationalized into 'emic' constructs for each culture. This, they aver, avoids the danger of imposing one 'emic' culture from one culture as an 'etic' construct on another culture (p. 375) (see also Aldridge and Fraser, 2000: 127). Essentially the authors are arguing for ensuring the relevance of the instrument for all the target cultures, by including 'emic' and 'etic' elements.

To address meaningfulness and relevance in cross-cultural research is important: whilst a construct or element of culture may be found in two cultures, it may have different meanings, weight or significance in the two cultures, i.e. the *presence* of a factor may not be sufficient in cross-cultural research. This introduces us to several concerns in cross-cultural research about validity.

Threats to validity in cross-cultural research may lie in many areas, for example:

- Failure to operationalize elements of cultures into researchable variables.
- Problems of whose construction of 'culture' to adopt: 'emic' and/or 'etic' research.
- False attribution of causality for differences found between groups to cultural factors rather than non-cultural factors (e.g. economic factors, affluence, demography, biological features of people, climate, personality, religion, educational practices, personal/subjective perceptions of the research, contextual but non-cultural variables (Alexander, 2000; Matsumoto and Yoo, 2006)).
- The ecological fallacy: the error of the ecological

fallacy is made where 'relationships that are found between aggregated data (e.g. mean scores) are assumed to apply to individuals, i.e. one infers an individual or particular characteristic from a generalization. It assumes that the individuals in a group exhibit the same features of the whole group taken together (a form of stereotyping)' (Morrison, 2009: 62). The caution here is to avoid assuming that what one finds at a group level is necessarily the same as that which one would find at an individual level.

- The directions of causality, for example, whether culture influences individual behaviour or vice versa, or both.
- Sampling (e.g. a lot of cross-cultural research involves using groups of university students, or – as in the case of Hofstede (1980) – individual companies, hence it is dangerous to generalize more widely from these. Further, some studies do not have samples that are matched in terms of size or characteristics of the sample).
- Instrument problems: different groups may not understand, or have different understandings of, the language/issues/instruments that are used for gathering data.
- Problems of convergent validity (where several items that are supposed to be measuring the same construct or variable do not yield strong inter-correlations).
- Problems of discriminant validity (where items that are supposed to be measuring different constructs or variables yield strong inter-correlations).
- Problems of equivalence (where the same meaning and significance is given to concepts, constructs, language, sampling, methods in different cultures, such that meaningful comparisons can be made between cultures):
  - problems of conceptual equivalence (where items are unrelated or relatively unimportant or meaningless to one or more groups) (e.g. Aldridge and Fraser, 2000: 111);
  - problems of psychological equivalence, where the psychological connotations or referents in the original language may be different from those in the translated language, giving rise to differences in results that are attributable to factors other than cultural (Liu, 2002; Riordan and Vandenburg, 1994);
  - problems of meaning equivalence: using similar words in the two languages but which connote different interpretations or meanings;
  - failure of the instruments to take account of the different frames of reference of the different cultural groups (Riordan and Vandenburg, 1994);

- failure of groups to understand the measures, instruments, language, meaning or research, i.e. the same items may be interpreted differently by different groups;
- failure to accord equal significance to items (factors might be found to be present in different cultures, but some cultures accord those factors much more importance than others (e.g. in measures of personality such as the Big Five factors of personality (Matsumoto and Yoo, 2006: 240));
- failure to accord equal relevance and meaning to the same construct or item in different cultures;
- measurement equivalence;
- linguistic equivalence (where translated versions of an instrument carry the same meaning as in the original, and which will be understood in the same way by members of different cultures).

- Response bias, in which members of different cultures respond in systematically different ways to items, elements, constructs or scales in the instrument in ways that are meaningful to their own cultures, situations or contexts (Riordan and Vandenburg, 1994; Aldridge and Fraser, 2000: 127) (e.g. (a) some cultures may give more weight to socially desirable responses or to responses that make the participants look good (Liu, 2002: 82); (b) some cultures may give more weight to categories of 'agree' rather than 'disagree' in responses; (c) some cultures may consider it undesirable to use extreme ends of a measurement scale (e.g. 'strongly agree', 'strongly disagree') or, indeed, some cultures may deliberately value the use of extreme categories (e.g. those that emphasize status, masculinity and power) (Matsumoto and Yoo, 2006)).
- Preparation of participants – giving advance organizers or suggestions to participants before administering an instrument ('priming') (Matsumoto and Yoo, 2006) – may give rise to different responses.
- Problems with the researcher who may not speak the language(s) of the participants, or whose participants may be insufficiently articulate or literate to engage in respondent validation.

To address problems of validity in cross-cultural research there are several techniques that researchers can use. For instruments such as questionnaires, a common practice is to use 'back translation', undertaken by bilinguals or those with a sound ability in the second as well as the first language (cf. Brislin, 1970; Vallerand *et al*., 1992; Banville *et al*., 2000; Cardinal *et al*., 2003). Here the original version of the instrument (say a questionnaire in English) is translated into the other language required (say Chinese). Then the

Chinese version is given to a third party who does not have sight of the original English version, and that third party translates the Chinese version back into English. The two English versions (the original and the resultant back-translation) are then compared to check whether the meanings (and, in a few cases, the exact language) are the same. If the meanings in the two English versions are the same then the Chinese version is said to be acceptable; if the meanings in the two English versions are discrepant then there is said to be a problem in the Chinese, and the Chinese translation is revisited to make changes to it.

Liu (2002) suggests that translators should be familiar not only with both languages, but also with the subject matter, and, if possible, instrumentation. Banville *et al*. (2000) report the use of professional translators instead of simply back-translation, in order to ensure discriminability of similar items in translation. Further, they indicate that translation should precede the conduct of the empirical research and that translated instruments should be piloted to determine their suitability for the target population.

A variant of this, to ensure even greater validity and reliability of the translated version, is to have more than one person doing the translation into the new language (each person is unknown to the other) and similarly for the back translation into English, as this avoids possible bias in having only a single translator at each stage (Banville *et al*., 2000: 379). In this instance, the two translators at each stage should compare their translations and discuss any differences found in meaning or language.

Aldridge and Fraser (2000) draw attention to the fact that there may be no equivalent words in the target translated language, and this may mean that there have to be rewordings of the original language in order to reach a compromise statement in the instrument (e.g. a questionnaire) that fits both languages. Whilst back-translation keeps the original language as the language of reference, 'decentring' suggests that, in fact compromises may have to be made in both the original and the translated language, in order to ensure communality or equivalence of meaning, i.e. the original and the translated language are equally important (Liu, 2002: 81) and must be user-friendly to all groups. Liu also suggests that it is useful to keep the original language in active rather than passive voice, simple and short sentences, avoiding colloquialisms, idioms and using specific terms and familiar rather than abstruse words (see also Hilton and Skrutkowski, 2002).

Banville *et al*. (2000) provide a useful seven-step approach from Vallerand (1989) to translating and using instruments in cross-cultural research:

Step 1: Prepare a preliminary version of the instrument using the back-translation technique.

Step 2: Evaluate the preliminary versions (to check that the back-translated version is acceptable, or to adjudicate between different versions of the back-translated items) and prepare an experimental version of the instrument using a committee of experts (three to five persons) to conduct such a review, thereby avoiding possible bias by a single researcher (see also Vallerand *et al.*, 1992; Liu, 2002: 82).

Step 3: Pre-test the experimental version using a random survey approach, to check the clarity of the instructions and the appropriateness of the instrument.

Step 4: Evaluate the content and concurrent validity of the instrument using bilingual participants to check whether they are answering both versions in the same way, and to check the appropriateness of the instrument (using between 20 and 30 participants). Participants answer both versions of the instrument (i.e. both languages). Content validity to be assessed qualitatively (expert review) and concurrent validity to be assessed quantitatively (t-tests).

Step 5: Conduct a reliability analysis to check for internal validity and stability over time (looking for high reliability coefficients: Cronbach alphas), and to check the suitability of the instrument. Remove items with low reliability.

Step 6: Evaluate the construct validity of the instruments (through factor analysis, inter-scale correlations and to test the hypothesis that stems from theory).

Step 7: Establish norms of the scales/measures by selecting the population from which the sample will be drawn, by statistical indices, and by calculating means standard deviations and z-scores, used with a large number of people in order to establish the stability of the norms.

Step 4 uses bilingual participants to undertake both versions (both languages), so that their two sets of answers can be compared to look for discrepancies (see also Liu, 2002: 81–2). This may not be feasible for sole researchers, who may not have access to a sufficiently large group of bilingual participants, but may only have access to people who can translate rather than be fully bilingual and expert in both cultures. For an example of the use of this technique see Cothran *et al.* (2005).

In order to avoid the risk of bias in cross-cultural research, the researcher can also use a multi-instrument approach with different sized samples for different instruments (Aldridge and Fraser, 2000; Aldridge *et al.*, 1999; Sumathipala and Murray, 2006). A multi-method approach provides triangulation and concurrent validity and gives a closer, more authentic meaning to the phenomenon or culture (particularly when qualitative data combine with quantitative data).

Qualitatively speaking, the researcher has to ensure: (a) that the meanings, definitions constructs that are being used are understood similarly by the members of the different cultures being investigated (the equivalence issue); (b) that these are given sufficient relevance, meaningfulness and weight in the different cultures for them to be suitable for investigation (or, indeed, the research may be intended to discover the relevance, meaningfulness and weight of these in the different cultures); (c) that the research includes items that are meaningful, relevant and significant to participants; and (d) the research draws on both 'emic' and 'etic' analysis and constructs as appropriate.

Quantitatively speaking, there are several ways in which the cross-cultural validity of measures can be addressed. We discuss these below. Essentially the purpose is to test the instrument on the different cultures to see if the reliability, items, clusters of items into factors, and suitability of the items are acceptable in both cultures; an instrument that is suitable, reliable and valid in one culture may not be in the other (Cothran *et al.*, 2005: 194).

Factor analysis enables the researcher to examine the factor structure of the instrument. A suitable instrument for cross-cultural research should ensure that: (a) the same *factors* are extracted from the same instrument with the different groups of participants; (b) the same *variables* are included onto these factors with the different groups of participants; (c) the same *loadings* (e.g. weightings) of each variable are loaded onto each factor (see Chapter 37, which discusses factor loadings). One has to exercise discretion here, as, clearly the results will not be identical for each group of participants. However, if there are gross discrepancies found between factors, variables included, and loadings of each variable, then the researcher will need to consider whether the instrument is sufficiently valid to use, or whether some items will need to be excluded or replaced.

Inter-correlations of variables (alphas) (discussed later in this chapter: reliability) can be conducted to see whether: (a) the item-to-whole reliability correlation coefficient is the same for the different groups of participants; (b) the overall reliability level (the alpha) is sufficiently high for items to be included (see Chapter 36). A suitable instrument will ensure that the coefficient of correlation for each item to the whole is sufficiently high (e.g. ≥ 0.67), or the overall alphas for the sections of the instrument are sufficiently high (e.g. ≥ 0.67) to be retained. Items that show low correlations should be considered for removal. Hence the researcher will need to test his/her instrument in the groups concerned (e.g. groups of members of different cultures) in order to conduct such pilot testing. In this case it is advisable to include no fewer than 30 people in each of the pilot groups.

Items that the researcher hypothesizes should be strongly correlated (i.e. convergent validity: measuring the same construct, factor or trait (Rohner and Katz, 1970: 1069)) should have high correlation coefficients. Items that the researcher hypothesizes should have very low correlation coefficients (i.e. discriminant validity: measuring unrelated constructs, factors or traits (Rohner and Katz, 1970: 1069)) should have low correlation coefficients. Alternatively instead of using correlations, the researcher can conduct difference testing (e.g. t-tests, see Chapter 36) to discover: (a) whether items that he/she hypothesizes should be similar to each other (convergent validity) in reality show no statistically significant difference; and (b) whether items that he/she hypothesizes should be different from each other (discriminant validity) in reality are statistically significantly different from each other (see Keet *et al.*, 1997 for an example of using correlational analysis, t-tests and factor analysis to establish validity in cross-cultural research).

Watkins (2007: 305–6) suggests that meta-analysis can be used to examine the cross-cultural relevance of variables to the participating groups. This is a statistical procedure in which the researcher selects and combines empirical studies that satisfy criteria for inclusion in respect of the hypotheses under investigation (e.g. they are quantitative, include relevant variables, include scales and measures that can be combined from different studies, include identified samples and include correlational analysis of items). Then the researcher calculates average correlations and effect sizes from the studies (bearing in mind the likely different sample sizes), and then judges whether the correlations and effect sizes found are sufficiently strong for items to be retained in the researcher's own research (see Glass *et al.*, 1981 for how to conduct a meta-analysis).

Cross-cultural validity, like other forms of research, has to be cautious in making generalizations from small samples, in avoiding claims about whole cultures or countries from limited or selective samples, and in imposing instruments from one culture onto another – however well they might be translated. Matsumoto and Yoo (2006) suggest that cross-cultural data are 'nested' (p. 246), i.e. there are data at several levels: individual, group, cultures, societies, ecologies. This points us to the statistical technique of multilevel modelling, which we introduce in Chapter 37.

Cultural validity

Related to cross-cultural research and ecological validity (see below) is cultural validity (Morgan, 1999). This is particularly an issue in cross-cultural, intercultural and comparative kinds of research, where the intention is to shape research so that it is appropriate to the culture of the researched, and where the researcher and the researched are members of different cultures. Cultural validity is defined as 'the degree to which a study is appropriate to the cultural setting where research is to be carried out' (Joy, 2003: 1) (see also Stutchbury and Fox, 2009: 494). Cultural validity, Morgan (1999) suggests, applies at all stages of the research, and affects its planning, implementation and dissemination. It involves a degree of sensitivity to the participants, cultures and circumstances being studied. Morgan (2005: 1) writes that:

> cultural validity entails an appreciation of the cultural values of those being researched. This could include: understanding possibly different target culture attitudes to research; identifying and understanding salient terms as used in the target culture; reviewing appropriate target language literature; choosing research instruments that are acceptable to the target participants; checking interpretations and translations of data with native speakers; and being aware of one's own cultural filters as a researcher.
>
> (Morgan, 2005: 1)

Joy (2003: 1) presents 12 important questions that researchers in different cultural contexts may face, to ensure that research is culture-fair and culturally sensitive:

1 Is the research question understandable and of importance to the target group?
2 Is the researcher the appropriate person to conduct the research?
3 Are the sources of the theories that the research is based on appropriate for the target culture?
4 How do researchers in the target culture deal with the issues related to the research question (including their method and findings)?
5 Are appropriate gatekeepers and informants chosen?
6 Are the research design and research instruments ethical and appropriate according to the standards of the target culture?
7 How do members of the target culture define the salient terms of the research?
8 Are documents and other information translated in a culturally appropriate way?

9 Are the possible results of the research of potential value and benefit to the target culture?

10 Does interpretation of the results include the opinions and views of members of the target culture?

11 Are the results made available to members of the target culture for review and comment?

12 Does the researcher accurately and fairly communicate the results in their cultural context to people who are not members of the target culture?

Ecological validity

In education, ecological validity is particularly important and useful in charting how policies are actually happening 'at the chalk face' (Brock-Utne, 1996: 617). It concerns examining and addressing the specific characteristics of a particular situation, for example how policies are actually impacting in practice (p. 617) rather than simply having surveys, interviews, observations and questionnaires that reproduce the 'rhetoric of policies' (p. 617), i.e. that assume that policies are implemented in the ways intended or in the ways that the powerful groups intended (those at 'the top of the hierarchy of credibility') (p. 618).

Ecological validity requires the specific factors of research sites – schools, universities, regions, etc. – to be included and taken into account in the research. In this respect it is far more sympathetic to qualitative research and 'thick description' (Geertz, 1973) than those forms of quantitative, positivist research variables that seek to isolate, control out and manipulate variables in contrived settings. The ethical tension is raised in ecological validity between the need to provide rich descriptions of characteristics of a situation or institution and the increased likelihood that this will lead to the situation or institution being able to be identified and anonymity breached (Brock-Utne, 1996: 618).

For qualitative, naturalistic research a fundamental premise is that the researcher deliberately does not try to manipulate variables or conditions, and that the situations in the research occur naturally. The intention here is to give accurate portrayals of the realities of social situations in their own terms, in their natural or conventional settings.

For ecological validity to be demonstrated it is important to include and address in the research as many as possible of the characteristics and factors of a given situation. The difficulty with this is that the more characteristics are included and described, the harder it is to abide by central ethical tenets of much research – non-traceability, anonymity and non-identifiability.

Ecological validity is also a form of external validity; it concerns the extent to which characteristics of one situation or behaviour observed in one setting can be transferred or generalized to another situation. This blends fidelity to one specific set of circumstances with the extent to which that situation can apply to others.

10.5 Triangulation

Triangulation may be defined as the use of two or more methods of data collection in the study of some aspect of human behaviour. The use of multiple methods, or the multi-method approach as it is sometimes called, contrasts with the ubiquitous but generally more vulnerable single-method approach that characterizes so much of research in the social sciences. In its original and literal sense, triangulation is a technique of physical measurement: maritime navigators, military strategists and surveyors, for example, use (or used to use) several locational markers in their endeavours to pinpoint a single spot or objective. By analogy, triangular techniques in the social sciences attempt to map out, or explain more fully, the richness and complexity of human behaviour by studying it from more than one standpoint and, in so doing, by making use of both quantitative and qualitative data. Triangulation is a powerful way of demonstrating concurrent validity, particularly in qualitative research (Campbell and Fiske, 1959).

The advantages of the mixed-method approach in social research are manifold and we examine two of them. First, whereas the single observation in fields such as medicine, chemistry and physics normally yields sufficient and unambiguous information on selected phenomena, it provides only a limited view of the complexity of human behaviour and of situations in which human beings interact. It has been observed that as research methods act as filters through which the environment is selectively experienced, they are never atheoretical or neutral in representing the world of experience (Smith, 1975). Exclusive reliance on one method, therefore, may bias or distort the researcher's picture of the particular slice of reality she is investigating. She needs to be confident that the data generated are not simply artefacts of one specific method of collection (Lin, 1976). Such confidence can be achieved, as far as nomothetic research is concerned, when different methods of data collection yield substantially the same results. (Where triangulation is used in interpretive research to investigate different actors' viewpoints, the same method, e.g. accounts, will naturally produce different sets of data.)

Further, the more the methods contrast with each other, the greater the researcher's confidence. If, for example, the outcomes of a questionnaire survey correspond to those of an observational study of the same phenomena, the more the researcher will be confident about the findings. Or, more extreme, where the results of a rigorous experimental investigation are replicated in, say, a role-playing exercise, the researcher will experience even greater assurance. If findings are artefacts of method, then the use of contrasting methods considerably reduces the chances of any consistent findings being attributable to similarities of method (Lin, 1976).

We come now to a second advantage: some theorists have been sharply critical of the limited use to which existing methods of enquiry in the social sciences have been put. One writer, for example, comments, 'Much research has employed particular methods or techniques out of methodological parochialism or ethnocentrism. Methodologists often push particular pet methods either because those are the only ones they have familiarity with, or because they believe their method is superior to all others' (Smith, 1975). The use of triangular techniques, it is argued, will help to overcome the problem of 'method-boundedness', as it has been termed; indeed Gorard and Taylor (2004) demonstrate the value of combining qualitative and quantitative methods.

In its use of mixed methods, triangulation may utilize either normative or interpretive techniques; or it may draw on methods from both these approaches and use them in combination.

Types of triangulation and their characteristics

We have just seen how triangulation is characterized by a mixed-method approach to a problem in contrast to a single-method approach. Denzin (1970) has, however, extended this view of triangulation to take in several other types as well as the mixed-method kind which he terms 'methodological triangulation', including:

- *time triangulation:* this type attempts to take into consideration the factors of change and process by utilizing cross-sectional and longitudinal designs. Kirk and Miller (1986) suggest that *diachronic reliability* seeks stability of observations over time, whilst *synchronic reliability* seeks similarity of data gathered in the same time;
- *space triangulation:* this type attempts to overcome the parochialism of studies conducted in the same country or within the same subculture by making use of cross-cultural techniques;
- *combined levels of triangulation:* this type uses more than one level of analysis from the three principal levels used in the social sciences, namely, the individual level, the interactive level (groups), and

the level of collectivities (organizational, cultural or societal);
- *theoretical triangulation:* this type draws upon alternative or competing theories in preference to utilizing one viewpoint only;
- *investigator triangulation:* this type engages more than one observer, data are discovered independently by more than one observer (Silverman, 1993: 99);
- *methodological triangulation:* this type uses either (a) the same method on different occasions, or (b) different methods on the same object of study.

Many studies in the social sciences are conducted at one point only in time, thereby ignoring the effects of social change and process. Time triangulation goes some way to rectifying these omissions by making use of cross-sectional and longitudinal approaches. Cross-sectional studies collect data at one point in time; longitudinal studies collect data from the same group at different points in the time sequence. The use of panel studies and trend studies may also be mentioned in this connection. The former compare the same measurements for the same individuals in a sample at several different points in time; and the latter examine selected processes continually over time. The weaknesses of each of these methods can be strengthened by using a combined approach to a given problem.

Space triangulation attempts to overcome the limitations of studies conducted within one culture or subculture. As one writer says, 'Not only are the behavioural sciences culture-bound, they are sub-culture-bound. Yet many such scholarly works are written as if basic principles have been discovered which would hold true as tendencies in any society, anywhere, anytime' (Smith, 1975). Cross-cultural studies may involve the testing of theories among different people, as in Piagetian and Freudian psychology; or they may measure differences between populations by using several different measuring instruments. We have addressed cultural validity earlier.

Social scientists are concerned in their research with the individual, the group and society. These reflect the three levels of analysis adopted by researchers in their work. Those who are critical of much present-day research argue that some of it uses the wrong level of analysis, individual when it should be societal, for instance, or limits itself to one level only when a more meaningful picture would emerge by using more than one level. Smith extends this analysis and identifies seven possible levels: the aggregate or individual level, and six levels that are more global in that 'they characterize the collective as a whole, and do not derive from an accumulation of individual characteristics' (Smith, 1975). The six include:

- group analysis (the interaction patterns of individuals and groups);
- organizational units of analysis (units which have qualities not possessed by the individuals making them up);
- institutional analysis (relationships within and across the legal, political, economic and familial institutions of society);
- ecological analysis (concerned with spatial explanation);
- cultural analysis (concerned with the norms, values, practices, traditions and ideologies of a culture); and
- societal analysis (concerned with gross factors such as urbanization, industrialization, education, wealth, etc.).

Where possible, studies combining several levels of analysis are to be preferred. Researchers are sometimes taken to task for their rigid adherence to one particular theory or theoretical orientation to the exclusion of competing theories. Indeed Smith (1975) recommends the use of research to test competing theories.

Investigator triangulation refers to the use of more than one observer (or participant) in a research setting. Observers and participants working on their own each have their own observational styles and this is reflected in the resulting data. The careful use of two or more observers or participants independently, therefore, can lead to more valid and reliable data (Smith, 1975), checking divergences between researchers leading to minimal divergence, i.e. reliability.

In this respect the notion of triangulation bridges issues of reliability and validity. We have already considered methodological triangulation earlier. Denzin (1970) identifies two categories in his typology: 'within methods' triangulation and 'between methods' triangulation. Triangulation within methods concerns the replication of a study as a check on reliability and theory confirmation. Triangulation between methods involves the use of more than one method in the pursuit of a given objective. As a check on validity, the between methods approach embraces the notion of convergence between independent measures of the same objective (Campbell and Fiske, 1959).

Of the six categories of triangulation in Denzin's typology, four are frequently used in education. These are: *time triangulation* with its longitudinal and cross-sectional studies; *space triangulation* as on the occasions when a number of schools in an area or across the country are investigated in some way; *investigator triangulation* as when two observers independently rate the same classroom phenomena; and *methodological triangulation*. Of these four, methodological triangulation is the one used most frequently and the one that possibly has the most to offer.

Triangular techniques are suitable when a more holistic view of educational outcomes is sought (e.g. Mortimore *et al.*'s (1988) search for school effectiveness), or where a complex phenomenon requires elucidation. Triangulation is useful when an established approach yields a limited and frequently distorted picture. Finally, triangulation can be a useful technique where a researcher is engaged in case study, a particular example of complex phenomena (Adelman *et al.*, 1980).

Triangulation is not without its critics. For example, Silverman (1985) suggests that the very notion of triangulation is positivistic, and that this is exposed most clearly in *data triangulation*, as it is presumed that a multiple data source (concurrent validity) is superior to a single data source or instrument. The assumption that a single unit can always be measured more than once violates the interactionist principles of emergence, fluidity, uniqueness and specificity (Denzin, 1997: 320). Further, Patton (1980) suggests that even having multiple data sources, particularly of qualitative data, does not ensure consistency or replication. Fielding and Fielding (1986) hold that methodological triangulation does not necessarily increase validity, reduce bias or bring objectivity to research.

With regard to investigator triangulation Lincoln and Guba (1985: 307) contend that it is erroneous to assume that one investigator will corroborate another, nor is this defensible, particularly in qualitative, reflexive enquiry. They extend their concern to include theory and methodological triangulation, arguing that the search for theory and methodological triangulation is epistemologically incoherent and empirically empty (see also Patton, 1980). No two theories, it is argued, will ever yield a sufficiently complete explanation of the phenomenon being researched.

These criticisms are trenchant, but they have been answered equally trenchantly by Denzin (1997).

In naturalistic enquiry, Lincoln and Guba (1985: 315) suggest that triangulation is intended as a check on data, whilst member checking, an element of credibility, is to be used as a check on members' constructions of data.

10.6 Validity in mixed methods research

Though each of the methods in mixed methods research (quantitative and qualitative) have to conform to their specific validity requirements, where research integrates quantitative and qualitative methods, there is an argument for identifying specific validity requirements for mixed methods research. Indeed Onwuegbuzie and Johnson (2006) argue that the term 'validity' be replaced by 'legitimation' in mixed methods research, and they identify nine main types of legitimation (discussed below). These nine methods, the authors aver (p. 52) constitute an attempt to overcome problems in mixed methods research of:

a   *representation* (using largely or only words and pictures to catch the dynamics of lived experiences and unfolding, emergent situations);

b   *legitimation* (ensuring that the results are dependable, credible, transferable, plausible, confirmable and trustworthy);

c   *integration* (using and combining quantitative and qualitative methods, each with their own, sometimes antagonistic, canons of validity, e.g. quantitative data may use large random samples whilst qualitative data may use small, purposive samples and yet they may have to be placed on an equal footing (p. 54)).

The nine types of legitimation in mixed methods research identified by Onwuegbuzie and Johnson (2006: 57) are:

1   *Sample integration* (how far different kinds and sizes of sample in combination, or the same samples in quantitative and qualitative research, can enable high-quality inferences to be made).

2   *Inside-outside* (how far researchers use, combine and balance both insiders' views ('emic' research) and outsiders' views ('etic' research) in the research in describing and explaining).

3   *Weakness minimization* (how far any weaknesses that stem from one approach are compensated by the strengths of the other approach, together with suitably weighting such strengths and weaknesses).

4   *Sequential* (how far one can minimize order effects (quantitative to qualitative and vice versa) in 'meta-inferences' made from data collection and analysis, such that one could reverse the order of the inferences made, or the order of the quantitative and qualitative data, without loss of power to the 'meta-inferences').

5   *Conversion* (how far qualitizing numerical data or quantitizing qualitative data can assist in yielding robust 'meta-inferences').

6   *Paradigmatic mixing* (how successful is the combination of the ontological, epistemological, axiological, methodological and rhetorical beliefs and practices in yielding useful results, particularly if the paradigms are in tension with each other).

7   *Commensurability* (how far any 'meta-inferences' made from the data catch a 'mixed worldview' (i.e. rejecting the incommensurability of paradigms) that is enabled by 'Gestalt switching' and integration of paradigms and their methodologies).

8   *Multiple validities* (fidelity to the canons of validity for each of the quantitative and qualitative data gathered).

9   *Political* (how accepted by the audiences are the 'meta-inferences' stemming from the combination of quantitative and qualitative methods).

10.7 Ensuring validity

It is very easy to slip into invalidity; it is both insidious and pernicious as it can enter at every stage of a piece of research. The attempt to build out invalidity is essential if the researcher is to be able to have confidence in the elements of the research plan, data acquisition, data processing analysis, interpretation and its ensuing judgement.

At the design stage threats to validity can be minimized by:

- choosing an appropriate timescale;
- ensuring that there are adequate resources for the required research to be undertaken;
- selecting an appropriate methodology for answering the research questions;
- selecting appropriate instrumentation for gathering the type of data required;
- using an appropriate sample (e.g. one which is representative, not too small or too large);
- demonstrating internal, external, content, concurrent and construct validity; 'operationalizing' the constructs fairly;
- ensuring reliability in terms of stability (consistency, equivalence, split-half analysis of test material);
- selecting appropriate foci to answer the research questions;
- devising and using appropriate instruments (for example, to catch accurate, representative, relevant and comprehensive data (King *et al.*, 1987); ensuring that readability levels are appropriate; avoiding any ambiguity of instructions, terms and questions; using instruments that will catch the complexity of issues; avoiding leading questions; ensuring that the level of test is appropriate, e.g. neither too easy nor too difficult; avoiding test items with little discriminability; avoiding making the instruments too short

or too long; avoiding too many or too few items for each issue);

■ avoiding a biased choice of researcher or research team (e.g. insiders or outsiders as researchers).

There are several areas where invalidity or bias might creep into the research at the stage of data gathering; these can be minimized by:

■ reducing the Hawthorne effect (see the accompanying website);
■ minimizing reactivity effects (respondents behaving differently when subjected to scrutiny or being placed in new situations, for example, the interview situation – we distort people's lives in the way we go about studying them (Lave and Kvale, 1995: 226));
■ trying to avoid drop-out rates amongst respondents;
■ taking steps to avoid non-return of questionnaires;
■ avoiding having too long or too short an interval between pre-tests and post-tests;
■ ensuring inter-rater reliability;
■ matching control and experimental groups fairly;
■ ensuring standardized procedures for gathering data or for administering tests;
■ building on the motivations of the respondents;
■ tailoring the instruments to the concentration span of the respondents and addressing other situational factors (e.g. health, environment, noise, distraction, threat);
■ addressing factors concerning the researcher (particularly in an interview situation); for example, the attitude, gender, race, age, personality, dress, comments, replies, questioning technique, behaviour, style and non-verbal communication of the researcher.

At the stage of data analysis there are several areas where invalidity lurks; these might be minimized by:

■ using respondent validation;
■ avoiding subjective interpretation of data (e.g. being too generous or too ungenerous in the award of marks), i.e. lack of standardization and moderation of results;
■ reducing the halo effect, where the researcher's knowledge of the person or knowledge of other data about the person or situation exerts an influence on subsequent judgements;
■ using appropriate statistical treatments for the level of data (e.g. avoiding applying techniques from interval scaling to ordinal data or using incorrect statistics for the type, size, complexity, sensitivity of data);

■ recognizing spurious correlations and extraneous factors which may be affecting the data (i.e. tunnel vision);
■ avoiding poor coding of qualitative data;
■ avoiding making inferences and generalizations beyond the capability of the data to support such statements;
■ avoiding the equating of correlations and causes;
■ avoiding selective use of data;
■ avoiding unfair aggregation of data (particularly of frequency tables);
■ avoiding unfair telescoping of data (degrading the data);
■ avoiding Type I and/or Type II errors.

At the stage of data reporting invalidity can show itself in several ways; the researcher must take steps to minimize this by, for example:

■ avoiding using data selectively and unrepresentatively (for example, accentuating the positive and neglecting or ignoring the negative);
■ indicating the context and parameters of the research in the data collection and treatment, the degree of confidence which can be placed in the results, the degree of context-freedom or context-boundedness of the data (i.e. the level to which the results can be generalized);
■ presenting the data without misrepresenting its message;
■ making claims which are sustainable by the data;
■ avoiding inaccurate or wrong reporting of data (i.e. technical errors or orthographic errors);
■ ensuring that the research questions are answered; releasing research results neither too soon nor too late.

Having identified where invalidity lurks, the researcher can take steps to ensure that, as far as possible, invalidity has been minimized in all areas of the research.

10.8 Reliability

Reliability is essentially a synonym for dependability, consistency and replicability over time, over instruments and over groups of respondents. It is concerned with precision and accuracy; some features, e.g. height, can be measured precisely, whilst others, e.g. musical ability, cannot. For research to be reliable it must demonstrate that if it were to be carried out on a similar group of respondents in a similar context (however defined), then similar results would be found. Guba and

Lincoln (1994) suggest that the concept of reliability is largely positivist. Whilst it may be true that widely held views of reliability seem to adhere to positivism rather than to qualitative research, it is not exclusively so; qualitative research has to be as reliable as positivist research, though in different ways: the canons of reliability and the types of reliability differ in quantitative and qualitative research. Similarly, it is simply not the case that qualitative research, per se, guarantees reliability or that it is an irrelevance in qualitative research (Brock-Utne, 1996: 613). Reliability, as a precondition or sine qua non of validity (Brock-Utne, 1996: 614), is relevant to both quantitative and qualitative research.

10.9 Reliability in quantitative research

In positivist and quantitative research (the two terms are different, as some qualitative research can also be positivist in seeking trends, patterns, predictability and control (e.g. Miles and Huberman, 1994)), there are three principal types of reliability: stability, equivalence and internal consistency (Carmines and Zeller, 1979). Here reliability concerns the research situation (e.g. the context of, or the conditions for, a test), factors affecting the researcher or participants, and the instruments for data collection themselves.

Reliability as stability

In this form reliability is a measure of consistency over time and over similar samples. A reliable instrument for a piece of research will yield similar data from similar respondents over time. A leaking tap which each day leaks one litre is leaking reliably whereas a tap which leaks one litre some days and two litres on others is not. In the experimental and survey models of research this would mean that if a test and then a re-test were undertaken within an appropriate time span, then similar results would be obtained. The researcher has to decide what an appropriate length of time is; too short a time and respondents may remember what they said or did in the first test situation, too long a time and there may be extraneous effects operating to distort the data (for example, maturation in students, outside influences on the students). A researcher seeking to demonstrate this type of reliability will have to choose an appropriate timescale between the test and re-test. Correlation coefficients can be calculated for the reliability of pre- and post-tests, using formulae which are readily available in books on statistics and test construction.

In addition to stability over time, reliability as stability can also be stability over a similar sample. For example, we would assume that if we were to adminis-

ter a test or a questionnaire simultaneously to two groups of students who were very closely matched on significant characteristics (e.g. age, gender, ability, etc. – whatever characteristics are deemed to have a significant bearing on the responses), then similar results (on a test) or responses (to a questionnaire) would be obtained. The correlation coefficient on this form of the test/re-test method can be calculated either for the whole test (e.g. by using the Pearson statistic or a t-test) or for sections of the questionnaire (e.g. by using the Spearman or Pearson statistic as appropriate or a t-test). The statistical significance of the correlation coefficient can be found and should be 0.05 or higher if reliability is to be guaranteed. This form of reliability over a sample is particularly useful in piloting tests and questionnaires.

In using the test/re-test method, care has to be taken to ensure (Cooper and Schindler, 2001: 216):

- the time period between the test and re-test is not so long that situational factors may change;
- the time period between the test and re-test is not so short that the participants will remember the first test;
- the participant may have become interested in the field and may have followed it up him/herself between the test and the re-test times.

Reliability as equivalence

Within this type of reliability there are two main sorts. Reliability may be achieved, first, through using equivalent forms (also known as 'alternative forms') of a test or data-gathering instrument. If an equivalent form of the test or instrument is devised and yields similar results, then the instrument can be said to demonstrate this form of reliability. For example, the pre-test and post-test in an experiment are predicated on this type of reliability, being alternate forms of instrument to measure the same issues. This type of reliability might also be demonstrated if the equivalent forms of a test or other instrument yield consistent results if applied simultaneously to matched samples (e.g. a control and experimental group or two random stratified samples in a survey). Here reliability can be measured through a t-test, through the demonstration of a high correlation coefficient and through the demonstration of similar means and standard deviations between two groups.

Second, reliability as equivalence may be achieved through inter-rater reliability. If more than one researcher is taking part in a piece of research then, human judgement being fallible, agreement between all researchers must be achieved, through ensuring that each researcher enters data in the same way. This would be particularly pertinent to a team of researchers gathering structured observational or semi-structured interview data where each member of the team would have to agree on which data would be entered in which categories. For observational data, reliability is addressed in the training sessions for researchers where they work on video material to ensure parity in how they enter the data.

At a simple level one can calculate the inter-rater agreement as a percentage:

$$\frac{\text{Number of actual agreements}}{\text{Number of possible agreements}} \times 100$$

Robson (2002: 341) sets out a more sophisticated way of measuring inter-rater reliability in coded observational data, and his method can be used with other types of data.

Reliability as internal consistency

Whereas the test/re-test method and the equivalent forms method of demonstrating reliability require the tests or instruments to be done twice, demonstrating internal consistency demands that the instrument or tests be run once only through the split-half method.

Let us imagine that a test is to be administered to a group of students. Here the test items are divided into two halves, ensuring that each half is matched in terms of item difficulty and content. Each half is marked separately. If the test is to demonstrate split-half reliability, then the marks obtained on each half should be correlated highly with the other. Any student's marks on the one half should match his or her marks on the other half. This can be calculated using the Spearman-Brown formula:

$$\text{Reliability} = \frac{2r}{1+r}$$

where
r = the actual correlation between the halves of the instrument.

This calculation requires a correlation coefficient to be calculated, e.g. a Spearman rank order correlation or a Pearson product moment correlation.

Let us say that using the Spearman-Brown formula the correlation coefficient is 0.85; in this case the formula for reliability is set out thus:

$$\text{Reliability} = \frac{2 \times 0.85}{1 + 0.85} = \frac{1.70}{1.85} = 0.919$$

Given that the maximum value of the coefficient is 1.00 we can see that the reliability of this instrument, calcu-

lated for the split-half form of reliability, is very high indeed.

This type of reliability assumes that the test administered can be split into two matched halves; many tests have a gradient of difficulty or different items of content in each half. If this is the case and, for example, the test contains 20 items, then the researcher, instead of splitting the test into two by assigning items one to ten to one half and items 11 to 20 to the second half may assign all the even-numbered items to one group and all the odd-numbered items to another. This would move towards the two halves being matched in terms of content and cumulative degrees of difficulty.

An alternative measure of reliability as internal consistency is the Cronbach alpha, frequently referred to simply as the alpha coefficient of reliability, or simply the alpha. The Cronbach alpha provides a coefficient of inter-item correlations, that is, the correlation of each item with the sum of all the other relevant items, and is useful for multi-item scales. This is a measure of the internal consistency amongst the *items* (not, for example, the people). We address the alpha coefficient and its calculation in Part 5.

Reliability, thus construed, makes several assumptions, e.g. that instrumentation, data and findings should be controllable, predictable, consistent and replicable. This presupposes a particular style of research, typically within the positivist paradigm. Cooper and Schindler (2001: 218) suggest that in this paradigm reliability can be improved by: minimizing any external sources of variation: standardizing and controlling the conditions under which the data collection and measurement take place; training the researchers in order to ensure consistency (inter-rater reliability); widening the number of items on a particular topic; excluding extreme responses from the data analysis (e.g. outliers, which can be done with SPSS).

10.10 Reliability in qualitative research

Whilst we discuss reliability in qualitative research here, the suitability of the term for qualitative research is contested (e.g. Winter, 2000; Stenbacka, 2001; Golafshani, 2003). Lincoln and Guba (1985) prefer to replace 'reliability' with terms such as 'credibility', 'neutrality', 'confirmability', 'dependability', 'consistency', 'applicability', 'trustworthiness' and 'transferability', in particular the notion of 'dependability'.

LeCompte and Preissle (1993: 332) suggest that the canons of reliability for quantitative research may be simply unworkable for qualitative research. Quantitative research assumes the possibility of replication; if the same methods are used with the same sample then the results should be the same. Typically quantitative methods require a degree of control and manipulation of phenomena. This distorts the natural occurrence of phenomena (see earlier: ecological validity). Indeed the premises of naturalistic studies include the uniqueness and idiosyncrasy of situations, such that the study cannot be replicated – that is their strength rather than their weakness.

On the other hand, this is not to say that qualitative research need not strive for replication in generating, refining, comparing and validating constructs. Indeed LeCompte and Preissle (1993: 334) argue that such replication might include repeating:

- the status position of the researcher;
- the choice of informant/respondents;
- the social situations and conditions;
- the analytic constructs and premises that are used;
- the methods of data collection and analysis.

Further, Denzin and Lincoln (1994) suggest that reliability as replicability in qualitative research can be addressed in several ways:

- *stability of observations* (whether the researcher would have made the same observations and interpretation of these if they had been observed at a different time or in a different place);
- *parallel forms* (whether the researcher would have made the same observations and interpretations of what had been seen if s/he had paid attention to other phenomena during the observation);
- *inter-rater reliability* (whether another observer with the same theoretical framework and observing the same phenomena would have interpreted them in the same way).

Clearly this is a contentious issue, for it is seeking to apply to qualitative research the canons of reliability of quantitative research. Purists might argue against the legitimacy, relevance or need for this in qualitative studies.

In qualitative research reliability can be regarded as a fit between what researchers record as data and what actually occurs in the natural setting that is being researched, i.e. a degree of accuracy and comprehensiveness of coverage (Bogdan and Biklen, 1992: 48). This is not to strive for uniformity; two researchers who are studying a single setting may come up with very different findings but both sets of findings might be reliable. Indeed Kvale (1996: 181) suggests that in interviewing there might be as many different interpretations of the qualitative data as there are researchers.

A clear example of this is the study of the Nissan automobile factory in the UK, where Wickens (1987) found a 'virtuous circle' of work organization practices that demonstrated flexibility, teamwork and quality consciousness, and where Garrahan and Stewart (1992), investigating the same practices, found a 'vicious circle' of exploitation, surveillance and control. Both versions of the same reality coexist because reality is multilayered. What is being argued for here is the notion of reliability through an eclectic use of instruments, researchers, perspectives and interpretations (echoing the comments earlier about triangulation) (see also Eisenhart and Howe, 1992).

Brock-Utne (1996) argues that qualitative research, being holistic, strives to record the multiple interpretations of, intention in and meanings given to situations and events. Here the notion of reliability is construed as *dependability* (Lincoln and Guba, 1985: 108–9; Anfara *et al.*, 2002), recalling the earlier discussion on internal validity. For them, dependability involves member checks (respondent validation), debriefing by peers, triangulation, prolonged engagement in the field, persistent observations in the field, reflexive journals, negative case analysis and independent audits (identifying acceptable processes of conducting the enquiry so that the results are consistent with the data). Audit trails enable the research to address the issue of confirmability of results, in terms of process and product (Golafshani, 2003: 601). These are a safeguard against the charge levelled against qualitative researchers, namely, that they respond only to the 'loudest bangs or the brightest lights'.

Dependability raises the important issue of *respondent validation* (see also McCormick and James, 1988). Whilst dependability might suggest that researchers need to go back to respondents to check that their findings are dependable, researchers also need to be cautious in placing exclusive store on respondents, for, as Hammersley and Atkinson (1983) suggest, they are not in a privileged position to be sole commentators on their actions.

Bloor (1978) suggests three means by which respondent validation can be addressed:

- researchers attempt to predict what the participants' classifications of situations will be;
- researchers prepare hypothetical cases and then predict respondents' likely responses to them;
- researchers take back their research report to the respondents and record their reactions to that report.

Kleven (1995) suggests that qualitative research can address reliability in part by asking three questions, particularly in observational research:

1 Would the same observations and interpretations have been made if observations had been conducted at different times? (The 'stability' version of reliability.)

2 Would the same observations and interpretations have been made if other observations had been conducted at the time? (The 'parallel forms' version of reliability.)

3 Would another observer, working in the same theoretical framework, have made the same observations and interpretations? (The 'inter-rater' version of reliability.)

The debate on reliability in quantitative and qualitative research rehearses the paradigm wars discussed in the opening chapters: quantitative measures are criticized for combining sophistication and refinement of process with crudity of concept (Ruddock, 1981) and for failing to distinguish between educational and statistical significance (Eisner, 1985); qualitative methodologies, whilst possessing immediacy, flexibility, authenticity, richness and candour, are criticized for being impressionistic, biased, commonplace, insignificant, ungeneralizable, idiosyncratic, subjective and short-sighted (Ruddock, 1981). This is an arid debate; rather the issue is one of fitness for purpose. For our purposes here we need to note that criteria of reliability in quantitative methodologies differ from those in qualitative methodologies. In qualitative methodologies reliability includes fidelity to real life, context- and

---

TABLE 10.2 COMPARING RELIABILITY IN QUANTITATIVE AND QUALITATIVE RESEARCH

Bases of reliability in quantitative research		Bases of reliability in qualitative research
Reliability	⟷	Dependability
Demonstrability	⟷	Trustworthiness
Stability	⟷	Stability
Isolation, control and manipulation of required variables	⟷	Fidelity to the natural situation and real life
Identification, control and manipulation of key variables	⟷	Thick description and high detail on required or important aspects
Singular, objective truths	⟷	Multiple interpretations/perceptions
Replicability	⟷	Replicability
Parallel forms	⟷	Parallel forms
Generalizability	⟷	Generalizability
Context-freedom	⟷	Context-specificity
Objectivity	⟷	Authenticity
Coverage of domain	⟷	Comprehensiveness of situation
Verification of data and analysis	⟷	Honesty and candour
Answering research questions	⟷	Depth of response
Meaningfulness to the research	⟷	Meaningfulness to respondents
Parsimony	⟷	Richness
Objectivity	⟷	Confirmability
Fidelity to 'etic' research	⟷	Fidelity to 'emic' research
Internal consistency	⟷	Credibility
Generalizability	⟷	Transferability
Parallel forms	⟷	Parallel forms
Inter-rater reliability	⟷	Inter-rater reliability
Accuracy	⟷	Accuracy
Precision	⟷	Accuracy
Replication	⟷	Replication
Neutrality	⟷	Multiple interests represented
Consistency	⟷	Consistency
Theoretical relevance	⟷	Applicability
Triangulation	⟷	Triangulation
Alternative forms (equivalence)		
Split-half		
Inter-item correlations (alphas)		

situation-specificity, authenticity, comprehensiveness, detail, honesty, depth of response and meaningfulness to the respondents.

We summarize some similarities and differences between reliability in quantitative and qualitative research in Table 10.2. This table shows that, whilst there are some areas of reliability that are exclusive to quantitative research (split-half testing, equivalent forms and Cronbach alphas), many features of reliability apply, *mutatis mutandis*, to both quantitative and qualitative research. Further, Table 10.2 also shows that there are some features that were found in validity (Table 10.1) that also appear in reliability (e.g. content validity that appears as coverage of domain and comprehensiveness, and concurrent validity that appears as triangulation). This suggests some blurring of the edges between validity and reliability in the literature.

10.11 Validity and reliability in interviews

In interviews, inferences about validity are made too often on the basis of face validity (Cannell and Kahn, 1968), that is, whether the questions asked look as if they are measuring what they claim to measure. One cause of invalidity is bias, defined as 'a systematic or persistent tendency to make errors in the same direction, that is, to overstate or understate the "true value" of an attribute' (Lansing *et al.*, 1961). One way of validating interview measures is to compare the interview measure with another measure that has already been shown to be valid. This kind of comparison is known as 'convergent validity'. If the two measures agree, it can be assumed that the validity of the interview is comparable with the proven validity of the other measure.

Perhaps the most practical way of achieving greater validity is to minimize the amount of bias as much as possible. The sources of bias are the characteristics of the interviewer, the characteristics of the respondent and the substantive content of the questions. More particularly, these will include:

- the attitudes, opinions and expectations of the interviewer;
- a tendency for the interviewer to see the respondent in her/his own image;
- a tendency for the interviewer to seek answers that support her/his preconceived notions;
- misperceptions on the part of the interviewer of what the respondent is saying;
- misunderstandings on the part of the respondent of what is being asked.

Studies have also shown that race, religion, gender, sexual orientation, status, social class and age in certain contexts can be potent sources of bias, i.e. interviewer effects (Lee, 1993; Scheurich, 1995). Interviewers and interviewees alike bring their own, often unconscious, experiential and biographical baggage with them into the interview situation. Indeed Hitchcock and Hughes (1989) argue that because interviews are interpersonal, humans interacting with humans, it is inevitable that the researcher will have some influence on the interviewee and, thereby, on the data. Fielding and Fielding (1986: 12) make the telling comment that even the most sophisticated surveys only manipulate data that at some time had to be gained by asking people! Interviewer neutrality is a chimera (Denscombe, 1995).

Lee (1993) indicates the problems of conducting interviews perhaps at their sharpest, where the researcher is researching sensitive subjects, i.e. research that might pose a significant threat to those involved (be they interviewers or interviewees). Here the interview might be seen as an intrusion into private worlds, or the interviewer might be regarded as someone who can impose sanctions on the interviewee, or as someone who can exploit the powerless; the interviewee is in the search-light that is being held by the interviewer (see also Scheurich, 1995). Indeed Gadd (2004) reports that an interviewee may reduce his/her willingness to 'open up' to an interviewer if the dynamics of the interview situation are too threatening, taking the role of the 'defended subject'. The issues also embrace *transference* and *counter-transference*, which have their basis in psychoanalysis. In transference the interviewees project onto the interviewer their feelings, fears, desires, needs and attitudes that derive from their own experiences (Scheurich, 1995). In counter-transference the process is reversed.

One way of controlling for reliability is to have a highly structured interview, with the same format and sequence of words and questions for each respondent (Silverman, 1993), though Scheurich (1995: 241–9) suggests that this is to misread the infinite complexity and open-endedness of social interaction. Controlling the wording is no guarantee of controlling the interview. Oppenheim (1992: 147) argues that wording is a particularly important factor in attitudinal questions rather than factual questions. He suggests that changes in wording, context and emphasis undermine reliability, because it ceases to be the same question for each respondent. Indeed he argues that error and bias can stem from alterations to wording, procedure, sequence, recording, rapport, and that training for interviewers is essential to minimize this. Silverman (1993) suggests that it is important for each interviewee to understand the question in the same way. He suggests that the reliability of interviews can be enhanced by: careful piloting of interview schedules; training of interviewers; inter-rater reliability in the coding of responses; and the extended use of closed questions.

On the other hand Silverman (1993) argues for the importance of open-ended interviews, as this enables respondents to demonstrate their unique way of looking at the world – their definition of the situation. It recognizes that what is a suitable sequence of questions for one respondent might be less suitable for another, and open-ended questions enable important but unanticipated issues to be raised.

Oppenheim (1992: 96–7) suggests several causes of bias in interviewing:

- biased sampling (sometimes created by the researcher not adhering to sampling instructions);
- poor rapport between interviewer and interviewee;
- changes to question wording (e.g. in attitudinal and factual questions);
- poor prompting and biased probing;
- poor use and management of support materials (e.g. show cards);
- alterations to the sequence of questions;
- inconsistent coding of responses;
- selective or interpreted recording of data/transcripts;
- poor handling of difficult interviews.

One can add to this the issue of 'acquiescence' (Breakwell, 2000: 254): the tendency that respondents may have to say 'yes', regardless of the question or, indeed, regardless of what they really feel or think.

There is also the issue of *leading questions*. A leading question is one which makes assumptions about interviewees or 'puts words into their mouths', i.e. where the question influences the answer perhaps illegitimately. For example (Morrison, 1993: 66–7) the question 'when did you stop complaining to the headteacher?' assumes that the interviewee had been a frequent complainer, and the question 'how satisfied are you with the new mathematics scheme?' assumes a degree of satisfaction with the scheme. The leading questions here might be rendered less leading by rephrasing, for example: 'how frequently do you have conversations with the headteacher?' and 'what is your opinion of the new mathematics scheme?' respectively.

In discussing the issue of leading questions we are not necessarily suggesting that there is not a place for them. Indeed Kvale (1996: 158) makes a powerful case *for* leading questions, arguing that they may be necessary in order to obtain information that the interviewer suspects the interviewee might be withholding. Here it might be important to put the 'burden of denial' onto the interviewee (e.g. 'when did you last stop beating your wife?'). Leading questions, frequently used in police interviews, may be used for reliability checks with what the interviewee has already said, or may be deliberately used to elicit particular non-verbal behaviours that give an indication of the sensitivity of the interviewee's remarks.

Hence reducing bias includes careful formulation of questions so that the meaning is crystal clear; thorough training procedures so that an interviewer is more aware of the possible problems; probability sampling of respondents; and sometimes matching interviewer characteristics with those of the sample being interviewed. Oppenheim (1992: 148) argues, for example, that interviewers seeking attitudinal responses have to ensure that people with known characteristics are included in the sample – the criterion group. We need to recognize that the interview is a shared, negotiated and dynamic social moment.

The notion of power is significant in the interview situation, for the interview is not simply a data collection situation but a social and frequently a political situation. Literally the word 'inter-view' is a view *between* people, mutually, not the interviewer extracting data, one-way, from the interviewee. Power can reside with interviewer and interviewee alike (Thapar-Björkert and Henry, 2004), though Scheurich (1995: 246) argues that, typically, more power resides with the interviewer: the interviewer generates the questions and the interviewee answers them; the interviewee is under scrutiny whilst the interviewer is not. Kvale (1996: 126), too, suggests that there are definite asymmetries of power as the interviewer tends to define the situation, the topics and the course of the interview.

Cassell (in Lee, 1993) suggests that elites and powerful people might feel demeaned or insulted when being interviewed by those with a lower status or less power. Further, those with power, resources and expertise might be anxious to maintain their reputation, and so will be more guarded in what they say, wrapping this up in well-chosen, articulate phrases. Lee (1993) comments on the asymmetries of power in several interview situations, with one party having more power and control over the interview than the other. Interviewers need to be aware of the potentially distorting effects of power, a significant feature of critical theory, as discussed in Chapter 2.

Neal (1995) draws attention to the feelings of powerlessness and anxieties about physical presentation and status on the part of interviewers when interviewing powerful people. This is particularly so for frequently lone, low-status research students interviewing powerful people; a low-status female research student might find that an interview with a male in a position of power (e.g. a university vice-chancellor, a senior politician or a senior manager) might turn out to be very different from an interview with the same person if conducted by a male university professor where it is perceived by the interviewee to be more of a dialogue between equals (see also Gewirtz and Ozga, 1993, 1994). Ball (1994b) comments that when powerful people are being interviewed, interviews must be seen as an extension of the 'play of power' – with its game-like connotations. He suggests that powerful people control the agenda and course of the interview, and are usually very adept at this because they have both a personal and professional investment in being interviewed (see also Batteson and Ball, 1995; Phillips, 1998).

The effect of power can be felt even before the interview commences, notes Neal (1995), where she instances being kept waiting, and subsequently being interrupted, being patronized and being interviewed by the interviewee (see also Walford, 1994b). Indeed Scheurich (1995) suggests that many powerful interviewees will rephrase or not answer the question. Connell et al. (1996) argue that a working-class female talking with a multinational director will be very different from a middle-class professor talking to the same person. Limerick et al. (1996) comment on occasions where interviewers have felt themselves to be passive, vulnerable, helpless and indeed manipulated. One way of overcoming this is to have two interviewers conducting each interview (Walford, 1994c: 227). On the other hand, Hitchcock and Hughes (1989) observe that if the researchers are known to the interviewees and they are peers, however powerful, then a degree of reciprocity might be taking place, with interviewees giving answers that they think the researchers might want to hear.

The issue of power has not been lost on feminist research (e.g. Thapar-Björkert and Henry, 2004), that is research that emphasizes subjectivity, equality, reciprocity, collaboration, non-hierarchical relations and emancipatory potential (catalytic and consequential validity) (Neal, 1995), echoing the comments about research that is influenced by the paradigm of critical theory. Here feminist research addresses a dilemma of interviews that are constructed in the dominant, male paradigm of pitching questions that demand answers from a passive respondent.

Limerick et al. (1996) suggest that, in fact, it is wiser to regard the interview as a gift, as interviewees have the power to withhold information, to choose the location of the interview, to choose how seriously to attend to the interview, how long it will last, when it will take place, what will be discussed – and in what

and whose terms – what knowledge is important, even how the data will be analysed and used (see also Thapar-Björkert and Henry, 2004). Echoing Foucault, they argue that power is fluid and is discursively constructed through the interview rather than being the province of either party.

Miller and Cannell (1997) identify some particular problems in conducting telephone interviews, where the reduction of the interview situation to just auditory sensory cues can be particularly problematical. There are sampling problems, as not everyone will have a telephone. Further, there are practical issues, for example, the interviewee can only retain a certain amount of information in her/his short-term memory, so bombarding the interviewee with too many choices (the non-written form of 'show cards' of possible responses) becomes unworkable. Hence the reliability of responses is subject to the memory capabilities of the interviewee – how many scale points and descriptors, for example, can an interviewee retain in her head about a single item? Further, the absence of non-verbal cues is significant, e.g. facial expression, gestures, posture, the significance of silences and pauses (Robinson, 1982), as interviewees may be unclear about the meaning behind words and statements. This problem is compounded if the interviewer is unknown to the interviewee.

Miller and Cannell report important research evidence to support the significance of the non-verbal mediation of verbal dialogue. As discussed earlier, the interview is a social situation; in telephone interviews the absence of essential social elements could undermine the salient conduct of the interview, and hence its reliability and validity. Non-verbal paralinguistic cues affect the conduct, pacing and relationships in the interview and the support, threat, confidence felt by the interviewees. Telephone interviews can easily slide into becoming mechanical and cold. Further, the problem of loss of non-verbal cues is compounded by the asymmetries of power that often exist between interviewer and interviewee; the interviewer will need to take immediate steps to address these issues (e.g. by putting interviewees at their ease).

On the other hand, Nias (1991) and Miller and Cannell (1997) suggest that the very factor that interviews are not face to face may strengthen their reliability, as the interviewee might disclose information that may not be so readily forthcoming in a face-to-face, more intimate situation. Hence, telephone interviews have their strengths and weaknesses, and their use should be governed by the criterion of fitness-for-purpose. They tend to be shorter, more focused and useful for contacting busy people (Harvey, 1988; Miller, 1995).

In his critique of the interview as a research tool, Kitwood (1977) draws attention to the conflict it generates between the traditional concepts of validity and reliability. Where increased reliability of the interview is brought about by greater control of its elements, this is achieved, he argues, at the cost of reduced validity. He explains,

> In proportion to the extent to which 'reliability' is enhanced by rationalization, 'validity' would decrease. For the main purpose of using an interview in research is that it is believed that in an interpersonal encounter people are more likely to disclose aspects of themselves, their thoughts, their feelings and values, than they would in a less human situation. At least for some purposes, it is necessary to generate a kind of conversation in which the 'respondent' feels at ease. In other words, the distinctively human element in the interview is necessary to its 'validity'. The more the interviewer becomes rational, calculating, and detached, the less likely the interview is to be perceived as a friendly transaction, and the more calculated the response also is likely to be.
>
> (Kitwood, 1977)

Kitwood suggests that a solution to the problem of validity and reliability might lie in the direction of a 'judicious compromise'.

A cluster of problems surround the person being interviewed. Tuckman (1972), for example, has observed that, when formulating her questions, an interviewer has to consider the extent to which a question might influence the respondent to show herself in a good light; or the extent to which a question might influence the respondent to be unduly helpful by attempting to anticipate what the interviewer wants to hear; or the extent to which a question might be asking for information about a respondent that she is not certain or likely to know herself. Further, interviewing procedures are based on the assumption that the person interviewed has insight into the cause of her behaviour. An insight of this kind may be rarely achieved and, when it is, it is after long and difficult effort, usually in the context of repeated clinical interviews.

In educational circles interviewing might be a particular problem in working with children. Simons (1982) and McCormick and James (1988) comment on particular problems involved in interviewing children, for example:

- establishing trust;
- overcoming reticence;
- maintaining informality;
- avoiding assuming that children 'know the answers';
- overcoming the problems of inarticulate children;
- pitching the question at the right level;
- choice of vocabulary;
- non-verbal cues;
- moving beyond the institutional response or receiving what children think the interviewer wants to hear;
- avoiding the interviewer being seen as an authority spy or plant;
- keeping to the point;
- breaking silences on taboo areas and those which are reinforced by peer-group pressure;
- children being seen as of lesser importance than adults (maybe in the sequence in which interviews are conducted, e.g. the headteacher, then the teaching staff, then the children).

These are not new matters. The studies by Labov in the 1960s showed how students reacted very strongly to contextual matters in an interview situation (Labov, 1969). The language of children varied according to the ethnicity of the interviewee, the friendliness of the surroundings, the opportunity for the children to be interviewed with friends, the ease with which the scene was set for the interview, the demeanour of the adult (e.g. whether the adult was standing or sitting), the nature of the topics covered. The differences were significant, varying from monosyllabic responses by children in unfamiliar and uncongenial surroundings to extended responses in the more congenial and less threatening surroundings – more sympathetic to the children's everyday world. The language, argot and jargon (Edwards, 1976), social and cultural factors of the interviewer and interviewee all exert a powerful influence on the interview situation.

The issue is also raised here (Lee, 1993) of whether there should be a single interview that maintains the detachment of the researcher (perhaps particularly useful in addressing sensitive topics), or whether there should be repeated interviews to gain depth and to show fidelity to the collaborative nature of research (a feature, as was noted above, which is significant for feminist research (Oakley, 1981)).

Kvale (1996: 148–9) suggests that a skilled interviewer should:

- know her subject matter in order to conduct an informed conversation;
- structure the interview well, so that each stage of the interview is clear to the participant;

- be clear in the terminology and coverage of the material;
- allow participants to take their time and answer in their own way;
- be sensitive and empathic, using active listening and being sensitive to how something is said and the non-verbal communication involved;
- be alert to those aspects of the interview which may hold significance for the participant;
- keep to the point and the matter in hand, steering the interview where necessary in order to address this;
- check the reliability, validity and consistency of responses by well-placed questioning;
- be able to recall and refer to earlier statements made by the participant;
- be ready to clarify, confirm and modify the participants' comments with the participant.

Walford (1994c: 225) adds to this the need for the interviewer to have done her homework when interviewing powerful people, as such people could well interrogate the interviewer – they will assume up-to-dateness, competence and knowledge in the interviewer. Powerful interviewees are usually busy people and will expect the interviewer to have read the material that is in the public domain.

The issues of reliability do not reside solely in the preparations for and conduct of the interview; they extend to the ways in which interviews are analysed. For example Lee (1993) and Kvale (1996: 163) comment on the issue of 'transcriber selectivity'. Here transcripts of interviews, however detailed and full they might be, remain selective, since they are interpretations of social situations. They become decontextualized, abstracted, even if they record silences, intonation, non-verbal behaviour, etc. The issue, then, is how useful they are to researchers overall rather than whether they are completely reliable.

One of the problems that has to be considered when open-ended questions are used in the interview is that of developing a satisfactory method of recording replies. One way is to summarize responses in the course of the interview. This has the disadvantage of breaking the continuity of the interview and may result in bias because the interviewer may unconsciously emphasize responses that agree with her expectations and fail to note those that do not. It is sometimes possible to summarize an individual's responses at the end of the interview. Although this preserves the continuity of the interview, it is likely to induce greater bias because the delay may lead to the interviewer forgetting some of the details. It is these forgotten details that are most likely to be the ones that disagree with the interviewer's own expectations.

10.12 Validity and reliability in experiments

As we have seen, the fundamental purpose of experimental design is to impose control over conditions that would otherwise cloud the true effects of the independent variables upon the dependent variables.

Clouding conditions that threaten to jeopardize the validity of experiments have been identified by Campbell and Stanley (1963), Bracht and Glass (1968) and Lewis-Beck (1993), conditions that are of greater consequence to the validity of quasi-experiments (more typical in educational research) than to true experiments in which random assignment to treatments occurs and where both treatment and measurement can be more adequately controlled by the researcher.

Threats to internal validity were introduced earlier in this chapter, and comprise:

- history
- maturation
- statistical regression
- testing
- instrumentation
- selection
- experimental mortality
- instrument reactivity
- selection-maturation interaction.

Several threats to external validity were discussed earlier in this chapter (Section 10.4) and the reader is advised to review these.

An experiment can be said to be internally valid to the extent that, within its own confines, its results are credible (Pilliner, 1973); but for those results to be useful, they must be generalizable beyond the confines of the particular experiment; in a word, they must be externally valid also (see also Morrison (2001) for a critique of randomized controlled experiments and the problems of generalizability). Pilliner points to a lop-sided relationship between internal and external validity (these terms have been discussed earlier in the chapter). Without internal validity an experiment cannot possibly be externally valid. But the converse does not necessarily follow; an internally valid experiment may or may not have external validity. Thus, the most carefully designed experiment involving a sample of Welsh-speaking children is not necessarily generalizable to a target population which includes non-Welsh-speaking subjects.

It follows, then, that the way to good experimentation in schools, or indeed any other organizational setting, lies in maximizing both internal and external validity.

10.13 Validity and reliability in questionnaires

Validity of postal questionnaires can be seen from two viewpoints (Belson, 1986). First, whether respondents who complete questionnaires do so accurately, honestly and correctly; and second, whether those who fail to return their questionnaires would have given the same distribution of answers as did the returnees. The question of accuracy can be checked by means of the intensive interview method, a technique consisting of 12 principal tactics that include familiarization, temporal reconstruction, probing and challenging. The interested reader should consult Belson (1986: 35–8).

The problem of non-response (the issue of 'volunteer bias' as Belson calls it) can, in part, be checked on and controlled for, particularly when the postal questionnaire is sent out on a continuous basis. It involves follow-up contact with non-respondents by means of interviewers trained to secure interviews with such people. A comparison is then made between the replies of respondents and non-respondents. Further, Hudson and Miller (1997) suggest several strategies for maximizing the response rate to postal questionnaires (and, thereby to increase reliability). They involve:

- including stamped addressed envelopes;
- multiple rounds of follow-up to request returns (maybe up to three follow-ups);
- stressing the importance and benefits of the questionnaire;
- stressing the importance of, and benefits to, the client group being targeted (particularly if it is a minority group that is struggling to have a voice);
- providing interim data from returns to non-returners to involve and engage them in the research;
- checking addresses and changing them if necessary;
- following up questionnaires with a personal telephone call;
- tailoring follow-up requests to individuals (with indications to them that they are personally known and/or important to the research – including providing respondents with clues by giving some personal information to show that they are known) rather than blanket generalized letters;
- features of the questionnaire itself (ease of completion, time to be spent, sensitivity of the questions asked, length of the questionnaire);
- invitations to a follow-up interview (face to face or by telephone);
- encouragement to participate by a friendly third party;
- understanding the nature of the sample population in depth, so that effective targeting strategies can be used.

The advantages of the questionnaire over interviews, for instance, are: it tends to be more reliable; it encourages greater honesty because it is anonymous (though, of course, dishonesty and falsification might not be able to be discovered in a questionnaire); it is more economical than the interview in terms of time and money; and there is the possibility that it may be mailed. Its disadvantages, on the other hand, are: there is often too low a percentage of returns; the interviewer is unable to answer questions concerning both the purpose of the interview and any misunderstandings experienced by the interviewee, for it sometimes happens in the case of the latter that the same questions have different meanings for different people; if only closed items are used, the questionnaire may lack coverage or authenticity; if only open items are used, respondents may be unwilling to write their answers for one reason or another; questionnaires present problems to people of limited literacy; and an interview can be conducted at an appropriate speed whereas questionnaires are often filled in hurriedly. There is a need, therefore, to pilot questionnaires and refine their contents, wording, length, etc. as appropriate for the sample being targeted.

One central issue in considering the reliability and validity of questionnaire surveys is that of sampling. An unrepresentative, skewed sample, one that is too small, can easily distort the data, and indeed, in the case of very small samples, prohibit statistical analysis (Morrison, 1993). The issue of sampling was covered in Chapter 8.

10.14 Validity and reliability in observations

There are questions about two types of validity in observation-based research. In effect, comments about the subjective and idiosyncratic nature of the participant observation study are about its external validity. How do we know that the results of this one piece of research are applicable to other situations? Fears that observers' judgements will be affected by their close involvement in the group relate to the internal validity of the method. How do we know that the results of this one piece of research represent the real thing, the genuine product? In Chapter 8 on sampling, we refer to a number of techniques (quota sampling, snowball sampling, purposive sampling) that researchers employ as a way of checking on the representativeness of the events that they observe and of cross-checking their interpretations of the meanings of those events.

In addition to external validity, participant observation also has to be rigorous in its internal validity checks. There are several threats to validity and reliability here, for example:

- the researcher, in exploring the present, may be unaware of important antecedent events;
- informants may be unrepresentative of the sample in the study;
- the presence of the observer might bring about different behaviours (reactivity and ecological validity);
- the researcher might 'go native', becoming too attached to the group to see it sufficiently dispassionately.

To address this Denzin (1989) suggests triangulation of data sources and methodologies. Chapter 23 discusses the principal ways of overcoming problems of reliability and validity in observational research in naturalistic enquiry. In essence it is suggested that the notion of 'trustworthiness' (Lincoln and Guba, 1985) replaces more conventional views of reliability and validity, and that this notion is devolved on issues of *credibility*, *confirmability*, *transferability* and *dependability*. Chapter 23 indicates how these areas can be addressed.

If observational research is much more structured in its nature, yielding quantitative data, then the conventions of intra- and inter-rater reliability apply. Here steps are taken to ensure that observers enter data into the appropriate categories consistently (i.e. intra- and inter-rater reliability) and accurately. Further, to ensure validity, a pilot must have been conducted to ensure that the observational categories themselves are appropriate, exhaustive, discrete, unambiguous and effectively operationalize the purposes of the research.

10.15 Validity and reliability in tests

The researcher will have to judge the place and significance of test data, not forgetting the problem of the Hawthorne effect operating negatively or positively on students who have to undertake the tests. There is a range of issues which might affect the reliability of the test – for example, the time of day, the time of the school year, the temperature in the test room, the perceived importance of the test, the degree of formality of the test situation, 'examination nerves', the amount of guessing of answers by the students (the calculation of *standard error* which the tests demonstrate feature here), the way that the test is administered, the way that the test is marked, the degree of closure or openness of test items. Hence the researcher who is considering

using testing as a way of acquiring research data must ensure that it is appropriate, valid and reliable (Carmines and Zeller, 1979; Linn, 1993; Borsboom *et al.*, 2004).

Wolf (1994) suggests four main factors that might affect reliability: the range of the group that is being tested, the group's level of proficiency, the length of the measure (the longer the test the greater the chance of errors), and the way in which reliability is calculated. Fitz-Gibbon (1997: 36) argues that, other things being equal, longer tests are more reliable than shorter tests. Additionally there are several ways in which reliability might be compromised in tests. Feldt and Brennan (1993) suggest four types of threat to reliability:

- *individuals* (e.g. their motivation, concentration, forgetfulness, health, carelessness, guessing, their related skills, e.g. reading ability, their usedness to solving the type of problem set, the effects of practice);
- *situational factors* (e.g. the psychological and physical conditions for the test – the context);
- *test marker factors* (e.g. idiosyncrasy and subjectivity);
- *instrument variables* (e.g. poor domain sampling, errors in sampling tasks, the realism of the tasks and relatedness to the experience of the testees, poor question items, the assumption or extent of unidimensionality in item response theory, length of the test, mechanical errors, scoring errors, computer errors).

Sources of unreliability

There are several threats to reliability in tests and examinations, particularly tests of performance and achievement, for example (Cunningham, 1998; Airasian, 2001) with respect to *examiners* and *markers*:

- errors in marking (e.g. attributing, adding and transfer of marks);
- inter-rater reliability (different markers giving different marks for the same or similar pieces of work);
- inconsistency in the marker (e.g. being harsh in the early stages of the marking and lenient in the later stages of the marking of many scripts);
- variations in the award of grades for work that is close to grade boundaries (some markers placing the score in a higher or lower category than other markers);
- the halo effect, wherein a student who is judged to do well or badly in one assessment is given undeserved favourable or unfavourable assessment respectively in other areas.

With reference to the *students* and *teachers* themselves, there are several sources of unreliability:

■ Motivation and interest in the task has a considerable effect on performance. Clearly, students need to be motivated if they are going to make a serious attempt at any test that they are required to undertake, where motivation is *intrinsic* (doing something for its own sake) or *extrinsic* (doing something for an external reason, e.g. obtaining a certificate or employment or entry into higher education). The results of a test completed in a desultory fashion by resentful pupils are hardly likely to supply the researcher with reliable information about the students' capabilities (Wiggins, 1998). Motivation to participate in test-taking sessions is strongest when students have been helped to see its purpose, and where the examiner maintains a warm, purposeful attitude toward them during the testing session (Airasian, 2001).

■ The relationship (positive to negative) between the assessor and the testee exerts an influence on the assessment. This takes on increasing significance in teacher assessment, where the students know the teachers personally and professionally – and vice versa – and where the assessment situation involves face-to-face contact between the teacher and the student. Both *test-takers* and *test-givers* mutually influence one another during examinations, oral assessments and the like (Harlen, 1994). During the test situation, students respond to such characteristics of the evaluator as the person's sex, age and personality.

■ The conditions – physical, emotional, social – exert an influence on the assessment, particularly if they are unfamiliar. Wherever possible, students should take tests in familiar settings, preferably in their own classrooms under normal school conditions. Distractions in the form of extraneous noise, walking about the room by the examiner and intrusions into the room, all have significant impact upon the scores of the test-takers, particularly when they are younger pupils (Gipps, 1994). An important factor in reducing students' anxiety and tension during an examination is the extent to which they are quite clear about what exactly they are required to do. Simple instructions, clearly and calmly given by the examiner, can significantly lower the general level of tension in the test-room. Teachers who intend to conduct testing sessions may find it beneficial in this respect to rehearse the instructions they wish to give to pupils *before* the actual testing session. Ideally, test instructions should be simple, direct and as brief as possible.

■ The Hawthorne effect, wherein, in this context, simply informing a student that this is an assessment situation will be enough to disturb her/his performance – for the better or the worse (either case not being a fair reflection of her/his usual abilities).

■ Distractions (including superfluous information).

■ Students respond to the tester in terms of their perceptions of what s/he expects of them (Haladyna, 1997; Tombari and Borich, 1999; Stiggins, 2001).

■ The time of the day, week, month will exert an influence on performance. Some students are fresher in the morning and more capable of concentration (Stiggins, 2001).

■ Students are not always clear on what they think is being asked in the question; they may know the right answer but not infer that this is what is required in the question.

■ The students may vary from one question to another – a student may have performed better with a different set of questions which tested the same matters. Black (1998) argues that two questions which, to the expert, may seem to be asking the same thing but in different ways, to the students might well be seen as completely different questions.

■ Students (and teachers) practise test-like materials, which, even though scores are raised, might make them better at taking tests although the results might not indicate increased performance.

■ A student may be able to perform a specific skill in a test but not be able to select or perform it in the wider context of learning.

■ Cultural, ethnic and gender background affect how meaningful an assessment task or activity is to students, and meaningfulness affects their performance.

■ Students' personalities may make a difference to their test performance.

■ Students' learning strategies and styles may make a difference to their test performance.

■ Marking practices are not always reliable, markers may be too generous, marking by effort and ability rather than performance.

■ The context in which the task is presented affects performance: some students can perform the task in everyday life but not under test conditions.

With regard to the *test items* themselves, there may be problems (e.g. test bias), e.g.

■ The task itself may be multidimensional, for example, testing 'reading' may require several components and constructs. Students can execute a mathematics operation in the mathematics class but they cannot perform the same operation in, for example, a physics class; students will disregard English grammar in a science class but observe it in an English class. This raises the issue of the number of contexts in which the behaviour must be demonstrated before a criterion is deemed to have been achieved (Cohen *et al.*, 2004). The question of transferability of knowledge and skills is also raised in this connection. The *context* of the task affects the student's performance.

■ The validity of the items may be in question.
■ The language of the assessment and the assessor exerts an influence on the testee, for example if the assessment is carried out in the testee's second language or in a 'middle-class' code (Haladyna, 1997).
■ The readability level of the task can exert an influence on the test, e.g. a difficulty in reading might distract from the purpose of a test which is of the use of a mathematical algorithm.
■ The size and complexity of numbers or operations in a test (e.g. of mathematics) that might distract the testee who actually understands the operations and concepts.
■ The number and type of operations and stages to a task – a student might know how to perform each element, but when they are presented in combination the size of the task can be overwhelming.
■ The form and presentation of questions affects the results, giving variability in students' performances.
■ A single error early on in a complex sequence may confound the later stages of the sequence (within a question or across a set of questions), even though the student might have been able to perform the later stages of the sequence, thereby preventing the student from gaining credit for all she or he can, in fact, do.
■ Questions might favour boys more than girls or vice versa.
■ Essay questions favour boys if they concern impersonal topics and girls if they concern personal and interpersonal topics (Haladyna, 1997; Wedeen *et al.*, 2002).
■ Boys perform better than girls on multiple choice questions and girls perform better than boys on essay-type questions (perhaps because boys are more willing than girls to guess in multiple-choice items), and girls perform better in written work than boys.
■ Questions and assessment may be culture-bound: what is comprehensible in one culture may be incomprehensible in another.
■ The test may be so long, in order to ensure coverage, that boredom and loss of concentration may impair reliability.

Hence specific contextual factors can exert a significant influence on learning and this has to be recognized in conducting assessments, to render an assessment as unthreatening and natural as possible.

Harlen (1994: 140–2) suggests that inconsistency and unreliability in teacher- and school-based assessment may derive from differences in: (a) interpreting the assessment purposes, tasks and contents, by teachers or assessors; (b) the actual task set, or the contexts and circumstances surrounding the tasks (e.g. time and place); (c) how much help is given to the test-takers during the test; (d) the degree of specificity in the marking criteria; (e) the application of the marking criteria and the grading or marking system that accompanies it; (f) how much additional information about the student or situation is being referred to in the assessment.

She advocates the use of a range of moderation strategies, both before and after the tests, including:

■ statistical reference/scaling tests;
■ inspection of samples (by post or by visit);
■ group moderation of grades;
■ *post hoc* adjustment of marks;
■ accreditation of institutions;
■ visits of verifiers;
■ agreement panels;
■ defining marking criteria;
■ exemplification;
■ group moderation meetings.

Whilst moderation procedures are essentially *post hoc* adjustments to scores, agreement trials and practice marking can be undertaken before the administration of a test, which is particularly important if there are large numbers of scripts or several markers.

The issue here is that the results as well as the instruments should be reliable. Reliability is also addressed by:

■ calculating coefficients of reliability, split-half techniques, the Kuder-Richardson formula, parallel/equivalent forms of a test, test/re-test methods, the alpha coefficient;
■ calculating and controlling the standard error of measurement;
■ increasing the sample size (to maximize the range and spread of scores in a norm-referenced test), though criterion-referenced tests recognize that scores may bunch around the high level (in mastery learning for example), i.e. that the range of scores might be limited, thereby lowering the correlation coefficients that can be calculated;

■ increasing the number of observations made and items included in the test (in order to increase the range of scores);

■ ensuring effective domain sampling of items in tests based on item response theory (a particular issue in Computer Adaptive Testing, introduced below (Thissen, 1990));

■ ensuring effective levels of item discriminability and item difficulty.

Reliability not only has to be achieved but be seen to be achieved, particularly in 'high stakes' testing (where a lot hangs on the results of the test, e.g. entrance to higher education or employment). Hence the procedures for ensuring reliability must be transparent. The difficulty here is that the more one moves towards reliability as defined above, the more the test will become objective, the more students will be measured as though they are inanimate objects, and the more the test will become decontextualized.

An alternative form of reliability which is premised on a more constructivist psychology, emphasizes the significance of context, the importance of subjectivity and the need to engage and involve the testee more fully than a simple test. This rehearses the tension between positivism and more interpretive approaches outlined in the first chapter of this book. Objective tests, as described in this chapter, lean strongly towards the positivist paradigm, whilst more phenomenological and interpretive paradigms of social science research will emphasize the importance of settings, of individual perceptions, of attitudes, in short, of 'authentic' testing (e.g. by using non-contrived, non-artificial forms of test data, for example portfolios, documents, course work, tasks that are stronger in realism and more 'hands on'). Though this latter adopts a view which is closer to assessment rather than narrowly 'testing', nevertheless the two overlap, both can yield marks, grades and awards, both can be formative as well as summative, both can be criterion-referenced.

With regard to validity, it is important to note here that an effective test will ensure adequate:

■ *Content validity* (e.g. adequate and representative coverage of programme and test objectives in the test items, a key feature of domain sampling) is achieved by ensuring that the content of the test fairly samples the class or fields of the situations or subject matter in question. Content validity is achieved by making professional judgements about the relevance and sampling of the contents of the test to a particular domain. It is concerned with coverage and representativeness rather than with patterns of response or scores. It is a matter of judgement rather than measurement (Kerlinger, 1986). Content validity will need to ensure several features of a test (Wolf, 1994): (a) test coverage (the extent to which the test covers the relevant field); (b) test relevance (the extent to which the test items are taught through, or are relevant to, a particular programme); (c) programme coverage (the extent to which the programme covers the overall field in question).

■ *Criterion-related validity* (where a high correlation coefficient exists between the scores on the test and the scores on other accepted tests of the same performance) is achieved by comparing the scores on the test with one or more variables (criteria) from other measures or tests that are considered to measure the same factor. Wolf (1994) argues that a major problem facing test devisers addressing criterion-related validity is the selection of the suitable criterion measure. He cites the example of the difficulty of selecting a suitable criterion of academic achievement in a test of academic aptitude. The criterion must be: (a) relevant (and agreed to be relevant); (b) free from bias (i.e. where external factors that might contaminate the criterion are removed); (c) reliable – precise and accurate; (d) capable of being measured or achieved.

■ *Construct validity* (e.g. the clear relatedness of a test item to its proposed construct/unobservable quality or trait, demonstrated by both empirical data and logical analysis and debate, i.e. the extent to which particular constructs or concepts can give an account for performance on the test) is achieved by ensuring that performance on the test is fairly explained by particular appropriate constructs or concepts. As with content validity, it is not based on test scores, but is more a matter of whether the test items are indicators of the underlying, latent construct in question. In this respect construct validity also subsumes content and criterion-related validity. It is argued (Loevinger, 1957) that in fact construct validity is the queen of the types of validity because it is subsumptive and because it concerns constructs or explanations rather than methodological factors. Construct validity is threatened by (a) under-representation of the construct, i.e. the test is too narrow and neglects significant facets of a construct, (b) the inclusion of irrelevancies – excess reliable variance.

■ *Concurrent validity* (where the results of the test concur with results on other tests or instruments that are testing/assessing the same construct/performance – similar to predictive validity but without the time dimension. Concurrent validity can occur simultaneously with another instrument rather than after some time has elapsed).

- *Face validity* (that, superficially, the test appears – at face value – to test what it is designed to test).
- *Jury validity* (an important element in construct validity, where it is important to agree on the conceptions and operationalization of an unobservable construct).
- *Predictive validity* (where results on a test accurately predict subsequent performance – akin to criterion-related validity).
- *Consequential validity* (where the inferences that can be made from a test are sound).
- *Systemic validity* (Fredericksen and Collins, 1989) (where programme activities both enhance test performance and enhance performance of the construct that is being addressed in the objective. Cunningham (1998) gives an example of systemic validity where, if the test with the objective of vocabulary performance leads to testees increasing their vocabulary, then systemic validity has been addressed).

To ensure test validity, then the test must demonstrate fitness for purpose as well as addressing the several types of validity outlined above. The most difficult for researchers to address, perhaps, is construct validity,

for it argues for agreement on the definition and operationalization of an unseen, half-guessed-at construct or phenomenon. The community of scholars has a role to play here. For a full discussion of validity see Messick (1993). To conclude this chapter, we turn briefly to consider validity and reliability in life history accounts.

10.16 Validity and reliability in life histories

Three central issues underpin the quality of data generated by life history methodology. They are to do with representativeness, validity and reliability. Plummer (1983) draws attention to a frequent criticism of life history research, namely that its cases are atypical rather than representative. To avoid this charge, he urges intending researchers to 'work out and explicitly state the life history's relationship to a wider population' by way of appraising the subject on a continuum of representativeness and non-representativeness.

Reliability in life history research hinges upon the identification of sources of bias and the application of techniques to reduce them. Bias arises from the informant, the researcher and the interactional encounter itself. Box 10.1, adapted from Plummer (1983), provides a checklist of some aspects of bias arising from these principal sources.

BOX 10.1   PRINCIPAL SOURCES OF BIAS IN LIFE HISTORY RESEARCH

Source: informant
Is misinformation (unintended) given?
Has there been evasion?
Is there evidence of direct lying and deception?
Is a 'front' being presented?
What may the informant 'take for granted' and hence not reveal?
How far is the informant 'pleasing you'?
How much has been forgotten?
How much may be self-deception?

Source: researcher
Attitudes of researcher: age, gender, class, race, religion, politics, etc.
Demeanour of researcher: dress, speech, body language, etc.
Personality of researcher: anxiety, need for approval, hostility, warmth, etc.
Scientific role of researcher: theory held (etc.), researcher expectancy.

Source: the interaction
The encounter needs to be examined. Is bias coming from:
The physical setting – 'social space'?
The prior interaction?
Non-verbal communication?
Vocal behaviour?

Source: Adapted from Plummer, 1983: 103, table 5.2

Several validity checks are available to intending researchers. Plummer (1983) identifies the following:

1 The subject of the life history may present an auto-critique of it, having read the entire product.
2 A comparison may be made with similar written sources by way of identifying points of major divergence or similarity.
3 A comparison may be made with official records by way of imposing accuracy checks on the life history.
4 A comparison may be made by interviewing other informants.

Essentially, the validity of any life history lies in its ability to represent the informant's subjective reality, that is to say, his or her definition of the situation.

 Companion Website

The companion website to the book includes PowerPoint slides for this chapter, which list the structure of the chapter and then provide a summary of the key points in each of its sections. In addition there is further information on the original Hawthorne experiments and measuring inter-rater reliability. These resources can be found online at **www.routledge.com/textbooks/cohen7e**.

Part 3
Styles of educational research

It is important to distinguish between design, methodology and instrumentation. Too often methods are confused with methodology and methodology is confused with design. Part Two provided an introduction to design issues and this part examines different methodologies of research, different styles, kinds of, and approaches to research, separating them from methods – instruments for data collection. We identify nine main styles of educational research in this part: a bundle of approaches that come under the umbrella of naturalistic/qualitative/ethnographic types of research; historical and documentary research (entirely rewritten by Gary McCulloch); different kinds of survey; case studies; *ex post facto* research; different kinds of experiment; a new chapter on meta-analysis, research syntheses and systematic reviews, which takes account of the increased prominence given to these in the research community; action research; and a new chapter on

virtual worlds in educational research (written by Stewart Martin). These chapters include more extended analysis of key issues and features of the different research styles that researchers can address in planning and implementing their research.

Although we recognize that these are by no means exhaustive, we suggest that they cover the major styles of research methodology. These take in quantitative as well as qualitative research, mixed methods, the emerging field of virtual worlds, together with small-scale and large-scale approaches. As with the previous parts, the key here is the application of the notion of *fitness for purpose*. We do not advocate slavish adherence to a single methodology in research; indeed combining methodologies may be appropriate for the research in hand. The intention here is to shed light on the different styles of research, locating them in the paradigms of research introduced in Part One.

Naturalistic, qualitative and ethnographic research

The title of this chapter indicates that a wide range of types and kinds of qualitative research are addressed here. The chapter addresses several key issues in planning and conducting qualitative research:

- foundations of naturalistic, qualitative and ethnographic enquiry (theoretical bases of these kinds of research)
- planning naturalistic, qualitative and ethnographic research
- features and stages of a qualitative study
- critical ethnography
- some problems with ethnographic and naturalistic approaches

There is no single blueprint for naturalistic, qualitative or ethnographic research, because there is no single picture of the world. Rather, there are many worlds and many ways of investigating them. In this chapter we set out a range of key issues in understanding these worlds. It is important to stress, at the outset, that, though there are many similarities and overlaps between naturalistic/ethnographic and qualitative methods, there are also differences between them. Here the former connotes long-term residence with an individual, group or specific community (cf. Swain, 2006: 206), whilst the latter, often being concerned with the nature of the data and the kinds of research question to be answered, is an approach that need not require naturalistic approaches or principles. That said, there are sufficient areas of commonality to render it appropriate to consider them in the same chapter, and we will tease out differences between them where relevant. The intention of this chapter is to provide guidance for qualitative researchers who are conducting either long-term ethnographic research or small-scale, short-term qualitative research.

There are many varieties of qualitative research, indeed Preissle (2006: 686) remarks that qualitative researchers cannot agree on the purposes of qualitative research, its boundaries and its disciplinary fields, or, indeed, its terminology ('interpretive', 'naturalistic', 'qualitative', 'ethnographic', 'phenomenological', etc.).

However, she does indicate that qualitative research is characterized by a 'loosely defined' group of designs that elicit verbal, aural, observational, tactile, gustatory and olfactory information from a range of sources including, amongst others, audio, film, documents and pictures, and that it draws strongly on direct experience and meanings, and that these may vary according to the style of qualitative research undertaken.

Qualitative research provides an in-depth, intricate and detailed understanding of meanings, actions, non-observable as well as observable phenomena, attitudes, intentions and behaviours, and these are well served by naturalistic enquiry (Gonzales *et al.*, 2008: 3). It gives voices to participants, and probes issues that lie beneath the surface of presenting behaviours and actions.

11.1 Foundations of naturalistic, qualitative and ethnographic enquiry

The social and educational world is a messy place, full of contradictions, richness, complexity, connectedness, conjunctions and disjunctions. It is multilayered, and not easily susceptible to the atomization process inherent in much numerical research. It has to be studied in total rather than in fragments if a true understanding is to be reached. Chapter 1 indicated that several approaches to educational research are contained in the paradigm of qualitative, naturalistic and ethnographic research. The characteristics of that paradigm (Boas, 1943; Blumer, 1969; Lincoln and Guba, 1985; Woods, 1992; LeCompte and Preissle, 1993) include:

- humans actively construct their own meanings of situations;
- meaning arises out of social situations and is handled through interpretive processes;
- behaviour and, thereby, data are socially situated, context-related, context-dependent and context-rich. To understand a situation researchers need to understand the context because situations affect behaviour and perspectives and vice versa;
- realities are multiple, constructed and holistic;
- knower and known are interactive, inseparable;

- only time- and context-bound working hypotheses (idiographic statements) are possible;
- all entities are in a state of mutual simultaneous shaping, so that it is impossible to distinguish causes from effects;
- enquiry is value-bound:
  - enquiries are influenced by enquirer values as expressed in the choice of a problem, evaluand or policy option, and in the framing, bounding and focusing of that problem, evaluand or policy option;
  - enquiry is influenced by the choice of the paradigm that guides the investigation into the problem;
  - enquiry is influenced by the choice of the substantive theory utilized to guide the collection and analysis of data and in the interpretation of findings;
  - enquiry is influenced by the values that inhere in the context;
  - enquiry is either value-resident (reinforcing or congruent) or value-dissonant (conflicting). Problem, evaluand or policy option, paradigm, theory and context must exhibit congruence (value-resonance) if the enquiry is to produce meaningful results;
- research must include 'thick descriptions' (Geertz, 1973) of the contextualized behaviour; for descriptions to be 'thick' requires inclusion not only of detailed observational data but data on meanings, participants' interpretations of situations and unobserved factors;
- the attribution of meaning is continuous and evolving over time;
- people are deliberate, intentional and creative in their actions;
- history and biography intersect – we create our own futures but not necessarily in situations of our own choosing;
- social research needs to examine situations through the eyes of the participants – the task of ethnographies, as Malinowski (1922: 25) observed, is to grasp the point of view of the native [sic], his [sic] view of the world and in relation to his life;
- researchers are the instruments of the research (Eisner, 1991);
- researchers generate rather than test hypotheses;
- researchers do not know in advance what they will see or what they will look for;
- humans are anticipatory beings;
- human phenomena seem to require even more conditional stipulations than do other kinds;
- meanings and understandings replace proof;

- generalizability is interpreted as generalizability to identifiable, specific settings and subjects rather than universally;
- situations are unique;
- the processes of research and behaviour are as important as the outcomes;
- people, situations, events and objects have meaning conferred upon them rather than possessing their own intrinsic meaning;
- social research should be conducted in natural, uncontrived, real-world settings with as little intrusiveness as possible by the researcher;
- social reality, experiences and social phenomena are capable of multiple, sometimes contradictory interpretations and are available to us through social interaction;
- all factors, rather than a limited number of variables, have to be taken into account;
- data are analysed inductively, with constructs deriving from the data during the research;
- theory generation is derivative – grounded (Glaser and Strauss, 1967) – the data suggest the theory rather than vice versa.

Lincoln and Guba (1985: 39–43) tease out the implications of these axioms:

- studies must be set in their natural settings as context is heavily implicated in meaning;
- humans are the research instrument;
- utilization of tacit knowledge is inescapable;
- qualitative methods sit more comfortably than quantitative methods with the notion of the human-as-instrument;
- purposive sampling enables the full scope of issues to be explored;
- data analysis is inductive rather than a priori and deductive;
- theory emerges rather than is pre-ordinate. A priori theory is replaced by grounded theory;
- research designs emerge over time (and as the sampling changes over time);
- the outcomes of the research are negotiated;
- the natural mode of reporting is the case study;
- nomothetic interpretation is replaced by idiographic interpretation;
- applications are tentative and pragmatic;
- the focus of the study determines its boundaries;
- trustworthiness and its components replace more conventional views of reliability and validity.

Qualitative research can be used in systematic reviews (Dixon-Woods *et al.*, 2001) to:

- identify and refine questions, fields, foci and topics of the review, i.e. to act as a precursor to a full review;
- provide data in their own right for a research synthesis;
- indicate and identify the outcomes that are of interest, and for whom;
- complement and augment data from quantitative reviews;
- fill out any gaps in quantitative reviews;
- explain the findings from quantitative reviews and data;
- provide alternative perspectives on topics;
- contribute to the drawing of conclusions from the review;
- be part of a multi-methods research synthesis;
- suggest how to turn evidence into practice.

Whilst the lack of controls in much qualitative research renders it perhaps unattractive for research syntheses, this is perhaps unjustified, as it suggests that qualitative research has to abide by the rules of the game of quantitative approaches. Qualitative methods have their own tenets, and these complement very well those of numerical research. As with quantitative studies, qualitative studies have to be weighted, downgraded, upgraded or excluded according to the quality of the evidence and sampling that they contain. They also have to overcome the problem that, by stripping out the context in order to obtain themes and key concepts, they destroy the heart of qualitative research – context (Dixon-Woods *et al.*, 2001: 131).

LeCompte and Preissle (1993) suggest that ethnographic research is a process involving methods of enquiry, an outcome and a resultant record of the enquiry. The intention of the research is to create as vivid a reconstruction as possible of the culture or groups being studied (p. 235). There are several purposes of qualitative research, for example, description and reporting, the creation of key concepts, theory generation and testing. LeCompte and Preissle (1993) indicate several key elements of ethnographic approaches:

- phenomenological data are elicited (p. 3);
- the world view of the participants is investigated and represented – their 'definition of the situation' (Thomas, 1923);
- meanings are accorded to phenomena by both the researcher and the participants; the process of research therefore is hermeneutic, uncovering meanings (LeCompte and Preissle, 1993: 31–2);
- the constructs of the participants are used to structure the investigation;

- empirical data are gather in their naturalistic setting (unlike laboratories or in controlled settings as in other forms of research where variables are manipulated);
- observational techniques are used extensively (both participant and non-participant) to acquire data on real-life settings;
- the research is holistic, that is, it seeks a description and interpretation of 'total phenomena';
- there is a move from description and data to inference, explanation, suggestions of causation and theory generation;
- methods are 'multimodal' and the ethnographer is a 'methodological omnivore' (p. 232).

Hitchcock and Hughes (1989: 52–3) suggest that ethnographies involve:

- the production of descriptive cultural knowledge of a group;
- the description of activities in relation to a particular cultural context from the point of view of the members of that group themselves;
- the production of a list of features constitutive of membership in a group or culture;
- the description and analysis of patterns of social interaction;
- the provision as far as possible of 'insider accounts';
- the development of theory.

Lofland (1971) suggests that naturalistic methods are intended to address three major questions:

- What are the characteristics of a social phenomenon?
- What are the causes of the social phenomenon?
- What are the consequences of the social phenomenon?

In this one can observe: (a) the environment; (b) people and their relationships; (c) behaviour, actions and activities; (d) verbal behaviour; (e) psychological stances; (f) histories; (g) physical objects (Baker, 1994: 241–4).

There are several key differences between the naturalistic approach and that of the positivists to whom we made reference in Chapter 1. LeCompte and Preissle (1993: 39–44) suggest that ethnographic approaches are concerned more with description rather than prediction, induction rather than deduction, generation rather than verification of theory, construction rather than enumeration, and subjectivities rather than objective knowledge. With regard to the latter the authors distinguish between *emic* approaches (as in the term 'phonemic', where the concern is to catch the subjective meanings placed on situations by participants) and *etic* approaches (as in the term 'phonetic', where the intention is to identify and understand the objective or researcher's meaning and constructions of a situation) (p. 45).

Woods (1992), however, argues that some differences between quantitative and qualitative research have been exaggerated. He proposes, for example (p. 381), that the 1970s witnessed an unproductive dichotomy between the two, the former being seen as strictly in the hypothetico-deductive mode (testing theories) and the latter being seen as the inductive method used for generating theory. He suggests that the epistemological contrast between the two is overstated, as qualitative techniques can be used both for generating and testing theories.

Indeed Dobbert and Kurth-Schai (1992) urge that ethnographic approaches become not only more systematic but that they study and address regularities in social behaviour and social structure (pp. 94–5). The task of ethnographers is to balance a commitment to catch the diversity, variability, creativity, individuality, uniqueness and spontaneity of social interactions (e.g. by 'thick descriptions' (Geertz, 1973)) with a commitment to the task of social science to seek regularities, order and patterns within such diversity (Dobbert and Kurth-Schai, 1992: 150). As Durkheim (1982) noted, there are 'social facts'.

Following this line, it is possible, therefore, to suggest that ethnographic research can address issues of generalizability – a tenet of positivist research – interpreted as 'comparability' and 'translatability' (LeCompte and Preissle, 1993: 47). For comparability the characteristics of the group that is being studied need to be made explicit so that readers can compare them with other similar or dissimilar groups. For translatability the analytic categories used in the research as well as the characteristics of the groups are made explicit so that meaningful comparisons can be made to other groups and disciplines.

Spindler and Spindler (1992: 72–4) put forward several hallmarks of effective ethnographies:

- Observations have contextual relevance, both in the immediate setting in which behaviour is observed and in further contexts beyond.
- Hypotheses emerge in situ as the study develops in the observed setting.
- Observation is prolonged and often repetitive. Events and series of events are observed more than once to establish reliability in the observational data.

- Inferences from observation and various forms of ethnographic enquiry are used to address insiders' views of reality.
- A major part of the ethnographic task is to elicit sociocultural knowledge from participants, rendering social behaviour comprehensible.
- Instruments, schedules, codes, agenda for interviews, questionnaires, etc. should be generated in situ, and should derive from observation and ethnographic enquiry.
- A transcultural, comparative perspective is usually present, although often it is an unstated assumption, and cultural variation (over space and time) is natural.
- Some sociocultural knowledge that affects behaviour and communication under study is tacit/implicit, and may not be known even to participants or known ambiguously to others. It follows that one task for an ethnography is to make explicit to readers what is tacit/implicit to informants.
- The ethnographic interviewer should not frame or predetermine responses by the kinds of questions that are asked, because the informants themselves have the emic, native cultural knowledge.
- In order to collect as much live data as possible, any technical device may be used.
- The ethnographer's presence should be declared and his or her personal, social and interactional position in the situation should be described.

With 'mutual shaping and interaction' between the researcher and participants taking place (Lincoln and Guba, 1985: 155) the researcher becomes, as it were, the 'human instrument' in the research (p. 187), building on her tacit knowledge in addition to her propositional knowledge, using methods that sit comfortably with human enquiry, e.g. observations, interviews, documentary analysis and 'unobtrusive' methods (p. 187). The advantage of the 'human instrument' is her adaptability, responsiveness, knowledge, ability to handle sensitive matters, ability to see the whole picture, ability to clarify and summarize, to explore, to analyse, to examine atypical or idiosyncratic responses (pp. 193–4).

The main *kinds* of naturalistic enquiry are (Arsenault and Anderson, 1998: 121; Flick, 2004a, 2004b):

- *case study* (an investigation into a specific instance or phenomenon in its real-life context);
- *comparative studies* (where several cases are compared on the basis of key areas of interest);
- *retrospective studies* (which focus on biographies of participants or which ask participants to look back on events and issues);

- *snapshots* (analyses of particular situations, events or phenomena at a single point in time);
- *longitudinal studies* (which investigate issues or people over time);
- *ethnography* (a portrayal and explanation of social groups and situations in their real-life contexts);
- *grounded theory* (developing theories to explain phenomena, the theories emerging from the data rather than being prefigured or predetermined);
- *biography* (individual or collective);
- *phenomenology* (seeing things as they are really like and establishing the meanings of things through illumination and explanation rather than through taxonomic approaches or abstractions, and developing theories through the dialogic relationships of researcher to researched).

The main *methods* for data collection in naturalistic enquiry are (Hammersley and Atkinson, 1983):

- participant observation;
- interviews and conversations;
- documents and field notes;
- accounts;
- notes and memos.

11.2 Planning naturalistic, qualitative and ethnographic research

In many ways the issues in naturalistic research are not exclusive; they apply to other forms of research, for example: identifying the problem and research purposes; deciding the focus of the study; identifying the research questions; selecting the research design and instrumentation; addressing validity and reliability; ethical issues; approaching data analysis and interpretation. These are common to all research. More specifically Wolcott (1992: 19) suggests that naturalistic researchers should address the stages of watching, asking and reviewing, or, as he puts it, experiencing, enquiring and examining. In naturalistic enquiry it is possible to formulate a more detailed set of stages that can be followed (Hitchcock and Hughes, 1989: 57–71; Bogdan and Biklen, 1992; LeCompte and Preissle, 1993). These are presented in Figure 11.1 and are subsequently dealt with in the later pages of this chapter.

One has to be cautious here: Figure 11.1 suggests a linearity in the sequence; in fact the process is often more complex that this, and there may be a backwards-and-forwards movement between the several stages over the course of the planning and conduct of the research. The process is iterative and recursive, as dif-

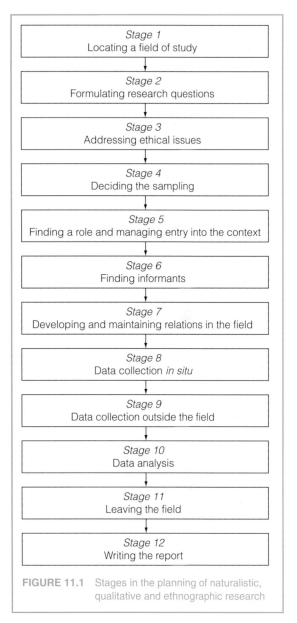

FIGURE 11.1 Stages in the planning of naturalistic, qualitative and ethnographic research

ferent elements will come into focus and interact with each other in different ways at different times. Indeed Flick (2009: 133) suggests a circularity or mutually informing nature of elements of a qualitative research design. In this instance the stages of Figure 11.1 might be better presented as interactive elements as in Figure 11.2.

Further, in some smaller-scale qualitative research not all of these stages may apply, as the researcher may not always be staying for a long time in the field but might

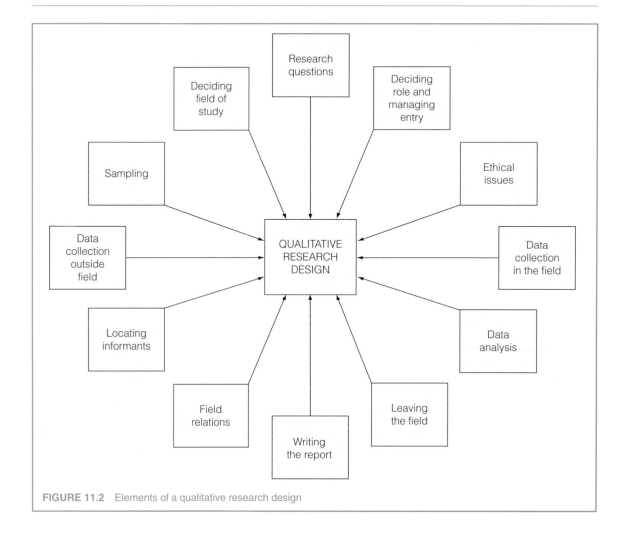

FIGURE 11.2 Elements of a qualitative research design

only be gathering qualitative data on a 'one-shot' basis (e.g. a qualitative survey, qualitative interviews). However, for several kinds of naturalistic and ethnographic study in which the researcher intends to remain in the field for some time, the several stages set out above, and commented upon in the following pages, may apply.

These stages are shot through with a range of issues that will affect the research, e.g.:

■ personal issues (the disciplinary sympathies of the researcher, researcher subjectivities and characteristics, personal motives and goals of the researcher). Hitchcock and Hughes (1989: 56) indicate that there are several serious strains in conducting fieldwork because the researcher's own emotions, attitudes, beliefs, values, characteristics enter the research; indeed, the more this happens the less will be the

likelihood of gaining the participants' perspectives and meanings;
■ the kinds of participation that the researcher will undertake;
■ issues of advocacy (where the researcher may be expected to identify with the same emotions, concerns and crises as the members of the group being studied and wishes to advance their cause, often a feature that arises at the beginning and the end of the research when the researcher is considered to be a legitimate spokesperson for the group);
■ role relationships;
■ boundary maintenance in the research;
■ the maintenance of the balance between distance and involvement;
■ ethical issues;
■ reflexivity.

Reflexivity recognizes that researchers are inescapably part of the social world that they are researching (Hammersley and Atkinson, 1983: 14), and, indeed, that this social world is an already interpreted world by the actors, undermining the notion of objective reality. Researchers are in the world and of the world. They bring their own biographies to the research situation and participants behave in particular ways in their presence. Qualitative enquiry is not a neutral activity, and researchers are not neutral; they have their own values, biases and world views, and these are lenses through which they look at and interpret the already-interpreted world of participants (cf. Preissle, 2006: 691). Reflexivity suggests that researchers should acknowledge and disclose their own selves in the research, seeking to understand their part in, or influence on, the research. Rather than trying to eliminate researcher effects (which is impossible, as researchers are part of the world that they are investigating), researchers should hold themselves up to the light, echoing Cooley's (1902) notion of the 'looking glass self'. As Hammersley and Atkinson say:

> He or she [the researcher] is the research instrument *par excellence*. The fact that behaviour and attitudes are often not stable across contexts and that the researcher may play a part in shaping the context becomes central to the analysis.... The theories we develop to explain the behaviour of the people we study should also, where relevant, be applied to our own activities as researchers.
>
> (Hammersley and Atkinson, 1983: 18 and 19)

Highly reflexive researchers will be acutely aware of the ways in which their selectivity, perception, background and inductive processes and paradigms shape the research. They are research instruments. McCormick and James (1988: 191) argue that combating reactivity through reflexivity requires researchers to monitor closely and continually their own interactions with participants, their own reaction, roles, biases and any other matters that might affect the research. This is addressed more fully in Chapter 10 on validity, encompassing issues of triangulation and respondent validity.

Lincoln and Guba (1985: 226–47) set out ten elements in research design for naturalistic studies:

1 Determining a focus for the enquiry.
2 Determining the fit of paradigm to focus.
3 Determining the 'fit' of the enquiry paradigm to the substantive theory selected to guide the enquiry.
4 Determining where and from whom data will be collected.
5 Determining successive phases of the enquiry.
6 Determining instrumentation.
7 Planning data collection and recording modes.
8 Planning data analysis procedures.
9 Planning the logistics:

  a prior logistical considerations for the project as a whole;
  b the logistics of field excursions prior to going into the field;
  c the logistics of field excursions while in the field;
  d the logistics of activities following field excursions;
  e the logistics of closure and termination.

10 Planning for trustworthiness.

These elements can be set out into a sequential, staged approach to planning naturalistic research (see, for example, Schatzman and Strauss, 1973; Delamont, 1992). Spradley (1979) sets out the stages of: (i) selecting a problem; (ii) collecting cultural data; (iii) analysing cultural data; (iv) formulating ethnographic hypotheses; (v) writing the ethnography. We offer a fuller, 12-stage model earlier in the chapter.

Like other styles of research, naturalistic and qualitative methods will need to formulate research questions which should be clear and unambiguous but open to change as the research develops. Strauss (1987) terms these 'generative questions': they stimulate the line of investigation, suggest initial hypotheses and areas for data collection, yet they do not foreclose the possibility of modification as the research develops. A balance has to be struck between having research questions that are so broad that they do not steer the research in any particular direction, and so narrow that they block new avenues of enquiry (Flick, 2004b: 150).

Miles and Huberman (1994) identify two types of qualitative research design: loose and tight. Loose research designs have broadly defined concepts and areas of study, and, indeed, are open to changes of methodology. These are suitable, they suggest, when the researchers are experienced and when the research is investigating new fields or developing new constructs, akin to the flexibility and openness of theoretical sampling of Glaser and Strauss (1967). By contrast, a tight research design has narrowly restricted research questions and predetermined procedures, with limited flexibility. These, the authors suggest, are useful when the researchers are inexperienced, when the research is intended to look at particular specified issues, constructs, groups or individuals, or when the research brief is explicit.

Even though, in naturalistic research, issues and theories emerge from the data, this does not preclude the value of having research questions. Flick (1998: 51) suggests three types of research questions in qualitative research, namely those that are concerned with: (a) describing states, their causes and how these states are sustained; (b) describing processes of change and consequences of those states; (c) how suitable they are for supporting or not supporting hypotheses and assumptions or for generating new hypotheses and assumptions (the 'generative questions' referred to above).

Should one have a hypothesis in qualitative research?

We mentioned in Chapter 1 that positivist approaches typically test pre-formulated hypotheses and that a distinguishing feature of naturalistic and qualitative approaches is its reluctance to enter the hypothetico-deductive paradigm (e.g. Meinefeld, 2004: 153), not least because there is a recognition that the researcher influences the research and because the research is much more open and emergent in qualitative approaches. Indeed, Meinefeld, citing classic studies like Whyte's (1955) *Street Corner Society*, suggests that it is impossible to predetermine hypotheses, whether one would wish to or not, as prior knowledge cannot be presumed. Glaser and Strauss (1967) suggest that researchers should deliberately free themselves from all prior knowledge, even suggesting that it is impossible to read up in advance, as it is not clear what reading will turn out to be relevant – the data speak for themselves. Theory is the end point of the research, not its starting point.

One has to be mindful that the researcher's own background interest, knowledge and biography precede the research and that though initial hypotheses may not be foregrounded in qualitative research, nevertheless the initial establishment of the research presupposes a particular area of interest, i.e. the research and data for focus are not theory-free; knowledge is not theory-free. Indeed Glaser and Strauss (1967) acknowledge that they brought their own prior knowledge to their research on dying.

The resolution of this apparent contradiction – the call to reject an initial hypothesis in qualitative research, yet a recognition that all research commences with some prior knowledge or theory that gives rise to the research, however embryonic – may lie in several fields. These include: an openness to data (Meinefeld, 2004: 156–7); a preparedness to modify one's initial presuppositions and position; a declaration of the extent to which the researcher's prior knowledge may be influencing the research (i.e. reflexivity); a recognition of the tentative nature of one's hypothesis; a willing-

ness to use the research to generate a hypothesis; and, as a more extreme position, an acknowledgement that having a hypothesis may be just as much a part of qualitative research as it is of quantitative research.

An alternative to research hypotheses in qualitative research is a set of research questions, and we consider these below. For qualitative research, Miles and Huberman (1994: 74) also suggest the replacement of 'hypotheses' with 'propositions', as this indicates that the qualitative research is not necessarily concerned with testing a predetermined hypothesis as such but, nevertheless, is concerned to be able to generate and test a theory (e.g. grounded theory that is tested).

11.3 Features and stages of a qualitative study

An effective qualitative study has several features (Creswell, 1998: 20–2), and these can be addressed in evaluating qualitative research:

- It uses rigorous procedures and multiple methods for data collection.
- The study is framed within the assumptions and nature of qualitative research.
- Enquiry is a major feature, and can follow one or more different traditions (e.g. biography, ethnography, phenomenology, case study, grounded theory).
- The project commences with a single focus on an issue or problem rather than a hypothesis or the supposition of a causal relationship of variables. Relationships may emerge later, but that is open.
- Criteria for verification are set out, and rigour is practised in writing up the report.
- Verisimilitude is required, such that readers can imagine being in the situation.
- Data are analysed at different levels; they are multilayered.
- The writing engages the reader and is replete with unexpected insights, whilst maintaining believability and accuracy.

Maxwell (2005: 21) argues that qualitative research should have both *practical* goals (e.g. that can be accomplished, that deliver a specific outcome and meet a need) and *intellectual* goals (e.g. to understand or explain something). His practical goals (p. 24) are: (a) to generate 'results and theories' that are credible and that can be understood by both participants and other readers; (b) to conduct formative evaluation in order to improve practice; and (c) to engage in 'collaborative and action research' with different parties. His intellectual goals (pp. 22–3) are: (a) to understand the meanings attributed to events and situations by participants; (b) to understand particular contexts in which participants are located; (c) to identify unanticipated events, situations and phenomena and to generate grounded theories that incorporate these; (d) to understand processes that contribute to situations, events and actions; and (e) to develop causal explanations of phenomena.

Maxwell (2005: 23) suggests that, whilst quantitative research is interested in discovering the *variance* – and regularity – in the effects of one or more particular independent variables on an outcome, qualitative research is interested in the causal processes at work in understanding how one or more interventions or factors lead to an outcome, the mechanisms of their causal linkages. Quantitative research can tell us correlations, how much, whether and 'what', whilst qualitative research can tell us the 'how' and 'why' – the processes – involved in understanding how things occur.

Maxwell also argues that qualitative research should be based on a suitable theoretical or paradigmal basis. Quoting Becker (1986), Maxwell (2005: 37) argues that if a researcher bases his or her research in an inappropriate theory or paradigm it is akin to a worker wearing the wrong clothes: it inhibits comfort and the ability to work properly. Maxwell cautions researchers to recognize that theoretical premises may not always be clear at the outset of the research; they may emerge, change, be added to and so on over time as the qualitative research progresses. We have discussed theories and paradigms in Chapter 1. Theory, Maxwell avers (p. 43) can provide a supporting set of principles, world view or sense-making referent, and it can be used as a 'spotlight', illuminating something very specific in a particular event or phenomenon. He advocates a cautious approach to the use of theory (p. 46), steering between, on the one hand, having it unnecessarily constrain and narrow a field of investigation and being accepted too readily and uncritically, and, on the other hand, not using it enough to ground rigorous research. Theories used in qualitative research should not only be those of the researcher, but also those of the participants. He suggests that theory can provide the conceptual and justificatory basis for the qualitative research being undertaken, and it can also inform the methods and data sources for the study (p. 55).

Stage 1 Locating a field of study

Bogdan and Biklen (1992: 2) suggest that research questions in qualitative research are not framed by simply operationalizing variables as in the positivist paradigm. Rather, research questions are formulated *in situ* and in response to situations observed, i.e. that topics are investigated in all their complexity, in the naturalistic context. The field, as Arsenault and Anderson (1998: 125) state, 'is used generically in qualitative research and quite simply refers to where the phenomenon exists'.

In some qualitative studies, the selection of the research field will be informed by the research purposes, the need for the research, what gave rise to the research, the problem to be addressed, and the research questions and sub-questions. In other qualitative studies these elements may only emerge after the researcher has been immersed for some time in the research site itself.

Stage 2 Formulating research questions

Research questions are an integral and driving feature of qualitative research. They must be able to be answered concretely, specifically and with evidence. They must be achievable and finite (cf. Maxwell, 2005: 65–78) and they are often characterized by being closed rather than open questions. Whereas research purposes can be open and less finite, motivated by a concern for 'understanding', research questions, by contrast, though they are informed by research purposes, are practical and able to be accomplished (Maxwell, 2005: 68–9).

Hence instead of asking a non-directly answerable question such as 'how should we improve online learning for biology students?' we can ask a specific, focused, bounded and answerable question such as 'how has the introduction of an online teacher–student chat room improved Form 5 students' interest in learning biology?'. Here the word 'should' (as an open question) has been replaced with 'has', the general terminology of 'online learning' has been replaced with 'an online teacher–student chat room', and the open-endedness of the first question has been replaced with the closed nature of the second (cf. Maxwell, 2005: 21).

Whereas in quantitative research, a typical research question asks 'what' and 'how much' (e.g. 'how much do male secondary students prefer female teachers of mathematics, and what is the relative weighting of the factors that account for their preferences?'), a qualitative research question often asks more probing, process-driven research questions (e.g. 'how do secondary school students in school X decide their preferences for male or female teachers of mathematics?').

Maxwell (2005: 75) suggests that qualitative research questions are suitable for answering questions about: (a) the *meanings* attributed by participants to situations, events, behaviours and activities; (b) the influence of *context* (e.g. physical, social, temporal, interpersonal) on participants' views, actions and behaviours; and (c) the *processes* by which actions, behaviours, situations and outcomes emerge.

Whilst in quantitative research, the research questions (or hypotheses to be tested) typically drive the research and are determined at the outset, in qualitative research a more iterative process occurs (Light *et al.*, 1990: 19). Here the researcher may have an initial set of research purposes, or even questions, but these may change over the course of the research, as the researcher finds out more about the research setting, participants, context and phenomena under investigation, i.e. the setting of research questions is not a once-and-for-all affair. This is not to say that qualitative research is an unprincipled, aimless activity; rather it is to say that, whilst the researcher may have clear purposes, the researcher is sensitive to the emergent situation in which she finds herself, and this steers the research questions. Research questions are the consequence, not the driver, of the situation and the interactions that take place within it. Indeed, in Chapters 6 and 7 we noted that the research questions are the consequence of the interaction between the goals, conceptual framework, methods and validity of the research (Maxwell, 2005: 11). It is important for the qualitative researcher to ask the right questions rather than to ask about what turn out to be irrelevancies to the participants. As Tukey (1962: 13) remarked, it is better to have approximate, inexact or imprecise answers to the right question than to have precise answers to the wrong question. The qualitative researcher has to be sensitized to the emergent key features of a situation before firming up the research questions.

Stage 3 Addressing ethical issues

Deyle *et al.* (1992: 623) identify several critical ethical issues that need to be addressed in approaching the research: How does one present oneself in the field? As whom does one present oneself? How ethically defensible is it to pretend to be somebody that you are not in order to: (a) gain knowledge that you would otherwise not be able to acquire; (b) obtain and preserve access to places which otherwise you would be unable to secure or sustain?

The issues here are several. First, there is the matter of *informed consent* (to participate and for disclosure), whether and how to gain participant assent (see also LeCompte and Preissle, 1993: 66). This uncovers another consideration, namely *covert* or *overt* research. On the one hand there is a powerful argument for informed consent. However, the more participants know about the research the less naturally they may behave (LeCompte and Preissle, 1993: 108), and naturalism is self-evidently a key criterion of the naturalistic paradigm.

Mitchell (1993) catches the dilemma for researchers in deciding whether to undertake overt or covert research. The issue of informed consent, he argues, can lead to the selection of particular forms of research – those where researchers can control the phenomena under investigation – thereby excluding other kinds of research where subjects behave in less controllable, predictable, prescribed ways, indeed where subjects may come in and out of the research over time.

Mitchell argues that in the real social world access to important areas of research is prohibited if informed consent has to be sought, for example in researching those on the margins of society or the disadvantaged. It is to the participants' own advantage that secrecy is maintained as, if secrecy is not upheld, important work may not be done and 'weightier secrets' (Mitchell, 1993: 54) may be kept which are of legitimate public concern and in the participants' own interests. He makes a powerful case for secrecy, arguing that informed consent may excuse social scientists from the risk of confronting powerful, privileged and cohesive groups who wish to protect themselves from public scrutiny. Secrecy and informed consent are moot points. The researcher, then, has to consider her loyalties and responsibilities (LeCompte and Preissle, 1993: 106), for example what is the public's right to know and what is the individual's right to privacy (Morrison, 1993; De Laine, 2000: 13).

In addition to the issue of overt or covert research, LeCompte and Preissle (1993) indicate that the problems of *risk* and *vulnerability* to subjects must be addressed; steps must be taken to prevent risk or harm to participants (non-maleficence – the principle of *primum non nocere*). Bogdan and Biklen (1992: 54) extend this to include issues of embarrassment as well as harm to those taking part. The question of vulnerability is present at its strongest when participants in the research have their freedom to choose limited, e.g. by dint of their age, by health, by social constraints, by dint of their lifestyle (e.g. engaging in criminality), social acceptability, experience of being victims (e.g. of abuse, of violent crime) (p. 107). As the authors comment, participants rarely initiate research, so it is the responsibility of the researcher to protect them. Relationships between researcher and the researched are rarely symmetrical in terms of power; it is often the case that those with more power, information and resources research those with less.

A standard protection is often the guarantee of *confidentiality*, withholding participants' real names and other identifying characteristics. The authors contrast this with anonymity, where identity is withheld because it is genuinely unknown (Bogdan and Biklen, 1992: 106). The issues are raised of identifiability and traceability. Further, participants might be able to identify themselves in the research report though others may not be able to identify them. A related factor here is the *ownership* of the data and the results, the control of the release of data (and to whom, and when) and what rights respondents have to veto the research results. Patrick (1973) indicates this point at its sharpest, when as an ethnographer of a Glasgow gang, he was witness to a murder; the dilemma was clear – to report the matter (and, thereby, also to 'blow his cover', consequently endangering his own life) or to stay as a covert researcher.

Bogdan and Biklen (1992: 54) add to this discussion the need to respect participants as subjects, not simply as research objects to be used and then discarded. Mason (2002: 41) suggests that it is important for researchers to consider the parties, bodies, practices that might be interested in, or affected by, the research and the implications of the answer to these questions for the conduct, reporting and dissemination of the enquiry. We address ethics in Chapters 2 and 5 and we advise readers to refer to these.

Stage 4 Deciding the sampling

In an ideal world the researcher would be able to study a group in its entirety. This was the case in Goffman's (1968) work on 'total institutions' – e.g. hospitals, prisons and police forces (see also Chapter 31). It was also the practice of anthropologists who were able to explore specific isolated communities or tribes. That is rarely possible nowadays because such groups are no longer isolated or insular. Hence the researcher is faced with the issue of sampling, that is deciding which people it will be possible to select to represent the wider group (however defined). The researcher has to decide the groups for which the research questions are appropriate, the contexts which are important for the research, the time periods that will be needed, and the possible artefacts of interest to the investigator. In other words decisions are necessary on the sampling of people, contexts, issues, time frames, artefacts and data sources. This takes the discussion beyond conventional notions of sampling.

In several forms of research, sampling is fixed at the start of the study, though there may be attrition of the sample through 'mortality' (e.g. people leaving the study). Mortality is seen as problematic. Ethnographic research regards this as natural rather than irksome. People come into and go from the study. This impacts on the decision whether to have a synchronic investigation occurring at a single point in time, or a diachronic study where events and behaviour are monitored over time to allow for change, development and evolving situations. In ethnographic enquiry sampling is recur-

sive and ad hoc rather than fixed at the outset; it changes and develops over time. Let us consider how this might happen.

LeCompte and Preissle (1993: 82–3) point out that ethnographic methods rule out statistical sampling, for a variety of reasons:

- the characteristics of the wider population are unknown;
- there are no straightforward boundary markers (categories or strata) in the group;
- generalizability, a goal of statistical methods, is not necessarily a goal of ethnography;
- characteristics of a sample may not be evenly distributed across the sample;
- only one or two subsets of a characteristic of a total sample may be important;
- researchers may not have access to the whole population;
- some members of a subset may not be drawn from the population from which the sampling is intended to be drawn.

Hence other types of sampling are required. A criterion-based selection requires the researcher to specify in advance a set of attributes, factors, characteristics or criteria that the study must address. The task then is to ensure that these appear in the sample selected (the equivalent of a stratified sample). There are other forms of sampling (discussed in Chapter 8) that are useful in ethnographic research (Bogdan and Biklen, 1992: 70; LeCompte and Preissle, 1993: 69–83), such as:

- convenience sampling (opportunistic sampling, selecting from whoever happens to be available);
- critical-case sampling (e.g. people who display the issue or set of characteristics in their entirety or in a way that is highly significant for their behaviour);
- extreme-case sampling (the norm of a characteristic is identified, then the extremes of that characteristic are located, and finally, the bearers of that extreme characteristic are selected);
- typical-case sampling (where a profile of attributes or characteristics that are possessed by an 'average', typical person or case is identified, and the sample is selected from these conventional people or cases);
- unique-case sampling, where cases that are rare, unique or unusual on one or more criteria are identified, and sampling takes places within these. Here whatever other characteristics or attributes a person might share with others, a particular attribute or characteristic sets that person apart;

- reputational-case sampling, a variant of extreme-case and unique-case sampling, is where a researcher chooses a sample on the recommendation of experts in the field;
- snowball sampling – using the first interviewee to suggest or recommend other interviewees.

Patton (1980) identifies several types of sampling that are useful in naturalistic research, including

- sampling extreme/deviant cases. This is done in order to gain information about unusual cases that may be particularly troublesome or enlightening;
- sampling typical cases. This is done in order to avoid rejecting information on the grounds that it has been gained from special or deviant cases;
- snowball sampling. This is where one participant provides access to a further participant and so on;
- maximum variation sampling. This is done in order to document the range of unique changes that have emerged, often in response to the different conditions to which participants have had to adapt. It is useful if the aim of the research is to investigate the variations, range and patterns in a particular phenomenon or phenomena (Guba and Lincoln, 1989: 178; Ezzy, 2002: 74);
- sampling according to the intensity with which the features of interest are displayed or occur;
- sampling critical cases. This is done in order to permit maximum applicability to others – if the information holds true for critical cases (e.g. cases where all the factors sought are present), then it is likely to hold true for others;
- sampling politically important or sensitive cases. This can be done to draw attention to the case;
- convenience sampling. This saves time and money and spares the researcher the effort of finding less amenable participants.

One can add to this list types of sample from Miles and Huberman (1994: 28):

- homogenous sampling (which focuses on groups with similar characteristics);
- theoretical sampling (in grounded theory, discussed below, where participants are selected for their ability to contribute to the developing/emergent theory);
- confirming and disconfirming cases (akin to the extreme and deviant cases indicated by Patton (1980), in order to look for exceptions to the rule, which may lead to the modification of the rule);
- random purposeful sampling (when the potential sample is too large, a smaller subsample can be used which still maintains some generalizability);
- stratified purposeful sampling (to identify subgroups and strata);
- criterion sampling (all those who meet some stated criteria for membership of the group or class under study);
- opportunistic sampling (to take advantage of unanticipated events, leads, ideas, issues).

Miles and Huberman make the point that these strategies can be used in combination as well as in isolation, and that using them in combination contributes to triangulation.

Patton (1980: 181) and Miles and Huberman (1994: 27–9) also counsel researchers on the dangers of convenience sampling, arguing that, being 'neither purposeful nor strategic' (Patton, 1980: 88), it cannot demonstrate representativeness even to the wider group being studied, let alone to a wider population.

Maxwell (2005: 89–90) indicates four possible purposes of 'purposeful selection':

- to achieve representativeness of the activities, behaviours, events, settings and individuals involved;
- to catch the breadth and heterogeneity of the population under investigation (i.e. the range of the possible variation: the 'maximum variation' sampling discussed above);
- to examine critical cases or extreme cases that provide a 'crucial test' of theories or that can illuminate a situation in ways which representative cases may not be able to do;
- to identify reasons for similarities and difference between individuals or settings (comparative research).

Maxwell (2005: 91) is clear that methods of data collection are not a logical corollary of, nor an analytically necessary consequence of, the research questions. Research questions and data collection are two conceptually separate activities, though, as we have mentioned earlier in this book, the researcher needs to ensure that they are mutually informing, in order to demonstrate cohesion and fitness for purpose. Methods cannot simply be cranked out, mechanistically, from research questions. Both the methods of data collection and the research questions are strongly influenced by the setting, the participants, the relationships and the research design as they unfold over time.

We discuss below two other categories of sample: 'primary informants' and 'secondary informants'

(Morse, 1994: 228), those who completely fulfil a set of selection criteria and those who fill a selection of those criteria respectively.

Lincoln and Guba (1985: 201–2) suggest an important difference between conventional and naturalistic research designs. In the former the intention is to focus on similarities and to be able to make generalizations, whereas in the latter the objective is informational, to provide such a wealth of detail that the uniqueness and individuality of each case can be represented. To the charge that naturalistic enquiry, thereby, cannot yield generalizations because of sampling flaws the writers argue that this is necessarily though trivially true. In a word, it is unimportant.

Patton (1980: 184) takes a slightly more cavalier approach to sampling, suggesting that 'there are no rules for sample size in qualitative enquiry', with the size of the sample depending on what one wishes to know, the purposes of the research, what will be useful and credible, and what can be done within the resources available, e.g. time, money, people, support – important considerations for the novice researcher.

In much qualitative research, it may not be possible or, indeed, desirable, to know in advance whom to sample or whom to include. One of the features of qualitative research is its emergent nature. Hence the researcher may only know which people to approach or include as the research progresses and unfolds (Flick, 2009: 125). In this case the nature of sampling is determined by the emergent issues in the study; this is termed 'theoretical sampling': once data have been collected, the researcher decides where to go next, in light of the analysis of the data, in order to gather more data in order to develop his or her theory (Flick, 2009: 118).

Ezzy (2002: 74) underlines the notion of 'theoretical sampling' from Glaser and Strauss (1967) in his comment that, unlike other forms of research, qualitative enquiries may not always commence with the full knowledge of whom to sample, but that the sample is determined on an ongoing, emergent basis. Theoretical sampling starts with data and then, having reviewed these, the researcher decides where to go next to collect data for the emerging theory (Glaser and Strauss, 1967: 45). We discuss this more fully in Chapter 33.

In theoretical sampling, individuals and groups are selected for their potential – or hoped for – ability to offer new insights into the emerging theory, i.e. they are chosen on the basis of their significant contribution to theory generation and development. As the theory develops, so the researcher decides whom to approach to request their participation. Theoretical sampling does not claim to know the population characteristics or to represent known populations in advance, and sample

size is not defined in advance; sampling is only concluded when theoretical saturation (discussed below) is reached.

Ezzy (2002) gives as an example of theoretical sampling his own work on unemployment (pp. 74–5) where he developed a theory that levels of distress experienced by unemployed people were influenced by their levels of financial distress. He interviewed unemployed low-income and high-income groups with and without debt, to determine their levels of distress. He reported that levels of distress were not caused so much by absolute levels of income but levels of income in relation to levels of debt.

In the educational field one could imagine theoretical sampling in an example thus: interviewing teachers about their morale might give rise to a theory that teacher morale is negatively affected by disruptive student behaviour in schools. This might suggest the need to sample teachers working with many disruptive students in difficult schools, as a 'critical case sampling'. However, the study finds that some of the teachers working in these circumstances have high morale, not least because they have come to expect disruptive behaviour from students with so many problems, and so are not surprised or threatened by it, and because the staff in these schools provide tremendous support for each other in difficult circumstances – they all know what it is like to have to work with challenging students.

So the study decides to focus on teachers working in schools with far fewer disruptive students. The researcher discovers that it is these teachers who experience far lower morale, and she hypothesizes that this is because this latter group of teachers has higher expectations of student behaviour, such that having only one or two students who do not conform to these expectations deflates staff morale significantly, and because disruptive behaviour is regarded in these schools as teacher weakness, and there is little or no mutual support. Her theory, then, is refined, to suggest that teacher morale is affected more by teacher expectations than by disruptive behaviour, so she adopts a 'maximum variation sampling' of teachers in a range of schools, to investigate how expectations and morale are related to disruptive behaviour. In this case the sampling emerges as the research proceeds and the theory emerges; this is theoretical sampling, the 'royal way for qualitative studies' (Flick, 2004b: 151). Schatzman and Strauss (1973: 38ff.) suggest that sampling within theoretical sampling may change according to time, place, individuals and events.

The above procedure accords with Glaser and Strauss's (1967) view that sampling involves continuously gathering data until practical factors (boundaries) put an end to data collection, or until no amendments have to be made to the theory in light of further data – their stage of 'theoretical saturation' – where the theory fits the data even when new data are gathered. Theoretical saturation is described by Glaser and Strauss (1967: 61) as being reached when any additional data collected do not advance, amend, refine or lead to the adjustment of the theory or its categories. That said, the researcher has to be cautious to avoid premature cessation of data collection; it would be too easy to close off research with limited data, when, in fact, further sampling and data collection might lead to a reformulation of the theory.

An extension of theoretical sampling is 'analytic induction', a process advanced by Znaniecki (1934). Here the researcher starts with a theory (that may have emerged from the data as in grounded theory) and then deliberately proceeds to look for deviant or discrepant cases, to provide a robust defence of the theory. This accords with Popper's notion of a rigorous scientific theory having to stand up to falsifiability tests. In analytic induction, the researcher deliberately seeks data which potentially could falsify the theory, thereby giving strength to the final theory.

We are suggesting here that, in qualitative research, sampling cannot always be decided in advance on a 'once and for all' basis. It may have to continue through the stages of data collection, analysis and reporting. This reflects the circular process of qualitative research, in which data collection, analysis, interpretation and reporting and sampling do not necessarily have to proceed in a linear fashion; the process is recursive and iterative. Sampling is not decided *a priori* – in advance – but may be decided, amended, added to, increased and extended as the research progresses.

Whilst sampling often refers to *people*, in qualitative research it also refers to *events*, *places*, *times*, *behaviours*, *activities*, *settings* and *processes* (cf. Miles and Huberman, 1984: 36). Many researchers will be concerned with short-term, small-scale qualitative research (e.g. qualitative interviews) rather than extended or large-scale ethnographic research, perhaps because they only have access to a small sample (too small to conduct meaningful statistical analysis) or because 'fitness for purpose' requires only a short-term qualitative study. In this case, it is important for careful boundaries to be drawn in the research, indicating clearly what can and cannot legitimately be said from the research.

For example, a fundamental question might be for the researcher to decide how long to stay in a situation. Too short, and she may miss an important outcome, too long and key features may become a blur. For example,

let us imagine a situation of two teachers in the same school. Teacher A introduces collaborative group work to a class, in order to improve their motivation for, say, learning a foreign language. She gives them a pre-test on motivation, and finds that it is low; she conducts the intervention and then, at the end of two months, gives them another test of motivation, and finds no change. She concludes that the intervention has failed. However, months later, after the intervention has finished, the students tell her that in fact their overall motivation to learn that foreign language had improved, but it took time for them to realize it after the intervention. Teacher B tries the same intervention, but decides to administer the post-test one year after the intervention has ended; she finds no change to motivation levels of the students, but had she conducted the post-test sooner, she would have found a difference. Timing and sampling of timing are important (cf. Maxwell, 2005: 33).

Stage 5 Finding a role and managing entry into the context

This involves matters of access and permission, establishing a reason for being there, developing a role and a persona, identifying the 'gatekeepers' who facilitate entry and access to the group being investigated (see LeCompte and Preissle, 1993: 100 and 111). The issue here is complex, for the researcher will be both a member of the group and yet studying that group, so it is a delicate matter to negotiate a role that will enable the investigator to be both participant and observer. The authors comment (p. 112) that the most important elements in securing access are the willingness of researchers to be flexible and their sensitivity to nuances of behaviour and response in the participants. Indeed De Laine (2000: 41) remarks that an ability to get on with people in the situation in question, and a willingness to join in with and share experiences in the activities in question are important criteria for gaining and maintaining access and entry into the field.

Wolff (2004: 195–6) suggests that there are two fundamental questions to be addressed in considering access and entry into the field:

a How can the researcher succeed in making contact and securing cooperation from informants?

b How can the researcher position herself/himself in the field so as to secure the necessary time, space, social relations to be able to carry out the research?

Flick (1998: 57) summarizes Wolff's work in identifying several issues in entering institutions for the purpose of conducting research:

1 Research is always an intrusion and intervention into a social system, and, so, disrupts the system to be studied, such that the system reacts, often defensively.

2 There is a 'mutual opacity' between the social system under study and the research project, which is not reduced by information exchange between the system under study and the researcher; rather this increases the complexity of the situation and, hence, 'immune reactions'.

3 Rather than striving for mutual understanding at the point of entry, it is more advisable to strive for an agreement as a process.

4 Whilst it is necessary to agree storage rights for data, this may contribute to increasing the complexity of the agreement to be reached.

5 The field under study only becomes clear when one has entered it.

6 The research project usually has nothing to offer the social system; hence no great promises for benefit or services can be made by the researcher, yet there may be no real reason why the social system should reject the researcher.

As Flick (1998: 57) remarks, the research will disturb the system and disrupt routines without being able to offer any real benefit for the institution.

The issue of managing relations is critical for the qualitative researcher. We discuss issues of access, gatekeepers and informants in Chapter 8. The researcher is seen as coming 'without history' (Wolff, 2004: 198), a 'professional stranger' (Flick, 1998: 59), one who has to be accepted, become familiar and yet remain distant from those being studied. Indeed Flick (1998: 60) suggests four roles of the researcher: stranger, visitor, insider and initiate. The first two essentially maintain the outsider role, whilst the latter two attempt to reach into the institution from an insider's perspective. These latter two become difficult to manage if one is dealing with sensitive issues (see Chapter 9). This typology resonates with the four roles typically cited for observers:

OUTSIDER ⟵——————————⟶ INSIDER				
Detached as observer	Observer	Observer as participant	Participant	Complete participant

Swain (2006), researching junior schools in an ethnography, comments that the researchers may often have to switch roles, from being completely passive observers to being completely active participants, as the situation demands, i.e. he or she will draw on the complete continuum of observations and roles.

Role negotiation, balance and trust are significant and difficult. For example, if one were to research a school, what role should one adopt: a teacher, a researcher, an inspector, a friend, a manager, a provider of a particular service (e.g. extra-curricular activities), a counsellor, a social worker, a resource provider, a librarian, a cleaner, a server in the school shop or canteen, and so on? The issue is that one has to try to select a role that will provide access to as wide a range of people as possible, preserve neutrality (not being seen as on anybody's side) and enable confidences to be secured.

Role conflict, strain and ambiguity are to be expected in qualitative research. For example, De Laine (2000: 29) comments on the potential conflicts between the researcher *qua* researcher, therapist, friend. She indicates that diverse role positions are rarely possible to plan in advance, and are an inevitable part of fieldwork, giving rise to ethical and moral problems for the researcher, and, in turn, requiring ongoing negotiation and resolution.

Roles change over time. Walford (2001: 62) reports a staged process wherein the researcher's role moved through five phases: newcomer, provisional acceptance, categorical acceptance, personal acceptance and imminent migrant. He also reports (p. 71) that it is almost to be expected that managing different roles not only throws the researcher into questioning his/her ability to handle the situation, but brings considerable emotional and psychological stress, anxiety and feelings of inadequacy. This is thrown into sharp relief when researchers have to conceal information, take on different roles in order to gain access, retain neutrality, compromise personal beliefs and values, and handle situations where they are seeking information from others but not divulging information about themselves. Walford suggests that researchers may have little opportunity to negotiate roles and manoeuvre roles, as they are restricted by the expectations of those being researched.

A related issue is the timing of the point of entry, so that researchers can commence the research at appropriate junctures (e.g. before the start of a programme, at the start of a programme, during a programme, at the end of a programme, after the end of a programme). The issue goes further than this, for the ethnographer will need to ensure acceptance into the group, which will be a matter of dress, demeanour, persona, age, colour, ethnicity, empathy and identification with the group, language, accent, argot and jargon, willingness to become involved and to take on the group's values and behaviour, etc. (see Patrick's (1973) fascinating study of a Glasgow gang). The researcher, then, has to be aware of the significance of 'impression management' (Hammersley and Atkinson, 1983: 78ff.). In covert research these factors take on added significance, as one slip could 'blow one's cover' (Patrick, 1973).

Lofland (1971) suggests that the field researcher should attempt to adopt the role of the 'acceptable incompetent', balancing intrusion with knowing when to remain apart. Such balancing is an ongoing process. Hammersley and Atkinson (1983: 97–9) suggest that researchers have to handle the management of 'marginality': they are in the organization but not of it. They comment that the ethnographer must be intellectually poised between 'familiarity' and 'strangeness', while socially he or she is poised between 'stranger' and 'friend'. They also comment that this management of several roles, not least the management of marginality, can engender 'a continual sense of insecurity' (p. 100).

Gaining access and entry should be regarded as a process (Walford, 2001: 31) that unfolds over time, rather than a once and for all matter. Walford charts the several setbacks, delays and modifications that occur and have to be expected in gaining entry to qualitative research sites.

Stage 6 Finding informants

This involves identifying those people who have the knowledge about the society or group being studied. This places the researcher in a difficult position, for she has to be able to evaluate key informants, to decide:

- whose accounts are more important than others;
- which informants are competent to pass comments;
- which are reliable;
- what the statuses of the informants are;
- how representative are the key informants (of the range of people, of issues, of situations, of views, of status, of roles, of the group);
- how to see the informants in different settings;
- how knowledgeable informants actually are – do they have intimate and expert understanding of the situation;
- how central to the organization or situation the informant is (e.g. marginal or central);
- how to meet and select informants;
- how critical the informants are as gatekeepers to other informants, opening up or restricting entry to people (Hammersley and Atkinson, 1983: 73);
- the relationship between the informant and others in the group or situation being studied.

Selecting informants and engaging with them is problematical; LeCompte and Preissle (1993: 95), for example, suggest that the first informants that an eth-

nographer meets might be self-selected people who are marginal to the group, have a low status, and who, therefore, might be seeking to enhance their own prestige by being involved with the research. Indeed Lincoln and Guba (1985: 252) argue that the researcher must be careful to use informants rather than informers, the latter possibly having 'an axe to grind'. Researchers who are working with gatekeepers, they argue, will be engaged in a constant process of bargaining and negotiation.

A 'good' informant, Morse (1994: 228) declares, is one who has the necessary knowledge, information and experience of the issue being researched, is capable of reflecting on that knowledge and experience, has time to be involved in the project, is willing to be involved in the project, and, indeed, can provide access to other informants. An informant who fulfils all these criteria is termed a 'primary informant'. Morse also cautions that not all these features may be present in the informants, but that they may still be useful for the research, though the researcher would have to decide how much time to spend with these 'secondary' informants.

Stage 7 Developing and maintaining relations in the field

This involves addressing interpersonal and practical issues, for example:

- building participants' confidence in the researcher;
- developing rapport, trust, sensitivity and discretion;
- handling people and issues with which the researcher disagrees or finds objectionable or repulsive;
- being attentive and empathizing;
- being discreet;
- deciding how long to stay. Spindler and Spindler (1992: 65) suggest that ethnographic validity is attained by having the researcher *in situ* long enough to see things happening repeatedly rather than just once, that is to say, observing regularities.

LeCompte and Preissle (1993: 89) suggest that fieldwork, particularly because it is conducted face to face, raises problems and questions that are less significant in research that is conducted at a distance, including: (a) how to communicate meaningfully with participants; (b) how they and the researcher might be affected by the emotions evoked in one another, and how to handle these; (c) differences and similarities between the researcher and the participants (e.g. personal characteristics, power, resources), and how these might affect relationships between parties and the course of the investigation; (d) the researcher's responsibilities to the participants (*qua* researcher and member of their community), even if the period of residence in the community is short; (e) how to balance responsibilities to the community with responsibilities to other interested parties.

Critically important in this area is the maintenance of trust and rapport (De Laine, 2000: 41), showing interest, assuring confidentiality (where appropriate) and avoiding being judgemental. De Laine adds to these (p. 97) the ability to tolerate ambiguity, to keep self-doubt in check, to withstand insecurity, and to be flexible and accommodating. Such features are not able to be encapsulated in formal agreements, but they are the lifeblood of effective qualitative enquiry. They are process matters.

Qualitative research recognizes that relationships emerge over time, they are not a one-off affair or in which access is negotiated and achieved on a once-and-for-all basis; rather, relationships, trust, intimacy, reciprocity, intrusion, consideration and access have to be constantly negotiated, renegotiated and agreed as time, relationships and events move on, as in real life (De Laine, 2000: 83–5). In this context Maxwell (2005: 83) suggests that 'rapport' is a problematic concept in discussing relationships, as it is not a unitary concept concerning its *amount* or *degree* (indeed one may have too much or too little of it (Seidman, 1998: 80–2)), but its nature and kind changes over time, as people and events evolve.

Rapport and relationships influence the data collection, sampling and research design (Maxwell, 2005: 83). Indeed, in longitudinal qualitative research, Thomson and Holland (2003: 235) report that maintaining and sustaining positive relationships over time can contribute significantly to lower attrition rates amongst both participants and researchers (and attrition is a problem in longitudinal research as people move out of the area, leave as they grow older, lose contact, become too busy and so on (Thomson and Holland, 2003: 241)). Similarly, Gordon and Lahelma (2003: 246), researching the transition of participants from being secondary school students into becoming adults, comment that maintaining rapport is a critical factor in longitudinal ethnographic research. Rapport, they aver (p. 248) is signified in attention to non-verbal communication as well as in the sensitive handling of verbal communication.

Rapport is not easy to maintain, as it can be overlaid with power relations. For example Swain (2006: 205) comments that, as an adult conducting an ethnography with junior school children, he felt obliged, at times, to take the 'adult', controlling position in the research, and that he could not act as a young child, indeed that

the children would find it odd if he did (p. 207), so he made no pretence of being less adult-centric as the occasion demanded. He was not a child – he was older, taller, had a deeper voice and dressed differently, and he could not pretend to be other than this, even though he gave the children freedom to respond to his questions as they wished. That said, Swain commented that he tried to adopt a role that made it clear to the children that he was not a teacher.

The issue here is that the data collection process is itself socially situated; it is neither a clean, antiseptic activity nor always a straightforward negotiation.

Stage 8 Data collection *in situ*

The qualitative researcher is able to use a variety of techniques for gathering information. There is no single prescription for which data collection instruments to use; rather the issue here is of 'fitness for purpose' because, as was mentioned earlier, the ethnographer is a methodological omnivore! Some qualitative research can be highly structured, with the structure being determined in advance of the research (pre-ordinate and nomothetic research), for example in order to enable comparisons to be made – similarities and differences (e.g. Miles and Huberman's (1984) cross-site analysis of several schools).

Less structured approaches to qualitative research enable specific, unique and idiographic accounts to be given, in which the research is highly sensitive to the specific situation, the specific participants, the relationships between the researcher and the participants (Maxwell, 2005: 82), and the emergent most suitable ways of conducting the data analysis.

There are several types of data collection instruments that are used more widely in qualitative research than others. The researcher can use field notes, participant observation, journal notes, interviews, diaries, life histories, artefacts, documents, video recordings, audio recordings, etc. Several of these are discussed elsewhere in this book. Lincoln and Guba (1985: 199) distinguish between 'obtrusive' (e.g. interviews, observation, non-verbal language) and 'unobtrusive' methods (e.g. documents and records), on the basis of whether another human typically is present at the point of data collection.

Field notes can be written both *in situ* and away from the situation. They contain the results of observations. The nature of observation in ethnographic research is discussed fully in Chapter 23. Accompanying observation techniques is the use of interviews, documentary analysis and life histories. These are discussed separately in Chapters 12 and 21. The popularly used interview technique employed in qualitative research is the semi-structured interview, where a schedule is prepared that is sufficiently open-ended to enable the contents to be reordered, digressions and expansions made, new avenues to be included, and further probing to be undertaken. Carspecken (1996: 159–60) describes how such interviews can range from the interrogator giving bland encouragements, 'non-leading' leads, active listening and low-inference para-phrasing to medium- and high-inference paraphrasing. In interviews the researcher might wish to further explore some matters arising from observations. In nat-uralistic research the canons of validity in interviews include: honesty, depth of response, richness of response and commitment of the interviewee (Oppen-heim, 1992).

Lincoln and Guba (1985: 268–70) propose several purposes for interviewing, including: *present construc-tions* of events, feelings, persons, organizations, activities, motivations, concerns, claims, etc.; *recon-structions* of past experiences; *projections* into the future; *verifying, amending and extending data.*

Further, Silverman (1993: 92–3) adds that inter-views in qualitative research are useful for: (a) gather-ing facts; (b) accessing beliefs about facts; (c) identifying feelings and motives; (d) commenting on the standards of actions (what could be done about situ-ations); (e) exploring present or previous behaviour; (f) eliciting reasons and explanations.

Lincoln and Guba (1985) emphasize that the plan-ning of the conduct of the interview is important, including the background preparation, the opening of the interview, its pacing and timing, keeping the con-versation going and eliciting knowledge, and rounding off and ending the interview. Clearly, it is important that careful consideration be given to the several stages of the interview. For example at the planning stage, attention will need to be given to the number (per person), duration, timing, frequency, setting/location, number of people in a single interview situation (e.g. individual or group interviews) and respondent styles (LeCompte and Preissle, 1993: 177). At the implemen-tation stage the conduct of the interview will be import-ant, for example, responding to interviewees, prompting, probing, supporting, empathizing, clarifying, crystalliz-ing, exemplifying, summarizing, avoiding censure, accepting. At the analysis stage there will be several important considerations, for example (LeCompte and Preissle, 1993: 195), the ease and clarity of communica-tion of meaning; the interest levels of the participants; the clarity of the question and the response; the preci-sion (and communication of this) of the interviewer; how the interviewer handles questionable responses (e.g. fabrications, untruths, claims made).

The qualitative interview tends to move away from a pre-structured, standardized form towards an open-ended or semi-structured arrangement (see Chapter 21), which enables respondents to project their own ways of defining the world. It permits flexibility rather than fixity of sequence of discussions, allowing participants to raise and pursue issues and matters that might not have been included in a pre-devised schedule (Denzin, 1970; Silverman, 1993).

The use of interviews is not automatic for qualita-tive research. Some participants may find it alien to their culture; they may feel uncomfortable with inter-views, or, indeed, with any such formal verbal commu-nication (Maxwell, 2005: 93). The qualitative researcher has to find a culturally appropriate and cul-turally sensitive way of gathering data. Maxwell (echoing Whyte, 1993: 303, discussed in Chapters 8 and 9) cites research in sensitive settings (e.g. heroin users) that indicates that it is unwise or not 'hip' to ask too many questions, and that conducting formal inter-views is an alienating activity, better to be replaced with informal conversations and field notes.

In addition to interviews, Lincoln and Guba (1985) discuss data collection from non-human sources, including:

i documents and records (e.g. archival records, private records). These have the attraction of being always available, often at low cost, and being factual. On the other hand they may be unrepresentative, they may be selective, lack objectivity, be of unknown validity, and may possibly be deliberately deceptive (see Finnegan, 1996);

ii unobtrusive informational residues. These include artefacts, physical traces and a variety of other records. Whilst they frequently have face validity, and whilst they may be simple and direct, gained by non-interventional means (hence reducing the prob-lems of reactivity), they may also be very heavily inferential, difficult to interpret, and may contain elements whose relevance is questionable.

Qualitative data collection is not hidebound to a few named strategies; it is marked by eclecticism and fitness for purpose. It is not to say that 'anything goes' but 'use what is appropriate' is sound advice. Mason (2002: 33–4) advocates the integration of methods, for several reasons:

■ To explore different elements or parts of a phenom-enon, ensuring that the researcher knows how they interrelate.

■ To answer different research questions.

- To answer the same research question but in different ways and from different perspectives.
- To give greater or lesser depth and breadth to analysis.
- To triangulate – corroborate – by seeking different data about the same phenomenon.

Mason (2002) argues that integration can take many forms. She suggests that it is necessary for researchers to consider whether the data are to complement each other, to be combined, grouped and aggregated, and to contribute to an overall picture. She also argues (p. 35) that it is important for the data to complement each other ontologically, to be ontologically consistent, i.e. whether they are 'based on similar, complementary or comparable assumptions about the nature of social entities and phenomena'. Added to this she suggests that integration must be in an epistemological sense, i.e. where the data emanate from the same, or at least complementary, epistemologies, whether they are based on 'similar, complementary or comparable assumptions about what can legitimately constitute knowledge of evidence' (p. 36). Finally Mason argues that integration must occur at the level of explanation. By this she means that the data from different sources and methods must be able to be combined into a coherent, convincing and relevant explanation and argument (p. 36).

Data collection also relates to sampling. For example, in qualitative or ethnographic interviews, though the researcher may wish to include a range of participants, in fact some of those participants may be shy, inarticulate, marginalized, dominated, introverted, overwhelmed or fearful in the presence of others or of being censured, uninterested in participating (Swain, 2006: 202). In these circumstances the researcher may have to use alternative methods of gathering data, such as observations methods. Indeed Miller and Dingwall (1997), in discussing the role of context in qualitative research, point out that an interview may be very unsettling for some participants, being too formal or unnatural; it is not the same as a conversation, and some participants may not 'open up' in a non-conversational situation. We discuss interviews and interviewing in Chapter 21.

Stage 9 Data collection outside the field

In order to make comparisons and to suggest explanations for phenomena, researchers might find it useful to go beyond the confines of the groups in which they occur. That this is a thorny issue is indicated in the following example. Two students are arguing very violently and physically in a school. At one level it is simply a fight between two people. However, this is a common occurrence between these two students as they are neighbours outside school and they don't enjoy positive amicable relations as their families are frequently feuding. The two households have been placed next door to each other by the local authority because it has taken a decision to keep together families who are very poor at paying for local housing rent (i.e. a 'sink' estate). The local authority has taken this decision because of a government policy to keep together disadvantaged groups so that targeted action and interventions can be more effective, thus meeting the needs of whole communities as well as individuals.

The issue here is: how far out of (or indeed inside) a micro-situation does the researcher need to go to understand that micro-situation? This is an imprecise matter but it is not insignificant in educational research, for example it underpinned: (a) the celebrated work by Bowles and Gintis (1976) on schooling in capitalist America, in which the authors suggested that the hidden curricula of schools were preparing students for differential occupational futures that perpetuated an inegalitarian capitalist system; (b) research on the self-fulfilling prophecy (Hurn, 1978); (c) work by Pollard (1985: 110) on the social world of the primary school, where everyday interactions in school were preparing students for the individualism, competition, achievement orientation, hierarchies and self-reliance that characterize mass private consumption in wider society; (d) Delamont's (1981) advocacy that educationists should study similar but different institutions to schools (e.g. hospitals and other 'total' institutions) in order to make the familiar strange (see also Erickson, 1973).

Stage 10 Data analysis

Though we devote two chapters specifically to qualitative data analysis later in this book (Chapters 28 and 29), there are some preliminary remarks that we make here, by way of fidelity to the 12-stage process of qualitative research outlined at the start of the chapter. Data analysis involves organizing, accounting for and explaining the data; in short, making sense of data in terms of participants' definitions of the situation, noting patterns, themes, categories and regularities. Typically in qualitative research, data analysis commences during the data collection process. There are several reasons for this, and these are discussed below.

At a practical level, qualitative research rapidly amasses huge amounts of data, and early analysis reduces the problem of data overload by selecting out significant features for future focus. Miles and Huberman (1984) suggest that careful data display is an important element of data reduction and selection. 'Progressive focussing', according to Parlett and Hamilton

(1976), starts with the researcher taking a wide angle lens to gather data, and then, by sifting, sorting, reviewing and reflecting on them, the salient features of the situation emerge. These are then used as the agenda for subsequent focusing. The process is like funnelling from the wide to the narrow.

Maxwell (2005: 95) cites evidence to argue for data analysis not only to be built into the design of qualitative research, but to start as soon as each stage or round of data collection, or as soon as any data have been collected, i.e. without waiting for the next stage, round or piece of data to have taken place. He cites the analogy of the fox having to keep close to the hare: keeping the collection and the analysis close together ensures that the researchers can keep close to changes and their effects. He suggests that data analysis commences with careful reading and rereading of the data, then constructing memos, categorizations (e.g. coding into organizational, substantive – descriptive – and theoretical categories (related to prior theory, or 'etic' categories, or grounded theory), and thematic analysis) and 'connecting strategies' such as narrative analysis (p. 96) and vignettes, discourse analysis and profiles (p. 98) that set the data in context and indicate relationships between different parts of the data such that the integrity – the wholeness – of the original context is preserved (p. 98), rather than the fracturing and regrouping of the data that can occur in a coding exercise.

At a theoretical level a major feature of qualitative research is that analysis commences early on in the data collection process so that theory generation can be undertaken (LeCompte and Preissle, 1993: 238). LeCompte and Preissle (1993: 237–53) advise that researchers should set out the main outlines of the phenomena that are under investigation. They then should assemble chunks or groups of data, putting them together to make a coherent whole (e.g. through writing summaries of what has been found). Then they should painstakingly take apart their field notes, matching, contrasting, aggregating, comparing and ordering notes made. The intention is to move from description to explanation and theory generation.

Thomson and Holland (2003: 236) suggest that, in longitudinal qualitative research, data analysis should be both cross-sectional (in order to discover the discourses and themes at work in the construction of identities and interpretations at a particular point in time) and longitudinal (in order to chart the development of narrative(s) over time). However, they also recognize that cross-sectional approaches and longitudinal approaches may sit together uncomfortably, as the former chops up and reassembles text from different participants in order to present themes at the moment in time, whilst the latter seeks individual narratives that require the continuity that only emerges over time and within individuals (p. 239).

Longitudinal research that uses ethnographic techniques (e.g. life histories) can also be used to chart transitions in participants, e.g. from primary to secondary school, from secondary school to university, from school to work, from childhood to adulthood, etc. Gordon and Lahelma (2003) comment that, in such research, the reflexivity of the participants can increase over time, and that sensitivity and rapport (discussed earlier) are key elements for success. Indeed the authors go further, to argue that, as the research develops over time, so does the obligation to demonstrate reciprocity in the relationships between researcher(s) and participants, so that, just as the participants give information, so the researcher has an ethical obligation to ensure that the research offers something positive, in return, to the participants. This need not necessarily mean a material incentive or reward; it could mean an opportunity for the participants to reflect on their own situation, to learn more about themselves and to support their development (p. 249). In this case reflexivity is not confined to the researcher, but extends to the participants as well (p. 252). We discuss cross-sectional and longitudinal studies (surveys) in Chapter 13.

Thomson and Holland (2003) also indicate the frustration and intimidation that early analysis in longitudinal research can cause for researchers, as there is never complete closure on data analysis, as 'the next round of data' can challenge earlier interpretations made by researchers. Indeed they question when is the right time to commence writing up or make interpretations.

In addition to the problem of continual openness to interpretation as qualitative research unfolds is the related issue of whose views/voices one includes in the data analysis, given that, in the interests of practicality, it may not be possible to include everyone's voice, even though the canons of validity in qualitative research might call for multiple voices to be heard. Eisenhart (2001: 19) points out that researchers all too easily can privilege some voices at the expense of others and that the express, beneficent intention of protecting some participants can have the effect of silencing them. How will the researcher present different, even conflicting voices, accounts or interpretations? What are the politics surrounding inclusion and exclusion of voices? We return to this issue in Part 5 on qualitative data analysis.

For clarity, the process of data analysis can be portrayed in a sequence of seven steps which are set out in Figure 11.3 and addressed in subsequent pages.

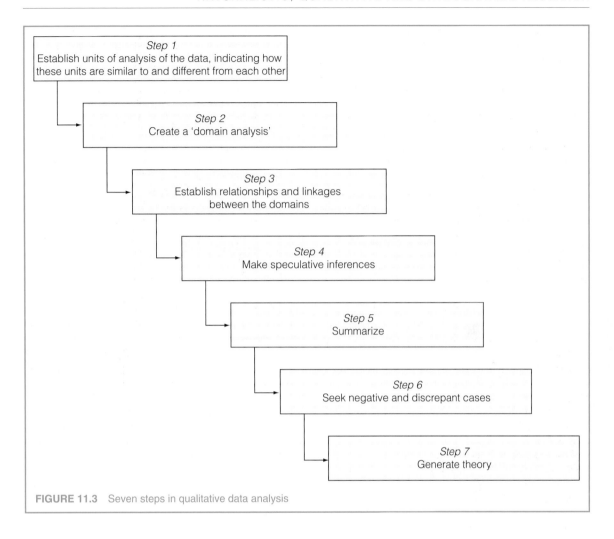

FIGURE 11.3 Seven steps in qualitative data analysis

Step 1 Establish units of analysis of the data, indicating how these units are similar to and different from each other

The criterion here is that each unit of analysis (category – conceptual, actual, classification element, cluster, issue) should be as discrete as possible whilst retaining fidelity to the integrity of the whole, i.e. that each unit must be a fair rather than a distorted representation of the context and other data. The creation of units of analysis can be done by ascribing *codes* to the data (Miles and Huberman, 1984). This is akin to the process of 'unitizing' (Lincoln and Guba, 1985: 203).

Step 2 Create a 'domain analysis'

A domain analysis involves grouping together items and units into related clusters, themes and patterns, a domain being a category which contains several other categories. We address domain analysis in more detail in Chapter 22.

Step 3 Establish relationships and linkages between the domains

This process ensures that the data, their richness and 'context-groundedness' are retained. Linkages can be found by identifying confirming cases, by seeking 'underlying associations' (LeCompte and Preissle, 1993: 246) and connections between data subsets. This helps to establish core themes, i.e. those themes which seem to underpin or to have reference made to them most frequently or most significantly in the data (Gonzales *et al.*, 2008: 5–6).

Step 4 Make speculative inferences

This is an important stage, for it moves the research from description to inference. It requires the researcher, on the basis of the evidence, to posit some explanations for the situation, some key elements and possibly even their causes. It is the process of hypothesis generation or the setting of working hypotheses that feeds into theory generation.

Step 5 Summarize

This involves the researcher in writing a preliminary summary of the main features, key issues, key concepts, constructs and ideas encountered so far in the research. We address summarizing in more detail in Chapter 29.

Step 6 Seek negative and discrepant cases

In theory generation it is important to seek not only confirming cases but to weigh the significance of disconfirming cases. LeCompte and Preissle (1993: 270) suggest that because interpretations of the data are grounded in the data themselves, results that fail to support an original hypothesis are neither discarded nor discredited; rather, it is the hypotheses themselves that must be modified to accommodate these data. Indeed Erickson (1992: 208) identifies progressive problem-solving as one key aspect of ethnographic research and data analysis. LeCompte and Preissle (1993: 250–1) define a negative case as an exemplar which disconfirms or refutes the working hypothesis, rule or explanation so far. It is the qualitative researcher's equivalent of the positivist's null hypothesis. The theory that is being developed becomes more robust if it addresses negative cases, for it sets the boundaries to the theory; it modifies the theory, it sets parameters to the applicability of the theory.

Discrepant cases are not so much exceptions to the rule (as in negative cases) as variants of the rule (LeCompte and Preissle, 1993: 251). The discrepant case leads to the modification or elaboration of the construct, rule or emerging hypothesis. Discrepant case analysis requires the researcher to seek out cases for which the rule, construct, or explanation cannot account or with which they will not fit, i.e. they are neither exceptions nor contradictions, they are simply different!

Step 7 Generate theory

Here the theory derives from the data – it is grounded in the data and emerges from it. As Lincoln and Guba (1985: 205) argue, grounded theory must fit the situation that is being researched. Grounded theory is an iterative process, moving backwards and forwards between data and theory until the theory fits the data. This breaks the linearity of much conventional research (Flick, 1998: 41, 43) in which hypotheses are formulated, sampling is decided, data are collected and then analysed and hypotheses are supported or not supported. In grounded theory a circular and recursive process is adopted, wherein modifications are made to the theory in light of data, more data are sought to investigate emergent issues (theoretical sampling), and hypotheses and theories emerge from the data.

Lincoln and Guba (1985: 354–5) urge the researcher to be mindful of several issues in analysing and interpreting the data, including: (a) data overload; (b) the problem of acting on first impressions only; (c) the availability of people and information (e.g. how representative these are and how to know if missing people and data might be important); (d) the dangers of only seeking confirming rather than disconfirming instances; (e) the reliability and consistency of the data and confidence that can be placed in the results.

Maxwell (2005: 108) draws attention to some important difficulties of validity for the qualitative data analyst, including researcher bias and reactivity. The former concerns the projection of the researcher's own values and judgements onto the situation, whilst the latter concerns the effect of the researcher on the participants, giving rise to unreliable behaviours or changes to the natural setting (a particular problem, for example, in interviewing or observing children). He sets out a useful checklist of eight ways in which attention can be given to validity in qualitative research:

1 *Intensive, long-term involvement*, as this enables the researcher to probe beneath immediate behaviours, for reactivity to be reduced and for causal processes to be revealed.
2 *'Rich' data*, sufficient to provide a sufficiently revealing, varied and full picture of the phenomenon, participants and settings.
3 *Respondent validation*, to solicit systematic feedback from participants on the interpretations made of, and conclusions from, the data.
4 *Intervention*, where the researcher intervenes formally or informally, in a small or a large way, in the natural setting in order to contribute positively to a situation (whether this is legitimate is a moot point,

as it disturbs the natural setting, even though its intention might be in the interests of serving the ethical issue of 'beneficence', see Chapter 5).

5 *Searching for discrepant evidence and negative cases*, in order to constitute a strong test of the theory or conclusions drawn.

6 *Triangulation*, in order to give reliability to the findings and data (see Chapter 10)

7 *Quasi-statistics*, where quasi-quantitative statements are interrogated, e.g. claims that a finding is rare, extreme, unusual, typical, frequent, dominant, prevalent and so on.

8 *Comparison*, between groups, subgroups, sites and settings, events and activities, times, contexts, behaviours and actions, etc., to look for consistency or inconsistency, similarity or difference across these.

Swain (2006: 202) comments that, in writing up an ethnography or piece of qualitative research, there is a significant discipline to be exercised by the researcher, in that a faithful account has to be written, yet, for manageability, the level of detail on the context, emerging situation and events has to be reduced. Indeed he argues that less than 1 per cent of the collected data may feature in the final report, and that, even if 100 per cent of the data that were collected were included, these would constitute less than 1 per cent of everything that took place or that was experienced by the researcher. Fidelity to the detail may stand in a relation of tension to the final, necessarily selective, use of data, and care has to be given to issues of reliability and validity in such a situation.

These are significant issues in addressing reliability, trustworthiness and validity in the research (see the discussions of reliability and validity in Chapter 5). The essence of this approach, that theory emerges from and is grounded in data, is not without its critics. For example Silverman (1993: 47) suggests that it fails to acknowledge the implicit theories which guide research in its early stages (i.e. data are not theory-neutral but theory-saturated) and that it might be strong on providing categorizations without necessarily explanatory potential. These are caveats that should feed into the process of reflexivity in qualitative research, perhaps.

Maxwell (2005: 115–16) also indicates that the process of data analysis, and the conclusions that are drawn from the data, should address the generalizability issue, i.e. to whom the results are generalizable. For example, internal generalizability will indicate that the results and conclusions are generalizable to the group in question, whilst external generalizability will indicate that the results and conclusions are generalizable to the wider population beyond the group under study. He suggests that, whilst the former may be applicable to qualitative research, the latter often may not. However, he also indicates that this by no means rules out the external generalizability of qualitative studies, as respondents themselves might have commented on the generalizability of their situation, or the researcher or readers might see similarities to other, comparable situations, constraints or dynamics, or the research might be corroborated by, or corroborate, other studies. He provides a caveat, to indicate that precision in external generalizability is not a strong feature, or indeed concern, for qualitative research.

Stage 11 Leaving the field

The issue here is how to conclude the research, how to terminate the roles adopted, how (and whether) to bring to an end the relationships that have built up over the course of the research, and how to disengage from the field in ways that bring as little disruption to the group or situation as possible (LeCompte and Preissle, 1993: 101). De Laine (2000: 142) remarks that some participants may want to maintain contact after the research is over, and not to do this might create, for them, a sense of disappointment, exploitation or even betrayal. One has to consider the after-effects of leaving and take care to ensure that nobody comes to harm or is worse off from the research, even if it is impossible to ensure that they have benefited from it.

Stage 12 Writing the report

There is a shift in emphasis in much research literature, away from the *conduct* of the research and towards the *reporting* of the research. It is often the case that the main vehicle for writing naturalistic research is the case study (see Chapter 9), whose 'trustworthiness' (Lincoln and Guba, 1985: 189) is defined in terms of credibility, transferability, dependability and confirmability – discussed in Chapter 10. Case studies are useful in that they can provide the thick descriptions that are useful in ethnographic research, and can catch and portray to the reader what it is like to be involved in the situation (Lincoln and Guba, 1985: 214). As Lincoln and Guba comment (p. 359), the case study is the ideal instrument for 'emic' enquiry. It also builds in and builds on the tacit knowledge that the writer and reader bring to the report, and, thereby, takes seriously their notion of the 'human instrument' in research, indicating the interactions of researcher and participants.

Lincoln and Guba provide several guidelines for writing case studies (1985: 365–6):

- the writing should strive to be informal and to capture informality;
- as far as possible the writing should report facts except in those sections where interpretation, evaluation and inference are made explicit;
- in drafting the report it is more advisable to opt for over-inclusion rather than under-inclusion;
- the ethical conventions of report writing must be honoured, e.g. anonymity, non-traceability;
- the case study writer should make clear the data that give rise to the report, so the readers have a means of checking back for reliability and validity and inferences;
- a fixed completion date should be specified.

Spradley (1979) suggests nine practical steps that can be followed in writing an ethnography:

1 Select the audience.
2 Select the thesis.
3 Make a list of topics and create an outline of the ethnography.
4 Write a rough draft of each section of the ethnography.
5 Revise the outline and create subheadings.
6 Edit the draft.
7 Write an introduction and a conclusion.
8 Reread the data and report to identify examples.
9 Write the final version.

Clearly there are several other aspects of case study reporting that need to be addressed. These are set out in Chapter 14.

The writing of a qualitative report can also consider the issue of the generalizability of the research. Whilst much qualitative research strives to embrace the uniqueness, the individual idiographic features, of the phenomenon and/or participants, rendering generalization irrelevant (though the study would still need to ensure that it contributes something that is worthwhile and significant for the research community), this need not preclude attention to generalization where it might be applicable in qualitative research. Indeed one can question the value or contribution of idiographic research that does not have any generalizable function or utility (Wolcott, 1994: 113).

Generalization takes many forms; it is not a unitary or singular concept, and it connotes far more than the familiar terms 'transferability' (Denzin and Lincoln, 1994) or 'external validity' (Cook and Campbell, 1979). Larsson (2009: 27) comments that generalization as that which is derived by strict sampling from a defined population is often irrelevant in qualitative

research. He also suggests that those single studies that seek to undermine 'universal' truths similarly do not need to aspire to be generalizable, as the single instance of falsification ('negative cases', p. 30) may be sufficient to bring down the theory (though the case would need to be made that the 'truths' ever claimed to be universal in the first place as social actions may not be susceptible to universal laws of behaviour). However, he suggests three kinds of reasoning on which generalization in qualitative research might be useful:

1 Enhancing the potential for generalization by maximizing the range of a sample's characteristics in exploring a particular issue (e.g. in theoretical sampling) or phenomenon, i.e. to ensure that as many different cases or categories of an issue as possible are included in the research. In this instance the uncommon cases have as equal a weight as the typical cases, and the variation that exists within the study should be expected to exist in the wider population, context or situation to which one wishes to generalize (p. 31). This, in turn, may require a larger sample than may be normal in qualitative research, in order to have as broad a variation and range of characteristics as possible included, and this may not be possible in some qualitative research, e.g. case studies. It also assumes that the researcher will know what the maximum variation will look like, so that he or she knows when it is reached, and this, too, may not be realistic (p. 32).

2 Generalization by ensuring the similarity of contexts between that of the qualitative research and the wider contexts to which it is wished to be applied (akin to the 'transferability' criterion of Guba and Lincoln (1994)). Here Strauss and Corbin (1990: 267) argue that generalizability might also be replaced by 'explanatory power' in the context of the research and the wider contexts. This view of generalizability assumes that the characteristics of the wider contexts are known, and this may not be for the researcher to judge, but, rather, for the outsider readers, audiences or users of the research to make such judgements (c.f. Wolcott, 1994: 113). Hence, Larsson (2009: 32) argues, the task of the researcher is to provide sufficient details and 'thick descriptions' for the audiences to come to an informed judgement about this form of generalizability. A problem is raised in this kind of generalizability, in deciding when, and on what – and how many – criteria the contexts of the research and the wider contexts are similar and when sufficient similarity of contexts has been reached for the research to be generalizable to those wider contexts (p. 33),

as the same kinds of people may act differently in different – or even the same – contexts.

3 Generalization by the recognition of similar patterns between the research and other contexts (Larsson, 2009: 33–5) in terms of, for example, theoretical constructions, themes, concepts, behaviours, assumptions made and processes, and in the interpretations of actions, events or descriptions. In this instance the problem of interpretation is raised, as interpretations of one context may be very different from the interpretations made of another – however similar – context. Whether a pattern is indeed a pattern, or whether a construction is an acceptable construction, is a matter of debate and interpretation. Researchers have to be sure that the patterns between both research and the wider context are, indeed, tenable. Interpretation is an inescapable feature of qualitative research, and it is this precise matter that renders difficult the applicability of research from one context to another, because it is not the context but the *interpretation* of the context that has to be similar to that to which it is being applied, and then one is faced with the added problem of identifying whose interpretation should stand (not only the issue of 'emic' and 'etic' research, but also whose 'etic' and 'emic' interpretations, given that there will be multiple variants of each type).

Larsson (2009: 36) is arguing powerfully that the responsibility for generalization from qualitative research resides with the audience rather than the researcher. However, to suggest this may be to invite the view that the researcher has no special expertise to offer here; if so, then how is the research justified? Perhaps the solution to this is to regard the research, as with other kinds of research, as raising working hypotheses rather than conclusions, i.e. about being 'work in progress' rather than unassailable truths.

11.4 Critical ethnography

An emerging branch of ethnography that resonates with the critical paradigm outlined in Chapter 3 is the field of critical ethnography – 'critical theory in action' (Madison, 2005: 13), which, as Thomas (1993: vii) suggests, adopts a 'subversive worldview' to conventional traditions of research.

Whereas conventional ethnography is concerned with what is, critical ethnography concerns itself with what could be (Thomas, 1993: 4). Here not only is qualitative, anthropological, participant, observer-based research undertaken, but its theoretical basis lies in critical theory (Quantz, 1992: 448; Carspecken, 1996). As was outlined in Chapter 3, this paradigm is concerned with the exposure of oppression and inequality in society with a view to emancipating individuals and groups towards collective empowerment. In this respect research is an inherently political enterprise; it is ethnography with a political intent (cf. Thomas, 1993: 4). Madison (2005: 5) indicates that critical ethnography has an explicit agenda, that it has an 'ethical responsibility' to promote freedom, social justice, equity and well-being. This, he avers, inevitably involves disturbing accepted meanings and disrupting the status quo and purported neutrality of research, together with exposing taken-for-granted, 'domesticated' (Thomas, 1993: 7) assumptions that perpetuate the power of the already powerful at the expense of the powerless and the dominated. It takes power, control and social exploitation as problematic, and to be changed, rather than simply to be interrogated and discovered (Thomas, 1993: 6). Like ethnography, it catches ethnographic data, but, beyond this, exposes this to the ideology critique that was set out in Chapter 2 of this volume.

Like Habermas's *emancipatory interest* (Chapter 3), research is not simply a scientific, technical exercise, nor is it simply a hermeneutic matter of understanding and interpreting a situation; it does not reject these, but it requires the researcher to move beyond them (Thomas, 1993: 19), to engage different ways of 'viewing the world' (Thomas, 1993: 67). Rather it is a political act, and it must play its part as activism against hegemonic oppression, and researchers have to consider their own 'positionality' in this enterprise (Madison, 2005: 7), i.e. how their research will help to break domination and inequality. Researchers and their research are neither neutral nor innocent. Both subjectivity and objectivity have to be interrogated for their political stances and effects (p. 8) in relation to those being researched (the 'Others' (p. 9)); the research has to make a positive difference to the worlds of the 'Others' (the participants). This moves the ethnographer beyond simply being reflexive to being an activist.

This is contentious: on the one hand it suggests that the researcher is an ideologist (rather than, say, a theorist); on the other hand the claim would be made that, like it or not, research is a political act, it is just that this has been hidden in much research.

Carspecken (1996: 4ff.) suggests several key premises of critical ethnography:

■ research and thinking are mediated by power relations;
■ these power relations are socially and historically located;

- facts and values are inseparable;
- relationships between objects and concepts are fluid and mediated by the social relations of production;
- language is central to perception;
- certain groups in society exert more power than others;
- inequality and oppression are inherent in capitalist relations of production and consumption;
- ideological domination is strongest when oppressed groups see their situation as inevitable, natural or necessary;
- forms of oppression mediate each other and must be considered together (e.g. race, gender, class).

Quantz (1992: 473–4) argues that research is inescapably value-laden in that it serves some interests, and that in critical ethnography researchers must expose these interests and move participants towards emancipation and freedom. The focus and process of research are thus political at heart, concerning issues of power, domination, voice and empowerment. In critical ethnography the cultures, groups and individuals being studied are located in contexts of power and interests. These contexts have to be exposed, their legitimacy interrogated and the value base of the research itself exposed. Reflexivity is high in critical ethnography. What separates critical ethnography from other forms of ethnography is that, in the former, questions of legitimacy, power, values in society and domination and oppression are foregrounded.

How does the critical ethnographer proceed? This is not an easy task, as critical ethnography focuses on, and challenges, taken-for-granted assumptions and meanings, and these may be difficult to expose simply because they are so taken-for-granted, i.e. embedded in our daily lifeworlds and behaviour. In this sense a critical ethnography is untidy, the study emerges rather than being planned in advance; areas of focus emerge as meanings are revealed and challenged from the position of ideology critique (Thomas, 1993: 35). It starts with unsettling issues in society and explores them further (Thomas gives the examples of prisons, the social construction of deviance, racism, prejudice and repressive legislation).

Carspecken and Apple (1992: 512–14) and Carspecken (1996: 41–2) identify five stages in critical ethnography (see Figure 11.4).

Stage 1 Compiling the primary record through the collection of monological data

At this stage the researcher is comparatively passive and unobtrusive – a participant observer. The task here is to acquire *objective* data and it is 'monological' in

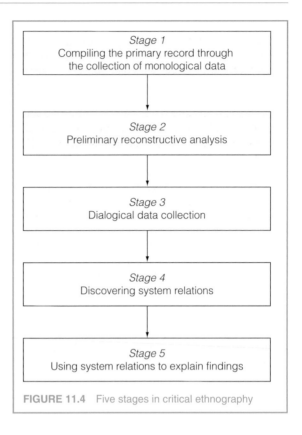

FIGURE 11.4 Five stages in critical ethnography

the sense that it concerns only the researcher writing her own notes to herself. Lincoln and Guba (1985) suggest that validity checks at this stage will include:

1 using multiple devices for recording together with multiple observers;
2 using a flexible observation schedule in order to minimize biases;
3 remaining in the situation for a long time in order to overcome the Hawthorne effect;
4 using low-inference terminology and descriptions;
5 using peer-debriefing;
6 using respondent validation.

Echoing Habermas's (1979, 1982, 1984) work on validity claims, validity here includes truth (the veracity of the utterance), legitimacy (rightness and appropriateness of the speaker), comprehensibility (that the utterance is comprehensible) and sincerity (of the speaker's intentions). Carspecken (1996: 104–5) takes this further in suggesting several categories of reference in objective validity: (i) that the act is comprehensible, socially legitimate and appropriate; (ii) that the actor has a particular identity and particular intentions or feelings when the action takes place; (iii) that objective, contextual factors are acknowledged.

Stage 2 Preliminary reconstructive analysis

Reconstructive analysis attempts to uncover the taken-for-granted components of meaning or abstractions that participants have of a situation. Such analysis is intended to identify the value systems, norms, key concepts that are guiding and underpinning situations. Carspecken (1996: 42) suggests that the researcher goes back over the primary record from stage one to examine patterns of interaction, power relations, roles, sequences of events and meanings accorded to situations. He asserts that what distinguishes this stage as 'reconstructive' is that cultural themes, social and system factors that are not usually articulated by the participants themselves are, in fact, reconstructed and articulated, making the undiscursive into discourse. In moving to higher level abstractions this stage can utilize high-level coding (see the discussion of coding in this chapter).

In critical ethnography Carspecken (1996: 141) delineates several ways of ensuring validity at this stage:

1 Use interviews and group discussions with the subjects themselves.
2 Conduct member checks on the reconstruction in order to equalize power relations.
3 Use peer debriefing (a peer is asked to review the data to suggest if the researcher is being too selective, e.g. of individuals, of data, of inference) to check biases or absences in reconstructions.
4 Employ prolonged engagement to heighten the researcher's capacity to assume the insider's perspective.
5 Use 'strip analysis' – checking themes and segments of extracted data with the primary data, for consistency.
6 Use negative case analysis.

Stage 3 Dialogical data collection

Here data are generated by, and discussed with, the participants (Carspecken and Apple, 1992). The authors argue that this is not-naturalistic in that the participants are being asked to reflect on their own situations, circumstances and lives and to begin to theorize about their lives. This is a crucial stage because it enables the participants to have a voice, to democratize the research. It may be that this stage produces new data that challenge the preceding two stages.

In introducing greater subjectivity by participants into the research at this stage Carspecken (1996: 164–5)

proffers several validity checks, e.g. (a) consistency checks on interviews that have been recorded; (b) repeated interviews with participants; (c) matching observation with what participants say is happening or has happened; (d) avoiding leading questions at interview, reinforced by having peer debriefers check on this; (e) respondent validation; (f) asking participants to use their own terms in describing naturalistic contexts, and encouraging them to explain these terms.

Stage 4 Discovering system relations

This stage relates the group being studied to other factors that impinge on that group, e.g. local community groups, local sites that produce cultural products. At this stage Carspecken (1996: 202) notes that validity checks will include: (i) maintaining the validity requirements of the earlier stages; (ii) seeking a match between the researcher's analysis and the commentaries that are provided by the participants and other researchers; (iii) using peer debriefers and respondent validation.

Stage 5 Using system relations to explain findings

This stage seeks to examine and explain the findings in light of macro-social theories (Carspecken, 1996: 202). In part, this is a matching exercise to fit the research findings within a social theory.

In critical ethnography, therefore, the move is from describing a situation, understanding it, to questioning it and to changing it. This parallels the stages of ideology critique set out in Chapter 2:

Stage 1 A description of the existing situation – a hermeneutic exercise.
Stage 2 A penetration of the reasons that brought the situation to the form that it takes.
Stage 3 An agenda for altering the situation.
Stage 4 An evaluation of the achievement of the new situation.

11.5 Some problems with ethnographic and naturalistic approaches

There are several difficulties in ethnographic and natural approaches. These might affect the reliability and validity of the research, and include:

1 *The definition of the situation* – the participants are being asked for their definition of the situation, yet they have no monopoly on wisdom. They may be 'falsely conscious' (unaware of the 'real' situation), deliberately distorting or falsifying information, or

being highly selective. The issues of reliability and validity here are addressed in Chapter 10 (see the discussions of triangulation).

2 *Reactivity* – the Hawthorne effect – the presence of the researcher alters the situation as participants may wish to avoid, impress, direct, deny or influence the researcher. Again, this is discussed in Chapter 10. Typically the problem of reactivity is addressed by careful negotiation in the field, remaining in the field for a considerable time, ensuring as far as possible a careful presentation of the researcher's self.

3 The *halo effect* – where existing or given information about the situation or participants might be used to be selective in subsequent data collection, or may bring about a particular reading of a subsequent situation (the research equivalent of the self-fulfilling prophecy). This is an issue of reliability, and can be addressed by the use of a wide, triangulated database and the assistance of an external observer. The *halo effect* commonly refers to the researcher's belief in the goodness of participants (the participants have haloes around their heads!), such that the more negative aspects of their behaviour or personality are neglected or overlooked. By contrast, the *horns effect* refers to the researcher's belief in the badness of the participants (the participants have devils' horns on their heads!), such that the more positive aspects of their behaviour or personality are neglected or overlooked.

4 The *implicit conservatism* of the interpretive methodology. The kind of research described in this chapter, with the possible exception of critical ethnography, accepts the perspective of the participants and corroborates the status quo. It is focused on the past and the present rather than on the future.

5 There is the difficulty of focusing on the *familiar*, participants (and, maybe researchers too) being so close to the situation that they neglect certain, often tacit, aspects of it. The task, therefore, is to make the familiar strange. Delamont (1981) suggests that this can be done by:

- studying unusual examples of the same issue (e.g. atypical classrooms, timetabling or organizations of schools);
- studying examples in other cultures;
- studying other situations that might have a bearing on the situation in hand (e.g. if studying schools it might be useful to look at other similar-but-different organizations, for instance hospitals or prisons);

- taking a significant issue and focusing on it deliberately, e.g. gendered behaviour.

6 The *open-endedness and diversity* of the situations studied. The drive towards focusing on specific contexts and situations might overemphasize the difference between contexts and situations rather than their gross similarity, their routine features. Researchers, should be as aware of regularities as of differences.

7 The *neglect of wider social contexts and constraints*. Studying situations that emphasize how highly context-bound they are, might neglect broader currents and contexts – micro-level research risks putting boundaries that exclude important macro-level factors. Wider – macro-contexts – cannot be ruled out of individual situations.

8 The issue of *generalizability*. If situations are unique and non-generalizable, as many naturalistic principles would suggest, how is the issue of generalizability going to be addressed? To which contexts will the findings apply, and what is the role and nature of replication studies?

9 How to write up *multiple realities* and explanations? How will a representative view be reached? What if the researcher sees things that are not seen by the participants?

10 Who *owns* the data, the report, and who has control over the release of the data?

Naturalistic and ethnographic research, then, are important, if challenging, research methods in education. Recently, the emerging field of autoethnography has been developed in research. Here the researcher compiles a personal, subjective narrative about his or her own life or situation, and this can include feelings, reactions, agentic and constrained behaviour, i.e. those elements of an ethnography that feature in conducting other-than-self ethnographies. It has been aligned to autobiography with a reflexive turn. For examples of this see Reed-Denahay (1997); Ellis (2004); and Chang (2008).

Useful websites for those commencing qualitative research are:

www.nova.edu/ssss/QR/web.html (which gives the websites of several hundred other sites providing materials on qualitative research);

www.esds.ac.uk/qualidata/about/introduction.asp (the UK's Economic and Social Data website);

www.esrc.ac.uk/ESRCInfoCentre/research/resources/index.aspx (the UK's Economic and Social Research Council's website);

http://caqdas.soc.surrey.ac.uk/ (the Computer Assisted Qualitative Data Analysis website);

www.data-archive.ac.uk/ (the UK data archive);

http://gsociology.icaap.org/methods/qual.htm (a source for accessing other websites for online materials and support).

Additionally Gobo and Diotti (2008) have compiled an extensive list of journals, newsletters, online fora, search engines, archives and thematic portals, training and research centres, interviews and software, all available on the internet.

 Companion Website

The companion website to the book includes PowerPoint slides for this chapter, which list the structure of the chapter and then provide a summary of the key points in each of its sections. This resource can be found online at **www.routledge.com/textbooks/cohen7e**.

Historical and documentary research in education

Gary McCulloch

This chapter is designed to provide an introduction to historical methods in education, and in particular to examine such matters as:

- what is a document?
- primary documents
- in the archive
- documentary analysis
- ethical and legal issues

(See also McCulloch (2004) for a more detailed treatment of these themes.)

12.1 Introduction

Historical and documentary research methods are intended to provide access to, and facilitate insights into, three related areas of knowledge about human social activity. The first of these is the past, whether that of modern history over the past two centuries or of earlier times. The second is that of processes of change and continuity over time, including the contestation and negotiation that is involved in these and the broader social, political, economic and other forms of context within which they take place. The third relates to the origins of the present that explains current structures, relationships and behaviours in the context of recent and longer term trends.

Education has a significant position in each of these broad areas of knowledge. National age-related systems of mass schooling, which are now familiar around the world, are a comparatively recent invention of the past two centuries. Schools for groups of pupils and students have existed for many centuries, although specific forms and practices such as subject-based curricula, examinations, desks and classrooms have developed to suit particular purposes. Universities and institutions of higher education for elite groups of students have also long been in existence. Informal processes of teaching and learning throughout society and the lifespan have taken place throughout recorded history. In all such cases we may investigate the activities of the past, the processes of change and continuity, and the origins of the present through historical research (see also McCulloch and Richardson, 2000). The history of education itself is a broad, eclectic and contested field of study (Reese and Rury, 2008). It characteristically examines the longer term development of education in relation to the broader society, including for example pertaining to social change and mobility, the economy, national traditions, gender, ethnicity and work (see for example McCulloch, 2005). The study of the history of education draws on historical, educational and social scientific methods and insights (Reese and Rury, 2008; McCulloch, in press), with a duty to both the people of the past and the current generation as well as to search for the truth (Aldrich, 2003).

Historical research in education employs a number of methods and makes use of a wide range of source materials. These include oral sources in relation to the recent past, based on interviews for example with teachers and pupils in which respondents recall their own experiences as historical evidence (for instance Humphries, 1981; Gardner, 2003). There has been increasing interest in such sources over the past 20 years. Nevertheless, analysis of documents has been the most characteristic and traditional method employed in modern historical research as distinct from social research. As John Scott (1990: 1) argued, handling documentary source material is widely seen as the hallmark of the professional historian. The established practices of working historians are therefore a key point of departure in addressing documentary research, although historians have tended not to reflect in detail or depth on this central aspect of their craft. One leading historian, John Tosh, in introducing his own useful contribution to the aims and methods of history, has noted that history students have not in the past generally had formal instruction on the nature of their discipline (Tosh, 2002: xix). At the same time, in educational research, as in other forms of social research, the use of documents has tended to appear less significant than interviews, questionnaires and techniques of direct observation (see for example Burton, 2000).

12.2 What is a document?

A document may be defined briefly as a record of an event or process. Such records may be produced by individuals or groups, and take many different forms. Broad distinctions may be drawn between types of documents and it is important for the researcher to observe these, although they are not always rigid typologies. One distinction that can be made, for example, is between the documents created by private individuals and family groups in their everyday lives, and the records produced by local, national and international authorities and small or large organizations (Hodder, 1998). The former class of personal or private documents might include diaries, letters, photographs, blogs, autobiographies and suicide notes (Plummer, 2001). The latter group of public and official records would include committee minutes, reports and memoranda, but also formal items such as birth, marriage and death certificates, driving licences and bank statements (Scott, 1990). Media documents, either printed like newspapers and magazines or visual such as television, operate at the interface of the private and public, and record aspects of both types of domain.

A distinction may also be drawn between documents that are based on written text and other forms produced through other means. Until very recently, most written documents were produced on paper or similar materials, either by hand or mechanically. In the mid-fifteenth century, the invention of the printing press with a movable print type by Johann Gutenberg led to the spread of 'print culture' (Briggs and Burke, 2002). The past two decades have witnessed the exponential growth of electronic documents such as electronic mail and data communicated and stored through the internet. This constitutes a contemporary revolution in the nature of documents, albeit that electronic documents may well retain and incorporate elements of the print culture developed over the past five centuries (McCulloch, 2004: 2). Such written, printed and electronic texts might be contrasted with visual documents such as photographs, cartoons, paintings and films (Prosser, 1998; Grosvenor, 2007), although it should be noted that texts in contemporary society have become increasingly multi-semiotic in combining and juxtaposing language and visual forms (Fairclough, 1995). They also differ from oral sources such as sound recordings of speeches. One may also distinguish textual records from material artefacts like fossils, slates, desks and buildings.

A further distinction is between documents produced independently of the researcher, for a range of possible purposes outside the researcher's control, and those produced by researchers themselves as data for their research. Transcripts of interviews or completed questionnaires are examples of documents prepared by researchers for the purposes of their research (Silverman, 2001: 119). Electronic technology facilitates the rapid interchange of solicited documents in a wide variety of formats. Documentary research typically makes use of documents produced previously and by others, rather than in the process of the research or by the researcher.

There is also an established difference between primary documents and secondary documents, although this difference is more complex than it may at first appear. Primary documents are produced as a direct record of an event or process by a witness or subject involved in it. Secondary documents are formed through an analysis of primary documents to provide an account of the event or process in question, often in relation to others. However, many documents do not fit easily into this basic dichotomy. For example, autobiographies are primary documents by virtue of the author being a witness or participant in the relevant events, but are often produced years or even decades later, and so may be affected by memory or selective recall. They might also be regarded as secondary documents to the extent that they seek to analyse the changing times through which the autobiographer has lived (for instance Hobsbawm, 2002). Some other documents might also be regarded as both 'primary' and 'secondary' depending on the way in which they are used. Scholarly works might be a contribution to their field and thus secondary documents, but at the same time reflect attitudes to issues in a particular time or context and so, in this sense, they are primary documents. Fred Clarke's short book *Education and Social Change* (1940) was a significant contribution to the sociology and history of education, and also expressed an approach to the social and political issues raised by the Second World War. The book may be read and understood in either or both of these ways, depending on the interests of the reader (McCulloch, 2004: 32–3).

Moreover, some documents are edited and collected versions of diaries, letters and autobiographies. These might be described as hybrid documents. These are more widely accessible than the original primary document, but have gone through an editing process which may alter some their characteristics, whether subtly or substantially. In producing a published work of this kind, editors may tend to emphasize particular types of material to make it more interesting or more or less flattering to the authors of the document, or else to reflect specific interests (Fothergill, 1974). In such cases, one might say that the primary features of the primary document have been compromised by the process of being edited and presented in this way.

Virtual documents, that is primary documents stored electronically for access through the internet, are available through 'the click of a mouse' (*Guardian*, 2003). These are often most valuable for researchers (Crook, 2000), although government and other organizational websites that store documents in this way may seek to cast the government or organization in a favourable light. Many historians are also not fully convinced of the merits of such digital documents, and point out that they lose the immediacy of the original paper document that they represent (for example Schama, 1999; see McCulloch, 2004: 34–42).

12.3 Primary documents

In this section we will consider in more detail the kinds of primary documents that may be used as the basis for historical and documentary research in education, and a few examples of how they have been examined in historical and educational research. These include books and textbooks; reports and proceedings; newspapers and other media sources; works of fiction such as novels and plays; and personal documents such as diaries, letters and autobiographies. These are often used in combination, or alongside other types of data collected by the researcher.

Over the past 500 years, books in their modern printed format have been repositories of knowledge and scholarship, besides also being a key means of challenging established orthodoxies. Tracts and treatises are important sources of documentary evidence that often embody the principal themes of debate in politics and society, although they do not always fully convey wider attitudes in a particular context, and their representative nature and influence are often exaggerated. The assumptions and arguments of the authors of such works need to be critically scrutinized rather than being accepted at their face value, while there is also increasing interest in the readership of books. Recent research has highlighted the relationship between books and their readers (for example J. Rose, 2001, 2007; Secord, 2000).

A specific type of book that is often useful for researchers in education is the textbook, produced for schools and other educational institutions since the 1830s when the term itself appeared (Stray, 1994: 2). They are generally used to support teachers, lecturers, pupils and students to follow a syllabus, and are signi-

ficant partly for the way in which they present information but also for how they project approved values and ideologies. Stuart Foster, for example, has investigated the treatment of ethnic groups in history textbooks in the United States in terms of a struggle for American identity, arguing that such works have represented the views and interests of a white, male, Protestant middle or upper class, and have tended to support the capitalist system, traditional lifestyles, and western traditions (Foster, 1999). Such textbooks have also often been susceptible to commercial pressures, becoming political and economic as well as pedagogical artefacts (Clark, 2009).

Published reports are a further significant source of research evidence in this area of study. Governments as well as organizations and pressure groups produce reports in order to examine particular defined problems and to propose solutions. The information that they provide is often very helpful, although it cannot be assumed that this is always accurate, and it should be checked against other sources. Policy reports are also important for revealing the kinds of assumptions that underlie policy reforms. They represent an outlook or ideology (Scott, 2000: 27), and also embody the contradictions and tensions that are inherent in state policy (Codd, 1988). Some reports are voluminous, taking up several volumes including appendices of oral and written evidence provided by witnesses, whereas in recent decades reports have tended to become shorter in length, more limited in focus and more reader-friendly in format to promote their public appeal. Again, care needs to be taken to resist assuming that such reports reflect educational practices in a straightforward manner.

The proceedings of parliamentary debates and committees provide another kind of official publication. In Britain, these are known as Hansard, after Thomas Hansard, who began publishing the debates of the House of Commons and House of Lords in 1812, and are now available online (www.parliament.the-stationery-office.co.uk; see also www.parliament.uk). In the USA, the Congressional Record provides a similar service, also available on the internet (www.gpoaccess.gov/crecord/index.html). This was first published in 1873, and provides up-to-date and complete proceedings of debates in the House of Representatives and the Senate. Many datasets produced by governments, organizations and research project teams are also readily accessible, and these lend themselves to secondary analysis. Hakim (1982) has defined this in terms of the further analysis of existing datasets which develops the original interpretations and findings of the enquiry in a different way. These include population census reports and datasets specially related to education such as that of the National Child Development Study in Britain (see for example www.esds.ac.uk).

The printed press embodies a further important source of primary documentary evidence. This provides a day-to-day public record very soon after the event being studied (Vella, 2009: 194), albeit one that caters for particular kinds of public taste and interest and by no means comprehensive in its coverage. Peter Cunningham (1992) has made interesting use of newspapers as a documentary source by examining the development of the image of the teacher in the British press from 1950 to 1990. Cunningham's work compares newspaper coverage of teachers in 1950, 1970 and 1990, using *The Times* in its unofficial capacity as a newspaper of record as well as major mass-circulation newspapers of the political left and right. This has been taken further in other work that examines political cartoons involving teachers in the British press since the 1970s (Warburton and Saunders, 1996). Other particular features of newspapers also offer interesting and useful material for researchers, including leading articles, letters columns and advertisements. More specialist magazines provide information and commentary, including in the case of Britain for example the *Times Educational Supplement* and *Times Higher Education*, both published weekly, and also the monthly magazine *Punch* (see Smith, 1998).

School magazines have a limited circulation in and around their own institution, but constitute a significant record on behalf of the institution itself, with detailed information on everyday life and interests as well as transmitting the received values of the school. J. A. Mangan's (1986) research on English public schools in the late nineteenth century demonstrated the role of school magazines as the official record of school life, reflecting in many cases an emphasis on games and sports as opposed to examinations. Nevertheless, unofficial magazines may also provide important clues to debates and differences within the school (see for example McCulloch, 2007, chapter 6).

Another source of evidence for historical and documentary research is that of fiction. Although this is not intended to convey the literal truth about particular events, it may represent deeper realities about social experiences. In relation to education, in particular, it can provide insights into everyday life from the imagined viewpoints of pupils and teachers, notwithstanding the dramatization and stereotyped forms that it generally depends upon for plots and characterization. The realist novels of the nineteenth century attracted many historians, although there has also been much scepticism about the use made of novels as a historical docu-

mentary source (Reid, 2009). In the area of education, many works of fiction since the work of Charles Dickens in the nineteenth century may be analysed as documentary sources (Collins, 1963). Novels and plays have been especially useful for their depiction of teachers and teaching. James Hilton's *Goodbye, Mr. Chips* (1934), for example, is a classic account of the life story of a male veteran teacher in an elite English boarding school, while the plays of Alan Bennett such as *Forty Years On* (1969) and *The History Boys* (2004) have evoked resilient cultural images (Weber and Mitchell, 1995; see also McCulloch, 2009). Susan Ellsmore (2005) has also explored representations of the teaching profession in films, including the film of *Goodbye, Mr. Chips* produced in 1939.

Diaries, letters and autobiographies are generally regarded as personal documents, although they can often reveal a great deal about public issues and debates. In some cases, they may provide commentary on contemporary social developments, and they often record meetings or other events in which the author has been involved. Diaries are generally produced soon after the event, although this varies, and may give detailed and intimate evidence of individuals and daily life for women no less than for men (Blodgett, 1988). Political diaries, such as those of the British politician Tony Benn, can be highly revealing about policy changes, as in the case of the self-styled 'Great Debate' on education in Britain in 1976 (Benn, 1990). They also reveal much, often unintentionally, about the diarists themselves (Pimlott, 2002). School log books have an official function in that they are generally required to include specific information about the pupils, teachers and management of the school, but in some cases they may reveal the everyday life and interactions of the headteacher concerned (see for example McCulloch, 1989, chapter 8).

Letter writing as a means of communication has generated a further type of documentary source, one that has been rivalled in recent times by devices such as the telephone and transformed through electronic media. They are interactive in character, forming explicitly part of a dialogue, and may again be both personal and formal in their style and substance (Earle, 1999; Dobson, 2009). Many letters relating to education, such as those from parents to a school or to a newspaper or to a Minister of Education, reflect the interaction between the personal or family domain and the concerns of an established institution (see for instance Heward, 1988). By contrast, autobiographies and memoirs are essentially introspective, and provide an inside account of lives and relationships. They often give particular emphasis to the early life and schooling.

For example, David Vincent's (1981) major study of working-class autobiographies in nineteenth-century England, based on 142 accounts of this kind, demonstrates the nature of their involvement in a social network of family, friends, colleagues and acquaintances.

12.4 In the archive

As we have seen, many documentary records are available quite readily through research libraries or the internet. In other cases, they are stored in organized format, usually numbered files for identification, in archives and record offices. These are the most recognized and characteristic source for historical and documentary researchers. Archives are repositories of accumulated knowledge, in many ways the institutional memory of modern societies, and they exist in a number of forms.

National archives preserve the official records of government departments, and local record offices those of the particular location where appropriate, and in many countries around the world these are preserved carefully and methodically to store the collective memory. In some cases they date from the nineteenth century or even earlier, and they often reflect the specific national and social characteristics (Joyce, 1999; Tyacke, 2001). The French Archives Nationales, set up in 1790, developed with a strong focus on the centralized state (Sheppard, 1980). The Kenya National Archives in Nairobi, established in 1956, have been described as 'a reservoir and living example of historical and ethnographic knowledge' (Carotenuto and Luongo, 2005: 445), offering more than 'dusty documents' but 'history in its very space and structure, in the aims and ideas of its users, and in the various forms of popular and professional practice carried out within its walls' (Carotenuto and Luongo, 2005: 446).

National and local archives contain much primary source material relating to education policy and administration. Education department files are naturally the principal focus for this, but often other government departments such as those responsible for public finances, employment, social services, health and the central coordinating authority may hold relevant material (Gosden, 1981). As an example of these official records, in New Zealand files held at the Northern Regional Office of the Department of Education in Auckland included papers of an investigating committee established in 1970 to examine the spread of juvenile gangs (files 26/1/88 and 26/1/89). File 26/1/88 contains a full and detailed set of the minutes of the committee, and 26/1/89 includes correspondence, reports and memoranda, with a draft of the final report.

Such records are most useful in understanding debates and tracing processes behind the scenes as it were (McCulloch 2004, chapter 4). They also in many cases provide evidence of interactions between rival interests, private individuals and the state relating to education, for example on policies of school zoning (see for example McCulloch, 1986). The papers of key politicians and policy makers can also shed much light on educational policy making. The diaries of the British Labour Party politician James Chuter Ede, covering his time at the Board of Education during the negotiations that led to the Education Act of 1944, are housed at the British Library in London.

Other archives, often based in institutions of higher education, maintain personal and institutional documents that have been donated to them. Examples of these include the Modern Records Centre based at the University of Warwick near Coventry, England, and the archive collection of the Institute of Education at the University of London. In other cases, the archive is not in an organized repository such as this, but has been kept by the individual or institution involved. Collections retained by an educational institution may be fully referenced and easily accessible, but in many cases may have been neglected and are not straightforward to research. Those pertaining to individuals are often the most difficult to locate but may be especially fruitful when encountered by the researcher, perhaps in an attic, cupboard or garage, awaiting discovery. For example, the archive of Jane Johnson, an English eighteenth-century educator, was left in a shoebox that was discovered in a cupboard in the United States in 1986 (Heath, 1997).

If such discoveries can be the most productive for historical and documentary researchers, there are also many potential frustrations along the way. Much documentary evidence has been lost for a number of reasons, whether due to being discarded by the original owners, or failing to survive changes of location, or for lack of space or resources. Thus the researcher is left with only the documents, whether recent or from earlier periods of time, that remain to be examined today. There are many silences in the documents that do survive, as Alison Andrew has noted: 'There is the frustration of events reported without follow up, individuals not clearly identified, ambiguous accounts or those which provide a wealth of detail except that which is desperately sought' (Andrew, 1985: 156). The experience of working in an archive can also be a challenge. Beyond the costs and the time that may be involved in reaching an archive, it is often difficult to anticipate the amount and quality of documentary material that is available on a particular topic. As Carolyn Steedman has observed,

'You sit all day long, reading in the particular manner of the trade, to save time and money, and in the sure knowledge that out of the thousand lines of handwriting you decipher, you will perhaps use one or two' (Steedman, 2001: 29).

At the same time, the establishment and spread of online archives over the past ten years have transformed the nature of archival research. In many cases the archive catalogue or inventory of holdings is available in searchable form on the internet so that the researcher is able to check in advance before travelling to the archive. Increasingly also the documents themselves may be researched digitally. For example in Britain the results of the census up to and including 1901 (www.1901censusonline.com), and more than 150 years of the newspaper the *Guardian* (www.guardian.co.uk/archive; see also the *Guardian*, 2007) have been made available online. Cabinet minutes and discussions are also accessible by this means (www.nationalarchives.gov.uk/documentsonline). For example Cabinet discussion of the Conservative government on education policy in the early 1970s (Cabinet file CAB.128/50/55) may be consulted in this way. However, there are some restrictions in terms of coverage and a subscription or other cost may often be applied.

12.5 Documentary analysis

Documents once located and examined do not speak for themselves but require careful analysis and interpretation. There are preliminary issues around ascertaining the authenticity of the document; that is verifying the author, place and date of its production. In some cases the document may have been forged, or the authorship in doubt. The researcher also seeks to take into account the reliability of the document, for example the credibility of the account of an event in terms of the bias of the author, the access to the event and the interpretation of the observer. The differential survival rate of documents creates a further issue of reliability, and raises questions about how representative, typical and generalizable the surviving documents may be (Scott, 1990: 7).

The reliability of documentary evidence raises particular problems in relation to education. Such sources tend in the main to record the approaches adopted by policy makers and administrators, and so may privilege a top-down view of education. This has often tended to undermine consideration of working-class children and youth, girls and women, and ethnic minorities (Timutimu *et al.*, 1998). Moreover, documentary sources have often been criticized for failing

to engage with the classroom, the learning context, and the interface between teachers and learners. Goodson (1988), for example, has argued that documentary sources have encouraged too great an emphasis on 'Acts and facts'.

Ascertaining the meaning of a document is a further important issue. This involves understanding the information relayed and the underlying values and assumptions of the author, as well as any arguments developed. In doing so, it is necessary to comprehend both the text and its wider context. So far as the text is concerned, increasing attention has been given to its language and form in determining a deeper meaning, following the principles of hermeneutics and influenced by literary criticism (Reinfandt, 2009). Some historians of education have made creative use of the 'linguistic turn', based on this recourse to detailed study of the language and discourse of the document. For example, Sol Cohen has proposed that documents should be understood in relation to 'the semiotics of text production, how meaning is made in text, how readers take meaning from text, the status of authorial intention versus the reader's interpretation, the role of the community of discourse in the reception of text, and so forth' (Cohen, 1999: 81).

The context of the documents being examined also requires close examination. This includes taking account of broad educational, social, political, economic and other relationships that help explain the contemporary meaning of the documents, that is, how they are to be understood in the context of their time. This is especially important for historical documents that engage with the issues of their own time, and it is anachronistic to consider them without an understanding of these. An appreciation of this external context also facilitates addressing three specific aspects of a document that are commonly at issue. The first of these is about the authorship of documents in a broad sense, which includes consideration of their origins, the processes by which they were created, and individuals and groups directly involved in this. The second relates to the audience of the documents – who is being addressed, and the constituent parts and dynamics of this group. The third concerns the outcomes of the document, and an assessment of its impact on debates, ideas and policies as well as of its longer term influence. Understanding an education policy document, for example, might mean addressing one or more of these broad issues about how it has related to its wider context.

Finally, the theorization of the document (or documents) also requires attention. Jupp and Norris (1993) suggest that there are three general traditions in documentary analysis – positivist, interpretive and critical – within which particular types of theoretical approach may be framed. A positivist approach asserts the objective, systematic, rational and quantitative nature of the study. For example, Halstead (1988) examines the case of the English headteacher Ray Honeyford and the debate over multicultural education through an exhaustive study of well over 1,000 articles in local and national newspapers, magazines and journals, but does not develop an analysis addressing differential power relations. An interpretive outlook argues for social phenomena such as documents as having been socially constructed. A critical approach involving for example Marxist, feminist or critical discourse theory would emphasize social conflict, power, control and ideology. Codd's (1988) discussion of educational policy documents includes interpretive and critical elements. It argues in favour of theories of discourse relating the use of language to the exercise of power, and seeks to deconstruct the official discourse of policy documents in the light of these. Purvis (1985) also demonstrates a critical interpretation of documents from a feminist standpoint. She presents her research as a challenge to male notions of knowledge, and seeks to make use of documentary evidence that has been ignored to promote greater awareness of the experiences of women both in the past and in the present.

12.6 Ethical and legal issues

In much historical and documentary research in education there is little direct interaction with those being researched, and so there can be a temptation to overlook ethical issues. However, these may arise for example when a prominent school or other educational institution is being named in the research or the reputation of particular teachers and headteachers is questioned. Insider research based on documentary sources may also raise ethical dilemmas, for instance where the material appears likely to cast an unfavourable light upon the institution which may have commissioned it in the first place (McCulloch, 2008).

Legal questions should also be borne in mind. The laws of copyright, freedom of information and data protection as they operate in different countries are highly relevant to historical and documentary research. In Britain, the Copyright, Designs and Patents Act of 1988, the Data Protection Act of 1998 and the Freedom of Information Act of 2005 regulate the use of documentary material, personal information, and government and institutional records. Until recently, access to official records in Britain was restricted through a 'Thirty Year Rule' under the Public Records Act of 1967 (it was previously restricted for 50 years), but this has been relaxed to some extent and the time period further reduced. In other countries such as New Zealand the restrictions on access have been much less onerous, making it possible to examine more contemporary records in many cases. Another area involving both ethical and legal issues relates to working in archives. Cases of theft of original and sometimes highly valuable documents from archives have led to greater security restrictions being put in place for researchers. Careful handling of fragile documents in archives is a matter of ethical and professional conduct for historical and documentary research.

12.7 Conclusions

This chapter has discussed and illustrated a range of approaches to historical and documentary research in education. Such research has the capacity to illuminate the past, patterns of continuity and change over time, and the origins of current structures and relationships. A number of types of document have been discussed, and their uses for historical and documentary research in education explored. Much research employs one or two of these kinds of document as the principal source of data, but different combinations may be applied depending on the problem being studied. For example, an education policy report may be examined through the study of the report itself, of the files of the committee that produced it, and of newspapers relating to its reception after publication. The changes in the curriculum at a university might be appraised through institutional records, lecture notes and student diaries where these exist (see for example Slee, 1986; Soffer, 1994). Moreover, documentary research may frequently be allied to good effect with other research methods in education (see for example Saran (1985) on combining archive and interview research). Interviews with teachers about their curriculum and pedagogic practices may be compared with documentary evidence of changing policy in these areas over the past 30 years, as in the case of research by McCulloch et al. (2000). Thus historical and documentary research offers a means of promoting methodological pluralism which seems especially appropriate in a field as diverse and challenging as education.

Useful websites

www.1901censusonline.com: British census
www.esds.ac.uk: Economic and Social Data Service, Britain

www.gpoaccess.gov/crecord/index.html: US Congressional Record

www.guardian.co.uk/archive: the *Guardian* newspaper

www.parliament.the-stationery-office.co.uk: British parliamentary debates (Hansard)

www.parliament.uk: British parliamentary committee proceedings, evidence and reports

www.nationalarchives.gov.uk/documentsonline/: British official records online

---

 Companion Website

The companion website to the book includes PowerPoint slides for this chapter, which list the structure of the chapter and then provide a summary of the key points in each of its sections. In addition there is further information in the form of 20 questions to ask when using narrative and documentary sources. These resources can be found online at **www.routledge.com/textbooks/cohen7e**.

CHAPTER 13

Surveys, longitudinal, cross-sectional and trend studies

There are many different kinds of survey; each has its own characteristics and key issues. We set these out in this chapter, addressing such matters as:

- what is a survey?
- some preliminary considerations
- planning a survey
- low response and non-response, and how to reduce them
- survey sampling
- longitudinal, cross-sectional and trend studies
- strengths and weaknesses of longitudinal, cohort and cross-sectional studies
- postal, interview and telephone surveys
- internet-based surveys
- comparing methods of data collection in surveys

We advise readers to take this chapter in conjunction with the chapters on sampling, questionnaires, interviews and data analysis techniques. Many researchers reading this book will probably be studying for higher degrees within a fixed and maybe short time frame; that may render longitudinal study out of the question for them. Nevertheless longitudinal study is an important type of research, and we introduce it here. More likely, researchers for higher degrees will find cross-sectional survey research appropriate, and it is widely used in higher degree research.

13.1 What is a survey?

Many educational research methods are descriptive; that is they set out to describe and to interpret what is. Such studies look at individuals, groups, institutions, methods and materials in order to describe, compare, contrast, classify, analyse and interpret the entities and the events that constitute their various fields of enquiry. We deal here with several types of descriptive survey research, including longitudinal, cross-sectional and trend or prediction studies.

Typically, surveys gather data at a particular point in time with the intention of describing the nature of existing conditions, or identifying standards against which existing conditions can be compared, or determining the relationships that exist between specific events. Thus, surveys may vary in their levels of complexity from those which provide simple frequency counts to those which present relational analysis.

Surveys may be further differentiated in terms of their scope. A study of contemporary developments in post-secondary education, for example, might encompass the whole of Western Europe; a study of subject choice, on the other hand, might be confined to one secondary school. The complexity and scope of surveys in education can be illustrated by reference to familiar examples.

A survey has several characteristics and several claimed attractions; typically it is used to scan a wide field of issues, populations, programmes, etc. in order to measure or describe any generalized features. It is useful (Morrison, 1993: 38–40) in that it usually:

- gathers data on a one-shot basis and hence is economical and efficient;
- represents a wide target population (hence there is a need for careful sampling, see Chapter 8);
- generates numerical data;
- provides descriptive, inferential and explanatory information;
- manipulates key factors and variables to derive frequencies (e.g. the numbers registering a particular opinion or test score);
- gathers standardized information (i.e. using the same instruments and questions for all participants);
- ascertains correlations (e.g. to find out if there is any relationship between gender and scores);
- presents material which is uncluttered by specific contextual factors;
- captures data from multiple choice, closed questions, test scores or observation schedules;
- supports or refutes hypotheses about the target population;
- generates accurate instruments through their piloting and revision;
- makes generalizations about, and observes patterns of response in, the targets of focus;
- gathers data which can be processed statistically;

- usually relies on large-scale data gathering from a wide population in order to enable generalizations to be made about given factors or variables.

Examples of surveys[1] are:

- opinion polls (which refute the notion that only opinion polls can catch opinions);
- test scores (e.g. the results of testing students nationally or locally);
- students' preferences for particular courses (e.g. humanities, sciences);
- reading surveys (e.g. Southgate *et al.*'s example of teaching practices in 1981 in the United Kingdom).

The websites for the National Child Development Study (NCDS) can be found at www.cls.ioe.ac.uk/text. asp?section=000100020003 and www.cls.ioe.ac.uk/.

Websites for the Centre for Longitudinal Studies (CLS) can be found at www.cls.ioe.ac.uk/, which includes the British Cohort Study and the Millennium Cohort Study.

Surveys in education often use test results, self-completion questionnaires and attitude scales. A researcher using this model typically will be seeking to gather large-scale data from as representative a sample population as possible in order to say with a measure of statistical confidence that certain observed characteristics occur with a degree of regularity, or that certain factors cluster together (see Chapter 37) or that they correlate with each other (correlation and covariance), or that they change over time and location (e.g. results of test scores used to ascertain the 'value-added' dimension of education, maybe using regression analysis and analysis of residuals to determine the difference between a predicted and an observed score), or regression analysis to use data from one variable to predict an outcome on another variable.

Surveys can be *exploratory*, in which no assumptions or models are postulated, and in which relationships and patterns are explored (e.g. through correlation, regression, stepwise regression and factor analysis). They can also be *confirmatory*, in which a model, causal relationship or hypothesis is tested (see the discussion of exploratory and confirmatory analysis in Chapter 37). Surveys can be descriptive or analytic (e.g. to examine relationships). Descriptive surveys simply describe data on variables of interest, whilst analytic surveys operate with hypothesized predictor or explanatory variables that are tested for their influence on dependent variables.

Most surveys will combine nominal data on participants' backgrounds and relevant personal details with other scales (e.g. attitude scales, data from ordinal, interval and ratio measures). Surveys are useful for gathering factual information, data on attitudes and preferences, beliefs and predictions, opinions, behaviour and experiences – both past and present (Weisberg *et al.*, 1996; Aldridge and Levine, 2001).

The attractions of a survey lie in its appeal to generalizability or universality within given parameters, its ability to make statements which are supported by large data banks and its ability to establish the degree of confidence which can be placed in a set of findings.

On the other hand, if a researcher is concerned to catch local, institutional or small-scale factors and variables – to portray the specificity of a situation, its uniqueness and particular complexity, its interpersonal dynamics, and to provide explanations of why a situation occurred or why a person or group of people returned a particular set of results or behaved in a particular way in a situation, or how a programme changes and develops over time, then a survey approach is probably unsuitable. Its degree of explanatory potential or fine detail is limited; it is lost to broad brush generalizations which are free of temporal, spatial or local contexts, i.e. its appeal largely rests on the basis of positivism. The individual instance is sacrificed to the aggregated response (which has the attraction of anonymity, non-traceability and confidentiality for respondents).

Surveys typically, though by no means exclusively, rely on large-scale data, e.g. from questionnaires, test scores, attendance rates, results of public examinations, etc., all of which enable comparisons to be made over time or between groups. This is not to say that surveys cannot be undertaken on a small-scale basis, as indeed they can; rather it is to say that the generalizability of such small-scale data will be slight. In surveys the researcher is usually very clearly an outsider, indeed questions of reliability must attach themselves to researchers conducting survey research on their own subjects, e.g. participants in a course that they have been running (e.g. Bimrose and Bayne (1995) and Morrison (1997)). Further, it is critical that attention is paid to rigorous sampling, otherwise the basis of the survey's applicability to wider contexts is seriously undermined. Non-probability samples tend to be avoided in surveys if generalizability is sought; probability sampling will tend to lead to generalizability of the data collected.

13.2 Some preliminary considerations

Three prerequisites to the design of any survey are: the specification of the exact purpose of the enquiry; the population on which it is to focus; and the resources that are available. Hoinville and Jowell's (1978) consideration of each of these key factors in survey planning can be illustrated in relation to the design of an educational enquiry.

The purpose of the enquiry

First, a survey's general purpose must be translated into a specific central aim. Thus, 'to explore teachers' views about in-service work' is somewhat nebulous, whereas 'to obtain a detailed description of primary and secondary teachers' priorities in the provision of in-service education courses' is reasonably specific.

Having decided upon and specified the primary objective of the survey, the second phase of the planning involves the identification and itemizing of subsidiary topics that relate to its central purpose. In our example, subsidiary issues might well include: the types of courses required; the content of courses; the location of courses; the timing of courses; the design of courses; and the financing of courses.

The third phase follows the identification and itemization of subsidiary topics and involves formulating specific information requirements relating to each of these issues. For example, with respect to the type of courses required, detailed information would be needed about the duration of courses (one meeting, several meetings, a week, a month, a term or a year), the status of courses (non-award bearing, award bearing, with certificate, diploma, degree granted by college or university), the orientation of courses (theoretically oriented involving lectures, readings, etc., or practically oriented involving workshops and the production of curriculum materials).

As these details unfold, note Hoinville and Jowell (1978), consideration would have to be given to the most appropriate ways of collecting items of information (interviews with selected teachers, postal questionnaires to selected schools, etc.).

The population upon which the survey is focused

The second prerequisite to survey design, the specification of the population to which the enquiry is addressed, affects decisions that researchers must make both about sampling and resources. In our hypothetical survey of in-service requirements, for example, we might specify the population as 'those primary and secondary teachers employed in schools within a 30-mile radius of Loughborough University'. In this case, the population is readily identifiable and, given sufficient resources to contact every member of the designated group, sam-

pling decisions do not arise. Things are rarely so straightforward, however. Often the criteria by which populations are specified ('severely challenged', 'under-achievers', 'intending teachers' or 'highly anxious') are difficult to operationalize. Populations, moreover, vary considerably in their accessibility; pupils and student teachers are relatively easy to survey, gypsy children and headteachers are more elusive. More importantly, in a large survey researchers usually draw a sample from the population to be studied; rarely do they attempt to contact every member. We deal with the question of sampling shortly.

The resources available

The third important factor in designing and planning a survey is the financial cost. Sample surveys are labour-intensive (see Davidson, 1970), the largest single expenditure being the fieldwork where costs arise out of the interviewing time, travel time and transport claims of the interviewers themselves. There are additional demands on the survey budget. Training and supervising the panel of interviewers can often be as expensive as the costs incurred during the time that they actually spend in the field. Questionnaire construction, piloting, printing, posting, coding, together with computer programming – all eat into financial resources.

Proposals from intending education researchers seeking governmental or private funding are often weakest in the amount of time and thought devoted to a detailed planning of the financial implications of the projected enquiries. (In this chapter we confine ourselves from this point to a discussion of surveys based on self-completion questionnaires. A full account of the interview as a research technique is given in Chapter 21.)

Mode of data collection

There are two main issues to be addressed here:

1 Will the researcher be completing the survey by entering data, or will the participants be self-administering the survey?
2 How will the survey be administered, e.g. a postal survey, a telephone survey, an internet survey, by face-to-face interviews, by email?

Self-reporting

There can be a significant difference in the responses gained from self-reporting and those obtained from face-to-face survey interviews or telephone interviews

(Dale 2006: 145). Many surveys ask respondents not only to administer the questionnaires themselves but also to report on themselves. This may introduce bias, as respondents may under-report (e .g. to avoid socially undesirable responses) or over-report (to give socially desirable answers). Self-reporting also requires the researcher to ensure that respondents all understand the question, understand it in the same way and understand it in the way intended by the researcher (Kenett, 2006: 406). The difficulty here is that words are inherently ambiguous (see Chapter 20 on questionnaire design), so the researcher should be as specific as possible. The researcher should also indicate how much contextual information the respondent should provide, what kind of answer is being sought (so that the respondent knows how to respond appropriately), how much factual detail is required, and what constitutes relevant and irrelevant data (e.g. the level of detail or focus on priority issues required) (Kenett, 2006: 407–8). Further, surveys that rely on respondents' memory may be prone to the bias of forgetting or selective recall.

13.3 Planning a survey

Whether the survey is large scale and undertaken by some governmental bureau or small scale and carried out by the lone researcher, the collection of information typically involves one or more of the following data-gathering techniques: structured or semi-structured interviews, self-completion or postal questionnaires, telephone interviews, internet surveys, standardized tests of attainment or performance, and attitude scales. Typically, too, surveys proceed through well-defined stages, though not every stage outlined in Figure 13.1 is required for the successful completion of a survey.

The process moves from the general to the specific. A general research topic is broken down into complementary issues and questions, and, for each component, questions are set. As will be discussed in questionnaires (Chapter 20), it is important, in the interests of reliability and validity, to have several items or questions for each component issue, as this does justice to the all-round nature of the topic. Sapsford (1999: 34–40) suggests that there are four main considerations in planning a survey:

■ *problem definition* (e.g. deciding what kinds and contents of answers are required; what hypotheses there are to be tested; what variables there are to explore);
■ *sample selection* (e.g. what is the target population; how can access and representativeness be assured;

what other samples will need to be drawn for the purpose of comparison);
■ *design of measurements* (e.g. what will be measured, and how (i.e. what metrics will be used – see Chapter 20 on questionnaires); what variables will be required; how reliability and validity will be assured);
■ *concern for participants* (e.g. protection of confidentiality and anonymity; avoidance of pain to the respondents; avoiding harm to those who might be affected by the results; avoiding over-intrusive questions; avoiding coercion; informed consent – see Chapter 5 on ethics).

A 14-stage process of planning a survey can be considered:

Stage 1: define the objectives;
Stage 2: decide the kind of survey required (e.g. longitudinal, cross-section, trend study; cohort study);
Stage 3: formulate research questions or hypotheses (if appropriate): the null hypothesis and alternative hypothesis;
Stage 4: decide the issues on which to focus;
Stage 5: decide the information that is needed to address the issues;
Stage 6: decide the sampling required;
Stage 7: decide the instrumentation and the metrics required;
Stage 8: generate the data collection instruments;
Stage 9: decide how the data will be collected (e.g. postal survey, interviews);
Stage 10: pilot the instruments and refine them;
Stage 11: train the interviewers (if appropriate);
Stage 12: collect the data;
Stage 13: analyse the data;
Stage 14: report the results.

Rosier (1997: 154–62) suggests that the planning of a survey will need to include clarification of:

■ the research questions to which answers need to be provided;
■ the conceptual framework of the survey, specifying in precise terms the concepts that will be used and explored;
■ operationalizing the research questions (e.g. into hypotheses);
■ the instruments to be used for data collection, e.g. to chart or measure background characteristics of the sample (often nominal data), academic achievements (e.g. examination results, degrees awarded), attitudes and opinions (often using ordinal data from rating scales) and behaviour (using observational techniques);

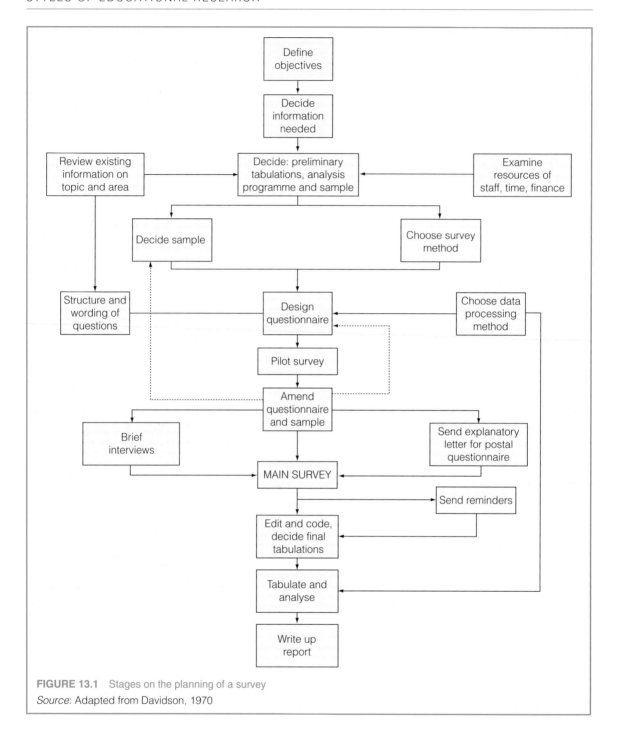

FIGURE 13.1 Stages on the planning of a survey

Source: Adapted from Davidson, 1970

- sampling strategies and subgroups within the sample (unless the whole population is being surveyed, e.g. through census returns or nationally aggregated test scores etc.);
- pre-piloting the survey;
- piloting the survey;
- data collection practicalities and conduct (e.g. permissions, funding, ethical considerations, response rates);
- data preparation (e.g. coding, data entry for computer analysis, checking and verification);
- data analysis (e.g. statistical processes, construction of variables and factor analysis, inferential statistics);
- reporting the findings (answering the research questions).

It is important to pilot and pre-pilot a survey. The difference between the pre-pilot and the pilot is significant. Whereas the pre-pilot is usually a series of open-ended questions that are used to generate categories for closed, typically multiple-choice questions, the pilot is used to test the actual survey instrument itself (see Chapter 20).

A rigorous survey, then, formulates clear, specific objectives and research questions, ensures that the instrumentation, sampling and data types are appropriate to yield answers to the research questions, ensures that as high a level of sophistication of data analysis is undertaken as the data will sustain (but no more!).

Some challenges in surveys

A survey is no stronger than its weakest point, and we consider a range of issues here in an endeavour to strengthen each aspect of a survey. Surveys have to minimize errors caused by:

- poor sampling (e.g. failure to represent or include sufficiently the target population);
- poor question design and wording (e.g. failure to catch accurately the views of, or meanings from, the respondents or to measure the factors of interest);
- incorrect or biased responses;
- low response or non-response.

The first of these – a sampling matter – may be caused by a failure correctly to identify the population and its characteristics, or a failure to use the correct sampling strategy, or systematically to bias the sample (e.g. using a telephone survey based on telephone directory entries, when key people in the population may not have a telephone (e.g. the poor), or may have a cellphone rather than a fixed line (e.g. the young, the middle aged but not the elderly), or using an internet or email based survey, when many respondents do not have access). We address the issue of sampling in Chapter 8 and below.

The second of these is a failure to operationalize the variables fairly (i.e. a validity issue) or a failure in the wording or meanings used or inferred, such that incorrect responses are collected (a reliability issue) (e.g. people may not understand a question, or may misinterpret it, or interpret it differently). We address this in Chapter 10 and below.

The third problem is that some participants may deliberately over-report or under-report the real situation in – often sensitive – matters (e.g. teenage alcohol, smoking or drug use, underage sexual relations, bullying, domestic violence, petty criminality may be *systematically* under-reported (i.e. biased), whereas popularity of a teacher or students might be over-reported (biased)). Bias obtains where there is a *systematic* skewing or distortion in the responses. Further, some questions may rely on memory, and memory can be selective and deceptive (e.g. people may not remember accurately). Also, some responses will depend on a person's state of mind at the time of completing the survey – asking a teacher about teacher stress and tiredness, late on a Friday afternoon in school with a difficult class, could well elicit a completely different response from asking her directly after a week's holiday. Some questions may be so general as to be unhelpful (e.g. 'how stressed do you feel?'), whereas others might be so specific as to prevent accurate recall (e.g. 'how many times have you shouted at a class of children in the past week?') (one solution to the latter might be to ask participants to keep a diary of instances).

Fowler (2009: 15) suggests that the answer that a respondent gives is a combination of the true response plus an error in the answer given, and he indicates that errors may come from many sources.

The fourth of these – low response or non-response – is a problem that besets researchers, and is so significant that we devote a separate section to it below.

13.4 Low response and non-response, and how to reduce them

Non-response to a whole questionnaire ('unit non-response' (Durrant, 2009: 293)) or to a specific item ('item non-response' (Durrant, 2009: 293)) is a serious problem for much survey research, though Denscombe (2009: 282) notes that online surveys tend to have lower item non-response than paper-based surveys, though there may be more dropouts before reaching the end of an online survey than in a paper-based survey.

Dale (2006: 148) suggests that 'non-respondents almost invariably differ from respondents', and that this affects the validity and reliability of the responses obtained, and their analysis. If non-response is received from a very homogenous sample then this might be less of a problem than if the sample is very varied. Further, if non-response is received randomly across a sample then this might be less of a problem than if the non-response was from a particular sub-sector of the respondents (e.g. a very low or a very high socio-economic group), as this would bias the results (cf. Dale, 2006: 148). A subset of non-response to a whole questionnaire is item non-response, and here missing data should not be ignored (Dale, 2006: 15).

Rubin (1987), Little and Rubin (1989), Allison (2001), Dale (2006: 149–50) and Durrant (2006, 2009) review a range of different 'imputation methods' for handling and weighting non-response (i.e. methods for filling in data with 'plausible values' in order to render a set of data complete and yet to reduce bias in the non-responses, i.e. that bias which might be caused by the non-responses having different values from the non-missing responses (Durrant, 2009: 295)). These depend on whether the non-response is largely confined to a single variable or many variables. The researcher has to determine whether there are patterns of non-response, as these affect the method for handling non-response. For example, if the non-response is randomly distributed across several variables, with no clear patterns of non-response, then this may be less problematic than if there is a systematic non-response to one or more variables in a survey (Durrant, 2009: 295). Durrant sets out several ways of calculating missing values, including, for example:

a calculating missing values from regression techniques using auxiliary variables (p. 296);
b 'hot deck' methods, in which subgroups of participants (based on their scores on auxiliary variables) are constructed and the researcher compares their results to the non-missing results of the respondent who had omitted a particular response (p. 297);
c 'nearest neighbour' techniques, in which the results from a person whose data diverge as little as possible from those of the missing person are used to replace the missing values.

Durrant (2006, 2009) identifies further, statistical methods of calculating missing scores, such as multiple and fractional imputation, and propensity score weighting. She makes the point that how one calculates the values of missing data depends on a range of factors such as the purpose of the analysis, the variable(s) in question, the kinds of data, any patterns of missing data, and the characteristics and fittingness of the assumptions on which the particular intended imputation method is based. For further guidance on this matter we refer the reader to the sources indicated above.

In some cases (e.g. when all the students in a class complete a questionnaire during a lesson) the response rate may be very high, but in other circumstances the response rate may be very low or zero, either for the whole survey or for individual items within it, for several reasons, e.g.

- the survey never reaches the intended people;
- people refuse to answer;
- people may not be available (e.g. for a survey administered by interview), for example they may be out at work when a telephone survey administrator calls;
- people may not be able to answer the questions (e.g. language or writing difficulties);
- people may not actually have the information requested;
- people may overlook some items in error;
- the survey was completed and posted but failed to return;
- the pressure of competing activities on the time of the respondent;
- potential embarrassment at their own ignorance if respondents feel unable to answer a question;
- ignorance of the topic/no background in the topic;
- dislike of the contents or subject matter of the interview;
- fear of possible consequences of the survey to himself/herself or others;
- lack of clarity in the instructions;
- fear or dislike of being interviewed;
- sensitivity of the topic, or potentially insulting or threatening topic;
- betrayal of confidences;
- losing the return envelope or return address;
- the wrong person may open the mail, and fail to pass it on to the most appropriate person.

Later in this chapter we discuss ways of improving response rates. However, here we wish to insert a note of caution: some researchers suggest that, for non-responders to an item, an average score for that item can be inserted. This might be acceptable if it can be shown that the sample or the population is fairly homogeneous, but, for heterogeneous populations or samples, or those where the variation in the sample or population is not known, it may be dangerous to assume homogeneity and hence to infer what the missing data may look like, as this could distort the results.

Let us suppose that out of a sample of 200 participants 90 per cent reply (180 participants) to a 'yes/no' type of question, e.g. for the question 'Do you agree with public examinations at age 11?', and let us say that 50 per cent (90 people) indicate 'yes' and 50 per cent indicate 'no'. If the 10 per cent who did not reply (20 people) would have said 'yes' then this would clearly swing the results as 110 people say 'yes' (55 per cent) and 90 people say 'no' (45 per cent). However, if the response rates vary, then the maximum variation could be very different, as in Table 13.1 (cf. Fowler, 2009: 55). Table 13.1 assumes that if a 100 per sample had replied, 50 per said 'yes' and 50 per cent said 'no; the rest of the table indicates the possible variation depending on response rate.

Table 13.1 indicates the possible variation in a simple 'yes/no' type of question. If a rating scale is chosen, for example a 5-point rating scale, the number of options increases from two to five, and, correspondingly, the possibility for variation increases even further.

Improving response rates in a survey

A major difficulty in survey research is securing a sufficiently high response rate to give credibility and reliability to the data. In some postal research, response rates can be as low as 20–30 per cent, and this compromises the reliability of the data very considerably. There is a difference between the *intended* and the *achieved* sample (Fogelman, 2002: 105). Punch (2003:

TABLE 13.1	MAXIMUM VARIATION FOR LOW RESPONSE RATES IN A YES/NO QUESTION FOR A 50/50 DISTRIBUTION
Response rate (%)	*Variation in the true value of 'yes' and 'no' votes (lowest % to highest % in each category)*
100	50–50
90	45–55
80	40–60
70	35–65
60	30–70
50	25–75
40	20–80
30	15–85
20	10–90
10	5–95

43) suggests that it is important to plan for poor response rates (e.g. by increasing the sample size) rather than trying to adjust sampling *post hoc*. He also suggests that access to the sample needs to be researched before the survey commences, maybe pre-notifying potential participants if that is deemed desirable. He argues that a poor response level may also be due to the careless omission of details of how and when the questionnaire will be returned or collected. This is a matter that needs to be made clear in the questionnaire itself. In the case of a postal survey a stamped addressed envelope should always be included.

Kenett (2006) and Fowler (2009: 52) report that responses rates increase when people are interested in the subject matter of the survey, or if the subject is very relevant to them, or if the completion of the survey brings a sense of satisfaction to the respondent. Denscombe (2009: 288) reports that response rates increase if the 'respondent burden' is low (i.e. the effort required by the respondent to answer a question).

Further, the design, layout and presentation of the survey may also exert an influence on response rate. It is important to include a brief covering letter that explains the research clearly and introduces the researcher. The timing of the survey is important, for example schools will not welcome researchers or surveys in examination periods or at special periods, e.g. Christmas or inspection times (Fogelman, 2002: 106). Finally, it is important to plan the follow-up to surveys, to ensure that non-respondents are called again and reminded of the request to complete the survey. Fowler (2009: 57) indicates that between a quarter and a third of people may agree to complete a survey if a follow-up is undertaken.

There are several possible ways of increasing response rates to mailed surveys, including, for example (e.g. Aldridge and Levine, 2001; Fowler, 2009: 56):

- follow-ups and polite reminders (e.g. by mail, email, telephone call) in which the reminder is short, polite, indicating the value of the respondent's participation and, if the reminder is postal, another clean copy of the questionnaire;
- advance notification of the survey (e.g. by telephone, post or email);
- pre-paid return stamped addressed envelopes;
- institutional affiliation, survey sponsorship or support from a high status agent;
- financial incentives (though increasing the financial incentive to a high figure does not bring commensurate returns in response rates);
- rewards for return;

- making surveys easy to read and to complete;
- making instructions about responses and return very clear;
- avoid open-ended questions unless these are really important (as the quality of responses is usually poor to open-ended questions: people tend not to write anything or to write very little);
- avoid placing open-ended questions at the start of a questionnaire;
- make the surveys attractive, with easy-to-follow instructions and spacing of the text;
- flatter the participants without being seen to flatter them;
- providing information about the research through a covering letter and/or advance notification;
- making the survey look very unlike junk mail;
- consider asking the respondents for an interview to complete the survey questionnaire;
- deliver the questionnaire personally rather than through mail;
- ensure that the questions or items are non-judgemental (e.g. in sensitive matters);
- assure confidentiality and anonymity.

Cooper and Schindler (2001: 314–15) and Fowler (2009: 58) report that the following factors make little or no appreciable difference to response rates:

- personalizing the introductory letter;
- writing an introductory letter;
- promises of anonymity;
- questionnaire length (it is not always the case that a short questionnaire produces more returns than a long questionnaire, but researchers will need to consider the effect of a long survey questionnaire on the respondents – they may feel positive or negative about it, or set it aside temporarily and forget to return it later);
- size, reproduction and colour of the questionnaire;
- deadline dates for return (it was found that these did not increase response rate but did accelerate the return of questionnaires).

Potential respondents may be persuaded to participate depending on, for example:

- the status and prestige of the institution or researcher carrying out the research;
- the perceived benefit of the research;
- the perceived importance of the topic;
- personal interest in the research;
- interest in being interviewed, i.e. the interview experience;

- personal liking for, or empathy with, the researcher;
- feelings of duty to the public and sense of civic responsibility;
- loneliness or boredom (nothing else to do);
- sense of self-importance.

Dillman (2007) suggests that response rates can be increased if, in sequence: (a) non-respondents are sent a friendly reminder after ten days, stressing the importance of the research; (b) non-respondents are sent a further friendly reminder ten days after the initial reminder, stressing the importance of the research; (c) a telephone call is made to the respondents shortly after the second reminder, indicating the importance of the research.

Fowler (2009: 60) suggests that the initial questionnaire might also include a statement to say that completion and return of the questionnaire will ensure that no follow-up reminders will be sent (though this may be regarded by some respondents as presumptuous).

13.5 Survey sampling

Sampling is a key feature of a survey approach, and we advise readers to look closely at Chapter 8 on sampling. Because questions about sampling arise directly from the second of our preliminary considerations, that is defining the population upon which the survey is to focus, researchers must take sampling decisions early in the overall planning of a survey (see Figure 13.1). We have already seen that due to factors of expense, time and accessibility, it is not always possible or practical to obtain measures from a population. Indeed Wilson *et al.* (2006: 352) draw attention to the tension between the need for large samples in order to conduct 'robust statistical analysis', and issues of resources such as cost and practicability (p. 353).

Researchers endeavour therefore to collect information from a smaller group or subset of the population in such a way that the knowledge gained is representative of the total population under study. This smaller group or subset is a 'sample'. Unless researchers identify the total population in advance, it is virtually impossible for them to assess how representative the sample is that they have drawn. Chapter 8 addresses probability and non-probability samples, and we refer readers to the detailed discussion of these in that chapter. The researcher will need to decide the sampling strategy to be used on the basis of fitness for purpose, e.g.

- a probability and non-probability sample;
- the desire to generalize, and to whom;

- the sampling frame (those who are eligible to be included);
- the sample size;
- the representativeness of the sample;
- access to the sample;
- the response rate.

Even if the researcher has taken extraordinary care with the sampling strategy, there may still be problems (e.g. response rate, respondent characteristics or availability) that may interfere with the best-laid strategies.

In addition to the sampling strategy to be used, there are the issues of sample size and selection. We discussed this in Chapter 8, but here we wish to address the issue of practicability. For example, let us say that, in the interests of precision, the researcher wishes to have a sample in which there are four strata (e.g. age groups in a primary school), and that each stratum comprised 50 students, i.e. 200 students. If that researcher wished to increase the sample size of one stratum by, say 20 students, this would necessitate an overall increase of 80 students (20 × 4) in the sample. Do the benefits outweigh the costs here?

An alternative to increasing the *total* size of the sample would be to increase the size of one stratum only, under certain conditions. For example, let us say that the researcher is studying attitudes of males and females to learning science, in a secondary school which had only recently moved from being a single-sex boys' school to a mixed sex school, so the ratio of male to female students is 4:1. The researcher wishes to include a minimum of 200 female students. This could require a total of 1,000 students in the sample (200 females + {200 × 4} male students in the sample); this could be unmanageable. Rather, the researcher could identify two female students for each male student (i.e. 400 females) and then, when analysing the data, could give one-quarter of the weight to the response of the female students, in order to gain a truer representation of the target population of the school. This would bring the total sample to 600 students, rather than 1,000, involved in the survey. Over-sampling a smaller group (in this case the females), and then weighting the analysis is frequently undertaken in surveys (cf. Fowler, 2009: 27).

In sampling, the probability might also exist of excluding some legitimate members of population in the target sample; however, the researcher will need to weigh the cost of excluding these members (e.g. the very-hard-to-reach) against the cost of ensuring that they are included – the benefit gained from including them may not justify the time, cost and effort (cf. Fowler, 2009: 179). Similarly, the precision gained

from stratified sampling (see Chapter 8) may not be worth the price to be paid in necessarily increasing the sample size in order to represent each stratum.

In many cases a sampling strategy may be in more than one stage. For example, let us consider the instance of a survey of 1,000 biology students from a population of 10,000 biology students in a city. In the first stage a group of, say, ten, schools is identified (A), then, within that, an age group of students (B), and then, within that the individuals in that group who are studying biology (C), and, finally, the sample (D) is taken from that group. The intention is to arrive at (D), but, in order to reach this point, a series of other steps has to be taken.

This raises the matter of deciding what are those steps to be taken. For example, the researcher could decide the sampling for the survey of the biology students by taking the random sample of 1,000 students from ten schools. The researcher lists all the 1,000 relevant students from the list of 10,000 students, and decides to select 100 students from each of the ten schools (a biology student, therefore, in one of these ten schools has a 1 in 10 chance of being selected). Alternatively the researcher could decide to sample from five schools only, with 200 students from each of the five schools, so students in each of these five schools have a 1 in 5 chance of being selected. Alternatively, the researcher could decide to sample from two schools, with 500 students, so students in each of these two schools have a 1 in 2 chance of being selected. There are other permutations. The point here is that, as the number of schools decreases, so does the possible cost of conducting the survey, but so does the overall reliability, as so few schools are included. It is a trade-off.

In order to reduce sampling error (the variation of the mean scores of the sample from the mean score of the population), a general rule is to increase the sample, and this is good advice. However, it has to be tempered by the fact that the effect of increasing the sample size in a small sample reduces sampling error more than in a large sample, e.g. increasing the sample size from 50 to 80 (30 persons) will have greater impact on reducing sampling error than increasing the sample size from 500 to 530 (30 persons). Hence it may be unprofitable simply to increase sample sizes in already large samples.

Further, the researcher has to exercise his or her judgement in attending to sampling. For example, if it is already known that a population is homogenous, then the researcher may feel it a needless exercise in having too large and unmanageable a sample if the results are not likely to be much different from those of a small sample of the same homogeneous group (though theoretical sampling (see Chapter 33) may suggest where a researcher needs to include participants from other small samples). As Fowler (2009: 44) remarks, the results of a sample of 150 people will describe a population of 15,000 or 25 million with more or less the same degree of accuracy. He remarks that samples of more than 150 or 200 may not yield more than modest gains to the precision of the data (p. 45), though this, of course, has to be addressed in relation to the population characteristics, the number, size and kind of strata to be included, and the type of sample being used. Sampling errors, he notes (p. 45) are more a function of sample size than of the proportions of the sample to the population. Further, he advocates probability rather than non-probability samples, unless there are persuasive reasons for non-probability samples to be used.

Whilst sample sizes can be calculated on the basis of statistics alone (e.g. confidence levels, confidence intervals, population size and so on, see Chapter 8), this is often not the sole criterion, as it accords a degree of precision to the sample which takes insufficient account of other sampling issues, for example access, variation or homogeneity in the population, levels of literacy in the population (e.g. in the case of a self-administered questionnaire survey) and costs.

Sampling is one of several sources of error in surveys, as indicated earlier in this chapter.

13.6 Longitudinal, cross-sectional and trend studies

The term 'longitudinal' is used to describe a variety of studies that are conducted over a period of time. Often, as we have seen, the word 'developmental' is employed in connection with longitudinal studies that deal specifically with aspects of human growth.

A clear distinction is drawn between longitudinal and cross-sectional studies.[2] The longitudinal study gathers data over an extended period of time; a short-term investigation may take several weeks or months; a long-term study can extend over many years. Where successive measures are taken at different points in time from the same respondents, the term 'follow-up study' or 'cohort study' is used in the British literature, the equivalent term in the United States being the 'panel study'. The term 'cohort' is a group of people with some common characteristic. A cohort study is sometimes differentiated from a panel study. In a cohort study a specific population is tracked over a specific period of time but selective sampling within that sample occurs (Borg and Gall, 1979: 291). This means that some members of a cohort may not be included

each time. By contrast, in a panel study each same individual is tracked over time.

Where different respondents are studied at different points in time, the study is called 'cross-sectional'. Where a few selected factors are studied continuously over time, the term 'trend study' is employed. One example of regular or repeated cross-sectional social surveys is the General Household Survey, in which the same questions are asked every year though they are put to a different sample of the population each time. The British Social Attitudes Survey is an example of a repeated cross-sectional survey, using some 3,600 respondents.

A famous example of a longitudinal (cohort) study is the National Child Development Study, which started in 1958. The British General Household Panel Survey interviewed individuals from a representative sample each year in the 1990s. Another example is the British Family Expenditure Survey. These latter two are cross-sectional in that they tell us about the population at a given point in time, and hence provide aggregated data.

By contrast, longitudinal studies can also provide individual level data, by focusing on the same individuals over time (e.g. the Household Panel Studies which follow individuals and families over time (Ruspini, 2002: 4). Lazarsfeld introduced the concept of a panel in the 1940s, attempting to identify causal patterns and the difficulties in tracing causal patterns (Ruspini, 2002: 13)).

Longitudinal studies

Longitudinal studies can be of the survey type or of other types (e.g. case study). Here we confine ourselves to the survey type. Such longitudinal studies can use repeated cross-sectional studies, which are 'carried out regularly, each time using a largely different sample or a completely new sample' (Ruspini, 2002: 3), or use the same sample over time. They enable researchers to: 'analyse the duration of social phenomena' (Ruspini, 2002: 24); highlight similarities, differences and changes over time in respect of one or more variables or participants (within and between participants); identify long-term ('sleeper') effects; and explain changes in terms of stable characteristics, e.g. sex, or variable characteristics, such as income. The appeal of longitudinal research is its ability to establish causality and to make inferences. Ruspini (2002) adds to these the ability of longitudinal research to 'construct more complicated behavioural models than purely cross-sectional or time-series data' (p. 26); they catch the complexity of human behaviour. Further, longitudinal studies can combine numerical and qualitative data.

Cohort studies and trend studies are *prospective* longitudinal methods, in that they are ongoing in their collection of information about individuals or their monitoring of specific events. *Retrospective* longitudinal studies, on the other hand, focus upon individuals who have reached some defined end-point or state. For example, a group of young people may be the researcher's particular interest (intending social workers, convicted drug offenders or university dropouts, for example), and the questions to which she will address herself are likely to include ones such as: 'Is there anything about the previous experience of these individuals that can account for their present situation?' Retrospective longitudinal studies will specify the period over which to be retrospective, e.g. one year, five years.

Retrospective analysis is not confined to longitudinal studies alone. For example Rose and Sullivan (1993: 185) and Ruane (2005: 87) suggest that cross-sectional studies can use retrospective factual questions, e.g. previous occupations, dates of birth within the family, dates of marriage, divorce, though Rose and Sullivan (1993: 185) advise against collecting other types of retrospective data in cross-sectional studies, as the quality of the data diminishes the further back one asks respondents to recall previous states or even facts.

It is important, in longitudinal studies, to decide when, and how frequently to collect data over time, and this is informed by issues of fitness for purpose as well as practicability. Further, in order to allow for attrition (dropout) of the sample, it is wise to have as large a sample as practicable and possible at the start of the study (Wilson *et al.*, 2006: 354).

Cross-sectional studies

A cross-sectional study is one that produces a 'snapshot' of a population at a particular point in time. The epitome of the cross-sectional study is a national census in which a representative sample of the population consisting of individuals of different ages, different occupations, different educational and income levels, and residing in different parts of the country is interviewed on the same day. More typically in education, cross-sectional studies involve indirect measures of the nature and rate of changes in the physical and intellectual development of samples of children drawn from representative age levels. The single 'snapshot' of the cross-sectional study provides researchers with data for either a retrospective or a prospective enquiry.

A cross-sectional study can also bear several hallmarks of a longitudinal study of parallel groups (e.g. age groups) which are drawn simultaneously from the population. For example, drawing students aged 5, 7, 9 and 11 at a single point in time would bear some characteristics of a longitudinal study in that developments over age groups could be seen, though, of course, it would not have the same weight as a longitudinal study conducted on the same age group over time. This is the case for international studies of educational achievement, requiring samples to be drawn from the same population (Lietz and Keeves, 1997: 122) and for factors that might influence changes in the dependent variables to remain constant across the age groups. Cross-sectional studies, catching a frozen moment in time, may be ineffective for studying change. If changes are to be addressed through cross-sectional surveys, then this suggests the need for repeated applications of the survey, or by the use of trend analysis.

Trend studies

Trend studies focus on factors rather than people, and these factors are studied over time. New samples are drawn at each stage of the data collection, but focusing on the same factors. By taking different samples the problem of reactivity is avoided (see below: 'pre-test sensitisation'), i.e. earlier surveys affecting the behaviour of participants in the later surveys. This is particularly useful if the research is being conducted on sensitive issues, as raising a sensitive issue early on in research may change an individual's behaviour, which could affect the responses in a later round of data collection. By drawing a different sample each time this problem is overcome.

Trend or prediction studies have an obvious importance to educational administrators or planners. Like cohort studies, they may be of relatively short or long duration. Essentially, the trend study examines recorded data to establish patterns of change that have already occurred in order to predict what will be likely to occur in the future. In trend studies two or more cross-sectional studies are undertaken with identical age groups at more than one point in time in order to make comparisons over time (e.g. the Scholastic Aptitude and Achievement tests in the United States) (Keeves, 1997a: 141) and the National Assessment of Educational Progress results (Lietz and Keeves, 1997: 122). A major difficulty that researchers face in conducting trend analyses is the intrusion of unpredictable factors that invalidate forecasts formulated on past data. For this reason, short-term trend studies tend to be more accurate than long-term analyses. Trend studies do not include the same respondents over time, so the possibility exists for variation in data due to the different respondents rather than the change in trends. Gorard (2001b: 87) suggests that this problem can be attenuated by a 'rolling sample' in which a proportion of the original sample is retained in the second wave of data

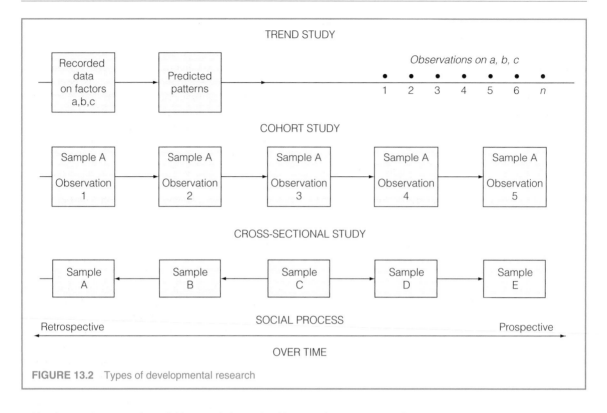

FIGURE 13.2 Types of developmental research

collection, and a proportion of this sample is retained in the third wave, and so on.

The distinctions we have drawn between the various terms used in developmental research are illustrated in Figure 13.2.

13.7 Strengths and weaknesses of longitudinal, cohort and cross-sectional studies

Longitudinal studies of the cohort analysis type have an important place in the research armoury of educational investigators. Longitudinal studies have considerable potential for yielding rich data that can trace changes over time, and with great accuracy (Gorard, 2001b: 86). On the other hand they suffer from problems of attrition (participants leaving the research over time, a particular problem in panel studies which research the same individuals over time), and they can be expensive to conduct in terms of time and money (Ruspini, 2002: 71). Gorard (2001b) reports a study of careers and identities that had an initial response rate of between 60 and 70 per cent in the first round, and then risked dropping to 25 per cent by the third round, becoming increasingly more middle class in each wave of the study. He also discusses a Youth Cohort Study (2001b) in which

only 45 per cent of the respondents took part in all three waves of the data collection. Ruspini (2002: 72) identifies an attrition rate of 78 per cent in the three waves of the European Community Household Panel survey of the UK in 1997.

Ruspini (2002) also indicates how a small measurement error in a longitudinal study may be compounded over time. She gives the example of an error in income occurring at a point in time (p. 72) that could lead to 'false transitions' appearing over time in regard to poverty and unemployment.

Further, long-term studies, Gorard (2001b: 86) avers, face 'a threat to internal validity' that stems from the need 'to test and re-test the same individuals'. Dooley (2001: 120) terms this 'pre-test sensitisation'; it is also termed 'panel conditioning' or 'time-in sample bias' (Ruspini, 2002: 73). Here the first interview in an interview survey can cause changes in the second interview, i.e. the first interview may set up a self-fulfilling prophecy that is recorded in the second interview. He gives the example of a health survey in the first round of data collection, which may raise participants' awareness of the dangers of smoking, such that they reduce or give up smoking by the time the second round takes place. Trend studies overcome this problem by drawing different populations at each stage of the data collection in the research.

Dooley (2001) also raises the issue of the difficulties caused by changes in the research staff over time in longitudinal surveys. Changes in interviewee response, he suggests, may be due to having different researchers rather than to the respondents themselves. Even using the same instruments, different researchers may use them differently (e.g. in interviewing behaviour).

To add to these matters, Ruspini (2002: 73) suggests that longitudinal data are affected by:

a   history (events occurring may change the observations of a group under study);

b   maturation (participants mature at different speeds and in different ways);

c   testing (test sensitization may occur – participants learn from exposure to repeated testing/interviews);

d   the timing of cause and effect (some causes may produce virtually instantaneous effects and others may take a long time for the effects to show);

e   the direction of causality not always being clear or singular.

A major concern in longitudinal studies concerns the comparability of data over time. For example, though public examinations may remain constant over time (e.g. GCSE, A levels), the contents and format of those examinations do not. (This rehearses the argument that public examinations like A levels are becoming easier over time.) This issue concerns the need to ensure consistency in the data collection instruments over time. Further, if comparability of data in a longitudinal study is to be addressed then this means that the initial rounds of data collection, in the earliest stage of the research, will need to anticipate and include all the variables that will be addressed over time.

Longitudinal studies are more prone to attrition than cross-sectional studies, and are more expensive to conduct in terms of time and cost. On the other hand, whereas trend studies change their populations, thereby disabling micro-level – individual-level – analysis from being conducted, longitudinal analysis enables such individual-level analysis to be performed. Indeed, whereas cross-sectional designs (even if they are repeated cross-sectional designs) may be unsuitable for studying developmental patterns and causality within cohorts, in longitudinal analysis this is a strength. Longitudinal data can supply 'satisfactory answers to questions concerning the dynamics and the determinants of individual behaviour' (Ruspini, 2002: 71), issues which are not easily addressed in cross-sectional designs.

Retrospective longitudinal studies rely on the memories of the participants. These may be faulty, and the further back one's memory reaches, the greater is the danger of distortion or inability to recall. Memory is affected by, for example (Ruspini, 2002: 97):

- the time that has elapsed since the event took place;
- the significance of the event for the participant;
- the amount of information required for the study – the greater the amount, the harder it is to provide;
- the contamination/interference effect of other memories of a similar event (i.e. the inability to separate similar events);
- the emotional content or the social desirability of the content;
- the psychological condition of the participant at interview.

Further, participants will look at past events through the lens of hindsight and subsequent events rather than what those events meant at the time. Further, it is not always easy for these participants to recall their emotional state at the time in question. Factually speaking, it may not be possible to gather data from some time past, as they simply do not exist, e.g. medical records, data on income, or they cannot be found or recovered.

Cohort studies of human growth and development conducted on representative samples of populations are uniquely able to identify typical patterns of development and to reveal factors operating on those samples which elude other research designs. They permit researchers to examine individual variations in characteristics or traits, and to produce individual growth curves. Cohort studies, too, are particularly appropriate when investigators attempt to establish causal relationships, for this task involves identifying changes in certain characteristics that result in changes in others.

Cross-sectional designs are inappropriate in causal research as they cannot sustain causal analysis unless they are repeated over time. Cohort analysis is especially useful in sociological research because it can show how changing properties of individuals fit together into changing properties of social systems as a whole. For example, the study of staff morale and its association with the emerging organizational climate of a newly opened school would lend itself to this type of developmental research. A further strength of cohort studies in schools is that they provide longitudinal records whose value derives in part from the known fallibility of any single test or assessment (see Davie, 1972). Finally, time, always a limiting factor in experimental and interview settings, is generally more readily available in cohort studies, allowing the researcher greater opportunity to observe trends and to distinguish 'real' changes from chance occurrences (see Bailey, 1994).

In longitudinal, cohort and trend studies there is the risk that characteristics of the respondents may affect the results (Robson, 1993: 128). For example, their memory, knowledge, motivation and personality may affect their responses, and, indeed, they may withhold information, particularly if it is sensitive.

Longitudinal research indicates the influence of biological factors over time (e.g. human development), environmental influences and intervention influences (Keeves, 1997a: 139) and their interactions. Addressing these, the appeal of longitudinal analysis is that it enables causal analysis to be undertaken. Time series studies in longitudinal research also enable emergent patterns to be observed over time, by examining a given range of variables over time, in addition to other factors. This permits individual and group profiles to be examined over time and development, indicating similarities and differences within and between individuals and groups in respect of given variables. As longitudinal studies do not concern themselves with time-specific influences, only those naturally occurring influences are included (Keeves, 1997a: 142).

Longitudinal studies suffer several disadvantages (though the gravity of these weaknesses is challenged by supporters of cohort analysis). The disadvantages are first, that they are time-consuming and expensive, because the researcher is obliged to wait for growth data to accumulate. Second, there is the difficulty of sample mortality. Inevitably during the course of a long-term cohort study, subjects drop out, are lost or refuse further cooperation. Such attrition makes it unlikely that those who remain in the study are as representative of the population as the sample that was originally drawn. Sometimes attempts are made to lessen the effects of sample mortality by introducing aspects of cross-sectional study design, that is, 'topping up' the original cohort sample size at each time of retesting with the same number of respondents drawn from the same population. The problem here is that differences arising in the data from one survey to the next may then be accounted for by differences in the persons surveyed rather than by genuine changes or trends.

A third difficulty has been termed 'control effect' (sometimes referred to as measurement effect). Often, repeated interviewing results in an undesired and confusing effect on the actions or attitudes under study, influencing the behaviour of subjects, sensitizing them to matters that have hitherto passed unnoticed, or stimulating them to communication with others on unwanted topics (see Riley, 1963). Fourth, cohort studies can suffer from the interaction of biological, environmental and intervention influences (Keeves, 1997a: 139). Finally, cohort studies in education pose considerable problems of organization due to the continuous changes that occur in pupils, staff, teaching methods and the like. Such changes make it highly unlikely that a study will be completed in the way that it was originally planned.

Cohort studies, as we have seen, are particularly appropriate in research on human growth and development. Why then are so many studies in this area cross-sectional in design? The reason is that they have a number of advantages over cohort studies; they are less expensive; they produce findings more quickly; they are less likely to suffer from control effects; and they are more likely to secure the cooperation of respondents on a 'one-off' basis. Generally, cross-sectional designs are able to include more subjects than are cohort designs.

The strengths of cohort analysis are the weaknesses of the cross-sectional design. The cross-sectional study is a less effective method for the researcher who is concerned to identify individual variations in growth or to establish causal relationships between variables. Sampling in the cross-sectional study is complicated because different subjects are involved at each age level and may not be comparable. Further problems arising out of selection effects and the obscuring of irregularities in growth weaken the cross-sectional study so much that one observer dismisses the method as a highly unsatisfactory way of obtaining developmental data except for the crudest purposes. Douglas (1976), who pioneered the first national cohort study to be undertaken in any country, makes a spirited defence of the method against the common criticisms that are levelled against it – that it is expensive and time-consuming. His account of the advantages of cohort analysis over cross-sectional designs is summarized in Box 13.1.

Cross-sectional studies require attention to be given to sampling, to ensure that the information on which the sample is based is comprehensive (Lietz and Keeves, 1997: 124). Further, there is a risk that some potential participants may decline to take part, thereby weakening the sample, or that some respondents may not answer specific questions, or, wittingly or unwittingly, give incorrect answers. Measurement error may also occur if the instrument is faulty, for example choosing inappropriate metrics or scales.

The comparative strengths and weaknesses of longitudinal studies (including retrospective studies), cross-section analysis and trend studies are summarized in Table 13.2 (see also Rose and Sullivan, 1993: 184–8).

Several of the strengths and weaknesses of retrospective longitudinal studies share the same characteristics as those of *ex post facto* research, discussed in Chapter 15.

BOX 13.1   ADVANTAGES OF COHORT OVER CROSS-SECTIONAL DESIGNS

1   Some types of information, for example on attitudes or assessment of potential ability, are only meaningful if collected contemporaneously. Other types are more complete or more accurate if collected during the course of a longitudinal survey, though they are likely to have some value even if collected retrospectively, for example length of schooling, job history, geographical movement.

2   In cohort studies, no duplication of information occurs, whereas in cross-sectional studies the same type of background information has to be collected on each occasion. This increases the interviewing costs.

3   The omission of even a single variable, later found to be important, from a cross-sectional study is a disaster, whereas it is usually possible in a cohort study to fill the gap, even if only partially, in a subsequent interview.

4   A cohort study allows the accumulation of a much larger number of variables, extending over a much wider area of knowledge than would be possible in a cross-sectional study. This is of course because the collection can be spread over many interviews. Moreover, information may be obtained at the most appropriate time, for example information on job entry may be obtained when it occurs even if this varies from one member of the sample to another.

5   Starting with a birth cohort removes later problems of sampling and allows the extensive use of subsamples. It also eases problems of estimating bias and reliability.

6   Longitudinal studies are free of one of the major obstacles to causal analysis, namely the reinterpretation of remembered information so that it conforms with conventional views on causation. It also provides the means to assess the direction of effect.

Source: Adapted from Douglas, 1976

13.8 Postal, interview and telephone surveys

Postal surveys

Robson (1993) indicates strengths and difficulties with postal and interview surveys. Postal surveys can reach a large number of people, gather data at comparatively low cost and quite quickly, and can give assurances of confidentiality (Bailey, 1994: 148). Similarly they can be completed at the respondents' own convenience and in their preferred surroundings and own time; this will enable them to check information if necessary (e.g. personal documents) and think about the responses. As standardized wording is used, there is a useful degree of comparability across the responses, and, as no interviewer is present, there is no risk of interviewer bias. Further, postal questionnaires enable widely scattered populations to be reached.

Postal surveys can also be used to gather detailed sensitive qualitative data (Beckett and Clegg, 2007), not least because the non-presence of another person (e.g. an interviewer) can increase the honesty and richness of the data (Beckett and Clegg, 2007), whereas the presence of an interviewer might inhibit the respondent. Further, in a postal survey, the relations of power between the researcher and the respondent are often more equal than in an interview situation (in which the former often controls the situation more than the latter) (Beckett and Clegg, 2007: 308).

On the other hand postal surveys typically suffer from a poor response rate, and, because one does not have any information about the non-respondents, one does not know whether the sample is representative of the wider population. Further, respondents may not take the care required to complete the survey carefully, and, indeed, may misunderstand the questions. There is no way of checking this. Bailey (1994: 149) suggests that the very issues that make postal surveys attractive might also render them less appealing, for example:

- the standardization of wording;
- the inability to catch anything other than a verbal response;
- the lack of control over the environment in which the survey questionnaire is completed;
- the lack of control over the order in which the questions are read and answered;
- the risk that some questions will not be answered;
- the inability to record spontaneous answers;
- the difficulty in separating non-response from bad response (the former being where the intended respondent receives the survey but does not reply to it, and the latter being where the intended recipient

does not receive the survey, e.g. because she/he has moved house);

■ the need for simplicity in format as there is no interviewer present to guide the respondent through a more complex format.

Postal surveys are an example of self-administered surveys. The anonymity and absence of face-to-face interaction between the interviewer and the respondent can render these useful for asking sensitive questions (Strange *et al.*, 2003: 337), though Fowler (2009: 74) also counsels that sensitive questions can sometimes be handled better in private face-to-face interviews. In self-administered surveys, Fowler (2009: 72) remarks that it is advisable to keep to closed questions and to make the response categories simple and explicit (e.g.

TABLE 13.2 THE CHARACTERISTICS, STRENGTHS AND WEAKNESSES OF LONGITUDINAL, CROSS-SECTIONAL, TREND ANALYSIS AND RETROSPECTIVE LONGITUDINAL STUDIES

Study type	Features	Strengths	Weaknesses
Longitudinal studies (cohort/panel studies)	1 Single sample over extended period of time. 2 Enables the same individuals to be compared over time (diachronic analysis). 3 Micro-level analysis.	1 Useful for establishing causal relationships and for making reliable inferences. 2 Shows how changing properties of individuals fit into systemic change. 3 Operates within the known limits of instrumentation employed. 4 Separates real trends from chance occurrence. 5 Brings the benefits of extended time frames. 6 Useful for charting growth and development. 7 Gathers data contemporaneously rather than retrospectively, thereby avoiding the problems of selective or false memory. 8 Economical in that a picture of the sample is built up over time. 9 In-depth and comprehensive coverage of a wide range of variables, both initial and emergent – individual specific effects and population heterogeneity. 10 Enables change to be analysed at the *individual/micro* level. 11 Enables the dynamics of change to be caught, the flows into and out of particular states and the transitions between states. 12 Individual-level data are more accurate than macro-level, cross-sectional data. 13 Sampling error reduced as the study remains with the same sample over time. 14 Enables clear recommendations for intervention to be made.	1 Time-consuming – it takes a long time for the studies to be conducted and the results to emerge. 2 Problems of sample mortality heighten over time and diminish initial representativeness. 3 Control effects – repeated interviewing of the same sample influences their behaviour. 4 Intervening effects attenuate the initial research plan. 5 Problem of securing participation as it involves repeated contact. 6 Data, being rich at an individual level, are typically complex to analyse.

continued

Study type	Features	Strengths	Weaknesses
Cross-sectional studies	1 Snapshot of different samples at one or more points in time (synchronic analysis). 2 Large-scale and representative sampling. 3 Macro-level analysis. 4 Enables different groups to be compared. 5 Can be retrospective and/or prospective.	1 Comparatively quick to conduct. 2 Comparatively cheap to administer. 3 Limited control effects as subjects only participate once. 4 Stronger likelihood of participation as it is for a single time. 5 Charts aggregated patterns. 6 Useful for charting population-wide features at one or more single points in time. 7 Enable researchers to identify the proportions of people in particular groups or states. 8 Large samples enable inferential statistics to be used, e.g. to compare subgroups within the sample.	1 Do not permit analysis of causal relationships. 2 Unable to chart individual variations in development or changes, and their significance. 3 Sampling not entirely comparable at each round of data collection as different samples are used. 4 Can be time-consuming as background details of each sample have to be collected each time. 5 Omission of a single variable can undermine the results significantly. 6 Unable to chart changing social processes over time. 7 They only permit analysis of overall, *net* change at the macro-level through aggregated data.
Trend analysis	1 Selected factors studied continuously over time. 2 Uses recorded data to predict future trends.	1 Maintains clarity of focus throughout the duration of the study. 2 Enables prediction and projection on the basis of identified and monitored variables and assumptions.	1 Neglects influence of unpredicted factors. 2 Past trends are not always a good predictor of future trends. 3 Formula-driven, i.e. could be too conservative or initial assumptions might be erroneous. 4 Neglects the implications of chaos and complexity theory, e.g. that long-range forecasting is dangerous. 5 The criteria for prediction may be imprecise.
Retrospective longitudinal studies	1 Retrospective analysis of history of a sample. 2 Individual- and micro-level data.	1 Useful for establishing causal relationships. 2 Clear focus (e.g. how did this particular end state or set of circumstances come to be?). 3 Enables data to be assembled that are not susceptible to experimental analysis.	1 Remembered information might be faulty, selective and inaccurate. 2 People might forget, suppress or fail to remember certain factors. 3 Individuals might interpret their own past behaviour in light of their subsequent events, i.e. the interpretations are not contemporaneous with the actual events. 4 The roots and causes of the end state may be multiple, diverse, complex, unidentified and unstraightforward to unravel. 5 Simple causality is unlikely. 6 A cause may be an effect and vice versa. 7 It is difficult to separate real from perceived or putative causes. 8 It is seldom easily falsifiable or confirmable.

ticking a box). If open questions are to be asked then, he indicates, it is better to gather the survey data in a face-to-face interview.

Further, Diaz de Rada (2005) reports that the design, size and colour of the paper used in postal surveys affects the response rates. He found that small sized questionnaires were mostly returned by males and those under 64 years of age (p. 69), whilst larger sized questionnaires were mostly returned by females and those over the age of 65 (p. 70). He recommends the use of paper size 14.85 cm × 21 cm (i.e. a sheet of A4 sized paper folded in half), with white paper, and with a cover page (p. 73) (though this inevitably increases the number of pages in a questionnaire, and this can be off-putting for respondents). He reports that paper size has no effect on the quality of the responses.

Interview surveys

Whereas postal surveys are self-administered, interview surveys are supervised, and, hence, potentially prone to fewer difficulties. Interview methods of gathering survey data are useful in that the presence of the interviewer can help clarify queries from the respondents and can stimulate the respondent to give full answers to an on-the-spot supervisor rather than an anonymous researcher known through an introductory letter (Robson, 1993). Indeed, there is evidence that face-to-face encounters improve response rates. Furthermore, as interviews can be flexible, questioners are able both to probe and explain more fully (Bailey, 1994: 174). Interviews are also useful when respondents have problems with reading and writing. Using non-verbal behaviour to encourage respondents to participate is also possible. Moreover, with interviews there are greater opportunities to control the environment in which the survey is conducted, particularly in respect of privacy, noise and external distractions.

The effective interviewer, Fowler (2009: 128) claims, is businesslike and assertive whilst being engaging, friendly and kind. Fowler argues for great care and training to be provided for interviewers, as much can hang on their behaviour.

The potential for trust, rapport and cooperation between the interviewer and the respondent is strong in face-to-face encounters (Dooley, 2001: 122; Gwartney, 2007: 16). Further, interviewers can either ensure that the sequence of the survey protocol is strictly adhered to or they can tailor the order of responses to individual participants, making certain, incidentally, that all questions are answered. Interview surveys, moreover, can guarantee that it is the respondent alone who answers the questions, whereas in postal surveys the researcher never knows what help or comments are solicited from

or given by other parties. Bailey (1994) adds that the opportunity for spontaneous behaviour and responses is also possible in interview surveys. Further, interviews can use more complex structures than postal questionnaires, the researcher being on hand to take participants through the schedule.

On the other hand, the very features which make interview methods attractive may also make them problematic. For example, interview survey methods may be affected by the characteristics of the interviewer (e.g. sex, race, age, ethnicity, personality, skills, social status, clothing and appearance). They may also be affected by the conduct of the interview itself (e.g. rapport between the interviewer and the interviewee), and interviewees may be reluctant to disclose some information if they feel that the interview will not be anonymous or if sensitive information is being requested. The flexibility which the interview gives also contributes to the potential lack of standardization of the interview survey, and this may render consistency and, thereby, reliability, a problem. Further, interview surveys are costly in time for the researcher and the interviewee, and, as they are conducted at a fixed time, they may prevent the interviewee from consulting records that may be important to answer the questions. Further, they may require the interviewer to travel long distances to reach interviewees, which can be expensive both in time and travel costs (Bailey, 1994: 175). If interviews are intended to be conducted in the participants' own homes, then participants may be unwilling to admit strangers. Moreover, neighbourhoods may be dangerous for some researchers to visit (e.g. a white researcher with a clipboard going into a non-white area of great deprivation, or a black researcher going into a conservative white area).

Telephone surveys

Telephone surveys lie between mailed questionnaires and personal interviews (Arnon and Reichel, 2009). They have the attraction of overcoming any bias in the researcher or the interviewee that may be caused by social characteristics, or matters of age, dress, race, ethnicity, appearance, etc. (e.g. Gwartney, 2007: 16). They also require the interviewer to be an articulate, clear speaker, a good listener and able to key in interviewee responses onto a computer whilst listening and speaking (Gwartney, 2007: 42–3).

It is suggested (Dooley, 2001: 122; Arnon and Reichel, 2009: 179) that telephone interviews have the advantage of reducing costs in time and travel, for where a potential respondent is not at home a call-back costs only a few coins and the time to redial. Re-visits to often distant locations, on the other hand, can incur considerable expense in time and travel. Furthermore, if the intended participant is unable or unwilling to respond, then it is a relatively easy matter to maintain the required sample size by calling a replacement. Again, where respondents are unable or unwilling to answer all the questions required, then their partial replies may be discarded and further substitutes sought from the sample listing. It is easy to see why telephone interviews must always have a much longer list of potential respondents in order to attain the required sample size.

On the other hand, not everyone has a telephone (e.g. the poor, the young, the less educated) and this may lead to a skewed sample (Arnon and Reichel, 2009: 179). Nor, for that matter, is everyone available for interview, particularly if they work. Furthermore, many people are 'ex-directory', i.e. their numbers are withheld from public scrutiny. In addition, Dooley (2001: 123) reports that others still (e.g. the younger, unmarried and higher occupational status groups) use answering machines that may screen out and delete researchers' calls. These could lead to a skewed sample. Indeed Fowler (2009: 75) indicates that telephone surveys tend to elicit more socially desirable answers than face-to-face interviews.

Even when the telephone is answered, the person responding may not be the most suitable one to take the call; she/he may not know the answer to the questions or have access to the kind of information required. For example, in an enquiry about household budgets, the respondent may simply be ignorant about a family's income or expenditure on particular items. A child may answer the call or an elderly person who may not be the householder. Interviewers will need to prepare a set of preliminary, screening questions or arrange a call-back time when a more appropriate person can be interviewed.

Telephone interviewing has its own strengths and weaknesses. For example, more often than not a respondent's sex will be clear from their voice, so particular questions may be inappropriate. On the other hand, it is unwise to have several multiple choices in a telephone interview, as respondents will simply forget the categories available, there being no written prompts to which the respondent can refer.

Similarly, order effects can be high: items appearing early in the interview exert an influence on responses to later ones, whilst items appearing early in a list of responses may be given greater consideration than those occurring later, a matter not confined to telephone surveys but to questionnaires in general. Dooley (2001: 136) indicates that 17 per cent difference in agreement was recorded to a general statement question when it appeared *before* rather than *after* a specific statement.

He cites further research demonstrating that responses to particular questions are affected by questions surrounding them. His advice is to ask *general* questions before *specific* ones. Otherwise, the general questions are influenced by earlier responses to specific questions. Once again, this is a matter not confined to telephone surveys but to questionnaires in general.

Further, if the questioning becomes too sensitive, respondents may simply hang up in the middle of the survey interview, tell lies or withhold information. Dooley (2001: 123) reports that, in comparison to face-to-face interviews, telephone respondents tend to produce more missing data, to be more evasive, more acquiescent (i.e. they tend to agree more with statements) and more extreme in their responses (e.g. opting for the extreme ends of rating scales).

Fowler (2009: 73–4) also indicates that, in a telephone survey, it is unwise to have too many response scale points, that it is better to avoid long lists of items, and that it is advisable to read the statement before indicating the response categories, unless a long list of items is to be given (i.e. is unavoidable) in which case he suggests that it is better to read and reread to the respondent the response categories before the list of statements. All of these points take account of the limits of the short-term memories on which respondents might rely in a telephone interview. He also suggests (p. 73) that complex questions can be approached in a staged manner. For example, if a researcher wishes to ask about a ten-category item (e.g. income level of the teacher), then the researcher could start with a general question (e.g. above or below a particular figure), and then, once that category has been identified, proceed to a sub-category, e.g. between such-and-such a figure; this avoids overload of asking a respondent to remember ten categories.

Because telephone interviews lack the sensory stimulation of visual or face-to-face interviews or written instructions and presentation, it is unwise to plan a long telephone survey call. Ten to 15 minutes is often the maximum time tolerable to most respondents, and, indeed 15 minutes for many may be too long. This means that careful piloting will need to take place in order to include those items, and only those items, that are necessary for the research. The risk to reliability and validity is considerable, as the number of items may be fewer than in other forms of data collection.

Procedures for telephone interviews also need to be decided (Gwartney, 2007), e.g.

- how many times to let the telephone ring before conceding that there is nobody to answer the call (Gwartney (2007: 99) suggests eight rings);

- how to introduce the caller and the project;
- what to say and how to introduce items and conduct the interview;
- how to determine who is receiving the call and whether he/she is the appropriate person to answer the call;
- whether to leave a message on an answer phone/ voice-mail/call-back facility and, if so, what that message will be;
- how to handle language problems (e.g. which language is being used, meanings/explanations/ vocabulary);
- how to handle the situation if the receiver asks to call back later;
- what to say and how to control the caller's voice/ tone/pitch/speed/pace of questions/repetitions/language/intonation/register;
- caller's pronunciation, enunciation and reading out loud;
- caller's ability to clarify, summarize, reiterate, probe (and when to stop probing), prompt (if the receiver does not understand), confirm, affirm, respond, give feedback, encourage respondents, keep respondents focused and to the point;
- how to conduct closed and open questions, sensitive, factual and opinion-based questions;
- how to indicate the nature and format of the responses sought;
- caller's ability to handle the called person's initial hostility, refusal, reluctance to take part, feelings of invasion of privacy, lack of interest, reluctance to disclose information, feelings of being harassed or singled out, anger, antagonism, lack of interest, incomplete answers, hurriedness to complete, slowness or hesitancy, mistrust, rudeness, abusive responses or simply saying that they are too busy;
- caller's ability to remain neutral, impartial and non-judgemental;
- how to record responses;
- how to end the interview.

It is advisable, also, in order to avoid the frequent responses to 'cold-calling' (whereby the called person simply slams down the telephone), for the interviewer to contact the person in advance of the call, perhaps by mail, to indicate that the call will come, when and what it is about, and to ask for the recipient's cooperation in the project.

It can be seen that many of the features of telephone interviewing are similar to those of effective interviewing per se, and we advise the reader to consult the comments on interviewing earlier and also in Chapter 21.

13.9 Internet-based surveys

Introduction

Using the internet for the conduct of surveys is becoming commonplace in many branches of social science (e.g. Virtual Surveys Limited, 2003). Though internet-based surveys have much in common with paper-based surveys, nevertheless they also have their own particular features.

Internet-based surveys have moved from being in the form of emails to emails-plus-attachments of the questionnaire itself, to emails directing potential respondents to a website, or simply to websites. Whilst emails have the attraction of immediacy, the potential for web-based surveys to include graphics has been too great for many researchers to resist. Often a combination of the two is used: emails direct potential participants to a website at which the survey questionnaire is located in HTML form. Though email surveys tend to attract greater response than web-based surveys, web-based surveys have the potential to reach greater numbers of participants, so web-based surveys are advisable; emails can be used as an addition, to contact participants to advise them to go to a particular website. Internet surveys have the added attraction of being cheap to administer. Though they take time to prepare, there are many online internet survey templates and (free) services available, e.g.

www.surveymonkey.com/
www.zoomerang.com/
www.surveymethods.com/
http://free-online-surveys.co.uk/
www.questionpro.com/internet-survey-software.html
www.esurveyspro.com/
www.freesurveysonline.com/
www.magicsurveytool.com/email_surveys.html
www.tucows.com/
www.my3q.com/misc/register/register.phtml

Several of these also automatically collate and present results.

Some principles for constructing internet-based surveys

Dillman *et al.* (1998a, 1998b, 1999) set out several principles of web-based surveys. Some of these are technical and some are presentational. For example, in terms of technical matters, they found that the difference between simple and 'fancy' (*sic*) versions of questionnaires (the former with few graphics, the latter with many, using sophisticated software) could be as much as three times the size of the file to be downloaded (317k in contrast to 959k), with a time of downloading of 225 seconds for the plain version and 682 seconds for the 'fancy' version. They found (1998a) that respondents with slow browsers or limited power either spent longer in downloading the file or, indeed, the machine crashed before the file was downloaded. They also found that recipients of plain versions were more likely to complete a questionnaire than those receiving fancy versions (93.1 per cent and 82.1 per cent respectively), as it took less time to complete the plain version. Utilizing advanced page layout features does not translate into higher completion rates, indeed, more advanced page layout reduced completion rates. This echoes the work of Fricker and Schonlau (2002) who report studies that indicate a 43 per cent response rate to an email survey compared to a 71 per cent response rate for the same mailed paper questionnaire. Indeed they report that it is only with specialized samples (e.g. undergraduates) that higher response rates can be obtained in an internet survey.

For presentational matters Dillman and his colleagues (1998a, 1999) make the point that in a paper-based survey the eyes and the hands are focused on the same area, whilst in a web-based survey the eyes are focused on the screen whilst the hands are either on the keyboard or on the mouse, and so completion is more difficult. This is one reason to avoid asking respondents to type in many responses to open-ended questions, and replacing these with radio buttons or clicking on a mouse that automatically inserts a tick into a box (Witte et al., 1999: 139). Further, some respondents may have less developed computer skills than others. They suggest a mixed mode of operation (paper-based together with web-based versions of the same questionnaire). The researchers also found that 'check-all-that-apply' lists of factors to be addressed had questionable reliability, as respondents would tend to complete those items at the top of the list and ignore the remainder. Hence they recommend avoiding the use of check-all-that-apply questions in a web-based survey.

Similarly they advocate keeping the introduction to the questionnaire short (no more than one screen), informative (e.g. of how to move on) and avoiding giving a long list of instructions. Further, as the first question in a survey tends to raise in respondents' minds a particular mindset, care is needed on setting the first question, to entice participants and not to put them off participating (e.g. not too difficult, not too easy, interesting, straightforward to complete, avoiding drop-down boxes and scrolling). Dillman et al. (1998a, 1998b, 1999) make specific recommendations about the layout of the screen, for example keeping the response categories close to the question for ease of following, using features like brightness, large fonts and spacing for clarity in the early parts of the survey. They also suggest following the natural movement of the eyes from the top left (the most important part of the screen, hence the part in which the question is located) to the bottom right quadrants of the screen (the least important part of the screen which might contain the researcher's logo). They comment that the natural movement of the eye is to read prose unevenly, with the risk of missing critical words, and that this is particularly true on long lines, hence they advocate keeping lines and sentences short (e.g. by inserting a hard break in the text or to use table-editing features, locating the text in a table frame). Taking this further, they also advocate the use of some marker to indicate to the respondent where he or she has reached in the questionnaire (e.g. a progress bar or a table that indicates what proportion of the questionnaire has been completed so far).

Respondents may not be familiar with web-based questionnaires, e.g. with radio buttons, scroll bars, the use of the mouse, the use of drop-down menus, where to insert open-ended responses, and the survey designer must not overestimate the capability of the respondent to use the software, though Roztocki and Lahri (2002) suggest that there is no relationship between perceived level of computer literacy and preference for web-based surveys. Indeed their use may have to be explained in the survey itself. Dillman et al. (1999) suggest that the problem of differential expertise in computer usage can be addressed in three ways:

1 by having the instructions for how to complete the item next to the item itself (not all placed together at the start of the questionnaire);
2 by asking the respondents at the beginning about their level of computer expertise, and, if they are more expert, offering them the questionnaire with certain instructions omitted, and if they are less experienced, directing them to instructions and further assistance;
3 having a 'floating window' that accompanies each screen and which can be maximized for further instructions.

Some web-based surveys prevent respondents from proceeding until they have completed all the items on the screen in question. Whilst this might ensure coverage, it can also both anger respondents – such that they give up and abandon the survey – or prevent them from having a deliberate non-response (e.g. if they do not wish to reveal particular information, or if in fact the question does not apply to them, or if they do not know the answer). Hence the advice of Dillman *et al.* (1999) is to avoid this practice. One way to address this matter is to give respondents the opportunity to answer an item with 'prefer not to answer' or 'don't know'. The point that relates to this is that it is much easier for participants in a web-based survey to abandon the survey – a simple click of a button – so more attention has to be given to keeping them participating than in a paper-based survey.

Redline *et al.* (2002) suggest that branching instructions (e.g. 'skip to item 13', 'go to item 10'; 'if "yes" go to item 12, if "no" then continue') can create problems in web-based surveys, as respondents may skip over items and series of questions that they should have addressed. This concerns the location of the instruction (e.g. to the right of the item, underneath the item, to the right of the answer box). Locating the instruction too far to the right of the answer box (e.g. more than nine characters of text to the right) can mean that it is outside the foveal view (2 degrees) of the respondent's vision, and, hence, can be overlooked. Further, they report that having a branching instruction in the same font size and colour as the rest of the text can result in it being regarded as unimportant, not least because respondents frequently expect the completion of a form to be easier than it actually is. Hence they advocate making the instruction easier to detect by locating it within the natural field of vision of the reader, printing it in a large font to make it bolder and using a different colour. They report that, for the most part, branching instruction errors occur because they are overlooked and respondents are unaware of them rather than deliberately disregarding them (p. 18).

The researchers also investigated a range of other variables that impacted on the success of using branching programs, and reported the following:

- the number of words in the question has an impact on the reader: the greater the number of words the less is the likelihood of correct branching processing by the reader, as the reader is too absorbed with the question than with the instructions;
- using large fonts, strategies and verbal design to draw attention to branching instructions leads to greater observance of these instructions;
- the number of answer categories can exert an effect on the reader: more than seven categories and the reader may make errors and also overlook branching instructions;
- having to read branching instructions at the same time as looking at answer categories results in overlooking the branching instructions;
- locating the branching instruction next to the final category of a series of answer boxes is a much safer

guarantee of it being observed than placing it further up a list; this may mean changing the order of the list of response categories, so that the final category naturally leads to the branching instruction;
- branching instructions should be placed where they are to be used and where they can be seen;
- response-order effects operate in surveys, such that respondents in a self-administered survey tend to choose earlier items in a list rather than later items in a list (the primacy effect), thereby erroneously acting on branching instructions that appear with later items in a list;
- questions with alternating branches (i.e. more than one branch) may be forgotten by the time they need to be acted upon after respondents have completed an item;
- if every answer has a branch then respondents may overlook the instructions for branching as all the branches appear to be similar;
- if respondents are required to write an open-ended response this may cause them to overlook a branching instruction as they are so absorbed in composing their own response and the branching instruction may be out of their field of vision when writing in their answer;
- items that are located at the bottom of a page are more likely to elicit a non-response than items further up a page, hence if branching instructions are located near the bottom of a page they are more likely to be overlooked; placing branching instructions at the bottom of the page should be avoided;
- if the branching instructions are located too far from the answer box then they may be overlooked.

These pieces of advice from the research can be applied not only to online survey questionnaires but are also useful in the construction of paper-based survey questionnaires.

Dillman *et al.* (1999) and Dillman and Bowker (2000: 10–11) suggest that successful web-based surveys: (a) take account of the inability of some respondents to access and respond to web questionnaires that include advanced programming features (e.g. that may require software that the respondents do not have or which download very slowly); and (b) match the expectations of the respondents in completing the questionnaire design and layout.

There are several 'principles' for designing web-based questionnaires (e.g. Dillman *et al.*, 1999; Dillman and Bowker, 2000: 10–11; Shropshire *et al.*, 2009):

- Start the web questionnaire with a welcome screen that will motivate the respondents to continue, which makes it clear that it is easy to complete and gives clear instructions on how to proceed.

- Provide a PIN number in order to limit access to those people sought in the sample.
- Ensure that that first question can be seen in its entirety on the first screen, and is easy to understand and complete.
- Embed visual images in a survey (as this reduces premature dropout from the survey).
- Place interest-based questions early on in the survey, as this, too, reduces premature dropout.
- Ensure that the layout of each question is as close as possible to a paper format, as respondents may be familiar with this.
- Ensure that the use of colour keeps the figure/ground consistency and readability, so that it is easy to navigate through the questionnaire and navigational flow is unimpeded, and so that the measurement properties of questions are clear and sustained.
- Avoid differences in the visual appearance of questions that may happen as a result of different computers, configurations, operating systems, screen displays (e.g. partial and wrap-around text) and browsers.
- Keep the line length short, to fit in with the screen size.
- Minimize the use of drop-down boxes, and direct respondents to them where they occur.
- Give clear instructions for how to move through the questionnaire using the computer.
- Make instructions for skipping parts very clear.
- Keep instructions for computer actions to be taken at the point where the action is needed, rather than placing them all at the start of the questionnaire.
- Avoid requiring respondents to answer each question before being able to move on to the next questions.
- Ensure that questionnaires scroll easily from question to question, unless order effects are important.
- If multiple choices are presented, try to keep them to a single screen; if this is not possible then consider double columns, providing navigational instructions.
- Provide graphical symbols or words to indicate where the respondent has reached in the questionnaire.
- Avoid the kinds of questions that cause problems in paper questionnaires (e.g. tick-all-those-that-apply kinds of question).

Additionally, Heerwegh *et al.* (2005) report that personalizing the e-survey (i.e. using the recipient's name in the salutation) increases response rates by 8.6 per-

centage points (e.g. starting an e-survey letter with Dear [name of specific person]), though care has to be taken to ensure consistency, e.g. it is counterproductive to start an e-survey letter with Dear [name of person] and then, later, to refer to 'student', 'colleague', etc. (i.e. a depersonalized version). The authors indicate that personalizing an e-survey increases the chances of a respondent *starting* the survey (p. 92) rather than dropout rates during the survey; whether participants continue and complete the survey depends on other factors, for example the difficulty in completing the items, the relevance of the topic to the respondents and the user-friendliness of the survey. They also report (p. 94) that personalizing an e-survey increases participant honesty on sensitive matters (e.g. number of sexual partners) and adherence to survey instructions (p. 96) and also increases the tendency of respondents to answer questions in a socially desirable way.

Denscombe (2009: 286–7) reports that, for online surveys, fixed choice questions tend to have a 'lower item-response rate than open-ended questions', and, for open-ended questions, item non-response is lower in online surveys than in paper-based surveys.

Christian *et al.* (2009) report that if a survey questionnaire presents the positive end of a scale first then, whilst it does not make a difference to the response, it does increase response time (which might lead to dropping out). They also note that if the positive categories are given lower numbers (e.g. '1' and '2'), and the negative categories are given high numbers (e.g. '4' and '5') then this can increase response times. Further, they report that displaying 'the categories in multiple columns' increases response time, as does giving the poles of rating scales numbers rather than words.

Toepoel *et al.* (2009) also suggest that account has to be taken of the 'cognitive sophistication' of the respondents, as those with less cognitive sophistication tend to be affected by contextual clues more than those respondents with more cognitive sophistication. Context effects occur when a particular item is affected by the items around it or which precede it, in effect providing cues for the respondent, or in which a particular mindset of responses is created in the respondent (Friedman and Amoo, 1999).

Some advantages of internet-based surveys

The most widely used data collection instrument for internet surveys is the questionnaire. There are several claimed advantages to using an internet questionnaire in comparison to a paper questionnaire (e.g. Watt, 1997; Dillman *et al.*, 1999; Dillman and Bowker, 2000; Aldridge and Levine, 2001; Roztocki and Lahri, 2002; Glover and Bush, 2005; Fowler, 2009):

- it reduces cost (e.g. of postage, paper, printing, keying in data, processing data, interviewer costs);
- it reduces the time taken to distribute, gather and process data (data entered onto a web-based survey can be processed automatically as soon as they are entered by the respondent rather than being keyed in later by the researcher);
- it enables a wider and much larger population to be accessed;
- it enables researchers to reach difficult populations under the cover of anonymity and non-traceability;
- it may have novelty value (though this decreases over time);
- respondents can complete the questionnaire from home (rather than, for example, in the workplace), i.e. in self-chosen and familiar settings;
- respondents can complete it at a time to suit themselves, thereby minimizing organizational constraints on the part of the researcher or the respondents;
- respondents can complete the survey over time (i.e. they do not need to do it all at one sitting);
- complex skip-patterns can be created and organized by the computer, so that participants do not have to understand complicated instructions, i.e. so that automated navigation through the questionnaire can occur;
- the software can prompt respondents to complete missed items or to correct errors (e.g. two ticks for a single item in a rating scale);
- the computer can check incomplete or inconsistent replies;
- for each screen, the computer can provide an on-screen indication of how much of the questionnaire has been completed (e.g. 50 per cent completed, 75 per cent completed);
- reduction of researcher effects;
- responses in web-based surveys show fewer missing entries than paper-based surveys;
- human error is reduced in entering and processing online data;
- additional features may make the survey attractive (e.g. graphics, colour, fonts and so on);
- greater generalizability may be obtained as internet users come from a wide and diverse population;
- because of volunteer participation (i.e. an absence of coercion), greater authenticity of responses may be obtained.

With regard to costs, Watt (1997) alerts us to the fact that cost savings always make a difference in comparison to a telephone survey, but that an internet-based survey is only slightly cheaper than a mail survey unless that web-based survey gathers data from more than around 500 participants, as the costs in terms of development and design time are considerable. Over 500, and the internet-based survey makes considerable cost savings. Further, Fricker and Schonlau (2002) suggest that the claims that internet-based surveys are cheaper and faster are not always borne out by the evidence, and that, if internet survey development, programming, testing and modification time, initial contact time and follow-up time to ensure an increased response rate are factored in, then the savings may not be as strong as the claims made. That said, they do acknowledge that as internet surveys develop they are likely to meet these claims. Reips (2002a, 2002b) suggests that though there may be costs in terms of laboratory space, equipment and administration, these have to be offset by development costs. The jury is still out on overall time cost savings.

Glover and Bush (2005) suggest that response rates for internet-based surveys are generally higher than for conventional approaches (though there is some evidence to challenge this), and that e-surveys overcome spatial and temporal constraints (e.g. researchers and participants can be separated from each other in time and physical distance). Further, they report (pp. 140–3) that participants tended to respond more quickly and more fully, reflectively and incisively than in conventional postal questionnaires, particularly when e-reminders were sent (see also Deutskens et al., 2005). Deutskens et al. (2005: 2), whilst reporting higher quality data, higher item completion and response, higher item variability and fewer missing values in online surveys, also report that these findings are not unequivocal, and that more extreme responses might be elicited.

In comparing online and conventional surveys, one has to examine not only the means, range and standard deviations of results, but also the factor structure (is it the same in both, i.e. when factor analysis is conducted are the same factors and variables extracted) and the variables loadings onto the factors (whether they are the same or similar in both online and paper surveys).

Key issues in internet-based surveys

On the other hand, internet-based surveys are not without their problems. Some of these are indicated below (Table 13.3), together with possible solutions (Coomber, 1997; Dillman et al., 1999; Dillman and Bowker, 2000; Witmer et al., 1999; Frick et al., 1999; Solomon, 2001; Reips, 2002a, 2002b; Dillman et al., 2003; Hewson et al., 2003; Smyth et al., 2004; Glover and Bush, 2005).

TABLE 13.3   PROBLEMS AND SOLUTIONS IN INTERNET-BASED SURVEYS

Problem (sampling)	Possible solution
Some subsample groups may be under-represented in the respondents	Adjust the results by weighting the sample responses (see the comments on a 'boosted sample' and 'weighting' in Chapter 4)
There may be coverage error (not everyone has a non-zero chance of being included)	Disclose the sample characteristics in reporting
Non-response and volunteer bias	Follow-up messages posted on websites and electronic discussion groups. Use emails to contact potential participants. Require the respondents to submit their replies screen by screen. (This enables the researcher not only to use some data from incomplete responses, but also enables her to identify in detail patterns of non-response, i.e. responding is not an all-or-nothing affair (either submit the whole questionnaire or none of it) but can be partial (a respondent may answer some questions but not others))

Problem (ethics)	Possible solution
Respondents may wish to keep their identity from the researcher, and an email address identifies the respondent (in the case of sensitive research, e.g. on child abuse or drug abuse, this may involve criminal proceedings if the identity of the respondent is known or able to be tracked by criminal investigators who break into the site). Non-traceability of respondents may be problematic	Direct respondents to a website rather than to using email correspondence. Provide advice on using non-traceable connections to access and return the survey (e.g. an internet café, a library, a university). Advise the respondent to print off the survey and return it by post to a given address. Avoid asking respondents to enter a password or to give an email address. Prevent access to unprotected directories and confidential data
Respondents may not know anything about the researcher, or if it is a *bona fide* piece of research and not simply a marketing ploy	Include the researcher's affiliation (e.g. university), with a logo if possible
Informed consent	Ensure that it is easy for respondents to withdraw at any time (e.g. include a 'Withdraw' button at the foot of each screen)

Problem (technical: hardware and software)	Possible solution
The configuration of the questionnaire may vary from one machine to another (because of web browsers, connection, hardware, software) and can lead to dropout	Opt for simplicity. Test the survey on different computer systems/browsers to ensure consistency. Avoid surveys that require real-time completion
The screen as set out by the survey designer may not appear the same as that which appears on the respondent's screen	Opt for simplicity. Use a commercial survey software system for generating the questionnaire. Avoid high level programs
Slow network connections or limited bandwidth can slow down loading	Keep the use of graphics to a minimum. Advise on the possible time it takes to load
Respondents may not have the same software, or the same version of the software as the sender, rendering downloading of the questionnaire either impossible or distorting the received graphics	Avoid the use of graphics and more advanced software programs

continued

Problem (technical: hardware and software)	Possible solution
Graphics may be corrupted/incompatible between the sender and the user, i.e. between one kind of machine, user platform and software and another. Hardware may differ between sender and receiver	Opt for simplicity. Use commercially available web-based surveying systems and packages. Use image files (e.g. .jpeg, .gif) to reduce loading time. Avoid pop-ups if possible as they reduce response rate
The greater the use of graphics and plug-ins (e.g. using Java and Applets), the longer it takes to download, and, particularly – though not exclusively – if respondents do not have broadband access then time-consuming downloads could result in either the respondent giving up and cancelling the download, or creating a bad mood in the respondent	Keep software requirements as low-tech as possible. Avoid questionnaires that use sophisticated computer graphics
There may be slow loading times due to internet congestion	Avoid sophisticated graphics and 'fancy' presentations as these take longer to download
The physical distance between points on an attitude scale may spread out because of configuration differences between machines	Indicate how best the questionnaire may be viewed (e.g. 800 × 400)
The construction procedures for wrap-around text may vary between computers	Keep lines of text short
Email questionnaires may distort the layout of the questionnaire (some email software uses HTML, others do not)	Avoid sending a questionnaire directly using email; rather, post it on a website (e.g. so that respondents visit a website and then click a box for immediate transfer to the questionnaire). Consider using an email to direct participants to a website (e.g. the email includes the website which can be reached by clicking in the address contained in the email). Use an email that includes an attachment which contains the more graphically sophisticated survey instrument itself

Problem (respondents)	Possible solution
Respondents may be unfamiliar or inexperienced with the internet and the media	Keep the questionnaire simple and easy to complete
Respondents may send multiple copies of their completed questionnaire from the same or different addresses	Have a security device that tracks and limits (as far as possible) respondents who may be returning the same questionnaire on more than one occasion. Use passwords (though this, itself, may create problems of identifiability). Collect personal identification items. Check for internal consistency across submissions
There may be more than one respondent to a single questionnaire (the same problem as in, for example, a postal questionnaire)	Include questions to cross-check the consistency of replies to similar items
Respondents may not be used to pull-down menus	Provide clear instructions
Drop-down boxes take up more space on a screen than conventional questionnaires	Avoid their overuse
Respondents dislike the situation where the computer prevents them from continuing to the next screen until all the items on a particular screen have been completed	Avoid this unless considered absolutely necessary

continued

Problem (respondents)	Possible solution
The language of email surveys can risk offending potential participants ('flaming')	Check the language used to avoid angering the participants
Respondents' difficulty in navigating the pages of the online survey	Keep instructions to the page in question. Make the instructions for branching very clear (font size, colour, etc.)

Problem (layout and presentation)	Possible solution
A page of paper is longer than it is wide, but a screen is wider than it is long, and a screen is smaller than a page, i.e. layout becomes a matter of concern	Remember that screen-based surveys take a greater number of screens than their equivalent number of pages in a paper copy. Sectionalize the questionnaire so that each section fills the screen, and does not take more than one screen
The layout of the text and instructions assumes greater importance than for paper questionnaires	Opt for clarity and simplicity
The layout uses a lot of grids and matrices	Avoid grids and matrices: they are a major source of non-response
The order of items affects response rates	Locate requests for personal information at the beginning of the survey. Include 'warm-ups' and early 'high hurdles' to avoid dropout
Respondents may be bombarded with too much information in an introductory message	Place the advertisement for the survey on user groups as well as for the general public, inviting participants to contact such-and-such a person or website for further information and the questionnaire itself, i.e. separate the questionnaire from the advertisement for/introduction to the questionnaire
Respondents may be overloaded with instructions at the beginning of the survey	Avoid placing all the instructions at the start of the questionnaire, but keep specific instructions for specific questions
Respondents may be overloaded with information at the beginning of the survey	Keep the initial information brief and embed further information deeper in the survey
Respondents may have to take multiple actions in order to answer each question (e.g. clicking on an answer, moving the scroll bar, clicking for the next screen, clicking to submit a screen of information)	Keep the number of actions required in order to move on to a minimum
Respondents may not be able to see all the option choices without scrolling down the screen	Ensure that the whole item and options are contained on a single screen
Respondents may not understand instructions	Provide a helpline, email address or contact details of the researcher. Pilot the instrument
Instructions about options may be unclear	Use radio buttons for single choice items, and try to keep layout similar to a paper layout
Respondents only read part of each question before going to the response category	Keep instructions and words to a necessary minimum

continued

Problem (reliability)	Possible solution
Respondents may alter the instrument itself. The researcher relinquishes a greater amount of control to the respondents than in conventional questionnaires	Include technological safeguards to prevent alteration and have procedures to identify altered instruments
Respondents may be forced to answer every question even when they consider some response categories inappropriate	Pilot the survey. Include options such as 'don't know' and 'do not wish to answer' and avoid forcing respondents to reply before they can move on
Respondents may not be telling the truth – they may misrepresent themselves	Include questions to cross-check replies (to try to reduce the problem of respondents not telling the truth)

Problem (dropout)	Possible solution
Respondents may lose interest after a while and abandon the survey, thereby losing all the survey data	Have a device that requires respondents to send their replies screen by screen (e.g. a 'Submit' button at the foot of each screen), section by section, or item by item. Put each question or each section on a separate screen, with 'submit' at the end of each screen. Adopt a 'one-item-one-screen' technique
Respondents may not know how long the questionnaire is, and so may lose interest	Include a device for indicating how far through the questionnaire the respondent has reached: a progress bar at the bottom or the side of the survey
Internet surveys take longer to complete than paper-based surveys	Keep the internet survey as short, clear and easy to complete as possible
People do not want to take part, and it is easier for someone to quit or cancel an internet-based survey than a paper-based survey (simply a click of a button)	Increase incentives to participate (e.g. financial incentives, lottery tickets (if they are permitted in the country))
Diminishing returns (the survey response drops off quite quickly). Newsgroup postings and electronic discussion group data are removed, relegated or archived after a period of time (e.g. a week), and readers do not read lower down the lists of postings	Ensure that the website is re-posted each week during the data collection period
Non-participation may be high (i.e. potential participants may not choose to start, in contrast to those who start and who subsequently drop out)	Increase incentives to participate. Locate personal informational questions at the start of the survey
Error messages (e.g. if an item has not been completed) cause frustration and may cause respondents to abandon the questionnaire	Avoid error messages if possible, but, if not possible, provide clear reasons why the error was made and how to rectify it

As suggested in these lists, the importance of the visual aspect of questionnaires is heightened in internet surveys (Smyth *et al.*, 2004), and this affects the layout of questions, instructions and response lists, the grouping of items, the colours used, the spacing of response categories, the formatting of responses (e.g. writing in words or ticking boxes). Smyth *et al.* (2004) report that respondents use 'preattentive processing' when approaching internet surveys, i.e. they try to take in and understand the whole scene (or screen) before attending to specific items, hence visual features are important,

e.g. emboldened words, large fonts, colours, brightness, section headings, spacing, placing boxes around items. This rests on Gestalt psychology that abides by the principles of: (a) *proximity* (we tend to group together those items that are physically close to each other); (b) *similarity* (we tend to group together those items that appear alike); (c) *prägnanz* (figures or items with simplicity, regularity and symmetry are more easily perceived and remembered).

Smyth *et al.* (2004: 21) also suggest that the use of headings and separation of sections take on added significance in internet-based surveys. They report that separating items into two sections with headings had a 'dramatic effect' on responses, as respondents felt compelled to answer both subgroups (70 per cent gave an answer in both subgroups whereas only 41 per cent did so when there were no headings or sectionalization). They also found that separating a vertical list of items into subgroups and columns (double-banking) was not a 'desirable construction practice' and should be avoided if possible. They report that asking respondents for some open-ended responses (e.g. writing their subject specialisms) can be more efficient than having them track down a long list of subjects to find the one that applies to them, though this can be mitigated by placing simple lists in alphabetical order. Finally they found that placing very short guides underneath the write-in box rather than at its side (e.g. dd/mm/yy for 'day/month/year', and using 'yy' for 'year' rather than 'yyyy') increased response rates, and that placing instructions very close to the answer box improved response rates.

Dillman *et al.* (2003) also found that having respondents use a yes/no format (a 'forced choice') for responding resulted in increased numbers of affirmative answers, even though this requires more cognitive processing than non-forced choice questions (e.g. 'tick[check]-all-that-apply' questions) (p. 23). This is because respondents may not wish to answer questions in the outright negative (p. 10); even if they do not really have an opinion or they are neutral or the item does not really apply to them, they may choose a 'yes' rather than a 'no' category. They may leave a blank rather than indicating a 'no'. The percentage of affirmative responses was higher in a paper-based survey than in an internet-based survey (11.3 per cent and 6.5 per cent respectively) (p. 22).

Similarly, as mentioned earlier, Dillman *et al.* (2003) report that respondents tend to select items higher up a list than lower down a list of options (the primacy effect), opting for the 'satisficing' principle (they are satisfied with a minimum sufficient response, selecting the first reasonable response in a list and then moving on rather than working their way down the list to find the optimal response), suggesting that item order is a significant feature, making a difference of over 39 per cent to responses (p. 7). This is particularly so, the authors aver, when respondents are asked for opinions and beliefs rather than topics seeking factual information. They also suggest that the more difficult the item is, the more respondents will move towards 'satisficing'. They found that 'satisficing' and the primacy effect were stronger in internet surveys than paper-based surveys (p. 22), and that changing 'check-all-

that-apply' to forced responses (yes/no) did not eliminate response order effects.

Dillman *et al.* (2003) also report that the order of response items can have an effect on responses, citing, as an example (p. 6), a study that found that asking college students whether their male or female teachers were more empathetic was affected by whether the 'male' option was placed before or after the 'female' option: 'respondents evaluated their female teachers more positively when they were asked to compare them to their male teachers than when they were asked to compare their male teachers to their female teachers'. Respondents compare the second item in light of the first item in a list rather than considering the items separately.

Internet-based surveys are subject to the same ethical rules as paper-based surveys. These include, for example, informed consent and confidentiality. Whilst the former may be straightforward to ensure, the issue of confidentiality on the internet is more troublesome for researchers. For example, on the one hand an email survey can be quick and uncomplicated, it can also reveal the identity and traceability of the respondent. As Witmer *et al.* (1999: 147) remark, this could stall a project. Security (e.g. through passwords and PIN numbers) is one possible solution, though this, too, can create problems in that respondents may feel that they are being identified and tracked, and, indeed, some surveys may deposit unwelcome 'cookies' onto the respondent's computer, for future contact.

Sampling in internet-based surveys

Sampling bias is a major concern for internet-based surveys (Coomber, 1997; Roztocki and Lahri, 2002; Schonlau *et al.*, 2009). Hewson *et al.* (2003: 27) suggest that 'internet-mediated research is immediately subject to serious problems concerning sampling representativeness and validity of data', e.g. that the internet researcher tends to tap into middle-class and well-educated populations, mainly from the United States, or undergraduate and college students. Survey2000 (Witte *et al.*, 1999) found that 92.5 per cent of respondents were white. However, this view of over-representation of some and under-representation of others is being increasingly challenged (Smith and Leigh, 1997; Witte *et al.*, 1999; Hewson *et al.*, 2003), with results showing that samples taken from users and non-users of the internet did not differ in terms of income, education, sexual orientation, marital status, ethnicity and religious belief. However, they did differ in terms of age, with the internet samples containing a wider age range than non-internet samples, and in terms of sex, with the internet samples containing more males. Hewson *et al.*

(2003) report overall a greater diversity of sample characteristics in internet-based samples, though they caution that this is inconclusive, and that the sample characteristics of internet samples, like non-internet samples, depend on the sampling strategy used. Stewart and Yalonis (2001) suggest that one can overcome the possible bias in sampling through simple stratification techniques.

A major problem in sampling for internet surveys is estimating the size and nature of the population from which the sample is drawn: a key feature of sampling strategy. Researchers have no clear knowledge of the population characteristics or size, and indeed the same applies to the sample. The number of internet users is not a simple function of the number of computers or the number of servers (e.g. many users can employ a single computer or server), though at the time of writing, a figure of over 500 million users has been suggested (Hewson *et al.*, 2003: 36). Further, it is difficult to know how many or what kind of people saw a particular survey on a website (e.g. more males than females), i.e. the sampling frame is unclear. Moreover, certain sectors of the population may still be excluded from the internet, for example those not wishing to, or unable to (e.g. because of cost or availability), gain access to the internet. The situation is changing rapidly. In 1997 it was reported (Coomber, 1997) that internet users tended to be white, relatively affluent and relatively well-educated males from the first world; more recent studies (e.g. Hewson *et al.*, 2003) suggest that the internet is attracting a much more diverse population that is closer to the general population.

There are further concerns about the sampling on internet-based surveys. Internet-based surveys are based largely on volunteer samples, obtained through general posting on the Web (e.g. an advertisement giving details and directing volunteers to a site for further information), or, more popular in the social sciences, through announcements to specific newsgroups and interest groups on the Web, e.g. contacting user groups (e.g. through the SchoolNet). Lists of different kinds of user (USENET) groups, newsgroups and electronic discussion groups (e.g. Listservs) can be found on the Web. Several search engines exist that seek and return web mailing lists, such as: www.liszt.com (categorized by subject); Catalist (the official catalogue of LISTSERV lists at www.lsoft.com/catalist.html); Mailbase (www.mailbase.ac.uk) which is a major collection of over 2,500 lists concerning the academic community in the UK; and Meta-List.net (www.meta-list.net) which searches a database of nearly a quarter of a million mailing lists. Dochartaigh (2002) provides useful material on web searching for educational and social researchers.

The issue here is that the researcher is using non-probability, volunteer sampling, and this may decrease the generalizability of the findings (though, of course, this may be no more a problem on internet-based surveys than on other surveys). Opportunity samples (e.g. of undergraduate or postgraduate students using the Web, or of particular groups) may restrict the generalizability of the research, but this may be no more than in conventional research, and may not be a problem so long as it is acknowledged. The issue of volunteer samples runs deeper, for volunteers may differ from non-volunteers in terms of personality (e.g. they may be more extravert or concerned for self-actualization (Bargh *et al.*, 2002)) and may self-select themselves into, or out of, a survey, again restricting the generalizability of the results.

One method to try to overcome the problem of volunteer bias is to strive for extremely large samples, or to record the number of hits on a website, though these are crude indices. Another method of securing the participation of non-volunteers in an internet survey is to contact them by email (assuming that their email addresses are known), e.g. a class of students, a group of teachers. However, email addresses themselves do not give the researcher any indication of the sample characteristics (e.g. age, sex, nationality, etc.).

Watt (1997) suggests that there are three types of internet sample:

- an unrestricted sample (anyone can complete the questionnaire, but it may have limited representativeness);
- a screened sample (quotas are placed on the subsample categories and types (e.g. gender, income, job responsibility, etc.));
- a recruited sample (where respondents complete a preliminary classification questionnaire and then, based on the data provided in them, are recruited or not).

Response rate for an internet survey is typically lower than for a paper-based survey, as is the rate of completion of the whole survey (Reips, 2002a). Witmer *et al.* (1999: 147) report that for a paper-based survey the response could be as high as 50 per cent and as low as 20 per cent; for an internet survey it could be as low as 10 per cent or even lower. Dillman *et al.* (1998b) report a study that found that 84 per cent of a sample completed a particular paper-based survey, whilst only 68 per cent of a sample completed the same survey online. Solomon (2001) reported that response rates to an internet-based survey are lower than for their equivalent mail surveys. However, this issue is compounded because in an internet-based survey, there is no real knowledge of the population or the sample, unless only specific people have been approached (e.g. through email). Witmer *et al.* (1999) found that short versions of an internet-based questionnaire did not produce a significantly higher response rate than the long version (p. 155). Solomon (2001) suggests that response rates can be improved through the use of personalized email, follow-up reminders, the use of simple formats and pre-notification of the intent to survey.

Reips (2002a) provides some useful guidelines for increasing response rates on an internet survey. He suggests that response rates can be increased by utilizing the multiple site entry technique, i.e. having several websites and postings on several discussion groups that link potential participants or web surfers to the website containing the questionnaire. He also suggests (p. 249) utilizing a 'high hurdle technique', where 'motivationally adverse factors are announced or concentrated as close to the beginning' as possible, so that any potential dropouts will self-select at the start rather than during the data collection. A 'high hurdle' technique, he suggests, comprises:

Seriousness:	inform the participants that the research is serious and rigorous;
Personalization:	ask for an email address or contact details and personal information;
Impression of control:	inform participants that their identity is traceable;
Patience: loading time:	use image files to reduce loading time of web pages;
Patience: long texts:	place most of the text in the first page, and successively reduce the amount on each subsequent page;
Duration:	inform participants how long the survey will take;
Privacy:	inform the participants that some personal information will be sought;
Preconditions:	indicate the requirements for particular software;
Technical pre-tests:	conduct tests of compatibility of software;
Rewards:	indicate that any rewards/incentives are contingent on full completion of the survey.

Of course, some of these strategies could backfire on the researcher (e.g. the disclosure of personal and traceable details), but the principle here is that it is better for the participant not to take part in the first place rather than then drop out during the process. Indeed Frick *et al.* (1999) found that early dropout was not increased by asking for personal information at the beginning. In relation to online experiments they found that 'the tendency of leaving the experiment when personal information is requested is higher after the experiment has already been finished' (p. 4), i.e. it is better to ask for personal information at the beginning.

Reips (2002a) also advocates the use of 'warm-up' techniques in internet-based research in conjunction with the 'high hurdle' technique (see also Frick *et al.*, 1999). He suggests that most dropouts occur earlier rather than later in data collection, or, indeed, at the very beginning (non-participation) and that most such initial dropouts occur because participants are overloaded with information early on. Rather, he suggests, it is preferable to introduce some simple-to-complete items earlier on to build up an idea of how to respond to the later items and to try out practice materials. Frick *et al.* (1999) report that offering financial incentives may be useful in reducing dropouts, ensuring that respondents continue an online survey to completion (up to twice as likely to ensure completion), and that they may be useful if intrinsic motivation is insufficient to guarantee completion.

Gwartney (2007: 17) suggests that online surveys might be most appropriate with 'closed populations', i.e. employees in a particular organization, as this will enable the researcher to know some of the characteristics and parameters of the respondents.

13.10 Comparing methods of data collection in surveys

Aldridge and Levine (2001: 51–4) and Fowler (2009: 80–3) offer useful summary guides to the advantages and disadvantages of several methods of data collection in surveys: personal face-to-face interviewing; telephone interviewing; self-administered/self-completion versus interviewer-administered; group administered; mailed surveys; delivered (distributed) surveys (e.g. personally delivered or delivered to an institution); internet surveys. We refer the reader to these useful sources. Additionally Fowler (2009) discusses the attractions of combining methods of data collection (e.g. face-to-face interviews with telephone interviews, internet surveys with postal surveys).

Case studies

Case studies are important sources of research data, either on their own or to supplement other kinds of data. This chapter sets out key areas for attention in case studies, and it addresses:

- what is a case study?
- generalization in case study
- reliability and validity in case studies
- what makes a good case study researcher?
- examples of kinds of case study
- why participant observation?
- planning a case study
- data in case studies
- recording observations
- writing up a case study

The intention here is to provide researchers with an overview of key issues in the planning, conduct and reporting of a case study.

14.1 What is a case study?

A case study is a specific instance that is frequently designed to illustrate a more general principle (Nisbet and Watt, 1984: 72), it is 'the study of an instance in action' (Adelman *et al.*, 1980); it is the study of a 'particular' (Stake, 1995). Whilst Creswell (1994: 12) defines the case study as a single instance of a bounded system, such as a child, a clique, a class, a school, a community, others would not hold to such a tight definition, for example Yin (2009: 18) argues that the boundary line between the phenomenon and its context is blurred, as a case study is a study of a case in a context and it is important to set the case within its context (i.e. rich descriptions and details are often a feature of a case study). A case study can be both: sometimes tightly bounded and other times less so; as Verschuren (2003: 123) argues, it is ambiguous.

A case study provides a unique example of real people in real situations, enabling readers to understand ideas more clearly than simply by presenting them with abstract theories or principles. Indeed a case study can enable readers to understand how ideas and abstract

principles can fit together (Yin, 2009: 72–3). Case studies can penetrate situations in ways that are not always susceptible to numerical analysis.

Case studies recognize and accept that there are many variables operating in a single case, and, hence, to catch the implications of these variables usually requires more than one tool for data collection and many sources of evidence. Case studies can blend numerical and qualitative data, and they are a prototypical instance of mixed methods research (see Chapter 1); they can explain, describe, illustrate and enlighten (Yin, 2009: 19–20).

Verschuren (2003: 124) reports a range of authors who argue that a distinguishing feature of case study research is 'holism' rather than 'reductionism'. Whilst for Yin (2009) 'holism' refers to conducting the research at the single 'unit of analysis' chosen (discussed below), which may be an individual, a group, an organization, etc., for Verschuren the term 'holism' is ambiguous, as it may not necessarily mean looking at a *whole* subject, person, group, organization but only at the relevant areas of interest.

Case studies can establish cause and effect ('how' and 'why'); indeed one of their strengths is that they observe effects in real contexts, recognizing that context is a powerful determinant of both causes and effects, and that in-depth understanding is required to do justice to the case. As Nisbet and Watt (1984: 78) remark, the whole is more than the sum of its parts. Sturman (1999: 103) argues that a distinguishing feature of case studies is that human systems have a wholeness or integrity to them rather than being a loose connection of traits, necessitating in-depth investigation. Further, contexts are unique and dynamic, hence case studies investigate and report the real-life, complex dynamic and unfolding interactions of events, human relationships and other factors in a unique instance. Hitchcock and Hughes (1995: 316) suggest that case studies are distinguished less by the methodologies that they employ than by the subjects/objects of their enquiry (though, as indicated below, there is frequently a resonance between case studies and interpretive methodologies). They further suggest (p. 322) that the case study approach is particularly valuable when the researcher has little control over events, i.e. behaviours cannot be manipulated or controlled. They consider (p. 317) that a case study has several hallmarks:

- it is concerned with a rich and vivid description of events relevant to the case;
- it provides a chronological narrative of events relevant to the case;
- it blends a description of events with the analysis of them;
- it focuses on individual actors or groups of actors, and seeks to understand their perceptions of events;
- it highlights specific events that are relevant to the case;
- the researcher is integrally involved in the case, and the case study may be linked to the personality of the researcher (cf. Verschuren, 2003: 133);
- an attempt is made to portray the richness of the case in writing up the report.

Case studies, they argue (Hitchcock and Hughes, 1995: 319): (a) are set in temporal, geographical, organizational, institutional and other contexts that enable boundaries to be drawn around the case; (b) can be defined with reference to characteristics defined by individuals and groups involved; and (c) can be defined by participants' roles and functions in the case. They also point out that case studies:

- will have temporal characteristics which help to define their nature;
- have geographical parameters allowing for their definition;
- will have boundaries which allow for definition;
- may be defined by an individual in a particular context, at a point in time;
- may be defined by the characteristics of the group;
- may be defined by role or function;
- may be shaped by organizational or institutional arrangements.

Case studies have the advantage over historical studies of including direct observation and interviews with participants (Yin, 2009: 11). They strive to portray 'what it is like' to be in a particular situation, to catch the close-up reality and 'thick description' (Geertz, 1973) of participants' lived experiences of, thoughts about and feelings for, a situation. They involve looking at a case or phenomenon in its real-life context, usually employing many types of data (Robson, 2002: 178). They are descriptive and detailed, with a narrow focus, and combining subjective and objective data

(Dyer, 1995: 48–9). It is important in case studies for events and situations to be allowed to speak for themselves, rather than to be largely interpreted, evaluated or judged by the researcher. In this respect the case study is akin to the television documentary.

This is not to say that case studies are unsystematic or merely illustrative; case study data are gathered systematically and rigorously. Indeed Nisbet and Watt (1984: 91) specifically counsel case study researchers to avoid:

- journalism (picking out more striking features of the case, thereby distorting the full account in order to emphasize these more sensational aspects);
- selective reporting (selecting only that evidence which will support a particular conclusion, thereby misrepresenting the whole case);
- an anecdotal style (degenerating into an endless series of low-level banal and tedious illustrations that take over from in-depth, rigorous analysis); one is reminded of Stake's (1978) wry comment that 'our scrapbooks are full of enlargements of enlargements', alluding to the tendency of some case studies to overemphasize detail to the detriment of seeing the whole picture;
- pomposity (striving to derive or generate profound theories from low-level data, or by wrapping up accounts in high-sounding verbiage);
- blandness (unquestioningly accepting only the respondents' views, or only including those aspects of the case study on which people agree rather than areas on which they might disagree).

Simons (1996) has argued that case study needs to address six paradoxes; it needs to:

- reject the subject–object dichotomy, regarding all participants equally;
- recognize the contribution that a genuine creative encounter can make to new forms of understanding education;
- regard different ways of seeing as new ways of knowing;
- approximate the ways of the artist;
- free the mind of traditional analysis;
- embrace these paradoxes, with an overriding interest in people.

There are several types of case study. Yin (1984) identifies three such types in terms of their outcomes: (i) exploratory (as a pilot to other studies or research questions); (ii) descriptive (providing narrative accounts); (iii) explanatory (testing theories). Exploratory case studies that act as a pilot can be used to generate hypotheses that are tested in larger scale surveys, experiments or other forms of research, e.g. observational. However Adelman *et al.* (1980) caution against using case studies solely as preliminaries to other studies, e.g. as pre-experimental or pre-survey; rather, they argue, case studies exist in their own right as a significant and legitimate research method.

Yin's (1984) classification accords with Merriam (1988) who identifies three types: (i) descriptive (narrative accounts); (ii) interpretive (developing conceptual categories inductively in order to examine initial assumptions); (iii) evaluative (explaining and judging). Merriam also categorizes four common domains or kinds of case study: ethnographic, historical, psychological and sociological. Sturman (1999: 107), echoing Stenhouse (1985), identifies four kinds of case study: (i) an ethnographic case study – single in-depth study; (ii) action research case study; (iii) evaluative case study; and (iv) educational case study. Stake (1994) identifies three main types of case study: (i) intrinsic case studies (studies that are undertaken in order to understand the particular case in question); (ii) instrumental case studies (examining a particular case in order to gain insight into an issue or a theory); (iii) collective case studies (groups of individual studies that are undertaken to gain a fuller picture). Because case studies provide fine grain detail they can also be used to complement other, more coarsely grained – often large-scale – kinds of research. Case study material in this sense can provide powerful human-scale data on macro-political decision making, fusing theory and practice, for example the work of Ball (1990), Bowe *et al.* (1992) and Ball (1994a) on the impact of government policy on specific schools.

Robson (2002: 181–2) suggests that there are: an individual case study; a set of individual case studies; a social group study; studies of organizations and institutions; studies of events, roles and relationships. All these, he argues, find expression in the case study method. He adds to these the distinction between a critical case study and an extreme or unique case. The former, he argues, is:

> when your theoretical understanding is such that there is a clear, unambiguous and non-trivial set of circumstances where predicted outcomes will be found. Finding a case which fits, and demonstrating what has been predicted, can give a powerful boost to knowledge and understanding.
>
> (Robson, 2002: 182)

One can add to the critical case study the issue that the case in question might possess all, or most of, the characteristics or features that one is investigating, more fully or distinctly than under 'normal' circumstances, for example a case study of student disruptive behaviour might go on in a *very* disruptive class, with students who are very seriously disturbed or challenging, rather than going into a class where the level of disruption is not so marked.

By contrast, Robson (2002: 182) argues that the extreme and the unique case can provide a valuable 'test bed'. Extremes include, he argues, the situation in which 'if it can work here it will work anywhere', or choosing an ideal set of circumstances in which to try out a new approach or project, maybe to gain a fuller insight into how it operates before taking it to a wider audience (e.g. the research and development model).

Yin (2009: 46ff.) identifies four main case study designs:

1 The *single-case design* can focus on a critical case, an extreme case, a unique case, a representative or typical case, a revelatory case (an opportunity to research a case heretofore unresearched, e.g. Whyte's Street Corner Society: see Chapter 11), a longitudinal case.

2 The *embedded, single-case design*, in which more than one 'unit of analysis' is incorporated into the design, e.g. a case study of a whole school might also use sub-units of classes, teachers, students, parents, and each of these might require different data collection instruments, e.g. a survey questionnaire, interviews, observations, etc.

3 The *multiple-case design*, e.g. comparative case studies within an overall piece of research, or replication case studies. Indeed Campbell (1975: 180), in arguing against single-case studies, suggests that having two case studies, for comparative purposes, is more than worth having double the amount of data on a single-case study! Here, for example, akin to a quasi-experiment, a regional education authority may want to see the effects of a new innovation, let us say in mathematics teaching, in three circumstances (conditions): one where teachers are given in-house staff development for the new mathematics, the other where they attend externally provided courses on the new mathematics, and the other where the teachers receive both kinds of staff development; here the case studies might look at the effects in the schools concerned (cf. Yin, 2009: 54–5).

4 The *embedded multiple-case design*, in which different sub-units may be involved in each of the different cases, and a range of instruments (e.g. a survey questionnaire, interviews, observations,

archival records, etc.) might be used for each sub-unit, and each is kept separate to each case.

A single case may be part of a multiple-case study design, and, by contrast, a particular data collection instrument (e.g. a survey) may be part of a cross-site case study. In considering multiple case studies, it is important to decide how many are required; typically, the more subtle is the issue under investigation, the more cases might be required (Yin, 2009: 58) in order to be able to rule out rival explanations. Yin also counsels caution in conducting a single-case design, in that this overlooks the possible benefits of multiples cases, e.g. replication and the avoidance of the criticism of being a unique, single case, and the researcher is 'putting all the eggs in one basket', which may be risky: an 'all-or-nothing' risk.

Case studies have several claimed strengths and weaknesses. These are summarized in Box 14.1 (Adelman *et al.*, 1980) and Box 14.2 (Nisbet and Watt, 1984).

Shaughnessy *et al.* (2003: 290–9) suggest that case studies often lack a high degree of control, and treatments are rarely controlled systematically, yet they are applied simultaneously, and with little control over extraneous variables. This, they argue, renders it difficult to make inferences to draw cause and effect conclusions from case studies, and there is potential for bias in some case studies as the therapist is both the participant and observer and, in that role, may overstate or understate the case. Case studies, they argue, may be impressionistic, and self-reporting may be biased (by the participant or the observer). Further, they argue that bias may be a problem if the case study relies on an individual's memory.

Dyer (1995: 50–2) remarks that, reading a case study, one has to be aware that a process of selection has already taken place, and only the author knows what has been selected in or out, and on what criteria, and, indeed, the participants themselves may not know what selection has taken place. Indeed he observes

---

BOX 14.1 POSSIBLE ADVANTAGES OF CASE STUDY

Case studies have a number of advantages that make them attractive to educational evaluators or researchers. Thus:

1 Case study data, paradoxically, is 'strong in reality' but difficult to organize. In contrast, other research data is often 'weak in reality' but susceptible to ready organization. This strength in reality is because case studies are down to earth and attention-holding, in harmony with the reader's own experience, and thus provide a 'natural' basis for generalization.

2 Case studies allow generalizations either about an instance or from an instance to a class. Their peculiar strength lies in their attention to the subtlety and complexity of the case in its own right.

3 Case studies recognize the complexity and 'embeddedness' of social truths. By carefully attending to social situations, case studies can represent something of the discrepancies or conflicts between the viewpoints held by participants. The best case studies are capable of offering some support to alternative interpretations.

4 Case studies, considered as products, may form an archive of descriptive material sufficiently rich to admit subsequent reinterpretation. Given the variety and complexity of educational purposes and environments, there is an obvious value in having a data source for researchers and users whose purposes may be different from our own.

5 Case studies are 'a step to action'. They begin in a world of action and contribute to it. Their insights may be directly interpreted and put to use; for staff or individual self-development, for within-institutional feedback; for formative evaluation; and in educational policy making.

6 Case studies present research or evaluation data in a more publicly accessible form than other kinds of research report, although this virtue is to some extent bought at the expense of their length. The language and the form of the presentation is hopefully less esoteric and less dependent on specialized interpretation than conventional research reports. The case study is capable of serving multiple audiences. It reduces the dependence of the reader upon unstated implicit assumptions ... and makes the research process itself accessible. Case studies, therefore, may contribute towards the 'democratization' of decision making (and knowledge itself). At its best, they allow readers to judge the implications of a study for themselves.

Source: Adapted from Adelman *et al.*, 1980

BOX 14.2 NISBET'S AND WATT'S (1984) STRENGTHS AND WEAKNESSES OF CASE STUDY

Strengths

1 The results are more easily understood by a wide audience (including non-academics) as they are frequently written in everyday, non-professional language.
2 They are immediately intelligible; they speak for themselves.
3 They catch unique features that may otherwise be lost in larger scale data (e.g. surveys); these unique features might hold the key to understanding the situation.
4 They are strong on reality.
5 They provide insights into other, similar situations and cases, thereby assisting interpretation of other similar cases.
6 They can be undertaken by a single researcher without needing a full research team.
7 They can embrace and build in unanticipated events and uncontrolled variables.

Weaknesses

1 The results may not be generalizable except where other readers/researchers see their application.
2 They are not easily open to cross-checking, hence they may be selective, biased, personal and subjective.
3 They are prone to problems of observer bias, despite attempts made to address reflexivity.

(pp. 48–9) that case studies combine knowledge and inference, and it is often difficult to separate these; the researcher has to be clear on which of these feature in the case study data.

From the preceding analysis it is clear that case studies frequently follow the interpretive tradition of research – seeing the situation through the eyes of participants – rather than the quantitative paradigm, though this need not always be the case. Its sympathy to the interpretive paradigm has rendered case study an object of criticism. Consider, for example, Smith (1991: 375) who argues that not only is the case study method the logically weakest method of knowing, but that studying individual cases, careers and communities is a thing of the past, and that attention should be focused on patterns and laws in historical research.

This is prejudice and ideology rather than critique, but signifies the problem of respectability and legitimacy that case study has to conquer amongst certain academics. Like other research methods, case study has to demonstrate reliability and validity. This can be difficult, for given the uniqueness of any situation, a case study may be, by definition, inconsistent with other case studies or unable to demonstrate this positivist view of reliability. Even though case studies do not have to demonstrate this form of reliability, nevertheless there are important questions to be faced in undertaking case studies, for example (Adelman *et al.*, 1980; Nisbet and Watt, 1984; Hitchcock and Hughes, 1995):

What exactly is a case?
How are cases identified and selected?

What kind of case study is this (what is its purpose)?
What is reliable evidence?
What is objective evidence?
What is an appropriate selection to include from the wealth of generated data?
What is a fair and accurate account?
Under what circumstances is it fair to take an exceptional case (or a critical event – see the discussion of observation in Chapter 23)?
What kind of sampling is most appropriate?
To what extent is triangulation required and how will this be addressed?
What is the nature of the validation process in case studies?
How will the balance be struck between uniqueness and generalization?
What is the most appropriate form of writing up and reporting the case study?
What ethical issues are exposed in undertaking a case study?

A key issue in case study research is the selection of information. Though it is frequently useful to record typical, representative occurrences, the researcher need not always adhere to criteria of representativeness. For example, it may be that infrequent, unrepresentative but critical incidents or events occur that are crucial to the understanding of the case. For example, a subject might only demonstrate a particular behaviour once, but it is so important as not to be ruled out simply because it occurred once; sometimes a single event might occur which sheds a hugely important insight into a person or situation (see the discussion of critical incidents in Chapter 29); it can be a key to understanding a situation (Flanagan, 1949).

For example, it may be that a psychological case study might happen upon a single instance of child abuse earlier in an adult's life, but the effects of this were so profound as to constitute a turning point in understanding that adult. A child might suddenly pass a single comment that indicates complete frustration with or complete fear of a teacher, yet it is too important to overlook. Case studies, in not having to seek frequencies of occurrences, can replace quantity with quality and intensity, separating the *significant few* from the *insignificant many* instances of behaviour. Significance rather than frequency is a hallmark of case studies, offering the researcher an insight into the real dynamics of situations and people.

In designing a case study Yin (2009: 27) provides a valuable set of five components that need to be addressed:

- The case study's questions (it was suggested earlier that case study is particularly powerful in answering the 'how' and 'why' type of questions, and Yin (2009: 29) argues that the more specific are the questions that the case study should answer, the stronger is the likelihood of the case study staying on track and within limits).
- The case study's propositions (if there are any) (e.g. a hypothesis to be tested).
- The case study's 'unit(s) of analysis' (this relates to the key issue in case study, which is defining what constitutes the case, and this can comprise an individual, a group, a community, an organization, a programme, a piece of innovation, a decision and its ramifications, an industry, an economy, etc.). What constitutes the case should be clear from the research questions that are asked (Yin, 2009: 30), as these should specify the 'unit of analysis'. Yin (2009: 32) suggests that the 'unit of analysis' should be concrete (a real-life phenomenon) rather than abstract (e.g. an argument or topic). Identifying the 'unit of analysis' can be used to identify the tricky question of what constitutes a case. Verschuren (2003: 126) provides a neat example of this: in a case study of a single business organization in which a sample of 500 employees is taken, this does not constitute a case study but, rather, a survey, as the unit of analysis is each of the individual 500 employees. For it to be constituted as a case study the unit of analysis here would have to be the whole organization.
- The logic that links the data gathered to the propositions set out in the case study (i.e. how the data will

be analysed, for example by looking for patterns, explanations, analysis of events as they unravel over time, cross-site and cross-case analysis (Yin, 2009: 34).
- The 'criteria for interpreting the findings' from the case study (which includes a clear indication of how the interpretation given is better than rival explanations of the data).

Yin (2009: 35) also adds that theory generation should be included in the research design phase of the case study, as this assists in the focusing of the case study, and such theories might be of the behaviour of individuals, groups, organizations, communities, societies (e.g. there are several levels of theory).

14.2 Generalization in case study

It is often heard that case studies, being idiographic, have limited generalizability (e.g. Yin, 2009: 15). Of course, the same could be said of single experiments (p. 15). However, just as the generalizability of single experiments can be extended by replication and multiple experiments, so, too, case studies can be part of a growing pool of data, with multiple case studies contributing to greater generalizability. However, more pertinent is the claim by Robson (2002: 183) and Yin (2009: 15), that case studies opt for 'analytic' rather than 'statistical' generalization.

In statistical generalization the researcher seeks to move from a sample to a population, based on, for example, sampling strategies, frequencies, statistical significance and effect size. However, in analytic generalization, the concern is not so much for a representative sample (indeed the strength of the case study approach is that the case only represents itself) so much as its ability to contribute to the expansion and generalization of theory (Yin, 2009: 15), which can help researchers to understand other similar cases, phenomena or situations, i.e. there is a logical rather than statistical connection between the case and the wider theory. A case is not a sample. Yin (2009: 43) makes the telling point that to assume that generalization is only from sample to population/universe is simply incorrect, irrelevant, inappropriate and inapplicable in respect of case studies. Rather, he makes the point (pp. 38–9) that case studies can help to generalize to a broader *theory*, in that the theory can be tested in one or more empirical cases (akin, in this respect, to a single experiment or quasi-experiment), and can be shown *not* to support rival, even if plausible, theories.

Generalization requires extrapolation, and the case study researcher, whilst not necessarily being able to extrapolate on the basis of typicality or representativeness, nevertheless can extrapolate to relevant theory (Macpherson *et al.*, 2000: 52) and, by implication, to the testing of that theory.

Case studies can make theoretical statements, but, like other forms of research and human sciences, these must be supported by the evidence presented. This requires the nature of generalization in case study to be clarified. Generalization can take various forms, for example:

- from the single instance to the class of instances that it represents (for example a single-sex selective school might act as a case study to catch significant features of other single-sex selective schools);
- from features of the single case to a multiplicity of classes with the same features;
- from the single features of part of the case to the whole of that case;
- from a single case to a theoretical extension or theoretical generalization.

A more robust defence of generalization from case studies than those mentioned above is made by Verschuren (2003: 136). First he argues that statistical generalization is made on the basis of the homogeneity (or variability) of the population and the sample, together with the level of certainty required in the sample (see Chapter 8). So, for example, if the population is highly standardized and invariant (he uses the example of a factory that makes the same, uniform, standardized machines) the sample used for quality control could well be very small, whereas in a very variable population (with many variables) the sample size would have to be large. He then turns to the number of case studies which might be required for generalizability to be secure, and he argues that, in fact, a very small number of case studies could be used, each of which embraces the range of variables in question, thereby reducing the number of overall cases required; this is because 'complex issues in general have a much lower variability than separate variables' (p. 137), i.e. the researcher can generalize from a small number of case studies that represent the complex issues in general. It is a sophisticated argument: case studies include many variables; multi-variable phenomena are characterized by homogeneity rather than high variability; therefore if the researcher can identify case studies that catch the range of variability then external validity – generalizability – can be demonstrated.

14.3 Reliability and validity in case studies

Whilst case studies may not have the external checks and balances that other forms of research enjoy or require, nevertheless they still have to abide by canons of validity and reliability, for example:

- *construct validity* (through employing accepted definitions and constructions of concepts and terms; operationalizing the research and its measures/criteria acceptably);
- *internal validity* (through ensuring agreements between different parts of the data, matching patterns of results, ensuring that findings and interpretations derive from the data transparently, and that causal explanations are supported by the evidence (alone), and that rival explanations and inferences have been weighed and found to be less acceptable than the explanation or inference made, again based on evidence);
- *external validity* (clarifying the contexts, theory and domain to which generalization can be made);
- *concurrent validity* (using multiple sources and kinds of evidence to address research questions and to yield *convergent validity*, e.g. triangulation of data, investigators, perspectives, methodologies, instruments);
- *ecological validity* (fidelity to the special features of the context in which the study is located);
- *reliability* (replicability and internal consistency);
- *avoidance of bias* (e.g. the case study simply being an embodiment or fulfilment of the researcher's initial prejudices or suspicions, with selective data being gathered or data being used selectively, i.e. a circular argument (Yin, 2009: 72), or with the researcher's bias being inevitable if the researcher is a participant observer whose personality may affect the research process (Verschuren, 2003: 122). This can be addressed by reflexivity, respondent checks or checks by external reviewers of the data and inferences/conclusions drawn).

Of note here is Yin's (2009: 41, 122–4) call for a 'chain of evidence' to be provided, such that an external researcher could track through every step of the case study from its inception to its research questions, design, data sources, instrumentation, data (evidence and the circumstances in which they were collected, e.g. time, place and functional interconnections of people, places, etc.) and conclusions. It is important to note the time and place in which case study data are collected, as, not only are many actions and events context-specific and are part of a 'thick description', but this will enable any replication research to be planned (Macpherson *et al.*, 2000: 56).

14.4 What makes a good case study researcher?

A case study requires in-depth data, a researcher's ability to gather data that address fitness for purpose, and a researcher's skills in probing beneath the surface of phenomena. These requirements imply that the researcher must be an effective questioner, listener (through many sources), prober, able to make informed inferences ('to read between the lines' (Yin, 2009: 70)) and adaptable to changing and emerging situations. Given that a case study uses a range of methods for data collection (e.g. observation, interview, artefacts, documents, survey), and that it may use different methodologies within it (e.g. action research, experiment, ethnography) the effective case study researcher must be versed in each of these, know how to draw on them at the most appropriate moment, able to keep a clear sense of direction in the data collection, so that the case study is kept on track rather than being side-tracked, and have a clear grasp of the issues for which the case study is being conducted (and keep to these). Clarity of focus, issues and direction are important elements here.

Further, the effective case study researcher will need to possess the ability to collate and synthesize data from different sources, to make inferences and interpretations based on evidence, to know how to test inferences and conclusions (and how to test them against rival explanations).

The case study researcher is often privy to confidential or sensitive material. Hence the researcher must be clear on: the ethics of the research; on his/her own stance in respect of disclosing private or sensitive data; how to protect people at risk or vulnerable groups; how to address matters of justified covert research; whether to report people anonymously or to identify them; how to address non-traceability and non-identifiability of participants, non-attributability of particular comments to individuals; and how to incorporate specific, important features into a cross-site analysis.

It is important for the case study researcher to have the subject knowledge and research expertise required to conduct the case study, to be highly prepared, to have a sense of realism about the situation being researched (as case study is a 'real-life' exercise), to be an excellent communicator (which may require training), and to have the appropriate personality characteristics that will enable access, empathy, rapport and trust to be built up with a diversity of participants. Not every researcher has all of these, yet each is vitally important.

14.5 Examples of kinds of case study

Unlike the experimenter who manipulates variables to determine their causal significance or the surveyor who asks standardized questions of large, representative samples of individuals, the case study researcher typically observes the characteristics of an individual unit – a child, a clique, a class, a school or a community. The purpose of such observation is to probe deeply and to analyse intensively the multifarious phenomena that constitute the life cycle of the unit with a view to establishing generalizations about the wider population to which that unit belongs.

Antipathy amongst researchers towards the statistical-experimental paradigm has led to much case study research. Gangs (Patrick, 1973), dropouts (Parker, 1974), drug-users (Young, 1971) and schools (King, 1979) attest to the wide use of the case study in contemporary social science and educational research. Such wide use is marked by an equally diverse range of techniques employed in the collection and analysis of both qualitative and quantitative data. Case studies are methodologically eclectic (i.e. embedded within them may be more than one kind of research such as ethnography, experiment, action research, survey, illuminative research, observational research, documentary research); they can use a range of methods of data collection, and indeed data types (quantitative and qualitative) and ways of analysing data (statistically and through qualitative tools), and they can be short term or long term. In short, case study is a hybrid (cf. Verschuren, 2003: 125). That said, at the heart of many case studies lies observation.

In Figure 14.1 we set out a typology of observation studies on the basis of which our six examples are selected. (For further explication of these examples, see the accompanying website.)

Acker's (1990) study is an ethnographic account that is based on several hundred hours of participant observation material, whilst Boulton's (1992) work, by contrast, is based on highly structured, non-participant observation conducted over five years. The study by Wild *et al.* (1992) used participant observation, loosely structured interviews that yielded simple frequency counts. Blease and Cohen's (1990) study of coping with computers used highly structured observation schedules, undertaken by non-participant observers, with the express intention of obtaining precise, quantitative data on the classroom use of a computer program.

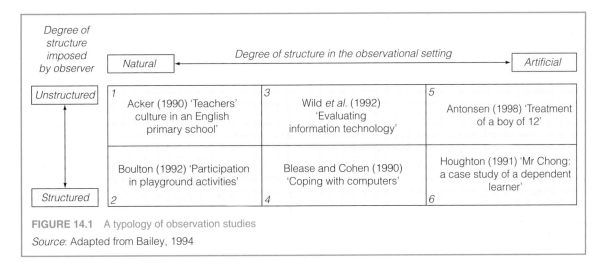

FIGURE 14.1 A typology of observation studies

Source: Adapted from Bailey, 1994

This was part of a longitudinal study in primary classrooms, and yielded typical profiles of individual behaviour and group interaction in students' usage of the computer program. Antonsen's (1988) study was of a single child undergoing psychotherapy at a Child Psychiatric Unit, and uses unstructured observation within the artificial setting of a psychiatric clinic and is a record of the therapist's non-directive approach. Finally Houghton's (1991) study uses data from structured sets of test materials together with focused interviews with those with whom an international student had contact. Together these case studies provide a valuable insight into the range and types of case study.

There are two principal types of observation – participant observation and non-participant observation. In the former, observers engage in the very activities they set out to observe. Often, their 'cover' is so complete that as far as the other participants are concerned, they are simply one of the group. In the case of Patrick, for example, born and bred in Glasgow, his researcher role remained hidden from the members of the Glasgow gang in whose activities he participated for a period of four months (see Patrick, 1973). Such complete anonymity is not always possible, however. Thus in Parker's (1974) study of downtown Liverpool adolescents, it was generally known that the researcher was waiting to take up a post at the university. In the meantime, 'knocking around' during the day with the lads and frequenting their pub at night rapidly established that he was 'OK'. The researcher was, in his own terms, 'a drinker, a hanger-arounder' who could be relied on to keep quiet in illegal matters.

Cover is not necessarily a prerequisite of participant observation. In an intensive study of a small group of working-class boys during their last two years at school and their first months in employment, Willis (1977)

attended all the different subject classes at school – 'not as a teacher, but as a member of the class' – and worked alongside each boy in industry for a short period.

Non-participant observers, on the other hand, stand aloof from the group activities they are investigating and eschew group membership – no great difficulty for King (1979), an adult observer in infant classrooms. King recalls how he firmly established his non-participant status with young children by recognizing that they regarded any adult as another teacher or surrogate teacher. Hence he would stand up to maintain social distance, and deliberately decline to show immediate interest, and avoided eye contact.

The best illustration of the non-participant observer role is perhaps the case of the researcher sitting at the back of a classroom coding up every three seconds the verbal exchanges between teacher and pupils by means of a structured set of observational categories.

Often the type of observation undertaken by the researcher is associated with the type of setting in which the research takes place. In Figure 14.1 we identify a continuum of settings ranging from the 'artificial' environments of the counsellor's and the therapist's clinics (cells 5 and 6) to the 'natural' environments of school classrooms, staffrooms and playgrounds (cells 1 and 2). Because our continuum is crude and arbitrary we are at liberty to locate studies of an information technology audit and computer usage (cells 3 and 4) somewhere between the 'artificial' and the 'natural' poles.

Although in theory each of the six examples of case studies in Figure 14.1 could have been undertaken either as a participant or as a non-participant observation study, a number of factors intrude to make one or other of the observational strategies the dominant mode of enquiry in a particular type of setting. Bailey (1994: 247) explains that it is hard for a researcher who wishes to undertake covert research not to act as a participant in a natural setting, as, if the researcher does not appear to be participating, then why is he/she there? Hence, in many natural settings the researchers will be participants. This is in contrast to laboratory or artificial settings, in which non-participant observation (e.g. through video recording) may take place.

What we are saying is that the unstructured, ethnographic account of teachers' work (cell 1) is the most typical method of observation in the natural surroundings of the school in which that study was conducted. Similarly, the structured inventories of study habits and personality employed in the study of Mr Chong (cell 6) reflect a common approach in the artificial setting of a counsellor's office.

14.6 Why participant observation?

The natural scientist, Schutz (1962) points out, explores a field that means nothing to the molecules, atoms and electrons therein. By contrast, the subject matter of the world in which the educational researcher is interested is composed of people and is essentially meaningful to them. That world is subjectively structured, possessing particular meanings for its inhabitants. The task of the educational investigator is very often to explain the means by which an orderly social world is established and maintained in terms of its shared meanings. How do participant observation techniques assist the researcher in this task? Bailey (1994: 243–4) identifies some inherent advantages in the participant observation approach:

1 Observation studies are superior to experiments and surveys when data are being collected on non-verbal behaviour.
2 In observation studies, investigators are able to discern ongoing behaviour as it occurs and are able to make appropriate notes about its salient features.
3 Because case study observations take place over an extended period of time, researchers can develop more intimate and informal relationships with those they are observing, generally in more natural environments than those in which experiments and surveys are conducted.
4 Case study observations are less reactive than other types of data-gathering methods. For example, in laboratory-based experiments and in surveys that depend upon verbal responses to structured questions, bias can be introduced in the very data that researchers are attempting to study.

Further, direct observation is faithful to the real-life, *in situ* and holistic nature of a case study (Verschuren, 2003: 131).

14.7 Planning a case study

In planning a case study there are several issues that researchers may find useful to consider (e.g. Adelman *et al.*, 1980):

■ The particular circumstances of the case, including: (a) the possible disruption to individual participants that participation might entail; (b) negotiating access to people; (c) negotiating ownership of the data; (d) negotiating release of the data.
■ The conduct of the study including: (a) the use of primary and secondary sources; (b) the opportunities to check data; (c) triangulation (including peer examination of the findings, respondent validation and reflexivity); (d) data collection methods – in the interpretive paradigm case studies tend to use certain data collection methods, e.g. semi-structured and open interviews, observation, narrative accounts and documents, diaries, maybe also tests, rather than other methods, e.g. surveys, experiments. Nisbet and Watt (1984) suggest that, in conducting interviews, it may be wiser to interview senior people later rather than earlier so that the most effective use of discussion time can be made, the interviewer having been put into the picture fully before the interview; (e) data analysis and interpretation, and, where appropriate, theory generation; (f) the writing of the report – Nisbet and Watt (1984) suggest that it is important to separate conclusions from the evidence, with the essential evidence included in the main text, and to balance illustration with analysis and generalization.
■ The consequences of the research (for participants). This might include the anonymizing of the research in order to protect participants, though such anonymization might suggest that a primary goal of case study is generalization rather than the portrayal of a unique case, i.e. it might go against a central feature of case study. Anonymizing reports might render them anodyne, and Adelman *et al.* (1980) suggest that the distortion that is involved in such anonymization – to render cases unrecognizable – might be too high a price to pay for going public.

Nisbet and Watt (1984: 78) suggest three main stages in undertaking a case study. Because case studies catch the dynamics of unfolding situations it is advisable to commence with a very wide field of focus, an open phase, without selectivity or prejudgement. Thereafter progressive focusing enables a narrower field of focus to be established, identifying key foci for subsequent study and data collection. At the third stage a draft interpretation is prepared which needs to be checked with respondents before appearing in the final form. Nisbet and Watt (p. 79) advise against the generation of hypotheses too early in a case study; rather, they suggest, it is important to gather data openly. Respondent validation can be particularly useful as respondents might suggest a better way of expressing the issue or may wish to add or qualify points.

There is a risk in respondent validation, however, that they may disagree with an interpretation. Nisbet and Watt (1984: 81) indicate the need to have negotiated rights to veto. They also recommend that researchers: (a) promise that respondents can see those sections of the report that refer to them (subject to controls for confidentiality, e.g. of others in the case study); (b) take full account of suggestions and responses made by respondents and, where possible, to modify the account; (c) in the case of disagreement between researchers and respondents, promise to publish respondents' comments and criticisms alongside the researchers' report.

Sturman (1997) places on a set of continua the nature of data collection, types and analysis techniques in case study research. These are presented in summary form (Table 14.1).

At one pole we have unstructured, typically qualitative data, whilst at the other we have structured, typically quantitative data. Researchers using case study approaches will need to decide which methods of data collection, which type of data and techniques of analysis to employ.

14.8 Data in case studies

We mentioned earlier that case studies are eclectic in the types of data that are used. Indeed many case studies will rely on mixed methods and a variety of data. Whilst observation and participant observation are often pre-eminent in case studies, they are by no means the only sources of data. For example Yin (2009: 101) identifies 'six sources of evidence':

- *Documents* (p. 103): e.g. letters, emails, memoranda, agendas, minutes, reports, records, diaries, notes, other studies, newspaper articles, website uploads, etc.
- *Archival records* (p. 105): e.g. public records, organizational records and reports, personal (maybe medical or behavioural) and personnel data stored in an organization (with due care to privacy legislation), charts and maps.
- *Interviews* (p. 106): in-depth, focused, and formal survey interviews (see Chapter 21).
- *Direct observation* (p. 109): i.e. non-participant observation of the natural setting and the target individual(s): groups *in situ*, artefacts, rooms, décor, layout.
- *Participant observation* (p. 111): in which the researcher takes on a role in the situation or context featured in the case study.
- *Physical artefacts* (p. 113): e.g. pictures, furniture, decorations, photographs, ornaments.

True to the principle of mixed methods research, the multiple sources of evidence can provide convergent and concurrent validity on a case, and they demand of the researcher an ability to handle and synthesize many

---

TABLE 14.1 CONTINUA OF DATA COLLECTION, TYPES AND ANALYSIS IN CASE STUDY RESEARCH

	Data Collection	
Unstructured (field notes)	⟷	Structured (survey, census data)
	(interviews – open to closed)	
	Data Types	
Narrative (field notes)	⟷	Numeric (ratio scale data)
	(coded qualitative data and non-parametric statistics)	
	Data Analysis	
Journalistic (impressionistic)	⟷	Statistical (inferential statistics)
	(content analysis)	

Source: Adapted from Sturman, 1997

kinds of data simultaneously. This, in turn, advocates the compilation of a case study database of evidence (Yin, 2009: 118) that comprises two main kinds of collection: the actual data gathered, recorded and organized by entry, and the researcher's ongoing analysis/report/comments/narrative on the data.

Not only do the diverse data provide the evidence needed for the researcher to draw conclusions, but they provide the evidential 'chain of evidence' that gives credibility, reliability and validity to the case study (Yin, 2009: 122). When writing the report, the researcher must allude – by direct reference – to the actual evidence that supports the point being made, and it is to the writing of the case study report that we turn below.

The researcher gathers data; this is only one stage of the case study, as those data still have to be analysed. Whilst the analysis is the task of the researcher, there are several computer-assisted software tools that can process the data ready for analysis, for example NVivo, NUD*IST, Ethnograph, ATLAS.ti, HyperRESEARCH. These can group, retrieve, organize and search single and multiple data sets, and return these ready for analysis and presentation in such forms as, for example (Miles and Huberman, 1984):

- matrices and arrays of data;
- patterns, themes and configurations;
- narratives;
- data displays;
- flowcharts;
- within-site and cross-site analyses;
- cause-and-effect diagrams and chains (e.g. where an effect becomes a subsequent cause);
- networks of relationships or linked events (i.e. rather than linear models of cause and effect (Morrison, 2009: chapter 7));
- chronologies and causal sequences;
- time-series and critical events;
- key issues and subordinate issues;
- explanations;
- tabulations;
- grounded theory.

We return to these in Part 5. Yin (2009: 143) makes the point that the analysis of data is an iterative process, i.e. the researcher has to go back through the data several times to ensure that all the data fit the interpretations given or conclusions drawn, i.e. without unexplained anomalies or contradictions (the constant comparison method), that all the data are accounted for (p. 160), that rival interpretations are considered (p. 160) and that the significance features of the case are highlighted (p. 161).

14.9 Recording observations

> I filled thirty-two notebooks with about half a million words of notes made during nearly six hundred hours [of observation].
>
> (King, 1979)

The recording of observations is a frequent source of concern to inexperienced case study researchers. How much ought to be recorded? In what form should the recordings be made? What does one do with the mass of recorded data? Lofland (1971) gives a number of useful suggestions about collecting field notes:

- Record the notes as quickly as possible after observation, since the quantity of information forgotten is very slight over a short period of time but accelerates quickly as more time passes.
- Discipline yourself to write notes quickly and reconcile yourself to the fact that although it may seem ironic, recording of field notes can be expected to take as long as is spent in actual observation.
- Dictating rather than writing is acceptable if one can afford it, but writing has the advantage of stimulating thought.
- Typing field notes is vastly preferable to handwriting because it is faster and easier to read, especially when making multiple copies.
- It is advisable to make at least two copies of field notes and preferable to type on a master for reproduction. One original copy is retained for reference and other copies can be used as rough draught to be cut up, reorganized and rewritten.
- The notes ought to be full enough adequately to summon up for one again, months later, a reasonably vivid picture of any described event. This probably means that one ought to be writing up, at the very minimum, at least a couple of single space typed pages for every hour of observation.

The sort of note-taking recommended by Lofland (1971) and actually undertaken by King (1979) and Wolcott (1973) in their ethnographic accounts grows out of the nature of the unstructured observation study. Note-taking, confessed Wolcott, helped him fight the acute boredom that he sometimes felt when observing the interminable meetings that are the daily lot of the school principal. Occasionally, however, a series of events would occur so quickly that Wolcott had time only to make cursory notes which he supplemented later with fuller accounts. One useful tip from this experienced ethnographer is worth noting: never resume your observations until the notes from the

---

BOX 14.3   THE CASE STUDY AND PROBLEMS OF SELECTION

Among the issues confronting the researcher at the outset of his case study are the problems of selection. The following questions indicate some of the obstacles in this respect:

1 How do you get from the initial idea to the working design (from the idea to a specification, to usable data)?
2 What do you lose in the process?
3 What unwanted concerns do you take on board as a result?
4 How do you find a site which provides the best location for the design?
5 How do you locate, identify and approach key informants?
6 How they see you creates a context within which you see them. How can you handle such social complexities?
7 How do you record evidence? When? How much?
8 How do you file and categorize it?
9 How much time do you give to thinking and reflecting about what you are doing?
10 At what points do you show your subject what you are doing?
11 At what points do you give them control over who sees what?
12 Who sees the reports first?

Source: Adapted from Walker, 1980

---

preceding observation are complete. There is nothing to be gained merely by your presence as an observer. Until your observations and impressions from one visit are a matter of record, there is little point in returning to the classroom or school and reducing the impact of one set of events by superimposing another and more recent set. Indeed, when to record one's data is but one of a number of practical problems identified by Walker, which are listed in Box 14.3 (Walker, 1980).

14.10 Writing up a case study

The writing up of a case study abides by the twin notions of 'fitness for purpose' and 'fitness for audience'. Robson (2002: 512–13) and Yin (2009: 176–9) suggests six forms of organizing the writing-up of a case study:

■ In the *suspense structure* the author presents the main findings (e.g. an executive summary) in the opening part of the report and then devotes the remainder of the report to providing evidence, analysis, explanations, justifications (e.g. for what is selected in or out, what conclusions are drawn, what alternative explanations are rejected) and argument that leads to the overall picture or conclusion.

■ In the *narrative report* a prose account is provided, interspersed with relevant figures, tables, emergent issues, analysis and conclusion.

■ In the *comparative structure* the same case is exam-

ined through two or more lenses (e.g. explanatory, descriptive, theoretical) in order either to provide a rich, all-round account of the case, or to enable the reader to have sufficient information from which to judge which of the explanations, descriptions or theories best fit(s) the data.

■ In the *chronological structure* a simple sequence or chronology is used as the organizational principle, thereby enabling not only cause and effect to be addressed, but also possessing the strength of an ongoing story. Adding to Robson's comments, the chronology can be sectionalized as appropriate (e.g. key events or key time frames), and intersperse (a) commentaries on, (b) interpretations of and explanations for, and (c) summaries of, emerging issues as events unfold (e.g. akin to 'memoing' in ethnographic research). The chronology becomes an organizing principle, but different kinds of contents are included at each stage of the chronological sequence.

■ In the *theory-generating structure*, the structure follows a set of theoretical constructs or a case that is being made. Here, Robson suggests, each succeeding section of the case study contributes to, or constitutes, an element of a developing 'theoretical formulation', providing a link in the chain of argument, leading eventually to the overall theoretical formulation.

■ In the *unsequenced structures* the sequence, e.g. chronological, issue-based, event-based, theory-based, is unimportant. Robson suggests that this approach renders it difficult for the reader to know which areas are important or unimportant, or whether there are any omissions. It risks the caprice of the writer.

Some case studies are of a single situation – a single child, a single social group, a single class, a single school. Here any of the above six approaches may be appropriate. Some case studies require an unfolding of events, some case studies operate under a 'snapshot' approach (e.g. of several schools, or classes, or groups at a particular point in time). In the former it may be important to preserve the chronology, whereas in the latter such a chronology may be irrelevant. Some case studies are divided into two main parts (e.g. Willis, 1977): the data reporting and then the analysis/interpretation/explanation.

Yin (2009: 133) makes the important point that a case study report should consider rival explanations of the findings and indicate how the explanation adopted is better than its rivals. Such rival explanations might include, for example (cf. Yin, 2009: 135):

- the role of chance/coincidence;
- experimenter effects or situation effects (reactivity);
- researcher bias;
- other influences on the case;
- covariance or the influence of another variable, i.e. a cause other than the intervention or situation reported explains the effects;
- alternative explanations of what the data show;
- the *process* of the intervention, rather than its contents, explain the outcome;
- a different theory can explain the findings more fully and fittingly;
- the intervention was part of a much bigger intervention that was already taking place at the time of the

case study, so is subsumed by that bigger intervention;
- observed changes might have happened anyway, without the intervention from the case study.

14.11 Conclusion

The different strategies we have illustrated in our six examples of case studies in a variety of educational settings suggest that participant observation is best thought of as a generic term that describes a methodological approach rather than one specific method.[1] What our examples have shown is that the representativeness of a particular sample often relates to the observational strategy open to the researcher. Generally speaking, the larger the sample, the more representative it is, and the more likely that the observer's role is of a participant nature.

Macpherson *et al.* (2000: 57–8) set out several principles to guide the practice of case study research. With regard to *purpose*, they suggest a collaborative approach between participants and researcher in order to address *contextuality*. With regard to *place*, they suggest *sensitivity* to the place (akin to ecological validity). With regard to both *purpose* and *process*, they suggest *authenticity* (fitness for purpose), *applicability* (thinking large but starting small) and *growth* (ensuring development and social transformation). With regard to *product*, they suggest *communicability* of the findings through networking (which they also apply to *purpose* and *process*).

Yin (2009: 185–9) suggests that an 'exemplary' case study must be 'significant', 'complete', considering of 'alternative perspectives', careful to include 'sufficient evidence' and 'engaging'. These precepts, surely, can provide a useful guide for researchers.

For examples of case studies, see, for example, Macpherson *et al.*'s (2000) study of schooling in Australia, and the accompanying website.

 Companion Website

The companion website to the book includes PowerPoint slides for this chapter, which list the structure of the chapter and then provide a summary of the key points in each of its sections. In addition there is further information in the form of case study examples. These resources can be found online at **www.routledge.com/ textbooks/cohen7e**.

Ex post facto research

This kind of research may be unfamiliar to novice researchers. Hence this chapter introduces *ex post facto* research, its key features and how to conduct such a project. It includes:

- co-relational and criterion groups designs
- characteristics of *ex post facto* research
- occasions when appropriate
- advantages and disadvantages of *ex post facto* research
- designing an *ex post facto* investigation
- procedures in *ex post facto* research

As an introduction to experiments in educational research in Chapter 16, this chapter indicates how researchers can work with data to construct forms of experimentation and to explore cause and effect in such studies.

15.1 Introduction

When translated literally, *ex post facto* means 'after the fact'; it signifies 'from what is done afterwards', 'from after the event' or 'from what has happened'. In the context of social and educational research the phrase means 'retrospectively' and refers to those studies which investigate possible cause-and-effect relationships by observing an existing condition or state of affairs and searching back in time for plausible causal factors. In terms of Chapter 4 on causation, this is examining the causes of effects, and we advise readers to refer to that chapter. Here researchers ask themselves what factors seem to be associated with certain occurrences, or conditions, or aspects of behaviour. As they have happened already, the researcher has to hypothesize possible causes and then test them against the evidence, for example by holding factors constant and by controlling and matching the samples.

Ex post facto research is a method of teasing out possible antecedents of events that have happened and cannot, therefore, be controlled, engineered or manipulated by the investigator (Cooper and Schindler, 2001: 136). Researchers can only report what has happened or what is happening, by trying to hold factors constant by careful attention to the sampling. Independent variables cannot be manipulated as in true experiments, as they have already happened. Hence the researcher is in the realms of probabilistic causation, inferring causes tentatively rather than being able to demonstrate causality unequivocally.

Ex post facto research can be used to study groups which are similar and which have had the same experience with the exception of one condition, and here the effect of the one differing condition on the dependent variable can be assessed. *Ex post facto* research, then, is a form of experiment, but without the stringent controls of a true experiment; there are control and 'experimental' groups (the latter where a particular condition has been applied), but, since there is little or no rigorous manipulation of the independent variables or conditions, and since there is no random allocation of subjects to groups, any inferences of causation are tentative.

The following example will illustrate the basic idea. Imagine a situation in which there has been a dramatic increase in the number of fatal road accidents in a particular locality. An expert is called in to investigate. Naturally, there is no way in which she can study the actual accidents because they have happened; nor can she turn to technology for a video replay of the incidents; nor can she require a participant to run under a bus or a lorry, or to stand in the way of a speeding motorcycle in order to discover the effects. What she can do, however, is to study hospital records to see which groups have experienced the greatest trauma – bus, lorry or motorcycle impact victims. Or she can attempt a reconstruction by studying the statistics, examining the accident spots, and taking note of the statements given by victims and witnesses. In this way the expert will be in a position to identify possible determinants of the accidents, looking at the outcomes and working backwards to examine possible causes. These may include excessive speed, poor road conditions, careless driving, frustration, inefficient vehicles, the effects of drugs or alcohol and so on. On the basis of her examination, she can formulate hypotheses as to the likely causes and submit them to the appropriate authority in the form of recommendations. These may include improving road conditions, or lowering the speed limit, or increasing police surveillance, for instance. The point of interest to us is that in identifying the causes retrospectively, the expert adopts an *ex post facto* perspective.

Ex post facto research is a method that can also be used instead of an experiment, to test hypotheses about cause and effect in situations where it is impossible, impractical or unethical to control or manipulate the dependent variable or, indeed, the independent variables. We cannot expose people, say, to an aeroplane crash or place emotionally stable children in controlled traumatic environments in order to study the effects (Lord, 1973: 2).

For example, let us say that we wish to test the hypothesis that family violence causes poor school performance. Here, ethically speaking, we should not expose a student to family violence. However, one could put students into two groups, matched carefully on a range of factors, with one group comprising those who have experienced family violence and the other whose domestic circumstances are more acceptable. If the hypothesis is supportable then the researcher should be able to discover a difference in school performance between the two groups when the other variables are matched or held as constant as possible.

Kerlinger (1970) has defined *ex post facto* research as that in which the independent variable or variables have already occurred and in which the researcher starts with the observation of a dependent variable or variables. She then studies the independent variable or variables in retrospect for their possible relationship to, and effects on, the dependent variable or variables. The researcher is thus examining retrospectively the effects of a naturally occurring event on a subsequent outcome with a view to establishing a causal link between them. The key to establishing the causes is the careful identification of those that are possible, testing each against the evidence, and then eliminating the ones that do not stand up to the test, ensuring that attention is paid to careful sampling and to controls – holding fixed some variables.

Some instances of *ex post facto* designs correspond to experimental research in reverse, for instead of taking groups that are equivalent and subjecting them to different treatments so as to bring about differences in the dependent variables to be measured, an *ex post facto* experiment begins with groups that are already different in some respect and searches in retrospect for the factor that brought about the difference. Indeed Spector (1993: 42) suggests that *ex post facto* research

is a procedure that is intended to transform a non-experimental research design into a pseudo-experimental form. An *ex post facto* experiment, then, is a form of quasi-experiment (see Chapter 16).

One can discern two approaches to *ex post facto* research. In the first approach one commences with subjects who differ on an *independent* variable, for example their years of study in mathematics, and then study how they differ on the dependent variable, e.g. a mathematics test. In a second approach, one can commence with subjects who differ on the *dependent* variable (e.g. their performance in a mathematics test) and discover how they differ on a range of independent variables (e.g. their years of study, their liking for the subject, the amount of homework they do in mathematics). The *ex post facto* research here seeks to discover the causes of a particular outcome (mathematics test performance) by comparing those students in whom the outcome is high (high marks on the mathematics test) with students whose outcome is low (low marks on the mathematics test), after the independent variable has occurred.

Ary *et al.* (2009: 335) discuss 'proactive' and 'retroactive' *ex post facto* research designs. In the former, the subjects are grouped on the basis of the presence or absence of an independent variable, and then the researcher compares the groups in terms of the outcomes – the dependent variable. In the latter, the dependent variable is constant, and the researcher seeks to discover the independent variables that might have contributed to the outcome, hypothesizing about these independent variables and then testing them against the evidence. Figure 15.1 indicates these two main types of *ex post facto research* designs.

An example of an *ex post facto piece* of research can be presented. It has been observed that staff at a very large secondary school have been absent on days when they teach difficult classes. An *ex post facto* piece of research was conducted to try to establish the causes of this. Staff absences on days when teaching difficult secondary classes were noted.

	Days when teaching difficult secondary classes	
Absences	Yes	No
High	26	30
Low	22	50
Total	48	80
Overall total: 128		

Here the question of time was important: were the staff absent only on days when they were teaching

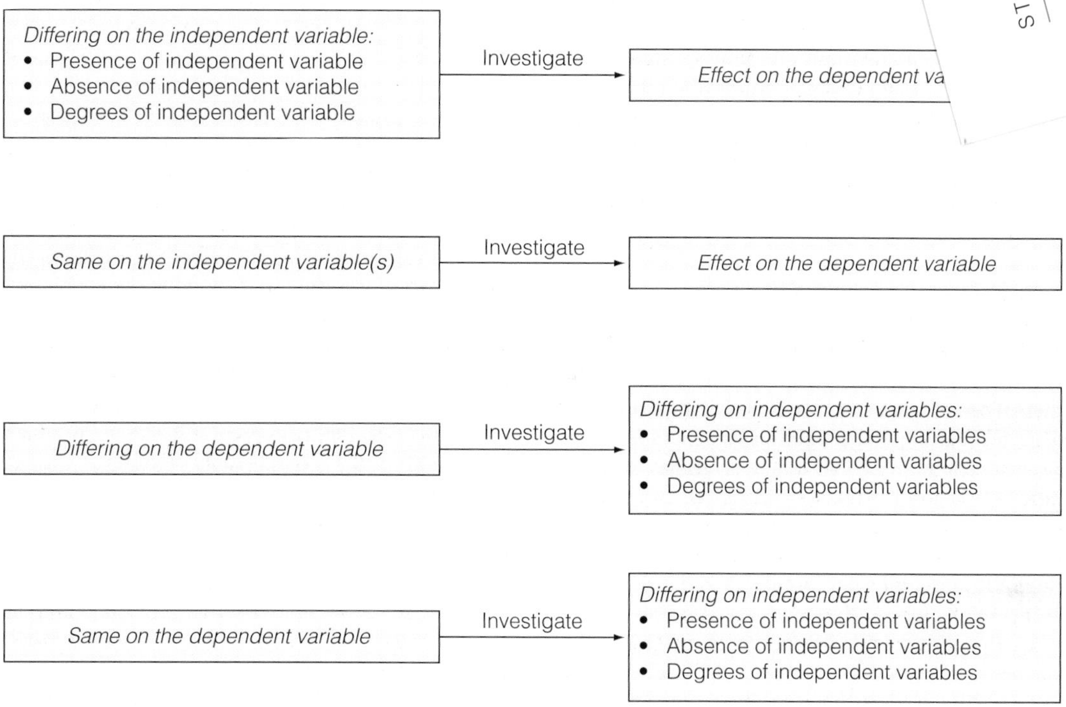

FIGURE 15.1 Four types of *ex post facto* research

difficult classes or at other times? Were there other variables that could be factored into the study, for example age groups? Hence the study was refined further, collecting more data.

	Days when teaching difficult secondary classes		Days when not teaching difficult secondary classes	
Age	High absence	Low absence	High absence	Low absence
<30 years old	30	6	16	10
30–50 years old	4	4	4	20
>50 years old	2	2	2	28
Total	36	12	22	58
Overall total: 128				

This shows that age was also a factor as well as days when teaching difficult secondary classes: younger people are more likely to be absent. Most teachers who were absent were under 30 years of age. Within age groups, it is also clear that young teachers have a higher incidence of excessive absence when teaching difficult secondary classes than teachers of the same (young) age group when they are not teaching difficult secondary classes.

Of course, a further check here would be to compare the absence rates of the same teachers when they do and do not teach difficult classes, and conduct difference tests (e.g. t-tests, ANOVA: see Chapter 36) to examine differences between the two sets of scores (days when difficult classes were taught and days when they were not taught; differences between age groups in respect of the days when difficult classes were and were not taught).

15.2 Co-relational and criterion groups designs

Two kinds of design may be identified in *ex post facto* research – the co-relational study and the criterion group study. The former is sometimes termed 'causal research' and the latter, 'causal-comparative research'. A co-relational (or causal) study is concerned with identifying the antecedents of a present condition. As

...s name suggests, it involves the collection of two sets of data, one of which will be retrospective, with a view to determining the relationship between them. The basic design of such an experiment may be represented thus (using the symbols from Campbell and Stanley, 1963, where X=the independent variable and O=the dependent variable, discussed below):

$$X \rightarrow O$$

A study by Borkowsky (1970) was based upon this kind of design. He attempted to show a relationship between the quality of a music teacher's undergraduate training (X) and his subsequent effectiveness as a teacher of his subject (O). Measures of the quality of a music teacher's college training can include grades in specific courses, overall grade average and self-ratings, etc. Teacher effectiveness can be assessed by indices of pupil performance, pupil knowledge, pupil attitudes and judgement of experts, etc. Correlations between all measures were obtained to determine the relationship. At most, this study could show that a relationship existed, after the fact, between the quality of teacher preparation and subsequent teacher effectiveness. Where a strong relationship is found between the independent and dependent variables, three possible interpretations are open to the researcher:

1 that the variable X has caused O;
2 that the variable O has caused X; or
3 that some third unidentified, and therefore unmeasured, variable has caused X and O.

It is often the case that a researcher cannot tell which of these is correct. This raises the issue of the direction of causality: it is difficult in an *ex post facto* experiment to determine what causes what: whether A causes B or B causes A.

The value of co-relational or causal studies lies chiefly in their exploratory or suggestive character for, as we have seen, while they are not always adequate in themselves for establishing causal relationships among variables, they are a useful first step in this direction in that they do yield measures of association.

In the criterion group (or causal-comparative) approach, the investigator sets out to discover possible causes for a phenomenon being studied, by comparing the subjects in which the variable is present with similar subjects in whom it is absent, i.e. noting the circumstances in which a given effect occurs and does not occur (Lord, 1973: 3). The basic design in this kind of study may be represented thus:

If, for example, a researcher chose such a design to investigate factors contributing to teacher effectiveness, the criterion group O_1 (the effective teachers) and its counterpart O_2 (a group *not* showing the characteristics of the criterion group) are identified by measuring the differential effects of the groups on classes of children. The researcher may then examine X, some variable or event, such as the background, training, skills and personality of the groups, to discover what might 'cause' only some teachers to be effective.

Morrison (2009: 181) gives an example of a criterion group piece of *ex post facto* research. He writes thus:

Let us imagine, for example, that the researcher is seeking to establish the cause of effective teaching, and hypothesizes that one cause is collegial curriculum planning with other members of the department. The research could be designed [as in Figure 15.2].

Here there are two criterion groups: (a) the presence of collegial curriculum planning; and (b) the absence of collegial curriculum planning. By examining the difference in teaching effectiveness between those teachers (however one wished to measure 'effective teaching') who did and did not plan their curriculum with colleagues (collegial curriculum planning) one could infer a possible causal difference. But one has to be cautious: at most this is a correlational study and causation is not the same as correlation. Indeed … a third cause may be influencing both the effective/ineffective teaching and the presence/absence of collegial curriculum planning, e.g. staff sociability.

(Morrison, 2009: 181)

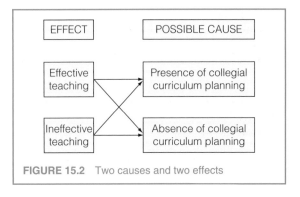

FIGURE 15.2 *Two causes and two effects*

The causal-comparative design is different from a historical design, in that the former is concerned with present events, whereas the latter traces the history of past events (Lord, 1973: 4).

Criterion group or causal-comparative studies may be seen as bridging the gap between descriptive research methods on the one hand and true experimental research on the other.

15.3 Characteristics of *ex post facto* research

In *ex post facto* research the researcher takes the effect (or dependent variable) and examines the data retrospectively to establish causes, relationships or associations, and their meanings.

Other characteristics of *ex post facto* research become apparent when it is contrasted with true experimental research. Kerlinger (1970) describes the *modus operandi* of the experimental researcher. ('If *x*, then *y*' in Kerlinger's usage. We have substituted *X* for *x* and *O* for *y* to fit in with Campbell and Stanley's (1963) conventions throughout the chapter.) Kerlinger hypothesizes: if *X*, then *O*; if frustration, then aggression. Depending on circumstances and his own predilections in research design, he uses some method to manipulate *X*. He then observes *O* to see if concomitant variation, the variation expected or predicted from the variation in *X*, occurs. If it does, this is evidence for the validity of the proposition, *X-O*, meaning 'If *X*, then *O*'. Note that the scientist here predicts from a controlled *X* to *O*. To help him achieve control, he can use the principle of randomization and active manipulation of *X* and can assume, other things being equal, that *O* is varying as a result of the manipulation of *X*.

In *ex post facto* designs, on the other hand, *O* is observed. Then a retrospective search for *X* ensues. An *X* is found that is plausible and agrees with the hypothesis. Due to lack of control of *X* and other possible *X*s, the truth of the hypothesized relation between *X* and *O* cannot be asserted with the confidence of the experimental researcher. Basically, then, *ex post facto* investigations have, so to speak, a built-in weakness: lack of control of the independent variable or variables. As Spector (1993: 43) suggests, it is impossible to isolate and control every possible variable, or to know with absolute certainty which are the most crucial variables.

This brief comparison highlights the most important difference between the two designs – control. In the experimental situation, investigators at least have manipulative control; they have as a minimum one active variable. If an experiment is a 'true' experiment, they can also exercise control by randomization. They can assign subjects to groups randomly; or, at the very least, they can assign treatments to groups at random. In the *ex post facto* research situation, this control of the independent variable is not possible, and, perhaps more important, neither is randomization. Investigators must take things as they are and try to disentangle them, though having said this, they can make use of selected procedures that will give them an element of control in this research. These we shall touch upon shortly.

By their very nature, *ex post facto* experiments can provide support for any number of different, perhaps even contradictory, hypotheses; they are so completely flexible that it is largely a matter of postulating hypotheses according to one's personal preference. The investigator begins with certain data and looks for an interpretation consistent with them; often, however, a number of interpretations may be at hand. Consider again the hypothetical increase in road accidents in a given town. A retrospective search for causes will disclose half a dozen plausible ones.

Experimental studies, by contrast, begin with a specific interpretation and then determine whether it is congruent with externally derived data. Frequently, causal relationships seem to be established on nothing more substantial than the premise that any related event occurring prior to the phenomenon under study is assumed to be its cause – the classical *post hoc, ergo propter hoc* fallacy ('after this, therefore because of this'); just because one variable precedes another in time, it does not follow that the first variable *causes* the second: I may drink coffee and then have a sleepless night, but it does not follow that drinking the coffee *caused* the sleepless night – there may have been other causes (Cohen and Nagel, 1961). Even when we do find a relationship between two variables, we must recognize the possibility that both are individual results of a common third factor rather than the first being necessarily the cause of the second.

As we have seen earlier, there is also the real possibility of reverse causation, e.g. that a heart condition promotes obesity rather than the other way around, or that they encourage each other. The point is that the evidence simply *illustrates* the hypothesis; it does not test it, since hypotheses cannot be tested on the same data from which they were derived. The relationship noted may actually exist, but it is not necessarily the only relationship, or perhaps the crucial one. Before we can accept that smoking is the primary cause of lung cancer, we have to rule out alternative hypotheses.

Further, a researcher may find that watching television correlates with poor school performance. Now, it may be there is a causal effect here: watching television causes poor school performance; or there may be reverse causality: poor school performance causes students to watch more television. However, there may be a third explanation: students who, for whatever reason (e.g. ability, motivation), do not do well at school also like watching television; it may be the third variable (the independent variable of ability or motivation) that is causing the other two outcomes (watching a lot of television or poor school performance).

We must not conclude from what has just been said that *ex post facto* studies are of little value; many of our important investigations in education and psychology are *ex post facto* designs. There is often no choice in the matter: an investigator cannot cause one group to become failures, delinquent, suicidal, brain-damaged or dropouts. Research must of necessity rely on existing groups. On the other hand, the inability of *ex post facto* designs to incorporate the basic need for control (e.g. through manipulation or randomization) makes them vulnerable from a scientific point of view and the possibility of their being misleading should be clearly acknowledged. *Ex post facto* designs are probably better conceived more circumspectly, not as experiments with the greater certainty that these denote, but more as surveys, useful as sources of hypotheses to be tested by more conventional experimental means at a later date.

15.4 Occasions when appropriate

Ex post facto designs are appropriate in circumstances where the more powerful experimental method is not possible. These arise when, for example, it is not possible to select, control and manipulate the factors necessary to study cause-and-effect relationships directly; or when the control of all variables except a single independent variable may be unrealistic and artificial, preventing the normal interaction with other influential variables; or when laboratory controls for many research purposes would be impractical, costly or ethically undesirable.

Ex post facto research is particularly suitable in social, educational and – to a lesser extent – psychological contexts where the independent variable or variables lie outside the researcher's control. Examples of the method abound in these areas: the research on cigarette smoking and lung cancer, for instance; or studies of teacher characteristics; or studies examining the relationship between political and religious affiliation and attitudes; or investigations into the relationship between school achievement and independent variables such as social class, race, sex and intelligence. Many of these may be divided into large-scale or small-scale *ex post*

facto studies, for example Stables' (1990) large-scale study of differences between students from mixed and single-sex schools and Arnold and Atkins's (1991) small-scale study of the social and emotional adjustment of hearing-impaired students.

Ayres (2008) demonstrates the power of probabilities and regularities in *ex post facto* designs (e.g. surveys), yielded by data sets from extremely large samples and subsamples, particularly when the analysis takes account of standard deviations (two standard deviations accounting for 95 per cent of the population). These are important in evidence-based education and may be more reliable than human intuition (e.g. Ayres 2008: chapter 10).

For educational research, public domain databases and data sets can be used for conducting *ex post facto* educational research, for example databases and data sets produced by:

- governments (e.g. http://data.gov.uk/data/all; www.dcsf.gov.uk/rsgateway/; http://data.gov.uk/data/list?keyword=education); www.hesa.ac.uk; www.gsr.gov.uk;
- research agencies (e.g. www.data-archive.ac.uk/);
- consortia (e.g. www.icpsr.umich.edu/icpsrweb/ICPSR/access/index.jsp; www.socsciresearch.com/r6.html);
- organizations (e.g:
  - The European Union: http://eacea.ec.europa.eu/portal/page/portal/Eurydice/EuryPresentation;
  - The OECD: http://stats.oecd.org/index.aspx; www.oecd.org/document/54/0,3343,en_2649_39263238_38082166_1_1_1_37455,00.html; www.oecd.org/statsportal/0,3352,en_2825_293564_1_1_1_1_1,00.html; www.oecd.org/document/54/0,3343,en_2649_39263238_38082166_1_1_1_37455,00.html; www.oecd.org/topicstatsportal/0,2647,en_2825_495609_1_1_1_1_1,00.html;
  - UNESCO (Institute for Statistics): www.uis.unesco.org/ev.php?URL_ID=2867&URL_DO=DO_TOPIC&URL_SECTION=201; http://stats.uis.unesco.org/unesco/TableViewer/document.aspx?ReportId=143&IF_Language=eng;
  - The PISA database (http://pisa2006.acer.edu.au/);
  - The World Bank: http://web.worldbank.org/WBSITE/EXTERNAL/DATASTATISTICS/0,,contentMDK:20519297~pagePK:64133150~piPK:64133175~theSitePK:239419,00.html;
  - The TIMSS database (http://nces.ed.gov/timss/datafiles.asp);
- individual data sets (e.g. www.bera.ac.uk/the-use-of-large-scale-data-sets-in-educational-research/);

■ data sets held in higher education institutions (e.g. www.bristol.ac.uk/cmpo/plug/; www.bristol.ac.uk/cmpo/plug/support-docs/; www.cls.ioe.ac.uk/text.asp?section=000100010002).

15.5 Advantages and disadvantages of *ex post facto* research

Among the advantages of the approach are the following:

■ *Ex post facto* research meets an important need of the researcher where the more rigorous experimental approach is not possible. In the case of the alleged relationship between smoking and lung cancer, for instance, this cannot be tested experimentally (at least as far as human beings are concerned).

■ The method yields useful information concerning the nature of phenomena – what goes with what and under what conditions. In this way, *ex post facto* research is a valuable exploratory tool.

■ Improvements in statistical techniques and general methodology have made *ex post facto* designs more defensible.

■ In some ways and in certain situations the method is more useful than the experimental method, especially where the setting up of the latter would introduce a note of artificiality into research proceedings.

■ *Ex post facto* research is particularly appropriate when simple cause-and-effect relationships are being explored.

■ The method can give a sense of direction and provide a fruitful source of hypotheses that can subsequently be tested by the more rigorous experimental method.

Among the limitations and weaknesses of *ex post facto* designs the following may be mentioned:

■ There is the problem of lack of control in that the researcher is unable to manipulate the independent variable or to randomize her subjects.

■ One cannot know for certain whether the causative factor has been included or even identified.

■ It may be that no single factor is the cause.

■ A particular outcome may result from different causes on different occasions.

■ When a relationship has been discovered, there is the problem of deciding which is the cause and which the effect; the possibility of reverse causation must be considered.

■ The relationship of two factors does not establish cause and effect.

■ The *ex post facto* hypothesis is generated after the data have been collected, so it is not possible to disconfirm it (Babbie, 2010: 462).

■ Classifying into dichotomous groups can be problematic.

■ There is the difficulty of interpretation and the danger of the *post hoc* assumption being made, that is believing that because *X* precedes *O*, *X* causes *O*.

■ As the researcher attempts to match groups on key variables, this leads to shrinkage of sample (Spector, 1993: 43). (Lewis-Beck (1993: 43) reports an example of such shrinkage from a sample of 1,194 to 46 after matching had been undertaken.)

■ It often bases its conclusions on too limited a sample or number of occurrences.

■ It frequently fails to single out the really significant factor or factors, and fails to recognize that events have multiple rather than single causes.

■ As a method it is regarded by some as too flexible.

■ It lacks nullifiability and confirmation.

15.6 Designing an *ex post facto* investigation

We earlier referred to the two basic designs embraced by *ex post facto* research – the co-relational (or causal) model and the criterion group (or causal-comparative) model. As we saw, the causal model attempts to identify the antecedent of a present condition and may be represented thus:

Independent variable	*Dependent variable*
X	*O*

Although one variable in an *ex post facto* study cannot be confidently said to depend upon the other as would be the case in a truly experimental investigation, it is nevertheless usual to designate one of the variables as independent (*X*) and the other as dependent (*O*). The left to right dimension indicates the temporal order, though having established this, we must not overlook the possibility of reverse causality.

In a typical investigation of this kind, then, two sets of data relating to the independent and dependent variables respectively will be gathered. As indicated earlier in the chapter, the data on the independent variable (*X*) will be retrospective in character and as such will be prone to the kinds of weakness, limitations and distortions to which all historical evidence is subject. Let us now translate the design into a hypothetical situation. Imagine a secondary school in which it is hypothesized that low staff morale (*O*) has come about as a direct result of reorganization some two years earlier, say. A number of key factors distinguishing the new organization from the previous one can be readily identified. Collectively these could represent or contain the independent variable X and data on them could be accumulated retrospectively. They could include, for example, the introduction of mixed ability and team teaching, curricular innovation, loss of teacher status, decline in student motivation, modifications to the school catchment area or the appointment of a new headteacher. These could then be checked against a measure of prevailing teachers' attitudes (O), thus providing the researcher with some leads at least as to possible causes of current discontent.

The second model, the causal-comparative, may be represented schematically as:

Group	Independent variable	Dependent variable
E	X	O_1
C		O_2

Using this model, the investigator hypothesizes the independent variable and then compares two groups, an experimental group (E) which has been exposed to the presumed independent variable X and a control group (C) which has not. (The dashed line in the model shows that the comparison groups E and C are not equated by random assignment.) Alternatively, she may examine two groups that are different in some way or ways and then try to account for the difference or differences by investigating possible antecedents. These two examples reflect two types of approach to causal-comparative research: the 'cause-to-effect' kind and the 'effect-to-cause' kind.

The basic design of causal-comparative investigations is similar to an experimentally designed study. The chief difference resides in the nature of the independent variable, X. In a truly experimental situation, this will be under the control of the investigator and may therefore be described as manipulable. In the causal-comparative model (and also the causal model), however, the independent variable is beyond her control, having already occurred. It may therefore be described in this design as non-manipulable.

15.7 Procedures in *ex post facto* research

Ex post facto research is concerned with discovering relationships among variables in one's data; and we have seen how this may be accomplished by using either a causal or causal-comparative model. We now examine the steps involved in implementing a piece of *ex post facto* research. We may begin by identifying the problem area to be investigated. This stage will be followed by a clear and precise statement of the hypothesis to be tested or questions to be answered. The next step will be to make explicit the assumptions on which the hypothesis and subsequent procedures will be based. A review of the research literature will follow. This will enable the investigator to ascertain the kinds of issues, problems, obstacles and findings disclosed by previous studies in the area. There will then follow the planning of the actual investigation and this will consist of three broad stages – identification of the population and samples; the selection and construction of techniques for collecting data; and the establishment of categories for classifying the data. The final stage will involve the description, analysis and interpretation of the findings.

Drawing on Lord (1973: 6) we can set out several stages in conducting an *ex post facto* piece of research:

Stage 1: Define the problem and survey the literature.
Stage 2: State the hypotheses and the assumptions or premises on which the hypotheses and research procedures are based.
Stage 3: Select the subjects (sampling) and identify the methods for collecting the data.
Stage 4: Identify the criteria and categories for classifying the data to fit the purposes of the study and which are as unambiguous as possible and which will enable relationships and similarities to be found.
Stage 5: Gather data on those factors which are always present in which the given outcome occurs, and discard the data in which those factors are not always present.
Stage 6: Gather data on those factors which are always present in which the given outcome does not occur.
Stage 7: Compare the two sets of data (i.e. subtract the former (Stage 5) from the latter (Stage 6), in order to be able to infer the causes that are responsible for the occurrence or non-occurrence of the outcome.
Stage 8: Analyse, interpret and report the findings.

One has to bear in mind that the evidence illustrates rather than tests the hypothesis here (Lord, 1973: 7). It was noted earlier that the principal weakness of *ex post facto* research is the absence of control over the independent variable influencing the dependent variable in the case of causal designs or affecting observed differences between dependent variables in the case of causal-comparative designs. Although the *ex post facto* researcher is denied not only this kind of control but also the principle of randomization, she can nevertheless utilize procedures that provide some measure of control in her investigation; it is to some of these that we now turn.

One of the commonest means of introducing control into this type of research is that of matching the subjects in the experimental and control groups where the design is causal-comparative. Ary *et al.* (2009) indicate that matched pair designs (see Chapter 16) are careful to match the participants on important and relevant characteristics that may have a bearing on the research (for an example of this see Leow, 2009).

There are difficulties with this procedure, however, for it assumes that the investigator knows what the relevant factors are, that is the factors that may be related to the dependent variable. Further, there is the possibility of losing those subjects who cannot be matched, thus reducing one's sample.

As an alternative procedure for introducing a degree of control into *ex post facto* research, Ary and his colleagues (2009) suggest building the extraneous independent variables into the design and then using an analysis of variance technique. For example, if intelligence is a relevant extraneous variable but it is not possible to control it through matching or other means, then it could be added to the research as another independent variable, with the participants being classified in terms of intelligence levels. Through analysis of variance techniques the dependent variable measures would then be analysed and this would reveal the main and interaction effects of intelligence, indicating any statistically significant differences between the groups on the dependent variable, even though no causal relationship between intelligence and the dependent variable could be assumed.

Yet another procedure which may be adopted for introducing a measure of control into *ex post facto* design is that of selecting samples that are as homogeneous as possible on a given variable. For example, Ary *et al.* (2009) suggest that if intelligence were a relevant extraneous variable, its effects could be controlled by including participants from only one intelligence level. This would disentangle the independent variable from other variables with which it is commonly associated, so that any effects found could be associated justifiably with the independent variable.

Finally, control may be introduced into an *ex post facto* investigation by stating and testing any alternative hypotheses that might be plausible explanations for the empirical outcomes of the study. A researcher has thus to beware of accepting the first likely explanation of relationships in an *ex post facto* study as necessarily the only or final one. A well-known instance to which reference has already been made is the presumed relationship between cigarette smoking and lung cancer. Health officials have been quick to seize on the explanation that smoking causes lung cancer. Tobacco firms, however, have put forward an alternative hypothesis – that both smoking and lung cancer are possibly the result of a third, as yet unspecified, factor, i.e. the possibility that both the independent and dependent variables are simply two separate results of a single common cause cannot be ignored.

 Companion Website

The companion website to the book includes PowerPoint slides for this chapter, which list the structure of the chapter and then provide a summary of the key points in each of its sections. This resource can be found online at **www.routledge.com/textbooks/cohen7e**.

CHAPTER 16

Experiments, quasi-experiments, single-case research and internet-based experiments

Whilst Chapter 15 provided an overview of a particular kind of experiment (the *ex post facto* experiment), this chapter constitutes a full exploration of key issues in experiments in education, indicating how they might address causality as a main target of much educational research. The chapter addresses:

- designs in educational experimentation
- true experimental designs
- a quasi-experimental design: the non-equivalent control group design
- single-case research: ABAB design
- procedures in conducting experimental research
- threats to internal and external validity in experiments
- the timing of the pre-test and the post-test
- examples from educational research
- the design experiment
- internet-based experiments

The intention here is not only to introduce different forms of experiment but to ensure that researchers are aware of the key issues to be addressed in their planning and conduct, and what might or might not legitimately be inferred from their results.

16.1 Introduction

The issue of *causality* and, hence, predictability has exercised the minds of researchers considerably (Smith, 1991: 177; Morrison, 2009). One response has been in the operation of *control*, and it finds its apotheosis in the experimental design. If rival causes or explanations can be eliminated from a study then clear causality can be established; the model can *explain* outcomes. Smith (1991: 177) and Morrison (2009) claim the high ground for the experimental approach, arguing that it is an important method that directly concerns itself with causality; this, clearly is contestable, as we make clear in Part 3 of the book.

In Chapter 15, we described *ex post facto* research as experimentation in reverse in that *ex post facto* studies start with groups that are already different with

regard to certain characteristics and then proceed to search, in retrospect, for the factors that brought about those differences. We then went on to cite Kerlinger's (1970: 22) description of the experimental researcher's approach: 'If *x*, then *y*; if frustration, then aggression ... the researcher uses some method to measure *x* and then observes *y* to see if concomitant variation occurs.'

The essential feature of experimental research is that investigators deliberately control and manipulate the conditions which determine the events in which they are interested, introduce an intervention and measure the difference that it makes. An experiment involves making a change in the value of one variable – called the independent variable – and observing the effect of that change on another variable – called the dependent variable. Using a fixed design, experimental research can be *confirmatory*, seeking to support or not to support a null hypothesis, or *exploratory*, discovering the effects of certain variables. An independent variable is the input variable, whereas the dependent variable is the outcome variable – the result; for example Kgaile and Morrison (2006) indicate seven independent variables that have an effect on the result (the effectiveness of the school), as shown in Figure 16.1.

In an experiment the post-test measures the dependent variable, and the independent variables are isolated and controlled carefully.

Imagine that we have been transported to a laboratory to investigate the properties of a new wonder fertilizer that farmers could use on their cereal crops, let us say wheat (Morrison, 1993: 44–5). The scientist would take the bag of wheat seed and randomly split it into two equal parts. One part would be grown under normal existing conditions – controlled and measured amounts of soil, warmth, water and light and no other factors. This would be called the control group. The other part would be grown under the same conditions – the same controlled and measured amounts of soil, warmth, water and light as the control group, *but*, additionally, the new wonder fertilizer. Then, four months later, the two groups are examined and their growth measured. The control group has

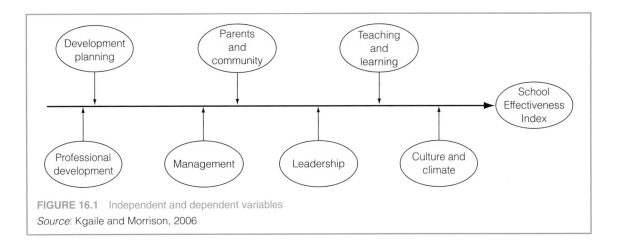

FIGURE 16.1 Independent and dependent variables
Source: Kgaile and Morrison, 2006

grown half a metre and each ear of wheat is in place but the seeds are small. The experimental group, by contrast, has grown half a metre as well but has significantly more seeds on each ear, the seeds are larger, fuller and more robust.

The scientist concludes that, because both groups came into contact with nothing other than measured amounts of soil, warmth, water and light, then it could not have been anything else but the new wonder fertilizer that caused the experimental group to flourish so well. The key factors in the experiment were:

- the random allocation of the whole bag of wheat into two matched groups (the control and the experimental group), involving the initial measurement of the size of the wheat to ensure that it was the same for both groups (i.e. the pre-test);
- the identification and isolation of key variables (soil, warmth, water and light);
- the control of the key variables (the same amounts to each group);
- the exclusion of any other variables;
- the giving of the special treatment (the intervention) to the experimental group (i.e. manipulating the independent variable) whilst holding every other variable constant for the two groups;
- ensuring that the two groups are entirely separate throughout the experiment (non-contamination);
- the final measurement of yield and growth to compare the control and experimental groups and to look at differences from the pre-test results (the post-test);
- the comparison of one group with another;
- the stage of generalization – that this new wonder fertilizer improves yield and growth under a given set of conditions.

Of true experiments Morrison writes:

Randomization is a key, critical element of the 'true' experiment; random sampling and random allocation to either a control or experimental group is a key way of allowing for the very many additional uncontrolled and, hence, unmeasured, variables that may be part of the make-up of the groups in question (c.f. Slavin 2007). It is an attempt to overcome the confounding effects of exogenous and endogenous variables: the *ceteris paribus* condition (all other things being equal); it assumes that the distribution of these extraneous variables is more or less even and perhaps of little significance. In short it strives to address Holland's (1986) 'fundamental problem of causal inference', which is that a person may not be in both a control group and an experimental group simultaneously.... As Schneider *et al.* (2007: 16) remark, because random allocation takes into account both observed and unobserved factors, controls on unobserved factors, thereby, are unnecessary.... If students are randomly allocated to control and experimental groups and are equivalent in all respects (by randomization) other than one group being exposed to the intervention and the other not being exposed to the intervention, then, it is argued, the researcher can attribute any different outcomes between the two groups to the effects of the intervention.

(Morrison, 2009: 143–4)

The 'true' experiment can be represented diagrammatically as in Figure 16.2.

Schneider *et al.* (2007: 13) suggest that Holland's (1986, 2004) 'fundamental problem of causal inference' comes into being once one accepts that a causal

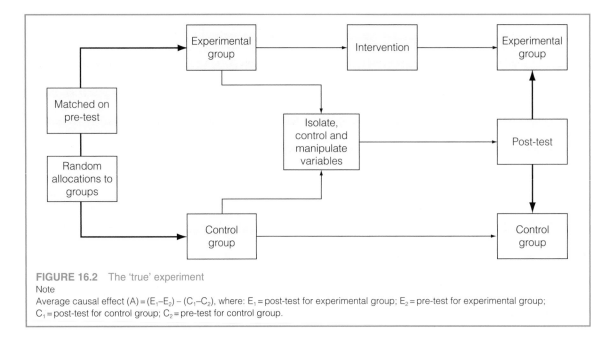

FIGURE 16.2 The 'true' experiment

Note

Average causal effect (A) = $(E_1 - E_2) - (C_1 - C_2)$, where: E_1 = post-test for experimental group; E_2 = pre-test for experimental group; C_1 = post-test for control group; C_2 = pre-test for control group.

effect is the difference between what would have happened to a person in an experiment if she had been in the experimental group (receiving the intervention) and if the same person had been in the control group. However, this is impossible to test empirically, as she cannot be in both groups.

Holland (1986: 947) suggests a statistical solution to this through randomization and the measurement of average effects, and Schneider *et al.* (2007: 13–15) make several suggestions to address Holland's problem:

- Place the same person in the control group, followed by placing her in the experimental groups (which assumes temporal stability (cf. Holland 1986: 948), i.e. the fact that there are two time periods should make no difference to the results, there being a constancy of response regardless of time), assuming or demonstrating that the placement of the person in the first group does not affect the person for long enough to contaminate (affect) the person's response to being in the second group (cf. Holland 1986: 948) (see the section 'Repeated measures designs' below).
- Assume that all the participants are identical in every respect (which may be able to be done in the physical sciences but questionably so in the human sciences, even in twin studies: Holland (1986: 947)).
- Focus on the *average* results (Holland, 1986: 948), for example the *average* scores on the pre-test and

post-test, which may be useful unless they mask important differences between subsets of the two samples, e.g. students with a high IQ and students with a low IQ may perform very differently, but this would be lost in an average, in which case stratification into subsample can be adopted.

This model of an experiment, premised on notions of randomization, isolation and control of variables in order to establish causality, may be appropriate for a laboratory, though whether, in fact, a social situation either ever *could become* the antiseptic, artificial world of the laboratory or *should become* such a world is both an empirical and a moral question respectively. Indeed, the discussion of the 'design experiment' later in this chapter notes that its early advocate (Brown, 1992) had moved away from laboratory experiments to naturalistic settings in order to catch the true interaction of a myriad of variables in the real world. Further, the ethical dilemmas of treating humans as manipulable, controllable and inanimate are considerable (see Chapter 5).

Hage and Meeker (1988: 55) suggest that the experimental approach may be fundamentally flawed in assuming that a single cause produces an effect. Further, it may be that the setting effects are acting causally, rather than the intervention itself, i.e. there is a 'setting effect' (where the results are largely a function of their context) (see Maxwell, 2004), for instance in the Milgram studies of obedience and the Stanford prison experiment reported in Chapter 26, and Zimbardo (2007a, 2007b).

However, despite these concerns about experiments, let us pursue the experimental model further.

Frequently in learning experiments in classroom settings the independent variable is a stimulus of some kind, a new method in arithmetical computation for example, and the dependent variable is a response, the time taken to do 20 sums using the new method. Most empirical studies in educational settings, however, are quasi-experimental rather than experimental. The single most important difference between the quasi-experiment and the true experiment is that in the former case, the researcher undertakes his study with groups that are intact, that is to say, the groups have been constituted by means other than random selection. In this chapter we identify the essential features of true experimental and quasi-experimental designs, our intention being to introduce the reader to the meaning and purpose of control in educational experimentation.

In experiments, researchers can remain relatively aloof from the participants, bringing a degree of objectivity to the research (Robson, 2002: 98). Observer effects can distort the experiment, for example researchers may record inconsistently, or inaccurately, or selectively, or, less consciously, they may be having an effect on the experiment. Further, participant effects might distort the experiment (see the discussion of the Hawthorne effect in Chapter 10); the fact of simply being in an experiment, rather than what the experiment is doing, might be sufficient to alter participants' behaviour.

In medical experiments these twin concerns are addressed by giving placebos to certain participants, to monitor any changes, and experiments are blind or double-blind. In blind experiments, participants are not told whether they are in a control group or an experimental group, though which they are is known to the researcher. In a double-blind experiment not even the researcher knows whether a participant is in the control or experimental group – that knowledge resides with a third party. These are intended to reduce the subtle effects of participants knowing whether they are in a control or experimental group. In educational research it is easier to conduct a blind experiment rather than a double-blind experiment, and it is even possible not to tell participants that they are in an experiment at all, or to tell them that the experiment is about X when in fact it is about Y, i.e. to 'put them off the scent'. This form of deception needs to be justified; a common justification is that it enables the experiment to be conducted under more natural conditions, without participants altering their everyday behaviour.

The term 'control' has been used in two main senses so far: the random allocation of participants to a control or an experimental group and the isolation and control of variables. Whilst the former is self-evident, the latter has a double meaning which can be explicated a little further, for the control of variables happens at two stages. First, so far the only stage mentioned has been in isolating key independent variables and controlling what happens to these, e.g. so that the same amounts of these are given to both the control group and the experimental group, i.e. the control group and experimental groups are matched in their exposure to these independent variables. This involves giving an identical, measured amount of exposure of both groups to these (whether this can actually be achieved in practice is a moot point, but for the purpose of the discussion here we assume it can). By holding the independent variable constant (giving the same amount to both the control group and the experimental group), it is argued that any changes brought about in the experimental group must be attributable to the intervention, the other variables having been held constant (controlled).

In *ex post facto* experiments (discussed in Chapter 15), it is not possible to control these variables in advance of the experiment, or during the experiment, the data being already in existence before the experiment has commenced. However, in this case, the controls can be applied at the stage of data analysis, where the researcher can manipulate the independent variables to hold them constant, i.e. to control for the relative effects of these. For an example of this we refer the reader to Chapter 4 on causation, and to Chapter 35 for an indication on how controls can be placed statistically (e.g. partial correlations and crosstabulations).

16.2 Designs in educational experimentation

There are several different kinds of experimental design, for example:

1 The controlled experiment in laboratory conditions (the 'true' experiment): two or more groups.
2 The field or quasi-experiment (in the natural setting rather than the laboratory, but where variables are isolated, controlled and manipulated).
3 The natural experiment (in which it is not possible to isolate and control variables).

We consider these in this chapter. The laboratory experiment (the classic true experiment) is conducted in a specially contrived, artificial environment, so that variables can be isolated, controlled and manipulated (as in the example of the wheat seeds above). The field experiment is similar to the laboratory experiment in that variables are isolated, controlled and manipulated, but the setting is the real world rather than the artificially constructed world of the laboratory.

Sometimes it is not possible, desirable or ethical to set up a laboratory or field experiment. For example, let us imagine that we wanted to investigate the trauma effects on people in road traffic accidents. We could not require a participant to run under a bus, or another to stand in the way of a moving lorry, or another to be hit by a motorcycle, and so on. Instead we might examine hospital records to see the trauma effects of victims of bus accidents, lorry accidents and motorcycle accidents, and see which group seems to have sustained the greatest traumas. It may be that the lorry accident victims had the greatest trauma, followed by the motorcycle victims, followed by the bus victims. Now, although it is not possible to say with 100 per cent certainty what caused the trauma, one could make an intelligent guess that those involved in lorry accidents suffer the worst injuries. Here we look at the outcomes and work backwards to examine possible causes. We cannot isolate, control or manipulate variables, but nevertheless we can come to some likely defensible conclusions.

In the outline of research designs that follows we use symbols and conventions from Campbell and Stanley (1963):

- *X* represents the exposure of a group to an experimental variable or event, the effects of which are to be measured.
- *O* refers to the process of observation or measurement.
- *X*s and *O*s in a given row are applied to the same persons.
- Left to right order indicates temporal sequence.
- *X*s and *O*s vertical to one another are simultaneous.
- *R* indicates random assignment to separate treatment groups.
- Parallel rows unseparated by dashes represent comparison groups equated by randomization, while those separated by a dashed line represent groups not equated by random assignment.

16.3 True experimental designs

There are several variants of the 'true' experimental design, and we consider many of these below:

the pre-test–post-test control and experimental group design;

the two control groups and one experimental group pre-test–post-test design;
the post-test control and experimental group design;
the post-test two experimental groups design;
the pre-test–post-test two treatment design;
the matched pairs design;
the factorial design;
the parametric design;
repeated measures designs.

The laboratory experiment typically has to identify and control a large number of variables, and this may not be possible. Further, the laboratory environment itself can have an effect on the experiment, or it may take some time for a particular intervention to manifest its effects (e.g. a particular reading intervention may have little immediate effect but may have a delayed effect in promoting a liking for reading in adult life, or may have a cumulative effect over time).

A 'true' experiment includes several key features:

- one or more control groups;
- one or more experimental groups;
- random allocation to control and experimental groups;
- pre-test of the groups to ensure parity;
- post-test of the groups to see the effects on the dependent variable;
- one or more interventions to the experimental group(s);
- isolation, control and manipulation of independent variables;
- non-contamination between the control and experimental groups.

If an experiment does not possess all of these features then it is a quasi-experiment: it may look *as if* it is an experiment ('quasi' means 'as if') but it is not a true experiment, only a variant on it.

An alternative to the laboratory experiment is the quasi-experiment or field experiment, including:

the one-group pre-test–post-test;
the non-equivalent control group design;
the time series design.

We consider these below. Field experiments have less control over experimental conditions or extraneous variables than a laboratory experiment, and, hence, inferring causality is more contestable, but they have the attraction of taking place in a natural setting. Extraneous variables may include, for example:

- participant factors (they may differ on important characteristics between the control and experimental groups);
- intervention factors (the intervention may not be exactly the same for all participants, varying, for example, in sequence, duration, degree of intervention and assistance, and other practices and contents);
- situational factors (the experimental conditions may differ).

These can lead to experimental error, in which the results may not be due to the independent variables in question.

The pre-test–post-test control and experimental group design

A complete exposition of experimental designs is beyond the scope of this chapter. In the brief outline that follows, we have selected one design from the comprehensive treatment of the subject by Campbell and Stanley (1963) in order to identify the essential features of what they term a 'true experimental' and what Kerlinger (1970) refers to as a 'good' design. Along with its variants, the chosen design is commonly used in educational experimentation (e.g. Schellenberg, 2004).

The pre-test–post-test control group design can be represented as:

| *Experimental* | RO_1 | X | O_2 |
| *Control* | RO_3 | | O_4 |

Kerlinger observes that, in theory, random assignment to E and C conditions controls all possible independent variables. In practice, of course, it is only when enough subjects are included in the experiment that the principle of randomization has a chance to operate as a powerful control. However, the effects of randomization even with a small number of subjects is well illustrated in Box 16.1.

Randomization, then, ensures the greater likelihood of equivalence, that is, the apportioning out between the experimental and control groups of any other factors or characteristics of the subjects which might conceivably affect the experimental variables in which the researcher is interested (cf. Torgerson and Torgerson, 2003a, 2003b). If the groups are made equivalent, then any so-called 'clouding' effects should be present in both groups.

So strong is this simple and elegant true experimental design, that all the threats to internal validity identified in Chapter 10 are, according to Campbell and Stanley (1963), controlled in the pre-test–post-test control group design. The causal effect of an intervention can be calculated thus:

Step 1: Subtract the pre-test score from the post-test score for the experimental group to yield score 1.
Step 2: Subtract the pre-test score from the post-test score for the control group to yield score 2.
Step 3: Subtract score 2 from score 1.

Using Campbell and Stanley's terminology, the effect of the experimental intervention is:

$$(O_2 - RO_1) - (O_4 - RO_3)$$

If the result is negative then the causal effect was negative.

BOX 16.1 THE EFFECTS OF RANDOMIZATION

Select 20 cards from a pack, ten red and ten black. Shuffle and deal into two ten-card piles. Now count the number of red cards and black cards in either pile and record the results. Repeat the whole sequence many times, recording the results each time.

You will soon convince yourself that the most likely distribution of reds and blacks in a pile is five in each: the next most likely, six red (or black) and four black (or red); and so on. You will be lucky (or unlucky for the purposes of the demonstration!) to achieve one pile of red and the other entirely of black cards. The probability of this happening is 1 in 92,378! On the other hand, the probability of obtaining a 'mix' of not more than six of one colour and four of the other is about 82 in 100.

If you now imagine the red cards to stand for the 'better' ten children and the black cards for the 'poorer' ten children in a class of 20, you will conclude that the operation of the laws of chance alone will almost probably give you close equivalent 'mixes' of 'better' and 'poorer' children in the experimental and control groups.

Source: Adapted from Pilliner, 1973

One problem that has been identified with this particular experimental design is the interaction effect of testing. Good (1963) explains that whereas the various threats to the validity of the experiments listed in Chapter 10 can be thought of as main effects, manifesting themselves in mean differences independently of the presence of other variables, interaction effects, as their name implies, are joint effects and may occur even when no main effects are present. For example, an interaction effect may occur as a result of the pre-test measure sensitizing the subjects to the experimental variable.[1] Interaction effects can be controlled for by adding to the pre-test–post-test control group design two more groups that do not experience the pre-test measures. The result is a four-group design, as suggested by Solomon below. Later in the chapter, we describe an educational study which built into a pre-test–post-test group design a further control group to take account of the possibility of pre-test sensitization.

Randomization, Smith (1991: 215) explains, produces equivalence over a whole range of variables, whereas matching produces equivalence over only a few named variables. The use of randomized controlled trials (RCTs), a method used in medicine, is a putative way of establishing causality and generalizability (though, in medicine, the sample sizes for some RCTs is necessarily so small – there being limited sufferers from a particular complaint – that randomization is seriously compromised).

A powerful advocacy of RCTs for planning and evaluation is provided by Boruch (1997). Indeed he argues (p. 69) that the problem of poor experimental controls has led to highly questionable claims being made about the success of programmes. Examples of the use of RCTs can be seen in Maynard and Chalmers (1997).

The randomized controlled trial is the 'gold standard' of many educational researchers, as it purports to establish controllability, causality and generalizability (Curriculum, Evaluation and Management Centre, 2000; Coe *et al.*, 2000). How far this is true is contested (Morrison, 2001). For example, complexity theory replaces simple causality with an emphasis on networks, linkages, holism, feedback, relationships and interactivity in context (Cohen and Stewart, 1995), emergence, dynamical systems, self-organization and an open system (rather than the closed world of the experimental laboratory). Even if we could conduct an experiment, its applicability to ongoing, emerging, interactive, relational, changing, open situations, in practice, may be limited (Morrison, 2001). It is misconceived to hold variables constant in a dynamical, evolving, fluid, open situation.

Further, the laboratory is a contrived, unreal and artificial world. Schools and classrooms are not the antiseptic, reductionist, analysed-out or analysable-out world of the laboratory. Indeed the successionist conceptualization of causality (Harré, 1972), wherein researchers make inferences about causality on the basis of observation, must admit its limitations. One cannot infer causes from effects or multiple causes from multiple effects. Generalizability from the laboratory to the classroom is dangerous, yet with field experiments, with their loss of control of variables, generalizability might be equally dangerous.

Classical experimental methods, abiding by the need for replicability and predictability, may not be particularly fruitful since, in complex phenomena, results are never clearly replicable or predictable: we never step into the same river twice. In linear thinking small causes bring small effects and large causes bring large effects, but in complexity theory small causes can bring huge effects and huge causes may have little or no effect. Further, to atomize phenomena into measurable variables and then to focus only on certain of these is to miss synergy and the spirit of the whole. Measurement, however acute, may tell us little of value about a phenomenon; I can measure every physical variable of a person but the nature of the person, what makes that person who she or he is, eludes atomization and measurement. Randomized controlled trials belong to a discredited view of science as positivism.

Though we address ethical concerns in Chapter 5, it is important here to note the common reservation that is voiced about the two-group experiment (e.g. Gorard, 2001b: 146), which is to question how ethical it is to deny a control group access to a treatment or intervention in order to suit the researcher (to which the counter-argument is, as in medicine, that the researcher does not know whether the intervention (e.g. the new drug) will work or whether it will bring harmful results, and, indeed, the purpose of the experiment is to discover this).

The two control groups and one experimental group pre-test–post-test design

This is the Solomon design, intended to identify the interaction effect that may occur if the subject deduces the desired result from looking at the pre-test and the post-test. It is the same as the randomized controlled trial above, except that there are two control groups instead of one. In the standard randomized controlled trial any change in the experimental group can be due to the intervention or the pre-test, and any change in the control group can be due to the pre-test. In the Solomon variant the second control group receives the intervention but no pre-test. This can be modelled thus:

Experimental	RO_1	X	O_2
Control	RO_3		O_4
Control$_2$		X	O_5

Thus any change in this second control group can only be due to the intervention. We refer readers to Bailey (1994: 231–4) for a full explication of this technique and its variants.

The post-test control and experimental group design

Here participants are randomly assigned to a control group and an experimental group, but there is no pre-test. The experimental group receives the intervention and the two groups are given only a post-test. The design is:

Experimental	R_1	X	O_1
Control	R_2		O_2

The post-test two experimental groups design

Here participants are randomly assigned to each of two experimental groups. Experimental group 1 receives intervention 1 and experimental group 2 receives intervention 2. Only post-tests are conducted on the two groups. The design is:

Experimental$_1$	R_1	X_1	O_1
Experimental$_2$	R_2	X_2	O_2

The pre-test–post-test two treatment design

Here participants are randomly allocated to each of two experimental groups. Experimental group 1 receives intervention 1 and experimental group 2 receives intervention 2. Pre-tests and post-tests are conducted to measure changes in individuals in the two groups. The design is:

Experimental$_1$	RO_1	X_1	O_2
Experimental$_2$	RO_2	X_2	O_4

The true experiment can also be conducted with one control group and two or more experimental groups. So, for example, the designs might be:

Experimental$_1$	RO_1	X_1	O_2
Experimental$_2$	RO_3	X_2	O_4
Control	RO_5	X	O_6

This can be extended to the post-test control and experimental group design and the post-test two experimental groups design, and the pre-test–post-test two treatment design.

The matched pairs design

As the name suggests, here participants are allocated to control and experimental groups randomly, but the basis of the allocation is that one member of the control group is matched to a member of the experimental group on the several independent variables considered important for the study (e.g. those independent variables that are considered to have an influence on the dependent variable, such as sex, age, ability). So, first, pairs of participants are selected who are matched in terms of the independent variable under consideration (e.g. whose scores on a particular measure are the same or similar), and then each of the pair is randomly assigned to the control or experimental group. Randomization takes place at the pair rather than the group level. Though, as its name suggests, this ensures effective matching of control and experimental groups, in practice it may not be easy to find sufficiently close matching, particularly in a field experiment, though finding such a close match in a field experiment may increase the control of the experiment considerably. Matched pairs designs are useful if the researcher cannot be certain that individual differences will not obscure treatment effects, as it enables these individual differences to be controlled.

Borg and Gall (1979: 547) set out a useful series of steps in the planning and conduct of an experiment:

Step 1: Carry out a measure of the dependent variable.
Step 2: Assign participants to matched pairs, based on the scores and measures established from Step 1.
Step 3: Randomly assign one person from each pair to the control group and the other to the experimental group.
Step 4: Administer the experimental treatment/intervention to the experimental group and, if appropriate, a placebo to the control group. Ensure that the control group is not subject to the intervention.
Step 5: Carry out a measure of the dependent variable with both groups and compare/measure them in order to determine the effect and its size on the dependent variable.

Borg and Gall (1979) indicate that difficulties arise in the close matching of the sample of the control and experimental groups. This involves careful identification of the variables on which the matching must take place. They suggest (p. 547) that matching on a number of variables that correlate with the dependent variable is more likely to reduce errors than matching on a single variable. The problem, of course, is that the greater the number of variables that have to be matched, the harder it is actually to find the sample of people who are matched. Hence the balance must be struck between having too few variables such that error can occur, and having so many variables that it is impossible to draw a sample. Instead of matched pairs, random allocation is possible, and this is discussed below.

Mitchell and Jolley (1988: 103) pose three important questions that researchers need to consider when comparing two groups:

- Are the two groups equal at the commencement of the experiment?
- Would the two groups have grown apart naturally, regardless of the intervention?
- To what extent has initial measurement error of the two groups been a contributory factor in differences between scores?

Borg and Gall draw attention to the need to specify the degree of exactitude (or variance) of the match. For example, if the subjects were to be matched on, say, linguistic ability as measured in a standardized test, it is important to define the limits of variability that will be used to define the matching (e.g. ± 3 points). As before, the greater the degree of precision in the matching here, the closer will be the match, but the greater the degree of precision the harder it will be to find an exactly matched sample.

One way of addressing this issue is to place all the subjects in rank order on the basis of the scores or measures of the dependent variable. Then the first two subjects become one matched pair (which one is allocated to the control group and which to the experimental group is done randomly, e.g. by tossing a coin), subjects three and four become the next matched pair, subjects five and six become the next matched pair, and so on until the sample is drawn. Here the loss of precision is counterbalanced by the avoidance of the loss of subjects.

The alternative to matching that has been discussed earlier in the chapter is randomization. Smith (1991: 215) suggests that matching is most widely used in quasi-experimental and non-experimental research, and is a far inferior means of ruling out alternative causal explanations than randomization.

The factorial design

In an experiment there may be two or more independent variables acting on the dependent variable. For example, performance in an examination may be a consequence of availability of resources (independent variable one: limited availability, moderate availability, high availability) and motivation for the subject studied (independent variable two: little motivation, moderate motivation, high motivation). Each independent variable is studied at each of its levels (in the example here it is three levels for each independent variable). Participants are randomly assigned to groups that cover all the possible combinations of levels of each independent variable, for example:

Independent variable	Level 1	Level 2	Level 3
Availability of resources	limited availability (1)	moderate availability (2)	high availability (3)
Motivation for the subject studied	little motivation (4)	moderate motivation (5)	high motivation (6)

Here the possible combinations are: 1+4, 1+5, 1+6, 2+4, 2+5, 2+6, 3+4, 3+5 and 3+6. This yields nine groups (3 × 3 combinations). Pre-tests and post-tests or post-tests only can be conducted. It might show, for example, that limited availability of resources and little motivation had a statistically significant influence on examination performance, whereas moderate and high availability of resources did not, or that high availability and high motivation had a statistically significant effect on performance, whereas high motivation and limited availability did not, and so on.

This example assumes that there are the same numbers of levels for each independent variable; this may not be the case. One variable may have, say, two levels, another three levels, and another four levels. Here the possible combinations are 2 × 3 × 4 = 24 levels and, therefore, 24 experimental groups. One can see that factorial designs quickly generate several groups of participants. A common example is a 2 × 2 design, in which two independent variables each have two values (i.e. four groups). Here experimental group 1 receives the intervention with independent variable 1 at level 1 and independent variable 2 at level 1; experimental group 2 receives the intervention with independent variable 1 at level 1 and independent variable 2 at level 2; experimental group 3 receives the intervention with independent variable 1 at level 2 and independent variable 2 at level 1; experimental group 4 receives the

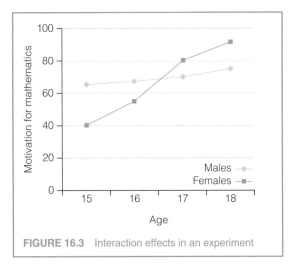

FIGURE 16.3 Interaction effects in an experiment

intervention with independent variable 1 at level 2 and independent variable 2 at level 2.

Factorial designs also have to take account of the interaction of the independent variables. For example one factor (independent variable) may be 'sex' and the other 'age' (Figure 16.3). The researcher may be investigating their effects on motivation for learning mathematics.

In Figure 16.3 one can see that the difference in motivation for mathematics is not constant between males and females, but that it varies according to the age of the participants. There is an interaction effect between age and sex, such that the effect of sex depends on age. A factorial design is useful for examining interaction effects.

At their simplest, factorial designs may have two levels of an independent variable, e.g. its presence or absence, but, as has been seen here, it can become more complex. That complexity is bought at the price of increasing exponentially the number of groups required.

The parametric design

Here participants are randomly assigned to groups whose parameters are fixed in terms of the levels of the independent variable that each receives. For example, let us imagine that an experiment is conducted to improve the reading abilities of poor, average, good and outstanding readers (four levels of the independent variable 'reading ability'). Four experimental groups are set up to receive the intervention, thus: experimental group 1 (poor readers); experimental group 2 (average readers), experimental group 3 (good readers) and experimental group 4 (outstanding readers). The control group (group 5) would receive no intervention.

The researcher could chart the differential effects of the intervention on the groups, and thus have a more sensitive indication of its effects than if there was only one experimental group containing a wide range of reading abilities; the researcher would know which group was most and least affected by the intervention. Parametric designs are useful if an independent variable is considered to have different levels or a range of values which may have a bearing on the outcome (confirmatory research) or if the researcher wishes to discover whether different levels of an independent variable have an effect on the outcome (exploratory research).

Repeated measures designs

Here participants in the experimental groups are tested under two or more experimental conditions. So, for example, a member of the experimental group may receive more than one 'intervention', which may or may not include a control condition. This is a variant of the matched pairs design, and offers considerable control potential, as it is exactly the same person receiving different interventions. Order effects raise their heads here: the order in which the interventions are sequenced may have an effect on the outcome; the first intervention may have an influence – a carry-over effect – on the second, and the second intervention may have an influence on the third and so on. Further, early interventions may have a greater effect than later interventions. To overcome this it is possible to randomize the order of the interventions and assign participants randomly to different sequences, though this may not ensure a balanced sequence. Rather, a deliberate ordering may have to be planned, for example, in a three-intervention experiment:

Group 1 receives intervention 1 followed by intervention 2, followed by intervention 3;
Group 2 receives intervention 2 followed by intervention 3, followed by intervention 1;
Group 3 receives intervention 3 followed by intervention 1, followed by intervention 2;
Group 4 receives intervention 1 followed by intervention 3, followed by intervention 2;
Group 5 receives intervention 2 followed by intervention 1, followed by intervention 3;
Group 6 receives intervention 3 followed by intervention 2, followed by intervention 1.

Repeated measures designs are useful if it is considered that order effects are either unimportant or unlikely (see Figure 16.4), or if the researcher cannot be certain that individual differences will not obscure treatment effects, as it enables these individual differences to be controlled.

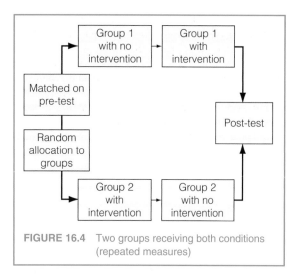

FIGURE 16.4 Two groups receiving both conditions (repeated measures)

16.4 A quasi-experimental design: the non-equivalent control group design

Often in educational research, it is simply not possible for investigators to undertake true experiments, e.g. in random assignation of participants to control or experimental groups. Quasi-experiments are the stuff of field experimentation, i.e. outside the laboratory. At best, they may be able to employ something approaching a true experimental design in which they have control over what Campbell and Stanley (1963) refer to as 'the who and to whom of measurement' but lack control over 'the when and to whom of exposure', or the randomization of exposures – essential if true experimentation is to take place. These situations are quasi-experimental and the methodologies employed by researchers are termed quasi-experimental designs. (Kerlinger (1970) refers to quasi-experimental situations as 'compromise designs', an apt description when applied to much educational research where the random selection or random assignment of schools and classrooms is quite impracticable.)

Quasi-experiments come in several forms, for example:

- pre-experimental designs: the one group pre-test–post-test design; the one-group post-tests only design; the non-equivalent post-test only design;
- pre-test–post-test non-equivalent group design;
- one-group time series.

We consider these below.

A pre-experimental design: the one group pre-test–post-test

Very often, reports about the value of a new teaching method or interest aroused by some curriculum innovation or other reveal that a researcher has measured a group on a dependent variable (O_1), for example, attitudes towards minority groups, and then introduced an experimental manipulation (X), perhaps a ten-week curriculum project designed to increase tolerance of ethnic minorities. Following the experimental treatment, the researcher has again measured group attitudes (O_2) and proceeded to account for differences between pre-test and post-test scores by reference to the effects of X.

The one group pre-test–post-test design can be represented as:

Experimental O_1 X O_2

Suppose that just such a project has been undertaken and that the researcher finds that O_2 scores indicate greater tolerance of ethnic minorities than O_1 scores. How justified is she in attributing the cause of O_1–O_2 differences to the experimental treatment (X), that is, the term's project work? At first glance the assumption of causality seems reasonable enough. The situation is not that simple, however. Compare for a moment the circumstances represented in our hypothetical educational example with those which typically obtain in experiments in the physical sciences. A physicist who applies heat to a metal bar can confidently attribute the observed expansion to the rise in temperature that she has introduced because within the confines of her laboratory she has excluded (i.e. controlled) all other extraneous sources of variation (Pilliner, 1973).

The same degree of control can never be attained in educational experimentation. At this point readers may care to reflect upon some possible influences other than the ten-week curriculum project that might account for the O_1–O_2 differences in our hypothetical educational example.

They may conclude that factors to do with the pupils, the teacher, the school, the classroom organization, the curriculum materials and their presentation, the way that the subjects' attitudes were measured, to say nothing of the thousand and one other events that occurred in and about the school during the course of the term's work, might all have exerted some influence upon the observed differences in attitude. These kinds of extraneous variables which are outside the experimenters control in one-group pre-test–post-test designs threaten to invalidate their research efforts. We later identify a number of such threats to the validity of educational experimentation.

A pre-experimental design: the one-group post-tests only design

Here an experimental group receives the intervention and then takes the post-test. Though this has some features of an experiment (an intervention and a post-test), the lack of a pre-test, of a control group, of random allocation and of controls renders this a flawed methodology.

A pre-experimental design: the post-tests only non-equivalent groups design

Again, though this appears to be akin to an experiment, the lack of a pre-test, of matched groups, of random allocation and of controls renders this a flawed methodology.

A quasi-experimental design: the pre-test–post-test non-equivalent group design

One of the most commonly used quasi-experimental designs in educational research can be represented as:

Experimental	O_1	X	O_2
Control	O_3		O_4

The dashed line separating the parallel rows in the diagram of the non-equivalent control group indicates that the experimental and control groups have not been equated by randomization – hence the term 'non-equivalent'. The addition of a control group makes the present design a decided improvement over the one group pre-test–post-test design, for to the degree that experimenters can make E and C groups as equivalent as possible, they can avoid the equivocality of interpretations that plague the pre-experimental design discussed earlier. The equivalence of groups can be strengthened by matching, followed by random assignment to E and C treatments.

Where matching is not possible, the researcher is advised to use samples from the same population or samples that are as alike as possible (Kerlinger, 1970). Where intact groups differ substantially, however, matching is unsatisfactory due to regression effects which lead to different group means on post-test measures.

The one-group time series

Here the one group is the experimental group, and it is given more than one pre-test and more than one post-test. The time series uses repeated tests or observations both before and after the treatment, which, in effect, enables the participants to become their own controls, which reduces the effects of reactivity. Time series allow for trends to be observed, and avoid reliance on only one single pre-testing and post-testing data collection point. This enables trends to be observed such as: no effect at all (e.g. continuing an existing upward, downward or even trend), a clear effect (e.g. a sustained rise or drop in performance), delayed effects (e.g. some time after the intervention has occurred). Time series studies have the potential to increase reliability.

16.5 Single-case research: ABAB design

At the beginning of Chapter 14, we described case study researchers as typically engaged in observing the characteristics of an individual unit, be it a child, a classroom, a school or a whole community. We went on to contrast case study researchers with experimenters whom we described as typically concerned with the manipulation of variables in order to determine their causal significance. That distinction, as we shall see, is only partly true.

Increasingly, in recent years, single-case research as an experimental methodology has extended to such diverse fields as clinical psychology, medicine, education, social work, psychiatry and counselling. Most of the single-case studies carried out in these (and other) areas share the following characteristics:

- they involve the continuous assessment of some aspect of human behaviour over a period of time, requiring on the part of the researcher the administration of measures on multiple occasions within separate phases of a study;
- they involve 'intervention effects' which are replicated in the same subject(s) over time.

Continuous assessment measures are used as a basis for drawing inferences about the effectiveness of intervention procedures.

The characteristics of single-case research studies are discussed by Kazdin (1982) in terms of ABAB designs, the basic experimental format in most single-case researches. ABAB designs, Kazdin observes, consist of a family of procedures in which observations of performance are made over time for a given client or group of clients. Over the course of the investigation, changes are made in the experimental conditions to which the client is exposed. The basic rationale of the ABAB design is illustrated in Figure 16.5. What it does is this. It examines the effects of an intervention by alternating the baseline condition (the A phase), when no intervention is in effect, with the intervention condition (the B phase). The A and B phases are then repeated to complete the four phases. As Kazdin says, the effects of the intervention are clear if performance improves during the first intervention phase, reverts to or approaches original baseline levels of performance when the treatment is withdrawn, and improves again when treatment is recommenced in the second intervention phase.

An example of the application of the ABAB design in an educational setting is provided by Dietz (1977) whose single-case study sought to measure the effect that a teacher could have upon the disruptive behaviour of an adolescent boy whose persistent talking disturbed his fellow classmates in a special education class.

In order to decrease the unwelcome behaviour, a reinforcement programme was devised in which the boy could earn extra time with the teacher by decreasing the number of times he called out. The boy was told that when he made three (or fewer) interruptions during any 55-minute class period the teacher would spend extra time working with him. In the technical language of behaviour modification theory, the pupil would receive reinforcing consequences when he was able to show a low rate of disruptive behaviour (in Figure 16.6 this is referred to as 'differential reinforcement of low rates' or DRL).

When the boy was able to desist from talking aloud on fewer than three occasions during any timetabled period, he was rewarded by the teacher spending 15 minutes with him helping him with his learning tasks. The pattern of results displayed in Figure 16.6 shows the considerable changes that occurred in the boy's behaviour when the intervention procedures were carried out and the substantial increases in disruptions towards baseline levels when the teacher's rewarding strategies were withdrawn. Finally, when the intervention was reinstated, the boy's behaviour is seen to improve again.

The single-case research design is uniquely able to provide an experimental technique for evaluating interventions for the individual subject. Moreover, such interventions can be directed towards the particular subject or group and replicated over time or across behaviours, situations or persons. Single-case research offers an alternative strategy to the more usual methodologies based on between-group designs. There are, however, a number of problems that arise in connection with the use of single-case designs having to do with ambiguities introduced by trends and variations in baseline phase data and with the generality of results from single-case research. The interested reader is directed to Kazdin (1982), Borg (1981) and Vasta (1979).[2]

16.6 Procedures in conducting experimental research

An experimental investigation must follow a set of logical procedures. Those that we now enumerate, however, should be treated with some circumspection. It is extraordinarily difficult (and foolhardy) to lay down clear-cut rules as guides to experimental research. At best, we can identify an ideal route to be followed, knowing full well that educational research rarely proceeds in such a systematic fashion.[3]

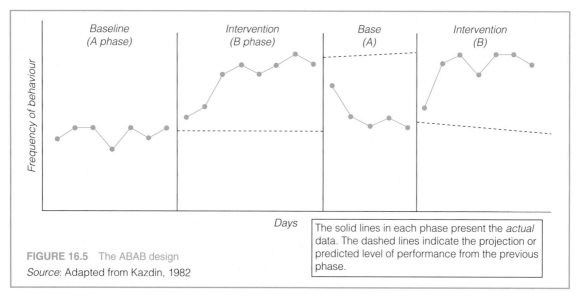

FIGURE 16.5   The ABAB design
Source: Adapted from Kazdin, 1982

The solid lines in each phase present the *actual* data. The dashed lines indicate the projection or predicted level of performance from the previous phase.

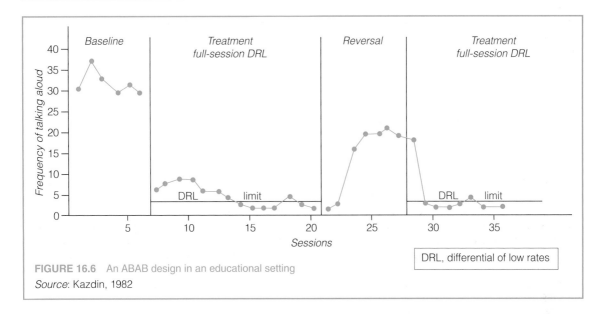

FIGURE 16.6 An ABAB design in an educational setting

Source: Kazdin, 1982

First, the researcher must identify and define the research problem as precisely as possible, always supposing that the problem is amenable to experimental methods.

Second, she must formulate hypotheses that she wishes to test. This involves making predictions about relationships between specific variables and at the same time making decisions about other variables that are to be excluded from the experiment by means of controls. Variables, remember, must have two properties. First, they must be measurable. Physical fitness, for example, is not directly measurable until it has been operationally defined. Making the variable 'physical fitness' operational means simply defining it by letting something else that is measurable stand for it – a gymnastics test, perhaps. Second, the proxy variable must be a valid indicator of the hypothetical variable in which one is interested. That is to say, a gymnastics test probably is a reasonable proxy for physical fitness; height on the other hand most certainly is not. Excluding variables from the experiment is inevitable, given constraints of time and money. It follows therefore that one must set up priorities among the variables in which one is interested so that the most important of them can be varied experimentally whilst others are held constant.

Third, the researcher must select appropriate levels at which to test the independent variables. By way of example, suppose an educational psychologist wishes to find out whether longer or shorter periods of reading make for reading attainment in school settings (see Simon, 1978). She will hardly select 5-hour and 5-minute periods as appropriate levels; rather, she is

more likely to choose 30-minute and 60-minute levels, in order to compare with the usual timetabled periods of 45 minutes' duration. In other words, the experimenter will vary the stimuli at such levels as are of practical interest in the real-life situation. Pursuing the example of reading attainment somewhat further, our hypothetical experimenter will be wise to vary the stimuli in large enough intervals so as to obtain measurable results. Comparing reading periods of 44 minutes, or 46 minutes, with timetabled reading lessons of 45 minutes is scarcely likely to result in observable differences in attainment.

Fourth, the researcher must decide which kind of experiment she will adopt, perhaps from the varieties set out in this chapter.

Fifth, in planning the design of the experiment, the researcher must take account of the population to which she wishes to generalize her results. This involves her in decisions over sample sizes and sampling methods. Sampling decisions are bound up with questions of funds, staffing and the amount of time available for experimentation. However, one general rule of thumb is to try to make the sample as large as possible so that even small effects can reveal themselves which might otherwise be lost with small samples, even though the trade-off here is that, with large samples, it is easier to achieve statistical significance (i.e. it is easier to find a statistically significant difference between the control group and the experimental group) than it is with a small sample (statistical significance being, in part, a function of sample size), though measures of effect size overcome this problem. Second, it is important, where possible, to use a random, probability sample, as this not only permits a greater range of statistics to be used (e.g. t-tests and analysis of variance, both of which are important in experiments, see Chapter 36), but it also enables the findings to have greater generalizability (external validity), i.e. to represent the wider population.

Sixth, with problems of validity in mind, the researcher must select instruments, choose tests and decide upon appropriate methods of analysis (typically t-tests and measures of effect size are used to determine whether there are any statistically significant or sizeable differences that are worthy of note, respectively, between the control and experimental groups).

Seventh, before embarking upon the actual experiment, the researcher must pilot test the experimental procedures to identify possible snags in connection with any aspect of the investigation. This is of crucial importance.

Eighth, during the experiment itself, the researcher must endeavour to follow tested and agreed-on procedures to the letter. The standardization of instructions, the exact timing of experimental sequences, the meticulous recording and checking of observations – these are the hallmark of the competent researcher.

With her data collected, the researcher faces the most important part of the whole enterprise. Processing data, analysing results and drafting reports are all extremely demanding activities, both in intellectual effort and time. Often this last part of the experimental research is given too little time in the overall planning of the investigation. Experienced researchers rarely make such a mistake; computer program faults and a dozen more unanticipated disasters teach the hard lesson of leaving ample time for the analysis and interpretation of experimental findings.

A ten-step model for the conduct of the experiment can be suggested:

Step 1: Identify the purpose of the experiment.
Step 2: Select the relevant variables.
Step 3: Specify the level(s) of the intervention (e.g. low, medium, high intervention).
Step 4: Control the experimental conditions and environment.
Step 5: Select the appropriate experimental design.
Step 6: Administer the pre-test.
Step 7: Assign the participants to the group(s).
Step 8: Conduct the intervention.
Step 9: Conduct the post-test.
Step 10: Analyse the results.

The sequence of steps 6 and 7 can be reversed; the intention in putting them in the present sequence is to ensure that the two groups are randomly allocated and matched. In experiments and fixed designs, data are aggregated rather than related to specific individuals, and data look for averages, the range of results, and their variation. In calculating differences or similarity between groups at the stages of the pre-test and the post-test, the t-test for independent samples is often used.

16.7 Threats to internal and external validity in experiments

Chapter 10 indicted several threats to the internal and external validity of experiments, and we refer the reader to this chapter. In that chapter threats to internal validity (the validity of the research design, process, instrumentation and measurement) were seen to reside in:

- history
- maturation
- statistical regression
- testing
- instrumentation
- selection
- experimental mortality
- instrument reactivity
- selection-maturation interaction
- Type I and Type II errors.

To this, Hammersley (2008: 4) adds the point that not all the confounding variables may be properly controlled in the randomization process.

In Chapter 10, too, threats to external validity (wider generalizability) were seen to reside in:

- failure to describe independent variables explicitly
- lack of representativeness of available and target populations
- Hawthorne effect
- inadequate operationalizing of dependent variables
- sensitization/reactivity to experimental/research conditions
- interaction effects of extraneous factors and experimental/research treatments
- invalidity or unreliability of instruments
- ecological validity
- multiple treatment validity.

To this, Hamnmersley (2008: 4) adds the point that, in principle, a laboratory trial, in which variables are controlled, misrepresents the 'real' world of the classroom in which the variables are far less controlled, i.e. the findings may not be transferable to wider conditions and situations.

One can add to these factors the matter that statistical significance can be found comparatively easily if sample sizes are large (Kline, 2004) (hence the need to consider placing greater reliance on effect size rather than statistical significance, discussed in Chapter 17). Further, Torgerson and Torgerson (2003a: 70–1) draw attention to the limits of small samples in experimental research, as small samples can fail to spot small effects, thereby risking a Type II error (failing to find an effect when, in fact, it exists). As they remark, in a time of evidence-based education and discussions of 'what works', small effects can be useful (p. 70), and they give the example where, if a small change in delivering the curriculum led to improved examination passes of only one child in each class in public examinations, then this could total up to between 20,000 and 30,000 students across the UK.

Torgerson and Torgerson (2003b) also identify several sources of bias in randomized controlled trials, for example:

a   Having a very selective sample (they give the example of an exclusive girls-only boarding school) and then seeking to generalize the results to a much wider population, e.g. an inner-city mixed sex comprehensive (non-selective) school (p. 37).

b   A selection bias, where the experimental group possesses a variable that is related to the outcome variable but which is not included in the intervention (pp. 37–8).

c   A dilution bias, where the control group, not being exposed to the intervention, deliberately seeks out a 'compensating treatment' (p. 38). For example, there may be an experiment to test the effects of increased attention to mathematics in the classroom on mathematics results in public examinations; the control group, not being exposed to what they see as a useful intervention (given that there has to be informed consent), may take private mathematics lessons in order to compensate, thereby disturbing or diluting the findings of the experiment.

d   Chance effects: the authors give an example of a group of 40 children learning spellings, in which four of them were dyslexic, and in which the likelihood of them being randomly allocated to the control group and experimental group evenly (two in each group) was very small, indeed all four could be in one group (either the experimental group or the control group). The researchers argue that this can be addressed through 'minimisation' (p. 40), deliberately ensuring an even split of such students into both groups (e.g. matched pairs allocation).

e   'Subversion bias' (p. 40), where researchers deliberately breach the requirements of random allocation (hence the need for double-blind experiments or where the researcher is not involved in the randomized allocation).

f   Attrition bias: Torgerson and Torgerson (2003a: 74–5) draw attention to the problem of attrition in experimental methods, where some students could drop out of the experimental group (they give the example of students who attend voluntary Saturday morning 'booster classes' and then who drop out of the class). Here, if the researchers only focused on the results of those students who remained in the Saturday morning classes, then they would obtain very different results from those which might have been found if the dropouts had not dropped out (e.g. in terms of measured motivation levels and, hence, achievement). There is a risk, the authors aver, of 'attrition bias' here (p. 75).

g   Reporting or detection bias: where different researchers or reporters for the control and experimental groups report with differing degrees of detail or inclusion of relevant observations (Torgerson and Torgerson, 2003b: 42).

h   Exclusion bias, where members of the experimental group for reasons other than attrition, do not actually take part in the experiment.

16.8 The timing of the pre-test and the post-test

Experiments typically suffer from the problem of only having two time points for measurement: the pre-test and the post-test. It is essential that the researcher plans the timing of the pre-test and the post-test appropriately. Morrison (2009: 168) writes that 'experimental procedures are prone to problems of timing – too soon and the effect may not be noticed; too late and the effect might have gone or been submerged by other matters'. The pre-test should be conducted as close to the start of the intervention as possible, to avoid the influence of confounding effects between the pre-test and the start of the intervention; that is quite straightforward.

More difficult is the issue of the timing of the post-test. On the one hand the argument is strong that it should be as close as possible to the end of the intervention, as this will reduce the possibility of the influence of confounding effects. On the other hand, it may well be that the effects of a particular intervention may not reveal themselves immediately, but much later, for example a student may study Shakespeare at age 15 and, on an outcome measure, may use it to say that she strongly dislikes English literature, but, years later, she may point back to her study of Shakespeare as sowing the seed for her eventual love of Shakespeare that only developed after she had left school. Too soon the post-test and that effect is lost, it goes unmeasured (and this is a serious problem for the 'what works' movement that appears to concern itself with short-term payback).

On the other hand, too long a time lapse, and it becomes impossible to determine whether it was a particular independent variable that caused a particular effect, or whether other factors have intervened since the intervention to produce the effect.

Further still, it is possible that an immediate post-test could easily find an effect, but the effect is not sustained to any worthwhile degree over time. A standard example of this is where an end of course examination is administered at the last session of the course, or within a week of its completion, and, unsurprisingly perhaps, given the 'recency effect' (in which most recently studied items are more easily recalled than items studied a long time previously), many students score well. However, let us imagine that the post-test (the examination) had been conducted one month later, in which case the students might well have bleached the subject matter from their minds. Or, more problematic in this instance is the familiar case of students revising hard before the post-test (the examination) is administered, and they score well, but this time it is not a consequence of the intervention but a rehearsal, practice or revision effect.

One way in which the researcher can overcome the difficulty of the timing of the post-test is to have more than one post-test (e.g. an 'equivalent form' of the post-test: see Chapter 10), with the post-test administered soon after the intervention has ended, and its equivalent form administered after a longer period of time – to determine more long-lasting effects.

16.9 Examples from educational research

Example 1: A pre-experimental design

A pre-experimental design was used in a study involving the 1991–92 Postgraduate Diploma in Education group following a course of training to equip them to teach social studies in senior secondary schools in Botswana. The researcher wished to find out whether the programme of studies he had devised would effect changes in the students' orientations towards social studies teaching. To that end, he employed a research instrument, the Barth/Shermis Studies Preference Scale (BSSPS) which has had wide use in differing cultures including America, Egypt and Nigeria, and whose construction meets commonly required criteria concerning validity and internal consistency reliability.

The BSSPS consists of 45 Likert-type items (Chapter 20), providing measures of what purport to be three social studies traditions or philosophical orientations, the oldest of which, Citizenship Transmission, involves indoctrination of the young in the basic values of a society. The second orientation, called the Social Science, is held to relate to the acquisition of knowledge-gathering skills based on the mastery of social science concepts and processes. The third tradition, Reflective Enquiry, is said to derive from John Dewey's pragmatism with its emphasis on the process of enquiry. Forty-eight Postgraduate Diploma students were administered the BSSPS during the first session of their one-year course of study. At the end of the programme, the BSSPS was again completed in order to determine whether changes had occurred in students' philosophical orientations. Briefly, the 'preferred orientation' in the pre-test and post-test was the criterion measure, the two orientations least preferred being ignored. Broadly speaking, students tended to move from a majority holding a Citizenship Transmission orientation at the beginning of the course to a greater affirmation of the Social Science and the Reflective Enquiry traditions. Using the symbols and conventions adopted earlier to represent research designs, we can illustrate the Botswana study as:

Experimental	O_1	X	O_2

The briefest consideration reveals inadequacies in the design. Indeed, Campbell and Stanley (1963) describe the one group pre-test–post-test design as 'a "bad example" to illustrate several of the confounded extraneous variables that can jeopardize internal validity'. The investigator is rightly cautious in his conclusions: 'it is possible to say that the social studies course *might* be responsible for this phenomenon, although other extraneous variables might be operating' (Adeyemi, 1992, emphasis added). Somewhat ingenuously he puts his finger on one potential explanation, that the changes could have occurred among his intending teachers because the shift from 'inculcation to rational decision-making was in line with the recommendation of the Nine Year Social Studies Syllabus issued by the Botswana Ministry of Education in 1989' (Adeyemi, 1992).

Example 2: A quasi-experimental design

Mason *et al.*'s (1992) longitudinal study took place between 1984 and 1992. Its principal aim was to test whether the explicit teaching of linguistic features of GCSE textbooks, coursework and examinations would produce an improvement in performance across the secondary curriculum. The title of their report, 'Illuminating English: how explicit language teaching improved public examination results in a comprehensive school', suggests that the authors were persuaded that they had achieved their objective. In light of the experimental design selected for the research, readers may ask themselves whether or not the results are as unequivocal as reported.

The design adopted in the Shevington study (Shevington is the location of the experiment in north-west England) may be represented as:

Experimental	O_1	X	O_2
Control	O_3		O_4

This is, of course, the non-equivalent control group design outlined earlier in this chapter in which parallel rows separated by dashed lines represent groups that have not been equated by random assignment.

In brief, the researchers adopted a methodology akin to teaching English as a foreign language and applied this to Years 7–9 in Shevington Comprehensive School and two neighbouring schools, monitoring the pupils at every stage and comparing their performance with control groups drawn both from Shevington and the two other schools. Inevitably, because experimental and control groups were not randomly allocated, there were significant differences in the performance of some groups on pre-treatment measures such as the York Language Aptitude Test. Moreover, because no standardized reading tests of sufficient difficulty were available as post-treatment measures, tests had to be devised by the researchers, who provide no details as to their validity or reliability. These difficulties notwithstanding, pupils in the experimental groups taking public examinations in 1990 and 1991 showed substantial gains in respect of the percentage increases of those obtaining GCSE Grades A to C. The researchers note that during the three years 1989 to 1991, 'no other significant change in the policy, teaching staff or organization of the school took place which could account for this dramatic improvement of 50 per cent' (Mason *et al.*, 1992).

Although the Shevington researchers attempted to exercise control over extraneous variables, readers may well ask whether threats to internal and external validity such as those alluded to earlier were sufficiently met as to allow such a categorical conclusion as, 'the pupils … achieved greater success in public examinations as a result of taking part in the project' (Mason *et al.*, 1992).

Example 3: A 'true' experimental design

Another investigation (Bhadwal and Panda, 1991) concerned with effecting improvements in pupils' performance as a consequence of changing teaching strategies used a more robust experimental design. In rural India, the researchers drew a sample of 78 pupils, matched by socio-economic backgrounds and non-verbal IQs, from three primary schools that were themselves matched by location, physical facilities, teachers' qualifications and skills, school evaluation procedures and degree of parental involvement. Twenty-six pupils were randomly selected to comprise the experimental group, the remaining 52 being equally divided into two control groups. Before the introduction of the changed teaching strategies to the experimental group, all three groups completed questionnaires on their study habits and attitudes. These instruments were specifically designed for use with younger children and were subjected to the usual item analyses, test-retest and split-half reliability inspections. Bhadwal and Panda's research design can be represented as:

Experimental	RO_1	X	RO_2
First control	RO_3		RO_4
Second control	RO_5		RO_6

Recalling Kerlinger's (1970) discussion of a 'good' experimental design, the version of the pre-test–post-test control design employed here (unlike the design used in Example 2 above) resorted to randomization which, in theory, controls all possible independent variables. Kerlinger adds, however, '*in practice*, it is only when enough subjects are included in the experiment that the principle of randomization has a chance to operate as a powerful control'. It is doubtful whether 26 pupils in each of the three groups in Bhadwal and Panda's study constituted 'enough subjects'.

In addition to the matching procedures in drawing up the sample, and the random allocation of pupils to experimental and control groups, the researchers also used analysis of covariance, as a further means of controlling for initial differences between E and C groups on their pre-test mean scores on the independent variables, study habits and attitudes.

The experimental programme involved improving teaching skills, classroom organization, teaching aids, pupil participation, remedial help, peer-tutoring and continuous evaluation. In addition, provision was also made in the experimental group for ensuring parental involvement and extra reading materials. It would be startling if such a package of teaching aids and curriculum strategies did not effect significant changes in their recipients and such was the case in the experimental results. The Experimental Group made highly significant gains in respect of its level of study habits as compared with Control Group 2 where students did not show a marked change. What did surprise the investigators, we suspect, was the significant increase in levels of study habits in Control Group 1. Maybe, they opined, this unexpected result occurred because Control Group 1 pupils were tested immediately prior to the beginning of their annual examinations. On the other hand, they conceded, some unaccountable variables might have been operating. There is, surely, a lesson here for all researchers! (For a set of examples of problematic experiments see the website material.)

16.10 The design experiment

The design experiment is perhaps more fittingly termed a 'design study', as it frequently does not conform to the requirements of an experiment (e.g. it does not have the hallmarks of a randomized controlled trial), as set out in the earlier part of this chapter. Design-based research is not the same as an experiment, though, in many circles, it has been termed (misleadingly) a design experiment. Hence it is included in this chapter because of its nomenclature rather than its affinity to experiments as described so far in this chapter, though, like an experiment, it involves a deliberate and planned intervention. It has appeared comparatively recently in education (e.g. Brown, 1992), and it was given the imprimatur of status in a special issue of *Educational Researcher* in 2003 (vol. 32 (1)).

It is more useful to focus on the word 'design' rather than 'experiment' here, as a design study owes some of its pedigree to engineering and science rather than to an experiment that has control and experimental groups. Brown (1992: 141) suggests that design studies attempt to 'engineeer innovative educational environments and simultaneously conduct experimental studies of those innovations'. Take the example of engineering: here the designer develops a product and then tests it in real conditions (Gorard *et al.*, 2004: 576), noting, during the testing (the experiment) what are the problems with the design, what needs to be improved, where there are faults and failures, and so on, gathering data from other participants and users. Then the engineer redesigns the product to address the faults found, refines the product and retests the improved product, noting faults, problems or failures; the engineer reworks the product to address these problems, and tests it out again, and so on. We can observe here:

1 The process is iterative; it has many cycles, trials, improvements and refinements over time.
2 It focuses on the processes involved in the workings of the product.
3 It communicates with different parties (theoreticians, designers, practitioners), about the design and development of the product (the designers, the engineers, the users), akin to a research-and-development model.
4 The product has to work in the 'real world' (an example of 'what works') and in non-laboratory conditions and contexts.
5 It is data-driven – the next cycle of refinement is based on data (e.g. observational data, measurement data, notes and records) derived from the previous round.

These points accord with key principles of design studies in education (Design-Based Research Collective, 2003: 5), for example in developing learning environments:

1 They intertwine theory, models and practice.
2 Research and development occur in cycles of refinement, testing and feedback ('design, enactment and analysis' (Design-Based Research Collective, 2003: 6)).
3 The findings must be communicated and shared with all parties, including the users.
4 The research and the outcomes must be tested and used in authentic, real-world settings respectively.
5 Reporting and development go together in developing a useable outcome.

Shavelson *et al.* (2003: 26) suggest that key principles of design studies are that they are: (a) 'iterative'; (b) 'process focused'; (c) 'interventionist'; (d) 'collaborative'; (e) 'multileveled'; (f) 'utility oriented'; and (g) 'theory driven'. Cobb *et al.* (2003: 9) suggest that theory generation is a key feature of design experiments; they are 'crucibles for the generation and testing of theory' (p. 9), their purpose is to generate theories of teaching and learning (p. 10), and this involves development, intervention and reflection. In having 'pragmatic roots' (p. 10), Cobb *et al.* point us to suggesting the affinity between design experiments and mixed methods research (see Chapter 1), and, indeed, this is echoed by Gorard *et al.* (2004: 579, 593).

The inception of design studies is often attributed to Brown (1992), whose autobiographical account of her years of research charts a movement away from the laboratory and into the classroom, in order to catch the authenticity of the real world in research and development. She recognizes that this is bought at the price of tidiness, and she justifies this in terms of the real world being 'rarely isolatable' in terms of its components, and in which 'the whole really is more than the sum of its parts' (p. 166). For her and her successors, interventions are based on theoretical claims (e.g. about teaching and learning) (for example Design-Based Research Collective, 2003: 5) and are inextricably linked to practices that improve the situation (e.g. of teaching and learning); they respond to 'emergent features' of the situation in which they are operating (Design-Based Research Collective, 2003: 6). Practitioners, researchers and developers work together to produce a useful intervention and innovation.

A design-base study is a study that focuses on changing practice, instead of the static, 'frozen' (Design-Based Research Collective, 2003: 7) input–output model of an intervention that one sees in much experimental and educational research, in a design study the 'product' changes over time, as refinements are made in response to feedback from all parties.

However, unlike an engineering product, a design-base study does not end with the perfecting of a particular product. Rather, as Brown (1992) indicated, it affects theory, e.g. of learning, of teaching. The design-based study can address and generate many kinds of knowledge (Design-Based Research Collective, 2003: 8):

■ investigating possibilities for new and innovative teaching environments;
■ developing theories of teaching and learning that are rooted in real-world contexts;
■ developing cumulative knowledge of design;
■ increasing capacity in humans for innovation.

To this Shavelson et al. (2003: 28) suggest that design studies can address research that asks 'what is happening?', 'is there a systematic effect?' and 'why or how is it happening?'.

The attraction of the approach is that it takes account of the complex, real, multivariate world of learning, teaching and education; as such they are 'messier' than conventional experiments, as they take account of many variables and contexts, the intervention develops and changes over time and involves several parties and strives to ensure that what works at the design stage really works in practice (Gorard et al., 2004: 578, 582). The design study develops a profile of multiple variables rather than testing a sole hypothesis (Lobato, 2003: 19).

On the other hand Shavelson et al. (2003) argue that design studies are not exempted the usual warrants of research, for example, they ask 'what is the basis of knowing in design studies' (p. 25), 'with so many confounding variables in a design study, can the knowledge claims be warranted' (p. 27), how generalizable the results can be, as they are so rooted in specific contexts (p. 27), and how have alternative explanations of the outcomes been considered (p. 27). To answer these questions, McCandliss et al. (2003: 15) also add that video recording can provide useful data over time, and Shavelson et al. (2003) suggest that longitudinal narrative data are particularly useful as they can track developments and causal developments over time in a way that catches the complexity and contextualization of the intervention which inheres in its very principles. However, narrative accounts risk circularity, and there need to be external checks and balances, controls and warrants, in validating the knowledge claims (p. 27).

Further, Sloane and Gorard (2003) indicate some difficulties that design studies have to address, including measurement problems, external validity, the lack of controls and control groups, the lack of failure criteria (and they argue that engineers include failure criteria as essential features of their research and development), and the need for appropriate modelling of causality at both the alpha stages (the designers) and the beta stages (the users). Hence researchers using a design study have to be clear on its purposes, intended contribution to theory generation, participants and communication processes between them, processes of intervention and debriefing/feedback, clear understanding of the local context of the intervention (Cobb et al., 2003: 12), and 'testable conjectures' that can be revised iteratively (Cobb et al., 2003: 11).

16.11 Internet-based experiments

A growing field in psychological research is the use of the internet for experiments (e.g. www.psych.unizh.ch/genpsy/Ulf/Lab/webExpPsyLab.html). Hewson et al. (2003: 48) classify these into four principal types: 'those that present static printed materials (for example, printed text or graphics); second are those that make use of non-printed materials (for example, video or sound); third are reaction-time experiments; and fourth are experiments that involve some form of interpersonal interaction'.

The first kind of experiment is akin to a survey in that it sends formulated material to respondents (e.g. graphically presented material) by email or by web page, and the intervention will be to send different groups different materials. Here all the cautions and comments that were made about internet-based surveys apply, particularly those problems of download times, different browsers and platforms. However, the matter of download time applies more strongly to the second type of internet-based experiments that use video clips or sound, and some software packages will reproduce higher quality than others, even though the original that is transmitted is the same for everyone. This can be addressed by ensuring that the material runs at its optimum even on the slowest computer (Hewson *et al.*, 2003: 49) or by stating the minimum hardware required for the experiment to be run successfully.

Reaction-time experiments, those that require very precise timing (e.g. to milliseconds) are difficult in remote situations, as different platforms and internet connection speeds and congestion on the internet through having multiple users at busy times can render standardization virtually impossible. One solution to this is to have the experiment downloaded and then run offline before loading it back onto the computer and sending it.

The fourth type involves interaction, and is akin to internet interviewing (discussed below), facilitated by chat rooms. However, this is solely a written medium and so intonation, inflection, hesitancies, non-verbal cues, extra-linguistic and paralinguistic factors are ruled out of this medium. It is, in a sense, incomplete, though the increasing availability and use of simple screen-top video cameras is mitigating this. Indeed this latter development renders observational studies an increasing possibility in the internet age.

Reips (2002a) reports that in comparison to laboratory experiments, internet-based experiments experienced greater problems of dropout, that the dropout rate in an internet experiment was very varied (from 1 per cent to 87 per cent), and that dropout could be reduced by offering incentives, e.g. payments or lottery tickets, bringing a difference of as much as 31 per cent to dropout rates. Dropout on internet-based research was due to a range of factors, for example motivation, how interesting the experiment was, not least of which was the non-compulsory nature of the experiment (in contrast, for example, to the compulsory nature of experiments undertaken by university student participants as part of their degree studies). The discussion of the 'high hurdle technique' earlier is applicable to experiments here. Reips (2002b: 245–6) also reports that greater variance in results is likely in an internet-based experiment than in a conventional experiment due to technical matters (e.g. network connection speed, computer speed, multiple software running in parallel). He also reports (Reips, 2009: 381) that internet experiments suffer from reducing the controls that the experimenter can place on the participant, and the problems of a biased, volunteer-only sample (p. 382) or recruitment biases.

On the other hand Reips (2002b: 247) also reports that internet-based experiments have an attraction over laboratory and conventional experiments in that they:

- have greater generalizability because of their wider sampling;
- demonstrate greater ecological validity as typically they are conducted in settings that are familiar to the participants and at times suitable to the participant ('the experiment comes to the participant, not vice versa'), though, of course, the obverse of this is that the researcher has no control over the experimental setting (p. 250);
- they have a high degree of voluntariness, such that more authentic behaviours can be observed.

How correct these claims are is an empirical matter. For example, the use of sophisticated software packages (e.g. Java) can reduce experimenter control as these packages may interact with other programming languages. Indeed Schwarz and Reips (2001) report that the use of Javascript led to a 13 per cent higher dropout rate in an experiment compared to an identical experiment that did not use Javascript. Further, multiple returns by a single participant could confound reliability (discussed above in connection with survey methods).

Reips (2002a, 2002b) provides a series of 'dos' and 'don'ts' in internet experimenting. In terms of 'dos' he gives five main points:

1 use dropout as a dependent variable;
2 use dropout to detect motivational confounding (i.e. to identify boredom and motivation levels in experiments);
3 place questions for personal information at the beginning of the internet study. Reips (2002b) suggests that asking for personal information may assist in keeping participants in an experiment, and that this is part of the 'high hurdle' technique, where dropouts self-select out of the study, rather than dropping out during the study;
4 use techniques that help ensure quality in data collection over the internet (e.g. the 'high hurdle' and 'warm-up' techniques discussed earlier, subsampling to detect and ensure consistency of results, using single passwords to ensure data integrity, providing contact information, reducing dropout);
5 use internet-based tools and services to develop and announce your study (using commercially produced software to ensure that technical and presentational problems are overcome). There are also websites (e.g. the American Psychological Society) that announce experiments.

In terms of 'don'ts' he gives five main points:

1 Do not allow external access to unprotected directories. This can violate ethical and legal requirements, as it provides access to confidential data. It also might allow the participants to have access to the structure of the experiment, thereby contaminating the experiment.
2 Do not allow public display of confidential participant data through URLs (a problem if respondents use the GET protocol), as this, again, violates ethical codes.
3 Do not accidentally reveal the experiment's structure (as this could affect participant behaviour). This might be done through including the experiment's details on a related file or a file in the same directory.
4 Do not ignore the technical variance inherent in the internet (configuration details, browsers, platforms, bandwidth and software might all distort the experiment, as discussed above).
5 Do not bias results through improper use of form elements (i.e. measurement errors, where, by omitting particular categories (e.g. 'neutral', 'do not want to respond', 'neither agree nor disagree') could distort the results).

Indeed, the points made in connection with internet surveys and questionnaires apply equally to internet experiments, and readers are advised to review these.

Reips (2002b) points out that it is a misconception to regard an internet-based experiment as the same as a laboratory experiment, as: (a) internet participants could choose to leave the experiment at any time; (b) they can conduct the experiment at any time and in their own settings; (c) they are often conducted with larger samples than conventional experiments; (d) they rely on technical matters, network connections and the computer competence of the participants; and (e) they are more public than most conventional experiments. On the other hand he also cautions against regarding the internet-based experiment as completely different from the laboratory experiment, as: (a) many laboratory experiments also rely on computers; (b) fundamental ideas are the same for laboratory and internet-based surveys; (c) similar results have been produced by both means. He suggests several issues in conducting internet-based experiments:

1 Consider a web-based software tool to develop the experimental materials.
2 Pilot the experiment on different platforms for clarity of instructions and availability on different platforms.

3 Decide the level of sophistication of HTML scripting and whether to use HTML or non-HTML.
4 Check the experiments for configuration errors and variance on different computers.
5 Place the experiment on several websites and services.
6 Run the experiment online and offline to make comparisons.
7 Use the 'warm-up' and 'high hurdle' techniques, asking filter questions (e.g. about the seriousness of the participant, their background and expertise, language skills).
8 Use dropout to ascertain whether there is motivational confounding.
9 Check for obvious naming of files and conditions (to reduce the possibility of unwanted access to files).
10 Consider using passwords and procedures (e.g. consistency checks) to reduce the possibility of multiple submissions.
11 Keep an experimental log of data for any subsequent analysis and verification of results.
12 Analyse and report dropout.
13 Keep the experimental details on the internet, to give a positive impression of the experiment.

Reips (2009: 375) also writes that the success of internet-based experimentation depends in part on the 'cues transmitted', the 'bandwidth', 'cost constraints', 'level and type of anonymity' and 'synchronicity and exclusivity' (see also Birnbaum, 2009).

At the time of writing, the internet-based experiment is currently more a child of psychology than of education. However, given the rise of evidence-based practice in education, and the advocacy of randomized controlled trials in education, this form of experimentation is set to become more widely used in education.

Details of the development of internet-based experimental software can be found at:

www.genpsylab.unizch/wextor/index.html
http://psych.hanover.edu.APS/exponnet.html
www.genpsy.unizch/Ulf.Lab/webexplist.html.

We also refer readers to Joinson *et al.* (2009), Part Five.

16.12 Conclusion

This chapter has introduced a range of different types of experiment. Starting with the 'true' experiment, it held this up as the clearest example of a full experiment, as it abides by all the features of an experiment, in particular it adheres to the tenets of a randomized controlled trial, which is intended to yield evidence of 'what works'. The strengths and limitations of the true experiment and the randomized controlled trial were set out. Further variants of a true experiment were set out. Moving further out of the laboratory and into the 'real world', the chapter then presented a discussion of different types of quasi-experiment, i.e. those kinds of experiment in which not all the requirements of a true experiment were met or, in the case of *ex post facto* experiments or those which could not be justified on ethical or practical grounds, where the requirements of a true experiment were impossible to meet. Rendering an experiment a quasi-experiment rather than a true experiment was seen to lie not only in design matters, but in issues of sampling and controls. Moving yet further into the 'real world' the chapter ended by introducing design experiments, or, as was argued to be more fittingly described, a design study.

 Companion Website

The companion website to the book includes PowerPoint slides for this chapter, which list the structure of the chapter and then provide a summary of the key points in each of its sections. In addition there is further information in the form of examples of experiments. These resources can be found online at **www.routledge. com/textbooks/cohen7e**.

CHAPTER 17

Meta-analysis, research syntheses and systematic reviews

This new chapter introduces key issues in the more established field of meta-analysis and the more recent field of research syntheses and systematic reviews, as part of the push towards evidence-based educational practice. The chapter addresses issues in:

- evidence-based research
- meta-analysis
- research syntheses and systematic reviews

As evidence-based education gathers pace (Coe, 1999), the fields of meta-evaluation and research syntheses come to take on increasing prominence as research methods in their own right. The use of meta-analysis and systematic reviews enables the cumulative effect of knowledge from educational research to be developed, as in, for example, medical sciences (Davies, 2000). Since the early days of reviews of research, gathering together a range of research studies and summarizing their main findings ('narrative reviews', e.g. in the journal *Review of Educational Research*), the field has advanced to include meta-analysis and research syntheses/systematic reviews, with the journal *Research Synthesis Methods* launched in 2009. This chapter introduces meta-analysis and research syntheses/systematic reviews.

17.1 Evidence-based research

In an age of evidence-based education, meta-analysis and research syntheses/systematic reviews are increasingly used methods of investigation, bringing together different studies to provide evidence to inform policy making and planning (Sebba, 1999; Thomas and Pring, 2004). That this is happening significantly is demonstrated in the establishment of:

- the EPPI-Centre (Evidence for Policy and Practice Information and Co-ordinating Centre) at the University of London (http://eppi.ioe.ac.uk/cms/);
- the Social, Psychological, Educational and Criminological Controlled Trials Register (SPECTR) (Milwain, 1998; Milwain *et al.*, 1999), later trans-

ferred to the Campbell Collaboration (www.campbellcollaboration.org), a parallel to the Cochrane Collaboration in medicine (www.cochrane.org/index0.htm), which undertakes systematic reviews and meta-analyses of, typically, experimental evidence in medicine;
- the Curriculum, Evaluation and Management (CEM) centre at the University of Durham (www.cemcentre.org/);
- the UK Centre for Evidence-based Policy (from the UK's Economic and Social Research Council) (www.esrcsocietytoday.ac.uk/ESRCInfoCentre/research/resources/centre_for_evidence_based_policy.aspx);
- the Evidence Network at King's College, London (www.evidencenetwork.org/);
- the What Works Clearinghouse in the USA (http://ies.ed.gov/ncee/wwc/ and http://ies.ed.gov/ncee/wwc/reports/), with recommendations made for practice (e.g. http://ies.ed.gov/ncee/wwc/publications/practiceguides/);
- the UK government's 'Research Informed Practice Site' (www.standards.dcsf.gov.uk/research/themes/).

'Evidence' here typically comes from randomized controlled trials (RCTs) of one hue or another (Tymms, 1999; Coe *et al.*, 2000; Thomas and Pring, 2004: 95), with their emphasis on careful sampling, control of variables, both extraneous and included, and measurements of effect size. It also comes from systematic reviews of qualitative research. The cumulative evidence from these sources is intended to provide a reliable body of knowledge on which to base policy and practice (Coe *et al.*, 2000). Such accumulated data, it is claimed, delivers evidence of 'what works', though Morrison (2001) suggests that this claim is suspect.

The roots of evidence-based practice lie in medicine, where the advocacy by Cochrane (1972) for randomized controlled trials together with their systematic review and documentation led to the foundation of the Cochrane Collaboration (Maynard and Chalmers, 1997), which is now worldwide. The careful, quantitative-based research studies that can contribute to the accretion of an evidential base are seen to be a powerful counter to the often untried and under-tested schemes that are injected into practice.

More recently evidence-based education has entered the worlds of social policy, social work (MacDonald, 1997) and education (Fitz-Gibbon, 1997). At the forefront of educational research in this area are the EPPI-Centre (Evidence for Policy and Practice Information and Co-ordinating Centre) at the University of London, and the Curriculum, Evaluation and Management Centre at the University of Durham, where the work of Fitz-Gibbon and Tymms shows how indicator systems can be used with experimental methods to provide clear evidence of causality and a ready answer to Fitz-Gibbon's own question: how do we know what works? (Fitz-Gibbon, 1999: 33).

Echoing Anderson and Biddle (1991), Fitz-Gibbon suggests that *policy makers* shun evidence in the development of policy and that *practitioners*, in the hurly-burly of everyday activity, call upon tacit knowledge rather than the knowledge which is derived from randomized controlled trials. However, in a compelling argument (1997: 35–6), she suggests that evidence-based approaches are necessary in order to: (a) challenge the imposition of unproven practices; (b) solve problems and avoid harmful procedures; (c) create improvement that leads to more effective learning. Further, such evidence, she contends, should examine effect sizes rather than statistical significance.

Meta-analysis argues that effect size, rather than statistical significance, should be calculated (Coe, 2000). This is useful, as the notion of effect size breaks the perceived stranglehold of statistical significance (Carver, 1978; Thompson, 1994, 1996, 1998, 2001, 2002; Thompson and Snyder, 1997; Coe, 2000), and replaces it with a more discerning, differentiated notion. It is commonplace to observe that statistical significance is easier to achieve with large samples than with small samples (Fitz-Gibbon, 1997: 118; Kline, 2004); effect size, as a more subtle function of sample size, is a more exact measure and feeds straightforwardly into the aggregation of data for meta-analyses (see, for example, Glass *et al.*, 1981; Lipsey, 1992; Coe, 2000, 2002). Whilst effect size might be a less blunt instrument than statistical significance, nevertheless it does raise the issue of the transferability of data from small samples into the larger picture as discussed above, i.e. the problem of generalizability of small samples does not disappear.

Whilst the nature of information in evidence-based education might be contested by researchers whose sympathies (for whatever reason) lie outside rand-

omized controlled trials, the message from Fitz-Gibbon (1996) will not go away: the educational community needs evidence on which to base its judgements and actions. The development of indicator systems worldwide attests to the importance of this, be it through assessment and examination data, inspection findings, national and international comparisons of achievement, or target setting. Rather than being a shot in the dark, evidence-based education suggests that policy formation should be informed, and policy decision making should be based on the best information to date rather than on hunch, ideology or political will. It is bordering on the unethical to implement untried and untested recommendations in educational practice, just as it is unethical to use untested products and procedures on hospital patients without their consent.

17.2 Meta-analysis

The study by Bhadwal and Panda (1991) is typical of research undertaken to explore the effectiveness of classroom methods. Often as not, such studies fail to reach the light of day, particularly when they form part of the research requirements for a higher degree. Meta-analysis is, simply, the analysis of other analyses. It involves aggregating and combining the results of comparable studies into a coherent account to discover main effects. This is often done statistically, though qualitative analysis is also advocated. Among the advantages of using meta-analysis, Fitz-Gibbon (1985: 46) cites the following:

■ Humble, small-scale reports which have simply been gathering dust may now become useful.
■ Small-scale research conducted by individual students and lecturers will be valuable since meta-analysis provides a way of coordinating results drawn from many studies without having to coordinate the studies themselves.
■ For historians, a whole new genre of studies is created – the study of how *effect sizes* vary over time, relating this to historical changes.

McGaw (1997: 371) suggests that *quantitative* meta-analysis replaces intuition, which is frequently reported narratively (Wood, 1995: 389), as a means of synthesizing different research studies transparently and explicitly (a *desideratum* in many synthetic studies (Jackson, 1980)), particularly when they differ very substantially. Narrative reviews, suggest Jackson (1980), Cook *et al.* (1992: 13) and Wood (1995: 390) are prone to:

- lack comprehensiveness, being selective and only going to subsets of studies;
- misrepresentation and crude representation of research findings;
- over-reliance on significance tests as a means of supporting hypotheses, thereby overlooking the point that sample size exerts a major effect on significance levels, and overlooking effect size;
- reviewers' failure to recognize that random sampling error can play a part in creating variations in findings amongst studies;
- overlook differing and conflicting research findings;
- reviewers' failure to examine critically the evidence, methods and conclusions of previous reviews;
- overlook the extent to which findings from research are mediated by the characteristics of the sample;
- overlook the importance of intervening variables in research;
- unreplicability because the procedures for integrating the research findings have not been made explicit.

A quantitative method for synthesizing research results has been developed by Glass *et al.* (1978, 1981) and others (e.g. Hedges and Olkin, 1985; Hedges, 1990; Rosenthal, 1991) to supersede narrative intuition. Meta-analysis, essentially the 'analysis of analysis', is a means of quantitatively (a) identifying generalizations from a range of separate and disparate studies, and (b) discovering inadequacies in existing research such that new emphases for future research can be proposed. It is simple to use and easy to understand, though the statistical treatment that underpins it is somewhat complex. It involves the quantification and synthesis of findings from separate studies on some common measure, usually an aggregate of effect size estimates, together with an analysis of the relationship between effect size and other features of the studies being synthesized. Statistical treatments are applied to attenuate the effects of other contaminating factors, e.g. sampling error, measurement errors and range restriction. Research findings are coded into substantive categories for generalizations to be made (Glass *et al.*, 1981), such that consistency of findings is discovered that through the traditional means of intuition and narrative review would have been missed.

Fitz-Gibbon (1985: 45) explains the technique by suggesting that in *meta-analysis* the effects of variables are examined in terms of their *effect size*, that is to say, in terms of *how much* difference they make rather than only in terms of whether or not the effects are statistically significant at some arbitrary level such as 5 per cent. Because with *effect sizes* it becomes easier to con-centrate on the educational significance of a finding rather than trying to assess its importance by its statistical significance, and we may finally see statistical significance kept in its place as just one of many possible threats to internal validity. The move towards elevating effect size over significance levels is very important (see also Chapter 34), and signals an emphasis on 'fitness for purpose' (the size of the effect having to be suitable for the researcher's purposes) over arbitrary cut-off points in significance levels as determinants of utility.

The term 'meta-analysis' originated in 1976 (Glass, 1976) and early forms of meta-analysis used calculations of combined probabilities and frequencies with which results fell into defined categories (e.g. statistically significant at given levels), though problems of different sample sizes confounded rigour (e.g. large samples would yield significance in trivial effects, whilst important data from small samples would not be discovered because they failed to reach statistical significance) (Light and Smith, 1971; Glass *et al.*, 1981; McGaw, 1997: 371). Glass (1976) and Glass *et al.* (1981) suggested three levels of analysis: (a) primary analysis of the data; (b) secondary analysis, a re-analysis using different statistics; (c) meta-analysis, analysing results of several studies statistically in order to integrate the findings. Glass *et al.* (1981) and Hunter *et al.* (1982) suggest several stages in the procedure:

Step 1: Identify the variables for focus (independent and dependent).
Step 2: Identify all the studies which feature the variables in which the researcher is interested.
Step 3: Code each study for those characteristics that might be predictors of outcomes and effect sizes (e.g. age of participants, gender, ethnicity, duration of the intervention).
Step 4: Estimate the effect sizes through calculation for each pair of variables (dependent and independent variable) (see Glass, 1977), weighting the effect size by the sample size.
Step 5: Calculate the mean and the standard deviation of effect sizes across the studies, i.e. the variance across the studies.
Step 6: Determine the effects of sampling errors, measurement errors and range of restriction.
Step 7: If a large proportion of the variance is attributable to the issues in Step 6, then the average effect size can be considered an accurate estimate of relationships between variables.
Step 8: If a large proportion of the variance is not attributable to the issues in Step 6, then review those characteristics of interest which correlate with the study effects.

Cook *et al.* (1992: 7–12) set out a four-stage model for an integrative review as a research process, covering:

- problem formulation (where a high-quality meta-analysis must be rigorous in its attention to the design, conduct and analysis of the review);
- data collection (where sampling of studies for review has to demonstrate fitness for purpose);
- data retrieval and analysis (where threats to validity in non-experimental research – of which integrative review is an example – are addressed). Validity here must demonstrate fitness for purpose, reliability in coding and attention to the methodological rigour of the original pieces of research;
- analysis and interpretation (where the accumulated findings of several pieces of research should be regarded as complex data points that have to be interpreted by meticulous statistical analysis).

Fitz-Gibbon (1984: 141–2) sets out four steps in conducting a meta-analysis:

Step 1: Finding studies (e.g. published/unpublished reviews) from which effect sizes can be computed.
Step 2: Coding the study characteristics (e.g. date, publication status, design characteristics, quality of design, status of researcher).
Step 3: Measuring the effect sizes (e.g. locating the experimental group as a *z*-score in the control group distribution) so that outcomes can be measured on a common scale, controlling for 'lumpy data' (non-independent data from a large data set).
Step 4: Correlating effect sizes with context variables (e.g. to identify differences between well-controlled and poorly controlled studies).

Effect size (e.g. Cohen's *d* and *eta* squared) are the preferred statistics over statistical significance in meta-analyses, and we discuss this in Part 5. Effect size is a measure of the degree to which a phenomenon is present or the degree to which a null hypothesis is not supported. Wood (1995: 393) suggests that effect size can be calculated by dividing the significance level by the sample size. Glass *et al.* (1981: 29, 102) calculate the effect size as:

$$\frac{\text{(mean of experimental group} - \text{mean of control group)}}{\text{Standard deviation of the control group}}$$

Hedges (1981) and Hunter *et al.* (1982) suggest alternative equations to take account of differential weightings due to sample size variations. The two most frequently used indices of effect sizes are standardized mean differences and correlations (Glass *et al.*, 1981: 373), though nonparametric statistics, e.g. the median, can be used. Lipsey (1992: 93–100) sets out a series of statistical tests for working on effect sizes, effect size means and homogeneity. It is clear from this that Glass and others assume that meta-analysis can only be undertaken for a particular kind of research – the experimental type – rather than for all types of research; this might limit its applicability.

Glass *et al.* (1981) suggest that meta-analysis is particularly useful when it uses unpublished dissertations, as these often contain weaker correlations than those reported in published research, and hence act as a brake on misleading, more spectacular generalizations. Meta-analysis, it is claimed (Cooper and Rosenthal, 1980), is a means of avoiding Type II errors (failing to find effects that really exist), synthesizing research findings more rigorously and systematically, and generating hypotheses for future research. However Hedges and Olkin (1980) and Cook *et al.* (1992: 297) show that Type II errors become more likely as the number of studies included in the sample increases.

Further, Rosenthal (1991) has indicated a method for avoiding Type I errors (finding an effect that, in fact, does not exist) that is based on establishing how many unpublished studies that average a null result would need to be undertaken to offset the group of published statistically significant studies. For one example he shows a ratio of 277:1 of unpublished to published research, thereby indicating the limited bias in published research.

Meta-analysis is not without its critics (e.g. Wolf, 1986; Elliott, 2001; Thomas and Pring, 2004). Wolf (1986: 14–17) suggests six main areas:

1. It is difficult to draw logical conclusions from studies that use different interventions, measurements, definitions of variables and participants.
2. Results from poorly designed studies take their place alongside results from higher quality studies.
3. Published research is favoured over unpublished research.
4. Multiple results from a single study are used, making the overall meta-analysis appear more reliable than it is, since the results are not independent.
5. Interaction effects are overlooked in favour of main effects.
6. Meta-analysis may have 'mischievous consequences' (p. 16) because its apparent objectivity and precision may disguise procedural invalidity in the studies.

Wolf (1986) provides a robust response to these criticisms, both theoretically and empirically. He also suggests (pp. 55–6) a ten-step sequence for carrying out meta-analyses rigorously, including, *inter alia*:

1 Make clear the criteria for inclusion and exclusion of studies.
2 Search for unpublished studies.
3 Develop coding categories that cover the widest range of studies identified.
4 Look for interaction effects and examine multiple independent and dependent variables separately.
5 Test for heterogeneity of results and the effects of outliers, graphing distributions of results.
6 Check for inter-rater coding reliability.
7 Use indicators of effect size rather than statistical significance.
8 Calculate unadjusted (raw) and weighted tests and effects sizes in order to examine the influence of sample size on the results found.
9 Combine qualitative and quantitative reviewing methods.
10 Report the limitations of the meta-analyses conducted.

One can add to this the need to specify the research questions being asked, the conceptual frameworks being used, the review protocols being followed, the search and retrieval strategies being used, and the ways in which the syntheses of the findings from several studies are brought together (Thomas and Pring, 2004: 54–5).

Gorard (2001b: 72–3) suggests a four-step model for conducting meta-analysis:

Step 1: Collect all the appropriate studies for inclusion.
Step 2: Weight each study 'according to its size and quality'.
Step 3: List the outcome measures used.
Step 4: Select a method for aggregation, based on the nature of the data collected (e.g. counting those studies in which an effect appeared and those in which an effect did not appear, or calculating the average effect size across the studies).

Subjectivity can enter into meta-analysis. Since so much depends upon the quality of the results that are to be synthesized, there is the danger that adherents may simply multiply the inadequacies of the database and the limits of the sample (e.g. trying to compare the incomparable). Hunter *et al.* (1982) suggest that sampling error and the influence of other factors has to be addressed, and that it should account for less than 75 per cent of the variance in observed effect sizes if the results are to be acceptable and able to be coded into categories. The issue is clear here: coding categories have to declare their level of precision, their reliability (e.g. inter-coder reliability – the equivalent of inter-rater reliability, see Chapter 10) and validity (McGaw, 1997: 376–7).

To the charge that selection bias will be as strong in meta-analysis – which embraces both published and unpublished research – as in solely published research, Glass *et al.* (1981: 226–9) argue that it is necessary to counter gross claims made in published research with more cautious claims found in unpublished research.

Because the quantitative mode of (many) studies demands only a few common variables to be measured in each case, explains Tripp (1985), the accumulation of the studies tends to increase sample size much more than it increases the complexity of the data in terms of the number of variables. Meta-analysis risks attempting to synthesize studies which are insufficiently similar to each other to permit this with any legitimacy (Glass *et al.*, 1981: 22; McGaw, 1997: 372) other than at an unhelpful level of generality. The analogy here might be to try to keep together oil and water as 'liquids'; meta-analysts would argue that differences between studies and their relationships to findings can be coded and addressed in meta-analysis. Eysenck (1978) suggests that early meta-evaluation studies mixed apples with oranges. Morrison asks:

How can we be certain that meta-analysis is fair if the hypotheses for the separate experiments were not identical, if the hypotheses were not operationalisations of the identical constructs, if the conduct of the separate RCTs (e.g. time frames, interventions and programmes, controls, constitution of the groups, characteristics of the participants, measures used) were not identical?

(Morrison, 2001: 78)

Though Smith and Glass (1977), Glass *et al.* (1981: 218–20), Slavin (1995) and Evans *et al.* (2000) address these kinds of charges, it remains the case (McGaw, 1997) that there is a risk in meta-analysis of dealing indiscriminately with a large and sometimes incoherent body of research literature. Evans *et al.* (2000: 221) argue that, nonetheless, weak studies can add up to a strong conclusion and that the differences in the size of experimental effects between high-validity and low-validity studies are surprisingly small (p. 226) (see also Glass *et al.*, 1981: 220–6).

It is unclear, too, how meta-analysis differentiates between 'good' and 'bad' research – e.g. between methodologically rigorous and poorly constructed research (Cook *et al.*, 1992: 297). Smith and Glass (1977) and Levačić and Glatter (2000) suggest that it is possible to use study findings, regardless of their methodological quality, though Glass and Smith (1978) and Slavin (1984a, 1984b), in a study of the effects of class size, indicate that methodological quality does make a difference.

Further, Wood (1995: 296) suggests that meta-analysis oversimplifies results by concentrating on overall effects to the neglect of the interaction of intervening variables. To the charge that because meta-analyses are frequently conducted on large data sets where multiple results derive from the same study (i.e. that the data are nonindependent) and are therefore unreliable, Glass *et al.* (1981) indicate how this can be addressed by using sophisticated data analysis techniques (pp. 153–216). Finally, a practical concern is the time required not only to use the easily discoverable studies (typically large-scale published studies) but to include the smaller-scale unpublished studies; the effect of neglecting the latter might be to build in bias in the meta-analysis.

Meta-analysis is an attempt to overcome the problems of small samples (see Maynard and Chalmers's (1997) review of the Cochrane Collaboration in medicine), yet the issue of sampling is complex. RCTs frequently use aggregated and averaged, rather than individual, data (Clarke and Dawson, 1999: 130), which might risk overlooking the distribution or spread of data or the possibilities of following up on individuals. In RCTs in the field of medicine, the issue of generalizability from the sample has been recognized as problematical (Clarke and Dawson, 1999: 131). The authors suggests that, here, in order to ensure that causality is clear, patients suffering from more than one illness might be deliberately excluded from the RCT. This results, characteristically, in small or very small samples, and, in this case, there are limits to generalizability, typicality and representativeness. The same problem can apply to education – in order to establish clear causality, the reduction of the sample to a subset might lead to very small samples. RCTs are inherently reductionist in their sampling. The results of the RCTs may be 'true' but trivially so, i.e. unable to be generalized to any wider population or circumstance. The problem here for RCTs is that, in terms of sampling, big is not necessarily beautiful, but neither is small! The simple accretion of results from RCTs through meta-analysis is, of course, a way of validating them, as is the prolongation of the duration of the RCT, but this is blind to the other consequences and activities taking place all around the RCT. A treatment for cancer in multiple RCTs might show it to be effective in redu-

cing cancer, and hence might justify its use; however it might bring a host of other effects which, on balance, and in the eyes of the sufferers, are worse than the cancer.

The issue of sampling is compounded by questions of ethics. For example, in medicine, ethical questions can be raised about the process of randomization, wherein control groups might be denied access to treatment (e.g. the teacher's attention or access to resources), or where participants might be subjected to potentially hazardous treatments. Fitz-Gibbon and Morris (1987) suggest that one way of addressing this is through the notion of drawing the sample from 'borderline cases' only for the control group: patients in greatest need of treatment/intervention are not deprived of it, and it is only those patients who are at the borders of needing treatment that are randomly assigned to control or experimental groups (Clarke and Dawson, 1999: 129). Whilst the borderline method might make for ethical practice, it limits the generalizability of the results. Further, if informed consent is to be obtained from participants, then this might skew the sampling to volunteers, who may or may not be representative of the wider population.

Randomization may not be appropriate in some circumstances. For example, let us imagine a situation where some form of punishment were to be tried in schools for a particular offence. How would one justify not making this a required punishment for all those in the school who committed the particular offence in question? It would contradict natural justice (Wilkins, 1969; see also Clarke and Dawson, 1999: 98) for some offenders to be exempted, in the interests of an experiment.

Clarke and Dawson (1999: 130) draw attention to the fact that in health care treatments may produce adverse reactions, in which case patients are withdrawn from the experiment. Others might simply leave the experiment. That this contributes to 'experimental mortality' or attrition rates has been long recognized (Campbell and Stanley, 1963). Less clear in education, however, is how the problem has been, or might be, addressed (cf. Rossi and Freeman, 1993). This might undermine putative parity between the control and experimental groups, a parity which, from earlier arguments about the range of participants and characteristics within and between groups, is already suspect. As the constitution of the groups changes, however slightly (and chaos theory reminds us that small changes can result in massive effects), so the dynamics of the situation change, and the consistency and comparability of the research protocol, conditions, contexts and contents are undermined. To address this involves identifying not only the exact factors on which assignation of the sample to control and experimental groups will take place, but also a recognition of significant ways in which the two groups differ. The judgement then becomes about the extent to which the dissimilarities between the two groups might outweigh their similarities (see the earlier discussion).

Further, in connection with changes to the sample, there is an 'arrow of time' (Prigogine and Stengers, 1985) that argues that situations evolve irreversibly and that to overlook this by holding time and situations constant in RCTs is to misrepresent reality. Though Campbell and Stanley's (1963) influential work on RCTs discusses the threats to internal validity caused by history and maturation (p. 5), and they suggest that randomization can overcome these (pp. 13–14), there is a nagging worry that the importance of these factors – of the people involved in the RCT – might be underestimated. How these can be addressed in education is an open question.

If meta-analysis is to be fair, in the traditions of natural science, it will need to gather and evaluate alternative, rival explanations and data that might refute the hypotheses under investigation. This is, as proponents of RCTs might agree, standard in scientific methodology. Though the advocates of meta-analysis in education (e.g. Fitz-Gibbon, 1984, 1985) suggest the need to utilize both published and unpublished research, there are serious practical problems in that published research may only report 'successes' and unpublished research may be difficult to locate, or ownership and release of data may be prohibited or restricted.

What we have, then, in meta-analysis, holds out the possibility of combining studies to provide a clear message about accumulated data from RCTs. The confidence that can be placed in these data, however, is a matter for judgement.

It is the traditional pursuit of generalizations from each quantitative study which has most hampered the development of a database adequate to reflect the complexity of the social nature of education. The cumulative effects of 'good' and 'bad' experimental studies is graphically illustrated in Figure 17.1.

An example of meta-analysis in educational research

Glass and Smith (1978) and Glass *et al.* (1981: 35–44) identified 77 empirical studies of the relationship between class size and pupil learning. These studies yielded 725 comparisons of the achievements of smaller and larger classes, the comparisons resting on data accumulated from nearly 900,000 pupils of all ages and aptitudes studying all manner of school subjects. Using regression analysis, the 725 comparisons were integrated into a single curve showing the relationship between class size and achievement in general. This curve revealed a definite inverse relationship between class size and pupil learning. When the researchers derived similar curves for a variety of circumstances that they hypothesized would alter the basic relationship (for example, grade level, subject taught, pupil ability, etc.), virtually none of these special circumstances altered the basic relationship. Only one

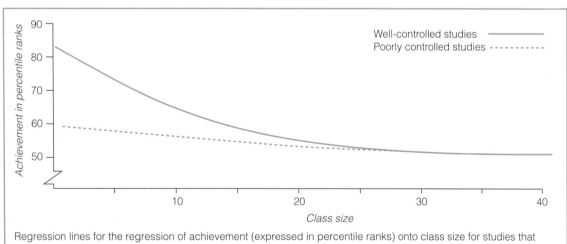

Regression lines for the regression of achievement (expressed in percentile ranks) onto class size for studies that were well-controlled and poorly controlled in the assignment of pupils to classes.

FIGURE 17.1   Class size and learning in well-controlled and poorly controlled studies

Source: Adapted from Glass and Smith, 1978

factor substantially affected the curve – whether the original study controlled adequately in the experimental sense for initial differences among pupils and teachers in smaller and larger classes. Adequate and inadequate control curves are set out in Figure 17.1.[1]

17.3 Research syntheses and systematic reviews

Whilst meta-analysis is one form of research synthesis, research syntheses and systematic reviews go broader, to include studies that are not solely randomized controlled trials. Research synthesis is an umbrella term which includes a range of styles of bringing together into a single expert review or report several studies and summaries on a particular topic. They often evaluate the quality of these studies, and draw conclusions that enable recommendations to be made for policy and practice.

Systematic reviews are a refinement of general research synthesis, by being more rigorous and less 'narrative' in character; they require the use of techniques to minimize bias, they follow protocols and criteria for searching for relevant primary, usually empirical, studies, their inclusion and exclusion, the standards for acceptable methodological rigour, their relevance to the topic in question, the scope of the studies included, team approaches to reviewing in order to reduce bias, the adoption of a consistent and clearly stated approach to combining information from across different studies, and the careful, relevant conclusions and recommendations drawn (Evans and Benefield, 2001: 529; Hemsley-Brown and Sharp, 2003). It is these criteria that separate them from the conventional 'narrative reviews', the latter being more wide-ranging and less explicit on their selection criteria (Evans and Benefield, 2001: 529).

Systematic reviews may include, for example, surveys, qualitative research, ethnographies and narrative studies (for an introduction to qualitative researcher syntheses we refer readers to Howell Major and Savin-Baden, 2010). They can combine qualitative and quantitative studies, using, for example: narrative reviews and summaries, vote-counting reviews (counting how many results are statistically significant in one direction and how many show no effect (Davies 2000: 367)), best evidence syntheses (based on clear criteria and methodologies for selection of studies), meta-ethnographies (which summarize and synthesize evidence from ethnographic and interpretive, qualitative studies (Slavin, 1986)), thematic analyses, grounded theory, meta-study, realist synthesis, qualitative data analysis techniques from Miles and Huberman (1984)

(e.g. within-site and cross-site analysis), content analyses, case surveys and qualitative comparative analysis (Davies, 2000; Dixon-Woods et al., 2005). Research syntheses seek to discover both consistencies in similar-appearing primary studies and also to account for the variability found between them (Cooper and Hedges, 1994: 4), leading to generalizations within the limits and contexts of the research studies used (Davies, 2000: 366).

The EPPI-Centre at the University of London indicates that systematic reviews are characterized by several criteria (http://eppi.ioe.ac.uk/cms/Default.aspx?tabid=67):

- they use explicit, rigorous and transparent methods, which must be applied systematically;
- they synthesize research studies, based on explicit criteria, in order to avoid bias;
- they follow a standard set of stages;
- they are accountable, able to be replicated and to be updated;
- they are required to be relevant and useful to users;
- they are intended to answer specific research questions;
- they are evidence-based.

Based on these criteria, the EPPI-Centre indicates several stages that a systematic review must follow (http://eppi.ioe.ac.uk/cms/Default.aspx?tabid=89), including:

- approaches to reviewing (including the involvement of users, different kinds of review, and methodological matters);
- getting started (including setting the scope and methods of the review and ensuring quality in the review);
- gathering and describing research (including locating and screening the studies for review, describing them and clarifying their scope);
- appraising and synthesizing the data (including appraising their quality and relevance, synthesizing the findings, drawing conclusions and making recommendations, and reporting);
- making use of the review (including disseminating the findings, with advice on how to use and apply the reports' findings).

The Centre also provides 'tools' for undertaking systematic reviews (http://eppi.ioe.ac.uk/cms/Default.aspx?tabid=184).

The British Educational Research Association also publishes its own guidelines for the conduct of systematic reviews (www.bera.ac.uk/systematic-review/

questions-conceptual-framework-and-inclusion-criteria/), which cover:

- systematic review questions;
- conceptual framework and inclusion/exclusion criteria; and
- further reading.

Evans and Benefield (2001: 533–7) set out six principles for undertaking systematic reviews of evidence:

1 a clear specification of the research question which is being addressed;
2 a systematic, comprehensive and exhaustive search for relevant studies;
3 the specification and application of clear criteria for the inclusion and exclusion of studies (including data extraction criteria: published; unpublished; citation details; language; keywords; funding support; type of study (e.g. process- or outcome-focused, prospective or retrospective); nature of the intervention; sample characteristics; planning and processes of the study; outcome evaluation) and descriptive data on the studies (e.g. from funded or non-funded research, the type of study (process- or outcome-focused), the intervention made, the population and sampling, the design and planning of the intervention and the study, the evaluation of the outcome) (Evans and Benefield, 2001: 537);
4 evaluations of the quality of the methodology used in each study (e.g. the kind of experiment and sample; reporting of outcome measures);
5 the specification of strategies for reducing bias in selecting and reviewing studies;
6 transparency in the methodology adopted for reviewing the studies.

Cooper (2010) sets out a seven-step sequence for undertaking systematic reviews:

1 formulating the problem (including identifying the kinds of research evidence that will be relevant to answer the research question or hypothesis in the area of interest, looking at research designs in the studies used, the treatment of the main effects, drawing on qualitative and quantitative research, identifying the kind of research (e.g. descriptive or causal), judging the conceptual relevance of the studies, screening the studies);
2 searching the literature (including searching, locating and retrieving relevant literature, different kinds of literature, the status of the literature, addressing the adequacy of the literature);
3 gathering information from studies (including how to develop a coding guide, identifying predictor and outcome variables, research designs used, sampling, context, statistics used, effect sizes, using a coding guide);
4 evaluating the quality of studies (deciding which studies to include and exclude, identifying problems in the research studies used, evaluating the suitability of the research design for the research synthesis, evaluating the quality and rigour of the research);
5 analysing and integrating the outcomes of studies;
6 interpreting the evidence;
7 presenting the results.

Davies (2000: 373) cautions researchers to ensure that systematic reviews do not use evidence selectively to provide overwhelming evidence of 'a positive effect of most educational interventions', i.e. that they are a consequence of the methodology of the review in question, and to ensure that statistical significance does not override educational significance. His comments apply equally appropriately to meta-analysis and research syntheses. Examples of studies that use meta-evaluation and research syntheses can be found from the websites indicated at the start of this chapter, and also in the references given throughout the chapter.

 Companion Website

The companion website to the book includes PowerPoint slides for this chapter, which list the structure of the chapter and then provide a summary of the key points in each of its sections. This resource can be found online at **www.routledge.com/textbooks/cohen7e**.

Action research

Action research is a popular way in which teachers research their own institutions, staff development facilitators bring about change, and groups and communities undertake research. This chapter introduces key issues in the planning, conduct and reporting of action research, including:

- defining action research
- principles and characteristics of action research
- participatory action research
- action research as critical praxis
- action research and complexity theory
- procedures for action research
- reporting action research
- reflexivity in action research
- some practical and theoretical matters

The chapter draws links between action research and critical theory, in particular in respect of participatory action research. It also notes the connections between action research and complexity theory.

18.1 Introduction

Action research, sometimes called practitioner based research (McNiff, 2002a: 6) is a powerful tool for change and improvement at the local level. Indeed, Kurt Lewin's own work (one of action research's founding fathers) was deliberately intended to change the life chances of disadvantaged groups in terms of housing, employment, prejudice, socialization and training. Its combination of *action* and *research* has contributed to its attraction to researchers, teachers and the academic and educational community alike.

The scope of action research as a method is impressive. It can be used in almost any setting where a problem involving people, tasks and procedures cries out for solution, or where some change of feature results in a more desirable outcome (cf. Bassey, 1998). It can be undertaken by the individual teacher, a group of teachers working cooperatively within one school, or a teacher or teachers working alongside a researcher or researchers in a sustained relationship, possibly with other interested parties like advisers, university departments and sponsors on the periphery (Holly and Whitehead, 1986). Action research can be used in a variety of areas, for example:

- *teaching methods* – replacing a traditional method by a discovery method;
- *learning strategies* – adopting an integrated approach to learning in preference to a single-subject style of teaching and learning;
- *evaluative procedures* – improving one's methods of continuous assessment;
- *attitudes and values* – encouraging more positive attitudes to work, or modifying pupils' value systems with regard to some aspect of life;
- *continuing professional development of teachers* – improving teaching skills, developing new methods of learning, increasing powers of analysis, of heightening self-awareness;
- *management and control* – the gradual introduction of the techniques of behaviour modification;
- *administration* – increasing the efficiency of some aspect of the administrative side of school life.

These examples do not mean, however, that action research can be typified straightforwardly; that is to distort its complex and multifaceted nature. Indeed Kemmis (1997) suggests that there are several schools of action research. That said, what unites different conceptions of action research is the desire for improvement to practice, based on a rigorous evidential trail of data and research.

Ferrance (2000: 1) argues that a powerful justification for action research is that teachers:

- work best on problems that they have identified for themselves;
- become more effective when they are encouraged to examine and assess their own work and then consider ways of working differently;
- help each other by working collaboratively;
- can help each other in their professional development by working together.

She suggests that action research builds on, and builds in, these principles. Indeed action research is a powerful form of participatory research, as discussed in Chapter 2 (see also Kapoor and Jordan, 2009). 'Commitment' is a feature of participatory research (see Chapter 2), and participatory action research both requires and builds commitment (David, 2002). Participatory research breaks the separation of the researcher and the participants; power is equalized and, indeed, they may all be part of the same community (*ibid.*). The research becomes a collective and shared enterprise, in many spheres, including: the research interests, agendas and problems; the generation and analysis of data; the equalization of power and control over the research outcomes, products and uses; the development of participant voice, authorship and ownership; a process-oriented and problem-solving approach; emancipatory agendas and political goals; and ethical responsibility and behaviour. We refer the reader to Chapter 2 for a fuller discussion of this.

18.2 Defining action research

The different conceptions of action research can be revealed in some typical definitions of action research, for example Hopkins (1985: 32) suggests that the combination of action and research renders that action a form of disciplined, rigorous enquiry, in which a personal attempt is made to understand, improve and reform practice. Ebbutt (1985: 156), too, regards action research as a systematic study that combines action and reflection with the intention of improving practice. Cohen and Manion (1994: 186) define it as 'a small-scale intervention in the functioning of the real world and a close examination of the effects of such an intervention'. The rigour of action research is attested by another of its founding fathers, Corey (1953: 6), who argues that it is a process in which practitioners study problems *scientifically* (our italics) so that they can evaluate, improve and steer decision making and practice. Indeed Kemmis and McTaggart (1992: 10) argue that 'to do action research is to plan, act, observe and reflect more carefully, more systematically, and more rigorously than one usually does in everyday life'.

A more philosophical stance on action research, that echoes the work of Habermas, is taken by Carr and Kemmis (1986: 162), who regard it as a form of 'self-reflective enquiry' by participants, which is undertaken in order to improve their understanding of their practices in context with a view to maximizing social justice. McNiff (2002: 17) suggests that action researchers support the view that people can 'create

their own identities' and that they should allow others to do the same. Grundy (1987: 142) regards action research as concerned with improving the 'social conditions of existence'. Kemmis and McTaggart (1992) suggest that:

Action research is concerned equally with changing *individuals*, on the one hand, and, on the other, the *culture* of the groups, institutions and societies to which they belong. The culture of a group can be defined in terms of the characteristic substance and forms of the language and discourses, activities and practices, and social relationships and organization which constitute the interactions of the group.

(Kemmis and McTaggart, 1992: 16)

Action research is designed to bridge the gap between research and practice (Somekh, 1995: 340), thereby striving to overcome the perceived persistent failure of research to impact on, or improve, practice (see also Rapoport, 1970: 499 and McCormick and James, 1988: 339). Stenhouse (1979) suggests that action research should contribute not only to practice but to a theory of education and teaching which is accessible to other teachers, making educational practice more reflective (Elliott, 1991: 54).

Action research combines diagnosis, action and reflection (McNiff 2002: 15), focusing on practical issues that have been identified by participants and which are somehow both problematic yet capable of being changed (Elliott, 1978: 355–6). McNiff (2002: 6) places self-reflection at the heart of action research, suggesting that whereas in some forms of research the researcher 'does research on other people', in action research the researcher does it to herself/himself. Zuber-Skerritt (1996b: 83) suggests that 'the aims of any action research project or program are to bring about practical improvement, innovation, change or development of social practice, and the practitioners' better understanding of their practices'.

The several strands of action research are drawn together by Kemmis and McTaggart (1988) in their all-encompassing definition:

Action research is a form of *collective* self-reflective enquiry undertaken by participants in social situations in order to improve the rationality and justice of the own social or educational practices, as well as their understanding of these practices and the situations in which these practices are carried out.... The approach is only action research when it is *collaborative*, though it is important to realize that the action research of the group is achieved through the *critically examined action* of individual group members.

(Kemmis and McTaggart, 1988: 5)

Kemmis and McTaggart (1992: 21–2) distinguish action research from the everyday actions of teachers:

- It is *not* the usual thinking teachers do when they think about their teaching. Action research is more systematic and collaborative in collecting evidence on which to base rigorous group reflection.
- It is *not* simply problem-solving. Action research involves problem-posing, not just problem-solving. It does not start from a view of 'problems' as pathologies. It is motivated by a quest to improve and understand the world by changing it and learning how to improve it from the effects of the changes made.
- It is *not* research done on other people. Action research is research by particular people on their own work, to help them improve what they do, including how they work with and for others.
- Action research is *not* 'the scientific method' applied to teaching. There is not just one view of 'the scientific method'; there are many.

Noffke and Zeichner (1987) make several claims for action research with teachers, namely that it:

- brings about changes in their definitions of their professional skills and roles;
- increases their feelings of self-worth and confidence;
- increases their awareness of classroom issues;
- improves their dispositions toward reflection;
- changes their values and beliefs;
- improves the congruence between practical theories and practices;
- broadens their views on teaching, schooling and society.

A significant feature here is that action research lays claim to the professional development of teachers; action research for professional development is a frequently heard maxim (e.g. Nixon, 1981; Oja and Smulyan, 1989; Somekh, 1995: 343; Winter, 1996). It is 'situated learning'; learning *in* the workplace and *about* the workplace (Collins and Duguid, 1989). The claims for action research, then, are several. Arising from these claims and definitions are several principles.

18.3 Principles and characteristics of action research

Hult and Lennung (1980: 241–50) and McKernan (1991: 32–3) suggest that action research:

- makes for practical problem-solving as well as expanding scientific knowledge;
- enhances the competencies of participants;
- is collaborative;
- is undertaken directly *in situ*;
- uses feedback from data in an ongoing cyclical process;
- seeks to understand particular complex social situations;
- seeks to understand the processes of change within social systems;
- is undertaken within an agreed framework of ethics;
- seeks to improve the quality of human actions;
- focuses on those problems that are of immediate concern to practitioners;
- is participatory;
- frequently uses case study;
- tends to avoid the paradigm of research that isolates and controls variables;
- is formative, such that the definition of the problem, the aims and methodology may alter during the process of action research;
- includes evaluation and reflection;
- is methodologically eclectic;
- contributes to a science of education;
- strives to render the research usable and shareable by participants;
- is dialogical and celebrates discourse;
- has a critical purpose in some forms;
- strives to be emancipatory.

Zuber-Skerritt (1996b: 85) suggests that action research is:

critical (and self-critical) collaborative enquiry by
reflective practitioners being
accountable and making results of their enquiry public
self-evaluating their practice and engaged in
participatory problem-solving and continuing professional development.

This latter view is echoed in Winter's (1996: 13–14) six key principles of action research:

- *reflexive critique*, which is the process of becoming aware of our own perceptual biases;

- *dialectical critique*, which is a way of understanding the relationships between the elements that make up various phenomena in our context;
- *collaboration*, which is intended to mean that everyone's view is taken as a contribution to understanding the situation;
- *risking disturbance*, which is an understanding of our own taken-for-granted processes and willingness to submit them to critique;
- *creating plural structures*, which involves developing various accounts and critiques, rather than a single authoritative interpretation;
- *theory and practice internalized*, which is seeing theory and practice as two interdependent yet complementary phases of the change process.

The several features that the definitions at the start of this chapter have in common suggest that action research has key principles. These are summarized by Kemmis and McTaggart (1992: 22–5):

- Action research is an approach to *improving education* by *changing* it and learning from the consequences of changes.
- Action research is *participatory*: it is research through which people work towards the improvement of *their own practices* (and only secondarily on other people's practices).
- Action research develops through *the self-reflective spiral*: a spiral of cycles of *planning, acting* (implementing plans), *observing* (systematically), *reflecting* … and then re-planning, further implementation, observing and reflecting.
- Action research is *collaborative*: it involves those responsible for action in improving it.
- Action research establishes *self-critical communities* of people participating and collaborating in all phases of the research process: the planning, the action, the observation and the reflection; it aims to build communities of people committed to *enlightening* themselves about the relationship between circumstance, action and consequence in their own situation, and *emancipating* themselves from the institutional and personal constraints which limit their power to live their own legitimate educational and social values.
- Action research is a *systematic learning process* in which people act deliberately, though remaining open to surprises and responsive to opportunities.
- Action research involves people in *theorizing* about their practices – being *inquisitive* about circumstances, action and consequences and coming to *understand* the relationships between circumstances, actions and consequences in their own lives.

- Action research requires that people put their practices, ideas and assumptions about institutions to the *test* by gathering *compelling evidence* which could convince them that their previous practices, ideas and assumptions were wrong or wrong-headed.
- Action research is open-minded about what counts as evidence (or data) – it involves not only *keeping records* which describe what is happening as accurately as possible … but also *collecting and analysing our own judgements, reactions and impressions* about what is going on.
- Action research involves keeping a *personal journal* in which we record our progress and our reflections about two parallel sets of learning: our learnings about the practices we are studying … and our learnings about the process (the practice) of studying them.
- Action research is a *political process* because it involves us in making changes that will affect others.
- Action research involves people in making *critical analyses* of the situations (classrooms, schools, systems) in which they work: these situations are *structured* institutionally.
- Action research *starts small*, by working through changes which even a single person (myself) can try, and works towards extensive changes – even critiques of ideas or institutions which in turn might lead to more general reforms of classroom, school or system-wide policies and practices.
- Action research starts with *small cycles* of planning, acting, observing and reflecting which can help to define issues, ideas and assumptions more clearly so that those involved can define more *power questions* for themselves as their work progresses.
- Action research starts with *small groups* of collaborators, but widens the community of participating action researchers so that it gradually includes more and more of those involved and affected by the practices in question.
- Action research allows us to build *records* of our improvements: (a) records of our changing *activities and practices*, (b) records of the changes in the *language and discourse* in which we describe, explain and justify our practices, (c) records of the changes in the *social relationships and forms of organization* which characterize and constrain our practices, and (d) records of the development in mastery of *action research*.
- Action research allows us to give a *reasoned justification* of our educational work to others because we can show how the evidence we have gathered and the critical reflection we have done have helped us

to create a *developed, tested and critically examined rationale* for what we are doing.

Though these principles find widespread support in the literature on action research, they require some comment. For example, there is a strong emphasis in these principles on action research as a cooperative, collaborative activity (e.g. Hill and Kerber, 1967). Kemmis and McTaggart (1992) locate this in the work of Lewin himself, commenting on his commitment to group decision making (p. 6). They argue, for example, that 'those affected by planned changes have the primary responsibility for deciding on courses of critically informed action which seem likely to lead to improvement, and for evaluating the results of strategies tried out in practice ... *action research is a group activity* [and] *action research is not individualistic'*. To 'lapse into individualism is to destroy the critical dynamic of the group' (p. 15) (italics in original).

The view of action research solely as a group activity, however, might be too restricting. It is possible for action research to be an individualistic matter as well, relating action research to the 'teacher-as-researcher' movement (Stenhouse, 1975). Whitehead (1985: 98) explicitly writes about action research in individualistic terms, and we can take this to suggest that a teacher can ask herself or himself: 'what do I see as my problem?' 'What do I see as a possible solution?' 'How can I direct the solution?' 'How can I evaluate the outcomes and take subsequent action?'

The adherence to action research as a group activity derives from several sources. *Pragmatically*, Oja and Smulyan (1989: 14), in arguing for collaborative action research, suggest that teachers are more likely to change their behaviours and attitudes if they have been involved in the research that demonstrates not only the need for such change but that it can be done – the issue of 'ownership' and 'involvement' that finds its parallel in management literature that suggests that those closest to the problem are in the best position to identify it and work towards its solution (e.g. Morrison, 1998).

Ideologically, there is a view that those experiencing the issue should be involved in decision making, itself hardly surprising given Lewin's own work with disadvantaged and marginalized groups, i.e. those groups with little voice (cf. David, 2002).

Politics and ideology are brought together in action research in *participatory action research* and *action research as critical praxis*, and it is to this that we turn.

18.4 Participatory action research

Participatory action research has attracted attention across the world, in its advocacy of empowerment and emancipation. McTaggart (1989) suggests 16 tenets of participatory action research, indicating that it:

- seeks to improve social practice by changing it;
- requires authentic participation;
- is collaborative;
- establishes self-critical communities;
- is a systematic process of learning;
- involves people in theorizing about their own practices and values;
- requires people to test their own assumptions, values, ideas and practices in real-life practice;
- requires records to be kept;
- requires participants to look at their own experiences objectively;
- is part of a political process (e.g. towards democracy);
- involves people in making critical analyses of a situation, research and practice;
- starts small;
- starts in small cycles;
- starts with small groups of people;
- requires and allows participants to build evidential records of practice, theory and reflection;
- requires and allows participants to provide a reasoned justification to others for their work.

That there is a coupling of the ideological and political debate here has been brought into focus with the work of Freire (1972) and Torres (1992: 56) in Latin America, the latter setting out several principles of participatory action research:

- it commences with explicit social and political intentions that articulate with the dominated and poor classes and groups in society;
- it must involve popular participation in the research process, i.e. it must have a social basis;
- it regards knowledge as an agent of social transformation as a whole, thereby constituting a powerful critique of those views of knowledge (theory) as somehow separate from practice;
- its epistemological base is rooted in critical theory and its critique of the subject/object relations in research;
- it must raise the consciousness of individuals, groups and nations.

Participatory action research does not mean that all participants need be doing the same. This recognizes a role for the researcher as facilitator, guide, formulator and summarizer of knowledge, raiser of issues (e.g. the possible consequences of actions, the awareness of structural conditions) (Weiskopf and Laske, 1996: 132–3).

Participatory action research is distinguished not only by its methodology (collective participation) and its outcomes (democracy, voice, emancipation) but by its areas of focus (inequalities of power, grassroots agendas for change and development, e.g. educational inequality, social exclusion, sexism and racism in education, powerlessness in decision making, student disaffection with a socially reproductive curriculum, elitism in education (cf. Wadsworth, 1998; Fine, 2010; INCITE, 2010)). Importantly here, the agendas and areas of focus are identified by the participants themselves, so they are rooted in reality, are authentic, and are 'owned' by the participants and communities themselves.

What is being argued here is that participatory action research – people acting and researching on, by, with and for themselves – is a democratic activity (Grundy, 1987: 142). This form of democracy is participatory (rather than, for example, representative), a key feature of critical theory (discussed below, see also Aronowitz and Giroux, 1986; Giroux, 1989). It is not merely a form of change theory, but addresses fundamental issues of power and power relationships, for, in according power to participants, action research is seen as an empowering activity (David, 2002). Elliott (1991: 54) argues that such empowerment has to be at a collective rather than individual level as individuals do not operate is isolation from each other, but they are shaped by organizational and structural forces.

The issue is important, for it begins to separate action research into different camps (Kemmis, 1997: 177). On the one hand are long-time advocates of action research such as Elliott (e.g. 1978, 1991) who are in the tradition of Schwab and Schön and who emphasize reflective practice; this is a particularly powerful field of curriculum research with notions of the 'teacher-as-researcher' (Stenhouse, 1975) and the reflective practitioner (Schön, 1983, 1987). On the other are advocates in the 'critical' action research model, e.g. Carr and Kemmis (1986).

18.5 Action research as critical praxis

Much of the writing in this field of action research draws on the Frankfurt School of critical theory (discussed in Chapter 2), in particular the work of Habermas. Indeed Weiskopf and Laske (1996: 123) locate action research, in the German tradition, squarely as a 'critical social science'. Using Habermas's early writing on knowledge-constitutive interests (1972, 1974) a threefold typology of action research can be constructed; the classification was set out in Chapter 2.

Grundy (1987: 154) argues that 'technical' action research is designed to render an existing situation more efficient and effective. In this respect it is akin to Argyris's (1990) notion of 'single-loop learning', being functional, often short term and technical. It is akin to Schön's (1987) notion of 'reflection-in-action' (Morrison, 1995a). Elliott (1991: 55) suggests that this view is limiting for action research since it is too individualistic and neglects wider curriculum structures, regarding teachers in isolation from wider factors.

By contrast, 'practical' action research is designed to promote teachers' professionalism by drawing on their informed judgement (Grundy, 1987: 154). This underpins the 'teacher-as-researcher' movement, inspired by Stenhouse. It is akin to Schön's 'reflection-on-action' and is a hermeneutic activity of understanding and interpreting social situations with a view to their improvement. Echoing this, Kincheloe (2003: 42) suggests that action research rejects positivistic views of rationality, objectivity, truth and methodology, preferring hermeneutic understanding and emancipatory practice. As he says (p. 108) the teacher-as-researcher movement is a political enterprise rather than the accretion of trivial cookbook remedies – a technical exercise.

Emancipatory action research has an explicit agenda which is as political as it is educational. Grundy (1987) provides a useful introduction to this view. She argues (pp. 146–7) that emancipatory action research seeks to develop in participants their understandings of illegitimate structural and interpersonal constraints that are preventing the exercise of their autonomy and freedom. These constraints, she argues, are based on illegitimate repression, domination and control. When participants develop a consciousness of these constraints, she suggests, they begin to move from unfreedom and constraint to freedom, autonomy and social justice.

Kincheloe (2003: 138–9) suggests a seven-step process of emancipatory action research:

- Constructing a system of meaning.
- Understanding dominant research methods and their effects.
- Selecting what to study.
- Acquiring a variety of research strategies.
- Making sense of information collected.
- Gaining awareness of the tacit theories and assumptions which guide practice.

■ Viewing teaching as an emancipatory, praxis-based act.

'Praxis' here is defined as action informed through reflection, and with emancipation as its goal.

Action research, then, empowers individuals and social groups to take control over their lives within a framework of the promotion, rather than the suppression of, generalizable interests (Habermas, 1976). It commences with a challenge to the illegitimate operation of power, hence in some respects (albeit more politicized because it embraces the dimension of power) it is akin to Argyris's (1990) notion of 'double-loop learning' in that it requires participants to question and challenge given value systems. For Grundy, praxis fuses theory and practice within an egalitarian social order, and action research is designed with the political agenda of improvement towards a more just, egalitarian society. This accords to some extent with Lewin's view that action research leads to equality and cooperation, an end to exploitation and the furtherance of democracy (see also Hopkins, 1985: 32; Carr and Kemmis, 1986: 163). Zuber-Skerritt suggests that:

> emancipatory action research ... is collaborative, critical and self-critical inquiry by practitioners ... into a major problem or issue or concern in their own practice. They own the problem and feel responsible and accountable for solving it through teamwork and through following a cyclical process of:
>
> 1 strategic *planning*;
> 2 *action*, i.e. implementing the plan;
> 3 *observation*, evaluation and self-evaluation;
> 4 critical and self-critical *reflection* on the results of points 1–3 and making decisions for the next cycle of action research.
>
> (Zuber-Skerritt, 1996a: 3)

Action research, she argues,

> is *emancipatory* when it aims not only at technical and practical improvement and the participants' better understanding, along with transformation and change within the existing boundaries and conditions, but also at changing the system itself or those conditions which impede desired improvement in the system/organization.... There is no hierarchy, but open and 'symmetrical communication'.
>
> (Zuber-Skerritt, 1996a: 5)

The emancipatory interest takes very seriously the notion of action researchers as participants in a community of equals. This, in turn is premised on the later

work of Habermas in his notion of the 'ideal speech situation'. Here:

■ action research is construed as reflective practice with a political agenda;
■ all participants (and action research is participatory) are equal 'players';
■ action research is necessarily dialogical – interpersonal – rather than monological (individual); and
■ communication is an intrinsic element, with communication being amongst the community of equals (Grundy and Kemmis, 1988: 87, term this 'symmetrical communication');
■ because it is a community of equals, action research is necessarily democratic and promotes democracy;
■ the search is for consensus (and consensus requires more than one participant), hence it requires collaboration and participation.

In this sense emancipatory action research fulfils the requirements of action research set out by Kemmis and McTaggart above; indeed it could be argued that *only* emancipatory action research (in the threefold typology) has the potential to do this.

Kemmis (1997: 177) suggests that the distinction between the two camps (the reflective practitioners and the critical theorists) lies in their interpretation of action research. For the former, action research is an improvement to professional practice at the local, perhaps classroom level, within the capacities of individuals and the situations in which they are working; for the latter, action research is part of a broader agenda of changing education, changing schooling and changing society.

A key term in action research is 'empowerment'; for the former camp, empowerment is largely a matter of the professional sphere of operations, achieving professional autonomy through professional development. For the latter, empowerment concerns taking control over one's life within a just, egalitarian, democratic society. Whether the latter is realizable or utopian is a matter of critique of this view. Where is the evidence that critical action research either empowers groups or alters the macro-structures of society? Is critical action research socially transformative? At best the jury is out; at worst the jury simply has gone away as capitalism overrides egalitarianism worldwide. The point at issue here is the extent to which the notion of emancipatory action research has attempted to hijack the action research agenda, and whether, in so doing (if it has), it has wrested action research away from practitioners and into the hands of theorists and the academic research community only.

More specifically, several criticisms have been levelled at this interpretation of emancipatory action research (Gibson, 1985; Morrison, 1995a, 1995b; Somekh, 1995; Melrose, 1996; Grundy, 1996; Weiskopf and Laske, 1996; Webb, 1996; McTaggart, 1996; Kemmis, 1997), including the views that:

- it is utopian and unrealizable;
- it is too controlling and prescriptive, seeking to capture and contain action research within a particular mould – it moves towards conformity;
- it adopts a narrow and particularistic view of emancipation and action research, and how to undertake the latter;
- it undermines the significance of the individual teacher-as-researcher in favour of self-critical communities. (Kemmis and McTaggart (1992: 152) pose the question 'why *must* action research consist of a *group* process?');
- the threefold typification of action research is untenable;
- it assumes that rational consensus is achievable, that rational debate will empower all participants (i.e. it understates the issue of power, wherein the most informed are already the most powerful – Grundy (1996: 111) argues that the better argument derives from the one with the most evidence and reasons, and that these are more available to the powerful, thereby rendering the conditions of equality suspect);
- it overstates the desirability of consensus-oriented research (which neglects the complexity of power);
- power cannot be dispersed or rearranged simply by rationality;
- action research as critical theory reduces its practical impact and confines it to the commodification of knowledge in the academy;
- it is uncritical and self-contradicting;
- will promote conformity through slavish adherence to its orthodoxies;
- is naive in its understanding of groups and celebrates groups over individuals, particularly the 'in-groups' rather than the 'out-groups';
- privileges its own view of science (rejecting objectivity) and lacks modesty;
- privileges the authority of critical theory;
- is elitist whilst purporting to serve egalitarianism;
- assumes an undifferentiated view of action research;
- is attempting to colonize and redirect action research.

This seemingly devastating critique serves to remind the reader that critical action research, even though it has caught the high ground of recent coverage, is highly problematical. It is just as controlling as those controlling agendas that it seeks to attack (Morrison, 1995b). Indeed Melrose (1996: 52) suggests that, because critical research is, itself, value-laden, it abandons neutrality; it has an explicit social agenda that, under the guise of examining values, ethics, morals and politics that are operating in a particular situation, is actually aimed at transforming the status quo.

For a simple introductory exercise for understanding action research see the accompanying website.

18.6 Action research and complexity theory

Not only does action research link with participatory research, but affinities have been drawn between action research and complexity theory. Phelps and Graham (2010: 184) argue that action research 'can readily accommodate the key tenets of complexity theory' and that there is a 'deep complementarity' between them. For example they note (p. 187) that action research:

- accepts that systems are unpredictable, open and non-linear;
- resonates with issues of adaptation to environment;
- can lead to bifurcation (see Chapter 1) (i.e. when a system moves from one 'point of stability to another' (p. 190));
- celebrates the interaction of participants;
- requires both feedback and feed forward;
- is reflective;
- shows an interests in 'exceptions' or outliers (which can lead to major change (p. 194));
- is not concerned with controlling variables;
- accepts that the systems in which it takes place are complex and dynamic.

This is reinforced by Davis and Sumara (2005: 455) in their comments that 'coherent collective behaviours and characters emerge in the activities and interactivities of individual agents', not least in the context of self-organization. Phelps and Graham (2010: 195) are concerned to show that action research, like complexity theory, has some aversion to positivism.

18.7 Procedures for action research

There are several ways in which the steps of action research have been analysed. Blum (National Education Association of the United States, 1959) casts action research into two simple stages: a diagnostic stage in which the problems are analysed and the hypotheses developed; and a therapeutic stage in which the hypotheses are tested by a consciously directed intervention or experiment *in situ*. Lewin (1946, 1948) codified the action research process into four main stages: planning, acting, observing and reflecting.

He suggests that action research commences with a general idea and data are sought about the presenting situation. The successful outcome of this examination is the production of a plan of action to reach an identified objective, together with a decision on the first steps to be taken. Lewin acknowledges that this might involve modifying the original plan or idea. The next stage of implementation is accompanied by ongoing fact-finding to monitor and evaluate the intervention, i.e. to act as a formative evaluation. This feeds forward into a revised plan and set of procedures for implementation, themselves accompanied by monitoring and evaluation. Lewin (1948: 205) suggests that such 'rational social management' can be conceived of as a spiral of planning, action and fact-finding about the outcomes of the actions taken.

The legacy of Lewin's work, though contested (e.g. McTaggart, 1996: 248) is powerful in the steps of action research set out by Kemmis and McTaggart:

In practice, the process begins with a *general idea* that some kind of improvement or change is desirable. In deciding just where to begin in making improvements, one decides on a *field of action* ... where the battle (not the whole war) should be fought. It is a decision on where it is possible to have an impact. The general idea prompts a '*reconnaissance*' of the circumstances of the field, and fact-finding about them. Having decided on the field and made a preliminary reconnaissance, the action researcher decides on a *general plan* of action. Breaking the general plan down into achievable steps, the action researcher settles on the *first action step*. Before taking this first step the action researcher becomes more circumspect, and devises a way of *monitoring* the effects of the first action step. When it is possible to maintain fact-finding by monitoring the action, the first step is taken. As the step is implemented, new data start coming in and the effect of the action can be described and *evaluated*. The general plan is then revised in the light of the new information about the field of action and the second action step can be planned along with appropriate monitoring procedures. The second step is then implemented, monitored and evaluated; and the spiral of action, monitoring, evaluation and replanning continues.

(Kemmis and McTaggart, 1981: 2)

McKernan (1991: 17) suggests that Lewin's model of action research is a series of spirals, each of which incorporates a cycle of analysis, reconnaissance, reconceptualization of the problem, planning of the intervention, implementation of the plan, evaluation of the effectiveness of the intervention. Ebbutt (1985) adds to this the view that feedback within and between each cycle is important, facilitating reflection. This is reinforced in the model of action research by Altricher and Gstettner (1993) where, though they have four steps (p. 343): (a) finding a starting point; (b) clarifying the situation;, (c) developing action strategies and putting them into practice; (d) making teachers' knowledge public – they suggest that steps (b) and (c) need not be sequential, thereby avoiding the artificial divide that might exist between data collection, analysis and interpretation.

Zuber-Skerritt (1996b: 84) sets emancipatory (critical) action research into a cyclical process of: '(1) strategic planning, (2) implementing the plan (action), (3) observation, evaluation and self-evaluation, (4) critical and self-critical reflection on the results of (1) – (3) and making decisions for the next cycle of research.' In an imaginative application of action research to organizational change theory she takes the famous work of Lewin (1952) on forcefield analysis and change theory (unfreezing → moving → refreezing) and the work of Beer *et al.* (1990) on task alignment, and sets them into an action research sequence that clarifies the steps of action research very usefully (Figure 18.1).

Bassey (1998) sets out eight stages in action research:

Stage 1: Defining the enquiry.
Stage 2: Describing the educational context and situation.
Stage 3: Collecting evaluative data and analysing them.
Stage 4: Reviewing the data and looking for contradictions.
Stage 5: Tackling a contradiction by introducing change.
Stage 6: Monitoring the change.
Stage 7: Analysing evaluative data about the change.
Stage 8: Reviewing the change and deciding what to do next.

McNiff (2002: 71), too, sets out an eight-stage model of the action research process:

- review your current practice;
- identify an aspect that you wish to improve;
- imagine a way forward in this;
- try it out;
- monitor and reflect on what happens;
- modify the plan in the light of what has been found, what has happened, and continue;

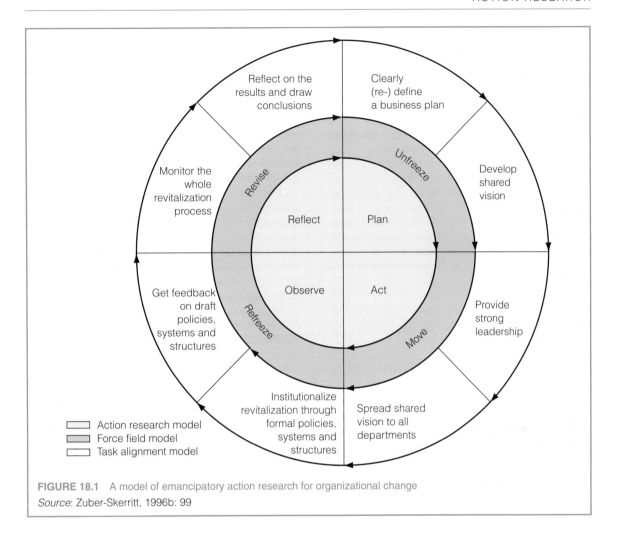

FIGURE 18.1 A model of emancipatory action research for organizational change

Source: Zuber-Skerritt, 1996b: 99

- evaluate the modified action;
- continue until you are satisfied with that aspect of your work (e.g. repeat the cycle).

Sagor (2005: 4) sets out a straightforward four-stage model of action research:

Stage 1: Clarify vision and targets.
Stage 2: Articulate appropriate theory.
Stage 3: Implement action and collect data.
Stage 4: Reflect on the data and plan informed action.

Another approach is to set out an eight-stage model:

Stage 1: Decide and agree one common problem that you are experiencing or need that must be addressed.
Stage 2: Identify some causes of the problem (need).

Stage 3: Brainstorm a range of possible practical solutions to the problem, to address the real problem and the real cause(s).
Stage 4: From the range of possible practical solutions decide *one* of the solutions to the problems, perhaps what you consider to be the most suitable or best solution to the problem. Plan how to put the solution into practice.
Stage 5: Identify some 'success criteria' by which you will be able to judge whether the solution has worked to solve the problem, i.e. how will you know whether the proposed solution, when it is put into practice, has been successful. Identify some practical criteria which will tell you how successful the project has been.
Stage 6: Put the plan into action; monitor, adjust and evaluate what is taking place.
Stage 7: Evaluate the outcome to see how well it has

addressed and solved the problem or need, using the success criteria identified in Stage 5.

Stage 8: Review and plan what needs to be done in light of the evaluation.

The key features of action research here are:

- it works on, and tries to solve, real, practitioner-identified problems of everyday practice;
- it is collaborative and builds in teacher involvement;
- it seeks causes and tries to work on those causes;
- the solutions are suggested by the practitioners involved;
- it involves a divergent phase and a convergent phase;
- it plans an intervention by the practitioners themselves;
- it implements the intervention;
- it evaluates the success of the intervention in solving the identified problem.

Tripp (2003) sets out a full action research cycle of reconnaissance, planning, acting, researching action, evaluating action, in Figure 18.2.

Put more skeletally, the action research process is set out in Figure 18.3.

We set out below an eight-stage process of action research that attempts to draw together the several strands and steps of the action research undertaking. The *first stage* will involve the identification, evaluation and formulation of the problem perceived as critical in an everyday teaching situation. 'Problem' should be interpreted loosely here so that it could refer to the need to introduce innovation into some aspect of a school's established programme.

The *second stage* involves preliminary discussion and negotiations among the interested parties – teachers, researchers, advisers, sponsors, possibly – which may culminate in a draft proposal. This may include a statement of the questions to be answered (e.g. 'Under what conditions can curriculum change be best effected?', 'What are the limiting factors in bringing about effective curriculum change?', 'What strong points of action research can be employed to bring about curriculum change?'). The researchers in their capacity as consultants (or sometimes as programme

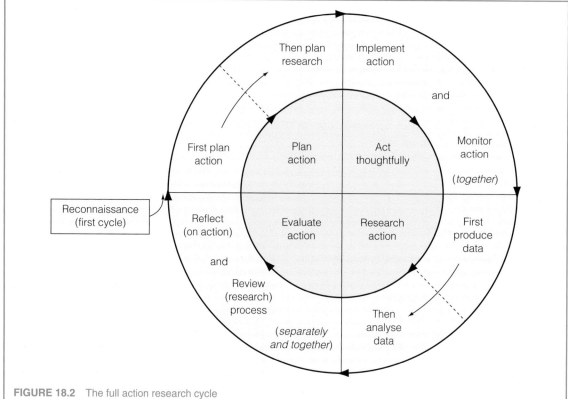

FIGURE 18.2 The full action research cycle

Source: Tripp, D. 2003. Action Inquiry. Action Research e-Reports 017. http://www2.fhs.usyd.edu.au/arow/arer/017. htm. Reproduced with permission of David Tripp

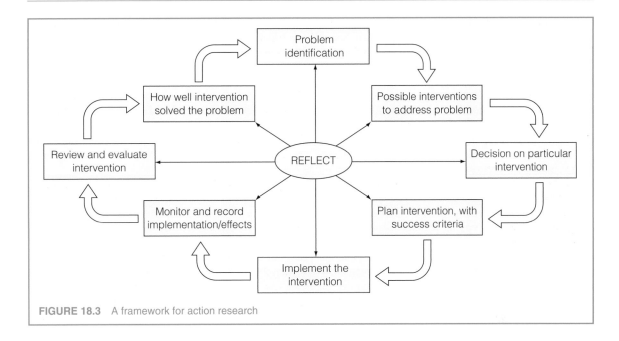

FIGURE 18.3 A framework for action research

initiators) may draw upon their expertise to bring the problem more into focus, possibly determining causal factors or recommending alternative lines of approach to established ones. This is often the crucial stage for the venture as it is at this point that the seeds of success or failure are planted, for, generally speaking, unless the objectives, purposes and assumptions are made perfectly clear to all concerned, and unless the role of key concepts is stressed (e.g. feedback), the enterprise can easily miscarry.

The *third stage* may in some circumstances involve a review of the research literature to find out what can be learned from comparable studies, their objectives, procedures and problems encountered.

The *fourth stage* may involve a modification or redefinition of the initial statement of the problem at stage one. It may now emerge in the form of a testable hypothesis; or as a set of guiding objectives. Sometimes change agents deliberately decide against the use of objectives on the grounds that they have a constraining effect on the process itself. It is also at this stage that assumptions underlying the project are made explicit (e.g. in order to effect curriculum changes, the attitudes, values, skills and objectives of the teachers involved must be changed).

The *fifth stage* may be concerned with the selection of research procedures – sampling, administration, choice of materials, methods of teaching and learning, allocation of resources and tasks, deployment of staff and so on. Here it must be stated that embedded within

the overall scope of the term 'action research' might be a number of different research designs that include different methods of gathering data. A piece of action research might include, for example:

- an initial and end-of-intervention survey (a pre- and post-survey);
- an experimental or quasi-experimental design (e.g. where some students/teachers are involved in the intervention and some are not, or where pre- and post-testing of students/teachers is undertaken);
- a longitudinal study (over the duration of the intervention);
- participant and non-participant observation;
- interviews and field notes;
- one or more case studies;
- documentation from, and about, participants;
- questionnaire data.

In this respect readers are advised to go to the chapters in this book that deal with these methods, in particular on case study, experiments and quasi-experiments, and observation. Many novice researchers are unsure whether their research is action research or a case study; indeed it may be both, but a distinguishing feature may be whether the research involves action/ collective action on the part of the researcher(s), or whether the data are largely only collected. If it is the former – concerning change, development and intervention, then it may be action research, whereas if it is largely the latter then it may be more of a case study; one has to be very cautious in making this distinction because there can be gross overlaps between the two.

As action research is intended to bring about a change, with an intervention involved, then the researcher may wish to use an experimental or quasi-experimental approach in the action research in an attempt to identify causality through a controlled intervention, with control and experimental groups (see Chapter 16).

The *sixth stage* will be concerned with the choice of the evaluation procedures to be used and will need to take into consideration that evaluation in this context will be continuous.

The *seventh stage* embraces the implementation of the project itself (over varying periods of time). It will include the conditions and methods of data collection (e.g. fortnightly meetings, the keeping of records, interim reports, final reports, the submission of self-evaluation and group-evaluation reports, etc.); the monitoring of tasks and the transmission of feedback to the research team; and the classification and analysis of data.

The *eighth and final stage* will involve the interpretation of the data; inferences to be drawn; and overall evaluation of the project (see Woods, 1989). Discussions on the findings will take place in the light of previously agreed evaluative criteria. Errors, mistakes and problems will be considered. A general summing-up may follow this in which the outcomes of the project are reviewed, recommendations made and arrangements for dissemination of results to interested parties decided.

As we stressed, this is a basic framework; much activity of an incidental and possibly ad hoc nature will take place in and around it. This may comprise discussions among teachers, researchers and pupils; regular meetings among teachers or schools to discuss progress and problems, and to exchange information; possibly regional conferences; and related activities, all enhanced by the range of current hardware and software.

Hopkins (1985), McNiff (1988), McNiff *et al.* (1996) and McNiff and Whitehead (2009) offer much practical advice on the conduct of action research, including 'getting started', operationalization, planning, monitoring and documenting the intervention, collecting data and making sense of them, using case studies, evaluating the action research, ethical issues and reporting. We urge readers to go to these helpful sources. These are essentially both introductory sources and manuals for practice. McNiff (2002: 85–91) provides useful advice for novice action researchers:

- Stay small, stay focused.
- Identify a clear research question.

- Be realistic about what you can do; be aware that wider change begins with you.
- Plan carefully.
- Set a realistic timescale.
- Involve others (as participants, observers, validators – including critical friends – potential researchers).
- Ensure good ethical practice.
- Concentrate on learning, not on the outcomes of action.
- The focus of the research is you, in company with others.
- Beware of happy endings.
- Be aware of political issues.

She makes the point (p. 98) that it is important to set evaluative criteria. Without success criteria it is impossible for the researcher to know whether, or how far, the action research has been successful. Action researchers could ask themselves 'How will we know whether we have been successful?'

Kemmis and McTaggart (1992: 25–7) offer a useful series of observations for beginning action research:

- Get an action research group together and *participate* yourself – be a model learner about action research.
- Be content to start to work with a *small group*.
- *Get organized.*
- *Start small.*
- *Establish a time line.*
- Arrange for *supportive work-in-progress discussions* in the action research group.
- Be tolerant and supportive – expect people to learn from experience.
- Be persistent about monitoring.
- Plan for a long haul on the bigger issues of changing classroom practices and school structures.
- Work to involve (in the research process) those who are involved (in the action), so that they share responsibility for the whole action research process.
- Remember that *how you think about things* – the language and understandings that shape your action – may need changing just as much as the specifics of what you do.
- *Register progress* not only with the participant group but also with the whole staff and other interested people.
- If necessary arrange *legitimizing rituals* – involving consultants or other outsiders.
- Make time to *write* throughout your project.
- Be explicit about what you have achieved by *reporting progress*.

- Throughout, keep in mind *the distinction between education and schooling*.
- Throughout, ask yourself whether your action research project is helping you (and those with whom you work) to improve the extent to which you are *living your educational values* [italics in original].

It is clear from this list that action research is a blend of practical and theoretical concerns; it is both action and research.

In conducting action research the participants can be both methodologically eclectic and can use a variety of instruments for data collection: questionnaires, diaries, interviews, case studies, observational data, experimental design, field notes, photography, audio and video recording, sociometry, rating scales, biographies and accounts, documents and records, in short the full *gamut* of techniques (for a discussion of these see Hopkins, 1985; McKernan, 1991, and the chapters in our own book here).

Additionally a useful way of managing to gain a focus within a group of action researchers is through the use of Nominal Group Technique (Morrison, 1993). The administration is straightforward and is useful for gathering information in a single instance. In this approach one member of the group provides the group with a series of questions, statements or issues. A four-stage model can be adopted:

Stage 1: A short time is provided for individuals to write down without interruption or discussion with anybody else their own answers, views, reflections and opinions in response to questions/statements/issues provided by the group leader (e.g. problems of teaching or organizing such-and-such, or an identification of issues in the organization of a piece of the curriculum, etc.).

Stage 2: The responses are entered onto a sheet of paper which is then displayed for others to view. The leader invites *individual* comments on the displayed responses to the questions/statements/issue, but no group discussion, i.e. the data collection is still at an individual level, and then notes these comments on the display sheet on which the responses have been collected. The process of inviting individual comments/contributions which are then displayed for everyone to see is repeated until no more comments are received.

Stage 3: At this point the leader asks the respondents to identify *clusters* of displayed comments and responses, i.e. to put some structure, order and priority into the displayed items. It is here that control of proceedings moves from the leader to the participants. A group discussion takes place since a process of clarification of

meanings and organizing issues and responses into coherent and cohesive bundles is required which then moves to the identification of priorities.

Stage 4: Finally the leader invites any further group discussion about the material and its organization.

The process of the Nominal Group Technique enables individual responses to be included within a group response, i.e. the individual's contribution to the group delineation of significant issues is maintained. This technique is very useful in gathering data from individuals and putting them into some order which is shared by the group (and action research is largely, though not exclusively, a group matter), e.g. of priority, of similarity and difference, of generality and specificity. It also enables individual disagreements to be registered and to be built into the group responses and identification of significant issues to emerge. Further, it gives equal status to all respondents in the situation, for example, the voice of the new entrant to the teaching profession is given equal consideration to the voice of the head teacher of several years' experience. The attraction of this process is that it balances writing with discussion, a divergent phase with a convergent phase, space for individual comments and contributions to group interaction. It is a useful device for developing collegiality. All participants have a voice and are heard.

The written partner to the Nominal Group Technique is the Delphi technique. This has the advantage that it does not *require* participants to meet together as a whole group. This is particularly useful in institutions where time is precious and where it is difficult to arrange a whole group meeting. The process of data collection resembles that of the Nominal Group Technique in many respects: it can be set out in a three-stage process:

Stage 1: The leader asks participants to respond to a series of questions and statements in writing. This may be done on an individual basis or on a small group basis – which enables it to be used flexibly, e.g. within a department, within an age phase.

Stage 2: The leader collects the written responses and collates them into clusters of issues and responses (maybe providing some numerical data on frequency of response). This analysis is then passed back to the respondents for comment, further discussion and identification of issues, responses and priorities. At this stage the respondents are presented with a *group response* (which may reflect similarities or record differences) and the respondents are asked to react to this *group response*. By adopting this procedure the individual has the opportunity to agree with the group response (i.e. to move from a possibly small private individual disagreement to a general group agreement) or to indicate a more substantial disagreement with the group response.

Stage 3: This process is repeated as many times as it is necessary. In saying this, however, the leader will need to identify the most appropriate place to stop the re-circulation of responses. This might be done at a group meeting which, it is envisaged, will be the plenary session for the participants, i.e. an endpoint of data collection will be in a whole group forum.

By presenting the group response back to the participants, there is a general progression in the technique towards a polarizing of responses, i.e. a clear identification of areas of consensus and dissensus (and emancipatory action research strives for consensus). The Delphi technique brings advantages of clarity, privacy, voice and collegiality. In doing so it engages the issues of confidentiality, anonymity and disclosure of relevant information whilst protecting participants' rights to privacy. It is a very useful means of undertaking behind-the-scenes data collection which can then be brought to a whole group meeting; the price that this exacts is that the leader has much more work to do in collecting, synthesizing, collating, summarizing, prioritizing and re-circulating data than in the Nominal Group Technique, which is immediate. As participatory techniques both the Nominal Group Technique and Delphi techniques are valuable for data collection and analysis in action research.

18.8 Reporting action research

McNiff and Whitehead (2009: 15) argue that, in reporting action research, it is important to note not only the action but the research element, including the rigorous methodology and interpretation of data. They suggest that it is important to state clearly:

- The research issue and how it came to become a research issue in the improvement of practice.
- The methodology of, and justification for, the intervention, and how it was selected from amongst other possible interventions.
- How the intervention derived from an understanding of the situation.
- What data were collected, when and from whom.
- How data were collected, processed and analysed.
- How the intervention was monitored and reviewed.
- How reflexivity was addressed.
- What were the standard and criteria for success, and how these criteria were derived.

- How conclusions were reached and how these were validated.
- What and how the researcher learnt as a consequence of the action research.
- How practice was changed as a consequence of the findings.

The authors note that validity is a key concern in reporting, that warrants have to be justified for the conclusions drawn, and that these warrants reside in the evidential trail provided in the research (e.g., p. 23), and that reflection and reflexivity are demonstrated (p. 28).

It was noted at the start of this chapter that the goal of action research is improvement; therefore the report must indicate not only what the improvement was, but that it was attributable to the intervention and not to other factors, i.e. that causality is demonstrated. This requires a level of rigour that is indicated in the 'research' part of the 'action research'. More than this, given that action research concerns research, the report should indicate not only how the research led to improvement in practice, but how the action research in question contributes to the expansion of knowledge, scholarship and scholarly enquiry, i.e. what significance the research has for both the academic and professional communities. The report, then, serves a dual set of criteria:

- criteria for the planning, conducting, reporting and evaluation of the research;
- criteria for the planning, conducting, reporting and evaluation of practice/action.

Given that the intervention was into a 'real-life' situation, it is important to include in the report some information about the real-life context of the intervention, so that the reader has a clear picture of this. This means that the report will include necessary descriptive data (McNiff and Whitehead, 2009: 37), together with scholarly enquiry (e.g. a literature review), explanations, reflections, research methodology, data collection, analysis and interpretation, consideration of alternative explanations and, of course, evidence that there has been an improvement in practice and in the development of the researcher (e.g. in terms of pedagogy, subject knowledge, researcher ability and skills, reflective capacity).

A piece of action research may be reported in narrative form (given that the researcher is an actor in the situation) (e.g. McNiff and Whitehead, 2009: 49), though it must be written with the reader in mind. An action research report should address (cf. McNiff and Whitehead, 2009: 56):

- The action researcher's concern and the reason for that concern.
- An indication of the presenting situation at the start of the action research.
- A review of what, how and why the action researcher moved into action and reflection.
- What methodology, design and data were used in the action research (e.g. it was suggested earlier that, embedded in action research might be a case study, an experimental or quasi-experimental approach, a survey, an ethnography).
- What were the research questions.
- What were the problems that the action research was intended to address/solve.
- What possible interventions were considered, and why some of these were rejected/accepted (e.g. on what criteria).
- How the intervention was planned and implemented.
- How ongoing data were gathered, processed and used during the action research.
- What were the roles of the action researcher.
- What was discovered during, and as a consequence of, the action research.
- What conclusions were drawn, and how they were valid (their warrants).
- An indication of the significance of the action research – for action and for research.
- An indication of how practice was modified and improved as a consequence of the action research.
- An indication of, and justification for, the success criteria used to evaluate the action research.
- The reflections of the action researcher, together with evidence of growth in reflective ability (and the criteria used to evaluate this).

It can be seen that the action researcher has to adopt a potentially schizophrenic stance to the action and the research, being both in it and of them, but also having to stand back from the situation and view it with as much objectivity as possible; subjectivity and objectivity (or, perhaps better, relative subjectivity and objectivity) are combined in a single action researcher.

18.9 Reflexivity in action research

The analysis so far has made much of the issue of reflection, be it reflection-in-action, reflection-on-action or critical reflection (Morrison, 1995a). Reflection, it has been argued, occurs at every stage of action research. Beyond this, the notion of *reflexivity* is central to action research, because the researchers are also the participants and practitioners in the action research –

they are part of the social world that they are studying (Hammersley and Atkinson, 1983: 14). Hall (1996: 29) suggests that reflexivity is an integral element and epistemological basis of emancipatory action research because it takes as its basis the view of the construction of knowledge in which: (a) data are authentic and reflect the experiences of all participants; (b) democratic relations exist between all participants in the research; the researcher's views (which may be theory-laden) do not hold precedence over the views of participants.

What is being required in the notion of reflexivity is a self-conscious awareness of the effects that the participants-as-practitioners-and-researchers are having on the research process, how their values, attitudes, perceptions, opinions, actions, feelings, etc. are feeding into the situation being studied (akin, perhaps, to the notion of counter-transference in counselling). The participants-as-practitioners-and-researchers need to apply to themselves the same critical scrutiny that they are applying to others and to the research. This issue is discussed in Chapter 10.

Reflexivity also links to awareness of possible bias, in that the practitioner is also the researcher, and may not be entirely disinterested (cf. Newby, 2010: 64), for example in an attempt to impress a senior manager, a teacher who is an action researcher may present a rosier picture of the outcome of the action research than is really the case, or, in contrast, a teacher who may be pressing for increased resources may present the outcome more negatively than it is. Here ethics, validity and political agendas coincide.

18.10 Some practical and theoretical matters

Much has been made in this chapter of the democratic principles that underpin a considerable amount of action research. The ramifications of this are several. For example, there must be a free flow of information between participants and communication must be extensive (Elliott, 1978: 356). Furthermore, communication must be open, unconstrained and unconstraining – the force of the better argument in Habermas's 'ideal speech situation'. That this might be problematic in some organizations has been noted by Holly (1984: 100), as action research and schools are often structured differently, schools being hierarchical, formal and bureaucratic whilst action research is collegial, informal, open, collaborative and crosses formal boundaries. In turn this suggests that, for action research to be successful, the conditions of collegiality have to be present, for example (Morrison, 1998: 157–8):

- participatory approaches to decision making;
- democratic and consensual decision making;
- shared values, beliefs and goals;
- equal rights of participation in discussion;
- equal rights to determine policy;
- equal voting rights on decisions;
- the deployment of subgroups who are accountable to the whole group;
- shared responsibility and open accountability;
- an extended view of expertise;
- judgements and decisions based on the power of the argument rather than the positional power of the advocates;
- shared ownership of decisions and practices.

It is interesting, perhaps, that these features, derived from management theory, can apply so well to action research – action research nests comfortably within certain management styles. Indeed Zuber-Skerritt (1996b: 90) suggests that the main barriers to emancipatory action research are: (a) single-loop learning (rather than double-loop learning (Argyris, 1990)); (b) overdependence on experts or seniors to the extent that independent thought and expression are stifled; (c) an orientation to efficiency rather than to research and development (one might add here 'rather than to reflection and problem-posing'); (d) a preoccupation with operational rather than strategic thinking and practice.

Zuber-Skerritt (1996a: 17) suggests four practical problems that action researchers might face:

- How can we formulate a method of work which is sufficiently economical as regards the amount of data gathering and data processing for a practitioner to undertake it alongside a normal workload, over a limited timescale?
- How can action research techniques be sufficiently specific that they enable a small-scale investigation by a practitioner to lead to genuinely new insights, and avoid being accused of being either too minimal to be valid, or too elaborate to be feasible?
- How can these methods, given the above, be readily available and accessible to anyone who wishes to practise them, building on the competencies which practitioners already possess?
- How can these methods contribute a genuine improvement of understanding and skill, beyond prior competence, in return for the time and energy expended – that is, a more rigorous process than that which characterizes positivist research?

She also suggests that the issue of the audience of action research reports is problematic:

The answer to the question 'who are action research reports written for?' is that there are three audiences – each of equal importance. One audience comprises those colleagues with whom we have collaborated in carrying out the research reported.... It is important to give equal importance to the second audience. These are interested colleagues in other institutions, or in other areas of the same institution, for whom the underlying structure of the work presented may be similar to situations in which they work.... But the third, and perhaps most important audience, is ourselves. The process of writing involves clarifying and exploring ideas and interpretations.

(Zuber-Skerritt, 1996a: 26)

We have already seen that the participants in a change situation may be either a teacher, a group of teachers working internally, or else teachers and researchers working on a collaborative basis. It is this last category, where action research brings together two professional bodies each with its own objectives and values, that we shall consider further at this point because of its inherent problematic nature. Both parties share the same interest in an educational problem, yet their respective orientations to it differ. It has been observed (e.g. Halsey, 1972) that research values precision, control, replication and attempts to generalize from specific events. Teaching, on the other hand, is concerned with action, with doing things, and translates generalizations into specific acts. The incompatibility between action and research in these respects, therefore, can be a source of problems (Marris and Rein, 1967).

Another issue of some consequence concerns head teachers' and teachers' attitudes to the possibility of change as a result of action research. Hutchinson and Whitehouse (1986), for example, having monitored teachers' efforts to form collaborative groups within their schools, discovered one source of difficulty to be not only resistance from heads but also, and in their view more importantly, from some teachers themselves to the action researcher's efforts to have them scrutinize individual and social practice, possibly with a view to changing it, e.g. in line with the head teacher's policies.

Action research is not exempted from the ethical issues that were identified in Chapter 5. It requires the informed consent of participants, options for teachers/students not to take part, and with no penalty (Nolen and Vander Putten, 2007), and confidentiality and autonomy of participants to be respected. Whilst referring the reader to Chapter 5, we also note that there is a blurred dividing line between the teacher *qua* teacher and the teacher *qua* researcher, and that effective teaching also concerns effective researching. Perhaps the fact that minors attend school on a compulsory basis already gives the teacher automatic right to research them as part of her everyday teaching? Where is the dividing line?

Finally, Winter (1982) draws attention to the problem of interpreting data in action research. He writes:

> The action research/case study tradition does have a methodology for the *creation* of data, but not (as yet) for the interpretation of data. We are shown how the descriptive journal, the observer's field notes, and the open-ended interview are utilized to create accounts of events which will *confront* the practitioner's current pragmatic assumptions and definitions; we are shown the potential value of this process (in terms of increasing teachers' sensitivity) and the problem it poses for individual and collective professional equilibrium. What we are *not* shown is *how* the teacher can or should handle the data thus collected.
>
> (Winter, 1982: 162)

The problem for Winter is how to carry out an interpretive analysis of restricted data, that is, data which can make no claim to be generally representative. In other words, the problem of validity cannot be sidestepped by arguing that the contexts are unique.

18.11 Conclusion

Action research has been seen as a significant vehicle for empowering teachers, though this chapter has questioned the extent of this. As a research device it combines six notions:

1 a straightforward cycle of: identifying a problem, planning an intervention, implementing the intervention, evaluating the outcome;
2 reflective practice;

3 political emancipation;
4 critical theory;
5 professional development; and
6 participatory practitioner research.

It is a flexible, situationally responsive methodology that offers rigour, authenticity and voice. That said, this chapter has tried to expose both the attractions and problematic areas of action research. In its thrust towards integrating action and research one has to question whether this is an optimistic way of ensuring that research impacts on practice for improvement, or whether it is a recessive hybrid.

There are several important and useful websites for action research:

Educational Action Research (journal): www.tandf.co.uk/journals/titles/09650792.asp

Action research links: http://ggsc.wnmu.edu/gap/ar.html

Action research resources: www.scu.edu.au/schools/gcm/ar/arhome.html

Action Research International (journal): www.scu.edu.au/schools/gcm/ar/ari/arihome.html

Participatory Action Research Network at Cornell University: http://sao.cornell.edu/SO/org/05–06/1265

Action research net: www.actionresearch.net

Action research websites: www.alliance.brown.edu/dnd/ar_websites.shtml and www.emtech.net/actionresearch.htm

Action research resources: http://carbon.cudenver.edu/~mryder/itc_data/act_res.html

University of Colorado action research site: http://carbon.cudenver.edu/~mryder/reflect/act_res.html

Leading action research in schools: www.fldoe.org/ESE/pdf/action-res.pdf

Participatory action research websites: http://www2.bc.edu/~lykes/research.htm

Jean McNiff's website: www.jeanmcniff.com/writings.html

Action research methodology: www.web.net/~robrien/papers/arfinal.html

---

 Companion Website

The companion website to the book includes PowerPoint slides for this chapter, which list the structure of the chapter and then provide a summary of the key points in each of its sections. In addition there is further information in the form of a plan to introduce action research. These resources can be found online at **www.routledge.com/textbooks/cohen7e**.

Virtual worlds in educational research

Stewart Martin

This chapter introduces computer simulations and virtual worlds and discusses:

- simulations and virtual worlds
- theoretical bases of simulations and virtual worlds
- applications of virtual worlds
- a worked example of virtual world research
- opportunities and limitations
- issues and problems in virtual world research
- using a virtual world and simulations in educational research
- ethical issues in virtual world research
- online tools for data collection from virtual worlds

19.1 Simulations and virtual worlds

A computer simulation is a representation of a real-world system. Simulations have two main components: a *system* of interrelated features in which the researcher is interested and that lends itself to be modelled or simulated, and a *model* of that system that is often a mathematical analogue (Wilcox, 1997).

In *deterministic* simulations all the mathematical relationships between the components of a system are known whereas in *stochastic* simulations, typically the main types used in educational research, at least one variable is random (Wilcox, 1997). A simulation is a model of the real world in which the relevant factors in the research can be included and manipulated. A model may operationalize a theory and convert it into a computer program (see Gilbert and Troitzsch, 2005: 3), making explicit its assumptions.

Gilbert and Troitzsch (2005: 6) suggest that the prime purposes of computer simulations are for discovery, proof and experiment. Beyond simply prediction, computer simulations enable an *understanding* and *explanation* to be gained of how processes operate and unfold over time, and the results of these. This explodes the value of *prediction* as a test of a theory; rather it argues that the test of a theory should be its explanatory and hermeneutic power, rather than its predictive value. Indeed computer simulations may be useful in developing rather than testing theories.

Virtual worlds are computer-based simulated environments in which the possibilities for developing and testing theories are enhanced by the *agency* of the participants, who join online communities and interact with each other.[1] These worlds are also often *persistent*, in that they may continue to exist and develop with possible consequences for an individual user, even when that user is not present online. Virtual worlds commonly feature multiple users interacting with each other and the environment in a dynamic way. They share with many computer and video games (including games using virtual worlds) the deployment of realistic three-dimensional environments but, unlike them, their rationale does not have to lie in scenarios of 'winning' and 'losing'. Nor do they need to have predefined objectives or rules of play, unlike, say, a computerized chess game played by participants or virtual worlds that exist to facilitate 'questing' or the 'levelling' of characters. The virtual worlds we are most concerned with here are created by the participants and the world emerges from the interaction of the participants. Participants create an 'avatar' for themselves, which represents them in the virtual world – this representation may take whatever form the participants wish (human, animal, object or creation of any sort) and may be changed at any time. Avatars are usually three-dimensional and interact with each other through communication and messaging, both private and public, both synchronous and diachronous.

In such virtual worlds individuals can project their own views and values on topics through their avatar and receive the feedback of others in the system. It is the participants who create their world and who affect each other. Such a projection technique enables authentic and honest views to be expressed and, where desired by the participants, to be modified. Topics can be both given and created – the environment is emergent – and they are sometimes for this reason described as 'synthetic worlds' (Castronova, 2005).

Pure (closed) computer simulations are characterized by:

- modelling and imitating the behaviour of systems and their major attributes;

- enabling researchers to see 'what happens if' the system is allowed to run its course or if variables are manipulated (e.g. to enable prediction);
- a mathematical formula that models key features of the reality;
- mathematical relationships that are assumed to be repeating in controlled, bounded and clearly defined situations, sometimes giving rise to unanticipated outcomes (Tymms, 1996);
- feedback and multiple iteration procedures for understanding the emergence of phenomena and behaviours;
- complex phenomena and behaviours derived from the repeated interplay of initial conditions/variables;
- deterministic laws (the repeated calculation of a formula) sometimes leading to unpredictable outcomes.

By enabling the researcher to control and manipulate the variables and components, these simulations are useful in addressing 'what if' questions, e.g. 'What happens if I change this parameter or that parameter?' 'What if the person behaves in such-and-such a way?' 'What happens if I change such-and-such a feature of the environment?' The relevant elements are put into the simulation and are then manipulated – set to different parameters – to see what the outcomes are.

Bailey (2007) suggests that simulations have advantages such as:

- economy (they are cheaper to run than the real-life situation);
- visibility (they can make a phenomenon more accessible and clear to the researcher);
- control (the researcher has more control over the simulation than in the real-life situation);
- safety (researchers can work on situations that may be too dangerous, sensitive, ethically questionable or difficult in real-life natural situations).

In the field of education what is being suggested is that environments for learning, whilst being complex, non-linear, dynamical systems, can be understood in terms of the working out of simple mathematical modelling. This may be at the level of analogy only (see Morrison, 2002a), but, as Tymms (1996: 130) remarks, if the analogue fits the reality then researchers have a powerful tool for understanding and prediction in terms of the interplay of key variables or initial conditions and a set of simple rules.

Computer simulations are powerful in that, as well as enabling researchers to *predict* the future (e.g. in economic forecasting), they also enable them to *under-*

stand and *explore* a phenomenon. They can act as a substitute for human expertise, sometimes enabling non-experts to conduct research that, prior to the advent of computers, would have been the exclusive preserve of experts. Gilbert and Troitzsch (2005: 5) cite the example of geologists, chemists and doctors and also suggest that computer simulations are useful for *training* purposes (e.g. pilots) and, indeed, for *entertainment*. However, they underline (p. 5) the prime importance of computer simulations as being *discovery* and *formalization* of theory (i.e. clarity, coherence, operationalization, inclusion of elements and completeness of a theory).

However Bailey (2007) notes several reservations about computer simulations:

- artificiality (they mimic life, rather than being the real thing);
- cost (computer simulations can be expensive);
- training of participants (simulations often require considerable training);
- quantitative problems (they may require programming expertise).

To concerns that computer simulations subvert human agency and freedom and produce limited outcomes constrained within and determined by the assumptions on which they are built, we can respond that simulations can reveal behaviours that occur 'behind the backs' of social actors to illuminate social facts and patterns (Durkheim, 1956) and can therefore tell us what we do not know (Simon, 1996). The charge that they artificially represent the world and are a *reductio ad absurdum* is an argument for refining simulations rather than abandoning them.

Other concerns are:

- The complexity and chaos theory underpinning many mathematical simulations might explain diverse, variable outcomes (as in school effectiveness research), but may not help us intervene to promote improvement (e.g. in schools) so explanation here is retrospective rather than prospective (Morrison, 2002a); however, researchers may be able to manipulate parameters and variables to see what happens when they do this.
- How we ascertain the key initial conditions set into the simulation (i.e. construct validity) and how do simulations from these lead to prescriptions for practice.
- How acceptable is it to regard systems as the recurring iteration and reiteration of the same formula/ model?

- Simulations work out and assume only the interplay of initial conditions, thereby neglecting the introduction of additional factors 'on the way', i.e. the process is too deterministic (that said, there are computer simulations in which the computer 'learns' during the simulation).
- Manipulating human variables is technicist.
- There is more to behaviour than the repeated iteration of the same mathematical model.
- There will always be a world of difference between the real world and the simulated world other than at an unhelpfully simplistic level.
- The agentic, moral and reflexive behaviour of humans is not as simple as what happens to simpler phenomena that have been studied in computer simulations (e.g. birds and ants, or the dynamics of sand dunes).
- As with other numerical approaches, simulations might combine refinement of process with crudity of concept (Ruddock, 1981: 49).
- If reality operates 'behind the backs' of players, where does responsibility (free will) for agentic actions lie?
- Reducing the world to numbers is quite simply wrong-headed; the world is too complicated for numbers.

These reservations at conceptual and practical levels do not argue against simulations but for their development and refinement. Simulations promise much and in areas of the sciences apart from education have already yielded much of value.

Virtual worlds can offer closer approximations to real-life situations than closed simulations, including the handing over of control to the human agent projections (avatars) which enables researchers to explore hitherto less accessible or inaccessible territory without losing the benefits offered by simulations. Hence, to explore issues using virtual worlds may risk both exposing areas of conflict and 'dangerous knowledge' (Giroux, 1983) in areas such as community and religious identity, statehood, values and politics, majorities and minorities and ethnicity and identity. The creation of a safe environment is one means of addressing this. And how can this be done? One response is through projection techniques. Whilst some of the pedigree for this lies in personal construct theory, developments in information technology have enabled newer methods to be adopted.

First, it is through simulation (Cohen *et al.*, 2007: 245–51). Simulations and virtual worlds offer the opportunity to explore situations, values and behaviours in a safe environment (though this is not guaranteed:

for example cases are reported of student suicide as a result of cyber-bullying through social networking). Second, it is through agent-based modelling in computers.

The use of virtual worlds can overcome to a significant degree many of the limitations of, and reservations about, pure simulations by providing features that can be exploited to offer unique educational and research opportunities difficult to replicate in conventional contexts. Their resemblances to visually realistic, imaginatively designed three-dimensional game worlds makes them useful in stimulating participants' imaginations, where the sense of being in a real place may be important as, for example, in creating greater engagement so as to convey difficult moral dilemmas which engage and retain the user's attention. Creating a sense of life as a fictional experience may also be valuable in characterization exploration and development at one remove (i.e. via the avatar). Such facilities makes virtual worlds attractive places to develop otherwise inaccessible or impossible environments to explore human interaction and human agency, values and perceptions, historical locations and experiences, future imagined scenarios or uninhabitable settings such as inside highly 'radioactive' spaces.

These features often make virtual worlds more effective training environments than simulations, where the depiction of a hostile environment (say in firefighter training for casualty location) can be enhanced to offer more realism because not all parameters are controlled or known in advance. Similarly, otherwise impossible experiences can be offered in virtual worlds to capitalize on human agency, especially when participants are acting anonymously (where neither the user nor the individuals being engaged by them know each other's identity), such as the experience of being immobile or disabled, or being a member of a different social or ethnic group.

The low risk and 'repeatability' of experience associated with virtual worlds offers advantages over models and mathematical simulations, not just by virtue of the safety they offer in environments characterized by essential unpredictability but also because, despite their creation of a heightened sense of realism over other approaches, virtual worlds afford the user discardable experiences which can carry relatively little personal, experiential or emotional cost (e.g. when training armed forces in decision making in pressured situations; training medics to treat 'real' casualties; or advancing views, proposals or identity depictions in hostile situations) (Waller and Hunt, 1998).

Virtual worlds also offer the participant control or even superhuman abilities such as the ability to fly.

Together with the configurable avatar these features make virtual worlds good technologies for studying and affording rehabilitation experiences such as enabling those who have undergone traumatic experiences such as domestic violence to explore how to deal with situations in future, or offering opportunities for participants to make otherwise unavailable choices regarding actions, gender or personality. Their potential for exploiting role/real playing and the blending of real-life activity with virtual activity offers the researcher wide scope for exploring innumerable scenarios.

Working in artificial/simulated/virtual worlds such as Second Life, using projection techniques with networking and social interaction, feedback and iteration involves the creation and development of virtual worlds that are safe environments, in which the participants themselves are responsible for their creation and development. These are environments in which participants can project, share and comment on their own and others' views, leading to the exposure and exploration of further, often sensitive, issues for investigation and possible resolution and to the resolution of potential conflict and disagreement and hence to the development and enlargement of understanding. Through the creation of safe, virtual worlds and communication in them, participants can be encouraged to be open, honest and authentic in disclosing their views, their values and their beliefs about given and created situations and issues, particularly about sensitive issues. A comparison of simulations and virtual worlds is made in Table 19.1.

The use of simulations and especially those identified as virtual worlds offer significant opportunities here for both practitioners and researchers. Exploring virtual worlds means that the researcher has to be open to a range of methodologies but has at the same time to re-examine the assumptions people may make when seeking to apply them to virtual environments. These environments offer higher levels of interaction and embodiment with participants than simulations constructed using purely mathematical models, and they offer unique features for data capture, including the ability to record sound, chat and text as well as images and video, all in real time.

In such scenarios we may need to modify, or at least revise, what we understand by ethnographic or qualitative approaches such as participant observation, focus groups and interviewing. We will need to examine the assumptions we make when deploying our methodological tools to verify that they are still applicable in these different communities, in which alternative values and different articulations of reality are to be found, in which participants may alter their displayed embodiment at will and in which we may simultaneously conduct our research with individuals in different locations around the world. In this way by exposing the researcher and practitioner to new constructions, expressions and transformations of identity, reality and community, virtual worlds offer unique opportunities to re-examine the nature of community and self in the virtual and the real world and also offer a unique opportunity to rethink, refine and

TABLE 19.1 FEATURES AND AFFORDANCES OF SIMULATIONS AND VIRTUAL WORLDS

Features and affordances	
Simulations	Virtual worlds
Modelling/imitating	Realizing/acting
'What if' modelling of known variables	Few known variables
An underlying mathematical construct	Minimal underlying constructs
Modelled and interpreted reality	Catching and manipulating the fine grain of reality
Bounded, defined parameters	Unbounded and undefined parameters
Iteration and feedback to reveal emergent phenomena	Human agency as the driver of emergence
Repeated interplay of set initial conditions	Any set initial conditions rapidly abandoned
Unpredictable outcomes sometimes	Unpredictable outcomes common
Limited simultaneous users	Multiple simultaneous users
Transience	Persistence

improve existing pedagogy and research methodology and instrumentation.

19.2 Theoretical bases of simulations and virtual worlds

For Laplace and Newton, the universe was rationalistic and deterministic, where effects were functions of causes and where predictability, causality, patterning, universality, linearity, continuity, stability and objectivity all contributed to a view of the universe as an ordered and internally harmonistic mechanism in a complex equilibrium. This was a rational, closed and deterministic system susceptible to comparatively straightforward scientific discovery and laws. Since the 1960s this view has been increasingly challenged with the rise of theories of chaos and complexity (see Chapter 1). Central to these theories are several principles (see also Chapter 1) (Gleick, 1987; Morrison, 1998, 2002a):

- small-scale changes in initial conditions can produce large and unpredictable changes in outcomes;
- very similar conditions can produce very dissimilar outcomes (e.g. using simple mathematical equations (Stewart, 1990));
- regularity, conformity and linear relationships between elements break down to irregularity, diversity and non-linear relationships between elements;
- even if the mathematical equations are very simple, the behaviour of the system that they are modelling may not be simple;
- effects are not straightforward continuous functions of causes;
- the universe is largely unpredictable;
- if something works once there is no guarantee that it will work in the same way a second time;
- determinism is replaced by indeterminism; deterministic, linear and stable systems are replaced by 'dynamical', changing, evolving systems and non-linear explanations of phenomena;
- continuity is replaced by discontinuity, turbulence and irreversible transformation;
- grand, universal, all-encompassing theories and large-scale explanations provide inadequate accounts of localized and specific phenomena;
- long-term prediction is impossible.

More recently, theories of chaos have been extended to complexity theory (Waldrop, 1992; Lewin, 1993) which argues that, in many respects, the real world, though highly complex, is built on comparatively simple rules that give rise to such complexity (see also

Gilbert and Troitzsch, 2005: 10) and the foundations of computer simulations including those we have identified as virtual worlds lie in complexity theory, providing a response to the charge that they oversimplify the real world.[2]

Determinism has given way to complexity theory and the ascendance of the latter is realized in virtual worlds where the inherent organic, unpredictable and irreplicable nature of the universe and human experience is mediated and celebrated. To the extent that virtual worlds are able to facilitate the creation of realities which hold true for participants and 'make sense' to them, these environments replace 'real' reality and meaning with symbols and signs to create a perceived reality (a simulacrum) which in some ways replaces human experience. For the educational researcher, virtual worlds offer opportunities to study identity, society and experience by means which do not replace the 'real' but afford means to better understand it by exploring it in alternate possibilities.

The use of media, either interactive or non-interactive, to externalize the self and create an impression of presence in an environment that we are not physically part of relies on the 'willing suspension of disbelief' (Coleridge, 1817) to create an 'illusory shift in point of view' (Dennett, 1978: 312) as well as the use of our own knowledge, imagination and enthusiasm in the experience (Zhao, 2003). Our sense of being present in the real world appears to be an essential component of consciousness but is not something we normally think about unless prompted by a displacement of our self-perception, for example through a dream, literature or cinema experience. Contemporary technology provides increasingly detailed and convincing simulations of reality and a sense of physical and/or social presence is now a commonplace feature of broadcast, cinema and virtual environments. *Co-presence* is the intersection of physical and social presence, where individuals have a sense of being together in a communal, shared environment.

A sense of presence is likely to be highly individual and conditional upon the sensory information presented within and the user's level of control over the environment (Sheridan, 1992; Ijsselsteijn *et al.*, 2000; Sadowski and Stanney, 2002). An *immersive* experience results when presence in an environment is augmented by its apparent overall fidelity to physical reality (Slater and Steed, 2000), although this does not have to be ego-centric or computer mediated; it appears when 'being there' is augmented by a total response of 'making sense there' (Schuemie *et al.*, 2001; Riva *et al.*, 2003).

Agent-based modelling simulates or facilitates the actions and interactions of agentic (i.e. freely choosing, autonomous, intentional, purposeful) individuals in a network of other agentic actors, which leads to a range of effects on a whole system (Bonabeau, 2002). This is a key distinction between modelling environments using simulations and those found in many virtual worlds. The background for this lies in the work of Holland (1992), Ulam (1992) and Kauffman (1993)[3] in developing computation-based and grid-based models to represent the actions of bounded rational agents in a system and to see how individual actions both pattern themselves and pattern the network. See, for example, the work of Reynolds[4] (1987) on the behaviour of flocking creatures ('boids'), where he identified three simple initial conditions (rules) which modelled behaviour:

- keep a minimum distance from other objects (including other boids);
- keep to the same speed as other boids;
- try to move towards the centre of the flock.

It is important to note here that complex, patterned behaviour emerges from simple rules, and that the patterns cannot be understood entirely in terms of the initial conditions that gave rise to them, they cannot be decomposed or atomized into the initial conditions – the new whole is greater than the sum of the parts. It is more than an aggregate model. A new situation emerges from the interaction of agents and behaviours, giving rise to Durkheim's *social facts*: ways of acting that can exert an external constraint over the individual or a society, and which have an existence of their own which is independent of their individual manifestations (Durkheim, 1982: 59).

What is being argued here is that macro-level behaviour emerges from micro-level agents; that is, complex, unpredictable virtual realities and norms emerge from the interactions of agents (individuals) within virtual worlds, just as they do between real people in real worlds. Agent-based modelling is therefore useful in exploring how individual behaviour and changes in individual behaviour contribute to new emergent patterns of behaviour in a system. These make virtual worlds useful technologies for research into human perception and interaction. Agent-based models place emergence through self-organization at their heart and in essence, therefore, a central feature of complexity theory underpins the field (see Chapter 1).

Whilst some agent-based models and forms of artificial life simulations have been criticized for oversimplifying the complexity that they are trying to model, and for being too mechanistic (e.g. in cellular automata)[5], nevertheless it is a powerful emergent methodol-

ogy for understanding larger scale, patterned behaviour, and it has been applied to fields as varied as: biology (Holland, 1992; Kauffman, 1993; Langton, 1984), political science (Axelrod, 1997); economics, cognition and neural networks (Sun, 2008); seasonal migration, pollution, sexual reproduction, wars, traffic jams, logistics, supply chains and transmission of disease (Epstein, 1996). The establishment of the European Social Simulation Association (www.essa.eu.org/) attests to the significance of such developments. Such models are less deterministic and more stochastic and emergent, faithful to central tenets of complexity theory.

The popularity of social networking sites indicates the significance of communication as a strong feature of contemporary society, where such communication leads to the emergence of key patterns, systems of thoughts, values and ideas. Communication via avatars offers a natural extension of such opportunities to circumvent traditional power games in face-to-face communication and are examples of the 'privatisation of sociability' (Castells, 2009: 389) that brings with it a greater likelihood that individuals will feel free to express themselves.

Such a model of communicative action accords with central tenets of the 'ideal speech situation' from Habermas (1979, 1982, 1984, 1987). The principles of Habermas's 'ideal speech situation' echo strongly through the view of exploration of issues through virtual worlds, for example (see the discussion of critical theory in Chapter 2) (Morrison, 1995a: 102):

- freedom to enter a discourse;
- freedom to check questionable claims;
- freedom to evaluate explanations;
- freedom to modify a given conceptual framework;
- freedom to assess justifications;
- freedom to alter norms;
- freedom to reflect on the nature of political will;
- mutual understanding between participants;
- equal opportunity to select and employ speech acts;
- recognition of the legitimacy of each subject to participate in the dialogue as an autonomous and equal partner;
- equal opportunity for discussion;
- the consensus resulting from discussion derives from the force of the better argument alone, and not from the positional or political power of the participants;
- all motives except for the cooperative search for truth are excluded;
- the speech-act validity claims of truth, legitimacy, sincerity and comprehensibility are all embodied.

19.3 Applications of virtual worlds

Virtual worlds can provide environments that reflect 'real-life' activities and facilitate greater social inclusion, especially in situations exploring sensitive or contentious issues, where the anonymity and 'ideal speech situations' offered by the use of an avatar can facilitate participant engagement.

Virtual worlds also allow researchers to collect more participant data than are often possible in the traditional classroom, through capturing text, chat and user-presentations from the 'inworld' environment, and by videoing activity.[6]

By providing a scaffolded vocabulary, researchers can also more easily collect data from individuals with communication difficulties, where the (currently) reduced amount of data involved in communication in these environments (lack of subtle facial or body-language communication, for example) and the slower pace of communication can be advantageous (Ravenscroft and McAllister, 2006).

The communication in virtual worlds via text, chat, voice and signing can all be captured for later analysis via recording and transcription and, because data can be time-stamped, it is possible to compare the outcomes from analysis from these different communication channels for data triangulation (Martin and Vallance, 2008; Vallance and Wiz, 2008). These data can be converted to numbers for quantitative analysis or can be used to provide a richer understanding through interpretive phenomenological analysis, which is a form of qualitative analysis that is useful when we are interested in describing how people negotiate, understand and make sense of the world. Both quantitative and qualitative data need to be used in light of the perspective we wish to adopt, the kind of information we seek to collect and the assumptions that underpin our approach as well as what we wish to achieve (prediction or interpretation, for example):

Quantitative	Qualitative
An outsider's view (*etic*)	An insider's view (*emic*)
Researcher objective	Researcher subjective
Objective reality (facts)	Subjective reality (reality socially constructed)
Numerical deductive approach	Naturalistic inductive approach
Hypothesis-oriented	Process-oriented
Prediction	Interpretation
Reliable/generalizable	Contextual
Classification and summary	Detail and richness
Larger samples	Smaller samples
Faster	Slower

Virtual worlds are useful for the study of human interaction, especially in dynamic, fluid, uncertain or contested contexts, for exploring complex behaviour variables and for monitoring developments over time. By their nature virtual worlds – especially the perceptually realistic ones that are increasingly common – offer the researcher an opportunity to exploit the participant's sense of immersion in the created world (a sense of being *there*) and also their sense of a shared experience with other individuals – a sense of presence and co-presence in a virtual world which responds to individual actions (a sense of *being* there). Both immersion and co-presence have been identified as important facilitators of user engagement in a time when media consumers demand more and deeper experiences (Riva *et al.*, 2003; Boellstorff, 2008) through artefacts exploiting 'the fluid boundaries between mechanism and flesh' (Turkle, 2000: 555).

Virtual worlds are valuable for studying interactions between individuals especially when we wish to explore contexts where sensitive or dangerous knowledge is important and where it is important for subjects to feel safe to participate and respond candidly. Virtual worlds can offer ways of exploring behaviours and attitudes towards others in such contexts, such as when studying contested opinions or beliefs, or individual perceptions (including those of oneself) in relation to others and in exploring how these might change over time as a result of interaction with them. This makes virtual worlds useful places for researching the development of understanding, of perception, of processes where negotiated meaning is important and of the development of consensus and the dynamics of discord.

19.4 A worked example of virtual world research

This section presents a worked example of using a virtual world as a safe environment in which researchers and participants explore sensitive issues in educational research and education itself. It reports how researchers can study how young people see themselves in relation to the society in which they live. It is based on work in progress at the time of writing, by Martin (2010), in exploring virtual worlds as safe environments for the study of sensitive issues, in this case of citizenship-related topics. Such a study might explore tensions between the internal image that individual young people have of themselves (their constructed identity) and the civic responsibilities and duties they are expected to discharge publicly, the loyalties which they are expected to defend and the behaviours which they are encouraged to display. A study of these elements of their 'citizenship' identity can explore: (a) individuals' perceptions of, and attitudes towards, others; (b) their relationship to the dominant values, laws and legal systems in their country; (c) the social expectations of other individuals and groups; and (d) their experience of discrimination or disempowerment. Many countries have significant groups in their population who have different cultural, religious and social values and associated backgrounds. These pluralistic societies are often concerned about social fragmentation and political (dis)engagement and, in some cases, the marginalization and radicalization of groups within them. A study would therefore be very likely to touch upon sensitive issues, explore areas of 'dangerous knowledge' (that knowledge which is unsettling and which could provoke social unrest), and highlight social and individual tensions.

Using a virtual world in this context, as with any other approach, would involve developing appropriate research questions, deciding on the data that would be needed to answer them and determining how the required data could best be collected and analysed.

Suppose our research interest is in exploring what kind of society young people in secondary education wish to become part of, where the context is an economically developed, pluralistic democracy. Our research question might be 'What do young people think it should mean to be a citizen in our country?', assuming that its basis should be tolerance and the empowerment of individuals. We might also be interested in exploring how citizenship education might be developed. To address our research question we would need to know what the sampled young people associated with citizenship and how they defined 'tolerance' and 'empowerment'. What values might they invoke and how could we discover how their definitions and understandings of these sometimes sensitive and contested issues emerged and operated?

In this study we might be interested in exploring the internal world of individuals and the way in which their values and feelings are externalized, projected, expressed and used, and how these drive behaviour. We might also wish to study how these can be shared and discussed in a safe environment. We therefore decide that we need not only to measure and ask our sample about the values and feelings they associate with a tolerant, empowered citizenship, but also that we wish to observe how these are deployed in practice, during discussion and negotiation with others, especially in situations where the values and acceptable behaviours might be contested. We might be interested in tracking emergent values and beliefs within discussions about citizenship.

Hence we decide to provide a number of inworld scenarios featuring 'moral dilemmas' of citizenship for our participants to discuss, so that we can observe how groups explore and discuss these, how different values and assumptions are brought into play and the relative weights that are accorded to each. Observing real-world group interaction in such circumstances would be unlikely, we conclude, to be ethically acceptable or practically useful because of the significant risk during discussion of self (or group) censorship, the influence of individual sensitivity to group expectations, individual's anxieties about exposure when offering contentious views or arguments and the associated risk of conflict or the fear of it. We decide that even if ethical concerns about placing subjects in environments in which they may fear personal threat or harm could be overcome, our data would be subject to too many uncontrolled variables for them to be useful. Given these difficulties, we can better conduct our experiment in a virtual environment, and address and minimize many of the problems that could be foreseen with real-world groups. In a virtual environment the participants would be able to project their feelings, values, arguments and evidence anonymously via their avatar and interact with others in live (synchronous) debate to explore issues that arise, but with fewer anxieties about potential conflict, and greater confidence in sharing thoughts openly.

To operationalize our study and collect our data we therefore select an appropriate population for our study – here we focus on young people in secondary education. For practical reasons we cannot involve every such young person in our study, so we wish to select a fair sample. If the sample is 'fair' (i.e. representative of the population) we will be able to generalize (apply) our findings reliably back to the wider population from which our sample was drawn. This is not straightforward because, in order to be representative of the population, the sample should include as many features as possible from the wider population, in the same proportions as they are found in that population. In our study we would need to include males and females in the right proportion, and, within these groups, also the range of ages, cultural backgrounds, religious beliefs and everything else we might consider to be important – each in the correct proportions. To prevent this from becoming unmanageable, we recognize that, unless we are going to have a very large sample, we will have to be measured in the claims made from the study. We will not be able to generalize fully (unless everyone in our defined population is included) and so we should narrow our study – say to secondary school pupils in a particular age-group or year of study – and be explicit about the population to which we are trying to generalize. For us this means restricting the range of features covered in the sample and being clear that our conclusions will apply less and less widely as the contexts to which our findings are being applied become increasingly dissimilar to those sampled.

Our participants will complete a questionnaire which collects basic demographic information for use as the independent variables in our analysis. It also measures appropriate citizenship-related attitudes. A questionnaire is developed from focus group discussions with individuals representative of our population. Such discussions identify relevant key themes and items associated with demographic factors, identity, citizenship, tolerance and empowerment. For each theme (i.e. 'tolerance' or 'the rule of law') we design a number of Likert-style questions to sample individual views and feelings, and then ask the focus group(s) to assess each of these items for relevance, clarity and 'fit' to each theme. After any necessary modifications, our questionnaire is completed by participants pre- and post-experiment.

Then we construct a virtual environment similar to Second Life but host this securely on our own computers and allow entry only via a secure password system so as to address concerns about access. In our environment we have an 'inventory' of relevant items developed from focus group discussions. Avatars access the inventory to select and use items, but every time they must attach a value and associated definition. Values and definitions are stored in a 'Values Dictionary', which is augmented over time as more avatars are created and discussion of scenarios proceeds.

Within our experimental environment we ask participants to create an avatar, and attach an associated biography/back story. Participants are asked to make their avatar depict how they see themselves as a citizen, using clothing and artefacts drawn from the inventory. Avatars are provided with a dwelling which participants are asked to furnish and decorate with inventory items in order to create an 'installation' depicting who they are and what is important to them as a citizen. These data will be used to understand the items and attached values drawn upon and how they are defined in relationship to citizenship identity.

Groups of avatars are subsequently offered a series of contentious scenarios, each designed to highlight known areas of difference, tension or controversy within debates about citizenship. Participants' avatars are invited to discuss these collectively and attempt to reach a consensus. Discussions are monitored discreetly to ensure civilized and courteous debates, but otherwise they are uncensored. Each avatar response must be accompanied by one or more attached values and the selection of an 'emoticon' that visually conveys to other avatars and their drivers the feelings attached to the response. Discussion continues until a majority view or impasse is reached.

Following each session, participants complete an online diary entry, unseen by other participants, where they talk about their feelings and views on the session. They are asked to reflect upon anything of significance they wish to identify, on suggestions for other scenarios for inclusion, on whether their experience would be likely to change their real-world behaviour, on how their experience within the experiment was different from the way in which they were normally taught about such topics in school, together with the advantages and disadvantages of each approach. These data are used to explore developing views and feelings as different scenarios unfold (e.g. views on how citizenship education might develop), and to discover topics for exploration during the experiment and exit interviews.

At the close of all the scenario discussions, a still image of each avatar is placed alongside its installation/dwelling together with its biography and attached values; each participant is then asked to review these and write a confidential note in their diary for each, in which they respond to these examples of citizenship identity. These data are used to gather reflections of others' constructed citizenship identity for thematic and correlational analysis.

Participants also create a 'Legacy Document' in which they leave a statement for future users, in which is recorded what they have learned from taking part in the experiment and in which they offer advice that they wish to give to new participants in the experiment. These data are used to improve subsequent experiences of participants and as an indicator of personal change.

Participants then complete again the initial questionnaire and undertake a real-world face-to-face exit interview in which they are asked to reflect on their experiences within the virtual world and to respond to the anonymous notes left by other avatars about their installation/dwelling and their created avatar. These data are used as participant confirmation for the extracted inferences and conclusions, and to enrich the data set.

We may analyse our data via correlation, factor analysis or by applying item response theory or thematic analysis, to discover relationships between the independent variables (demographics and initial views and values) and any changes in values, definitions and perceptions of what participants think it should mean to be a tolerant, empowered citizen in our country (dependent variables). Statistical and thematic analysis will provide us with measures of *internal validity* for our findings. We will also use one or more control groups to which we will compare our findings from the experimental group, to help ensure that outputs from our analysis are not unduly skewed by the experience of the experiment and its features which are unrelated to the study focus or exposure to the environment we have created, and are not just outcomes that arise simply because individuals know they are being studied.[7]

We may wish to compare findings from several of our sources so that, by the *triangulation* of our data, we may strengthen *internal* validity[8] and reliability in our conclusions. Demonstrating *external* validity[9] is more difficult but we could provide increasing support for this by repeated use of our experiment with more samples from our population.

For further material on this project and its developments, readers can refer to the project website at http://web.me.com/stewartmartin2/Stewart_Martin/Citizenship.html (see also Martin, 2010).

19.5 Opportunities and limitations

Simulation methods provide a means of alleviating a number of problems inherent in laboratory experiments. At the same time, they permit the retention of some of their virtues. Simulations, notes Palys (1978), share with the laboratory experiment the characteristic that the experimenter has complete manipulative control over every aspect of the situation, such as found in flight simulators, surgical simulators, training in dangerous environments and decision-making training, in which virtual world/reality applications are very varied and the experiences and skills involved can be simple, single, physical or abstract.

At the same time, the subjects' humanity is left intact in that they are given a realistic situation in which to act in whatever way they think appropriate. The inclusion of the time dimension is another important contribution of the simulation, allowing the subject to take an active role in interacting with the environment, and enabling the experimenter to observe a social system in action, with its feedback loops, multidirectional causal connections and so forth. Finally, Palys (1978) observes, the high involvement normally associated with participation in simulations shows that the self-consciousness usually associated with the laboratory experiment is more easily dissipated. Hence, in summary, the advantages of simulations and the use of virtual worlds are:

- experiential and active learning, so encouraging motivation and engagement;
- visualization, managing complex environments;
- access to impossible/difficult environments;
- flexibility, can be programmed to offer a wide range of situations/stimuli;
- monitoring, sessions can be recorded, examined – good for evaluation and assessment.

The advantages of virtual worlds over pure simulations lies in exploring contexts in which the experimenter neither desires nor is able to exert manipulative control over every aspect of the situation and where the researcher himself/herself desires the environment itself to be shaped by participants. Virtual worlds offer environments which enhance the agentic control and immersion of participants and therefore provide quantitatively and qualitatively different affordances for the researcher. Virtual worlds are highly suited to mixed methods approaches (with their inherent advantages and disadvantages), the development of research activity design, the exploitation of game theory and complexity/chaos theory and the general development of research methodology (Broadribb *et al.*, 2009). Worlds such as Second Life and Club Penguin are examples of collaborative environments using 'inclusive' research practices in which researchers and subjects collaborate on equal terms and therefore offer opportunities to develop scenarios of 'ideal speech' (Rybas and Gajjala, 2007; Sheehy, 2010).

19.6 Issues and problems in virtual world research

By their nature, virtual worlds lend themselves to projects which do not require participants or researchers to be physically located near to each other. Collaborative affordances are therefore just as important for the research team as for the participants, and being able to work together on analysis can be important for the research team. Synchronous and asynchronous researcher collaboration can be facilitated by technologies such as 'Google docs' or 'Dropbox' where individuals can share documents, spreadsheets and databases with colleagues and work synchronously on them to develop understandings, investigative approaches and dynamic trend-analysis, including motion-graphs such as those featured in Gapminder[10] software.

Challenges can emerge when creating common research protocols which must function in institutions which apply different procurement constraints, use dissimilar and sometimes incompatible IT infrastructures and with policies with very different embedded institutional and cultural assumptions about the nature of academic roles and responsibilities (including those towards, and for, students and research participants). International research into the effective use of immersive virtual environments which, by its very nature, offers the opportunity to annihilate conventional frames of space and time, also involves successfully navigating a combination of real-world and inworld assumptions, limitations and obstacles whilst exploiting their many opportunities and resources for exploration, innovation and progress.

Research difficulties in using virtual environments also relate to having sufficient expertise in their use within both researchers and participants, and training in this may be a prerequisite. Having computers with appropriate specifications is important (commercial virtual worlds have advice on their websites), as is having sufficient bandwidth and safe passage through institutional network firewalls.

Participant enthusiasm is common but cannot be assumed and some studies have found to their cost that participants who are initially enthusiastic find that time constraints, the relative complexity of virtual worlds and bandwidth demands (which can create operational slowness) proved the biggest disincentive for continuing engagement (see the case study in lifelong learning conducted by Jarmon *et al.*, 2009). Despite the visual and conceptual allure of virtual worlds, user acceptance remains one of the most significant challenges to be overcome (Fetscherin and Lattemann, 2007).

Evaluating virtual worlds will naturally focus on whether they achieve what is hoped for, but researchers should also seek unexpected outcomes and changes to practice or perceptions as a consequence of individual experiences of and within them (Lewis and Allan, 2005). Less often considered, but equally important, should be comparisons with existing practice, such as asking about ways in which the use of the virtual world has produced outcomes that could not equally well have been achieved by other or more conventional means.

The most effective use of a technology in a given context (for example in research or for teaching and learning), whether paper-based, physical, electronic or virtual, is always contingent upon exploiting its uniqueness – what it can do or provide which other means or technologies cannot. Using a technology to simply replicate existing practice or to copy what other technologies do is an example of cultural reproduction or 'first order change' which is unlikely to produce a fundamental or sustained difference (Cuban, 1986, 2003; Fullan, 2007). It also does not represent genuine

innovation and is likely to produce overly elaborate, less effective and efficient, and often more expensive, outcomes than the alternatives. So we may ask how educators are using virtual worlds and whether they are doing so as a result of novelty, personal enthusiasm, to aid student motivation (which may decline with familiarity) or because they have identified some unique affordance within this technology.

19.7 Using a virtual world and simulations in educational research

In addition to the usual decisions to be made when designing a research project, if researchers conclude that a virtual world or simulation will be both necessary and useful for their project then they will additionally have to set up and manage the environment they wish to use. Depending on their experience and proficiency they may decide to involve someone with technical expertise to help them choose whether to make use of an existing commercial product[11] or to create a purpose-built environment.[12] The former is more straightforward but the options available for customization may be more limited, so it is important for researchers to be clear in advance which features they require for their study, what data they wish to collect and how. A customized platform may be the ideal but often it will be better to use a commercial product first, starting simply and adding complexity and customization as needed and proficiency grows.

Virtual worlds offer both new opportunities and new obstacles for research. Whilst researchers can use many familiar research tools, they also need to have familiarity with the virtual world's technology and may find arranging the research venue more complicated and disseminating outcomes to the inworld community problematic, especially if using handheld devices.[13]

User engagement and scheduling of synchronous activity can also be difficult, due to time zone differences, technology differences and/or incompatibilities between user sites, and in terms of participant availability and technical skill.

When considering the design of educational research projects in virtual worlds, a number of factors should be taken into account (Moschini, 2010):

- Type of project: exclusively inworld, blended, distance-learning or comparative (i.e. where similar activities will be conducted inworld and in the physical world for comparison).
- Carefully define the activity to be investigated (e.g. focus on skill acquisition, collaborative work or communication).

- Carefully formulate the research question and the appropriate theoretical background.
- Venue: a 'closed' private environment or an 'open' space (such as in the public areas in Second Life).
- Participants: do they know (or will they get to know) each other in the physical world or is the project an exclusively inworld experience?
- Methodology: will evaluation use only inworld tools or will a blend of online and traditional research methods be used?
- Ethical issues: is the project complying with the virtual world's 'rules of behaviour' and with the researcher's institutional guidelines for online research?
- Data analysis: the tools to be used.
- Dissemination: identification of the best channels for dissemination to both the inworld and wider academic community.

Deciding on the appropriate methodology for using virtual worlds or simulations in educational research involves considering offline and online tools (Fielding *et al.*, 2008; Markham and Baym, 2008) and, as a result, mixed methods/mixed worlds approaches are common (Johnson *et al.*, 2007; Martin *et al.*, 2010), although these can exacerbate some problems, especially of maintaining user engagement and support (see the case study in Livingstone and Bloomfield, 2010).[14]

19.8 Ethical issues in virtual world research

Exploring virtual worlds is itself a sensitive issue and it bears the hallmarks of sensitive research, i.e. that research which 'potentially poses a substantial threat to those who are involved or have been involved in it' (Lee, 1993: 4), or when those studied view the research as somehow undesirable (Van Meter, 2000), a feature which Morrison (2006) notes particularly for totalitarian regimes. Sensitivity is dealt with in Chapter 9, and readers should refer to the list of sources of insensitivity contained in the opening pages of that chapter.

The main ethical issues here concern vulnerability, individual risk and informed consent, especially when dealing with: online identities (when individuals may (re)present themselves as machines, real or fantasy creatures, plants, objects, etc.); the nature of communication (is it public or private); security; confidentiality and privacy and the inworld standards and rules.

19.9 Online tools for data collection from virtual worlds

Virtual worlds present both new opportunities and challenges when collecting data, even where the data are then to be processed by conventional means. Lewis and Allen (2005) emphasize that collecting data from an online or virtual community requires the researcher to be clear from the start about what data are needed, so that they can be gathered throughout the project, preventing the need for a major collection task at the end. Reflective diaries are useful sources of information, thoughts, feelings and ideas, and social network and group communication software can provide tracking tools. These collection techniques can be supplemented by online survey tools such as the Bristol Online Survey, Survey Gizmo, Survey Monkey or Zoomerang.[15]

Surveys and questionnaires are relatively simple data collection devices but can be time-consuming to design and always require careful forethought and planning in terms of exactly what analysis is to be done with each piece of information gathered. Deciding in advance exactly how each piece of gathered information will be used in subsequent analysis helps ensure that all (and *only*) information that is required is collected.

Virtual worlds offer possibilities for collecting data over time in ways that may be more difficult by other means. As such they offer opportunities to conduct research in ways and on topics that have proved problematic in the past, particularly those where extended interactions are important. One of the challenges for the researcher is therefore how to interrogate data that are chronological or sequential in nature. Dynamic data depiction and analysis tools are becoming ever more important in such areas. When working with dynamic data (data where values change over time in ways not yet fully understood), it can be difficult for the researcher to identify the correct questions to ask, let alone identify which are the appropriate variables to analyse; here traditional static graphs, charts and tables may be insufficiently informative. One example of a valuable tool for researchers to use in working with dynamic data can be found in *Gapminder* software.[16] Gapminder was developed to explore trends over time, and it is useful for contextualizing data where chronology is important but where the relationships between variables over time are little understood.

In many virtual worlds inworld events and objects may also be connected to other online technologies such as blogs, wikis, questionnaires, rating-systems, databases, etc. and increasingly to inworld tools such as questionnaires.[17]

19.10 Conclusions

This chapter has argued that emergent, contentious or sensitive topics can be usefully explored using safe virtual environments applying an IT-facilitated form of projection technique, and this has been explicated in terms of computer-based simulation and agent-based modelling. These, it has been argued, are rooted in complexity theory which argues that new systems and patterns emerge through self-organization, through the effects of the parts/individuals on the emergent whole and on the parts/individuals themselves, and on the impossibility of understanding the whole as simply a sum of its parts. The process of emergence, from micro to macro and from macro to micro, requires adaptability, open systems, learning, feedback, communication and connectedness in order that individuals and systems develop their own identity (autopoiesis).

Further, this chapter has argued for the importance of including developments in behaviour and understanding behaviour such as understanding of networks and social networking, agentic behaviour and agent-based modelling and models, the micro–macro link and emergence through self-organization. How can such an understanding be addressed in research terms, whilst respecting the sensitivity of the research topic and embracing the safe environment of a computer-generated world? One way is through the creation of a virtual world in which agents create their own world and interact with each other in the creation of that world. This is akin to the stochastic simulation mentioned at the start of the chapter, which is emergent, unpredictable, but real, in that real people create the world and, within it, project their real opinions, values, identity and views.

 Companion Website

The companion website to the book includes PowerPoint slides for this chapter, which list the structure of the chapter and then provide a summary of the key points in each of its sections. This resource can be found online at **www.routledge.com/textbooks/cohen7e**.

Part 4
Strategies and instruments for data collection and researching

This part moves to a closer-grained account of instruments for collecting data, how they can be used and how they can be constructed. We identify eight main kinds of data collection instruments, with many variants included in each: questionnaires (with greater coverage of issues in questionnaire design and the developing field of online questionnaires); interviews; accounts; observations; tests; personal constructs (entirely rewritten by Richard Bell); role-playing (entirely rewritten by Carmel O'Sullivan); and a completely new chapter on visual media in educational research. We have expanded on discussion of material from the previous editions, particularly in respect of questionnaire design and interviews. The intention of this part is to enable researchers to decide on the most appropriate instruments for data collection, and to carry out the practical, careful design and use of such instru-

ments. The strengths and weaknesses of these instruments are set out, so that decisions on their suitability and the criterion of *fitness for purpose* can be addressed. Hence this part not only introduces underlying principles that underpin instruments, but also offers sound, tested, practical advice for their usage. This is intended to enable researchers to gather useful and usable data. In particular more recent forms of gathering data are considered, including telephonically and by internet usage, and the strengths and weaknesses of these different kinds are set out clearly for researchers. There is greater coverage of conducting research that involves children. The new chapter on visual media in educational research considers these not only as means but as ends in themselves. We provide practical advice to researchers who are collecting visual data in classrooms and educational locations.

Questionnaires

CHAPTER 20

The field of questionnaire design is vast. This chapter provides a straightforward introduction to its key elements, indicating the main issues to be addressed, some important problematical considerations and how they can be resolved. It follows a sequence in designing a questionnaire that, it is hoped, will be useful for researchers, thus:

- ethical issues
- approaching the planning of a questionnaire
- operationalizing the questionnaire
- structured, semi-structured and unstructured questionnaires
- types of questionnaire items
- closed and open questions compared
- scales of data
- the dangers of assuming knowledge
- dichotomous questions
- multiple choice questions
- rank ordering
- rating scales
- constant sum questions
- ratio data questions
- open-ended questions
- matrix questions
- contingency questions, filters and branches
- asking sensitive questions
- avoiding pitfalls in question writing
- sequencing questions
- questionnaires containing few verbal items
- the layout of the questionnaire
- covering letters/sheets and follow-up letters
- piloting the questionnaire
- practical considerations in questionnaire design
- administering questionnaires
- self-administered questionnaires
- postal questionnaires
- processing questionnaire data

It is suggested that researchers may find it useful to work through these issues in sequence, though, clearly, a degree of recursion is desirable.

We advise readers to take this chapter together with the other chapters in this book on surveys, sampling and interviewing. Indeed Chapter 13 (Surveys) addresses important materials on online questionnaires, and we advise readers to consult that in detail. Part 5 concerns data analysis, and this can include analysis of quantitative and qualitative data.

The questionnaire is a widely used and useful instrument for collecting survey information, providing structured, often numerical data, being able to be administered without the presence of the researcher, and often being comparatively straightforward to analyse (Wilson and McLean, 1994). These attractions have to be counterbalanced by the time taken to develop, pilot and refine the questionnaire, by the possible unsophistication and limited scope of the data that are collected, and from the likely limited flexibility of response (though, as Wilson and McLean (1994: 3) observe, this can frequently be an attraction). The researcher will have to judge the appropriateness of using a questionnaire for data collection, and, if so, what kind of questionnaire it should be.

20.1 Ethical issues

The questionnaire will always be an intrusion into the life of the respondent, be it in terms of time taken to complete the instrument, the level of threat or sensitivity of the questions, or the possible invasion of privacy. Questionnaire respondents are not passive data providers for researchers; they are subjects not objects of research. There are several sequiturs that flow from this.

Respondents cannot be coerced into completing a questionnaire. They might be strongly encouraged, but the decision whether to become involved and when to withdraw from the research is entirely theirs. Their involvement in the research is likely to be a function of:

a their *informed consent* (see Chapter 5 on the ethics of educational research);

b their *rights to withdraw* at any stage or *not to complete* particular items in the questionnaire;

c the potential of the research to improve their situation (the issue of *beneficence*);

d   the guarantees that the research will not harm them (the issue of *non-maleficence*);

e   the guarantees of *confidentiality, anonymity* and *non-traceability* in the research;

f   the degree of *threat* or *sensitivity* of the questions (which may lead to respondents' over-reporting or under-reporting (Sudman and Bradburn, 1982: 32 and Chapter 3));

g   factors in the questionnaire itself (e.g. its coverage of issues, its ability to catch what respondents want to say rather than to promote the researcher's agenda), i.e. the avoidance of bias and the assurance of validity and reliability in the questionnaire – the issues of *methodological rigour* and *fairness*. Methodological rigour is an ethical not simply a technical matter (Morrison, 1996b), and respondents have a right to expect reliability and validity;

h   the *reactions* of the respondent, for example, respondents will react if they consider an item to be offensive, intrusive, misleading, biased, misguided, irritating, inconsiderate, impertinent or abstruse.

These factors impact on every stage of the use of a questionnaire, to suggest that attention has to be given to the questionnaire itself, the approaches that are made to the respondents, the explanations that are given to the respondents, the data analysis and the data reporting.

20.2 Approaching the planning of a questionnaire

The overall plan

At this preliminary stage of design, it can sometimes be helpful to use a flow chart technique to plan the sequencing of questions. In this way, researchers are able to anticipate the type and range of responses that their questions are likely to elicit. In Figure 20.1 we illustrate a flow chart employed in a commercial survey based upon an interview schedule, though the application of the method to a self-completion questionnaire is self-evident.

On a more positive note, Sellitz and her associates (1976) have provided a fairly exhaustive guide to researchers in constructing their questionnaires which we summarize in Box 20.1.

These are introductory issues, and the remainder of this chapter takes each of these and unpacks them in greater detail. Additionally, one can set out a staged sequence for planning a questionnaire, thus:

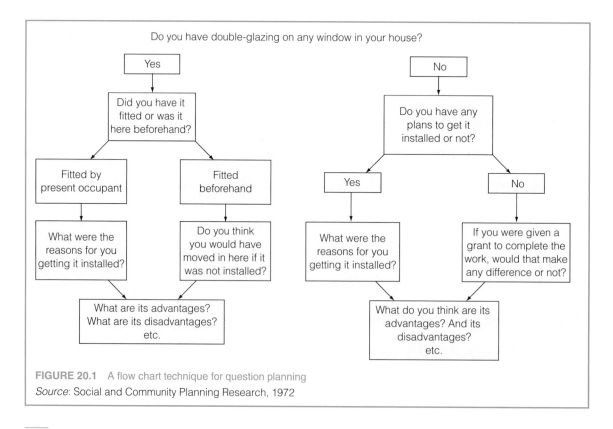

FIGURE 20.1   A flow chart technique for question planning
Source: Social and Community Planning Research, 1972

1 Decide the purposes/objectives of the questionnaire.
2 Decide the population and the sample (as questions about their characteristics will need to be included on the questionnaire under 'personal details').
3 Generate the topics/constructs/concepts/issues to be addressed and data required in order to meet the objectives of the research (this can be done from literature, or a pre-pilot, for example, focus groups and semi-structured interviews).
4 Decide the kinds of measures/scales/questions/responses required.
5 Write the questionnaire items.
6 Check that each issue from (3) has been addressed, using several items for each issue.

7 Pilot the questionnaire and refine items as a consequence.
8 Administer the final questionnaire.

Within these stages there are several sub-components, and this chapter addresses these.

Operationalizing the questionnaire

The process of operationalizing a questionnaire is to take a general purpose or set of purposes and turn these into concrete, researchable fields about which actual data can be gathered. First, a questionnaire's general purposes must be clarified and then translated into a specific, concrete aim or set of aims. Thus, 'to explore

---

BOX 20.1 A GUIDE FOR QUESTIONNAIRE CONSTRUCTION

A Decisions about question content
1 Is the question necessary? Just how will it be useful?
2 Are several questions needed on the subject matter of this question?
3 Do respondents have the information necessary to answer the question?
4 Does the question need to be more concrete, specific and closely related to the respondent's personal experience?
5 Is the question content sufficiently general and free from spurious concreteness and specificity?
6 Do the replies express general attitudes and only seem to be as specific as they sound?
7 Is the question content biased or loaded in one direction, without accompanying questions to balance the emphasis?
8 Will the respondents give the information that is asked for?

B Decisions about question wording
1 Can the question be misunderstood? Does it contain difficult or unclear phraseology?
2 Does the question adequately express the alternative with respect to the point?
3 Is the question misleading because of unstated assumptions or unseen implications?
4 Is the wording biased? Is it emotionally loaded or slanted towards a particular kind of answer?
5 Is the question wording likely to be objectionable to the respondent in any way?
6 Would a more personalized wording of the question produce better results?
7 Can the question be better asked in a more direct or a more indirect form?

C Decisions about form of response to the question
1 Can the question best be asked in a form calling for check answer (or short answer of a word or two, or a number), free answer or check answer with follow-up answer?
2 If a check answer is used, which is the best type for this question – dichotomous, multiple choice ('cafeteria' question), or scale?
3 If a checklist is used, does it cover adequately all the significant alternatives without overlapping and in a defensible order? Is it of reasonable length? Is the wording of items impartial and balanced?
4 Is the form of response easy, definite, uniform and adequate for the purpose?

D Decisions about the place of the question in the sequence
1 Is the answer to the question likely to be influenced by the content of preceding questions?
2 Is the question led up to in a natural way? Is it in correct psychological order?
3 Does the question come too early or too late from the point of view of arousing interest and receiving sufficient attention, avoiding resistance, and so on?

Source: Adapted from Sellitz *et al.*, 1976

teachers' views about in-service work' is somewhat nebulous, whereas 'to obtain a detailed description of primary and secondary teachers' priorities in the provision of in-service education courses' is reasonably specific.

Having decided upon and specified the primary objective of the questionnaire, the second phase of the planning involves the identification and itemizing of subsidiary topics that relate to its central purpose. In our example, subsidiary issues might well include: the types of courses required; the content of courses; the location of courses; the timing of courses; the design of courses; and the financing of courses.

The third phase follows the identification and itemization of subsidiary topics and involves formulating specific information requirements relating to each of these issues. For example, with respect to the type of courses required, detailed information would be needed about the duration of courses (one meeting, several meetings, a week, a month, a term or a year), the status of courses (non-award bearing, award bearing, with certificate, diploma, degree granted by college or university), the orientation of courses (theoretically oriented involving lectures, readings, etc., or practically oriented involving workshops and the production of curriculum materials).

What we have in the example, then, is a move from a generalized area of interest or purpose to a very specific set of features about which direct data can be gathered. Wilson and McLean (1994: 8–9) suggest an alternative approach which is to identify the research problem, then to clarify the relevant concepts or constructs, then to identify what kinds of measures (if appropriate) or empirical indicators there are of these, i.e. the kinds of data required to give the researcher relevant evidence about the concepts or constructs, e.g. their presence, their intensity, their main features and dimensions, their key elements, etc.

What unites these two approaches is their recognition of the need to ensure that the questionnaire: (a) is clear on its purposes; (b) is clear on what needs to be included or covered in the questionnaire in order to meet the purposes; (c) is exhaustive in its coverage of the elements of inclusion; (d) asks the most appropriate *kinds* of question (discussed below); (e) elicits the most appropriate *kinds* of data to answer the research purposes and sub-questions; (f) asks for empirical data.

Planning with the data analysis in mind

When planning a questionnaire it is important to plan so that the questionnaire is set up – structured – in such a way that the data analysis can proceed as planned. So, for example, if the researcher wishes to conduct multiple

regression (e.g. to find out the relative weights of a range of independents variables on a dependent variable, for example the relative strength of three independent variables – teaching preparation, teacher/student relationships and subject knowledge – on the dependent variable of teaching effectiveness) then both the independent and dependent variables must be included in the questionnaire. This might appear thus (though the questions below may appear to be leading questions, the student is given the option of scoring a zero, i.e. 'not at all'):

- A general question (dependent variable): 'Overall, how effective do you think the teaching is in this Mathematics department?'
- A specific question (independent variable): 'How well prepared for her/his teaching is the Mathematics teacher?'
- A specific question (independent variable): 'How positive are the teacher/student relationships in the Mathematics department?'
- A specific question (independent variable): 'How well do you think that the teacher knows his/her subject in the Mathematics department?'

Let us imagine that there is an 11-point scale, where zero ('0') means 'not at all' and 10 means 'very much'. Here the scales are the same (11 points), the dependent variable is included, and each independent variable is included. Whilst this sounds like common sense, our experience has led to us make this point, as too many times students omit the dependent variable.

As a second example, let us imagine that the researcher is investigating the reason why undergraduate students take part-time jobs (cf. Morrison and Tam, 2005). She asks the general question (dependent variable): 'What are your main reasons for taking part-time jobs? Please indicate the level of importance of each of the following reasons by encircling the appropriate rating (0–10), where 0="Of no importance" and 10="of very great importance"'. She then asks respondents to give a score out of 10 for the importance of each of several possible reasons for taking a part-time job (independent variables), for example:

- meet necessary study expenses
- meet living expenses
- purchase better consumer products
- support entertainment expenses
- for extra money to spend
- support family expenses
- gain job experience
- fill-in spare time
- affected by peer group.

She can then conduct a multiple regression to see the relative importance of each of these independent variables on the dependent variables (e.g. using standardized beta values, discussed in Part 5 of this book).

If the researcher wishes to conduct factor analysis then the variables must be at the ratio level of data (discussed below). If structural equation modelling is required then both variables and factors have to be calculated, and these have to be able to be calculated in the questionnaire. If simple frequencies, percentages and correlations are to be calculated then the questions must be framed in such a way that they can be calculated. This is a statement of the obvious, but, in our experience, too many students neglect the obvious.

A researcher may not wish to conduct such high-level data analysis, and often simple frequencies will suffice and will be very persuasive. This, too, can suggest causality (though not prove it – see Chapter 4), or, at least, correlation. Let us imagine that the researcher is looking into the effects of communication on leadership in a very large secondary school (160 teachers). She asks three simple questions:

1   Generally, how effective is the overall leadership in the school (tick one only):
    ☐ Good   ☐ Not Good

2   Generally, how effective is the principal's communication in the school (tick one only):
    ☐ Good   ☐ Not Good

3   Generally, how willing to communicate is the school principal (tick one only):
    ☐ Good   ☐ Not Good

These simple dichotomous questions require respondents to come to a judgement; they are not permitted to 'sit on the fence', they have to make up their minds. In tabular form, the results could be presented as shown in Table 20.1 (fictitious figures). In Table 20.1 'effective leadership' is reported by 82 respondents (51.2 per cent) (45+15+10+12); 'not good' leadership is reported by 78 respondents (48.8 per cent) (3+12+5+58). Table 20.1 indicates that, for 'good' leadership to be present in its strongest form requires the factors 'principal's communication' and 'willingness to communicate' to be present and 'good', and that if either or both of these factors is 'not good' then 'good' knowledge management drops dramatically.

The point to be made here is that the questionnaire is designed – set up – with the analysis in mind; the researcher knows in advance how she wants to analyse the data, and the structure and contents of the questionnaire follow from this.

Structured, semi-structured and unstructured questionnaires

Though there is a large range of types of questionnaire, there is a simple rule of thumb: the larger the size of the sample, the more structured, closed and numerical the questionnaire may have to be, and the smaller the size of the sample, the less structured, more open and word-based the questionnaire may be.

The researcher can select several types of questionnaire, from highly structured to unstructured. If a closed and structured questionnaire is used, enabling patterns to be observed and comparisons to be made, then the questionnaire will need to be piloted and refined so that the final version contains as full a range of possible responses as can be reasonably foreseen. Such a

TABLE 20.1   CROSSTABULATION OF RESPONSES TO TWO KEY FACTORS IN EFFECTIVE LEADERSHIP

Effective leadership	Principal's communication	Willingness to communicate	Frequency (% rounded)
Good	Good	Good	45 (28.1%)
Good	Good	Not good	15 (9.4%)
Good	Not good	Good	10 (6.2%)
Good	Not good	Not good	12 (7.5%)
Not good	Good	Good	3 (1.9%)
Not good	Good	Not good	12 (7.5%)
Not good	Not good	Good	5 (3.1%)
Not good	Not good	Not good	58 (36.3%)
Total			**160 (100%)**

questionnaire is heavy on time early in the research; however, once the questionnaire has been 'set up' then the mode of analysis might be comparatively rapid. For example, it may take two or three months to devise a survey questionnaire, pilot it, refine it and set it out in a format that will enable the data to be processed and statistics to be calculated. However, the 'trade-off' from this is that the data analysis can be undertaken fairly rapidly – we already know the response categories, the nature of the data and the statistics to be used; it is simply a matter of processing the data – often using computer analysis.

It is perhaps misleading to describe a questionnaire as being 'unstructured', as the whole devising of a questionnaire requires respondents to adhere to some form of given structure. That said, between a completely open questionnaire that is akin to an open invitation to 'write what one wants' and a completely closed, completely structured questionnaire, there is the powerful tool of the semi-structured questionnaire. Here a series of questions, statements or items are presented and the respondents are asked to answer, respond to or comment on them in a way that they think best. There is a clear structure, sequence, focus, but the format is open-ended, enabling respondents to reply in their own terms. The semi-structured questionnaire sets the agenda but does not presuppose the nature of the response.

20.3 Types of questionnaire items

Closed and open questions compared

There are several kinds of question and response modes in questionnaires, including, for example: dichotomous questions; multiple choice questions; rating scales; constant sum questions; ratio data and open-ended questions. These are considered below (see also Wilson, 1996). Closed questions prescribe the range of responses from which the respondent may choose. Highly structured, closed questions are useful in that they can generate frequencies of response amenable to statistical treatment and analysis. They also enable comparisons to be made across groups in the sample (Oppenheim, 1992: 115). They are quicker to code up and analyse than word-based data (Bailey, 1994: 118), and, often, they are directly to the point and deliberately more focused than open-ended questions. Indeed it would be almost impossible, as well as unnecessary, to try to process vast quantities of word-based data in a short time frame.

If a site-specific case study is required, then qualitative, less structured, word-based and open-ended questionnaires may be more appropriate as they can capture the specificity of a particular situation. Where measurement is sought then a quantitative approach is required; where rich and personal data are sought, then a word-based qualitative approach might be more suitable. Open-ended questions are useful if the possible answers are unknown or the questionnaire is exploratory (Bailey, 1994: 120), or if there are so many possible categories of response that a closed question would contain an extremely long list of options. They also enable respondents to answer as much as they wish, and are particularly suitable for investigating complex issues, to which simple answers cannot be provided. Open questions may be useful for generating items that will subsequently become the stuff of closed questions in a subsequent questionnaire (i.e. a pre-pilot).

In general closed questions (dichotomous, multiple choice, constant sum and rating scales) are quick to complete and straightforward to code (e.g. for computer analysis), and do not discriminate unduly on the basis of how articulate respondents are (Wilson and McLean, 1994: 21). On the other hand they do not enable respondents to add any remarks, qualifications and explanations to the categories, and there is a risk that the categories might not be exhaustive and that there might be bias in them (Oppenheim, 1992: 115).

Open questions enable participants to write a free account in their own terms, to explain and qualify their responses and avoid the limitations of pre-set categories of response. On the other hand open questions can lead to irrelevant and redundant information; they may be too open-ended for the respondent to know what *kind* of information is being sought; they may require much more time from the respondent to enter a response (thereby leading to refusal to complete the item), and they may make the questionnaire appear long and discouraging. With regard to analysis, the data are not easily compared across participants, and the responses are difficult to code and to classify.

We consider in more detail below the different kinds of closed and open questions.

Scales of data

The questionnaire designer will need to choose the metric – the scale of data – to be adopted. This concerns numerical data, and we advise readers to turn to Part 5 for an analysis of the different scales of data that can be gathered (nominal, ordinal, interval and ratio), and the different statistics that can be used for analysis. Nominal data indicate categories; ordinal data indicate order ('high' to 'low', 'first' to 'last', 'smallest' to 'largest', 'strongly disagree' to 'strongly agree', 'not at all' to 'a very great deal'); ratio data indicate continuous values and a true zero (e.g. marks in a test, number of attendances per year, hours spent on study). These are presented thus:

QUESTION TYPE	LEVEL OF DATA
Dichotomous questions	Nominal
Multiple choice questions	Nominal
Rank ordering	Ordinal
Rating scales	Ordinal
Constant sum questions	Ordinal
Ratio data questions	Ratio
Open-ended questions	Word-based data

The dangers of assuming knowledge or viewpoints

There is often an assumption that respondents will have the information or have an opinion about the matters in which researchers are interested. This is a dangerous assumption. It is particularly a problem when administering questionnaires to children, who may write anything rather than nothing. This means that the opportunity should be provided for respondents to indicate that they have no opinion, or that they don't know the answer to a particular question, or to state that that they feel the question does not apply to them. This is frequently a matter in surveys of customer satisfaction in social science, where respondents are asked, for example, to answer a host of questions about the services provided by utility companies (electricity, gas, water, telephone) about which they have no strong feelings, and, in fact, they are only interested in whether the service is uninterrupted, reliable, cheap, easy to pay for, and that their complaints are solved.

There is also the issue of choice of vocabulary and the concepts and information behind them. It is essential that, regardless of the type of question asked, the language and the concepts behind the language should be within the grasp of the respondents. Simply because the researcher is interested in, and has a background in, a particular topic is no guarantee that the respondents will be like-minded. The effect of the questionnaire on the respondent has to be considered carefully.

Dichotomous questions

A highly structured questionnaire will ask closed questions. These can take several forms. *Dichotomous* questions require a 'yes'/'no' response, e.g. 'have you ever had to appear in court?', 'do you prefer didactic methods to child-centred methods?'. The layout of a dichotomous question can be thus:

Sex (please tick): Male ☐ Female ☐

The dichotomous question is useful, for it compels respondents to 'come off the fence' on an issue. It provides a clear, unequivocal response. Further, it is possible to code responses quickly, there being only two categories of response. A dichotomous question is also useful as a funnelling or sorting device for subsequent questions, for example: 'if you answered "yes" to question X, please go to question Y; if you answered "no" to question X, please go to question Z' (see the section below on contingency questions). Sudman and Bradburn (1982: 89) suggest that if dichotomous questions are being used, then it is desirable to use several to gain data on the same topic, in order to reduce the problems of respondents 'guessing' answers.

On the other hand, the researcher must ask, for instance, whether a 'yes'/'no' response actually provides any useful information. Requiring respondents to make a 'yes'/'no' decision may be inappropriate; it might be more appropriate to have a range of responses, for example in a rating scale. There may be comparatively few complex or subtle questions which can be answered with a simple 'yes' or 'no'. A 'yes' or a 'no' may be inappropriate for a situation whose complexity is better served by a series of questions which catch that complexity. Further, Youngman (1984: 163) suggests that it is a natural human tendency to agree with a statement rather than to disagree with it; this suggests that a simple dichotomous question might build in respondent bias. Indeed people may be more reluctant to agree with a negative statement than to disagree with a positive question (Weems *et al.*, 2003).

In addition to dichotomous questions ('yes'/'no' questions), a piece of research might ask for information about dichotomous variables, for example gender (male/female), type of school (elementary/secondary), type of course (vocational/non-vocational). In these cases only one of two responses can be selected. This enables nominal data to be gathered, which can then be processed using the chi-square statistic, the binomial test, the G-test, and crosstabulations (see Cohen and Holliday (1996) for examples). Dichotomous questions are treated as nominal data (see Part 5).

Multiple choice questions

To try to gain some purchase on complexity, the researcher can move towards *multiple choice* questions, where the range of choices is designed to capture the likely range of responses to given statements. For example, the researcher might ask a series of questions about a new chemistry scheme in the school; a statement precedes a set of responses thus:

> The New Intermediate Chemistry Education (NICE) is:
>
> (a) a waste of time;
> (b) an extra burden on teachers;
> (c) not appropriate to our school;
> (d) a useful complementary scheme;
> (e) a useful core scheme throughout the school;
> (f) well-presented and practicable.

The categories would have to be discrete (i.e. having no overlap and being mutually exclusive) and would have to exhaust the possible range of responses. Guidance would have to be given on the completion of the multiple choice, clarifying, for example, whether respondents are able to tick only *one* response (a *single answer* mode) or *several* responses (*multiple answer* mode) from the list. Like dichotomous questions, multiple choice questions can be quickly coded and quickly aggregated to give frequencies of response. If that is appropriate for the research, then this might be a useful instrument.

The layout of a multiple choice question can be thus:

> Number of years in teaching
>   1–5 ☐   6–14 ☐   15–24 ☐   25+ ☐
>
> Which age group do you teach at present (you may tick more than one)?
>   Infant   ☐
>   Primary   ☐
>   Secondary (excluding sixth form) ☐
>   Sixth form only   ☐

Just as dichotomous questions have their parallel in dichotomous variables, so multiple choice questions have their parallel in *multiple elements of a variable*. For example, the researcher may be asking to which form a student belongs – there being up to, say, 40 forms in a large school, or the researcher may be asking which post-16 course a student is following (e.g. academic, vocational, manual, non-manual). In these cases only one response may be selected. As with the dichotomous variable, the listing of several categories or elements of a variable (e.g. form membership and course followed) enables nominal data to be collected and processed using the chi-square statis-

tic, the G-test, and crosstabulations (Cohen and Holliday, 1996). Multiple choice questions are treated as nominal data (see Part 5).

It may be important to include in the multiple choices those that will enable respondents to select the response that most closely represents their view, hence a pilot is needed to ensure that the categories are comprehensive, exhaustive and representative. On the other hand, the researcher may be only interested in certain features, and it is these that would figure in the response categories.

The multiple choice questionnaire seldom gives more than a crude statistic, for words are inherently ambiguous. In the example above of chemistry, the notion of 'useful' is unclear, as are 'appropriate', 'practicable' and 'burden'. Respondents could interpret these words differently in their own contexts, thereby rendering the data ambiguous. One respondent might see the utility of the chemistry scheme in one area and thereby say that it is useful – ticking (d). Another respondent might see the same utility in that same one area but because it is only useful in that single area may see this as a flaw and therefore not tick category (d). With an anonymous questionnaire this difference would be impossible to detect.

This is the heart of the problem of questionnaires – that different respondents interpret the same words differently. 'Anchor statements' can be provided to allow a degree of discrimination in response (e.g. 'strongly agree', 'agree', etc.) but there is no guarantee that respondents will always interpret them in the way that is intended. In the example above this might not be a problem as the researcher might only be seeking an index of utility – without wishing to know the areas of utility or the reasons for that utility. The evaluator might be wishing only for a crude statistic (which might be very useful statistically in making a decisive judgement about a programme). In this case this rough and ready statistic might be perfectly acceptable.

One can see in the example of chemistry above not only ambiguity in the wording but a very incomplete set of response categories which is hardly capable of representing all aspects of the chemistry scheme. That this might be politically expedient cannot be overlooked, for if the choice of responses is limited, then those responses might enable bias to be built into the research. For example, if the responses were limited to statements about the *utility* of the chemistry scheme, then the evaluator would have little difficulty in establishing that the scheme was useful. By avoiding the inclusion of negative statements or the opportunity to record a negative response the research will surely be biased. The issue of the wording of questions has been discussed earlier.

Multiple choice items are also prone to problems of word order and statement order. For example, Dillman *et al.* (2003: 6) report a study of sports, in which tennis was found to be less exciting than football when the tennis option was presented before the football option, and more exciting when the football option was placed before the tennis option. This suggests that respondents tend to judge later items in terms of the earlier items, rather than vice versa and that they overlook features specific to later items if these are not contained in the earlier items. This is an instance of the 'primacy effect' or 'order effect', wherein items earlier in a list are given greater weight than items lower in the list. Order effects are resilient to efforts to minimize them, and primacy effects are particularly strong in internet questionnaires (Dillman *et al.*, 2003: 22). Preceding questions and the answers given may influence responses to subsequent questions (Schwartz *et al.*, 1998: 177).

Order effects and the primacy effects are examples of context effects, in which some questions in the questionnaire (sometimes coming later in the questionnaire, as respondents do not always answer questions in the given sequence, and may scan the whole questionnaire before answering specific items) may effect the responses given to other questions in the questionnaire (Friedman and Amoo, 1999: 122), biasing the responses by creating a specific mindset, i.e. a predisposition to answering questions in a particular way.

Rank ordering

The rank order question is akin to the multiple choice question in that it identifies options from which respondents can choose, yet it moves beyond multiple choice items in that it asks respondents to identify priorities. This enables a *relative* degree of preference, priority, intensity, etc. to be charted. Rank ordering requires respondents to *compare* values across variables; in this respect they are unlike rating scales in which the values are entered independently of each other (Ovadia, 2004: 404), i.e. the category 'strongly agree' can be applied to a single variable without any regard to what one enters for any other variable. In a ranking exercise the respondent is required to take account of the other variables, because he/she is being asked to see their *relative* value, weighting or importance. This means that, in a ranking exercise, the task is fair, i.e. the variables are truly able to be compared and placed in a rank order, they lie on the same scale and/or can be judged on the same criteria.

In the rank ordering exercise a list of factors is set out and the respondent is required to place them in a rank order, for example:

> Please indicate your priorities by placing numbers in the boxes to indicate the ordering of your views, 1 = the highest priority, 2 = the second highest, and so on.
>
> The proposed amendments to the mathematics scheme might be successful if the following factors are addressed:
> - the appropriate material resources are in school; ☐
> - the amendments are made clear to all teachers; ☐
> - the amendments are supported by the mathematics team; ☐
> - the necessary staff development is assured; ☐
> - there are subsequent improvements to student achievement; ☐
> - the proposals have the agreement of all teachers; ☐
> - they improve student motivation; ☐
> - parents approve of the amendments; ☐
> - they will raise the achievements of the brighter students; ☐
> - the work becomes more geared to problem-solving. ☐

In this example ten items are listed. Whilst this might be enticing for the researcher, enabling fine distinctions possibly to be made in priorities, it might be asking too much of the respondents to make such distinctions. They genuinely might not be able to differentiate their responses, or they simply might not feel strongly enough to make such distinctions. The inclusion of too long a list might be overwhelming. Indeed Wilson and McLean (1994: 26) suggest that it is unrealistic to ask respondents to arrange priorities where there are more than five ranks that have been requested. In the case of the list of ten points above, the researcher might approach this problem in one of two ways. The list in the questionnaire item can be reduced to five items only, in which case the *range* and comprehensiveness of responses that fairly catches what the respondent feels is significantly reduced. Alternatively, the list of ten items can be retained, but the request can be made to the respondents only to rank their first five priorities, in which case the range is retained and the task is not overwhelming (though the problem of sorting the data for analysis is increased).

An example of a shorter list might be:

Please place these in rank order of the most to the least important, by putting the position (1–5) against each of the following statements, number one being the most important and number 5 being the least important:

Students should enjoy school	[ ]
Teachers should set less homework	[ ]
Students should have more choice of subjects in school	[ ]
Teachers should use more collaborative methods	[ ]
Students should be tested more, so that they work harder	[ ]

Rankings may also assume that the different items can truly be placed on a single scale. Consider the example above, where the respondent is required to place five items on a single scale of importance. Can these items really be differentiated according to the single criterion of 'importance'? Surely 'fitness for purpose' and context would suggest that a fairer answer is that 'it all depends' on what is happening in a specific context, i.e. even though one could place items in a rank order, in fact it may be meaningless to do so. The items may truly not be comparable (Ovadia, 2004: 405). As Ovadia (2004: 407) reports, valuing justice may say nothing about valuing love, so to place them in a single ranking scale of importance may be meaningless.

Rankings are useful in indicating *degrees* of response. In this respect they are like rating scales, discussed below. Ranking questions are treated as ordinal data (see Part 5 for a discussion of ordinal data). However, rankings do not enable sophisticated statistical analysis to be conducted (Ovadia, 2004: 405), as the ranks are interdependent rather than independent, and these vary for each respondent, i.e. not only does the rank '1st' mean different things to different respondents, but there are no equal intervals between each rank, and the rank of, say, '3rd' has a different meaning for different respondents, which is relative to their idea of what constitutes '2nd' and '4th', i.e. the rankings are interdependent; there is no truly common metric here. Further, because rankings force a respondent to place items in a rank order, differences between values may be overstated.

Rankings operate on a zero-sum model (Ovadia, 2004: 406), i.e. if one places an item in the 1st position then this means that another item drops in the ranking; this may or may not be desirable, depending on what the researcher wishes to find out. Researchers using rankings will need to consider whether it is fair to ask respondents really to compare items and to judge one item in relation to another; to ask 'are they really commensurable?' (able to be measured by the same single standard or criterion).

Rating scales

One way in which degrees of response, intensity of response and the move away from dichotomous questions have been managed can be seen in the notion of *rating scales* – Likert scales, semantic differential scales, Thurstone scales and Guttman scaling. These are very useful devices for the researcher, as they build in a degree of sensitivity and differentiation of response whilst still generating numbers. This chapter will focus on the first two of these, though readers will find the others discussed in Oppenheim (1992). A Likert scale (named after its deviser, Rensis Likert, 1932) provides a range of responses to a given question or statement, for example:

How important do you consider work placements to be for secondary school students?

1 = not at all
2 = very little
3 = a little
4 = quite a lot
5 = a very great deal

All students should have access to free higher education.

1 = strongly disagree
2 = disagree
3 = neither agree nor disagree
4 = agree
5 = strongly agree

Such a scale could be set out thus:

Please complete the following by placing a tick in one space only, as follows:

1 = strongly disagree; 2 = disagree;
3 = neither agree nor disagree;
4 = agree; 5 = strongly agree

Senior school staff should teach more

1	2	3	4	5
[ ]	[ ]	[ ]	[ ]	[ ]

In these examples the categories need to be discrete and to exhaust the range of possible responses which respondents may wish to give. Notwithstanding the problems of interpretation which arise as in the previous example – one respondent's 'agree' may be another's 'strongly agree', one respondent's 'very little' might be another's 'a little' – the greater subtlety of response which is built into a rating scale renders this a very attractive and widely used instrument in research.

These two examples both indicate an important feature of an attitude scaling instrument, namely the assumption of *unidimensionality* in the scale; the scale should only be measuring one thing at a time (Oppenheim, 1992: 187–8). Indeed this is a cornerstone of Likert's own thinking (1932).

It is a very straightforward matter to convert a dichotomous question into a multiple choice question. For example, instead of asking the 'do you?', 'have you?', 'are you?', 'can you?' type questions in a dichotomous format, a simple addition to wording will convert it into a much more subtle rating scale, by substituting the words 'to what extent?', 'how far?', 'how much?', 'how often?', etc.

A semantic differential is a variation of a rating scale which operates by putting an adjective at one end of a scale and its opposite at the other, for example:

How informative do you consider the new set of history textbooks to be?

	1	2	3	4	5	6	7	
useful	_	_	_	_	_	_	_	useless

Respondents indicate their opinion by circling or putting a mark on that position on the scale which most represents what they feel. Researchers devise their own terms and their polar opposites, for example:

Approachable ... Unapproachable
Generous   ... Mean
Friendly   ... Hostile
Caring   ... Uncaring
Attentive   ... Inattentive
Hard-working ... Lazy

Osgood *et al.* (1957), the pioneers of this technique, suggest that semantic differential scales are useful in three contexts: *evaluative* (e.g. valuable–valueless, useful–useless, good–bad); *potency* (e.g. large–small, weak–strong, light–heavy); and *activity* (e.g. quick–slow; active–passive, dynamic–lethargic).

There are several commonly used categories in rating scales, for example:

■ Strongly disagree/disagree/neither agree nor disagree/agree/strongly agree

■ Very seldom/occasionally/quite often/very often
■ Very little/a little/somewhat/a lot/a very great deal
■ Never/almost never/sometimes/often/very often
■ Not at all important/unimportant/neither important nor unimportant/important/very important
■ Very true of me/a little bit true of me/don't know/ not really true of me/very untrue of me
■ Strongly agree / agree / uncertain / disagree / strongly disagree.

To these could be added the category 'don't know' or 'have no opinion'. Rating scales are widely used in research, and rightly so, for they combine the opportunity for a flexible response with the ability to determine frequencies, correlations and other forms of quantitative analysis. They afford the researcher the freedom to fuse measurement with opinion, quantity and quality.

Though rating scales are powerful and useful in research, the investigator, nevertheless, needs to be aware of their limitations. For example, the researcher may infer a degree of sensitivity and subtlety from the data that they cannot bear. There are other cautionary factors about rating scales, be they Likert scales or semantic differential scales:

1 There is no assumption of equal intervals between the categories, hence a rating of 4 indicates neither that it is twice as powerful as 2 nor that it is twice as strongly felt; one cannot infer that the intensity of feeling in the Likert scale between 'strongly agree' and 'disagree' somehow matches the intensity of feeling between 'strongly disagree' and 'agree'. These are illegitimate inferences. The problem of equal intervals has been addressed in Thurstone scales (Thurstone and Chave, 1929; Oppenheim, 1992: 190–5). Friedman and Amoo (1999: 115) suggest that if the researcher wishes to assume equal intervals ('equal-sized gradations') between points in the rating scale, then he or she must ensure that the category descriptors are genuinely equal interval. Take, for example, the scale 'not at all', 'very little', 'a little', 'quite a lot', 'a very great deal'. Here the conceptual distance between 'a little' and 'quite a lot' is much greater than between 'very little' and 'a little', i.e. there are not equal intervals.

2 Numbers have different meanings for different respondents, so one person may use a particular criterion to award a score of '6' on a seven-point scale, whilst another person using exactly the same criterion would award a score of '5' on the same scale. Here '6' and '5' actually mean the same but the numbers are different. Alternatively, one person

looking at a score of, say, 7 marks out of 10 on a ten-point scale would consider that to be a high score, whereas another person looking at the same score would consider it to be moderate only. Similarly the same word has a different meaning for different respondents; one teacher may think that 'very poor' is a very negative descriptor, whereas another might think less negatively about it, and what one respondent might term 'poor', another respondent, using the same criterion, might term 'very poor'. Friedman and Amoo (1999: 115) report that there was greater consistency between subjects on the meanings of positive words rather than negative words, and they suggest that, therefore, researchers should use descriptors that have lesser strength at the negative pole of a scale (p. 3). Further, they suggest that temporal words (e.g. 'very often', 'seldom', 'fairly often', 'occasionally', etc.) are open to great variation in their meanings for respondents (p. 3).

3 Some rating scales are unbalanced, forcing unrealistic choices to be made, for example in the scale 'very acceptable', 'quite acceptable', 'a little acceptable' 'acceptable' and 'unacceptable', or in the scale 'excellent, 'very good', 'quite good', 'good' and 'poor', there are four positive categories and only one negative category (cf. Friedman and Amoo, 1999: 119). This can skew results. Such imbalance could even be called unethical.

4 Respondents are biased towards the left-hand side of a bipolar scale (Friedman and Amoo, 1999: 120; Hartley and Betts, 2010: 25). For example, if the scale 'extremely good' to 'extremely poor' runs from left to right respectively, then the results will be different if the same scale is reversed ('extremely poor' to 'extremely good') and runs from left to right (or, for example, 'strongly agree' on the left, to 'strongly disagree' on the right and *vice versa*). Typically, the authors report, the categories on the left-hand side of a scale are used more frequently than those on the right-hand side of a scale. Further, Hartley and Betts (2010: 25) found that those scales that had a positive label in the left-hand side would elicit higher scores than other orderings. Hence researchers must be cautious about putting all the positive categories on the left-hand side alone, as this can result in more respondents using those categories than if they were placed at the right-hand side of the scale, i.e. rating scales may want to mix the item scales so that sometimes there are positive scores on the left and sometimes positive scores on the right.

5 The 'direction of comparison' (Friedman and Amoo, 1999: 120) also makes a difference to results. The authors cite an example where students were asked how empathetic their male and female teachers were in regard to academic and personal problems. When the question asked 'would you say that female teachers were more empathetic ... than the male teachers?', the mean score of the responses on a nine-point scale was different from that when the question was 'would you say that male teachers were more empathetic ... than the female teachers?'. In the former, 41 per cent of responses indicated that female teachers were more empathetic, whereas in the latter only 9 per cent of responses indicated that female teachers were more empathetic.

6 We have no check on whether respondents are telling the truth. Some may be deliberately falsifying their replies.

7 We have no way of knowing if the respondent wishes to add any other comments about the issue under investigation. It might be the case that there is something far more pressing about the issue than the rating scale includes but which is condemned to silence for want of a category. A straightforward way to circumvent this issue is to run a pilot and also to include a category entitled 'other (please state)'.

8 Most of us would not wish to be called extremists; we often prefer to appear like each other in many respects. For rating scales this means that we might wish to avoid the two extreme poles at each end of the continuum of the rating scales, reducing the number of positions in the scales to a choice of three (in a five-point scale). That means that *in fact* there could be very little choice for us. The way round this is to create a larger scale than a five-point scale, for example a seven-point scale. To go beyond a seven-point scale is to invite a degree of detail and precision which might be inappropriate for the item in question, particularly if the argument set out above is accepted, namely that one respondent's scale point 3 might be another's scale point 4. Friedman and Amoo (1999: 120) suggest that five-point to 11-point scales might be most useful, whilst Schwartz *et al.* (1991: 571) suggest that seven-point scales seem to be best in terms of reliability, the ability of respondents to discriminate between the values in the scales, and the percentages of respondents who are 'undecided'.

9 Schwartz *et al.* (1991: 571) report that rating scales that have a verbal label for each point in the scale are more reliable than rating scales that provide labels only for the end points of the numerical scales.

10 If the researcher wishes to use ratio data (discussed in Part 5) in order to calculate more sophisticated level statistics (e.g. regressions, factor analysis, structural equation modelling), then a ratio scale must have a true zero ('0') and equal intervals. Many rating scales use an 11-point scale here that runs from 0 to 10, with 0 being 'not at all' (or something equivalent to this, depending on the question/item) and 10 being the highest score (e.g. 'completely' or 'excellent').

11 The end-point descriptors on a scale have a significant effect on the responses (Friedman and Amoo, 1999: 117). For example, if the end points of a scale are extreme (e.g. 'terrible' and 'marvellous') then respondents will avoid these extremes, whereas if the end points are 'very bad' and 'very good' then more responses in these categories are chosen.

12 The nature of the scaling may affect significantly the responses given and the range of responses actually given (Schwartz and Bienias, 1990: 63). Further, Schwartz et al. (1991) found that if a scale only had positive integers (e.g. 1 to 10) on a scale of 'extremely successful' to 'not at all successful' then 34 per cent of respondents chose values in the 1–5 categories. However, when the scale was set at –5 for 'not at all successful' and +5 for 'extremely successful', then only 13 per cent of respondents chose the equivalent lower 5 values (–5 to 0). The authors surmised that the former scale (0–10) was perceived by respondents to indicate degrees of success, whereas the latter scale (–5 to 0) was perceived by respondents to indicate not only the absence of success but the presence of the negative factor of failure (see also Schwartz et al., 1998: 177). Indeed they reported that respondents were reluctant to use negative scores (p. 572) and that responses to a –5 to +5 scale tended to be more extreme than responses to a 0–10 scale, even when they used the same scale verbal labels. They also suggest (p. 577) that, in a –5 to +5 scale, zero (0) indicates absence of an attribute, whereas in a 0–10 scale a zero (0) indicates the presence of the negative end of the bipolar scale, i.e. the zero has two different meanings, depending on the scale used. Hence researchers must be careful not only on the verbal labels that they use, but the scales and scale points that they use with those same descriptors. Kenett (2006: 409) also comments, in this respect, that researchers will need to consider whether they are asking about a bipolar dimension (e.g. 'very successful' to 'very unsuccessful') where an attribute and its opposite are included, or whether a single pole is being used (e.g. only degrees of positive response or presence of a factor). For a bipolar dimension a combination of negative and positive numbers on a scale may be useful (with the cautions indicated above), whereas for a singly polar dimension then only positive numbers should be used (cf. Schwartz et al., 1991: 577). In other words, if the researcher is looking to discover the intensity of a single attribute then it is better to use positive numbers only (p. 578).

13 Response alternative may signal the nature of the considerations to be borne in mind by respondents (Gaskell et al., 1994: 243). For example, if one is asking about how often there are incidents of indiscipline in a class, the categories 'several times each lesson', 'several times each morning', 'several times each day' may indicate that a more inclusive, wider definition of 'indiscipline' is required than if the categories of 'several times each week', 'several times each month' or 'several times each term' were used. The terms used may frame the nature of the thinking or responses that the respondent uses. The authors suggest that this is particularly the case if some vague phrases are included in the response categories (p. 242). Obtained responses, as Schwartz and Bienias (1990: 62) indicate, are a function of the response alternatives that the researcher has provided. Indeed Bless et al. (1992: 309) indicate that scales which offer higher response categories/values tend to produce higher estimates from the respondents (and that this tendency increases as questions become increasingly difficult (p. 312).

14 There is a tendency for participants to opt for the mid-point of a five- or seven-point scale (the central tendency). This is notably an issue in East Asian respondents, where the 'doctrine of the mean' is advocated in Confucian culture. One way to overcome this is to use an even number scaling system, as there is no mid-point. On the other hand, it could be argued that if respondents wish to 'sit on the fence' and choose a mid-point, then they should be given the option to do so.

15 Respondents tend to cluster their responses, e.g. around the centre, or around one end or another of the scale, and their responses to one item may affect their responses to another item (e.g. creating a single mindset).

16 Choices may be 'forced' by omitting certain categories (e.g. 'no opinion', 'undecided', 'don't know', 'neither agree nor disagree'). If the researcher genuinely believes that respondents do, or should, have an opinion then such omissions

may be justified. Alternatively, it may be unacceptable to force a choice for want of a category that genuinely lets respondents say what is in their minds, even if their minds are not made up about a factor or if they have a reason for concealing their true feelings. Forcing a choice may lead to respondents having an opinion on matters that they really have no opinion about, or, indeed, on matters that do not exist, e.g. phoney topics (Friedman and Amoo, 1999: 118).

17 On some scales there are mid-points; on the five-point scale it is category three, and on the seven point scale it is category four. The use of an odd number of points on a scale enables this to occur. However, choosing an even number of scale points, for example a six-point scale, might *require* a decision on rating to be indicated.

For example, suppose a new staffing structure has been introduced into a school and the head teacher is seeking some guidance on its effectiveness. A six-point rating scale might ask respondents to indicate their response to the statement:

The new staffing structure in the school has enabled teamwork to be managed within a clear model of line management.

(Circle one number)

	1	2	3	4	5	6	
strongly agree	_	_	_	_	_	_	strongly disagree

Let us say that one member of staff circled 1, eight staff circled 2, twelve staff circled 3, nine staff circled 4, two staff circled 5, and seven staff circled 6. There being no mid-point on this continuum, the researcher could infer that those respondents who circled 1, 2 or 3 were in some measure of agreement, whilst those respondents who circled 4, 5 or 6 were in some measure of disagreement. That would be very useful for, say, a head teacher, in publicly displaying agreement, there being 21 staff (1+8+12) agreeing with the statement and 18 (9+2+7) displaying a measure of disagreement. However, one could point out that the measure of 'strongly disagree' attracted seven staff – a very strong feeling – which was not true for the 'strongly agree' category, which only attracted one member of staff. The extremity of the voting has been lost in a crude aggregation.

Further, if the researcher were to aggregate the scoring around the two mid-point categories (3 and 4)

there would be 21 members of staff represented, leaving nine (1+8) from categories 1 and 2 and nine (2+7) from categories 5 and 6; adding together categories 1, 2, 5 and 6, a total of 18 is reached, which is less that the 21 total of the two categories 3 and 4. It seems on this scenario that it is far from clear that there was agreement with the statement from the staff; indeed taking the high incidence of 'strongly disagree', it could be argued that those staff who were perhaps ambivalent (categories 3 and 4), coupled with those who registered a 'strongly disagree' indicate not agreement but disagreement with the statement.

The interpretation of data has to be handled very carefully; ordering them to suit a researcher's own purposes might be very alluring but quite illegitimate. The golden rule here is that crude data can only yield crude interpretation; subtle statistics require subtle data. The interpretation of data must not distort the data unfairly. Rating scale questions are treated as ordinal data (see Part 5), using modal scores and non-parametric data analysis, though one can find very many examples where this rule has been violated, and non-parametric data have been treated as parametric data. This is unacceptable.

It has been suggested that the attraction of rating scales is that they provide more opportunity than dichotomous questions for rendering data more sensitive and responsive to respondents. This makes rating scales particularly useful for tapping attitudes, perceptions and opinions. The need for a pilot study to devise and refine categories, making them exhaustive and discrete, has been suggested as a necessary part of this type of data collection.

Questionnaires that are going to yield numerical or word-based data can be analysed using computer programs (for example SPSS or Ethnograph, SphinxSurvey, N-Vivo respectively). If the researcher intends to process the data using a computer package it is essential that the layout and coding system of the questionnaire is appropriate for that particular computer package. Instructions for layout in order to facilitate data entry are contained in manuals that accompany such packages.

Rating scales are more sensitive instruments than dichotomous scales. Nevertheless they are limited in their usefulness to researchers by their fixity of response caused by the need to select from a given choice. A questionnaire might be tailored even more to respondents by including *open-ended* questions to which they can reply in their own terms and own opinions. We consider these later. For further reviews of, and references to, rating scales we refer the reader to Hartley and Betts (2010).

Ranking or rating?

If the researcher wishes respondents to *compare* variables (items) and award scores for items in relation to each other, then rankings are suitable. If the researcher wishes respondents to give a response/score to variables (items) that are independent of the score awarded to any other variables (items), then ratings should be considered. In the latter, the score that one awards to one variable has no bearing or effect on the score that one awards to another. In practice, the results of many rating scales may enable the researcher to place items in a rank order (Ovadia, 2004: 405), but rating scales may also result in many variables having ties (the same score) in the values given, which may be coincidental or, indeed, the 'result of indifference' (Ovadia, 2004: 405) on the part of the respondent to the variable in question (e.g. respondents simply and quickly tick the middle box (e.g. '3' in a five-point scale) going down a list of items).

Rankings force the respondent to use the full range of the scale (the scale here being the number of items included, e.g. if there are ten items then ten rankings must be given). By contrast, ratings do not have such a stringent requirement; respondents may cluster their responses to all the items around one end of a scale (e.g. points '5', '6' and '7' in a seven-point scale, or point '3' in a five-point scale).

Let us imagine that a researcher asked respondents to indicate the importance of three items in respect of student success, and that the scale used was to award points out of ten. Here are the results for respondent A and respondent B (cf. Ovadia, 2004: 407):

Respondent A: working hard (9 points); family pressure (6 points); enjoyment of the subject (5 points).

Respondent B: working hard (6 points); family pressure (4 points); enjoyment of the subject (2 points).

A ranking exercise would accord the same positioning of the items on these two scores: in first place comes 'working hard', then 'family pressure' and in the lowest position, 'enjoyment of the subject'. However, as we can see, the *actual* scores are very different, and respondent A awards much higher scores than respondent B, i.e. for respondent A these items are much more important than for respondent B, and any single item is much more important for respondent A than for respondent B. Whilst rankings and ratings here will yield equally valid results, the issue is one of 'fitness for purpose': if the researcher wishes to *compare* then rankings might be useful, whereas if the researcher wishes to examine actual values then ratings might be more useful.

Further, let us imagine that for respondent A in this example, the score for 'working hard' drops by two points over time, the score for 'family pressure' drops by one point, and the score for 'enjoyment of the subject'; drops by three points over time. The result of the ranking, however, remains the same, i.e. even though the level of importance has dropped for these three items; the ranking is insensitive to these changes.

Constant sum questions

In this type of question respondents are asked to distribute a given number of marks (points) between a range of items. For example:

'Please distribute a total of ten points among the sentences that you think most closely describe your behaviour. You may distribute these freely: they may be spread out, or awarded to only a few statements, or all allocated to a single sentence if you wish.'

I can take advantage of new opportunities	[ ]
I can work effectively with all kinds of people	[ ]
Generating new ideas is one of my strengths	[ ]
I can usually tell what is likely to work in practice	[ ]
I am able to see tasks through to the very end	[ ]
I am prepared to be unpopular for the good of the school	[ ]

This enables priorities to be identified, comparing highs and lows, and for equality of choices to be indicated, and, importantly, for this to be done in the respondents' own terms. It requires respondents to make comparative judgements and choices across a range of items. For example, we may wish to distribute ten points for aspects of an individual's personality:

Talkative	[ ]
Cooperative	[ ]
Hard-working	[ ]
Lazy	[ ]
Motivated	[ ]
Attentive	[ ]

This means that the respondent has to consider the *relative* weight of each of the given aspects before coming to a decision about how to award the marks. To accomplish this means that the all-round nature of the person, in the terms provided, has to be considered, to see, on balance, which aspect is stronger when compared to another.[1]

The difficulty with this approach is to decide how many marks can be distributed (a round number, for example ten makes subsequent calculation easily comprehensible) and how many statements/items to include, e.g. whether to have the same number of statements as there are marks, or more or fewer statements than the total of marks. Having too few statements/items does not do justice to the complexity of the issue, and having too many statements/items may mean that it is difficult for respondents to decide how to distribute their marks. Having too few marks available may be unhelpful, but, by contrast, having too many marks and too many statements/items can lead to simple computational errors by respondents. Our advice is to keep the number of marks to ten and the number of statements to around six to eight. Constant sum data are ordinal, and this means that non-parametric analysis can be performed on the data (see Part 5).

Ratio data questions

We discuss ratio data in Part 5 and we refer the reader to the discussion and definition there. For our purposes here we suggest that ratio data questions deal with continuous variables where there is a true zero, e.g.

How much money do you have in the bank?	____
How many times have you been late for school?	____
How many marks did you score in the mathematics test?	____
How old are you (in years)?	____

Here no fixed answer or category is provided, and the respondent puts in the numerical answer that fits his/her exact figure, i.e. the accuracy is higher, much higher than in *categories* of data. This enables averages (means), standard deviations, range, and high-level statistics to be calculated, e.g. regression, factor analysis, structural equation modelling (see Part 5).

An alternative form of ratio scaling is where the respondent has to award marks out of, say, ten, for a particular item. This is a device that has been used in business and commerce for measuring service quality and customer satisfaction, and is being used in education by Kgaile and Morrison (2006), for example Table 20.2.

This kind of scaling is often used in telephone interviews, as it is easy for respondents to understand. The argument could be advanced that this is a sophisticated form of rating scale, but the terminology used in the instruction clearly suggests that it asks for ratio scale data.

Open-ended questions

The open-ended question is a very attractive device for smaller scale research or for those sections of a questionnaire that invite an honest, personal comment from respondents in addition to ticking numbers and boxes. The questionnaire simply puts the open-ended questions and leaves a space (or draws lines) for a free response. It is the open-ended responses that might contain the 'gems' of information that otherwise might not be caught in the questionnaire. Further, it puts the responsibility for and ownership of the data much more firmly into respondents' hands.

It is useful for the researcher to provide some support for respondents, so that they know the kind of reply being sought. For example, an open question that includes a prompt could be:

'Please indicate the most important factors that reduce staff participation in decision making';
'Please comment on the strengths and weaknesses of the mathematics course';
'Please indicate areas for improvement in the teaching of foreign languages in the school'.

This is not to say that the open-ended question might well not frame the answer, just as the stem of a rating

---

TABLE 20.2   A TEN-POINT MARKING SCALE IN A QUESTIONNAIRE

'Please give a mark from 0 to 10 for the following statements, with 10 being excellent and 0 being very poor. Please circle the appropriate number for each statement.'

Teaching and learning	Very poor									Excellent	
1 The attention given to teaching and learning at the school	0 1 2 3 4 5 6 7 8 9 10										
2 The quality of the lesson preparation	0 1 2 3 4 5 6 7 8 9 10										
3 How well learners are cared for, guided and supported	0 1 2 3 4 5 6 7 8 9 10										
4 How effectively teachers challenge and engage learners	0 1 2 3 4 5 6 7 8 9 10										
5 The educators' use of assessment for maximizing learners' learning	0 1 2 3 4 5 6 7 8 9 10										
6 How well students apply themselves to learning	0 1 2 3 4 5 6 7 8 9 10										
7 Discussion and review by educators of the quality of teaching and learning	0 1 2 3 4 5 6 7 8 9 10										

scale question might frame the response given. However, an open-ended question can catch the authenticity, richness, depth of response, honesty and candour which, as is argued elsewhere in this book, are the hallmarks of qualitative data.

Oppenheim (1992: 56–7) suggests that a sentence-completion item is a useful adjunct to an open-ended question, for example:

Please complete the following sentence in your own words:

An effective teacher…

or

The main things that I find annoying with disruptive students are…

Open-endedness also carries problems of data handling. For example, if one tries to convert opinions into numbers (e.g. so many people indicated some degree of satisfaction with the new principal's management plan), then it could be argued that the questionnaire should have used rating scales in the first place. Further, it might well be that the researcher is in danger of violating one principle of word-based data, which is that they are not validly susceptible to aggregation, i.e. that it is trying to bring to word-based data the principles of numerical data, borrowing from one paradigm (quantitative, positivist methodology) to inform another paradigm (qualitative, interpretive methodology).

Further, if a genuinely open-ended question is being asked, it is perhaps unlikely that responses will bear such a degree of similarity to each other so as to enable them to be aggregated too tightly. Open-ended questions make it difficult for the researcher to make comparisons between respondents, as there may be little in common to compare. Moreover, to complete an open-ended questionnaire takes much longer than placing a tick in a rating scale response box; not only will time be a constraint here, but there is an assumption that respondents will be sufficiently or equally capable of articulating their thoughts and committing them to paper.

In practical terms, Redline *et al.* (2002) report that using open-ended questions can lead to respondents overlooking instructions, as they are occupied with the more demanding task of writing in their own words than reading instructions.

Despite these cautions, the space provided for an open-ended response is a window of opportunity for the respondent to shed light on an issue or course.

Thus, an open-ended questionnaire has much to recommend it.

Matrix questions

Matrix questions are not types of questions but concern the layout of questions. Matrix questions enable the same kind of response to be given to several questions, for example 'strongly disagree' to 'strongly agree'. The matrix layout helps to save space, for example:

Please complete the following by placing a tick in one space only, as follows:

1=not at all; 2=very little; 3=a moderate amount; 4=quite a lot; 5=a very great deal

How much do you use the following for assessment purposes?

		1	2	3	4	5
a	commercially published tests	[]	[]	[]	[]	[]
b	your own made-up tests	[]	[]	[]	[]	[]
c	students' projects	[]	[]	[]	[]	[]
d	essays	[]	[]	[]	[]	[]
e	samples of students' work	[]	[]	[]	[]	[]

Here five questions have been asked in only five lines, excluding, of course, the instructions and explanations of the anchor statements. Such a layout is economical of space.

A second example indicates how a matrix design can save a considerable amount of space in a questionnaire. Here the size of potential problems in conducting a piece of research is asked for, and data on how much these problems were soluble are requested. For the first issue (the size of the problem) 1=no problem, 2=a small problem, 3=a moderate problem, 4=a large problem, 5=a very large problem. For the second issue (how much the problem was solved) 1=not solved at all, 2=solved only a very little, 3=solved a moderate amount, 4=solved a lot, 5=completely solved. In Table 20.3 30 questions (15 × 2) have been able to be covered in just a short amount of space.

Laying out the questionnaire like this enables the respondent to fill in the questionnaire rapidly. On the other hand, it risks creating a mindset in the respondent (a 'response set' (Baker, 1994: 181)) in that the respondent may simply go down the questionnaire columns and write the same number each time (e.g. all number 3) or, in a rating scale, tick all number 3. Such response sets can be detected by looking at patterns of replies and eliminating response sets from subsequent analysis.

The conventional way of minimizing response sets has been by reversing the meaning of some of the

TABLE 20.3 POTENTIAL PROBLEMS IN CONDUCTING RESEARCH		
Potential problems in conducting research	Size of the problem (1–5)	How much the problem was solved (1–5)
1 Gaining access to schools and teachers;		
2 Gaining permission to conduct the research (e.g. from principals);		
3 Resentment by principals;		
4 People vetting what could be used;		
5 Finding enough willing participants for your sample;		
6 Schools suffering from 'too much research' by outsiders and insiders;		
7 Schools/people not wishing to divulge information about themselves;		
8 Schools not wishing to be identifiable, even with protections guaranteed;		
9 Local political factors that impinge on the school;		
10 Teachers' fear of being identified/traceable, even with protections guaranteed;		
11 Fear of participation by teachers (e.g. if they are critical of the school or others they could lose their contracts);		
12 Unwillingness of teachers to be involved because of their workload;		
13 The principal deciding on whether to involve the staff, without consultation with the staff;		
14 Schools'/institutions' fear of criticism/loss of face;		
15 The sensitivity of the research: the issues being investigated.		

questions so that the respondents will need to read them carefully. However Weems *et al.* (2003) argue that using positively and negatively worded items within a scale is not measuring the same underlying traits. They report that some respondents will tend to disagree with a negatively worded item, that the reliability levels of negatively worded items are lower than for positively worded items, and that negatively worded items receive greater non-response than positively worded items. Indeed the authors argue against mixed-item formats, and supplement this by reporting that inappropriately worded items can induce an artificially extreme response which, in turn, compromises the reliability of the data. Mixing negatively and positively worded items in the same scale, they argue, compromises both validity and reliability. Indeed they suggest that respondents may not read negatively worded items as carefully as positively worded items.

Contingency questions, filters and branches

Contingency questions depend on responses to earlier questions, for example: 'if your answer to question (1) was "yes" please go to question (4)'. The earlier question acts as a filter for the later question, and the later question is contingent on the earlier, and is a branch of the earlier question. Some questionnaires will write in words the number of the question to which to go (e.g. 'please go to question 6'); others will place an arrow to indicate the next question to be answered if your answer to the first question was such-and-such.

Contingency and filter questions may be useful for the researcher, but they can be confusing for the respondent as it is not always clear how to proceed through the sequence of questions and where to go once a particular branch has been completed. Redline *et al.* (2002) found that respondents tend to ignore, misread and incorrectly follow branching instructions, such that item non-response occurs for follow-up questions that are only applicable to certain subsamples, and respondents skip over, and therefore fail to follow-up on those questions that they should have completed. The authors found that the increased complexity of the questionnaire brought about by branching instructions negatively influenced its correct completion.

The authors report (Redline *et al.*, 2002: 7) that the number of words in the question affects the respondents' ability to follow branching instructions – the greater the number of words in the question, the greater is the likelihood of the respondents overlooking the branching instructions. The authors report that up to seven items, and no more, can be retained in the short-term memory. This has implications for the number of items in a list of telephone interviews, where there is no visual recall or checking possible. Similarly, the greater the number of answer categories, the greater is the likelihood of making errors, e.g. overlooking branching instructions (p. 19). They report that respondents tend to see branching instructions when they are placed by the last category, particularly if they have chosen that last category.

Further, Redline *et al.* (2002: 8) note that sandwiching branching instructions between items that do not branch is likely to lead to errors of omission and commission being made: omitting to answer all the questions and answering the wrong questions. Further, locating the instructions for branching some distance away from the preceding answer box can also lead to errors in following the instructions. They report (p. 17) that 'altering the visual and verbal design of branching instructions has a substantial impact on how well respondents read, comprehend, and act upon the branching instructions'. It follows from this that the *clear location* and *visual impact* of instructions are important for successful completion of branching instructions. Most respondents, they acknowledge, do not deliberately ignore branching instructions; they simply are unaware of them.

The implications of the findings from Redline *et al.* (2002) are that instructions should be placed where they are to be used and where they can be seen.

We would advise judicious and limited use of filtering and branching devices. It is particularly important to avoid having participants turning pages forwards and backwards in a questionnaire in order to follow the sequence of questions that have had filters and branches following from them. It is a particular problem in internet surveys where the screen size is much smaller than the length of a printed page. One way of overcoming the problem of branches is to sectionalize the questionnaire, keeping together conceptually close items and keeping the branches within that section.

20.4 Asking sensitive questions

Sudman and Bradburn (1982: chapter 3) draw attention to the important issue of including sensitive items in a questionnaire. Whilst the anonymity of a questionnaire and, frequently, the lack of face-to-face contact between the researcher and the respondents in a questionnaire might facilitate responses to sensitive material, the issues of sensitivity and threat cannot be avoided, as they might lead to under-reporting (non-disclosure and withholding data) or over-reporting (exaggeration) by participants. Some respondents may be unwilling to disclose sensitive information, particularly if it could harm themselves or others. Why should they share private matters (e.g. about family life and opinions of school managers and colleagues) with a complete stranger (Cooper and Schindler, 2001: 341)?

Even details of age, income, educational background, qualifications and opinions can be regarded as private and/or sensitive matters.

Sudman and Bradburn (1982: 55–6) identify several important considerations in addressing potentially threatening or sensitive issues, for example socially undesirable behaviour (e.g. drug abuse, sexual offences, violent behaviour, criminality, illnesses, employment and unemployment, physical features, sexual activity, behaviour and sexuality, gambling, drinking, family details, political beliefs, social taboos). They suggest that:

- Open rather than closed questions might be more suitable to elicit information about socially undesirable behaviour, particularly frequencies.
- Long rather than short questions might be more suitable for eliciting information about socially undesirable behaviour, particularly frequencies.
- Using familiar words might increase the number of reported frequencies of socially undesirable behaviour.
- Using data gathered from informants, where possible, can enhance the likelihood of obtaining reports of threatening behaviour.
- Deliberately loading the question so that overstatements of socially desirable behaviour and understatements of socially undesirable behaviour are reduced might be a useful means of eliciting information.
- With regard to socially undesirable behaviour, it might be advisable first to ask whether the respondent has engaged in that behaviour previously, and then move to asking about his or her current behaviour. By contrast, when asking about socially acceptable behaviour the reverse might be true, i.e. asking about current behaviour before asking about everyday behaviour.
- In order to defuse threat, it might be useful to locate the sensitive topic within a discussion of other more or less sensitive matters, in order to suggest to respondents that this issue might not be too important.
- Use alternative ways of asking standard questions, for example sorting cards, or putting questions in sealed envelopes, or repeating questions over time (this has to be handled sensitively, so that respondents do not feel that they are being 'checked'), and in order to increase reliability.
- Ask respondents to keep diaries in order to increase validity and reliability.
- At the end of an interview ask respondents their views on the sensitivity of the topics that have been discussed.

■ If possible, find ways of validating the data.

Indeed the authors suggest (Sudman and Bradburn, 1982: 86) that, as the questions become more threatening and sensitive, it is wise to expect greater bias and unreliability. They draw attention to the fact (p. 208) that several nominal, demographic details might be considered threatening by respondents. This has implications for their location within the questionnaire (discussed below). The issue here is that sensitivity and threat are to be viewed through the eyes of respondents rather than the questionnaire designer; what might appear innocuous to the researcher might be highly sensitive or offensive to participants. We refer readers to Chapter 9 on sensitive educational research.

20.5 Avoiding pitfalls in question writing

Though there are several kinds of questions that can be used, there are some caveats about the framing of questions in a questionnaire:

i   Avoid leading questions, that is, questions which are worded (or their response categories presented) in such a way as to suggest to respondents that there is only one acceptable answer, and that other responses might or might not gain approval or disapproval respectively. For example:

Do you prefer abstract, academic-type courses, or down-to-earth, practical courses that have some pay-off in your day-to-day teaching?

The guidance here is to check the 'loadedness' or possible pejorative overtones of terms or verbs.

ii   Avoid highbrow questions even with sophisticated respondents. For example:

What particular aspects of the current positivistic/interpretive debate would you like to see reflected in a course of developmental psychology aimed at a teacher audience?

Where the sample being surveyed is representative of the whole adult population, misunderstandings of what researchers take to be clear, unambiguous language are commonplace. Therefore it is important to use clear and simple language.

iii Avoid complex questions. For example:

Would you prefer a short, non-award bearing course (3, 4 or 5 sessions) with part-day release (e.g. Wednesday afternoons) and one evening per week attendance with financial reimbursement for travel, or a longer, non-award bearing course (6, 7 or 8 sessions) with full-day release, or the whole course designed on part-day release without evening attendance?

iv   Avoid irritating questions or instructions. For example:

Have you ever attended an in-service course of any kind during your entire teaching career?

If you are over 40, and have never attended an in-service course, put one tick in the box marked *NEVER* and another in the box marked *OLD*.

v   Avoid questions that use negatives and double negatives (Oppenheim, 1992: 128). For example:

How strongly do you feel that no teacher should enrol on the in-service, award-bearing course who has not completed at least two years' full-time teaching?

Or:

Do you feel that without a parent/teacher association teachers are unable to express their views to parents clearly?

In this case, if you feel that a parent/teacher association *is* essential for teachers to express their views, do you vote 'yes' or 'no'? The hesitancy involved in reaching such a decision, and the possible required rereading of the question could cause the respondent simply to leave it blank and move on to the next question. The problem is the double negative: 'without' and 'unable'; it creates confusion.

vi   Avoid too many open-ended questions on self-completion questionnaires. Because self-completion questionnaires cannot probe respondents to find out just what they mean by particular responses, open-ended questions are a less satisfactory way of eliciting information. (This caution does not hold in the interview situation, however.) Open-ended questions, moreover, are too demanding of most respondents' time. Nothing can be more off-putting than the following format:

Use pages 5, 6 and 7 respectively to respond to each of the questions about your attitudes to in-service courses in general and your beliefs about their value in the professional life of the serving teacher.

vii Avoid extremes in rating scales, e.g. 'never', 'always', 'totally', 'not at all' unless there is a good reason to include them. Most respondents are reluctant to use such extreme categories (Anderson and Arsenault, 1998: 174).

viii Avoid pressuring/biasing by association, for example: 'Do you agree with your head teacher that boys are more troublesome than girls?' In this case the reference to the head teacher should simply be excised.

ix Avoid statements with which people tend either to disagree or agree (i.e. that have built-in skewedness (the 'base-rate' problem, in which natural biases in the population affect the sample results)).

x   Avoid ambiguous questions or questions that could be interpreted differently from the way that is intended. The problem of ambiguity in words is intractable; at best it can be minimized rather than eliminated altogether. The most innocent of questions is replete with ambiguity (Youngman, 1984: 158–9; Morrison, 1993: 71–2). Take the following examples:

■ Does your child regularly do homework?

What does 'regularly' mean – once a day; once a year; once a term; once a week?

■ How many students are there in the school?

What does this mean: on roll, on roll but absent; marked as present but out of school on a field trip; at this precise moment or this week (there being a difference in attendance between a Monday and a Friday), or between the first term of an academic year and the last term of the academic year for secondary school students as some of them will have left school to go into employment and others will be at home revising for examinations or have completed them?

■ How many computers do you have in school?

What does this mean: present but broken; including those out of school being repaired; the property of the school or staffs' and students' own computers; on average or exactly in school today?

■ Have you had a French lesson this week?

What constitutes a 'week': the start of the school week (i.e. from Monday to a Friday), since last Sunday (or Saturday depending on one's religion), or, if the question were put on a Wednesday, since last Wednesday; how representative of all weeks is this week – there being public examinations in the school for some of the week?

■ How old are you?

15–20
20–30
30–40
40–50
50–60

The categories are not discrete; will an old-looking 40-year-old flatter himself and put himself in the 30–40 category, or will an immature 20-year-old seek the maturity of being put into the 20–30 category? The rule in questionnaire design is to avoid any overlap of categories.

■ Vocational education is only available to the lower ability students but it should be open to every student.

This is, in fact, a double question. What does the respondent do who agrees with the first part of the sentence – 'vocational education is only available to the lower ability students' – but disagrees with the latter part of the sentence, or vice versa? The rule in questionnaire design is to ask only one question at a time.

Though it is impossible to legislate for the respondents' interpretation of wording, the researcher, of course, has to adopt a common-sense approach to this, recognizing the inherent ambiguity but nevertheless still feeling that it is possible to live with this indeterminacy.

An ideal questionnaire possesses the same properties as a good law, being clear, unambiguous and practicable, reducing potential errors in participants and data analysts, being motivating for participants and ensuring as far as possible that respondents are telling the truth (Davidson, 1970).

The golden rule is to keep questions as short and as simple as possible.

20.6 Sequencing questions

To some extent the order of questions in a schedule is a function of the target sample (e.g. how they will react to certain questions), the purposes of the questionnaire (e.g. to gather facts or opinions), the sensitivity of the research (e.g. how personal and potentially disturbing the issues are that will be addressed) and the overall balance of the questionnaire (e.g. where best to place sensitive questions in relation to less threatening questions, and how many of each to include).

The ordering of the questionnaire is important, for early questions may set the tone or the mindset of the respondent to later questions. For example, a questionnaire that makes a respondent irritated or angry early on is unlikely to have managed to enable that respondent's irritation or anger to subside by the end of the questionnaire. As Oppenheim remarks (1992: 121) one covert purpose of each question is to ensure that the respondent will continue to cooperate.

Further, a respondent might 'read the signs' in the questionnaire, seeking similarities and resonances between statements so that responses to early statements will affect responses to later statements and vice versa. Whilst multiple items may act as a cross-check, this very process might be irritating for some respondents.

Krosnick and Alwin (1987) found a 'primacy effect' (discussed earlier), i.e. respondents tend to choose items that appear earlier in a list rather than items that appear later in a list. This is particularly important for branching instructions, where the instruction, because it appears at the bottom of the list, could easily be overlooked. Krosnick (1991, 1999) also found that the more difficult a question is, the greater is the likelihood of 'satisficing', i.e. choosing the first reasonable response option in a list, rather than working through a list methodically to find the most appropriate response category.

The key principle, perhaps, is to avoid creating a mood-set or a mindset early on in the questionnaire. For this reason it is important to commence the questionnaire with non-threatening questions that respondents can readily answer. After that it might be possible to move towards more personalized questions.

Completing a questionnaire can be seen as a learning process in which respondents become more at home with the task as they proceed. Initial questions should therefore be simple, have high interest value and encourage participation. This will build up the confidence and motivation of the respondent. The middle section of the questionnaire should contain the difficult questions; the last few questions should be of high interest in order to encourage respondents to return the completed schedule.

A common sequence of a questionnaire is:

a   to commence with unthreatening factual questions (that, perhaps, will give the researcher some nominal data about the sample, e.g. age group, sex, occupation, years in post, qualifications, etc.);

b   to move to closed questions (e.g. dichotomous, multiple choice, rating scales, constant sum questions) about given statements or questions, eliciting responses that require opinions, attitudes, perceptions, views;

c   to move to more open-ended questions (or, maybe, to intersperse these with more closed questions) that seek responses on opinions, attitudes, perceptions and views, together with reasons for the responses given. These responses and reasons might include sensitive or more personal data.

The move is from objective facts to subjective attitudes and opinions through justifications and to sensitive, personalized data. Clearly the ordering is neither as discrete nor as straightforward as this. For example, an apparently innocuous question about age might be offensive to some respondents; a question about income is unlikely to go down well with somebody who has just become unemployed, and a question about religious belief might be seen as an unwarranted intrusion into private matters. Indeed, many questionnaires keep questions about personal details until the very end.

The issue here is that the questionnaire designer has to anticipate the sensitivity of the topics in terms of the respondents, and this has a large socio-cultural dimension. What is being argued here is that the *logical* ordering of a questionnaire has to be mediated by its *psychological* ordering. The instrument has to be viewed through the eyes of the respondent as well as the designer.

In addition to the *overall* sequencing of the questionnaire, Oppenheim (1992: chapter 7) suggests that the sequence *within* sections of the questionnaire is important. He indicates that the questionnaire designer can use *funnels* and *filters* within the question. A funnelling process moves from the general to the specific, asking questions about the general context or issues and then moving toward specific points within that. A filter is used to include and exclude certain respondents, i.e. to decide if certain questions are relevant or irrelevant to them, and to instruct respondents about how to proceed (e.g. which items to jump to or proceed to). For example, if respondents indicate a 'yes' or a 'no' to a certain question, then this might exempt them from certain other questions in that section or subsequently.

20.7 Questionnaires containing few verbal items

The discussion so far has assumed that questionnaires are entirely word-based. This might be off-putting for many respondents, particularly children. In these circumstances a questionnaire might include visual information and ask participants to respond to this (e.g. pictures, cartoons, diagrams) or might include some projective visual techniques (e.g. to draw a picture or diagram, to join two related pictures with a line, to write the words or what someone is saying or thinking in a 'bubble' picture), to tell the story of a sequence of pictures together with personal reactions to it. The issue here is that in tailoring the format of the questionnaire to the characteristics of the sample, a very wide embrace might be necessary to take in non-word-based techniques. This is not only a matter of *appeal* to respondents, but, perhaps more significantly, is a matter of *accessibility* of the questionnaire to the respondents, i.e. a matter of reliability and validity.

20.8 The layout of the questionnaire

The appearance of the questionnaire is vitally important. It must look easy, attractive and interesting rather than complicated, unclear, forbidding and boring. A compressed layout is uninviting and it clutters everything together; a larger questionnaire with plenty of space for questions and answers is more encouraging to respondents. Verma and Mallick (1999: 120) suggest the use of high quality paper if funding permits.

Dillman *et al.* (1999) found that respondents tend to expect less of a form-filling task than is actually required. They expect to read a question, read the response, make a mark and move on to the next question, but in many questionnaires it is more complicated than this. The rule is simple: keep it as uncomplicated as possible.

It is important, perhaps, for respondents to be introduced to the purposes of each section of a questionnaire, so that they can become involved in it and maybe identify with it. If space permits, it is useful to tell the respondent the purposes and focuses of the sections/of the questionnaire, and the reasons for the inclusion of the items.

Clarity of wording and simplicity of design are essential. Clear instructions should guide respondents – 'Put a tick', for example, invites participation, whereas complicated instructions and complex procedures intimidate respondents. Putting ticks in boxes by way of answering a questionnaire is familiar to most respondents, whereas requests to circle precoded numbers at the right-hand side of the questionnaire can be a source of confusion and error. In some cases it might also be useful to include an example of how to fill in the questionnaire (e.g. ticking a box, circling a statement), though, clearly, care must be exercised to avoid leading the respondents to answering questions in a particular way by dint of the example provided (e.g. by suggesting what might be a desired answer to the subsequent questions). Verma and Mallick (1999: 121) suggest the use of emboldening to draw the respondent's attention to significant features.

Ensure that short, clear instructions accompany each section of the questionnaire. Repeating instructions as often as necessary is good practice in a postal questionnaire. Since everything hinges on respondents knowing exactly what is required of them, clear, unambiguous instructions, boldly and attractively displayed, are essential.

Clarity and presentation also impact on the numbering of the questions. For example a four-page questionnaire might contain 60 questions, broken down into four sections. It might be off-putting to respondents to number each question (1–60) as the list will seem interminably long, whereas to number each section (1–4) makes the questionnaire look manageable. Hence it is useful, in the interests of clarity and logic, to break down the questionnaire into subsections with section headings. This will also indicate the overall logic and coherence of the questionnaire to the respondents, enabling them to 'find their way' through the questionnaire. It might be useful to preface each subsection with a brief introduction that tells them the purpose of that section.

The practice of sectionalizing and sublettering questions (e.g. Q9 (a) (b) (c) and so on) is a useful technique for grouping together questions about a specific issue. It is also a way of making the questionnaire look smaller than it actually is!

This previous point also requires the questionnaire designer to make it clear if respondents are exempted from completing certain questions or sections of the questionnaire (discussed earlier in the section on filters). If so, then it is vital that the sections or questions are numbered so that the respondent knows exactly where to move to next. Here the instruction might be, for example: 'if you have answered "yes" to question 10 please go to question 15, otherwise continue with question 11', or, for example: 'if you are the school principal please answer this section, otherwise proceed to section three'.

Arrange the contents of the questionnaire in such a way as to maximize cooperation. For example, include questions that are likely to be of general interest. Make sure that questions which appear early in the format do not suggest to respondents that the enquiry is not intended for them. Intersperse attitude questions throughout the schedule to allow respondents to air their views rather than merely describe their behaviour. Such questions relieve boredom and frustration as well as providing valuable information in the process.

Coloured pages can help to clarify the overall structure of the questionnaire and the use of different colours for instructions can assist respondents.

It is important to include in the questionnaire, perhaps at the beginning, assurances of confidentiality, anonymity and non-traceability, for example by indicating that respondents need not give their name, that the data will be aggregated, that individuals will not be able to be identified through the use of categories or details of their location, etc. (i.e. that it will not be possible to put together a traceable picture of the respondents through the compiling of nominal, descriptive data about them). In some cases, however, the questionnaire might ask respondents to put their names so that they can be traced for follow-up interviews in the research

(Verma and Mallick, 1999: 121); here the guarantee of eventual anonymity and non-traceability will still need to be given.

Redline *et al.* (2002) indicate that the placing of the response categories to the immediate right of the text increases the chance of it being answered (the visual *location*), and making the material more salient (e.g. through emboldening and capitalization) can increase the chances of it being addressed (the *visibility* issue). This is particularly important for branching questions and instructions.

Redline *et al.* (2002) also note that questions placed at the bottom of a page tend to receive more non-response than questions placed further up on the page. Indeed they found that putting instructions at the bottom of the page, particularly if they apply to items on the next page, can easily lead to those instructions being overlooked. It is important, then, to consider what should go at the bottom of the page, perhaps the inclusion of less important items at that point. The authors suggest that questions with branching instructions should not be placed at the bottom of a page.

Finally, a brief note at the very end of the questionnaire can: (a) ask respondents to check that no answer has been inadvertently missed out; (b) solicit an early return of the completed schedule; (c) thank respondents for their participation and cooperation, and offer to send a short abstract of the major findings when the analysis is completed.

20.9 Covering letters/sheets and follow-up letters

The purpose of the covering letter/sheet is to indicate the aim of the research, to convey to respondents its importance, to assure them of confidentiality and to encourage their replies. The covering letter/sheet should:

- provide a title to the research;
- introduce the researcher, her/his name, address, organization, contact telephone/fax/email address, together with an invitation to feel free to contact the researcher for further clarification or details;
- indicate the purposes of the research;
- indicate the importance and benefits of the research;
- indicate why the respondent has been selected for receipt of the questionnaire;
- indicate any professional backing, endorsement, or sponsorship of, or permission for, the research (e.g. university, professional associations, government departments). The use of a logo can be helpful here;

- set out how to return the questionnaire (e.g. in the accompanying stamped addressed envelope, in a collection box in a particular institution, to a named person; whether the questionnaire will be collected – and when, where and by whom);
- indicate the address to which to return the questionnaire;
- indicate what to do if questions or uncertainties arise;
- indicate a return-by date;
- indicate any incentives for completing the questionnaire;
- provide assurances of confidentiality, anonymity and non-traceability;
- indication of how the results will and will not be disseminated, and to whom;
- thank respondents in advance for their cooperation.

Verma and Mallick (1999: 122) suggest that, where possible, it is useful to personalize the letter, avoiding 'Dear colleague', 'Dear Madam/Ms/Sir', etc., and replacing these with exact names.

With these intentions in mind, the following practices are to be recommended:

The appeal in the covering letter must be tailored to suit the particular audience. Thus, a survey of teachers might stress the importance of the study to the profession as a whole.

Neither the use of prestigious signatories, nor appeals to altruism, nor the addition of handwritten postscripts affects response levels to postal questionnaires.

The name of the sponsor or the organization conducting the survey should appear on the letterhead as well as in the body of the covering letter.

A direct reference should be made to the confidentiality of respondents' answers and the purposes of any serial numbers and codings should be explained.

A pre-survey letter advising respondents of the forthcoming questionnaire has been shown to have substantial effect on response rates.

A short covering letter is most effective; aim at no more than one page. An example of a covering letter for teachers and senior staff might be:

Dear Colleague,

IMPROVING SCHOOL EFFECTIVENESS

We are asking you to take part in a project to improve school effectiveness, by completing this short research questionnaire. The project is part of your school development, support management and monitoring of school effectiveness, and the project will facilitate a change management programme that will be tailor-made for the school. This questionnaire is seeking to identify the nature, strengths and weaknesses of different aspects of your school, particularly in respect of those aspects of the school over which the school itself has some control. It would be greatly appreciated if you would be involved in this process by completing the sheets attached, and returning them to me. Please ***be as truthful as possible*** in completing the questionnaire.

You do not need to write your name, and no individuals will be identified or traced from this, i.e. confidentiality and anonymity are assured. If you wish to discuss any aspects of the review or this document please do not hesitate to contact me. I hope that you will feel able to take part in this project.

Thank you.

Signed

Contact details (address, fax, telephone, email)

Another example might be:

Dear Colleague,

PROJECT ON CONDUCTING EDUCATIONAL RESEARCH

I am conducting a small-scale piece of research into issues facing researchers undertaking investigations in education. The topic is very much under-researched in education, and that is why I intend to explore the area.

I am asking you to be involved as you yourself have conducted empirical work as part of a Master's or doctorate degree. No one knows the practical problems facing the educational researcher better than you.

The enclosed questionnaire forms part of my investigation. May I invite you to spend a short time in its completion?

If you are willing to be involved, please complete the questionnaire and return it to XXX by the end of November. You may either place it in the collection box at the General Office at my institution or send it by post (stamped addressed envelope enclosed), or by fax or email attachment.

The questionnaire will take around fifteen minutes to complete. It employs rating scales and asks for your comments and a few personal details. You <u>do not need to write your name</u>, and you will not be able to be identified or traced. ANONYMITY AND NON-TRACEABILITY ARE ASSURED. When completed, I intend to publish my results in an education journal.

If you wish to discuss any aspects of the study then please do not hesitate to contact me.

I very much hope that you will feel able to participate. May I thank you, in advance, for your valuable cooperation.

Yours sincerely,

Signed

Contact details (address, fax, telephone, email)

For a further example of a questionnaire see the accompanying website.

20.10 Piloting the questionnaire

It bears repeating that the wording of questionnaires is of paramount importance and that pre-testing is crucial to their success. A pilot has several functions, principally to increase the reliability, validity and practicability of the questionnaire (Oppenheim, 1992; Morrison, 1993: Wilson and McLean, 1994: 47):

- to check the clarity of the questionnaire items, instructions and layout;
- to gain feedback on the validity of the questionnaire items, the operationalization of the constructs and the purposes of the research;
- to eliminate ambiguities or difficulties in wording;
- to check readability levels for the target audience;
- to gain feedback on the type of question and its format (e.g. rating scale, multiple choice, open, closed, etc.);
- to gain feedback on response categories for closed questions and multiple choice items, and for the appropriateness of specific questions or stems of questions;
- to identify omissions, redundant and irrelevant items;
- to gain feedback on leading questions;
- to gain feedback on the attractiveness and appearance of the questionnaire;
- to gain feedback on the layout, sectionalizing, numbering and itemization of the questionnaire;
- to check the time taken to complete the questionnaire;
- to check whether the questionnaire is too long or too short, too easy or too difficult;
- to generate categories from open-ended responses to use as categories for closed-response modes (e.g. rating scale items);
- to identify how motivating/non-motivating/sensitive/threatening/intrusive/offensive items might be;
- to identify redundant questions (e.g. those questions which consistently gain a total 'yes' or 'no' response (Youngman, 1984: 172)), i.e. those questions with little discriminability;
- to identify which items are too easy, too difficult, too complex or too remote from the respondents' experience;
- to identify commonly misunderstood or non-completed items (e.g. by studying common patterns of unexpected response and non-response (Verma and Mallick, 1999: 120));
- to try out the coding/classification system for data analysis.

In short, as Oppenheim (1992: 48) remarks, *everything* about the questionnaire should be piloted; nothing should be excluded, not even the type face or the quality of the paper.

The above outline describes a particular kind of pilot: one that does not focus on data, but on matters of coverage and format, gaining feedback from a limited number of respondents and experts on the items set out above.

There is a second type of pilot. This is one which starts with a long list of items and, through statistical analysis and feedback, reduces those items (Kgaile and Morrison, 2006). For example, a researcher may generate an initial list of, for example, 120 items to be included in a questionnaire, and wish to know which items to excise. A pilot is conducted on a sizeable and representative number of respondents (e.g. 50–100) and this generates real data – numerical responses. These data can be analysed for:

a *reliability*: those items with low reliability (Cronbach's alpha for internal consistency: see Part 5) can be removed;
b *collinearity*: if items correlate very strongly with others then a decision can be taken to remove one or more of them, provided, of course, that this does not result in the loss of important areas of the research (i.e. human judgement would have to prevail over statistical analysis);
c *multiple regression*: those items with low betas (see Part 5) can be removed, provided, of course, that this does not result in the loss of important areas of the research (i.e. human judgement would have to prevail over statistical analysis);
d *factor analysis*: to identify clusters of key variables and to identify redundant items (see Part 5).

As a result of such analysis, the items for removal can be identified, and this can result in a questionnaire of manageable proportions. It is important to have a good-sized and representative sample here in order to generate reliable data for statistical analysis; too few respondents to this type of pilot and this may result in important items being excluded from the final questionnaire.

20.11 Practical considerations in questionnaire design

Taking the issues discussed so far in questionnaire design, a range of practical implications for designing a questionnaire can be highlighted:

- Operationalize the purposes of the questionnaire carefully.
- Be prepared to have a pre-pilot to generate items for a pilot questionnaire, and then be ready to modify the pilot questionnaire for the final version.
- If the pilot includes many items, and the intention is to reduce the number of items through statistical

analysis or feedback, then be prepared to have a second round of piloting, after the first pilot has been modified.

■ Decide on the most appropriate *type* of question – dichotomous, multiple choice, rank orderings, rating scales, constant sum, ratio, closed, open.

■ Ensure that every issue has been explored exhaustively and comprehensively; decide on the content and explore it in depth and breadth.

■ Use several items to measure a specific attribute, concept or issue.

■ Ensure that the data acquired will answer the research questions.

■ Ask more closed than open questions for ease of analysis (particularly in a large sample).

■ Balance comprehensiveness and exhaustive coverage of issues with the demotivating factor of having respondents complete several pages of a questionnaire.

■ Ask only one thing at a time in a question. Use single sentences per item wherever possible.

■ Keep response categories simple.

■ Avoid jargon.

■ Keep statements in the present tense wherever possible.

■ Strive to be unambiguous and clear in the wording.

■ Be simple, clear and brief wherever possible.

■ Clarify the kinds of responses required in open questions.

■ Balance brevity with politeness (Oppenheim, 1992: 122). It might be advantageous to replace a blunt phrase like 'marital status' with a gentler 'please indicate whether you are married, living with a partner, or single…' or 'I would be grateful if would tell me if you are married, living with a partner, or single.'

■ Ensure a balance of questions which ask for facts and opinions (this is especially true if statistical correlations and crosstabulations are required).

■ Avoid leading questions.

■ Try to avoid threatening questions.

■ Do not assume that respondents know the answers, or have information to answer the questions, or will always tell the truth (wittingly or not). Therefore include 'don't know', 'not applicable', 'unsure', 'neither agree not disagree' and 'not relevant' categories.

■ Avoid making the questions too hard.

■ Balance the number of negative questions with the number of positive questions (Black, 1999: 229).

■ Consider the readability levels of the questionnaire and the reading and writing abilities of the respondents (which may lead the researcher to conduct the questionnaire as a structured interview).

■ Put sensitive questions later in the questionnaire in order to avoid creating a mental set in the mind of respondents, but not so late in the questionnaire that boredom and lack of concentration have set in.

■ Intersperse sensitive questions with non-sensitive questions.

■ Be very clear on the layout of the questionnaire so that it is unambiguous and attractive (this is particularly the case if a computer program is going to be used for data analysis).

■ Avoid, where possible, splitting an item over more than one page, as the respondent may think that the item from the previous page is finished.

■ Ensure that the respondent knows how to enter a reply to each question, e.g. by underlining, circling, ticking, writing; provide the instructions for introducing, completing and returning (or collection of) the questionnaire (provide a stamped addressed envelope if it is to be a postal questionnaire).

■ Pilot the questionnaire, using a group of respondents who are drawn from the possible sample but who will not receive the final, refined version.

■ With the data analysis in mind, plan so that the appropriate scales and kinds of data (e.g. nominal, ordinal, interval and ratio) are used.

■ Decide how to avoid falsification of responses (e.g. introduce a checking mechanism into the questionnaire responses to another question on the same topic or issue).

■ Be satisfied if you receive a 50 per cent response to the questionnaire; decide what you will do with missing data and what is the significance of the missing data (that might have implications for the strata of a stratified sample targeted in the questionnaire), and why the questionnaires have not been completed and returned (e.g. were the questions too threatening?, was the questionnaire too long? – this might have been signalled in the pilot).

■ Include a covering explanation, thanking the potential respondent for anticipated cooperation, indicating the purposes of the research, how anonymity and confidentiality will be addressed, who you are and what position you hold, and who will be party to the final report.

■ If the questionnaire is going to be administered by someone other than the researcher, ensure that instructions for administration are provided and that they are clear.

A key issue that permeates this lengthy list is for the reader to pay considerable attention to respondents; to see the questionnaire through their eyes, and envisage how they will regard it (e.g. from hostility to suspicion to apathy to grudging compliance to welcome, from easy to difficult, from motivating to boring, from straightforward to complex, etc.).

20.12 Administering questionnaires

Questionnaires can be administered in several ways, including:

- self-administration
- post
- face-to-face interview
- telephone
- internet.

Here we discuss only self-administered and postal questionnaires. Chapter 21 covers administration by face-to-face interview, telephone, and administration by the internet. We also refer readers to Chapter 13 on surveys, to the section on conducting surveys by interview.

The setting in which the questionnaire is completed can also exert an influence on the results. Strange *et al.* (2003: 343), for example, found that asking students to complete a questionnaire in silence in a classroom or in a hall set out in an examination style might be very challenging for some; some students did not want to complete a questionnaire 'on their own' and wanted clarification from other students, some wanted a less 'serious' atmosphere to prevail whilst completing the questionnaire, and some (often boys) simply did not complete a questionnaire in conditions that they did not like (p. 344). Researchers will need to consider how best to achieve reliability by taking into account the setting and preferences of the respondents, and this includes, for example, with reference to schools (p. 345):

- the timing of the completion;
- the school timetable
- the space available;
- the layout of the room;
- the size of the school;
- the relationships between the students and the researchers;
- the culture of the school and classrooms;
- the duration of lessons.

Self-administered questionnaires

There are two types of self-administered questionnaire: those that are completed in the presence of the researcher and those that are filled in when the researcher is absent (e.g. at home, in the workplace).

Self-administered questionnaires in the presence of the researcher

The presence of the researcher is helpful in that it enables any queries or uncertainties to be addressed immediately with the questionnaire designer. Further, it typically ensures a good response rate (e.g. undertaken with teachers at a staff meeting or with students in one or more classes). It also ensures that all the questions are completed (the researcher can check these before finally receiving the questionnaire) and filled in correctly (e.g. no rating scale items that have more than one entry per item, and no missed items). It means that the questionnaires are completed rapidly and on one occasion, i.e. it can gather data from many respondents simultaneously.

On the other hand, having the researcher present may be threatening and exert a sense of compulsion, where respondents may feel uncomfortable about completing the questionnaire, and may not want to complete it or even start it. Respondents may also want extra time to think about and complete the questionnaire, maybe at home, and they are denied the opportunity to do this.

Having the researcher present also places pressure on the researcher to attend at an agreed time and in an agreed place, and this may be time-consuming and require the researcher to travel extensively, thereby extending the time frame for data collection. Travel costs for conducting the research with dispersed samples could also be expensive.

Self-administered questionnaires without the presence of the researcher

On the other hand, the absence of the researcher is helpful in that it enables respondents to complete the questionnaire in private, to devote as much time as they wish to its completion, to be in familiar surroundings, and to avoid the potential threat or pressure to participate caused by the researcher's presence. It can be inexpensive to operate, and is more anonymous than having the researcher present. This latter point, in turn, can render the data more or less honest: it is perhaps harder to tell lies or not to tell the whole truth in the presence of the researcher, and it is also easier to be very honest and revealing about sensitive matters without the presence of the researcher.

The down side, however, is that the researcher is not there to address any queries or problems that respondents may have, and they may omit items or give up rather than try to contact the researcher. They may also wrongly interpret and, consequently, answer questions inaccurately. They may present an untrue picture to the researcher, for example answering what they would like a situation to be rather than what the actual situation is, or painting a falsely negative or positive picture of the situation or themselves. Indeed, the researcher has no control over the environment in which the questionnaire is completed, e.g. time of day, noise distractions, presence of others with whom to discuss the questions and responses, seriousness given to the completion of the questionnaire, or even whether it is completed by the intended person.

Postal questionnaires

Frequently, the postal questionnaire is the best form of survey in an educational enquiry. Take, for example, the researcher intent on investigating the adoption and use made of a new curriculum series in secondary schools. An interview survey based upon some sampling of the population of schools would be both expensive and time-consuming. A postal questionnaire, on the other hand, would have several distinct advantages. Moreover, given the usual constraints over finance and resources, it might well prove the only viable way of carrying through such an enquiry.

What evidence we have about the advantages and disadvantages of postal surveys derives from settings other than educational. Many of the findings, however, have relevance to the educational researcher. Here, we focus upon some of the ways in which educational researchers can maximize the response level that they obtain when using postal surveys.

A number of myths about postal questionnaires are not borne out by the evidence (see Hoinville and Jowell, 1978). Response levels to postal surveys are not invariably less than those obtained by interview procedures; frequently they equal, and in some cases surpass, those achieved in interviews. Nor does the questionnaire necessarily have to be short in order to obtain a satisfactory response level. With sophisticated respondents, for example, a short questionnaire might appear to trivialize complex issues with which they are familiar. Hoinville and Jowell (1978) identify a number of factors in securing a good response rate to a postal questionnaire.

Initial mailing

■ Use good-quality envelopes, typed and addressed to a named person wherever possible.
■ Use first-class – rapid – postage services, with stamped rather than franked envelopes wherever possible.
■ Enclose a first-class stamped envelope for the respondent's reply.
■ In surveys of the general population, Thursday is the best day for mailing out; in surveys of organizations, Monday or Tuesday are recommended.
■ Avoid at all costs a December survey (questionnaires will be lost in the welter of Christmas postings in the western world).

Follow-up letter

Of the four factors that Hoinville and Jowell (1978) discuss in connection with maximizing response levels, the follow-up letter has been shown to be the most productive. The following points should be borne in mind in preparing reminder letters:

■ All of the rules that apply to the covering letter apply even more strongly to the follow-up letter.
■ The follow-up should re-emphasize the importance of the study and the value of the respondents' participation.
■ The use of the second person singular, the conveying of an air of disappointment at non-response and some surprise at non-cooperation have been shown to be effective ploys.
■ Nowhere should the follow-up give the impression that non-response is normal or that numerous non-responses have occurred in the particular study.
■ The follow-up letter must be accompanied by a further copy of the questionnaire together with a first-class stamped addressed envelope for its return.
■ Second and third reminder letters suffer from the law of diminishing returns, so how many follow-ups are recommended and what success rates do they achieve? It is difficult to generalize, but the following points are worth bearing in mind. A well-planned postal survey should obtain at least a 40 per cent response rate and with the judicious use of reminders, a 70 per cent to 80 per cent response level should be possible. A preliminary pilot survey is invaluable in that it can indicate the general level of response to be expected. The main survey should generally achieve at least as high as and normally a higher level of return than the pilot enquiry. The Office of Population Censuses and Surveys recommends the use of three reminders which, they say, can increase the original return by as much as 30 per cent in surveys of the general public. A typical pattern of responses to the three follow-ups is as follows:

Original despatch	40 per cent
First follow-up	+20 per cent
Second follow-up	+10 per cent
Third follow-up	+5 per cent
Total	75 per cent

Bailey (1994: 163–9) shows that follow-ups can be both by mail and by telephone. If a follow-up letter is sent, then this should be around three weeks after the initial mailing. A second follow-up is also advisable (Bailey, 1994), and this should take place one week after the first follow-up. He reports research (p. 165) that indicates that a second follow-up can elicit up to a

95.6 per cent response rate compared to a 74.8 per cent response with no follow-up. A telephone call *in advance* of the questionnaire can also help in boosting response rates (by up to 8 per cent).

Incentives

An important factor in maximizing response rates is the use of incentives. Although such usage is comparatively rare in British surveys, it can substantially reduce non-response rates particularly when the chosen incentives accompany the initial mailing rather than being mailed subsequently as rewards for the return of completed schedules. The explanation of the effectiveness of this particular ploy appears to lie in the sense of obligation that is created in the recipient. Care is needed in selecting the most appropriate type of incentive. It should clearly be seen as a token rather than a payment for the respondent's efforts and, according to Hoinville and Jowell (1978), should be as neutral as possible. In this respect, they suggest that books of postage stamps or ballpoint pens are cheap, easily packaged in the questionnaire envelopes and appropriate to the task required of the respondent.

The preparation of a flow chart can help the researcher to plan the timing and the sequencing of the various parts of a postal survey. One such flow chart suggested by Hoinville and Jowell (1978) is shown in Figure 20.2. The researcher might wish to add a chronological chart alongside it to help plan the exact timing of the events shown here.

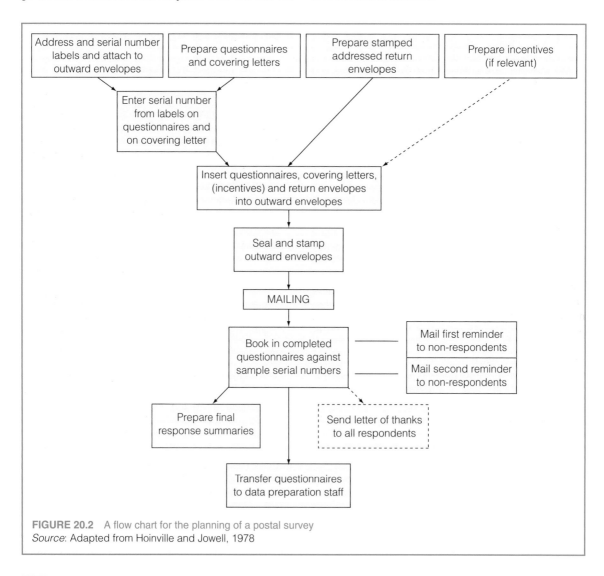

FIGURE 20.2 A flow chart for the planning of a postal survey
Source: Adapted from Hoinville and Jowell, 1978

Validity

Our discussion, so far, has concentrated on ways of increasing the response rate of postal questionnaires; we have said nothing yet about the validity of this particular technique.

Validity of postal questionnaires can be seen from two viewpoints according to Belson (1986). First, whether respondents who complete questionnaires do so accurately and second, whether those who fail to return their questionnaires would have given the same distribution of answers as did the returnees.

The question of accuracy can be checked by means of the intensive interview method, a technique consisting of 12 principal tactics that include familiarization, temporal reconstruction, probing and challenging. The interested reader should consult Belson (1986: 35–8).

The problem of non-response (the issue of 'volunteer bias' as Belson calls it) can, in part, be checked on and controlled for, particularly when the postal questionnaire is sent out on a continuous basis. It involves follow-up contact with non-respondents by means of interviewers trained to secure interviews with such people. A comparison is then made between the replies of respondents and non-respondents.

20.13 Processing questionnaire data

Let us assume that researchers have followed the advice we have given about the planning of postal questionnaires and have secured a high response rate to their surveys. Their task is now to reduce the mass of data they have obtained to a form suitable for analysis. 'Data reduction', as the process is called, generally consists of coding data in preparation for analysis – by hand in the case of small surveys; by computers when numbers are larger. First, however, prior to coding, the questionnaires have to be checked. This task is referred to as *editing*.

Editing questionnaires is intended to identify and eliminate errors made by respondents. (In addition to the clerical editing that we discuss in this section, editing checks are also performed by the computer. For an account of computer-run structure checks and valid coding range checks, see Hoinville and Jowell (1978: 150–5)). Moser and Kalton (1977) point to three central tasks in editing:

1 *Completeness*: a check is made that there is an answer to every question. In most surveys, interviewers are required to record an answer to every question (a 'not applicable' category always being available). Missing answers can sometimes be cross-

checked from other sections of the survey. At worst, respondents can be contacted again to supply the missing information.

2 *Accuracy*: as far as is possible a check is made that all questions are answered accurately. Inaccuracies arise out of carelessness on the part of either interviewers or respondents. Sometimes a deliberate attempt is made to mislead. A tick in the wrong box, a ring round the wrong code, an error in simple arithmetic – all can reduce the validity of the data unless they are picked up in the editing process.

3 *Uniformity*: a check is made that interviewers have interpreted instructions and questions uniformly. Sometimes the failure to give explicit instructions over the interpretation of respondents' replies leads to interviewers recording the same answer in a variety of answer codes instead of one. A check on uniformity can help eradicate this source of error.

The primary task of data reduction is *coding*, that is assigning a code number to each answer to a survey question. Of course, not all answers to survey questions can be reduced to code numbers. Many open-ended questions, for example, are not reducible in this way for computer analysis. Coding can be built into the construction of the questionnaire itself. In this case, we talk of precoded answers. Where coding is developed after the questionnaire has been administered and answered by respondents, we refer to post-coded answers. Precoding is appropriate for closed-ended questions – male 1, female 2, for example; or single 1, married 2, separated 3, divorced 4. For questions such as those whose answer categories are known in advance, a coding frame is generally developed before the interviewing commences so that it can be printed into the questionnaire itself. For open-ended questions (Why did you choose this particular in-service course rather than XYZ?), a coding frame has to be devised after the completion of the questionnaire. This is best done by taking a random sample of the questionnaires (10 per cent or more, time permitting) and generating a frequency tally of the range of responses as a preliminary to coding classification. Having devised the coding frame, the researcher can make a further check on its validity by using it to code up a further sample of the questionnaires. It is vital to get coding frames right from the outset – extending them or making alterations at a later point in the study is both expensive and wearisome.

There are several computer packages that will process questionnaire survey data. At the time of writing one such is SphinxSurvey. This package, like others of its type, assists researchers in the design, administration and processing of questionnaires, either for paper-based or for onscreen administration. Responses can be entered rapidly, and data can be examined automatically, producing graphs and tables, as well as a wide range of statistics. (The Plus edition offers lexical analysis of open-ended text, and the Lexica Edition has additional functions for qualitative data analysis.) A website for previewing a demonstration of this program can be found at www.scolari.co.uk and is typical of several of its kind.

Whilst coding is usually undertaken by the researcher, Sudman and Bradburn (1982: 149) also make the case for coding by the respondents themselves, to increase validity. This is particularly valuable in open-ended questionnaire items, though, of course, it does assume not only the willingness of respondents to become involved *post hoc* but, also, that the researcher can identify and trace the respondents, which, as was indicated earlier, is an ethical matter.

 Companion Website

The companion website to the book includes PowerPoint slides for this chapter, which list the structure of the chapter and then provide a summary of the key points in each of its sections. This resource can be found online at **www.routledge.com/textbooks/cohen7e**.

Interviews

Interviews are a widely used instrument for data collection. This chapter sets out a range of key issues to be considered in planning, conducting and reporting interviews, including:

- conceptions of the interview
- purposes of the interview
- types of interview
- planning interview-based research procedures
- group interviewing
- interviewing children
- interviewing minority and marginalized people
- focus groups
- non-directive, focused, problem-centred and in-depth interviews
- telephone interviewing
- ethical issues in interviewing

This chapter indicates different kinds of interview, and argues for 'fitness for purpose' to be addressed in deciding which kind of interview and interview questions to employ.

21.1 Introduction

The use of the interview in research marks a move away from seeing human subjects as simply manipulable and data as somehow external to individuals, and towards regarding knowledge as generated between humans, often through conversations (Kvale, 1996: 11). Regarding an interview, as Kvale (1996: 14) remarks, as an *inter-view*, an interchange of views between two or more people on a topic of mutual interest, sees the centrality of human interaction for knowledge production, and emphasizes the social situatedness of research data. As we suggested in Chapter 5, knowledge should be seen as constructed between participants, generating *data* rather than *capta* (Laing, 1967: 53). As such, the interview is not exclusively either subjective or objective, it is intersubjective (Laing, 1967: 66). Interviews enable participants – be they interviewers or interviewees – to discuss their interpretations of the world in which they live, and to express how they regard situations from their own point of view. In these senses the interview is not simply concerned with collecting data about life: it is part of life itself, its human embeddedness is inescapable.

The interview is a flexible tool for data collection, enabling multi-sensory channels to be used: verbal, non-verbal, spoken and heard. The order of the interview may be controlled whilst still giving space for spontaneity, and the interviewer can press not only for complete answers but for responses about complex and deep issues. In short, the interview is a powerful implement for researchers. On the other hand the researcher using interviews has to be aware that they are expensive in time, they are open to interviewer bias, they may be inconvenient for respondents, issues of interviewee fatigue may hamper the interview, and anonymity may be difficult. We explore these several issues in this chapter.

An interview is not an ordinary, everyday conversation (Dyer, 1995: 56–8). For example, in contrast to an everyday conversation, it has a specific purpose, it is often question-based, with the questions being asked by the interviewer; the interviewer alone may express ignorance (and not the interviewee), and the responses must be as explicit and often as detailed as possible. The interview is a constructed and usually a specifically planned event rather than naturally occurring situation, and this renders it different from an everyday conversation; therefore the researcher has an obligation to set up, and abide by, the different 'rules of the game' in an interview.

21.2 Conceptions of the interview

Kitwood (1977) lucidly contrasts three conceptions of an interview. The first conception is that of a potential means of pure information transfer. He explains that:

> if the interviewer does his job well (establishes rapport, asks questions in an acceptable manner, etc.), and if the respondent is sincere and well-motivated, accurate data may be obtained. Of course all kinds of bias are liable to creep in, but

with skill these can largely be eliminated. In its fullest expression, this view accords closely with that of the psychometricians, who apparently believe that there is a relatively permanent, consistent, 'core' to the personality, about which a person will give information under certain conditions. Such features as lying, or the tendency to give a socially desirable response, are to be eliminated where possible.

(Kitwood, 1977)

This conception of the interview appears to be widely held.

A second conception of the interview is that of a transaction which inevitably has bias, that needs to be recognized and controlled. According to this viewpoint, Kitwood (1977) explains that 'each participant in an interview will define the situation in a particular way. This fact can be best handled by building controls into the research design, for example by having a range of interviewers with different biases.' The interview is best understood in terms of a theory of motivation which recognizes a range of non-rational factors governing human behaviour, like emotions, unconscious needs and interpersonal influences. Kitwood points out that both these views of the interview regard the inherent features of interpersonal transactions as if they were 'potential obstacles to sound research, and therefore to be removed, controlled, or at least harnessed in some way'.

The third conception of the interview sees it as an encounter necessarily sharing many of the features of everyday life (see for example, Box 21.1). Kitwood (1977) suggests that what is required, according to this view, is not a technique for dealing with bias, but a theory of everyday life that takes account of the relevant features of interviews. These may include role-playing, stereotyping, perception and understanding. As Walford (2001: 90) remarks, 'interviewers and interviewees co-construct the interview'. The interview is a social encounter, not simply a site for information exchange, and researchers would be well advised to keep this in the forefront of their minds when conducting an interview.

One of the strongest advocates of this latter viewpoint is Cicourel (1964) who lists five of the unavoidable features of the interview situation that would normally be regarded as problematic.

1 There are many factors which inevitably differ from one interview to another, such as mutual trust, social distance and the interviewer's control.
2 The respondent may well feel uneasy and adopt avoidance tactics if the questioning is too deep.
3 Both interviewer and respondent are bound to hold back part of what it is in their power to state.
4 Many of the meanings which are clear to one will be relatively opaque to the other, even when the intention is genuine communication.
5 It is impossible, just as in everyday life, to bring every aspect of the encounter within rational control.

The message that proponents of this view would express is that no matter how hard an interviewer may try to be systematic and objective, the constraints of everyday life will be a part of whatever interpersonal transactions she initiates. Kitwood concludes:

The solution is to have as explicit a theory as possible to take the various factors into account. For those who hold this view, there are not good interviews and bad in the conventional sense. There are simply social encounters; goodness and badness are

---

BOX 21.1 ATTRIBUTES OF ETHNOGRAPHERS AS INTERVIEWERS

Trust: There would have to be a relationship between the interviewer and interviewee that transcended the research, that promoted a bond of friendship, a feeling of togetherness and joint pursuit of a common mission rising above personal egos.
Curiosity: There would have to be a desire to know, to learn people's views and perceptions of the facts, to hear their stories, discover their feelings. This is the motive force, and it has to be a burning one, that drives researchers to tackle and overcome the many difficulties involved in setting up and conducting successful interviews.
Naturalness: As with observation one endeavours to be unobtrusive in order to witness events as they are, untainted by one's presence and actions, so in interviews the aim is to secure what is within the minds of interviewees, uncoloured and unaffected by the interviewer.

Source: Adapted from Woods, 1986

predicates applicable, rather, to the theories within which the phenomena are explained.

(Kitwood, 1977)

Indeed Barker and Johnson (1998: 230) argue that the interview is a particular medium for enacting or displaying people's knowledge of cultural forms, as questions, far from being neutral, are couched in the cultural repertoires of all participants, indicating how people make sense of their social world and of each other.[1]

21.3 Purposes of the interview

The purposes of the interview in the wider context of life are many and varied, for example:

- to evaluate or assess a person in some respect;
- to select or promote an employee;
- to effect therapeutic change, as in the psychiatric interview;
- to test or develop hypotheses;
- to gather data, as in surveys or experimental situations;
- to sample respondents' opinions, as in door-step interviews.

Although in each of these situations the respective roles of the interviewer and interviewee may vary and the motives for taking part may differ, a common denominator is the transaction that takes place between seeking information on the part of one and supplying information on the part of the other.

As a distinctive research technique, the interview may serve three purposes. First, it may be used as the principal means of gathering information having direct bearing on the research objectives. As Tuckman (1972) describes it, 'By providing access to what is "inside a person's head", [it] makes it possible to measure what a person knows (knowledge or information), what a person likes or dislikes (values and preferences), and what a person thinks (attitudes and beliefs).' Second, it may be used to test hypotheses or to suggest new ones; or as an explanatory device to help identify variables and relationships. And third, the interview may be used in conjunction with other methods in a research undertaking. In this connection, Kerlinger (1970) suggests that it might be used to follow up unexpected results, for example, or to validate other methods, or to go deeper into the motivations of respondents and their reasons for responding as they do.

As our interests lie primarily in reviewing research methods and techniques, we will subsequently limit ourselves to the use of the interview as a specific research tool. Interviews in this sense range from the formal interview in which set questions are asked and the answers recorded on a standardized schedule through less formal interviews in which the interviewer is free to modify the sequence of questions, change the wording, explain them or add to them to the completely informal interview where the interviewer may have a number of key issues which she raises in conversational style instead of having a set questionnaire. Beyond this point is located the non-directive interview in which the interviewer takes on a subordinate role.

The research interview has been defined as 'a two-person conversation initiated by the interviewer for the specific purpose of obtaining research-relevant information, and focused by him on content specified by research objectives of systematic description, prediction, or explanation' (Cannell and Kahn, 1968). It is an unusual method in that it involves the gathering of data through direct verbal interaction between individuals. In this sense it differs from the questionnaire where the respondent is required to record in some way her responses to set questions.

As the interview has some things in common with the self-administered questionnaire, it is frequently compared with it. Each has advantages over the other in certain respects. The advantages of the questionnaire, for instance, are: it tends to be more reliable because it is anonymous; it encourages greater honesty; it is more economical than the interview in terms of time and money and there is the possibility that it may be mailed. Its disadvantages, on the other hand, are: there is often too low a percentage of returns; the interviewer is able to answer questions concerning both the purpose of the interview and any misunderstandings experienced by the interviewee, for it sometimes happens in the case of the latter that the same questions have different meanings for different people; if only closed items are used, the questionnaire will be subject to the weaknesses already discussed; if only open items are used, respondents may be unwilling to write their answers for one reason or another; questionnaires present problems to people of limited literacy; and an interview can be conducted at an appropriate speed whereas questionnaires are often filled in hurriedly.

By way of interest, we illustrate the relative merits of the interview and the questionnaire in Table 21.1. It has been pointed out that the direct interaction of the interview is the source of both its advantages and disadvantages as a research technique (Borg, 1963). One advantage, for example, is that it allows for greater depth than is the case with other methods of data collection. A disadvantage, on the other hand, is that it is prone to subjectivity and bias on the part of the interviewer.

TABLE 21.1 SUMMARY OF RELATIVE MERITS OF INTERVIEW VERSUS QUESTIONNAIRE

Consideration	Interview	Questionnaire
1 Personal need to collect data	Requires interviewers	Requires a secretary
2 Major expense	Payment to interviewers	Postage and printing
3 Opportunities for response-keying (personalization)	Extensive	Limited
4 Opportunities for asking	Extensive	Limited
5 Opportunities for probing	Possible	Difficult
6 Relative magnitude of data reduction	Great (because of coding)	Mainly limited to rostering
7 Typically, the number of respondents who can be reached	Limited	Extensive
8 Rate of return	Good	Poor
9 Sources of error	Interviewer, instrument, coding, sample	Limited to instrument and sample
10 Overall reliability	Quite limited	Fair
11 Emphasis on writing skill	Limited	Extensive

Source: Tuckman, 1972

Oppenheim (1992: 81–2) suggests that interviews have a higher response rate than questionnaires because respondents become more involved and, hence, motivated; they enable more to be said about the research than is usually mentioned in a covering letter to a questionnaire, and they are better than questionnaires for handling more difficult and open-ended questions.

21.4 Types of interview

The number of types of interview given is frequently a function of the sources one reads! For example LeCompte and Preissle (1993) give six types: (i) standardized interviews; (ii) in-depth interviews; (iii) ethnographic interviews; (iv) elite interviews; (v) life history interviews; (vi) focus groups. Bogdan and Biklen (1992) add to this: (vii) semi-structured interviews; (viii) group interviews. Lincoln and Guba (1985) add: (ix) structured interviews; and Oppenheim (1992: 65) adds to this: (x) exploratory interviews. Patton (1980: 206) outlines four types: (xi) informal conversational interviews; (xii) interview guide approaches; (xiii) standardized open-ended interviews; (xiv) closed quantitative interviews. Patton sets these out clearly as shown in Table 21.2.

How is the researcher to comprehend the range of these various types? Kvale (1996: 126–7) sets the several forms of interview along a series of continua, arguing that interviews differ in the openness of their purpose, their degree of structure, the extent to which they are exploratory or hypothesis-testing, whether they seek description or interpretation, or whether they are largely cognitive-focused or emotion-focused. A major difference appears to lie in the degree of structure in the interview, which, itself, reflects the purposes of the interview, for example, to generate numbers of respondents' feelings about a given issue or to indicate unique, alternative feelings about a particular matter. Lincoln and Guba (1985: 269) suggest that the structured interview is useful when the researcher is aware of what she does not know and therefore is in a position to frame questions that will supply the knowledge required, whereas the unstructured interview is useful when the researcher is not aware of what she does not know, and therefore relies on the respondents to tell her!

The issue here is of 'fitness for purpose'; the more one wishes to gain comparable data – across people, across sites – the more standardized and quantitative one's interview tends to become; the more one wishes to acquire unique, non-standardized, personalized information about how individuals view the world, the more one veers towards qualitative, open-ended, unstructured interviewing. Indeed, this is true not simply of interviews but of their written counterpart – questionnaires. Oppenheim (1992: 86) indicates that standardization should refer to *stimulus equivalence*, i.e. that every respondent should *understand* the interview question in the same way, rather than replicating the exact wording, as some respondents might have difficulty with, or interpret very differently, and perhaps irrelevantly, particular questions. (He also adds that as soon as the wording of a question is altered, however minimally, it becomes, in effect, a different question!)

Oppenheim (1992: 65) suggests that *exploratory* interviews are designed to be essentially heuristic and seek to develop hypotheses rather than to collect facts and numbers. He notes that these frequently cover

TABLE 21.2   STRENGTHS AND WEAKNESSES OF DIFFERENT TYPES OF INTERVIEW

Type of interview	Characteristics	Strengths	Weaknesses
1 Informal conversational interview	Questions emerge from the immediate context and are asked in the natural course of things; there is no predetermination of question topics or wording.	Increases the salience and relevance of questions; interviews are built on and emerge from observations; the interview can be matched to individuals and circumstances.	Different information collected from different people with different questions. Less systematic and comprehensive if certain questions don't arise 'naturally'. Data organization and analysis can be quite difficult.
2 Interview guide approach	Topics and issues to be covered are specified in advance, in outline form; interviewer decides sequence and working of questions in the course of the interview.	The outline increases the comprehensiveness of the data and makes data collection somewhat systematic for each respondent. Logical gaps in data can be anticipated and closed. Interviews remain fairly conversational and situational.	Important and salient topics may be inadvertently omitted. Interviewer flexibility in sequencing and wording questions can result in substantially different responses, thus reducing the comparability of responses.
3 Standardized open-ended interviews	The exact wording and sequence of questions are determined in advance. All interviewees are asked the same basic questions in the same order.	Respondents answer the same questions, thus increasing comparability of responses; data are complete for each person on the topics addressed in the interview. Reduces interviewer effects and bias when several interviewers are used. Permits decision makers to see and review the instrumentation used in the evaluation. Facilitates organization and analysis of the data.	Little flexibility in relating the interview to particular individuals and circumstances; standardized wording of questions may constrain and limit naturalness and relevance of questions and answers.
4 Closed quantitative interviews	Questions and response categories are determined in advance. Responses are fixed; respondent chooses from among these fixed responses.	Data analysis is simple; responses can be directly compared and easily aggregated; many short questions can be asked in a short time.	Respondents must fit their experiences and feelings into the researcher's categories; may be perceived as impersonal, irrelevant and mechanistic. Can distort what respondents really mean or experienced by so completely limiting their response choices.

Source: Patton, 1980: 206

emotionally loaded topics and, hence, require skill on the part of the interviewer to handle the interview situation, enabling respondents to talk freely and emotionally and to have candour, richness, depth, authenticity, honesty about their experiences.

Morrison (1993: 34–6) sets out five continua of different ways of conceptualizing interviews. At one end of the first continuum are numbers, statistics, objective facts, quantitative data; at the other end are transcripts of conversations, comments, subjective accounts, essentially word-based qualitative data.

At one end of the second continuum are closed questions, multiple choice questions where respondents have to select from a given, predetermined range of responses that particular response which most accurately represents what they wish to have recorded for them; at the other end of the continuum are much more open-ended questions which do not require the selection from a given range of responses – respondents can answer the questions in their own way and in their own words, i.e. the research is responsive to participants' own frames of reference and response.

At one end of the third continuum is a desire to measure responses, to compare one set of responses with another, to correlate responses, to see how many people said this, how many rated a particular item as such-and-such; at the other end of the continuum is a desire to capture the uniqueness of a particular situation, person or programme – what makes it different from others, i.e. to record the quality of a situation or response.

At one end of the fourth continuum is a desire for formality and the precision of numbers and prescribed categories of response where the researcher knows in advance what is being sought; at the other end is a more responsive, informal intent where what is being sought is more uncertain and indeterminate – we only know what we are looking for when we have found it! The researcher goes into the situation and responds to what emerges.

At one end of the fifth continuum is the attempt to find regularities – of response, opinions, etc. – in order to begin to make generalizations from the data, to describe what is happening; at the other end is the attempt to portray and catch uniqueness, the quality of a response, the complexity of a situation, to understand why respondents say what they say, and all of this in their own terms.

One can cluster the sets of poles of the five continua thus:

Quantitative approaches	Qualitative approaches
numbers	words
predetermined, given	open-ended, responsive
measuring	capturing uniqueness
short-term, intermittent	long-term, continuous
comparing	capturing particularity
correlating	valuing quality
frequencies	individuality
formality	informality
looking at	looking for
regularities	uniqueness
description	explanation
objective facts	subjective facts
describing	interpreting
looking in from the outside	looking from the inside
structured	unstructured
statistical	ethnographic, illuminative

The left-hand column is much more formal and pre-planned to a high level of detail, whilst the right-hand column is far less formal and the fine detail only emerges once the researcher is *in situ*. Interviews in the left-hand column are front-loaded, that is, they require all the categories and multiple choice questions to be worked out in advance. This usually requires a pilot to try out the material and refine it. Once the detail of this planning is completed the analysis of the data is relatively straightforward because the categories for analysing the data have been worked out in advance, hence data analysis is rapid.

The right-hand column is much more end-loaded, that is, it is quicker to commence and gather data because the categories do not have to be worked out in advance, they emerge once the data have been collected. However, in order to discover the issues that emerge and to organize the data presentation, the analysis of the data takes considerably longer.

Kvale (1996: 30) sets out key characteristics of qualitative research interviews, namely that they should:

■ engage, understand and interpret the key feature of the lifeworlds of the participants;
■ use natural language to gather and understand qualitative knowledge;
■ be able to reveal and explore the nuanced descriptions of the lifeworlds of the participants;
■ elicit descriptions of specific situations and actions, rather than generalities;
■ adopt a deliberate openness to new data and phenomena, rather than being too pre-structured;
■ focus on specific ideas and themes, i.e. have direction, but avoid being too tightly structured;
■ accept the ambiguity and contradictions of situations where they occur in participants, if this is a fair reflection of the ambiguous and contradictory situation in which they find themselves;
■ accept that the interview may provoke new insights and changes in the participants themselves;
■ regard interviews as an interpersonal encounter, with all that this entails;
■ be a positive and enriching experience for all participants.

There are four main kinds of interview that we discuss here that may be used specifically as research tools: (i) the structured interview; (ii) the unstructured interview; (iii) the non-directive interview; and (iv) the focused interview. The structured interview is one in which the content and procedures are organized in advance. This means that the sequence and wording of the questions are determined by means of a schedule and the interviewer is left little freedom to make modifications. Where some leeway is granted her, it too is specified in advance. It is therefore characterized by being a closed situation. In contrast to it in this respect, the unstructured interview is an open situation, having greater flexibility and freedom. As Kerlinger (1970) notes, although the research purposes govern the questions asked, their content, sequence and wording are entirely in the hands of the interviewer. This does not mean, however, that the unstructured interview is a more casual affair, for in its own way it also has to be carefully planned.

The non-directive interview as a research technique derives from the therapeutic or psychiatric interview. The principal features of it are the minimal direction or control exhibited by the interviewer and the freedom the respondent has to express her subjective feelings as fully and as spontaneously as she chooses or is able. Moser and Kalton (1977: 297) argue that respondents should be encouraged to talk about the subject under investigation (e.g. themselves) and to be free to guide the interview, with few set questions or pre-figured frameworks. The interviewer should prompt and probe, pressing for clarity and elucidation, rephrasing and summarizing where necessary and checking for confirmation of this, particularly if the issues are complex or vague.

The need to introduce rather more interviewer control into the non-directive situation led to the development of the focused interview. The distinctive feature of this type is that it focuses on a respondent's subjective responses to a known situation in which she has been involved and which has been analysed by the interviewer prior to the interview. She is thereby able to use the data from the interview to substantiate or reject previously formulated hypotheses. As Merton and Kendall explain,

> In the usual depth interview, one can urge informants to reminisce on their experiences. In the focused interview, however, the interviewer can, when expedient, play a more active role: he can introduce more explicit verbal cues to the stimulus pattern or even *represent* it. In either case this usually activates a concrete report of responses by informants.
>
> (Merton and Kendall, 1946: 542)

We shall be examining both the non-directive interview and the focused interview in more detail later in the chapter.

21.5 Planning interview-based research procedures

Kvale (1996: 88) sets out seven stages of an interview investigation that can be used to plan this type of research: thematizing; designing; interviewing; transcribing; analysing; verifying; and reporting. We use these to structure our comments here about the planning of interview-based research.

Thematizing

The preliminary stage of an interview study will be the point where the purpose of the research is decided. It may begin by outlining the theoretical basis of the study, its broad aims, its practical value and the reasons why the interview approach was chosen. There may then follow the translation of the general goals of the research into more detailed and specific objectives. This is the most important step, for only careful formulation of objectives at this point will eventually produce the right kind of data necessary for satisfactory answers to the research problem.

Designing

There follows the preparation of the interview schedule itself. This involves translating the research objectives into the questions that will make up the main body of the schedule. This needs to be done in such a way that the questions adequately reflect what it is the researcher is trying to find out. It is quite usual to begin this task by writing down the variables to be dealt with in the study. As one commentator says, 'The first step in constructing interview questions is to *specify your variables by name*. Your variables are what you are trying to measure. They tell you where to begin' (Tuckman, 1972).

Before the actual interview items are prepared, it is desirable to give some thought to the question format and the response mode. The choice of question format, for instance, depends on a consideration of one or more of the following factors:

- the objectives of the interview;
- the nature of the subject matter;
- whether the interviewer is dealing in facts, opinions or attitudes;
- whether specificity or depth is sought;
- the respondent's level of education;
- the kind of information she can be expected to have;
- whether or not her thought needs to be structured;
- some assessment of her motivational level;
- the extent of the interviewer's own insight into the respondent's situation;
- the kind of relationship the interviewer can expect to develop with the respondent.

Having given prior thought to these matters, the researcher is in a position to decide whether to use open and/or closed questions, direct and/or indirect questions, specific and/or non-specific questions and so on.

Construction of schedules

Three kinds of items are used in the construction of schedules used in research interviews (see Kerlinger, 1970). First, 'fixed-alternative' items allow the respondent to choose from two or more alternatives. The most frequently used is the dichotomous item which offers two alternatives only: 'yes/no' or 'agree/disagree', for instance. Sometimes a third alternative such as 'undecided' or 'don't know' is also offered.

Example: Do you feel it is against the interests of a school to have to make public its examination results?

Yes

No

Don't know

Kerlinger has identified the chief advantages and disadvantages of fixed-alternative items. They have, for example, the advantage of achieving greater uniformity of measurement and therefore greater reliability; of making the respondents answer in a manner fitting the response category; and of being more easily coded.

Disadvantages include their superficiality; the possibility of irritating respondents who find none of the alternatives suitable; and the possibility of forcing responses that are inappropriate, either because the alternative chosen conceals ignorance on the part of the respondent or because she may choose an alternative that does not accurately represent the true facts. These weaknesses can be overcome, however, if the items are written with care, mixed with open-ended ones, and used in conjunction with probes on the part of the interviewer.

Second, 'open-ended items' have been succinctly defined by Kerlinger (1970) as 'those that supply a frame of reference for respondents' answers, but put a minimum of restraint on the answers and their expression'. Other than the subject of the question, which is determined by the nature of the problem under investigation, there are no other restrictions on either the content or the manner of the interviewee's reply.

Example: What kind of television programmes do you most prefer to watch?

Open-ended questions have a number of advantages: they are flexible; they allow the interviewer to probe so that she may go into more depth if she chooses, or to clear up any misunderstandings; they enable the interviewer to test the limits of the respondent's knowledge; they encourage cooperation and help establish rapport;

and they allow the interviewer to make a truer assessment of what the respondent really believes. Open-ended situations can also result in unexpected or unanticipated answers which may suggest hitherto unthought-of relationships or hypotheses. A particular kind of open-ended question is the 'funnel' to which reference has been made earlier. This starts, the reader will recall, with a broad question or statement and then narrows down to more specific ones. Kerlinger (1970) quotes an example from the study by Sears *et al.* (1957):

All babies cry, of course. Some mothers feel that if you pick up a baby every time it cries, you will spoil it. Others think you should never let a baby cry for very long. How do you feel about this? What did you do about it? How about the middle of the night?

(Sears *et al.*, 1957: 157)

Third, the 'scale' is, as we have already seen, a set of verbal items to each of which the interviewee responds by indicating degrees of agreement or disagreement. The individual's response is thus located on a scale of fixed alternatives. The use of this technique along with open-ended questions is a comparatively recent development and means that scale scores can be checked against data elicited by the open-ended questions.

Example: Attendance at school after the age of 14 should be voluntary:

Strongly agree   Agree   Undecided
Disagree   Strongly disagree

It is possible to use one of a number of scales in this context: attitude scales, rank-order scales, rating scales and so on. We touch upon this subject again subsequently.

In devising questions for the interview, attention has to be given to (Arksey and Knight, 1999: 93–5):

- the vocabulary to be used (keeping it simple);
- the avoidance of prejudicial language;
- the avoidance of ambiguity and imprecision;
- leading questions (a decision has to be taken whether it is justified to use them);
- the avoidance of double-barrelled questions (asking more than one point at a time);
- questions that make assumptions (e.g. do you go to work in your car?);
- hypothetical or speculative questions;
- sensitive or personal questions (whether to ask or avoid them);

- assuming that the respondent has the required knowledge/information;
- recall (how easy it will be for the respondent to recall memories).

Question formats

We now look at the kinds of questions and modes of response associated with interviewing. First, the matter of question format: how is a question to be phrased or organized? (see Wilson, 1996). Tuckman (1972) has listed four such formats that an interviewer may draw upon. Questions may, for example, take a direct or indirect form. Thus an interviewer could ask a teacher whether she likes teaching: this would be a direct question. Or else she could adopt an indirect approach by asking for the respondent's views on education in general and the ways schools function. From the answers proffered, the interviewer could make inferences about the teacher's opinions concerning her own job. Tuckman suggests that by making the purpose of questions less obvious, the indirect approach is more likely to produce frank and open responses.

There are also those kinds of questions which deal with either a general or specific issue. To ask a child what she thought of the teaching methods of the staff as a whole would be a general or non-specific question. To ask her what she thought of her teacher as a teacher would be a specific question. There is also the sequence of questions designated the funnel in which the movement is from the general and non-specific to the more specific. Tuckman (1972) comments, 'Specific questions, like direct ones, may cause a respondent to become cautious or guarded and give less-than-honest answers. Non-specific questions may lead circuitously to the desired information but with less alarm by the respondents.'

A further distinction is that between questions inviting factual answers and those inviting opinions. To ask a person what political party he supports would be a factual question. To ask her what she thinks of the current government's foreign policy would be an opinion question. Both fact and opinion questions can yield less than the truth, however: the former do not always produce factual answers; nor do the latter necessarily elicit honest opinions. In both instances, inaccuracy and bias may be minimized by careful structuring of the questions.

There are several ways of categorizing questions, for example (Spradley, 1979; Patton, 1980):

- descriptive questions;
- experience questions;
- behaviour questions;
- knowledge questions;

- construct-forming questions;
- contrast questions (asking respondents to contrast one thing with another);
- feeling questions;
- sensory questions;
- background questions;
- demographic questions.

These concern the *substance* of the question. Kvale (1996: 133–5) adds to these what might be termed the *process* questions, i.e. questions that:

- introduce a topic or interview;
- follow up on a topic or idea;
- probe for further information or response;
- ask respondents to specify and provide examples;
- directly ask for information;
- indirectly ask for information;
- interpret respondents' replies.

We may also note that an interviewee may be presented with either a question or a statement. In the case of the latter she will be asked for her response to it in one form or another.

Example question: Do you think homework should be compulsory for all children between 11 and 16?

Example statement: Homework should be compulsory for all children between 11 and 16 years old.

Agree   Disagree   Don't know

Stylianou (2008) discusses the 'interview control question'. In experimental and survey designs, variables are often controlled, i.e. held 'constant and unvarying so that one can see the true effects of other variables' after the effects of others have been neutralized (controlled out), i.e. what effects remain after all the other variables have been controlled out (Morrison, 2009: 65). Morrison continues:

For example, we might be interested in examining the effects of gender on earnings, but these earnings are also affected by, for example, education level, type of work, qualifications, ethnicity, previous job experience, social behaviour and personality factors. If we wish to see the effects of gender then we have to control these other factors. This means that, in the case of gender for example, we would have to keep the males and females matched on the other variables, so that we could gain a true picture of the effects of gender rather than, say, education or job experience.

(Morrison, 2009: 65)

He suggests that controlling for the effects of other variables can be undertaken, *inter alia*, through randomization and random allocation (see Chapter 16), and isolation and control of independent variables of those other than the one(s) in which the researcher is interested (e.g. holding them constant). Controlling for the effects of other variables enables the researcher to see the true effect(s) of a single independent variable in which she or he is interested, i.e. what is left after other variables have been controlled out of the situation. Stylianou (2008) suggests that the same can be done in interviews, i.e. by isolating and controlling out the effects of other variables the researcher can see the true effect of a particular variable in which she or he is interested, i.e. when the effects of others have been removed. Interview control questions are a form of a probe (discussed below).

Let us give an example of an interview control question in an imaginary interview concerning a parent who expresses a negative attitude towards mixed ability classes in a primary school:

1 *Interviewer*: Why are you not in favour of mixed ability classes in the school?

2 *Respondent*: The less able students will slow down the more able students in the class, and the teacher will have to work very hard to keep up with the wide range of different abilities in the class.

3 *Interviewer*: But we know that many more capable students slow down anyway, for two reasons: firstly, if they finish work quickly then they are given more work to do, and they want an easy life, and secondly, many of the more able students don't want to stand out as being exceptional in their class, so they slow down. And next, the teacher has to work hard anyway, as she has a range of tasks to do as part of her daily work. In fact the teacher can have a classroom assistant to work with students of different abilities.

4 *Respondent*: But having a classroom assistant still doesn't make sure that all the students get their fair share of the teacher's attention – only the less able and more able children get the extra attention from the classroom assistant.

5 *Interviewer*: But that's the case anyway, as not all the students get the same amount of attention by the teacher, regardless of their abilities, as some students prefer to work quietly on their own without the teacher. Students have to work by themselves anyway, for example, in their mathematics lessons only they can do the work and the teacher cannot do it for them. And, anyway, it's important for stu-

dents to learn to work by themselves; isn't that a good thing?

6 *Respondent*: But some students aren't good at working by themselves and they may need the teacher's help at critical moments, and having so many mixed abilities will prevent the teacher from being there at critical moments.

7 *Interviewer*: But the teacher will be there to help them at critical moments anyway, that's part of their job, and they are trained to recognize critical moments. Teachers have to be present at critical moments in a student's thinking, prompting them to take the next step in their thinking or learning.

8 *Respondent*: But some students will want to have an easy life, so they won't let the teacher know that they need help or prompting, and they will ask their friend to help them.

9 *Interviewer*: But students do that anyway, as they often help each other, surely that's a good thing, to work collaboratively and help each other, and students learn well from each other.

10 *Respondent*: Look, I just don't want my child to have to work with less able children, and that's all.

In the example, the interviewer is carefully stripping away the possible causes of the parent's negative attitude: (a) slowing down the more capable students (lines 2 and 3); (b) students having fair access to adult help (lines 4 and 5); (c) students having to learn by themselves (lines 5 and 6); (d) the presence of teachers at critical moments (lines 6 and 7); (e) students working with friends (lines 8 and 9). The interviewer is raising alternative applications of each of the possible causes, i.e.

■ there are reasons other than the one given here as to why the teacher has to work hard anyway (i.e. not only a matter of having the more and less able students in the same class), and why the more able students may slow down their rate of learning, not only the presence of less able students;

■ there are reasons other than the one given here as to why having a classroom assistant will not help to solve the problem of students' access to the teacher's attention (i.e. there are other things that a classroom assistant has to do);

■ there are reasons other than the one given here as to why students work by themselves, not only a matter of having or not having the teacher's attention;

■ there are reasons other than the one given here as to why the teacher may be present at critical moments;

■ there are reasons other than the one given here as to why students work together.

The interviewer is finding that the reasons that the respondent gives for objecting to mixed ability classes are not substantial, as these reasons operate in other contexts as well, and not solely mixed ability contexts, and so they have to be controlled out: teacher working hard; access to teacher's attention; students working on their own; teacher's non-presence at critical moments; students working collaboratively.

In line 10, the respondent, having had a range of variables controlled (neutralized) here (a) to (e), becomes exasperated and ends that part of the interview. The researcher might conclude here that the parent is simply prejudiced, other key variables having been removed (controlled) from the reasoning. (Indeed Stylianou (2008: 244) suggests that this kind of probing is useful for studying attitudes and prejudice.) Here the interview control question assumes that the variables are dichotomous (e.g. the presence or absence of a variable are the only options); however, within that limitation, the interview control question is useful for identifying causal factors in an interviewees' responses.

Response modes

If there are varied ways of asking questions, it follows there will be several ways in which they may be answered. It is to the different response modes that we now turn. In all, Tuckman (1972) lists eight such modes.

The first of these is the 'unstructured response'. This allows the respondent to give her answer in whatever way she chooses.

Example: Why did you not go to university?

A 'structured response', by contrast, would limit her in some way.

Example: Can you give me two reasons for not going to university?

Although the interviewer has little control over the unstructured response, it does ensure that the respondent has the freedom to give her own answer as fully as she chooses rather than being constrained in some way by the nature of the question. The chief disadvantage of the unstructured response concerns the matter of quantification. Data yielded in the unstructured response are more difficult to code and quantify than data in the structured response.

A 'fill-in response' mode requires the respondent to supply rather than choose a response, though the response is often limited to a word or phrase.

Example: What is your present occupation?

or:

How long have you lived at your present address?

The differences between the fill-in response and the unstructured response is one of degree.

A 'tabular response' is similar to a fill-in response though more structured. It may demand words, figures or phrases, for example:

University	Subject	Degree	Dates	
			From	To

It is thus a convenient and short-hand way of recording complex information.

A 'scaled response' is one structured by means of a series of gradations. The respondent is required to record her response to a given statement by selecting from a number of alternatives.

Example: What are your chances of reaching a top managerial position within the next five years?

Excellent   Good   Fair   Poor   Very poor

Tuckman draws our attention to the fact that, unlike an unstructured response which has to be coded to be useful as data, a scaled response is collected in the form of usable and analysable data.

A 'ranking response' is one in which a respondent is required to rank order a series of words, phrases or statements according to a particular criterion.

Example: Rank order the following people in terms of their usefulness to you as sources of advice and guidance on problems you have encountered in the classroom. Use numbers 1 to 5, with 1 representing the person most useful.

Education tutor
Subject tutor
Class teacher
Head teacher
Other student

Ranked data can be analysed by adding up the rank of each response across the respondents, thus resulting in an overall rank order of alternatives.

A 'checklist response' requires that the respondent selects one of the alternatives presented to her. In that they do not represent points on a continuum, they are nominal categories.

Example: I get most satisfaction in college from:

the social life
studying on my own
attending lectures
college societies
giving a paper at a seminar

This kind of response tends to yield less information than the other kinds considered.

Finally, the 'categorical response' mode is similar to the checklist but simpler in that it offers respondents only two possibilities.

Example: Material progress results in greater happiness for people

True   False

or:

In the event of another war, would you be prepared to fight for your country?

Yes   No

Summing the numbers of respondents with the same responses yields a nominal measure.

As a general rule, the kind of information sought and the means of its acquisition will determine the choice of response mode. Data analysis, then, ought properly to be considered alongside the choice of response mode so that the interviewer can be confident that the data will serve her purposes and analysis of them can be duly prepared. Table 21.3 summarizes the relationship between response mode and type of data.

Once the variables to be measured or studied have been identified, questions can be constructed so as to reflect them. If, for example, one of the variables was to be a new social education project that had recently been attempted with 15-year-olds in a comprehensive school, one obvious question would be: 'How do you think the project has affected the pupils?' Or, less directly, 'Do you think the children have been given too much or too little responsibility?' It is important to bear in mind that more than one question format and more than one response mode may be employed when building up a schedule. The final mixture will depend on the kinds of factors mentioned earlier – the objectives of the research, and so on.

Where an interview schedule is to be used as part of a field survey in which a number of trained interviewers are to be used, it will of course be necessary to include in it appropriate instructions for both interviewer and interviewees.

The framing of questions for a semi-structured interview will also need to consider *prompts* and *probes* (Morrison, 1993: 66). Prompts enable the interviewer to clarify topics or questions, particularly if the interviewee seems not to have understood, or to have misunderstood, or wishes to ask for clarification or more guidance from the interviewer. Probes enable the interviewer to ask respondents to extend, elaborate, add to, provide detail for, clarify or qualify their response, thereby addressing richness, depth of response, comprehensiveness and honesty that are some of the hallmarks of successful interviewing (see also Patton, 1980: 238).

A probe may be simply the follow-up 'why' question. It could comprise simply repeating the question, repeating the answer in a questioning tone, showing interest and understanding, asking for clarification or an example or further explication, or, indeed, simply

TABLE 21.3   THE SELECTION OF RESPONSE MODE

Response mode	Type of data	Chief advantages	Chief disadvantages
Fill-in	Nominal	Less biasing; greater response flexibility	More difficult to score
Scaled	Interval	Easy to score	Time-consuming; can be biasing
Ranking	Ordinal	Easy to score; forces discrimination	Difficult to complete
Checklist or Categorical	Nominal (may be interval when totalled)	Easy to score; easy to respond	Provides less data and fewer options

Source: Tuckman, 1972

pausing. Aldridge and Levine (2001: 119) suggest two types of probe: one in which more detailed factual information is sought, and another in which the respondent is encouraged to elaborate on accounts that they have given or opinions that they hold. Probes can range from the less intrusive (e.g. pausing for the respondent to say more, or making a sound such as 'mmm' to indicate that the interviewer is following closely) to the more intrusive (e.g. repeating a phrase or idea that the respondent said and then following it up with a request for further information, or summarizing ('am I right in thinking that you were saying…', or 'can I just check that I have understood correctly?') and then questioning, or asking for an example or instance, or asking for clarification, or even politely and respectfully challenging, or checking) (cf. Aldridge and Levine, 2001: 120).

Fowler (2009: 139) offers a cautionary note, suggesting that the more the interviewer prompts and probes, the greater is the chance of bias entering the interview. His argument favours standardized wording, with the possibility of further explanation if respondents are unclear.

Hence an interview schedule for a semi-structured interview (i.e. where topics and open-ended questions are written but the exact sequence and wording does not have to be followed with each respondent) might include:

- the topic to be discussed;
- the specific possible questions to be put for each topic;
- the issues within each topic to be discussed, together with possible questions for each issue;
- a series of prompts and probes for each topic, issue and question.

It would be incomplete to end this section without some comment on sampling in addition to question type, for the design of the interview has to consider who is being interviewed. 'How many interviews do I need to conduct?' is a frequent question of novice researchers, asking both about the numbers of people and the number of interviews with each person. The advice here echoes that of Kvale (1996: 101) that one conducts interviews with as many people as necessary in order to gain the information sought. There is no simple rule of thumb, as this depends on the purpose of the interview, for example, whether it is to make generalizations, to provide in-depth, individual data, to gain a range of responses. Though the reader is directed to Chapter 8 on sampling for fuller treatment of these matters, the issue here is that the interviewer must ensure that the interviewees selected will be able to furnish the researcher with the information, i.e. that they possess the information.

Interviewing

Setting up and conducting the interview will make up the next stage in the procedure. Where the interviewer is initiating the research herself, she will clearly select her own respondents; where she is engaged by another agent, then she will probably be given a list of people to contact. Tuckman (1972) has succinctly reviewed the procedures to adopt at the interview itself. He writes that the interviewer should inform the participant of the nature or purpose of the interview, being honest yet without risking biasing responses, and should strive to put the participant at ease. The conduct of the interview should be explained (what happens, and how, and the structure and organization of the interview), how responses may be recorded (and to seek permission if this is to happen), and these procedures should be observed throughout (cf. Fowler, 2009: 140). During the interview the biases and values of the interviewer should not be revealed, and the interviewer should avoid being judgemental. The interviewer may have to steer respondents if they are rambling off the point, without being impolite. Aldridge and Levine (2001: 119) suggest that factual, personal data should be kept until later in the interview, or at the end, rather than at the beginning of the interview.

It is crucial to keep uppermost in one's mind the fact that the interview is a social, interpersonal encounter, not merely a data collection exercise. In this respect one has to bear in mind that different socio-cultural contexts exert different influences on an interview (not least the linguistic factor in which the researcher may be conducting the interview in a language that is not his/her first language or the respondent's first language). Miltiades (2008) notes that, in some cultures, the influence of culture manifests itself in having not only the presence of other members of an extended family at the interview (p. 281), but in those other members actively participating in the interview, giving answers, censoring information (p. 282), interrupting, preventing information from being spoken, and passing comments, i.e. adopting a gate-keeping role (p. 283). As she remarks (p. 282), in some cultures the self is a 'we-self' (rather than an 'I-self') in a collective family, and, indeed, she notes that the Bengali language has no word for 'private'. Just as the researcher brings his or her own cultural background to the interview, so do the respondents (p. 278), and this might affect the nature, substance and amount of data given, the possible biases towards social desirability of answers (the tendency of respondents to give what they believe will be a socially desirable response, or indeed to self-censor (p. 283)), and, indeed, in some cultures, the tendency for elders – as authority figures – to give answers rather than the initially targeted interviewees (p. 278). As she remarks (p. 281), in some cultures, the interview becomes a social event.

As the interview is a social encounter, Kvale (1996: 125) suggests that an interview follows an unwritten script for interactions, the rules for which only surface when they are transgressed. Hence the interviewer must be at pains to conduct the interview carefully and sensitively. Kvale (1996: 147) adds that, as the researcher is the research instrument, the effective interviewer is not only knowledgeable about the subject matter but is also an expert in interaction and communication. The interviewer will need to establish an appropriate atmosphere such that the participant can feel secure to talk freely. This operates at several levels.

For example there is the need to address the *cognitive* aspect of the interview, ensuring that the interviewer is sufficiently knowledgeable about the subject matter that she or he can conduct the interview in an informed manner, and that the interviewee does not feel threatened by lack of knowledge. That this is a particular problem when interviewing children has been documented by Simons (1982) and Lewis (1992), who indicate that children will tend to say anything rather than nothing at all, thereby limiting the possible reliability of the data. The interviewer must also be vigilant to the fact that respondents may not always be what they seem; they may be providing misinformation, telling lies, evading the issue, putting on a front (Walford, 2001: 91), settling scores and being malicious.

Further, the ethical dimension of the interview needs to be borne in mind, ensuring, for example, informed consent, guarantees of confidentiality, beneficence and non-maleficence (i.e. that the interview may be to the advantage of the respondent and will not harm her). The issues of ethics also needs to take account of what is to count as data, for example, it is often after the cassette recorder or video camera has been switched off that the 'gems' of the interview are revealed, or people may wish to say something 'off the record'; the status of this kind of information needs to be clarified before the interview commences. The ethical aspects of interviewing are discussed later in the chapter.

Then there is a need to address the *interpersonal, interactional, communicative* and *emotional* aspects of the interview. For example, the interviewer and interviewee communicate non-verbally, by facial and bodily expression. Something as slight as a shift in position in a chair might convey whether the researcher is inter-

ested, angry, bored, agreeing, disagreeing and so on. Here the interviewer has to be adept at 'active listening'.

Further, the onus is on the interviewer to establish and maintain a good rapport with the interviewee. This concerns being clear, polite, non-threatening, friendly and personable, to the point without being too assertive. It also involves being respectful, e.g. some respondents may or may not wish to be called by their first name, family name or title; being dressed too casually may not inspire confidence. Rapport also requires the interviewer to communicate very clearly and positively the purpose, likely duration, nature and conduct and contents of the interview, to give the respondent the opportunity to ask questions, to be sensitive to any emotions in the respondent, to avoid giving any signs of annoyance, criticism or impatience, and to leave the respondent feeling better than, or at least no worse than, she or he felt at the start of the interview. This requires the interviewer to put himself/herself in the shoes of the respondent, and to be sensitive to how it must feel to be interviewed. Rapport does not mean 'liking' the respondent (Dyer, 1995: 62); it means handling the situation sensitively and professionally.

The interviewer is also responsible for considering the *dynamics* of the situation, for example, how to keep the conversation going, how to motivate participants to discuss their thoughts, feelings and experiences, how to overcome the problems of the likely asymmetries of power in the interview (where the interviewer typically defines the situation, the topic, the conduct, the introduction, the course of the interview and the closing of the interview) (Kvale, 1996: 126). As Kvale suggests, the interview is not usually a reciprocal interaction between two equal participants. That said, it is important to keep the interview moving forward, and how to achieve this needs to be anticipated by the interviewer, for example by being clear on what one wishes to find out, asking those questions that will elicit the kinds of data sought, giving appropriate verbal and non-verbal feedback to the respondent during the interview. It extends even to considering when the interviewer should keep silent (p. 135).

The 'directiveness' of the interviewer has been scaled by Whyte (1982), where a six-point scale of directiveness and responding was devised (1=the least directive, and 6=the most directive):

1 Making encouraging noises.
2 Reflecting on remarks made by the informant.
3 Probing on the last remark made by the informant.
4 Probing an idea preceding the last remark by the informant.

5 Probing an idea expressed earlier in the interview.
6 Introducing a new topic.

This is not to say that the interviewer should avoid being too directive or not directive enough; indeed on occasions a confrontational style might yield much more useful data than a non-confrontational style. Further, it may be in the interests of the research if the interview is sometimes quite tightly controlled, as this might facilitate the subsequent analysis of the data. For example, if the subsequent analysis will seek to categorize and classify the responses, then it might be useful for the interviewer to clarify meaning and even suggest classifications during the interview (see Kvale, 1996: 130).

Patton (1980: 210) suggests that it is important to maintain the interviewee's motivation, hence the interviewer must keep boredom at bay, for example by keeping to a minimum demographic and background questions. The issue of the *interpersonal* and *interactional* elements reaches further, for the language of all speakers has to be considered, for example, translating the academic language of the researcher into the everyday, more easy-going and colloquial language of the interviewee, in order to generate rich descriptions and authentic data. Patton (1980: 225) goes on to underline the importance of clarity in questioning, and suggests that this entails the interviewer finding out what terms the interviewees use about the matter in hand, what terms they use amongst themselves, and avoiding the use of academic jargon. The issue here is not only that the language of the interviewer must be understandable to interviewees but that it must be part of their frame of reference, such that they feel comfortable with it.

This can be pursued even further, suggesting that the age, gender, race, class, dress, language of the interviewers and interviewees will all exert an influence on the interview itself. Bailey (1994: 183) reports that many interviewers are female, middle-class, white-collar workers, yet those they interview may have none of these characteristics. He reports that having women interviewers elicited a greater percentage of honest responses than having male interviewers (p. 182), that having white interviewers interviewing black respondents yielded different results from having black interviewers interview black respondents (pp. 180–1). He also suggests that having interviewers avoiding specific identity with particular groups or counter-cultures in their dress (e.g. rings, pins, etc.) should be eschewed (p. 185) as this can bias the interview; rather some unobtrusive clothing should be worn so as to legitimize the role of the interviewer by fitting in with the respondents' expectations of an interviewer's appear-

ance. One can add here that people in power may expect to be interviewed by interviewers in powerful positions and it is more likely that an interview with a powerful person may be granted to a higher status interviewer. This is discussed fully in Chapter 9.

The *sequence* and *framing* of the interview questions will also need to be considered, for example, ensuring that easier and less threatening, non-controversial questions are addressed earlier in the interview in order to put respondents at their ease (see Patton, 1980: 210–11). This might mean that the 'what' questions precede the more searching and difficult 'how' and 'why' questions (though, as Patton reminds us (1980: 211), knowledge questions – 'what'-type questions – can be threatening). The interviewer's questions should be straightforward and brief, even though the responses need not be (Kvale, 1996: 132). He/she will also need to consider the *kinds* of questions to be put to interviewees, discussed earlier.

There are several problems in the actual conduct of an interview that can be anticipated and, possibly, prevented, ensuring that the interview proceeds comfortably, for example (see Field and Morse, 1989):

■ avoiding interruptions from outside (e.g. telephone calls, people knocking on the door);
■ minimizing distractions;
■ minimizing the risk of 'stage fright' in interviewees and interviewers;
■ avoiding asking embarrassing or awkward questions;
■ jumping from one topic to another;
■ giving advice or opinions (rather than active listening);
■ summarizing too early or closing off an interview too soon;
■ being too superficial;
■ handling sensitive matters (e.g. legal matters, personal matters, emotional matters).

Arksey and Knight (1999: 53) suggest that the interviewer should:

■ appear to be interested;
■ keep to the interview schedule in a structured interview;
■ avoid giving signs of approval or disapproval of responses received;
■ be prepared to repeat questions at the respondent's request;
■ be prepared to move on to another question without irritation, if the respondent indicates unwillingness or inability to answer the question;

- ensure that he/she (the interviewer) understands a response, checking if necessary (e.g. 'am I right in thinking that you mean…?');
- if a response is inadequate, but the interviewer feels that the respondent may have more to say, thank the respondent and add 'and could you please tell me…?';
- give the respondent time to answer (i.e. avoid answering the question for the respondent).

Gadd (2004: 397) reports the significance of how the interviewer responds to the interviewee, as an unsupportive, unsympathetic or negative response (even if not intended) could discourage a respondent from proceeding.

There is also the issue of how to record the interview as it proceeds. For example, an audiotape recorder might be unobtrusive but might constrain the respondent; a videotape might yield more accurate data but might be even more constraining, with its connotation of surveillance. Merton *et al.* (1956) comment on the tendency of taping to 'cool things down'. It might be less threatening not to have any mechanical means of recording the interview, in which case the reliability of the data might rely on the memory of the interviewer (though, as Gadd (2004: 384) remarks, memory is *motivated* in nature, and may be subject to selective recall). An alternative might be to have the interviewer make notes *during* the interview, but this could be highly off-putting for some respondents. The issue here is that there is a trade-off between the need to catch as much data as possible and yet to avoid having so threatening an environment that it impedes the potential of the interview situation.

What is being suggested here is that the interview, as a social encounter, has to take account of, and plan for, the whole range of other possibly non-cognitive factors that form part of everyday conduct. The 'ideal' interview, then, meets several 'quality criteria' (Kvale, 1996: 145):

- The extent of spontaneous, rich, specific and relevant answers from the interviewee.
- The shorter the interviewer's questions and the longer the subject's answers, the better.
- The degree to which the interviewer follows up and clarifies the meanings of the relevant aspects of the answers.
- The ideal interview is to a large extent interpreted throughout the interview.
- The interviewer attempts to verify his or her interpretations of the subject's answers in the course of the interview.

- The interview is 'self-communicating' – it is a story contained in itself that hardly requires much extra descriptions and explanations.

People may refuse to be interviewed (Bailey, 1994: 186–7; Cooper and Schindler, 2001: 301), e.g. they may:

- not give a reason for refusing;
- be hostile to what they see as intrusion.
- hold anti-authoritarian feelings;
- feel that surveys are a waste of time;
- speak a foreign language;
- take an instant dislike to the interviewer;
- say that they are too busy;
- feel embarrassed or ignorant;
- dislike the topic under review;
- be afraid of the consequences of participating;
- feel inadequate or that they do not know the right answer.

The onus is on the interviewer to try to overcome these factors, whilst recognizing, of course, that they may be legitimate, in which case no further attempt can be made to conduct the interview. It is important for the interviewer to render the interview a positive, pleasant and beneficial experience, and to convince the participant of their own worth and the importance of the topic. If there is a significant difference between the interviewer and the respondent (e.g. gender, age, ethnicity, race, social status, class), then it might be advisable to have another interviewer try to conduct the interview.

So far the assumption has been that there is only one interviewer present at the interview. There is an argument for having more than one interviewer present, not only so that one can transcribe or observe features that might be overlooked by the other interviewer whilst engaging the respondent (and these roles have to be signalled clearly to the respondent at the interview), but also to share the interviewing. Joint interviews can provide two versions of the interview – a cross-check – and one can complement the other with additional points, leading to a more complete and reliable record. It also enables one interviewer to observe non-verbal features such as the power and status differentials and social dynamics, and, if there is more than one respondent present at the interview, the relationships between the respondents, e.g. how they support, influence, complement, agree and disagree with each other, or, indeed, contradict each other, the power plays at work, and so on.

On the other hand having more than one interviewer present is not without its difficulties. For example, the roles of the two interviewers may be unclear to the respondents (and it is the job of the interviewers to make this clear), or it may be intimidating to have more than one interviewer present. Researchers will need to weigh carefully the strengths and weaknesses of having more than one interviewer present, and what their roles will be.

We give readers a list of guidelines for conduct during the interview in Box 21.2.

BOX 21.2 GUIDELINES FOR THE CONDUCT OF INTERVIEWS

- Interviews are an interpersonal matter.
- Avoid saying 'I want to know…'; the interviewee is doing you a favour, not being interrogated.
- How to follow up on questions/answers.
- How to keep people on track and how to keep the interview moving forward.
- How to show respect.
- How to divide your attention as interviewer and to share out the interviewees' responses – giving them all a chance to speak in a group interview.
- Do you ask everyone in a group interview to give a response to a question?
- If there is more than one interviewer, what are the roles of the 'silent' interviewer, and do the interviewees know the roles of the interviewers?
- Who is looking at whom.
- If you need to look at your watch then maybe comment on this publicly.
- Try not to refer to your interview schedule; if you need to refer to it then comment on this publicly (e.g. 'let me just check that I have covered the points that I wanted').
- Avoid using your pen as a threatening weapon, pointing it at the interviewee.
- Consider your non-verbal communication, eye contact, signs of anxiety, showing respect.
- Give people time to think – don't interrupt yourself if there is silence.
- How to pass over from one interviewer to another and from one interviewee to another if there is more than one interviewer or interviewee.
- How to give feedback and acceptance to the interviewees.
- Should you write responses down – what messages does this give?
- Put yourself in the shoes of the interviewee.
- What are the effects of losing eye contact or of maintaining it for too long?
- Think of your body posture – not too laid back and not too menacing.
- How to interpret and handle silence.
- Avoid looking away from the respondent if possible.
- Avoid interrupting the respondent.
- Avoid judging the respondent or his/her response.
- The interviewer should summarize and crystallize issues and build on them – that is a way of showing respect.
- How to give signs of acceptance of what people are saying, and how to avoid being judgemental.
- Take care of timing – not too long to be boring.
- Give interviewees the final chance to add any comments, and thank them at the end.
- Plan how to hand over the questions to the next interviewer.
- How to arrange the chairs and tables – do you have tables (they may be a barrier or a protection)?
- Identify who controls the data, and when the control of the data passes from the interviewee to the interviewer.
- What to do with 'off the record' data.
- Take time to 'manage' the interview and keep interviewees aware of what is happening and where it is going.
- Vary the volume/tone of your voice.
- Avoid giving your own view or opinion; be neutral.
- Who is working harder – the interviewer or the interviewee?
- Who is saying more – the interviewer or the interviewee?
- If there is more than one interviewer, how to avoid one interviewer undermining another.
- Think of prompts and probes.
- How to respond to people who say little?
- Consider the social (and physical) distance between the interviewer and interviewee(s).
- Consider the layout of the furniture – circle/oval/straight line or what?
- Have a clear introduction which makes it clear how the interview will be conducted and how the interviewees can respond (e.g. turn taking).

continued

- Make sure you summarize and crystallize every so often.
- How to handle interviewees who know more about the topic than you do.
- Do you have males interviewing females and vice versa (think of age/gender/race, etc. of interviewers and interviewees)?
- Give some feedback to respondents every so often.
- What is the interview doing that cannot be done in a questionnaire?
- If there are status differentials then don't try to alter them in the space of an interview.
- Plan what to do if the interviewee 'turns the tables' and tries to be the interviewer.
- Plan what to do with aggressive or angry interviewees.
- Plan what to do if powerful interviewees don't answer your questions (maybe you need to admit that you haven't understood very well, and ask for clarification, i.e. that it is your fault).
- Be very prepared, so that you don't need to look at your schedule.
- Know your subject matter well.
- If people speak fast then try to slow down everything.
- As an interviewer, you have the responsibility for making sure the interview runs well.

Interviewers have to be sensitive to their own effect on the interview. For example (Cooper and Schindler, 2001: 307), they may fail to secure full cooperation or keep to procedures, they may establish an inappropriate environment (physical, cognitive, interpersonal), they may be exerting undue influence or pressure on the respondent, or they may be selective in recording the data; we consider the issue of reliability in Chapter 10.

It is important for the interviewer to explain to the respondent the purpose, scope, nature and conduct of the interview, the use to be made of the data, ethical issues, the likely duration of the interview, i.e. to explain fully the 'rules of the game' so that the interviewee is left in no doubt as to what will happen during and after the interview. It is important for the interviewer to introduce herself/himself properly and fully to the respondent (maybe even providing identification). The interviewer has to set the scene appropriately, for example, to say that there are no right and wrong answers, that some of the topics may be deep but that they are not designed to be a test, to invite questions and interruptions, and to clear permission for recording. During the interview it is important, also, for the interviewee to speak more than the interviewer, for the interviewer to listen attentively and to be seen by the respondent to be listening attentively, and for the interviewer to be seen to be enjoying, or at ease with, the interview.

Transcribing

This is a crucial step in interviewing, for there is the potential for massive data loss, distortion and the reduction of complexity. It has been suggested throughout that the interview is a social encounter, not merely a data collection exercise; the problem with much transcription is that it becomes solely a record of data rather than a record of a social encounter.

Indeed this problem might have begun at the data collection stage, for example audiotape is selective, it filters out important contextual factors, neglecting the visual and non-verbal aspects of the interview (Mishler, 1986). Moreover, it is frequently the non-verbal communication that gives more information than the verbal communication. Morrison (1993: 63) recounts the incident of an autocratic head teacher extolling the virtues of collegiality and democratic decision making whilst shaking her head vigorously from side to side and pressing the flat of her hand in a downwards motion away from herself as if to silence discussion! To replace audio recording with video recording might make for richer data and catch non-verbal communication, but this then becomes very time-consuming to analyse.

Transcriptions inevitably lose data from the original encounter. This problem is compounded, for a transcription represents the translation from one set of rule systems (oral and interpersonal) to another very remote rule system (written language). As Kvale (1996: 166) suggests the prefix *trans* indicates a change of state or form; transcription is selective transformation. Therefore it is unrealistic to pretend that the data on transcripts are anything but *already interpreted* data. As Kvale (1996: 167) remarks, the transcript can become an opaque screen between the researcher and the original live interview situation.

Hence there can be no single 'correct' transcription; rather the issue becomes whether, to what extent and how a transcription is useful for the research. Transcriptions are decontextualized, abstracted from time and space, from the dynamics of the situation, from the live form, and from the social, interactive, dynamic and fluid dimensions of their source; they are frozen.

The words in transcripts are not necessarily as solid as they were in the social setting of the interview.

Scheurich (1995: 240) suggests that even conventional procedures for achieving reliability are inadequate here, for holding constant the questions, the interviewer, the interviewee, the time and place does not guarantee stable, unambiguous data. Indeed Mishler (1991: 260) suggests that data and the relationship between meaning and language are contextually situated; they are unstable, changing and capable of endless reinterpretation.

We are not arguing against transcriptions, rather we are cautioning against the researcher believing that they tell everything that took place in the interview. This might require the researcher to ensure that different *kinds* of data are recorded in the transcript of the audiotape, for example:

- what was being said;
- the tone of voice of the speaker(s) (e.g. harsh, kindly, encouraging);
- the inflection of the voice (e.g. rising or falling, a question or a statement, a cadence or a pause, a summarizing or exploratory tone, opening or closing a line of enquiry);
- emphases placed by the speaker;
- pauses (short to long) and silences (short to long);
- interruptions;
- the mood of the speaker(s) (e.g. excited, angry, resigned, bored, enthusiastic, committed, happy, grudging);
- the speed of the talk (fast to slow, hurried or unhurried, hesitant to confident);
- how many people were speaking simultaneously;
- whether a speaker was speaking continuously or in short phrases;
- who is speaking to whom;
- indecipherable speech;
- any other events that were taking place at the same time that the researcher can recall.

If the transcript is of videotape, then this enables the researcher to comment on all of the non-verbal communication that was taking place in addition to the features noted from the audiotape. The issue here is that it is often inadequate to transcribe only spoken words; other data are important. Of course, as soon as other data are noted, this becomes a matter of interpretation (what is a long pause, what is a short pause, was the respondent happy or was it just a 'front', what gave rise to such-and-such a question or response, why did the speaker suddenly burst into tears). As Kvale (1996: 183) notes, interviewees' statements are not simply collected by the interviewer, they are, in reality, co-authored.

Analysing

Once data from the interview have been collected, the next stage involves analysing them, often by some form of coding or scoring. In qualitative data the data analysis here is almost inevitably interpretive, hence the data analysis is less a completely accurate representation (as in the numerical, positivist tradition) but more of a reflexive, reactive interaction between the researcher and the decontextualized data that are already interpretations of a social encounter. The researcher has to consider whether to focus on those items that the participant mentions or reiterates the most, or whether to deem important those items that arise when the participant wanders from the point or changes the subject, or – in the case of two respondents – whether they actually mean the same even if they are using the same words to describe similar experiences or the same experience (Gadd, 2004: 385). At issue here is the unavoidable integration of analysis and interpretation.

The great tension in data analysis is between maintaining a sense of the holism of the interview and the tendency for analysis to atomize and fragment the data – to separate them into constituent elements, thereby losing the synergy of the whole, and in interviews often the whole is greater than the sum of the parts. There are several stages in analysis, for example:

- generating natural units of meaning;
- classifying, categorizing and ordering these units of meaning;
- structuring narratives to describe the interview contents;
- interpreting the interview data.

These are comparatively generalized stages. Miles and Huberman (1994) suggest 12 tactics for generating meaning from transcribed and interview data:

- counting frequencies of occurrence (of ideas, themes, pieces of data, words);
- noting patterns and themes (Gestalts), which may stem from repeated themes and causes or explanations or constructs;
- seeing plausibility – trying to make good sense of data, using informed intuition to reach a conclusion;
- clustering – setting items into categories, types, behaviours and classifications;
- making metaphors – using figurative and connotative language rather than literal and denotative language, bringing data to life, thereby reducing data, making patterns, decentring the data, and connecting data with theory;
- splitting variables to elaborate, differentiate and

'unpack' ideas, i.e. to move away from the drive towards integration and the blurring of data;

- subsuming particulars into the general (akin to Glaser's (1978) notion of 'constant comparison' – see Chapter 33 in this book) – a move towards clarifying key concepts;
- factoring – bringing a large number of variables under a smaller number of (frequently) unobserved hypothetical variables;
- identifying and noting relations between variables;
- finding intervening variables – looking for other variables that appear to be 'getting in the way' of accounting for what one would expect to be strong relationships between variables;
- building a logical chain of evidence – noting causality and making inferences;
- making conceptual/theoretical coherence – moving from metaphors to constructs to theories to explain the phenomena.

This progression, though perhaps positivist in its tone, is a useful way of moving from the specific to the general in data analysis. Running through the suggestions from Miles and Huberman (1994) is the importance that they attach to coding of responses in interviews, partially as a way of reducing what is typically data overload from qualitative data.

Coding has been defined by Kerlinger (1970) as the translation of question responses and respondent information to specific categories for the purpose of analysis. As we have seen, many questions are precoded, that is, each response can be immediately and directly converted into a score in an objective way. Rating scales and checklists are examples of precoded questions. Coding is the ascription of a category label to a piece of data, with the category label either decided in advance or in response to the data that have been collected.

We discuss coding more fully in Chapter 33, and we refer the reader to that discussion.

Content analysis involves reading and judgement; Brenner et al. (1985) set out several steps in undertaking a content analysis of open-ended data:

1 Briefing (understanding the problem and its context in detail).
2 Sampling (of people, including the types of sample sought, see Chapter 8).
3 Associating (with other work that has been done).
4 Hypothesis development.
5 Hypothesis testing.
6 Immersion (in the data collected, to pick up all the clues).

7 Categorizing (in which the categories and their labels must: (a) reflect the purpose of the research; (b) be exhaustive; (c) be mutually exclusive).
8 Incubation (e.g. reflecting on data and developing interpretations and meanings).
9 Synthesis (involving a review of the rationale for coding and an identification of the emerging patterns and themes).
10 Culling (condensing, excising and even reinterpreting the data so that they can be written up intelligibly).
11 Interpretation (making meaning of the data).
12 Writing (including (pp. 140–3): giving clear guidance on the incidence of occurrence; proving an indication of direction and intentionality of feelings; being aware of what is not said as well as what it said – silences; indicating salience (to the readers and respondents).
13 Rethinking.

This process, the authors suggest (Brenner et al., 1985: 144), requires researchers to address several factors:

- Understand the research brief thoroughly.
- Evaluate the relevance of the sample for the research project.
- Associate their own experiences with the problem, looking for clues from the past.
- Develop testable hypotheses as the basis for the content analysis (the authors name this the 'Concept Book').
- Test the hypotheses throughout the interviewing and analysis process.
- Stay immersed in the data throughout the study.
- Categorize the data in the Concept Book, creating labels and codes.
- Incubate the data before writing up.
- Synthesize the data in the Concept Book, looking for key concepts.
- Cull the data, being selective is important because it is impossible to report everything that happened.
- Interpret the data, identifying its meaning and implication.
- Write up the report.
- Rethink and rewrite: have the research objectives been met?

Hycner (1985) sets out procedures that can be followed when phenomenologically analysing interview data. We saw in Chapter 1 that the phenomenologist advocates the study of direct experience taken at face value and sees behaviour as determined by the phenomena of experience rather than by external, objective and physically described reality. Hycner points out that there is a reluctance on the part of phenomenologists to focus too much on specific steps in research methods for fear that they will become reified. The steps suggested by Hycner, however, offer a possible way of analysing data which allays such fears. As he himself explains, his guidelines 'have arisen out of a number of years of teaching phenomenological research classes to graduate psychology students and trying to be true to the phenomenon of interview data while also providing concrete guidelines' (Hycner, 1985). In summary, the guidelines are as follows:

1 *Transcription*: having the interview tape transcribed, noting not only the literal statements but also non-verbal and paralinguistic communication.

2 *Bracketing and phenomenological reduction*: for Hycner (1985) this means, 'suspending (bracketing) as much as possible the researcher's meaning and interpretations and entering into the world of the unique individual who was interviewed'. The researcher thus sets out to understand what the interviewee is saying rather than what she expects that person to say.

3 *Listening to the interview for a sense of the whole*: this involves listening to the entire tape several times and reading the transcription a number of times in order to provide a context for the emergence of specific units of meaning and themes later on.

4 *Delineating units of general meaning*: this entails a thorough scrutiny of both verbal and non-verbal gestures to elicit the participant's meaning. Hycner (1985) says, 'It is a crystallization and condensation of what the participant has said, still using as much as possible the literal words of the participant.' (See Box 21.3 for Hycner's own example. This is the second page of transcription describing an experience of wonderment and awe. On the previous page, the participant discussed the background where he and his girlfriend were up in the mountains on vacation. The scene being described is the beginning of an experience of wonder.)

BOX 21.3 DELINEATING UNITS OF GENERAL MEANING

[1]I was looking at Mary and [2]all of a sudden I knew [3]I was looking at her like I never looked at anybody in my whole life – and [4]my eyes were sort of just kind of staring at her and the reason that [5]I realized that it was tremendous was that she said to me – what are you doing – [6]and I just said I'm looking at you – [7]and so we just sat there and she [8]sort of watched me look at her – and [9]she was getting kind of uncomfortable [10]and yet also kept saying – what's going on [11]but not really wanting to hear – [12]just letting me – have enough sensitivity to let me experience it – [13] a lot was going on – [14]I didn't realize what – what it was – [15]I was just sort of sitting there – [16]*I couldn't move* – [17]I didn't want to move – [18]I just want to continue looking at her.

[1]Was looking at Mary
[2]suddenly he knew
[3]He was looking at her like he never looked at anybody in his whole life
[4]His eyes were just staring at her
[5]Realized it was tremendous when she said 'What are you doing?'
[6]He just said, 'I'm looking at you.'
[7]Both just sat there
[8]She sort of watched him look at her
[9]She was getting kind of uncomfortable
[10]She kept saying 'What's going on?'
[11]She didn't seem to want a response
[12]She had enough sensitivity to let him experience it
[13]A lot was going on
[14]He didn't realize what was going on
[15]He continued to just sit there
[16]He *couldn't move*
[17]Didn't want to move
[18]Just wanted to continue looking at her.

Source: Hycner, 1985

5 *Delineating units of meaning relevant to the research question*: once the units of general meaning have been noted, they are then reduced to units of meaning relevant to the research question. In the case of Hycner's (1985) study, the original 18 general units (see Box 21.3) are reduced to 13 units of meaning relevant to the research question (see Box 21.4).

6 *Training independent judges to verify the units of relevant meaning*: findings can be verified by using other researchers to carry out the above procedures. Hycner's own experience in working with graduate students well trained in this type of research is that there are rarely significant differences in the findings.

7 *Eliminating redundancies*: at this stage, the researcher checks the lists of relevant meaning and eliminates those clearly redundant to others previously listed.

8 *Clustering units of relevant meaning*: the researcher now tries to determine if any of the units of relevant meaning naturally cluster together; whether there seems to be some common theme or essence that unites several discrete units of relevant meaning. Box 21.5 gives an example of clustering units of relevant meaning.

9 *Determining themes from clusters of meaning*: the researcher examines all the clusters of meaning to determine if there is one (or more) central theme(s) which expresses the essence of these clusters.

10 *Writing a summary of each individual interview*: it is useful at this point, Hycner suggests, to go back to the interview transcription and write up a summary of the interview incorporating the themes that have been elicited from the data.

11 *Return to the participant with the summary and themes, conducting a second interview*: this is a check to see whether the essence of the first interview has been accurately and fully captured.

12 *Modifying themes and summary*: with the new data from the second interview, the researcher looks at all the data as a whole and modifies or adds themes as necessary.

13 *Identifying general and unique themes for all the interviews*: the researcher now looks for the themes common to most or all of the interviews as well as the individual variations. The first step is to note if there are themes common to all or most of the interviews. The second step is to note when there are themes that are unique to a single interview or a minority of the interviews.

14 *Contextualization of themes*: at this point it is helpful to place these themes back within the overall contexts or horizons from which these themes emerged.

15 *Composite summary*: Hycner considers it useful to write up a composite summary of all the interviews which would accurately capture the essence of the phenomenon being investigated. He concludes, 'Such a composite summary describes the "world" in general, as experienced by the participants. At the end of such a summary the researcher might want to note significant individual differences' (Hycner, 1985).

Issues arising from this procedure are discussed in some detail in the second part of Hycner's (1985) article.

BOX 21.4   UNITS OF RELEVANT MEANING

[1]Was looking at Mary
[2]Suddenly he knew
[3]He was looking at her like he never looked at anybody in his whole life
[4]His eyes were just staring at her
[5]Realized it was tremendous when she said 'What are you doing?'
[6]He just said, 'I'm looking at you.'
[7]Both just sat there
[12]She had enough sensitivity to let him experience it
[13]A lot was going on
[14]He didn't realize what was going on
[15]He continued to just sit there
[16]He *couldn't move* –
[17]Didn't want to move
[18]Just wanted to continue looking at her

Source: Hycner, 1985

BOX 21.5 CLUSTERS OF RELEVANT MEANING

I The tremendousness of the looking at Mary
A Looking at Mary in a way totally different than he had ever looked at anyone in his life.[1,3]
B His eyes were just staring.[4]
C Realized it was tremendous when she said 'What are you doing?'[5]
D Was (just) looking at her.[6]
E A lot was going on.[13]
F Just wanted to continue looking at her.[16]

II Realization
A A sudden realization[2] (Almost like it breaks in).
B Realized how tremendous it was (through her question).[5]
C A lot was going on and he didn't realize what was going on[13,14] (rhythm of awareness).

III Continuation of what was happening
A Both just (continued) to sit there.[7]
B He continued to sit.[15]

IV Inability to move
A *Couldn't move*[16] (issue of volition).
B Didn't want to move[17] (didn't desire to move).

V Interpersonal dimension
A Was looking at Mary in a way he had never looked at anyone in his whole life.[1,3]
B Her question elicited the realization of how tremendous it was.[5]
C He just said 'I'm looking at you.'[6]
D Both just sat there.[7]

Source: Hycner, 1985

Verifying

Chapter 10 discusses at length the issues of reliability, validity and generalizability of the data from interviews, and so these issues will not be repeated here. The reader is advised to explore not only that section of Chapter 10, but, indeed, the whole chapter. Kvale (1996: 237) makes the point that validation must take place at all seven stages of the interview-based investigation, set out earlier in this chapter. For example: (a) the theoretical foundation of the research must be rigorous and there must be a logical link between such theory and the research questions; (b) all aspects of the research design must be sound and rigorous; (c) the data must be accurate, reliable and valid (with consistency and reliability checks undertaken); (d) the translation of the data from an oral to a written medium must demonstrate fidelity to the key features of the interview situation; (e) data analysis must demonstrate fidelity to the data; (f) validation procedures should be in place and used; (g) the reporting should be fair and seen to be fair by readers.

One main issue here is that there is no single canon of validity; rather the notion of fitness for purpose within an ethically defensible framework should be adopted, giving rise to different kinds of validity for different kinds of interview-based research (e.g. structured to unstructured, qualitative to quantitative, nomothetic to idiographic, generalizable to unique, descriptive to explanatory, positivist to ethnographic, pre-ordinate to responsive).

Reporting

The nature of the reporting will be decided to some extent by the nature of the interviewing. For example a standardized, structured interview may yield numerical data that may be reported succinctly in tables and graphs, whilst a qualitative, word-based, open-ended interview will yield word-based accounts that take up considerably more space.

Kvale (1996: 263–6) suggests several elements of a report: (i) an introduction that includes the main themes and contents; (ii) an outline of the methodology and methods (from designing to interviewing, transcription and analysis); (iii) the results (the data analysis, interpretation and verification); (iv) a discussion.

If the report is largely numerical then figures and tables might be appropriate; if the interview is more faithfully represented in words rather than numbers then this presents the researcher with the issue of how to present particular quotations. Here Kvale (1996: 266) suggests that direct quotations should: (a) illuminate and relate to the general text whilst maintaining a balance with the main text; (b) be contextualized and be accompanied by a commentary and interpretation; (c) be particularly clear, useful and the 'best' of the data (the 'gems'!); (d) should include an indication of how they have been edited; and (e) be incorporated into the natural written style of the report.

For sample interview data, see the accompanying website.

21.6 Group interviewing

One technique within the methodology of interviewing to have grown in popularity is that of group interviewing. Watts and Ebbutt (1987), for example, have considered the advantages and disadvantages of group interviewing as a means of collecting data in educational research. The advantages the authors identify include the potential for discussions to develop, thus yielding a wide range of responses. They explain, 'such interviews are useful ... where a group of people have been working together for some time or common purpose, or where it is seen as important that everyone concerned is aware of what others in the group are saying' (Watts and Ebbutt, 1987). The group interview, the paper argues, can generate a wider range of responses than in individual interviews. Bogdan and Biklen (1992: 100) add that group interviews might be useful for gaining an insight into what might be pursued in subsequent individual interviews. There are practical and organizational advantages, too. Pre-arranged groups can be used for the purpose in question by teachers with minimum disruption. Group interviews are often quicker than individual interviews and hence are time-saving. The group interview can also bring together people with varied opinions, or as representatives of different collectivities.

Arksey and Knight (1999: 76) suggest that having more than one interviewee present can provide two versions of events – a cross-check – and one can complement the other with additional points, leading to a more complete and reliable record. It is also possible to detect how the participants support, influence, complement, agree and disagree with each other, and the relationships between them. On the other hand, one respondent may dominate the interview (particularly if one respondent is male and another female (p. 76)). Further, Arksey and Knight suggest that antagonisms

may be stirred up at the interview, individuals may be reticent in front of others, particularly if they are colleagues or if the matter is sensitive. They also suggest that a 'public line' may be offered instead of a more honest, personal response, and, indeed, that participants may collude in withholding information. Watts and Ebbutt (1987) note that group interviews are of little use in allowing personal matters to emerge, or in circumstances where the researcher has to aim a series of follow-up questions at one specific member of the group. As they explain, 'the dynamic of a group denies access to this sort of data' (Watts and Ebbutt, 1987). Group interviews may produce 'group think', discouraging individuals who hold a different view from speaking out in front of the other group members. Further, Lewis (1992) comments on the problem of coding up the responses of group interviews. For further guidance on this topic and the procedures involved, we refer the reader to Simons (1982), Watts and Ebbutt (1987), Hedges (1985), Breakwell (1990), Spencer and Flin (1990), Lewis (1992) and Arksey and Knight (1999).

Several issues have to be addressed in the conduct of a group interview, for example:

1. How to divide your attention as interviewer and to share out the interviewees' responses – giving them all a chance to speak in a group interview?
2. Do you ask everyone in a group interview to give a response to a question?
3. How to handle people who are too quiet, too noisy, who monopolize the conversation, who argue and disagree with each other?
4. What happens if people become angry with you or with each other?
5. How to make people be quiet/stop talking whilst being polite?
6. How to handle differences in how talkative people are?
7. How to arrange turn-taking (if appropriate)?
8. Do you ask named individuals questions?
9. How can you have individuals answer without forcing them?
10. How to handle a range of very different responses to the same question?
11. Why have you brought together the particular people in the group?
12. Do you want people to answer in a particular sequence?
13. What to do if the more experienced people always answer first in a group interview?
14. As an interviewer, be vigilant to pick up on people who are trying to speak.

It must be borne in mind when conducting group interviews that the unit of analysis is the view of the whole group and not the individual member; a collective group response is being sought, even if there are individual differences or a range of responses within the group. This ensures that no individual is either unnecessarily marginalized or subject to blame or being ostracized for holding a different view.

Group interviews are also very useful when interviewing children, and it is to this that we now turn.

21.7 Interviewing children

Children have been regarded as 'the best sources of information about themselves' (Docherty and Sandelowski, 1999: 177), but it is important for the interviewer to be able to enter their world and childhood culture and to see the situation through their eyes (Docherty and Sandelowski, 1999: 177). It is important to understand the world of children through their own eyes rather than the lens of the adult. Children differ from adults in cognitive and linguistic development, attention and concentration span, ability to recall, life experiences, what they consider to be important, status and power (Arksey and Knight, 1999: 116). All these have a bearing on the interview. Arksey and Knight also indicate (pp. 116–18) that it is important to establish trust with children, to put the child at ease quickly and to help him/her to feel confident, to avoid overreacting (e.g. if the child is distracted), to make the interview non-threatening and enjoyable, to use straightforward language and child's language, to ask questions that are appropriate for the age of the child (e.g. to keep to the 'here and now', to avoid using 'why', 'when' and 'how' questions with very young children, e.g. below five years old), to ensure that children can understand abstract questions (often for older children), to allow time to think, and to combine methods and activities in an interview (e.g. drawing, playing, writing, speaking, playing a game, using pictures, newspapers, toys or photographs).

Group interviewing can be useful with children, as it encourages interaction between the group rather than simply a response to an adult's question. Group interviews of children might also be less intimidating for them than individual interviews (Greig and Taylor, 1999: 132). Eder and Fingerson (2003: 34) suggest that a power and status dynamic is heavily implicated in interviewing children; they have little in comparison to the adult. Indeed, Thorne (1994) uses the term 'kids' rather than 'children', as the former is the term used by the children themselves, whereas 'children', she argues, is a term used exclusively by adults, denoting subordi-

nacy (cf. Eder and Fingerson, 2003: 34). Mayall (1999) suggests regarding children as a 'minority group', in that they lack power and control over their own lives. If this is the case, then it is important to take steps to ensure that children are given a voice and an interview setting in which they feel comfortable (cf. Maguire, 2005). Group interviewing is such a setting, taking place in as close to a natural surrounding as possible (Greig and Taylor, 1999: 131); indeed Eder and Fingerson (2003: 45) report the successful use of a high status child as the interviewer with a group of children.

Group interviewing with children enables them to challenge each other and participate in a way that may not happen in a one-to-one, adult–child interview and using language that the children themselves use. For example, Lewis (1992) found that ten-year-olds' understanding of severe learning difficulties was enhanced in group interview situations, the children challenging and extending each other's ideas and introducing new ideas into the discussion. Further, having the interview as part of a more routine, everyday activity can also help to make it less unnatural, as can making the interview more like a game (e.g. by using props such as toys and pictures). For example, it could be part of a 'show and tell' or 'circle time' session, or part of group discussion time. The issue here is to try to make the interview as informal as possible. Of course, sometimes it may be more useful to formalize the session, so that children have a sense of how important the situation is, and they can respond to this positively. It can be respectful to have an informal or, indeed, a formal interview; the former maybe for younger children and the latter for older children.

Whilst group interviews may be useful with many children, it is also the case that individual interviews with children may also be valuable. For example, Eder and Fingerson (2003: 43–4) report the value of individual interviews with adolescents, particularly about sensitive matters, for example relationships, family, body issues, sexuality, love. Indeed they report examples where individual interviews yielded different results from group interviews with the same people about the same topics, and where the individuals valued greatly the opportunity for a one-to-one conversation.

Interviews with children should try to employ openended questions, to avoid a single answer type of response (Greig and Taylor, 1999; Wright and Powell, 2006), as answers to open-ended questions are usually more accurate than answers to closed questions (Wright and Powell, 2006: 317) since they are respondent-driven and respondent-focused, and they can take greater account of children with limited linguistic or cognitive abilities. Closed questions can lead to response bias in that children may provide answers without thinking (Wright and Powell, 2006: 317). Waterman *et al.* (2001) report that children gave clear answers to yes/no closed questions even when such question types were deliberately given in respect of unanswerable questions (i.e. where insufficient information had been given for the question to be answered), in other words, the format of the question artificially skewed the response. Clearly, however, specific questions may be needed to elicit specific, e.g. factual, details (Wright and Powell, 2006: 320).

Another strategy for interviewing children is to use a projection technique. Here, instead of asking direct questions, the interviewer can show a picture or set of pictures, and then ask the children for their responses to it/them (cf. Greig and Taylor, 1999: 132–3). For example, a child may first comment on the people's race in the pictures, followed by their sex, suggesting that race may be more important in their mind than their sex. This avoids a direct question and may reduce the possibility of a biased answer – where the respondent may be looking for cues as to how to respond. Other projection techniques include the use of dolls or puppets, photographs of a particular scene which the respondents have to comment upon (e.g. what is happening? What should be done here?) and the 'guess who?' technique (Wragg, 2002: 157) (which people might fit a particular description).

Simons (1982), Lewis (1992), Bailey (1994: 447–9), Breakwell (2000: 245–6) and Breakwell *et al.* (2006: 245–6), however, chart some difficulties in interviewing children, for example how to:

- overcome children being easily distracted (e.g. some interviewers provide toys or pictures, or children may be fascinated by something as simple as the researcher's pen, or there may be a passing vehicle outside, and these distract the children);
- avoid the researcher being seen as an authority figure (e.g. a teacher, a parent or an adult in a powerful position);
- understand what children mean and what they say (particularly with very young children);
- gather a lot of information in a short time, children's attention span being limited;
- have children reveal what they really think and feel rather than what they think the researcher wants to hear;
- avoid the situation being seen by the child as a test;
- keep the interview relevant;
- overcome young children's unwillingness to contradict an adult or assert themselves, or, in the case of adolescents, deliberately being oppositional in their views;

- interview inarticulate, hesitant and nervous children;
- get the children's teacher away from the children;
- respond to the child who says something then immediately wishes she hadn't said it;
- elicit genuine responses from children rather than simply responses to the interview situation;
- get beyond the institutional, head teacher's or 'expected' response;
- avoid receiving a socially desirable response;
- ensure that the child is giving a true opinion;
- keep children to the point;
- avoid children being too extreme or destructive of each other's views;
- pitch language at the appropriate level;
- overcome the children (particularly young children) taking a question too literally (hence the need to avoid metaphors, similes or analogies);
- enable the children to see a situation through other people's eyes;
- avoid the interview being an arduous bore;
- overcome children's poor memories;
- avoid children being too focused on particular features or situations;
- avoid the situation where the child will say 'yes' to anything (an 'acquiescence bias') addressed, for example, by avoiding 'yes/no' questions in favour of open-ended questions;
- overcome the situation of the child saying anything in order to please;
- overcome the unwillingness of children to contradict an adult or to assert themselves in the presence of an adult;
- overcome the proclivity of some children to say that they 'don't know' (for a variety of reasons, e.g. they are not interested, they genuinely don't know, they don't understand the question, they think that the interviewer might expect them not to know, they are unwilling to disclose what they do know, they are too shy to speak, they cannot explain themselves very well), or simply to shrug their shoulders and remain silent;
- overcome the problem that some children will say anything rather than feel they do not have 'the answer';
- overcome the problem that some children dominate the conversation;
- avoid the problem of children feeling very exposed in front of their friends;
- avoid children feeling uncomfortable or threatened (addressed, perhaps, by placing children with their friends);
- avoid children telling lies.

Clearly these problems are not exclusive to children; they apply equally well to some adult group interviews. Group interviews require skilful chairing and attention to the physical layout of the room so that everyone can see everyone else. Group size is also an issue; too few and it can put pressure on individuals, too large and the group fragments and loses focus. Lewis (1992) summarizes research to indicate that a group of around six or seven is an optimum size, though it can be smaller for younger children. The duration of an interview may not be for longer than, at most, 15 minutes, and it might be useful to ensure that distractions are kept to a minimum. Simple language to the point and without ambiguity (e.g. avoiding metaphors) is important. It is crucial to keep in mind that an interview is a social encounter, and children may be very sensitive to the social dynamics and social context of the interview (Morison *et al.*, 2000), and not only its cognitive element (Maguire (2005: 4) suggests that 'children have good social radar'. Children will be sensitive to the sex and ethnicity of the interviewer; the very fact that the interviewer is an adult will affect the interview (Morison *et al.*, 2000: 113). For further information we refer the reader to Wilson and Powell (2001) and Mukerji and Albon (2010).

21.8 Interviewing minority and marginalized people

Not all the methods of interviewing set out so far will apply to interviewing marginalized people, i.e. those who are 'on the edge' of society (Barron, 1999), e. g. economically, socially, politically, or who are 'invisible': stigmatized groups, the unemployed, the elderly, refugees, asylum seekers, travellers, those with special needs, those with a low status in society, those with limited linguistic, cognitive or intellectual abilities, those whose first language is a minority language, the disabled, the chronically ill, children with cerebral palsy, victims of crime, the oppressed, the subordinate and so on. That this is an area of increasing educational concern is attested by Parker and Lynn (2002: 13), who argue that much educational research has ignored marginalized groups by not addressing their concerns or including them as areas of research, or that regard them as minorities that do not merit research, and, where, if research is conducted with/on them, it uses culturally inappropriate methods of investigation (p. 13). Similarly Kelly (2007: 22) argues that researchers can no longer 'exclude learning disabled children' from research on the grounds that they pose challenges to conventional research methods.

In interviewing marginalized groups, the interviewer will need to consider greater use of informal, open-ended interviews (which follow the train of thought and response of the respondent and which use age-appropriate and context-appropriate language) rather than highly structured interviews (Swain *et al.*, 1998: 26). Further, the authors recommend the use of narrative, qualitative and in-depth interviews (discussed later in this chapter), enabling self-disclosure (both by the interviewer and the interviewee) (Swain *et al.*, 1998: 26), wherein participants 'tell their stories' (Barron, 1999: 38) in their own words, and recount their subjective experiences and feelings. This gives them a 'voice', where otherwise they would either not be heard or listened to (see also Swain *et al.*, 1998). This accords with the emancipatory potential or intent of research that was set out as a key feature of critical educational research in Chapter 2 (see also Barron, 1999: 40, 44–6) Barron suggests that it is important for the respondent to feel safe, secure, supported, close to the interviewer, and to know that he/she has the undivided attention of the interviewer (p. 41) and a non-judgemental and non-evaluative stance by the interviewer, with built-in opportunities for respondent validation and clearance (respondents may wish, upon reflection, to withdraw comments initially made at interview).

The researcher must take care not to exploit what are likely to be (perceived) asymmetries of power in the interview (where the researcher may be regarded as having more than the respondent) (Swain *et al.*, 1998: 26). Indeed Swain *et al.* (1998: 25) remind researchers that the interviews and research on marginalized groups should bring benefit to them, i.e. they do not continue to be exploited or marginalized.

An interview is a communicative encounter, and, for some marginalized groups (e.g. the physically disabled or those with communication difficulties) this is precisely the challenge to be faced by researchers: how to communicate with those who cannot communicate easily or at all (e.g. those who cannot speak, elective mutes, the deaf, children with degrees of autism, children with Down's syndrome or attention deficit disorder). Here Kelly (2007: 25–6) notes the use of communication cards, pictorial cards (e.g. that indicate feelings), drawing frames, picture books, toys, puppets, photographs of familiar people or places, respecting and working with – and in – the language used by the participant and keeping within their frame of reference, considering the greater use of yes/no questions than open questions (e.g. for students who cannot speak but who can point). She also advocates the use of projection techniques (p. 28) such as 'three wishes', asking participants to draw a picture to represent the matter in hand, and the use of 'feeling cards' (cards with pictures of feelings).

Kelly (2007: 24) comments that gaining access to marginalized groups may be difficult, and that, in the case of those with disabilities, it is likely to be necessary to gain access through gatekeepers, e.g. parents, social workers, health team members, carers and the suchlike, and, indeed, to have them present during the interview or to speak on the respondents' behalf (e.g. to protect the respondents' rights directly or in acting as proxies/advocates). This is important, as Kelly (p. 23) reports the dangers of 'suggestibility' of participants in interviews, and it leads to her comment that skilful and sensitive questioning are essential, drawing on participants' actual experiences, and taking care not to project the researcher's own interests. Bourne-Day and Lee-Treweek (2008) also indicate that issues of privacy and identity may be highly significant in researching marginalized groups.

In conducting interviews, Kelly (2007) makes the point that it may be necessary to hold several short interviews rather than a single long interview, in order for the participants to be able to concentrate, retain their attention (p. 25) and not become tired. She also emphasizes the importance of waiting longer for an answer to be given, and to be alert to different ways in which children can communicate other than through speech (p. 28), e.g. facial expression, writing, signing, gestures and non-verbal communication, symbols (see also Mitchell and Sloper, 2008: 11), drawing and game playing. There has to be a shift, Kelly avers, away from a deficit model in which children cannot speak, and towards a positive model of how they can communicate through other means.

Morgan (1996) suggests that interviewing marginalized groups can be addressed usefully through group interviewing and with focus groups, and it is to focus groups that we turn now.

21.9 Focus groups

As an adjunct to group interviews, the use of focus groups is growing in educational research, albeit more slowly than, for instance, in business and political circles. Focus groups are a form of group interview, though not in the sense of a backwards and forwards between interviewer and group. Rather, the reliance is on the interaction within the group who discuss a topic supplied by the researcher (Morgan, 1988: 9), yielding a collective rather than an individual view. Hence the participants interact with each other rather than with the interviewer, such that the views of the participants can emerge – the participants' rather than the researcher's

agenda can predominate. It is from the *interaction* of the group that the data emerge. Focus groups are contrived settings, bringing together a specifically chosen sector of the population, previously unknown to each other (Hydén and Bülow, 2003) to discuss a particular given theme or topic, where the interaction with the group leads to data and outcomes (Smithson, 2000; Hydén and Bülow, 2003). Their contrived nature is both their strength and their weakness: they are unnatural settings yet they are very focused on a particular issue and, therefore, will yield insights that might not otherwise have been available in a straightforward interview; they are economical on time, producing a large amount of data in a short period of time, but they tend to produce less data than interviews with the same number of individuals on a one-to-one basis (Hydén and Bülow, 2003: 19).

Focus groups (Morgan, 1988; Krueger, 1988; Bailey, 1994: 192–3; Robson, 2002: 284–5) are useful for:

- orientation to a particular field of focus;
- developing themes, topic and schedules flexibly for subsequent interviews and/or questionnaires;
- generating hypotheses that derive from the insights and data from the group;
- generating and evaluating data from different sub-groups of a population;
- gathering qualitative data;
- generating data quickly and at low cost;
- gathering data on attitudes, values and opinions;
- empowering participants to speak out, and in their own words;
- encouraging groups, rather than individuals, to voice opinions;
- encouraging non-literate participants;
- providing greater coverage of issues than would be possible in a survey;
- gathering feedback from previous studies.

Focus groups might be useful to triangulate with more traditional forms of interviewing, questionnaire, observation, etc. There are several issues to be addressed in running focus groups, for example (Morgan, 1988: 41–8):

- deciding the number of focus groups for a single topic (one group is insufficient, as the researcher will be unable to know whether the outcome is unique to the behaviour of the group);
- deciding the size of the group (too small and intra-group dynamics exert a disproportionate effect, too large and the group becomes unwieldy and hard to

manage; it fragments). Morgan (1988: 43) suggests between four and 12 people per group, whilst Fowler (2009: 117) suggests between six and eight people;

- how to allow for people not 'turning up' on the day. Morgan (1988: 44) suggests the need to over-recruit by as much as 20 per cent;

- taking extreme care with the sampling, so that every participant is the bearer of the particular characteristic required or that the group has homogeneity of background in the required area, otherwise the discussion will lose focus or become unrepresentative. Sampling is a major key to the success of focus groups;

- ensuring that participants have something to say and feel comfortable enough to say it;

- chairing the meeting so that a balance is struck between being too directive and veering off the point, i.e. keeping the meeting open-ended but to the point.

Newby (2010: 350–1) indicts that focus groups should be clear on the agenda and the focus, take place in a setting that is conducive to discussion, have a skilled moderator who can prompt people to speak, promote thinking and reflection, and should have a record kept.

Unlike group interviewing with children, discussed above, focus groups operate more successfully if they are composed of relative strangers rather than friends unless friendship, of course, is an important criterion for the focus (e.g. that the group will discuss something that is usually only discussed amongst friends).

Focus groups are not without their drawbacks. For example they tend not to yield numerical, quantifiable or generalizable data; the data may be difficult to analyse succinctly; the number of people involved tends to be small; they may yield less information than a survey; and the group dynamics may lead to non-participation by some members and dominance by others (e.g. status differentials may operate); the number of topics to be covered may be limited; intra-group disagreement and even conflicts may arise; inarticulate members may be denied a voice; the data may lack overall reliability. Further, Smithson (2000) suggests that there is a problem of only one voice being heard, particularly if there is a dominant member of the group, and for the group dynamics to suppress dissenting voices or different views on controversial topics, even though the group moderator may try to prevent this.

Although its potential is considerable, the focus group, as a particular kind of group interviewing, still has to find its way into educational circles to the extent that it has in other areas of life. Focus groups require skilful facilitation and management by the researcher.

21.10 Non-directive, focused, problem-centred and in-depth interviews

Originating from psychiatric and therapeutic fields with which it is most readily associated, the non-directive interview is characterized by a situation in which the respondent is responsible for initiating and directing the course of the encounter and for the attitudes she expresses in it (in contrast to the structured or research interview we have already considered, where the dominating role assumed by the interviewer results in, to use Kitwood's (1977) phrase, 'an asymmetry of commitment'). It has been shown to be a particularly valuable technique because it gets at the deeper attitudes and perceptions of the person being interviewed in such a way as to leave them free from interviewer bias. We shall examine briefly the characteristics of the therapeutic interview and then consider its usefulness as a research tool in the social and educational sciences.

The non-directive interview as it is currently understood grew out of the pioneering work of Freud and subsequent modifications to his approach by later analysts. His basic discovery was that if one can arrange a special set of conditions and have a patient talk about his difficulties in a certain way, behaviour changes of many kinds can be accomplished. The technique developed was used to elicit highly personal data from patients in such a way as to increase their self-awareness and improve their skills in self-analysis. By these means they became better able to help themselves. As Madge (1965) observes, it is these techniques which have greatly influenced contemporary interviewing techniques, especially those of a more penetrating and less quantitative kind.

The present-day therapeutic interview has its most persuasive advocate in Carl Rogers who has on different occasions testified to its efficacy. Basing his analysis on his own clinical studies, he has identified a sequence of characteristic stages in the therapeutic process, beginning with the client's decision to seek help. He is met by a counsellor who is friendly and receptive, but not didactic. The next stage is signalled when the client begins to give vent to hostile, critical and destructive feelings, which the counsellor accepts, recognizes and clarifies. Subsequently, and invariably, these antagonistic impulses are used up and give way to the first expressions of positive feeling. The counsellor likewise accepts these until suddenly and spontaneously 'insight and self-understanding come bubbling through' (Rogers, 1942). With insight comes the realization of possible courses of action and also the power to make decisions. It is in translating these into practical terms that the client frees himself from dependence on the counsellor.

Rogers (1945) subsequently identified a number of qualities in the interviewer which he deemed essential: that she bases her work on attitudes of acceptance and permissiveness; that she respects the client's responsibility for his own situation; that she permits the client to explain his problem in his own way; and that she does nothing that would in any way arouse the client's defences.

Such then are the principal characteristics of the non-directive interview technique in a therapeutic setting. But what of its usefulness as a purely research technique in societal and educational contexts? There are a number of features of the therapeutic interview which are peculiar to it and may well be inappropriate in other settings: for example, as we have seen, the interview is initiated by the respondent; his motivation is to obtain relief from a particular symptom; the interviewer is primarily a source of help, not a procurer of information; the actual interview is part of the therapeutic experience; the purpose of the interview is to change the behaviour and inner life of the person and its success is defined in these terms; and there is no restriction on the topics discussed.

A researcher has a different order of priorities, however, and what appear as advantages in a therapeutic context may be decided limitations when the technique is used for research purposes, even though she may be sympathetic to the spirit of the non-directive interview. As Madge (1965) explains, increasingly there are those 'who wish to retain the good qualities of the non-directive technique and at the same time are keen to evolve a method that is economical and precise enough to leave a residue of results rather than merely a posse of cured souls'.

One attempt to meet this need is to be found in a programme reported by Merton and Kendall (1946) in which the *focused interview* was developed. While seeking to follow closely the principle of non-direction, the method did introduce rather more interviewer control in the kinds of questions used and sought also to limit the discussion to certain parts of the respondent's experience.

The focused interview differs from other types of research interview in certain respects. These have been identified by Merton and Kendall (1946) as follows:

1 The persons interviewed are known to have been involved in a particular situation: they may, for example, have watched a TV programme; or seen a film; or read a book or article; or have been a participant in a social situation.

2 By means of the techniques of content analysis, elements in the situation which the researcher deems significant have previously been analysed by her. She has thus arrived at a set of hypotheses relating to the meaning and effects of the specified elements.

3 Using her analysis as a basis, the investigator constructs an interview guide. This identifies the major areas of enquiry and the hypotheses which determine the relevant data to be obtained in the interview.

4 The actual interview is focused on the subjective experiences of the people who have been exposed to the situation. Their responses enable the researcher both to test the validity of her hypotheses, and to ascertain unanticipated responses to the situation, thus giving rise to further hypotheses.

From this it can be seen that the distinctive feature of the focused interview is the prior analysis by the researcher of the situation in which subjects have been involved. The advantages of this procedure have been cogently explained by Merton and Kendall:

> Foreknowledge of the situation obviously reduces the task confronting the investigator, since the interview need not be devoted to discovering the objective nature of the situation. Equipped in advance with a content analysis, the interviewer can readily distinguish the objective facts of the case from the subjective definitions of the situation. He thus becomes alert to the entire field of 'selective response'. When the interviewer, through his familiarity with the objective situation, is able to recognize symbolic or functional silences, 'distortions', avoidances, or blockings, he is the more prepared to explore their implications.
>
> (Merton and Kendall, 1946: 541)

In the quest for what Merton and Kendall (1946) term 'significant data', the interviewer must develop the ability to evaluate continuously the interview while it is in progress. To this end, they established a set of criteria by which productive and unproductive interview material can be distinguished. Briefly, these are:

1 *Non-direction*: interviewer guidance should be minimal.

2 *Specificity*: respondents' definitions of the situation should find full and specific expression.

3 *Range and scope*: the interview should maximize

the range of evocative stimuli and responses reported by the subject.

4   *Depth and personal context*: the interview should bring out the affective and value-laden implications of the subjects' responses, to determine whether the experience has central or peripheral significance. It should elicit the relevant personal context, the idiosyncratic associations, beliefs and ideas.

Witzel (2000) advocates the use of the problem-centred interview for gathering objective evidence on human behaviour and subjective views on social phenomena. He indicates three principles underpinning the problem-centred interview:

- a 'problem-centred orientation' toward socially relevant problems (p. 2);
- methodological flexibility (e.g. group interviews, individual interviews, the biographical interview, structured and less structured interviews) in the 'object-orientation' (i.e. in order to address different kinds of problem) (p. 3);
- a 'process orientation', i.e. attempting to reconstruct the actions and orientations of the participant (p. 3).

The problem-centred interview, Witzel (2000) avers, can use: (a) a structured, *short questionnaire* at interview in order to gather factual data about the participants (e.g. age, sex, occupation, education); (b) an *interview schedule* (guidelines) in order to structure the interview, with lead questions; (c) *recording equipment* to ensure accuracy of the account and to avoid the interviewers having to take notes (i.e. able to concentrate on the discussion); and (d) a *postscript* (pp. 3–4), written directly after the interview, to contain reflections, key points, observations and interpretations.

The in-depth interview, as its name suggests, is conducted to explore issues, personal biographies, and what is meaningful to, or valued by, participants, how they feel about particular issues, how they look at particular issues, their attitudes, opinions and emotions (cf. Newby, 2010: 243–4). They tend to be semi-structured, to enable the course of the respondents' responses to dictate the direction of the interview, though the researcher also has an interview schedule to keep an interview on track, and may operate probes to enquire further into issues. They may feature in case studies, action research and, as the work of Ball (1990, 1994a, 1994b) and Bowe *et al.* (1992) testify, they may feature in interviewing powerful people and policy makers. On the other hand, they may be useful in gathering data from marginalized or stigmatized groups in society (Newby (2010: 243–4) gives the example of migrants and refugees). Given the intensive and extensive nature of these interviews, gaining access and permission may be difficult, not least as they may take time to conduct.

21.11 Telephone interviewing

We advise the reader to take this section in conjunction with Chapter 13 on telephone interviews in surveys. The use of telephone interviewing has long been recognized as an important method of data collection and is common practice in survey research, though, as Arksey and Knight (1999: 79) aver, telephone interviews do not feel like interviews, as both parties are deprived of several channels of communication and the establishment of a positive relationship (e.g. non-verbal). We explore this here. Dicker and Gilbert (1988), Nias (1991), Oppenheim (1992), Borg and Gall (1996), Shaughnessy *et al.* (2003) and Shuy (2003) suggest several attractions to telephone interviewing:

- It is sometimes cheaper and quicker than face-to-face interviewing.
- It enables researchers to select respondents from a much more dispersed population than if they have to travel to meet the interviewees.
- Travel costs are omitted.
- It is particularly useful for brief surveys.
- It may protect the anonymity of respondents more than a personal interview.
- It is useful for gaining rapid responses to a structured questionnaire.
- Monitoring and quality control are undertaken more easily since interviews are undertaken and administered centrally, indeed there are greater guarantees that the researcher actually carries out the interview as required.
- Interviewer effects are reduced.
- There is greater uniformity in the conduct of the interview and the standardization of questions.
- There is greater interviewer control of the interview.
- The results tend to be quantitative.
- They are quicker to administer than face-to-face interviews because respondents will only usually be prepared to speak on the telephone for, at most, 15 minutes.
- Callback costs are so slight as to enable frequent callbacks, enhancing reliability and contact.
- Many groups, particularly of busy people, can be reached at times more convenient to them than if a visit were to be made.
- They are safer to undertake than, for example, having to visit dangerous neighbourhoods.

- They can be used to collect sensitive data, as possible feelings of threat of face-to-face questions about awkward, embarrassing or difficult matters are absent.
- It does not rely on the literacy of the respondent (as, for example, in questionnaires).
- The use of the telephone may put a little pressure on the respondent to respond, and it is usually the interviewer rather than the interviewee who terminates the call.
- Response rate is higher than, for example, questionnaires.

More recently, the use of smartphones in interviewing has increased (Raento *et al.*, 2009), and is a powerful tool, as increasing numbers of people carry them around on a permanent basis and hence can be contacted easily, regardless of their location. Further, with increasing additional functionality, the smartphone offers a potentially powerful tool for researchers. Smartphones, the authors (Raento *et al.*, 2009: 428) aver, have the attraction of flexibility (many uses and computer-like functions on a single smartphone, e.g. video and image recording for (self-) documentation, and cost-efficiency; they enable easy access and relatively unobtrusive data collection as data can be collected in real time or stored (increasing ecological validity); and they enable high granularity of data to be gathered (p. 442)).

Taking forward the use of electronic media, James and Busher (2007) and James (2007) argue for the power of email interviewing as a qualitative method in educational research, as it enables the researcher to contact hard-to-reach groups (e.g. by virtue of practical constraints such as time and availability of both parties to meet face-to-face, location and travelling, geographical dispersion, disability and language or communication (James, 2007: 966)) (see also Bampton and Cowton, 2002). Indeed James and Busher (2007: 405) argue that email interviews can generate fuller, richer, more reflective, thoughtful and longer answers than telephone interviewing.

Email interviews also reduce transcription time as the email is already transcribed, and the interviewee, therefore, has the opportunity to check what data are being given, thereby overcoming the possibility of respondents in a face-to-face interview saying something they later wish to withdraw (Bampton and Cowton, 2002: 4). Whether or not the absence of face-to-face contact, the visibility of the participants and the absence of non-verbal cues increases or reduces reliability is a moot point (p. 969). Similarly, the researcher will need to make continual efforts to ensure that the respondent:

- keeps to the point;
- fully understands the nature, focus and purpose of the interview;
- knows the number of questions that will be asked (particularly if there are several email exchanges);
- knows that they should not delete previous emails that are part of the interview;
- knows the time frame in which to reply to an email (cf. James and Busher, 2006: 407–9).

Email interviews can be conducted synchronously, in real time, or asynchronously (James and Busher, 2006: 970) (the latter can afford the interviewee some time to consider his/her responses (Bampton and Cowton, 2002: 3), and they 'democratise narrative exchanges' between the interviewer and the respondent (p. 970) (though James and Busher (2007: 416) contest this latter point). That said, Bampton and Cowton (2002: 5) caution against bombarding the respondent with too many questions in a single interview; rather, they suggest, the questions could be spaced over more than one email. Further, they indicate the need to signal to the respondent when the email interview is nearing its close. E-interviewing is susceptible to technological problems (e.g. unstable connectivity, slow connections (particularly in video-conferencing) mailbox being full), and these must be explored before the e-interview is conducted.

Telephone interviewing is not as cut-and-dried as the claims made for it, as there are several potential problems with telephone interviewing, for example:

- It is very easy for respondents simply to hang up on the caller.
- Motivation to participate may be lower than for a personal interview.
- There is a chance of skewed sampling, as not all of the population have a telephone (often those lower income households – perhaps the very people that the researcher wishes to target) or can hear (e.g. the old and second language speakers in addition to those with hearing difficulties).
- There is a lower response rate at weekends.
- The standardized format of telephone interviews may prevent thoughtful or deep answers from being provided.
- Some people have a deep dislike of telephones, that sometimes extends to a phobia, and this inhibits their responses or willingness to participate.
- Respondents may not disclose information because of uncertainty about actual (even though promised) confidentiality.
- Respondents may come to snap judgements without

the adequate or deeper reflection necessary for a full answer to serious issues.

■ Respondents may not wish to spend a long time on the telephone, so telephone interviews tend to be briefer than other forms of interview.

■ Concentration spans are shorter than in a face-to-face interview.

■ The interviewer has to remain bright and focused, listen very carefully and respond – it is tiring.

■ Questions tend to be closed, fixed and simple.

■ There is a limit on the complexity of the questions that can be put.

■ Response categories must be very simple or else respondents will forget what they are.

■ Many respondents (up to 25 per cent (Oppenheim, 1992: 97)) will be 'ex-directory' and so their numbers will not be available in telephone directories.

■ Respondents may withhold important information or tell lies, as the non-verbal behaviour that frequently accompanies this is not witnessed by the interviewer.

■ It is often more difficult for complete strangers to communicate by telephone than face-to-face, particularly as non-verbal cues are absent.

■ Respondents are naturally suspicious (e.g. of the caller trying to sell a product).

■ One telephone might be shared by several people.

■ Some respondents feel that telephone interviews afford less opportunity for them to question or rebut the points made by the interviewer.

■ There may be distractions for the respondent (e.g. a television may be switched on, children may be crying, others may be present).

■ Responses are difficult to write down or record during the interview.

That said, Sykes and Hoinville (1985) and also Borg and Gall (1996) suggest that telephone interviewing reaches nearly the same proportion of many target populations as 'standard' interviews, that it obtains nearly the same rate of response, and produces comparable information to 'standard' interviews, sometimes at a fraction of the cost. The response rate issue is contested: Weisberg *et al.* (1996: 122) and Shuy (2003: 181) report lower response rates to telephone interviews.

Harvey (1988), Oppenheim (1992) and Miller (1995) consider that: (a) telephone interviews need careful arrangements for timing and duration (typically that they are shorter and quicker than face-to-face interviews) – a preliminary call may be necessary to fix a time for a longer call to be made; (b) the interviewer

will need to have ready careful prompts and probes, including more than usual closed questions and less complex questions, in case the respondent 'dries up' on the telephone; (c) both interviewer and interviewee need to be prepared in advance of the interview if its potential is to be realized; and that (d) sampling requires careful consideration, using, for example, random numbers or some form of stratified sample. In general, however, many of the issues from 'standard' forms of interviewing apply equally well to telephone interviewing. Further, Houtkoop-Steenstra and van den Bergh (2000) report that an agenda-based introduction (in which interviewers formulated their own introductions based on a small number of key words) is more effective in securing higher response rates than standardized, scripted introductions.

Face-to-face interviews may be more suitable than telephone interviews (Weisberg *et al.*, 1996: 122; Shuy, 2003: 179–82) if: (a) the interviewer wishes to address complex issues or sensitive questions; (b) a natural context might yield greater accuracy; (c) deeper and self-generated answers are sought (i.e. where the question does not frame the answer too strongly); (d) issues requiring probing, deep reflection and, thereby, a longer time is sought; (e) greater equality of power between interviewer and respondent is sought; (f) older, second language speakers and hearing-impaired respondents are being interviewed; (g) marginalized respondents are being sought.

It is not uncommon for telephone interviewing to be outsourced, and this might be an advantage or a disadvantage. On the one hand it takes pressure off the researcher, not only because of the time involved but also because a 15-minute telephone interview might be more exhausting than a 15-minute face-to-face interview, there being more social and non-verbal cues in face-to-face interaction. On the other hand in outsourced telephone interviews care has to be taken on standardization of the conduct of the interview, the content of questions, the entry of responses and, indeed, to check that the interviews have been done and response not simply fabricated.

In conducting telephone interviews it is important to consider several issues, for example:

1 Will the people have the information that you require? Who will you need to speak to on the telephone? If the person answering the call is not the most suitable person then you need to talk to somebody else.

2 There is a need to pilot the interview schedule and to prepare and train the telephonists, and to discover the difficult/sensitive/annoying/personal questions,

the questions over which the respondents hesitate and answer very easily; the questions that will need prompts and explanations.

3 Keep to the same, simple response categories for several questions, so that the respondents become used to these and keep in the same mindset for responding.

4 Keep personal details, if any, until the end of the interview, in order to reduce a sense of threat.

5 Keep to no more than, at the most, 35 questions, and to no more than, at the most, 15 minutes, and preferably ten minutes.

6 Clear with the respondents at the start of the interview that they have the time to answer and that they have the information sought (i.e. that they are suitable respondents). If they are not the most suitable respondents then ask if there is someone present on the premises who can answer the questions, or try to arrange callback times when the most suitable person can be reached. Ask to speak to the most suitable person.

7 Keep the terminology simple and to the point, avoiding jargon and confusion.

8 You should be able to tell the gender of the respondent by his or her voice, i.e. there may be no need to ask a particular question.

9 Keep the response categories very simple and use them consistently (e.g. a mark out of ten, 'strongly agree' to 'strongly disagree', a 1–5 scale, etc.);

10 Rather than asking direct personal questions (unless you are confident of an answer), e.g. about age, income, ask about groups (e.g. which age group do they fall into (and give the age groups) or income brackets (and give them)).

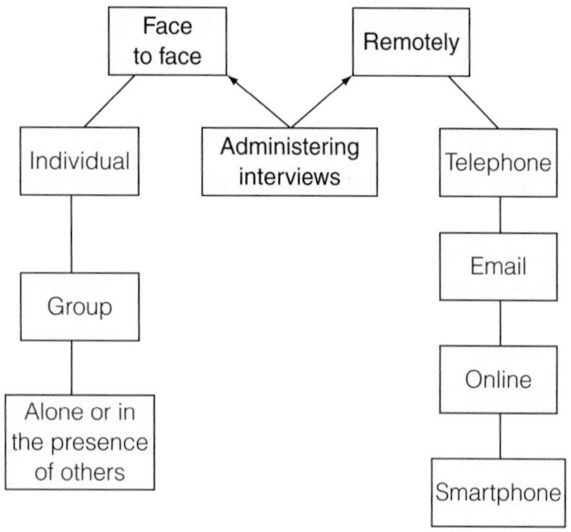

Telephone interviewing is a useful, but tricky art.

We sum up the different forms of administering interviews in Figure 21.1.

21.12 Ethical issues in interviewing

Interviews have an ethical dimension; they concern interpersonal interaction and produce information about the human condition. Though one can identify three main areas of ethical issues here – informed consent, confidentiality and the consequences of the interviews – these need to be 'unpacked' a little, as each is not unproblematic (Kvale, 1996: 111–20). For instance, who should give the informed consent (e.g. participants, their superiors), and for whom and what? How much information should be given, and to whom? What is legitimate private and public knowledge? How might the research help or harm the interviewees? Does the interviewer have a duty to point out the possible harmful consequences of the research data or will this illegitimately steer the interview?

It is difficult to lay down hard and fast ethical rules, as, by definition, ethical matters are contestable. Nevertheless it is possible to raise some ethical questions to which answers need to be given before the interviews commence:

■ Has the informed consent of the interviewees been gained?
■ Has this been obtained in writing or orally?
■ How much information should be given in advance of the study?
■ How can adequate information be provided if the study is exploratory?
■ Have the possible consequences of the research been made clear to the participants?
■ Has care been taken to prevent any harmful effects of the research to the participants (and to others)?
■ To what extent do any potential benefits outweigh the potential harm done by the research, and how justifiable is this for conducting the research?
■ How will the research benefit the participants?
■ Who will benefit from the research?
■ To what extent is there reciprocity between what participants give to and receive from the research?
■ Have confidentiality, anonymity, non-identifiability and non-traceability been guaranteed? Should participants' identities be disguised?
■ How do Data Protection Acts and laws operate in interview situations?

FIGURE 21.1 Methods of administering interviews

- Who will have access to the data?
- What has been done to ensure that the interview is conducted in an appropriate, non-stressful, non-threatening, manner?
- How will the data and transcriptions be verified, and by whom?
- Who will see the results of the research? Will some parts be withheld? Who own the data? At what stage does ownership of the data pass from interviewees to interviewers? Are there rights of veto for what appears? To whom should sensitive data be made available (e.g. should interview data on child abuse or drug taking be made available with or without consent to parents and the police)?
- How far should the researcher's own agenda and views predominate? What if the researcher makes a different interpretation from the interviewee? Should the interviewees be told, even if they have not asked for these interpretations?

These issues, by no means an exhaustive list, are not exclusive to the research interview, though they are highly applicable here. For further reading on ethical issues we refer readers to Chapter 5. The personal safety of interviewers must also be addressed: it may be important, for example, for the interviewer to be accompanied, to leave details of where he or she is going, to take a friend, to show identification, to take a mobile phone, to reconnoitre the neighbourhood, to learn how to behave with fierce dogs, to use the most suitable transport. It is perhaps a sad indictment on society that these considerations have to be addressed, but they do.

For further information on interviewing we refer the reader to the following websites:

www.bera.ac.uk/data-collection-interviews-in-research/
http://fds.oup.com/www.oup.co.uk/
    pdf/0-19-874204-5chap15.pdf
www.edu.plymouth.ac.uk/resined/interviews/inthome.
    htm
http://libraries.uta.edu/dillard/subfiles/SocWSocSciInter-
    viewingBib.htm
http://pareonline.net/getvn.asp?v=5&n=12
www.eric.ed.gov/ERICDocs/data/ericdocs2sql/content_
    storage_01/0000019b/80/27/f2/8d.pdf
www.utexas.edu/academic/diia/assessment/iar/research/
    plan/method/interview.php
www.public.asu.edu/~ifmls/artinculturalcontextsfolder/
    qualintermeth.html
www.public.asu.edu/~kroel/www500/Interview%20Fri.
    pdf
www.sasked.gov.sk.ca/docs/social/psych30/support_
    materials/research_methods.htm
www.sociology.org.uk/methfi.pdf
www.gerardkeegan.co.uk/resource/interviewmeth1.htm
http://owl.english.purdue.edu/owl/resource/559/06/
http://owl.english.purdue.edu/owl/resource/559/04/
www.vanuatu.usp.ac.fj/student_resources/Resources_
    Main/interviews.html
http://managementhelp.org/evaluatn/intrview.htm
http://ppa.aces.uiuc.edu/KeyInform.htm
www.scu.edu.au/schools/gcm/ar/arp/iview.html

 Companion Website

The companion website to the book includes PowerPoint slides for this chapter, which list the structure of the chapter and then provide a summary of the key points in each of its sections. In addition there is further information in the form of an example of interviewing and interview transcripts. These resources can be found online at **www.routledge.com/textbooks/cohen7e**.

Accounts

This short chapter introduces accounts in educational research. It can be taken in conjunction with Chapter 31 on discourses. This chapter proceeds in several stages:

- characteristics of the ethogenic approach
- characteristics of accounts and episodes
- procedures in eliciting, analysing and authenticating accounts
- network analysis
- discourse analysis
- analysing social episodes
- account gathering in educational research
- problems in gathering and analysing accounts
- an introduction to handling quantitative and qualitative accounts
- strengths and weaknesses of ethogenic approaches
- a note on stories

In discussing these points we provide worked examples for clarification. We recognize that the field of language and language use is vast, and to try to do justice to it here is the 'optimism of ignorance' (Edwards, 1976). Rather, we attempt to indicate some important ways in which researchers can use accounts in collecting data for their research.

22.1 Introduction

Accounts focus on language in context. Their study can range from speech acts (Austin, 1962) and ethnomethodology (Garfinkel, 1967) to conversation analysis and discourse analysis (Wooffitt, 1993). Accounts include descriptive, analytic and explanatory features of language, be it in everyday language or the language used in extreme cases. Accounts feature language in action and talk as a 'form of, and a vehicle for, social action' (Wooffitt, 1993: 303).

The rationale of much of this chapter is located in the interpretive, ethnographic paradigm which strives to view situations through the eyes of participants, to catch their intentionality and their interpretations of frequently complex situations, their meaning systems and the dynamics of the interaction as it unfolds. This is akin to the notion of 'thick description' from Geertz (1973).

Although each of us sees the world from our own point of view, we have a way of speaking about our experiences which we share with those around us. Explaining our behaviour towards one another can be thought of as accounting for our actions in order to make them intelligible and justifiable to our fellow beings. Thus, saying 'I'm terribly sorry, I didn't mean to bump into you', is a simple case of the explication of social meaning, for by locating the bump outside any planned sequence and neutralizing it by making it intelligible in such a way that it is not warrantable, it ceases to be offensive in that situation (Harré, 1978).

Accounting for actions in those larger slices of life called social episodes is the central concern of a participatory psychology which focuses upon actors' intentions, their beliefs about what sorts of behaviour will enable them to reach their goals and their awareness of the rules that govern those behaviours. Studies carried out within this framework have been termed 'ethogenic', an adjective which expresses a view of the human being as a person, that is, a plan-making, self-monitoring agent, aware of goals and deliberately considering the best ways to achieve them. Ethogenic studies represent another approach to the study of social behaviour and their methods stand in bold contrast to those commonly employed in much of the educational research which we describe in Chapters 1–3. Before discussing the elicitation and analysis of accounts we need to outline the ethogenic approach in more detail. This we do by reference to the work of one of its foremost exponents, Rom Harré (1974, 1976, 1977a, 1977b, 1978).

22.2 The ethogenic approach

Harré (1978) identifies five main principles in the ethogenic approach. They are set out in Box 22.1.

BOX 22.1   PRINCIPLES IN THE ETHOGENIC APPROACH

1   An explicit distinction is drawn between *synchronic analysis*, that is, the analysis of social practices and institutions as they exist at any one time, and *diachronic analysis*, the study of the stages and the processes by which social practices and institutions are created and abandoned, change and are changed. Neither type of analysis can be expected to lead directly to the discovery of universal social psychological principles or laws.

2   In social interactions, it is assumed that action takes place through endowing intersubjective entities with meaning; the ethogenic approach therefore concentrates upon the *meaning system*, that is, the whole sequence by which a social act is achieved in an episode. Consider, for example, the action of a kiss in the particular episodes of (a) leaving a friend's house; (b) the passing-out parade at St Cyr; and (c) the meeting in the garden of Gethsemane.

3   The ethogenic approach is concerned with speech which accompanies action. That speech is intended to make the action intelligible and justifiable in occurring at the time and the place it did in the whole sequence of unfolding and coordinated action. Such speech is *accounting*. In so far as accounts are socially meaningful, it is possible to derive *accounts of accounts*.

4   The ethogenic approach is founded upon the belief that human beings tend to be the kind of individuals their language, their traditions, their tacit and explicit knowledge tell them they are.

5   The skills that are employed in ethogenic studies therefore make use of commonsense understandings of the social world. As such the activities of the poet and the playwright offer the ethogenic researcher a better model than those of the physical scientist.

Source: Adapted from Harré, 1978

22.3 Characteristics of accounts and episodes

The discussion of accounts and episodes that now follows develops some of the ideas contained in the principles of the ethogenic approach outlined above.

We have already noted that accounts must be seen within the context of social episodes. The idea of an episode is a fairly general one. The concept itself may be defined as any coherent fragment of social life. Being a natural division of life, an episode will often have a recognizable beginning and end, and the sequence of actions that constitute it will have some meaning for the participants. Episodes may thus vary in duration and reflect innumerable aspects of life. A student entering primary school at seven and leaving at 11 would be an extended episode. A two-minute television interview with a political celebrity would be another. The contents of an episode which interest the ethogenic researcher include not only the perceived behaviour such as gesture and speech, but also the thoughts, the feelings and the intentions of those taking part. And the 'speech' that accounts for those thoughts, feelings and intentions must be conceived of in the widest connotation of the word. Thus, accounts may be personal records of the events we experience in our day-to-day lives, our conversations with neighbours, our letters to friends, our entries in diaries. Accounts serve to explain our past, present and future oriented actions.

Providing that accounts are authentic, it is argued, there is no reason why they should not be used as scientific tools in explaining people's actions.

22.4 Procedures in eliciting, analysing and authenticating accounts: an example

The account-gathering method proposed by Brown and Sime (1977) is summarized in Box 22.2. It involves attention to informants, the account-gathering situation, the transformation of accounts and researchers' accounts, and sets out control procedures for each of these elements.

Problems of eliciting, analysing and authenticating accounts are further illustrated in the following outlines of two educational studies. The first is concerned with valuing among older boys and girls; the second is to do with the activities of pupils and teachers in using computers in primary classrooms.

Kitwood (1977) developed an experience-sampling method, that is, a qualitative technique for gathering and analysing accounts based upon tape-recorded interviews that were themselves prompted by the 15 situations listed in Box 22.3.

BOX 22.2 ACCOUNT GATHERING

Research strategy	*Control procedure*
1 INFORMANTS	
Definition of episode and role groups representing domain of interest	rationale for choice of episode and role groups
Identification of exemplars	degree of involvement of potential informants
Selection of individual informants	contact with individuals to establish motive for participation, competence and performance
2 ACCOUNT-GATHERING SITUATION	
Establishing venue	contextual effects of venue
Recording the account	appropriateness and accuracy in documenting account
Controlling relevance of account	accounts agenda
Authenticating account	negotiation and internal consistency
Establishing role of interviewer and interviewee	degree of direction
Post account authentication	corroboration
3 TRANSFORMATION OF ACCOUNTS	
Provision of working documents	transcription reliability; coder reliability
Data reduction techniques	appropriateness of statistical and content analyses
4 RESEARCHERS' ACCOUNTS	
Account of the account summary, overview, interpretation	description of research operations
	explanatory scheme and theoretical background

Source: Brown and Sime, 1981: 163

BOX 22.3 EXPERIENCE-SAMPLING METHOD

Below are listed 15 types of situation which most people have been in at some time. Try to think of something that has happened in your life in the last year or so, or perhaps something that keeps on happening, which fits into each of the descriptions. Then choose the ten of them which deal with the things that seem to you to be most important, which cover your main interests and concerns, and the different parts of your life. When we meet we will talk together about the situations you have chosen. Try beforehand to remember as clearly as you can what happened, what you and others did, and how you yourself felt and thought. Be as definite as you can. If you like, write a few notes to help you keep the situation in mind.

1 When there was a misunderstanding between you and someone else (or several others)...
2 When you got on really well with people...
3 When you had to make an important decision...
4 When you discovered something new about yourself...
5 When you felt angry, annoyed or resentful...
6 When you did what was expected of you...
7 When your life changed direction in some way...
8 When you felt you had done something well...
9 When you were right on your own, with hardly anyone taking your side...
10 When you 'got away with it', or were not found out...
11 When you made a serious mistake...
12 When you felt afterwards that you had done right...
13 When you were disappointed with yourself...
14 When you had a serious clash or disagreement with another person...
15 When you began to take seriously something that had not mattered much to you before...

Source: Adapted from Kitwood, 1977

Because the experience-sampling method avoids interrogation, the material which emerges is less organized than that obtained from a tightly structured interview. Successful handling of individual accounts therefore requires the researcher to know the interview content extremely well and to work toward the gradual emergence of tentative interpretive schemata which he then modifies, confirms or falsifies as the research continues. Kitwood (1977) identifies eight methods for dealing with the tape-recorded accounts. Methods 1–4 are fairly close to the approach adopted in handling questionnaires; and Methods 5–8 are more in tune with the ethogenic principles that we identified earlier:

1 *The total pattern of choice* The frequency of choice of various items permits some surface generalizations about the participants, taken as a group. The most revealing analyses may be those of the least and most popular items.

2 *Similarities and differences* Using the same technique as in Method 1, it is possible to investigate similarities and differences within the total sample of accounts according to some characteristic(s) of the participants such as age, sex, level of educational attainment, etc.

3 *Grouping items together* It may be convenient for some purposes to fuse together categories that cover similar subject matter. For example, items 1, 5 and 14 in Box 22.3 relate to conflict; items 4, 7 and 15, to personal growth and change.

4 *Categorization of content* The content of a particular item is inspected for the total sample and an attempt is then made to develop some categories into which all the material will fit. The analysis is most effective when two or more researchers work in collaboration, each initially proposing a category system independently and then exchanging views to negotiate a final category system.

5 *Tracing a theme* This type of analysis transcends the rather artificial boundaries which the items themselves imply. It aims to collect as much data as possible relevant to a particular topic regardless of where it occurs in the interview material. The method is exacting because it requires very detailed knowledge of content and may entail going through taped interviews several times. Data so collected may be further analysed along the lines suggested in Method 4 above.

6 *The study of omissions* The researcher may well have expectations about the kind of issues likely to occur in the interviews. When some of these are absent, that fact may be highly significant. The absence of an anticipated topic should be explored to discover the correct explanation of its omission.

7 *Reconstruction of a social lifeworld* This method can be applied to the accounts of a number of people who have part of their lives in common, for example, a group of friends who go around together. The aim is to attempt some kind of reconstruction of the world which the participants share in analysing the fragmentary material obtained in an interview. The researcher seeks to understand the dominant modes of orienting to reality, the conceptions of purpose and the limits to what is perceived.

8 *Generating and testing hypotheses* New hypotheses may occur to the researcher during the analysis of the tape-recordings. It is possible to do more than simply advance these as a result of tentative impressions; one can loosely apply the hypothetico-deductive method to the data. This involves putting the hypothesis forward as clearly as possible, working out what the verifiable inferences from it would logically be, and testing these against the account data. Where these data are too fragmentary, the researcher may then consider what kind of evidence and method of obtaining it would be necessary for more thorough hypothesis testing. Subsequent sets of interviews forming part of the same piece of research might then be used to obtain relevant data.

In the light of the weaknesses in account gathering and analysis (discussed later), Kitwood's (1977) suggestions of safeguards are worth mentioning. First he calls for cross-checking between researchers as a precaution against consistent but unrecognized bias in the interviews themselves. Second he recommends member tests, that is, taking hypotheses and unresolved problems back to the participants themselves or to people in similar situations to them for their comments. Only in this way can researchers be sure that they understand the participants' own grounds for action. Since there is always the possibility that an obliging participant will readily confirm the researcher's own speculations, every effort should be made to convey to the participant that one wants to know the truth as he or she sees it, and that one is as glad to be proved wrong as right.

A study by Blease and Cohen (1990) used cross-checking as a way of validating the classroom observation records of co-researchers, and member tests to authenticate both quantitative and qualitative data derived from teacher and pupil informants. Thus, in the case of cross-checking, the classroom observation schedules of research assistants and researchers were compared and discussed, to arrive at definitive accounts of the range and duration of specific computer activities occurring within observation sessions. Member tests arose when interpretations of interview data were taken back to participating teachers for their comments. Similarly, pupils' scores on certain self-concept scales were discussed individually with respondents in order to ascertain why children awarded themselves high or low marks in respect of a range of skills in using computer programs.

22.5 Network analysis

Accounts are given and are about social contexts and the behaviour of people in them. It is important, then, to identify the contexts of accounts and the agentic, intentional behaviours of actors in them and the constraints under which they are operating: the macro-micro-link of sociology.

A technique that has been successfully employed here in the analysis of qualitative data is described by its originators as 'systematic network analysis' (Bliss *et al.*, 1983). Drawing upon developments in artificial intelligence, Bliss and her colleagues employed the concept of 'relational network' to represent the content and structuring of a person's knowledge of a particular domain.

Since the early work of Bliss *et al.* (1983), network analysis has taken off dramatically with the arrival of the internet and social networking sites. The work of Barabási (2002), Buchanan (2003) and Watts (2003) draws attention to the essential connectedness of humans in different social contexts. This was inspired in part by the 'small world' experiment of Milgram (Travers and Milgram, 1969) and his findings that many people are connected by only six degrees of separation (number of links in the chain of 'who-knows-whom' or 'who has worked with whom'). It has also been inspired by early work in sociometry (e.g. Moreno, 1934, 1960; Hoffman, 2001) on the measurement of the strength of social relations, e.g. which people are chosen by many others as would-be friends ('stars'), which pairs choose each other ('dyads'), which three people choose each other ('triads'), which people make no choices and are not chosen ('ghosts'), which people are not chosen by anyone ('isolates'), and which people choose others, who then choose others, but these choices are not reciprocated ('chains') (see Figure 22.1).

Indeed internet search engines use 'hubs' as major organizing and searching principles. The advent of social networking has been brought into the educational arena with teachers and students contacting each other synchronously and asynchronously through networking sites, for academic discussion, discussion threads, professional development, blogs, e-portfolios and a host of other communications (see also www.leeds.ac.uk/bei/COLN/COLN_default.html for recent conference

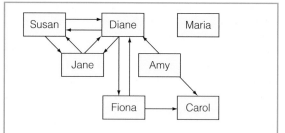

Diane is a 'star' (chosen by many people).
Diane and Fiona are a 'dyad' (a pair who choose each other).
Susan, Diane and Jane are a 'triad' (three people who choose each other).
Amy → Diane → Fiona → Carol are a 'chain' (choices are made that link people, but which are not necessarily reciprocated).
Amy is an 'isolate' (chooses but is not chosen).
Maria is a 'ghost' (does not choose and is not chosen).

FIGURE 22.1 A sociogram in sociometry

papers on networking in educational research). A search of the ERIC database at the time of writing (www.eric.ed.gov/) produced over 1,000 references to social networking papers, articles, dissertations, etc.

Essentially, network analysis involves the development of a system of categories by way of classifying qualitative data and preserving the essential complexity and subtlety of the materials under investigation. A notational technique is employed to generate network-like structures that show the interdependencies of the categories as they are developed. More recently, network analysis has involved the identification of key actors and their connectedness to other key actors ('nodes'), their own circles of contacts ('egos'), and their influence on the behaviour of other actors ('alters'). In the internet community, social networking sites such as Facebook, MySpace, Twitter and LinkedIn are enabling individuals and groups to connect with each other in ways, and at speeds, never previously imagined or possible. Analysing and understanding these is a breakthrough topic in social and educational research.

Network mapping is akin to cognitive mapping,[1] an example of which can be seen in the work of Bliss *et al.* (1983). The arrival of computer packages such as UCINET and StOCNET to analyse and present social networks is reviewed in Knoke and Yang (2008).

Knoke and Yang (2008) indicate that a principle underpinning networks is that there are 'structural regularities' (regular patterns) (p. 4) in social relations between entities (defined as individuals, groups, organizations, etc.), and that these macro-structural relations influence people's agentic decisions, actions, values and behaviours. Network analysis is an attempt to measure and chart these (e.g. through graphic means). The authors argue that these relations are more powerful in explaining behaviours than are, for example, conventional categories such as age, sex, values, class, status (pp. 4–5), and that these relations are context-specific and dynamic, i.e. we behave in one way in one context and another way in another context (p. 5), hence it is important to identify the context in which social relations occur. As with complexity theory (see Chapter 1), the whole cannot be explained simply as the sum of its parts, it has its own identity and properties – a social network – which is different from simply being an aggregate of the individuals within it. This, the authors aver (p. 9), enables explanations to be given of variations in structural relations, in individual, agentic behaviour, and in linking macro- and micro-levels of analysis. In other words, individuals shape social networks but are also shaped by them.

Knoke and Yang (2008: 6–7) suggest that there are two main elements of networks: the *actors* (members of the social network, units, e.g. individuals or collective groups and organizations, associations, parties) and *relations* (kinds of connections, e.g. dyads, triads (see above: sociometry) which may be one way ('directed') or two-way (mutual': 'nondirected')). Together actors and relations give rise to social networks which have their own features (which are different from the sum of the constituent elements). They also comprise nodes (key members) and ties (connections, which may be strong to weak, directed or nondirected), and which are contingent on the social sphere in which they are set, e.g. a network of friends may be different from a network of employees in an organization. A network analysis, then, involves identifying vectors: nodes and actors that have strength/magnitude and direction of connections.

Researching social networks, then, involves identifying (Knoke and Yang, 2008):

- The units: the actors.
- The 'relational form': (a) the dyads, triads, stars, chains, etc.; (b) the nature of the relationship (e.g. subordinate, superordinate competitive, cooperative, harmonious, conflictual); (c) the strength, intensity and frequency of the relationship (p. 11).
- The relational content: (a) the purposes, motives and interests of actors, which influence their behaviour and interaction; (b) the substance of the relationship, e.g. the context in which the relationship is being constructed, such as friends to whom to turn for per-

sonal support ('friendship': p. 11), or people to turn to for professional, work-related advice ('mentors').
- The 'type of tie' (p. 11): this concerns the field of the relationship, e.g. a political network, a social network, a professional network, a personal network.
- The 'level of data analysis' (pp. 13–15): individual ('egocentric network'); dyadic (as defined above); triadic (as defined above); 'complete network' (the macro-level). Knoke and Yang (2008: 14) stress that each level of analysis has to be conducted in its own terms, i.e. as in complexity theory, a level of analysis cannot be explained solely or completely by the elements of analysis from a lower level.

Knoke and Yang (2008: 12) set out a typology of relations, including: transactions (giving and receiving of actual or symbolic gifts); communications (media through which messages are given and received); boundary penetration (two or more networks involved simultaneously); instrumental (to secure something desired); sentiment (feelings towards others); authority/power (rights to give or receive orders); and kinship and descent (family or blood ties and relations).

There are several ways of portraying social networks, for example sociograms (Figure 22.1), or graphic displays that identify different strengths or types of relationship (Figure 22.2).

Knoke and Yang (2008) also suggest a range of other methods of display and measures, including matrices (p. 49), relationship measures (p. 51), directional and non-directional graphs (pp. 56–62), measures of centrality and prestige of participants (actors) (pp. 62–72), cliques (pp. 72–6), structural equivalence (pp. 76–9), visual displays (e.g. dendrograms) (pp. 79–85), and block models (pp. 85–91) and we refer the reader to these.

Bliss *et al.* (1983) point out that there cannot be one overall account of criteria for judging the merits of a particular network. They do, however, attempt to identify a number of factors that ought to feature in any

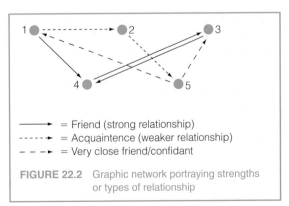

FIGURE 22.2 Graphic network portraying strengths or types of relationship

discussion of the standards by which a network might fairly be judged as adequate.

First, any system of description needs to be valid and reliable: valid in the sense that it is appropriate in kind and, within that kind, sufficiently complete and faithful; reliable in the sense that there exists an acceptable level of agreement between people as to how to use the network system to describe data.

Second, there are properties that a network description should possess such as clarity, completeness and self-consistency. These relate to a further criterion of 'network utility', the sufficiency of detail contained in a particular network. A third property that a network should possess is termed 'learnability'. Communicating the terms of the analysis to others, say the authors, is of central importance. It follows therefore that much hinges on whether networks are relatively easy or hard to teach to others. A fourth aspect of network acceptability has to do with its 'testability'. Bliss *et al.* (1983) identify two forms of testability, the first having to do with testing a network as a 'theory' against data, the second with testing data against a 'theory' or expectation via a network.

Finally, the terms 'expressiveness' and 'persuasiveness' refer to qualities of language used in developing the network structure. And here, the authors proffer the following advice. 'Helpful as the choice of an expressive coding mood or neat use of indentation or brackets may be, *the code actually says no more than the network distinguishes'* (our italics).

To conclude, network analysis has a growing role to play in educational research by providing a technique for dealing with the bulk and the complexity of the accounts that are typically generated in qualitative studies, and for using social networks to identify key players and their influence in groups and organizations. Social network analysis is often highly structured and the consequence of structured questions such as 'from such-and-such [e.g. a class, a group] a group of people, who would you go to for advice on such-and-such [e.g. professional, personal advice]?' or 'from such-and-such [e.g. a class, a group] a group of people, who would you say is your professional colleague with whom you can share your professional concerns?'. For advice on software analysis of social networks, we refer the reader to Knoke and Yang (2008).

22.6 Discourse analysis

Discourse researchers explore the organization of ordinary talk and everyday explanations and the social actions performed in them. Collecting, transcribing and analysing discourse data constitutes a kind of psycho-logical 'natural history' of the phenomena in which discourse analysts are interested (Edwards and Potter, 1993). Discourses can be regarded as sets of linguistic material that are coherent in organization and content and enable people to construct meaning in social contexts (Coyle, 1995: 245). The emphasis on the *construction* of meaning indicates the action perspective of discourse analysis (*ibid.*).

Further, the focus on discourse and speech acts links this style of research to Habermas's critical theory set out at the start of this book. Habermas argues that utterances are never simply sentences (Habermas, 1970: 368) that are disembodied from context, but, rather, their meaning derives from the intersubjective contexts in which they are set. A speech situation has a double structure, the propositional content (the locutionary aspect – what is being said) and the performatory content (the illocutionary and perlocutionary aspect – what is being done or achieved through the utterance). For Habermas (1979, 1984) each utterance has to abide by the criteria of legitimacy, truth, rightness, sincerity and comprehensibility. His concept of the 'ideal speech situation' argues that speech and – for our purposes here – discourse, should seek to be empowering and not subject to repression or ideological distortion. His ideal speech situation is governed by several principles, not the least of which are: mutual understanding between participants, freedom to enter a discourse, an equal opportunity to use speech acts, discussion to be free from domination, the movement towards consensus resulting from the discussion alone and the force of the argument alone (rather than the position power of speakers). For Habermas, then, discourse analysis would seek to uncover, through ideology critique (see Chapter 2) the repressive forces which 'sytematically distort' communication. For our purposes, we can take from Habermas the need to expose and interrogate the dominatory influences that not only thread through the discourses which researchers are studying, but the discourses that the research itself produces.

Recent developments in discourse analysis have made important contributions to our understanding of children's thinking, challenging views (still common in educational circles) of 'the child as a lone organism, constructing a succession of general models of the world as each new stage is mastered' (Edwards, 1991). Rather than treating children's language as representative of an inner cognitive world to be explored experimentally by controlling for a host of intruding variables, discourse analysts treat that language as action, as 'situated discursive practice'.

By way of example, Edwards (1993) explores discourse data emanating from a visit to a greenhouse by five-year-old pupils and their teacher, to see plants

---

BOX 22.4   CONCEPTS IN CHILDREN'S TALK

81	*Sally*	Cuttings can grow to plants.
82	*Teacher*	[*writing*] 'Cuttings can grow –', instead of saying 'to
83		plants', you can say 'grow,=*in*: to plants'.
84	*Sally*	= You wrote Christina.
85	*Teacher*	Oops. Thank you. I'll do this again. 'Cuttings can
86		grow into plants'. That's also good. What is a cutting,
87		Christina?
88	*Christina*	A cutting is, umm, I don't know.
89	*Teacher*	Who knows what a cutting is besides Sally? Sam.
90	*Sam*	It's when you cut off a –, it's when you cut off a piece
91		of a plant.
92	*Teacher*	Exactly, and when you cut off a piece of a plant, what do
93		you then do with it to make it grow? If you leave
94		It –,
95	*X*	Put it in soil.
96	*Teacher*	Well, sometimes you can put it in soil.
97	*Y*	And plant it,
98	*Teacher*	But what –, wait, what else could you put it in?
99	*Sam*	Put it in a pot?
100	*Teacher*	Pot, with soil, or…? There's another way.
101	*Sally*	I know another way. =
102	*Teacher*	= Wait. Sam, do you know? No? =
103	*Sam*	= Dirt.
104	*Teacher*	No, it doesn't have to do with s –, it's not a solid, it's
105		a liquid. What liquid –,
106	*Meredith*	Water.
107	*Teacher*	Right. […]

Source: Edwards, 1993

---

being propagated and grown. His analysis shows how children take understandings of adults' meanings from the words they hear and the situations in which those words are used. And in turn, adults (in this case, the teacher) take from pupils' talk, not only what they might mean but also what they could and should mean. What Edwards describes as 'the discursive appropriation of ideas' (Edwards 1991) is illustrated in Box 22.4.

Discourse analysis requires a careful reading and interpretation of textual material, with interpretation being supported by the linguistic evidence. The inferential and interactional aspects of discourse and discourse analysis suggest the need for the researcher to be highly sensitive to the nuances of language (Coyle, 1995: 247). In discourse analysis, as in qualitative data analysis generally (Miles and Huberman, 1984) the researcher can use coding at an early stage of analysis, assigning codes to the textual material being studied

(Parker, 1992; Potter and Wetherell, 1987). This enables the researcher to discover patterns and broad areas in the discourse. With this achieved the researcher can then re-examine the text to discover intentions, functions and consequences of the discourse (examining the speech act functions of the discourse, e.g. to impart information, to persuade, to accuse, to censure, to encourage, etc.). By seeking *alternative explanations* and the *degree of variability* in the discourse, it is possible to rule out rival interpretations and arrive at a fair reading of what was actually taking place in the discourse in its social context.

The application of discourse analysis to our understanding of classroom learning processes is well exemplified in a study by Edwards and Mercer (1987). Rather than taking the classroom talk as evidence of children's thought processes, the researchers explore it as 'contextualized dialogue with the teacher. The discourse itself is the educational reality and the issue becomes that of examining how teacher and children construct a shared account, a common interpretative framework for curriculum knowledge and for what happens in the classroom' (Edwards, 1991).

Overriding asymmetries between teachers and pupils, Edwards concludes, both cognitive (in terms of knowledge) and interactive (in terms of power), impose different discursive patterns and functions. Indeed Edwards (1980) suggests that teachers control classroom talk very effectively, reproducing asymmetries of power in the classroom by telling the students when to talk, what to talk about, and how well they have talked.

Discourse analysis has been criticized for its lack of systematicity (Coyle, 1995: 256), for its emphasis on the linguistic construction of a social reality, and the impact of the analysis in shifting attention away from what is being analysed and towards the analysis itself, i.e. the risk of losing the independence of phenomena. Discourse analysis risks reifying discourse. One must not lose sight of the fact that the discourse analysis, itself, is a text, a discourse, that in turn can be analysed for its meaning and inferences, rendering the need for reflexivity to be high (Ashmore, 1989).[2]

Edwards and Westgate (1987) show what substantial strides have been made in recent years in the development of approaches to the investigation of classroom dialogue. Some methods encourage participants to talk; others wait for talk to emerge and sophisticated audio/video techniques record the result by whatever method it is achieved. Thus captured, dialogue is reviewed, discussed and reflected upon; moreover, that reviewing, discussing and reflecting is usually undertaken by researchers. It is they, generally, who read 'between the lines' and 'within the gaps' of classroom talk by way of interpreting the intentionality of the participating discussants (O'Neill and McMahon, 1990).

22.7 Analysing social episodes

A major problem in the investigation of that natural unit of social behaviour, the 'social episode', has been the ambiguity that surrounds the concept itself and the lack of an acceptable taxonomy by which to classify an interaction sequence on the basis of empirically quantifiable characteristics. Several quantitative studies have been undertaken in this field. For example Magnusson (1971), Ekehammer and Magnusson (1973) and McQuitty (1957) use factor analysis and linkage analysis respectively, whilst Forgas (1976, 1978), Peevers and Secord (1973) and Secord and Peevers (1974) use multidimensional scaling and cluster analysis.

22.8 Account gathering in educational research: an example

The 'free commentary' method that Secord and Peevers (1974) recommend as a way of probing for explanations of people's behaviour lies at the very heart of the ethnographer's skills. In the example of ethnographic research that now follows, one can detect the attempt of the researcher to get below the surface data and to search for the deeper, hidden patterns that are only revealed when attention is directed to the ways that group members interpret the flow of events in their lives.

Heath – 'Questioning at home and at school' (1982)

Heath's study of misunderstandings existing between black children and their white teachers in classrooms in the south of the United States brought to light teachers' assumptions that pupils would respond to language routines and the uses of language in building knowledge and skills just as other children (including their own) did (Heath, 1982). Specifically, she sought to understand why these particular children did *not* respond just as others did. Her research involved eliciting explanations from both the children's parents and teachers. 'We don't talk to our children like you folks do', the parents observed when questioned about their children's behaviour. Those children, it seemed to Heath, were not regarded as information givers or as appropriate conversational partners for adults. That is not to say that the children were excluded from language participation. They did, in fact, participate in a language that Heath describes as rich in styles, speakers and topics. Rather, it seemed to the researcher that the teachers' characteristic mode of questioning was 'to pull attributes of things out of context, particularly out of the context of books and name them – queens, elves, police, red apples' (Heath, 1982). The parents did *not* ask these kinds of questions of their children, and the children themselves had their own ways of deflecting such questions, as the example in Box 22.5 well illustrates.

Heath elicited both parents' and teachers' accounts of the children's behaviour and their apparent communication 'problems' (see Box 22.6). Her account of accounts arose out of periods of participation and observation in classrooms and in some of the teachers' homes. In particular, she focused upon the ways in which 'the children learned to use language to satisfy their needs, ask questions, transmit information, and convince those around them that they were competent communicators' (Heath, 1982). This involved her in a much wider and more intensive study of the total fabric

---

BOX 22.5 'AIN'T NOBODY CAN TALK ABOUT THINGS BEING ABOUT THEIRSELVES'

This comment by a nine-year-old boy was directed to his teacher when she persisted in interrogating him about the story he had just completed in his reading group.

Teacher: What is the story about?
Children: (*silence*)
Teacher: Uh … Let's … Who is it the story talks about?
Children: (*silence*)
Teacher: *Who* is *the* main character? … What *kind* of story is it?
Child: Ain't nobody can talk about things being about theirselves.

The boy was saying 'There's no way anybody can talk (and ask) about things being about themselves'.

Source: Adapted from Heath, in Spindler, 1982

BOX 22.6 PARENTS AND TEACHERS: DIVERGENT VIEWPOINTS ON CHILDREN'S COMMUNICATIVE COMPETENCE

Parents

The teachers won't listen. My kid, he too scared to talk, 'cause nobody play by the rules he know. At home, I can't shut 'im up.

  Miss Davis, she complain 'bout Ned not answerin' back. He say she asks dumb questions she already know 'bout.

Teachers

They don't seem to be able to answer even the simplest questions.

  I would almost think some of them have a hearing problem; it is as though they don't hear me ask a question. I get blank stares to my questions. Yet when I am making statements or telling stories which interest them, they always seem to hear me.

  The simplest questions are the ones they can't answer in the classroom; yet on the playground, they can explain a rule for a ballgame or describe a particular kind of bait with no problem. Therefore, I know they can't be as dumb as they seem in my class.

  I sometimes feel that when I look at them and ask a question I'm staring at a wall I can't break through. There's something there; yet in spite of all the questions I ask, I'm never sure I've gotten through to what's inside that wall.

Source: Adapted from Heath, in Spindler, 1982

---

of life in Trackton, the southern community in which the research was located. She comments that she was able to collect data from a wide range of contexts and situations, tracking children longitudinally and in several contexts, taking care to record language used and the social contexts of the language, and the communicative competence of participants.[3]

22.9 Problems in gathering and analysing accounts

The importance of the meaning of events and actions to those who are involved in them is now generally recog-nized in social research. The implications of the etho-genic stance in terms of actual research techniques, however, remain problematic. Menzel (1978) discusses a number of ambiguities and shortcomings in the etho-genic approach, arising out of the multiplicity of mean-ings that may be held for the same behaviour. Most behaviour, Menzel observes, can be assigned meanings and more than one of these may very well be valid simultaneously. It is fallacious therefore, he argues, to insist upon determining 'the' meaning of an act. Nor can it be said that the task of interpreting an act is done when one has identified one meaning of it, or the one meaning that the researcher is pleased to designate as the true one.

A second problem that Menzel (1978) raises is to do with actors' meanings as sources of bias. How central a place, he asks, ought to be given to actors' meanings in formulating explanations of events? Should the researcher exclusively and invariably be guided by these considerations? To do so would be to ignore a whole range of potential explanations which few researchers would wish to see excluded from consideration.

These are far-reaching, difficult issues though by no means intractable. What solutions does Menzel (1978) propose? First we must specify 'to whom' when asking what acts and situations mean. Second, researchers must make choices and take responsibility in the assignment of meanings to acts; moreover, problem formulations must respect the meaning of the act to us, the researchers. And third, explanations should respect the meanings of acts to the actors themselves but need not invariably be centred around these meanings.

Menzel's (1978) plea is for the usefulness of an outside observer's account of a social episode alongside the explanations that participants themselves may give of that event. A similar argument is implicit in McIntyre and MacLeod's (1978) justification of objective, systematic observation in classroom settings. Their case is set out in Box 22.7.

22.10 Strengths of the ethogenic approach

The advantages of the ethogenic approach to the educational researcher lie in the distinctive insights that are made available to her through the analysis of accounts of social episodes. The benefits to be derived from the exploration of accounts are best seen by contrasting the ethogenic approach with a more traditional educational technique such as the survey which we discussed in Chapter 13.

There is a good deal of truth in the assertion of the ethogenically oriented researcher that approaches which employ survey techniques such as the questionnaire take for granted the very things that should be treated as problematic in an educational study. Too often the phenomena that ought to be the focus of attention are taken as given, that is, they are treated as the starting point of the research rather than becoming the centre of the researcher's interest and effort to discover how the phenomena arose or came to be important in the first place. Numerous educational studies, for example, have identified the incidence and the duration of disciplinary infractions in school; only relatively recently, however, has the meaning of classroom disorder, as opposed to its frequency and type, been subjected to intensive investigation. Unlike the survey, which is a cross-sectional technique that takes its data at a single point in time, the ethogenic study employs an ongoing observational approach that focuses upon processes rather than products. Thus it is the process of becoming deviant in school which would capture the attention of the ethogenic researcher rather than the frequency and type of misbehaviour among k types of ability in children located in n kinds of school.

22.11 A note on stories

A comparatively neglected area in educational research is the field of stories and storytelling. Bauman (1986:

BOX 22.7   JUSTIFICATION OF OBJECTIVE SYSTEMATIC OBSERVATION IN CLASSROOM SETTINGS

When Smith looks at Jones and says, 'Jones, why does the blue substance spread through the liquid?' (probably with a particular kind of voice inflection), and then silently looks at Jones (probably with a particular kind of facial expression), the observer can unambiguously categorize the event as 'Smith asks Jones a question seeking an explanation of diffusion in a liquid.' Now Smith might describe the event as 'giving Jones a chance to show he knows something', and Jones might describe the event as 'Smith trying to get at me'; but if either of them denied the validity of the observer's description, they would be simply wrong, because the observer would be describing at least part of what the behaviour which occurred means in English in Britain. No assumptions are made here about the effectiveness of classroom communication; but the assumption is made that ... communication is dependent on the system of conventional meanings available within the wider culture. More fundamentally, this interpretation implies that the systematic observer is concerned with an objective reality (or, if one prefers, a shared intersubjective reality) of classroom events. This is not to suggest that the subjective meanings of events to participants are not important, but only that these are not accessible to the observer and that *there is an objective reality to classroom activity which does not depend on these meanings* [our emphasis].

Source: McIntyre and MacLeod, in McAleese and Hamilton, 1978

3) suggests that stories are oral literature whose meanings, forms and functions are situationally rooted in cultural contexts, scenes and events which give meaning to action. This recalls Bruner (1986) who, echoing the interpretive mode of educational research, regards much action as 'storied text', with actors making meaning of their situations through narrative. Stories have a legitimate place as an enquiry method in educational research (Parsons and Lyons, 1979), and, indeed, Jones (1990), Crow (1992), Dunning (1993) and Thody (1997) place them on a par with interviews as sources of evidence for research. Thody (1997: 331) suggests that, as an extension to interviews, stories – like biographies – are rich in authentic, live data; they are, she avers, an 'unparalleled method of reaching practitioners' mindsets'. She provides a fascinating report on stories as data sources for educational management research as well as for gathering data from young children (pp. 333–4).

Thody (1997: 331) indicates how stories can be analysed, using, for example, conventional techniques such as: categorizing and coding of content; thematization; concept building. In this respect stories have their place alongside other sources of primary and secondary documentary evidence (e.g. case studies, biographies). They can be used in *ex post facto* research, historical research, as accounts or in action research; in short they are part of the everyday battery of research instruments that are available to the researcher. The rise in the use of oral history as a legitimate research technique in social research can be seen here to apply to educational research. Though they might be problematic in that verification is difficult (unless other people were present to verify events reported), stories, being rich in the subjective involvement of the storyteller, offer an opportunity for the researcher to gather authentic, rich and 'respectable' data (Bauman, 1986).

 Companion Website

The companion website to the book includes PowerPoint slides for this chapter, which list the structure of the chapter and then provide a summary of the key points in each of its sections. This resource can be found online at **www.routledge.com/textbooks/cohen7e**.

Observation

Observation is a widely used means of data collection, and it takes many forms. This chapter addresses several different kinds of observation and how to plan, conduct and report them. Given the spread of types of observation and the issues related to them, we address:

- structured observation
- the need to practise structured observation
- analysing data from structured observations
- critical incidents
- naturalistic and participant observation
- data analysis for less structured observations
- natural and artificial settings for observation
- the use of technology in recording observations
- timing and causality with observational data
- ethical considerations
- some cautionary comments

This chapter can also be read with Chapters 11 and 27.

23.1 Introduction

Observation is more than just looking. It is looking (often systematically) and noting systematically (always) people, events, behaviours, settings, artefacts, routines and so on (Marshall and Rossman, 1995; Simpson and Tuson, 2003: 2). The distinctive feature of observation as a research process is that it offers an investigator the opportunity to gather 'live' data from naturally occurring social situations. In this way, the researcher can look directly at what is taking place *in situ* rather than relying on second-hand accounts. The use of immediate awareness, or direct cognition, as a principle mode of research thus has the potential to yield more valid or authentic data than would otherwise be the case with mediated or inferential methods. And this is observation's unique strength. There are other attractions in its favour: as Robson says (2002: 310), what people do may differ from what they say they do, and observation provides a reality check; observation also enables a researcher to look afresh at everyday behaviour that otherwise might be taken for granted, expected or go unnoticed (Cooper and Schindler, 2001:

374); and the approach with its carefully prepared recording schedules avoids problems caused when there is a time gap between the act of observation and the recording of the event – selective or faulty memory, for example. Finally, on a procedural point, some participants may prefer the presence of an observer to an intrusive, time-consuming interview or questionnaire.

Observation can be of *facts*, e.g. the number of books in a classroom, the number of students in a class, the number of students who visit the school library in a given period. It can also focus on *events* as they happen in a classroom, e.g. the amount of teacher and student talk; the amount of off-task conversation; the amount of group collaborative work. Further, it can focus on *behaviours* or qualities, e.g. the friendliness of the teacher; the degree of aggressive behaviour; the extent of unsociable behaviour amongst students.

One can detect here a putative continuum from the observation of uncontestable facts to the researcher's interpretation and judgement of situations, which are then recorded as observations. What counts as evidence immediately becomes cloudy in observation, because what we observe depends on when, where and for how long we look, how many observers there are, and how we look. It also depends on what is taken to be evidence of, or a proxy for, an underlying, latent construct. What counts as acceptable evidence of unsociable behaviour in the example above requires an operational definition that is valid and reliable. Observers need to decide 'what is the observation evidence', for example: is the degree of wear and tear on a book in the school library an indication of its popularity, or carelessness by its readers, or of destructive behaviour by students? One cannot infer cause from effect, intention from observation, stimulus from response.

Observational data are sensitive to contexts and demonstrate strong ecological validity (Moyles, 2002). This enables researchers to understand the context of programmes, to be open-ended and inductive, to see things that might otherwise be unconsciously missed, to discover things that participants might not freely talk about in interview situations, to move beyond perception-based data (e.g. opinions in interviews) and to access personal knowledge. Because observed incidents are less predictable there is a certain freshness to this form of data collection that is often denied in other forms, e.g. a questionnaire or a test.

Observation is a highly flexible form of data collection that can enable the researcher to have access to interactions in a social context and to yield systematic records of these in many forms and contexts, to complement other kinds of data (Simpson and Tuson, 2003: 17).

Observations (Morrison, 1993: 80) enable the researcher to gather data on:

- the *physical setting* (e.g. the physical environment and its organization);
- the *human setting* (e.g. the organization of people, the characteristics and make up of the groups or individuals being observed, for instance, gender, class);
- the *interactional setting* (e.g. the interactions that are taking place, formal, informal, planned, unplanned, verbal, non-verbal, etc.);
- the *programme setting* (e.g. the resources and their organization, pedagogic styles, curricula and their organization).

Additionally, observational data may be useful for recording non-verbal behaviour, behaviour in natural or contrived settings, and longitudinal analysis (Bailey, 1994: 244). On the other hand, the lack of control in observing in natural settings may render observation less useful, coupled with difficulties in measurement, problems of small samples, difficulties of gaining access and negotiating entry, and difficulties in maintaining anonymity (Bailey, 1994: 245–6). Observation can be a powerful research tool, but it is not without its difficulties, and this chapter exposes and addresses these.

Patton (1990: 202) suggests that observational data should enable the researcher to enter and understand the situation that is being described. The kind of observations available to the researcher lie on a continuum from unstructured to structured, responsive to pre-ordinate. A *highly structured* observation will know in advance what it is looking for (i.e. pre-ordinate observation) and will have its observation categories worked out in advance. A *semi-structured observation* will have an agenda of issues but will gather data to illuminate these issues in a far less predetermined or systematic manner. An *unstructured observation* will be far less clear on what it is looking for and will therefore have to go into a situation and observe what is taking place before deciding on its significance for the research. In a nutshell, a structured observation will already have its hypotheses decided and will use the

observational data to conform or refute these hypotheses. On the other hand, a semi-structured and, more particularly, an unstructured observation, will be hypothesis-generating rather than hypothesis-testing. The semi-structured and unstructured observations will review observational data before suggesting an explanation for the phenomena being observed.

Though it is possible to argue that all research is some form of participant observation since we cannot study the world without being part of it (Adler and Adler, 1994), nevertheless Gold (1958) offers a well-known classification of researcher roles in observation, that lie on a continuum:

- The *complete participant* (a member of the group who conceals her/his role as an observer, whose knowledge of the group/situation may be intimate and who may gain 'insider knowledge', but who may be viewed with suspicion or resentment by the other members when his/her true role comes to light and who may lack the necessary objectivity to observe reliably).
- The *participant-as-observer* (a member of the group who reveals her/his role as an observer, whose knowledge of the group/situation may be intimate and who may gain 'insider knowledge', but who may lack the necessary objectivity to observe reliably and with whom confidences and confidential data may not be shared or given respectively).
- The *observer-as-participant* (not a member of the group, but who may participate a little or peripherally in the group's activities, and whose role as researcher is clear and overt, as unobtrusive as possible, without those being observed always knowing who is the researcher, and whose access to information and people may be incomplete or restricted).
- The *complete observer* (who only observes (overt or covert) and is detached from the group, e.g. an outside observer, or where the observer is not covert but whose presence is unnoticed by the group e.g. an observer at a crowded rail station).

The move is from complete participation to complete detachment. The mid-points of this continuum strive to balance involvement with detachment, closeness with distance, familiarity with strangeness. The role of the complete observer is typified in the two-way mirror, the video recording, the audio recording and the photograph, whilst complete participation involves researchers taking on membership roles (overt or covert).

Traditionally observation has been characterized as non-interventionist, where researchers do not seek to manipulate the situation or subjects, they do not pose questions for the subjects, nor do they deliberately create 'new provocations' (Adler and Adler, 1994: 378). Quantitative research tends to have a small field of focus, fragmenting the observed into minute chunks that can subsequently be aggregated into a variable. Qualitative research, on the other hand, draws the researcher into the phenomenological complexity of participants' worlds; here situations unfold, and connections, causes and correlations can be observed as they occur over time. The qualitative researcher aims to catch the dynamic nature of events, to see intentionality, to seek trends and patterns over time.

If we know in advance what we wish to observe, i.e. if the observation is concerned to chart the *incidence, presence* and *frequency* of elements and maybe wishes to compare one situation with another, then it may be more efficient in terms of time to go into a situation with a prepared observation schedule. If, on the other hand, we want to go into a situation and let the elements of the situation speak for themselves, perhaps with no concern with how one situation compares with another, then it may be more appropriate to opt for a less structured observation.

The former, structured observation, takes much time to prepare but the data analysis is fairly rapid, the categories having already been established, whilst the latter, less structured approach, is quicker to prepare but the data take much longer to analyse. The former approach operates within the agenda of the researcher and hence might neglect aspects of the four settings above if they do not appear on the observation schedule, i.e. it looks selectively at situations. On the other hand, the latter operates within the agenda of the participants, i.e. it is responsive to what it finds and therefore, by definition, is honest to the situation as it unfolds. Here selectivity derives from the *situation* rather than from the *researcher* in the sense that the key issues which emerge follow from the observation rather

than the researcher knowing in advance what those key issues will be. Structured observation is useful for testing hypotheses, whilst unstructured observation provides a rich description of a situation which, in turn, can lead to the subsequent generation of hypotheses.

Flick (1998: 137) suggests that observation has to be considered along five dimensions:

- structured, systematic and quantitative observation versus unstructured and unsystematic and qualitative observation;
- participant observation versus non-participant observation;
- overt versus covert observation;
- observation in natural settings versus observation in unnatural, artificial settings (e.g. a 'laboratory' or contrived situation);
- self-observation versus observation of others.

Cooper and Schindler (2001: 375) suggest that observation can be considered along three dimensions:

- whether the observation is direct or indirect (the former requiring the presence of the observer; the latter requiring recording devices, e.g. video cameras);
- whether the presence of the observer is known or unknown (overt or covert research, whether the researcher is concealed (e.g. through a two-way mirror or hidden camera) or partially concealed, i.e. the researcher is seen but not known to be a researcher, e.g. the researcher takes up a visible role in the school);
- the role taken by the observer (participant to non-participant observation, discussed below).

We address these throughout the chapter, and present these dimensions and others in Figure 23.1.

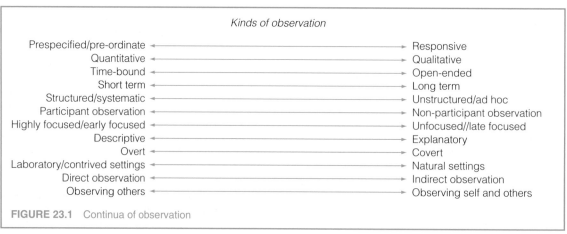

Kinds of observation

Prespecified/pre-ordinate ←——————————→ Responsive
Quantitative ←——————————→ Qualitative
Time-bound ←——————————→ Open-ended
Short term ←——————————→ Long term
Structured/systematic ←——————————→ Unstructured/ad hoc
Participant observation ←——————————→ Non-participant observation
Highly focused/early focused ←——————————→ Unfocused//late focused
Descriptive ←——————————→ Explanatory
Overt ←——————————→ Covert
Laboratory/contrived settings ←——————————→ Natural settings
Direct observation ←——————————→ Indirect observation
Observing others ←——————————→ Observing self and others

FIGURE 23.1 Continua of observation

Observation, in general, is not only time-consuming but is prone to bias – in terms of what, why, when, where, who and how the observer is observing. Observations are inevitably selective, and, in part, depend as much on the observer's attention and opportunity to observe as they do on the observational instruments and data collection techniques used. Hence great caution and reflexivity are requisites for this form of data collection. As with other forms of data collection, observational data must be collected that enable research questions to be answered. Indeed Simpson and Tuson (2003: chapter 2) suggest that observers need to consider:

- the focus of the observation(s);
- why you are observing (e.g. looking for regularities, similarities, evolution of a situation, irregularities, patterns, key features, etc.);
- the research questions that the observational data will address;
- the boundaries of the observation (what to include and exclude);
- how to record the observations;
- where to observe (e.g. key social places);
- what to observe (e.g. significant objects, setting, events, people, etc.);
- whom to observe (e.g. key people, everyday participants, marginalized people);
- how many people, events, settings to observe (i.e. sampling);
- how systematic, structured, descriptive to be;
- what is the 'unit' of observation (e.g. a teacher, a student, a pair, a small group, a class);
- what resources are necessary (e.g. human observers, video cameras, audio recording);
- problems that might be encountered;
- additional information that may be needed to complement the observational record; and
- the processing and analysis of observational data.

There is also the need to consider who the observer will be, as observation (particularly participant observation) can be affected by the sex, sexuality, ethnicity class, appearance, age, language, personality, temperament, attitude, interpersonal behaviour, familiarity with the situation, involvement and concern, etc. of the observer (cf. Kawulich, 2005: 7).

On a practical level the researcher has to decide fundamental points such as whether to stand or sit, whether to move around a setting (e.g. in order to track a student), and where to stand or sit. If a researcher is located too close he/she might be intrusive, inhibiting, or the researcher might lose the observation if a student

moves away; if the researcher is too far away he/she might miss what is happening in detail (cf. Simpson and Tuson, 2003: 54–5).

23.2 Structured observation

A structured observation is very systematic and enables the researcher to generate numerical data from the observations. Numerical data, in turn, facilitate the making of comparisons between settings and situations, and frequencies, patterns and trends to be noted or calculated. The observer adopts a passive, non-intrusive role, merely noting down the incidence of the factors being studied. Observations are entered on an observational schedule. An example of this is shown in Table 23.1. This is an example of a schedule used to monitor student and teacher conversations over a ten-minute period. The upper seven categories indicate who is speaking to whom, whilst the lower four categories indicate the nature of the talk. Looking at the example of the observation schedule, several points can be noted:

- The categories for the observation are discrete, i.e. there is no overlap between them. For this to be the case requires a pilot to have been developed and tested in order to iron out any problems of overlap of categories.
- Each column represents a 30-second time interval, i.e. the movement from left to right represents the chronology of the sequence, and the researcher has to enter data in the appropriate cell of the matrix every 30 seconds (see below: instantaneous sampling).
- Because there are so many categories which have to be scanned at speed (every 30 seconds), the researcher will need to practise completing the schedule until he or she becomes proficient and consistent in entering data (i.e. that the observed behaviours, settings, etc. are entered into the same categories consistently), achieving reliability. This can be done either through practising with video material or through practising in a live situation with participants who will not subsequently be included in the research. If there is to be more than one researcher then it may be necessary to provide training sessions so that the team of researchers proficiently, efficiently and consistently enter the same sort of data in the same categories, i.e. that there is inter-rater reliability.
- The researcher will need to decide what entry is to be made in the appropriate category, for example: a tick ($\checkmark$), a forward slash (/), a backward slash (\), a

TABLE 23.1 A STRUCTURED OBSERVATION SCHEDULE

	1	2	3	4	5	6	7	8	9	10	11	12	13	14	15	16	17	18	19	20
Student to Student	/	/	/	/																
Student to Students					/	/														
Student to Teacher												/	/	/	/					
Students to Teacher							/	/	/	/	/									
Teacher to Student																/	/			
Teacher to Students																		/	/	/
Student to Self																				
Task in hand					✓	✓						✓	✓	✓	✓	✓	✓	✓	✓	✓
Previous task						✓	✓	✓	✓	✓	✓									
Future task																				
Non-task	✓	✓	✓	✓																

Notes
/ = participants in the conversation
✓ = nature of the conversation.

figure (1, 2, 3, etc.), a letter (a, b, c, etc.), a tally mark (|). Whatever code or set of codes is used, it must be understood by all the researchers (if there is a team) and must be simple and quick to enter (i.e. symbols rather than words). Bearing in mind that every 30 seconds one or more entries must be made in each column, the researcher will need to become proficient in fast and accurate data entry of the appropriate codes.[1]

The need to pilot a structured observation schedule, as in the example, cannot be overemphasized. Categories must be mutually exclusive and must be comprehensive. The researcher, then, will need to decide:

i   the foci of the observation (e.g. people as well as events);
ii the frequency of the observations (e.g. every 30 seconds, every minute, every two minutes);
iii the length of the observation period (e.g. one hour, 20 minutes);
iv what counts as evidence (e.g. how a behaviour is defined and operationalized);
v   the nature of the entry (the coding system).

The criterion of 'fitness for purpose' is used for making decisions on these four matters. Structured observation will take much time in preparation but the analysis of the data should be rapid as the categories for analysis will have been built into the schedule itself. So, for example, if close, detailed scrutiny is required then the time intervals will be very short, and if less detail is required then the intervals may be longer.

Dyer (1995: 181–4) suggests that structured observation must address several key principles:

■ the choice of the environment (such that there will be opportunities for the behaviour to be observed to be actually occurring – the availability and frequency of the behaviour of interest to the observer: a key feature if unusual or special behaviour is sought);
■ the need for clear and unambiguous measures (particularly if a latent characteristic or construct is being operationalized);
■ a manageable number of variables (a sufficient number for validity to be demonstrated, yet not so many as to render data entry unreliable);
■ overt or covert observation;
■ continuous, time-series or random observation;
■ the different categories of behaviour to be observed;
■ the number of people to be observed;
■ the number of variables on which data must be gathered;
■ the kind of observation schedule to be used.

He provides a checklist (p. 186) for planning a structured observation (Box 23.1).

There are five principal ways of entering data onto a structured observation schedule: event sampling, instantaneous sampling, interval recording, rating scales and duration recording.

Event sampling

Event sampling, also known as a sign system, requires a tally mark to be entered against each statement each time it is observed, for example:

BOX 23.1   NON-PARTICIPANT OBSERVATION – A CHECKLIST OF DESIGN TASKS

1 The preliminary tasks

Have you

- Clearly described the research problem?
- Stated the precise aim of the research?
- Developed an explanation which either links your research to a theory or says why the observations should be made?
- Stated the hypotheses (if any) to be tested?
- Identified the appropriate test statistic (if needed)?

2 The observational system

Have you

- Identified the type(s) of behaviour to be observed?
- Developed clear and objective definitions of each category of behaviour?
- Checked that the categories are complete, and cover all the target behaviours?
- Checked that each category is clearly distinct from the others?
- Checked that the differences between each category are easily seen in the observing situation?

3 The observational process

Have you

- Identified an appropriate location to make your observations?
- Decided which data sampling procedure to use?
- Decided whether to use overt or covert observation?
- Decided whether to use one or more observers to collect information?

4 And finally…

Have you

- Designed the data collection sheet?
- Reviewed the ethical standards of the investigation?
- Run a pilot study and made any necessary amendments to the observation system, or procedure?
- If more than one observer has been used, made a preliminary assessment of inter-observer reliability?

Source: Dyer, 1995: 186

---

teacher shouts at the child	/////
child shouts at the teacher	///
parent shouts at the teacher	//
teacher shouts at the parent	//

The researcher will need to devise statements that yield the data that answer the research questions. This method is useful for finding out the frequencies or incidence of observed situations or behaviours, so that comparisons can be made; we can tell, for example, that the teacher does most shouting and that the parent shouts least of all. However, whilst these data enable us to chart the incidence of observed situations or behaviours, the difficulty with them is that we are unable to determine the chronological order in which they occurred. For example, two different stories could be

told from these data if the sequence of events were known. If the data were presented in a chronology, one story could be seen as follows, where the numbers 1–7 are the different periods over time (e.g. every 30 seconds):

	1	2	3	4	5	6	7
teacher shouts at the child		/	/	/	/		/
child shouts at the teacher	/	/				/	
parent shouts at the teacher	/			/			
teacher shouts at the parent						/	/

Imagine the scene: a parent and his child arrive late for school one morning and the child slips into the classroom; an event quickly occurs which prompts the child to shout at the teacher, the exasperated teacher is very cross when thus provoked by the child; the teacher shouts at the child who then brings in the parent (who has not yet left the premises); the parent shouts at the teacher for unreasonable behaviour and the teacher shouts back at the child. It seems in this version that the teacher only shouts when provoked by the child or parent.

If the same number of tally marks were distributed in a different order, a very different story might emerge, for example:

	1	2	3	4	5	6	7
teacher shouts at the child	/	/	/	/		/	
child shouts at the teacher					/	/	/
parent shouts at the teacher					/	/	
teacher shouts at the parent		/	/				

In this scene it is the teacher who is the instigator of the shouting, shouting at the child and then at the parent; the child and the parent only shout back when they have been provoked!

Instantaneous sampling

If it is important to know the chronology of events, then it is necessary to use instantaneous sampling, sometimes called time sampling. Here the researcher enters what she observes at standard intervals of time, for example every 20 seconds, every minute. On the stroke of that interval she notes what is happening at that precise moment and enters it into the appropriate category on the schedule. For example, imagine that the sampling will take place every 30 seconds; numbers 1–7 represent each 30-second interval thus:

	1	2	3	4	5	6	7
teacher smiles at the child	/	/	/	/			
child smiles at the teacher			/	/	/	/	
teacher smiles at the parent	/	/	/	/			
parent smiles at the teacher			/	/	/	/	

In this scene the researcher notes down what is happening on the 30-second point and notices from these precise moments that the teacher initiates the smiling but that all parties seem to be doing quite a lot of smiling, with the parent and the child doing the same amount of smiling each! Instantaneous sampling involves recording what is happening on the instant and entering it in the appropriate category. The chronology of events is preserved.

Interval recording

This method charts the chronology of events to some extent and, like instantaneous sampling, requires the data to be entered in the appropriate category at fixed intervals. However, instead of charting what is happening on the instant, it charts what has happened during the preceding interval. So, for example, if recording were to take place every 30 seconds, then the researcher would note down in the appropriate category what had happened during the preceding 30 seconds. Whilst this enables frequencies to be calculated, simple patterns to be observed and an approximate sequence of events to be noted, because it charts what has taken place in the preceding interval of time, some elements of the chronology might be lost. For example, if three events took place in the preceding 30 seconds of the example, then the order of the three events would be lost; we would know simply that they had occurred.

Wilkinson (2000: 236) distinguishes between *whole* interval recording and *partial* interval recording. In the former, behaviour is recorded only if it lasts for the whole of the interval; in the latter, behaviour is recorded if it occupies only a part of the interval in question. In the case of the partial interval recording, the researcher will need to specify how to record this.

Rating scales

In this method the researcher is asked to make some judgement about the events being observed, and to enter responses into a rating scale. For example, Wragg (1994) suggests that observed teaching behaviour might be entered onto rating scales by placing the observed behaviour onto a continuum:

	1	2	3	4	5	
Warm	__	__	__	__	__	Aloof
Stimulating	__	__	__	__	__	Dull
Businesslike	__	__	__	__	__	Slipshod

An observer might wish to enter a rating according to a five-point scale of observed behaviour, for example:

1 = not at all	2 = very little	3 = a little
4 = a lot	5 = a very great deal	

	1	2	3	4	5
Child seeks teacher's attention					
Teacher praises the child					
Teacher intervenes to stop misbehaviour					

What is required here is for the researcher to move from low inference (simply reporting observations) to a higher degree of inference (making judgements about events observed). This might introduce a degree of unreliability into the observation (for example through: (a) the halo effect; (b) the central tendency wherein observers will avoid extreme categories; (c) recency – where observers are influenced by more recent events than less recent events). That said, this might be a helpful summary way of gathering observational data.

Simpson and Tuson (2003: 42–4) suggest that researchers ensure that:

■ the categories to be included in ratings adequately cover the 'range of behaviours or features' (p. 42) of interest in the target group for observation;
■ the anchor statements (descriptor) on each scale point adequately describe the 'range of possibilities' (p. 43) in the item for observation;
■ sufficient specification of what and how to observe are given to researchers in the completion of the observational schedule, such that two independent observers would complete the schedule of the 'same observed activities in the same way' (p. 44).

The duration of behaviour

So far we have concerned ourselves with single events and their recording. This is very suitable for single and usually short-lived behaviours. However, sometimes certain behaviours last a long time and would 'overrun' the interval categories or event categories described above, i.e. it is continuous behaviour rather than a single event. For example, a child may remove her shoes only once, but she may continue to be without her shoes for a 20-minute period; a child may delay starting to do any writing for ten minutes, again a single behaviour but which continues for longer than each of the intervals in interval or instantaneous recording; a child may have a single tantrum which continues for 20 minutes, and so on. What we need is an indication of the *duration* of a particular behaviour. The observation is driven by the event, not the frequency of the observation. This means that the observer needs to structure the recording schedule to indicate the total duration of a single continuous behaviour.

For all the kinds of schedules discussed above, a decision will have to have been agreed in advance on how to enter data. Consistency of entering by a single and multiple observers will need to be founded on what counts as evidence, when, where and how to observe, and how many people on whom to focus. For example, how will the observation schedule distinguish between one person being observed demonstrating the same behaviour 12 times (1 person × 12) and many people demonstrating the same behaviour fewer times (e.g. 2 people × 6 times each, or 4 people × 3 times each), i.e. is the focus to be on *people* or on *behaviour*?

Whilst structured observation can provide useful numerical data (e.g. Bennett *et al.*, 1984; Galton and Simon, 1980), there are several concerns which must be addressed in this form of observation, for example:

■ the method is behaviourist, excluding any mention of the intentions or motivations of the people being observed;
■ the individual's subjectivity is lost to an aggregated score;
■ there is an assumption that the observed behaviour provides evidence of underlying feelings, i.e. that concepts or constructs can be crudely measured in observed occurrences.

This latter point is important, for it goes to the very heart of the notion of validity, since it requires researchers to satisfy themselves that it is valid to infer that a particular behaviour indicates a particular state of mind or particular intention or motivation. The desire to operationalize concepts and constructs can easily lead researchers to provide overly simple indicators of complex concepts.

Further, structured observation neglects the significance of contexts – temporal and spatial – thereby overlooking the fact that behaviours may be context-specific. In their concern for the overt and the observable, researchers may overlook unintended outcomes which may have significance; they may be unable to show how significant are the behaviours of the participants being observed in their own terms. If we accept that behaviour is developmental, that interactions evolve over time and, therefore, are, by definition, fluid, then the methods of structured observation outlined above appear to take a series of 'freeze-frame' snapshots of behaviour, thereby violating the principle of fluidity of action. Captured for an instant in time, it is difficult to infer a particular meaning to one or more events (Stubbs and Delamont, 1976), just as it is impossible to say with any certainty what is taking place when we study a single photograph or a set of photographs of a particular event. Put simply, if structured observation is to hold water, then the researcher may need to gather additional data from other sources to inform the interpretation of observational data.

This latter point is a matter not only for structured observation but, equally, for unstructured observation, for what is being suggested here is the notion that *triangulation* (of methods, of observers, of time and space) can assist the researcher to generate reliable evidence. There is a risk that observations will be selective, and the effects of this can be attenuated by triangulation. One way of gathering more reliable data (for example about a particular student or group of students) is by *tracking* them through the course of a day or a week, following them from place to place, event to event. It is part of teaching folklore that students will behave very differently for one teacher than for another, and a full picture of students' behaviour might require the observer to see the students in different contexts.

23.3 The need to practise structured observation

It may sound like a naive truism to say that researchers need to practise observation, but they do! For example, they may need to practise entering data in the appropriate categories in the structured observation schedule, and at speed (Simpson and Tuson, 2003: 10). They may need to practise where to locate themselves when observing, what to focus on, where to look, what to record (e.g. the level of detail), where to move around the setting, whether to stand or sit, how to code *in situ*, and how to observe without those observed being too conscious of the observation taking place or the observation being too intrusive, what role to take in the classroom or setting, how to avoid eye-contact (as this can be threatening or disturbing to the setting or the person being observed), how to observe discreetly or indirectly (e.g. without directly looking intently at a person or group, or without being seen to be looking directly or to be watching or tracking specific persons). Further, they need to practise and pilot their structured observational instruments in order to find the optimum time intervals for observation schedules for instantaneous sampling, interval recording and duration recording (e.g. five seconds, one minute, two minutes, ten minutes, etc.).

23.4 Analysing data from structured observations

For structured observations researchers can count *frequencies*, and with references to individuals, groups, classes, events, activities, behaviours and so on. One can observe *patterns* (e.g. in *sequences* of behaviours, or sequences of conversations or interactions, e.g. discourse analysis or question and answer sequences in classroom talk), or *frequently occurring* combinations of events/behaviours/people/kinds of interaction, or *aggregated data* (e.g. from individuals to groups to

classes, from individuals to males/females, from individual lessons to courses or subjects, from individual behaviours to categories of behaviour, from individual units of talk to kinds of talk (e.g. closed questions/open questions, extended responses/one-word responses, teacher-initiated talk/student-initiated talk), on-task/off-task behaviour). Further, since the data can be converted into numbers, the panoply of suitable statistical analyses can be utilized (see Part 5).

In addition to data from structured observations being 'quantitized', they can be turned into narrative accounts, descriptions and themes i.e. 'qualitized', and we refer readers to Part 5 on this.

23.5 Critical incidents

There will be times when reliability as consistency in observations is not always necessary. For example, a student might only demonstrate a particular behaviour once, but it is so important as not to be ruled out simply because it occurred once. One only has to commit a single murder to be branded a murderer! Sometimes one event can occur which reveals an extremely important insight into a person or situation. Critical incidents (Flanagan, 1949) and critical events (Wragg, 1994) are particular events or occurrences that might typify or illuminate very starkly a particular feature of a teacher's behaviour or teaching style for example. Wragg (1994: 64) writes that these are events that appear to the observer to have more interest than other ones, and therefore warrant greater detail and recording than other events; they have an important insight to offer. For example, a child might unexpectedly behave very aggressively when asked to work with another child – that might reveal an insight into the child's social tolerance; a teacher might suddenly overreact when a student produces a substandard piece of work – the straw that breaks the camel's back – that might indicate a level of frustration tolerance or intolerance and the effects of that threshold of tolerance being reached. These events are critical in that they may be non-routine but very revealing; they offer the researcher an insight that would not be available by routine observation. They are frequently unusual events.[2]

23.6 Naturalistic and participant observation

Whilst some observations take place in a context in which the researcher knows clearly and in advance what to look for, with categories and coding worked out before the observation takes place, this is not always the case. It is here that ethnographic and naturalistic observation come into pre-eminence (we advise readers to read this in combination with Chapter 11). Here the intention is to observe participants in their natural settings, their everyday social settings and their everyday behaviour in them. Participant observation here has a wider embrace, including visual observation, document analysis, interviewing, direct observation and introspection (Flick, 2009: 226). It is a process, moving from *descriptive observation* (orientation to a field) to *focused observation* (narrowing one's field of observation to focus in on those problems and processes that are most germane to the research purpose and questions), and on to *selective observation* (to find further evidence for those items identified in the previous step) (Flick, 2009: 227).

Participant observation, as Simpson and Tuson (2003: 14) argue, is 'the most subtly intrusive' form of observation since it requires the researcher to be an empathic, sympathetic member of a group, in order to gain access to insiders' behaviours and activities, whilst still acting as a researcher with a degree of detachment. Indeed Merriam (1998: 103) suggests that the participant observer is somewhat 'schizophrenic', as he/she has to balance participation in order to absorb the situation, with sufficient detachment to be able to analyse and observe it in a detached way. Further, it is usually very time-consuming, as not only does the researcher have to join in many activities and spend a long time with the group, but he/she has to write up field notes away from the activity itself (e.g. in the evening).

Participant observation is useful for enabling researchers to check their definitions of key terms that are used by participants, to observe events or behaviours that might not be mentioned in interviews, to gather data on sensitive, unspoken topics (Kawulich, 2005). Participant observation can help in guiding relationships with participants and informants, enable the researcher to 'get a feel' of a situation and how matters are organized in a group or subculture, find out about interactions and relationships, raise questions for further investigation (Schensul *et al.*, 1999), sensitize and familiarize a researcher to a context, and reduce the reactivity caused by a short observation (Bernard, 1994). It enables rich descriptions of 'backstage culture' (DeMunck and Sobo, 1998: 43) to be gathered.

As mentioned at the start of this chapter, there are degrees of participation in observation (LeCompte and Preissle, 1993: 93–4). The 'complete participant' is a researcher who takes on an insider role in the group being studied, and maybe who does not even declare that she is a researcher (discussed later in comments about the ethics of covert research). The 'participant-as-observer', as its name suggests, is part of the social

life of participants and documents and records what is happening for research purposes. The 'observer-as-participant', like the participant-as-observer, is known as a researcher to the group, and maybe has less extensive contact with the group. With the 'complete observer' participants do not realize that they are being observed (e.g. using a two-way mirror), hence this is another form of covert research.

Hammersley and Atkinson (1983: 93–5) suggest that comparative involvement may come in the forms of the complete participant and the participant-as-observer, with a degree of subjectivity and sympathy, whilst comparative detachment may come in the forms of the observer-as-participant and the complete observer, where objectivity and distance are key characteristics. Both complete participation and complete detachment are as limiting as each other. As a complete participant the researcher dare not go outside the confines of the group for fear of revealing her identity (in covert research), and as a complete observer there is no contact with the observed, so inference is dangerous. That said, both complete participation and complete detachment minimize reactivity, though in the former there is the risk of 'going native' – where the researcher adopts the values, norms and behaviours of the group as her own, i.e. ceases to be a researcher or ceases to be objective (Kawulich, 2005: 4) and becomes a member of the group.

Participant observation may be particularly useful in studying small groups, or for events and processes that only last a short time or are frequent, for activities that lend themselves to being observed, for researchers who wish to reach inside a situation and have a long time available to them to 'get under the skin' of behaviour or organizations (as in an ethnography), and when the prime interest is in gathering detailed information about what is happening (i.e. is descriptive). Indeed participation may be required in order to understand a situation (there is a Chinese saying that if you want to understand something you have to chew it in your mouth!).

In participant observational studies the researcher stays with the participants for a substantial period of time to reduce reactivity effects (the effects of the researcher on the researched, changing the behaviour of the latter), recording what is happening, whilst taking a role in that situation. In schools this might be taking on some particular activities, sharing supervisions, participating in school life, recording impressions, conversations, observations, comments, behaviour, events and activities and the views of all participants in a situation. Participant observation, then, requires careful attention to gaining access, building trust, identifying a suitable role and being careful about with whom to be seen or with whom to 'hang out' (e.g. the school principal, a marginalized or fringe member of the group) (Kawulich, 2005: 12–13). Indeed this latter point extends to the need for care in working with informants, so as not to be at the mercy of informants and gatekeepers and to recognize that informants may only provide selective access to people and to data, and, indeed, depending on the views of other members of the group on the informant, they may prevent access to key people (Flick, 2009: 229).

Participant observation is often combined with other forms of data collection that, together, elicit the participants' definitions of the situation and their organizing constructs in accounting for situations and behaviour. By staying in a situation over a long period the researcher is also able to see how events evolve over time, catching the dynamics of situations, the people, personalities, contexts, resources, roles, etc. Morrison (1993: 88) argues that by 'being immersed in a particular context over time not only will the salient features of the situation emerge and present themselves but a more holistic view will be gathered of the interrelationships of factors'. Such immersion facilitates the generation of 'thick descriptions', particularly of social processes and interaction, which lend themselves to accurate explanation and interpretation of events rather than relying on the researcher's own inferences. The data derived from participant observation are 'strong on reality'.

Components of 'thick descriptions' involve recording (Carspecken, 1996: 47), for example: speech acts; non-verbal communication; descriptions in low-inference vocabulary; careful and frequent recording of the time and timing of events; the observer's comments that are placed into categories; detailed contextual data.

Observations are recorded in field notes; these can be written at several levels. At the level of *description* they might include, for example (Spradley, 1980; Bogdan and Biklen, 1992: 120–1; LeCompte and Preissle, 1993: 224):

■ quick, fragmentary jottings of key words/symbols;
■ transcriptions and more detailed observations written out fully;
■ descriptions that, when assembled and written out, form a comprehensive and comprehensible account if what has happened;
■ pen portraits of participants;
■ reconstructions of conversations;
■ descriptions of the physical settings of events;
■ descriptions of events, behaviour and activities;
■ description of the researcher's activities and behaviour.

Lincoln and Guba (1985: 273) suggest a variety of elements or types of observations that include:

■ ongoing notes, either verbatim or categorized *in situ*;
■ logs or diaries of field experiences (similar to field notes though usually written some time after the observations have been made);
■ notes that are made on specific, predetermined themes (e.g. that have arisen from grounded theory);
■ 'chronologs', where each separate behavioural episode is noted, together with the time at which it occurred, or recording an observation at regular time intervals, e.g. every two or three minutes;
■ context maps – maps, sketches, diagrams or some graphic display of the context (usually physical) within which the observation takes place, such graphics enabling movements to be charted;
■ entries on predetermined schedules (including rating scales, checklists and structured observation charts), using taxonomic or categoric systems, where the categories derive from previous observational or interview data;
■ sociometric diagrams (indicating social relationships, e.g. isolates (whom nobody chooses), stars (whom everyone chooses); and dyads (who choose each other));
■ debriefing questionnaires from respondents that are devised for, and by, the observer only, to be used for reminding the observer of main types of information and events once she or he has left the scene;
■ data from debriefing sessions with other researchers, again as an aide-memoire.

LeCompte and Preissle (1993: 199–200) provide a useful set of guidelines for directing observations of specific activities, events or scenes, suggesting that they should include answers to the following questions:

■ Who is in the group/scene/activity – who is taking part?
■ How many people are there, their identities and their characteristics?
■ How do participants come to be members of the group/event/activity?
■ What is taking place?
■ How routine, regular, patterned, irregular and repetitive are the behaviours observed?
■ What resources are being used in the scene?
■ How are activities being described, justified, explained, organized, labelled?
■ How do different participants behave towards each other?

- What are the statuses and roles of the participants?
- Who is making decisions, and for whom?
- What is being said, and by whom?
- What is being discussed frequently/infrequently?
- What appears to be the significant issues that are being discussed?
- What non-verbal communication is taking place?
- Who is talking and who is listening?
- Where does the event take place?
- When does the event take place?
- How long does the event take?
- How is time used in the event?
- How are the individual elements of the event connected?
- How are change and stability managed?
- What rules govern the social organization of, and behaviour in, the event?
- Why is this event occurring, and occurring in the way that it is?
- What meanings are participants attributing to what is happening?
- What are the history, goals and values of the group in question?

That this list is long (and by no means exhaustive) reflects the complexity of even the apparently most mundane activity.

In an earlier volume, Lofland (1971) suggests that there are six main categories of information in participant observation:

- acts (specific actions);
- activities (which last a longer time, for instance, a week, a term, months, e.g. attendance at school, membership of a club);
- meanings (e.g. how participants explain the causes of, meanings of and purposes of particular events and actions);
- participation (what the participants do, e.g. membership of a family group, school groups, peer group, clubs and societies, extra-curricular groups);
- relationships (those which are observed in the several settings and contexts in which the observation is undertaken);
- settings (descriptions of the settings of the actions and behaviours observed).

Spradley (1980: 78) suggests a checklist of the content of field notes:

- space: the physical setting;
- actors: the people in the situation;
- activities: the sets of related acts that are taking place;

- objects: the artefacts and physical things that are there;
- acts: the specific actions that participants are doing;
- events: the sets of activities that are taking place;
- time: the sequence of acts, activities and events;
- goals: what people are trying to achieve;
- feelings: what people feel and how they express this.

Moyles (2002: 181) suggests that researchers need to record the physical and contextual setting of the observation, the participants (e.g. number, who they are, who comes and goes, what they do and what are their roles), the time of day of the observation, the layout of the setting (e.g. seating arrangements, arrangement of desks), the chronology of the events observed, and any critical incidents that happened.

At the level of *reflection*, field notes might include (Bogdan and Biklen, 1992: 122):

- reflections on the descriptions and analyses that have been done;
- reflections on the methods used in the observations and data collection and analysis;
- ethical issues, tensions, problems and dilemmas;
- the reactions of the observer to what has been observed and recorded – attitude, emotion, analysis, etc.;
- points of clarification that have been and/or need to be made;
- possible lines of further enquiry.

Lincoln and Guba (1985: 327) indicate three main types of item that might be included in a journal:

- a daily schedule, including practical matters, e.g. logistics;
- a personal diary, for reflection, speculation and catharsis;
- notes on and a log of methodology.

In deciding what to focus on, Wilkinson (2000: 228) suggests an important distinction between observing *molecular* and *molar* units of behaviour. Small units of behaviour are molecular, e.g. gestures, non-verbal behaviour, short actions, short phrases of a conversation. Whilst these yield very specific data, they risk being taken out of context, such that their meanings and, thereby, their validity, are reduced. By contrast, the molar approach deals in large units of behaviour, the size of which is determined by the theoretical interests of the researcher. The researcher must ensure that the units of focus are valid indicators of the issues of concern to the researcher.

From all this we suggest that the data should be comprehensive enough to enable the reader to reproduce the analysis that was performed. It should focus on the observable and make explicit the inferential, and that the construction of abstractions and generalizations might commence early but should not starve the researcher of novel channels of enquiry (Sacks, 1992).

The context of observation is important (Silverman, 1993: 146). Indeed Spradley (1979) and Kirk and Miller (1986) suggest that observers should keep four sets of observational data to include:

1 notes made *in situ*;
2 expanded notes that are made as soon as possible after the initial observations;
3 journal notes to record issues, ideas, difficulties, etc. that arise during the fieldwork;
4 a developing, tentative running record of ongoing analysis and interpretation.

The intention here is to introduce some systematization into observations in order to increase their reliability. In this respect Silverman (1993) reminds us of the important distinction between *etic* and *emic* analysis. *Etic* analysis uses the conceptual framework of the researcher, whilst *emic* approaches use the conceptual frameworks of those being researched. Structured observation uses *etic* approaches, with predefined frameworks that are adhered to unswervingly, whilst *emic* approaches sit comfortably within qualitative approaches, where the definitions of the situations are captured through the eyes of the observed.

Participant observation studies are not without their critics. The accounts that typically emerge from participant observations echo the criticisms of qualitative data outlined earlier, being described as subjective, biased, impressionistic, idiosyncratic and lacking in the precise quantifiable measures that are the hallmark of survey research and experimentation. Whilst it is probably true that nothing can give better insight into the life of a gang of juvenile delinquents than going to live with them for an extended period of time, critics of participant observation studies will point to the dangers of 'going native' as a result of playing a role within such a group. How do we know that observers do not lose their perspective and become blind to the peculiarities that they are supposed to be investigating?

Further, Johnson and Sackett (1998) suggest that participant observation risks being highly selective, unrepresentative and more concerned with the agenda of the researcher rather than the real situation (they report that researchers were more concerned with political and religious behaviours than with eating and sleeping behaviours, yet political and religious behaviours accounted for only 3 per cent of time whilst eating and sleeping accounted for 60 per cent of the participants' time), i.e. there is skewing of the descriptions.

Adler and Adler (1994: 380) suggest several stages in an observation. Commencing with the selection of a setting on which to focus, the observer then seeks a means of gaining entry to the situation (for example, taking on a role in it). Having gained entry the observer can then commence the observation proper, be it structured or unstructured, focused or unfocused. If quantitative observation is being used then data are gathered to be analysed *post hoc*; if more ethnographic techniques are being used then *progressive focusing* requires the observer to undertake analysis *during* the period of observation itself (discussed earlier).

The question that researchers frequently ask is 'how much observation to do', or 'when do I stop observation?'. Of course, there is no hard and fast rule here, though it may be appropriate to stop when 'theoretical saturation' has been reached (Adler and Adler, 1994: 380), i.e. when the situations that are being observed appear to be repeating data that have already been collected. Of course, it may be important to carry on collecting data at this point, to indicate overall frequencies of observed behaviour, enabling the researcher to find the most to the least common behaviours observed over time. Further, the greater the number of observations, the greater the reliability of the data might be, enabling emergent categories to be verified. What is being addressed here is the reliability of the observations (see the earlier discussion of triangulation).

23.7 Data analysis for less structured observations

For less structured observational data (e.g. from field notes), the tools of qualitative analysis can be used, e.g. coding and categorizing, nodes and connections, summarizing, narrative accounts (of individuals, groups, behaviours, events), constant comparison, theoretical saturation, thematic analysis and patterning (see Part 5). This includes use of computer-based software for analysing qualitative data (e.g. NUD*IST, NVivo, ATLAS.ti, MAXqda).

Simpson and Tuson (2003: 83–5) and Miles and Huberman (1984) indicate several strategies for data analysis of field notes and qualitative data, including:

■ reviewing, analysing and coding early rather than accumulating too much data before analysis;
■ coding densely at first (i.e. avoiding moving too quickly into summarizing);

- keeping track of the data analysis over time (e.g. key codes and what they embrace, key people observed, keeping to the research questions (if appropriate, i.e. depending on the nature of the research));
- verifying intuitions with data;
- identifying themes and patterns (sometimes by counting frequencies or consistencies);
- looking for clusters of events, activities, people, behaviours, etc.;
- writing metaphors to catch the essence of features;
- being prepared to disaggregate as well as aggregate data in order to preserve fidelity to the events/people/situations;
- putting codes into hierarchies (some codes are subsumed by others);
- ensuring conceptual coherence to the analysis.

Merriam (1998) suggests that it is useful for researchers to identify key words, not only in the observed events, but in their analysis, together with attention to the start and end of conversations as these are often significant and most easily remembered. Kawulich (2005) reports the value of 'quantitizing' data, looking for frequencies, together with narrative descriptions of settings, participants, activities and behaviours. She commends the use of two types of field notes for analysis: (a) observed data, including verbatim conversations, and (b) reflections, questions to be asked, issues for further exploration, and comments (i.e. observations on observations). Hence observations data can be both mixed methods in themselves and in conjunction with other methods of data collection and analysis.

23.8 Natural and artificial settings for observation

Most observations by educational researchers will be undertaken in natural settings: schools, classrooms, playgrounds, lessons and suchlike. In studies of a psychological flavour it may be that a contrived, artificial setting is set up in order to give greater observational power to the observers. In Chapter 26 we describe two classic studies in the field of social psychology, both of which use contrived settings – the Milgram study of obedience and the Stanford Prison experiment. Similarly psychological researchers may wish to construct a classroom with a two-way mirror in order to observe children's behaviour without the presence of the observer. This raises the ethical issue of overt and covert research. The advantage of a contrived, artificial setting is the degree of control that the researcher can exert over the situation – typically as large a degree of control as in a laboratory experiment. To the charge that this is an unrealistic situation and that humans should neither be controlled nor manipulated, we refer the reader to the ethical issues addressed in Chapter 5.

One can place settings for observation along a continuum from structured to unstructured and from natural to artificial, as shown in Table 23.2. Settings may be classified by the degree of structure that is imposed on the environment by the observer/researcher, and by the degree of structure inherent in the environment itself (Cooper and Schindler, 2001: 378).

Clearly the researcher will need to be guided by the notion of 'fitness for purpose' in the type of setting and the amount of structure imposed. There is fuzziness between the boundaries here. Structured settings may be useful in testing hypotheses whilst unstructured settings may be useful for generating hypotheses.

23.9 The use of technology in recording observations

Observations include both oral and visual data. In addition to the observer writing down details in field notes, a powerful recording device is through audio-visual

TABLE 23.2	STRUCTURED, UNSTRUCTURED, NATURAL AND ARTIFICIAL SETTINGS FOR OBSERVATIONS	
	Natural setting	*Artificial setting*
Structured	Structured field studies (e.g. Sears *et al.*'s (1965) study of *Identification and Child Rearing*)	Completely structured laboratory (e.g. the Stanford Prison experiment, the Milgram experiment on obedience, see Chapter 26). Experiments with one-way mirrors or video recordings
Unstructured	Completely unstructured field study (e.g. Whyte's (1993) celebrated study of *Street Corner Society*, and ethnographic studies)	Unstructured laboratory (e.g. Axline's (1964) celebrated study of *Dibs in Search of Self*. Observations with one-way mirrors or video recordings)

recording (Erickson, 1992: 209–10). Comprehensive audio-visual recording can overcome the partialness of the observer's view of a single event and can overcome the tendency towards only recording the frequently occurring events. Video recording can offer a more 'unfiltered' observational record than human observation (Simpson and Tuson, 2003: 51), and the record can be viewed several times; it is not a 'once-and-for' all observation. Audio-visual data collection has the capacity for completeness of analysis and comprehensiveness of material, reducing the dependence on prior interpretations by the researcher. Video recording also enables several playbacks to be conducted, to scrutinize the data more fully.

On the other hand, one has to be cautious here, for installing video cameras might create the problem of reactivity. If fixed cameras are used they might be as selective as participant observers, and even if movable, they might still be highly selective (Morrison, 1993: 91). Whilst a human observer can turn his/her attention to an event that occurs, for example, in a different part of the classroom, a fixed video camera cannot, and, indeed, a movable camera that changes direction to focus on that event or group of students might be very intrusive. Further, students, unintentionally, might block the camera's eye or move across the classroom and 'get in the way' of the focus of the camera, such that the observation is lost, whereas a human can see much more easily. Whilst having a second camera in the classroom might overcome this, it is costly not only in terms of equipment but in terms of time needed to review and analyse the recordings. Further, video cameras may need to be set in close-up focus to catch certain details (e.g. facial expressions), but this rules out the benefits of a panoramic focus (e.g. to catch other class members or activities); on the other hand, a panoramic focus may not have the degree of focus required for close-up detail. There is also the issue of when to start and stop the video recording (Flick, 2009: 251).

Some observational behavioural research frequently uses a two-way mirror, in which those being observed see a mirror on a wall through which unseen observers watch what is happening without disturbing the 'natural' (or contrived) setting under observation (e.g. counsellor training, young children interacting with each other, parents with their children) and, thereby, causing anxiety amongst the participants. Often rooms are specifically prepared for this, and they may also include video camera installations. It raises questions of the ethics of covert research, discussed below.

23.10 Timing and causality with observational data

Observation in experimental procedures is prone to problems of timing – too soon and the effect may not be noticed; too late and the effect might have gone or been submerged by other matters. Experiments typically suffer from the problem of only having two time points for observational measurement: the pre-test and the post-test, and this offers researchers little opportunity for identifying causal *processes* and *mechanisms* at work. The choice of timing of observation for establishing causation is crucial and it varies with the purposes of the research. The frequency of the observational data collection varies with the phenomenon under investigation, the scope of the phenomenon, the overall timescale of the phenomenon, the speed at which the dependent variable is likely to change and the level of detailed causal explanation required.

Sometimes micro-time is important (e.g. the intervals of just a few seconds as in the data collection for the ORACLE studies in the 1980s (Galton and Simon, 1980)). In other research a longer time frame is more suitable. Rather than fixing a specific time, it may be the events themselves that dictate the timing of the data collection, so that, for example, changes are reported when they occur, which may vary in time.

The rule of thumb here is that the more accurately we wish to know the causal sequences, the more frequently and closer together must be the observational data collection points. As the number of time points for data collection increases, so does the likelihood of making correct causal inferences and establishing correct causal processes and causation (Morrison, 2009: 168). The second rule of thumb is that the more complex is the phenomenon under investigation, i.e. the more possible causal lines there are in a network of causation, the more time points for observational data collection might be necessary in order to understand the causation at work. Hage and Meeker (1988: 177) comment that most causal processes are either not observable or not easily observable, i.e. inference overrules description. The shorter and more frequent are the time intervals and times of data collection respectively, the more the causal inferences become a matter of fact rather than of faith.

If we wish to understand causation at work then rich data are necessary. Hence, concomitant with the first two rules of thumb comes the third rule of thumb: the more we wish to understand causation and causal processes, then the more it is that qualitative observational data may be useful, as they often have much greater explanatory potential than numerical data. Qualitative observational data can be ongoing and in-depth, and they can indicate causation at work, action narratives and agency within broader conditions and constraints. Consider clinical case studies of individuals, which may have masses of rich qualitative, observational data and field notes that, thereby, enable researchers to understand the processes and mechanisms of causation at work. Participant observation, rather than being an epiphenomenon in the battery of data collection methods, becomes important in understanding causation at work. This is potentiated when used in combination with other qualitative methods (e.g. Hage and Meeker 1988: 179), not least because observation on its own does not establish causation as much causation is unobservable.

Ethnography may have the edge over experimentation in understanding causation in the real world of education rather than the laboratory. The case for qualitative observational data in the understanding of causation and causal processes is powerful, even pre-eminent.

23.11 Ethical considerations

Though observation frequently claims neutrality by being non-interventionist, there are several ethical considerations that surround it, and typically ethics committees for research located in higher education institutions will need to give clearance for the observation(s) to take place. To undertake observation, as with many other forms of data collection requires the informed consent of participants, the right not to be observed, permission from the school and the parents, and, in the UK, clearance concerning your reliability and safety to work with young people in schools (e.g. criminal checks and disclosure form completion). All of these take on even greater significance if the researcher is to conduct participant observation or if the research involves close-up observation (e.g. that which might invade the personal space of participants or any sense of threat (Simpson and Tuson, 2003: 61)). Informed consent also has to attend to the cultural dimension of observation, for example knowing whom to approach, how to address them, how to secure permission in a culturally appropriate manner, and so on.

In addition to informed consent, there is a well-documented literature on the dilemma surrounding overt and covert observation. Whereas in overt research the subjects know that they are being observed, in covert research they do not. On the one hand this latter form of research appears to violate the principle of informed consent, invades the privacy of subjects and private space, treats the participants instrumentally – as

research objects – and places the researcher in a position of misrepresenting her/his role (Mitchell, 1993), or rather, of denying it. However, on the other hand, it is argued (Mitchell, 1993) that there are some forms of knowledge that are legitimately in the public domain but access to which is only available to the covert researcher (see, for example, the fascinating account of the lookout 'watch queen' in the homosexual community (Humphreys, 1975)). Covert research might be necessary to gain access to marginalized and stigmatized groups, or groups who would not willingly accede to the requests of a researcher to become involved in research. This might include those groups in sensitive positions, for example drug users and suppliers, HIV sufferers, political activists, child abusers, police informants and racially motivated attackers.

Mitchell (1993) makes a powerful case for covert research, arguing that not to undertake covert research is to deny access to powerful groups who operate under the protection of silence, to neglect research on sensitive but important topics and to reduce research to mealy-mouthed avoidance of difficult but strongly held issues and beliefs, i.e. to capitulate when the going gets rough! In a series of examples from research undertaken covertly, he makes the case that not to have undertaken this kind of research would be to deny the public access to areas of legitimate concern, the agendas of the powerful (who can manipulate silence and denial of access to their advantage) and the public knowledge of poorly understood groups or situations.

Covert research can also be justified on the grounds that it overcomes problems of reactivity, in particular if the researcher believes that individuals would change their natural behaviour if they knew that they were being observed. In some cases covert research can produce more reliable, less biased results than overt research, and, indeed, may be justified where the safety of the researcher may be at risk (Pearson, 2009).

That covert research can be threatening is well documented from Patrick's (1973) study of a Glasgow gang, where the researcher had to take extreme care not to 'blow his cover' when witness to a murder, to Mitchell's (1993) account of the careful negotiation of role required to undertake covert research into a group of 'millennialists' – ultra-right-wing armed political groups in America who were bound by codes of secrecy, and to his research on mountaineers, where membership of the group involved initiation into the rigours and pains of mountaineering (the researcher had to become a fully fledged mountaineer himself to gain acceptance by the group).

Ethical issues also have to address the problem that observations often disturb the natural setting. Indeed

Bernard (1994) suggests that participation may involve some deception, pretence, impression management in order to achieve rapport, access, immersion, objectivity and an ability to blend into the community or context, even if the researcher is overt rather than covert. Maybe the observer has to feign ignorance or willingness to be involved and to gain access to sensitive or confidential data (thereby using persons as objects rather than as subjects).

The ethical dilemmas of covert research are numerous, charting the tension between invasion and protection of privacy and the public's legitimate 'right to know', between informed consent and its violation in the interests of a wider public, between observation as a superficial, perhaps titillating, spectator sport and as important social research. At issue is the dilemma that arises between protecting the individual and protecting the wider public, posing the question 'whose beneficence?' – whom does the research serve, whom does the research protect, is the greater good the protection and interests of the individual or the protection and interests of the wider public, will the research harm already damaged or vulnerable people, will the research improve their lot, will the research have to treat the researched instrumentally in the interests of gathering otherwise unobtainable yet valuable research data? Should the researcher disclose all the data (Kawulich, 2005) or keep some private? (Kawulich (2005: 14) reports being told that she should not request additional funding for research if the research was not publishable, and she decided not to publish some data, in order to retain good relationships with the group she was studying; her loyalty was to the group rather than to the public.) The researcher has inescapable moral obligations to consider, and, whilst codes of ethical conduct abound, each case might have to be judged on its own merits.

The need for covert research, with due protections, is justified ethically in guidelines and codes of ethics. For example the British Sociological Association (2002: para. 31) indicates that 'the use of covert methods may be justified in certain circumstances' and that 'covert methods violate the principles of informed consent and may invade the privacy of those being studied. Covert researchers might need to take into account the emerging legal frameworks surrounding the right to privacy' (para. 32). The British Educational Research Association (2004) writes that 'researchers must therefore avoid deception or subterfuge unless their research design specifically requires it to ensure that the appropriate data is collected or that the welfare of the researcher is not put in jeopardy' (para. 12). The American Educational Research Association (2000)

appears more stringent, writing that 'Deception is discouraged; it should be used only when clearly necessary for scientific studies, and should then be minimized. After the study, the researcher should explain to the participants and institutional representatives the reasons for the deception' (para. 3); here the requirement for full subsequent disclosure might prevent certain kinds of research from being done. Pearson (2009: 244) comments that in considering covert research 'proportionality' has to be addressed, whereby the potential harm done to individuals and organizations is minimal, and much less than the public benefit to be gained from the research.

Further, the issue of non-intervention is, itself, problematical. Whilst the claim for observation as being non-interventionist was made at the start of this chapter, the issue is not as clear as this, for researchers inhabit the world that they are researching, and their influence may not be neutral (the Hawthorne and halo effects discussed in Chapter 10). This is clearly as issue in, for example, school inspections, where the presence of an inspector in the classroom exerts a powerful influence on what takes place; it is disingenuous to pretend otherwise. Observer effects can be considerable.

Moreover, the non-interventionist observer has to consider her/his position very closely. In the example mentioned above of Patrick's (1973) witness to a murder, should the researcher have 'blown his cover' and reported the murder? What if not acting on the witnessed murder might have yielded access to further sensitive data? Should a researcher investigating drug or child abuse report the first incident or 'hang back' in order to gain access to further, more sensitive data? Should a witness to abuse simply report it or take action about it? If I see an incident of racial abuse, or bullying, do I maintain my non-interventionist position? Do I 'turn a blind eye' to breaches of discipline or school rules, or even criminal acts or plans for criminal acts (Pearson, 2009: 246) (e.g. an individual's or group's plans to bully a student, to physically assault someone, to steal and so on)? Do I undertake criminal acts in order to be an insider to a group? Is the observer merely a journalist, providing data for others to judge? When does non-intervention become morally reprehensible? These are issues for which one cannot turn to codes of conduct for a clear adjudication.

23.12 Some cautionary comments

Many observation situations carry the risk of bias (e.g. Wilkinson, 2000: 228; Moyles, 2002: 179; Robson, 2002: 324–5; Shaughnessy *et al.*, 2003: 116–17; Flick, 2009: chapter 17), for example by:

- *Selective attention* of the observer (what we see is a function of where we look, what we look at, how we look, when we look, what we think we see, whom we look at; what is in our minds at the time of observation; what are our own interests and experiences).

- *Reactivity* (participants may change their behaviour if they know that they are being observed, e.g. they may try harder in class, they may feel more anxious, they may behave much better or much worse than normal, they may behave in ways in which they think the researcher wishes or in ways for which the researcher tacitly signals approval: 'demand characteristics' (Shaughnessy *et al.*, 2003: 113)).

- *Attention deficit* (what if the observer is distracted, or looks away and misses an event?).

- *Validity of constructs* (decisions have to be taken on what counts as valid evidence for a judgement. For example, is a smile a relaxed smile, a nervous smile, a friendly smile, a hostile smile? Does looking at a person's non-verbal gestures count as a valid indicator of interaction? Are the labels and indicators used to describe the behaviour of interest valid indicators of that behaviour?).

- *Selective data entry* (what we record is sometimes affected by our personal judgement rather than the phenomenon itself; we sometimes interpret the situation and then record our interpretation rather than the phenomenon).

- *Selective memory* (if we write up our observations after the event our memory neglects and selects data, sometimes overlooking the need to record the contextual details of the observation; notes should be written either during or immediately after the observation).

- *Interpersonal matters and counter-transference* (our interpretations are affected by our judgements and preferences – what we like and what we don't like about people and their behaviour, together with the relationships that we may have developed with those being observed and the context of the situation; researchers have to deliberately distance themselves from the situation and address reflexivity).

- *Expectancy effects* (the observer knows the hypotheses to be tested, or the findings of similar studies, or has expectations of finding certain behaviours, and these may influence her/his observations).

- *Decisions on how to record* (the same person in a group under observation may be demonstrating the behaviour repeatedly, but nobody else in the group may be demonstrating that behaviour: there is a need to record how many different people show the behaviour).

- *Number of observers* (different observers of the same situation may be looking in different directions, and so there may be inconsistency in the results. Therefore there is a need for training, for consistency, for clear definition of what constitutes the behaviour, of entry/judgement, and for kinds of recording).

- *The problem of inference* (observations can only record what happens and what can be seen, and it may be dangerous, without any other evidence, e.g. triangulation, to infer the reasons, intentions and causes and purposes that lie behind actors' behaviours. One cannot always judge intention from observation: for example, a child may intend to be friendly, but it may be construed by an inexperienced observer as selfishness; a teacher may wish to be helpful but the researcher may interpret it as threatening. It is dangerous to infer a stimulus from a response, an intention from an observation. Similarly one may not see certain phenomena emerging over time (e.g. biographical processes)).

The issues here concern validity and reliability. With regard to the validity of the observation, researchers have to ensure that the indicators of the construct under investigation are fair and operationalized, for example, so that there is agreement on what counts as constituting qualities such as 'friendly', 'happy', 'aggressive', 'sociable' and 'unapproachable'. The matter of what to observe is problematic. For example, do you only focus on certain people rather than the whole group, on certain events and at certain times rather than others, on molar or molecular units? Do you provide a close-grained, close-up observation or a holistic, wider-focused and wider-ranging observation, i.e. do you use a zoom lens and obtain high definition of a limited scope, or a wide-angle lens and obtain a full field but lacking in detail, or somewhere between the two? How do you decide on what to focus?

Expectancy effects can be overcome by ensuring that the observers do not know the purpose of the research, the 'double-blind' approach.

With regard to reliability, the indicators have to be applied fully, consistently and securely, with no variation in interpretation. Not only is this a matter for one observer – consistency in his or her observation and recording – but it is also a matter if there are several observers. A formula for calculating the degree of agreement (as a percentage) between observers can be used thus:

$$\frac{\text{Number of times two observers agree}}{\text{Number of possible opportunities to agree}} \times 100$$

In measuring inter-rater reliability one should strive for a high percentage (over 90 per cent minimum). Other measures of inter-rater reliability use correlations, and here coefficients of >0.90 (i.e. over 90 per cent) should be sought (Shaughnessy *et al.*, 2003: 111).

To ensure the researcher's or researchers' reliability, it is likely that training is required, so that, for example, researchers:

- use the same operational definitions;
- record the same observations in the same way;
- have good concentration;
- can focus on detail;
- can be unobtrusive but attentive;
- have the necessary experience to make informed judgements from the observational data.

These qualities are essential in order to avoid fatigue, 'observer drift' (Cooper and Schindler, 2001: 380) and halo effects, all of which can reduce the reliability of the data.

With regard to the issue of reactivity, one suggestion is to adopt covert observation, though this raises ethical issues which have been addressed in Chapter 5. Another suggestion is to adopt habituation, i.e. the researcher remains in the situation for such a long time that participants not only become used to his/her presence but revert to their natural behaviour.

Lofland (1971: 104–6) suggests that, to overcome problems of reliability in the research, it is also important for the observer to write up notes as soon after the event as possible, to write quickly yet to expect to take a long time to write notes, to consider dictating notes (though writing may stimulate more thought), to use a word-processing facility as it aids later analysis through software packages, and to make two copies: one of the original data and another for manipulation and analysis (e.g. cutting and pasting data).

23.13 Conclusion

Observation methods are powerful tools for gaining insight into situations. As with other data collection techniques, they are beset by issues of validity and reliability. Even low inference observation, perhaps the safest form of observation, is itself highly selective, just as perception is selective. Higher forms of inference, whilst moving towards establishing causality, rely on greater levels of interpretation by the observer, wherein the observer makes judgements about intentionality and motivation. In this respect it has been suggested that additional methods of gathering data might be employed, to provide corroboration and triangulation,

in short, to ensure that reliable inferences are derived from reliable data.

In planning observations one has to consider:

- When, where, how and what to observe.
- How much degree of structure is necessary in the observation.
- The duration of the observation period, which must be suitable for the behaviour to occur and be observed.
- The timing of the observation period (e.g. morning, afternoon, evening).
- The context of the observation (a meeting, a lesson, a development workshop, a senior management briefing, etc.).
- The nature of the observation (structured, semi-structured, open, molar, molecular, etc.).
- The need for there to be an opportunity to observe, for example to ensure that there is the presence of the people to be observed of the behaviour to be observed.
- The merging of subjective and objective observation, even in a structured observation: an observation schedule can become highly subjective when it is being completed, as interpretation, selection and counter-transference may enter the observation, and operational definitions may not always be sufficiently clear.
- The value of covert participant observation in order to reduce reactivity.
- Threats to reliability and validity.
- The need to operationalize the observation so that what counts as evidence is consistent, unambiguous and valid, for example what constitutes a particular quality (e.g. anti-social behaviour: what counts as antisocial behaviour – one person's 'sociable' is another's 'unsociable' and vice versa).
- The need to choose the appropriate kind of structured observation and recording (e.g. event sampling, instantaneous sampling, whole interval/partial interval recording, duration recording, dichotomous/rating scale recording).
- How to go under cover, or whether informed consent is necessary.
- Whether deception is justified.
- Which role(s) to adopt on the continuum of complete participant, to participant-as-observer, to observer as participant, to complete observer.

Observation can be a very useful research tool. On the other hand it exacts its price, for example: it may take a long time to catch the required behaviour or phenomenon, it can be costly in time and effort, and it is prone to difficulties of interpreting or inferring what the data mean. This chapter has outlined several different types of observation and the premises that underlie them, the selection of the method to be used depending on 'fitness for purpose'. Overriding the issues of which specific method of observation to use, this chapter has suggested that observation places the observer into the moral domain, that it is insufficient simply to describe observation as a non-intrusive, non-interventionist technique and thereby to abrogate responsibility for the participants involved. Like other forms of data collection in the human sciences, observation is not a morally neutral enterprise. Observers, like other researchers, have obligations to participants as well as to the research community.

For examples of observational data see the accompanying website.

 Companion Website

The companion website to the book includes PowerPoint slides for this chapter, which list the structure of the chapter and then provide a summary of the key points in each of its sections. In addition there is further information in the form of sample observation notes. These resources can be found online at **www.routledge. com/textbooks/cohen7e**.

Tests

The field of testing is so extensive that the comments that follow must needs be of an introductory nature and the reader seeking a deeper understanding will need to refer to specialist texts and sources on the subject. Limitations of space permit no more than a brief outline of a small number of key issues to do with tests and testing. This includes:

- what are we testing?
- parametric and non-parametric tests
- norm-referenced, criterion-referenced and domain-referenced tests
- commercially produced tests and researcher-produced tests
- constructing a test
- software for preparation of a test
- devising a pre-test and post-test
- ethical issues in testing
- computerized adaptive testing

Since the spelling test of Rice (1897), the fatigue test of Ebbinghaus (1897) and the intelligence scale of Binet (1905), the growth of tests has proceeded at an extraordinary pace in terms of volume, variety, scope and sophistication. In tests, researchers have at their disposal a powerful method of data collection, an impressive array of tests for gathering data of a numerical rather than verbal kind. In considering testing for gathering research data, several issues need to be borne in mind, not the least of which is why tests are being used at all:

- What are we testing (e.g. achievement, aptitude, attitude, personality, intelligence, social adjustment, etc.)?
- Are we dealing with parametric or non-parametric tests?
- Are they norm-referenced or criterion-referenced?
- Are they available commercially for researchers to use or will researchers have to develop home-produced tests?
- Do the test scores derive from a pre-test and post-test in the experimental method?
- Are they group or individual tests?
- Do they involve self-reporting or are they administered tests?

Let us unpack some of these issues.

24.1 What are we testing?

There is a myriad of tests, to cover all aspects of a student's life and for all ages (young children to old adults), for example:

ability
achievement
anxiety
aptitude
attainment
attitudes and values
behavioural disorders
competence-based assessment
computer-based assessment
creativity
critical thinking
cross-cultural adjustment
depression
diagnostic assessment
diagnosis of difficulties
higher order thinking
intelligence
interest inventories
introversion and extraversion
language proficiency tests
learning disabilities
locus of control
motivation and interest
neuropsychological assessment
performance
performance in school subjects
personality
potential
projective tests
reading readiness
self-esteem

sensory and perceptual tests
social adjustment
spatial awareness
special abilities and disabilities
stress and burnout
university entrance tests
verbal and non-verbal reasoning

The *Handbook of Psychoeducational Assessment* (Sak-lofske *et al.*, 2001) includes sections on ability assessment, achievement assessment, behaviour assessment, cross-cultural cognitive assessment and neuropsychological assessment. The *Handbook of Psychological and Educational Assessment of Children: Intelligence, Aptitude and Achievement* (Reynolds and Kamphaus, 2003) provides a clear overview of, *inter alia*:

- the history of psychological and educational assessment;
- a practical model of test development;
- legal and ethical issues in the assessment of children;
- measurement and design issues in the assessment of children;
- intelligence testing, both verbal and non-verbal;
- memory testing;
- neuropsychological and biological perspectives on the assessment of children;
- assessment of academic skills;
- criterion-referenced testing;
- diagnostic assessment;
- writing abilities and instructional needs;
- assessment of learning disabilities;
- bias in aptitude assessment;
- assessment of culturally and linguistically diverse children;
- assessment of creativity;
- assessment of language impairment;
- assessment of psychological and educational needs of children with severe mental retardation and brain injury;
- computer-based assessment.

The purpose in providing this comprehensive list is to indicate not only that there is a copious amount of assessment and testing material available but that it covers a very wide spectrum of topics. *The Eighteenth Mental Measurements Yearbook* (Spies *et al.*, 2010) and *Tests in Print VII* (Murphy *et al.*, 2010) are useful sources of published tests, as are specific publishers such as Harcourt Assessment and John Wiley. The American Psychological Association also produces on its website *Finding Information about Psychological*

Tests: (www.apa.org/science/programs/testing/find-tests.aspx) and the British Psychological Society (www.bps.org.uk; www.psychtesting.org.uk and www.psychtesting.org.uk/directories/directories_home.cfm) produces lists of tests and suppliers. Standard texts that detail copious tests, suppliers and websites include: Gronlund and Linn (1990); Kline (2000); Loewenthal (2001); Saklofske *et al.* (2001); Reynolds and Kamphaus (2003); and Aiken (2003). The British Psychological Society also produces a glossary of terms connected with testing, at www.psychtesting.org.uk/download$.cfm?file_uuid=A1FBEA7D-1143-DFD0–7EAB-C510B9D1DC1A&siteName=ptc

24.2 Parametric and non-parametric tests

Parametric tests are designed to represent the wide population, e.g. of a country or age group. They make assumptions about the wider population and the characteristics of that wider population, i.e. the parameters of abilities are known. They assume (Morrison, 1993):

- that there is a normal curve of distribution of scores in the population (the bell-shaped symmetry of the Gaussian curve of distribution seen, for example, in standardized scores of IQ or the measurement of people's height or the distribution of achievement on reading tests in the population as a whole),
- that there are continuous and equal intervals between the test scores, and, with tests that have a true zero (see Chapter 34), the opportunity for a score of, say, 80 per cent to be double that of 40 per cent; this differs from the ordinal scaling of rating scales discussed earlier in connection with questionnaire design where equal intervals between each score could not be assumed.

Parametric tests will usually be published tests which are commercially available and which have been piloted and standardized on a large and representative sample of the whole population. They usually arrive complete with the backup data on sampling, reliability and validity statistics which have been computed in the devising of the tests. Working with these tests enables the researcher to use statistics applicable to interval and ratio levels of data.

On the other hand, non-parametric tests make few or no assumptions about the distribution of the population (the parameters of the scores) or the characteristics of that population. The tests do not assume a regular bell-shaped curve of distribution in the wider population; indeed the wider population is perhaps irrelevant as these tests are designed for a given specific population – a class in school, a chemistry group, a primary school year group. Because they make no assumptions about the wider population, the researcher must work with non-parametric statistics appropriate to nominal and ordinal levels of data. Parametric tests, with a true zero and marks awarded, are the stock-in-trade of classroom teachers – the spelling test, the mathematics test, the end-of-year examination, the mock examination.

The attraction of non-parametric statistics is their utility for small samples because they do not make any assumptions about how normal, even and regular the distributions of scores will be. Furthermore, computation of statistics for non-parametric tests is less complicated than that for parametric tests. Non-parametric tests have the advantage of being tailored to particular institutional, departmental and individual circumstances. They offer teachers a valuable opportunity for quick, relevant and focused feedback on student performance.

Parametric tests are more powerful than non-parametric tests because they not only derive from standardized scores but enable the researcher to compare sub-populations with a whole population (e.g. to compare the results of one school or local education authority with the whole country, for instance in comparing students' performance in norm-referenced or criterion-referenced tests against a national average score in that same test). They enable the researcher to use powerful statistics in data processing (see Chapters 34–8), and to make *inferences* about the results. Because non-parametric tests make no assumptions about the wider population a different set of statistics is available to the researcher (see Part 5). These can be used in very specific situations – one class of students, one year group, one style of teaching, one curriculum area – and hence are valuable to teachers.

24.3 Norm-referenced, criterion-referenced and domain-referenced tests

A norm-referenced test compares students' achievements relative to other students' achievements (e.g. a national test of mathematical performance or a test of intelligence which has been standardized on a large and representative sample of students between the ages of six and 16). A criterion-referenced test does not compare student with student but, rather, requires the student to fulfil a given set of criteria, a predefined and absolute standard or outcome (Cunningham, 1998). For example, a driving test is usually criterion-referenced

since to pass it requires the ability to meet certain test items – reversing round a corner, undertaking an emergency stop, avoiding a crash, etc. *regardless* of how many others have or have not passed the driving test. Similarly many tests of playing a musical instrument require specified performances – e.g. the ability to play a particular scale or arpeggio, the ability to play a Bach Fugue without hesitation or technical error. If the student meets the criteria, then he or she passes the examination.

A criterion-referenced test provides the researcher with information about exactly what a student has learned, what she can do, whereas a norm-referenced test can only provide the researcher with information on how well one student has achieved in comparison to another, enabling rank orderings of performance and achievement to be constructed. Hence a major feature of the norm-referenced test is its ability to discriminate between students and their achievements – a well constructed norm-referenced test enables differences in achievement to be measured acutely, i.e. to provide variability or a great range of scores. For a criterion-referenced test this is less of a problem, the intention here is to indicate whether students have achieved a set of given criteria, regardless of how many others might or might not have achieved them, hence variability or range is less important here.

More recently an outgrowth of criterion-referenced testing has been the rise of domain-referenced tests (Gipps, 1994: 81). Here considerable significance is accorded to the careful and detailed specification of the content or the domain which will be assessed. The domain is the particular field or area of the subject that is being tested, for example, light in science, two-part counterpoint in music, parts of speech in English language. The domain is set out very clearly and very fully, such that the full depth and breadth of the content are established. Test items are then selected from this very full field, with careful attention to sampling procedures so that representativeness of the wider field is ensured in the test items. The student's achievements on that test are computed to yield a proportion of the maximum score possible, and this, in turn, is used as an index of the proportion of the overall domain that she has grasped. So, for example, if a domain has 1,000 items and the test has 50 items, and the student scores 30 marks from the possible 50 then it is inferred that she has grasped 60 per cent ($\{30 \div 50\} \times 100$) of the domain of 1,000 items. Here inferences are being made from a limited number of items to the student's achievements in the whole domain; this requires careful and representative sampling procedures for test items.

24.4 Commercially produced tests and researcher-produced tests

There is a battery of tests in the public domain which cover a vast range of topics and which can be used for evaluative purposes (references are indicated at the start of this chapter).

Most schools will have used published tests at one time or another. There are several attractions to using published tests:

■ they are objective;
■ they have been piloted and refined;
■ they have been standardized across a named population (e.g. a region of the country, the whole country, a particular age group or various age groups) so that they represent a wide population;
■ they declare how reliable and valid they are (mentioned in the statistical details which are usually contained in the manual of instructions for administering the test);
■ they tend to be parametric tests, hence enabling sophisticated statistics to be calculated;
■ they come complete with instructions for administration;
■ they are often straightforward and quick to administer and to mark;
■ guides to the interpretation of the data are usually included in the manual;
■ researchers are spared the task of having to devise, pilot and refine their own test.

On the other hand Howitt and Cramer (2005) suggest that commercially produced tests are expensive to purchase and to administer; they are often targeted to special, rather than general, populations (e.g. in psychological testing), and they may not be exactly suited to the purpose required. Further, several commercially produced tests have restricted release or availability, hence the researcher might have to register with a particular association or be given clearance to use the test or to have copies of it. For example, Harcourt Assessment and McGraw-Hill publishers not only hold the rights to a worldwide battery of tests of all kinds but require registration before releasing tests. In this example Harcourt Assessment also has different levels of clearance, so that certain parties or researchers may not be eligible to have a test released to them because they do not fulfil particular criteria for eligibility.

Published tests by definition are not tailored to institutional or local contexts or needs; indeed their claim to objectivity is made on the grounds that they are deliberately supra-institutional. The researcher wishing to use published tests must be certain that the purposes, objectives and content of the published tests match the purposes, objectives and content of the evaluation. For example, a published diagnostic test might not fit the needs of the evaluation to have an achievement test, a test of achievement might not have the predictive quality which the researcher seeks in an aptitude test, a published reading test might not address the areas of reading that the researcher is wishing to cover, a verbal reading test written in English might contain language which is difficult for a student whose first language is not English. These are important considerations. A much-cited text on evaluating the utility for researchers of commercially available tests is produced by the American Psychological Association (1999) in the *Standards for Educational and Psychological Testing* (www.apa.org/science/programs/testing/standards.aspx).

The golden rule for deciding to use a published test is that it must demonstrate *fitness for purpose*. If it fails to demonstrate this, then tests will have to be devised by the researcher. The attraction of this latter point is that such a 'home-grown' test will be tailored to the local and institutional context very tightly, i.e. that the purposes, objectives and content of the test will be deliberately fitted to the *specific* needs of the researcher in a specific, given context. In discussing fitness for purpose Cronbach (1949) and Gronlund and Linn (1990) set out a range of criteria against which a commercially produced test can be evaluated for its suitability for specific research purposes.

Researchers should be cautious, perhaps, in considering whether to employ commercially produced tests, particularly in the case of having to use them with individuals and groups that are different from those in which the test was devised, as many tests show cultural bias. Further, there is the issue of the language medium of the test – for example using the Wechsler tests of intelligence (in English medium) with students who are not native speakers of English or who do not know about certain aspects of English culture turns the test away from a test on intelligence and towards a test of English language ability and English cultural knowledge.

Many commercially produced tests might be available in languages other than the original, but not only should the translations be checked to see if they are correct but the cultural significance of the test items themselves should be checked to see that they hold the same meaning and connotations in the target language as they do in the original language. It is often dangerous to import tests developed in one language and one culture into another language and another culture, as there are problems of validity, bias and reliability.

Against these advantages of course there are several important considerations in devising a 'homegrown' test. Not only might it be time-consuming to devise, pilot, refine and then administer the test but, because much of it will probably be non-parametric, there will be a more limited range of statistics which may be applied to the data than in the case of parametric tests.

The scope of tests and testing is far-reaching; no areas of educational activity are untouched by them. Achievement tests, largely summative in nature, measure achieved performance in a given content area. Aptitude tests are intended to predict capability, achievement potential, learning potential and future achievements. However, the assumption that these two constructs – achievement and aptitude – are separate has to be questioned (Cunningham, 1998); indeed it is often the case that a test of aptitude for, say, geography, at a particular age or stage will be measured by using an achievement test at that age or stage. Cunningham (1998) has suggested that an achievement test might include more straightforward measures of basic skills whereas aptitude tests might put these in combination, e.g. combining reasoning (often abstract) and particular knowledge, i.e. achievement and aptitude tests differ according to what they are testing.

Not only do the tests differ according to what they measure, but, since both can be used predictively, they differ according to what they might be able to predict. For example, because an achievement test is more specific and often tied to a specific content area, it will be useful as a predictor of future performance in that content area but will be largely unable to predict future performance out of that content area. An aptitude test tends to test more generalized abilities (e.g. aspects of 'intelligence', skills and abilities that are common to several areas of knowledge or curricula), hence it is able to be used as a more generalized predictor of achievement. Achievement tests, Gronlund (1985) suggests, are more linked to school experiences whereas aptitude tests encompass out-of-school learning and wider experiences and abilities. However Cunningham (1998), in arguing that there is a considerable overlap between the two types, is suggesting that the difference is largely cosmetic. An achievement test tends to be much more specific and linked to instructional programmes and cognate areas than an aptitude test, which looks for more general aptitudes (Hanna, 1993) (e.g. intelligence or intelligences (Gardner, 1993)).

24.5 Constructing a test

Researchers considering constructing a test of their own will need to be aware of classical test theory (CTT) and

Item Response Theory (IRT). Classical test theory assumes that there is a 'true score', which is the score which an individual would obtain on that test if the measurement was made without error and the expected score that would be gained over an infinite number of independent test administrations. It is the score that would be found by calculating the mean score that the individual test-taker would obtain on that same test if that person took it on an infinite number of occasions.

However, CTT recognizes that, in fact, errors do arise in the real world, due to, for example, cultural and socio-economic backgrounds and bias in the test, administration and marking of the test, and attitudes to the test by the test-takers. Hence tests provide an 'observed score' rather than a 'true score'; the observed score (X) is the true score (T) plus the error (E) (X = T + E). A true score in CTT depends on the contents of the test rather than the characteristics of the test-taker, and the difficulty of the items might depend on the characteristics of the sample (a sampling issue) rather than on the item itself, i.e. it may be difficult to compare the results of different test-takers on different tests. Readers are advised to review classical test theory and reliability in connection with this formula and the calculation of the error (e.g. Kline, 2005).

By contrast, Item Response Theory (IRT) is based on the principle that it is possible to measure single, specific latent traits, abilities, attributes that, themselves, are not observable, i.e. to determine observable quantities of unobservable quantities (e.g. Hambleton, 1993). The theory/model assumes a relationship between a person's possession or level of a particular attribute, trait or ability and his/her response to a test item. IRT is also based on the view that it is possible:

- to identify objective levels of difficulty of an item, e.g. the Rasch model (Wainer and Mislevy, 1990);
- to devise items that will be able to discriminate effectively between individuals;
- to describe an item independently of any particular sample of people who might be responding to it, i.e. is not group-dependent (i.e. the item difficulty and item discriminability are independent of the sample);
- to describe a testee's proficiency in terms of his or her achievement of an item of a known difficulty level;
- to describe a person independently of any sample of items that has been administered to that person (i.e. a testee's ability does not depend on the particular sample of test items);

- to specify and predict the properties of a test before it has been administered;
- for traits to be unidimensional (single traits are specifiable, e.g. verbal ability, mathematical proficiency) and to account for test outcomes and performance in terms of that unidimensional trait, i.e. for an item to measure a single, undimensional trait;
- for a set of items to measure a common trait or ability;
- for a testee's response to any one test item not to affect his or her response to another test item;
- that the probability of the correct response to an item does not depend on the number of testees who might be at the same level of ability;
- that it is possible to identify objective levels of difficulty of an item;
- that a statistic can be calculated that indicates the precision of the measured ability for each testee, and that this statistic depends on the ability of the testee and the number and properties of the test items.

In devising a test the researcher will have to consider not only the foundations of the test (e.g. in CTT or IRT) but also:

- the *purposes* of the test (for answering evaluation questions and ensuring that it tests what it is supposed to be testing, e.g. the achievement of the objectives of a piece of the curriculum);
- the *type* of test (e.g. diagnostic, achievement, aptitude, criterion-referenced, norm-referenced);
- the *objectives* of the test (cast in very specific terms so that the content of the test items can be seen to relate to specific objectives of a programme or curriculum);
- the *content* of the test (what is being tested and what the test items are);
- the *construction* of the test, involving *item analysis* in order to clarify the *item discriminability* and *item difficulty* of the test (see below);
- the *format* of the test – its layout, instructions, method of working and of completion (e.g. oral instructions to clarify what students will need to write, or a written set of instructions to introduce a practical piece of work);
- the nature of the *piloting* of the test;
- the *validity and reliability* of the test;
- the provision of a *manual of instructions* for the administration, marking and data treatment of the test (this is particularly important if the test is not to be administered by the researcher or if the test is to be administered by several different people, so that reliability is ensured by having a standard procedure).

In planning a test the researcher can proceed through the following headings.

Identify the purposes of the test

The purposes of a test are several, for example to *diagnose* a student's strengths weaknesses and difficulties, to measure *achievement*, to measure *aptitude* and *potential*, to identify *readiness* for a programme (Gronlund and Linn (1990) term this 'placement testing' and it is usually a form of pre-test, normally designed to discover whether students have the essential prerequisites to begin a programme, e.g. in terms of knowledge, skills, understandings). These types of tests occur at different stages. For example, the placement test is conducted prior to the commencement of a programme, and will identify starting abilities and achievements – the initial or 'entry' abilities in a student. If the placement test is designed to assign students to tracks, sets or teaching groups (i.e. to place them into administrative or teaching groupings), then the entry test might be criterion-referenced or norm-referenced; if it is designed to measure detailed starting points, knowledge, abilities and skills then the test might be more criterion-referenced as it requires a high level of detail. It has its equivalent in 'baseline assessment' and is an important feature if one is to measure the 'value-added' component of teaching and learning: one can only assess how much a set of educational experiences has added value to the student if one knows that student's starting point and starting abilities and achievements.

- *Formative* testing is undertaken during a programme, and is designed to monitor students' progress during that programme, to measure achievement of sections of the programme, and to diagnose strengths and weaknesses. It is typically criterion-referenced.
- *Diagnostic* testing is an in-depth test to discover particular strengths, weaknesses and difficulties that a student is experiencing, and is designed to expose causes and specific areas of weakness or strength. This often requires the test to include several items about the same feature, so that, for example, several types of difficulty in a student's understanding will be exposed; the diagnostic test will need to construct test items that will focus on each of a range of very specific difficulties that students might be experiencing, in order to identify the exact problems that they are having from a range of possible problems. Clearly this type of test is criterion-referenced.
- *Summative* testing is the test given at the end of the programme, and is designed to measure achievement,

outcomes or 'mastery'. This might be criterion-referenced or norm-referenced, depending to some extent on the use to which the results will be put (e.g. to award certificates or grades, to identify achievement of specific objectives).

Identify the test specifications

The test specifications include:

- which programme objectives and student learning outcomes will be addressed;
- which content areas will be addressed;
- the relative weightings, balance and coverage of items;
- the total number of items in the test;
- the number of questions required to address a particular element of a programme or learning outcomes;
- the exact items in the test.

To ensure validity in a test it is essential to ensure that the objectives of the test are fairly addressed in the test items. Objectives, it is argued (Mager, 1962; Wiles and Bondi, 1984), should: (a) be specific and be expressed with an appropriate degree of precision; (b) represent intended learning outcomes; (c) identify the actual and observable behaviour which will demonstrate achievement; (d) include an active verb; (e) be unitary (focusing on one item per objective).

The test must measure what it purports to measure. It should demonstrate several forms of validity (e.g. construct, content, concurrent, predictive, criterion-related), discussed later.

One way of ensuring that the objectives are fairly addressed in test items can be done through a matrix frame that indicates the *coverage* of content areas, the coverage of *objectives* of the programme and the *relative weighting* of the items on the test. Such a matrix is

set out in Table 24.1 taking the example from a secondary school history syllabus.

Table 24.1 indicates the main areas of the programme to be covered in the test (*content areas*); then it indicates which objectives or detailed content areas will be covered (1a–3c) – these numbers refer to the identified specifications in the syllabus; then it indicates the marks/percentages to be awarded for each area. This indicates several points:

- the least emphasis is given to the build-up to and end of the war (10 marks each in the 'total' column);
- the greatest emphasis is given to the invasion of France (35 marks in the 'total' column);
- there is fairly even coverage of the objectives specified (the figures in the 'total' row only vary from 9–13);
- greatest coverage is given to objectives 2a and 3a, and least coverage is given to objective 1c;
- some content areas are not covered in the test items (the blanks in the matrix).

Hence we have here a test scheme that indicates relative weightings, coverage of objectives and content, and the relation between these two latter elements. Gronlund and Linn (1990) suggest that relative weightings should be addressed by first assigning percentages at the foot of each column, then by assigning percentages at the end of each row, and then completing each cell of the matrix within these specifications. This ensures that appropriate sampling and coverage of the items are achieved. The example of the matrix refers to specific objectives as column headings; of course these could be replaced by factual knowledge, conceptual knowledge and principles, and skills for each of the column headings. Alternatively they could be replaced with specific aspects of an activity, for example (Cohen

---

TABLE 24.1 A MATRIX OF TEST ITEMS

Content areas	Objective/area of programme content			Objective/area of programme content			Objective/area of programme content			
Aspects of the 1939–45 war	1a	1b	1c	2a	2b	2c	3a	3b	3c	Total
The build-up to the 1939–45 world war	1	2		2	1	1	1	1	1	10
The invasion of Poland	2	1	1	3	2	2	3	3	3	20
The invasion of France	3	4	5	4	4	3	4	4	4	35
The allied invasion	3	2	3	3	4	3	3	2	2	25
The end of the conflict	2	1		1	1	1	2	2		10
Total	11	10	9	13	12	10	13	12	10	100

TABLE 24.2   COMPILING ELEMENTS OF TEST ITEMS

Content area	Identifying key concepts and principles	Practical skills	Evaluative skills	Recording results	Total
Designing a crane	2	1	1	3	7
Making the crane	2	5	2	3	12
Testing the crane	3	3	1	4	11
Evaluating the results	3		5	4	12
Improving the design	2	2	3	1	8
Total	12	11	12	15	50

et al., 2004: 339): designing a crane, making the crane, testing the crane, evaluating the results, improving the design. Indeed these latter could become content (row) headings, as shown in Table 24.2. Here one can see that practical skills will carry fewer marks than recording skills (the column totals), and that making and evaluating carry equal marks (the row totals).

This exercise also enables some indication to be gained on the number of items to be included in the test, for instance in the example of the history test above the matrix is 9 × 6 = 54 possible items, and in the 'crane' activity above the matrix is 5 × 4 = 20 possible items. Of course, there could be considerable variation in this, for example more test items could be inserted if it were deemed desirable to test one cell of the matrix with more than one item (possible for cross-checking), or indeed there could be fewer items if it were possible to have a single test item that serves more than one cell of the matrix. The difficulty in matrix construction is that it can easily become a runaway activity, generating very many test items and, hence, leading to an unworkably long test – typically the greater the degree of specificity required, the greater the number of test items there will be. One skill in test construction is to be able to have a single test item that provides valid and reliable data for more than a single factor.

Having undertaken the test specifications, the researcher should have achieved clarity on (a) the exact test items that test certain aspects of achievement of objectives, programmes, contents, etc.; (b) the coverage and balance of coverage of the test items; and (c) the relative weightings of the test items.

Address validity and reliability

Validity concerns the extent to which the test tests what it is supposed to test; it must measure what it purports to measure. It should demonstrate several forms of validity (see also Chapter 10):

- construct validity (the extent to which the test measures a particular construct, trait, behaviour, evidenced through convergent validity and discriminant, divergent validity, and by correlating the test with other published tests with the same purposes and similar contents);
- content validity (by adequate and representative coverage of the domain, field, tasks, behaviours, knowledge, etc., without interference from extraneous variables);
- concurrent validity (the extent to which the test correlates with other tests in a similar field);
- predictive validity (that it applies to the situation under consideration, e.g. that it accurately predicts final scores);
- criterion-related validity (the extent to which the performance on the test enables the researcher to infer the individual's performance on a particular criterion of interest, often calculated as a correlation between the score on a test and a score in another indication of the item that the test was intended to measure, e.g. a test of performance on a job-specific matter and the individual's actual performance on that job-specific item in the real situation);
- cultural validity (fairness to the language and culture of the individual test-takers, and avoidance of cultural bias: a feature of all research instruments, not solely tests);
- consequential validity (that the results of the test are used fairly and ethically (discussed later in this chapter), and are only for the purpose of, and ways in which, the test was constructed).

Reliability concerns the degree of confidence that can be placed in the results and the data, which is often a matter of statistical calculation and subsequent test redesigning. Reliability is addressed through the forms and techniques set out in Chapter 10: test/re-test, parallel forms, split-half and internal consistency (Cronbach's alpha).

Select the contents of the test

Here the test is subject to *item analysis*. Gronlund and Linn (1990) suggest that an item analysis will need to consider:

- the suitability of the format of each item for the (learning) objective (appropriateness);
- the ability of each item to enable students to demonstrate their performance of the (learning) objective (relevance);
- the clarity of the task for each item;
- the straightforwardness of the task;
- the unambiguity of the outcome of each item, and agreement on what that outcome should be;
- the cultural fairness of each item;
- the independence of each item (i.e. where the influence of other items of the test is minimal and where successful completion of one item is not dependent on successful completion of another);
- the adequacy of coverage of each (learning) objective by the items of the test.

In moving to test construction the researcher will need to consider how each element to be tested will be *operationalized*: (a) what indicators and kinds of evidence of achievement of the objective will be required; (b) what indicators of high, moderate and low achievement there will be; (c) what will the students be doing when they are working on each element of the test; (d) what the outcome of the test will be (e.g. a written response, a tick in a box of multiple choice items, an essay, a diagram, a computation). Indeed the Task Group on Assessment and Testing in the UK (1988) suggest that attention will have to be given to the *presentation*, *operation* and *response* modes of a test: (a) how the task will be introduced (e.g. oral, written, pictorial, computer, practical demonstration); (b) what the students will be doing when they are working on the test (e.g. mental computation, practical work, oral work, written); and (c) what the outcome will be – how they will show achievement and present the outcomes (e.g. choosing one item from a multiple choice question, writing a short response, open-ended writing, oral, practical outcome, computer output). Operationalizing a test from objectives can proceed by stages:

- identify the objectives/outcomes/elements to be covered;
- break down the objectives/outcomes/elements into constituent components or elements;

- select the components that will feature in the test, such that, if possible, they will represent the larger field (i.e. domain-referencing, if required);
- recast the components in terms of specific, practical, observable behaviours, activities and practices that fairly represent and cover that component;
- specify the kinds of data required to provide information on the achievement of the criteria;
- specify the success criteria (performance indicators) in practical terms, working out marks and grades to be awarded and how weightings will be addressed;
- write each item of the test.

Item analysis, Gronlund and Linn (1990: 255) aver, is designed to ensure that: (a) the items function as they are intended, for example, that criterion-referenced items fairly cover the fields and criteria and that norm-referenced items demonstrate *item discriminability* (discussed below); (b) the level of difficulty of the items is appropriate (see below: *item difficulty*); (c) the test is reliable (free of distractors – unnecessary information and irrelevant cues, see below: *distractors*) (see Millman and Greene, 1993). An item analysis will consider the accuracy levels available in the answer, the item difficulty, the importance of the knowledge or skill being tested, the match of the item to the programme and the number of items to be included. The foundation for item analysis lies in Item Response Theory, discussed earlier.

In constructing a test the researcher will need to undertake an item analysis to clarify the item discriminability and item difficulty of each item of the test. *Item discriminability* refers to the potential of the item in question to be answered correctly by those students who have a lot of the particular quality that the item is designed to measure and to be answered incorrectly by those students who have less of the particular quality that the same item is designed to measure. In other words, how effective is the test item in showing up differences between a group of students? Does the item enable us to discriminate between students' abilities in a given field? An item with high discriminability will enable the researcher to see a potentially wide variety of scores on that item; an item with low discriminability will show scores on that item poorly differentiated. Clearly a high measure of discriminability is desirable, and items with low discriminability should be discarded.

Suppose the researcher wishes to construct a test of mathematics for eventual use with 30 students in a particular school (or with class A in a particular school). The researcher devises a test and *pilots* it in a different school or class B respectively, administering the test to

30 students of the same age (i.e. she matches the sample of the pilot school or class to the sample in the school which eventually will be used). The scores of the 30 pilot children are then split into three groups of ten students each (high, medium and low scores). It would be reasonable to assume that there will be more correct answers to a particular item amongst the high scorers than amongst the low scorers. For each item compute the following:

$$\frac{A - B}{\frac{1}{2}(N)}$$

where

A = the number of *correct* scores from the high scoring group;

B = the number of *correct* scores from the low scoring group;

N = the *total* number of students in the two groups.

Suppose all ten students from the high scoring group answered the item correctly and two students from the low scoring group answered the item correctly. The formula would work out thus:

$$\frac{8}{\frac{1}{2}(10+10)} = 0.80 \text{ (index of discriminability)}$$

The maximum index of discriminability is 1.00. Any item whose index of discriminability is less than 0.67, i.e. is too undiscriminating, should be reviewed first to find out whether this is due to ambiguity in the wording or possible clues in the wording. If this is not the case, then whether the researcher uses an item with an index lower than 0.67 is a matter of judgement. It would appear, then, that the item in the example would be appropriate to use in a test. For a further discussion of item discriminability see Linn (1993) and Aiken (2003).

One can use the discriminability index to examine the effectiveness of *distractors*. This is based on the premise that an effective distractor should attract more students from a low scoring group than from a high scoring group. Consider the following example, where low and high scoring groups are identified:

	A	B	C
Top 10 students	10	0	2
Bottom 10 students	8	0	10

In example A, the item discriminates positively in that it attracts more correct responses (10) from the top ten students than the bottom ten (2) and hence is a poor

distractor; here, also, the discriminability index is 0.20, hence is a poor discriminator and is also a poor distractor. Example B is an ineffective distractor because nobody was included from either group. Example C is an effective distractor because it includes far more students from the bottom ten students (10) than the higher group (2). However, in this case any ambiguities must be ruled out before the discriminating power can be improved.

Distractors are the stuff of multiple choice items, where incorrect alternatives are offered, and students have to select the correct alternatives. Here a simple frequency count of the number of times a particular alternative is selected will provide information on the effectiveness of the distractor: if it is selected many times then it is working effectively; if it is seldom or never selected then it is not working effectively and it should be replaced.

If we wish to calculate the *item difficulty* of a test, we can use the following formula:

$$\frac{A}{N} \times 100$$

where

A = the number of students who answered the item correctly;

N = the *total* number of students who attempted the item.

Hence if 12 students out of a class of 20 answered the item correctly, then the formula would work out thus:

$$\frac{12}{20} \times 100 = 60\%$$

The maximum index of difficulty is 100 per cent. Items falling below 33 per cent and above 67 per cent are likely to be too difficult and too easy respectively. It would appear, then, that this item would be appropriate to use in a test. Here, again, whether the researcher uses an item with an index of difficulty below or above the cut-off points is a matter of judgement. In a norm-referenced test the item difficulty should be around 50 per cent (Frisbie, 1981). For further discussion of item difficulty see Linn (1993) and Hanna (1993).

Given that the researcher can only know the degree of item discriminability and difficulty once the test has been undertaken, there is an unavoidable need to pilot home-grown tests. Items with limited discriminability and limited difficulty must be weeded out and replaced, those items with the greatest discriminability and the most appropriate degrees of difficulty can be retained;

this can only be undertaken once data from a pilot have been analysed.

Item discriminability and item difficulty take on differential significance in norm-referenced and criterion-referenced tests. In a norm-referenced test we wish to compare students with each other, hence item discriminability is very important. In a criterion-referenced test, on the other hand, it is not important per se to be able to compare or discriminate between students' performance. For example, it may be the case that we wish to discover whether a group of students has learnt a particular body of knowledge, that is the objective, rather than, say, finding out how many have learned it better than others. Hence it may be that a criterion-referenced test has very low discriminability if all the students achieve very well or achieve very poorly, but the discriminability is less important than the fact than the students have or have not learnt the material. A norm-referenced test would regard such a poorly discriminating item as unsuitable for inclusion, whereas a criterion-referenced test would regard such an item as providing useful information (on success or failure).

With regard to item difficulty, in a criterion-referenced test the level of difficulty is that which is appropriate to the task or objective. Hence if an objective is easily achieved then the test item should be easily achieved; if the objective is difficult then the test item should be correspondingly difficult. This means that, unlike a norm-referenced test where an item might be reworked in order to increase its discriminability index, this is less of an issue in criterion-referencing. Of course, this is not to deny the value of undertaking an item difficulty analysis, rather it is to question the centrality of such a concern. Gronlund and Linn (1990: 265) suggest that where instruction has been effective the item difficulty index of a criterion-referenced test will be high.

In addressing the item discriminability, item difficulty and distractor effect of particular test items, it is advisable, of course, to pilot these tests and to be cautious about placing too great a store on indices of difficulty and discriminability that are computed from small samples.

In constructing a test with item analysis, item discriminability, item difficulty and distractor effects in mind, it is important also to consider the actual requirements of the test (Nuttall, 1987; Cresswell and Houston, 1991), for example:

- are all the items in the test equally difficult;
- which items are easy, moderately hard, hard, very hard;
- what kinds of task each item is addressing (e.g. is it

(a) a practice item – repeating known knowledge, (b) an application item – applying known knowledge, (c) a synthesis item – bringing together and integrating diverse areas of knowledge);
- if not, what makes some items more difficult than the rest;
- whether the items are sufficiently within the experience of the students;
- how motivated students will be by the contents of each item (i.e. how relevant they perceive the item to be, how interesting it is).

The contents of the test will also need to take account of the notion of *fitness for purpose*, for example in the types of test items. Here the researcher will need to consider whether the kinds of data to demonstrate ability, understanding and achievement will be best demonstrated in, for example (Lewis, 1974; Cohen *et al.*, 2004, chapter 16):

- an open essay,
- a factual and heavily directed essay;
- short answer questions;
- divergent thinking items;
- completion items;
- multiple choice items (with one correct answer or more than one correct answer);
- matching pairs of items or statements;
- inserting missing words;
- incomplete sentences or incomplete, unlabelled diagrams;
- true/false statements;
- open-ended questions where students are given guidance on how much to write (e.g. 300 words, a sentence, a paragraph);
- closed questions.

These items can test recall, knowledge, comprehension, application, analysis, synthesis and evaluation, i.e. different orders of thinking. These take their rationale from Bloom (1956) on hierarchies of thinking – from low order (comprehension, application), through middle order thinking (analysis, synthesis) to higher order thinking (evaluation, judgement, criticism). Clearly the selection of the form of the test item will be based on the principle of gaining the maximum amount of information in the most economical way. This is evidenced in the use of machine-scorable multiple choice completion tests, where optical mark readers and scanners can enter and process large-scale data rapidly.

In considering the contents of a test the test writer must also consider the *scale* for some kinds of test. The notion of a scale (a graded system of classification) can be created in two main ways (Howitt and Cramer, 2005: 203):

- a list of items whose measurements go from the lowest to highest (e.g. an IQ test, a measure of sexism, a measure of aggressiveness), such that it is possible to judge where a student has reached on the scale by seeing the maximum level reached on the items;
- the method of 'summated scores' in which a pool of items is created, and the student's score is the total score gained by summing the marks for all the items.

Further, many psychological tests used in educational research will be *unidimensional*, that is, the items all measure a single element or dimension (Howitt and Cramer (2005: 204) liken this to weighing 30 people using ten bathroom scales, in which one would expect a high intercorrelation to be found between the bathroom scales). Other tests may be *multidimensional*, i.e. where two or more factors or dimensions are being measured in the same test (Howitt and Cramer (2005: 204) liken this to weighing 30 people using ten bathroom scales and then their heights using five different tape measures. Here one would expect a high intercorrelation to be found between the bathroom scale measures, a high intercorrelation to be found between the measurements from the tape measures, and a low intercorrelation to be found between the bathroom scale measures and the measurements from the tape measures, because they are measuring different things/dimensions).

Test constructors, then, need to be clear whether they are using a unidimensional or a multidimensional scale. Many texts, whilst advocating the purity of using a unidimensional test that measures a single construct or concept, also recognize the efficacy, practicality and efficiency in using multidimensional tests. For example, though one might regard intelligence casually as a unidimensional factor, in fact a stronger measure of intelligence would be obtained by regarding it as a multidimensional construct, thereby requiring multidimensional scaling. Of course, some items on a test are automatically unidimensional, for example age, hours spent on homework.

Further, the selection of the items needs to be considered in order to have the highest reliability. Let us say that we have ten items that measure students' negative examination stress. Each item is intended to measure stress, for example:

Item 1 Loss of sleep at examination time;
Item 2 Anxiety at examination time;
Item 3 Irritability at examination time;

Item 4 Depression at examination time;
Item 5 Tearfulness at examination time;
Item 6 Unwillingness to do household chores at examination time;
Item 7 Mood swings at examination time;
Item 8 Increased consumption of coffee at examination time;
Item 9 Positive attitude and cheerfulness at examination time;
Item 10 Eager anticipation of the examination.

You run a reliability test (see Chapter 36 on SPSS reliability) of internal consistency and find strong intercorrelations between items 1–5 (e.g. around 0.85), negative correlations between items 9 and 10 and all the other items (e.g. −0.79), and a very low intercorrelation between items 6 and 8 and all the others (e.g. 0.26). Item-to-total correlations (one kind of item analysis in which the item in question is correlated with the sum of the other items) vary here. What do you do? You can retain items 1–5. For items 9 and 10 you can reverse the scoring (as these items looked at positive rather than negative aspects), and for items 6 and 8 you can consider excluding them from the test, as they appear to be measuring something else. Such item analysis is designed to include items that measure the same construct and to exclude items that do not. We refer readers to Howitt and Cramer (2005: chapter 12) for further discussion of this.

An alternative approach to deciding which items to retain or exclude from the list of ten items above is to use factor analysis (see Chapter 37), a method facilitated greatly by SPSS. Factor analysis will group together a cluster of similar items and keep that cluster separate from clusters of other items. So, for our example above, the factor analysis could have found, by way of illustration, three factors:

- positive feelings (items 9 and 10);
- negative psychological states (items 2, 3, 4, 5, 7);
- physical, behavioural changes (items 1, 6, 8).

By looking at the factor loadings (see Chapter 37) the researcher would have to decide which were the most appropriate factors to retain, and, thereby, which items to include and exclude. As a general rule, items with low factor loadings (e.g. <0.3) should be considered for exclusion, as they do not contribute sufficiently to the factor. Factor analysis will indicate, also, whether the construct is unidimensional or multidimensional (if there is only one factor it is probably unidimensional).

Consider the form of the test

Much of the discussion in this chapter assumes that the test is of the pen-and-paper variety. Clearly this need not be the case, for example tests can be written, oral, practical, interactive, computer-based, dramatic, diagrammatic, pictorial, photographic, involve the use of audio and video material, presentational and role-play, simulations. Oral tests, for example, can be conducted if the researcher feels that reading and writing will obstruct the true purpose of the test (i.e. it becomes a reading and writing test rather than, say, a test of mathematics). This does not negate the issues discussed in this chapter, for the form of the test will still need to consider, for example, reliability and validity, difficulty, discriminability, marking and grading, item analysis, timing. Indeed several of these factors take on an added significance in non-written forms of testing; for example: (a) reliability is a major issue in judging live musical performance or the performance of a gymnastics routine – where a 'one-off' event is likely; (b) reliability and validity are significant issues in group performance or group exercises – where group dynamics may prevent a testee's true abilities from being demonstrated. Clearly the researcher will need to consider whether the test will be undertaken individually, or in a group, and what form it will take.

Write the test item

The test will need to address the intended and unintended clues that might be provided in it, for example (Morris *et al.*, 1987):

- the number of blanks might indicate the number of words required;
- the number of dots might indicate the number of letters required;
- the length of blanks might indicate the length of response required;
- the space left for completion will give cues about how much to write;
- blanks in different parts of a sentence will be assisted by the reader having read the other parts of the sentence (anaphoric and cataphoric reading cues).

Hanna (1993: 139–41) and Cunningham (1998) provide several guidelines for constructing short answer items to overcome some of these problems:

- make the blanks close to the end of the sentence;
- keep the blanks the same length;
- ensure that there can be only a single correct answer;

- avoid putting several blanks close to each other (in a sentence or paragraph) such that the overall meaning is obscured;
- only make blanks of key words or concepts, rather than of trivial words;
- avoid addressing only trivial matters;
- ensure that students know exactly the kind and specificity of the answer required;
- specify the units in which a numerical answer is to be given;
- use short answers for testing knowledge recall.

With regard to multiple choice items there are several potential problems:

- the number of choices in a single multiple choice item (and whether there is one or more right answer(s));
- the number and realism of the distractors in a multiple choice item (e.g. there might be many distractors but many of them are too obvious to be chosen – there may be several redundant items);
- the sequence of items and their effects on each other;
- the location of the correct response(s) in a multiple choice item.

Gronlund and Linn (1990), Hanna (1993: 161–75), Cunningham (1998) and Aiken (2003) set out several suggestions for constructing effective multiple choice test items:

- ensure that they catch significant knowledge and learning rather than low-level recall of facts;
- frame the nature of the issue in the stem of the item, ensuring that the stem is meaningful in itself (e.g. replace the general 'sheep': (a) 'are graminivorous, (b) are cloven footed, (c) usually give birth to one or two lambs at a time' with 'how many lambs are normally born to a sheep at one time?');
- ensure that the stem includes as much of the item as possible, with no irrelevancies;
- avoid negative stems to the item;
- keep the readability levels low;
- ensure clarity and unambiguity;
- ensure that all the options are plausible so that guessing of the only possible option is avoided;
- avoid the possibility of students making the correct choice through incorrect reasoning;
- include some novelty to the item if it is being used to measure understanding;
- ensure that there can only be a single correct option (if a single answer is required) and that it is unambiguously the right response;

- avoid syntactical and grammatical clues by making all options syntactically and grammatically parallel and by avoiding matching the phrasing of a stem with similar phrasing in the response;
- avoid including in the stem clues as to which may be the correct response;
- ensure that the length of each response item is the same (e.g. to avoid one long correct answer from standing out);
- keep each option separate, avoiding options which are included in each other;
- ensure that the correct option is positioned differently for each item (e.g. so that it is not always option 2);
- avoid using options like 'all of the above' or 'none of the above';
- avoid answers from one item being used to cue answers to another item – keep items separate.

The response categories of tests need to be considered, and we refer readers to our discussion of this topic in Chapter 20 on questionnaires (e.g. Likert scales, Guttman scales, semantic differential scales, Thurstone scales).

Morris *et al.* (1987: 161), Gronlund and Linn (1990), Hanna (1993: 147), Cunningham (1998) and Aiken (2003) also indicate particular problems in true/false questions:

- ambiguity of meaning;
- some items might be partly true or partly false;
- items that polarize – being too easy or too hard;
- most items might be true or false under certain conditions;
- it may not be clear to the student whether facts or opinions are being sought;
- as this is dichotomous, students have an even chance of guessing the correct answer;
- an imbalance of true to false statements;
- some items might contain 'absolutes' which give powerful clues, e.g. 'always', 'never', 'all', 'none'.

To overcome these problems the authors suggest several points that can be addressed:

- avoid generalized statements (as they are usually false);
- avoid trivial questions;
- avoid negatives and double negatives in statements;
- avoid over-long and over-complex statements;
- ensure that items are rooted in facts;
- ensure that statements can be either only true or false;

- write statements in everyday language;
- decide where it is appropriate to use 'degrees' – 'generally', 'usually', 'often' – as these are capable of interpretation;
- avoid ambiguities;
- ensure that each statement only contains one idea;
- if an opinion is to be sought then ensure that it is attributable to a named source;
- ensure that true statements and false statements are equal in length and number.

Morris *et al.* (1987), Hanna (1993: 150–2), Cunningham (1998) and Aiken (2003) also indicate particular potential difficulties in matching items:

- it might be very clear to a student which items in a list simply cannot be matched to items in the other list (e.g. by dint of content, grammar, concepts), thereby enabling the student to complete the matching by elimination rather than understanding;
- one item in one list might be able to be matched to several items in the other;
- the lists might contain unequal numbers of items, thereby introducing distractors – rendering the selection as much a multiple choice item as a matching exercise.

The authors suggest that difficulties in matching items can be addressed thus:

- ensure that the items for matching are homogenous – similar – over the whole test (to render guessing more difficult);
- avoid constructing matching items to answers that can be worked out by elimination (e.g. by ensuring that: (a) there are different numbers of items in each column so that there are more options to be matched than there are items; (b) students can avoid being able to reduce the field of options as they increase the number of items that they have matched; (c) the same option may be used more than once);
- decide whether to mix the two columns of matched items (i.e. ensure, if desired, that each column includes both items and options);
- sequence the options for matching so that they are logical and easy to follow (e.g. by number, by chronology);
- avoid over-long columns and keep the columns on a single page;
- make the statements in the options columns as brief as possible;
- avoid ambiguity by ensuring that there is a clearly suitable option that stands out from its rivals;

- make it clear what the nature of the relationship should be between the item and the option (on what terms they relate to each other);
- number the items and letter the options.

With regard to essay questions, there are several advantages that can be claimed. For example, an essay, as an open form of testing, enables complex learning outcomes to be measured, it enables the student to integrate, apply and synthesize knowledge, to demonstrate the ability for expression and self-expression, and to demonstrate higher order and divergent cognitive processes. Further, it is comparatively easy to construct an essay title. On the other hand, essays have been criticized for yielding unreliable data (Gronlund and Linn, 1990; Cunningham, 1998), for being prone to unreliable (inconsistent and variable) scoring, neglectful of intended learning outcomes and prone to marker bias and preference (being too intuitive, subjective, holistic and time-consuming to mark). To overcome these difficulties the authors suggest that:

- the essay question must be restricted to those learning outcomes that are unable to be measured more objectively;
- the essay question must ensure that it is clearly linked to desired learning outcomes; that it is clear what behaviours the students must demonstrate;
- the essay question must indicate the field and tasks very clearly (e.g. 'compare', 'justify', 'critique', 'summarize', 'classify', 'analyse', 'clarify', 'examine', 'apply', 'evaluate', 'synthesize', 'contrast', 'explain', 'illustrate');
- time limits are set for each essay;
- options are avoided, or, if options are to be given, ensure that, if students have a list of titles from which to choose, each title is equally difficult and equally capable of enabling the student to demonstrate achievement, understanding, etc.
- marking criteria are prepared and are explicit, indicating what must be included in the answers and the points to be awarded for such inclusions or ratings to be scored for the extent to which certain criteria have been met;
- decisions are agreed on how to address and score irrelevancies, inaccuracies, poor grammar and spelling;
- the work is double-marked, blind and, where appropriate, without the marker knowing (the name of) the essay writer.

Clearly these are issues of reliability (see Chapter 10). The issue here is that layout can exert a profound effect on the test. For a general introduction to writing test items see Cohen and Wollack (2010) and http://cte.umdnj.edu/student_evaluation/evaluation_constructing.cfm.

Consider the layout of the test

This will include (Gronlund and Linn, 1990; Hanna, 1993; Linn, 1993; Cunningham, 1998):

- the nature, length and clarity of the instructions, e.g. what to do, how long to take, how much to do, how many items to attempt, what kind of response is required (e.g. a single word, a sentence, a paragraph, a formula, a number, a statement, etc.), how and where to enter the response, where to show the 'working out' of a problem, where to start new answers (e.g. in a separate booklet), is one answer only required to a multiple choice item, or is more than one answer required;
- spread out the instructions through the test, avoiding overloading students with too much information at first, and providing instructions for each section as they come to it;
- what marks are to be awarded for which parts of the test;
- minimizing ambiguity and taking care over the readability of the items;
- the progression from the easy to the more difficult items of the test (i.e. the location and sequence of items);
- the visual layout of the page, for example, avoiding overloading students with visual material or words;
- the grouping of items – keeping together items that have the same contents or the same format;
- the setting out of the answer sheets/locations so that they can be entered onto computers and read by optical mark readers and scanners (if appropriate).

The layout of the text should be such that it supports the completion of the test and that this is done as efficiently and as effectively as possible for the student.

Consider the timing of the test

This refers to two areas: (a) when the test will take place (the day of the week, month, time of day), and (b) the time allowances to be given to the test and its component items. With regard to the former, in part this is a matter of reliability, for the time of day, week, etc. might influence how alert, motivated, capable a student might be. With regard to the latter, the researcher will need to decide what time restrictions are being imposed and why (for example, is the pressure of a time constraint desirable – to show what a student can do under time pressure (a speed test) – or an unnecessary impediment, putting a time boundary around something that need not be bounded – was Van Gogh put under a time pressure to produce the painting of sunflowers?) (see also Kohn, 2000).

Though it is vital that the student knows what the overall time allowance is for the test, clearly it might be helpful to a student to indicate notional time allowances for different elements of the test; if these are aligned to the relative weightings of the test (see the discussions of weighting and scoring) they enable a student to decide where to place emphasis in the test – she may want to concentrate her time on the high scoring elements of the test. Further, if the items of the test have exact time allowances, this enables a degree of standardization to be built into the test, and this may be useful if the results are going to be used to compare individuals or groups.

Plan the scoring of the test

The awarding of scores for different items of the test is a clear indication of the relative significance of each item – the weightings of each item are addressed in their scoring. It is important to ensure that easier parts of the test attract fewer marks than more difficult parts of it, otherwise a student's results might be artificially inflated by answering many easy questions and fewer more difficult questions (Gronlund and Linn, 1990). Additionally, there are several attractions to making the scoring of tests as detailed and specific as possible (Cresswell and Houston, 1991; Gipps, 1994; Aiken, 2003), awarding specific points for each item and sub-item, for example:

- it enables partial completion of the task to be recognized – students gain marks in proportion to how much of the task they have completed successfully (an important feature of domain-referencing);
- it enables a student to compensate for doing badly in some parts of a test by doing well in other parts of the test;
- it enables weightings to be to be made explicit to the students;
- it enables the rewards for successful completion of parts of a test to reflect considerations such as the length of the item, the time required to complete it, its level of difficulty, its level of importance;
- it facilitates moderation because it is clear and specific;
- it enables comparisons to be made across groups by item;
- it enables reliability indices to be calculated (see discussions of reliability);

- scores can be aggregated and converted into grades straightforwardly.

Ebel (1979) argues that the more marks that are available to indicate different levels of achievement (e.g. for the awarding of grades), the greater the reliability of the grades will be, though clearly this could make the test longer. Scoring will also need to be prepared to handle issues of poor spelling, grammar and punctuation – is it to be penalized, and how will consistency be assured here? Further, how will issues of omission be treated, e.g. if a student omits the units of measurement (miles per hour, dollars or pounds, metres or centimetres)?

Related to the scoring of the test is the issue of reporting the results. If the scoring of a test is specific then this enables variety in reporting to be addressed, for example, results may be reported item by item, section by section, or whole test by whole test. This degree of flexibility might be useful for the researcher, as it will enable particular strengths and weaknesses in groups of students to be exposed.

The desirability of some of the above points is open to question. For example, it could be argued that the strength of criterion-referencing is precisely its specificity, and that to aggregate data (e.g. to assign grades) is to lose the very purpose of the criterion-referencing (Gipps, 1994: 85). For example, if I am awarded a grade E for spelling in English, and a grade A for imaginative writing, this could be aggregated into a C grade as an overall grade of my English language competence, but what does this C grade mean? It is meaningless, it has no frame of reference or clear criteria, it loses the useful specificity of the A and E grades, it is a compromise that actually tells us nothing. Further, aggregating such grades assumes equal levels of difficulty of all items.

Of course, raw scores are still open to interpretation – which is a matter of judgement rather than exactitude or precision (Wiliam, 1996). For example, if a test is designed to assess 'mastery' of a subject, then the researcher is faced with the issue of deciding what constitutes 'mastery' – is it an absolute (i.e. very high score) or are there gradations, and if the latter, then where do these gradations fall? For published tests the scoring is standardized and already made clear, as are the conversions of scores into, for example, percentiles and grades.

Underpinning the discussion of scoring is the need to make it unequivocally clear exactly what the marking criteria are – what will and will not score points. This requires a clarification of whether there is a 'checklist' of features that must be present in a student's answer.

Clearly criterion-referenced tests will have to declare their lowest boundary – a cut-off point – below which the student has been deemed to fail to meet the criteria. A compromise can be seen in those criterion-referenced tests which award different grades for different levels of performance of the same task, necessitating the clarification of different cut-off points in the examination. A common example of this can be seen in the GCSE examinations for secondary school pupils in the United Kingdom, where students can achieve a grade between A and F for a criterion-related examination.

The determination of cut-off points has been addressed by Nedelsky (1954), Angoff (1971), Ebel (1979) and Linn (1993). Angoff (1971) suggests a method for dichotomously scored items. Here judges are asked to identify the proportion of minimally acceptable persons who would answer each item correctly. The sum of these proportions would then be taken to represent the minimally acceptable score.

An elaborated version of this principle comes from Ebel (1979). Here a difficulty by relevance matrix is constructed for all the items. Difficulty might be assigned three levels (e.g. easy, medium and hard), and relevance might be assigned three levels (e.g. highly relevant, moderately relevant, barely relevant). When each and every test item has been assigned to the cells of the matrix the judges estimate the proportion of items in each cell that minimally acceptable persons would answer correctly, with the standard for each judge being the weighted average of the proportions in each cell (which are determined by the number of items in each cell). In this method judges have to consider two factors – relevance and difficulty (unlike Angoff, where only difficulty featured). What characterizes these approaches is the trust that they place in experts in making judgements about levels (e.g. of difficulty, or relevance or proportions of successful achievement), i.e. they are based on fallible human subjectivity.

Ebel (1979) argues that one principle in assignation of grades is that they should represent equal intervals on the score scales. Reference is made to median scores and standard deviations, median scores because it is meaningless to assume an absolute zero on scoring, and standard deviations as the unit of convenient size for inclusion of scores for each grade (see also Cohen and Holliday, 1996). One procedure is thus:

Step 1 Calculate the median and standard deviation of the scores.
Step 2 Determine the lower score limits of the mark intervals using the median and the standard deviation as the unit of size for each grade.

However, the issue of cut-off scores is complicated by the fact that they may vary according to the different purposes and uses of scores (e.g. for diagnosis, for certification, for selection, for program evaluation), as these purposes will affect the number of cut-off points and grades, and the precision of detail required. For a full analysis of determining cut-off grades see Linn (1993).

The issue of scoring takes in a range of factors, for example: grade norms, age norms, percentile norms and standard score norms (e.g. z-scores, T-scores, stanine scores, percentiles). These are beyond the scope of this book to discuss, but readers are referred to Cronbach (1970), Gronlund and Linn (1990), Cohen and Holliday (1996), Hopkins *et al.* (1996).

Pilot the test

Piloting can be done in several ways:

a a small group of experts can examine the items in the test, their suitability, validity, relevance, possible cultural biases and sources of invalidity and unreliability, remoteness from the test-takers' experiences;

b a small group of test-takers, asking them to give feedback on:
  ■ the clarity of the items, instructions and layout;
  ■ ambiguities or difficulties in wording;
  ■ readability levels and language problems for the target audience;
  ■ the *type* of question and its format (e.g. rating scale, multiple choice, open, closed, etc.);
  ■ response categories for closed questions and multiple choice items, and for the appropriateness of specific questions or stems of questions;
  ■ omissions, redundant and irrelevant items;
  ■ the clarity of the layout of the test;
  ■ the time taken to complete the test;
  ■ the complexity of the test items;

c a larger group of test-takers, to be able to gather sufficiently large-scale data to calculate reliability levels (alphas), item difficulty and item discriminability, to identify commonly misunderstood or non-completed items, and to check which items are consistently omitted or not reached (i.e. if the time was too short so that test-takers run out of time), and to be able to test out the marking scheme.

24.6 Software for preparation of a test

There are very many websites that researchers can visit to download software (either free or for inexpensive purchase) for test preparation, construction, layout, marking, and for collation and weighting of marks, for example:

www.easytestmaker.com/
www.classbuilder.com/
www.testshop.com/
www.centronsoftware.com/tcpage.html
www.aditsoftware.com/
www.classbuilder.com/
www.classmarker.com/
www.bestshareware.net/test-construction-kit.htm
www.educational-software-directory.net/teacher/test-
    making (a website that links researchers to several
    software tools for test preparation).

Of course, these do not exonerate the researcher/test deviser from the thinking that goes into the test construction; rather, they follow from that thinking and preparation, and turn it into practical formats for administration either in hard copy or online. Further, the use of software and online testing can remove some of the burden of marking, data entry and analysis, as online tests can perform these calculations automatically (e.g. for closed/multiple choice items), and optical mark scanners can also be used to read in marks from hard copy into a computer file.

These kinds of software packages do not address validity and reliability, and the researcher will need to pilot and refine the test before final use.

24.7 Devising a pre-test and post-test

The construction and administration of tests is an essential part of the experimental model of research, where a pre-test and a post-test have to be devised for the control and experimental groups. The pre-test and post-test must adhere to several guidelines:

■ The pre-test may have questions which differ in form or wording from the post-test, though the two tests must test the same content, i.e. they will be alternate forms of a test for the same groups.
■ The pre-test must be the same for the control and experimental groups.
■ The post-test must be the same for both groups.
■ Care must be taken in the construction of a post-test to avoid making the test easier to complete by one group than another.
■ The level of difficulty must be the same in both tests.

Test data feature centrally in the experimental model of research; additionally they may feature as part of a questionnaire, interview and documentary material.

24.8 Ethical issues in testing

A major source of unreliability of test data derives from the extent and ways in which students have been prepared for the test. These can be located on a continuum from direct and specific preparation, through indirect and general preparation, to no preparation at all. With the growing demand for test data (e.g. for selection, for certification, for grading, for employment, for tracking, for entry to higher education, for accountability, for judging schools and teachers) there is a perhaps understandable pressure to prepare students for tests. This is the 'high-stakes' aspect of testing (Harlen, 1994), where much hinges on the test results. At one level this can be seen in the backwash effect of examinations on curricula and syllabuses; at another level it can lead to the direct preparation of students for specific examinations. Preparation can take many forms (Mehrens and Kaminski, 1989; Gipps, 1994):

■ ensuring coverage, amongst other programme contents and objectives, of the objectives and programme that will be tested;
■ restricting the coverage of the programme content and objectives to those only that will be tested;
■ preparing students with 'exam technique';
■ practice with past/similar papers;
■ directly matching the teaching to specific test items, where each piece of teaching and content is the same as each test item;
■ practise on an exactly parallel form of the test;
■ telling students in advance what will appear on the test;
■ practise on, and preparation of, the identical test itself (e.g. giving out test papers in advance) without teacher input;
■ practise on, and preparation of, the identical test itself (e.g. giving out the test papers in advance), with the teacher working through the items, maybe providing sample answers.

How ethical it would be to undertake the final four of these is perhaps questionable, or indeed any apart from the first on the list. Are they cheating or legitimate test preparation? Should one teach to a test; is not to do so a dereliction of duty (e.g. in criterion- and domain-referenced tests) or giving students an unfair advantage and thus reducing the reliability of the test as a true and fair measure of ability or achievement? In high-stakes assessment (e.g. for public accountability and to compare schools and teachers) there is even the issue of not entering for tests students whose performance will be low (see, for example Haladyna et al., 1991).

There is a risk of a correlation between the 'stakes' and the degree of unethical practice – the greater the stakes, the greater the incidence of unethical practice. Unethical practice, observes Gipps (1994), occurs where scores are inflated but reliable inference on performance or achievement is not, and where different groups of students are prepared differentially for tests, i.e. giving some students an unfair advantage over others. To overcome such problems, she suggests, it is ethical and legitimate for teachers to teach to a broader domain than the test, that teachers should not teach directly to the test, and the situation should only be that better instruction rather than test preparation is acceptable (Cunningham, 1998).

One can add to this list of considerations (Cronbach, 1970; Hanna, 1993; Cunningham, 1998) the view that:

- tests must be valid and reliable (see Chapter 10);
- the administration, marking and use of the test should only be undertaken by suitably competent/qualified people (i.e. people and projects should be vetted);
- access to test materials should be controlled, for instance: test items should not be reproduced apart from selections in professional publication; the tests should only be released to suitably qualified professionals in connection with specific professionally acceptable projects;
- tests should benefit the testee (beneficence);
- clear marking and grading protocols should exist (the issue of transparency is discussed in Chapter 5);
- test results are only reported in a way that cannot be misinterpreted;
- the privacy and dignity of individuals should be respected (e.g. confidentiality, anonymity, non-traceability);
- individuals should not be harmed by the test or its results (non-maleficence);
- informed consent to participate in the test should be sought.

Whilst the use of tests in research is bound by the same ethical requirements as other forms of data collection (e.g. informed consent, non-maleficence, anonymity and confidentiality, rights to non-participation and withdrawal, etc.), a further major ethical issue concerns the use made of the test data (consequential validity). Here the test data should only be used for the purpose for which the test was constructed; too often test data become used for purposes other than these, and this is ethically highly questionable.

24.9 Computerized adaptive testing

Computerized adaptive testing (Wainer, 1990; Aiken, 2003: 50–2; Wainer and Dorans, 2000) is the decision on which particular test items to administer, which is based on the subjects' responses to previous items. It is particularly useful for large-scale testing, where a wide range of ability can be expected. Here a test must be devised that enables the tester to cover this wide range of ability; hence it must include some easy to some difficult items – too easy and it does not enable a range of high ability to be charted (testees simply getting all the answers right), too difficult and it does not enable a range of low ability to be charted (testees simply getting all the answers wrong). We find out very little about a testee if we ask a battery of questions which are too easy or too difficult for her. Further, it is more efficient and reliable if a test can avoid the problem for high ability testees of having to work through a mass of easy items in order to reach the more difficult items and for low ability testees of having to try to guess the answers to more difficult items. Hence it is useful to have a test that is flexible and that can be adapted to the testees. For example, if a testee found an item too hard the next item could adapt to this and be easier, and, conversely, if a testee was successful on an item the next item could be harder.

Wainer indicates that in an adaptive test the first item is pitched in the middle of the assumed ability range; if the testee answers it correctly then it is followed by a more difficult item, and if the testee answers it incorrectly then it is followed by an easier item. Computers here provide an ideal opportunity to address the flexibility, discriminability and efficiency of testing. Aiken (2003: 51) suggests that computer adaptive testing can reduce the number of test items present to around 50 per cent of those used in conventional tests. Testees can work at their own pace, they need not be discouraged but can be challenged, the test is scored instantly to provide feedback to the testee, a greater range of items can be included in the test and a greater degree of precision and reliability of measurement can be achieved; indeed test security can be increased and the problem of understanding answer sheets is avoided.

Clearly the use of computer adaptive testing has several putative attractions. On the other hand it requires different skills from traditional tests, and these might compromise the reliability of the test, for example:

- the mental processes required to work with a computer screen and computer program differ from those required for a pen-and-paper test;
- motivation and anxiety levels increase or decrease when testees work with computers;

- the physical environment might exert a significant difference, e.g. lighting, glare from the screen, noise from machines, loading and running the software;
- reliability shifts from an index of the variability of the test to an index of the standard error of the testee's performance. The usual formula for calculating standard error assumes that error variance is the same for all scores, whereas in item response theory it is assumed that error variance depends on each testee's ability – the conventional statistic of error variance calculates a single average variance of summed scores, whereas in item response theory this is at best very crude, and at worst misleading as variation is a function of ability rather than test variation and cannot fairly be summed (see Thissen (1990) for an analysis of how to address this issue);

- having so many test items increases the chance of inclusion of poor items.

Computer adaptive testing requires a large item pool for each area of content domain to be developed (Flaugher, 1990), with sufficient numbers, variety and spread of difficulty. All items must measure a single aptitude or dimension, and the items must be independent of each other, i.e. a person's response to an item should not depend on that person's response to another item. The items have to be pre-tested and validated, their difficulty and discriminability calculated, the effect of distractors reduced, the capability of the test to address unidimensionality and/or multidimensionality clarified, and the rules for selecting items enacted.

 Companion Website

The companion website to the book includes PowerPoint slides for this chapter, which list the structure of the chapter and then provide a summary of the key points in each of its sections. This resource can be found online at **www.routledge.com/textbooks/cohen7e**.

Personal constructs

CHAPTER 25

Richard Bell

This chapter introduces personal constructs and discusses:

- strengths of repertory grid technique
- working with personal constructs
- grid analysis
- some examples of the use of repertory grid in educational research
- difficulties in the use of repertory grid technique in research
- resources

25.1 Introduction

Personal constructs are the basic units of analysis in a complete and formally stated theory of personality proposed by George Kelly in his book *The Psychology of Personal Constructs* (1955). Kelly's own clinical experiences led him to the view that there is no objective, absolute truth and that events are meaningful only in relation to the ways that are construed by individuals. Kelly's primary focus is on the way individuals perceive their environment, the way they interpret what they perceive in terms of their existing mental structure, and the way in which, as a consequence, they behave towards it.

In *The Psychology of Personal Constructs*, Kelly proposes a view of people actively engaged in making sense of and extending their experience of the world. Personal constructs are the dimensions that we use to conceptualize aspects of our day-to-day world, and, as Kelly writes, people differ from each other in their construction of events. The constructs that we create are used by us to forecast events and rehearse situations before their actual occurrence, and are sometimes organized into groups which embody subordinate and super-ordinate relationships. According to Kelly, we take on the role of scientist seeking to predict and control the course of events in which we are caught up. For Kelly, the ultimate explanation of human behaviour 'lies in scanning man's [*sic*] undertakings, the questions he asks, the lines of inquiry he initiates and the strategies he employs' (Kelly, 1969). Education, in Kelly's view, is necessarily experimental. Its ultimate goal is individual fulfilment and the maximizing of individual potential, capitalizing on the need of each individual to question and explore.

Kelly's theory was very formally constructed, with a 'fundamental postulate' and 11 corollaries that followed from this. Later, even in volume 2 of this work, but more obviously even later (Kelly, 1969), he moved away from this very formal statement. Butt (2008) provides a good introduction to this broader view of Kelly and his theory. Nevertheless the formal statement provides the model for the repertory grid. The fundamental postulate is:

A person's processes are psychologically channelized by the ways in which he or she anticipates events.

One key component in the above statement is *the ways in which*; for Kelly, these *ways* are called constructs. The person's repertoire of constructs are the basis by which the person construes or understands his/her world and makes predictions about the future. What is to be construed or understood are the *events*. What are these events? It is rather an ambiguous term. In one sense they really are events such as 'going to a party' or 'teaching a class', but Kelly uses the term much more broadly to encompass all psychological objects such as 'ideal self' or 'teacher I looked up to'. In the repertory grid technique, these objects are termed *elements*.

A repertory grid then is simply a representation of the relationship between these elements and constructs. As such it provides information that we can use to understand how *'a person's processes are psychologically channelized by the ways in which he or she anticipates events'*. Figure 25.1 shows a simple grid layout for collecting data and Figure 25.2 shows the grid with data.

Kelly's theory then has a number of corollaries to this fundamental postulate that relate to the constructs. An important one from a repertory grid perspective, is that constructs are essentially bipolar, that is capable of being defined in terms of polar adjectives (good–bad) or polar phrases (makes me feel happy–makes me feel sad).

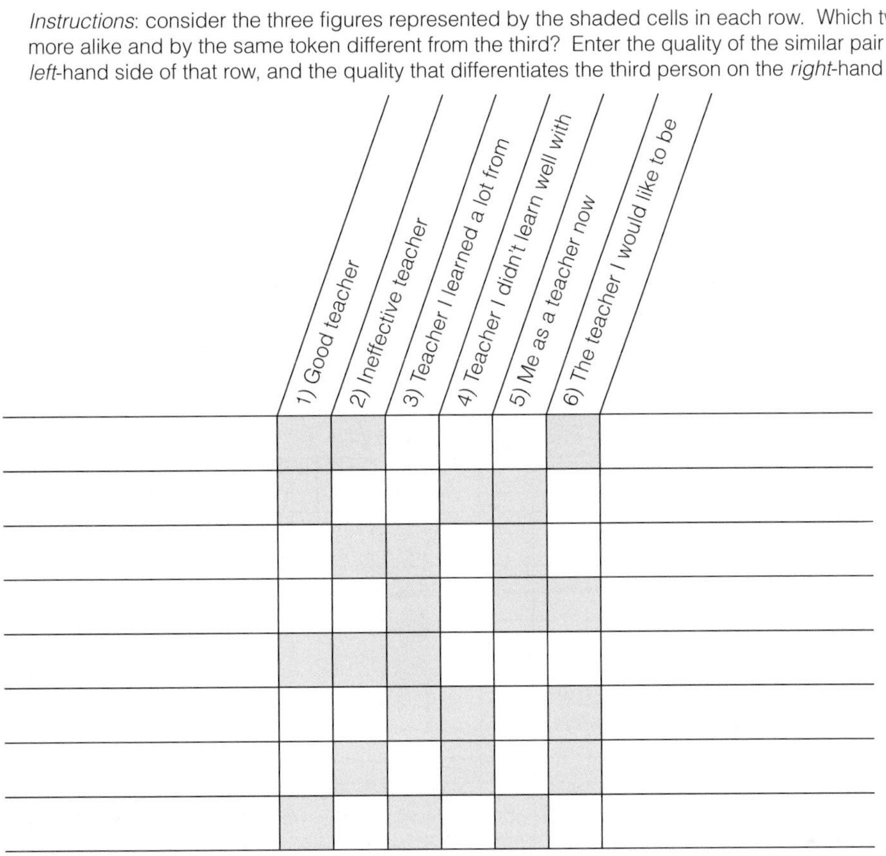

Instructions: consider the three figures represented by the shaded cells in each row. Which two are more alike and by the same token different from the third? Enter the quality of the similar pair on the *left*-hand side of that row, and the quality that differentiates the third person on the *right*-hand side.

Column headers:
1) Good teacher
2) Ineffective teacher
3) Teacher I learned a lot from
4) Teacher I didn't learn well with
5) Me as a teacher now
6) The teacher I would like to be

FIGURE 25.1 Simple grid layout

Other corollaries can also affect the ways in which we can use the repertory grid technique, as we shall see later. In addition to the corollaries there are other formal aspects of the theory that play roles in relating constructs to behaviour. Fransella (2003: 455–7) provides a concise summary of all components of the theory.

A number of different forms of repertory grid technique have been developed since Kelly's first formulation. All have the two essential characteristics in common that we have already identified, that is, constructs – the dimensions used by a person in conceptualizing aspects of his or her world – and elements – the stimulus objects that a person evaluates in terms of the constructs she employs.

Since Kelly's (1955) original account of what he called 'The Role Construct Repertory Grid Test', several variations of repertory grid have been developed and used in many different areas of research. In a chapter entitled 'Some uses to which grids have been put' Fransella *et al.* (2004) provide an annotated bibliography of a wide range of areas including 'working with children', 'teachers and teaching', 'construing of professionals' and 'those with learning difficulties'.

25.2 Strengths of repertory grid technique

The repertory grid technique draws its strength from two particular features. The obvious one is that it is an individualized technique where the respondent provides the framework as well as the responses. For example, Suto and Nádas (2009) used grids with two principal examiners to identify features of examination questions that differed in the difficulty of marking. The other, perhaps more important, strength derives from the two-way nature of the data where elements are related to

Instructions: consider how the qualities in each row apply to each of the six figures. To the extent that the quality on the *left* applies more to the person, give a rating closer to *1*. And to the extent that the quality on the *right* applies more to the person, give a rating closer to *5*.

	1) Good teacher	2) Ineffective teacher	3) Teacher I learned a lot from	4) Teacher I didn't learn well with	5) Me as a teacher now	6) The teacher I would like to be	
Quiet	1	5	2	2	3	1	Loud
Sociable	4	1	5	5	1	2	Aloof
Open	2	4	1	3	1	2	Private
Creative	2	4	1	5	5	1	Follow set plans
Independent	1	5	1	3	5	1	Dependent
Listens	1	5	1	5	3	1	Doesn't listen
Reject ideas	5	1	4	1	3	5	Accepts
Strict	1	3	1	5	5	2	Lax

FIGURE 25.2 A completed grid

constructs. This enables relationships between elements to be assessed, since there is information about each element provided by the set of constructs. Conversely the relationships between constructs can be examined through the information provided for each construct by the set of elements. Even if the individuality of the grid is restricted by the use of provided constructs or elements (as discussed below) the two-way data allows for within-respondent analyses to be carried out.

25.3 Working with personal constructs

Choosing elements

The key issue in choosing elements, is that they should be a homogeneous set to ensure that the constructs elicited from some of them, will also be relevant to other elements. Yorke (1978) and Wright and Lam (2002)

draw attention to problems that can arise when this requirement is not met.

In Kelly's original technique, elements were usually chosen by the client to fit 'role titles' provided by the clinician. Some role titles allowed no choice: 'me as I am now'; some allowed a possible choice: 'your mother (or the person who filled that role in your life)'; and some allowed wide choice: 'a teacher you admired'. Some recent research (Bell *et al.*, 2002; Haritos *et al.*, 2004) suggests that value-laden role titles such as the teacher role above or 'a girl you did not like' tend to polarize the grid by making constructs subsequently elicited more similar to one another than when role titles are neutral such as 'a significant person in your life'.

Eliciting constructs

Kelly originally suggested six ways in which constructs could be elicited from elements, the most familiar being to choose three elements and to ask the participant to specify *some important way in which two of them are alike and thereby different from the third*. The way in which two were alike formed one pole (the similarity pole); the way in which the third differed formed the other pole. Another way involves asking the participant for the opposite to the similarity pole. Another way suggested by Kelly was to always have the 'as I am now' element included. This is more widely used in psychotherapy settings since it ensures that all constructs are relevant to the self.

The task of triadic comparison is cognitively demanding, and it has been found that simply using two elements is better for children (e.g. Salmon, 1976) or those with learning difficulties (Barton *et al.*, 1976).

'Elicited' versus 'provided' constructs

One form of repertory grid technique now in common use represents a significant departure from Kelly's original procedure in that they provide constructs to subjects rather than elicit constructs from them. Eliciting constructs from individuals follows from Kelly's *individuality corollary: persons differ from each other in their construction of events*. Supplying constructs contravenes this. However Kelly also posited a *commonality corollary: to the extent that one person employs a construction of experience which is similar to that employed by another, his or her psychological processes are similar to those of the other person*. This suggests that there will be constructs which are common to a number of individuals.

Can the practice of providing constructs to subjects be reconciled with the individuality corollary assumptions? Despite much research, the answer is still unclear and of course is further clouded by the more recently discovered effect of value-laden role titles in elicited constructs. As Fransella *et al.* (2004: 48) point out however, that 'Constructs have to be supplied in a group context if group data is required.' Bell (2000) has shown how the commonality corollary may be simply tested by examining each supplied construct in turn for unidimensionality of the element ratings.

But the issue of supplied or elicited constructs is not necessarily an all-or-none situation. Bannister and Mair (1968) support the use of supplied constructs in experiments where hypotheses have been formulated and in those involving group comparisons. The use of elicited constructs alongside supplied ones can serve as a useful check on the meaningfulness of those that are provided; substantially lower inter-correlations between elicited and supplied constructs suggesting, perhaps, the lack of relevance of those provided by the researcher.

Allocating elements to constructs

In Kelly's original technique, participants were allowed to classify as many or as few elements at the similarity or the contrast pole, giving a very lopsided construct. Originally this was seen as a problem since measures of association between constructs could be affected by this (e.g. Bannister and Mair, 1968: 59) and strategies were proposed to overcome this. These strategies had problems of their own, in that they forced the participant to allocate elements to constructs in a fixed fashion, as removed from Kelly's individual focus as are supplied constructs.

More recently Bell (2004a) has shown that lopsidedness is associated with the super- and sub-ordinate relationships implied by Kelly's organizational corollary. The common method now of allotting elements is the 'rating form'. Here, the subject is required to judge each element on a multi-point scale, where one extreme (say 7) is aligned with one pole ('notices when I am having problems') and the other extreme (1) is aligned with the other pole ('doesn't notice when I am having problems'). As with most rating scale formats, questions arise as to the meaning of a midpoint rating (where an odd number of rating points are specified).

Another of Kelly's corollaries was the range corollary: *a construct is convenient for the anticipation of a finite range of events* only. In a rated grid then, does a midpoint rating mean neither or both poles are relevant? Or more generally, does a grid allow missing data? Kelly's range corollary would suggest 'yes' but the computation of summary measures to represent grids would usually say 'no'. In practice this problem can be ameliorated if not overcome by the careful nomination of a homogeneous set of elements. The midpoint issue remains intriguing. Winter *et al.* (2010) found in a psychotherapy study, constructs, where either 'self now' or 'ideal self' was located at the midpoint, were associated with more complex cognitive structures in the grid. The rating form is the third example illustrated in Figure 25.2.

Other techniques: laddering and pyramid construct elicitation and other forms of grids

The technique known as laddering arises out of Hinkle's (1965) linking of the notion of implication with the organization corollary (*Each person characteristically evolves for his or her convenience in anticipating events, a construction system embracing ordinal relationships between constructs*). Hinkle's innovation was to replace 'anticipation' with 'implication'. The linking of implication with ordinal relationships enables logical relationships to be specified between poles of different constructs.

'Laddering' is an exploratory technique using implication to move from a pole of a given construct to a pole of an as yet unelicited construct. It usually proceeds by asking the participant to indicate which pole of the given construct is preferred. (This is linked to Kelly's *choice corollary: a person chooses that alternative ... through which he anticipates the greater possibility for the extension and definition of his system.*) Having identified the preferred pole, the participant is then asked 'Why?' The response to this forms one preferred pole of the higher order or implied superordinate construct. The construct can then be completed by asking the participant for the contrasting pole of the new construct. In turn the participant can then be asked for the preferred pole of this new construct and again asked 'Why?' to produce the first pole of the next higher order construct.

Although he never published his development of the technique of laddering, it has been used widely in many fields, particularly research into consumer perceptions (Reynolds and Gutman (1988) provide practical advice in using this technique in the context of laddering from product properties to consumer values).

Laddering is a technique for eliciting constructs in terms of a single element, the self ('Which pole do you prefer and why?'). Pyramiding, a somewhat similar procedure developed by Landfield (1971), also uses a single element. Respondents are asked to think of a particular 'element', a person, and then to specify an attribute which is characteristic of that person. Then the respondent is asked to identify what kind of person would *not* have that characteristic. The researcher then returns to the first characteristic and asks 'What more can you tell me about a person who has that characteristic?' and again 'What is the opposite of that characteristic?' The enquiry is then repeated similarly for the opposite pole of the first characteristic. According to Landfield, the enquiry then proceeds to similarly enquire of the four construct poles thus elicited. Landfield termed this a 'pyramid' since it starts from one element to produce two construct poles which in turn produce four construct poles and finally eight construct poles. This kind of enquiry asks for elaborations (What more can you say?) rather than implications (Why?) and thus does not identify super-ordinate relationships between constructs as does Hinkle's procedure.

Landfield saw his technique as purely qualitative and informing the psychotherapeutic process. Hinkle (1965) however went on to develop an Implication Grid or Impgrid, in which the subject is required to compare each of his/her constructs with every other to see which implies the other. Table 25.1 illustrates a laddering conversation.

Exchange grids are procedures developed to enhance the quality of conversational exchanges. Basically, one person's construing provides the format for an empty grid which is offered to another person for completion. The empty grid consists of the first person's verbal descriptions from which his/her ratings have been deleted. The second person is then invited to test his/her comprehending of the first person's point of view by filling in the grid as s/he believes the other has already completed it. Various computer programs ('Pairs', 'Cores' and 'Difference') are available to assist analysis of the processes of negotiation elicited in exchange grids.

In the 'Pairs' analysis, all constructs in one grid are compared with all constructs in the other grid and a measure of commonality in construing is determined. 'Pairs' analysis leads on to 'Sociogrids' in which the pattern of relationships between the grids of one group can be identified. In turn, 'Sociogrids' can provide a mode grid for the whole group or a number of mode grids identifying cliques. 'Socionets' which reveal the pattern of shared construing can also be derived.

Grid administration

The way in which a grid is administered depends in part on the purpose and nature of the research. Where the researcher wants detailed information from few respondents, then administration is best carried out with one-on-one interviews. This has the advantage of allowing the researcher to monitor the constructs elicited for duplication or difficult to understand pole labels. Such administration usually begins with some discussion of the area to which the grid will relate and a simple trial run of two or three constructs elicited from half a dozen elements not related to the main task. Clarifications can be sought, and the preferred pole identified as the constructs are elicited.

Grids can also be collected in group testing. This usually requires a somewhat smaller grid (the study of Haritos *et al.* (2004) used this approach) and a proforma form that allows spaces for element and construct labels as well as grid ratings, and uses shading or some other method of identifying which elements are to form the triads (see Figure 25.1). Here overheads or PowerPoint are needed to illustrate how the grid is to be completed.

Where grids are to be collected with supplied elements and constructs (perhaps following on from some individually elicited grids, as in Reid and Holley's (1972) study of choice of university) the grid data can be collected in a simpler questionnaire-type format. Should

TABLE 25.1   A LADDERING DIALOGUE

Okay so **good teacher** and **teacher I learned a lot from** are alike in that they are both 'alert' while **an ineffective teacher** is… *'has his mind on other things'*	The opening construct dialogue
So if you had to choose between 'having your mind on other things' or 'being alert', which would you choose *obviously I'd choose being 'alert'*	Choosing the preferred pole
Why? *well, 'being alert' means you can pick up on where each kid is at in their work but having your mind on other things means you just see the class as a whole*	Laddering up to next higher construct
Why is it important to 'pick up on where each kid is at in their work'? *Because kids don't all learn in the same way or at the same rate …* *they're…* They're individuals? *Right*	Laddering up again to next higher construct. Notice the interviewer doesn't look for the opposite pole of this construct
Why is important to treat them as individuals? *So they can each reach their potential*	Notice the interviewer doesn't look for the opposite pole of 'individuals' but keeps laddering from this pole
Why is that important? *It's important because that is why I want to be a teacher – to enable kids to realize their potential*	The interviewer stops here, sensing perhaps that this is far enough up this ladder for the moment
Can I just go back to what you said as the opposite of 'pick up on where each kid is at in their work', you said 'just see the class as a whole' *Mmm*	The interviewer now goes back to the contrast pole of the first laddered construct
What do you think seeing the class as a whole implies? *You mean about a teacher who does that?* Yes *I guess it means that they don't really care about the kids*	Laddering up to next higher construct from this contrast pole
And what would that mean? *They would be thinking about themselves – it might be temporary like some problem at home – or it might be that they want an easy life, not have to work as hard*	Laddering up to next higher construct. Notice the respondent gives two consequences
Yes, I guess there are times when temporary problems affect our work. But what about wanting an easy life – what does that imply? *Unambitious – I don't mean about promotion or things like that, but not being ambitious about being a good teacher*	The interviewer chooses one to ladder from
And the opposite of 'not being ambitious about being a good teacher' is? *Being ambitious about being a good teacher*	Here the interviewer switches attention across from this negative pole to the contrast positive pole
Is that important to you? *Yes*	And checks that it is the preferred pole
Which is more important to you: 'enabling kids to reach their potential' or 'being ambitious about being a good teacher'? *They're the same thing really; a good teacher is one who enables kids to reach their potential*	The interviewer now draws the higher level positive poles together
And the 'being ambitious'? *Yeah, it's also important to try to improve your teaching*	The interviewer notices that part of one of the poles has been left out and draws that in

the ratings be collected construct by construct, rating each element in turn, or element by element, rating each construct in turn? Evidence suggests (Bell *et al.*, 2002; Neimeyer and Hagans, 2002) that it does not matter.

In this century it is to be expected that computer administration is to be a major way in which grid data is collected. A web version can be found at http://gigi.cpsc. ucalgary.ca:2000/ for the Gaines and Shaw program Webgrid 5 that allows relatively simple grids to be elicited. Idiogrid (at the website www.idiogrid.com/) is a freeware program that allows quite complex grid elicitations to be structured and subsequently used to collect data from respondents. Both of these resources provide for data analysis of the grids collected.

25.4 Grid analysis

Before we analyse the grid data, we need to be aware that the orientation of the data in the grid will be a function of the way in which the constructs were elicited. If the two elements that are alike are both positive figures (e.g. 'ideal self' and 'best friend') then the pole corresponding to their similarity will reflect this (e.g. generous). If the two figures are negative ones (such as 'person I dislike' and 'worst teacher') then the pole corresponding to their similarity (e.g. stingy) will – and the correlations with other constructs would be opposite.

A preliminary step in analysing a grid should often be to make all the constructs similarly aligned. This can be done by asking the respondent to indicate their 'preferred' pole. (This is also done in a related personal construct technique, called laddering.) Another way of doing this is when the grid contains the element 'ideal self'. Whichever pole of each construct is aligned with the 'ideal self' is the preferred pole. Of course, this may not be of any use when the 'ideal self' is located at or near the midpoint. There is also an automatic way of doing this. We can analyse the correlations between the constructs and identify those constructs which generally correlate negatively with other constructs, and reverse these constructs.

How do we extract information from a repertory grid? There are a number of ways in which we can look at the numerical information in a grid, and these are discussed below.

Looking at relationships between elements and between constructs

Even in an individual grid, there is replicated information for elements (across constructs) and constructs (across elements). We can use this to make comparisons between constructs or between elements, or to create indices to represent these comparisons. One of

the oldest of these is Bieri's (1955) index of cognitive complexity/simplicity. This was originally a matching coefficient calculated for each pair of constructs and summed for the whole grid.

These days it is usually based on the average correlation among constructs. If this is a large value, then it means all constructs are highly correlated and relate to the elements in much the same way. The person might thus be said to be construing their world in a simple way. If the average correlation is low, then the constructs are differentiated and the person might be said to be construing in a complex fashion.

We can also compute such averages for each construct to determine which constructs are like the others and which are different. Table 25.2 shows the average (root-mean-squared) correlations for each construct in the same grid. This output was obtained from the freeware DOS program GRIDSTAT available at www. repgrid.unimelb.edu.au/grids.htm. It can be seen that the construct 'sociable – aloof' is less related to other constructs, while overall there is a consistent and substantial similarity in the ways these constructs are applied.

Of course the construct correlations that form the basis of this index can also be analysed in other ways, such as with principal components. Table 25.2 also shows that one principal component accounted for nearly 66 per cent of the variance in construct correlations. The component loadings also show constructs where the poles are reversed with respect to the orientation of the other constructs. All construct loadings have negative signs except for 'sociable – aloof' and 'rejects ideas – accepts'. While the latter construct poles can easily be seen to be unaligned with the others (where the left-hand pole is the positive quality), *sociable* rather than *aloof* would normally be seen as positive. For this grid however *aloof* is perceived as the more positive quality in a teacher.

Cluster analysis is another way of depicting relationships in a matrix of measures of association among elements or constructs. Figure 25.3 shows element Euclidean distances and a hierarchical clustering of these. *Good teacher* and *ideal teacher (teacher I would like to be)* are similar, while *teacher I learned a lot from* is also similar to these two. *Me as a teacher now* is weakly associated with an *ineffective teacher* and somewhat less associated with *teacher I did not learn from*.

Particularly useful elements where grids involve the self as an element, are the elements *self now* and *ideal self*. The discrepancy between these two can be taken as a measure of self-esteem or used to generate a self-identity plot (as in Figure 25.4, taken from the Idiogrid program) where self and ideal are reference axes against which are plotted the other elements.

TABLE 25.2   GRID SUMMARY MEASURES

Average [Root-Mean-Squared (RMS)] Correlations

Mean	S. Dev.	
0.59	0.47	1 quiet – loud
0.29	0.34	2 sociable – aloof
0.45	0.43	3 open – private
0.66	0.57	4 creative – follows set plans
0.68	0.51	5 independent – dependent
0.70	0.56	6 listens – doesn't listen
0.68	0.55	7 rejects ideas – accepts
0.58	0.55	8 strict – lax
0.58	0.50	Average of Statistic
0.13	0.07	St. Dev. of Statistic

Construct Component Loadings

quiet – loud	–0.82
sociable – aloof	0.36
open – private	–0.62
creative – follows set plans	–0.90
independent – dependent	–0.93
listens – doesn't listen	–0.96
rejects ideas – accepts	0.93
strict – lax	–0.80
Percentage Variance	65.98

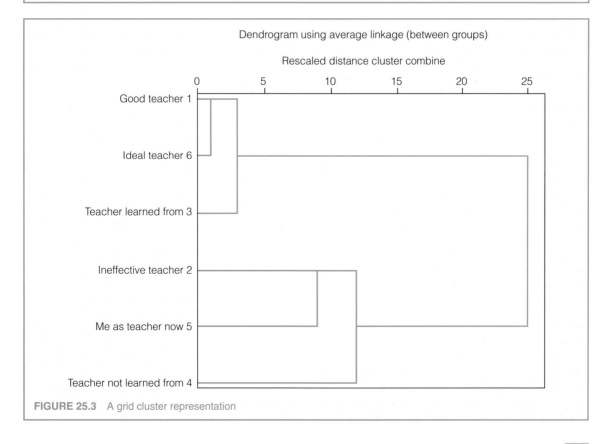

FIGURE 25.3   A grid cluster representation

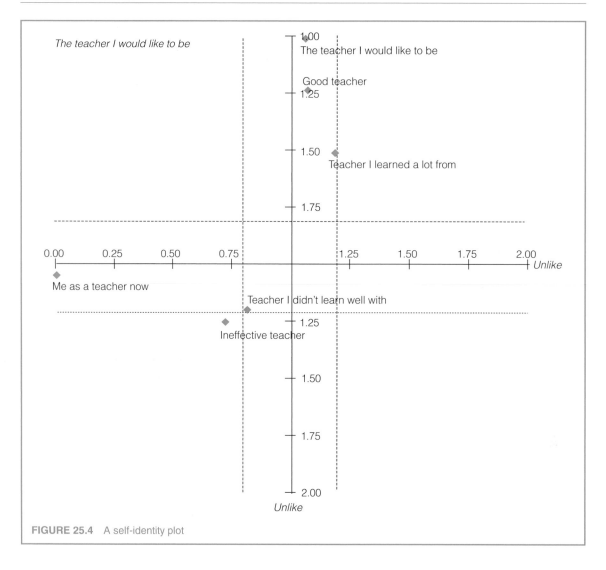

FIGURE 25.4   A self-identity plot

Looking at the overall grid

In the 1960s Patrick Slater (Slater, 1964) introduced a technique (that he called 'principal components') we now know as singular-value-decomposition which enables both elements and constructs to be represented together. There have been a number of different ways of representing the constructs and elements in these maps. Elements always appear as points in the map. Constructs however, are shown in different ways. The construct data are like a principal component solution with two columns of coordinates which define a point in the space. However representations differ. Often the point is reflected back through the origin to make a line symmetric about the origin, the two ends of which represent the construct poles. Other representations (such as that originally used by Slater) show the construct poles as points on a circle encompassing the elements.

Figure 25.5 shows a spatial representation of our sample grid using the program Idiogrid with elements shown as points and constructs shown as vectors (lines) symmetric about the origin. The longer the line, the more important the construct. The horizontal dimension separates better and poorer teachers, with constructs similarly aligned, while the vertical axis is aligned with the isolated construct *aloof – sociable* distinguishing principally between *teacher I didn't learn well with* and *me as a teacher now*.

Another way of representing the whole grid is by a technique known in the repertory grid world as 'focusing'. This means the rows (constructs) and columns

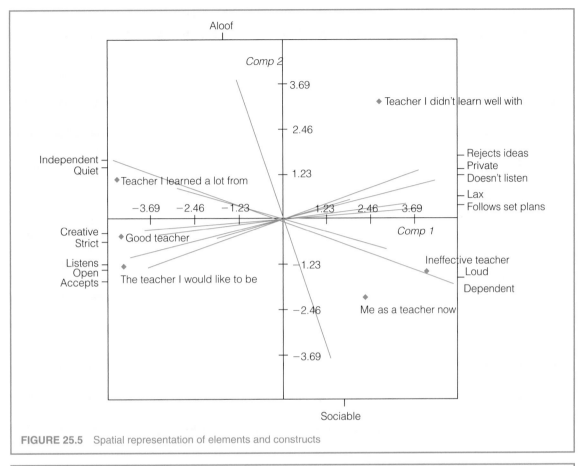

FIGURE 25.5 Spatial representation of elements and constructs

TABLE 25.3 FOCUSED GRID DATA SHOWING EFFECT OF CONSTRUCT ALIGNMENT

Misaligned constructs reversed							Original construct orientation						
Focused grid							*Focused grid*						
Element:	1	3	6	2	5	4	Element:	1	3	6	4	2	5
Cluster:	1	1	1	2	2	3	Cluster:	1	1	1	2	3	3
1 sociable – aloof	3	5	2	1	1	5	1 open – private	2	1	2	3	4	1
1 open – private	2	1	2	4	1	3	2 creative – follows s	2	1	1	5	4	5
1 rejects ideas – ace	5	4	5	1	3	1	2 independent – depend	1	1	1	3	5	5
2 quiet – loud	1	2	1	5	3	2	2 listens – doesn't li	1	1	1	5	5	3
2 creative – follows s	2	1	1	4	5	5	2 accepts – rejects id	1	2	1	5	5	3
2 independent – depend	1	1	1	5	5	3	2 strict – lax	1	1	2	5	3	5
2 listens – doesn't li	1	1	1	5	3	5	3 aloof – sociable	3	1	4	1	5	5
2 strict – lax	1	1	2	3	5	5	4 quiet – loud	1	2	1	2	5	3

Element clusters		*Element Clusters*	
Cluster	Element	Cluster	Element
1	Good teacher	1	Good teacher
1	Teacher I learned a lot from	1	Teacher I learned a lot from
1	The teacher I would like to be	1	The teacher I would like to be
2	Ineffective teacher	2	Teacher I didn't learn well with
2	Me as a teacher now	3	Ineffective teacher
3	Teacher I didn't learn well with	3	Me as a teacher now

(elements) are reordered and the grid data and labels shown in this reordering. This approach was originally devised by Shaw and Thomas (1978) and employs single-linkage hierarchical clustering to align constructs and elements. Other clustering such as *k-means* can be used and Table 25.3 shows such a rearrangement of the sample grid from the GRIDSTAT program referred to earlier. The focused grid is shown in two forms. On the left is shown the grid with two misaligned constructs, 'sociable – aloof' and 'rejects ideas – accepts' realigned as 'aloof – sociable' and 'accepts – rejects ideas' while on the right, the grid as elicited is shown. The original grid has four groups of constructs but in the aligned form there are only two.

25.5 Some examples of the use of repertory grid in educational research

Jones (1999) used repertory grids alongside interviews and participant observation to elicit head teachers' views of their roles and agenda in changing times. While the study found an increase in their management activities (one construct), it also found that not only did their changing role not lead to their deprofessionalization but also their core values were rooted in their values in, and views of, education (a second construct). The super-ordinate constructs for the primary head teachers were child-centred and management, in that order, i.e. the management systems were there to serve the child-centred values and vision. Constructs elicited included, for example: child-centred problem-solving, implementation policy, evaluation, involving other agencies, problem-solving and paperwork.

Bezzi (1999) used repertory grids to explore the perceptions of the images of the geosciences held by a university geology lecturer and five undergraduates at the beginning and end of the academic year. Participants were provided with six names of science subjects (e.g. physics, geography, geology) as elements and 15 constructs were elicited by Kelly's triadic method separately at the beginning and the end of the year. Construct labels were treated as qualitative data and were classified into five categories by the author: (i) nature of science (e.g. *objective/subjective*); (ii) aspects of investigation (e.g. *use of maps or charts/no such use*); (iii) application of science and its professional aspects (e.g. *more employment opportunities/less, modifies environment/preserves environment*); (iv) affective aspects (e.g. *like/dislike, difficult/easy*); and (v) characteristics of the courses (*with lab/without lab*).

Bezzi (1999) found constructs to be predominantly of the first two kinds, that is dealing with the scientific

essence of the disciplines. He used principal component representations of both elements and constructs (as in Figure 25.5) to identify constructs associated with the elements 'geology' and 'geography' both before and after the course of instruction for each of the five students and the lecturer to show how their perceptions of these two subjects had shifted over the year. Bezzi (1999) was able to conclude that simply studying the content of science did not lead to a greater understanding of the role of science in society or how to make good public decisions about scientific issues confronting society.

Lui and Lee (2005) showed how repertory grids could be incorporated into a learning programme in an examination of conceptual understanding in computer-mediated peer discourse. Twelve graduate students rated each of six database design methodologies on 11 supplied database design concepts. The course instructor also completed this task. Use of supplied elements and constructs enabled the researchers to feedback information to students about conflicts between their perspectives and for the students to take these differences into account during a week of online unstructured discourse in which students were required to reach a consensus perspective. Following this, students again completed the grids, and it was found that student concepts became significantly more aligned with the instructor's perspective. Lui and Lee (2005) conclude by suggesting that the methodology could be extended to using student-derived constructs although this would require more complex procedures.

Yeung and Watkins (2000) employed the repertory grid technique to investigate how student teachers in Hong Kong developed a personal sense of teaching efficacy. A pilot study was used to generate elements such as 'self-efficacy', 'teaching practice', 'teaching practice supervisors', 'pupils' and 'lessons'. Constructs were then individually elicited from 27 students using the triadic procedure with cards. Yeung and Watkins (2000) matched constructs between student teachers to identify core constructs and create networks of similarity among student teachers using the REPGRID software of Shaw and Gaines (REPGRID 2, 1993). They found that third-year students' perceptions were more homogeneous than those of first-year students.

Suto and Nádas (2009) used repertory grids to investigate why some GCSE examination questions in maths and physics were harder to mark accurately than others. Two highly experienced principal examiners generated constructs of question features for triads of questions (elements) and rated each question (i.e. the elements) on these constructs. The study examined the constructs generated in detail and related this to marking accuracy.

In a similar vein Johnson (2008) used the repertory grid procedure with assessors of vocationally related portfolios to elicit constructs of differentiation among portfolios. Six assessors generated 131 constructs over six assessment objectives. There was generally agreement between the assessors about the qualities of the commonly identified constructs, but Johnson (2008) did identify some potentially problematic linguistic issues, usually between the notions of quality and quantity.

Madill and Latchford (2005) explored identity change in four medical students over their first year of medical training, particularly in relation to their experience of human dissection. Each participant completed two repertory grids (one oriented towards their identity construction, the other drawing out their experience of human dissection) at two time points, early in term 1 and towards the end of term 3. The identity constructs elicited involved three common themes: dedication, competence and responsibility as well as negative reactions, such as feeling driven and stressed. Three major themes were apparent in their experience of human dissection: involvement, emotional coping and ability. Complex patterns of relationships between the grids and between occasions led the authors to see a development of a vulnerable sense of professionalism alongside a frustration of losing out potentially on wider aspects of personal development.

Lown *et al.* (2009) similarly investigated medical students' perceptions of their personal and professional development. However they used an inventory adapted from a form of the repertory grid devised by Button (1994) to measure self-esteem that focused on the ideal and actual self. This adaptation of a grid was necessary because the large sample size (n=339) required a more constrained version of the grid than is possible in individual-based studies and is a good example of a 'repertory grid influenced' study. All students generated five qualities that distinguished between an 'ideal medical student' and a 'less than ideal medical student' and rated themselves on this quality. The 1,531 attributes generated were reduced to a pool of 100 through the elimination of redundancies, etc., and 49 of these were selected for a freesort grouping by a subset of the students. Multidimensional scaling was then used to identify clusters from the co-occurrences produced by the freesort grouping. Seven clusters were identified and the original 1,531 terms classified under these. Most common categories were Personal and Professional Conduct, Committed Work Ethic and Time and Self Management.

There are also some examples of the use of laddering in research. Crudge and Johnson (2007) used the repertory grid to elicit a set of constructs relevant to web search engines (such as Google) from ten information science undergraduates. They then used laddering to determine the reasons for a construct's importance within the user's mental model. Using standard qualitative techniques they identified three hierarchical strata that conveyed the interrelations between basic system description, evaluative description and the key evaluations of ease, efficiency, effort and effectiveness. Two additional layers related to the perceived process and the experience of emotion. They concluded that their model of key evaluations with the conjunctions of procedural elements provided a framework for further research to evaluate search engines from the user perspective.

In another use of laddering Voss *et al.* (2007) used two laddering techniques (personal interviews and laddering questionnaires) to identify desired qualities of lecturers in a sample of 82 business management students. They found that personal interviewing led to more complex ladder structures with more components. Among the substantive findings they found that students' academic interests motivated them less than the vocational aspects of their studies.[1]

25.6 Difficulties in the use of repertory grid technique in research

The major overarching difficulty in repertory in research is the tension between individuality and commonality. A grid which is elicited wholly from the respondent is the most valid representation of that person's construing. However research often demands replications across subjects, so that for some purposes there needs to be commonality across respondents. Where the researcher's interests are qualitative, then individual grids form a useful way of collecting qualitative data.

However when the structure of the grid data is of interest, the quantitative aspects of the grid become important. When these are specific to an individual because of the individualized specification of elements and elicitation of constructs, the quantitative component of an individual's grid cannot be related to that of others. In such situations the only way these individualized grids can be compared is through the use of grid summary measures, such as 'cognitive complexity'. When grids have some aspects in common, for example role-specified elements or supplied constructs, it is possible to analyse the common aspects of such grids (see Fransella *et al.*, 2004: 98–101).

There are also some important issues to consider concerning aspects of the grids themselves, particularly relating to the issue of bipolarity in the grid. When only one pole of the construct is used, unwarranted inferences about constructs' polar opposites may be made. Yorke's (1978) illustration of the possibility of the researcher obtaining 'bent' constructs suggests the usefulness of the opposite method (Epting *et al.*, 1971) in ensuring the bipolarity of elicited constructs. There is also the previously mentioned uncertainty about the meaning attached to midpoint ratings. Value-laden element role titles (such as 'A teacher I disliked') can affect the structure of the grid (see Haritos et al., 2004), as can the orientation of construct poles. A number of practical problems experienced in collecting grid data (although it should be said these problems are not confined to grid methodology) are identified by Yorke (1978):

- Variable perception of elements of low personal relevance.
- Varying the context in which the elements are perceived during the administration of the grid.
- Halo effect intruding into the ratings where the subject sees the grid matrix building up.
- Accidental reversal of the rating scale (mentally switching from 5=high to 1=high, perhaps because '5 points' and 'first' are both ways of describing high quality). This can happen both within and between constructs, and is particularly likely where a negative or implicitly negative property is ascribed to the pair during triadic elicitation.

The size of the grid can also present problems. Even the simple grid in Figure 25.2 with only six elements and eight constructs contains 16 pieces of qualitative data and 48 pieces of quantitative data. It is unlikely that such a small grid could represent the ways in which a person sees a complex aspect of their world such as a person's view of their teaching world. But a substantially sized grid (in the psychotherapy world, a 15 element 15 construct grid is common and has 225 pieces of quantitative data) takes a substantial amount of time to collect. Laddering has its own problems, both in process (Butt, 1995) and in the hierarchical implications that follow (van Rekom and Wierenga, 2007).

Another problem is the continuing tension between theory and method in the repertory grid. Major works devoted to the repertory grid technique (Bannister and Mair, 1968; Fransella and Bannister, 1977; Jankowicz, 2003; Fransella et al., 2004) have all been written from a personal construct theory perspective and emphasize the importance and relevance of Kelly's theory to the usage of the technique. Yet most research with the repertory grid is carried out with the grid being used in a purely methodological and atheoretical fashion that is content with a passing reference to Kelly as the originator of the grid. As this chapter demonstrates, the theory can be used to understand what is happening in the grid, but of course it is not essential to its use. The real drawback to the personal construct theory background of writers in this area is often with the jargon employed,

particularly for indices or measures developed to summarize structures in the grid. For example, the average correlation used to summarize relationships between constructs was originally termed 'intensity' by Bannister and is often referred to by that name.

25.7 Resources

It might be thought that the repertory grid is unchanging. However, there has been continuing research to inform the technique itself (some details of such developments have been mentioned in this chapter) as well as new measures that can be derived from grid data (for example Bell (2004b) has devised a new index of inconsistency in ratings in the grid) that could have applications in educational research. Most, if not all, of these developments occur through the work of researchers identified with personal construct psychology. Accordingly a number of resources available on the Web are listed as follows:

General resources

A very general and comprehensive site with many resources and links:
www.pcp-net.org/
another comprehensive site:
www.enquirewithin.co.nz/
Personal Construct Psychology searchable database:
www.uow.edu.au/health/psyc/research/pcp/database/index.html
Online journal *Personal Construct Theory and Practice*:
www.pcp-net.org/journal/

Organizations

Europe:
www.epca-net.org/
North America:
www.constructivistpsych.org/
Australia:
www.pcp-net.org/aus/

Freeware programs

Webgrid 5, the current web-based software of Shaw and Gaines:
http://tiger.cpsc.ucalgary.ca/
Idiogrid, a comprehensive windows-based program:
www.idiogrid.com/
Gridstat, the author's comprehensive DOS grid program (Italian version available). Also a comprehensive document on using SPSS syntax with grids is available here:
www.repgrid.unimelb.edu.au/grids.htm

Software for purchase

Gridsuite, a grid program available in German or English:
www.gridsuite.de/
Gridcor, a grid program available in Spanish or English:
www.terapiacognitiva.net/record/gridcor.htm

Rep 5, the Shaw and Gaines comprehensive program:
http://repgrid.com/
Scivesco, analyses multiple grids with sophisticated graphics:
http://elementsandconstructs.de/en/home

 Companion Website

The companion website to the book includes PowerPoint slides for this chapter, which list the structure of the chapter and then provide a summary of the key points in each of its sections. In addition there is further information on repertory grids and triadic elicitation. These resources can be found online at **www.routledge.com/textbooks/cohen7e**.

Role-playing

CHAPTER 26

Carmel O'Sullivan

This chapter introduces role-playing as a research technique, and discusses issues such as:

- what is role-play?
- why use role-play in research?
- issues to be aware of when using role-play
- role-play as a research method
- how does it work?
- important strategies for successful role-play
- three examples of research using role-play

26.1 Introduction

Erving Goffman (1969: 78) has famously claimed that 'Life itself is a dramatically enacted thing', and although he recognized that 'all the world' is not a stage, he argued that 'the crucial ways in which it isn't are not easy to specify'.

Drama, in some form or other, touches most people's lives, but typically in contemporary society, through watching television soap operas, going to the movies or attending the theatre. However, drama has been recognized for many years as a useful training method in the fields of business, psychology and education. Harriet Finlay-Johnson (1912) and Henry Caldwell Cook (1917) were using dramatic play in schools as a teaching and learning method in England at the turn of the twentieth century, while Jacob Levy Moreno was similarly exploring its use with children in Vienna, before later developing its application in therapeutic procedures known as psychodrama (Moreno, 1939). Owing to the immediacy of its impact, drama can affect people in different ways, and historically it has been viewed unfavourably by dominant hegemonies wishing to suppress its ability to move audiences and mould attitudes (Banham, 1995).

As is the case with all art which has the power to 'move people', the educational use of drama has the potential to connect with people both emotionally and cognitively, resulting in what we might call 'felt understanding'; a type of knowing which results in people taking a personal interest in issues and wanting to effect change. This potentially subversive power has been recognized throughout the ages by different ruling elites and oppressive regimes, who sought to diminish or eradicate its power through banning or severely censoring it. For example, from as early as the fifth century BC, Aristophanes' *Lysistrata* attracted censors for exploring themes of a moral and sexual nature (Sova, 2004), and until the Theatres Act of 1968, the British Lord Chamberlain's Examiner of Plays expunged and refused dramatic texts on a weekly basis (Nicholson, 1906), fearing the connection between political radicalism and social unrest, and the powerful role of theatricality in everyday life (Worrall, 2006). Drama censorship occupied a great deal of the ruling class's time and energy in nineteenth-century Europe, as they viewed the theatre as a form of mass entertainment/communication which potentially threatened the existing political, legal and social order (Goldstein, 2009). Similar concerns are evident in American, African, Austral-Asian and Latin American contexts where censorship of the theatre and dramatic performativity in people's daily lives remained active throughout most of the twentieth century (see Houchin, 2003 and Banham, 1995).

However, its potential as a valuable educational method has endured, and with the publication of Maier, Solem and Maier's training manual for role-playing in 1957, an ever-increasing number of researchers have been motivated to use role-play as part of their research design. Described as 'a pioneering attempt to portray industrial conflicts in role-playing format' (Mee, 1957: 135), the authors (1957: xi) recognize that understanding the 'principles of human behavior has little value unless it is supplemented with skill practice'. Maier *et al.* (1957) describe one of the benefits of using role-play as being able to demonstrate the gap between thinking and doing. The innovative approach was well received at the time by researchers in a number of applied areas including sociology, education, management science and industrial relations (see Berg, 1957; Mee, 1957; Borgatta, 1957; and Argyris, 1958), and researchers recognized in this fusion of case study method with role-playing techniques, a rich potential to analyse aspects of social behaviour and social interaction implicit in ordinary living.

In the succeeding 50 years, role-play has been widely used in education and training, and increasingly in the field of corporate training, where it is used to explore such issues as change management, negotiation skills, communication skills, leadership skills, team building, presentation skills, management training, public speaking, assertiveness training, performance management, customer service, interview skills, stress management, appraisals training and media training. Role-playing, gaming and computer simulation are three related strands of activity in this wider field, but it is beyond the scope of this chapter to explore the last two categories, and the focus here is on the use of role-play as a technique of educational research.

Similarly, the area of online role-play is currently burgeoning, with many people engaging in online roles through their experiences with playing video games or participating in virtual worlds on sites such as SimCity, Second Life and Whyville (Beach and Doerr-Stevens, 2009). These experiences, while usually recreational, can also offer valuable educational outcomes, such as the acquisition of the literacy practices of collective intelligence, problem-solving, strategic thinking, interpreting contexts and imaginative play (Beach and Doerr-Stevens, 2009; see also Gee, 2004; and Shaffer, 2006), but online role-playing will not be discussed here.

It is arguable that the use of role-play has had mixed success to date, much of it owing to a degree of confusion over what it is, and how to define it, as revealed in the report from the *British Medical Journal* in Box 26.1.

We begin by taking a closer look at drama and role-play in order to increase our understanding of what it is, and how it works.

BOX 26.1 A ROLE-PLAYING EXPERIENCE

It's Wednesday morning again, and time for our clinic sisters' teaching session. Anybody who thinks this gives me a relaxing two hour break from the rigours of outpatients is sorely deluded. Seeing a hundred patients seems quite a soft option compared with facing our four most senior sisters, exercise books open and pens poised to take down my every word.

Thinking up suitable topics is not easy. But harder is the actual task of teaching. British medical training provides ample case studies in how not to teach, and I've wasted many hours trying to find a comfortable sleeping position while a well intentioned lecturer starts on yet another new piece of chalk. Surely I can do better than that?

So I've put away the blackboard. And I've got the chairs rearranged in a circle. Dividing up for group work is tricky when there's only five of us all together. 'Brainstorming' with the flip chart is a bit of a non-starter with a group that's as talkative as a bunch of Trappist monks. But for today's session, on AIDS counselling, there is only one possible option. I must introduce them to the joys of role-play.

After a prolonged discussion about counselling in general, we kick off with a simple scenario. I am heading the bill with a stirring performance as Sipho, a young Zulu man who will need to be told that he is HIV positive. I have been rehearsing my lines for sometime, and I am all ready to bring the audience to its feet with my impassioned soliloquy. Sister Gumede has bravely volunteered to star in the lead role as, well, a clinic sister. After all, it is the first time they have ever done role-play, and I don't want to put them off.

So I reel off my performance, standing up, gesticulating, groaning, and clutching my head as I hear the bad news. Only the glycerine tears are missing. But the audience is not moved. They watch with bemused perplexity, and take copious notes. Sister takes her cue, and improvises her lines deadpan: 'Sipho, your HIV test is positive. We don't have any cure for AIDS so you are going to die.'

Now I have real cause to groan and clutch my head. What sort of a way is that to counsel someone who is HIV positive? Where are the open ended questions, the active listening, the non-verbal communication? My Balint colleagues in Lisson Grove would throw up their hands in horror.

But this is Africa, not north London. Maybe sister's performance is the one that should win the Oscar. After all it is exactly the way most of the sisters talk to patients, and probably the way that patients expect to be spoken to. And whoever saw a Zulu man behaving anything like my performance? Maybe this role-play business is not so simple. Maybe teaching is not so simple. So next time, sisters, bring your pillows; I am going to write notes on the blackboard.

Duncan Curr, Medical Officer, Mosvold Hospital, Ingwavuma, South Africa

Source: Curr, 1994: 725

26.2 What is role-play?

Deriving its theoretical basis from the field of psycho-drama, role-play is a 'spontaneous, dramatic, creative teaching strategy in which individuals overtly and consciously assume the roles of others' (Sellers, 2002: 498). Sellers (2002: 498) argues that it involves 'multi-level communication', and as a powerful teaching strategy, is capable of influencing participants' attitudes and emotions, whilst simultaneously promoting higher order cognitive skills. This definition supports the claim that role-play is an effective strategy for learning because it forces participants to think about the person whose role is being assumed, is connected to real-life situations, and promotes active, personal involvement in learning (Billings and Halstead, 2005). Errington (1997: 3) defines role-play as 'a planned learning activity designed to achieve specific educational purposes'. He suggests that it is based on three major aspects of the experiences that most people have of role in every day life:

- role-taking (the roles we hold in accordance with social expectations and in social circumstances, i.e. how police officers should act – Goffman, 1976);
- role making (the ability to create, switch and modify roles as required – Roberts, 1991);
- role-negotiation (negotiation and social interaction with other role holders – Hare, 1985).

For educational researchers, these categories offer a wealth of possibilities for accessing and exploring people's behaviour and responses to situations and stimuli in a diverse range of contexts and settings. For example, a researcher investigating a new coaching and mentoring training approach for senior managers in schools, may involve participants in varying aspects of role-taking, role making and role-negotiation as part of his overall research design to gather relevant data.

Role-play consists of three major stages: briefing, acting and debriefing. The first stage focuses on introducing the participants to the activity by clarifying the learning objectives and 'setting the scene'. In the second stage, the educator must encourage the participants to 'act out' the role in a spontaneous, accurate and realistic manner. Debriefing, the final stage, allows participants to discuss, analyse and evaluate the role-play and insights gained (Billings and Halstead, 2005).

Working in drama involves stepping into an imagined world, a fictional reality, and in order to make this imaginary world more meaningful and purposeful in an educational research context, it must have aspects of the real world in it. Thus, human relationships are a central component of role-play situations, and exist in the form of:

1 relationships between people;
2 the relationship between people and ideas; and
3 the relationship between people and the environment (O'Toole and Haseman, 1992: 3).

These categories provide a useful framework for researchers interested in using role-play to identify who and what their research should focus on. Thus a researcher who wishes to explore whether teenagers empathize with bullied peers, may use role-play to determine the extent to which young people:

1 discuss the issue among themselves, and if/how they would approach the subject with a peer in school who they know is being bullied;
2 engage with training sessions and resources they have received in school on the issue of bullying, and if/how they put these into practice;
3 demonstrate an awareness of their role in the creation of a culture that does not accept or tolerate bullying in their school environment and wider social community.

Taking on roles allows participants to set up and explore the different dynamics of the relationships cited above, but differs from traditional understandings of theatre in that the role-taker is not required to demonstrate elaborate acting skills, rather, simply to represent a point of view. Ideally, the role should be portrayed honestly and without elaborate costumes or props, where participants place themselves 'as if' they are that person, temporarily identifying with and exploring a set of attitudes and values, which may not identify closely with their own. It is therefore important that participants respect the role being played, as it represents another person's perspective or point of view (O'Toole and Haseman, 1992: 3). Heathcote (1980: 42) defines the educational use of drama as people involved in active role-taking, where their attitude to the situation, not their ability to portray a character, is the chief concern. The role-play must be lived at life-rate (i.e. in that moment), and aim to create a living picture of life, which provides a learning opportunity for the participant as much as for any onlookers, including the researcher.

Role-play is improvisational in nature and increasingly unscripted, although role cards may be supplied to provide sufficient background information to participants to enable them to comfortably 'step into the shoes' of another, and feel what it might be like to be that person in that situation for a little while. Wagner (1998: 60) defines improvisational drama as taking on 'a role in a particular moment in time and creating with others a plausible world'. She argues that when working in role, as in all learning contexts, participants make meaning by connecting their prior experiences to the challenge of the moment.

26.3 Why use role-play in research?

Cabral (1987: 470) describes role-playing as a valuable technique that 'has been broadly adapted for use in academic research and applied settings'. Before presenting the arguments related to the particular use of role-play in research contexts, it is worth taking a brief look at the general educational claims made in its name. In their aptly titled book *So You Want to Use Role-Play?*, Bolton and Heathcote (1999) provide six major categories which summarize the use and value of role-play in education.

1   Behaviour modification. It is a concrete form of learning, and particularly suitable for giving participants practice in behavioural procedures (for example, training reception staff or police officers to handle particular situations according to an established procedure).
2   Acquiring information.
3   Using information.
4   Training in seeking information.
5   Attention to detail (role work can generate in participants a disposition to attend to detail, an alertness to particulars).
6   Fosters a change in values, perceptions or attitudes.
   (Adapted from Bolton and Heathcote, 1999: 178–85)

The arts, and role-play in this particular discussion, work by revealing truths about people and the world they live in, and they do this through the creation of a fictional situation, a make-believe world, but one that is closely connected to reality. This is the difference between fiction and fantasy, and in most research situations where role-play is used, the emphasis is on working in and through fiction: uncovering and exploring truths about reality, and about how we respond individually to such situations, as we each construct our own understanding of experiences. Bolton and Heathcote (1999: ix) are concerned with broadening the traditionally perceived use of role-play, away from a strictly behavioural emphasis to the communication of meaning. Thus, an educational researcher interested in investigating social skills education with children with

an Autistic Spectrum Disorder, may use role-play to create a baseline assessment of participants' 'theory of mind' (i.e. their ability to perceive and understand the thoughts of others), through placing the children in role as detectives, observing a crime as it unfolds, and trying to predict what the characters are thinking at that time (see O'Sullivan *et al.*, 2010).

There are many uses and types of role-play, but the single criterion underpinning all role-play activity according to Bolton and Heathcote (1999: 57), is that it demands participants to step into an 'as if' fiction: a fiction that has been 'conceived of by a tutor, teacher, or researcher in terms of *learning*'. It poses a unique challenge to participants, as it involves 'embracing knowledge', an act which is not just a matter of instruction or absorption, but is achieved by entering the fiction in such a way as to make the required knowledge one's own. Thus, role-players are not just receiving or acquiring knowledge as in a typical instructional context; they are making it, practising it and embodying it: they know what they know (Bolton and Heathcote, 1999: 57, 58). This highlights the importance of accurately setting up and structuring the role-play to record these truths and attitudes, and thereby increase the reliability and validity of the data retrieved.

Roslyn Arnold (1998: 111) claims that the arts, and in particular drama, uniquely explore the dynamics between affect and cognition, two significant aspects of human existence. The use of role-play in research contexts is a rich source of insight into the role and function of such dynamics. Thus, when participating in role, we articulate both physically and verbally, and this active engagement promotes 'emotional, cognitive, social and ego development. We are, metaphorically speaking, sitting on a research gold mine' (Arnold, 1998: 111).

One of the main reasons for considering the use of role-play in research is because of its ability to help participants consider ideas from different perspectives, to think of possibilities. Role-play is concerned with representing and exploring different people's points of view, and different points of view forge different types of knowledge. It places participants at the centre of the learning experience, and allows them to build their own bridges of understanding. As a result of this informed consideration, they are better able to resolve problems and issues. For example, role-play as a research method has been successfully used with young people in a designated disadvantaged school to elicit the extent to which they use an elaborate or restricted linguistic code (public versus private use of language), and whether through the use of role-playing, they can explore and develop different linguistic registers and codes as appropriate to a range of communication contexts (see O'Sullivan and Heeran-Flynn, 2010).

The following list identifies the range of possibilities in which role-play can be employed as an effective research method. Specifically, role-play can allow participants to:

- experience how people behave in particular circumstances by exploring a variety of social situations and social interactions;
- explore a range of human feelings and responses to situations;
- explore choices and moral dilemmas;
- make decisions which are tested out in the role-play and later reflected on;
- develop a sense of responsibility and confidence as decision makers and problem solvers;
- improve the social health of their group and foster improved relationships with peers or colleagues;
- interact with peers and learn to compromise in order to sustain and develop activities;
- extend, enrich and prompt the use of authentic language use in simulated real-life contexts where language use arises out a genuine need to communicate;
- explore the skills and processes involved in conflict, negotiation and resolution of difficulties and problems in their environment;
- develop personal creativity;
- develop agency and an increased awareness of self;
- improve visual and spatial skills through responding to a range of stimuli and situations.

Role-play situations as described above can be observed by the researcher, and/or digitally recorded, and replayed to participants to elicit their responses and perspectives according to predetermined or emerging research themes and issues, thereby assisting in the triangulation and interpretation of data. Such an approach was used when investigating social skills education with children and young people with Asperger's Syndrome. Role-play was used as a core research method in a longitudinal study to initially create a baseline measure of participants' literal and metaphorical language competencies, and then to assess the extent to which improvements in participants' social skills were revealed and practised during subsequent role-play episodes (see O'Sullivan et al., 2009).

Role-play operates in a 'no-penalty zone', where people are freer to explore and try out a range of solutions to problems and issues, without having to worry about the outcome. Drama functions as a way of making the world simpler and more understandable. It

can be a kind of 'playing at' or practice of living in real-life situations. It enables participants to put into practice skills they have learnt in the fictional context of the drama world. It is a tool that can affect participants' fundamental reactions to everyday situations. Augusto Boal (1979, 2002) refers to this type of dramatic activity as a 'rehearsal for reality'. In professional disciplines, such as health care, education, engineering and social care practice, both pre- and in-service education models rely on problem-based and enquiry-based approaches to teaching, learning and research. Role-play offers enormous potential in these areas to enhance case study method and facilitate research on models of best practice. For example, in a comparative study exploring integrated approaches to teaching the curriculum in an early years educational setting versus the use of more traditional pedagogies, the teacher-researcher and young learners were engaged in a sustained role-play throughout the school day for several weeks (see O'Sullivan and Murphy, 2006).

The notion of learning through play tends to be associated with early years education, and opportunities for imaginative and dramatic play decline as a child progresses through the school system and into adult life. An unfounded belief that academic content standards cannot be met through creative and imaginative activities still persists, and has caused playful methods of learning to virtually disappear from classrooms (Bergen, 2009). The following is a brief summary from the literature reflecting the use of role-play in a process of life-long education (see Oberle, 2004).

- Role-play develops participants' transferable skills and content knowledge (Cutler and Hay, 2000).
- The integrated nature of role-play allows for individual differences in development (Frost et al., 2008).
- Role-playing is fun and motivating for students (Isenberg and Jalongo, 2006).
- Role-play successfully energizes students and promotes in-depth understanding of traditional educational issues (Montgomery et al., 1997).
- Meaningful, motivating contexts help students better internalize their learning and improve their recall (Hickey and Zuiker, 2005).
- Role-play facilitates student participation in active learning (Freeman, 2003; Kerr et al., 2003).
- Role-playing in science classrooms develops deeper student understanding, improves student motivation, and facilitates learning across a range of ability levels (Aubusson et al., 1997).
- Role-play in school enhances the creative and innovative potential of future scientists (Bergen, 2009),

and encourages creativity and imagination (Johnson 1998); essential skills for scientists (Bergen, 2009).

- Role-playing is in accord with the pedagogical framework established by the Association of American Colleges and Universities and other organizations that seek to foster a more dynamic university-level general education curriculum (Oberle, 2004; AACU, 2002).

- Role-playing activities complement traditional lectures because they simulate real-world experiences and enhance students' retention of information (DeNeve and Heppner, 1997).

- Role-playing activities enhance students' understanding of concepts, develop students' key-skills, which are transferable to other endeavours outside of the classroom; and increase students' level of motivation and participation in the learning process (Livingstone, 1999).

- Role-playing activities can engage students in projects that challenge gender, class and racial stereotypes; diminish the hierarchical relationship between students and instructors; and encourage students to engage in democratic participation (Maddrell, 1994).

Many of the reports above used role-play as a key research method in their studies.

26.4 Issues to be aware of when using role-play

Much of the early history relating to the use of role-play in research settings was mired in controversy and notoriety, mainly relating to issues around deception in experimental social psychology (see Milgram's obedience to authority experiments, 1974; Mixon's role-playing replications of the Milgram experiment, 1974), and to overt/covert forms of research. Bolton (1996: 187) discusses the case of James Patrick [a pseudonym], a young teacher at an approved school who in the late 1950s obtained entry into a Glaswegian gang for four months, in order to record and analyse how a city gang functions (see Patrick, 1973). He made friends with a pupil in his school called Tim, and through this acquaintance, joined his pupil's gang. In deciding to open his teacher's eyes to gang life, Tim understood the risks more clearly than Patrick did. Tim was extremely well behaved when in school, but at weekends he participated fully in the violent incidents that regularly erupted at a moment's notice (Douglas Home, 2007). After having been placed in several uncompromising situations, Patrick left Glasgow quickly when the violence became too severe and he

felt threatened by it. As he was so afraid of the gang members, he did not publish his research until many years later.

Bolton (1996) describes this act of infiltration and deception as a blatantly unethical form of enquiry. Although, researchers may well have to ask themselves whether the same information could have been gained by overt means. In contrast to this covert approach, William Foote Whyte (1993) conducted a similar research exercise in a poor Italian district in Boston from 1937 onwards called 'Street Corner Society'. He was interested in the activities of the adolescent boys who hung around street corners and got involved in gang activities. However, his research approach was not covert, and he began almost as an observer, having informed the group that he was writing a book about their activities (Whyte, 1993). Perhaps one of the most controversial examples of a study involving the use of role-play is the well-known Stanford Prison Experiment carried out by Philip Zimbardo in 1971 (2007a, 2007b, 2008; Zimbardo et al., 2000; see also Haney and Zimbardo, 1998), a brief overview of which is given in Box 26.2.

Early enthusiasts of role-playing as a research methodology cite experiments such as the Stanford Prison Experiment to support their claim that where realism and spontaneity can be introduced into role-play, then such experimental conditions do, in fact, simulate both symbolically and phenomenologically, the real-life analogues that they purport to represent. Such advocates of role-play would concur with the conclusions of Zimbardo and his research associates that the simulated prison developed into a psychologically compelling prison environment and they, too, would infer that the dramatic differences in the behaviour of prisoners and guards arose out of their location in different positions within the institutional structure of the prison and the social psychological conditions that prevailed there, rather than from personality differences between the two groups of subjects (see Banuazizi and Movahedi, 1975). In discussing the Stanford Prison Experiment, Bolton (1996: 188) argues that the disregard of ethical standards in this research results from 'the tacit permission that role-playing a power-position gives', and not from deception. Although the researchers anticipated the risk of physical abuse and changed the rules to reflect this, they failed to predict the pleasure that some guards might derive from employing psychological abuse, 'even when they could perceive … the genuine discomfort of their victims' (Bolton, 1996: 188).

Bolton (1996) expresses concern that the use of role-play in such circumstances can appear to give permission to participants to behave outside their normal

---

BOX 26.2   THE STANFORD PRISON EXPERIMENT

The study was conducted in the summer of 1971 in a mock prison constructed in the basement of the psychology building at Stanford University. The subjects were selected from a pool of 75 respondents to a newspaper advertisement asking for paid volunteers to participate in a psychological study of prison life. On a random basis half of the subjects were assigned to the role of guard and half to the role of prisoner. Prior to the experiment subjects were asked to sign a form, agreeing to play either the prisoner or the guard role for a maximum of two weeks. Those assigned to the prisoner role should expect to be under surveillance, to be harassed, but not to be physically abused. In return, subjects would be adequately fed, clothed and housed and would receive 15 dollars per day for the duration of the experiment. The outcome of the study was quite dramatic. In less than two days after the initiation of the experiment, violence and rebellion broke out. The prisoners ripped off their clothing and their identification numbers and barricaded themselves inside the cells while shouting and cursing at the guards. The guards, in turn, began to harass, humiliate and intimidate the prisoners. They used sophisticated psychological techniques to break the solidarity among the inmates and to create a sense of distrust among them. In less than 36 hours one of the prisoners showed severe symptoms of emotional disturbance, uncontrollable crying and screaming and was released. On the third day, a rumour developed about a mass escape plot. The guards increased their harassment, intimidation and brutality towards the prisoners. On the fourth day, two prisoners showed symptoms of severe emotional disturbance and were released. On the fifth day, the prisoners showed symptoms of individual and group disintegration. They had become mostly passive and docile, suffering from an acute loss of contact with reality. The guards on the other hand, had kept up their harassment, some behaving sadistically. Because of the unexpectedly intense reactions generated by the mock prison experience, the experimenters terminated the study at the end of the sixth day.

Source: Adapted from Banuazizi and Movahedi, 1975

---

moral constraints. Grumet (1998: 8, 9) acknowledges that taking on a role is complex and provocative, and when working in role, researchers should be aware of 'the power of a role to extend or constrict meaning and exploration'. If we accept the Latin word for role as *dramatis personae*, there is a danger that the participant may hide behind the mask of a role, taking on 'actions and ideas that would be difficult to assume within his or her daily identity' (Grumet, 1998: 8). Thus, playing a role in this context may result in behaviours and attitudes that extend imagination and expression beyond the individual's usual capacity, and 'the imaginative extension of ego into role' might have the effect of constraining rather than enlarging understanding (Grumet, 1998: 9).

On the other hand, Grumet (1998: 9) argues, when a role is used in a naturalized scene, untrained participants may 'fail to fill it with the complex and multiple possibilities that a real life situation' would demand, choosing instead to adopt a more stereotypical action in the improvisation than might exist in real life. The researcher must therefore look for opportunities to break the often powerful grip of a scene and role, and encourage critical reflection on the choices that are being taken in the role-play. The aim is to shift, alter, interrupt and possibly distort the focus of the role-play (during it if necessary), to allow participants to explore

and experience different aspects of the situation under consideration, thereby 'avoiding a reductive metonymy that would substitute the improvisational situation for the world', with its infinite colour and myriad of possibilities (Grumet, 1998: 9). This can often be achieved by following step 8 (the hidden objective) as described in Box 26.3.

Wagner (1998: 58) suggests that working in drama requires the same intelligence it takes to live one's life in the real world, in order to be able to cope with the many possibilities, choices, decisions, ambiguities, changes, etc. that face people on a daily basis. The challenge in drama is to engage with those issues without losing the capacity to analyse situations responsibly and carefully, choose between alternatives that are not always clear, 'act on those choices and live with consequences. In other words, to think before, during, and after one acts' (Wagner, 1998: 58). For the researcher interested in exploring the intricacies and complexities of life, the key is to set up and organize the role-play event so that it accurately reflects, not mirrors, the situation under scrutiny (see the guidelines provided in Box 26.3).

In using role-play in research trials such as the Stanford Prison Experiment, where none of the preliminary documentation given to participants refers explicitly to the act of role-playing, or provides them with

---

BOX 26.3 MANAGING ROLE-PLAY EFFECTIVELY

1 *Set the scene*: when the participants are settled, the researcher should introduce the activity and outline what is going to happen during the session.

2 *Narrate the dramatic frame*: describe the context and background to the fictional situation by outlining any necessary information, i.e. what has happened up to this point in the story, where is this scene set, who is present, when does it take place, etc. It familiarizes the participant with the context, and removes some of the awkwardness associated with starting a role-play 'cold'.

3 *Provide a 'second dimension' for each role*: the researcher must provide adequate information about each of the characters in the role-play in order to 'flesh out' their profile sufficiently for the role-player to be able to 'step into the role' safely, confidently and with integrity. The 'first dimension' of role specifies only the character's broad profile, such as being 'a father', 'a teacher', 'a prisoner', 'a doctor', but does not indicate what kind of doctor is to be represented, what training she has had, what are her dominant personality traits (kind, generous, short-tempered, even-handed), etc. Talk about 'the character' as if you know her (it will increase participants' interest and investment in her situation).

4 *Dilemma*: the researcher must outline the dilemma or problem which is to be explored (and/or resolved) in the scene (usually consisting of conflicting choices where decisions have to be made and consequences dealt with). In planning the research, the dilemma or problem selected for enquiry may be of a personal nature (my family comes before my job); social nature (everyone goes to the nightclub at weekends); or of a moral nature (if we restructure the company in this manner, many workers will lose their jobs).

5 *Dramatic tension*: all drama, by virtue of its definition, relies on dramatic tension to propel the action forward. Tension may occur as follows: in relationships; as a result of a task that has to be undertaken; in not knowing what is going to happen (surprise and/or mystery); or in exploring ways of behaving not typical in participants' daily lives. A successful role-play must have dramatic tension to sustain character belief and investment in the situation ('as if it could be real'). A well-chosen dilemma will lead to dramatic tension in the scene.

6 *Objective*: the researcher must ensure that *each* participant in the role-play has an objective. For example, as human resources manager, invite the union representative to lunch, and your objective is to find out who is driving the proposed work stoppage among the workers. The person playing the part of the union worker may be given a different objective, possibly one that counters yours (i.e. reveal nothing), or operates at a more devisive or subtle level (provide misleading information, or play along with the game). Selecting the right objectives will impact on the focus of action in the scene, and thereby facilitate the researcher to gather data on his/her area(s) of interest. It will also impact upon the mood generated by the participants in response to their attempts to achieve their objectives, which may further alter or intensify the dramatic tension as a result.

7 *Constraint*: the researcher must formulate appropriate and purposeful constraints for each participant in the role-play before it begins. Constraints help to make a scene more realistic, and slow the action down, allowing for greater opportunity for negotiation and interaction. To be meaningful, constraints must be related to the dominant political, economic, historical, social or personal realities in the scene. For example, in the scene above, the union representative may be aware that he is being 'pressed' for information, but has to maintain a calm and vaguely pleasant demeanour as he is aware that greater harm could result if he were to have an outburst at a lunch table with the human resources manager. The constraint for the HR manager could be that she is not allowed to ask the union rep. directly about staff members' activities, and has to exercise caution in how she gently probes over a long and leisurely lunch. Without effective constraints, a role-player may ignore the social and professional 'niceties' in the scene above, demand the required information and conclude the scene rather swiftly, thereby missing out on the learning possibilities that this activity has to offer.

continued

8 *Hidden objective*: while the information in principles 1–7, should be shared with all role-play participants openly, the researcher may decide to add additional information or instructions to complicate, enrich or develop a scene. It involves giving a piece of information or instruction to one participant in the role-play, and giving a different piece of information or instruction to the other role-player(s). This information is not shared with the full group but delivered privately, and thus when the characters come together to improvise the scene, their objectives may clash overtly (or covertly) as set up by the researcher. A hidden objective can be used successfully to replay the same scene, but altering some of the detail in the second and subsequent runnings. For example, in a rerun of a scene between a marriage guidance counsellor and a client, the researcher may call the counsellor to one side of the room to additionally inform her that this client has already seen another counsellor in the same organization, and made an official complaint about her. The client is not aware of this additional information being applied to the scene, and it would be interesting to gather data from both participants, comparing how the two scenes may (or may not) differ. It is possible to give a hidden objective to both parties, which can result in a lively interaction when the scene recommences.

information or guidance on how to safely 'enter a role', 'step into the shoes of another person', and behave as if they are that person for the duration of the activity (see www.prisonexp.org for copies of the original documentation), there is an implicit assumption that the person in charge of organizing the game is taking on ultimate responsibility for what might happen. Bolton (1996: 188) suggests that this effectively provides temporary release to the participants to regard the experiment as 'only a game and, what's more, someone else has asked us to play it'.

However, Bolton (1996) makes an interesting observation when he claims that this seeming release from responsibility rarely extends to breaking the rules of a game, and he recommends that researchers interested in using role-play may need to pay particular attention to this by 'delineating participant goals and delimiting strategies'. It may have been a very different prison experiment had the responsibility been altered during the role-play by telling the warders that they had been nominated for promotion within the prison service on the basis of their ability to combine authority and respect in their dealings with prisoners (Bolton, 1996: 188). The flexibility of role-play as a research method can provide a researcher with valuable opportunities to shift variables and explore other angles/perspectives, all within the framework of the existing role-play, thus saving time and resources (with due attention being paid to ethical issues and constraints as relevant).

There is recognition that all acting is, by definition, 'not real'. The extent of the illusion is reflected in the different versions of reality and humanity portrayed, and in role-play, it is possible to show both the inner and outer voices of a participant. This is referred to as the self-spectator, where participants are able to monitor their performance in the role, and are not overwhelmed by it (see Heathcote, 1991). They are empowered through the initial setting up of the exercise to be able to maintain a dual personality: they are watching themselves as they play the role, and can learn from the experience. This is particularly useful for researchers as it allows them to gather data from a dual perspective, i.e. what it was like for participants to play the role of someone else, and to compare that experience to participants' own realities. Such data can be used by the researcher to inform and create a multilayered approach to the research.

In the Stanford Prison Experiment however, the participants appear to have been fully submerged in the role, or as Sartre (1976: 162) might put it 'devoured by the imaginary'. This led to its own consequences as presented in Box 26.2, and serves to highlight the necessity of thorough planning and preparation for the use of role-playing in research contexts, particularly in the field of social psychology. O'Neill (1995: 70) suggests that anyone who publicly takes on a fictional role changes in response to the alteration in interpretive attitude of the viewer to the viewed. They become 'both more and less than an individual', acquiring what Roland Barthes (1972: 49) calls a 'corporeal exemplarity'. A role can protect and conceal participants within the dramatic world, and they can be simultaneously 'both more and less than themselves. They embody both present meaning and future possibility' (O'Neill, 1995: 144). For this reason, role-play can provide an experimental setting in which questions of identity and the power and limitations of the roles we inhabit may be explored (O'Neill, 1995: 144).

26.5 Role-play as a research method

The approach to role-play advocated in this chapter represents a move away from a strictly behaviourist system to one which emphasizes process, and is involved in the creation and communication of meaning. Thus, role-play as presented here offers particular advantages to a researcher who is interested in exploring and analysing data which may not be easily accessed through other methods. It is a unique blending with case study method, and offers a rare opportunity to critically examine aspects of social behaviour and social interaction in relationships between people, ideas and the environment.

Using role-play in research allows researchers to:

■ explore the principles of human behaviour in real-life settings, lived at life-pace;
■ access and assess how people make sense of their lives, and the structures of the natural world;
■ prioritize the process of engagement;
■ explore different points of view, and forge different types of knowledge;
■ adopt multiple viewing points within a data set;
■ study multi-level communication;
■ identify and explore the development and manifestation of participants' attitudes, decisions, strategies, values, higher-level cognitive and affective thinking skills, and emotions;
■ shift and alter variables as the research unfolds, to explore subtleties and nuances in human interactions and situations, in an uncomplicated and undemanding manner, without having to schedule additional sessions or devise alternative methods to collect the data required;
■ provide planned or spontaneous physical, emotional, personal, social or intellectual prompts and stimuli to participants, in comparison to the use of predominantly intellectual prompts in other methods such as interviews and questionnaires;
■ engage with a fully diverse research population through the use of an inclusive method to explore and access relevant data;
■ explore meanings and the ways in which people understand things;
■ investigate patterns of behaviour;
■ provide a somewhat objective lens through which to interpret the material, and thus distance themselves from the topic of enquiry, facilitating an objective mode of analysis;
■ examine ready-made, visually and narratively rich research data, which evoke layers of meaning through reflection;
■ capture visual data, adding immediacy and authenticity to the research;
■ involve participants as co-researchers;
■ engage in meaningful interaction with participants.

Role-play as a research method – special features

■ Participants are actively involved in the research process through the three major stages of briefing, acting and debriefing. The use of role-play in a well-structured research process has the potential to create a reciprocal relationship, a valuable learning experience for both researcher and participant, which may ultimately impact upon the quality of resulting data.
■ Helps participants to consider ideas from different perspectives. It can place participants at the centre of the research experience, and allow them to construct their own bridges of understanding. As a result, they are often better able to respond to questions and comments from researchers about the experience.
■ Supports participants during the research process, owing to the group and social nature of the activity. It tends to be much less isolating than completing a questionnaire, for example.
■ Engages the whole person through the process, and reduces the danger of intellectual speculation or 'navel gazing' (what I would do if I were in that situation…). It places participants 'in situ', at that moment, and demands a holistic response.
■ The role-play can be structured to become incrementally more challenging or complex as participants are eased into the activity and prepared to engage with the issues under examination.
■ It is an enjoyable activity and fosters positive relations between the researcher and participants.
■ It is a spontaneous, dramatic, creative research strategy in which participants overtly and consciously assume the roles of others.
■ The role-play may stimulate related memories and experiences, and can be used as a naturally occurring springboard to explore other relevant experiences or situations without the researcher probing too deeply or overtly.
■ It can both relax and poise participants simultaneously, who may respond more openly and freely without overt direction from the researcher.
■ It can be controlled by participants, and they can stop, pause or extend the activity at will.
■ Debriefing and de-roling activities can increase reflection, and provide rich data that is not easily accessed using other methods, or within such an economic time frame.
■ It can provide an added dimension to the research in that participants are engaged in reflexive praxis; they are learning and doing at the same time, i.e.

research as a combination of both experience and reasoning.

- Like other forms of empirical data, role-playing may not provide researchers with unbiased, objective documentation, but it can show characteristic attributes that are often missed in other forms of data collection.

A note of caution

Like much research in the qualitative tradition, role-playing as a research method caters for issues concerning moral responsibility, individuality, freedom and choice, resulting in the collation of rich and personal data. While quantitative research is characterized by presupposed outcomes, qualitative analysis encourages an organic development, with much more flexibility offered to the overall process (see Taylor, 1996). However, it is important to note that role-playing is always context-bound and localized. It does not lend easily to mass generalization, unlike quantitative techniques. The conclusions are usually derived from intensive, small-scale experiences drawing on a rich and deep data set, but they may be highly selective depending on the researcher's objectives. In this approach, the researcher turns away from statistical analysis in favour of in-depth analytical accounts of human behaviour.

If using role-play as a research method, the researcher must ask herself, what impact does the interplay of art with reality have? In addition to those issues identified in the previous section, Ginsburg (1978) summarizes the argument against role-playing as a device for generating scientific knowledge when he notes that:

- role-playing is unreal with respect to the variables under study in that the subject reports what she would do, and that is taken as though she did do it;
- the behaviour displayed is not spontaneous even in the more active forms of role-playing;
- the verbal reports in role-playing are very susceptible to artefactual influence such as social desirability; and
- role-playing procedures are not sensitive to complex interactions.

Ginsburg's (1978) critique relates to a form of practice that underpins a behaviourist approach to role-playing. It is noteworthy that many of his concerns have been addressed in the intervening years through the development of a systematic approach to role-play methodology as described in the following sections.

26.6 How does it work?

Maier *et al.* (1957: 14) state that leading role-playing is not a difficult task, and does not require special training by the trainer. However, this is disputed by Argyris (1958: 321) who claims that role-playing requires skilful leaders who have a high degree of self-awareness, confidence and self-worth. As alluded to earlier, the shift in role-play from a typical transactional model of passing on of knowledge, to the 'making' of it, 'calls on one's humanness in a way not normally associated with an instructional context': it can be both demanding and revealing (Bolton and Heathcote, 1999: 58). This was evident in the response of the participants in the Stanford Prison Experiment, and the challenge for researchers is to get the balance right between maximizing opportunities for research, and protecting participants. If one over or under protects, it may stifle learning. Many people are nervous about role-play, and associate it with being required to 'act' in front of their peers or colleagues. Taking on a role is like an actor working to create a character in a play or film. However, whereas the actor is required to build a complex personality through a process called characterization, the role-player focuses only on the following:

1 the purpose of taking on the role;
2 the status or level of power of the role – high, low or equal status in relation to the others in the role-play;
3 the attitude of the role; and
4 the participant's motivation in the role-play (O'Toole and Haseman, 1992: 7–13).

The researcher should determine these in advance according to the issues or themes being investigated, and brief participants fully on these four points before they engage in the role-play. This will facilitate transparency about the research exercise, and ensure greater clarity and depth in the activity itself, thereby improving the reliability of the data by more closely reflecting the real-life situation and reducing any tendency to superficiality.

Unscripted or improvised role-play increases flexibility, encourages varied discourse and allows for natural turn-taking in a conversational exchange, but educators and researchers should be aware that a loosely structured role-play places more demands on participants, and thus requires greater preparation in advance. A more structured, scripted role-play may also be used, but it does not allow for the same level of discourse and flexible response as open role-play (see Kasper and Roever, 2005). Occasionally, the educator or researcher may play a role (often called Teacher in Role in the literature), but most roles are usually assumed by participants.

Although no set method or standardized approach exists for role-play, McKeachie and Svinicki (2006) indicate that the effectiveness of role-play is dependent on careful planning and the educator's ability to convey confidence to participants that role-play can be a valuable strategy. The eight principles outlined in Box 26.3 are designed to support the researcher as she endeavours to plan for a rich and well-designed role-playing episode. Without adhering to some general guidelines, an improvisation or role-play is in danger of becoming stereotypical, overacted, simplistic and may skew resulting data. Such an activity may also peter out after a few moments if participants lack sufficient information about the situation or the characters they are playing. Depending on the researcher's objectives, it is possible to alter some of these principles to elicit, monitor and assess a specific response. The following guidelines are useful to encourage active participation in most role-play situations, and should be attended to during the initial planning stage of the research, and communicated to the participants, either orally, much as a narrator in a film or play might do at the outset to fill in missing information, or through the use of written briefs or role cards (which are commercially available or written by the researcher in accordance with her objectives).

26.7 Important strategies for successful role-play

Inserting dramatic tension and awakening participants' self-spectator

Irrespective of the many types and genre of drama, one of its key defining characteristics is dramatic tension. Role-play, devoid of any tension, is sometimes used in educational and research contexts, and results in little more than rote learning or drill practice. While a behaviourist mode of training is appropriate in some areas, it can ignore the intricacies of real life where interactions with other people occur. If, as is suggested, dramatic tension is a key feature of successful role-play, then Heathcote (1991: 34) argues for the importance of focusing on the *quality* of dramatic tension, and by this she is not referring to 'huge terrifying events such as earthquakes, mutinies, armies and so on' which can characterize some forms of drama, but rather to localized incidents operating at a subtle level within a human circumstance. Tension is often manifest in situations where there is an incomplete task with a deadline looming, and related to power games and status in rela-

tionships. By inserting low-level or insipid dramatic tension into a role-play, it can motivate participants, build investment in the fictional situation, and it 'has the effect of making the most hackneyed situations spring into new focus and create new awareness' (Heathcote, 1991: 34).

Being cognizant of the fact that role-play operates in a fictional realm, and employs the art form of drama as its vehicle to achieve new insights, participants must not be allowed to become emotionally and intellectually consumed by a situation, or it will reduce the possibilities for reflection on their actions and related consequences. In addition to good planning for role-playing episodes, the concept of the 'self-spectator' (see Heathcote, 1991 and Bolton and Heathcote, 1999) is closely linked with protecting participants in drama, and allowing for greater reflection and deepening of the experience. The concept implies that participants are observing themselves when in role, are aware of what they are doing and of what is happening to them, and do not become overly immersed in the action. This is achieved by monitoring their emotional and cognitive responses to the dramatic stimulus, so that they are aware that they are playing a part. They are simultaneously themselves and also representing a character.

Self-spectation implies becoming the critical audience of your own performance, and facilitates an ability to change if required. Failure to monitor one's participation in a role-play may result in missed learning opportunities, reduced flexibility in responding to a situation, and increases the risk of dangerous emotional engagement (i.e. getting carried away with the action). Regular moments of reflection both during and after the role-play are important to allow for self-spectation to be activated and employed. These can be facilitated by researcher interventions during the activity, such as questioning, judicious use of praise and encouraging participants to be responsible and to look for implications and consequences of their actions at all times. It is important to encourage the participants to document their experiences of the role-play, whilst in-, and/or out-of-role. It can allow for the emergence of important insights and form the basis for later reflection and evaluation. Writing or drawing whilst inside or outside the dramatic situation, can facilitate the formulation and expression of both private and public responses, and also stimulate self-spectation.

Protection into role and protection into emotion

Emotion is the underlying currency of drama, because any imaginary act is necessarily accompanied by emotion (Davis and Lawrence, 1987). It fosters participant investment where the characters begin to care about the situation, and work collaboratively towards exploring creative and meaningful solutions. If we take the emotion out of drama, there is only the 'burden' or 'hard grind' of life left. There are many ways to categorize and discuss emotion, but in educational drama and role-play we are broadly concerned with the notion of first and second order emotions. The former describes raw emotion as experienced in real life, and the latter refers to filtered emotion, as may be experienced in art (see Witkin, 1974; Best, 1992). It is generally agreed that first order emotion has no place in art, as it is transitory and fleeting, and may at times be overwhelming and uncontrollable. But the advantage of using the arts in educational research is that they allow us to slow down time, pausing and dwelling a little on experiences that might otherwise be lost to us. This can be a useful approach in gathering valuable data for research. For example, when working with children who were prone to public release of inappropriate behaviours, such as tantrums or meltdowns, a role-play methodology was employed to investigate whether such children could learn to mediate and manage their emotional state using an experiential rather than a behaviourist intervention (O'Sullivan, 2005).

In drama and role-play, the aim is not to protect participants *from* emotion, but *into* emotion, in order to maximize engagement and extend learning opportunities. There are several highly effective strategies, including the aforementioned self-spectatorship and second dimension of role, which serve to maintain and increase the objective distance between participants' real lives and the fictional scenario they are working in. The challenge is to induct people comfortably and carefully into role to ensure that they are equipped to play that part responsibly.

Whereas a professional actor will develop a whole technique to accommodate this, role-play facilitators and researchers who use this methodology typically ask participants to 'just be a…' (pensioner, waiter, taxi-driver or prisoner) with little or no preparation for what it might mean to 'just be a…'. Without adequate preparation, participants may have little or no option but to fall back on a stereotype, as they have been given nothing else to work from. Thus, if asking children 'to be pirates', they tend to rely on stereotyped images from film and television to base their representation on. The use of context and second dimension of role (and the principles discussed in Box 26.3), can considerably reduce this risk, and in this case, encourage the children to explore what type of pirate they are playing. In building an initial profile, children can be encouraged to think about what they might have done (as a pirate) to be outlawed. Preliminary discussion to elicit

information about what type of people pirates are, why they may have been forced into that way of life, and what it means to be a pirate historically and in today's world, are effective strategies to build belief and investment ('I care about the role'), protect the participants into role and subsequently into emotion, and activate their self-spectator.

Attention to detail and responsible planning should always incorporate these strategies in order to simultaneously challenge and protect participants when engaged in role-playing. Paying careful attention to how we induct people safely and responsibly into role will elicit more reliable and ethical research findings, and serve to limit any possible skewing of data. It would appear that while every attention was paid to organizing the research component in the Stanford Prison Experiment (via consent forms and university ethical approval), a major weakness in the design was evident in the lack of attention to the practicalities of using role-play as a method in this case study. Unfortunately, a review of the literature would suggest that this is commonly reflected in many studies using role-play. Box 26.4 indicates several practical points when setting up a multiple role-play procedure.

26.8 Three examples of research using role-play

Role-playing versus lecturing

In an empirical study designed to compare the effectiveness of role-playing and collaborative activities to teacher-centered discussions and lectures, with history and political science college students, McCarthy and Anderson (2000) report that the experimental group who participated in the role-plays and collaborative exercises did substantially better on subsequent standard evaluations than the control group, their traditionally instructed peers: the difference in the mean performance of the experimental group in political science was +0.8, while that in history was +1.0. The authors acknowledge the limitations of the experimental design in that it did not involve the use of randomly selected samples, nor did they control for potentially confounding factors such as differences in instructor performance or the academic levels of the students in the groups. Despite these limitations, the results provide suggestive evidence about the potential utility of active learning in the classroom relative to the lecture and teacher-centred discussion formats. Significantly, they report that role-play consumed the same amount of classroom time as traditional pedagogies. The data revealed that the difference between the test and control groups came from the preparation for the role-play as

---

BOX 26.4   PRACTICAL POINTS WHEN SETTING UP A MULTIPLE ROLE-PLAYING PROCEDURE

1   If the researcher is using 'a multiple role-playing procedure', where there are a number of pairs or groups conducting the role-play in the same space at the same time, begin by organizing the groups according to the number of people required in the scene (i.e. 'get into groups of three please').

2   Using the eight principles of role-play cited in Box 26.3, give the group the requisite information and instructions for the ensuing role-play. Ask them to take a moment to discuss who is going to be who and what the characters' names are (if this has not already been predetermined). It is good idea to write the names of the characters on a clearly visible flip chart which participants can refer to if they forget, without stopping the action.

3   Ask the participants to find a space in the room and organize it in preparation for the role-play (i.e. loosely demarcate it as an office space, a jewellery shop, a university classroom, etc. according to easily available objects and resources). Invite them to use a chair or bag to section off their space. This helps to establish belief in what they are doing and makes their space semi-private so that they can focus on the task in hand.

4   Inform them that the role-play will begin at the same time for all groups, and that when theirs has run its natural course, they should remain *in situ*, and quietly observe until the other groups have finished. On average, role-plays will run for between five and ten minutes.

5   Where the role-play begins with all players *in situ* (i.e. sitting opposite each other in an office-type setting), the researcher should invite them to adopt an appropriate position for their role, such as scanning through a list on the desk, fiddling with a watch to signal nervousness, or concluding a phone call. Ask them to place their eye contact on an object rather than on their partner(s), freeze this gaze and their physical action for a moment, and on a clearly audible count of three from the researcher, all groups begin at the same time. It is a good idea to provide the opening words of the scene, such as, 'Now then, Mr Hayes, why did you come to see us today?', which all groups use to get them started. It reduces tension and any nervousness that may be present, and can usefully serve to focus the direction, the tone and the mood of the role-play.

   If the role play begins with one person entering a room and the other(s) already *in situ*, ask the person entering to stand about a metre away from their role-play partner(s), to lower their gaze as if preparing to knock on a door and enter on a given signal. In this situation, the person/people inside the room should adopt an appropriate action and eye gaze, away from the imaginary door and their role-play partner standing 'outside', and wait for the facilitator to count aloud and knock physically on a table or wall on everyone's behalf. The opening words provided here may usefully be 'Come in please', or 'One moment please, I'm on the phone/finishing off a document', etc. Deciding to leave a person waiting outside an office door for 10–20 seconds can create an interesting power dynamic that will impact upon the remainder of the role-play as it unfolds.

6   Allow the role-play to run its natural course, and if most pairs/groups are finished, you can gently intervene by inviting those still going to finish up shortly.

7   Provide an opportunity for the pair/group to reflect and discuss initially, and then open up the discussion as a whole group exercise. This will be structured according to the individual research requirements. Participant diaries can be a useful tool to gather participants' perspectives.

8   Scenes can be replayed as required, giving participants a different experience by shifting or altering any of the principles outlined in Box 26.3.

---

much as from the role-play itself. Students were devoting extra class time to prepare for the process, and video recorded evidence indicated that students in the role-play groups were three times more likely than the control group to speak and participate in class. Students reported a greater individual investment in the material and that they had become more comfortable with the content by discussing it in smaller peer groups at the

beginning of class. However, the researchers testify to the importance of debriefing after a role-play, whereby the instructors can help students contextually organize the information and perspectives explored during the activity. In their study, it was found that a role-play's effectiveness would be severely diminished unless the students could carefully review it under the instructor's guidance (McCarthy and Anderson, 2000: 285).

Role-playing as a final examination

This study of graduate nurse education (Sellers, 2002: 498) examined the use of role-play in the two-hour final examination of students' knowledge of the nursing theory curriculum. Each student was allocated a particular theorist (unidentified to their peers), and invited to present the role in a creative, accurate and realistic manner to their peers, who subsequently completed an assessment sheet after the oral examination (this technique is also known as 'hot seating', see Neelands and Goode, 2000). A series of pre-established theoretical questions devised by the course tutors, in addition to students' own, were posed to each student being 'hot seated', in an attempt to identify the theorist being represented.

Sellers (2002: 499) notes that involvement in role-play activity requires students to know the major tenets of the nursing theories and models, and to demonstrate the relevance of nursing theory to clinical practice. The active learning approach serves to reinforce students' awareness of the historical contributions that a range of relevant theorists made to the discipline. Having been administered on six occasions, the findings indicate that the learning outcomes are satisfactorily achieved; students adopt collaborative-responsibility and self-responsibility for their own learning; engage in substantial extra-curricular reading to meet the challenges of the role activity; positive attitudes toward nursing theory are fostered; and students are encouraged to think critically about the applicability of nursing theory to advanced nursing practice. Students' ranking of the effectiveness of the role-play final examination in evaluating their knowledge shows that group mean scores ranged from 6.68 to 7.0 (with 7 being outstanding).

Using role-play and digital video to develop reflection

Robinson and Kelley (2007) write about the additional benefits of using streamed video technology in a special education pre-service teacher education programme, which already uses role-playing methods to develop reflective practice. In a quasi-experimental, time-series design, participants were divided into two groups. The first group participated in three role-plays, reflected on their actions and then wrote reflections after each role-play. The second group participated in three role-plays that were recorded digitally and placed on a streaming server. Students watched each video, reflected on their actions and then wrote reflections. Other than the use of video-recorded role-plays, the groups were comparable in terms of student variables and the type of instruction delivered. It is interesting to note that every student also participated in an additional initial practice role-play session that was not videotaped or included in the analyses. The contexts of the role-plays included an introductory meeting, parent–teacher conference, special education referral meeting and an individual education programme (IEP) planning meeting. Each role-playing session consisted of participation in two role-plays, with students occupying a number of roles, including both professionals and family members.

In this study, all aspects of the 'families', such as family members, family member characteristics, and family needs and strengths, were developed by the students; no scripts or case studies were used. The focus of the course, the role-plays and the reflections was professional collaboration, and the students' collaboration skills as professionals were analysed, not their performance or skills as family members. All students were given a schedule of the role-plays as an advance organizer, which included cumulative collaboration topics such as effective listening skills, effective communication, family diversity, conducting meetings, paraprofessional collaboration and problem-solving. Students, as professionals, were responsible for demonstrating effective communication and collaboration skills within each role-play. A developmental coding rubric was used to score and analyse the written reflections following the role-plays. A sentence by sentence analysis was conducted for each role-play reflection from both groups, and following a two-step process, inter-rater reliability was established (a mean of 89 per cent), and each role-play was individually analysed by both researchers, and the results compared.

In summary, the quantitative and qualitative data revealed that Group 1 students tended to describe what they saw, with little higher level reflection and no progression in their skill development, whereas Group 2 students were more likely to briefly describe what they saw and then engage in critical reflective thought, with significant evidence of a growth in reflection skills between role-play 1 and 3. Notwithstanding the limitations of this study (small sample size, difficulties relating to generalizability owing to the nature of the investigation, and variances in participants' writing skills), the results indicate a relationship between recording performance in a role-play, reviewing it at a later date, and an increase in reflective thought.

Further examples in summary form

The literature in almost every discipline contains many examples of creative, innovative and active teaching and learning methods, and role-play is high on the list of most commonly used strategies in this regard. Table 26.1 provides a brief summary (illustrative only) of some of the most recent uses of role-playing method, both as a research tool and as an effective approach to teaching and learning, as reported in the literature.

TABLE 26.1 EXAMPLES OF THE USE OF ROLE-PLAY IN THE LITERATURE

Title of article	Publication details	Use of role-play	Major findings	Issues for consideration
Building Personal and Social Competence Through Cancer-Related Issues	Donovan, O. M. (2009) *Journal of School Health*, 79 (3), 138–43.	To prepare young people in schools to competently and sensitively interact with peers who have had cancer treatment.	Role-play is proposed as being effective in situating learners in real-life contexts in which accurate cancer information is used.	As preliminary work, teachers should review the problem scenarios, anticipate the likely need for information, and identify sources of that information to support student enquiry that are age and developmentally appropriate. The teacher should model the process of giving feedback and the types of feedback that are acceptable.
Role-Playing Lecturing: A Method for Teaching Neuroscience to Medical Students	Kumar, S. R. Narayanan, S. N. (2008) *Advances in Physiology Education*, 32 (4), 329–31. [Published by the American Physiological Society]	To help first-year medical students better understand the concepts and features of various neurological abnormalities relating to different parts of the brain by incorporating role-playing in lectures.	Quantitative data revealed better visualization of the disorders, improved ability to retrieve the most important features in neurological abnormalities, and students are better able to recollect the key points of lectures.	Active engagement in sessions. A cost-effective method, as published visual aids can be expensive. Effective and easily reproducible method for helping students better understand the core concepts and features involved in different neurological diseases.
HIV/AIDS Role-Play Activity	Penny, K. (2008) *Journal of Nursing Education*, 47 (9), 435–6.	Student nurses are required to role-play living with an HIV diagnosis for 24 hours (including role-playing the medication regimen), and to keep a written journal of personal experiences and feelings related to the role-play scenario.	Students were motivated to investigate all aspects of living with HIV/AIDS, such as laundry, relationships, services, medication costs and insurance. 62% of participants reported increased feelings of empathy for clients diagnosed with HIV.	The value of role-play, journaling and reflection are noted in the promotion of experiential learning and the transference of information and skills from one context to another.
Understanding Public Land Management through Role-Playing	Oberle, A. P. (2004) *Journal of Geography*, 103 (5), 199–210.	College geography students use role-play to explore public land management as an example of human–environmental interaction. Real-world stakeholders are represented in whole class role-plays. Follow-up written activities and the role-plays are assessed.	Pre- and post-test data revealed advances in students' understanding of public land issues, development of independent research skills and improved ability to engage in an informed debate.	Students requested additional time to discuss and reflect on outcomes after role-plays, and to relate knowledge acquired to broader regional issues. Instructor reported the need to provide adequate closure to each session, by updating students on issues relating to the real case study.

continued

Teaching Case. A Systems Analysis Role Play Case: We Sell Stuff, Inc.	Mitri, M. and Cole, C. (2007) *Journal of Information Systems Education*, 18 (2), 163–8.	To give students an active experience and appreciation of the differing perspectives that end users, managers and system developers bring to software projects in a fictional company.	Provided an enjoyable break from the usual lecture-oriented classroom activity, and gave students an idea of real-world issues in IS development.	Students reported: time needed for clarification of role briefs once distributed, results in a heavy work load requiring a lot of thinking and planning. Researchers noted difficulties in large classes, some negative student attitudes, and extra time required to grade the assignments.
Methods and Strategies: Role-Play in the Science Classroom	Worch, E. A., Scheuermann, A. M. and Haney, J. J. (2009) *Science and Children*, 47 (1), 54–9.	An animal role-playing game for early years children, designed to explore the basic needs (food, shelter, water) of different types of animals, and to reinforce that animals acquire their needs in different ways.	Pre- and post-test data revealed a growth in children's understanding, increased curiosity and motivation to learn, and an ability to articulate their findings as a result of the role-play.	The importance of discussing children's findings with them afterwards is highlighted. Role-play helped extend children's learning beyond merely memorizing information and facts.
Learning Argument Practices through Online Role-Play: Toward a Rhetoric of Significance and Transformation	Beach, R. and Doerr-Stevens, C. (2009) *Journal of Adolescent & Adult Literacy*, 52 (6), 460–8.	Students adopted fictional roles, such as lawyers, education advisers and internet users, to research, formulate and argue their cases in online role-play activities based on such topics as nuclear power, lowering the drinking age and single-sex classrooms.	Online role-plays facilitated perspective taking through adopting different roles and espousing beliefs that differ from students' own personal beliefs, creating links, formulating positions, reflecting on their posts and developing increased agency.	Initial formulation of arguments on a discussion forum, and construction of roles through a biographical sketch and an avatar image, are important preparations for online role-playing.
The Impact of Simulation Training on Call Center Agent Performance: A Field-Based Investigation	Murthy, N. N., Challagalla, G. N., Vincent, L. H. and Shervani, T. A. (2008) *Management Science*, 54 (2), 384–99.	Using role-play and simulation, this study evaluates the effectiveness of simulation training as a behaviour modelling technique versus role-play training in a real-world call centre environment, focusing on call accuracy and call duration.	Results show that simulation training outperforms role-playing based training in terms of both accuracy and speed of processing customer calls, and improves at higher levels of task complexity.	Unlike role-play, simulation training incorporates behaviour modelling enhancements such as providing an in-built feedback mechanism for individual learning, mimicking actual tasks, and relieving cognitive load in processing complex tasks.
Role-Play Training at 'Violent Disneyland'. The FBI Academy's Performance Paradigms	Colborn-Roxworthy, E. (2004) *The Drama Review*, 48 (4) (T184), 81–108.	Use of role-players (with and without professional acting backgrounds) by the Federal Bureau of Investigation (FBI) to train new agents.	The use of live role-playing actors (as opposed to simulation software) results in authentic, dynamic and spontaneous reactions that facilitates agents' training.	Importance of using a diverse group of actors to realistically represent the population. Issues of effectiveness between professionally trained and untrained actors. Use of simulation software versus training via role-playing.

Companion Website

The companion website to the book includes PowerPoint slides for this chapter, which list the structure of the chapter and then provide a summary of the key points in each of its sections. This resource can be found online at **www.routledge.com/textbooks/cohen7e**.

CHAPTER 27

Visual media in educational research

We are surrounded by visual data. How researchers can use them is introduced in this chapter, which addresses a core of issues in the planning and conduct of data collection using visual media of different types. The chapter raises a series of issues concerning:

- photographs and still images
- video and moving images
- artefacts
- ethical practices in visual research

This chapter should also be read in conjunction with Chapter 32, on the analysis of visual data.

27.1 Introduction

Educational researchers can draw on a host of visual media in their research. These include, but are not limited to: film, video, photographs, television, advertisements, pictures, artefacts, objects of fine art, memorabilia, moving images, still images, media images, maps, drawings and sketches, illustrations, graphical representations, cartoons, everyday objects and deliberately non-commonplace, and so on. In short, anything we see, watch or look at counts as a visual image; we are surrounded by visual images, and these can be used in educational research. They are the commonplace stuff of ethnographic and anthropological educational research (witness, for example, the attention given to artefacts and visual images in studying organizational culture, and the messages about the organization that are conveyed in such images, discussed later in this chapter). Prosser and Loxley (2008) identify four main kinds of visual data: found data; researcher-created data; respondent-created data; and 'representations'. These will be addressed in this chapter.

Using visual media concerns the production of the image, the image itself, and the audiences of the image. Visual media are not neutral; they give messages, deliberately or not, and we interpret them in many different ways. They have their own forms and effects (e.g. compositions and technical properties) and these have an effect on the viewer. They are constructions of social events and perspectives, of power and power relations, of social relations and social difference. More than that, we look at them in different ways, i.e. we bring our own values, biographies, cultures and background to bear on images (Rose, 2007: 11). Images, then, cannot be viewed outside the social and cultural contexts (Banks, 1995: 2) of the production of the image to the observing and interpretation of the image, or outside the consideration of who are the audiences, intended or otherwise, of the image. An essential feature of an image is its audience and the way in which the audience views and 'reads' the image (Fiske, 1995). As Berger (1972) made clear, we have 'ways of seeing'.

Further, images are made, kept and displayed in different places, from museums, cinemas and galleries to each person's home, each of which confers its own required social behaviours and audience reactions (as Bourdieu and Darbel (1991) indicated: middle-class, educated visitors to art galleries stand in quiet contemplation of paintings). Some visual media have texts, others do not. An image is the product of certain *technologies* (oil paintings, video production, photographic materials, computer software), certain *compositional features* (e.g. visual form, material form, presentational form, structure, colour (e.g. hue, saturation, lightness/darkness), texture, abstraction, expressive content, spatial arrangement, symbolism, etc.), and certain *social contexts* (cf. Rose, 2007: 26). Some images balance colour and content harmoniously; others scream at us. Some are close up, some are distant or wide-angle. Some shots are deliberately taken from an elevated position, a low position, a side position, a frontal position and are posed; others are snapshots taken as the opportunity arises. Some are in focus; others are not. Some are geometrically structured (e.g. with perspective); others are free of geometric form. Some images are meticulously planned; others are fleeting snapshots taken on the spur of the moment. Some are part of a series or a collection; some stand alone. Some are part of a recognizable genre; others are not. Some are made by amateurs; others by professionals. Some are deliberately designed to give messages; others are not. Some are reflections of culture and society; others are in the vanguard of social and cultural change. Some are part of normal living (e.g. food); others are deliberate constructions that are out of the ordinary (the oil painting). Some are faded and fuzzy (the 'materiality' of the image (Rose, 2007: 234)); others are crisp and sharp. As Rose (2007: 26) remarks, visual images are never innocent; they are wrapped up in many layers of meaning and interpretation. They are not only 'reproductions of reality' (Flick, 2009: 240) but, rather, as 'presentations of reality', themselves, are then interpreted by viewers. All of this renders images difficult to interpret, and, indeed, exposes them to multiple interpretations.

Nowadays huge proportions of the population can take still and moving images, not only with conventional and video cameras but with both of these on a single cell phone. Cameras can present an immediate, comprehensive and holistic image of situations, objects, people, events, lifestyles, contexts, conditions and so on, that happen very quickly or suddenly (maybe too quickly or with too many details or with too great a level of complexity for conventional observational recording to be able to catch). Such images are easy to transport, and enable the researcher to review them repeatedly (particularly useful for fleeting, short-lived and ephemeral moments) and, indeed, to have their reviews checked by a third party. Further, such images can be taken non-intrusively, reducing observer effects and reactivity (cf. Denzin, 1989: 203; Flick, 2009: 241).

It may be the researcher who takes the image, or, indeed, the researched, e.g. the researcher asks participants to take images, maybe even providing them with the camera so that they can decide what they consider to be important to be kept as a still or moving image (Flick, 2009: 242). Indeed research that uses images may be both collaborative and participatory in involving participants as partners in the creation, production and discussion of images, both still and moving, though, of course, setting up a concealed camera is far from collaborative (Banks, 1995: 3). Further, as online communication increases, so the ability to share images has become part of everyday life for many people. Indeed Banks (1995: 1) argues that the dichotomy between the researcher and participants, the observed and the observer, has started to collapse.

It may be that the researcher provides the already-taken images (and, for example, uses them as a starting point for discussion), or asks the participants to bring images that they possess and which they have or have not taken themselves (e.g. family photographs), and which can be used, for example, in interviews, as starting points for interviews or as main elements of interviews (the 'photo-elicitation interview' (Harper, 2000: 725)). Here consideration has to be given to the taking of the image and the derivation of data from the image (cf. Denzin, 1989: 210).

In considering visual images, Denzin (1989: 213–14) indicates that whilst cameras report what they see and what really happens (rather than the selective observation of the human observer), nevertheless images are selective, in that the image maker has already decided what to include or not to include (Becker, 1986: 241–2), what to focus on and what not to focus on, where to point the camera and where not to point the camera. Images also create their own representational and symbolic forms and they are time-bound – they catch a particular moment (or several). Given this, it is perhaps wiser to regard visual images as telling a story – a discourse – rather than being a singular objective reality. Indeed it is commonplace to have written text – a commentary or analysis – accompanying the image, and this text, too, tells a selective story or has a selective focus.

Visual data catch and store a wealth of data in a single image or video sequence and, like other forms of observational data, they are selective in their focus and contents (e.g. deriving from the researcher's agenda, interests, research questions, etc.). This presents issues of data overload, selectivity and manageability. Whilst this may present problems in the stage of data analysis, it is not unusual for visual data to be part of a range of different types of data (e.g. written, aural, oral, observational) in a research project. Rather than standing on their own, visual data are one element in triangulated data and, as will be seen in Chapter 32, can be subjected to analytical techniques used with other kinds of data, as well as having their own methods of analysis.

In contemplating images the researcher has to consider the extent to which they are natural, contrived/arranged/posed or staged. In this respect there is an argument, perhaps, for covert research and/or a fixed camera as it leaves the natural situation undisturbed.

27.2 Photographs and still images

Photographs have a central place in educational research. They can be taken by the researcher or the researched, or they can be acquired or viewed by the researcher (e.g. historical photographs). They carry meanings that words alone, be they spoken or written, cannot. They convey real life, flesh and blood (witness Sutcliffe's nineteenth-century photographs of the fishing port of Whitby in the UK and everyday lives that he photographed, or the photographic work of Forsyth in the poor districts of twentieth-century

Newcastle upon Tyne in the UK). Photographs evoke meanings and reflections as well as information and factual data. They catch the texture, the mood, the atmosphere, the 'feel' of real life and different places, emotions and flesh-and-blood drama. They are both *emic* and *etic*. They carry documentary and interpretive meaning, either posed or natural. They can support and supplement other sources of data and text, or they can stand alone. They are less time-consuming to study than film footage or video materials. Indeed they are highly time-efficient and researcher-efficient, as they can convey far more in a single image than many pages of text ('a picture paints a thousand words').

In using photographs, researchers can take photographs and ask the participants to comment on them, or, indeed, the researcher can ask participants either to take their own photographs (and the researcher might supply the camera) or to bring along to an interview (e.g. individual or group) one or more photographs that have meaning to them, to discuss them, or to provide a commentary on them. Such interviews or textual material can then be subject to the normal methods of data analysis introduced in this book, e.g. analysis of transcripts, field notes, software packages for textual analysis (e.g. ATLAS.ti, see Chapter 30), or coding, content analysis, grounded theory approaches, constant comparison of images and codes, looking for patterns and genre, and moving towards generalization where appropriate.

In the photo-elicitation technique, the photograph, or set of photographs, or sequence of photographs, is used to invoke, prompt and promote discussion, reflections, comments, observations and memories (Banks, 2007: 65). The interview or meeting between the researcher and participant(s) can start with photographs, what they show, who took them, when, where, what is the story behind them, and so on. Indeed using photographs in an interview can overcome any awkward silences or any need to maintain direct eye contact in an interview (Banks, 2007: 66), as this can be a little intimidating for some participants (e.g. children), not least because of the potential power and status differentials between the researcher and participants. Further, having a focus on a photograph or different photographs can offset any feelings that the interview is some kind of 'test' or 'grilling' for the participants (p. 65), particularly if the photograph comes from, or has been taken by, the participant(s). Having a common/shared focus in the photograph introduces a 'neutral' third party (the photograph) into the interview (p. 66).

Whilst the researcher can strive to have high quality photographs and reproduction, this is not always possible: old photographs fade over time; they can become damaged and fuzzy. On the one hand this may impede the interpretation of the photograph; on the other it may give added authenticity or poignancy to the photograph.

In deciding which images to use, the researcher can ask the participants to select images from their own or researcher-provided images, or the images may be selected on the basis of sampling techniques, e.g. random stratified sampling of images, representative sampling, convenience sampling, probability and non-probability sampling from a given population and so on. Strict sampling may not be possible if the still images are in very short supply (e.g. only one or two images are available). Nonetheless, as with other forms of data and participants, the selection of which images to use is subject to specification of criteria; the selection may be made on objective grounds (e.g. researcher-specified criteria or those which derive from the research questions), or subjectively from the participants themselves (e.g. their preferences or selections). The researcher should specify and justify the selection made.

27.3 Video and moving images

Taking and viewing moving images (e.g. through film and nowadays, pre-eminently through video), are part of the everyday lives of everyday people, be they members of a family, the public, researchers, security and surveillance services or others. Video material catches the non-verbal data that audio recordings cannot, which may be particularly useful, for example in detailed case study data collection (e.g. of children at work, at play, interacting with each other and with adults, for example using a fixed camera). Video material is live, and is a superb medium for recording evolving situations and interactions, details that the observer may miss, and non-verbal matters (e.g. facial expressions, aggressive behaviour) (e.g. Greig and Taylor, 1999: 66–7). It allows for repeated viewing and checking, though this exacts its price in terms of the time required to watch and re-watch the video.

Flick (2009: 249) reports the use of video materials for catching: (a) natural social situations; (b) contrived situations, e.g. experimental conditions and situations, events and activities as recorded by the participants themselves and/or the researcher; (c) posed situations (such as video diaries); (d) special events; or (e) commissioned materials (for instance a DVD of a celebration of commemorative activity). As with photographs, the researcher has to be aware of the selective bias inherent in moving images, i.e. the images recorded are a function of the focus and location of the camera, as well as the editing of the material. Hence the researcher must consider not only the images themselves and where, how, why, for whom, how and under what conditions they were produced, but also the interpretations that he or she (or indeed others) make or may make of the moving images, and how these interpretations are influenced by the interpreters' own backgrounds, values and purposes, i.e. the issue of reflexivity.

Moving images are powerful in a range of methodologies of educational research, from experimental research to ethnography. They can catch both the everyday routines and practices of participants and also special events. They exact their price: on the one hand they are rich in detail, and on the other hand this raises problems of how to analyse complex and detailed, often superfluous, multimedia data, in ways that do justice to the different media (sound and vision) both separately and together. On the one hand the data are rich but, on the other, they are also selective, depending on the focus and angle of the camera, whether it is a fixed camera (the 'eye in the classroom': see Chapter 23) or a moving camera that is moved round the location and focused by a moving operator, a wide-angle lens or a lens with close-up focus, and, indeed, when and for how long the camera is taking the moving images. On the one hand they are rich in detail and on the other hand this presents issues of how to conduct and write up an analysis of the data. Flick (2009: 250) also draws attention to the important legal and ethical matters of permission, data protection, privacy, covert research (on the public and on identified persons) and permission to film (see the discussion below on the ethics of taking and using visual data).

A fixed camera in a classroom is not neutral; it has its field and focus predetermined. A wide-angle lens might catch gross behaviours but miss important detail – an eye movement, a facial expression, a small hand movement, a finger gesture. A fixed camera may be less intrusive, as it does not need the presence of an operator and, indeed, may be located in a ceiling-level corner of the classroom. However, people move in and out of the field and focus of a fixed camera. Sometimes the video camera might be supplemented by a microphone situated on the table(s) at which children/participants are seated.

Whereas having a moving camera that is operated by a person *in situ*, whilst it may catch close-up detail, is highly intrusive and artificial. In taking moving images, consideration will need to be given to the location, height, visibility and intrusiveness of the camera, the field of focus, the lighting in the area to be filmed and so on. Given their selectivity, researchers often use them in conjunction with other kinds of data, as part of triangulation. Indeed Flick (2009: 252) advocates the use of video material as part of a wider database and methods rather than being stand-alone. Here data from

moving images can be used retrospectively, as points of discussion (e.g. in subsequent interviews), to ask for video participants to reflect on the material, to corroborate data from other sources, and to exemplify and illustrate themes, issues and events.

Useful sources for using moving and still images in research can be found in: Heath and Hindmarsh (2002); Flick *et al.* (2004); Knoblauch *et al.* (2006); Banks (2007); Pink (2007); Rose (2007); Konecki (2009), and on www.lboro.ac.uk/departments/ss/visualising_ethnography/. For guidelines on conducting video research more specifically in education we refer readers to:

http://drdc.uchicago.edu/what/video-research-
    guidelines.pdf
http://drdc.uchicago.edu/what/video-research.html
http://net.educause.edu/ir/library/pdf/nmm09video.pdf
http://eprints.ncrm.ac.uk/481/1/0606_researching_
    visual_images.pdf

As with still images, in deciding which images to use, the criteria for selection (i.e. sampling criteria) should demonstrate fitness for purpose, fairness and defensibility. Moving images may focus on, for example, critical incidents, turning points, key events, representative behaviours, extreme examples and so on. The criteria for the choice of video clips must be justified. As with still images, the moving image clips may be selected by the researcher or the participants, and, as with still images, strict sampling may not be possible if the moving images are in very short supply (e.g. only one or two image clips are available). The researcher should specify and justify the selection made.

27.4 Artefacts

As with other visual data, objects/artefacts can convey messages, even if those messages may be unclear. Artefacts include, for example, objects in interior design and equipment (Higgins and McAllaster, 2004), desks, tables, chairs, textbooks, exercise books, equipment, ornaments, display materials, clothing, pictures, maps, notice boards, lesson plans, smart boards, athletics equipment, science materials, etc. They include children's toys, reading materials, DVDs, clothes, etc., and, indeed, these give indications of gender stereotyping in young children and how such stereotyping occurs and how boys and girls are inducted into differently gendered worlds (e.g. Francis, 2010).

They have been shown to be useful in educational research (e.g. Boston, 2008; Francis, 2010), and, indeed, have been widely used in ethnographic, anthropological and historical research.

Artefacts have been widely used in studies of organizational culture (e.g. Schein, 1992). For example, dress codes, architecture, status symbols, signs, furniture, office areas, space, technology, mission statements and physical premises (Buch and Wetzel, 2001). Indeed Schein (1992) considers artefacts to be one of the three main levels and manifestations of organizational culture. Artefacts are the observable level of organizational culture (the other two levels being values and deep-seated norms); they are the outward manifestations of culture, for example executive rooms, dress codes, level of technology utilized (and where it is utilized), the physical layout of work spaces, the objects provided or observed in the workplace. All may be visible indicators of culture, but they are difficult to interpret; artefacts may suggest what a group is doing, but not why.

For example, consider a dull, dark, sparsely fitted classroom with no real amenities or decoration, with a few dried pot plants in a corner, and no surplus ornaments or displays. Contrast this with the brightly lit, interesting, multi-equipped classroom with notices, displays, samples of students' work and the latest interactive whiteboard in use. The objects can make a point here very tellingly, but what is that point? Is it that:

- some classrooms are dull, dispiriting places whilst others are energizing and interesting;
- some schools don't care about the teaching room whilst others take pains to present a stimulating environment;
- some schools are financially poor whilst others are rich;
- some classrooms exude a focus on learning from the teacher whilst others emphasize learning from the environment;
- some classrooms do not care about students' emotions whilst others are concerned to make the environment a happy place;
- some classrooms are very old and off-putting whilst others are new and engaging?

Inferring a total picture from the artefacts alone may be dangerous as they may signify very different or discrepant realities; hence it may be wise for the researcher to use artefacts alongside other sources of data.

Or take the example of the school in which the principal's office is private, separated from the main part of the school, large, beautifully carpeted, airy and spacious, with trophies, pictures, gifts, a huge working desk and an ergonomically designed chair, maybe a glass cabinet or two, works of art, a photograph of the family and of a meeting with an important dignitary, an up-to-date computer and colour printer, and a personal bathroom. Contrast this with the working space of the staff, who each have a small cubicle as part of a large room which has been sectioned off into workspaces for a dozen or more staff, with eye-level partitions, like a typing pool, a small chair and desk, no room to put anything personal, with workstations squashed into an egg-crate arrangement and with no personal space, no superfluous ornaments, not a picture in sight, bare walls except for notices, shared equipment and piles of books in each cubicle waiting to be marked. The messages – the not-so-hidden curriculum – of power, status, care and respect for people and humanity are very clear.

Or take the example of a staff room in the school, which may be untidy, with piles of books strewn around in different places, unwashed cups all over the room, notices peeling off the notice boards, cushions crumpled up on chairs, boxes of sports equipment lying in the corners, box files piled up alongside tables, comfortable chairs in very short supply and pieces of computer equipment cluttering up several tables. What can the researcher infer from this scene: that staff are extremely casual and careless or that they are extremely busy? Very different interpretations can be made of the same scene and artefacts.

As with other visual materials, artefacts can give researchers messages. The irony is that artefacts, like other visual objects, are easy to observe but difficult to interpret, and there are multiple interpretations (e.g. the pyramids of Egypt are easy to observe but it is difficult to understand what they mean). In other cases artefacts may be easier to interpret, e.g. the images presented in children's books may indicate sex role or ethnic stereotyping, or may portray positive images of some groups and negative images of others.

Artefacts can be seen, heard, smelt, touched, felt, even tasted and heard, so the researcher can brings to bear a multi-sensory analysis. They can be used by the researcher to stimulate discussion (see the comments above about the use of photographs), to glimpse into the past or, indeed, the present, to reconstruct or help to imagine a scene, to remind people and bring back memories. They can be observed *in situ* (and the location and placing of the object in a spatial context itself will carry meaning, e.g. in a home, a museum, at the back of a room, in a dark corner, in a prominent position, etc.). As with still and moving images, the artefact may be provided by the researcher or by the participants.

The researcher can examine artefacts on their own or in combination. For instance, in the example of the messages about the organizational culture of the principal's and staff's office areas, a single object may not say very much, but taken together the objects can make a persuasive case. Objects may also be grouped into categories, for example, ornaments, books, furniture, space; each category can be examined on its own and/or in combination (akin to the different kinds of coding exercise in grounded theory, where individual codes are combined into categories).

In looking at artefacts, the researcher can consider what was the purpose of the production and location of the artefact, what it was used for and by whom, who produced it, when was it made, what materials have been used in its making, what was its actual and/or symbolic purpose or function, how has it been preserved and in what condition, and what value it has to the provider or user. This has particular significance in historical, anthropological, ethnographic and archaeological research in educational and social science.

In some kinds of research (e.g. on child abuse) artefacts (e.g. dolls with lifelike features or sexual organs) can be used to encourage children to speak out about their experiences, displacing the highly sensitive personal threat or embarrassment onto the doll in question. Indeed Greig and Taylor (1999: 64) advocate the use of familiar artefacts with children – dolls, puppets, drawings, pictures – as this not only sets them at their ease but helps them to make concrete their ideas. This technique is particularly useful with young children, where dolls or puppets can have a series of facial expressions (happy, sad, angry, afraid) and where non-verbal postures can be manipulated on puppets (e.g. dolls, manikins, glove puppets) to enable the researcher to investigate emotions in young children (Greig and Taylor, 1999: 120–2). Greig and Taylor indicate how puppets can be used to research situations of conflict in young children. For example the researcher can ask what puppets A and B want, how they feel, why they are fighting, who is winning, whether the fight is justified, what each puppet should do, what the child would do in a similar situation, why puppet A or B was wrong, how the situation could end, and how the situation could be resolved (p. 122).

How researchers use artefacts depends on their research questions. Similarly, just as one uses sampling procedures to decide, for example, which people to approach to be involved in the research, so one has to consider the criteria to be used for deciding the sampling and selection of artefacts (cf. Lodico et al., 2010: 164). As with still and moving images, in deciding which artefacts to use, the criteria for selection (i.e. sampling criteria) should demonstrate fitness for purpose, fairness and defensibility. This operates in two ways: researcher- or participant-provided artefacts, or researcher observation of existing artefacts (e.g. the objects in a classroom, staff room, principal's office and so on). The researcher should specify and justify the selection made for the artefacts included, and, to be faithful to the multiple interpretation that can be made of artefacts, the researcher should consider – and provide – alternative interpretations of the artefacts where appropriate.

27.5 Ethical practices in visual research

Taking visual images is subject to the same ethical concerns and requirements as other forms of educational research, and we refer readers to Chapter 5 in connection with this. In particular, the issue of informed consent may prove difficult in the case of historical images, images of the general public or deliberately covert research. It is important to consider the indiscriminate taking of photographic or visual images of children without their consent and that of their teacher, the school, parents, helpers, guardians and staff. Permission concerns not only the site of the image itself (e.g. the taking of the photograph, filming in public places), but permission for reproduction (e.g. from individuals, from institutions), indicating the uses to which the image will be put, and, indeed, for altering the image in some way. In the case of public places (and Prosser et al. (2008: 6) argue that what constitutes a public place is unclear), permission may need to be sought from the official bodies or parties responsible for that public place as well as individuals (e.g. the informed consent of people in the street or in a building). Not only are there issues of legally and illegally taking images (e.g. of military establishments) or storing images, there is the issue of preferred and non-preferred sites for taking pictures (Prosser et al., 2008: 6), such as police stations, hospitals, schools, leisure facilities, surgeries, even rail stations, airports and libraries.

Further, the issues of identification, anonymization and obscuring of individuals and places relate not only to the ethical sphere but to matters of legal regulation on data protection. (On the other hand some participants may deliberately wish to be identified (Prosser et al., 2008: 11)).

Prosser et al. (2008) contend that 'visual methods, and the data they produce, challenge some of the ethical practices associated with word and number based research, in particular around informed consent, anonymity and confidentiality, and dissemination strategies' (p. 2), and they note that ethics in visual research are less well developed than in numerical and text-based research. They give an example of 'informed consent' (pp. 12–14), a cornerstone of much educational research, indicating seven challenges that visual researchers face in gaining informed consent:

■ it may not always be appropriate to gain informed consent (e.g. in covert research or surveillance work);
■ what 'informed' and 'consent' mean may be different in different cultures or with different groups (e.g. children);
■ it is not always clear who is actually in a position to give the consent sought (e.g. in the case of children or teachers);
■ it may not be practically possible to gain the consent of those who feature in visual images (e.g. in public places), for instance in the case of photo-journalism;
■ it may be difficult to gain the consent of those featured in a visual image if the provider of the image (e.g. a participant) has not gained that consent;
■ it is important to ensure that participants know to what they are giving their consent, e.g. to the taking of the image, to the reproduction of that image (and where);
■ it is not always clear what to do with 'found images', where the provenance of the image is unknown, or with images which were not originally produced for the purposes used in the research (see the analysis of the photograph in Chapter 32).

Prosser *et al.* (2008: 15) indicate that anonymity and confidentiality may be highly problematic in visual images, as the whole purpose of the image lies in the person, place or institution in question, without disguise. The authors discuss ways of anonymizing images (e.g. blurring of identifying features, using pseudonyms, taking the image showing only the back of the person, or with shaded, back-lit lighting), and Clark (2006) provides detailed guidance on anonymization.

Whilst Clark (2006) and Prosser *et al.* (2008) regard collaborative research (between researcher and participants) as one way of addressing complex ethical issues, this does not cover all situations, and researchers need to consider the ethical principles set out in Chapter 5.

A statement on ethical practice in visual research can be found from the British Sociological Association (2006) on: www.visualsociology.org.uk/about/ethical_statement.php. This includes statements on: professional integrity; legal considerations (including data protection, copyright and libel laws); ownership of images; images of illegal activities; morally questionable practices; beneficence and non-maleficence; non-breaching of trust; informed consent; relations with and responsibilities towards research participants; sensitivity to local cultures; procedures for sharing images; covert research; researching vulnerable groups; anonymity, privacy and confidentiality; dangers of intrusion into private worlds and lives; working with children and images of children; internet-based research; relations with and responsibilities towards sponsors and/or funders; and clarification of rights to publish.

The UK's Economic and Social Research Council (2008) has produced a comprehensive analysis of ethical issues in visual research, available on: http://eprints.ncrm.ac.uk/421/1/MethodsReviewPaperNCRM-011.pdf. This includes material on frameworks, professional guidance, regulation and legal rights and duties for visual researchers. It covers: ethics; issues of consent; researcher-generated and respondent-generated images; anonymizing and obscuring visual data; photo-elicitation and informed consent; anonymity and confidentiality; photographs and films that identify individuals; images of place and how to anonymize these; the construction and consumption of images; and guidelines for practice. We strongly advise researchers to consider carefully the contents of these ethical guidelines, as they indicate the very careful boundaries within which researchers with visual data must work. We also refer readers to ethical issues concerning visual research, discussed in:

http://in-visio.org/events/seeingisbelieving/the-ethics-of-visual-research-methods/
www.socialsciences.manchester.ac.uk/realities/publications/workingpapers/10–2008–11-realities-prosseretal.pdf
http://eprints.ncrm.ac.uk/480/1/0706_anonymising_research_data.pdf

We also refer readers to Clark (2006), Wiles *et al.* (2008), Prosser *et al.* (2008) and Skåreus (2009).

 Companion Website

The companion website to the book includes PowerPoint slides for this chapter, which list the structure of the chapter and then provide a summary of the key points in each of its sections. This resource can be found online at **www.routledge.com/textbooks/cohen7e**.

Part 5
Data analysis

In this edition we extend very considerably the material on qualitative and quantitative data analysis. This has led to a much-revised organization of this part, which starts with qualitative data analysis and then moves to quantitative data analysis. In qualitative data analysis we take readers from first principles to content analysis and grounded theory, making the point that texts – data – are multilayered and open to a variety of interpretations. We indicate in practical terms how researchers can analyse and present qualitative data, including an introduction to the foundational principles of such approaches. The material on qualitative data analysis in this edition gives much greater coverage to qualitative data analysis which is not conducted through coding and grounded theory, including conversational analysis and new material on narrative analysis, discourse analysis and autobiographies. We provide new and extensive, worked examples of each of these, indicating how to approach and conduct analyses of different kinds of textual material, and the need for reflexive authorship of the analyses provided. We include an entirely new chapter on analysing visual data, including artefacts, moving images and photographs, and we introduce several different methods for analysing them, including an extended worked example of the analysis of photographic material.

In quantitative data we assume that researchers will not only have no experience of statistics but may even be frightened off by them! Hence we take readers by the hand from very first principles to more complex sta-tistical processes. We take care to explain the founda-tions, principles and concepts underlying the statistical procedures, and we deliberately avoid introducing for-mulae and numbers, except where they are helpful. We have reorganized these chapters on quantitative data analysis. We start with some introductory issues in numerical analysis, including new material on distribu-tions and curves of distribution. We then introduce descriptive statistics and reliability testing. Following this we introduce several inferential statistics at ele-mentary levels, including difference tests and regres-sion (Chapter 36), and then higher levels of inferential statistics, such as factor analysis, together with new introductory material on structural equation modelling and multilevel modelling (Chapter 37). Given the number of statistics available to researchers, the final chapter organizes these carefully and clearly using charts and tables, so that researchers can see how to select appropriate statistics for their purposes and to fit the kinds of data collected. In these chapters we give precise instructions and commands for using SPSS in quantitative data analysis, and the accompanying website includes an easy-to-use manual to introduce novice researchers to SPSS.

These chapters are accompanied by extensive mater-ials on the companion website. For both the qualitative and quantitative data analysis we provide practical advice – including sample phrases and choice of words – on how to report results and findings.

CHAPTER 28

Approaches to qualitative data analysis

This chapter discusses several forms of qualitative data analysis. Subsequent chapters focus more specifically on content analysis and grounded theory. We deal here with different approaches to qualitative data analysis, including:

- data analysis, thick description and reflexivity
- ethics in qualitative data analysis
- computer assisted qualitative data analysis (CAQDAS)

This chapter sets the scene for more in-depth considerations of different ways of analysing data in Chapters 29 to 33.

28.1 Introduction

Qualitative data analysis involves organizing, accounting for and explaining the data; in short, making sense of data in terms of the participants' definitions of the situation, noting patterns, themes, categories and regularities.

There is no one single or correct way to analyse and present qualitative data; how one does it should abide by the issue of *fitness for purpose*. Further, qualitative data analysis, as we shall see here, is often heavy on interpretation, and one has to note that there are frequently multiple interpretations to be made of qualitative data – that is their glory and their headache! Qualitative data analysis is distinguished by its merging of analysis and interpretation and often by the merging of data collection with data analysis (Gibbs, 2007: 3) in an iterative, back-and-forth process (Teddlie and Tashakkori, 2009: 251); indeed the results of the analysis also constitute data for further analysis. As researchers write down notes, memos, thoughts, reflections, in the field or during an interview or observation, these, too, become data.

Qualitative data derive from many sources, for example:

- interviews (transcribed or not transcribed);
- observation (participant to non-participant);

- field notes;
- documents and reports;
- memos;
- emails and online conversations;
- diaries;
- audio, and video and film materials;
- website data;
- advertisements, and print materials;
- pictures and photographs;
- artefacts.

Researchers will need to consider whether to transcribe interview data for analysis. On the one hand transcriptions can provide important detail and an accurate verbatim record of the interview. On the other hand they omit non-verbal aspects, and, indeed, what may take place before or after the interview, and the contextual features of the interview. Further, on a practical level, they are very time-consuming to prepare (e.g. one hour of interview may take up to five or six hours to transcribe, even with a transcription machine (a machine that can be paused (e.g. by a foot pedal) whilst the transcriber writes down the words, or software that will enable a researcher to pause to enter data into, for example, a dialogue box)). The researcher will need to consider the costs and benefits of transcription. An alternative to transcription is to write the analysis of the data directly from the video or audio recording, selecting out the important materials directly from the original source rather than from the mediated source of transcription, thereby avoiding becoming so caught up in detail that sight of the bigger picture is lost.

If transcription is used, then the researcher must make clear the transcription conventions being followed (see also Chapter 30), for example:

- give each speaker a name or pseudonym (and keep a list separately of which speaker has which pseudonym);
- record hesitations, small to long pauses, and silences (e.g. through dots (…) in the text);
- recording inflections and tone of voice (rising to falling), e.g. writing down the mood of the speaker

or the speech at the time: anger, anxiety, sadness, excitement, questioning, hesitance, etc.;

- volume of the speaker (quiet to loud, whispering to shouting);
- recording the speed of the speech (slow to fast, hurried to calm);
- breaks (sudden to considered) in speech;
- stresses and phases in the speech;
- audible breathing out or breathing in;
- non-verbal activity (e.g. standing up, leaning back, etc.);
- record uninterpretable noise (e.g. the words in brackets 'noise' or 'unclear noise');
- record several speakers who are all speaking at the same time (e.g. the word 'together' after each speaker's name);
- record non-verbal behaviours (if transcribing from video recording);
- being consistent in spelling (so that search and retrieval can be facilitated, particularly if software for this is used, discussed later);
- ensuring that each line or section/paragraph is numbered (in Word this can be done through the 'Layout' or 'Page Layout' menu (depending on the version of Word being used));
- ensuring that wide margins and double spacing are used for annotating text in hard copy form.

For a fuller description of these see Atkinson and Heritage (1999), Flick (2009: 300–2) and Woods (2010). The transcriber will need to check the accuracy of the transcription, as it is not uncommon for speech to be heard incorrectly or for words to be confused (Gibbs (2007: 19) gives many examples of such confusions).

Voice recognition software is becoming available that will both recognize and transcribe speech, and this can save time, though the reliability of the transcription is influenced by the accuracy of the speech recognition.

Researchers can analyse 'threaded' electronic conversations or communications, in which topics are linked together or the ongoing communications between the same parties are entered onto email inboxes. For example Figure 28.1 provides an edited screen shot of a deliberately prepared sequence of emails sent through Gmail by one of our authors to himself, for the purpose of illustrating how emails can indicate a threaded conversation. Here one can see eight emails in a single thread, and Gmail records the opening words of each of the previous emails in the thread (above the email currently opened), with times (i.e. a chronology) at which the earlier emails were sent.

28.2 Data analysis, thick description and reflexivity

In abiding by the principle of *fitness for purpose*, the researcher must be clear what s/he wants the data analysis to do as this will determine the kind of analysis that is undertaken. The researcher can set out, for example:

- to describe;
- to portray;
- to summarize;
- to interpret;
- to discover patterns;
- to generate themes;
- to understand individuals and idiographic features;
- to understand groups and nomothetic features (e.g. frequencies, norms, patterns, 'laws');
- to raise issues;

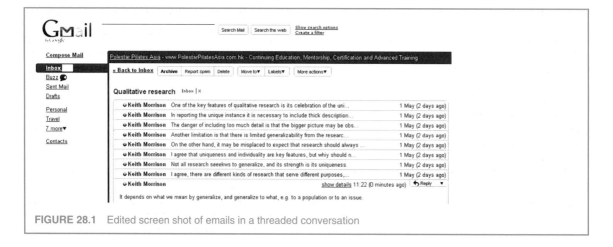

FIGURE 28.1   Edited screen shot of emails in a threaded conversation

- to prove or demonstrate;
- to explain and seek causality;
- to explore;
- to test;
- to discover commonalities, differences and similarities;
- to examine the application and operation of the same issues in different contexts.

The significance of deciding the purpose is that it will determine the kind of analysis performed on the data. This, in turn, will influence the way in which the analysis is written up. The data analysis will also be influenced by the kind of qualitative study that is being undertaken. For example, a biography and a case study may be most suitably written as descriptive narrative, often chronologically, with issues raised throughout. An ethnography may be written as narrative or stories, with issues raised, but not necessarily conforming to a chronology of events, and including description, analysis, interpretation and explanation of the key features of a group or culture. A grounded theory and content analysis will proceed through a systematic series of analyses, including coding and categorization, until theory emerges that explains the phenomena being studied or which can be used for predictive purposes.

The analysis will also be influenced by the number of data sets and people from whom data have been collected. Qualitative data often focus on smaller numbers of people than quantitative data, yet the data tend to be detailed and rich. Researchers will need to decide, for example, whether to present data individual by individual, and then, if desired, to amalgamate key issues emerging across the individuals, or whether to proceed by working within a largely predetermined analytical frame of issues that crosses the individuals concerned. Some qualitative studies (e.g. Ball, 1990, 1994a; Bowe et al., 1992) deliberately focus on individuals and the responses of significant players in a particular scenario, often quoting verbatim responses in the final account; others are content to summarize issues without necessarily identifying exactly from whom the specific data were derived. Later on here we discuss methods to be used with respect to people and issues.

Some studies include a lot of verbatim conversations; others use fewer verbatim data. Some researchers feel that it is important to keep the flavour of the original data, so they report direct phrases and sentences, not only because they are often more illuminative and direct than the researchers' own words, but also because they feel that it is important to be faithful to the exact words used. Indeed, as reported in the example later, direct conversations can be immensely

rich in data and detail. Ball (1990) and Bowe et al. (1992) use a lot of verbatim data, not least because those whom they interviewed were powerful people and justice needed to be done to the exact words that they used. By contrast Walford (2001: 92), commenting on the 'fetish of transcription', admits that he 'rarely fully transcribed more than a few interviews for any of [his] research studies', not least because of the time that it took for transcription (Walford suggests a ratio of 5 to 1 – five hours to transcribe one hour of interviews, though it can take much longer than this).

At a theoretical level, a major feature of qualitative research is that analysis often begins early on in the data collection process so that theory generation can be undertaken (LeCompte and Preissle, 1993: 238). LeCompte and Preissle (1993: 237–53) advise that researchers should set out the main outlines of the phenomena that are under investigation. They should then assemble blocks or groups of data, putting them together to make a coherent whole (e.g. through writing summaries of what has been found). Then they should painstakingly take apart their field notes, matching, contrasting, aggregating, comparing and ordering notes made. The intention is to move from description to explanation and theory generation.

At a practical level, qualitative research rapidly amasses huge amounts of data, and early analysis can reduce the problem of data overload by selecting out significant features for future focus. Indeed Miles and Huberman (1984) advise researchers to start writing and analysing early and frequently (i.e. as soon as the first data have been collected, even in a longitudinal study), rather than to leave all the writing and analysis until the data collection is over, as this enables 'progressive focusing', and selection of key issues for further investigation to be conducted. As Gibbs (2007: 25) remarks, 'writing is thinking'. Such analysis should, itself, be given a date and time, and could be included in a diary of field notes which record, for example, what the researcher was doing, where the researcher was, what was happening at the time, who was present, what the data were, particular or notable features of the event, context or situation, reflections and observation (Miles and Huberman, 1994: 50–4).

'Progressive focussing', according to Parlett and Hamilton (1976), starts with the researcher taking a wide-angle lens to gather data, and then, by sifting, sorting, reviewing and reflecting on them, the salient features of the situation emerge. These are then used as the agenda for subsequent focusing. The process is akin to funnelling from the wide to the narrow. Miles and Huberman (1984) suggest that careful data display is an important element of data reduction and selection. On the other hand Gibbs (2007: 4) argues that qualitative data analysis, far from reducing data, actually increases its 'bulk, density and complexity' as it creates more texts such as notes, reflections, memos (discussed later), summaries, reflexive insights and further notes, in short, in its attempt to generate 'thick descriptions' (Geertz, 1973): data that not only describe events in context, but participants' intentions, strategies and agency.

Geertz (1973) argues that thick descriptions include reflections on meanings attributed to situations and phenomena. As he writes: 'The ethnographer "inscribes" social discourse; *he writes it down*. In so doing, he turns it from a passing event, which exists only in its own moment of occurrence, into an account, which exists in its inscriptions and can be reconsulted' (p. 19). Doing ethnography, he writes, 'is like trying to read (in the sense of "construct a reading of") a manuscript – foreign, faded, full of ellipses, incoherencies, suspicious emendations, and tendentious commentaries, but written not in conventionalized graphs of sound but in transient examples of shaped behavior' (p. 10).

The qualitative data, yielded by research instruments such as interviews, observations and accounts, present several challenges. First, data are so rich that analysis involves much selecting and ordering on the part of the researcher. This, as a result, might involve some personal bias to which the researcher needs to be alert. Second, since the data obtained are all couched in 'social events', reporting involves a double *hermeneutic process* (Giddens, 1976) by which the researcher *interprets* the data from participants who have already interpreted their world, and then *relates* them to the audience in his/her own words. Hence the reporting and analysis should strive to catch the different definitions of the situation from the different participants, and to combine *etic* and *emic* analysis. This naturally may subject the data to criticisms of lack of objectivity, which is attenuated by reflexivity on the part of the researcher. Given this, qualitative data analysis is often written in the first person, and with colloquial language rather than the conventional third-person, passive voice and past tense of many pieces of reported research.

In selecting, organizing, analysing, reporting and interpreting data the researcher is faced with several decisions and issues. For example, there is a risk that, since data and interpretation are unavoidably combined (the double hermeneutic), the subjective views of the researcher might lead to him or her being over-selective, unrepresentative and unfair to the situation in hand in the choice of data and the interpretation placed on them. Fact and interpretation are inseparable, and the selection of which events and data to include are, to some extent, under the control of the researcher. Indeed, as participants (including the researcher), act on interpretations, interpretations may, themselves, become facts in the situation, i.e. an interpretation can constitute a fact or data. As Geertz (1973: 14) writes: 'in short, anthropological writings are themselves interpretations, and second and third order ones to boot.... They are, thus, fictions; fiction in the sense that they are "something made".'

The issue concerns validity and reliability in qualitative data analysis, as there may be limited external points of appeal other than respondent validation. The researcher's choice of which data and events to include inevitably involves a personal choice, but this choice has to be fair to the phenomena under investigation. As Geertz (1973: 13) writes: 'finding our feet, an unnerving business which never more than distantly succeeds, is what ethnographic research consists of as a personal experience'.

Geertz's view is echoed in the later edition of Whyte's (1993) Appendix A to his celebrated study of *Street Corner Society*, where he writes that:

> it seemed as if the academic world had imposed a conspiracy of silence regarding the personal experiences of field workers.... It was impossible to find realistic accounts that revealed the errors and confusions and the personal involvements that a field worker must experience. I decided to do my bit to fill this gap. In undertaking this task it seemed to me important to be as honest about myself as I could possibly be.
>
> (Whyte, 1993: 358–9)

Indeed he writes that 'participatory action research (PAR) provides one important means of bridging the gap between professional researchers and members of the organization we study' (Whyte, 1993: 364).

Further, he reports commentaries that the researcher:

> abandons any hope of establishing scientific conclusions, and speaks rather of 'rendering your account credible through rendering your person so'.... Ethnography takes ... more and more openly today, a rather introspective turn. To be a customary 'I-witness' one must, so it seems, first become a convincing 'I'. Ethnological writing thus comes to depend on persuasion of the reader.... I have come to recognize that the objective-subjective distinction is not as clear as I once thought.... We seek to observe behavior that is significant to our research purposes. Selection therefore depends upon some

implicit or explicit theory – a process which is in large part subjective. But the choice is not random. If we specify our theoretical assumptions and the research methods we use, others can utilize the same assumptions and methods to either verify or challenge our conclusions.

(Whyte, 1993: 366–7)

Further, in the same volume Whyte (1993: 362) even questions the practicality of, or necessity for, respondent validation, particularly if the researcher discovers something that might contradict or upset the values and practices of the group. There is 'the right of the researcher to publish conclusions and interpretations as he or she sees them' (p. 362).

Respondent validation may be problematic as, for example, respondents:

- may change their minds as to what they wished to say, or meant, or meant to say but did not say, or wished to have included or made public;
- may have faulty memories and may have recalled events over-selectively, or incorrectly, or not at all;
- may disagree with the interpretations made by the researcher;
- may wish to withdraw comments made in light of subsequent events in their lives;
- may have said what they said in the heat of the moment or because of peer pressure or authority pressure;
- may feel embarrassed by, or nervous about, what they said.

If respondents are asked to validate the data and the data analysis and interpretation, then, as Gibbs (2007: 95) remarks, their responses may then become data. For example, if respondents wish to withdraw their comments (and they may be entitled to do this if informed consent was given for *all stages* of the research, but they may not be entitled to do this if the informed consent was given to participate in the research but not to alter the reporting, i.e. the researcher owns the data, once given), or change them, or prevent their public disclosure, then the researcher may wish to explore the reasons for this, and this, too, may become part of the research.

Further, whilst many qualitative data derive from field notes, some of these, given the exigencies of the moment (the 'personal convenience' of the researcher (Hammersley and Atkinson, 1983: 173)) and the press for time, also may use the researcher's own memory, and this might be fallible, selective and over-interpreting a situation (Hammersley and Atkinson,

1983: 172). The same authors also indicate that 'there is no single correct way of retrieving the data for analysis' (p. 173). Indeed, to repeat Geertz (1973: 19), 'the ethnographer "inscribes" social discourse; *he writes it down*'. He adds:

So, there are three characteristics of ethnographic description: it is interpretive; what it is interpretive of is the flow of social discourse; and the interpreting involved consists in trying to rescue the "said" of such discourse from its perishing occasions and fix it in perusable terms.… But there is, in addition, a fourth characteristic of such description…: it is microscopic.

(Geertz, 1973: 20–1)

Hence it is important not only to examine a situation and events through the eyes of the researcher, but also to use a range of data and to ensure that these data include the views of other participants in a situation, in order to give some 'externality' to the situation and to focus on actual things that happened and which can be corroborated by other participants. The process is inductive and reflexive, yet true to the indicators and constructs of the interpretation made.

Further, Hammersley and Atkinson (1983: 173) indicate the importance of reflexivity in addressing validity and reliability in the analysis qualitative data. They write that:

When it comes to writing up, the principle of reflexivity implies a number of things. The construction of the researcher's account is, in principle, no different from other varieties of account: just as there is no neutral language of description, so there is no neutral mode of report. The reflexive researcher, then, must remain self-conscious as an author, and the chosen modes of writing should not be taken for granted. There can be no question, then, of viewing writing as a purely technical matter … [as a qualitative analysis or account; it] is more informal and impressionistic and thus written in the first person.

(Hammersley and Atkinson, 1983: 207–8)

Hammersley and Atkinson (1983) suggest that a qualitative data analysis itself becomes a text, i.e. as constructed interpretations, and that their organization, ordering, chronology chosen, selection of themes and narrative style have to be subject to reflexivity (pp. 212–17). Hence, the validity of the selection, analysis and interpretation of events and the data that are included in analysis, whilst being inductively and reflexively chosen, and whilst being unavoidably personal and partly impressionistic, are not only that – they are subject to the validity checks of having other participants' views included and a faithful record made of actual events which involve more than the single researcher.

Qualitative data can be analysed for their nomothetic properties (patterns, themes (both emergent and pre-ordinate/a priori), trends, commonalities, generalizations, similarities, laws of behaviour) and their idiographic properties (individual, unique events, people, behaviours, contexts, actions, intentions). Nomothetic approaches to data analysis are well represented in the work of Miles and Huberman (1994), whilst idiographic approaches are well represented in life histories, case studies, individual biographies and narratives.

28.3 Ethics in qualitative data analysis

Given that qualitative data analysis frequently concerns individual cases and unique instances, and may involve personal and sensitive matters, it raises the question of identifiability, confidentiality and privacy of individuals. Whilst numerical data can be aggregated so that individuals are not traceable, this may not be the case in qualitative data analysis, even if individuals are not named or are given pseudonyms. The researcher has an ethical obligation to reflect on the principles of non-maleficence, loyalties (and to whom) and beneficence set out in Chapter 5, and to ensure that the principle of *primum non nocere* is addressed – do no harm to participants. This may call not only for respondent validation but respondent clearance for what is included, which, in turn, places the researcher in a dilemma of whether to include material that has not been cleared or which participants indicate they do not wish to have included or with which they disagree (e.g. in the case of an interpretation).

Given that some qualitative data may be sensitive or personal, the researcher will not only need to consider who will perform any transcription, but the ethical conditions (e.g. of confidentiality) to which the transcriber must be subject.

28.4 Computer assisted qualitative data analysis (CAQDAS)

LeCompte and Preissle (1993) provide a summary of ways in which information technology can be utilized in supporting qualitative research (see also Tesch, 1990 and Gibbs, 2007: chapter 8) in Computer Assisted

Qualitative Data Analysis Software (CAQDAS). As can be seen from the list below, its uses are diverse. Data have to be processed, and as word data are laborious to process, and as several powerful packages for data analysis and processing exist, researchers will find it useful to make full use of computing facilities. These can be used as follows (LeCompte and Preissle, 1993: 280–1; Flick, 2009: 360–1):

- To make notes.
- To transcribe field notes and audio data.
- To manage and store data in an ordered and organized way (e.g. by ascribing data to specific addresses).
- For search and retrieval of text.
- To edit, extend or revise field notes.
- To code data (i.e. words or very short phrases which describe the textual data in question, for later ordering, combining or retrieval) and to arrange codes into hierarchies (trees) and nodes (key codes).
- To conduct content analysis (e.g. in terms of frequencies, meanings, sequences, locations, people, etc.).
- To store and check (e.g. proofread) data.
- To collate and segment data and to make numerous copies of data.
- To enable memoing to take place, together with details of the circumstances in which the memos were written.
- To conduct a search for words or phrases in the data and to retrieve text.
- To attach identification labels to units of text, (e.g. questionnaire responses), so that subsequent sorting can be undertaken.
- To annotate and append text.
- To partition data into units which have been determined either by the researcher or in response to the natural language itself.
- To enable preliminary coding of data to be undertaken.
- To sort, re-sort, collate, classify and reclassify pieces of data to facilitate constant comparison and to refine schemas of classification.
- To code memos and bring them into the same schema of classification.
- To assemble, reassemble and recall data into categories.
- To display data in different ways.
- To undertake frequency counts (e.g. of words, phrases, codes).
- To cross-check data to see if they can be coded into more than one category, enabling linkages between categories and data to be discovered.

■ To establish the incidence of data that are contained in more than one category.

■ To retrieve coded and noded data segments from subsets (e.g. by sex) in order to compare and contrast data.

■ To search for pieces of data which appear in a certain (e.g. chronological) sequence.

■ To filter, assemble and relate data according to preferred criteria (e.g. words, codes, themes, nodes).

■ To establish linkages between coding categories.

■ To display relationships of categories (e.g. hierarchical, temporal, relational, subsumptive, superordinate).

■ To draw conclusions and to verify conclusions and hypotheses.

■ To quote data in the final report.

■ To generate and test theory.

■ To communicate with other researchers or participants.

Flick (2009: 362) suggests that CAQDAS software can be grouped into several types:

■ those that act as word processors (e.g. entering, editing and searching text);

■ those that retrieve text (searching, summarizing, listing sequences of words);

■ those that manage text (e.g. searching, sorting and organizing passages of text);

■ those that code and retrieve text (i.e. which enable text to be split into smaller units and segments by relevant code and which list and organize and order codes and nodes);

■ those that enable theory building (e.g. through coding and the categorization and classification of codes and taxonomies to enable relations and superordinate and subordinate categories to be constructed);

■ those that enable conceptual networks to be plotted and visualized.

Which software one uses, he avers (pp. 364–5), depends on what questions one wishes to ask of the data, what kinds of data one has, what one wishes to do with the data, what processes of analysis one wishes to conduct, the technical requirements of the software, the competence level of the researcher/user of the software, the costs and the level of detail required in the analysis.

Kelle (1995) suggests that computers are particularly effective at coping with the often-encountered problem of data overload and retrieval in qualitative research. Computers, it is argued, enable the researcher to use codes, memos, hypertext systems, selective retrieval, co-occurring codes, and to perform quantitative counts of qualitative data types (see also Seidel and Kelle, 1995). In turn, these authors suggest, this enables linkages of elements to be undertaken, the building of networks and, ultimately, theory generation to be undertaken. Indeed Lonkila (1995) indicates how computers can assist in the generation of grounded theory through coding, constant comparison, linkages, memoing, annotations and appending, use of diagrams, verification and, ultimately, theory building. For a full discussion of coding we refer the reader to Chapter 30.

Kelle and Laurie (1995: 27) suggest that computer-aided methods can enhance: (a) validity (by the management of samples); and (b) reliability (by retrieving all the data on a given topic, thereby ensuring trustworthiness of the data), without losing contextual factors (Gibbs, 2007: 106). An important feature here is the speed of organized and systematic data collation and retrieval; though data entry is time-consuming, a great advantage of software is its ability subsequently to process data rapidly.

Coding the data is part of a six-step sequence of using software (Kelle, 2000: 295):

Step 1: Entering and formatting the text data.

Step 2: Coding the data.

Step 3: Memoing (with reference to specific segments of data).

Step 4: Comparison of textual segments which have the same codes, to check for consistency.

Step 5: Integrating the codes that have been generated, and memoing the codes.

Step 6: Developing the core category – a feature of grounded theory (see Chapter 33 here).

There are several computer packages for qualitative data (see Kelle, 1995), for example: AQUAD, HyperQuad2, HyperRESEARCH, Hypersoft, Kwaliton, Martin, MAXqda, QSR.NUD*IST, NVivo, QUALPRO, Textbase Alpha, Ethnograph, ATLAS.ti, Code-A-Text, Decision Explorer, Diction. Some of these are reviewed by Prein *et al.* (1995: 190–209), Gibbs (2007: 105–42), Lewins and Silver (2004, 2009) and García-Horta and Guerra-Ramos (2009); these authors indicate how to choose software and which to choose. These do not actually perform the analysis (in contrast to packages for quantitative data analysis) but facilitate and assist it. As Kelle (2004: 277) remarks, they do not analyse text so much as organize and structure text for subsequent analysis. Though there are many software packages available, Gibbs (2007) focuses on three: NVivo, MAXqda and ATLAS.ti; these share common features such as:

(a) the ability to import, work with and display rich texts; (b) the ability to code text into key codes (nodes) and to arrange codes and nodes into hierarchies, clusters and (c) the ability to sort, combine and retrieve text using different combinations and search strings/terms; (d) the ability to work with original documents using codes or to combine selected extracts from documents using codes; (e) the ability to annotate, add memos, comments or additional documents to existing data files and documents; (f) the ability to sort material using codes. Some software allows researchers to combine different kinds of data (e.g. NVivo and ATLAS.ti allow the researcher to combine word data with images, video material and sound recordings) and to code these different kinds of data (cf. Gibbs, 2007: 114).

These programs have the attraction of coping with large quantities of text-based material rapidly and without any risk of human error in computation and retrieval, and releasing researchers from some mechanical tasks. With respect to words, phrases, codes, nodes and categories they can:

a search for and return text, codes, nodes and categories;
b search for specific terms and codes, singly or in combination;
c filter text;
d return counts;
e present the grouped data according to the selection criterion desired, both within and across texts;
f perform the qualitative equivalent of statistical analyses, such as:

- Boolean searches (intersections of text which have been coded by more than one code or node, using 'and', 'not' and 'or'; looking for overlaps and co-occurrences);
- proximity searches (looking at clustering of data and related contextual data either side of, or near to, or preceding, or following, a node or code);
- restrictions, trees, crosstabs (including and excluding documents for searching, looking for codes subsumed by a particular node, and looking for nodes which subsume others).

g construct dendrograms (tree structures) of related nodes and codes;
h present data in sequences and locate the text in surrounding material in order to provide the necessary context;
i locate and return similar passages of text;
j look for negative cases (Gibbs, 2007: 126);
k look for terms in context (lexical searching) (Gibbs, 2007: 126);
l select text on combined criteria (e.g. joint occurrences, collocations);
m enable analyses of similarities, differences and relationships between texts and passages of text;
n annotate text and enable memos to be written about text.

Additionally, dictionaries and concordances of terms can be employed to facilitate coding, searching, retrieval and presentation.

Since the rules for coding and categories are public and rule-governed, computer analysis can be particularly useful for searching, retrieving and grouping text, both in terms of specific words and in terms of words with similar meanings. Single words and word counts can overlook the importance of context. Hence computer software packages have been developed that look at Key-Words-In-Context. Most software packages have advanced functions for memoing, i.e. writing commentaries to accompany text that are not part of the original text but which may or may not be marked as incorporated material into the textual analysis. Additionally many software packages include an annotation function, which lets the researcher annotate and append text, and the annotation is kept in the text but marked as an annotation.

Computers do not do away with 'the human touch', as humans are still needed to decide and generate the codes and categories, to verify and interpret the data. Similarly 'there are strict limits to algorithmic interpretations of texts' (Kelle, 2004: 277), as texts contain more than that which can be examined mechanically. Further, Kelle (2004: 283) suggests that there may be problems where assumptions behind the software may not accord with those of the researchers or correspond to the researcher's purposes, and that the software does not enable the range and richness of analytic techniques that are associated with qualitative research. He argues that software may be more closely aligned to the technique of grounded theory than to other techniques (e.g. hermeneutics, discourse analysis) (Coffey *et al.*, 1996), that it may drive the analysis rather than vice versa (Fielding and Lee, 1998) and that it has a preoccupation with coding categories (Seidel and Kelle, 1995). One could also argue that the software for qualitative data analysis does not give the same added value that one finds in quantitative data analysis software that automatically yields statistics, and the textual input is a highly laborious process; qualitative data analysis software does not *perform* the analysis but only *supports* the researcher doing the analysis by organizing data and recording codes and nodes, etc. It is more like a word processor and collator than an analytical software tool (Flick, 2009: 359).

The use of CAQDAS is not without its concerns. For example Gibbs (2007) reports that researchers may feel distanced from their data (p. 106), that software is too strongly linked to grounded theory rather than other forms of qualitative data analysis (p. 107) (though this is also questioned by newer software packages that are more methodologically eclectic (p. 107)). Indeed Flick (2009: 370) suggests that qualitative data analysis software is best suited to data which require coding and categorization for developing grounded theory. However, Kelle (1997: para. 3.2) has suggested that the software Ethnograph is rooted in ethnographic and phenomenological research, that MAXqda has its roots in Weberian 'ideal types' and AQUAD has its roots in Popperian methodology. Richards (2002) remarks on the tendency of many software packages to focus on 'code and retrieve' techniques (p. 266), with the risk that software encourages researchers to opt for coding and patterning to the neglect of more complex interrogation of texts (p. 269), and, indeed, that many researchers do not wish to use coding techniques with their qualitative data but are more concerned to review their texts iteratively (p. 270).

Gibbs (2007) also worries that too great an emphasis is placed on coding and its applications (p. 107), and that some important context may be stripped out of the data when they are assembled by codes alone (p. 122), a view shared by Crowley *et al.* (2002), who argue that the software drives the analysis rather than vice versa. Gibbs (2007: 140) reminds researchers that the use of much of the software is only as good as the codes that have been used and the careful coding of the data, i.e. if poor codes or poor coding has been undertaken (e.g. inconsistent coding, or coding that overlooks some text, or miscoding, or using a different code for the same kind or meaning of data) then poor results are likely to ensue (i.e. a problem of reliability). This applies similarly to the searching codes, terms or combinations that have been undertaken. Flick (2009: 370) worries that the practicalities of data entry, coding and retrieval with software might detract researchers from the 'real' task of hermeneutically understanding, thinking about and explaining the meanings of the research and the texts.

Further, as mentioned earlier, the 'added value' of software packages may not be as great as their statistical counterparts, for they require a significant amount of time and effort in entering transcribed and other word data, and then the software only searches, organizes, retrieves and collates the data, leaving the researcher still to analyse the data. Whilst statistical packages (e.g. SPSS) only process data, and whilst the researcher still has to analyse these data, the return on effort is much greater, as the software gives test results that do not have their simple equivalent in qualitative data analysis software. As García-Horta and Guerra-Ramos (2009: 152) argue, qualitative software is no substitute for the requirement and capability of the researcher to 'assign meaning, identify similarities and differences, establish relations' between data. Indeed they suggest that, whilst software for qualitative data analysis might be useful for working with structure, to date there have been no software packages that can handle the making of meaning, the interpretations of data, the working out of categories, the making of decisions on coding and the interpretation of the outcomes of the analysis and processing (p. 153).

There are many websites that contain useful materials on qualitative data analysis, e.g.

http://qualitative-research.net/fqs
http://ualberta.ca/~iiqm
www.esds.ac.uk/qualidata/support/teaching.asp
www.nova.edu/ssss/QR/text.html
www.nova.edu/ssss/QR/web.html
www.qualitative-research.net/fqs/fqs-e/rubriken-e.htm
www.qualitativeresearch.uga.edu/QualPage/
www.ringsurf.com/netring?ring=QualitativeResearch;
action=list
http://caqdas.soc.surrey.ac.uk/
www.intute.ac.uk/education/
www.textanalysis.info
http://onlineqda.hud.ac.uk
http://onlineqda.hud.ac.uk/resources.php
www.unm.edu/~jka/qualres.html
www.edu.plymouth.ac.uk/resined/
www.esds.ac.uk/qualidata/about/introduction.asp
www.data-archive.ac.uk/

Many of these provide links to a host of other websites providing guidance and resources for qualitative data analysis.

For working with audio and visual data (e.g. annotating and incorporating) the following are websites for software:

www.eval.org/resources/qda.htm
www.transana.org/
www.ideaworks.com/qualrus/index.html
www.researchware.com/
www.qsrinternational.com/
www.aquad.de/eng/index.html
www.kwalitan.nl/engels/index.html
http://maxqda.com/
www.anvil-software.de/

We advise readers to go to the papers by Lewins and Silver (2004, 2009) for a fuller guide as to which software to select.

The accompanying website contains an introductory manual for using QSR NUD*IST (the principles of which apply to NVivo). The website also contains a full set of word-based data files specifically prepared for QSR, concerning a single project of assessment and testing (these have also been saved into Word documents).

 Companion Website

The companion website to the book includes PowerPoint slides for this chapter, which list the structure of the chapter and then provide a summary of the key points in each of its sections. In addition there is further information on presenting qualitative data in tabular form. These resources can be found online at **www. routledge.com/textbooks/cohen7e**.

CHAPTER 29

Organizing and presenting qualitative data

There are several ways in which qualitative data can be organized and presented. In this chapter we introduce some important, useful and widely used ways. These address several issues, including:

- tabulating data
- seven ways of organizing and presenting data analysis
- narrative and biographical approaches to data analysis
- systematic approaches to data analysis
- methodological tools for analysing qualitative data

We provide several worked examples here, for clarification. It is also important for the researcher to index and provide a record of the provenance of the data, i.e. to record the dates, context, time, participants, researcher, location and so on, so that the setting for the data, and indeed their chronology, can be determined – the latter being useful in charting how situations emerge, evolve, change, lead to other situations, how networks emerge and how causality might be established.

29.1 Tabulating data

We outline several examples of data analysis and presentation in this chapter and the next. The first of these illustrates simple summary and clear, tabulated data presentation and commentary. It derives from a doctorate thesis.

Example: Chinese children learning English. An example of analysing and presenting interview data

The interview data are presented question by question. In what follows, where the data for respondents in each age phase are similar they are grouped into a single set of responses by row; where there are dissimilar responses they are kept separate. The left-hand column in each table below indicates the number of the respondent (1–12) and the level which the respondent

taught (e.g. P1, F3, etc.), so, for example, '1–3: P1' means the responses of respondents 1–3, who taught P1 classes; the right-hand column indicates the responses. In many cases it can be seen that respondents *all* gave similar responses in terms of the actual items mentioned and the coverage of items specified. A brief summary comment is provided after each table.

The data here derive from a doctorate thesis concerning the problems that school children experience in learning English in China. The data set reproduced is incomplete and has been selected for illustrative purposes only. Note that the data are not verbatim, but have already been summarized by the researcher, i.e. what is presented here is not the first stage of the data analysis, as the first stage would be transcription.

The coding is as follows:

> P1–P6 = Primary forms (1–6), P1 = year one, P2 = year two, etc.
>
> F = Secondary forms (1–5), F1 = Form 1 (first year of secondary school), F2 = Form 2 (second year of secondary school, etc.)

The numbers preceding each letter in the left-hand column refers to the number ascribed to the teacher (Table 29.1). There were 12 teachers in all, six from primary and six from secondary schools.

English teaching and learning at school have not really achieved their intended purposes. Students: (a) are poor at understanding written or spoken English, speaking, reading, listening and writing; (b) this limits their abilities, regardless of the number of years of learning English; (c) low-level memorization model leads to superficial learning; (d) teaching and learning are poor; (e) students can enter university, even though their standard is poor, as there are many universities to take students; (f) students do not require English to gain employment.

Comment: The primary English teachers had a wider range of views than the secondary teachers; there was greater unanimity between the primary teachers in comparison to the secondary teachers; all the Form 3

TABLE 29.1   THE EFFECTIVENESS OF ENGLISH TEACHING

Q6: The effectiveness of English teaching

1–3: P1	■ Students neither understood written or spoken English nor were able to speak or write very well. ■ Though students started learning English at a very young age, their standard was still very low as they could not really understand or use English.
4–6: P6	■ Students could not speak, read or write English well. ■ Students had a low standard as they could not read, write or speak English. ■ They used memorization to learn and thus the English knowledge was very superficial and confined to limited vocabulary.
7–9: F3	■ On the whole, students' standard was low. English teaching and learning was not very successful. ■ Even with a poor knowledge of English students still managed to get jobs. ■ This was not an international city; English was not really that important even if students did not learn well.
10: F5	English teaching and learning were not very effective as students were not working hard and they resorted to memorization to learn English. However, students managed to get into universities.
11: F5	Students had learned at least some basic knowledge about English.
12: F5	It was effective to some extent as some students became English teachers themselves, having finished their university education.

secondary teachers were unanimous in their comments, and all the Form 5 secondary teachers had different views.

Table 29.2 indicates that the strengths of English teaching were that: (a) students start to learn English very young; (b) schools had autonomy over the design of syllabuses. The weaknesses in English teaching were that: (a) insufficient emphasis was placed on understanding; (b) students were too young to learn English; (c) syllabuses were unrealistic in their demands, being too rich, leading teachers to a 'spoon-feeding' mentality in their teaching; (d) undue pressure was put on teachers and students because of the demands of the syllabus; (e) English had to compete with other languages for curriculum space. Hence students did not learn well, despite years of learning English.

Comment: Apart from one primary teacher, the other 11 teachers, drawn from both primary and secondary schools, were unanimous in the comments they gave.

It was clear that high class size (between 30 and 50 students, rising to 60) and tight syllabuses exerted a significant impact on teaching methods and restrictions of class activities, because of control issues (Table 29.3). The nature of this influence is to adopt largely didactic and grammar-translation methods, with little extended recourse to using or 'thinking in' English. Teaching utilized some group activity, but this was very limited. Teachers used Chinese to explain English.

Comment: All the teachers here were unanimous in their comments which fell mainly into two sets of points.

TABLE 29.2   THE STRENGTHS AND WEAKNESSES OF ENGLISH LANGUAGE TEACHING

Q7: Strengths and weaknesses of English language teaching

1: P1	Students started learning English at a very young age and they should be good at it. However, this could also be a disadvantage as students were too young to learn English and to understand what they were taught.
2–6: P6 7–9: F3 10–12: F5	These respondents all commented that individual schools had great autonomy over syllabus design. Consequently, some syllabus contents were too rich to be covered within the limited time span. Therefore, it was hard to make adjustments, though students could not cope with the learning requirements. This put pressure on both teachers and students. Worse still, some schools made students learn other foreign languages apart from English, and that made the learning of English more difficult.

TABLE 29.3   TEACHING METHODS

Q9: Teaching methods

1–3: P1 4–6: P6 7–9: F3 10–12: F5	■ All respondents replied that teaching was mostly conducted on a didactic approach though they utilized visual aids and group activities to arouse students' interest, as they had a very tight syllabus to cover within the fixed number of periods. This method also gave them more control over the class, which was necessary as classes were usually big, between 30 and 50 students, and could rise to 60. ■ Whenever these teachers taught grammar, they relied heavily on the grammar-translation method. They used mostly Chinese (could be as much as 80%) to explain grammar, as that would make it easier for students to understand the explanation.

Students contributed significantly to their own success or failure in learning English (Table 29.4), they: (a) were shy, afraid of making mistakes and of losing face, (b) had little interest in learning at all, let alone English; (c) were overloaded with other subjects, a situation exacerbated by their poor time management; (d) held negative attitudes to the bookish nature of learning English and its unrelatedness to other curriculum subjects; (e) had too many other distractions; (f) had limited abilities in English; (g) had little incentive to learn fast as they could repeat courses; (h) gave little priority to English; (i) had poor foundations for learning English; (j) had limited motivation or positive attitudes to learning English; (k) were given limited direction in their learning; (l) had limited incentive to learn English well, as universities required only a low standard of English.

Comment: There was a great variety of comments here. There were degrees of agreement: the teachers of the younger primary children agreed with each other; the teachers of the older primary children agreed with each other; and the teachers of the older secondary children agreed with each other. The teachers of the younger secondary children raised different points from each other. However, the four groups of teachers (younger primary, older primary, younger secondary and older secondary) raised different points from each other.

For an example of the layout of tabulated word-based data and supporting analysis see the accompanying website.

TABLE 29.4   STUDENT-RELATED FACTORS

Q11: Student-related factors

1–3: P1 4–6: P6	■ Students were shy and were afraid of 'losing face' when they made mistakes in front of the class. ■ Students basically had no interest in learning anything, especially a foreign language. ■ Students had too many subjects to learn, and learning English was too bookish. ■ There were too many other distractions such as surfing the internet or going out with friends.
7: F3	■ Students could not relate learning English to other things they learned at school, so they had no interest. ■ Students' language learning ability was poor and they feared learning English. ■ Students were allowed to repeat programmes, so they could become lazy and indifferent.
8: F3	■ Students spent too much time surfing the Net. ■ Students put more time into science rather than language subjects.
9: F3	■ Students' foundation was weak.
10–12: F5	■ Students lacked enthusiasm and 'proper' learning attitudes. ■ Students had poor time management. ■ Students were afraid of 'losing face' when they made mistakes in front of the class. They were shy as well. ■ Students had no direction in their learning and they had no plan for their future. Therefore, they did not learn well, especially a foreign language. ■ Students had many opportunities to enter universities, despite having a low standard of English.

Summary of the interview data

The issues that emerge from the interview data are striking in several ways. What characterizes the data is the widespread agreement of the respondents on the issues. For example:

1 There was absolute unanimity in the responses to questions 9, 12.
2 There was very considerable, though not absolute, unanimity on question 11.
3 In addition to the unanimity observed in point (1), there was additional unanimity amongst the primary teachers in respect of question 11.
4 In addition to the considerable, though not absolute, unanimity observed in point (2), there was much unanimity amongst the primary teachers concerning question 6.

Such a degree of unanimity gives considerable power to the results, even though, because of the sampling used, they cannot be said to be representative of the wider population. However, the sample of experienced teachers was deliberately selected to provide an informed overview of the key issues to be faced. It must be remembered that, though the unanimity is useful, the main purpose of the interview data was to identify key issues, regardless of unanimity, convergence or frequency of mention. That the respondents articulated similar issues, however, signals that these may be important elements.

Further, the issues themselves are seen to lie in a huge diversity of fields, such that there is no single or simplistic set of problems or solutions. Hence, to complement the considerable unanimity of voice is a similar consensus in identifying the scope of the problem, yet the range of the problems is vast. Both singly and together, the issues of English language teaching, learning and achievement in Macau are complex. The messages are clear in respect of F5 students and their English teaching and learning:

i English performance is weak in all its aspects – reading, writing, speaking and listening – but it is particularly weak in speaking and writing.
ii Local cultural factors exert an influence on learning English:

- students do not wish to lose face in public (and the Chinese emphasis on gaining and maintaining face is powerful);
- students are shy and afraid of making mistakes;
- the pressure of examination success is universal and severe;
- the local culture is not English; it is Chinese and, if anything else, is Portuguese rather than English, though this latter is very limited; there is little need for people to speak or use English at present.

iii In some quarters knowledge of English culture is seen to be an important element in learning English; this was refuted by the teachers in this sample.
iv English is seen instrumentally, but this message has to be qualified, as many students gain employment and university entrance even though their English is weak. The fact of English being an international language has limited effect on student motivation or achievement.
v Poor teaching and learning are significant contributors to poor performance, in several areas:

- the emphasis on drill, rote learning and memorization;
- the predominance of passive rather than active learning, with teaching as the delivery of facts rather than the promotion of learning and understanding;
- the use of traditional didactic methods;
- the reliance on a very limited range of teaching and learning styles;
- the limited subject and pedagogical knowledge of English teachers, compounded by the lack of adequate initial and post-initial teacher education;
- frequently the careful laying of foundations of English teaching and learning are absent;
- students use so much Chinese during English lessons that they have little chance to think in English – they translate rather than think in English.

From the interview data it can be seen that the size of the problems and issues to be faced in English language teaching and learning is vast. In this example, tables are carefully laid out to draw together similar sets of responses. The tables enable the reader to see, at a glance, where similarities and differences lie between the two groups of respondents. Note also that after each table there is a summary of the main points to which the researcher wishes to draw the reader's attention, and that these comprise both substantive and overall comments (e.g. on the topic in hand and on the similarities and differences between the groups of respondents respectively). Finally, note that an overall summary of 'key messages' has been provided at the end of all the tables and their commentaries. This is a very abridged and selective example, and justice has not been done to the whole of the data that the original researcher used. Nevertheless the point is clearly illustrated here that summarizing and presenting data in tabular form can address the twin issues of qualitative research: data reduction through careful data display and commentary.

29.2 Seven ways of organizing and presenting data analysis

We present seven ways of organizing and presenting analysis as follows: the first two methods are by *people*, and the next two methods are by *issue* or *theme*, the fifth method is by *instrument*, the sixth is by *case studies* and the final method is by *narrative account*.

One can observe in the example of teaching English in Macau that the data have been organized and presented by respondents, in response to particular issues. Indeed, where the respondents said the same, they have been organized by groups of respondents in relation to a given issue. The groups of respondents were also organized by their membership of different strata in a stratified sample: teachers of younger primary children, older primary children, younger secondary children and older secondary children. This is only *one* way of organizing a qualitative data analysis – by *groups*. The advantage of this method is that it automatically groups the data and enables themes, patterns and similarities to be seen at a glance. Whilst this is a useful method for summarizing similar responses, the collective responses of an individual participant are dispersed across many categories and groups of people, and the integrity and coherence of the individual respondent risks being lost to a collective summary. Further, this method is often used in relation to a single-instrument approach, otherwise it becomes unwieldy (for example, trying to put together the data derived from qualitative questionnaires, interviews and observations could be very cumbersome in this approach). So, researchers may find it helpful to use this approach instrument by instrument.

A *second* way of organizing the data analysis is by *individuals*. Here the total responses of a single participant are presented, and then the analysis moves on to the next individual. This preserves the coherence and integrity of the individual's response and enables a whole picture of that person to be presented, which may be important for the researcher. On the other hand, this integrity exacts its price, in that, unless the researcher is only interested in individual responses, it often requires him/her then to put together the issues arising *across* the individuals (a second level of analysis) in order to look for themes, shared responses, patterns of response, agreement and disagreement, to

compare individuals and issues that each of them has raised, i.e. to summarize the data.

Whilst approaches that are concerned with people strive to be faithful to those involved in terms of the completeness of the picture of them *qua* people, unless case study approaches are deemed to be driving the research, they are usually accompanied by a second round of analysis, which is of the issues that arise from the people, and it is to the matter of issues that we turn now.

A *third* way of organizing data is to present all the data that are relevant to a particular *issue* or *theme*. This is the method that was used in the example of Chinese students learning English. Whilst it is economical in making comparisons across respondents (the issue of data reduction through careful data display, mentioned earlier), again the wholeness, coherence and integrity of each individual respondent risks being lost.

The derivation of the issue/theme for which data are gathered needs to be clarified. For example, it could be that the issue has been decided *pre-ordinately*, in advance of the data collection. Then all the relevant data for that issue are simply collected together into that single basket – the issue in question. Whilst this is an economical approach to handling, summarizing and presenting data, it raises three main concerns:

a the integrity and wholeness of each individual can be lost, such that comparisons across the whole picture from each individual is almost impossible;

b the data can become decontextualized. This may occur in two ways; first in terms of their place in the emerging sequence and content of the interview or the questionnaire (e.g. some data may require an understanding of what preceded a particular comment or set of comments), and second in terms of the overall picture of the relatedness of the issues, as this approach can fragment the data into relatively discrete chunks, thereby losing their interconnectedness;

c having had its framework and areas of interest already decided pre-ordinately, the analysis may be unresponsive to additional relevant factors that could emerge *responsively* in the data. It is akin to lowering a magnet onto data – the magnet picks up relevant data for the issue in question but it also leaves behind data not deemed relevant and these risk being lost. The researcher, therefore, has to trawl through the residual data to see if there are other important issues that have emerged that have not been caught in the pre-ordinate selection of categories and issues for attention.

The researcher, therefore, has to be mindful of the strengths and weaknesses not only of pre-ordinate categorization (and, by implication, include responsive categorization), but she must also decide whether it is or is not important to consider the whole set of responses of an individual, i.e. to decide whether the data analysis is driven by people/respondents or by issues.

A *fourth* method of organizing the analysis is by *research question*. This is a very useful way of organizing data, as it draws together all the relevant data for the exact issue of concern to the researcher, and preserves the coherence of the material. It returns the reader to the driving concerns of the research, thereby 'closing the loop' on the research questions that typically were raised in the early part of an enquiry. In this approach all the relevant data from various data streams (interviews, observations, questionnaires, etc.) are collated to provide a collective answer to a research question. There is usually a degree of systematization here, in that, for example, the numerical data for a particular research question will be presented, followed by the qualitative data, or vice versa. This enables patterns, relationships, comparisons and qualifications across data types to be explored conveniently and clearly.

A *fifth* method of organizing the data is by *instrument*. Typically this approach is often used in conjunction with another approach, e.g. by issue or by people. Here the results of each instrument are presented, e.g. all the interview data are presented and organized, and then all the data from questionnaires are presented, followed by all the documentary data and field notes and so on. Whilst this approach retains fidelity to the coherence of the instrument and enables the reader to see clearly which data derive from which instrument, one has to observe that the instrument is often only a means to an end, and that further analysis will be required to analyse the *content* of the responses – by issue and by people. Hence if it is important to know from which instrument the data are derived then this is a useful method; however, if that is not important then this could be adding an unnecessary level of analysis to the data. Further, connections between data could be lost if the data are presented instrument by instrument rather than across instruments.

In analysing qualitative data, a major tension may arise from using contrasting holistic and fragmentary/atomistic modes of analysis. The example of teaching English in Macau is clearly atomistic, breaking down the analysis into smaller sections and units. It could be argued that this violates the wholeness of the respondents' evidence, and there is some truth to this, though one has to ask whether this is a problem or not. Sectionalizing and fragmenting the analysis can make for easy reading. On the other hand, holistic approaches to

qualitative data presentation will want to catch the wholeness of individuals and groups, and this may lead to a more narrative, almost case study or story style of reporting with issues emerging as they arise during the narrative! Neither approach is better than the other; researchers need to decide how to present data with respect to their aims and intended readership.

A *sixth* way of organizing and writing up a qualitative data is by one or more (e.g. a series) of case studies, or by combining case studies into an overall study that sets out common and singular features and properties of the cases (see also Miles and Huberman (1994) on within site and cross-site analysis). Or a series of individual case studies can be followed by an analysis that draws together common findings from the different case studies and also indicates the exclusive features of each. The researcher can also identify common themes in and across the case studies, or, if a theme has been decided in advance (pre-ordinately) or indeed responsively when reading through all the case studies (see content analysis and coding, discussed in later chapters), then materials from case studies can be used selectively to illustrate specific themes (whilst adhering to the principle of fidelity to the case in question).

A *seventh* way of organizing the analysis is by constructing a narrative that may be in the form of a chronology, a logical analysis, a thematic analysis, a series of 'stories' about the research findings. This is an important approach, and we address it in further detail below.

Clearly these seven ways are not all mutually exclusive, and they may be used in combination, so as to better answer the research questions.

29.3 Narrative and biographical approaches to data analysis

Bruner (1986) remarks that humans make meaning and think in terms of 'storied text' which catch the human condition, human intentionality, the vividness of human experience very fully (pp. 14 and 19) and the multiple perspectives and lived realities ('subjective landscapes') of participants (p. 29). They model the world (p. 7), starting as metaphors and metamorphosing into empirical statements by verifiable data. They make the familiar strange, 'rescue it from obviousness' (p. 24) and require the reader to fill in the gaps, i.e. they are an interactive medium (p. 24).

Stories personalize generalizations (Gibbs, 2007: 57) and are evidence-based. Further, they catch the chronology of events as they unfold over time, and this can enable the researcher to infer causality, coupled with the dramatic and dramaturgical power of carefully chosen words. Narrative not only conveys information but brings information to life. As the poet Pasternak remarks, events 'catch fire' on their way, through the reporting of personal experiences, dramatic events and even the simple unfolding of a sequence of activities, behaviours or people over time. Gibbs (2007: 60) comments that narratives not only pass on information but they meet people's psychological needs in coping with life, or help a group to crystallize or define an issue, view, stance or perspective, or they can persuade or create a positive image, they can help researchers and readers to understand the experiences of participants and cultures, and contribute to the structuring of identity (as, indeed, is the case with life histories and biographies). Narratives are a foil to the supremacy of coding and coding-derived analysis.

Biographies, too, tend to follow a chronology, to report critical or key events and moments, to report key decisions and people, and to establish causality. Indeed, for their authors, they may even be restorative of broken identities or shattered futures (Gibbs, 2007: 67).

Both narratives and biographies may have a chronology (but this is not a requirement, as some narratives are structured by logical relations or psychological coherence rather than chronology). They may have a beginning, a middle and an end, they may include critical moments and decisions, complicating factors, evaluation and outcomes (cf. Labov's (1972) characteristics of a narrative as having an abstract, orientation (context), complicating actions (sequences of events that decide the course of the narrative), evaluation (indicating the significance of the narrative and its main points), resolution (outcomes), and a coda (a rounding off of the narrative)).

Narratives and biographies cannot record all the events; rather a selective focus should be adopted, based on the criteria that the researcher wishes to use. These may include, for example: key decision points in the story or narrative, or key, critical (or meaningful to the participants) events, themes, behaviours, actions, decisions, people, points in the chronology, or meaningful events to the participants, reconstruction of the case history (Flick, 2009: 347), key places, key experiences. Once the researcher has identified the textual units in the biography or narrative, based on the criteria that are fit for the researcher's purpose, the researcher can then analyse and interpret the text for the meanings contained in it, develop working hypotheses to explain what is taking place, check these hypotheses against the data and the remainder of the text, see the text as a whole rather than as discrete units, and ensure that different interpretations of the text have been considered

and the one(s) chosen are the most secure in terms of fidelity to the text.

Following these stages of text selection, analysis, interpretation and checking, the process of construction of the final narrative takes place. This can be undertaken in several ways, for example:

- by temporal sequence (a chronology);
- by a sequence of causal relations;
- by key participants;
- by key behaviours or actions;
- by emergent or key themes;
- by key issues and clusters of issues;
- by biographies of the participants;
- by critical or key events;
- by turning points in a life history or biography;
- by different perspectives;
- by key decision points;
- by key behaviours;
- by individual case studies or a collective analysis of the unfolding of events for many cases/participants over time.

In constructing a narrative analysis (as, indeed, in other forms of qualitative data analysis), the researcher can introduce verbatim quotations from participants where relevant and illuminative; these can add life to the narrative and often convey the point very expressively – without it being mediated or softened by the academic language of the researcher. It is important to keep them short enough to convey the main point without distortion or exclusion of relevant details and context, but not so long that the reader does not know what is the point of the quotation (i.e. having to perform an analysis of the data for herself/himself (Gibbs, 2007: 97)). When using verbatim quotations from participants, it is often useful to accompany them with the researcher's interpretive commentary. Quotations are often chosen for their ability to crystallize or exemplify an issue or example really well, or typically, or extremely, and the researcher will need to decide whether to identify the person who said it (see the discussion of ethics in Chapter 28).

Narrative analysis, together with biographical data, can give the added dimension of realism, authenticity, humanity, personality, emotions, views and values in a situation, and the researcher must ensure that these are featured in the narratives that have been constructed. By 'telling a story' a narrative account, case study or biography breaks with the strictures of coding and the risk of disembodied text that can too easily result from coding and retrieval exercise; it keeps text and content together, it retains the integrity of people rather than fragmenting bits of them into common themes or codes, it enables evolving situations, causes and consequences to be charted. It enables events to 'catch fire' as they unfold. Narratives are powerful, human and integrated; truly qualitative.

29.4 Systematic approaches to data analysis

Data analysis can be very systematic. Becker and Geer (1960) indicate how this might proceed:

1 comparing different groups simultaneously and over time;
2 matching the responses given in interviews to observed behaviour;
3 analysing deviant and negative cases;
4 calculating frequencies of occurrences and responses;
5 assembling and providing sufficient data that keeps separate raw data from analysis.

In qualitative data the analysis here is almost inevitably interpretive, hence the data analysis is less a completely accurate representation (as in the numerical, positivist tradition) but more of a reflexive, reactive interaction between the researcher and the decontextualized data that are already interpretations of a social encounter. Indeed reflexivity is an important feature of qualitative data analysis, and we discuss this separately (Chapter 11). The issue here is that the researcher brings to the data her own preconceptions, interests, biases, preferences, biography, background and agenda. As Walford (2001: 98) writes: 'all research is researching yourself'. In practical terms it means that the researcher may be selective in her focus, or that the research may be influenced by the subjective features of the researcher. Robson (1993: 374–5) and Lincoln and Guba (1985: 354–5) suggest that these can include:

■ data overload (humans may be unable to handle large amounts of data);
■ first impressions (early data analysis may affect later data collection and analysis);
■ availability of people (e.g. how representative these are and how to know if missing people and data might be important);
■ information availability (easily accessible information may receive greater attention than hard-to-obtain data);
■ positive instances (researchers may overemphasize confirming data and under-emphasize disconfirming data);

■ internal consistency (the unusual, unexpected or novel may be under-treated);
■ uneven reliability (the researcher may overlook the fact that some sources are more reliable/unreliable than others);
■ missing data (that issue for which there are incomplete data may be overlooked or neglected);
■ revision of hypotheses (researchers may overreact or under-react to new data);
■ confidence in judgement (researchers may have greater confidence in their final judgements than is tenable);
■ co-occurrence may be mistaken for association;
■ inconsistency (subsequent analyses of the same data may yield different results); a notable example of this is Bennett (1976) and Aitken et al. (1981).

The issue here is that great caution and self-awareness must be exercised by the researcher in conducting qualitative data analysis, for the analysis and the findings may say more about the researcher than about the data. For example, it is the researcher who sets the codes and categories for analysis, be they pre-ordinate or responsive (decided in advance of or in response to the data analysis respectively). It is the researcher's agenda that drives the research and she who chooses the methodology.

As the researcher analyses data, she will have ideas, insights, comments, reflections to make on data. These can be noted down in memos, and, indeed, these can become data themselves in the process of reflexivity (though they should be kept separate from the primary data themselves). Glaser (1978) and Robson (1993: 387) argue that memos are not data in themselves but help the process of data analysis; this is debatable, for if reflexivity is part of the data analysis process then memos may become legitimate secondary data in the process or journey of data analysis. Many computer packages for qualitative data analysis (discussed later) have a facility not only for the researcher to write a memo, but also to attach it to a particular piece of datum. There is no single nature or format of a memo; it can include subjective thoughts about the data, with ideas, theories, reflections, comments, opinions, personal responses, suggestions for future and new lines of research, reminders, observations, evaluations, critiques, judgements, conclusions, explanations, considerations, implications, speculations, predictions, hunches, theories, connections, relationships between codes and categories, insights and so on. Memos can be reflections on the past, present and the future, thereby beginning to examine the issue of causality. There is no required minimum or maximum length, though memos should be dated not only for ease of reference but also for a marking of the development of the researcher as well as of the research.

Memos are an important part of the self-conscious reflection on the data and have considerable potential to inform the data collection, analysis and theorizing processes. They should be written whenever they strike the researcher as important – during and after analysis. They can be written at any time, indeed some researchers deliberately carry a pen and paper with them wherever they go, so that ideas that occur can be written down before they are forgotten. They enable the researcher to comment and theorize on events, situations, behaviours and so on as they are being analysed, and can focus on observations, methodological and theoretical matters, or personal matters (cf. Gibbs, 2007: 30–1).

The great tension in data analysis is between maintaining a sense of the holism of the data – the text – and the tendency for analysis to atomize and fragment the data – to separate them into constituent elements, thereby losing the synergy of the whole, and often the whole is greater than the sum of the parts. There are several stages in analysis, e.g.

- generating natural units of meaning;
- classifying, categorizing and ordering these units of meaning;
- structuring narratives to describe the contents;
- interpreting the data.

These are comparatively generalized stages. Miles and Huberman (1994) suggest 12 tactics for generating meaning from transcribed data:

- counting frequencies of occurrence (of ideas, themes, pieces of data, words);
- noting patterns and themes (Gestalts), which may stem from repeated themes and causes or explanations or constructs;
- seeing plausibility – trying to make good sense of data, using informed intuition to reach a conclusion;
- clustering – setting items into categories, types, behaviours and classifications;
- making metaphors – using figurative and connotative language rather than literal and denotative language, bringing data to life, thereby reducing data, making patterns, decentring the data and connecting data with theory;
- splitting variables to elaborate, differentiate and 'unpack' ideas, i.e. to move away from the drive towards integration and the blurring of data;
- subsuming particulars into the general (akin to

Glaser's (1978) notion of 'constant comparison' – see Chapter 33 in this book) – a move towards clarifying key concepts;

- factoring – bringing a large number of variables under a smaller number of (frequently) unobserved hypothetical variables;
- identifying and noting relations between variables;
- finding intervening variables – looking for other variables that appear to be 'getting in the way' of accounting for what one would expect to be strong relationships between variables;
- building a logical chain of evidence – noting causality and making inferences;
- making conceptual/theoretical coherence – moving from metaphors to constructs, to theories to explain the phenomena.

This progression, though perhaps positivist in its tone, is a useful way of moving from the specific to the general in data analysis. Running through the suggestions from Miles and Huberman (1994) is the importance that they attach to coding of data, partially as a way of reducing what is typically data overload from qualitative data. Huberman and Miles suggest that analysis through coding can be performed both within-site and cross-site, enabling causal chains, networks and matrices to be established, all of these addressing what they see as the major issue of reducing data overload through careful data display.

Content analysis involves reading and judgement; Brenner *et al.* (1985) set out several steps in undertaking a content analysis of open-ended data:

1 briefing (understanding the problem and its context in detail);
2 sampling (of people, including the types of sample sought, see Chapter 4);
3 associating (with other work that has been done);
4 hypothesis development;
5 hypothesis testing;
6 immersion (in the data collected, to pick up all the clues);
7 categorizing (in which the categories and their labels must: (a) reflect the purpose of the research; (b) be exhaustive; (c) be mutually exclusive);
8 incubation (e.g. reflecting on data and developing interpretations and meanings);
9 synthesis (involving a review of the rationale for coding and an identification of the emerging patterns and themes);
10 culling (condensing, excising and even reinterpreting the data so that they can be written up intelligibly);

11 interpretation (making meaning of the data);

12 writing (including (pp. 140–3): giving clear guidance on the incidence of occurrence; proving an indication of direction and intentionality of feelings; being aware of what is not said as well as what is said – silences; indicating salience (to the readers and respondents));

13 rethinking.

Content analysis is addressed more fully in the next chapter. This process, Brenner *et al.* (1985: 144), requires researchers to address several factors:

1 Understand the research brief thoroughly.

2 Evaluate the relevance of the sample for the research project.

3 Associate their own experiences with the problem, looking for clues from the past.

4 Develop testable hypotheses as the basis for the content analysis (the authors name this the 'Concept Book').

5 Test the hypotheses throughout the interviewing and analysis process.

6 Stay immersed in the data throughout the study.

7 Categorize the data in the Concept Book, creating labels and codes.

8 Incubate the data before writing up.

9 Synthesize the data in the Concept Book, looking for key concepts.

10 Cull the data; being selective is important because it is impossible to report everything that happened.

11 Interpret the data, identifying its meaning and implication.

12 Write up the report.

13 Rethink and rewrite: have the research objectives been met?

Hycner (1985) sets out procedures that can be followed when phenomenologically analysing interview data. We saw in Chapter 1 that the phenomenologist advocates the study of direct experience taken at face value and sees behaviour as determined by the phenomena of experience rather than by external, objective and physically described reality. Hycner points out that there is a reluctance on the part of phenomenologists to focus too much on specific steps in research methods for fear that they will become reified. The steps suggested by Hycner, however, offer a possible way of analysing data which allays such fears. As he himself explains, his guidelines 'have arisen out of a number of years of teaching phenomenological research classes to graduate psychology students and trying to be true to the phenomenon of interview data while also providing

concrete guidelines' (Hycner, 1985). In summary, the guidelines are as follows:

- *Transcription*: having the interview tape transcribed, noting not only the literal statements but also non-verbal and paralinguistic communication.

- *Bracketing and phenomenological reduction*: for Hycner (1985) this means, 'suspending (bracketing) as much as possible the researcher's meaning and interpretations and entering into the world of the unique individual who was interviewed'. The researcher thus sets out to understand what the interviewee is saying rather than what she expects that person to say.

- *Listening to the interview for a sense of the whole*: this involves listening to the entire tape several times and reading the transcription a number of times in order to provide a context for the emergence of specific units of meaning and themes later on.

- *Delineating units of general meaning*: this entails a thorough scrutiny of both verbal and non-verbal gestures to elicit the participant's meaning. Hycner (1985) says, 'It is a crystallization and condensation of what the participant has said, still using as much as possible the literal words of the participant.'

- *Delineating units of meaning relevant to the research question*: once the units of general meaning have been noted, they are then reduced to units of meaning relevant to the research question.

- *Training independent judges to verify the units of relevant meaning*: findings can be verified by using other researchers to carry out the above procedures. Hycner's own experience in working with graduate students well trained in this type of research is that there are rarely significant differences in the findings.

- *Eliminating redundancies*: at this stage, the researcher checks the lists of relevant meaning and eliminates those clearly redundant to others previously listed.

- *Clustering units of relevant meaning*: the researcher now tries to determine if any of the units of relevant meaning naturally cluster together; whether there seems to be some common theme or essence that unites several discrete units of relevant meaning.

- *Determining themes from clusters of meaning*: the researcher examines all the clusters of meaning to determine if there is one (or more) central theme(s) which expresses the essence of these clusters.

- *Writing a summary of each individual interview*: it is useful at this point, the author suggests, to go back to the interview transcription and write up a summary of the interview incorporating the themes that have been elicited from the data.

■ *Return to the participant with the summary and themes, conducting a second interview*: this is a check to see whether the essence of the first interview has been accurately and fully captured.

■ *Modifying themes and summary*: with the new data from the second interview, the researcher looks at all the data as a whole and modifies them or adds themes as necessary.

■ *Identifying general and unique themes for all the interviews*: the researcher now looks for the themes common to most or all of the interviews as well as the individual variations. The first step is to note if there are themes common to all or most of the interviews. The second step is to note when there are themes that are unique to a single interview or a minority of the interviews.

■ *Contextualization of themes*: at this point it is helpful to place these themes back within the overall contexts or horizons from which they emerged.

■ *Composite summary*: the author considers it useful to write up a composite summary of all the interviews which would accurately capture the essence of the phenomenon being investigated. Hycner (1985) concludes, 'Such a composite summary describes the "world" in general, as experienced by the participants. At the end of such a summary the researcher might want to note significant individual differences.'

29.5 Methodological tools for analysing qualitative data

There are several procedural tools for analysing qualitative data. LeCompte and Preissle (1993: 253) see analytic induction, constant comparison, typological analysis and enumeration as valuable techniques for the qualitative researcher to use in analysing data and generating theory.

Analytic induction is a term and process that was introduced by Znaniecki (1934) in deliberate opposition to statistical methods of data analysis. LeCompte and Preissle (1993: 254) suggest that the process is akin to the several steps set out above, in that: (a) data are scanned to generate categories of phenomena; (b) relationships between these categories are sought; (c) working typologies and summaries are written on the basis of the data examined; (d) these are then refined by subsequent cases and analysis; (e) negative and discrepant cases are deliberately sought to modify, enlarge or restrict the original explanation/theory. Denzin (1970: 192) uses the term 'analytical induction' to describe the broad strategy of participant observation that is set out below:

1 A rough definition of the phenomenon to be explained is formulated.
2 A hypothetical explanation of that phenomenon is formulated.
3 One case is studied in the light of the hypothesis, with the object of determining whether or not the hypothesis fits the facts in that case.
4 If the hypothesis does not fit the facts, either the hypothesis is reformulated or the phenomenon to be explained is redefined, so that the case is excluded.
5 Practical certainty may be attained after a small number of cases has been examined, but the discovery of negative cases disproves the explanation and requires a reformulation.
6 This procedure of examining cases, redefining the phenomenon and reformulating the hypothesis is continued until a universal relationship is established, each negative case calling for a redefinition of a reformulation.

A more deliberate seeking of disconfirming (negative) cases is advocated by Bogdan and Biklen (1992: 72). Here the researcher searches for cases which do not fit the other data, or cases, or that do not fit expected patterns of findings. They can be used to extend, expand or modify the existing or emerging hypothesis. Bogdan and Biklen (1992) also enumerate five main stages in analytic induction:

1 In the early stages of the research a rough definition and explanation of the particular phenomenon is developed.
2 This definition and explanation is examined in the light of the data that are being collected during the research.
3 If the definition and/or explanation that have been generated need modification in the light of new data (e.g. if the data do not fit the explanation or definition) then this is undertaken.
4 A deliberate attempt is made to find cases that may not fit into the explanation or definition.
5 The process of redefinition and reformulation is repeated until the explanation is reached that embraces all the data, and until a generalized relationship has been established, which will also embrace the negative cases.

In *constant comparison* the researcher compares newly acquired data with existing data and categories and theories that have been devised and which are emerging, in order to achieve a perfect fit between these and the data. Hence negative cases or data which challenge these existing categories or theories lead to their modification until they can fully accommodate all the data. We discuss this technique more fully in the next chapter, as it is a major feature of qualitative techniques for data analysis.

Typological analysis is essentially a classificatory process (LeCompte and Preissle, 1993: 257) wherein data are put into groups, subsets or categories on the basis of some clear criterion (e.g. acts, behaviour, meanings, nature of participation, relationships, settings, activities). It is the process of *secondary coding* (Miles and Huberman, 1984) where descriptive codes are then drawn together and put into subsets. Typologies are a set of phenomena that represent subtypes of a more general set or category (Lofland, 1970). Lazarsfeld and Barton (1951) suggest that a typology can be developed in terms of an underlying dimension or key characteristic. In creating typologies Lofland insists that the researcher must: (a) deliberately assemble all the data on how a participant addresses a particular issue – what strategies are being employed; (b) disaggregate and separate out the variations between the ranges of instances of strategies; (c) classify these into sets and subsets; and (d) present them in an ordered, named and numbered way for the reader.

The process of *enumeration* is one in which categories and the frequencies of codes, units of analysis, terms, words or ideas are counted. This enables incidence to be recorded, and, indeed, statistical analysis of the frequencies to be undertaken (e.g. Monge and Contractor, 2003). This is a method used in conventional forms of content analysis, and we address this topic in the next chapter.

This chapter has suggested several approaches to analysing and presenting qualitative data. It should be read in conjunction with the next chapter, as they complement each other.

 Companion Website

The companion website to the book includes PowerPoint slides for this chapter, which list the structure of the chapter and then provide a summary of the key points in each of its sections. This resource can be found online at **www.routledge.com/textbooks/cohen7e**.

Coding and content analysis

CHAPTER 30

Many researchers who have gathered qualitative data undertake forms of content analysis. This chapter addresses coding and content analysis. It provides a straightforward introduction to key issues in coding and content analysis, including:

- coding
- what is content analysis?
- how does content analysis work?
- a worked example of content analysis
- reliability in content analysis

One of the enduring problems of qualitative data analysis is the reduction of copious amounts of written data to manageable and comprehensible proportions. Data reduction is a key element of qualitative analysis, performed in a way that attempts to respect the *quality* of the qualitative data. One common procedure for achieving this is content analysis, a process by which the 'many words of texts are classified into much fewer categories' (Weber, 1990: 15). The goal is to reduce the material in different ways (Flick, 1998: 192). Categories are usually derived from theoretical constructs or areas of interest devised in advance of the analysis (pre-ordinate categorization) rather than developed from the material itself, though these may be modified, of course, by reference to the empirical data. Before we turn to content analysis, it is important to consider the matter of coding, and we address this in the next section.

30.1 Coding

A major feature of qualitative data analysis is coding (e.g. Strauss and Corbin, 1990; Kelle, 1995: 62–104; Gibbs, 2007: 38–55; Flick, 2009: 305–32). There are several kinds of codes (e.g. Lonkila, 1995; Strauss and Corbin, 1990; Kelle, 1995: 62–104; Gibbs, 2007: 38–55; Flick, 2009: 305–32) and we explore these below. Texts may be lightly coded or densely coded (e.g. where a single piece of text has several codes attached to it). A code is simply a name or label that the researcher gives to a piece of text that contains an idea

or a piece of information. Gibbs (2007: 38) catches the nature of a code neatly when he writes that the same code is given to an item of text that says the same thing or is about the same thing. Seidel and Kelle (1995) suggest that codes can denote a text, passage or fact, and can be used to construct data networks.

Coding has been defined by Kerlinger (1970) as the translation of question responses and respondent information to specific categories for the purpose of analysis. Coding is the ascription of a category label to a piece of data, that is either decided in advance or in response to the data that have been collected. Newby (2010: 467) refers to this as 'tagging'. The same piece of text may have more than one code ascribed to it, depending on the richness and contents of that piece of text.

Coding enables the researcher to identify similar information. More than this, it enables the researcher to search and retrieve the data in terms of those items that bear the same code. Codes can be regarded as an indexing or categorizing system, akin to the index in a book, which gives all the references to that index entry in the book, and the data can be stored under the same code, with an indexed entry for that code. A list of codes can be stored, accompanied by data such as who coded the data, when the coding was undertaken and what the code means (Gibbs, 2007: 41).

Coding can be performed on many kinds of data, focusing on, for example (cf. Gibbs, 2007: 47–8): specific acts, conversations, reports, behaviours, events, interactions, activities, contexts, settings, conditions, actions, strategies, practices, tactics, meanings, intentions, states, symbols, participation, relationships, constraints, causes, consequences and issues concerning the researcher's reflexivity. In short, nothing is ruled out.

Codes can be at different levels of specificity and generality when defining content and concepts. There may be some codes which subsume others, thereby creating a hierarchy of subsumption – subordination and superordination – in effect creating a tree diagram of codes. Some codes are very general; others are more specific. Codes are astringent, pulling together a wealth of material into some order and structure. They keep words as words; they maintain context specificity. Codes may be *descriptive* and might include (Bogdan and Biklen, 1992: 167–72): situation codes; perspectives held by subjects; ways of thinking about people and objects; process codes; activity codes; event codes; strategy codes; relationship and social structure codes; methods codes. However, to be faithful to the data, the codes themselves derive from the data responsively rather than being created pre-ordinately. Hence the researcher will go through the data ascribing codes to each piece of datum. A code is a word or abbreviation sufficiently close to that which it is describing for the researcher to see at a glance what it means (in this respect it is unlike a number). For example, the code 'trust' might refer to a person's trustworthiness; the code 'power' might refer to the status or power of the person in the group. This enables meanings to be seen at a glance, memorized and recalled easily.

Miles and Huberman (1994) advise that codes should be kept as discrete as possible and that coding should start earlier rather than later as late coding enfeebles the analysis, though there is a risk that early coding might influence too strongly any later codes. It is possible, they suggest, for as many as 90 codes to be held in the working memory whilst going through data, though clearly, there is a process of iteration and re-iteration whereby some codes that are used in the early stages of coding might be modified subsequently and vice versa, necessitating the researcher to go through a data set more than once to ensure consistency, refinement, modification and exhaustiveness of coding (some codes might become redundant, others might need to be broken down into finer codes). By coding up the data the researcher is able to detect frequencies (which codes are occurring most commonly) and patterns (which codes occur together).

In coding a piece of transcription the researcher goes through the data systematically, typically line by line, and writes a descriptive code by the side of each piece of datum, for example:

Text	Code
The students will undertake problem-solving in science	PROB
I prefer to teach mixed ability classes	MIXABIL

One can see here that the codes are frequently abbreviations, enabling the researcher to understand immediately the issue that they denote because they resemble that issue (rather than, for example, ascribing a number as a code for each piece of datum, where the number provides no clue as to what the datum or category concerns). Where they are not abbreviations, Miles and Huberman (1994) suggest that the coding label should bear sufficient resemblance to the original data so that the researcher can know, by looking at the code, what the original piece of datum concerned. We give a full worked example of a coding exercise later in this chapter.

There are several computer packages that can help the coder here (e.g. MAXqda, ATLAS.ti, NVivo, NUD*IST, Ethnograph), though they require the original transcript to be entered onto the computer. One such, Code-A-Text, is particularly useful for analysing dialogues both quantitatively and qualitatively (the system also accepts sound and video input).

Although Miles and Huberman (1994) suggest that it is possible to keep as many as 90 codes in the working memory at any one time, they make the point that data might be recoded on a second or third reading, as codes that were used early on might have to be refined in light of codes that are used later, either to make the codes more discriminating or to conflate codes that are unnecessarily specific. Codes, they argue, should enable the researcher to catch the complexity and comprehensiveness of the data. Codes are derived through the dual processes of induction and deduction (p. 111); codes should be verifiable by data (p. 108).

It is important for codes to be applied consistently, so that relevant data are coded consistently, that no data are excluded, that the same code is used. This enables retrieval, categorization, collation and separation of data (particularly if software is being used). Often, in the first coding attempt, many new codes are generated, and the subtlety of difference of codes may be unclear as the researcher goes further through the text, or the earlier codes may turn out to be unhelpful (e.g. too general), or the later codes may be too strongly influenced (or driven) by the earlier codes, or later coding may make the researcher feel that she or he wishes to alter the earlier coding, or there may be duplication or overlap of codes (e.g. the same kind of meaning but given slightly different codes), or there may be redundant codes (e.g. codes that only appear once or twice and which are more fittingly replaced by other codes in light of the remainder of the text). The point here is that coding is not a 'one-off' exercise; it requires reading and rereading, assigning and reassigning codes, placing and replacing codes, refining codes and coded data; the process is iterative and requires the researcher to go back and forth through the data on maybe several occasions, to ensure consistency and coverage of codes and data. Once the initial coding has been undertaken and checked then emergent themes, frequencies of codes, patterns of combinations of codes, key points, similarities and differences, variations and so on can be conducted, and we discuss these in this chapter and the next.

Coding, argues Flick (2009: 310), can address fundamental questions such as 'who', 'why' 'what', 'where', 'how', 'when', 'how long', 'how much', 'how strong', 'what for' and 'by which'. These, he suggests, are useful questions in steering the coding exercise, particularly for open coding (discussed below).

There are different kinds of code: an open code, an analytic code, an axial code, a selective code, and we discuss these next. Though there is a suggestion in what follows that there is a temporal sequence in coding, this need not be the case, as the different codes are different procedures and operate at different levels, and these are not necessarily driven by time-order (Flick, 2009: 307).

Open coding

An open code is simply a new label that the researcher attaches to a piece of text to describe and categorize that piece of text (Strauss and Corbin, 1990: chapter 5). Open coding generates categories and defines their properties (the characteristics of a category or phenomenon or its attributes) and dimensions (the location of a property along a given continuum) (Strauss and Corbin, 1990: 69). Strauss and Corbin (1990: 70) give an example of the category/code 'colour', which has properties of hue, shade and intensity. These properties, in turn, have dimensions: hue can be light to dark; shade can be light to dark, and intensity from high to low. Each category can have several properties, each of which has its own dimensional continuum (p. 70). The authors give an example of properties and dimensions for the category/code/label 'watching' (p. 72): property: 'frequency'; dimension: often to never; property: 'extent'; dimension: more to less; property: 'intensity': dimension: high to low; property: 'duration': dimension: long to short.

Coding is the process of breaking down segments of text data into smaller units (based on whatever criteria are relevant), and then examining, comparing, conceptualizing and categorizing the data (Strauss and Corbin, 1990: 61). The researcher goes through the text, marking the text with codes (labels) that describe that text. The code name might derive from the researcher's own creation, or it may derive from the words used in the text or spoken by one of the participants in the transcribed data (e.g. if the participant remarks that she is bored with the science lesson, the code may be 'bored': a short term that catches the essence of the text in question).

Open coding can be performed on a line-by-line, phrase-by-phrase, sentence-by-sentence, paragraph-by-paragraph or unit-of text-by-unit-of-text basis. Then the codes can be grouped into categories, with the categories given a title or name by the researcher, based on criteria that are decided by the researcher (e.g. concerning a specific theme, based on similar words, similar concepts, similar meanings, etc.). The title of the category should be more abstract than the specific concepts or contents of the codes that it subsumes (Strauss and Corbin, 1990: 69). In undertaking such grouping it is important that all the data fit into the group consistently, that there are no negative cases.

Open coding is usually the earliest, initial form of coding undertaken by the researcher.

Analytic coding

As its name suggests, an analytic code is more than a descriptive code. It becomes more interpretive. For example, whereas 'experimenting', 'controlling variables', 'testing' and 'measuring' are descriptive codes (e.g. in describing science activities), an analytic code here could be 'working like a scientist', 'doing science' or 'active science'; it draws together and gives more explanatory and analytic meaning to a group of descriptive codes.

Another example might be where the descriptive codes given to teacher behaviour might be 'ignores disruption' (for when a teacher ignores disruptive behaviour), 'interested students' (for when a teacher only concentrates on those students who are interested in the lesson contents) and 'no response' (for when a teacher does not respond to students shouting in class). The category might be 'teacher behaviour' and the analytic – more inferential – code might be 'teacher resignation' or 'teacher denial'.

An analytic code might derive from the theme or topic of the research (e.g. Gibbs, 2007: 45), the literature, or, responsively, from the data themselves.

Axial coding

An axial code is a category label ascribed to a group of open codes whose referents (the phenomena being described) are similar in meaning (e.g. concern the same concept). Axial coding is that set of procedures that the researcher follows, whereby the data that were originally segmented into small units of fractions of a whole text are recombined in new ways following the open coding (Strauss and Corbin, 1990: 96). An axial code refers to (Strauss and Corbin, 1990):

- causal conditions: events, activities, behaviours or incidents that lead to the occurrence of a phenomenon (p. 100);
- a phenomenon: an event, idea, activity, action, behaviour, etc. (p. 100);

- context: a specific set of properties or conditions that obtain in a phenomenon, action or interaction (p. 101);
- intervening conditions: the broad, general conditions that have a bearing on the action or interaction in question (p. 103);
- actions and interactions: purposeful, goal-oriented processes, strategies or behaviours obtaining in an action (p. 104);
- consequences: outcomes for people, events, places, etc., which may or may not have been predicted, and which, in turn, may become the causes or conditions of further actions and interactions (p. 106).

For a worked example of these six areas we refer readers to Buckley and Waring (2009), in which they diagrammatize the six areas and insert relevant data into them for their study of physical activity in children.

Axial coding connects related codes and subcategories into a larger category of common meaning that is shared by the group of codes in question (thereby creating a hierarchy in which some codes are subsumed into the large axial category); an axial code, as its name suggests, is a category or axis around which several codes revolve.

Axial coding works within one category, making connections between subgroups of that category and between one category and another. This might be in terms of the phenomena that are being studied, the causal conditions that lead to the phenomena, the context of the phenomena and their intervening conditions, and the actions and interactions of, and consequences for, the actors in situations.

Selective coding

Selective coding identifies the core categories of text data, integrating them to form a theory. It is the process of identifying the core category in a text, i.e. that central category or phenomenon around which all the other categories identified and created are integrated (Strauss and Corbin, 1990: 116), and to which other categories are systematically related and by which it is validated. Strauss and Corbin (1990) argue that, in fact, a selective code is very similar to an axial code, except that it is at a greater level of abstraction than an axial code. Creating the selective code requires: (a) a deep understanding of the main 'story line' (p. 117) (the descriptive overview of the main phenomenon being described and analysed, and its salient features); then moves to (b) creating the core category; then (c) relating categories at the level of the dimensions identified; then (d) validating those relations in terms of the data

that gave rise to them; and then (e) filling in any gaps in categories (pp. 116–17) to ensure the 'conceptual density' (p. 141) of the category, based on data collected. Though set out in a linear sequence, the authors indicate that, in fact, the process is iterative, and researchers move back and forth between the steps (a) to (e).

Once codes have been assigned, ordered and grouped, they can be structured into hierarchies of subsumption, in which lower order (e.g. descriptive codes) are subsumed under analytic and axial codes, which, in turn, are subsumed under a selective code. Hierarchies order codes and keep them tidy (Gibbs, 2007: 75), and, indeed, the creation of a hierarchy is, itself, part of data analysis, as the researcher ascribes meanings to the data. This is a pre-eminent function of CAQDAS software, in the creation of nodes, node trees and hierarchies. The advice from Gibbs (2007: 77) is to keep hierarchies 'shallow' rather than 'deep', i.e. not too many levels. It is important, too, to ensure that the data contained in each code at each level are consistent with each other, hence the researcher has to constantly check and make comparisons across the data (the 'constant comparison' of grounded theory (Glaser and Strauss, 1967)) to ensure that they all fit together, with no exceptions or disconfirming data. Gibbs (2007: 78–83) suggests that this can be done easily with tabulated data, and Chapter 29 provides examples of this, where data in columns can be compared or data in rows can be compared, to look for consistency, patterns, commonalities, relationships, similarities and differences (e.g. Tables 29.1 to 29.4). In such tabulated data (often where individuals are the rows and the issue is the column), it is possible to examine and compare individual cases (the rows) and different interpretations of the issues (the columns), for example Table 30.1, with fictitious data from a primary school.

In this example, looking across the rows we can see that the children have positive attitudes but their interest is thwarted by distractions, lack of 'voice' and level of demand in the lessons; they all prefer practical work but this is not always done. One child seems to be more accommodating to the teacher's decisions than the other two, and one seems to be much less accommodating, i.e. there is variation on this dimension. Looking down the columns, we see very different attitudes within and between the two lessons. The table enables comparisons to be made, looking for similarities, differences, consistencies and inconsistencies, variations and homogeneity of responses, and deviant and extreme cases (cf. Gibbs, 2007: 96).

Though coding is a central feature in many forms of qualitative data analysis, researchers need to ensure that

TABLE 30.1	TABULATED DATA FOR COMPARATIVE ANALYSIS	
Name	*Attitudes to science lessons*	*Attitudes to music lessons*
Jane	Finds them difficult, but interesting. Too much homework which is not addressed in the class. Enjoys experiments but is not very good at them.	Enjoys listening to music, but there is too much singing to be done in class, and not enough playing or practical activity. The teacher only concentrates on those who are in the school choir.
John	Cannot concentrate because he finds the work boring and too 'bookish'. Prefers experiments but never has the chance to do them.	We are never allowed to choose the music to listen to, and the teacher's music is boring and old. Why do we have to use babyish instruments?
Stephen	Thoroughly enjoys the practical activities and the idea of exploring what went wrong in the experiments, and why.	I liked it when we were making up our own tunes in groups, but the class was very noisy. I don't like singing. I wish we were taught how to read and write proper music. Lots of children just 'mess around' in the music lesson, and that's horrible.

it is the most appropriate way to analyse the data, as there is a risk of losing temporality, context and sequence in the coding and retrieval of text. For example, there is a temptation, perhaps, to ascribe the same code to an observed behaviour regardless of the setting, the time (e.g. in a longitudinal study or a study that involves observation over several weeks), the prevalent conditions, states of mind, actors involved, intervening events and so on, when, in fact, the meaning and significance of the behaviour is not the same in different contexts or points in time. In this case, the researcher may wish to write a narrative account rather than to abstract data from the several contexts in which they are set.

We return to coding and constant comparison in Chapter 31, as they are integral to grounded theory.

30.2 What is content analysis?

Having introduced coding, we are now in a position to consider content analysis. The term 'content analysis' is often used sloppily. In effect, it simply defines the process of summarizing and reporting written data – the main contents of data and their messages. More strictly speaking, it defines a strict and systematic set of procedures for the rigorous analysis, examination and verification of the contents of written data (Flick, 1998: 192; Mayring, 2004: 266). Krippendorp (2004: 18) defines it as 'a research technique for making replicable and valid inferences from texts (or other meaningful matter) to the contexts of their use'. Texts are defined as any written communicative materials which are intended to be read, interpreted and understood by people other than the analysts (Krippendorp, 2004: 30).

Originally deriving from analysis of mass media and public speeches, the use of content analysis has spread to examination of any form of communicative material, both structured and unstructured. It may be 'applied to substantive problems at the intersection of culture, social structure, and social interaction; used to generate dependent variables in experimental designs; and used to study groups as microcosms of society' (Weber, 1990: 11). Content analysis can be undertaken with any written material, from documents to interview transcriptions, from media products to personal interviews. It is often used to analyse large quantities of text, facilitated by the systematic, rule-governed nature of content analysis, not least because this enables computer assisted analysis to be undertaken. It often uses categorization as an essential feature in reducing large quantities of data (Flick, 2009: 323).

Content analysis has several attractions. It is an unobtrusive technique (Krippendorp, 2004: 40), in that one can observe without being observed (Robson, 1993: 280). It focuses on language and linguistic features, meaning in context, is systematic and verifiable (e.g. in its use of codes and categories), as the rules for analysis are explicit, transparent and public (Mayring, 2004: 267–9). Further, as the data are in a permanent form (texts), verification through re-analysis and replication is possible.

Many researchers see content analysis as an alternative to numerical analysis of qualitative data. But this is not so, although it is widely used as a device for extracting numerical data from word-based data. Indeed Anderson and Arsenault (1998: 101–2) suggest that content analysis can describe the *relative frequency* and importance of certain topics as well as to evaluate bias, prejudice or propaganda in print materials.

Weber (1990: 9) sees the purposes of content analysis as including: (a) the coding of open-ended questions in surveys; (b) the revealing of the focus of individual, group, institutional and societal matters; (c) the description of patterns and trends in communicative content. The latter suggestion indicates the role of statistical techniques in content analysis; indeed Weber (p. 10) suggests that the highest quality content-analytic studies use both quantitative and qualitative analysis of texts (texts defined as any form of written communication).

Content analysis takes texts and analyses, reduces and interrogates them into summary form through the use of both pre-existing categories and emergent themes in order to generate or test a theory. It uses systematic, replicable, observable and rule-governed forms of analysis in a theory-dependent system for the application of those categories.

Krippendorp (2004: 22–4) suggests that there are several features of texts that relate to a definition of content analysis, including the fact that texts have no objective reader-independent qualities; rather they have multiple meanings and can sustain multiple readings and interpretations. There is no one meaning waiting to be discovered or described in them. Indeed, the meanings in texts may be personal and are located in specific contexts, discourses and purposes, and, hence, meanings have to be drawn in context. Content analysis, then: (a) describes the manifest characteristics of communication (Krippendorp, 2004: 46) (asking who is saying what to whom, and how); (b) infers the antecedents of the communication (the reasons for, and purposes behind, the communication, and the context of communication (Mayring, 2004: 267)); (c) infers the consequences of the communication (its effects). Krippendorp suggests (pp. 75–7) that content analysis is at its most successful when it can break down 'linguistically constituted facts' into four classes: attributions, social relationships, public behaviours and institutional realities.

30.3 How does content analysis work?

Ezzy (2002: 83) suggests that content analysis starts with a sample of texts (the units), defines the units of analysis (e.g. words, sentences) and the categories to be used for analysis, reviews the texts in order to code them and place them into categories, and then counts and logs the occurrences of words, codes and categories. From here statistical analysis and quantitative methods are applied, leading to an interpretation of the results. Put simply, content analysis involves coding, categorizing (creating meaningful categories into which the units of analysis – words, phrases, sentences, etc. – can be placed), comparing (categories and making links between them), and concluding – drawing theoretical conclusions from the text.

Anderson and Arsenault (1998: 102) indicate the quantitative nature of content analysis when they state that 'at its simplest level, content analysis involves counting concepts, words or occurrences in documents and reporting them in tabular form'. This succinct statement catches essential features of the process of content analysis:

- breaking down text into units of analysis;
- undertaking statistical analysis of the units;
- presenting the analysis in as economical a form as possible.

This masks some other important features of content analysis, including, for example, examination of the interconnectedness of units of analysis (categories), the emergent nature of themes and the testing, development and generation of theory.

Flick (2009: 326) summarizes several stages of content analysis:

- defining the units of analysis;
- paraphrasing the relevant passages of text;
- defining the level of abstraction required of the paraphrasing;
- data reduction and deletion (e.g. removing paraphrases that duplicate meaning);
- data reduction by combing and integrating paraphrases at the level of abstraction required;
- putting together the new statements into a category system;
- reviewing the new category system against the original data.

More fully, the whole process of content analysis can follow several steps.

Step 1: Define the research questions to be addressed by the content analysis

This will also include what one wants from the texts to be content-analysed. The research questions will be informed by, indeed may be derived from, the theory to be tested.

Step 2: Define the population from which units of text are to be sampled

The population here refers not only to people but also, and mainly, to text – the domains of the analysis. For example, is it to be newspapers, programmes, interview transcripts, textbooks, conversations, public domain documents, examination scripts, emails, online conversations and so on?

Step 3: Define the sample to be included

Here the rules for sampling people can apply equally well to documents. One has to decide whether to opt for a probability or non-probability sample of documents, a stratified sample (and, if so, the kind of strata to be used), random sampling, convenience sampling, domain sampling, cluster sampling, purposive, systematic, time sampling, snowball and so on (see Chapter 8). Robson (1993: 275–9) indicates the careful delineation of the sampling strategy here, for example, such-and-such a set of documents, such-and-such a time frame (e.g. of newspapers), such-and-such a number of television programmes or interviews. The key issues of sampling apply to the sampling of texts: representativeness, access, size of the sample and generalizability of the results.

Krippendorp (2004: 145) indicates that there may be 'nested recording units', where one unit is nested within another, for example, with regard to newspapers that have been sampled it may be thus: 'the issues of a newspaper sampled; the articles in an issue of a newspaper sampled; the paragraphs in an article in an issue of a newspaper sampled; the propositions constituting a paragraph in an article in an issue of a newspaper sampled'. This is the equivalent of stage sampling, discussed in Chapter 8.

Step 4: Define the context of the generation of the document

This will examine, for example: how the material was generated (Flick 1998: 193); who was involved; who was present; where the documents come from; how the material was recorded and/or edited; whether the person was willing to, able to and did tell the truth; whether the data are accurately reported (Robson 1993: 273); whether the data are corroborated; the authenticity and credibility of the documents; the context of the generation of the document; the selection and evaluation of the evidence contained in the document.

Step 5: Define the units of analysis

This can be at very many levels, for example, a word, phrase, sentence, paragraph, whole text, people, and themes. Robson (1993: 276) includes here, for newspaper analysis, the number of stories on a topic, column inches, size of headline, number of stories on a page, position of stories within a newspaper, the number and type of pictures. His suggestions indicate the careful thought that needs to go into the selection of the units of analysis. Different levels of analysis will raise different issues of reliability, and these are discussed later. It is assumed that the units of analysis will be classifiable into the same category text with the same or similar meaning in the context of the text itself (semantic validity) (Krippendorp, 2004: 296), though this can be problematic (discussed later). The description of units of analysis will also include the units of measurement and enumeration.

The *coding unit* defines the smallest element of material that can be analysed, whilst the *contextual unit* defines the largest textual unit that may appear in a single category

Krippendorp (2004: 99–101) distinguishes three kinds of units. *Sampling units* are those units that are included in, or excluded from, an analysis; they are units of selection. *Recording/coding units* are units that are contained within sampling units and are smaller than sampling units, thereby avoiding the complexity that characterizes sampling units; they are units of description. *Context units* are 'units of textual matter that set limits on the information to be considered in the description of recording units' (p. 101); they are units that 'delineate the scope of information that coders need to consult in characterizing the recording units' (p. 103).

Krippendorp (2004) continues by suggesting a further five kinds of sampling units: physical (e.g. time, place, size); syntactical (words, grammar, sentences, paragraphs, chapters, series, etc.); categorical (members of a category have something in common); propositional (delineating particular constructions or propositions); and thematic (putting texts into themes and combinations of categories). The issue of categories signals the next step.

The criterion here is that each unit of analysis (category – conceptual, actual, classification element, cluster, issue) should be as discrete as possible whilst retaining fidelity to the integrity of the whole, i.e. that each unit must be a fair rather than a distorted representation of the context and other data. The creation of units of analysis can be done by ascribing *codes* to the data (Miles and Huberman, 1984). This is akin to the process of 'unitizing' (Lincoln and Guba, 1985: 203).

Step 6: Decide the codes to be used in the analysis

Hammersley and Atkinson (1983: 177–8) propose that the first activity here is to read and reread the data to become thoroughly familiar with them, noting also any interesting patterns, any surprising, puzzling or unexpected features, any apparent inconsistencies or contradictions (e.g. between groups, within and between individuals and groups, between what people say and what they do). Then, having become familiar with the text, the process of coding can take place, following the principles and mechanics of coding as set out earlier in this chapter.

Step 7: Construct the categories for analysis

Categories are the main groupings of constructs or key features of the text, showing links between units of analysis. For example, a text concerning teacher stress could have groupings such as 'causes of teacher stress', 'the nature of teacher stress', 'ways of coping with stress' and 'the effects of stress'. The researcher will have to decide whether to have mutually exclusive categories (preferable but difficult), how broad or narrow each category will be, the order or level of generality of a category (some categories may be very general and subsume other more specific categories, in which case analysis should only operate at the same level of each category rather than having the same analysis which combines and uses different levels of categories). Categories are inferred by the researcher, whereas specific words or units of analysis are less inferential; the more one moves towards inference, the more reliability may be compromised, and the more the researcher's agenda may impose itself on the data.

Categories will need to be exhaustive in order to address content validity; indeed Robson (1993: 277) argues that a content analysis 'is no better than its system of categories' and that these can include: subject matter; direction (how a matter is treated – positively or negatively); values; goals; method used to achieve goals; traits (characteristics used to describe people); actors (who is being discussed); authority (in whose name the statements are being made); location; conflict (sources and levels); and endings (how conflicts are resolved).

This stage of constructing the categories is sometimes termed the creation of a 'domain analysis'. This involves grouping the units into domains, clusters, groups, patterns, themes and coherent sets to form domains. A domain is any symbolic category that includes other categories (Spradley, 1979: 100). At this stage it might be useful for the researcher to recode the data into domain codes, or to review the codes used to see how they naturally fall into clusters, perhaps creating overarching codes for each cluster. Hammersley and Atkinson (1983) show how items can be assigned to more than one category, and, indeed, see this as desirable as it maintains the richness of the data. This is

akin to the process of 'categorization' (Lincoln and Guba, 1985), putting 'unitized' data to provide descriptive and inferential information. Unitization is the process of putting data into meaning units for analysis, examining data, and identifying what those units are. A meaning unit is simply a piece of datum which the researcher considers to be important; it may be as small as a word or phrase, or as large as a paragraph, groups of paragraphs, or, indeed, a whole text, provided that it has meaning in itself.

Spradley (1979) suggests that establishing domains can be achieved by four analytic tasks: (a) selecting a sample of verbatim interview and field notes; (b) looking for the names of things; (c) identifying possible terms from the sample; (d) searching through additional notes for other items to include. He identifies six steps to achieve these tasks: (i) select a single semantic relationship; (ii) prepare a domain analysis sheet; (iii) select a sample of statements from respondents; (iv) search for possible cover terms and include those that fit the semantic relationship identified; (v) formulate structural questions for each domain identified; (vi) list all the hypothesized domains. Domain analysis, then, strives to discover relationships between symbols (Spradley, 1979: 157).

Like codes, categories can be at different levels of specificity and generality. Some categories are general and overarching; others are less so. Typically codes are much more specific than categories. This indicates the difference between *nodes* and *codes*. A code is a label for a piece of text; a node is a category into which different codes fall or are collected. A node can be a concept, idea, process, group of people, place or, indeed, any other grouping that the researcher wishes it to be; it is an organizing category. Whereas codes describe specific textual moments, nodes draw together codes into a categorical framework, making connections between coded segments and concepts. It is rather like saying that a text can be regarded as a book, with the chapters being the nodes and the paragraphs being the codes, or the content pages being the nodes and the index being the codes. Nodes can be related in several ways, for example: one concept can define another; they can be logically related; and they can be empirically related (found to accompany each other) (Krippendorp, 2004: 296).

One has to be aware that the construction of codes and categories might steer the research and its findings, i.e. that the researcher may enter too far into the research process. For example, a researcher may have been examining the extra-curricular activities of a school and discovered that the benefits of these are to be found in non-cognitive and non-academic spheres rather than in academic spheres, but this may be fallacious. It could be that it was the codes and categories themselves rather than the data in the minds of the respondents that caused this separation of cognitive/academic spheres and issues from the non-cognitive/non-academic, and that if the researcher had specifically asked about, or established codes and categories which established the connection between the academic and non-academic, then s/he would have found more than s/he did. This is the danger of using codes and categories to predefine the data analysis.

Step 8: Conduct the coding and categorizing of the data

Once the codes and categories have been decided the analysis can be undertaken. This concerns the actual ascription of codes and categories to the text, as described earlier in this chapter. Mayring (2004: 268–9) suggests that *summarizing content analysis* reduces the material to manageable proportions whilst maintaining fidelity to essential contents, and that *inductive category formation* proceeds through summarizing content analysis by inductively generating categories from the text material. This is in contrast to *explicit content analysis*, the opposite of summarizing content analysis, which seeks to add in further information in the search for intelligible text analysis and category location. The former reduces contextual detail, the latter retains it. *Structuring content analysis* filters out parts of the text in order to construct a cross-section of the material using specified pre-ordinate criteria.

It is important to decide whether to code simply for the existence or the incidence of the concept. This is important, as it would mean that, in the case of the former – existence – the frequency of a concept would be lost, and frequency may give an indication of the significance of a concept in the text. Further, the coding will need to decide whether it should code only the exact words or those with a similar meaning. The former will probably result in significant data loss, as words are not often repeated in comparison to the concepts that they signify; the latter may risk losing the nuanced sensitivity of particular words and phrases. Indeed some speechmakers may deliberately use ambiguous words or those with more than one meaning.

Having performed the first round of coding the researcher is able to detect patterns, themes and begin to make generalizations (e.g. by counting the frequencies of codes). The researcher can also group codes into more general clusters, each with a code, i.e. begin the move towards factoring the data.

Perhaps the biggest problem concerns the coding and scoring of open-ended questions. Two solutions are possible here. Even though a response is open-ended, an interviewer, for example, may precode her interview schedule so that while an interviewee is responding freely, the interviewer is assigning the content of her responses, or parts of it, to predetermined coding categories. Classifications of this kind may be developed during pilot studies.

Alternatively, data may be postcoded. Having recorded the interviewee's response, for example, either by summarizing it during or after the interview itself, or verbatim by tape recorder, the researcher may subject it to content analysis and apply it to one of the available scoring procedures – scaling, scoring, rank scoring, response counting, etc.

Step 9: Conduct the data analysis

Once the data have been coded and categorized, the researcher can count the frequency of each code or word in the text, and the number of words in each category. This is the process of retrieval, which may be in multiple modes, for example words, codes, nodes and categories. Some words may be in more than one category, for example where one category is an overarching category and another is a subcategory. To ensure reliability, Weber (1990: 21–4) suggests that it is advisable at first to work on small samples of text rather than the whole text, to test out the coding and categorization, and make amendments where necessary. The complete texts should be analysed, as this preserves their semantic coherence.

Words and single codes on their own have limited power, and so it is important to move to associations between words and codes, i.e. to look at categories and relationships between categories. Establishing relationships and linkages between the domains ensures that the data, their richness and 'context-groundedness' are retained. Linkages can be found by identifying confirming cases, by seeking 'underlying associations' (LeCompte and Preissle, 1993: 246) and connections between data subsets.

Weber (1990: 54) suggests that it is preferable to retrieve text based on categories rather than single words, as categories tend to retrieve more than single words, drawing on synonyms and conceptually close meanings. One can make category counts as well as word counts. Indeed, one can specify at what level the counting can be conducted, for example, words, phrases, codes, categories and themes.

The implication here is that the frequency of words, codes, nodes and categories provides an indication of their significance. This may or may not be true, since subsequent mentions of a word or category may be difficult in certain texts (e.g. speeches). Frequency does not equal importance, and not saying something (withholding comment) may be as important as saying something. Content analysis only analyses what is present rather than what is missing or unsaid (Anderson and Arsenault, 1998: 104). Further, as Weber (1990: 73) says: 'pronouns may replace nouns the further on one goes through a passage; continuing raising of the issue may cause redundancy as it may be counter-productive repetition; constraints on text length may inhibit reference to the theme; some topics may require much more effort to raise than others'.

The researcher can summarize the inferences from the text, look for patterns, regularities and relationships between segments of the text, and test hypotheses. The summarizing of categories and data is an explicit aim of statistical techniques, for these permit trends, frequencies, priorities and relationships to be calculated. At the stage of data analysis there are several approaches and methods that can be used. Krippendorp (2004: 48–53) suggests that these can include:

- extrapolations (trends, patterns and differences);
- standards (evaluations and judgements);
- indices (e.g. of relationships, frequencies of occurrence and co-occurrence, number of favourable and unfavourable items);
- linguistic re-presentations.

Once frequencies have been calculated, statistical analysis can proceed, using, for example:

- factor analysis (to group the kinds of response);
- tabulation (of frequencies and percentages);
- crosstabulation (presenting a matrix where the words or codes are the column headings and the nominal variables, e.g. the newspaper, the year, the gender, are the row headings);
- correlation (to identify the strength and direction of association between words, between codes and between categories);
- graphical representation (for example to report the incidence of particular words, concepts, categories over time or over texts);
- regression (to determine the value of one variable/word/code/category in relationship to another): a form of association that gives exact values and the gradient or slope of the goodness of fit line of relationship – the regression line;
- multiple regression (to calculate the weighting of independents on dependent variables);
- structural equation modelling and LISREL analysis (to determine the multiple directions of causality and the weightings of different associations in a pathway analysis of causal relations);

- dendrograms (tree diagrams to show the relationship and connection between categories and codes, codes and nodes).

The calculation and presentation of statistics is discussed in Chapters 35–38. At this stage the argument here suggests that what starts as qualitative data – words – can be converted into numerical data for analysis.

If a less quantitative form of analysis is required then this does not preclude a qualitative version of the statistical procedures indicated here. For example, one can establish linkages and relationships between concepts and categories, examining their strength and direction (how strongly they are associated and whether the association is positive or negative respectively). Many computer packages will perform the qualitative equivalent of statistical procedures.

It is also useful to try to pursue the identification of core categories (see the later discussion of grounded theory). A core category is that which has the greatest explanatory potential and to which the other categories and subcategories seem to be repeatedly and closely related (Strauss, 1987: 11). Robson (1993: 401) suggests that drawing conclusions from qualitative data can be undertaken by counting, patterning (noting recurrent themes or patterns), clustering (of people, issues, events, etc. which have similar features), relating variables, building causal networks and relating findings to theoretical frameworks.

Whilst conducting qualitative data analysis using numerical approaches or paradigms may be criticized for being positivistic, one should note that one of the founders of grounded theory – Glaser – is on record (1996) as saying that not only did grounded theory develop out of a desire to apply a quantitative paradigm to qualitative data, but that paradigmal purity was unacceptable in the real world of qualitative data analysis, in which *fitness for purpose* should be the guide. Further, one can note that Miles and Huberman (1994) strongly advocate the graphic display of data as an economical means of reducing qualitative data. Such graphics might serve both to indicate causal relationships as well as simply summarizing data.

Step 10: Summarizing

By this stage the investigator will be in a position to write a summary of the main features of the situation that have been researched so far. The summary will identify key factors, key issues, key concepts and key areas for subsequent investigation. It is a watershed stage during the data collection, as it pinpoints major themes, issues and problems that have arisen, so far, from the data (responsively) and suggests avenues for further investigation.

The concepts used will be a combination of those derived from the data themselves and those inferred by the researcher (Hammersley and Atkinson, 1983: 178).

At this point, the researcher will have gone through the preliminary stages of theory generation. Patton (1980) sets these out for qualitative data:

i   finding a focus for the research and analysis;
ii   organizing, processing, ordering and checking data;
iii writing a qualitative description or analysis;
iv   inductively developing categories, typologies and labels;
v   analysing the categories to identify where further clarification and cross-clarification are needed;
vi   expressing and typifying these categories through metaphors (see also Pitman and Maxwell, 1992: 747);
vii making inferences and speculations about relationships, causes and effects.

Bogdan and Biklen (1992: 154–63) identify several important factors that researchers need to address at this stage, including: forcing oneself to take decisions that will focus and narrow the study and decide what kind of study it will be; developing analytical questions; using previous observational data to inform subsequent data collection; writing reflexive notes and memos about observations, ideas, what is being learned; trying out ideas with subjects; analysing relevant literature whilst conducting the field research; generating concepts, metaphors and analogies and visual devices to clarify the research.

Step 11: Making speculative inferences

This is an important stage, for it moves the research from description to inference. It requires the researcher, on the basis of the evidence, to posit some explanations for the situation, some key elements and possibly even their causes. It is the process of hypothesis generation or the setting of working hypotheses that feeds into theory generation.

The stage of theory generation is linked to grounded theory, and we turn to this later in the chapter. Here we provide an example of content analysis that does not use statistical analysis but which nevertheless demonstrates the systematic approach to analysing data that is at the heart of content analysis.

30.4 A worked example of content analysis

In this example the researcher has already transcribed data concerning stress in the workplace from, let us say, a limited number of accounts and interviews with a few teachers, and these have already been summarized

into key points. It is imagined that each account/interview has been written up onto a separate file (e.g. computer file), and now they are all being put together into a single data set for analysis. What we have are already-interpreted, rather than verbatim, data.

Stage 1: Extract the interpretive comments that have been written on the data

By the side of each, a code/category/descriptor word has been inserted (in capital letters), i.e. the summary data have already been collected together into 33 summary sentences.

1   Stress is caused by deflated expectation i.e. stress is caused by annoyance with other people not pulling their weight or not behaving as desired, or teachers letting themselves down. **CAUSE**
2   Stress is caused by having to make greater demands on personal time to meet professional concerns. So, no personal time/space as a cause of stress. Stress is caused by having to compromise one's plans/desires. **CAUSE**
3   Stress comes from having to manage several demands simultaneously, **CAUSE** but the very fact that they are simultaneous means that they can't be managed at once, so stress is built into the problem of coping – it's an insoluble situation. **NATURE**
4   Stress from one source brings additional stress which leads to loss of sleep – a sign that things are reaching a breaking point. **OUTCOME**
5   Stress is a function of the importance attached to activities/issues by the person involved. **NATURE** Stress is caused when one's own integrity/values are not only challenged but called into question. **CAUSE**
6   Stress comes from 'frustration'– frustration leads to stress leads to frustration leads to stress, etc. – a vicious circle. **NATURE**
7   When the best-laid plans go wrong this can be stressful. **CAUSE**
8   The vicious circle of stress, inducing sleep irregularity which, in turn, induces stress. **NATURE**
9   Reducing stress often works on symptoms rather than causes – may be the only thing possible **CAUSE**, given that the stressors will not go away, but it allows the stress to fester. **CAUSE**
10 The effects of stress are physical which, in turn, causes more stress – another vicious circle. **OUTCOMES**
11 Stress from lowering enthusiasm/commitment/aspiration/expectation. **CAUSE**
12 Pressure of work lowers aspiration which lowers stress. **CAUSE**

13 Stress reduction through companionship. **HAND-LING**

14 Stress because of things out of one's control. **CAUSE**

15 Stress through handling troublesome students. **CAUSE**

16 Stress because of a failure of management/leadership. **CAUSE**

17 Stress through absence of fulfilment. **CAUSE**

18 Stress rarely happens on its own, it is usually in combination – like a rolling snowball, it is cumulative. **NATURE**

19 Stress through worsening professional conditions that are out of the control of the participant. **CAUSE** Stress through loss of control and autonomy. **CAUSE**

20 Stress through worsening professional conditions is exponential in its effects. **NATURE**

21 Stress is caused when professional standards are felt to be compromised. **CAUSE**

22 Stress because matters are not resolved. **CAUSE**

23 Stress through professional compromise which is out of an individual's control. **CAUSE**

24 The rate of stress is a function of its size – a big bomb causes instant damage. **NATURE**

25 Stress is caused by having no escape valve; it's bottled up and causes more stress, like a kettle with no escape valve, it will stress the metal and then blow up. **CAUSE**

26 Stress through overload and frustration – a loss of control. Stress occurs when people cannot control the circumstances with which they have to work. **CAUSE**

27 Stress through overload. **CAUSE**

28 Stress through seeing one's former work being undone by others' incompetence. **CAUSE**

29 Stress because nothing has been possible to reduce the level of stress. So, if the boil of stress is not lanced, it grows and grows. **CAUSE NATURE**

30 Handling stress through relaxation and exercise. **HANDLING**

31 Trying to relieve stress through self-damaging behaviour – taking alcohol and smoking. **HAND-LING NATURE**

32 Stress is a function of the importance attached to activities by the participants involved. **NATURE**

33 The closer the relationship to people who cause stress, the greater the stress. **NATURE**

The data have been coded very coarsely, in terms of three or four main categories. It may have been possible to have coded the data far more specifically, e.g. each specific cause has its code, indeed one school of thought would argue that it is important to generate the specific codes first. One can code for words (and, thereafter, the frequency of words) or meanings – it is sometimes dangerous to go for words rather than meanings, as people say the same things in different ways.

Stage 2: Sort data into key headings/areas

The codes that have been used fall into four main areas:

a causes of stress
b nature of stress
c outcomes of stress
d handling stress.

Stage 3: List the topics within each key area/heading and put frequencies in which items are mentioned

For each main area the relevant data are presented together, and a tally mark (/) is placed against the number of times that the issue has been mentioned by the teachers.

a Causes of stress
  ■ Deflated expectation/aspiration /
  ■ Annoyance /
  ■ Others not pulling weight /
  ■ Others letting themselves down /
  ■ Professional demands, e.g. troublesome students /
  ■ Demands on personal time from professional tasks /
  ■ Difficulties of the job /
  ■ Loss of personal time and space /
  ■ Compromising oneself/one's professional standards and integrity ///
  ■ Plans go wrong /
  ■ Stress itself causes more stress /
  ■ Inability to reduce causes of stress /
  ■ Lowering enthusiasm/commitment/aspiration /
  ■ Pressure of work /
  ■ Things out of one's control //
  ■ Failure of management/leadership /
  ■ Absence of fulfilment /
  ■ Worsening professional conditions /
  ■ Loss of control and autonomy //
  ■ Inability to resolve situation /
  ■ Having no escape valve /
  ■ Overload at work /
  ■ Seeing one's work undone by others /
b Nature of stress
  ■ Stress is a function of the importance attached to activities issues by the participants /
  ■ Stress is inbuilt when too many simultaneous demands are made, i.e. it is insoluble /
  ■ It is cumulative (like a snowball) until it reaches a breaking point /

- Stress is a vicious circle //
- The effects of stress are exponential /
- The rate of stress is a function of its size /
- If stress has no escape valve then that causes more stress //
- Handling stress can lead to self-damaging behaviour (smoking/alcohol) /
- Stress is a function of the importance attached to activities issues by the participants /
- The closer the relationship to people who cause stress, the greater the stress /

c Outcomes of stress
- Loss of sleep/physical reaction //
- Effects of stress themselves cause more stress /
- Self-damaging behaviour /

d Handling stress
- Physical action/exercise /
- Companionship /
- Alcohol and smoking /

Stage 4: Go through the list generated in Stage 3 and put the issues into groups (avoiding category overlap)

Here the grouped data are re-analysed and re-presented according to possible groupings of issues under the four main heading (causes, nature, outcomes and handling of stress: (a) – (d) below).

a *Causes of Stress*:
  i Personal factors
   - Deflated expectation/aspiration /
   - Annoyance /
   - Demands on personal time from professional tasks /
   - Loss of personal time and space /
   - Stress itself causes more stress /
   - Inability to reduce causes of stress /
   - Lowering enthusiasm/commitment/aspiration /
   - Things out of one's control //
   - Absence of fulfilment /
   - Loss of control and autonomy //
   - Inability to resolve situation /
   - Having no escape valve /
  ii Interpersonal factors
   - Annoyance /
   - Others not pulling weight /
   - Others letting themselves down /
   - Compromising oneself/one's professional standards and integrity ///
   - Seeing one's work undone by others /
  iii Management
   - Pressure of work /
   - Things out of one's control //

- Failure of management/leadership /
- Worsening professional conditions /
- Seeing one's work undone by others /

iv Professional matters
- Others not pulling weight /
- Professional demands, e.g. troublesome students /
- Demands on personal time from professional tasks /
- Difficulties of the job /
- Compromising oneself/one's professional standards and integrity ///
- Plans go wrong /
- Pressure of work /
- Worsening professional conditions /
- Loss of control and autonomy //
- Overload at work /

b *Nature of Stress*:
  i Objective
   - It is a function of the importance attached to activities issues by the participants /
   - Stress is inbuilt when too many simultaneous demands are made, i.e. it is insoluble /
   - It is cumulative (like a snowball) until it reaches a breaking point /
   - Stress is a vicious circle //
   - The effects of stress are exponential /
   - The rate of stress is a function of its size /
   - If stress has no escape valve then that causes more stress //
   - Handling stress can lead to self-damaging behaviour (smoking/alcohol) /
  ii Subjective
   - Stress is a function of the importance attached to activities issues by the participants /
   - The closer the relationship to people who cause stress, the greater the stress /

c *Outcomes of Stress*:
  i Physiological
   - Loss of sleep /
  ii Physical
   - Physical reactions //
   - Increased smoking /
   - Increased alcohol /
  iii Psychological
   - Annoyance /

d *Handling Stress*:
  i Physical
   - Physical action/exercise /
  ii Social
   - Social solidarity, particularly with close people ///
   - Companionship /

Stage 5: Comment on the groups or results in Stage 4 and review their messages

Once the previous stage has been completed, the researcher is then in a position to draw attention to general and specific points, e.g.

1 There is a huge number of causes of stress (give numbers).
2 There are very few outlets for stress, so it is inevitable, perhaps, that stress will accumulate.
3 Causes of stress are more rooted in personal factors than any others – management, professional, etc. (give frequencies here).
4 The demands of the job tend to cause less stress than other factors (e.g. management), i.e. people go into the job knowing what to expect, but the problem lies elsewhere, with management (give frequencies).
5 Loss of control is a significant factor (give frequencies).
6 Challenges to people and personal integrity/self-esteem are very stressful (give frequencies).
7 The nature of stress is complex, with several interacting components (give frequencies).
8 Stress is omnipresent.
9 Not dealing with stress compounds the problem; dealing with stress compounds the problem.
10 The subjective aspects of the nature of stress are as important as its objective nature (give frequencies).
11 The outcomes of stress tend to be personal rather than outside the person (e.g. systemic, or system-disturbing) (give frequencies).
12 The outcomes of stress are almost exclusively negative rather than positive (give frequencies).
13 The outcomes of stress tend to be felt non-cognitively, e.g. emotionally and psychologically, rather than cognitively (give frequencies).
14 There are few ways of handling stress (frequencies), i.e. opportunities for stress reduction are limited.

The stages of this analysed example embody several of the issues raised in the preceding discussion of content analysis, though the example here does not undertake word counts or statistical analysis, and, being fair to content analysis, this could – some would argue even 'should' – be a further kind of analysis. What has happened in this analysis raises several important issues:

- The researcher has looked within and across categories and groupings for patterns, themes, generalizations, as well as exceptions, unusual observations, etc.

- The researcher has had to decide whether frequencies are important, or whether an issue is important even if it is only mentioned once or a few times.
- The researcher has looked for, and reported, disconfirming as well as confirming evidence for statements.
- The final stage of the analysis is that of theory generation, to account for what is being explained about stress. It might also be important, in further analysis, to try to find causal relationships here: what causes what and the directions of causality; it may also be useful to construct diagrams (with arrows) to show the directions, strength and positive/negative nature of stress.

30.5 Reliability in content analysis

There are several issues to be addressed in considering the reliability of texts and their content analysis; indeed in analysing qualitative data using a variety of means, for example:

- Witting and unwitting evidence (Robson, 1993: 273): witting evidence is that which was intended to be imparted; unwitting evidence is that which can be inferred from the text, and which may not be intended by the imparter.
- The text may not have been written with the researcher in mind and may have been written for a very different purpose from that of the research (a common matter in documentary research); hence the researcher will need to know or be able to infer the intentions of the text.
- The documents may be limited, selective, partial, biased, non-neutral and incomplete because they were intended for a different purpose other than that of research (an issue of validity as well as of reliability).
- It may be difficult to infer the direction of causality in the documents – they may have been the cause or the consequence of a particular situation.
- Classification of text may be inconsistent (a problem sometimes mitigated by computer analysis), because of human error, coder variability (within and between coders) and ambiguity in the coding rules (Weber, 1990: 17).
- Texts may not be corroborated or able to be corroborated.
- Words are inherently ambiguous and polyvalent (the problem of homographs), for example, what does the word 'school' mean? A building; a group of people; a particular movement of artists (e.g. the impressionist school); a department (a medical school); a noun; a verb (to drill, to induct, to

educate, to train, to control, to attend an institution); a period of instructional time ('he stayed after school to play sports'); a modifier (e.g. a school day); a sphere of activity (e.g. 'the school of hard knocks'); a collection of people adhering to a particular set of principles (e.g. the utilitarian school); a style of life (e.g. 'a gentleman from the old school'); a group assembled for a particular purpose (e.g. a gambling school), and so on. This is a particular problem for computer programs which may analyse words devoid of their meaning.

- Coding and categorizing may lose the nuanced richness of specific words and their connotations.
- Category definitions and themes may be ambiguous, as they are inferential.
- Some words may be included in the same overall category but they may have more or less significance in that category (and a system of weighting the words may be unreliable).
- Words that are grouped together into a similar category may have different connotations and their usage may be more nuanced than the categories recognize.
- Categories may reflect the researcher's agenda and imposition of meaning more than the text may sustain or the producers of the text (e.g. interviewees) may have intended.
- Aggregation may compromise reliability. Whereas sentences, phrases and words and whole documents may have the highest reliability in analysis, paragraphs and larger but incomplete portions of text have lower reliability (Weber, 1990: 39).
- A document may deliberately exclude something for mention, overstate an issue or understate an issue (Weber, 1990: 73).

At a wider level, the limits of content analysis are suggested by Ezzy (2002: 84) where he argues that, due to the pre-ordinate nature of coding and categorizing, content analysis is useful for testing or confirming a pre-existing theory rather than for building a new one, though this perhaps understates the ways in which content analysis can be used to generate new theory, not least through a grounded theory approach (discussed later). In many cases content analysts know in advance what they are looking for in text, and perhaps what the categories for analysis will be. Ezzy (p. 85) suggests that this restricts the extent to which the analytical categories can be responsive to the data, thereby confining the data analysis to the agenda of the researcher rather than the 'other'. In this way it enables pre-existing theory to be tested. Indeed Mayring (2004: 269) argues that if the research question is very open or if the study is exploratory, then more open procedures than content analysis, e.g. grounded theory, may be preferable.

However, inductive approaches may be ruled out of the early stages of a content analysis, but this does not keep them out of the later stages, as themes and interpretations may emerge inductively from the data and the researcher, rather than only or necessarily from the categories or pre-existing theories themselves. Hence to suggest that content analysis denies induction or is confined to the testing of pre-existing theory (Ezzy, 2002: 85) is uncharitable; it is to misrepresent the flexibility of content analysis. Indeed Flick (1998) suggests that pre-existing categories may need to be modified if they do not fit the data.

 Companion Website

The companion website to the book includes PowerPoint slides for this chapter, which list the structure of the chapter and then provide a summary of the key points in each of its sections. In addition there is further information in the form of a screen-print manual for using QSR N6 NUD*IST, exportable to N-Vivo, plus data files of qualitative data for analysis that can be read NUD*IST and N-Vivo, using Word files and OSR data files. These resources can be found online at **www.routledge.com/textbooks/cohen7e**.

Discourses

Conversations, narratives and autobiographies as texts

Whilst coding represents one major approach to analysing qualitative data (discussed in the previous chapter), nevertheless it is only one way. In this chapter we provide very different methods of analysing qualitative data, founded in part on discourse analysis, and including:

- what is a discourse?
- a conversational analysis
- a narrative discourse
- autobiography

These approaches do not use coding, and keep together the text rather than fragmenting them as in coding. In each instance we provide a worked example, so that readers can understand the issues more clearly.

31.1 What is a discourse?

Words carry many meanings; they are nuanced and highly context-sensitive. In qualitative data analysis it is often the case that interpretation and analysis are fused and, indeed, concurrent. It is naive to suppose that the qualitative data analyst can separate analysis from interpretation, because words themselves are interpretations and are to be interpreted. In this chapter we show how qualitative researchers can analyse discourses, be they in written texts or transcriptions of spoken conversations.

'Discourse' is a very slippery term. We use it here to indicate the meanings that are given to texts which create and shape knowledge and behaviour, not least by the exercise of power through texts and conversations. A discourse is a way of thinking, perhaps culturally or institutionally conditioned, which, like a paradigm, is legitimated by communities, often those with power. Discourses shape, and are shaped by, different meanings and people are members of different discourse communities – those communities which hold similar values, views, ideas and ways of looking at the world. The familiar slogan that 'knowledge is power' is a central element in much discourse analysis, and discourse analysis reveals how power operates and is legitimated or challenged in and through discourses (e.g. Fraser, 2004). As Foucault (1998: 101) remarks, 'discourse can be both an instrument and an effect of power'; it is the 'tactical dimension' of the operation of power in individuals, groups and organizations. Power is immanent in discourse; it is one of its defining features. Indeed the three examples in this chapter (a conversation, a narrative and an autobiographical text) all concern power – its possession, its denial, it operations, its fluidity, its negotiation, its relations, its absence and so on.

Any text can be the bearer of several discourses, and a single text can be deconstructed into several meanings. Texts are set in social contexts, and reality is a social construction, so discourse analysis has to take account of the social contexts in which the texts are set.

To constitute a discourse Renkema (2004) suggests that a text – spoken or written – must fulfil seven main criteria:

- cohesion: there must be a grammatical relationship between the different parts of the text or conversation;
- coherence: the sequence and structure of the text must make sense and 'hang together';
- intentionality: the text or conversation must be written or spoken intentionally;
- acceptability: it has to be accepted or acceptable to its intended audience;
- informativeness: it must include new information;
- situationality: the context, conditions and circumstances in which it is embedded must be known and made explicit;
- intertextuality: the text or conversation must go beyond simply the text and to an outer world of the reader, interpreter, researcher and other agents.

Whilst discourse analysis is a scrutiny of any text, conversation analysis is a subset of this, looking at a conversation between two or more people. Discourse analysis examines how meaning in constructed through texts at beyond the single sentence level, and, indeed, the different meanings that can be constructed. In particular (but by no means exclusively) it focuses on issues of power, domination and the constructions and reproduction of power in texts and conversations, language in social contexts and interactions. It regards talk and texts as social practices (Potter and Wetherell, 1994: 48), agentic, interactive and socially constructivist (Clifton, 2006). Discourse analysis is influenced by speech act theory (Austin, 1962; Searle, 1969) of locutions (what is uttered), illocutions (doing something whilst saying something) and perlocutions (achieving something by saying something), by textual analysis, ideological analysis and ideology critique (Potter and Wetherell, 1994: 47).

Wetherell *et al.* (2001) identify four methods of discourse analysis:

■ analysing words in context (e.g. cultural, social, group) as ways in which people express themselves and in which context influences the language used, i.e. how context affects meaning and language;
■ analysing interactions conducted through language;
■ analysing patterns of language use (e.g. language used to express wishes, emotions, reactions, to create scenarios, to give information);
■ analysing the links between language and the constitution, structure and nature of society, often focusing on differentials of power and their reproduction.

Texts themselves carry many levels of meaning, and the qualitative researcher has to strive to catch these different levels or layers. Further, researchers are often part of the world that they are actually writing about, and, even if not, bring their own culture, norms, values to bear in conducting, analysing, interpreting and reporting the research. The issues of projection and counter-transference are important: the researcher's analysis may say as much about the researcher as about the text being analysed, both in the selection of the levels of analysis, the actual analysis, and the imputation of intention and function of discourses in the text, with their corollary in the key issue of reflexivity.

In this chapter we take three examples of ways in which researchers can analyse and interpret discourse: a conversation, a narrative and an autobiographical text. A conversation involves more than one person; a narrative is written by a single person and an autobiography is a narrative that is written by, and in, the first person.

31.2 A conversational analysis

The following example of a conversational analysis exposes the multilevelled interpretations that can be made of conversations as discourses (Sacks, 1984). Conversational analysis is a rigorous investigation of features of a conversation, how it is generated and constructed, how it operates, what are its distinguishing features and how participants construct their own meanings in the conversational situation (Clifton, 2006: 203).

The example is of a transcript of a short conversation in an infant classroom (Cummings, 1985) which contains the potential for several levels of analysis; several meanings can be deconstructed from this conversation, and some of them concern power. The analysis also raises the issue of reflexivity in the researcher.

This is a class of 27 5–6-year-old children, with the children (CC) seated on a carpet and the teacher (T) seated on a chair. A new set of class books has arrived for the children's free use. After a few days the teacher feels that the class and the teacher should look at them together.

1	T	Right. Let's have a look at this book – 'cause these are – smashing books. Are you enjoying them?
2	CC	Yes// Yes// Yes.
3	T	What's it called this one? Can anyone tell me?
4	CC	Splosh//
5	C	//Splish//
6	CC	//Splosh//
7	T	Splosh not splish. It's got an 'o' in the middle. Splosh.
8	CC	Splish splosh//
9	C	//Splosh//
10	T	Splosh it says. (Reading) A dog, a pig, a cow, a bear, a monkey, a donkey, all in the –

11	T & CC	Air
12	T	((Showing pictures)) There's the dog and the pig and the cow and the bear and the monkey and the donkey all in the air. What are they in the air in?
13	CC	()//
14	T	//Put up your hand if you know. Vicky. ((Buzz of children trying to get in))
15	C	The cow's popped it.
16	Vicky	// A hot air balloon.
17	T	A hot air balloon.
18	C (as 15)	The cow's popped it.
19	T	What's the cow popped it with?
20	CC	Horn//horn//ear//horn//his horn.
21	T	His horn – it's not his ear is it – his ears//
22	CC	((Laughing))//
23	T	are down here. It's his horn that's sticking up.
24	CC	((Laughing))
25	T	What does this mean then? ((showing stylized drawings of air escaping))
26	C	Air's coming out//
27	C	//Air//
28	T	The air coming out of the balloon isn't it. Can you really see the air coming out of a balloon?
29	CC	No. No. No.
30	T	No – very often in cartoons it looks like that doesn't it.
31	C	I can see gas coming out of my mouth when I () on the windows.
32	T	When can you see it?
33	C	When it's steamed up.
34	T	Yes. And if//
35	C	//When it's cold.
36	T	When it's cold. When you hhh//
37	C	//When your breath – when your breath turns over and it steams on the – steams on the window.
38	T	Yes//
39	C	And it//
40	T	But only when it's –
41	CC	Cold.
42	T	Cold. Only when it's cold.

43	C	I saw a airship.
44	T	Did you. When? Where?
45	C	On the park.
46	T	Really.
47	CC	I have // I saw// Mrs. Cummings
48	T	Shh – Yes, Luke.
49	Luke	When we – when the airship was aft – when it was finished and the Pope was on we took the telly outside – and – we took the telly outside – and – and we saw – we saw the good old airship.
50	T	Did you.
51	Luke	An air balloon as well.
52	T	It's not good old airship – it's Goodyear – the Goodyear airship.
53	CC	Good year // Mrs. Cummmings
54	T	Good year. Yes.
55	C	I seed the airship. ((Many children talking at once))
56	T	Just a moment because I can't hear Luke because other people are chattering. You'll have your turn in a minute.
57	Luke	I said Mummy, what's that thing with the 'X' on the back and she didn't answer me but when I () it off () an air balloon.
58	T	Yes. It was an airship. Yes. Actually I think we saw it at school one day last summer, didn't we.
59	CC	Yes.
60	T	We all went outside and had a look at it. It was going through the sky.
61	CC	()//
62	Luke	Mrs Cummings //
63	C	()
64	T	Uuhm – Ben
65	Ben	I remember that time when it came () over the school.
66	T	Did you. Y-//
67	Ben	//() the same one came over my house when I went home.
68	T	Yes. Paul.
69	Paul	I went to a airship where they did //
70	Luke	//It flew over my house ()//
71	T	//Just a moment Paul because Luke is now interrupting. We listened to him very carefully. Now it's his turn to listen to us.
72	Paul	I went to see a airship where they take off and when I – when I got there I saw () going around.
73	T	Oh … What keeps an airship up in the air?
74	CC	Air//air//gas//

75	Luke	Mrs Cummings.
76	T	Air or gas. Yes. If it's air, it's got to be hot air to keep it up – or gas. Now put your hands down for a minute and we'll have a look at the rest of the book. ((Reading)) Help said Pig. There he is saying help. ((There is a cartoon-like 'bubble' from his mouth with 'help' written in)) Help said –
77	CC	Monkey
78	T	Help said donkey. It's gone wonky.
79	CC	h-h-h ((untranscribable talk from several children))
80	T	Look as though it had gone wonky once before. What makes me say that?
81	C	Because – because there's – something on the balloon.
82	T	Mmm. There's already a patch on it isn't there to cover a hole ((reading)) A bear, a cow, a pig, a dog, a donkey and a monkey all – in – a – and this is the word you got wrong before – all in a –
83	C	Bog
84	T	Bog – Who said it said dog at the end and it shouldn't?
85	James	Me.
86	T	James! James, what does it start with?
87	James	'b' for 'bog'.
88	T	'b'. It only goes to show how important it is to get them the right way round//
89	C	//Toilet//
90	T	No. I don't think it means toilet.
91	CC	((Laughter))
92	T	I don't think they're in a toilet.
93	CC	((Laughter))
94	T	What's a bog when it isn't a toilet?
95	Gavin	My brother call it the bog.
96	T	Yes. Lots of people do – call a toilet a bog but I don't think that's what this means.
97	Paul	(fall in) something when – when it sticks to you.
98	T	Yes, you're quite right Paul. It's somewhere that's very sticky. If you fall in its very sticky //
99	C	()
100	T	It's not glue.
101	C	It's called a swamp.
102	T	Swamp is another word for it, good boy – but it's not glue, it's usually mud or somewhere. It's usually somewhere – somewhere in the countryside that's very wet. ((Many children talking))
103	C	Mrs. Cummings what ()
104	T	Just a moment you are forgetting to listen. You are remembering to think and to talk but you're forgetting to listen and take your turn. Now Olga.
105	Olga	Once my daddy –

Let us explore the levels of analysis here. If we ask 'what is being learned here by the children?' there are several kinds of response. At a formal level, first, there is a *curricular* response: the children are learning a little bit of language (reading, speaking, listening, vocabulary, spelling, letter orientation (e.g. 'bog' and 'dog')), science (condensation, hot and cold, hot air rising, hot air and gas-filled balloons) and soil (a muddy swamp). That concerns the academic curriculum, as it were.

However, at a second level the children are learning other aspects of development, not just academic but personal, social, emotional and interpersonal, for example turn-taking, cooperation, shared enjoyment, listening to each other, contributing to a collective activity, taking risks with language (the risqué joke about the word 'bog' with its double-entendre of a swamp and an impolite term for a toilet).

At a third level one can notice language rights in the classroom. Here the text usefully provides numbered lines to assist analysis and to preserve the chronology of events. One can observe the following, using a closer textual analysis:

- A great deal of the conversation follows the sequence of teacher → student → teacher → student and so on (e.g. lines 28–48).
- It is rare for the sequence to be broken, for instance teacher→student→student (e.g. lines 3–7 and 14–16).
- Where the sequence is broken, it is at the teacher's behest, and with individual children only (lines 48–52, 64–9, 84–8, 94–8).
- Where the conventional sequence is broken without the teacher's blessing the teacher intervenes to restore the sequence or to control the proceedings (lines 54–6, 70–1, 103–4).
- It appears that many of the 27 children are not joining in very much – the teacher only talks directly to, or encourages to talk, a few named children individually: Vicky, Luke, Ben, Paul, James and Olga.
- There are almost no instances of children *initiating* conversations (e.g. lines 43, 65, 101); most of the conversations are in *response* to the teacher's initiation (e.g. lines 3, 11, 20, 25, 28, 32, 34, 36, etc.).
- The teacher only follows up on a child's initiation when it suits her purposes (lines 43–6).
- Nearly everything goes through, or comes from the teacher who mediates everything.
- Where a child says something that the teacher likes or is in the teacher's agenda for the lesson then that child is praised (e.g. lines 34, 42, 54, 58, 76 and 96, 98 (the word 'yes'), 102) and the teacher repeats the child's correct answer (e.g. lines 16–17, 20–1, 29–30, 35–6, 41–2).
- The teacher feeds the children with clues as to the expected answer (lines 10–11, 40–1, 76–7, 82–3).
- Where the conversation risks being out of the teacher's control the teacher becomes much more explicit in the classroom rules (e.g. lines 56, 71, 104).
- When the teacher decides that it is time to move on to get through her agenda she closes off further discussion and moves on (line 76).
- The teacher is prepared to share a joke (lines 90–3) to maintain a good relationship but then moves the conversation on (line 94).
- Most of the conversation, in speech act terms, is perlocutionary (achieving the teacher's intended aim of the lesson) rather than illocutionary (an open-ended and free-range, multi-directional discussion where the outcome is unpredictable).
- The teacher talks a lot more than the children.

At a fourth level, employing speech act theory we can see how some utterances in the conversation are intended not only to involve the children but thereby to control them. Lines 76, 82 and 102 show the teacher taking charge of the conversation by talking a lot – it has the effect of keeping the children quiet and of reining in the children's talk: a perlocutionary speech act that reasserts classroom control through talk (and it is noticeable that this is later in the conversation rather than earlier, as the children may be starting to become restless). Then, in line 104, when that strategy has not worked so effectively the teacher takes a more overt control strategy and tells the children to listen and take turns.

At a fifth level, one can begin to theorize from the materials here. It could be argued, for example, that the text discloses the overt and covert operations of power, to suggest, in fact, that what the children are learning very effectively is the hidden curriculum in which power is a major feature, for instance:

- The teacher has the power to decide who will talk, when they will talk, what they will talk about and how well they have talked (cf. Edwards, 1980).
- The teacher has the power to control a mass of children (27 children sitting on the floor whilst she, the teacher, sits on a chair, i.e. physically above them).
- The teacher controls and disciplines *through* her control of the conversation and its flow, and, when this does not work (e.g. lines 56, 71, 104) then her control and power become more overt and naked. What we have here is an example of Bernstein's (1975) 'invisible pedagogy', e.g. where the control

of the teacher over the child is implicit rather than explicit; where, ideally, the teacher arranges the *context* which the children are expected to rearrange and explore; where there is a reduced emphasis upon the transmission and acquisition of specific skills.

- What we have here is a clear example of the importance of the children learning the hidden curriculum of classrooms (Jackson, 1968), wherein they have to learn how to cope with power and authority, praise, denial, delay, membership of a crowd, loss of individuality, rules, routines and socially acceptable behaviour. As Jackson says, if children are to do well in school then it is equally, if not more important, that they learn, and abide by, the hidden curriculum rather than the formal curriculum.

- What we have here is also an example of Giddens's (1976, 1984) structuration theory, wherein the conversation in the classroom is the cause, the medium and the outcome of the perpetuation of the status quo of power asymmetries and differentials in the classroom, reinforcing the teacher's control, power and authority.

- The teacher has been placed in a difficult position by being the sole adult with 27 children, and so her behaviour, motivated perhaps benevolently, is, in fact, a coping or survival strategy to handle and manage the discipline with large numbers of young and demanding children – crowd control.

- The children are learning to be compliant and that their role is to obey, and that if they are obedient to a given agenda then they will be rewarded.

- The 'core variable' (in terms of grounded theory') is power: the teacher is acting to promote and sustain her power; when it can be asserted and reinforced through an invisible pedagogy then it is covert; when this does not work it becomes overt.

Now, one has to ask whether, at the fourth level, the researcher is reading too much into the text, over-interpreting it, driven by her own personal hang-ups or negative experiences of power and authority, and over-concerned with the issue of discipline, projecting too much of herself onto the data interpretation. Maybe the teacher is simply teaching the children socially acceptable behaviour and moving the conversation on productively, exercising her professional task sensitively and skilfully, building in the children's contributions, and her behaviour has actually nothing to do with power. Further, one can observe at level four that several theories are being promulgated to try to explain the messages in the text, and one has to observe the fertility of a simple piece of transcription to support several grounded or pre-ordinate/pre-existing theories. The dif-ficult question here is 'which interpretation is correct?'. Here there is no single answer; they are all perhaps correct.

The classroom transcription only records what is said. People will deliberately withhold information; some children will give way to more vocal children, and others may be off task. What we have here is only one medium that has been recorded. Even though the transcription tries to note a few other features (e.g. children talking simultaneously), it does not catch all the events in the classroom. How do we know, for example, whether most children are bored, or if some are asleep, or some are fighting, or some are reading another book and so on? All we have here is a selection from what is taking place, and the selection is made on what is transcribable.

One can see in this example that the text is multilay-ered. At issue here are the levels of analysis that are required, or legitimate, and how analysis is intermin-gled with interpretation. In qualitative research, ana-lysis and interpretation frequently merge. This raises the issues of validity and reliability. What we have here is a problem of the 'double hermeneutic' – as research-ers we are members of the world that we are research-ing, so we cannot be neutral; we live in an already-interpreted world. More extensively Morrison (2003) suggests that the problem extends beyond this. Look at the example above:

- The teacher and the children act on the basis of their interpretations of the situation (their 'definitions of the situation').

- The lived actions are converted from one medium (observations, actions and live events) to another (written) by choosing to opt only for transcription – an interpretation of their interpretation.

- The researcher then interprets the written data (a third hermeneutic) and writes an unavoidably selec-tive account (a fourth – quadruple – hermeneutic – an interpretation of an interpretation of an interpretation of an interpretation!).

- The reader then brings his/her own biography and background to interpret the researcher's written interpretation (a fifth – quintuple – hermeneutic).

Given the successive interpretations it is difficult not to suggest that reliability and validity can easily be compromised in qualitative research. Reflexivity as the disclosure of one's possible biased interpretations does little to reduce them – I can state my possible biases and interpretations but that does not necessarily stop them from being selective and biased. This suggests, perhaps, the limits of reflexivity. In connection with increasing reliability and validity, reflexivity is not enough.

31.3 A narrative discourse

Discourse analysis looks for meanings and themes in texts. The second example of discourse analysis that follows, is of a narrative text that has been constructed from field notes into an 'omniscient, authorial voice' (Bruner, 2004: 702), a third-person, continuous narrative report. A narrative analysis reports personal experiences or observations and brings fresh insights to often familiar situations. It is strongly interpretivist, with meanings constructed through observations and language, indeed it is sometimes difficult to separate facts from observations, as many narratives can use data selectively and report them in non-neutral terms (as in the example that follows). As with other forms of discourse analysis, narrative analysis is rooted in a social constructivist paradigm in which behaviours and their meanings are socially situated and socially interpreted.

Though this example is taken from Goffman's (1968) *Asylums* (a study of a psychiatric hospital), nevertheless the 'asylums' – hospitals – bear many similarities to schools, particularly boarding schools, in being 'total institutions'. By taking a non-school example here, it is intended to 'make the familiar strange' (Blumer, 1969): to make the familiar world of schools 'strange' to the researcher (i.e. to see schools with a new eye) by comparing them to another similar but also different institution.

Goffman (1968: 17–19) writes that a total institution (e.g. a hospital, an army, a boarding school, a prison), is characterized by several features:

- The institution is convened for a specific purpose.
- All aspects of life take place in the same place and under the same single authority.
- Every part of the member's normal daily activities takes place in the company of many others.
- All members are treated the same and are required to do the same things together.
- The daily activities are precisely and tightly scheduled by a controlling authority and officials, and through formal rules that are tightly enforced.
- The several activities are part of a single, overall plan that is intended to fulfil the aims of the organization.
- There is a division between the managers and the managed (e.g. the inmates and the hospital staff; the teachers and the students).
- The inmates have limited or no contact with the outside world but the officials do have contact with the outside world.
- Access to the outside world for inmates may be physically or institutionally restricted, controlled or forbidden.
- There is some antagonism between the two groups, who hold hostile stereotypes of each other and act on the basis of those stereotypes, often based on inequalities of power.
- Officials tend to feel superior and powerful whilst inmates tend to feel inferior and powerless.
- The cultures and cultural worlds of the officials and the inmates are separate.
- The two worlds – of officials and inmates – have limited penetration of each other.
- There is a considerable social distance between the two groups.
- Inmates tend to be excluded from knowledge of decisions made about them.
- Incentives (for work, behaviour) and privileges have greater significance within the institution than they would in the outside world.
- There are limited and formal channels of communication between the members of the two worlds.
- Release from the institution is often part of the privilege system.

It can be seen that these features can apply to several different total institutions, of which schools are an example.

Goffman (1968: 220–5) presents a narrative account of his field notes on the psychiatric hospital, synthesized into a single text.

> In everyday life, legitimate possessions employed in primary adjustments are typically stored, when not in use, in special places of safekeeping which can be gotten to at will, such as foot-lockers, cabinets, bureau drawers, and safe-deposit boxes. These storage places protect the object from damage, misuse, and misappropriation, and allow the user to conceal what he possesses from others. (p. 220).

> (pp. 222–5) When patients entered Central Hospital, especially if they were excited or depressed on admission, they were denied a private, accessible place to store things. Their personal clothing, for example, might be stored in a room that was beyond their discretionary use. Their money was kept in the administration building, unobtainable without medial and/or their legal agents'; permission. Valuable or breakables, such as false teeth, eyeglasses, wrist watches, often an integral part of body image, might be locked up safely out of their owners' reach.

Official papers of self-identification might also be retained by the institution. Cosmetics, needed to present oneself properly to others, were collectivized, being made accessible to patients only at certain times. On convalescent wards, bed boxes were available, but since they were unlocked they were subject to theft from other patients and from staff, and in any case were often located in rooms locked to patients during the day.

If people were selfless, or were required to be selfless, there would of course be a logic to having no private storage places, as a British ex-mental patient suggests:

> I looked for a locker, but without success. There appeared to be none in this hospital; the reason soon [became] abundantly clear; they were quite unnecessary – we had nothing to keep in them – everything being shared, even the solitary face cloth which was used for a number of other purposes, a subject on which my feelings became very strong.

But all have some self. Given the curtailment implied by loss of places of safekeeping, it is understandable that patients in Central Hospital developed places of their own.

It seemed characteristic of hospital life that the most common form of stash was one that could be carried around on one's person wherever one went. One such device for female patients was a large handbag; a parallel technique for a man was a jacket with commodious pockets, worn even in the hottest weather. While these containers are quite usual ones in the wider community, there was a special burden placed upon them in the hospital: books, writing materials, washcloths, fruit, small valuables, scarves, playing cards, soap, shaving equipment (on the part of men), containers of salt, pepper, and sugar, bottles of milk – these were some of the objects sometimes carried in this manner. So common was this practice that one of the most reliable symbols of patient status in the hospital was bulging pockets. Another portable storage device was a shopping bag lined with another shopping bag. (When partly full, this frequently employed stash also served as a cushion and back rest.) Among men, a small stash was sometimes created out of a long sock: by knotting the open end and twisting this end around a belt, the patient could let a kind of moneybag inconspicuously hang down inside his trouser leg. Individual variations of these portable containers were also found. One young engineering graduate fash-

ioned a purse out of discarded oilcloth, the purse being stitched in separate, well-measured compartments for comb, toothbrush, cards, writing paper, pencil, soap, small face cloth, toilet paper – the whole attached by a concealed clip to the underside of his belt. The same patient had also sewn an extra pocket on the inside of his jacket to carry a book. Another male patient, an avid newspaper reader, invariably wore a suit jacket, apparently to conceal his newspapers, which he carried folded over his belt. Still another made effective use of a cleaned-out tobacco pouch for transporting food; whole fruit, unpeeled, could easily be put in one's pocket to be taken back to the ward from the cafeteria, but cooked meat was better being carried in a grease-proof stash.

I would like to repeat that there were some good reasons for these bulky carryings-on. Many of the amenities of life, such as soap, toilet paper, or cards, which are ordinarily available in many depots of comfort in civil society, are thus not available to patients, so that the day's needs had to be partly provided for at the beginning of the day.

Fixed stashes, as well as portable ones, were employed, too; they were most often found in free places and territories. Some patients attempted to keep their valuables under their mattresses but, as previously suggested, the general hospital rule making dormitories off-limits during the day reduced the usefulness of this device. The half-concealed lips of window sills were sometimes used. Patients with private rooms and friendly relations with the attendant used their rooms as stashes. Female patients sometimes hid matches and cigarettes in the compacts they left in their rooms. And a favourite exemplary tale in the hospital was of an old man who was claimed to have hidden his money, $1,200 in a cigar box in a tree on the hospital grounds.

It would be plain that some assignments also provided stashes. Some of the patients who worked in the laundry availed themselves of the individual lockers officially allocated only to non-patient workers. The patients who worked in the kitchen of the recreation building used the cupboards and the refrigerator as places in which to lock up the food and drink they saved from the various socials, and other indulgences they had managed to acquire.

(Goffman, 1968: 220–5)

The narrative account tells a story, quite a gripping, disturbing story in much more graphic detail than would be possible through the often decontextualized world of extracted, codified and reassembled data; the narrative makes the most of the virtues of a story: an account that 'catches fire' through the language used, that persuades, that is human, that is rich in detail and that tells a story. What is that story?

At first sight the patients' behaviour may seem very odd, they seem fixated on minute matters, they dress bizarrely, their clothing bulges with a range of objects that normal people would not carry around, they are obsessive about hoarding, they trust nobody and what they take so many pains to carry around is almost worthless. They might be rightly accused of not being in their right mind, and therefore that they are rightly incarcerated in the secure hospital so that they are no danger to themselves and to others. That is one version, one discourse.

However, when one looks at the constructed narrative in detail, an alternative explanation can be offered, an alternative discourse is at work. Here one can see why their behaviour is as it is. For example, if we look at the descriptions of what the patients were experiencing we can observe:

- their personal clothing was available at the discretion of the staff;
- valuables were kept locked away from the patients;
- self-identification papers were held by the institution;
- cosmetics were made available only at certain times;
- everyday amenities of life in civil society were not available to the patients;
- bed boxes were kept unlocked;
- everything was shared;
- there were no free places;
- private spaces (dormitories) were off-limits during the day;
- individual lockers were for non-patients.

What we see in both an actual and metaphorical sense is the stripping away of identity, personality, individuality, privacy, power, freedom, autonomy, humanity and decision making, and all by those with power over the inmates. Goffman (1968) terms this the processes of *depersonalization* and *mortification*. Nothing personal is left to the patients; nothing is private, nothing is safe.

If we look at the vocabulary that Goffman has used in connection with the patients, we see very many terms about these same points: 'stash', 'possessions', 'protect', 'conceal', 'stored', 'storage', 'safekeeping', 'valuables', 'hidden', 'hid', 'half-concealed', 'lock up', 'containers', 'saved'. They have actual and metaphorical meaning: at both an actual and metaphorical level

the patients are trying to retain their lost personalities, identities, rights, autonomy and freedoms, even their sanity. It is little wonder, then, that metaphors of storage, protection, privacy, keeping things safe and containment become realized in practice. Indeed it could be argued that, far from being disturbed or out of their minds, the patients were behaving very sanely and sensibly in an insane or disturbing situation. How often do we find the same situation in schools, where students behave very sensibly in the face of extreme or unacceptable behaviour by teachers (but often the blame is placed on 'disruptive' students who dare to disrupt the disruptively power-and-control oriented, boring and dominatory behaviour of teachers)? Sanity and madness are, to some degree perhaps, a social construct rather than an objective reality.

Descriptive data in this narrative form enable the researcher to understand the situation vividly from the perspective of the participants – their 'definition of the situation'. The hospital staff might have put a very different interpretation on their own behaviour, arguing that they were removing sources of distress and danger from the patients, and caring for them very extensively. That may be true also; reality is multifaceted. Through an analysis of the narrative, the descriptive data help the researcher to explain why situations are the way that they are. In fact one could argue that the patients are behaving very rationally and reasonably in an unreasonable, power-stripping and depersonalizing situation, even though their behaviour at first might seem strange.

The extract is powerfully written; the structured silence on the less antagonistic or depersonalizing behaviour of the staff and the regime is presented highly selectively, if at all, but the force of the narrative is the stronger for this. The well-chosen examples of the hiding of even everyday objects are given extraordinary semiological, symbolic power in indicating how power reaches right to the heart of commonplace, almost taken-for-granted matters. The narrative is a well-worked example of how the taken-for-granted, everyday world and its artefacts can have extraordinary meaning in certain contexts. When these everyday objects are used to make grotesque shapes in the clothing of the patients, rendering them instantly recognizable as patients by their freakish garb, the contrastive power of this juxtaposition is startling. Whilst this is not the place to go into semiotics, narrative analysis can use semiotic analysis – the interpretation of signs and symbols as signifiers of meaning – as one of its strategies.

In examining the narrative, the researcher can look for what is happening, what are the main features that are being reported, why the behaviours were as they were (and on what basis of evidence the researcher is making that judgement), what other inferences and explanations might be made of the data provided, and what other data might be needed to support or refute the inferences and explanations given.

31.4 Autobiography

Bruner (2004) argues that we regard 'lived time' as a narrative (p. 692), a story that has meaning for us and which shapes our lives (as he remarks: 'we become the autobiographical narratives by which we "tell about" our lives' (p. 694); our own stories direct our future lives (p. 708)). As Eisner (1997: 6) puts it: 'first, we tell stories. Stories have particular features. Stories instruct, they reveal, they inform in special ways.' Or, as Sartre (1964: 39) writes: 'a man [sic] is surrounded by his own stories and those of others, and he sees everything that happens to him in terms of these stories and he tries to live his life as if he were recounting it'. Indeed Plummer (1995; 2001) argues that an essential feature of being human is our creation of stories to ourselves and others, and that these are essential features of research enquiry.

An autobiography is, as Bruner (2004: 693) writes, 'a privileged but troubled narrative because it is both subjective and objective, reflective and reflexive, and in which the narrator is also the central figure'. Given this, an autobiographical narrative, for all it is multilayered and selective, can be deconstructed at many levels: personal, cultural, interpersonal, ideological, linguistic and so on. It has facts, themes, actors, a sequence, agency, coherence, situatedness and a sense of audience, all of which are elements of a true discourse as set out at the start of this chapter.

In the example that follows, the fictitious autobiography tells a personal story in a highly selective and authentic way. Imagine that the researcher had asked the teacher to write a brief autobiography of his experiences as a teacher; what we have here is the teacher's own views, and this indicates the significance that the writer gives to the events selected.

I had always wanted to teach music to secondary school students. I had played in a school band when I was at secondary school, and had taken piano lessons for ten years, and had passed all the Grades, and I thought that it would be really good to teach. I thought it would be good for students to be exposed to the great classics, or modern music, and I thought that it would be even better if I could teach them how to read, write and compose music. I thought

that this would be particularly interesting for downtown kids who had not had access to such music, so I was keen to work in an inner city school.

I had been working in business for 25 years, ten years with a printing company and then 15 years in a commercial company selling paper products. But I felt dissatisfied with my life, so I decided to do what I had always wanted to do, which was to train to be a secondary school music teacher. So I discussed it with my family and gave up my job to take a teacher training course. I was very keen and worked hard on my studies.

I was very happy when the course began; we were introduced into all sorts of ways in which students could learn to write, read and play music, how they could work in pairs and groups to devise musical compositions, how to read non-standard musical scores, how to use the electronic instruments that had not been around when I was at school, and how to teach students to appreciate all different kinds and genres of music.

I passed my course and went to a downtown school. What a total let down! The students didn't care about music – they saw it as a waste of time and boring. They thought that the music syllabus was old fashioned, that it did not represent the music that they were interested in. All they wanted to do was to play their own downloads of the latest music releases and albums from the ridiculous groups and so called 'artists' which they had seen gyrating sexily on the television, to the whole class. When I tried to change the activities, so that they were playing musical instruments and composing their own music, they either just made a whole lot of noise with them, and the din was awful, or they thought that the instruments and the activity were just babyish, so they did nothing except fooling around in the class. Everything that I had been taught about discipline in my teacher training didn't work. At first I thought that it was that my class control wasn't very good, so I asked my mentor how to improve this, but it did not help – the students just sat and laughed, shouted, or refused to do anything.

So I tried a different approach – I told them that they had to learn several musical 'facts' such as information about the lives of composers and the names of pieces of music of certain composers. In fact this wasn't so much a music lesson as a reading lesson. I told them that I was going to give them a test on this, and that those who didn't score highly enough on the test would be punished. I thought that by making the lesson more like a 'high status' area of the curriculum, and coupled this with a test, it would make the students take this more seriously, but it didn't. All they said was that they didn't care, that music was a waste of time, and that it wouldn't help them to get a job. I felt very frustrated.

It didn't get better and I was worn out, stressed, and felt as if I were in a job that was completely unrewarding. So, in the end I looked for job in a private secondary all-boys boarding school, thinking that at least the students would be more motivated and well behaved. I was hopeful and felt good. I got a job in a small private secondary school where the students had to learn a music instrument at school, as well as taking class music lessons. I hoped that this would be the answer, and that I would be happy again and able to teach 'real' music.

However, I quickly found out that this wasn't the solution. Whilst some of the students were motivated and very nice indeed, some of them were arrogant and treated me as a hired servant whom they could control by threatening to report me to the Senior Teacher if I raised my voice to them or set them too much work to do. I felt insulted.

I didn't like their attitude to me or to the subject – I had been told to follow a more traditional curriculum, and I was very happy to do this, but I found that the students thought that the music lessons were 'beneath their dignity', trivial, and 'tame' compared to the other subjects on the curriculum. In turn, at first I thought that they were just upper class 'Sloane Rangers' [a young, fashionable, upper-class or would-be upper class person who has a superior attitude and self-confident manner, who is wealthy, privately educated, privileged, brash, indulgent, with an expensive lifestyle and high living, a love of country sports, and even a shared way of speaking], and I humoured them, but, the longer it went on the more it irritated me, as I felt that they were looking down on me and on the music lessons.

In fact they weren't all like that, and some of them were from poor, middle class and working class homes, whose parents wanted to give their children the chances that had not been available to them, and some students had been thrown out of other schools and had been put into this school by anxious and overwrought parents or by parents who were at their wits end in trying to cope with their badly behaved child. These students continued to be badly behaved, but I was told to 'put up with it', as they brought in a lot of money to the school.

I couldn't take it. One day I exploded with them. I insulted them very strongly, called them all upper class idiots, called the others 'layabouts', shouted that they should treat teachers with a shred of decency, and basically 'lost it'. The class laughed loud and long – they had won. I left the class and walked out of the job.

I feel very dispirited and let down. I feel as though I have a lot to offer to teaching, but there's no way I can offer it under the present system, so I'm getting out. I'm going back to find another job in business and maybe I'll do some part-time music tuition and give piano lessons in the evenings, with motivated kids and in a situation that is under my control, and where my students will learn something other than how to behave badly.

The autobiography has several *themes* (and themes or *leitmotivs* are a feature of narratives): optimism turning to resentment turning to disillusionment; positive to negative; empowerment turning to disempowerment; dreams turning to dust; power shifts (from the writer to the students); achievement and loss; aspiration turning to deterministic frustration; ignorance turning to knowledge; power turning to loss of control; false expectations to growing realism; and so on.

Further, we can observe that the narrative employs a chronological, linear sequence which is interrupted only very occasionally to break off into reflection or comment. The writer has chosen to focus on critical events and decisive moments, all of which are autonomously chosen and life-changing. This is an existential, journey in which agentic choice struggles to realize itself as planned and which, in the end, leads to resignation in several senses.

If we examine the text we can observe the overwhelming preponderance of the active rather than the passive voice – here is a writer who is existentially alert. We can note the absence of metaphor, the emphasis on the 'facts' of the events, and a 'no nonsense' approach to getting on with life (albeit selectively chosen and interpreted) rather than reflections, indeed it is only towards the end of the extract that we can detect a sense of deeper reflection in the writer – that the writer has learned from experience and the reflection on that experience, and has gained a truer knowledge of the 'real' rather than the perceived or desired situation.

We can note the presence of many stative verbs, phrases and their accompanying adjectives to indicate feelings: 'I thought it would be good'; 'I thought it would be even better'; 'I felt dissatisfied'; 'I was very keen'; 'I felt very frustrated'; 'I was in a job that was completely unrewarding'; 'I was hopeful and felt good'; 'I didn't like'; 'I felt insulted'; 'I felt that they were looking down on me'; 'I feel very dispirited and let down.' Here is a writer who is seeking authenticity, self-realization, emotional fulfilment, who is concerned with feelings.

One interpretation of the texts is that it reveals a writer who seeks control and the realization of a personal agenda for happiness; when this is challenged, he finds it hard to come to terms with the situation, to accept it or to accommodate to it. Points of conflict chart the movement in the text from 'me' to 'them', from the writer's agenda to the student. The word 'I' is used 54 times in the extract, whereas the word 'them' occurs only 15 times. Indeed one can suggest that using the contrast of 'I' and 'them' can denote a perhaps antagonistic stance of the writer, a significant divide between the teacher and the student, a power struggle for control of the agenda. Indeed the word 'them' occurs more frequently whenever things are going wrong for the writer.

We can see a distinctly sympathetic choice of prose, in which the writer's own situation is presented sympathetically and in which the report on the students is almost entirely negative: they are the ones who 'let down' the writer, who 'didn't care' about music, who only wanted to play 'music from the ridiculous groups and so called "artists" which they had seen gyrating sexily on the television', who 'did nothing except fooling around', who 'just made a whole lot of noise' and 'just sat and laughed' or who were 'just upper class Sloane Rangers' (note the use of the word 'just' – a negative term here), who didn't take the lesson seriously, and so on. The pejorative tone of the writer – sympathetic to one party and highly unsympathetic to the others – constitutes a very one-sided text. Indeed, as Riessman (1993) remarks, silence – what is not spoken or included, what is left out – is as important as what is said or included. The question is whether this is a problem, as the text is authentic, strong in reality and revealing of the intense emotions at play in the situation; that surely catches the 'quality' of the situation so prized by qualitative research.

There are a few tell-tale verbs: the early part of the text includes positive, hopeful verbs such as 'wanted', 'worked hard', 'passed', whereas by the final paragraph we have the dramatic verbs 'getting out', 'going back' (the use of 'back' is perhaps a sign of defeat and a retrograde step).

Do we have sympathy with the writer? Do we think that the writer is a 'control freak' who deserves to come to the kind of self-knowledge that becomes clear by the end of the extract? Did the writer simply receive his just desserts or were the outcomes undeserved and a pity? Did the writer deserve what happened? Has the writer really taken any account of the students? Do we think that the writer has been treated badly by the students? Is the writer controlled, weak, strong, too strong, too controlling a person?

This is one reading of the text. But a discourse permits many interpretations. The interpretation above has operated at the level of the personal perspective of the writer, and has suggested that issues of power, control and self-realization feature strongly in the text. An alternative reading is that this is an accurate and authentic account of a horrible situation in which a decent, hard-working and committed person is treated very badly by two groups of distasteful students. Another reading could focus on the quality and contents of teacher training and false aspirations that the teacher training might have led the writer to hold. Another reading might be of the text as an insight into the problems of teaching, e.g. indicating that teachers face huge problems of stress, disruptive behaviour and appalling treatment by students, that these constitute a major reason for the flight out of teaching and problems of teacher recruitment and retention, and that there are insufficient support systems for teachers in school. Another reading might be that of social class in education, and the perpetuation of deep-seated class structures through the provision and uptake of different kinds of schooling, curricula and education. We bring our own agenda to the reading and deconstruction of texts. Texts are multilayered.

And who is the writer? Is the writer male, female, young, old, single, in a relationship, living with parents or living alone, able-bodied or disabled, easy-going, temperamental, outgoing, introverted, sociable or antisocial, politically left-wing or right-wing, working class or middle class, and with what views on education and music, and so on? We don't know. Perhaps if we had known some of these details our reading of the text would have been different.

31.5 Conclusion

This chapter has introduced alternatives to coding and the collation of segmented data in qualitative data analysis. It has suggested that the holism of complete texts can constitute discourses, and that variants of discourse analysis have to recognize that discourses and texts are multilayered and open to a range of interpretations and deconstructions. The chapter has given three different examples of these, selected not only for their content but also for their exemplification of three main kinds of discourse: a conversation, a narrative text and an autobiographical extract. Discourse analysis has been seen to have many meanings, included in which is the recurrent theme of power and its operations (Foucault, 1998; Fraser, 2004). Whilst discourses have the attraction of *emic* research, authenticity and rich language, the researcher has to be mindful not only of the effects of this on the reader, but of the reader's own effects on the text. As Riessman (1993: 70) explains, how a person relates his or her story 'shapes how we can legitimately interpret it'. The chapter has indicated that analysis of narrative, discourse-based data has to attend to the fine-grained details of texts (Potter and Wetherell, 1994: 58), together with situating these in the social context and milieu in which they are set (e.g. Clifton, 2006). In combining different narratives, patterns, themes, similarities, commonalities and differences can be noted (Fraser, 2004), not only in content, but in terms of tone, style, register, genre, vocabulary, audience, settings, contexts, metaphors and intentions. Given this, there is no single privileged, definitive way of analysing discourse nor of the meanings that surface from it.

 Companion Website

The companion website to the book includes PowerPoint slides for this chapter, which list the structure of the chapter and then provide a summary of the key points in each of its sections. This resource can be found online at **www.routledge.com/textbooks/cohen7e**.

Analysing visual media CHAPTER 32

This chapter provides researchers with an introduction to key issues in analysing different kinds of visual image, including still and moving images, and artefacts. It uses tools of analysis that have been introduced in previous chapters, such as content analysis, discourse analysis, and it provides an entrée into the next chapter on grounded theory. With reference to analysing visual data, the chapter introduces:

- content analysis
- discourse analysis
- grounded theory
- interpreting images
- interpreting an image: an example
- analysing moving images

We provide an extended worked example of an analysis, of a photograph, to clarify key issues in this kind of analysis.

32.1 Introduction

Chapter 31 introduced discourse analysis. Visual media are a form of text or discourse. Hence they are susceptible to some of the same kinds of analytical tools that are available to quantitative and qualitative data analysts, including, for example: content analysis (both numerical and qualitative), discourse analysis and grounded theory. We address these below. Further, some computer software (e.g. NVivo, ATLAS.ti) works with visual data as well as textual data.

32.2 Content analysis

We can analyse visual images in a similar way to that of analysing texts, e.g. through 'reading' the meanings, through disclosing our own views, perspectives, backgrounds and values (reflexivity). Here content analysis – purportedly an 'objective' form of analysis – can be performed in ways similar to those in qualitative and, indeed, quantitative data analysis. A possible sequence is set out below:

- start with research questions that determine which images (sampling) will be used in the analysis;
- retrieve the appropriate images;
- devise a coding system and codes (which must be mutually exclusive, exhaustive and enlightening (Rose, 2007: 65));
- code the images according to the codes;
- count codes and their frequencies;
- reflect on what the coding and the frequencies have indicated.

A celebrated example of this approach is from Lutz and Collins (1993), who examined some 600 visual images in the magazine *National Geographic*. They devised 22 predetermined codes to analyse the photographs (e.g. smiling, gender of adults, group size, skin colour, activity, surroundings of people, wealth indicators, etc.). Codes were used in relation to each other as well as 'stand alone'. From their analysis they concluded that Westerners defined non-Westerners in terms that made them very different from Westerners and 'as everything that the West is not' (Rose, 2007: 67) (akin to Edward Said's (1978) notion of the 'other'), as 'natural', less advanced technologically, more attuned to their environment, more spiritual, more exotic and, indeed, naked. The photographs avoided negative imagery (e.g. of poverty, wars, starvation, conflict, illness, physical deformity); in short a sanitized, non-disturbing, non-upsetting, and, of course, unreal view of non-Westerners was portrayed. Issues of power, of dissatisfaction were simply excluded; a structured silence that acted ideologically to reproduce the status quo of inequality within and across countries.

Content analysis, as its name suggests, is more concerned with the contents of the image rather than the production or 'audiencing' of the image (Rose, 2007: 61); hence it may not be able to comment on the cultural significance of the images made or caught.

In content analysis of texts, the whole is more than the sum of the parts, and this is particularly so in visual data, as the effect of the whole and the combination of parts can be greater than each item of composition. As part of content analysis, coding risks losing this wholeness, as it is atomistic and fragmentizing. Rose (2007: 72) argues that content analysis: (a) does not discriminate between weaker and stronger instances of the code; (b) loses important interconnections between elements of an image. Further, codes miss the mood that an image might be trying to create. Indeed she argues that, fundamentally, they overlook the important point that different people view images in different ways and with different interpretations. Whilst content analysis, conducted through coding, lends itself to the scientifically approved maxim of replicability, this may miss important features of the researcher working with visual data.

In summary, then, content analysis risks overlooking any ideology-critical way of viewing an image; it builds out such an approach, and yet ideology critique is an important element of deconstructing a visual image. Ideology, defined as the views of the ruling, dominant groups who succeed – by force or by consent (hegemony) – in having their views and values 'count' or seen as legitimate, is all powerfully pervasive, and the views and values of others are relegated or discredited, i.e. ideology serves to reproduce social inequalities in society and to have those social inequalities played out in the everyday lives of participants. Ideology is 'lived experience', legitimating the power of the powerful at the expense of the powerless. Ideology critique is a powerful way of looking at visual data, exposing illegitimate operations and functions of power, and how these are produced and reproduced through images, how images legitimize social inequality. This takes place, for example, in the selection, focus, exclusion, inclusion and interpretation of images and their contents. This is evidenced in semiological studies (studies of signs – signifiers – and the meaning given to that which they signify – the signified – for the viewer of the image), how meaning is encoded in the image and decoded by the viewer. In this context it is interesting for researchers to look at school prospectuses and websites; for example look at the images on the front page of school websites (e.g. Eton College: www.etoncollege.com/ and Winchester College: www.winchestercollege.co.uk/, both of them private schools for the privileged) to see the images of the school that are selected, given or received by the school and the viewer, to see what the images denote or connote.

Content analysis is a useful way of examining images, then, but its limitations have to be recognized. That is not to say that the outcomes of content analysis cannot be subject to ideology critique (indeed the study by Lutz and Collins (1993) is an example of this).

32.3 Discourse analysis

Visual images can also be read as discourses, and here the discussion of discourse analysis in Chapter 31 can apply very strongly, as images can be 'read' for the meanings that they convey to, or elicit from, the viewer. A discourse, as Rose (2007: 142) remarks, is a group of statements which structure how we think about things and how we act on the basis of those thoughts. As Chapter 31 makes clear, discourses structure and define what is valuable knowledge, how to know and how to think, and this is linked to Foucault's (1998) view that discourse is an instrument and an effect of power. Discourses, like ideology, are saturated by power; hence in understanding images we have to engage in an analysis, and critique, of power, how it operates and with what effects (a worked example of this is presented below in an analysis of a photograph).

Discourse, as Rose (2007: 146) remarks, operates in several spheres, be they individual (the viewer or the producer of the image) or institutional (the items that galleries, museums, etc. hold, display and how they present them): 'the social production and the effects of discourses' (p. 147). We can 'read' images for their symbolism, their messages and their iconography. This may involve trying to set on one side our own interpretations or views, and endeavouring to see the image as it might have been intended by the producer of the image, to look at the image anew, to review and review again the image iteratively and reiteratively, as Rose (2007: 157) remarks, to immerse ourselves in the image.

One can review the image on the basis of the structured approach of content analysis, or to discover key themes or features, or to identify interesting features or messages, or to look for contradictions, discontinuities or complex issues in the image, or to look at what the image has omitted (deliberately or not), i.e. to consider silences and absences as well as the items that have been included. In conducting this kind of discourse analysis, as with the conversational analysis in Chapter 31, there is a high level of detail in the focus and the analysis. Further, one can consider the purpose of the image in terms of its effects on the audience – intended audience or unintended audience, intended effects or unintended effects. This engages consideration of the production of the image as well as the audience of the image.

As discourse analysis and the interpretation of images involve a large element of subjectivity as intrinsic to the activity, it is incumbent on the researcher to be highly reflexive in the account given, indeed to regard his or her own interpretation as itself a discourse.

Not only is discourse analysis conducted at the level of the individual image, but at the level of the institution which holds the image, e.g. the gallery, the museum, the newspaper, the film archive, the school, the broadcasting network. Rose (2007: 175) particularly cites this in her examples of photographs, where the use of the image may be giving messages about the institution and its values and, indeed, the intended message behind the institution's selection and use of the image, not least because institutions are sites of the operations of power (a central feature of discourses) in deciding what visual images to display or to give, together with considerations of to whom, how and where to display the images. Were the images commissioned, bought, donated, acquired and from whom – families, philanthropists, other institutions, and how and why, and so on? How did they change hands? Here we can consider the near instantaneous transfer of digital images in contrast to the protracted transfer of many valuable oil paintings. Indeed images have their own social lives and biographies (for a clear example of this see the 1998 film *The Red Violin*). What labels and captions accompany the image (e.g. the painting, the photograph), and what does it say about the priorities that the institution gives to the image? How are images stored, labelled, catalogued, archived and indexed? What are the visitor rules that have to be obeyed in the viewing institution (e.g. no touching, no approaching the image too close, no eating, no talking, no undesirable clothing (if the image is in a place of worship), how and in what order to move around the institution, where to sit, etc.)?

In terms of moving images, the researcher can investigate the kinds of films that come out of film companies and studios, the kinds of programmes that television channels put out, for whom and in what format. For example the easy-going, familiar, polite, superficial and chatty style of television talk shows, that always end on a happy note and take pains not to touch on sensitive or dangerous knowledge, can be contrasted to the gritty documentary about child prostitution or the raw film genre such as *Raging Bull* (Cormack, 1992). Here 'audiencing' features large: examining which audiences watch which films or which programmes, or go to see which images and where. In educational research the techniques of discourse analysis can be applied to still and moving images taken by, or provided by, the researcher and/or the participants.

Discourses and discourse analysis can apply to artefacts as well as to images. For example Francis (2010) analysed the discourses of gendered worlds into which young boys and girls are inducted through commercially produced toys and films.

32.4 Grounded theory

Both the tools and the outcomes of grounded theory can be used in analysing images. The tools of grounded theory, as discussed in Chapter 33, include induction, open coding, axial coding (relating conceptually similar codes to a code that embraces them all), selective coding (looking at relationships between axial codes), categorizing, theoretical sampling, constant comparison, memoing, generation of core categories, theoretical saturation and the generation of the theory itself as the end point of the analysis (i.e. derived from the data not driving the data). We refer the reader to Chapter 33 for a fuller overview of these techniques. The researcher gathers together the visual data, then codes the data, moving to generating categories, themes, key issues and features, thence to writing a memo about these, thence to formulating general concepts, thence to saturating the category and theoretical sampling, 'visual contrasting of time perspectives and co-constructed sequences of visual images of time' (Konecki, 2009: 85) and onwards to the generation of the grounded theory itself. For a worked example of this we refer the reader to Konecki (2009).

Figueroa (2008) argues that, although there is a large battery of analytical tools available for qualitative data analysis, these tend to focus on interactional studies. She argues for a variant of grounded theory to be used in analysing audio-visual texts, in the context of looking at audio-visual texts and narratives in their own right (as phenomena themselves) rather than solely regarding the audio-visual medium as the means for collecting data on a phenomenon. Texts, she avers, are 'crystallised pieces of this symbolic social net of meanings' (p. 4) and have to be examined in their own right. This entails looking at the actors' behaviours and strategies, and the consequences of these. But who are the actors – the people who have been filmed or the producers of the final image? Regarding audio-visual media simply as the means or instruments for observing a phenomenon will look at actors' behaviours and interactions; however, she suggests that it is not always easy to identify who the actors are. For example, in a piece of television journalism, the actors may be the cameraman, the journalist in the film, the chief editor, the television presenter, eyewitnesses or other people in the film, the film editor or, indeed, others. Hence it is not always easy to see who is 'speaking' in the text.

Given this difficulty, Figueroa (2008) argues that researchers have to look at texts in their own right as a single product, to see the text as a single-perspective narrative. If the researcher regards texts as the medium to another end, rather than as the product in itself, then this will lead the researcher to look at individual actors and their different behaviours, interactions, strategies, etc. However, if texts are regarded as ends in themselves, then they will be analysed and coded differently, and, not least, interrogated for what they omit as well as what they include. Such texts and their associated readings are recognized to be: (a) already selective (having *created* a world, not only *reflected* one); (b) fictional (because they are constructed narratives); and (c) affected by the manner of their construction (they are dramaturgical and framed in a certain way, e.g. by news editors and news presenters) (p. 6).

Reading audio-visual products as texts, to be analysed through grounded theory, Figueroa (2008: 7) suggests, breaks down elements into smaller 'microscopic' units of coded fragments too soon, usually at the beginning of the analysis. This, she argues, risks losing sight of the whole text and the force of the whole text, in which that whole is more than the sum of its parts. She makes the point that such early coding analysis loses the impact of the whole when it is undertaken before any 'deep interpretation' and analysis of the overall structure of the text has been made.

Hence Figueroa (2008) suggests that, whilst grounded theory of texts (as products rather than as media for studying other phenomena) is useful, it should be undertaken differently from the normal sequence of open coding moving to axial coding and categorizing and, through constant comparison and the generation of core categories, to the generation of the grounded theory. Rather, she suggests that the researcher needs to turn 'this paradigm [of grounded theory] on its head' (p. 8). Here an analysis of audio-visual texts should start by looking at the whole, with the overall picture and 'global impressions', as these influence the more detailed analysis that can follow. Only after the overall impression has been formed should the researcher move to the more detailed analysis and coding, i.e. with the overall picture in mind, together with an insight into the interconnections and interrelationships between different parts of the text. Echoing Blumer's (1969: 41) advocacy of moving from the broad view to a sharper, close-up focus, this recognizes that the text is not simply a collection of independent, coded units but a whole, which has a structure and overall impact. The textual analysis becomes an 'exploration' (Figueroa, 2008: 9) to provide a comprehensive overall picture and account of what is 'going on' in the audio-visual text, rather than simply being a coding exercise. To accompany

such 'exploration', she argues for Blumer's (1969: 43) use of 'inspection': 'an intensive focused examination of the empirical content of whatever analytical elements' arise from, and come out in the text, i.e. smaller units and pieces of the text. Indeed she writes that a more suitable way of interpreting Blumer's 'inspection' is not as examination of analytical units, but as 'exemplification' of analytical elements and emergent constructs and hypotheses.

In moving from the global to the detailed levels, macro to micro, the emergent hypotheses that are a feature of grounded theory take account of the audio-visual texts as a whole and are exemplified in the text, thus enabling the researcher to come to the close-up focus more slowly, after undertaking an overall view (Figueroa, 2008: 10). This, Figueroa avers, does greater justice to the nature of audio-visual texts and the structures of meaning within them. Though her comments are intended to apply to audio-visual texts of moving images, they can apply equally well to still images and visual data.

In advocating grounded theory, then, the researcher can start with the overall, general impression and awareness of the broad-based structures and interlocking elements of the whole, then move to the fine-grained, micro-analysis in coding and then through the several stages of the generation of the grounded theory, informed and influenced by the overall impression and messages gained at the early stages of approaching the analysis.

32.5 Interpreting images

Images are 'compressed performances' (Pinney, 2004: 8), they take place in a social milieu, both at the sites of production and 'consumption', and the sites of 'consumption' (viewing) may change over time. They are produced for one set of purposes but often used with other intentions. The researcher has to be alert not to over-interpret photographs or to read into them meanings which are barely supportable by the material itself, i.e. he or she needs to be highly reflexive. In this respect educational researchers should accompany the photograph in question with text, for verification, for third-party validation of interpretations, for contextualizing the photograph and, not least, for ensuring that the photograph is not 'read' in entirely different ways from those of the researcher.

In examining images we can suggest several questions that can be asked (cf. Rose, 2007: 258–9):

■ Why, when, where, by whom, for whom, how is/ was the image made?

- Who is/was/are/were the originally intended audiences of the image?
- How is/was the image displayed?
- What do we know about the maker, the owner(s) and the people (if any) on the image?
- What were the relations (if any) between the producer, the subjects and the owner(s) of the image?
- What is the image about, and what/whom does the image show?
- What are the features of the image (e.g. compositional, genre, style, colour, elements, structure, format, arrangement, symmetry, etc.)?
- What is the medium of the image?
- What are the striking features of the image?
- Is the image 'stand-alone', is it part of a set or series, is it part of a collection?
- Should the image be seen on its own or in the context of a set or series?
- From where was the image taken?
- What do the different elements of the image signify, and how do we know?
- What interpretations can be made of the image?
- Do the interpretations made of the image accord with the intentions of the producer of the image (do we know of the original intentions)?
- What different interpretations of the image are made by different audiences (and from different backgrounds, e.g. related to ethnicity, age group, sex, sexuality, social class, income groups, geographical location, etc.)?
- What and whose knowledge is included in or excluded from the image?
- Who is empowered/disempowered in or by the image?
- What contradictions, if any, exist within the image?
- Where is the image kept/stored/displayed?
- Who has/had access to the image?
- How can/could the image be viewed?
- How is the image described, labelled, indexed, catalogued, archived?
- Is there a written commentary on the image, and, if so, what does it contain?
- What is the intended and actual relation between the image and those who view it?

There is a wealth of literature on examining images in educational research, particularly in the history of education, and we refer readers to O'Donoghue (2010) for comprehensive references to this. His paper also suggests that images, including photographs, can be regarded as 'installation art', i.e. those artworks that are produced at an exhibition site (he gives an example of period rooms that have been constructed as 'immersive spaces' (p. 413) in an exhibition, into which the public can walk, look, touch, feel and smell, and in which they interact as more than spectators as participators). Regarding photographs as 'photographs of installations' (p. 411) invites researchers not only to imagine the three-dimensional nature of the classroom but how it must feel to be inside that classroom.

32.6 Interpreting an image: a worked example

A worked example of a 'reading' of an image (Figure 32.1) is presented in this section. This is a still image, a photograph.

This fascinating historical photograph of a UK schoolroom in the north-east of England carries the museum label thus: 'Children possibly at Woodland school, taken during an art class. Note sculptured trees on desks.' It is a typical photograph of its time (early twentieth century), and it is part of the genre of this type of photograph in which each child's head is turned to the left, the teacher is at the back of the class, and the photographer is on one side of the room in order to include all the children in the photograph. In places the photograph is faded and the image is a little fuzzy: the ravages of time. It has also been preserved in digital form by the museum, so that further image quality loss is prevented.

If we examine the picture, what can we notice?

The people

- There are 60 children in the class (there may have been just a few more, out of the camera shot on the right; the presence of light from the right suggests that the last row in the right may be next to a window).
- There are more girls than boys.
- The sexes sit together, and in some places a boy is wedged between two girls.
- All the children are white Caucasians.
- The teacher is female.
- Nearly all the children are dressed smartly in the style of the day; it is unclear whether there is a uniform, or clothing for the special event of the photograph, but there is a homogeneity or standardization of clothing.
- Some boys are wearing expensive lace collars, others are wearing stiff 'Eton' collars, but the school is probably not for rich children (who would be in much smaller classes and with different uniforms; perhaps here the parents wanted the best for their children's schooling).
- Clothing is clearly differentiated by sex.
- The children are wearing warm clothing.

FIGURE 32.1   An early twentieth-century photograph of children in an art lesson

Source: Image courtesy of Beamish Museum Limited, image copyright Beamish Museum Limited

- The only person not looking at the camera is the teacher, and, like a military officer, she is looking imperiously, sternly and unsmilingly at the children, and is the only one standing in the photograph, i.e. physically and metaphorically above the students.
- All the children are facing the camera; no child is looking away.
- The picture is 'posed' and serious, not light-hearted; clearly the children have been told what to do, how to sit (hands behind their backs) and where to look. Some are trying to smile, one or two seem to be smiling more naturally, and yet most are not.
- The situation seems unusual for the children, to have a photographer in the classroom, as many of them have an air of curiosity in their look.

The classroom and the furniture

- Proportional to the number of people, the classroom is quite small and the children are tightly packed.
- The back of the classroom is raised up (by one step, visible on the upper right of the photograph), so that the children at the back can see the teacher at the front, and be seen by that teacher.
- There are no windows out of which children can look (the windows are too high or are blocked out).

- The children are sitting in solid desks, three to a desk.
- The desks are standardized, the same, dark (black iron and dark wood), heavy (too heavy to move easily) and unable to be adjusted.
- The desks are large, taking up all the classroom space, yet the children are small. The desks are bigger than the children.
- The desks are fixed, made of strong wood and cast iron.
- The desks are hard, strong and large, in contrast to the students who are fragile and small.
- There is little room for movement in the desks; the position of the seats is fixed, as they are joined to the desk by the iron bar at the base.
- The seating arrangement suggests that all the inter-actions go through the teacher.
- The seating arrangements may be designed to control children, not least the boys (mixing the sexes and having some boys sitting between two girls).
- The children sit in rows, and columns, each row facing the front. It is very regimented, and oriented to a single focal point – the teacher at the front.
- There appears to be a gap between the front row of children and the teacher's desk (out of the image).

- There are some unusual objects in the class: the large thermometer hanging from the light fitting (a science instrument?), the large portraits high up around the room (not all completely contained within the photograph), with dignitaries looking down on the children.
- There is bare, but varnished, brickwork in the classroom.
- Some work that is on the walls is too high for children to read – it is for decoration only.
- The children's pictures are nearly all the same, and are about the same topic – flowers; all are nearly identical.
- The pictures by the children, on the walls, are stylized and almost the same.
- There is an almost exclusive focus on nature in the children's pictures and not other work on display (indicative, perhaps, of an alternative to the hardness of the real world inside and outside the classroom).
- This is an art lesson, yet there is no evidence of drawing materials. There is evidence of what the children should be looking at in the art lesson (the jar of flowers on their desk or the sculptured trees). It is unclear whether this is an art/drawing lesson or an art appreciation lesson.
- All the objects on the desks are the same.

The photograph and the photographer

- The photograph is old, and, in parts, the focus is not always sharp or even, the images are slightly unclear in places, and the contrast is uneven and, in parts, the image is faded. Hence the researcher has to be careful not to over-interpret those parts of the photograph which are unclear, or to read into the analysis any points that are not supportable by the evidence. This is a commonplace problem with old materials, and argues for the value of a third party to examine the photograph.
- The photographer must have been standing some distance from the children (nearly two desks' length from the front row of desks if we calculate the ratios) and higher than floor level. Standing higher than the children makes them look smaller – the symbolism is striking.
- The way in which, taken as a two-dimensional image, the teacher is at the apex and the children are below, a visual hierarchy reflecting a positional/role hierarchy.
- Why was the picture taken? For whom? For what purpose?
- There is no clear single focal point in the photograph; the conventional 'rule of the thirds' (where the focus is one third or two thirds of the way into the picture) is not there, nor is there a clear centre to the image.

- There are many points of focus, for example:
  a The girls' bright dresses in the first complete right-hand row.
  b The staring eyes of the boy sitting at the front, or the worried look of the little girl in the second row, or the haughty teacher at the back.
  c The children who are more in the image's sharp focus towards the rear of the second row of desks.
  d The bright lace collar of the boy in the centre rear.
  e The near-rhomboid symmetry in terms of the rows and columns of children's heads, which suggests order, regulation and regularity.
  f The use of diagonals here, rather than a front shot (whether simply out of the requirements to include all the children seated in their desks, or for artistic effect, or to make the most of the natural light, or some other reason), which brings a sense of inclusiveness to the picture and which draws the viewer into the picture.
  g The field of vision of the viewer (from a single point outwards), which is matched by the shape of the classroom and the view of the arrangement of the desks and children (almost a rhombus, see Figure 32.2).
  h The match between the direction of the walls of the classroom and the layout of the rows and columns of the desks (the children are triply 'contained': (a) within their desk; (b) with the rows and columns of the desk arrangement; and (c) within the confines of the classroom walls, all of which is supervised by the overriding presence of the teacher. There is a scalability to the picture: each desk is a scaled-down version of the arrangement of all the desks (into rows and columns) and the arrangement of all the desks is a scaled-down version of the proportions and layout of the classroom walls.
  i The contrast between the foreground and the background – the foreground shows powerless children whilst the background shows the powerful teacher keeping watch.

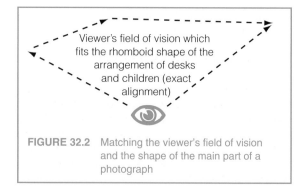

FIGURE 32.2 Matching the viewer's field of vision and the shape of the main part of a photograph

j The contrast between the dowdy walls/gloomy far reaches of the classroom and the humanity and clothed children/models sitting in the centre of the picture.

k The contrast between the harsh brick walls and the soft children.

l The contrast between the staid and very formally dressed teacher and the relatively innocent children's faces and clothing.

m The emphasis on regularity (rows and columns) and the repeated motifs of the three children sitting at a desk, multiplied 18 times (18 complete desks in the picture).

n The contrast between the static pose rather than the dynamic potential of the photograph, there being 61 potentially dynamic agents (people) in the photograph.

■ The way in which the picture's background is cut off at crucial points.

■ The old, faded and fuzzy parts of photograph.

■ The observation that there are almost no shadows, everything is open to scrutiny and nothing is shaded or hidden.

What we see is often what we look for; this makes us look selectively and construe what we see through the interpretive lenses of our own subjectivity and ideological frameworks and values. Researchers bring their own subjectivities and cultural backgrounds to the photograph (hence the issues of reflexivity and disclosure of possible subjectivity assume a high profile here).

For example, one researcher might 'read' this picture as presenting stark messages and themes of:

■ lack of freedom and no room for freedom;

■ power (the teacher has it all and the children seem to have none): asymmetrical relations of power;

■ lack of creativity;

■ standardization, sameness and uniformity;

■ surveillance, control, domination, authoritarianism and containment;

■ conformity, obedience, passivity and loss of individuality.

Though the formal curriculum here may be art (which, perhaps, concerns individuality and creativity), the hidden curriculum (that which is learnt without being taught; the unspoken messages that children must learn very thoroughly if they are to survive in school, e.g. about being one of a crowd, about differentials of power, about delay, denial and domination (Jackson, 1968)) is the exact opposite. As O'Donoghue (2010) suggests, photographs concern the 'Layout, design and associated disciplinary practices' embedded in the space.

Of course, this interpretation might say more about the researcher than the researched: the researcher may be attuned to looking for dominatory forms of schooling, to the neglect of its more positive aspects. For example, another researcher may interpret the photograph as showing:

■ a clear, undistracted focus on the teacher and children's own work, designed to promote learning and concentration;

■ clear understanding by all parties of roles and behaviours, so that learning can take place beneficially, willingly and without disruption.

Here the researcher may feel that the clarity of role specifications and expected behaviours are not at all negative, but are designed to promote the effective learning of children (and the current layout of rows and columns in East Asian classrooms follows this pattern and has produced outstanding results in world-class tests). Indeed the power of this arrangement for learning and its outcomes could be immense, e.g. for children to be able to climb the social ladder in the future – education as a great emancipatory force in society.

Further, initially we have the photograph's title attached to it by the museum: 'School Children in Art Class', with the museum's own label reading: 'Children possibly at Woodland school, taken during an art class. Note sculptured trees on desks.' Immediately the reader's attention is drawn to the fact that this concerns an art lesson, and that there are some art materials. Why were these features included in the text, and not others? Is that really the purpose or key message of the image, or is the museum, in a positive endeavour to be helpful, drawing attention to points that otherwise might go unnoticed? Is it trying not to be pejorative in its comments, or is it simply that the museum wanted a short label for indexing and referencing purposes? The point here is the labels can frame the researcher's or the viewer's insights, and the researcher needs to be aware of this. It is not only the focus of the text label, but the tone of those words: the label used by the museum may appear to be couched in neutral terms, but it has already decided what to comment on and what to ignore. Guidelines on inclusion and exclusion can be both useful and dangerous.

In considering the photograph, indeed any visual image, we can focus on the subject matter, its form, its genre, its meanings, its composition, its style and technical matters. However, we can go further, to examine the context of the photograph, its audience, its provenance, why it was taken, its usages and, indeed, the ethical issues that are raised by the photograph.

It is interesting, perhaps, to speculate on the history of the photograph in question, why it was taken, for whom it was taken, and what use was intended to be made of it, or, indeed, was made of it. Was it designed to impress parents, school governors, inspectors, local officials (and, if so, why was an art lesson chosen)? Was it designed to be simply a document of record of the school's history, and, if so, why this scene in particular? Was it designed to be a celebratory record (the children may have been dressed very smartly for the occasion, in clothes that they would not normally wear for school)? Who was the intended audience: the children themselves (e.g. in later life), their parents, education officials, researchers, visitors, historians, the families in question?

We can also ask how and why the photograph came to be in the museum in question (an award-winning national museum of social and industrial history). For example, was it a donation, a purchase, did it arrive by happenstance, or deliberately, or as part of a large collection, or what?

The photograph raises several ethical questions, for example:

- Are the people still alive?
- Was informed consent gained from the people in the photograph to be photographed (or was it simply an accepted part of being at school)?
- What informed consent was gained by the museum, and from whom, to release the document into the public domain, or has the passage of time obviated the need for this?
- Is it acceptable and fair of the researcher to portray the school, the teacher and the students in question in a perhaps negative way, and, if not, then who actually suffers?
- Will the use of the photograph bring harm or good, and to whom?

What we have here encapsulates the problem that often adheres to documentary evidence: that it is prepared (or in this case taken) for one set of purposes and audiences, but it is used for other reasons and intentions.

Photographs, like other visual materials, are multi-layered and capable of sustaining several interpretations. Hence the visual researcher, just like the textual researcher, has to disclose his or her own reflexivity and the possible influence that this has on the analysis and interpretation made. Though a picture may be worth a thousand words, photographs, on their own, may be relatively inert; it is only in the interaction between producer of the image, the image itself, and the audience that it comes alive.

Not only can we read a photograph like a text, but it is often the case that text is useful to accompany the image. Text and photograph run together. A commentary can be useful to accompany, explain, interpret and contextualize the image, and, in research terms, this can tie the image into other evidence – visual or textual – that the researcher is using.

32.7 Analysing moving images

The term 'moving images' here is taken to include video and film material. Denzin (1990: 102) remarks that 'films do not faithfully reproduce reality'; rather, they are ideological interpretations and selections from reality; they are a particular version or view of reality. Hence the researcher has to interrogate the moving images in light of the research questions and to undertake a more valuative and ideology-critical reading of their content. This includes selecting, and justifying the selection of, particular parts of the moving images (what to focus on and what to overlook) (which may be informed by the research questions and purposes).

Denzin (2004) suggests that films (and we can include video material here) should be considered initially at their 'textual realism' level, i.e. the story that the material is telling and how it is telling that story. At a second level, which he terms a 'subversive' level (p. 240), he suggests that a film can be read for its ideological content and effects, i.e. how the film functions to reproduce the (dominant) values and beliefs of everyday life and society. Hence the researcher starts with an overall view of the film as a whole, noting themes, impressions, key points, rather as one would 'read' a text. Having gained an overall view, the researcher can then go into details, e.g. scenes, events, sequences and so on, in short, a micro-analysis of the material (Flick, 2009: 247). In this, the methods and tools of grounded theory can be used, working not only with the visual images but also, where relevant, transcriptions of the spoken words. As Flick remarks (p. 249), films can be regarded as visual texts, and so the range of tools for textual analysis can be brought into play here. He argues (p. 247) that researchers can look for patterns in the film. Having conducted a first level and second level analysis, the researcher can then look for points of resonance, consonance, dissonance and contradiction between the two levels of analysis.

As with much qualitative data analysis, exploration and interpretation run together; hence researchers have to be acutely aware of the influence of their own values, cultures, interests, background in the selection and interpretation of the data, in short they have to be reflexive. In this respect the repeatability of moving image material is useful in being able to be viewed by a third party, to check for alternative interpretations of the material.

Analysing moving images is very costly in terms of time, as they have to be watched and re-watched many times, in order to extract fair and suitable data and interpretations (e.g. for coding and constant comparison). This can be exacting and demanding of the researcher's insight and persistence.

32.8 Concluding remarks

This chapter has suggested that analysis and interpretation of images are often inextricably linked, raising the need for considerable reflexivity on the part of the researcher. It has suggested that the processes of content analysis (both numerical and qualitative), dis-course analysis and a modified form of grounded theory can be used in the analysis and interpretation of visual images. It has provided a worked example of the analysis and interpretation of a single still image – a photograph. It has used this not only to indicate the processes and kinds of observations and interpretations that can be made, but to indicate that interpretations are multiple, sometimes conflicting, and subjective. The interpretation used elements of ideology critique in its exposure and disclosure of power in the image and its explanation. The authority of the researcher to determine the focus, analysis and interpretation of a still or moving image is, itself, subject to ideology critique and interrogation of power within a discourse. Visual images invite researchers to consider 'alternate forms of data representation' and the 'variety of questions that we can ask about the educational systems we study' and 'new ways of seeing things' (Eisner, 1997: 6). That is a powerful challenge for researchers.

 Companion Website

The companion website to the book includes PowerPoint slides for this chapter, which list the structure of the chapter and then provide a summary of the key points in each of its sections. This resource can be found online at **www.routledge.com/textbooks/cohen7e**.

Grounded theory

CHAPTER 33

A mainstream intention or outcome of analysing qualitative data is the generation of grounded theory. We unpack key issues in grounded theory and, along the way, introduce several tools for analysing qualitative data which yield the grounded theory. The chapter includes:

- the tools of grounded theory
- developing grounded theory
- evaluating grounded theory
- preparing to work in grounded theory

Readers may find it helpful to refer, also, to Chapters 11 and 30.

33.1 Introduction

Theory generation in qualitative data can be emergent, and grounded theory is an important method of theory generation. It is more inductive than content analysis, as the theories emerge from, rather than exist before, the data. Strauss and Corbin (1994: 273) remark: 'grounded theory is a general methodology for developing theory that is grounded in data systematically gathered and analysed'. The theory is derived inductively from the analysis and study of, and reflection on, the phenomena under scrutiny (cf. Strauss and Corbin, 1990: 23). Grounded theory, as Moghaddam (2006) avers, is a set of relationships amongst data and categories that proposes a plausible and reasonable explanation of the phenomenon under study, i.e. it explains by drawing on the data generated. It is a method or set of procedures for the generation of theory or for the production of a certain kind of knowledge (Greckhamer and Koro-Ljungberg, 2005: 729). (For a summary sheet of grounded theory principles see the accompanying website.) Though there are different versions of grounded theory, and variations in its forms and epistemologies (Greckhamer and Koro-Ljungberg, 2005: 731; Buckley and Waring, 2009: 318), nevertheless there are several features in common in these definitions:

- theory is *emergent* rather than predefined and tested;
- theory emerges from the *data* rather than vice versa;

- theory generation is a consequence of, and partner to, *systematic* data collection and analysis;
- patterns and theories are implicit in data, waiting to be discovered;
- grounded theory is both inductive and deductive, it is iterative and close to the data that give rise to it.

Glaser (1996) suggests that 'grounded theory is the systematic generation of a theory from data'; it is an inductive process in which everything is integrated and in which data pattern themselves rather than having the researcher pattern them, as actions are integrated and interrelated with other actions. Glaser and Strauss's (1967) seminal work rejects simple linear causality and the decontextualization of data, and argues that the world which participants inhabit is multivalent, multivariate and connected. As Glaser (1996) says: 'the world doesn't occur in a vacuum' and the researcher has to take account of the interconnectedness of actions. In everyday life, actions are interconnected and people make connections naturally; it is part of everyday living, and hence grounded theory catches the naturalistic element of research and formulates it into a systematic methodology. In seeking to catch the complexity and interconnectedness of everyday actions grounded theory is faithful to how people act; it takes account of apparent inconsistencies, contradictions, discontinuities and relatedness in actions. As Glaser (1996) says: 'grounded theory is appealing because it tends to get at exactly what's going on'. Flick (1998: 41) writes that 'the aim is not to reduce complexity by breaking it down into variables but rather to increase complexity by including context'.

Grounded theory is a systematic theory, using systematized methods (discussed below) of theoretical sampling, coding constant comparison, the identification of a core variable and saturation. Grounded theory is not averse to quantitative methods, it arose out of them (Glaser, 1996) in terms of trying to bring to qualitative data some of the analytic methods applied in statistical techniques (e.g. multivariate analysis). In grounded theory the researcher discovers what is relevant; indeed Glaser and Strauss's (1967) work is entitled *The Discovery of Grounded Theory*.

However, where grounded theory parts company with much quantitative, positivist research is in its view of theory. In positivist research the theory pre-exists its testing and the researcher deduces from the data whether the theory is robust and can be confirmed. The data are 'forced' into a fit with the theory. Grounded theory, on the other hand, does not force data to fit with a predetermined theory (Glaser and Strauss, 1967: 3); indeed the difference between inductive and deductive research is less clear than it appears to be at first sight. For example, before one can deduce, one has to generate theory and categories inductively. The intention of grounded theory is to build and generate theory rather than to test an existing theory, to provide researchers with tools that they can use to generate this theory through data analysis, to weigh up alternative explanation (e.g. through constant comparison) and to relate concepts in the development of theory (Moghaddam, 2006).

Grounded theory starts with data, which are then analysed and reviewed to enable the theory to be generated from them; it is rooted in the data and little else. Here the theory derives from the data – it is grounded in the data and emerges from it. As Lincoln and Guba (1985: 205) argue, grounded theory must fit the situation that is being researched.

Glaser (1996) writes that 'forcing methodologies were too ascendant', not least in positivist research and that grounded theory had to reject forcing or constraining the nature of a research investigation by pre-existing theories. As grounded theory sets aside any preconceived ideas, letting the data themselves give rise to the theory, certain abilities are required of the researcher, for example:

- tolerance and openness to data and what is emerging;
- tolerance of confusion and regression (feeling stupid when the theory does not become immediately obvious);
- resistance to premature formulation of theory;
- ability to pay close attention to data;
- willingness to engage in the process of theory generation rather than theory testing; it is an experiential methodology;
- ability to work with emergent categories rather than preconceived or received categories.

As theory is not predetermined, the role of targeted pre-reading is not as strong as in other kinds of research (e.g. using literature reviews to generate issues for the research), indeed it may be dangerous as it may prematurely close off or determine what one sees in data; it may cause one to read data through given lenses rather than anew. As one does not know what one will find, one cannot be sure what one should read before undertaking grounded theory. One should read widely, both within and outside the field, rather than narrowly and in too focused a direction.

There are several elements of grounded theory that contribute to its systematic nature, and it to these that we now turn.

33.2 The tools of grounded theory

There are several common practices that researchers use in grounded theory: theoretical sampling, coding (discussed in the previous chapter), constant comparison, the core variable(s) and 'saturation'. We discuss these below.

Theoretical sampling

In theoretical sampling, data are collected on an ongoing, iterative basis, and the researcher keeps on adding to the sample until she has enough data to describe what is going on in the context or situation under study and until 'theoretical saturation' is reached (discussed below). As one cannot know in advance when this point will be reached, one cannot determine the sample size or representativeness until one is actually doing the research. In theoretical sampling, data collection continues until sufficient data have been gathered to create a theoretical explanation of what is happening and what constitutes its key features. It is not a question of representativeness, but, rather, a question of allowing the theory to emerge. As Chapter 8 reported, Glaser and Strauss (1967: 45) write that theoretical sampling is where, during the data collection process as part of theory generation, the researcher collects data, codes the data and analyses them, and this analysis influences what data to collect next, from whom and where. The data collection process, then, is determined by the emerging theory and its categories. Hence theoretical relevance (how the data contribute to the emerging theory and its categories) is a key criterion for further data collection and sampling, rather than, for example, conventional sampling strategies and criteria.

Coding

Coding is 'the process of disassembling and reassembling the data. Data are disassembled when they are broken apart into lines, paragraphs or sections. These fragments are then rearranged, through coding, to produce a new understanding that explores similarities, differences, across a number of different cases. The early part of coding should be confusing, with a mass of apparently unrelated material. However, as coding progresses and themes emerge, the analysis becomes more organized and structured (Ezzy, 2002: 94).

In grounded theory there are three types of coding: *open*, *axial* and *selective* coding, the intention of which is to deconstruct the data into manageable chunks in order to facilitate an understanding of the phenomenon in question. *Open coding* involves exploring the data and identifying units of analysis to code for meanings, feelings, actions, events and so on. The researcher codes up the data, creating new codes and categories and subcategories where necessary, and integrating codes where relevant until the coding is complete. *Axial coding* seeks to make links between categories and codes, 'to integrate codes around the axes of central categories' (Ezzy, 2002: 91); the essence of axial coding is the interconnectedness of categories (Creswell, 1998: 57). Hence codes are explored, their interrelationships are examined, and codes and categories are compared to existing theory. In *selective coding* a core code is identified, the relationship between that core code and other codes is made clear (Ezzy, 2002: 93), and the coding scheme is compared with pre-existing theory. Creswell (1998: 57) writes that 'in selective coding, the researcher identifies a "story line" and writes a story that integrates the categories in the axial coding model'.

As coding proceeds the researcher develops concepts and makes connections between them. Flick *et al.* (2004: 19) argue that 'repeated coding of data leads to denser concept-based relationships and hence to a theory', i.e. that the richness of the data is included in the theoretical formulation.

Constant comparison

The application of open, axial and selective coding adopts the method of constant comparison. In constant comparison the researcher compares the new data with existing data and categories, so that the categories achieve a perfect fit with the data. If there is a poor fit between data and categories, or indeed between theory and data, then the categories and theories have to be modified until all the data are accounted for. New and emergent categories are developed in order to be able to incorporate and accommodate data in a good fit, with no discrepant cases. Glaser and Strauss (1967: 102) write that the constant comparative method, in which coding and analysis take place together, even simultaneously, is conducted in order to assist in the process of theory generation; that is its purpose. Further, they argue that theory does not concern itself with universality or any 'proof' of putative causation; rather constant comparison seeks only theoretical saturation rather than any intention to consider all available data.

To accompany the constant comparison, and to aid reflexivity, Glaser and Strauss (1967) suggest the value of memoing: where the researcher writes ideas, notes, comments, notes on surprising matters, themes or metaphors, reminders, hunches, draft hypotheses, references to literature, diagrams, questions, draft theories, methodological points, personal points, suggestions for further enquiry, etc. that occur to him/her during the process of constant comparison and data analysis (Lempert, 2007: 245; Flick, 2009: 434). They can be long or short, with verbatim quotations or just notes and jottings, with key points underlined, or simply observations made (Strauss and Corbin, 1990: 202–3). Memos should be dated and referenced to data and codes. Software also enables memos to be written and attached to text.

In constant comparison, discrepant, negative and disconfirming cases are important in assisting the categories and emergent (grounded) theory to fit all the data. Constant comparison is the process 'by which the properties and categories across the data are compared continuously until no more variation occurs' (Glaser, 1996), i.e. saturation is reached. In constant comparison data are compared across a range of situations, times, groups of people, and through a range of methods. The process resonates with the methodological notion of triangulation.

Glaser and Strauss (1967: 105–13) suggest that the constant comparison method involves four stages: (i) comparing incidents and data that are applicable to each category; (ii) integrating these categories and their properties; (iii) bounding the theory; (iv) setting out the theory. The first stage here involves coding of incidents and comparing them with previous incidents in the same and different groups and with other data that are in the same category. For this to happen they suggest that *unitizing* has to be undertaken – dividing the narrative into the smallest pieces of information or text that are meaningful in themselves, e.g. phrases, words, paragraphs. It also involves *categorizing*: bringing together those unitized texts that relate to each other, that can be put into the same category, together with devising rules to describe the properties of these categories, and checking that there is internal consistency within the unitized text contained in those categories. The second stage involves memoing and further coding. Here 'the constant comparative units change from comparison of incident with incident to comparison of incident with properties of the category that resulted from initial comparisons of incidents' (p. 108). The third stage – of delimitation – occurs at the levels of the theory and the categories (p. 110), and in which the major modifications reduce as underlying uniformities and properties are discovered and in which theoretical saturation takes place. The final stage – of writing theory – occurs when the researcher has gathered and generated coded data, memos and a theory, and this is then written in full.

By going through the previous sections of data, particularly the search for confirming, negative and discrepant cases, the researcher is able to keep a 'running total' of these cases for a particular theory. The researcher also generates alternative theories for the phenomena under investigation and performs the same count of confirming, negative and discrepant cases. Lincoln and Guba (1985: 253) argue that the theory with the greatest incidence of confirming cases and the lowest incidence of negative and discrepant cases is the most robust.

Constant comparison, LeCompte and Preissle (1993: 256) opine, combines the elements of inductive category coding (discussed above) with simultaneously comparing these with the other events and social incidents that have been observed and coded over time and location. This enables social phenomena to be compared across categories, where necessary giving rise to new dimensions, codes and categories. Glaser (1978) indicates that constant comparison can proceed from the moment of starting to collect data, to seeking key issues and categories, to discovering recurrent events or activities in the data that become categories of focus, to expanding the range of categories. This process can continue during the writing-up period, which should be ongoing, so that a model or explanation of the phenomena can emerge that accounts for fundamental social processes and relationships.

The core variable

Through the use of constant comparison a core variable (or core category) is identified: that variable/category which accounts for most of the data and to which as much as possible is related; that variable around which most data are focused (Strauss and Corbin, 1990: 116). As Flick *et al.* (2004: 19) suggest: 'the successive integration of concepts leads to one or more key categories and thereby to the core of the emerging theory'. The core variable is that variable that integrates the greatest number of codes, categories and concepts, and to which most of them are related and with which they are connected. It has the greatest explanatory power; as Glaser (1996) remarks: 'a concept has to earn its way into the theory by pulling its weight'.

A core variable/category must be central to the category system and the phenomena rather than peripheral to these; it must appear frequently in the data and must fit comfortably and logically to the data rather than be a strained fit. It should have an abstract title but one that is close to the categories and data in question, and it

must enable variations to be explained (Strauss and Corbin, 1994).

Saturation

Saturation is reached when no new insights, properties, dimensions, relationships, codes or categories are produced even when new data are added, when all of the data are accounted for in the core categories and sub-categories (Glaser and Strauss, 1967: 61; Creswell, 2002: 450), and when the variable covers variations and processes (Moghaddam, 2006). As Ezzy (2002: 93) remarks: 'saturation is achieved when the coding that has already been completed adequately supports and fills out the emerging theory'. Of course one can never know for certain that the categories are saturated, as there are limits to induction, i.e. fresh data may come along that refute the existing theory. The partner of saturation is theoretical completeness, when the theory is able to explain the data fully and satisfactorily.

33.3 Developing grounded theory

As a consequence of theoretical sampling, coding, constant comparison, the identification of the core variable and the saturation of data, categories and codes, the grounded theory (of whatever is being theorized) emerges from the data in an unforced manner, accounting for all the data. How adequate the derived theory is can be evaluated against several criteria. Glaser and Strauss (1967: 237) suggest four main criteria:

- the closeness of the *fit* between the theory and the data;
- how readily *understandable* the theory is by the lay persons working in the field, i.e. that it makes sense to them;
- the ability of the theory to be *general* to a 'multitude of diverse daily situations within the substantive area, not just to a specific type of situation';
- the theory must enable partial control to be exercised over the processes and the structures of day-to-day situations that evolve over time, such that the researcher who is using the theory can have sufficient control of such situations to render it worthwhile to apply the theory to these (p. 245).

Strauss and Corbin (1994: 253–6) suggest several criteria for evaluating the theory:

- How adequately and powerfully the theory accounts for the main concerns of the data.
- The relevance and utility of the theory for the participants.

- The closeness of the fit of the theory to the data and phenomenon being studied, and under what conditions the theory holds true.
- The fit of the axial coding to the categories and codes.
- The ability of the theory to embrace negative and discrepant cases.
- The fit of the theory to literature.
- How the original sample was selected, and on what basis.
- What major categories emerged?
- What were some of the events, incidents, actions, and so on (as indicators) that pointed to some of the major categories?
- On the basis of what categories did theoretical sampling proceed? Was it representative of the categories?
- What were some of the hypotheses pertaining to conceptual relations (that is, among categories), and on what grounds were they formulated and tested?
- Were there instances when hypotheses did not hold up against what was actually seen? How were these discrepancies accounted for? How did they affect the hypotheses?
- How and why was the core category selected (sudden, gradual, difficult, easy)? On what grounds?
- Were concepts generated and systematically related?
- Were there many conceptual linkages between concepts, and were the categories well developed?
- Was much variation built into the theory? Are variations explained? Were the broader conditions built into its explanation?
- Were change or movement taken into account in the development of the theory?

The essence of this approach, that theory emerges from and is grounded in data, is not without its critics. For example Silverman (1993: 47) suggests that it fails to acknowledge the implicit theories which guide research in its early stages (i.e. data are not theory-neutral but theory saturated) and that it might be strong on providing categorizations without necessarily explanatory potential. These are caveats that should feed into the process of reflexivity in qualitative research.

33.4 Evaluating grounded theory

Strauss and Corbin (1990) indicate that the grounded theory that has been generated should be judged against several criteria:

- the reliability, validity and credibility of the data (p. 252);

- the adequacy of the research process (p. 252);
- the empirical grounding of the research findings (p. 252);
- the sampling procedures (p. 253);
- the major categories that emerged (p. 253);
- the adequacy of the evidence base for the categories that emerged (p. 253);
- the adequacy of the basis in the categories that led to the theoretical sampling (p. 253);
- the formulation and testing of hypotheses and their relationship to the conceptual relations amongst the categories (p. 253);
- the adequacy of the way in which discrepant data were handled (p. 253);
- the adequacy of the basis on which the core category was selected (p. 253);
- the generation of the concepts (p. 254);
- the extent to which the concepts are systematically related (p. 254);
- the number and strength of the linkages between categories, and their conceptual density, leading to their explanatory power (p. 255);
- the extent of variation that is built into the theory (p. 255);
- the extent to which the explanations take account of the broader conditions that affected the phenomenon being studied (p. 255);
- the account taken of emergent processes over time in the research (p. 256);
- the significance of the theoretical findings (p. 256).

One can note here the emphasis on the procedures and not only on the outcomes of the grounded theory research.

To this can be added the criteria of originality, resonance (the data, the phenomenon, the participants' experiences and views) and usefulness (for different people and groups, for identifying generic processes, for further research, for advancing the field (Charmaz, 2006: 182–3)), and the criteria of 'workability' (practicality and explanatory power), fit with the data, 'relevance' (to the situation, to groups, to researchers, to the field) and 'modifiability' (in light of additional data) (Glaser and Strauss, 1967).

It can be seen here that grounded theory is not exempted from the conventional criteria of rigorous research.

33.5 Preparing to work in grounded theory

Glaser (1996) offers some useful practical and personal advice for researchers working in the field of grounded theory. He suggests that researchers need to be able to tolerate uncertainty (there is no preconceived theory), confusion (see also Buckley and Waring, 2009: 330), setbacks (e.g. when data disconfirm an emergent theory) and to avoid premature formulation of the theory, but, by constant comparison, enable the final theory to emerge. They need to be open to what is emerging, and not to try to force data to fit a theory but, rather, to ensure that data and theory fit together in an unstrained manner. As he says, 'forcing is a con-sequence of an inability to handle confusion and regression [feeling stupid] while you study'. Grounded theory, he avers, is an 'experiential methodology', and he advises researchers to 'just do it'! He also indicates that it might not be useful to do much pre-reading since, as he says 'you never know what you're going to find, so how do you know what to read?'. He makes the point that, since grounded theory is not easy, the researcher has to be prepared to work hard to be faithful to the rigour of the process.

 Companion Website

The companion website to the book includes PowerPoint slides for this chapter, which list the structure of the chapter and then provide a summary of the key points in each of its sections. In addition there is further information on grounded theory. These resources can be found online at **www.routledge.com/textbooks/ cohen7e**.

Approaches to quantitative data analysis

Many research data are numerical, and many numerical data are bewildering to researchers. Before moving to specific statistical tests for analysing data, we introduce some important foundational concepts in this chapter. These include:

- scales of data
- parametric and non-parametric data
- descriptive and inferential statistics
- kinds of variables
- hypotheses
- one-tailed and two-tailed tests
- distributions
- statistical significance
- hypothesis testing
- effect size
- a note on symbols

The prospect of analysing numerical data sends shivers down the spines of many novice researchers who not only baulk at the thought of statistics but hold fundamental objections to what they see as 'the mathematization of nature' (Horkheimer, 1972). Most concepts in education, some will assert, are simply not reducible to numerical analysis. Statistics, they will object, combine refinement of process with crudity of concept.

We do not hold with any of this. Quantitative data analysis has no greater or lesser importance than qualitative analysis. Its use is entirely dependent on *fitness for purpose*. Arbitrary dismissal of numerical analysis is mere ideology or prejudice.

Quantitative data analysis is a powerful research form, emanating in part from the positivist tradition. It is often associated with large-scale research, but can also serve smaller-scale investigations, with case studies, action research, correlational research and experiments. In the following chapters we will show how numerical data can be reported and introduce some of the most widely used statistics that can be employed in their analysis.

Numerical analysis can be performed using software, for example the Statistical Package for the Social Sciences (SPSS, Minitab, Excel). Software packages apply statistical formulae and carry out computations. With this in mind, we avoid extended outlines of statistical formulae though we do provide details where considered useful. Our primary aim is to explain the concepts that underpin statistical analyses and to do this in as user-friendly a way as possible. Lest our approach should raise purist eyebrows, we provide extended treatments in greater detail, signalled where appropriate by website references. Our outline commentary is closely linked to SPSS, the most widely used statistical package for social sciences. An introductory SPSS manual to this volume is located in an accompanying website (including printouts of data analysis together with comments on what they show). It is often the case that such outputs can clarify issues more straightforwardly than extended prose. We also include a guide to all the SPSS files held on the website. See the list of websites at the end of this chapter.

We begin by identifying some key concepts in numerical analysis (scales of data, parametric and non-parametric data, descriptive and inferential statistics, dependent and independent variables). We then address the concept of statistical significance. We finally conclude with a brief outline of some simple descriptive statistics. Throughout this chapter and the next we indicate how to report analysis; these are collected together in a single file on the accompanying website. Material in the accompanying website also refers to statistical tables, and these tables can also be found on the website.

In this chapter we introduce some basic concepts and terms, then the following chapters move to descriptive statistics, thence to inferential statistics. Bearing in mind the range of statistics covered, the final chapter reviews key statistics that are available to the researcher.

34.1 Scales of data

Before one can advance very far in the field of data analysis one needs to distinguish the kinds of numbers with which one is dealing. This takes us to the commonly reported issue of scales or levels of data, and four are identified, each of which, in the order given below, subsumes its predecessor.

The *nominal* scale simply denotes categories, 1 means such-and-such a category, 2 means another and so on, for example, '1' might denote males, '2' might denote females. The categories are mutually exclusive and have no numerical meaning. For example, consider numbers on a football shirt: we cannot say that the player wearing number 4 is twice as anything as a player wearing a number 2, nor half as anything as a player wearing a number 8; the number 4 simply identifies a category, and, indeed, nominal data are frequently termed categorical data. The data classify, but have no order. Nominal data include items such as sex, age group (e.g. 30–35, 36–40), subject taught, type of school, socio-economic status. Nominal data denote discrete variables, entirely separate categories, e.g. according females the number 1 category and males the number 2 category (there cannot be a 1.25 or a 1.99 position). The figure is simply a conveniently short label.

The *ordinal* scale classifies but also introduces an order into the data. These might be rating scales where, for example, 'strongly agree' is stronger than 'agree', or 'a very great deal' is stronger than 'very little'. It is possible to place items in an order, weakest to strongest, smallest to biggest, lowest to highest, least to most and so on, but there is still an absence of a metric – a measure using calibrated or equal intervals. Therefore one cannot assume that the distance between each point of the scale is equal, i.e. the distance between 'very little' and 'a little' may not be the same as the distance between 'a lot' and 'a very great deal' on a rating scale. One could not say, for example, that, in a five-point rating scale (1=strongly disagree; 2=disagree; 3=neither agree nor disagree; 4=agree; 5=strongly agree) point 4 is in twice as much agreement as point 2, or that point 1 is in five times more disagreement than point 5. However, one could place them in an order: 'not at all', 'very little', 'a little', 'quite a lot', 'a very great deal', or 'strongly disagree', 'disagree', 'neither agree nor disagree', 'agree', 'strongly agree', i.e. it is possible to rank the data according to rules of 'lesser than' or 'greater than', in relation to whatever the value is included on the rating scale. Ordinal data include items such as rating scales and Likert scales, and are frequently used in asking for opinions and attitudes.

The *interval* scale introduces a metric – a regular and equal interval between each data point – as well as keeping the features of the previous two scales of classification and order. This lets us know 'precisely how far apart are the individuals, the objects or the events that form the focus of our inquiry' (Cohen and Holli-day, 1996: 9). As there is an exact and same interval between each data point, interval level data are sometimes called *equal-interval scales* (e.g. the distance between 3 degrees Celsius and 4 degrees Celsius is the same as the distance between 98 degrees Celsius and 99 degrees Celsius). However, in interval data, there is no true zero. Let us give two examples. In Fahrenheit degrees the freezing point of water is 32 degrees, not zero, so we cannot say, for example, that 100 degrees Fahrenheit is twice as hot as 50 degrees Fahrenheit, because the measurement of Fahrenheit did not start at zero. In fact twice as hot as 50 degrees Fahrenheit is 68 degrees Fahrenheit (({50–32} $\times$ 2) + 32). Let us give another example. Many IQ tests commence their scoring at point 70, i.e. the lowest score possible is 70. We cannot say that a person with an IQ of 150 has twice the measured intelligence as a person with an IQ of 75 because the starting point is 70; a person with an IQ of 150 has twice the measured intelligence as a person with an IQ of 110, as one has to subtract the initial starting point of 70 ({150–70}/2). In practice, the interval scale is rarely used, and the statistics that one can use with this scale are, to all extents and purposes, the same as for the fourth scale: the ratio scale.

The *ratio* scale embraces the main features of the previous three scales – classification, order and an equal interval metric – but adds a fourth, powerful feature: a true zero. This enables the researcher to determine proportions easily – 'twice as many as', 'half as many as', 'three times the amount of' and so on. Because there is an absolute zero, all the arithmetical processes of addition, subtraction, multiplication and division are possible. Measures of distance, money in the bank, population, time spent on homework, years teaching, income, Celsius temperature, marks on a test and so on are all ratio measures as they are capable of having a 'true' zero quantity. If I have 1,000 dollars in the bank then it is twice as much as if I had 500 dollars in the bank; if I score 90 per cent in an examination then it is twice as many as if I had scored 45 per cent. The opportunity to use ratios and all four arithmetical processes renders this the most powerful level of data. Interval and ratio data are continuous variables that can take on any value within a particular, given range. Interval and ratio data typically use more powerful statistics than nominal and ordinal data.

The delineation of these four scales of data is important, as the consideration of which statistical test to use is dependent on the scale of data: it is incorrect to apply statistics which can only be used at a higher scale of data to data at a lower scale. For example, one should not apply averages (means) to nominal data, nor use t-tests and analysis of variances (discussed later) to ordinal data. Which statistical tests can be used with which data are set out clearly later. To close this section we record Wright's (2003: 127) view that the scale of measurement is not inherent to a particular variable, but something that researchers 'bestow on it based on our theories of that variable. It is a belief we hold about a variable.' What is being suggested here is that we have to justify classifying a variable as nominal, ordinal, interval or ratio, and not just assuming that it is self-evident.

34.2 Parametric and non-parametric data

Non-parametric data are those which make no assumptions about the population, usually because the characteristics of the population are unknown. Parametric data assume knowledge of the characteristics of the population, in order for inferences to be able to be made securely; they often assume a normal, Gaussian curve of distribution, as in reading scores, for example (though Wright (2003: 128) suggests that normal distributions are actually rare in psychology). In practice this distinction means: nominal and ordinal data are considered to be non-parametric, whilst interval and ratio data are considered to be parametric data. The distinction, as for the four scales of data, is important, as the consideration of which statistical test to use is dependent on the kinds of data: it is incorrect to apply parametric statistics to non-parametric data, though it is possible to apply non-parametric statistics to parametric data (though it is not widely done, as the statistics are usually less powerful). Non-parametric data are often derived from questionnaires and surveys (though these can also gain parametric data), whilst parametric data tend to be derived from experiments and tests (e.g. examination scores). (For the power efficiency of a statistical test see the accompanying website.)

34.3 Descriptive and inferential statistics

Descriptive statistics do exactly what they say: they describe and present data, for example in terms of summary frequencies. No attempt is made to infer or predict population parameters, and they are concerned simply with enumeration and organization. This will include, for example:

- the mode (the score obtained by the greatest number of people);
- the mean (the average score);
- the median (the score obtained by the middle person

in a ranked group of people, i.e. it has an equal number of scores above it and below it);
- minimum and maximum scores;
- the range (the distance between the highest and the lowest scores);
- the variance (a measure of how far scores are from the mean, calculated as the average of the squared deviations of individual scores from the mean);
- the standard deviation (a measure of the dispersal or range of scores, calculated as the square root of the variance);
- the standard error (the standard deviation of sample means);
- the skewness (how far the data are asymmetrical in relation to a 'normal' curve of distribution);
- kurtosis (how steep or flat is the shape of a graph or distribution of data; a measure of how peaked a distribution is and how steep is the slope or spread of data around the peak).

Such statistics make no inferences or predictions, they simply report what has been found, in a variety of ways.

Inferential statistics, by contrast, strive to make inferences and predictions based on the data gathered. They infer or predict population parameters or outcomes from simple measures, e.g. from sampling and from statistical techniques, and use information from a sample to reach conclusions about a population, based on probability. These will include, for example, hypothesis testing, correlations, regression and multiple regression, difference testing (e.g. t-tests and analysis of variance, factor analysis and structural equation modelling). Sometimes simple frequencies and descriptive statistics may speak for themselves, and the careful portrayal of descriptive data may be important. However, often it is the inferential statistics that are more valuable for researchers, and typically these are more powerful.

34.4 Kinds of variables

A variable is a condition, factor or quality that, as its name suggests, can vary from one case to another; it is the opposite of a constant, which does not vary between cases.

Dependent and independent variables

Research often concerns relationships between variables (a variable can be considered as a construct, operationalized construct or particular property in which the researcher is interested). An independent variable is an input variable, that which causes, in part or in total, a particular outcome; it is a stimulus that influences a response, an antecedent or a factor which may be modified (e.g. under experimental or other conditions) to affect an outcome. A dependent variable, on the other hand, is the outcome variable, that which is caused, in total or in part, by the input, antecedent variable. It is the effect, consequence of, or response to, an independent variable. This is a fundamental concept in many statistics.

For example, we may wish to see if doing more homework (independent variable) increases students' performance in, say, mathematics (dependent variable). We increase the homework and measure the result and, we notice, for example, that the performance increases on the mathematics test. The independent variable has produced a measured outcome. Or has it? Maybe: (a) the threat of the mathematics test increased the students' concentration, motivation and diligence in class; (b) the students liked mathematics and the mathematics teacher, and this caused them to work harder, not the mathematics test itself; (c) the students had a good night's sleep before the mathematics test and hence were refreshed and alert; (d) the students' performance in the mathematics test, in fact, influenced how much homework they did – the higher the marks, the more they were motivated to doing mathematics homework; (e) the increase in homework increased the students' motivation for mathematics and this, in turn, may have caused the performance increase in the mathematics test; (f) the students were told that if they did not perform well on the test then they would be punished, in proportion to how poorly they scored.

What one can observe here is important. In respect of (a) there are other *extraneous* variables which have to be factored into the causal relationship (i.e. in addition to the homework). In respect of (b) the assumed relationship is not really present; behind the coincidence of the rise in homework and the rise in the test result is a stronger causal relationship of the liking of the subject and the teacher which caused the students to work hard, a by-product of which was the rise in test scores. In respect of (c) an *intervening* variable was at work (a variable which affected the process of the test but which was not directly observed, measured or manipulated). In respect of (d) in fact the test caused the increase in homework, and not vice versa, i.e. the direction of causality was reversed. In respect of (f), the amount of increase was negatively correlated with the amount of punishment: the greater the mark, the lesser the punishment. In fact, what may be happening here is that causality may be less in a linear model and more multi-directional and multi-related, more like a web than a line.

This example indicates a range of issues in the discussion of dependent and independent variables:

- the direction of causality is not always clear (an independent variable may, in turn, become a dependent variable and vice versa);
- the direction of causality may be bi-directional;
- assumptions of association may not be assumptions of causality;
- there may be a range of other factors which have a bearing on an outcome;
- there may be causes (independent variables) behind the identified causes (independent variables) that have a bearing on the dependent variable;
- the independent variable may cause something else, and it is the something else that causes the outcome (dependent variable);
- causality may be non-linear rather than linear;
- the direction of the relationship may be negative rather than positive;
- the strength/magnitude of the relationship may be unclear.

Many statistics operate with dependent and independent variables (e.g. experiments using t-tests and analysis of variance, regression and multiple regression); others do not (e.g. correlational statistics, factor analysis). If one uses tests which require independent and dependent variables, great caution has to be exercised in assuming which is or is not the dependent or independent variable, and whether causality is as simple as the test assumes. Further, many statistical tests are based on linear relationships (e.g. correlation, regression and multiple regression, factor analysis) when in fact the relationships may not be linear (some software programs, e.g. SPSS, have the capability for handling non-linear relationships). The researcher has to make a fundamental decision about whether, in fact, the relationships are linear or non-linear, and select the appropriate statistical tests with these considerations in mind.

To draw these points together, the researcher will need to consider:

- What scales of data are there?
- Are the data parametric or non-parametric?
- Are descriptive or inferential statistics required?
- Do dependent and independent variables need to be identified?
- Are the relationships considered to be linear or non-linear?

The prepared researcher will need to consider the mode of data analysis that will be employed. This is very important as it has a specific bearing on the form of the instrumentation. For example a researcher will need to plan the layout and structure of a questionnaire survey very carefully in order to assist data entry for computer reading and analysis; an inappropriate layout may obstruct data entry and subsequent analysis by computer. The planning of data analysis will need to consider:

■ What needs to be done with the data when they have been collected – how will they be processed and analysed?
■ How will the results of the analysis be verified, cross-checked and validated?

Decisions will need to be taken with regard to the statistical tests that will be used in data analysis as this will affect the layout of research items (for example in a questionnaire), and the computer packages that are available for processing quantitative and qualitative data, e.g. SPSS and NUD*IST respectively.

Categorical, discrete and continuous variables

A categorical variable is a variable which has categories of values. For example, the variable 'sex' has two values: male and female, it is a dichotomous variable. In a rural community with, say, four local schools, the variable 'school attended' will have four values, one for each school. If we are looking at the types of food in school meals we may want to have three categories: carbohydrates, proteins and fats; each of these is a category of the variable 'food'.

A discrete variable has a finite number of values of the same item, with no intervals or fractions of the value (e.g. the number of illnesses a person has had, the number of mealtimes a person has each day). Here there are no fractions of a value – a person cannot have half an illness or half a mealtime; they either have the illness or not, they either have the mealtime or do not have it.

A continuous variable, as its name suggests, can vary in quantity, e.g. money in the bank, monthly earnings, numbers of students present in a class. Here there are equal intervals, and, usually, a zero (it is possible to have no money in the bank, or to have no earnings, or for a class of students to have none present that day).

Categorical variables match categorical data. Continuous variables match interval and ratio data. Depending on the kind of variable one has will be the kinds of statistics that can be used. This will be addressed in subsequent chapters.

Kinds of analysis

Univariate analysis examines differences amongst cases within one variable. Bivariate analysis looks for a relationship between two variables. Multivariate analysis looks for a relationship between two or more variables.

34.5 Hypotheses

Research in a hypothetico-deductive mode, and research that uses statistics, often commences with one or more hypotheses. This is the essence of hypothesis testing in quantitative research. Typically hypotheses fall into different types. The *null hypothesis*, a major type of hypothesis states that, for example, there is *no* relationship between two variables, or that there has been *no* change in participants between a pre-test and a post-test, or that there is *no* difference between three school districts in respect of their examination results, or that there is *no* difference between the voting of males and females on such-and-such a factor.

The point here is that by casting the hypothesis in a null form the burden of proof is placed on the researcher *not* to confirm that null hypothesis. The task is akin to a jury starting with a presumption of innocence and having to prove guilt beyond reasonable doubt. Not only is it often easier simply to support a straightforward positive hypothesis, but, more seriously, even if that positive hypothesis is supported, there may be insufficient grounds for accepting that hypothesis, as the finding may be consistent with other hypotheses. For example, let us imagine that our hypothesis is that a coin is weighted and, therefore, unfair. We flip the coin 100 times, and find that 60 times out of the hundred it comes out as heads. It would be easy to jump to the conclusion that the coin is weighted, but, equally easy, other reasons may account for the result. Of course, if the coin were to come out as heads 99 times out of the hundred then perhaps there would be greater truth in the hypothesis. The null hypothesis is a stronger version of evidence, requiring not only that the negative hypothesis be 'not supported', but also indicating a cut-off point only above which the null hypothesis is 'not supported', and below which the null hypothesis is supported. In our coin example it may be required to find that heads comes up 95 times out of a hundred, or 99 times out of a hundred, or even 999 times out of a thousand, to say, with increasing confidence in respect of these three sets of figures, that the null hypothesis is not supported.

We use terminology carefully here. Some researchers state that the null hypothesis is 'rejected'; others say that it is 'confirmed' or 'not confirmed'; others say that it is 'accepted' or 'not accepted'. We prefer the terminology of 'supported' or 'not supported'. This is not mere semantics or pedantry; rather it signals caution. Rejecting a null hypothesis is not the same as 'not confirming' or 'not supporting' that null hypothesis, rejection implying an absolute and universal state which the research will probably not be able to demonstrate, being bounded within strict parameters and not being applicable to all cases. Further, 'confirming' and 'not confirming', like 'rejecting', is too strong, absolute and universal a set of terms for what is, after all, research that is bounded and within delineated boundaries. Similarly, one cannot 'accept' a null hypothesis as a null hypothesis can never be proved unequivocally.

A second type of hypothesis is termed the *alternative hypothesis*. Whereas the null hypothesis states that there is *no* such-and-such (e.g. change, relationship, difference), the alternative hypothesis states that there *is* such-and-such, for example: there *is* a change in behaviour of the school students; there *is* a difference between students' scores on mathematics and science; there *is* a difference between the examination results of five school districts; there *is* a difference between the pre-test and post-test results of such-and-such a class. This weaker form of hypothesis is often supported when the null hypothesis is 'not supported', i.e. if the null hypothesis is not supported then the alternative hypothesis is.

The two kinds of hypothesis are usually written thus:

H_0: the null hypothesis
H_1: the alternative hypothesis

Sometimes the alternative hypothesis is written as H_A. So, for example the researcher could have null hypotheses and alternative hypotheses thus:

H_0: There is no difference between the results of the control group and experimental group in the post-test of mathematics
or There is no statistically significant difference between males and females in the results of the English examination
or There is no statistically significant correlation between the importance given to a subject and the amount of support given to it by the headteacher
H_1: There is a statistically significant difference between the control group and experimental groups in the post-test of mathematics
or There is a statistically significant difference between males and females in the results of the English examination

or There is a statistically significant positive correlation between examination scores in mathematics and science

The null hypothesis is the stronger hypothesis, requiring rigorous evidence *not* to support it. The alternative hypothesis is, perhaps, a fall-back position, taken up when the first – null – hypothesis is not confirmed. The latter is the logical opposite of the former. One should commence with the former and cast the research in the form of a null hypothesis, only turning to the latter in the case of finding the null hypothesis not to be supported.

A hypothesis can be directional or non-directional. A directional hypothesis states the kind of difference or relationship between two conditions or two groups of participants. For example:

■ Students who do homework *without* the television switched on in their room whilst working produce *better* results than those who do homework with the television switched on.
■ Students who have a computer at home do better in exams than those who do not.
■ People remember the words that appear early in a list better than the words that appear later.
■ People who are given a list of emotionally charged words recall more than participants given a list of neutral words.

Here one can see the direction of the hypothesis ('better', 'more than').

By contrast, a non-directional hypothesis simply predicts that there will be a difference or relationship between two conditions or two groups of participants, but it does not state the direction of the difference (e.g. 'more than', 'less than', 'better than', 'worse than'). For example:

■ Students who do homework without the television switched on in their room whilst working produce different results from those who do homework with the television switched on.
■ Students who have a computer at home perform differently in exams than people who do not.
■ People remember a different number of words that appear early in a list from the words that appear later.
■ People who are given a list of emotionally charged words recall a different number than participants given a list of neutral words.

Here there is a difference, but the *direction* of that difference is not made explicit. The stronger of these two types of hypothesis is the directional hypothesis because it makes a stronger claim than the non-directional hypothesis. In hypothesis testing the researcher:

1 Formulates a hypothesis.
2 Measures the variables involved and examines the relationship between them.
3 Calculates the probability of obtaining such a relationship if there were no relationship by chance, i.e. if there were no relationship in the population (if the null hypothesis is true). If the calculated probability is small enough, it suggests that the pattern of findings is unlikely to have arisen by chance, and probably reflects a genuine relationship in the population.

34.6 One-tailed and two-tailed tests

In using statistics, researchers are sometimes confronted with the decision whether to use a one-tailed or a two-tailed test. Which to use is a function of the kind of result one might predict. In a one-tailed test one predicts, for example, that one group will score more highly than the other, whereas in a two-tailed test one makes no such prediction. The one-tailed test is a stronger test than the two-tailed test as it makes assumptions about the population and the direction of the outcome (i.e. that one group will score more highly than another), and hence, if supported, is more powerful than a two-tailed test. A one-tailed test will be used with a directional hypothesis (e.g. 'Students who do homework *without* the TV on produce *better* results than those who do homework with the TV playing'). A two-tailed test will be used with a non-directional hypothesis (e.g. 'There is a *difference* between homework done in noisy or silent conditions'). The directional hypothesis indicates 'more' or 'less', whereas the non-directional hypothesis indicates only difference, and not where the difference may lie.

For example, let us imagine that we run a 'true experiment' to see if students who do homework *without* the TV on produce *better* results than those who do homework with the TV playing. The results are shown in Figure 34.1. We can see here that there is an overlap between the two sets of scores, but that the scores of the group that did not have the television switched on whilst doing homework are much higher than the scores of the group whose television is switched on whilst doing homework. Our directional hypothesis is supported, and we have used a one-tailed test to test the hypothesis.

In graphical terms, we can portray the results of a

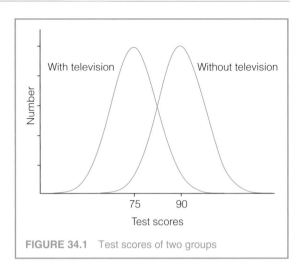

FIGURE 34.1 Test scores of two groups

one-tailed test that predicts high scores as in Figure 34.2. Here the prediction is that those students who work without the television switched on score more highly (the black area, that is at one end (tail) of the graph). The '5%' indicates that we are predicting with a 95 per cent degree of certainty that the results will be higher.

By contrast, we can portray the results of a one-tailed test that predicts low scores in Figure 34.3. Here the prediction is that those students who work with the television switched on score lower (the black area, that is at one end (tail) of the graph). Again, because we predict the direction of the result, we use a one-tailed test. Here the '5%' indicates that we are predicting with a 95 per cent degree of certainty that the results will be lower.

Figure 34.4 indicates the results for a two-tailed test. Here we can see that there are two black areas, one at each end (tail) of the graph. Because we have not predicted the direction of the result (it could be higher or lower, the burden of proof is higher, i.e. instead of

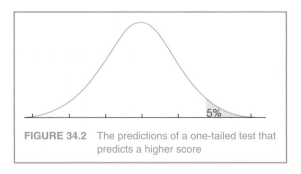

FIGURE 34.2 The predictions of a one-tailed test that predicts a higher score

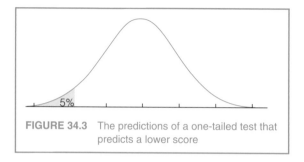

FIGURE 34.3 The predictions of a one-tailed test that predicts a lower score

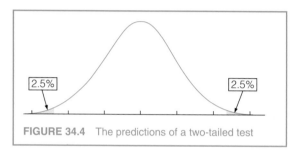

FIGURE 34.4 The predictions of a two-tailed test

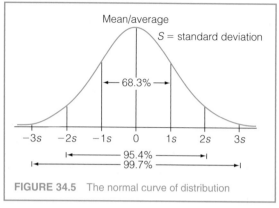

FIGURE 34.5 The normal curve of distribution

having a 95 per cent certainty (the 5 per cent of the two previous figures), we distribute that 5 per cent between the two tails, each of which is 2.5 per cent, i.e. we need to demonstrate a 97.5 per cent certainty level in the result.

34.7 Distributions

In everyday life many variables tend to be normally distributed. For example, we may say that most men are about such-and-such an average height. Some of course will be taller, and some shorter – there is a range. A smaller number will be much taller or much shorter; an even smaller number will be very much taller or very much shorter; a very small number will be extremely tall or extremely short. We can present the results on a normal curve of distribution (Figure 34.5).

The normal curve of distribution is a smooth, perfectly symmetrical (bell-shaped) curve; it is symmetrical about the mean and its tails are assumed to meet the x-axis at infinity. Here 68.3 per cent of people will fall within one standard deviation of the mean (a measure of variance from the mean (the average)). In our example we might assume that the majority of men (68.3 per cent) will be either just about or just below the mean height. Then, if we look at Figure 34.5, we can see that a smaller proportion (95.4 per cent minus 68.3 per cent=27.1 per cent) are much taller or much

shorter (between one standard deviation and two standard deviations away from the mean), and an even smaller proportion (99.7 per cent minus 95.4 per cent=4.3 per cent) are very tall or very short (even further away from the mean; between two and three standard deviations), and only a very tiny proportion (100 per cent minus 99.7 per cent=0.3 per cent) are extremely tall or extremely short (more than three standard deviations away from the mean).

In educational research that uses statistics, the statistical calculations often assume that the population is distributed normally and then compare the data collected from the sample to the population, allowing inferences to be made about the population (e.g. in random sampling). The assumption of the normal curve of distribution enables researchers to measure all normal distributions of a variable, regardless of the units in which that variable is initially measured.

Of course this is not always the case; rarely, if ever, in real life are data distributed so neatly. Rather than being symmetrical, data might be skewed in different ways. They may be positively or negatively skewed, as in Figure 34.6.

Skewed distributions are not symmetrical; a positively skewed distribution has the tail skewed to the right, whilst a negatively skewed distribution has the tail skewed to the left. This has important implications for even the simplest statistics calculated. For example whilst the mean (average) may be useful for normal distributions, in skewed distributions it is an unreliable measure, as it is affected by the long tail (positive or negative). Similarly the mode (the particular score registered by the greatest number) may not be an accurate measure of the distributions, being too strongly influenced by the positive or negative tails. In both of these cases, the median score (the score which

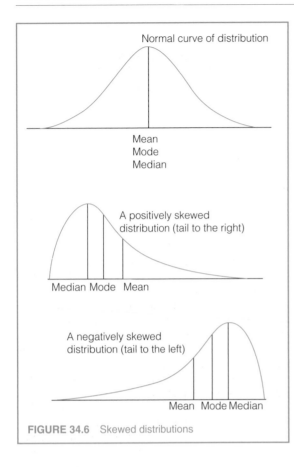

FIGURE 34.6   Skewed distributions

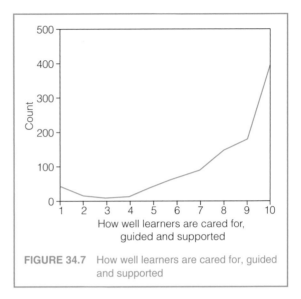

FIGURE 34.7   How well learners are cared for, guided and supported

is given by the middle person, e.g. in a test) is more reliable.

For example, Figure 34.7 is a line graph to show how respondents voted on how well learners are guided and supported in their learning, awarding marks out of ten for the voting, with a sample size of 400 respondents. Here the data are skewed, with more votes being received at the top end of the scale. There is a long tail going to the negative end of the scores, so, even though the highest scores are given at the top end of the scale, we say that this table has a negative skew because there is a long tail down.

By contrast, let us look at Figure 34.8, a graph of how much staff take on voluntarily roles in the school, with 150 votes received and awarding marks out of ten. Here a long tail goes toward the upper end of the scores, and the bulk of the scores are in the lower range. Even though most of the scores are in the lower range, because the long tail is towards the upper end of the scale this is termed a positive skew. The skewness of the data is an important feature to observe in data, and to which to draw attention.

Further, a graph of distribution may not always have the same bell-shaped features of the normal curve. For example it may be flatter than normal (platykurtic) or steeper than normal (leptokurtic), see Figure 34.9.

The measure of steepness of the curve is termed 'kurtosis', and many statistics packages calculate the measure of kurtosis. Normal distributions have a skewness of zero and a measure of kurtosis of zero: a platykurtic distribution has a negative value of kurtosis, whilst a leptokurtic distribution has a positive value of kurtosis. The degree of kurtosis may affect the reliability of the statistics that are used or the inferences that

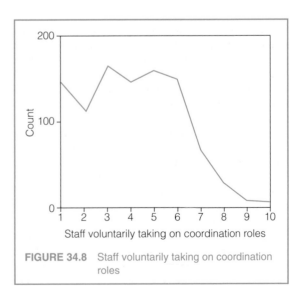

FIGURE 34.8   Staff voluntarily taking on coordination roles

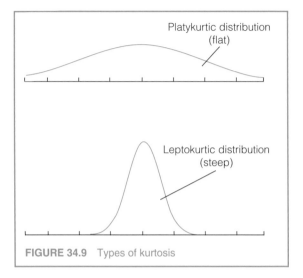

FIGURE 34.9   Types of kurtosis

are made from them. For example a platykurtic distribution may not have a problem with outliers, whilst a leptokurtic distribution may, and, further, many statistics assume normal kurtosis, rather than unduly flat or steep kurtosis.

34.8 Statistical significance

Much statistical analysis hinges on the notion of statistical significance. Kirk (1999: 337) indicates that 'a statistically significant result is one for which chance is an unlikely explanation'. Let us take an example from correlational research to unpack further the notion of statistical significance. A correlation enables a researcher to ascertain whether, and to what extent, there is a degree of association between two variables (this is discussed much more fully later in this chapter). Let us imagine that we observe that many people with large hands also have large feet and that people with small hands also have small feet (see Morrison, 1993: 136–40). We decide to conduct an investigation to see if there is any correlation or degree of association between the size of feet and the size of hands, or whether it is just chance that some people have large hands and large feet. We measure the hands and the feet of 100 people and observe that 99 times out of a hundred people with large feet also have large hands. Convinced that we have discovered an important relationship, we run the test on 1,000 people, and find that the relationship holds true in 999 cases out of the thousand. That seems to be more than mere coincidence; it would seem that we could say with some certainty that if a person has large hands then s/he will also have large feet. How do we know when we can make that

assertion? When do we know that we can have confidence in this prediction?

For statistical purposes, if we observe this relationship occurring 95 times out of a hundred, i.e. that chance only accounts for 5 per cent of the difference, then we could say with some confidence that there seems to be a high degree of association between the two variables hands and feet; it would occur by chance in five people in every hundred, reported as the 0.05 level of significance (0.05 being five hundredths). If we observe this relationship occurring 99 times out of every hundred (as in the example of hands and feet), i.e. that chance only accounts for 1 per cent of the difference, then we could say with even greater confidence that there seems to be a very high degree of association between the two variables; it would occur by chance once in every hundred, reported as the 0.01 level of significance (0.01 being one hundredth). If we observe this relationship occurring 999 times out of every thousand (as in the example of hands and feet), i.e. that chance only accounts for 0.1 per cent of the difference, then we could say with even greater confidence that there seems to be a very high degree of association between the two variables; it would occur only once in every thousand, reported as the 0.001 level of significance (0.001 being one thousandth).

We begin with a null hypothesis, which states that there is no relationship between the size of hands and the size of feet. The task is not to support the hypothesis, i.e. the burden of responsibility is not to support the null hypothesis. If we can show that the hypothesis is not supported for 95 per cent or 99 per cent or 99.9 per cent of the population, then we have demonstrated that there is a statistically significant relationship between the size of hands and the size of feet at the 0.05, 0.01 and 0.001 levels of significance respectively. These three levels of significance – the 0.05, 0.01 and 0.001 levels – are the levels at which statistical significance is frequently taken to have been demonstrated, usually the first two of these three levels. The researcher would say that the null hypothesis (that there is no statistically significant relationship between the two variables) has not been supported and that the level of significance observed (ρ) is at the 0.05, 0.01 or 0.001 level. Note here that we have used the terms 'statistically significant', and not simply 'significant'; this is important, for we are using the term in a specialized way.

Let us take a second example. Let us say that we have devised a scale of 1–8 which can be used to measure the sizes of hands and feet. Using the scale we make the following calculations for eight people, and set out the results thus:

	Hand size	Foot size
Subject A	1	1
Subject B	2	2
Subject C	3	3
Subject D	4	4
Subject E	5	5
Subject F	6	6
Subject G	7	7
Subject H	8	8

We can observe a perfect correlation between the size of the hands and the size of feet, from the person who has a size one hand and a size one foot to the person who has a size eight hand and also a size eight foot. There is a perfect positive correlation (as one variable increases, e.g. hand size, so the other variable – foot size – increases, and as one variable decreases so does the other). We can use the mathematical formula for calculating the Spearman correlation (this is calculated automatically in SPSS):

$$r = 1 - \frac{6\Sigma d^2}{N(N^2 - 1)}$$

where d = the difference between each pair of scores, Σ = the sum of, and N = the size of the population. We calculate that this perfect correlation yields an index of association – a coefficient of correlation – which is +1.00.

Suppose that this time we carry out the investigation on a second group of eight people and report the following results:

	Hand size	Foot size
Subject A	1	8
Subject B	2	7
Subject C	3	6
Subject D	4	5
Subject E	5	4
Subject F	6	3
Subject G	7	2
Subject H	8	1

This time the person with a size one hand has a size eight foot and the person with the size eight hand has a size one foot. There is a perfect negative correlation (as one variable increases, e.g. hand size, the other variable – foot size – decreases, and as one variable decreases, the other increases). Using the same mathematical formula we calculate that this perfect negative correlation yields an index of association – a coefficient of correlation – which is –1.00.

Now, clearly it is very rare to find a perfect positive or a perfect negative correlation; the truth of the matter is that looking for correlations will yield coefficients of correlation which lie somewhere between –1.00 and +1.00. How do we know whether the coefficients of correlation are statistically significant or not?

Let us say that we take a third sample of eight people and undertake an investigation into their hand and foot size. We enter the data case by case (Subject A to Subject H), indicating their rank order for hand size and then for foot size. This time the relationship is less clear because the rank ordering is more mixed, for example Subject A has a hand size of two and one for foot size, Subject B has a hand size of one and a foot size of two, etc.

	Hand size	Foot size
Subject A	2	1
Subject B	1	2
Subject C	3	3
Subject D	5	4
Subject E	4	5
Subject F	7	6
Subject G	6	7
Subject H	8	8

Using the mathematical formula for calculating the correlation statistic, we find that the coefficient of correlation for the eight people is 0.7857. Is it statistically significant? From a table of significance, we read off whether the coefficient is statistically significant or not for a specific number of cases, for example:

Number of cases	Level of significance	
	0.05	0.01
6	0.93	0.96
7	0.825	0.92
8	0.78	0.875
9	0.71	0.83
10	0.65	0.795
20	0.455	0.595
30	0.36	0.47

We see that for eight cases in an investigation the correlation coefficient has to be 0.78 or higher, if it is to be significant at the 0.05 level, and 0.875 or higher, if it is to be significant at the 0.01 level of significance. As the correlation coefficient in the example of the third experiment with eight subjects is 0.7857 we can see that it is higher than that required for significance at the 0.05 level (0.78) but not as high as that required for significance at the 0.01 level (0.875). We are safe, then, in stating that the degree of association between the hand and foot sizes does not support the null hypothesis and demonstrates statistical significance at the 0.05 level.

The first example above of hands and feet is very neat because it has 100 people in the sample. If we have more or less than 100 people how do we know if a relationship between two factors is statistically significant? Let us say that we have data on 30 people; in this case, because sample size is so small, we might hesitate to say that there is a strong association between the size of hands and size of feet if we observe it occurring in 27 people (i.e. 90 per cent of the population). On the other hand, let us say that we have a sample of 1,000 people and we observe the association in 700 of them. In this case, even though only 70 per cent of the sample demonstrate the association of hand and foot size, we might say that because the sample size is so large we can have greater confidence in the data than in the case of the small sample.

Statistical significance varies according to the size of the number in the sample (as can be seen also in the section of the table of significance reproduced above). In order to be able to determine significance we need to have two facts in our possession: the size of the sample and, in correlational research, the coefficient of correlation or, in other kinds of research, the appropriate coefficients or data (there are many kinds, depending on the test being used). Here, as the selection from the table of significance reproduced above shows, the coefficient of correlation can decrease and still be statistically significant as long as the sample size increases. (This resonates with Krejcie's and Morgan's (1970) principles for sampling, observed in Chapter 8, namely as the population increases the sample size increases at a diminishing rate in addressing randomness.) This is a major source of debate for critics of statistical significance, who argue that it is almost impossible *not* to find statistical significance when dealing with large samples, as the coefficients can be very low and still attain statistical significance.

To ascertain statistical significance from a table, then, is a matter of reading off the significance level from a table of significance according to the sample size, or processing data on a computer program to yield the appropriate statistic. In the selection from the table of significance for the third example above concerning hand and foot size, the first column indicates the number of people in the sample and the other two columns indicate significance at the two levels. Hence, if we have 30 people in the sample then, for the correlation to be statistically significant at the 0.05 level, we would need a correlation coefficient of 0.36, whereas, if there were only ten people in the sample, we would need a correlation coefficient of 0.65 for the correlation to be statistically significant at the same 0.05 level. Most statistical packages (e.g. SPSS) automatically calculate the level of statistical significance, indeed SPSS automatically asterisks each case of statistical significance at the 0.05 and 0.01 levels or smaller. We discuss correlational analysis in more detail later in Chapter 36, and we refer the reader to that discussion.

34.9 Hypothesis testing

The example that we have given above from correlational analysis illustrates a wider issue of hypothesis testing. This follows four stages.

Stage 1

In quantitative research, as mentioned above, we commence with a null hypothesis, for example:

- there is *no* statistical significance in the distribution of the data in a contingency table (crosstabulation);
- there is *no* statistically significant correlation between two factors;
- there is *no* statistically significant difference between the means of two groups;
- there is *no* statistically significant difference between the means of a group in a pre-test and a post-test;
- there is *no* statistically significant difference between the means of three or more groups;
- there is *no* statistically significant difference between two subsamples;
- there is *no* statistically significant difference between three or more subsamples;
- there is *no* significant prediction capability between one independent variable X and dependent variable Y;
- there is *no* significant prediction capability between two or more independent variable X, Y, Z … and dependent variable A.

The task of the researcher is to support or not to support the null hypothesis.

Stage 2

Having set the null hypothesis, the researcher then sets the level of significance (α) that will be used to support or not to support the null hypothesis; this is the alpha (α) level. The level of alpha is determined by the researcher. Typically it is 0.05, i.e. for 95 per cent of the time the null hypothesis is not supported. In writing this we could say 'Let $\alpha = 0.05$'. If one wished to be more robust then one would set a higher alpha level ($\alpha = 0.01$ or $\alpha = 0.001$). This is the level of risk that one wishes to take in supporting or not supporting the null hypothesis.

Stage 3

Having set the null hypothesis and the level at which it will be supported or not supported, one then computes the data in whatever form is appropriate for the research in question (e.g. measures of association, measures of difference, regression and prediction measures).

Stage 4

Having analysed the data one is then in a position to support or not to support the null hypothesis, and this is what would be reported.

It is important to distinguish two types of hypothesis (Wright, 2003: 132): a *causal* hypothesis and an *associative* hypothesis. As its name suggests, a causal hypothesis suggests that input X will affect outcome Y, as in, for example, an experimental design. An associative hypothesis describes how variables may relate to each other, not necessarily in a causal manner (e.g. in correlational analysis). One has to be careful not to describe an associative hypothesis (e.g. gender) as a causal hypothesis, as gender may not be actually having a causal effect.

In hypothesis testing one has to avoid Type I and Type II errors. A Type I error occurs when one does not support the null hypothesis when it is in fact true. This is a particular problem as the sample increases, as the chances of finding a significant association increase, irrespective of whether a true association exists (Rose and Sullivan, 1993: 168), requiring the researcher, therefore, to set a higher alpha (α) limit (e.g. 0.01 or 0.001) for statistical significance to be achieved). A Type II error occurs when one supports the null hypothesis when it is in fact not true (often the case if the levels of significance are set too stringently, i.e. requiring the researcher to lower the alpha level (α) of significance (e.g. 0.1 or 0.2) required). Type I and Type II can be represented as in Table 34.1.

TABLE 34.1 TYPE I AND TYPE II ERRORS

Decision	H_0 True	H_0 False
Support H_0	Correct	Type II error (β)
Do not support H_0	Type I error (α)	Correct

34.10 Effect size

One has to be cautious in using statistical significance. Statistical significance is not the same as educational significance. For example, I might find a statistically significant correlation between the amount of time spent on mathematics and the amount of time spent in watching television. This may be completely unimportant. Similarly I might find that there is no statistically significant difference between males and females in their liking of physics. However, close inspection might reveal that there is a difference. Say, for example, that males prefer physics to females, but that the difference does not reach the 'cut-off' point of the 0.05 level of significance; maybe it is 0.065. To say that there is no difference, or simply to support the null hypothesis here might be inadvisable. There are two issues here: (a) the cut-off level of significance is comparatively arbitrary, though high; (b) one should not ignore coefficients that fall below the conventional cut-off points. This leads us into a discussion of effect size as an alternative to significance levels.

Statistical significance on its own has come to be seen as an unacceptable index of effect (Thompson, 1994, 1996, 1998, 2001, 2002; Thompson and Snyder, 1997; Rozeboom, 1997: 335; Fitz-Gibbon, 1997: 43; Wilkinson and the Task Force on Statistical Inference, APA Board of Scientific Affairs, 1999; Olejnik and Algina, 2000; Capraro and Capraro, 2002; Wright, 2003; Kline, 2004) because it depends on both sample size and the coefficient (e.g. of correlation). Statistical significance can be attained *either* by having a large coefficient together with a small sample *or* having a small coefficient together with a large sample. The problem is that one is not able to deduce which is the determining effect from a study using statistical significance (Coe, 2000: 9). It is important to be able to tell whether it is the sample size or the coefficient that is making the difference. The effect size can do this.

What is required either to accompany or replace statistical significance is information about *effect size* (American Psychological Association, 1994: 18; 1999; Wilkinson and the Task Force on Statistical Inference, APA Board of Scientific Affairs, 1999; Kline, 2004). Indeed effect size is seen as much more important than significance, and many international journals have either abandoned statistical significance reporting in favour of effect size, or have insisted that statistical significance be accompanied by indications of effect size (Olejnik and Algina, 2000; Capraro and Capraro, 2002; Thompson, 2002). Statistical significance is seen as arbitrary in its cut-off points and unhelpful – a 'corrupt form of the scientific method' (Carver, 1978), an obstacle rather than a facilitator in educational research. It commands slavish adherence rather than addressing the subtle, sensitive and helpful notion of effect size (see Fitz-Gibbon, 1997: 118). Indeed common sense should tell the researcher that a differential measure of effect size is more useful than the blunt edge of statistical significance.

An effect size is 'simply a way of quantifying the difference between two groups. For example, if one group has had an "experimental treatment" and the other has not (the "control"), then the Effect Size is a measure of the effectiveness of the treatment' (Coe, 2000: 1). It tells the reader 'how big the effect is, something that the p value [statistical significance] does not do' (Wright, 2003: 125). An effect size (Thompson, 2002: 25) 'characterizes the degree to which sample results diverge from the null hypothesis'; it operates through the use of standard deviations.

Wood (1995: 393) suggests that effect size can be calculated by dividing the significance level by the sample size. Glass *et al.* (1981: 29, 102) calculate the effect size as:

$$\frac{\text{(mean of experimental group} - \text{mean of control group)}}{\text{standard deviation of the control group}}$$

Coe (2000: 7), whilst acknowledging that there is a debate on whether to use the standard deviation of the experimental or control group as the denominator, suggests that that of the control group is preferable as it provides 'the best estimate of standard deviation, since it consists of a representative group of the population who have not been affected by the experimental intervention'. However, he also suggests that it is perhaps preferable to use a 'pooled' estimate of standard deviation, as this is more accurate than that provided by the control group alone. To calculate the pooled deviation he suggests that the formula should be:

$$\text{SD pooled} = \sqrt{\frac{(N_E - 1)SD_E^2 + (N_C - 1)SD_C^2}{N_E + N_C - 2}}$$

where N_E=number in the experimental group, N_C=number in the control group, SD_E=standard deviation of the experimental group and SD_C=standard deviation of the control group.

The formula for the pooled deviation then becomes (Muijs, 2004: 136):

$$\frac{\text{(mean of experimental group} - \text{mean of control group)}}{\text{pooled standard deviation}}$$

where the pooled standard deviation=(standard deviation of group 1+standard deviation of group 2).

There are several different calculations of effect size, for example (Richardson, 1996; Capraro and Capraro, 2002: 771): r^2, adjusted R^2, η^2, ω^2, Cramer's V, Kendall's W, Cohen's d, and Eta. Different kinds of statistical treatments use different effect size calculations. For example, the formula given by Muijs (2004) here yields the statistic termed Cohen's d. Further details of this, together with a facility which calculates it automatically, can be found at www.uccs.edu/~lbecker/psy590/escalc3.htm.

An effect size can lie between 0 to 1 (some formulae yield an effect size that is larger than 1 – see Coe, 2000). In using Cohen's d:

$$0\text{--}0.20 = \text{weak effect}$$
$$0.21\text{--}0.50 = \text{modest effect}$$
$$0.51\text{--}1.00 = \text{moderate effect}$$
$$>1.00 = \text{strong effect}$$

In correlational data the coefficient of correlation is used as the effect size in conjunction with details of the direction of the association (i.e. a positive or negative correlation). The coefficient of correlation (effect size) is interpreted thus:

$<0 +/-1$	weak
$<0 +/-3$	modest
$<0 +/-5$	moderate
$<0 +/-8$	strong
$\geq +/-0.8$	very strong

We provide more detail on interpreting correlation coefficients later in this chapter. However, Thompson (2001, 2002) argues forcibly against simplistic interpretations of effect size as 'small', 'medium' and 'large', as to do this commits the same folly of fixed benchmarks as that of statistical significance. He writes that 'if people interpret effect sizes with the same rigidity that $\alpha =.05$ has been used in statistical testing, we would merely be being stupid in another metric' (Thompson, 2001, 82–3). Rather, he avers, it is important to avoid fixed benchmarks (i.e. cut-off points), and relate the effect sizes found to those of prior studies, confidence intervals and power analyses. Wright (2003: 125) also suggests that it is important to report the units of measurement of the effect size, for example in the units of measure of the original variables as well as in standardized units (e.g. standard deviations), the latter being useful if different scales of measures are being used for the different variables.

We discussed *confidence intervals* in Chapter 8. It is the amount of the 'true population value of the parameter'

(Wright, 2003: 126), e.g. 90 per cent of the population, 95 per cent of the population, 99 per cent of the population. A confidence interval is reported as $1-\alpha$, i.e. the level of likelihood that a score falls within a pre-specified range of scores (e.g. 95 per cent, 99 per cent likelihood). Software for calculating confidence intervals for many measures can be found at http://glass.ed.asu/stats/analysis/.

The *power of a test* is 'an estimate of the ability of the test to separate the effect size from random variation' (Gorard, 2001b: 14), the 'probability of rejecting a specific effect size for a specific sample size at a particular α level (i.e. the critical level to reject H_0)' (Wright, 2003: 126). Wright suggests that it should be a minimum of 80 per cent and to be typically with an α level at 5 per cent. Software for calculating power analysis can be found at www.psycho.uni-duesseldorf.de/ abteilungen/aap/gpower3/download-and-register.

In calculating the effect size (Eta squared) for independent samples in a t-test (discussed later) the following formula can be used.

$$\text{Eta squared} = \frac{t^2}{t^2 + (N_1 + N_2 - 2)}$$

Here t=the t-value (calculated by SPSS); N_1=the number in the sample of group one and N_2=the number in the sample of group 2. Let us take an example of the results of an evaluation item in which the two groups are (a) leaders/senior managers (SMT) of schools, and (b) teachers, shown in Tables 34.2 and 34.3.

Here the t-value is 1.923, N_1 is 347 and N_2 is 653. Hence the formula is:

$$\frac{t^2}{t^2 + (N_1 + N_2 - 2)} = \frac{1.923^2}{1.923^2 + (347 + 653 - 2)}$$

$$= \frac{3.698}{3.698 - 998} = 0.0037$$

The guidance here from Cohen (1988) is that 0.01=a very small effect; 0.06=a moderate effect; and 0.14=a very large effect. Here the result of 0.003 is a tiny effect, i.e. only 0.3 per cent of the variance in the variable 'How well learners are cared for, guided and supported' is explained by whether one is a leader/SMT member or a teacher.

For a paired sample t-test (discussed later) the effect size (Eta squared) is calculated by the following formula:

$$\text{Eta squared} = \frac{t^2}{t^2 + (N_1 - 1)}$$

Let us imagine that the same group of students had scored marks out of a hundred in 'Maths' and 'Science', as shown in Tables 34.4 and 34.5.

TABLE 34.2 MEAN AND STANDARD DEVIATION IN AN EFFECT SIZE (SPSS OUTPUT)

Group Statistics

	who are you	N	Mean	Std. Deviation	Std. Error Mean
How well learners are cared for, guided and supported	leader/member of the SMT	347	8.37	2.085	.112
	teachers	653	8.07	2.462	.096

TABLE 34.3 THE LEVENE TEST FOR EQUALITY OF VARIANCES (SPSS OUTPUT)

Independent Samples Test

		Levene's Test for Equality of Variances		t-test for Equality of Means					95% Confidence Interval of the Difference	
		F	Sig.	t	df	Sig. (2-tailed)	Mean Difference	Std. Error Difference	Lower	Upper
How well learners are cared for, guided and supported	Equal variances assumed	8.344	.004	1.923	998	.055	.30	.155	-.006	.603
	Equal variances not assumed			2.022	811.922	.044	.30	.148	.009	.589

The effect size can be worked out thus (using SPSS):

$$\frac{t^2}{t^2 + (N_1 - 1)} = \frac{16.588^2}{16.588^2 + (1000 - 1)} = \frac{275.162}{275.162 + 999}$$
$$= 0.216$$

In this example the effect size is 0.216, a very large effect, i.e. there was a very substantial difference between the scores of the two groups.

For analysis of variance (discussed in Chapter 36) the effect size is calculated thus:

$$\text{Eta squared} = \frac{\text{Sum of squares between groups}}{\text{Total sum of squares}}$$

In SPSS this is given as 'partial eta squared'. For example, let us imagine that we wish to compute the effect size of the difference between four groups of schools on mathematics performance in a public examination. The fours groups of schools are: (a) rural primary; (b) rural secondary; (c) urban primary; (d) urban secondary. Analysis of variance yields the result as shown in Table 34.6.

Working through the formula yields the following:

$$\frac{\text{Sum of squares between groups}}{\text{Total sum of squares}} = \frac{7078.619}{344344.8} = 0.021$$

The figure of 0.021 indicates a small effect size, i.e. that there is a small difference between the four groups in their mathematics performance (note that this is a much smaller difference than that indicated by the significance level of .006, which suggests a statistically highly

---

TABLE 34.4   MEAN AND STANDARD DEVIATION IN A PAIRED SAMPLE TEST (SPSS OUTPUT)

Paired Samples Statistics

		Mean	N	Std. Deviation	Std. Error Mean
Pair 1	MATHS	81.71	1000	23.412	.740
	SCIENCE	67.26	1000	27.369	.865

TABLE 34.5   DIFFERENCE TEST FOR A PAIRED SAMPLE (SPSS OUTPUT)

Paired Samples Test

		Paired Differences							
					95% Confidence Interval of the Difference				Sig. (2-tailed)
		Mean	Std. Deviation	Std. Error Mean	Lower	Upper	t	df	
Pair 1	MATHS - SCIENCE	14.45	27.547	.871	12.74	16.16	16.588	999	.000

TABLE 34.6   EFFECT SIZE IN ANALYSIS OF VARIANCE (SPSS OUTPUT)

ANOVA

MATHS

	Sum of Squares	df	Mean Square	F	Sig.
Between Groups	7078.619	3	2359.540	4.205	.006
Within Groups	337266.2	601	561.175		
Total	344344.8	604			

significant difference between the four groups of schools.

In regression analysis (discussed in Chapter 36) the effect size of the predictor variables is given by the beta weightings. In interpreting effect size here Muijs (2004: 194) gives the following guidance:

0–0.1	weak effect
0.1–0.3	modest effect
0.3–0.5	moderate effect
>0.5	strong effect

For a discussion of the importance of attending to both small effect sizes as well as large effect sizes, see Wang (2008). Wang argues that small effect sizes could indicate an important finding (p. 130), i.e. effect size and importance are two separate concepts.

Hedges (1981) and Hunter *et al.* (1982) suggest alternative equations to take account of differential weightings due to sample size variations. The two most frequently used indices of effect sizes are standardized mean differences and correlations (Hunter *et al.*, 1982: 373), though non-parametric statistics, e.g. the median, can be used. Lipsey (1992: 93–100) sets out a series of statistical tests for working on effect sizes, effect size means and homogeneity.

Muijs (2004: 126) indicates that a measure of effect size for crosstabulations, instead of chi-square, should be *phi*, which is the square root of the calculated value of chi-square divided by the overall valid sample size. He gives an example: 'if chi-square $= 14.810$ and the sample size is 885 then phi $= 14.810/885 = 0.0167$ and then take the square root of this $= 0.129$'.

Effect sizes are susceptible to a range of influences. These include (Coe: 2000):

- *Restricted range*: the smaller the range of scores, the greater is the possibility of a higher effect size, therefore it is important to use the standard deviation of the whole population (and not just one group), i.e. a pooled standard deviation, in calculating the effect size. It is important to report the possible restricted range or sampling here (e.g. a group of highly able students rather than, for example, the whole ability range).
- *Non-normal distributions*: effect size usually assumes a normal distribution, so any non-normal distributions would have to be reported.
- *Measurement reliability*: the reliability (accuracy, stability and robustness) of the instrument being used (e.g. the longer the test, or the more items that are used to measure a factor, the more reliable it could be).

There are downloadable software programs available that will calculate effect size simply by the researcher keying in minimal amounts of data, for example:

- http://web.uccs.edu/lbecker/Psy590/escalc3.htm
- www.cedu.niu.edu/~walker/calculators/effect.asp
- www.uccs.edu/~faculty/lbecker/
- www.cognitiveflexibility.org/effectsize/
- http://davidmlane.com/hyperstat/effect_size.html
- www.danielsoper.com/statcalc/calc05.aspx
- www.danielsoper.com/statcalc/
- http://freewareapp.com/effect-size-generator_download/
- www.public.asu.edu/~mwwatkin/Watkins3.html

More information on effect sizes can be found at: www.latrobe.edu.au/psy/esci and www.cemcentre.org/evidence-based-education/effect-size-calculator, Leech and Onwuegbuzie (2004) and Kline (2004).

34.11 A note on symbols

It is commonplace to see a range of Greek letters used in statistics. These may appear forbidding to the novice researcher, hence Table 34.7 presents the main letters used, together with an explanation of these.

Additionally there are many English letters used in statistics. The main ones are:

df	=	degrees of freedom
F	=	f-ratio value (in analysis of variance (ANOVA))
H_0	=	null hypothesis
H_1	=	alternative hypothesis
i as subscript	=	(number of) specific observations in a data set
N	=	population size
n	=	sample size
R^2	=	multiple coefficients of determination in a multiple regression
R_1	=	Spearman rank order correlation
r	=	correlation
SD	=	standard deviation
SS_i	=	sum of squares
t	=	t-value in a t-test
$\bar{x}$	=	arithmetic mean (x-bar)

We meet some of these signs, symbols and letters in the following chapters.

TABLE 34.7 FREQUENTLY USED GREEK LETTERS IN STATISTICS

Greek letter	Name	Use in statistics
α	Alpha	Probability of making a Type I error. The statistical significance level
β	Beta	Probability of making a Type II error. The beta value in multiple regression is a measure of how strongly each independent (predictor) variable influences the dependent variable
Δ δ	Delta	Difference: Δ. Standard deviation: δ
η	Eta	The partial regression coefficient, measure of effect size: η (usually used as 'partial eta squared' η^2)
Λ λ	Lambda	A test of mean differences in multivariate analyses (Wilks's lambda)
μ	Mu	Population mean: μ
ν	Nu	Degrees of freedom: ν
π	Pi	Population proportion: π
ρ	Rho	Correlation coefficient. Significance level: ρ
Σ σ	Sigma	The sum of: Σ. Population standard deviation (lower case: σ). Population variance: σ^2
Φ φ ϕ	Phi	The phi coefficient is a measure of the degree of association between two binary variables (a binary variable has only two values, e.g. male/female)
χ	Chi	Goodness of fit and independence of two or more variables (chi-square: χ^2)

 Companion Website

The companion website to the book includes PowerPoint slides for this chapter, which list the structure of the chapter and then provide a summary of the key points in each of its sections. This resource can be found online at **www.routledge.com/textbooks/cohen7e**.

Additionally readers are recommended to access the online resources for Chapter 36 as these contain materials that apply to the present chapter, such as the SPSS Manual which guides readers through the SPSS commands required to run statistics in SPSS, together with data files of different data sets.

Descriptive statistics

This chapter introduces descriptive statistics. Descriptive statistics do what they say: they describe, so that researchers can then analyse and interpret what these descriptions mean. This chapter introduces some key descriptive statistics and how to use them. This includes:

- frequencies, percentages and crosstabulations
- measures of central tendency and dispersal
- taking stock
- correlations and measures of association
- partial correlations
- reliability

Descriptive statistics include frequencies, measures of dispersal (standard deviation), measures of central tendency (means, modes, medians), standard deviations, crosstabulations and standardized scores. We address all these in this chapter, with the exception of standardized scores, which we keep for Chapter 36.

35.1 Frequencies, percentages and crosstabulations

Frequencies and percentages

In descriptive statistics much is made of visual techniques of data presentation. Hence frequencies and percentages, and forms of graphical presentation are often used. A host of graphical forms of data presentation are available in software packages, including, for example:

- frequency and percentage tables;
- bar charts (for nominal and ordinal data);
- histograms (for continuous – interval and ratio – data);
- line graphs;
- pie charts;
- high and low charts;
- scatterplots;
- stem and leaf displays;
- boxplots (box and whisker plots).

With most of these forms of data display there are various permutations of the ways in which data are displayed within the type of chart or graph chosen. Whilst graphs and charts may look appealing, it is often the case that they tell the reader no more than could be seen in a simple table of figures, and figures take up less space in a report. Pie charts, bar charts and histograms are particularly prone to this problem, and the data in them could be placed more succinctly into tables. Clearly the issue of fitness for audience is important here: some readers may find charts more accessible and able to be understood than tables of figures, and this is important. Other charts and graphs can add greater value than tables, for example line graphs, boxplots and scatterplots with regression lines, and we would suggest that these are helpful. Here is not the place to debate the strengths and weaknesses of each type, though the following list presents some guides:

- bar charts are useful for presenting categorical and discrete data, highest and lowest;
- avoid using a third dimension (e.g. depth) in a graph when it is unnecessary; a third dimension to a graph must provide additional information;
- histograms are useful for presenting continuous data;
- line graphs are useful for showing trends, particularly in continuous data, for one or more variables at a time;
- multiple line graphs are useful for showing trends in continuous data on several variables in the same graph;
- pie charts and bar charts are useful for showing proportions;
- interdependence can be shown through crosstabulations (discussed below);
- boxplots are useful for showing the distribution of values for several variables in a single chart, together with their range and medians;
- stacked bar charts are useful for showing the frequencies of different groups within a specific variable for two or more variables in the same chart;
- scatterplots are useful for showing the relationship between two variables or several sets of two or more variables on the same chart.

At a simple level one can present data in terms of frequencies and percentages, as shown in Table 35.1 (a piece of datum about a course evaluation). From this simple table we can tell that:

- 191 people completed the item;
- most respondents thought that the course was 'a little' too hard (with a clear modal score of 98, i.e. 51.3%); the modal score is that category or score which is given by the highest number of respondents;
- the results were skewed, with only 10.5 per cent being in the categories 'quite a lot' and 'a very great deal';
- more people thought that the course was 'not at all too hard' than thought that the course was 'quite a lot' or 'a very great deal' too hard;
- overall the course appears to have been slightly too difficult but not much more.

Crosstabulations

Let us imagine that we wished to explore this piece of datum further. We may wish to discover, for example, the voting on this item by males and females. This can be presented in a simple crosstabulation, following the convention of placing the nominal data (male and female) in rows and the ordinal data (the five-point scale) in the columns (or independent variables as row data and dependent variables as column data). A crosstabulation is simply a presentational device, whereby one variable is presented in relation to another, with the relevant data inserted into each cell (automatically generated by software packages, such as SPSS) (Table 35.2).

Table 35.2 shows that, of the total sample, nearly three times more females (38.2%) than males (13.1%) thought that the course was 'a little' too hard, between two-thirds and three-quarters more females (19.9%) than males (5.8%) thought that the course was a 'very little' too hard, and around three times more males (1.6%) than females (0.5%) thought that the course was 'a very great deal' too hard. However, one also has to observe that the size of the two subsamples was uneven. Around three-quarters of the sample was female (73.8%) and around one-quarter (26.2%) was male.

There are two ways to overcome the problem of uneven subsample sizes. One is to adjust the sample, in this case by multiplying up the subsample of males by an exact figure in order to make the two subsamples the same size (141/50=2.82). Another way is to examine the data by each row rather than by the overall totals, i.e. to examine the proportion of males voting such-and-such, and, separately, the proportion of females voting for the same categories of the variable, as shown in Table 35.3.

TABLE 35.1 FREQUENCIES AND PERCENTAGES FOR A COURSE EVALUATION (SPSS OUTPUT)

The course was too hard

		Frequency	Percentage
Valid	not at all	24	12.6
	very little	49	25.7
	a little	98	51.3
	quite a lot	16	8.4
	a very great deal	4	2.1
	Total	191	100.0

TABLE 35.2 CROSSTABULATION BY TOTALS (SPSS OUTPUT)

sex * The course was too hard: crosstabulation

		the course was too hard					
		not at all	very little	a little	quite a lot	a very great deal	Total
male	Count	7	11	25	4	3	50
	% of Total	3.7%	5.8%	13.1%	2.1%	1.6%	26.2%
female	Count	17	38	73	12	1	141
	% of Total	8.9%	19.9%	38.2%	6.3%	.5%	73.8%
Total	Count	24	49	98	16	4	191
	% of Total	12.6%	25.7%	51.3%	8.4%	2.1%	100.0%

TABLE 35.3 CROSSTABULATION BY ROW TOTALS (SPSS OUTPUT)

Sex * The course was too hard: crosstabulation

		the course was too hard					
		not at all	very little	a little	quite a lot	a very great deal	Total
male	Count	7	11	25	4	3	50
	% within sex	14.0%	22.0%	50%	8.0%	6.0%	100%
female	Count	17	38	73	12	1	141
	% within sex	12.1%	27.0%	52%	8.5%	.7%	100%
Total	Count	24	49	98	16	4	191
	% within sex	12.6%	25.7%	51%	8.4%	2.1%	100%

If you think that these two calculations and recalculations are complicated or difficult (overall-percentaged totals and row-percentaged totals), then be reassured: many software packages, e.g. SPSS (the example used here) will do this at one keystroke.

In this second table (Table 35.3) one can observe that:

- there was consistency in the voting by males and females in terms of the categories 'a little' and 'quite a lot';
- more males (6%) than females (0.7%) thought that the course was 'a very great deal' too hard;
- a slightly higher percentage of females (91.1%: {12.1%+27%+52%}) than males (86%: {14%+22%+50%}) indicated, overall, that the course was not too hard;
- the overall pattern of voting by males and females was similar, i.e. for both males and females the strong to weak categories in terms of voting percentages were identical.

We would suggest that this second table is more helpful than the first table, as, by including the row percentages, it renders fairer the comparison between the two groups: males and females. Further, we would suggest that it is usually preferable to give *both* the actual frequencies and percentages, but to make the comparisons by percentages. We say this, because it is important for the reader to know the actual numbers used. For example, in the first table (Table 35.2), if we were simply to be given the percentage of males voting that the course was a 'very great deal' too hard (1.6%), as course planners we might worry about this. However, when we realize that 1.6% is actually only three out of 141 people then we might be less worried.

Had the 1.6% represented, say, 50 people of a sample, then this would have given us cause for concern. Percentages on their own can mask the real numbers, and the reader needs to know the real numbers.

It is possible to comment on particular cells of a crosstabulated matrix in order to draw attention to certain factors (e.g. the very high 52% in comparison to its neighbour 8.5% in the voting of females in Table 35.3). It is also useful, on occasions, to combine data from more than one cell, as we have done in the list above. For example, if we combine the data from the males in the categories 'quite a lot' and 'a very great deal' (8%+6%=14%) we can observe that not only is this equal to the category 'not at all', but it contains fewer cases than any of the other single categories for the males, i.e. the combined category shows that the voting for the problem of the course being too difficult is still very slight.

Combining categories can be useful in showing the general trends or tendencies in the data. For example, in Tables 35.1–35.3, combining the measures 'not at all', 'very little' and 'a little' indicates that it is only a very small problem of the course being too hard, i.e. generally speaking the course was not too hard.

TABLE 35.4 RATING SCALE OF AGREEMENT AND DISAGREEMENT

Strongly disagree	Disagree	Neither agree nor disagree	Agree	Strongly agree
30	40	70	20	40
15%	20%	35%	10%	20%

TABLE 35.5   SATISFACTION WITH A COURSE

Satisfaction with course

	Low (1–3)	Medium (4–5)	High (6–7)	Total
Male	60 (41.4%)	70 (48.3%)	15 (10.3%)	145 (100%)
Female	35 (43.7%)	15 (18.8%)	30 (37.5%)	80 (100%)
Total	95 (42.2%)	85 (37.8%)	45 (20%)	225 (100%)

Combining categories can also be useful in rating scales of agreement to disagreement. For example, consider the results in Table 35.4 in relation to a survey of 200 people on a particular item. There are several ways of interpreting the table, for example: (a) more people 'strongly agreed' (20%) than 'strongly disagreed' (15%); (b) the modal score was for the central neutral category (a central tendency) of 'neither agree nor disagree'. However one can go further. If one wishes to ascertain an overall indication of disagreement and agreement, then adding together the two disagreement categories yields 35% (15%+20%) and adding together the two agreement categories yields 30% (10%+20%), i.e. there was more disagreement than agreement, despite the fact that more respondents 'strongly agreed' than 'strongly disagreed', i.e. the *strength* of agreement and disagreement has been lost. By adding together the two disagreement and agreement categories it gives us a general rather than a detailed picture; this may be useful for our purposes. However, if we do this then we also have to draw attention to the fact that the total of the two disagreement categories (35%) is the same as the total in the category 'neither agree nor disagree', in which case one could suggest that the modal category of 'neither agree nor disagree' has been superseded by bi-modality, with disagreement being one modal score and 'neither agree nor disagree' being the other.

Combining categories can be useful though it is not without its problems, for example let us consider three tables (Tables 35.5–35.7). The first presents the overall results of an imaginary course evaluation, in which three levels of satisfaction have been registered (low, medium, high) (Table 35.5). Here one can observe that the modal category is 'low' (95 votes, 42.2%) and the lowest category is 'high' (45 votes, 20%), i.e. overall the respondents are dissatisfied with the course. The females seem to be more satisfied with the course than the males, if the category 'high' is used as an indicator, and the males seem to be more moderately satisfied with the course than the females.

TABLE 35.6   COMBINED CATEGORIES OF RATING SCALES

Satisfaction with course

	Low (1–5)	High (6–7)	Total
Male	130 (89.7%)	15 (10.3)	145 (100%)
Female	50 (62.5%)	30 (37.5%)	80 (100%)
Total	180 (76.1%)	45 (23.9%)	225 (100%)
Difference	+27.2%	−27.2%	

TABLE 35.7   REPRESENTING COMBINED CATEGORIES OF RATING SCALES

Satisfaction with course

	Low (1–3)	High (4–7)	Total
Male	60 (41.4%)	85 (58.6%)	145 (100%)
Female	35 (43.7%)	45 (56.3%)	80 (100%)
Total	95 (42.6%)	130 (57.4%)	225 (100%)
Difference	−2.1%	+1.9%	

However, if one combines categories (low and medium) then a different story could be told, as in Table 35.6. By looking at the percentages, here it appears that the females are more satisfied with the course overall than males, and that the males are more dissatisfied with the course than females.

However, if one were to combine categories differently (medium and high) then a different story again could be told, as in Table 35.7. By looking at the percentages, here it appears that there is not much difference between the males and the females, and that both males and females are highly satisfied with the course.

At issue here is the notion of combining categories, or collapsing tables, and we advocate great caution in

TABLE 35.8   A BIVARIATE CROSSTABULATION (SPSS OUTPUT)

form * the contents are interesting Crosstabulation

			the contents are interesting				Total
			strongly agree	agree	no comment	disagree	
form	Primary 3	Count	12	7	1	2	22
		% within form	54.5%	31.8%	4.5%	9.1%	100.0%
	Primary 4	Count	35	18	11		64
		% within form	54.7%	28.1%	17.2%		100.0%
	Total	Count	47	25	12	2	86
		% within form	54.7%	29.1%	14.0%	2.3%	100.0%

doing this. Sometimes it can provide greater clarity, and sometimes it can distort the picture. In the example here it is wiser to keep with the original table (Table 35.5) rather than collapsing it into fewer categories.

Crosstabulations used for categorical data can be bivariate (two variables presented), for example Table 35.8, in which two forms of primary students (Primary 3 and Primary 4) are asked how interesting they find a course. The rows are the nominal, categorical variable and the columns are the values of the ordinal variable. This is a commonplace organization.

Let us give another example, let us suppose that we wished to examine the views of parents from socially advantaged and disadvantaged backgrounds of primary school children on traditional school examinations (in favour/against), using simple dichotomous variables

TABLE 35.9   A BIVARIATE ANALYSIS OF PARENTS' VIEWS ON PUBLIC EXAMINATIONS

Acceptability of formal, written public examinations

Formal, written public examinations	Socially advantaged	Socially disadvantaged
In favour	70%	35%
Against	30%	65%
Total per cent	100%	100%

TABLE 35.10   A TRIVARIATE CROSSTABULATION

Acceptability of formal, written public examinations

Formal, written public examinations	Traditionalist		Progressivist/child-centred	
	Socially advantaged	Socially disadvantaged	Socially advantaged	Socially disadvantaged
In favour	65%	70%	35%	20%
Against	35%	30%	65%	80%
Total per cent	100%	100%	100%	100%

(two values only in each variable). Table 35.9 presents the results. It shows us clearly that parents from socially advantaged backgrounds are more in favour of formal, written public examinations than those from socially disadvantaged backgrounds.

Additionally, a trivariate crosstabulation can be constructed (and SPSS enables researchers to do this), with three variables included. In the example here, let us say that we are interested in their socio-economic status (socially advantaged/socially disadvantaged) and their philosophies of education (traditionalist/child-centred). Our results appear as in Table 35.10.

The results here are almost the reverse of Table 35.9: now the socially advantaged are more likely than socially disadvantaged parents to favour forms of assessment other than formal, written public examinations, and socially disadvantaged parents are more likely than socially advantaged parents to favour formal, written public examinations. The educational philosophies of each of the two groups (socially advantaged and socially disadvantaged) have dramatically altered the scenario. A trivariate analysis can give greater subtlety to the data and their analysis. (They can be used as control variables, and we address this in the discussion of correlations.)

35.2 Measures of central tendency and dispersal

Central tendency: means, modes and medians

The central tendency of a set of scores is the way in which they tend to cluster round the middle of a set of scores, or where the majority of scores are located. For categorical data the measure of central tendency is the mode: that score which is given by the most people, that score which has the highest frequency (there can be more than one mode: if there are two clear modal scores then this is termed 'bimodal'; if there are three then this is termed 'tri-modal'). For continuous data (ratio data), in addition to the mode, the researcher can calculate the mean (the average score) and the median: the midpoint score of a range of data; half of the scores fall above it and half below it (the median is also sometimes used for ordinal data). If there is an even number of observations then the median is the average of the two middle scores. We cannot calculate the median score for nominal data, as the data have to be ranked-ordered from the lowest to the highest in terms of the quantity of the variable under discussion. Measures of central tendency are used with univariate data, and indicate the typical score (the mode), the middle score (the median) and the average score (the mean).

As a general rule, the mean is a useful statistic if the data are not skewed (i.e. if they are not bunched at one end or another of a curve of distribution) or if there are no outliers that may be exerting a disproportionate effect. One has to recall that the mean, as a statistical calculation only, can sometime yield some strange results, for example fractions of a person!

The median is useful for ordinal data, but, to be meaningful, there have to be many scores rather than just a few. The median overcomes the problem of outliers, and hence is useful for skewed results. The modal score is useful for all scales of data, particularly nominal and ordinal data, i.e. discrete and categorical data, rather than continuous data, and it is unaffected by outliers, though it is not strong if there are many values and many scores which occur with similar frequency (i.e. if there are only a few points on a rating scale).

The standard deviation

Are scores widely dispersed around the mean, do they cluster close to the mean, or are they at some distance from the mean? The measures used to determine this are measures of dispersal. If we have interval and ratio data then, in addition to the modal score and crosstabulations, we can calculate the mean (the average) and the standard deviation. The standard deviation is the average distance that each score is from the mean, i.e. the average difference between each score and the mean, and how much the scores, as a group, deviate from the mean. It is a standardized measure of dispersal. For small samples (fewer than 30 scores), or for samples rather than populations, it is calculated as:

$$\text{S.D.} = \frac{\Sigma d^2}{N-1}$$

where
d^2 = the deviation of the score from the mean (average), squared
Σ = the sum of
N = the number of cases

For populations rather than samples, it is calculated as:

$$\text{S.D.} = \sqrt{\frac{\Sigma d^2}{N}}$$

A low standard deviation indicates that the scores cluster together, whilst a high standard deviation indicates that the scores are widely dispersed. This is calculated automatically by software packages such as SPSS at the simple click of a single button.

Let us imagine that we have the test scores for 1,000 students, on a test that was marked out of ten, as shown

TABLE 35.11	DISTRIBUTION OF TEST SCORES (SPSS OUTPUT)	

Test scores

		Frequency	Valid Percent
Valid	2	1	.1
	3	223	22.3
	4	276	27.6
	5	32	3.2
	6	69	6.9
	7	149	14.9
	8	185	18.5
	9	39	3.9
	10	26	2.6
	Total	1000	100.0

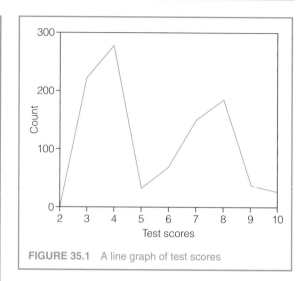

FIGURE 35.1   A line graph of test scores

in Table 35.11. Here we can calculate that the average score was 5.48. We can also calculate the standard deviation. In the example here the standard deviation in the example of scores was 2.134. What does this tell us? First, it suggests that the marks were not very high (an average of 5.48). Second, it tells us that there was quite a variation in the scores. Third, one can see that the scores were unevenly spread, indeed there was a high cluster of scores around the categories of 3 and 4, and another high cluster of scores around the categories 7 and 8. This is where a line graph could be useful in representing the scores, as it shows two peaks clearly, as in Figure 35.1.

It is important to report the standard deviation. For example, let us consider the following. Look at these three sets of numbers:

(1)	1	2	3	4	20	mean=6
(2)	1	2	6	10	11	mean=6
(3)	5	6	6	6	7	mean=6

If we were to plot these points on to three separate graphs we would see very different results (Figures 35.2–35.4).

Figure 35.2 shows the mean being heavily affected by the single score of 20 (an 'outlier' – an extreme score a long way from the others); in fact all the other four scores are some distance below the mean. The score of 20 is exerting a disproportionate effect on the

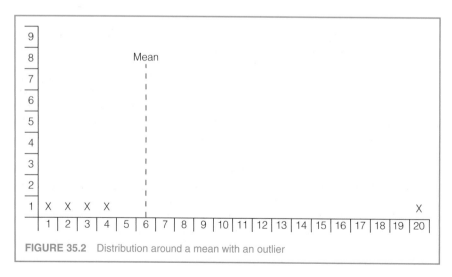

FIGURE 35.2   Distribution around a mean with an outlier

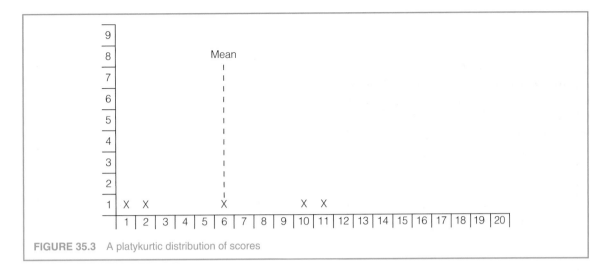

FIGURE 35.3 A platykurtic distribution of scores

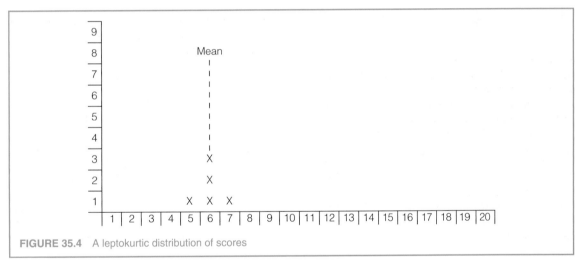

FIGURE 35.4 A leptokurtic distribution of scores

data and on the mean, raising it. Some statistical packages (e.g. SPSS) can take out outliers. If the data are widely spread then it may be more suitable not to use the mean but to use the median score; SPSS performs this automatically at a click of a button.

Figure 35.3 shows one score actually on the mean but the remainder some distance away from it. The scores are widely dispersed and the shape of the graph is flat (a platykurtic distribution).

Figure 35.4 shows the scores clustering very tightly around the mean, with a very peaked shape to the graph (a leptokurtic distribution).

The point at stake is this: it is not enough simply to calculate and report the mean; for a fuller picture of the data we need to look at the dispersal of scores. For this we require the statistic of the standard deviation, as this

will indicate the range and degree of dispersal of the data, though the standard deviation is susceptible to the disproportionate effects of outliers. Some scores will be widely dispersed (Figure 35.2), others will be evenly dispersed (Figure 35.3), and others will be bunched together (Figure 35.4). A high standard deviation will indicate a wide dispersal of scores, a low standard deviation will indicate clustering or bunching together of scores.

The range

A second way of measuring dispersal is to calculate the range, which is the difference between the lowest (minimum) score and the highest (maximum) score in a set of scores. This incorporates extreme scores, and is susceptible to the distorting effect of outliers: a wide range may be given if there are outliers, and if these outliers are removed then the range may be much reduced. Further, the range tells the researcher nothing about the distributions within the range.

The interquartile range

Another measure of dispersion is the interquartile range. If we arrange a set of scores in order, from the lowest to the highest, then we can divide that set of scores into four equal parts: the lowest quarter (quartile) that contains the lowest quarter of all the scores, the lower middle quartile, the upper middle quartile, and the highest quarter (quartile) that contains the highest quarter of the scores. The interquartile range is the difference between the first quartile and the third quartile, or, more precisely the difference between the 25th and the 75th percentile, i.e. the middle 50 per cent of scores (the second and third quartiles). This, thereby, ignores extreme scores and, unlike the simple range, does not change significantly if the researcher adds some scores that are some distance away from the average. For example let us imagine that we have a set of test scores thus, ordered into quartiles:

FIRST QUARTILE	SECOND QUARTILE	THIRD QUARTILE	FOURTH QUARTILE
40	50	65	83
41	55	70	86
43	58	75	90
47	63	77	93

The interquartile range is $65-47=18$. There are other ways of calculating the interquartile range (e.g. the difference between the medians of the first and third quartiles), and the reader may wish to explore these.

Though there are several ways of calculating dispersal, by far the most common is the standard deviation.

35.3 Taking stock

What we do with simple frequencies and descriptive data depends on the scales of data that we have (nominal, ordinal, interval and ratio). For all four scales we can calculate frequencies and percentages, and we can consider presenting these in a variety of forms. We can also calculate the mode and present crosstabulations, both bivariate and trivariate crosstabulations. We can consider combining categories and collapsing tables into smaller tables, providing that the sensitivity of the original data has not been lost. We can calculate the median score, which is particularly useful if the data are spread widely or if there are outliers. For interval and ratio data we can also calculate the mean and the standard deviation; the mean yields an average and the standard deviation indicates the range of dispersal of scores around that average, i.e. to see whether the data are widely dispersed (e.g. in a platykurtic distribution), or close together with a distinct peak (in a leptokurtic distribution). We can use other measures of dispersal such as the range and the interquartile range. In examining frequencies and percentages one also has to investigate whether the data are skewed, i.e. over-represented at one end of a scale and under-represented at the other end. A positive skew has a long tail at the positive end and the majority of the data at the negative end, and a negative skew has a long tail at the negative end and the majority of the data at the positive end.

35.4 Correlations and measures of association

Much educational research is concerned with establishing interrelationships among variables. We may wish to know, for example, how delinquency is related to social class background; whether an association exists between the number of years spent in full-time education and subsequent annual income; whether there is a link between personality and achievement. What, for example, is the relationship, if any, between membership of a public library and social class status? Is there a relationship between social class background and placement in different strata of the secondary school curriculum? Is there a relationship between gender and success/failure in 'first-time' driving test results?

There are several simple measures of association readily available to the researcher to help him or her test these sorts of relationships. We have selected the most widely used ones here and set them out in Table 35.12.

Of these, the two most commonly used correlations are the Spearman rank order correlation for ordinal data and the Pearson product moment correlation for interval and ratio data, and we advise readers to use these as the main kinds of correlation statistics. At this point it is pertinent to say a few words about some of the terms used in Table 35.12 to describe the nature of variables. Cohen and Holliday (1982, 1996) provide worked examples of the appropriate use and limitations of the correlational techniques outlined in Table 35.12, together with other measures of association such as Kruskal's *gamma*, Somer's *d* and Guttman's *lambda*.

Look at the words used at the top of the table to explain the nature of variables in connection with the measure called the Pearson product moment, *r*. The variables, we learn, are 'continuous' and at the 'interval' or the 'ratio' scale of measurement.

A continuous variable is one that, theoretically at least, can take any value between two points on a scale.

TABLE 35.12   COMMON MEASURES OF RELATIONSHIP

Measure	Nature of variables	Comment
Spearman's rho	Two ordinal variables	Relationship linear
Pearson product moment, r	Two continuous variables; interval or ratio scale	Relationship linear
Rank order or Kendall's tau	Two continuous variables; ordinal scale	
Correlation ratio, η (eta)	One variable continuous, other either continuous or discrete	Relationship non-linear
Intraclass	One variable continuous; other discrete; interval or ratio scale	Purpose: to determine within-group similarity
Biserial, r_{bis} Point biserial, $r_{pt\,bis}$	One variable continuous; other (a) continuous but dichotomized. r_{bis} or (b) true dichotomy, $r_{pt\,bis}$	Index of item discrimination (used in item analysis)
Phi coefficient, φ	Two true dichotomies; nominal or ordinal series	
Partial correlation $r_{12.3}$	Three or more continuous variables	Purpose: to determine relationship between two variables, with effect of third held constant
Multiple correlation $r_{1.234}$	Three or more continuous variables	Purpose: to predict one variable from a linear weighted combination of two or more independent variables
Kendall's coefficient of concordance (W)	Three or more continuous variables; ordinal series	Purpose: to determine the degree of (say, inter-rater) agreement

Source: Mouly, 1978.

Weight, for example, is a continuous variable; so too is time, so also is height. Weight, time and height can take on any number of possible values between nought and infinity, the feasibility of measuring them across such a range being limited only by the variability of suitable measuring instruments.

Turning again to Table 35.12, we read in connection with the next measure shown there (rank order or Kendall's tau) that the two continuous variables are at the ordinal scale of measurement.

The variables involved in connection with the phi coefficient measure of association (halfway down Table 35.12) are described as 'true dichotomies' and at the nominal scale of measurement. Truly dichotomous variables (such as sex or driving test result) can take only two values (male or female; pass or fail).

To conclude our explanation of terminology, readers should note the use of the term 'discrete variable' in the description of the fourth correlation ratio (eta) in Table 35.12. We said earlier that a continuous variable can take on any value between two points on a scale. A discrete variable, however, can only take on numerals or values that are specific points on a scale. The number of players in a football team is a discrete variable. It is usually 11; it could be fewer than 11, but it could never be seven and a quarter!

The percentage difference

The percentage difference is a simple asymmetric measure of association. An *asymmetric* measure is a measure of *one-way association*. That is to say, it estimates the extent to which one phenomenon implies the other but not vice versa. Gender, as we shall see shortly, may imply driving test success or failure. The association could never be the other way round! Measures which are concerned with the extent to which two phenomena imply each other are referred to as *symmetric* measures. Table 35.13 reports the percentage of public library members by their social class origin.

TABLE 35.13   PERCENTAGE OF PUBLIC LIBRARY MEMBERS BY THEIR SOCIAL CLASS ORIGIN

Public library membership	Social class status	
	Middle class	Working class
Member	86	37
Non-member	14	63
Total	100	100

What can we discover from the data set out in Table 35.13? By comparing percentages in different columns of the same row, we can see that 49% more middle-class persons are members of public libraries than working-class persons. By comparing percentages in different rows of the same columns we can see that 72% more middle-class persons are members rather than non-members. The data suggest, do they not, an association between the social class status of individuals and their membership of public libraries.

A second way of making use of the data in Table 35.13 involves the computing of a *percentage ratio* (%R). Look, for example, at the data in the second row of Table 35.13. By dividing 63 by 14 (%R=4.5) we can say that four and a half times as many working-class persons are not members of public libraries as are middle-class persons.

The *percentage difference* ranges from 0% when there is complete independence between two phenomena to 100% when there is complete association in the direction being examined. It is straightforward to calculate and simple to understand. Notice, however, that the percentage difference as we have defined it can only be employed when there are only two categories in the variable along which we percentage and only two categories in the variable in which we compare. In SPSS, using the 'Crosstabs' command can yield percentages, and we indicate this in the website manual that accompanies this volume.

In connection with this issue, on the accompanying website we discuss the phi coefficient, the correlation coefficient tetrachoric r (r_t), the contingency coefficient C, and combining independent significance tests of partial relations.

Explaining correlations

In our discussion of the principal correlational techniques shown in Table 35.12, three are of special interest to us and these form the basis of much of the rest of the chapter. They are the Pearson product moment correlation coefficient, multiple correlation and partial correlation.

Correlational techniques are generally intended to answer three questions about two variables or two sets of data. First, 'Is there a relationship between the two variables (or sets of data)?' If the answer to this question is 'yes', then two other questions follow: 'What is the direction of the relationship?' and 'What is the magnitude?'

Relationship in this context refers to any tendency for the two variables (or sets of data) to vary consistently. Pearson's product moment coefficient of correlation, one of the best-known measures of association, is a statistical value ranging from −1.0 to +1.0 and expresses this relationship in quantitative form. The coefficient is represented by the symbol r.

Where the two variables (or sets of data) fluctuate in the same direction, i.e. as one increases so does the other, or as one decreases so does the other, a positive relationship is said to exist. Correlations reflecting this pattern are prefaced with a plus sign to indicate the positive nature of the relationship. Thus, +1.0 would indicate perfect positive correlation between two factors, as with the radius and diameter of a circle, and +0.80 a high positive correlation, as between academic achievement and intelligence, for example. Where the sign has been omitted, a plus sign is assumed.

A negative correlation or relationship, on the other hand, is to be found when an increase in one variable is accompanied by a decrease in the other variable. Negative correlations are prefaced with a minus sign. Thus, −1.0 would represent perfect negative correlation, as between the number of errors children make on a spelling test and their score on the test, and −0.30 a low negative correlation, as between absenteeism and intelligence, say. There is no other meaning to the signs used; they indicate nothing more than which pattern holds for any two variables (or sets of data).

Generally speaking, researchers tend to be more interested in the magnitude of an obtained correlation than

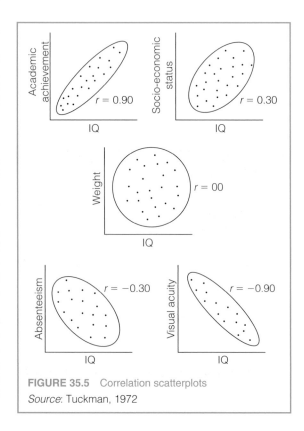

FIGURE 35.5 Correlation scatterplots

Source: Tuckman, 1972

they are in its direction. Correlational procedures have been developed so that no relationship whatever between two variables is represented by zero (or 0.00), as between body weight and intelligence, possibly. This means that a person's performance on one variable is totally unrelated to her performance on a second variable. If she is high on one, for example, she is just as likely to be high or low on the other. Perfect correlations of +1.00 or −1.00 are rarely found and, as we shall see, most coefficients of correlation in social research are around +0.50 or less. The correlation coefficient may be seen then as an indication of the predictability of one variable given the other: it is an indication of covariation. The relationship between two variables can be examined visually by plotting the paired measurements on graph paper with each pair of observations being represented by a point. The resulting arrangement of points is known as a scatterplot and enables us to assess graphically the degree of relationship between the characteristics being measured. Figure 35.5 gives some examples of scatterplots in the field of educational research.

Whilst correlations are widely used in research, and they are straightforward to calculate and to interpret,

the researcher must be aware of four caveats in undertaking correlational analysis:

i   do not assume that correlations imply causal relationships (i.e. simply because having large hands appears to correlate with having large feet does not imply that having large hands causes one to have large feet);

ii there is a need to be alert to a Type I error – not supporting the null hypothesis when it is in fact true;

iii there is a need to be alert to a Type II error – supporting the null hypothesis when it is in fact not true;

iv statistical significance must be accompanied by an indication of effect size.

In SPSS a typical print-out of a correlation coefficient is given in Table 35.14. In this fictitious example using 1,000 cases there are four points to note:

1   The cells of data to the right of the cells containing the figure 1 are the same as the cells to the left of the

TABLE 35.14   A PEARSON PRODUCT MOMENT CORRELATION (SPSS OUTPUT)

		The attention given to teaching and learning at the school	How well students apply themselves to learning	Discussion and review by educators of the quality of teaching, learning and classroom practice
The attention given to teaching and learning at the school	Pearson Correlation	1	.060	.066*
	Sig. (2-tailed)	.	.058	.036
	N	1000	1000	1000
How well students apply themselves to learning	Pearson Correlation	.060	1	.585**
	Sig. (2-tailed)	.058	.	.000
	N	1000	1000	1000
Discussion and review by educators of the quality of teaching, learning and classroom practice	Pearson Correlation	.066*	.585**	1
	Sig. (2-tailed)	.036	.000	.
	N	1000	1000	1000

*. Correlation is significant at the 0.05 level (2-tailed).

**. Correlation is significant at the 0.01 level (2-tailed).

cells containing the figure 1, i.e. there is a mirror image, and, if very many more variables were being correlated then, in fact, one would have to decide whether to look at only the variables to the right of the cell with the figure 1 (the perfect correlation, since it is one variable being correlated with itself), or to look at the cells to the left of the figure 1.

2 In each cell where one variable is being correlated with a different variable there are three figures: the top figure gives the correlation coefficient, the middle figure gives the significance level and the lowest figure gives the sample size.

3 SPSS marks with an asterisk those correlations which are statistically significant.

4 All the correlations are positive, since there are no negative coefficients given.

What these tables give us is the magnitude of the correlation (the coefficient), the direction of the correlation (positive and negative), and the significance level. The correlation coefficient can be taken as the effect size. The significance level, as mentioned earlier, is calculated automatically by SPSS, based on the coefficient and the sample size: the greater the sample size, the lower the coefficient of correlation has to be in order to be statistically significant, and, by contrast, the smaller the sample size, the greater the coefficient of correlation has to be in order to be statistically significant.

In reporting correlations one has to report the test used, the coefficient, the direction of the correlation (positive or negative) and the significance level (if considered appropriate). For example, one could write:

Using the Pearson product moment correlation, a statistically significant correlation was found between students' attendance at school and their examination performance ($r=0.87$, $\rho=0.035$). Those students who attended school the most tended to have the best examination performance, and those who attended the least tended to have the lowest examination performance.

Alternatively, there may be occasions when it is important to report when a correlation has *not* been found, for example:

There was no statistically significant correlation found between the amount of time spent on homework and examination performance ($r=0.37$, $\rho=0.43$).

In both these examples of reporting, exact significance levels have been given, assuming that SPSS has calculated these. An alternative way of reporting the signifi-

cance levels (as appropriate) are: $\rho<0.05$; $\rho<0.01$; $\rho<0.001$; $\rho=0.05$; $\rho=0.01$, $\rho=0.001$. In the case of statistical significance not having been found one could report this as $\rho>0.05$ or $\rho=$N.S.

Curvilinearity

The correlations discussed so far have assumed linearity, that is the more we have of one property, the more (or less) we have of another property, in a direct positive or negative relationship. A straight line can be drawn through the points on the scatterplots (a regression line). However, linearity cannot always be assumed. Consider the case, for example, of stress: a little stress might enhance performance ('setting the adrenalin running') positively, whereas too much stress might lead to a downturn in performance. Where stress enhances performance there is a positive correlation, but when stress debilitates performance there is a negative correlation. The result is not a straight line of correlation (indicating linearity) but a curved line (indicating curvilinearity). This can be shown graphically, as shown in Figure 35.6. It is assumed here, for the purposes of the example, that muscular strength can be measured on a single scale. It is clear from the graph that muscular strength increases from birth until 50 years, and thereafter it declines as muscles degenerate. There is a positive correlation between age and muscular strength on the left-hand side of the graph and a negative correlation on the right-hand side of the graph, i.e. a curvilinear correlation can be observed.

Hopkins *et al.* (1996: 92) provide another example of curvilinearity: room temperature and comfort. Raising the temperature a little can make for greater comfort – a positive correlation – whilst raising it too greatly can make for discomfort – a negative correlation. Many correlational statistics assume linearity (e.g. the Pearson product moment correlation). However, rather than using correlational statistics arbitrarily or blindly, the researcher will need to consider whether, in fact, linearity is a reasonable assumption to make, or

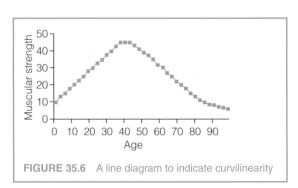

FIGURE 35.6 A line diagram to indicate curvilinearity

whether a curvilinear relationship is more appropriate (in which case more sophisticated statistics will be needed, e.g. η ('eta')) (Glass and Hopkins, 1996, section 8.7; Cohen and Holliday, 1996: 84; Fowler *et al.*, 2000: 81–9) or mathematical procedures will need to be applied to transform non-linear relations into linear relations. Examples of curvilinear relationships might include:

- pressure from the principal and teacher performance;
- pressure from the teacher and student achievement;
- degree of challenge and student achievement;
- assertiveness and success;
- age and muscular strength;
- age and physical control;
- age and concentration;
- age and sociability;
- age and cognitive abilities.

Hopkins *et al.* (1996) suggest that the variable 'age' frequently has a curvilinear relationship with other variables. The authors also point out (p. 92) that poorly constructed tests can give the appearance of curvilinearity if the test is too easy (a 'ceiling effect' where most students score highly) or if it is too difficult, but that this curvilinearity is, in fact, spurious, as the test does not demonstrate sufficient item difficulty or discriminability.

In planning correlational research, then, attention will need to be given to whether linearity or curvilinearity is to be assumed.

Coefficients of correlation

The coefficient of correlation, then, tells us something about the relations between two variables. Other measures exist, however, which allow us to specify relationships when more than two variables are involved. These are known as measures of 'multiple correlation' and 'partial correlation'.

Multiple correlation measures indicate the degree of association between three or more variables simultaneously. We may want to know, for example, the degree of association between delinquency, social class background and leisure facilities. Or we may be interested in finding out the relationship between academic achievement, intelligence and neuroticism. Multiple correlation, or 'regression' as it is sometimes called, indicates the degree of association between *n* variables. It is related not only to the correlations of the independent variable with the dependent variables, but also to the intercorrelations between the dependent variables.

Partial correlation aims at establishing the degree of association between two variables after the influence of a third has been controlled or partialled out. Guilford and Fruchter (1973) define a partial correlation between two variables as one which nullifies the effects of a third variable (or a number of variables) on the variables being correlated. They give the example of correlation between the height and weight of boys in a group whose age varies, where the correlation would be higher than the correlation between height and weight in a group comprised of boys of only the same age. Here the reason is clear – because some boys will be older they will be heavier and taller. Age, therefore, is a factor that increases the correlation between height and weight. Of course, even with age held constant, the correlation would still be positive and significant because, regardless of age, taller boys often tend to be heavier.

Consider, too, the relationship between success in basketball and previous experience in the game. Suppose, also, that the presence of a third factor, the height of the players, was known to have an important influence on the other two factors. The use of partial correlation techniques would enable a measure of the two primary variables to be achieved, freed from the influence of the secondary variable.

Correlational analysis is simple and involves collecting two or more scores on the same group of subjects and computing correlation coefficients. Many useful studies have been based on this simple design. Those involving more complex relationships, however, utilize multiple and partial correlations in order to provide a clearer picture of the relationships being investigated.

One final point: it is important to stress again that correlations refer to measures of association and do not necessarily indicate causal relationships between variables. Correlation does not imply cause.

Interpreting the correlation coefficient

Once a correlation coefficient has been computed, there remains the problem of interpreting it. A question often asked in this connection is how large should the coefficient be for it to be meaningful. The question may be approached in three ways: by examining the strength of the relationship; by examining the statistical significance of the relationship; and by examining the square of the correlation coefficient.

Inspection of the numerical value of a correlation coefficient will yield clear indication of the strength of the relationship between the variables in question. Low or near zero values indicate weak relationships, while those nearer to +1 or –1 suggest stronger relationships. Imagine, for instance, that a measure of a teacher's success in the classroom after five years in the profession is correlated with her final school experience grade as a student and that it was found that $r=+0.19$. Suppose now that her score on classroom success is correlated with a measure of need for professional achievement and that this yielded a correlation of 0.65. It could be concluded that there is a stronger relationship between success and professional achievement scores than between success and final student grade.

Where a correlation coefficient has been derived from a sample and one wishes to use it as a basis for inference about the parent population, the statistical significance of the obtained correlation must be considered. Statistical significance, when applied to a correlation coefficient, indicates whether or not the correlation is different from zero at a given level of confidence. As we have seen earlier, a statistically significant correlation is indicative of an actual relationship rather than one due entirely to chance. The level of statistical significance of a correlation is determined to a great extent by the number of cases upon which the correlation is based. Thus, the greater the number of cases, the smaller the correlation need be to be significant at a given level of confidence.

Exploratory relationship studies are generally interpreted with reference to their statistical significance, whereas prediction studies depend for their efficacy on the strength of the correlation coefficients. These need to be considerably higher than those found in exploratory relationship studies and for this reason rarely invoke the concept of significance.

The third approach to interpreting a coefficient is provided by examining the square of the coefficient of correlation, r^2. This shows the proportion of variance in one variable that can be attributed to its linear relationship with the second variable. In other words, it indicates the amount the two variables have in common. If, for example, two variables A and B have a correlation of 0.50, then $(0.50)^2$ or 0.25 of the variation shown by

the B scores can be attributed to the tendency of B to vary linearly with A. Figure 35.7 shows graphically the common variance between reading grade and arithmetic grade having a correlation of 0.65.

There are three cautions to be borne in mind when one is interpreting a correlation coefficient. First, a coefficient is a simple number and must not be interpreted as a percentage. A correlation of 0.50, for instance, does not mean 50 per cent relationship between the variables. Further, a correlation of 0.50 does not indicate twice as much relationship as that shown by a correlation of 0.25. A correlation of 0.50 actually indicates more than twice the relationship shown by a correlation of 0.25. In fact, as coefficients approach $+1$ or -1, a difference in the absolute values of the coefficients becomes more important than the same numerical difference between lower correlations would be.

Second, a correlation does not necessarily imply a cause-and-effect relationship between two factors, as we have previously indicated. It should not therefore be interpreted as meaning that one factor is causing the scores on the other to be as they are. There are invariably other factors influencing both variables under consideration. Suspected cause-and-effect relationships would have to be confirmed by subsequent experimental study.

Third, a correlation coefficient is not to be interpreted in any absolute sense. A correlational value for a given sample of a population may not necessarily be the same as that found in another sample from the same population. Many factors influence the value of a given correlation coefficient and if researchers wish to extrapolate to the populations from which they drew their samples they will then have to test the significance of the correlation.

We now offer some general guidelines for interpreting correlation coefficients. They are based on Borg's (1963) analysis and assume that the correlations relate to a hundred or more subjects.

Correlations ranging from 0.20 to 0.35
Correlations within this range show only very slight relationship between variables although they may be statistically significant. A correlation of 0.20 shows that only 4 per cent ($\{0.20 \times 0.20\} \times 100$) of the variance is common to the two measures. Whereas correlations at this level may have limited meaning in exploratory relationship research, they are of no value in either individual or group prediction studies.

Correlations ranging from 0.35 to 0.65
Within this range, correlations are statistically significant beyond the 1 per cent level. When correlations are

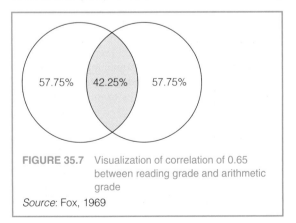

FIGURE 35.7   Visualization of correlation of 0.65 between reading grade and arithmetic grade

Source: Fox, 1969

around 0.40, crude group prediction may be possible. As Borg (1963) notes, correlations within this range are useful, however, when combined with other correlations in a multiple regression equation. Combining several correlations in this range in some cases can yield individual predictions that are correct within an acceptable margin of error. Correlations at this level used singly are of little use for individual prediction because they yield only a few more correct predictions than could be accomplished by guessing or by using some chance selection procedure.

Correlations ranging from 0.65 to 0.85
Correlations within this range make possible group predictions that are accurate enough for most purposes. Nearer the top of the range, group predictions can be made very accurately, usually predicting the proportion of successful candidates in selection problems within a very small margin of error. Near the top of this correlation range individual predictions can be made that are considerably more accurate than would occur if no such selection procedures were used.

Correlations over 0.85
Correlations as high as this indicate a close relationship between the two variables correlated. A correlation of 0.85 indicates that the measure used for prediction has about 72 per cent variance in common with the performance being predicted. Prediction studies in education very rarely yield correlations this high. When

correlations at this level are obtained, however, they are very useful for either individual or group prediction.

35.5 Partial correlations

Many researchers wish to control for the effects of other variables. As was discussed in Chapter 4, controlling for the effects of variables means holding them constant whilst manipulating other variables. Let us imagine that we have 1,000 students in a survey, and that we wish to investigate the effects of working part time on their degree classification (high/low) after we have controlled for the effects of socio-economic status (high/low).

First, a crosstabulation can be calculated (e.g. in SPSS), controlled for socio-economic status, which indicates the distributions of the categories, set out by part-time work and socio-economic status as the row variables (and with the class of degree as the column variable), as in Table 35.15.

Using SPSS software, partial correlations can be calculated straightforwardly. Partial correlations enable the researcher to control for a third variable, i.e. to see the correlation between two variables of interest once the effects of a third variable have been removed, hence rendering more accurate the relationship between the two variables of interest. As Turner (1997: 33) remarks: partialling can rule out special or specific relationships that do not hold true when variables have been controlled. In

---

TABLE 35.15 PART-TIME WORK AND CLASS OF DEGREE, CONTROLLED FOR SOCIO-ECONOMIC STATUS (SPSS OUTPUT)

Part-time Work by Class of Degree, Controlled for Socio-economic Status (SES)

SES				Class of degree		Total
				High class of degree	Low class of degree	
High	Part-time work	Working part-time	Frequency	75	57	132
			% within Part-time work	56.8%	43.2%	100.0%
		Not working part-time	Frequency	246	107	353
			% within Part-time work	69.7%	30.3%	100.0%
	Total		Frequency	321	164	485
			% within Part-time work	66.2%	33.8%	100.0%
Low	Part-time work	Working part-time	Frequency	96	219	315
			% within Part-time work	30.5%	69.5%	100.0%
		Not working part-time	Frequency	46	154	200
			% within Part-time work	23.0%	77.0%	100.0%
	Total		Frequency	142	373	515
			% within Part-time work	27.6%	72.4%	100.0%

```
- - -  P A R T I A L    C O R R E L A T I O N    C O E F F I C I E N T S  - -

Zero Order Partials
                   WORK        DEGREE         SES
WORK            1.0000       -.1451        -.3413
                (    0)      (   998)      (   998)
                P= .        P= .000       P= .000

DEGREE          -.1451       1.0000         .3870
                (   998)     (    0)       (   998)
                P= .000      P= .         P= .000

SES             -.3413        .3870        1.0000
                (   998)     (   998)      (    0)
                P= .000      P= .000       P= .

(Coefficient / (D.F.) / 2-tailed Significance)
" . " is printed if a coefficient cannot be computed

- - -  P A R T I A L    C O R R E L A T I O N    C O E F F I C I E N T S  - -

Controlling for..    SES
                   WORK        DEGREE
WORK            1.0000       -.0150
                (    0)      (   997)
                P= .        P= .636

DEGREE          -.0150       1.0000
                (   997)     (    0)
                P= .636      P= .

(Coefficient / (D.F.) / 2-tailed Significance)
" . " is printed if a coefficient cannot be computed
```

FIGURE 35.8 SPSS output from partial correlation, controlling for socio-economic status

```
- - -  P A R T I A L    C O R R E L A T I O N    C O E F F I C I E N T S  -

Zero Order Partials
                   DEGREE       SES          WORK
DEGREE          1.0000        .3870        -.1451
                (    0)      (   998)      (   998)
                P= .        P= .000       P= .000

SES              .3870       1.0000        -.3413
                (   998)     (    0)       (   998)
                P= .000      P= .         P= .000

WORK            -.1451       -.3413        1.0000
                (   998)     (   998)      (    0)
                P= .000      P= .000       P= .

(Coefficient / (D.F.) / 2-tailed Significance)
" . " is printed if a coefficient cannot be computed

- - -  P A R T I A L    C O R R E L A T I O N    C O E F F I C I E N T S  -

Controlling for..    WORK
                   DEGREE       SES
DEGREE          1.0000        .3629
                (    0)      (   997)
                P= .        P= .000

SES              .3629       1.0000
                (   997)     (    0)
                P= .000      P= .

(Coefficient / (D.F.) / 2-tailed Significance)
" . " is printed if a coefficient cannot be computed
```

FIGURE 35.9 SPSS output for partial correlations, controlling for part-time work

our example we have socio-economic status, part-time working and class of degree. We may be interested in investigating the effect of part-time working on class of degree, controlling for the effects of socio-economic status. SPSS enables us to do this at the touch of a button, producing output on partial correlations (Figure 35.8).

The SPSS output (Figure 35.8) indicates that in the second of the tables, the correlation coefficients have been controlled for socio-economic status (marked as 'Controlling for .. SES'). The top row for each variable presents the correlation coefficient; the middle row indicates the numbers of people who responded; and the bottom row presents the level of statistical significance ($\rho = 0.000$). Here the results indicate that there is a very little partial correlation between part-time working and class of degree ($r = -0.0150$, degrees of freedom $= 997$, $\rho = 0.636$), but that this is not statistically significant, i.e.

there is no significant correlation between part-time work and class of degree, when controlled for socio-economic status. However, when we examine the correlation coefficient for socio-economic status, in the first table there was a very different correlation coefficient (r=−0.1451), and this was highly statistically significant (ρ=0.000). This suggests to us that controlling for socio-economic status has a very considerable effect on the strength of the relationship between the variables 'part-time work' and 'class of degree'. Had the two coefficients here been close then one could have suggested that controlling for socio-economic status had very little effect on the strength of the relationship between the variables 'part-time work' and 'class of degree'.

This time let us imagine that we wish to explore the relationship between socio-economic status and class of degree, controlling for part-time working (Figure 35.9). The SPSS output indicates that the correlation coefficients have been controlled for part-time work (marked as 'Controlling for .. Work'). Here the results indicate that there is a very strong partial correlation between socio-economic status and class of degree (r=0.3629, degrees of freedom=997, ρ=0.000), i.e. that this is statistically significant. When we examine the correlation coefficient for socio-economic status, in the first table we see that the correlation coefficient (r=0.3870) is very similar to the correlation coefficient

found when the variable 'part-time work' has been controlled (the coefficient before being controlled being 0.3870 and the coefficient after being controlled being 0.3629). This suggests that controlling for part-time work status has very little effect on the strength of the relationship between the variables 'socio-economic status' and 'class of degree'. Partial correlation enables relationships to be calculated after controlling for one or more variables.

35.6 Reliability

We need to know how reliable is our instrument for data collection. Reliability in quantitative analysis takes two main forms, both of which are measures of internal consistency: the split-half technique and the alpha coefficient. Both calculate a coefficient of reliability that can lie between 0 and 1. The formula for calculating the Spearman-Brown split-half reliability (discussed in Chapter 10) is:

$$r = \frac{2r}{1+r}$$

where r=the actual correlation between the halves of the instrument (this requires the instrument to be able to be divided into two matched halves in terms of content and difficulty). So, for example, if the correlation coefficient

---

TABLE 35.16   IDENTIFYING UNRELIABLE ITEMS IN CRONBACH'S ALPHA (SPSS OUTPUT)

Item-Total Statistics

	Scale Mean if Item Deleted	Scale Variance if Item Deleted	Corrected Item-Total Correlation	Cronbach's Alpha if Item Deleted
How hard do you feel you are working in your job?	17.71	51.379	.272	.642
How much do you feel exhausted by the end of the workday?	17.99	43.902	.472	.553
How much do you feel that you cannot cope with your job any longer?	21.02	38.863	.567	.495
How much do you feel that you treat colleagues as impersonal objects?	23.52	50.959	.242	.658
How much do you feel that working with colleagues all day is really a strain for you?	22.08	43.084	.436	.569

Overall alpha: .642

---

between the two halves is 0.85 then the formula would be worked out thus:

$$r = \frac{2(0.85)}{1+0.85} = \frac{1.70}{1.85} = 0.919$$

Hence the split-half reliability coefficient is 0.919, which is very high. SPSS automatically calculates split-half reliability at the click of a button.

An alternative calculation of reliability as internal consistency can be found in Cronbach's alpha, frequently referred to simply as the alpha coefficient of reliability. The Cronbach alpha provides a coefficient of inter-item correlations. What it does is to calculate the average of all possible split-half reliability coefficients. It is a measure of the internal consistency amongst the *items* (not, for example, the people) and is used for multi-item scales. SPSS calculates Cronbach's alpha at the click of a button, the formula for alpha is:

$$alpha = \frac{nr_{ii}}{1+(n-1)r_{ii}}$$

where n = the number of items in the test or survey (e.g. questionnaire) and r_{ii} = the average of all the inter-item correlations. Let us imagine that the number of items in the survey is ten, and that the average correlation is 0.738. The alpha correlation can be calculated thus:

$$alpha = \frac{nr_{ii}}{1+(n-1)r_{ii}} = \frac{10(0.738)}{1+(10-1)0.738} = \frac{7.38}{7.64} = 0.97$$

This yields an alpha coefficient of 0.97, which is very high. For the split-half coefficient and the alpha coefficient the following guidelines can be used:

>0.90 very highly reliable
0.80–0.90 highly reliable
0.70–0.79 reliable
0.60–0.69 marginally/minimally reliable
<0.60 unacceptably low reliability.

Bryman and Cramer (1990: 71) suggest that the reliability level is acceptable at 0.8, though others suggest that it is acceptable if it is 0.67 or above.

If the researcher is using SPSS then there is a function that enables items to be discovered that might be exerting a negative influence on the Cronbach alpha. Table 35.16 provides an example of this, which indicates in the final column what the Cronbach alpha would be if any of the items were to be removed as unreliable.

In the example, the overall alpha is given as 0.642, but it can be seen that if the item 'How much do you feel that you treat colleagues as impersonal objects?' were removed, then the overall reliability would rise to 0.658. The researcher, then, may wish to remove that item – this is particularly true where the researcher is conducting a pilot to see which items are reliable and which are not.

 Companion Website

The companion website to the book includes PowerPoint slides for this chapter, which list the structure of the chapter and then provide a summary of the key points in each of its sections. This resource can be found online at **www.routledge.com/textbooks/cohen7e**.

Additionally readers are recommended to access the online resources for Chapter 36 as these contain materials that apply to the present chapter, such as the SPSS Manual which guides readers through the SPSS commands required to run statistics in SPSS, together with data files of different data sets.

Inferential statistics

The previous chapter introduced descriptive statistics. This chapter moves to inferential statistics, those statistics that enable researchers to make inferences about the wider population (discussed in Chapter 34). Here we introduce difference tests, regression and multiple regression, and, arising from both difference testing and regression analysis, the need for standardized scores, and how they can be calculated. The chapter covers:

- measures of difference between groups
- the t-test (a test of difference for parametric data)
- analysis of variance (a test of difference for parametric data)
- the chi-square test (a test of difference and a test of goodness of fit for non-parametric data)
- degrees of freedom (a statistic that is used in calculating statistical significance in considering difference tests)
- the Mann-Whitney and Wilcoxon tests (tests of difference for non-parametric data)
- the Kruskal-Wallis and Friedman tests (tests of difference for non-parametric data)
- regression analysis (prediction tests for parametric data)
- simple linear regression (predicting the value of one variable from the known value of another variable)
- multiple regression (calculating the different weightings of independent variables on a dependent variable)
- standardized scores (used in calculating regressions and comparing sets of data with different means and standard deviations)

Both separately and together, these statistics constitute powerful tools in the arsenal of statistics for analysing numerical data. We give several worked examples for clarification, and take the novice reader by the hand through these.

36.1 Measures of difference between groups

Researchers will sometimes be interested to find whether there are differences between two or more groups of subsamples, answering questions such as: 'Is there a significant difference between the amount of homework done by boys and girls?' 'Is there a significant difference between test scores from four similarly mixed-ability classes studying the same syllabus?' 'Does school A differ significantly from school B in the stress level of its sixth form students?' Such questions require measures of difference. This section introduces measures of difference and how to calculate difference. The process commences with the null hypothesis, stating that 'there is no statistically significant difference between the two groups', or 'there is no statistically significant difference between the four groups', and, if this is not supported, then the alternative hypothesis is supported, namely 'there is a statistically significant difference between the two (or more) groups'. We discuss difference tests for parametric and non-parametric data.

Before going very far one has to ascertain:

a the kind of data with which one is working, as this affects the choice of statistic used;
b the number of groups being compared, to discover whether there is a difference between them. Statistics are usually divided into those which measure differences between two groups and those which measure differences between more than two groups;
c whether the groups are related or independent. Independent groups are entirely unrelated to each other, e.g. males and females completing an examination; related groups might be the same group voting on two or more variables or the same group voting at two different points in time (e.g. a pre-test and a post-test).

Decisions on these matters will affect the choice of statistics used. Our discussion will proceed thus: *first* (in section 36.2) we look at a simple difference test for two groups using parametric data, which is the t-test; *second* (36.3) we look at differences between three or more groups using parametric data (analysis of variance (ANOVA) with a *post hoc* test (the Tukey test)); *third* (36.4) we look at a test of difference for categorical data (the chi-square test). Then, *fourth* (36.5), we introduce the 'degrees of freedom'. *Fifth* (36.6) we look at differences between two groups using non-parametric data (the Mann-Whitney and Wilcoxon tests); *sixth* (36.7) we look at differences between three or more groups using non-parametric data (the Kruskal-Wallis and the Friedman tests). *Seventh* (36.8) we move from difference testing to prediction, using regression analysis. *Eighth* (36.11), as regression analysis often uses standardized scores, we introduce standardized scores. As in previous examples, we will be using SPSS to illustrate our points.

36.2 The t-test

The t-test is used to discover whether there are statistically significant differences between the means of two groups, using parametric data drawn from random samples with a normal distribution. It is used to compare the means of two groups randomly assigned, for example on a pre-test and a post-test in an experiment.

The t-test has two variants: the t-test for independent samples and the t-test for related (or 'paired') samples. The former assumes that the two groups are unrelated to each other; the latter assumes that it is the same group either voting on two variables or voting at two different points in time about the same variable. We will address the former of these first. The t-test assumes that one variable is categorical (e.g. males and females) and one is a continuous variable (e.g. marks on a test). The formula used calculates a statistic based on:

$$t = \frac{\text{Sample one mean} - \text{sample two mean}}{\text{Standard error of the difference in means}}$$

Let us imagine that we wish to discover whether there is a statistically significant difference between the leader/senior management team (SMT) of a group of randomly chosen schools and the teachers, concerning how well learners are cared for, guided and supported. The data are ratio, the participants having had to award a mark out of ten for their response, the higher the mark the greater is the care, guidance and support offered to the students. The t-test for two independent samples presents us with two tables in SPSS. First it provides the average (mean) of the voting for each group: 8.37 for the leaders/senior managers and 8.07 for the teachers, i.e. there is a difference of means between the two groups. Is this difference statistically significant, i.e. is the null hypothesis ('there is no statistically significant difference between the leaders/SMT and the teachers') supported or not supported? We commence with the null hypothesis ('there is no statistically significant difference between the two means') and then we set the level of significance (α) to use for supporting or not supporting the null hypotheses; for example we could say 'Let $\alpha = 0.05$'. Then the data are computed as in Table 36.1.

In running the t-test SPSS gives us back what, at first glance, seems to be a morass of information. Much of this is superfluous for our purposes here. We will concern ourselves with the most important pieces of data for introductory purposes here: the Levene test and the significance level for a two-tailed test (Sig. 2-tailed) (Table 36.2).

The Levene test is a guide as to which row of the two to use ('equal variances assumed' and 'equal variances not assumed'). Look at the column 'Sig.' in the Levene test (0.004). If the probability value is statistically significant (as in this case (0.004)) then variances are *unequal* and the researcher needs to use the second row of data ('Equal variances not assumed'); if the probability value is not significant ($\rho > 0.05$) then equal variances *are* assumed and s/he uses the first row of data ('Equal variances assumed'). Once s/he has decided which row to use then the Levene test has served its purpose and s/he can move on. For our commentary here the purpose of the Levene test is only there to determine which row to look at of the two presented.

TABLE 36.1   MEANS AND STANDARD DEVIATIONS FOR A t-TEST (SPSS OUTPUT)

Group Statistics

	who are you	N	Mean	Std. Deviation	Std. Error Mean
How well learners are cared for, guided and supported	leader/member of the SMT	347	8.37	2.085	.112
	teachers	653	8.07	2.462	.096

TABLE 36.2   THE LEVENE TEST FOR EQUALITY OF VARIANCES IN A t-TEST (SPSS OUTPUT)

Independent Samples Test

		Levene's Test for Equality of Variances		t-test for Equality of Means						
		F	Sig.	t	df	Sig. (2-tailed)	Mean Difference	Std. Error Difference	95% Confidence Interval of the Difference	
									Lower	Upper
How well learners are cared for, guided and supported	Equal variances assumed	8.344	.004	1.92	998	.055	.30	.155	-.006	.603
	Equal variances not assumed			2.02	811.922	.044	.30	.148	.009	.589

Having discovered which row to follow, in our example it is the second row, we go along to the column 'Sig. (2-tailed)'. This tells us that there is a statistically significant difference between the two groups – leaders/SMT and the teachers – because the significance level is 0.044 (i.e. $\rho < 0.05$). Hence we can say that the null hypothesis is not supported, that there is a statistically significant difference between the means of the two groups ($\rho = 0.044$), and that the mean of the leaders/SMT is statistically significantly higher (8.37) than the mean of the teachers (8.07), i.e. the leaders/ SMT of the schools think more highly than the teachers in the schools that the learners are well cared for, guided and supported.

Look at Table 36.2 again, and at the column 'Sig. (2-tailed)'. Had equal variances been assumed (i.e. if the Levene test had indicated that we should remain on the top row of data rather than the second row of data) then we would *not* have found a statistically significant difference between the two means ($\rho = 0.055$, i.e. $\rho > 0.05$). Hence it is sometimes important to know whether equal variances are to be assumed or not to be assumed.

In the example here we find that there *is* a statistically significant difference between the means of the two groups, i.e. the leaders/SMT do not share the same perception as the teachers that the learners are well cared for, guided and supported, typically the leaders/ SMT are more generous than the teachers. This is of research interest, e.g. to discover the reasons for, and impact of, the differences of perception. It could be, for example, that the leaders/SMT have a much rosier picture of the situation than the teachers, and that the teachers – the ones who have to work with the students on a close daily basis – are more in touch with the students and know that there are problems, a matter to which the senior managers may be turning a blind eye.

In reporting the t-test here the following form of words can be used:

The mean score of the leaders/SMT on the variable 'How well learners are cared for, guided and supported' ($M = 8.37$, $SD = 2.085$) is statistically significantly higher ($t = 2.02$, $df = 811.922$), two-tailed ($\rho = 0.044$) than those of teachers on the same variable ($M = 8.07$, $SD = 2.462$).

Let us take a second example. Here the leaders/SMT and teachers are voting on 'the attention given to teaching and learning at the school', again awarding a mark out of ten, i.e. ratio data. The mean for the leaders/SMT is 5.53 and for the teachers it is 5.46. Are these means statistically significantly different (Tables 36.3 and 36.4)?

If we examine the Levene test (Sig.) we find that equal variances *are* assumed ($\rho = 0.728$), i.e. we remain on the top row of the data output. Running along to the column headed 'Sig. (2-tailed)' we find that $\rho = 0.610$, i.e. there is no statistically significant difference between the means of the two groups, therefore the null hypothesis (there is no statistically significant difference between the means of the two groups) is supported. This should not dismay the researcher; finding or *not* finding a statistically significant difference is of equal value in research – a win-win situation. Here, for example, one can say that there is a shared perception between the leaders/managers and the teachers on the attention given to teaching and learning in the school, even though it is that the attention given is poor (means of 5.53 and 5.46 respectively). The fact that there is a shared perception – that both parties see the same problem in the same way – offers a positive prospect for development and a shared vision, i.e. even though the picture is poor, nevertheless it is perhaps more positive than if there were very widely different perceptions.

In reporting the t-test here the following form of words can be used:

TABLE 36.3   A t-TEST FOR LEADERS AND TEACHERS (SPSS OUTPUT)

Group Statistics

	who are you	N	Mean	Std. Deviation	Std. Error Mean
The attention given to teaching and learning at the school	leader/member of the SMT	347	5.53	2.114	.113
	teachers	653	5.46	2.145	.084

TABLE 36.4   THE LEVENE TEST FOR EQUALITY OF VARIANCES BETWEEN LEADERS AND TEACHERS (SPSS OUTPUT)

Independent Samples Test

		Levene's Test for Equality of Variances		t-test for Equality of Means						95% Confidence Interval of the Difference	
		F	Sig.	t	df	Sig. (2-tailed)	Mean Difference	Std. Error Difference		Lower	Upper
The attention given to teaching and learning at the school	Equal variances assumed	.121	.728	.510	998	.610	.07	.142		-.206	.351
	Equal variances not assumed			.513	714.630	.608	.07	.141		-.205	.350

The mean score for the leaders/SMT on the variable 'The attention given to teaching and learning at the school' (M=5.53, SD=2.114) did not differ statistically significantly (t=0.510, df=998, two-tailed $p=0.610$) from that of the teachers (M=5.46, SD = 2.145).

The t-test for independent examples is a very widely used statistic, and we support its correct use very strongly.

Less frequently used is the t-test for a paired (related) sample, i.e. where the same group votes on two variables (e.g. liking for mathematics and music), or the same sample group is measured on two occasions (e.g. the pre-test and the post-test) or under two conditions, or the same variable is measured at two points in time. In Table 36.5 two variables are paired, with marks awarded by the same group.

One can see here that we are looking to see if the mean of the 1,000 respondents who voted on 'the attention given to teaching and learning at the school' (mean=5.48) is statistically significantly different from the mean of the same group voting on the variable 'the quality of the lesson preparation' (mean=7.17) using Table 36.6.

Here we can move directly to the final column ('Sig. (2-tailed)') where we find that $p=0.000$, i.e. $p<0.001$,

telling us that the null hypothesis is not supported, and that there is a statistically significant difference between the two means, even though it is the same group that is awarding the marks.

The issue of testing the difference between two proportions is set out on the accompanying website.

To replace statistical significance in difference measurement, calculating effect size can be conducted using 'partial eta squared' and Cohen's d. (In SPSS the command sequence is: Analyze → General Linear Model → Univariate → Estimates of effect size.) Eta squared is the proportion of the total variance that can be attributed to a particular effect, whilst partial eta squared is the proportion of the effect plus error variance that can be attributed to a particular effect. Partial eta squared and Cohen's d are the preferred measures here.

36.3 Analysis of variance

The t-test is useful for examining differences between *two* groups of respondents, or the same group on either two variables or two occasions, using parametric data from a random sample and assuming that each datum value is independent of the others. However, in much educational research we may wish to investigate

TABLE 36.5   MEANS AND STANDARD DEVIATIONS IN A PAIRED SAMPLES t-TEST (SPSS OUTPUT)

Paired Samples Statistics

		Mean	N	Std. Deviation	Std. Error Mean
Pair 1	The attention given to teaching and learning at the school	5.48	1000	2.134	.067
	The quality of the lesson preparation	7.17	1000	1.226	.039

TABLE 36.6   THE PAIRED SAMPLES t-TEST (SPSS OUTPUT)

Paired Samples Test

		Paired Differences							
					95% Confidence Interval of the Difference				
		Mean	Std. Deviation	Std. Error Mean	Lower	Upper	t	df	Sig. (2-tailed)
Pair 1	The attention given to teaching and learning at the school - The quality of the lesson preparation	-1.69	2.430	.077	-1.84	-1.54	-21.936	999	.000

differences between *more than two* groups. For example we may wish to look at the examination results of four regions or four kinds of schools. In this case the t-test will not suit out purposes, and we must turn to analysis of variance. Analysis of variance (ANOVA) is premised on the same assumptions as t-tests, namely random sampling, a normal distribution of scores and parametric data, and it can be used with three or more groups. There are several kinds of analysis of variance; here we introduce only the two most widely used versions: the one-way analysis of variance and the two-way analysis of variance. Analysis of variance, like the t-test, assumes that the independent variable(s) is/are categorical (e.g. teachers, students, parents, governors) and one is a continuous variable (e.g. marks on a test). It calculates the F ratio, given as:

$$\text{F ratio} = \frac{\text{Between-groups variance}}{\text{Within-groups variance}}$$

ANOVA calculates the means for all the groups, then it calculates the average of these means. For each group separately it calculates the total deviation of each individual's score from the mean of the group (within-groups

variation). Finally it calculates the deviation of each group mean from the grand mean (between-groups variation).

One-way analysis of variance

Let us imagine that we have four types of school:

- rural primary
- rural secondary
- urban primary
- urban secondary.

Let us imagine further that all the schools in these categories have taken the same standardized test of mathematics, and the results have been given as a percentage, as shown in Table 36.7. This gives us the means, standard deviations, standard error, confidence intervals, and the minimum and maximum marks for each group. At this stage we are only interested in the means:

rural primary: mean = 59.85%
rural secondary: mean = 60.44%
urban primary: mean = 50.64%
urban secondary: mean = 51.70%

Are these means statistically significantly different? Analysis of variance (ANOVA) will tell us whether they are. We commence with the null hypothesis ('there is no statistically significant difference between the four means') and then we set the level of significance (α) to use for supporting or not supporting the null hypothesis; for example we could say 'Let $\alpha = 0.05$'. Table 36.8 shows the SPSS calculations.

This tells us that, for three degrees of freedom (df), the F-ratio is 8.976. The F-ratio is the *between*-group mean square (variance) divided by the *within*-group mean square (variance), i.e.

$$F = \frac{\text{Between-group variance}}{\text{Within-group variance}} = \frac{3981.040}{443.514} = 8.976$$

By looking at the final column ('Sig.') ANOVA tell us that there is a statistically significant difference between the means ($\rho = 0.000$). This does *not* mean that all the means are statistically significantly different from each other, but that some are. For example, it may be that the means for the rural primary and rural secondary schools (59.85% and 60.44% respectively) are not sta-

tistically significantly different, and that the means for the urban primary schools and urban secondary schools (50.64% and 51.70% respectively) are not statistically significantly different. However it could be that there is a statistically significant difference between the scores of the rural (primary and secondary) and the urban (primary and secondary) schools. How can we find out which groups are different from each other? The purpose of a *post hoc* test is to find out exactly where those differences are.

There are several tests that can be employed here, though we will only concern ourselves with a very commonly used test: the Tukey honestly significant difference test, sometimes called the 'Tukey hsd' test, or simply (as in SPSS) the Tukey test. Others include the Bonferroni and Scheffé test; they are more rigorous than the Tukey test and tend to be used less frequently. The Scheffé test is very similar to the Tukey hsd test, but it is more stringent that the Tukey test in respect of reducing the risk of a Type I error, though this comes with some loss of power: one may be less likely to find a difference between groups in the Scheffé test. The

TABLE 36.7 DESCRIPTIVE STATISTICS FOR ANALYSIS OF VARIANCE (SPSS OUTPUT)

Descriptives

Standardised Mathematics scores (percentages)

	N	Mean	Std. Deviation	Std. Error	95% Confidence Interval for Mean		Minimum	Maximum
					Lower Bound	Upper Bound		
Rural primary	134	59.85	21.061	1.819	56.25	63.45	30	100
Rural secondary	136	60.44	19.470	1.669	57.14	63.74	30	100
Urban primary	141	50.64	22.463	1.892	46.90	54.38	30	100
Urban secondary	194	51.70	21.077	1.513	48.72	54.69	30	100
Total	605	55.22	21.473	.873	53.51	56.94	30	100

TABLE 36.8 SPSS OUTPUT FOR ONE-WAY ANALYSIS OF VARIANCE (SPSS OUTPUT)

ANOVA

Standardised Mathematics scores (percentages)

	Sum of Squares	df	Mean Square	F	Sig.
Between Groups	11943.119	3	3981.040	8.976	.000
Within Groups	266551.8	601	443.514		
Total	278494.9	604			

Tukey test groups together subsamples whose means are *not* statistically significantly different from each other and places them in a different group from a group whose means *are* statistically significantly different from the first group. Let us see what this means in our example of the mathematics results of four types of school.

Table 36.9 takes each type of school and compares it with the other three types, in order to see where there may be statistically significant differences between them. Here the rural primary school is first compared with the rural secondary school (row one of the left-hand column cell named 'Rural primary'), and no statistically significant difference is found between them (Sig.=0.996, i.e. $\rho>0.05$). The rural primary school is then compared with the urban primary school and a statistically significant difference is found between them (Sig.=0.002, i.e. $\rho<0.05$). The rural primary school is then compared with the urban secondary school, and, again, a statistically significant difference is found between them (Sig.=0.003, i.e. $\rho<0.05$). The next cell of the left-hand column commences with the rural secondary school, and this is compared with the rural primary school, and no statistically significant difference is found (Sig.=0.996, i.e. $\rho>0.05$). The rural secondary school is then compared to the urban primary school and a statistically significant difference is found between them (Sig.=0.001, i.e. $\rho<0.05$). The rural secondary school is then compared with the urban secondary school, and, again, a statistically significant difference is found between them (Sig.=0.001, i.e. $\rho<0.05$). The analysis is continued for the urban primary and the urban secondary school. One can see that the two types of rural school do *not* differ statistically significantly from each other, that the two types of urban school do *not* differ statistically significantly from each other, but that the rural and urban schools *do* differ statistically significantly from each other. We can see where the null hypothesis *is* supported and where it is *not* supported.

In fact the Tukey test in SPSS presents this very clearly, as shown in Table 36.10. Here one group of similar means (i.e. those not statistically significantly different from each other: the urban primary and urban secondary) is placed together (the column labelled '1') and the other group of similar means (i.e. those not statistically significantly different from each other: the rural primary and rural secondary) is placed together (the column labelled '2'). SPSS automatically groups these and places them in ascending order (the group with the lowest means appears in the first column, and the group with the highest means is in the second

---

TABLE 36.9 THE TUKEY TEST (SPSS OUTPUT)

Multiple Comparisons

Dependent Variable: Standardised Mathematics scores (percentages)

Tukey HSD

(I) Grouping of school	(J) Grouping of school	Mean Difference (I-J)	Std. Error	Sig.	95% Confidence Interval Lower Bound	95% Confidence Interval Upper Bound
Rural primary	Rural secondary	-.59	2.563	.996	-7.19	6.01
	Urban primary	9.21*	2.541	.002	2.67	15.76
	Urban secondary	8.15*	2.366	.003	2.06	14.24
Rural secondary	Rural primary	.59	2.563	.996	-6.01	7.19
	Urban primary	9.80*	2.531	.001	3.28	16.32
	Urban secondary	8.74*	2.355	.001	2.67	14.81
Urban primary	Rural primary	-9.21*	2.541	.002	-15.76	-2.67
	Rural secondary	-9.80*	2.531	.001	-16.32	-3.28
	Urban secondary	-1.06	2.331	.968	-7.07	4.94
Urban secondary	Rural primary	-8.15*	2.366	.003	-14.24	-2.06
	Rural secondary	-8.74*	2.355	.001	-14.81	-2.67
	Urban primary	1.06	2.331	.968	-4.94	7.07

*. The mean difference is significant at the .05 level.

column). So, one can see clearly that the difference between the schools lies *not* in the fact that some are primary and some are secondary, but that some are rural and some are urban, i.e. the differences relate to geographical location rather than age group in the school. The Tukey test helps us to locate exactly where the similarities and differences between groups lie. It places the means into homogeneous subgroups, so that we can see which means are close together but different from other groups of means.

Analysis of variance here tells us that there are or are not statistically significant differences between groups; the Tukey test indicates where these differences lie, if they exist. We advise using the two tests together. Of course, as with the t-test, it is sometimes equally important if we do *not* find a difference between groups as if we *do* find a difference. For example, if we were to find that there was no difference between four groups (parents, teachers, students and school governors/leaders) on a particular issue, say the move towards increased science teaching, then this would give us greater grounds for thinking that a proposed innovation – the introduction of increased science teaching – would stand a greater chance of success than if there had been statistically significant differences between the groups. Finding no difference can be as important as finding a difference.

In reporting analysis of variance and the Tukey test one could use a form of words thus:

Analysis of variance found that there was a statistically significant difference between rural and urban schools $(F_{14}=8.975, \rho<0.001)$. The Tukey test found that the means for rural primary schools and rural secondary schools (59.85 and 60.44 respectively) were not statistically significantly different from each other, and that the means for urban primary schools and urban secondary schools (50.64 and 51.70 respectively) were not statistically significantly different from each other. The homogeneous subsets calculated by the Tukey test reveal two subsets in respect of the variable 'Standardized mathematics scores': (a) urban primary and urban secondary schools; (b) rural primary and rural secondary scores. The two subsets reveal that these two groups were distinctly and statistically significantly different from each other in respect of this variable. The means of the rural schools were statistically significantly higher than the means of the urban schools.

For repeated measures in ANOVA (i.e. the same groups under three or more conditions), with the Tukey test and a measure of effect size, the SPSS command sequence is: Analyze → General Linear Model → Repeated Measures → In the box 'Within-Subject Factor Name' name a new variable → In the box 'Number of Levels' insert the number of dependent variables that you wish to include → Click on 'Add' → Click on 'Define' → Send over the dependent variables that you wish to include (the number of variables must be the same as the 'Number of Levels') into the box 'Within-Subjects Variables' → Send over the independent variable into the box 'Between-Subjects Factors' → Click on 'Options' → Click on 'Estimates of effect size' → Click on 'Continue' → Click 'Post Hoc' → Send over the factor from the 'Factor(s)' box to the 'Post Hoc Tests for' box → Click on 'Tukey' → Click 'Continue' (which returns you to the original screen) → Click 'OK'. This will give you several boxes in the output. Go to 'Multivariate Tests'; the furthest right-hand column has the partial eta squared. Go to the row that contains the last box, and look at the partial eta squared (e.g. 'Pillai's Trace' and Wilks's Lamda'); this gives the partial eta squared.

Two-way analysis of variance

The example of ANOVA above illustrates one-way analysis of variance, i.e. the difference between the means of three or more groups on a single independent variable. Additionally ANOVA can take account of more than one independent variable. Two-way analysis of variance is used 'to estimate the effect of two independent variables (factors) on a single variable' (Cohen and Holliday, 1996: 277). Let us take the example of how examination performance in science is affected by

---

TABLE 36.10 HOMOGENEOUS GROUPINGS IN THE TUKEY TEST (SPSS OUTPUT)

Standardised Mathematics scores (percentages)

Tukey HSD[a,b]

Grouping of school	N	Subset for alpha = .05	
		1	2
Urban primary	141	50.64	
Urban secondary	194	51.70	
Rural primary	134		59.85
Rural secondary	136		60.44
Sig.		.973	.995

Means for groups in homogeneous subsets are displayed.

a. Uses Harmonic Mean Sample Size = 147.806.

b. The group sizes are unequal. The harmonic mean of the group sizes is used. Type I error levels are not guaranteed.

TABLE 36.11 MEANS AND STANDARD DEVIATIONS IN A TWO-WAY ANALYSIS OF VARIANCE (SPSS OUTPUT)

Descriptive Statistics

Dependent Variable: SCIENCE

sex	Age group	Mean	Std. Deviation	N
male	15-20	71.92	24.353	125
	21-25	63.33	31.459	111
	26-45	70.95	28.793	21
	46 and above	64.69	28.752	128
	Total	66.99	28.390	385
female	15-20	70.33	25.768	182
	21-25	68.82	25.396	221
	26-45	69.59	28.059	49
	46 and above	61.66	28.464	163
	Total	67.43	26.731	615
Total	15-20	70.98	25.173	307
	21-25	66.99	27.646	332
	26-45	70.00	28.079	70
	46 and above	62.99	28.581	291
	Total	67.26	27.369	1000

both age group and sex. Two-way ANOVA enables the researcher not only to examine the effect of each independent variable but also the interaction effects on each other of the two independent variables, i.e. how sex effects are influenced or modified when combined with age group effects. We may discover, for example, that age group has a differential effect on examination performance according to whether one is male or female, i.e. there is an interaction effect.

For two-way analysis of variance the researcher requires two independent categorical (nominal) variables (e.g. sex, age group) and one continuous dependent variable (e.g. performance on examinations). Two-way ANOVA enables one to calculate three effects. In the example here they are:

■ difference in examination performance by sex;
■ difference in examination performance by age group;
■ the interaction of sex and age group on examination, e.g. is there a difference in the effects of age group on examination performance for males and females?

We will use SPSS to provide an example of this. SPSS first presents descriptive statistics, for example

Table 36.11. This simply presents the data, with means and standard deviations. Next SPSS calculates the Levene test for equality of error variances, degrees of freedom and significance levels, as shown in Table 36.12.

This test enables the researcher to know whether there is equality across the means. She needs to see if

TABLE 36.12 THE LEVENE TEST OF EQUALITY OF VARIANCES IN A TWO-WAY ANALYSIS OF VARIANCE (SPSS OUTPUT)

Levene's Test of Equality of Error Variances [a]

Dependent Variable: SCIENCE

F	df1	df2	Sig.
3.463	7	992	.001

Tests the null hypothesis that the error variance of the dependent variable is equal across groups.

a. Design: Intercept+SEX+AGE GROUP +SEX * AGE GROUP

TABLE 36.13 BETWEEN-SUBJECT EFFECTS IN TWO-WAY ANALYSIS OF VARIANCE (SPSS OUTPUT)

Tests of Between-Subjects Effects

Dependent Variable: SCIENCE

Source	Type III Sum of Squares	df	Mean Square	F	Sig.	Partial Eta Squared	Noncent. Parameter	Observed Power[a]
Corrected Model	13199.146[b]	7	1885.592	2.545	.013	.018	17.812	.888
Intercept	2687996.888	1	2687996.9	3627.42	.000	.785	3627.421	1.000
SEX	2.218	1	2.218	.003	.956	.000	.003	.050
AGE GROUP	10124.306	3	3374.769	4.554	.004	.014	13.663	.887
SEX * AGE GROUP	3089.630	3	1029.877	1.390	.244	.004	4.169	.371
Error	735093.254	992	741.021					
Total	5272200.000	1000						
Corrected Total	748292.400	999						

a. Computed using alpha = .05

b. R Squared = .018 (Adjusted R Squared = .011)

the significance level is greater than 0.05. The researcher is looking for a significance level *greater than* 0.05, i.e. *not* statistically significant, which supports the null hypothesis that holds that there is no statistically significant difference between the means and variances across the groups (i.e. to support the assumptions of ANOVA). In our example this is not the case as the significance level is 0.001. This means that she has to proceed with caution as equality of variances cannot be assumed. SPSS provides her with important information, as shown in Table 36.13.

Here one can see the three sets of independent variables listed (SEX, AGE GROUP, SEX*AGE GROUP). The column headed 'Sig.' shows that the significance levels for the three sets are, respectively: 0.956, 0.004 and 0.244. Hence one can see that sex does not have a statistically significant effect on science examination performance. Age group does have a statistically significant effect on the performance in the science examination ($p=0.004$). The interaction effect of sex and age group does not have a statistically significant effect on performance, i.e. there is no difference in the effect on science performance for males and females ($p=0.244$). SPSS also computes the effect size (Partial Eta squared). For the important variable AGE GROUP this is given as 0.014, which shows that the effect size is very small indeed, suggesting that, even though statistical significance has been found, the actual difference in the mean values is very small.

As with one-way ANOVA, the Tukey test can be applied here to present the homogeneous groupings of the subsample means. SPSS can also present a graphic plot of the two sets of scores, which gives the researcher a ready understanding of the effects of the males and females across the four age groups in their science examination, as shown in Figure 36.1.

In reporting the results of the two-way analysis of variance one can use the following form of words:

A two-way between-groups analysis of variance was conducted to discover the impact of sex and age group on performance in a science examination. Subjects were divided into four groups by age: Group 1: 15–20 years; Group 2: 21–25 years; Group 3: 26–45 years; and Group 4: 46 years and above. There was a statistically significant main effect for age group (F=4.554, $p=0.004$), however the effect size was small (partial eta squared=0.014). The main effect for sex (F=0.003, $p=0.956$) and the interaction effect (F=1.390, $p=0.244$) were not statistically significant.

To run two-way ANOVA in SPSS the command sequence is: 'Analyze' → Click on 'General Linear Model' → Click on 'Univariate' → Send the dependent variable to the box 'Dependent Variable' → Send the independent variables to the box 'Fixed Factors' → Click on the 'Options' box; in the 'Display' area, check the boxes 'Descriptive Statistics' and 'Estimates of effect size' → Click 'Continue' → Click on the 'Post Hoc' box, and send over from the 'Factors' box to the 'Post Hoc tests for' box those factors that you wish to investigate in the *post hoc* tests → Click the *post hoc* test that you wish to use (e.g. 'Tukey') → Click

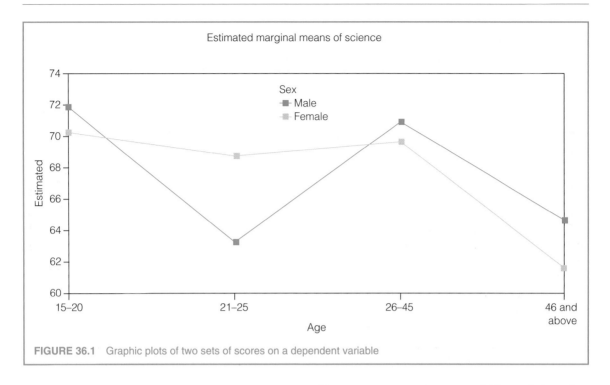

FIGURE 36.1 Graphic plots of two sets of scores on a dependent variable

'Continue' → Click the 'Plots' box → Move to the 'Horizontal' box the factor that has the most groups → Move to the 'Separate lines' box the factor the other independent variable → Click on 'Add' → Click on 'Continue' → Click on 'OK'.

Multiple analysis of variance

Multiple analysis of variance (MANOVA) is designed to see the effects of one categorical independent variable on two or more continuous variables (e.g. 'do males score more highly than females in terms of how hard they work and their IQ').

To run MANOVA, the SPSS command sequence is: 'Analyze' → Click on 'General Linear Model' → Click on 'Multivariate' → Send to the box 'Dependent Variables' the dependent variables that you wish to include → Send to the 'Fixed Factors' box the independent variable that you wish to use → Click on 'Model' and ensure that the 'Full factorial' (in the 'Specify Model' box) and the 'Type III' (in the 'Sum of Squares') boxes are selected → Click on 'Continue' → Click on the 'Options' box and send to the 'Display Means for' box the independent variable that you wish to include → In the 'Display' section, click on 'Descriptive Statistics', 'Estimates of effect size' and 'Homogeneity tests' → Click on 'Continue' → If you want a *post hoc* test click on 'Post Hoc' → Send over the independent variable from the 'Factor(s)' box to the 'Post Hoc tests for' box

(if you want a *post hoc* test and if your independent variable has three or more values) → Click on 'Tukey' → Click on 'Continue' → Click on 'OK'.

The standard text on one-way and two-way analysis of variance (ANOVA) and multiple analysis of variance (MANOVA) is Tabachnick and Fidell (2007), and we refer readers to this text. For further guidance on running SPSS for these matters and interpreting the SPSS output, we refer readers to Pallant (2007).

36.4 The chi-square test

Difference testing is an important feature in understanding data. We can conduct a statistical test to investigate difference; it is the chi-square test (χ^2) (pronounced 'kigh', as in 'high'). The chi-square test is a test of difference that can be conducted for a univariate analysis (one categorical variable), and between two categorical variables. The chi-square test measures the difference between a statistically generated expected result and an actual (observed) result to see if there is a statistically significant difference between them, i.e. to see if the frequencies observed are significant; it is a measure of 'goodness of fit' between an expected and an actual, observed result or set of results. The expected result is based on a statistical process discussed below. The chi-square statistic addresses the notion of statistical significance, itself based on notions of probability. Here is not the place to go into the mathematics of the test, not least because computer packages automatically calculate the results. That said, the formula for calculating chi-square is:

$$\chi^2 = \sum \frac{(O-E)^2}{E}$$

where
O = observed frequencies
E = expected frequencies
$\sum$ = the sum of

For univariate data let us take the example of 120 students who were asked which of four teachers they preferred. We start with the null hypothesis that states that there is no difference in the preferences for four teachers, i.e. that the 120 scores are spread evenly across the four teachers, thus:

Frequencies	Teacher A	Teacher B	Teacher C	Teacher D
Observed	20	70	10	20
Expected	30	30	30	30
Residual (difference between observed and expected frequencies)	−10	40	−20	−10

Using the formula above we compute the chi-square figure thus:

$$\chi^2 = \sum \frac{(O-E)^2}{E} = \sum \frac{(-10)^2}{30} + \frac{(40)^2}{30} + \frac{(-20)^2}{30} + \frac{(-10)^2}{30}$$

$$= \frac{100+1600+400+100}{30} = \frac{2200}{30} = 73.3$$

The chi-square value here is 73.3, with three degrees of freedom (explained below). In a table of critical values for chi-square distributions (usually in the appendices of most statistics books and freely available on the internet) we look up the level of statistical significance for three degrees of freedom:

Degrees of freedom	Level of significance	
	0.05	0.01
2	5.99	9.21
3	7.81	11.34
4	9.49	13.28
5	11.07	15.09
6	12.59	16.81

We find that, at 73.3, the chi-square value is considerably larger than 11.34, i.e. it has a probability level stronger than 0.01, i.e. of 0.000, i.e. there is a statistically significant difference between the observed and expected frequencies, i.e. not all teachers are equally preferred (more people preferred Teacher B, and this was statistically significant).

If all the teachers were equally popular then the observed frequencies would not differ much from the expected frequencies. However, if the observed frequencies differ a lot from the expected frequencies, then it is likely that all teachers are not equally preferred, and this is what was found here.

For bivariate data a similar procedure can be followed. Here the chi-square test is a test of independence, to see whether there is a relationship or association between two categorical variables. Let us say that we have a crosstabulation of males and females and their liking for maths (like/dislike). We start with the null hypothesis that states that there is *no* statistically significant difference between the males and females (variable 1) in their (dis)liking for mathematics (variable 2), and the onus on the data is *not* to support this. We then set the level of significance (α) that we wish to use for supporting or not supporting the null hypothesis; for example we could say 'Let $\alpha = 0.05$'. Having found out the true voting we set out a 2×2 crosstabulation thus, with the observed frequencies in the cells:

	Male	Female	Total
Like mathematics	60	25	85
Dislike mathematics	35	75	110
Total	95	100	195

These are the observed frequencies. To find out the expected frequencies for each cell we use the formula:

$$\text{Expected value of a cell} = \frac{\text{row total} \times \text{column total}}{\text{Overall total}}$$

Hence we can calculate the expected frequencies for each thus (figures rounded):

	Male	Female	Total
Like mathematics	(85 × 95)/195 = 41.4	(85 × 100)/195 = 43.6	85
Dislike mathematics	(110 × 95)/195 = 53.6	(110 × 100)/195 = 56.4	110
Total	95	100	195

The chi-square value, using the formula above is:

$$\chi^2 = \Sigma \frac{(O-E)^2}{E} = \Sigma \frac{(18.6)^2}{41.4} + \frac{(-18.6)^2}{53.6}$$

$$+ \frac{(-18.6)^2}{43.6} + \frac{(18.6)^2}{56.4} = \frac{345.96}{41.4} + \frac{345.96}{53.6}$$

$$+ \frac{345.96}{43.6} + \frac{345.96}{56.4}$$

$$= 8.36 + 6.45 + 7.93 + 6.13 = 28.87$$

When we look up the chi-square value of 28.87 in the tables of the critical values of the chi-square distribution, with two degrees of freedom we observe that the figure of 28.87 is larger than the figure of 9.21 required for statistical significance at the 0.01 level. Hence we conclude that the distribution of likes and dislikes for mathematics by males and females is not simply by chance but that there is a real, statistically significant difference between the voting of males and females here. Hence the null hypothesis is not supported and the alternative hypothesis, that there is a statistically significant difference between the voting of the two groups, is supported.

We do not need to perform these calculations by hand. Computer software such as SPSS will do all the calculations at the press of a button.

We recall that the conventionally accepted minimum level of significance is usually 0.05, and we used this level in the example; the significance level of our data here is smaller than either the 0.05 and 0.01 levels, i.e. it is highly statistically significant.

One can report the results of the chi-square test thus, for example:

> When the chi-square statistic was calculated for the distribution of males and females on their liking for mathematics, a statistically significant difference was found between the males and the females ($\chi^2 = 28.87$, d.f. $= 2$, $\rho = 0.000$).

We use Yates's correction (a continuity correction) to compensate for the overestimate of the chi-square in a 2×2 table, and this can be activated by a single button in SPSS or other software.

The chi-square statistic is normally used with nominal (categorical) data, and our example in Table 36.14 illustrates this. This is a further example of the chi-square statistic, with data that are set into a contingency table, this time in a 2×3 contingency table, i.e. two horizontal rows and three columns (contingency tables may contain more than this number of variables). The example in Table 36.14 presents data concerning 60 students' entry

TABLE 36.14	A 2 × 3 CONTINGENCY TABLE FOR CHI-SQUARE			
	Science subjects	Arts subjects	Humanities subjects	
Males	7.6 14	8 4	8.4 6	24
Females	11.4 5	12 16	12.6 15	36
	19	20	21	60

into science, arts and humanities, in a college, and whether the students are male or female (Morrison, 1993: 132–4). The lower of the two figures in each cell is the number of actual students who have opted for the particular subjects (sciences, arts, humanities). The upper of the two figures in each cell is what might be expected purely by chance to be the number of students opting for each of the particular subjects. The figure is arrived at by statistical computation, hence the decimal fractions for the figures. What is of interest to the researcher is whether the actual distribution of subject choice by males and females differs significantly from that which could occur by chance variation in the population of college entrants.

The researcher begins with the null hypothesis that there is no statistically significant difference between the actual results noted and what might be expected to occur by chance in the wider population. When the chi-square statistic is calculated, if the observed, actual distribution differs from that which might be expected to occur by chance alone, then the researcher has to determine whether that difference is statistically significant, i.e. not to support the null hypothesis.

In our example of 60 students' choices, the chi-square formula yields a final chi-square value of 14.64. This we refer to the tables of the critical values of the chi-square distribution (an extract from which is set out for the first example above) to determine whether the derived chi-square values indicate a statistically significant difference from that occurring by chance.

The researcher will see that the 'degrees of freedom' (a mathematical construct that is related to the number of restrictions that have been placed on the data) have to be identified. In many cases, to establish the degrees of freedom, one simply takes 1 away from the total number of rows of the contingency table and 1 away from the total number of columns and adds them; in this case it is $(2-1)+(3-1)=3$ degrees of freedom. Degrees of freedom are discussed in the next section. (Other formulae for ascertaining degrees of freedom hold that the number is the total number of cells minus one.) The researcher looks along the table from the entry for the three degrees of freedom and notes that the derived chi-square value calculated (14.64) is statistically significant at the 0.01 level, i.e. is higher than the required 11.34, indicating that the results obtained – the distributions of the actual data – could not have occurred simply by chance. The null hypothesis is not supported, at the 0.01 level of significance. Interpreting the specific numbers of the contingency table (Table 36.14) in educational rather than statistical terms, noting (a) the low incidence of females in the science subjects and the high incidence of females in the arts and humanities subjects, and (b) the high incidence of males in the science subjects and low incidence of males in the arts and humanities, the researcher would say that this distribution is statistically significant – suggesting, perhaps, that the college needs to consider action possibly to encourage females into science subjects and males into arts and humanities.

The chi-square test is one of the most widely used tests, and is applicable to nominal data in particular. More powerful tests are available for ordinal, interval and ratio data, and we discuss these separately. However, one has to be cautious of the limitations of the chi-square test. Look at the following example in Table 36.15.

If one were to perform the chi-square test on this table then one would have to be extremely cautious. The chi-square statistic assumes that no more than 20 per cent of the total number of cells contain fewer than five cases. In the example here we have one cell with four cases, another with three, and another with only one case, i.e. three cells out of the ten (two rows – males and females – with five cells in each for each of the rating categories). This means that 30 per cent of the cells contain less than five cases; even though a computer will calculate a chi-square statistic, it means that the result is unreliable. This highlights the point made in Chapter 8 about sampling, namely that the subsample size has to be large. For example, if each category here were to contain five cases then it would mean that the minimum sample size would

be 50 (10×5), assuming that the data are evenly spread. In the example here, even though the sample size is much larger (191) it still does not guarantee that the 20 per cent rule will be observed, as the data are unevenly spread. When calculating the chi-square statistic, the researcher can use the Fisher Exact Probability Test if more than 25 per cent of the cells have fewer than five cases, and this is automatically calculated and printed as part of the normal output in the chi-square calculation in SPSS.

Because of the need to ensure that at least 80 per cent of the cells of a chi-square contingency table contain more than five cases if confidence is to be placed in the results, it may not be feasible to calculate the chi-square statistic if only a small sample is being used. Hence the researcher would tend to use this statistic for larger-scale survey data. Other tests could be used if the problem of low cell frequencies obtains, e.g. the binomial test and, more widely used, the Fisher Exact Probability Test (Cohen and Holliday, 1996: 218–20). The required minimum number of cases in each cell renders the chi-square statistic problematic, and, apart from with nominal data, there are alternative statistics that can be calculated and which overcome this problem (e.g. the Mann-Whitney, Wilcoxon, Kruskal-Wallis and Friedman tests for non-parametric – ordinal – data, and the t-test and analysis of variance test for parametric – interval and ratio – data).

As the use of statistical significance is being increasingly questioned, it is being replaced with measures of effect size (discussed in Chapter 34). Calculations of effect size for categorical tables use two main statistics:

- Phi coefficient for 2×2 tables (in which Cohen's d indicates small effect for 0.10, a medium effect for 0.30 and a large effect for 0.50).
- Cramer's V for contingency tables larger than 2×2, which takes account of degrees of freedom.

Two significance tests for very small samples are given in the accompanying website.

TABLE 36.15 A 2 × 5 CONTINGENCY TABLE FOR CHI-SQUARE

	Music	Physics	Maths	German	Spanish	
Males	7 14.0%	11 22.0%	25 50%	4 8.0%	3 6%	50 100%
Females	17 12.1%	38 27.0%	73 52%	12 8.5%	1 0.7%	141 100%
Total	24 12.6%	49 25.7%	98 51%	16 8.4%	4 2.1%	191 100%

36.5 Degrees of freedom

The chi-square statistic introduces the term *degrees of freedom*. Gorard (2001b: 233) suggests that 'the degrees of freedom is the number of scores we need to know before we can calculate the rest'. Cohen and Holliday (1996: 113) explain the term clearly:

Suppose we have to select any five numbers. We have complete freedom of choice as to what the numbers are. So, we have five degrees of freedom. Suppose however we are then told that the five numbers must have a total value of 25. We will have complete freedom of choice to select four numbers but the fifth will be dependent on the other four. Let's say that the first four numbers we select are 7, 8, 9, and 10, which total 34, then if the total value of the five numbers is to be 25, the fifth number must be –9.

$$7+8+9+10-9=25$$

A restriction has been placed on one of the observations; only four are free to vary; the fifth has lost its freedom. In our example then d.f.$=4$, that is $N-1=5-1=4$.

Suppose now that we are told to select any five numbers, the first two of which have to total 9, and the total value of all five has to be 25. Our restriction is apparent when we wish the total of the first two numbers to be 9. Another restriction is apparent in the requirement that all five numbers must total 25. In other words we have lost two degrees of freedom in our example. It leaves us with d.f.$=3$, that is, $N-2=5-2=3$.

For a cross-tabulation (a contingency table), degrees of freedom refer to the freedom with which the researcher is able to assign values to the cells, given fixed marginal totals, usually given as (number of rows –

1)+(number of columns – 1). There are many variants of this, and readers will need to consult more detailed texts to explore this issue. We do not dwell on degrees of freedom here, as it is automatically calculated and addressed in subsequent calculations by most statistical software packages such as SPSS.

36.6 The Mann-Whitney and Wilcoxon tests

The non-parametric equivalents of the t-test are the Mann-Whitney U test for two independent samples and the Wilcoxon test for two related samples, both for use with one categorical variable and a minimum of one ordinal variable. These enable us to see, for example, whether there are differences between males and females on a rating scale.

The Mann-Whitney test is based on ranks, 'comparing the number of times a score from one of the samples is ranked higher than a score from the other sample' (Bryman and Cramer, 1990: 129) and hence overcomes the problem of low cell frequencies in the chi-square statistic. Let us take an example. Imagine that we have conducted a course evaluation, using five-point rating scales ('not at all', 'very little', 'a little', 'quite a lot', 'a very great deal'), and we wish to find if there is a statistically significant difference between the voting of males and females on the variable 'The course gave you opportunities to learn at your own pace'. We commence with the null hypothesis ('there is no statistically significant difference between the two rankings') and then we set the level of significance (α) to use for supporting or not supporting the null hypothesis; for example we could say 'Let $\alpha=0.05$'. A crosstabulation is shown in Table 36.16.

Are the differences between the two groups statistically significant? Using SPSS, the Mann-Whitney statistic is given in Tables 36.17 and 36.18.

TABLE 36.16   A CROSSTABULATION FOR A MANN-WHITNEY U TEST (SPSS OUTPUT)

sex * the course gave you opportunities to learn at your own pace Crosstabulation

| | | the course gave you opportunities to learn at your own pace | | | | | |
		strongly disagree	disagree	neither agree nor disagree	agree	strongly agree	Total
male	Count	1	2	16	21	9	49
	% within sex	2.0%	4.1%	32.7%	42.9%	18.4%	100.0%
female	Count	4	11	61	57	8	141
	% within sex	2.8%	7.8%	43.3%	40.4%	5.7%	100.0%
Total	Count	5	13	77	78	17	190
	% within sex	2.6%	6.8%	40.5%	41.1%	8.9%	100.0%

TABLE 36.17   RANKINGS FOR THE MANN-WHITNEY U TEST (SPSS OUTPUT)

Ranks

	sex	N	Mean Rank	Sum of Ranks
the course gave you opportunities to learn at your own pace	male	49	110.23	5401.50
	female	141	90.38	12743.50
	Total	190		

Mann-Whitney using ranks (as in Table 36.17) yields a U value of 2,732.500 (as in Table 36.18) from the formula it uses for the calculation (SPSS does this automatically). The important information in Table 36.18 is the 'Asymp. Sig. (2-tailed)', i.e. the statistical significance level of any difference found between the two groups (males and females). Here the significance level ($\rho = 0.019$, i.e. $\rho < 0.05$) indicates that the voting by males and females is statistically significantly different and that the null hypothesis is not supported. In the t-test and the Tukey test researchers could immediately find exactly where differences might lie between the groups (by looking at the means and the homogeneous subgroups respectively). Unfortunately the Mann-Whitney test does not enable the researcher to identify clearly where the differences lie between the two groups, so the researcher would need to go back to the crosstabulation to identify where differences lie. In the example above, it appears that the males feel more strongly than the females that the course in question has afforded them the opportunity to learn at their own pace.

In reporting the Mann-Whitney test one could use a form of words such as the following:

When the Mann-Whitney Wallis statistic was calculated to determine whether there was any statistically significant difference in the voting of the two groups ($U = 2,732.500$, $\rho = 0.019$), a statistically

TABLE 36.18   THE MANN-WHITNEY U VALUE AND SIGNIFICANCE LEVEL (SPSS OUTPUT)

Test Statistics [a]

	the course gave you opportunities to learn at your own pace
Mann-Whitney U	2732.500
Wilcoxon W	12743.500
Z	-2.343
Asymp. Sig. (2-tailed)	.019

a. Grouping Variable: sex

TABLE 36.19   FREQUENCIES AND PERCENTAGES OF VARIABLE ONE IN A WILCOXON TEST (SPSS OUTPUT)

the course was just right

	Valid					
	strongly disagree	disagree	neither agree nor disagree	agree	strongly agree	Total
Frequency	2	14	65	76	34	191
Valid Percent	1.0	7.3	34.0	39.8	17.8	100.0

TABLE 36.20   FREQUENCIES AND PERCENTAGES OF VARIABLE TWO IN A WILCOXON TEST (SPSS OUTPUT)

the lecturer was well prepared

	Valid						Total
	strongly disagree	disagree	neither agree nor disagree	agree	strongly agree	Total	
Frequency	3	5	25	85	72	190	191
Valid Percent	1.6	2.6	13.2	44.7	37.9	100.0	

TABLE 36.21   RANKS AND SUMS OF RANKS IN A WILCOXON TEST (SPSS OUTPUT)

Ranks

		N	Mean Rank	Sum of Ranks
the lecturer was well prepared - the course was just right	Negative Ranks	20 [a]	50.30	1006.00
	Positive Ranks	89 [b]	56.06	4989.00
	Ties	81 [c]		
	Total	190		

a. the lecturer was well prepared < the course was just right

b. the lecturer was well prepared > the course was just right

c. the course was just right = the lecturer was well prepared

significant difference was found between the males and females. A crosstabulation found that males felt more strongly than the females that the course in question had afforded them the opportunity to learn at their own pace.

For two related samples (e.g. the same group voting for more than one item, or the same grouping voting at two points in time) the Wilcoxon test is applied, and the data are presented and analysed in the same way as the Mann-Whitney test. For example in Tables 36.19 and 36.20 there are two variables ('The course was just right' and 'The lecturer was well prepared'), voted on by the same group. The frequencies are given. Is there a statistically significant difference in the voting?

As it is the same group voting on two variables, the sample is not independent, hence the Wilcoxon test is used. Using SPSS output, the data analysis shows that the voting of the group on the two variables is statistically significantly different (Tables 36.21 and 36.22).

TABLE 36.22   SIGNIFICANCE LEVEL IN A WILCOXON TEST (SPSS OUTPUT)

Test Statistics [b]

	the lecturer was well prepared - the course was just right
Z	-6.383 [a]
Asymp. Sig. (2-tailed)	.000

a. Based on negative ranks.

b. Wilcoxon Signed Ranks Test

TABLE 36.23   CROSSTABULATION FOR THE KRUSKAL-WALLIS TEST (SPSS OUTPUT)

number of years teaching * the teaching and learning tasks and activities consolidate learning through application Crosstabulation

| | | | the teaching and learning tasks and activities consolidate learning through application | | | | |
			disagree	neither agree nor disagree	agree	strongly agree	Total
number of years teaching	<16	Count		2	3		5
		% within number of years teaching		40.0%	60.0%		100.0%
	16-18	Count		29	52	14	95
		% within number of years teaching		30.5%	54.7%	14.7%	100.0%
	19-21	Count	6	40	34	7	87
		% within number of years teaching	6.9%	46.0%	39.1%	8.0%	100.0%
	>21	Count			2		2
		% within number of years teaching			100%		100.0%
Total		Count	6	71	91	21	189
		% within number of years teaching	3.2%	37.6%	48.1%	11.1%	100.0%

TABLE 36.24   RANKINGS FOR THE KRUSKAL-WALLIS TEST (SPSS OUTPUT)

Ranks

	number of years teaching	N	Mean Rank
the teaching and learning tasks and activities consolidate learning through application	<16	5	90.60
	16-18	95	106.53
	19-21	87	82.02
	>21	2	123.00
	Total	189	

The reporting of the results of the Wilcoxon test can follow that of the Mann-Whitney test.

For both the Mann-Whitney and Wilcoxon tests, *not* finding a statistically significant difference between groups can be just as important as finding a statistically significant difference between them, as the former suggests that nominal characteristics of the sample make no statistically significant difference to the voting, i.e. the voting is consistent, regardless of particular features of the sample.

36.7 The Kruskal-Wallis and Friedman tests

The non-parametric equivalents of analysis of variance are the Kruskal-Wallis test for three or more independent samples and the Friedman test for three or more related samples, both for use with one categorical variable and one ordinal variable. These enable us to see, for example, whether there are differences between three or more groups (e.g. classes, schools, groups of teachers) on a rating scale.

These tests operate in a very similar way to the Mann-Whitney test, being based on rankings. Let us take an example. Teachers in different groups, according to the number of years that they have been teaching, have been asked to evaluate one aspect of a particular course that they have attended ('The teaching and learning tasks and activities consolidate learning through application'). One of the results is the crosstabulation in Table 36.23. Are the groups of teachers statistically significantly different from each other? We commence with the null hypothesis ('there is no statistically significant difference between the four groups') and then we set the level of significance (α) to use for supporting or not supporting the null hypothesis; for example we could say 'Let $\alpha = 0.05$'.

Is the difference in the voting between the four groups statistically significantly different? The Kruskal-Wallis test calculates and presents results in SPSS as shown in Tables 36.24 and 36.25 .

The important figure to note here is the 0.009 ('Asymp. Sig.') – the significance level. Because this is less than 0.05 we can conclude that the null hypothesis ('there is no statistically significant difference between the voting by the different groups of years in teaching') is not supported, and that the results vary according to

the number of years in teaching of the voters. As with the Mann-Whitney test, the Kruskal-Wallis test tells us only that there *is* or *is not* a statistically significant difference, not *where* the difference lies. To find out where the difference lies, one has to return to the cross-tabulation and examine it. In the example here in Table 36.23 it appears that those teachers in the group which had been teaching from 16–18 years are the most positive about the aspect of the course in question.

TABLE 36.25   SIGNIFICANCE LEVELS IN A KRUSKAL-WALLIS TEST (SPSS OUTPUT)

Test Statistics [a,b]

	the teaching and learning tasks and activities consolidate learning through application
Chi-Square	11.595
df	3
Asymp. Sig.	.009

a. Kruskal Wallis Test

b. Grouping Variable: number of years teaching

TABLE 36.26   FREQUENCIES FOR VARIABLE ONE IN THE FRIEDMAN TEST (SPSS OUTPUT)

the course encouraged and stimulated your motivation and willingness to learn

	Valid						Total
	not at all	very little	a little	quite a lot	a very great deal	Total	
Frequency	1	13	64	79	32	189	191
Valid Percent	.5	6.9	33.9	41.8	16.9	100.0	

TABLE 36.27   FREQUENCIES FOR VARIABLE TWO IN THE FRIEDMAN TEST (SPSS OUTPUT)

the course encouraged you to take responsibility for your own learning

	Valid						Total
	not at all	very little	a little	quite a lot	a very great deal	Total	
Frequency	1	9	64	85	30	189	191
Valid Percent	.5	4.8	33.9	45.0	15.9	100.0	

TABLE 36.28   FREQUENCIES FOR VARIABLE THREE IN THE FRIEDMAN TEST (SPSS OUTPUT)

the teaching and learning tasks and activities consolidate learning through application

	Valid				
	very little	a little	quite a lot	a very great deal	Total
Frequency	6	71	92	22	191
Valid Percent	3.1	37.2	48.2	11.5	100.0

TABLE 36.29   RANKINGS FOR THE FRIEDMAN TEST (SPSS OUTPUT)

Ranks

	Mean Rank
the course encouraged and stimulated your motivation and willingness to learn	1.98
the course encouraged you to take responsibility for your own learning	2.03
the teaching and learning tasks and activities consolidate learning through application	1.99

TABLE 36.30   SIGNIFICANCE LEVEL IN THE FRIEDMAN TEST (SPSS OUTPUT)

Test Statistics [a]

N	187
Chi-Square	.353
df	2
Asymp. Sig.	.838

a. Friedman Test

In reporting the Kruskal-Wallis test one could use a form of words such as the following:

When the Kruskal-Wallis statistic was calculated to determine whether there was any statistically significant difference in the voting of the four groups ($\chi^2 = 11.595$, $\rho = 0.009$), a statistically significant difference was found between the groups which had different years of teaching experience. A crosstabulation found that those teachers in the group that had been teaching from 16–18 years were the most positive about the variable 'the teaching and learning tasks and activities consolidate learning through application'.

For more than two related samples (e.g. the same group voting for three or more items, or the same grouping voting at three points in time), the Friedman test is applied. For example in Tables 36.26–36.28 are three variables ('The course encouraged and stimulated your motivation and willingness to learn'; 'The course encouraged you to take responsibility for your own learning'; and 'The teaching and learning tasks and activities consolidate learning through application'), all of which are voted on by the same group. The frequencies are given. Is there a statistically significant difference between the groups in their voting?

The Friedman test reports the mean rank and then the significance level; in the examples here the SPSS output has been reproduced in Tables 36.29 and 36.30.

Here one can see that, with a significance level of 0.838 (greater than 0.05), the voting by the same group on the three variables is not statistically significantly different, i.e. the null hypothesis is supported. The reporting of the results of the Friedman test can follow that of the Kruskal-Wallis test.

For both the Kruskal-Wallis and the Friedman tests, as with the Mann-Whitney and Wilcoxon tests, *not* finding a statistically significant difference between groups can be just as important as finding a statistically significant difference between them, as the former suggests that nominal characteristics of the sample make no statistically significant difference to the voting, i.e. the voting is consistent, regardless of particular features of the sample.

36.8 Regression analysis

Regression analysis enables the researcher to predict 'the specific value of one variable when we know or assume values of the other variable(s)' (Cohen and Holliday, 1996: 88). It is a way of modelling the relationship between variables. We will concern ourselves here with simple linear regression and simple multiple regression, though we will also reference stepwise multiple regression and logistic regression.

36.9 Simple linear regression

In simple linear regression the model includes one explanatory variable (the independent variable) and one explained variable (the dependent variable). For example, we may wish to see the effect of hours of study on levels of achievement in an examination, to be able to see how much improvement will be made to an examination mark by a given number of hours of study. Hours of study is the independent variable and level of achievement is the dependent variable. Conventionally, as in the example below, one places the independent

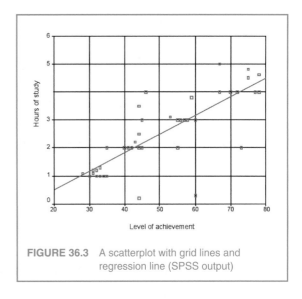

FIGURE 36.3   A scatterplot with grid lines and regression line (SPSS output)

variable in the vertical axis and the dependent variable in the horizontal axis.

In the example in Figure 36.2 we have taken 50 cases of hours of study and student performance, and have constructed a scatterplot to show the distributions (SPSS performs this function at the click of two or three keys). We have also constructed a line of best fit (SPSS will do this easily) to indicate the relationship between the two variables. The line of best fit is the closest straight line that can be constructed to take account of variance in the scores, and strives to have the same number of cases above it and below it and making each point as close to the line as possible; for example, one can see that some scores are very close to the line and others are some distance away. There is a formula for its calculation, but we do not explore that here.

One can observe that the greater the number of hours spent in studying, generally the greater is the level of achievement. This is akin to correlation. The line of best fit indicates not only that there is a positive relationship, but that the relationship is strong (the slope of the line is quite steep). However, where regression departs from correlation is that regression provides an exact prediction of the value – the amount – of one variable when one knows the value of the other. One could read off the level of achievement, for example, if one were to study for two hours (43 marks out of 80) or for four hours (72 marks out of 80), of course, taking no account of variance. To help here scatterplots (e.g. in SPSS) can insert grid lines, for example as shown in Figure 36.3.

It is dangerous to predict *outside* the limits of the line; simple regression is only to be used to calculate

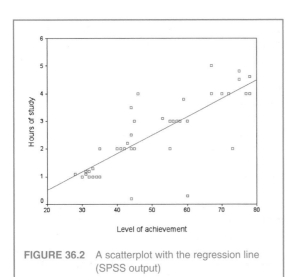

FIGURE 36.2   A scatterplot with the regression line (SPSS output)

TABLE 36.31   A SUMMARY OF THE R, R SQUARE AND ADJUSTED R SQUARE IN REGRESSION
ANALYSIS (SPSS OUTPUT)

Model Summary

Model	R	R Square	Adjusted R Square	Std. Error of the Estimate
1	.795[a]	.632	.625	9.200

a. Predictors: (Constant), Hours of study

values within the limits of the actual line, and not beyond it. One can observe, also, that though it is possible to construct a straight line of best fit (SPSS does this automatically), some of the data points lie close to the line and some lie a long way from the line; the distance of the data points from the line is termed the residuals, and this would have to be commented on in any analysis (there is a statistical calculation to address this but we do not go into it here).

Where the line strikes the vertical axis is named the *intercept*. We return to this later, but at this stage we note that the line does not go through the origin but starts a little way up the vertical line. In fact this is all calculated automatically by SPSS.

Let us look at a typical SPSS output, as shown in Table 36.31. This table provides the R square. The R square tells us how much variance in the dependent variable is explained by the independent variable in the calculation. First it gives us an R square value of 0.632, which indicates that 63.2% of the variance is accounted for in the model, which is high. The adjusted R square is more accurate, and we advocate its use, as it automatically takes account of the number of independent variables. The adjusted R square is usually smaller than the unadjusted R square, as it also takes account of the fact that one is looking at a sample rather than the whole population. Here the adjusted R square is 0.625, and this, again, shows that, in the regression model that we have constructed, the independent variable accounts for 62.5% of the variance in the dependent variable, which is high, i.e. our regression model is robust. Muijs (2004: 165) suggests that, for a goodness of fit with an adjusted R square:

< 0.1: poor fit
0.11–0.3: modest fit
0.31–0.5: moderate fit
> 0.5: strong fit.

SPSS then calculates the analysis of variance (ANOVA), as shown in Table 36.32. At this stage we will not go into all of the calculations here (typically SPSS prints out far more than researchers may need; for a discussion of df (degrees of freedom) we refer readers to our previous discussion, especially section 36.5). We go to the final column here, marked 'Sig.'; this is the significance level, and, because the significance is 0.000, we have a very statistically significant relationship (stronger than 0.001) between the independent variable (hours of study) and the dependent variable (level of achievement).

This tells us that it is useful to proceed with the analysis, as it contains important results. SPSS then gives us

TABLE 36.32   SIGNIFICANCE LEVEL IN REGRESSION ANALYSIS (SPSS OUTPUT)

ANOVA[b]

Model		Sum of Squares	df	Mean Square	F	Sig.
1	Regression	6988.208	1	6988.208	82.573	.000[a]
	Residual	4062.292	48	84.631		
	Total	11050.500	49			

a. Predictors: (Constant), Hours of study

b. Dependent Variable: Level of achievement

TABLE 36.33   THE BETA COEFFICIENT IN A REGRESSION ANALYSIS (SPSS OUTPUT)

Coefficients[a]

Model		Unstandardized Coefficients		Standardized Coefficients	t	Sig.
		B	Std. Error	Beta		
1	(Constant)	26.322	2.982		8.828	.000
	Hours of study	9.567	1.053	.795	9.087	.000

a. Dependent Variable: Level of achievement

a table of coefficients, both unstandardized and standardized. We advise to opt for the standardized coefficients, the Beta weightings. The Beta weight (β) is the amount of standard deviation unit of change in the dependent variable for each standard deviation unit of change in the independent variable. In the example in Table 36.33, the Beta weighting is 0.795; this tell us that, for every standard deviation unit change in the independent variable (hours of study), the dependent variable (level of achievement) will rise by 0.795 (79.5%) of one standard deviation unit, i.e. in lay person's terms, for every one unit rise in the independent variable there is just over three-quarters of a unit rise in the dependent variable. This also explains why the slope of the line of best fit is steep but not quite 45 degrees – each unit of one is worth only 79.5% of a unit of the other.

Table 36.33 also indicates that the results are highly statistically significant (the 'Sig.' column (0.000) reports a significance level stronger than 0.001). Note also that Table 36.33 indicates a 'constant'; this is an indication of where the line of best fit strikes the vertical axis, the intercept; the constant is sometimes taken out of any subsequent analyses.

In reporting the example of regression one could use a form of words thus:

a scattergraph of the regression of hours of study on levels of achievement indicates a linear positive relationship between the two variables, with an adjusted R square of 0.625. A standardized Beta coefficient of 0.795 is found for the variable 'hours of study', which is statistically significant ($\rho < 0.001$).

36.10   Multiple regression

In linear regression we were able to calculate the effect of one independent variable on one dependent variable. However, it is often useful to be able to calculate the effects of two or more independent variables on a depend-

ent variable. Multiple regression enables us to predict and weight the relationship between two or more *explanatory* – independent – variables and an *explained* – dependent – variable. We know from the previous example that the Beta weighting (β) gives us an indication of how many standard deviation units will be changed in the dependent variable for each standard deviation unit of change in each of the independent variables.

Let us take a worked example. An examination mark may be the outcome of study time and intelligence (Figure 36.4), i.e. the formula is:

Examination mark $= \beta$ study time $+ \beta$ intelligence

Let us say that the β for study time is calculated by SPSS to be 0.65, and the β for intelligence is calculated to be 0.30. These are the relative weightings of the two independent variables. We wish to see how many marks in the examination a student will obtain who has an intelligence score of 110 and who studies for 30 hours per week. The formula becomes:

Examination mark
$= (0.65 \times 30) + (0.30 \times 110) = 19.5 + 33 = 52.5$

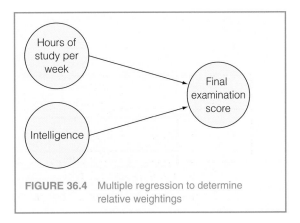

FIGURE 36.4   Multiple regression to determine relative weightings

If the same student studies for 40 hours then the examination mark could be predicted to be:

Examination mark
$$= (0.65 \times 40) + (0.30 \times 110) = 26 + 33 = 59$$

This enables the researcher to see exactly the predicted effects of a particular independent variable on a dependent variable, when other independent variables are also present. In SPSS the constant is also calculated and this can be included in the analysis, to give the following, for example:

Examination mark
$$= \text{constant} + \beta \text{ study time} + \beta \text{ intelligence}$$

Let us give an example with SPSS of more than two independent variables. Let us imagine that we wish to see how much improvement will be made to an examination mark by a given number of hours of study together with measured intelligence (for example, IQ) and level of interest in the subject studied. We know from the previous example that the Beta weighting (β) gives us an indication of how many standard deviation units will be changed in the dependent variable for each standard deviation unit of change in each of the independent variables. The equation is:

Level of achievement in the examination
$$= \text{constant} + \beta \text{ Hours of study} + \beta \text{ IQ} + \beta \text{ Level of interest in the subject}$$

The constant is calculated automatically by SPSS. Each of the three independent variables – hours of study, IQ and level of interest in the subject – has its own Beta (β) weighting in relation to the dependent variable: level of achievement.

If we calculate the multiple regression using SPSS we obtain the results (using fictitious data on 50 students) shown in Table 36.34. The adjusted R square is

very high indeed (0.975), indicating that 97.5% of the variance in the dependent variable is explained by the independent variables, which is extremely high. Similarly the analysis of variance shown in Table 36.35 is highly statistically significant (0.000), indicating that the relationship between the independent and dependent variables is very strong.

The Beta (β) weighting of the three independent variables is given in Table 36.36 in the 'Standardized coefficients' column. The constant is given as 21.304.

It is important to note here that the Beta weightings for the three independent variables are calculated *relative to* each other rather than independent of each other. Hence we can say that, relative to each other:

- the independent variable 'hours of study' has the strongest positive effect on ($\beta = 0.920$) on the level of achievement, and that this is statistically significant (the column 'Sig.' indicates that the level of significance, at 0.000, is stronger than 0.001);
- the independent variable 'intelligence' has a negative effect on the level of achievement ($\beta = -0.062$) but that this is not statistically significant (at 0.644, $\rho > 0.05$);
- the independent variable 'level of interest in the subject' has a positive effect on the level of achievement ($\beta = 0.131$), but this is not statistically significant (at 0.395, $\rho > 0.05$);
- the only independent variable that has a statistically significant effect on the level of achievement is 'hours of study'.

So, for example, with this knowledge, if we knew the hours of study, the IQ and the level of measured interest of a student, we could predict his or her expected level of achievement in the examination.

To run multiple regression in SPSS, the command sequence is thus: Analyze → Regression → Linear. Send over dependent variable to Dependent box. Send over independent variables to Independent box → Click

---

TABLE 36.34   A SUMMARY OF THE R, R SQUARE AND ADJUSTED R SQUARE IN MULTIPLE REGRESSION ANALYSIS (SPSS OUTPUT)

Model Summary

Model	R	R Square	Adjusted R Square	Std. Error of the Estimate
1	.988[a]	.977	.975	2.032

a. Predictors: (Constant), Level of interest in the subject, Intelligence, Hours of study

TABLE 36.35   SIGNIFICANCE LEVEL IN MULTIPLE REGRESSION ANALYSIS (SPSS OUTPUT)

ANOVA[b]

Model		Sum of Squares	df	Mean Square	F	Sig.
1	Regression	7969.607	3	2656.536	643.116	.000[a]
	Residual	190.013	46	4.131		
	Total	8159.620	49			

a. Predictors: (Constant), Level of interest in the subject, Intelligence, Hours of study

b. Dependent Variable: Level of achievement

TABLE 36.36   THE BETA COEFFICIENTS IN A MULTIPLE REGRESSION ANALYSIS (SPSS OUTPUT)

Coefficients[a]

Model		Unstandardized Coefficients		Standardized Coefficients	t	Sig.
		B	Std. Error	Beta		
1	(Constant)	21.304	10.675		1.996	.052
	Hours of study	9.637	1.863	.920	5.173	.000
	Intelligence	-6.20E-02	.133	-.062	-.466	.644
	Level of interest in the subject	.116	.135	.131	.858	.395

a. Dependent Variable: Level of achievement

on Statistics. Tick the boxes Estimates, Confidence Intervals, Model fit, Descriptives, Part and partial correlations, Collinearity diagnostics, Casewise diagnostics and Outliers outside 3 standard deviations → Click Continue → Click on Options → Click on Exclude cases pairwise → Click Continue → Click on Plots. Send over *ZRESID to the Y box. Send over *ZPRED to the X box → Click on Normal probability plots → Click Continue → Click on Save → Click the Mahalanobis box and the Cook's box → Click Continue → Click OK. For further discussion of the SPSS commands and analysis of output we refer the reader to Pallant (2007: chapter 13) and Tabachnick and Fidell (2007: chapter 5).

Multiple regression is useful in that it can take in a range of variables and enable us to calculate their relative weightings on a dependent variable. However, one has to be cautious: adding or removing variables affects their relative Beta weightings. Morrison (2009: 40–1) gives the example of Beta coefficients concerning the

relative effects of independent variables on teacher stress, as shown in Table 36.37.

Here one can see the relative strengths (i.e. when one factor is considered in relation to the others included) of the possible causes of stress. In the example, it appears that 'teacher voice and support' exert the strongest influence on the outcome (levels of stress) (Beta of 0.323), followed by 'benefits and rewards' of teaching (Beta of 0.205), then 'stress reproducing stress' (Beta of 0.164) (i.e. the feeling of stress causes yet more stress), followed by 'burnout' (Beta of 0.157), 'managing students' (Beta of 0.116) and so on down the list. However, if we remove those variables connected with family ('family pressures', 'balancing work, family and cultural expectations' and 'stress from family') then the relative strengths of the remaining factors alters, as shown in Table 36.38.

In this revised situation, the factor 'teacher voice and support' has slightly less weight, 'benefits and rewards of teaching' have added strength, and 'control and relationships' take on much greater strength.

TABLE 36.37   RELATIVE BETA WEIGHTINGS OF INDEPENDENT VARIABLES ON TEACHER
STRESS (SPSS OUTPUT)

Beta Coefficients

	Standardized Coefficients	Significance level
	Beta	
Teacher voice and support	.323	.000
Workload	.080	.000
Benefits and rewards of teaching	.205	.000
Managing students	.116	.000
Challenge and debate	.087	.000
Family pressures	.076	.000
Considering leaving teaching	.067	.000
Emotions and coping	.044	.000
Burnout	.157	.000
Balancing work, family and cultural expectations	.100	.000
Local culture	.071	.000
Stress from family	.058	.000
Stress reproducing stress	.164	.000
Control and relationships	.092	.000

TABLE 36.38   ALTERED WEIGHTINGS IN BETA COEFFICIENTS (SPSS OUTPUT)

Beta Coefficients

	Standardized Coefficients	Significance level
	Beta	
Teacher voice and support	.316	.000
Workload	.096	.000
Benefits and rewards of teaching	.219	.000
Managing students	.114	.000
Challenge and debate	.099	.000
Considering leaving teaching	.102	.000
Emotions and coping	.091	.000
Burnout	.156	.000
Local culture	.131	.000
Stress reproducing stress	.162	.000
Control and relationships	.130	.000

TABLE 36.39 FURTHER ALTERED WEIGHTINGS IN BETA COEFFICIENTS (SPSS OUTPUT)

Beta Coefficients

	Standardized Coefficients	Significance level
	Beta	
Principal behaviour	.270	.000
Clarity of jobs and goals	.087	.000
Teacher voice and support	.154	.000
Workload	.109	.000
Benefits and rewards of teaching	.124	.000
Managing students	.102	.000
Challenge and debate	.095	.000
Family pressures	.071	.000
Considering leaving teaching	.081	.000
Emotions and coping	.084	.000
Burnout	.129	.000
Balancing work, family and cultural expectations	.098	.000
Local culture	.088	.000
Stress from family	.067	.000
Stress reproducing stress	.150	.000
Control and relationships	.086	.000

On the other hand, if one adds in new independent variables ('principal behaviour' and 'clarity of jobs and goals') then the relative strengths of the variables alter again, as shown in Table 36.39. Here 'principal behaviour' greatly overrides the other factors, and the order of the relative strengths of the other factors alters.

The point to emphasize is that the Beta weightings vary according to the independent variables included.

Further, variables may interact with each other and may be intercorrelated (the issue of multicollinearity), for example Gorard (2001b: 172) suggests that 'poverty and ethnicity are likely to have some correlation between themselves, so using both together means that we end up using their *common* variance twice. If collinearity is discovered (e.g. if correlation coefficients between variables are higher than .80) then one can either remove one of the variables or create a new variable that combines the previous two that were highly intercorrelated'. Indeed SPSS will automatically remove variables where there is strong covariance (collinearity).[1] For further discussion of

collinearity, collinearity diagnostics and tolerance of collinearity, we refer the reader to Pallant (2007: 156).

The SPSS command sequence for running multiple regression with collinearity diagnostics is: Analyze → Regression → Linear → Statistics → Click 'Collinearity diagnostics' → Click 'Continue' → Enter dependent and independent variables → In the box marked 'Method' click 'Enter'→ Click OK.

Stepwise multiple regression enters variables one at a time, in a sequence, to see which adds to the explanatory power of a model, by looking at its impact on the R-squared – whether it increases the R-square value. This alternative way of entering variables and running the SPSS analysis in a 'stepwise' sequence is the same as above, except that in the 'Method' box the word 'Enter' should be replaced, in the dropdown box, with 'Stepwise'.

Logistic regression enables the researcher to work with categorical variables in a multiple regression where the dependent variable is a categorical variable. Here the independent variables may be categorical, discrete or continuous. To run logistic regression in SPSS, the command sequence is: Analyze → Regression → Binary Logistic → Insert dependent variable in the 'Dependent' box → Insert independent variables into the 'Covariates' box → Click on 'Categorical' → Move your first categorical variable into the 'Categorical Covariates' box → Click the radio button 'First' → Click the 'Change' button → Repeat this for every categorical variable → Click 'Continue' to return to the first screen → Click 'Options' → Click the boxes 'Classification plots', 'Hosmer-Lemeshow goodness of fit', 'Casewise listing of residuals' and 'CI for Exp(B)' → Click 'Continue' to return to first screen → Click 'OK'. For more on logistic regression we refer the reader to Pallant (2007: chapter 14) and Tabachnick and Fidell (2007: chapter 10).

In reporting multiple regression, in addition to presenting tables (often of SPSS output), one can use a form of words thus, for example (using Table 36.36):

Multiple regression was used, and the results include the adjusted R square (0.975), ANOVA ($\rho < 0.001$) and the standardized β coefficient of each component variable ($\beta = 0.920$, $\rho < 0.001$; $\beta = -0.062$, $\rho = 0.644$; $\beta = 0.131$, $\rho = 0.395$). One can observe that, relative to each other, 'hours of study' exerted the greatest influence on level of achievement, that 'level of interest' exerted a small and statistically insignificant influence on level of achievement, and that; 'intelligence' exerted a negative but statistically insignificant influence on level of achievement.

In using regression techniques, one has to be faithful to the assumptions underpinning them. Gorard (2001b: 213), Pallant (2007: 148–9) and Tabachnick and Fidell (2007: 121–8, 161–7) set these out as follows:

- The measurements are from a random sample (or at least a probability-based one).
- All variables used should be real numbers (ratio data) (or at least the dependent variable must be).
- There are no extreme outliers (i.e. outliers are removed).
- All variables are measured without error.
- There is an approximate linear relationship between the dependent variable and the independent variables (both individually and grouped).
- The dependent variable is approximately normally distributed (or at least the next assumption is true).
- The residuals for the dependent variable (the differences between calculated and observed scores) are approximately normally distributed.

- The variance of each variable is consistent across the range of values for all other variables (or at least the next assumption is true).
- The residuals for the dependent variable at each value of the independent variables have equal and constant variance.
- The residuals are not correlated with the independent variables.
- The residuals for the dependent variable at each value of the independent variables have a mean of zero (or they are approximately linearly related to the dependent variable).
- No independent variable is a perfect linear combination of another (not perfect 'multicollinearity').
- Interaction effects of independent variables are measured.
- Collinearity is avoided.
- For any two cases the correlation between the residuals should be zero (each case is independent of the others).

Though regression and multiple regression are most commonly used with interval and ratio data, more recently some procedures have been devised for undertaking regression analysis for ordinal data (e.g. in SPSS). This is of immense value for calculating regression from rating scale data.

Pallant (2001: 136) suggests that attention has to be given to the sample size in using multiple regression. She suggests that 15 cases for each independent variable are required, and that a formula can be applied to determine the minimum sample size required thus: sample size $\geq 50 + (8 \times$ number of independent variables), i.e. for ten independent variables one would require a minimum sample size of 130 (i.e. $50 + 80$).

36.11 Standardized scores

Many forms of difference tests and regression analysis with parametric data prefer to work with standardized scores, and we introduce these here. Imagine the following scenes:

- A child comes home from school and tells his parents that he scored a mark of 75 for a mathematics test; his parents scold him.
- A child comes home from school and tells his parents that he scored a mark of eight for a history test; his parents praise him.
- A child comes home from school and tells his parents that he scored a mark of 25 for an English test and a mark of 60 for a physics test; his parents praise him for both.

■ A child comes home from school and tells his parents that he scored a mark of 80 for a geography test and a mark of 120 for a chemistry test; his parents scold him for both.

How can we explain these apparent discrepant behaviours? In the examples here we do not know the scales used, the range of scores, the means and the distributions around the means. For example the first child who scored 75 for his maths test was scolded because the mean score was 144 and the range was from 75–200, i.e. he scored very low on the test. On the other hand, the child who scored eight for his history test was praised because that was the highest mark in the test, with an average mark of four out of a possible ten, and a range of one to eight. In the case of the child who was praised for scoring two very different marks (25 for English and 60 for physics), this was because the scales and range for the two tests varied, whereas the child who scored 80 for geography and 120 for chemistry was scolded because both tests were marked out of 300 and the average marks for both were 220.

These examples show the need for researchers to compare like with like in using numerical data and scores. We need to know how to judge whether a mark is high or low and how to compare marks between one test and another. Therefore we need to know the *scale* of the marks, the *range* of the marks, the *mean* of the marks, and the *distribution* of the marks either side of the mean. We need to know how to compare marks from a test which:

■ uses one *scale* with marks from a test which uses another scale;
■ has one *range* of marks with marks from a test that has another range of marks;
■ has a *mean* which is different from the mean of another test;
■ has a *distribution* around the mean which is different from the distribution of another test.

This is addressed by converting scores into standardized scores. Standardizing scores enables the researcher to judge whether a mark is high or low; it enables the researcher to compare marks between one test and another when two different tests have different scales, range, means and distributions around the mean. To standardize scores means to convert them into z-scores. Z-scores have the same mean and standard deviation, even though the original sets of scores had different means and standard deviations, i.e. z-scores let researchers compare scores fairly. A z-score tells us how many standard deviations some-

one's scores lies above or below the mean. By standardizing different sets of scores (usually either a mean of zero and a standard deviation of one), this enables the researcher to compare like with like, to compare scores fairly.

To calculate the z-score we subtract the mean from the raw score and divide that answer by the standard deviation. The formula is thus:

$$z = \frac{\text{the actual score} - \text{the mean of the sample}}{\text{standard deviation of the sample}} = \frac{x_i - \bar{x}}{s}$$

For example if the raw (unadjusted) score is 15, the mean is 10, and the standard deviation is 4, then $15 - 10 = 5$ and $5 \div 4 = 1.25$. Here the z-score tells us that the person's score is 1.25 standard deviations above the mean. However, we do not know whether this is a good score, a bad score, or, indeed, what it means. We need to see how this compares with other scores on the same distribution. Figure 36.5 plots the standardized scores on the normal curve of distribution, with the mean score of 0 (zero) and the standard deviation of 1.

Looking at Figure 36.5, in our example, the person who scores 1.25 has scored very well indeed. Had she scored 1 then she would have been better than 84.12 per cent of the population ($34.13 + 34.13 + 13.59 + 2.14 + 0.13 = 84.12$): the percentage of people below her (see the lines marked 'Percentage of cases in 8 portions of the curve', 'Cumulative percentages' and 'Percentiles' in Figure 36.5). We know that she is higher than 1 standard deviation above the mean (she has scored 1.25, not 1), so we need to find where her score places her in terms of the rest of the population. For an exact indication of where she stands in relation to the rest of the population we can turn to statistics tables concerning 'areas under the normal curve' (on the internet and in the appendices of most statistics books). Then we can simply read off the results (see Table 36.40 for an extract from such a table).

She has a z-score of 1.25, so in Table 36.40 we go to the left-hand column, to the row marked '1.2'. Then we go to the column marked '0.05', as this gives us the second decimal place of the '1.25'. Then we see the value 0.3944 (emboldened and shaded), i.e. the person is 39.44 per cent above the mean of zero. We know from Figure 36.5 that 49.99 per cent of people are below zero ($34.13 + 13.59 + 2.14 + 0.13 = 49.99$); now we add to that the 39.44 per cent above zero, giving a total of 89.43 per cent. This tells us that, for the person with the z-score of 1.25, only 10.56 per cent (100 per cent minus 89.43 per cent) of the population is above her, so her score is very high.

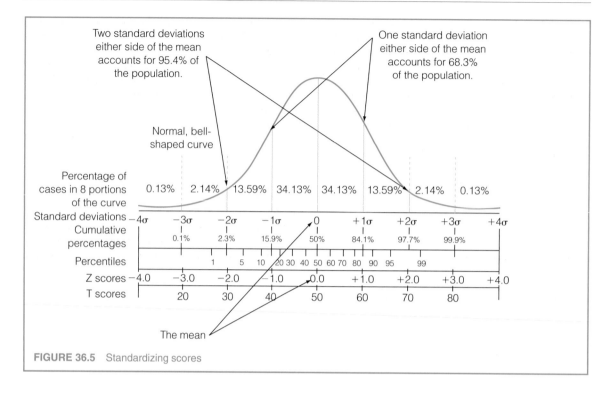

FIGURE 36.5 Standardizing scores

Using Table 36.40 for another example, if a person receives a z-score of 1.56 then the table gives us a reading of 0.4406, i.e. 44.06 per cent. We know from Figure 36.5 that 49.99 per cent of people are below zero (34.13 + 13.59 + 2.14 + 0.13 = 49.99); now we add to that the 44.06 per cent above zero, giving a total of 94.05 per cent. This tells us that, for the person with the z-score of 1.56 only 4.85 per cent (100 per cent minus 94.05 per cent) of the population is above that score, so the score is extremely high.

An online calculator of this is at: www.danielsoper. com/statcalc/calc02.aspx. This calculator gives the cumulative area under the curve (a figure as a decimal fraction that is less than 1 (let us call it X)). To find the area under the curve beyond that one point simply sub-

tract this figure from 1 (the formula, then, is $1 - X$) and, for a percentage, multiply it by 100. Another equally straightforward free online calculator of the area under the curve, and the position of a given z-score in that curve is given at http://stattrek.com/Tables/Normal. aspx.

To calculate z-scores with SPSS, the command sequence is: Analyze → Descriptive Statistics → Descriptives → Variables → Click the box 'Save standardized values as variables' → Click OK→ Two new variables will be created of the standardized scores.

Some people are uncomfortable with z-scores, as they do not like negative scores nor do they like an average being 0 (zero). To overcome this, z-scores can be converted to T-scores. To convert a z-score to a

TABLE 36.40 EXTRACT FROM AREA UNDER THE NORMAL CURVE OF DISTRIBUTION

z	0.00	0.01	0.02	0.03	0.04	0.05	0.06	0.07	0.08	0.09
1.0	0.3413	0.3438	0.3461	0.3485	0.3508	0.3531	0.3554	0.3577	0.3599	0.3621
1.1	0.3643	0.3665	0.3686	0.3708	0.3729	0.3749	0.3770	0.3790	0.3810	0.3830
1.2	0.3849	0.3869	0.3888	0.3907	0.3925	**0.3944**	0.3962	0.3980	0.3997	0.4015
1.3	0.4032	0.4049	0.4066	0.4082	0.4099	0.4115	0.4131	0.4147	0.4162	0.4177
1.4	0.4192	0.4207	0.4222	0.4236	0.4251	0.4265	0.4279	0.4292	0.4306	0.4319
1.5	0.4332	0.4345	0.4357	0.4370	0.4382	0.4394	0.4406	0.4418	0.4429	0.4441

T-score, multiply the z-score by 10 and add 50 to the result. For example a z-score of 0.5, multiplied by 10 gives 5, and then, with 50 added, gives 55. The T-score is 55. Many IQ tests and standardized tests convert z-scores. For example a common conversion in IQ tests is to multiply the z-score by 15 and add 100. So a z-score on an IQ test might be 0.5, multiplied by 15 gives 7.5, with 100 added gives 107.5, i.e. the IQ z-score converts to a T-score of 107.5.

Standardized scores are widely used in simple regression, as they enable researchers to compare different sets of scores on a fair basis.

36.12 Closing remarks

This chapter has introduced several inferential statistics and their related concepts:

- measures of difference for parametric data (t-test and ANOVA (one-way, two-way, multiple analysis of variance and *post hoc* tests of difference);

- measures of difference for non-parametric data (Mann-Whitney, Wilcoxon tests, Kruskal-Wallis, Friedman);
- the chi-square test of independence and goodness of fit for univariate and bivariate categorical and ordinal variables, as a measure of difference between observed and expected values;
- degrees of freedom;
- simple regression and multiple regression (typical usage, stepwise regression and logistic regression);
- standardized scores and T-scores.

Where relevant, it has also included SPSS command sequences to run these statistics. The statistics covered here are not exhaustive, and, indeed, we introduce several more in the following chapter. However, they do represent the key starting statistics that researchers use.

 Companion Website

The companion website to the book includes PowerPoint slides for this chapter, which list the structure of the chapter and then provide a summary of the key points in each of its sections. In addition there is further information in the form of how to report statistics, a selection of statistical tables, data files and a sample questionnaire for use with a range of statistics in SPSS, plus a full manual on using SPSS, with screen-prints. These resources can be found online at **www.routledge.com/textbooks/cohen7e**.

CHAPTER 37

Multidimensional measurement and factor analysis

This chapter introduces some high level statistics and the principles that underpin them. The statistics covered here are:

- elementary linkage analysis
- factor analysis
- what to look for in factor analysis output
- cluster analysis
- examples of studies using multidimensional scaling and cluster analysis
- multidimensional data: some words on notation
- a note on structural equation modelling
- a note on multilevel modelling

Some of these materials have significant coverage (e.g. factor analysis), whilst others are more by way of introduction (e.g. structural equation modelling and multilevel modelling).

37.1 Introduction

However limited our knowledge of astronomy, most of us have learned to pick out certain clusterings of stars from the infinity of those that crowd the Northern skies and to name them as the familiar Plough, Orion and the Great Bear. Few of us would identify constellations in the Southern Hemisphere that are instantly recognizable by those in Australia.

Our predilection for reducing the complexity of elements that constitute our lives to a more simple order does not stop at star gazing. In numerous ways, each and every one of us attempts to discern patterns or shapes in seemingly unconnected events in order to better grasp their significance for us in the conduct of our daily lives. The educational researcher is no exception.

As research into a particular aspect of human activity progresses, the variables being explored frequently turn out to be more complex than was first realized. Investigation into the relationship between teaching styles and pupil achievement is a case in point. Global distinctions between behaviour identified as progressive or traditional, informal or formal, are vague and

woolly and have led inevitably to research findings that are at worse inconsistent, at best, inconclusive. In reality, epithets such as informal or formal in the context of teaching and learning relate to 'multidimensional concepts', that is concepts made up of a number of variables. 'Multidimensional scaling', on the other hand, is a way of analysing judgements of similarity between such variables in order that the dimensionality of those judgements can be assessed (Bennett and Bowers, 1977). As regards research into teaching styles and pupil achievement, it has been suggested that multidimensional typologies of teacher behaviour should be developed. Such typologies, it is believed, would enable the researcher to group together similarities in teachers' judgements about specific aspects of their classroom organization and management, and their ways of motivating, assessing and instructing pupils.

Techniques for grouping such judgements are many and various. What they all have in common is that they are methods for 'determining the number and nature of the underlying variables among a large number of measures', a definition which Kerlinger (1970) uses to describe one of the best-known grouping techniques, 'factor analysis'. We begin the chapter by illustrating elementary linkage analysis which can be undertaken by hand, and move to factor analysis. We move to a brief note on cluster analysis as a way of organizing people/groups rather than variables, and then close with some introductory remarks on structural equation modelling and multilevel modelling.

37.2 Elementary linkage analysis: an example

Elementary linkage analysis (McQuitty, 1957) is one way of exploring the relationship between the teacher's personal constructs, that is, of assessing the dimensionality of the judgements that she makes about her pupils. It seeks to identify and define the clusterings of certain variables within a set of variables. Like factor analysis which we shortly illustrate, elementary linkage analysis searches for interrelated groups of correlation coefficients. The objective of the search is to identify 'types'.

By type, McQuitty (1957) refers to 'a category of people or other objects (personal constructs in our example) such that the members are internally self-contained in being like one another'.

Seven constructs were elicited from an infant school teacher who was invited to discuss the ways in which she saw the children in her class. She identified favourable and unfavourable constructs as follows: 'intelligent' (+), 'sociable' (+), 'verbally good' (+), 'well behaved' (+), 'aggressive' (−), 'noisy' (−) and 'clumsy' (−) (see also Cohen, 1977).

Four boys and six girls were then selected at random from the class register and the teacher was asked to place each child in rank order under each of the seven constructs, using rank position 1 to indicate the child most like the particular construct, and rank position 10, the child least like the particular construct. The teacher's rank ordering is set out in Table 37.1. Notice that

---

TABLE 37.1   RANK ORDERING OF TEN CHILDREN ON SEVEN CONSTRUCTS

	Intelligent		*Sociable*
(*favourable*)	1 Heather	(*favourable*)	1 Caroline
	2 Richard		2 Richard
	3 Caroline		3 Sharon
	4 Tim		4 Jane
	5 Patrick		5 Tim
	6 Sharon		6 Janice
	7 Janice		7 Heather
	8 Jane		8 Patrick
	9 Alex		9 Karen
(*unfavourable*)	10 Karen	(*unfavourable*)	10 Alex
	Aggressive		*Noisy*
(*unfavourable*)	10 Alex	(*unfavourable*)	10 Alex
	9 Patrick		9 Patrick
	8 Tim		8 Karen
	7 Karen		7 Tim
	6 Richard		6 Caroline
	5 Caroline		5 Richard
	4 Heather		4 Heather
	3 Jane		3 Janice
	2 Sharon		2 Sharon
(*favourable*)	1 Janice	(*favourable*)	1 Jane
	Verbally good		*Clumsy*
(*favourable*)	1 Richard	(*unfavourable*)	10 Alex
	2 Caroline		9 Patrick
	3 Heather		8 Karen
	4 Janice		7 Tim
	5 Patrick		6 Richard
	6 Tim		5 Sharon
	7 Alex		4 Jane
	8 Sharon		3 Janice
	9 Jane		2 Caroline
(*unfavourable*)	10 Karen	(*favourable*)	1 Heather
	Well behaved		
(*favourable*)	1 Janice		
	2 Jane		
	3 Sharon		
	4 Caroline		
	5 Heather		
	6 Richard		
	7 Tim		
	8 Karen		
	9 Patrick		
(*unfavourable*)	10 Alex		

Source: Cohen, 1977

on three constructs, the rankings have been reversed in order to maintain the consistency of Favourable = 1, Unfavourable = 10.

Table 37.2 sets out the intercorrelations between the seven personal construct ratings shown in Table 37.1 (Spearman's *rho* is the method of correlation used in this example).

Elementary linkage analysis enables the researcher to cluster together similar groups of variables by hand.

Steps in elementary linkage analysis

1 In Table 37.2, underline the strongest, that is the highest, correlation coefficient in each column of the matrix. Ignore negative signs.
2 Identify the highest correlation coefficient in the entire matrix. The two variables having this correlation constitute the first two of Cluster 1.
3 Now identify all those variables which are most like the variables in Cluster 1. To do this, read along the rows of the variables which emerged in Step 2, selecting any of the coefficients which are underlined in the rows. Table 37.3 illustrates diagrammatically the ways in which these new cluster members are related to the original pair which initially constituted Cluster 1.

4 Now identify any variables which are most like the variables elicited in Step 3. Repeat this procedure until no further variables are identified.
5 Excluding all those variables which belong within Cluster 1, repeat Steps 2 to 4 until all the variables have been accounted for.

37.3 Factor analysis

Factor analysis is a method of grouping together variables which have something in common. It is a process which enables the researcher to take a set of variables and reduce them to a smaller number of underlying factors which account for as many variables as possible. It detects structures and commonalities in the relationships between variables. Thus it enables researchers to identify where different variables in fact are addressing the same underlying concept. For example, one variable could measure somebody's height in centimetres; another variable could measure the same person's height in inches; the underlying factor that unites both variables is height; it is a latent factor that is indicated by the two variables.

Factor analysis can take two main forms: *exploratory factor analysis* and *confirmatory factor analysis*.

TABLE 37.2 INTERCORRELATIONS BETWEEN SEVEN PERSONAL CONSTRUCTS

		(1)	*(2)*	*(3)*	*(4)*	*(5)*	*(6)*	*(7)*
Intelligent	(1)		53	−10	−16	<u>83</u>	−52	13
Sociable	(2)	53		−50	−59	44	−56	61
Aggressive	(3)	−10	−50		91	−07	79	−96
Noisy	(4)	−16	−59	91		−01	73	−93
Verbally good	(5)	<u>83</u>	44	−07	−01		−43	12
Clumsy	(6)	−52	−56	79	73	−43		−81
Well behaved	(7)	13	<u>61</u>	<u>−96</u>	<u>−93</u>	12	−81	
(Decimal points omitted)								

Source: Cohen, 1977

TABLE 37.3 THE STRUCTURING OF RELATIONSHIPS AMONG THE SEVEN PERSONAL CONSTRUCTS

	Badly behaved	⇌	Aggressive
CLUSTER 1	Noisy	Clumsy	Unsociable
CLUSTER 2	Verbally good	⇌	Intelligent

⇌ Denotes a reciprocal relationship between two variables

Source: Cohen, 1977

The former refers to the use of factor analysis (principal components analysis in particular) to explore previously unknown groupings of variables, to seek underlying patterns, clusterings and groups. By contrast *confirmatory factor analysis* is more stringent, testing a found set of factors against a hypothesized model of groupings and relationships. This section introduces the most widely used form of factor analysis: principal components analysis. We refer the reader to further books on statistics for a fuller discussion of factor analysis and its variants.

The analysis here uses SPSS output, as it is the most commonly used way of undertaking principal components analysis by educational researchers.

As an example of factor analysis, one could have the following variables in a piece of educational research:

1 Student demotivation.
2 Poor student concentration.
3 Undue pressure on students.
4 Narrowing effect on curriculum.
5 Punishing the weaker students.
6 Overemphasis on memorization.
7 Testing only textbook knowledge.

These seven variables can be grouped together under the single overarching factor of 'negative effects of examinations'. Factor analysis, working through multiple correlations, is a method for grouping together several variables under one or more common factor(s).

To address factor analysis in more detail we provide a worked example. Consider the following variables concerning school effectiveness:

1 The clarity of the direction that is set by the school leadership.
2 The ability of the leader to motivate and inspire the educators.
3 The drive and confidence of the leader.
4 The consultation abilities/activities of the leader.
5 The example set by the leader.
6 The commitment of the leader to the school.
7 The versatility of the leader's styles.
8 The ability of the leader to communicate clear, individualized expectations.
9 The respect in which the leader is held by staff.
10 The staff's confidence in the Senior Management Team.
11 The effectiveness of the teamwork of the Senior Management Team.
12 The extent to which the vision for the school impacts on practice.

13 Educators given opportunities to take on leadership roles.
14 The creativity of the Senior Management Team.
15 Problem-posing, problem-identifying and problem-solving capacity of Senior Management Team.
16 The use of data to inform planning and school development.
17 Valuing of professional development in the school
18 Staff consulted about key decisions.
19 The encouragement and support for innovativeness and creativity.
20 Everybody is free to make suggestions to inform decision making.
21 The school works in partnership with parents.
22 People take positive risks for the good of the school and its development.
23 Staff voluntarily taking on coordination roles.
24 Teamwork amongst school staff.

Here we have 24 different variables. The question here is 'are there any underlying groups of factors' ('latent variables') that can embrace several of these variables, or of which the several variables are elements or indicators? Factor analysis will indicate whether there are. We offer a three-stage model for undertaking factor analysis. In what follows we distinguish *factors* from *variables*; a factor is an underlying or latent feature under which groups of variables are included; a variable is one of the elements that can be a member of an underlying factor. In our example here we have 24 variables and, as we shall see, five factors.

Stage 1

Let us imagine that we have gathered data from 1,000 teachers in several different schools, and we wish to see how the 24 variables above can be grouped, based on their voting (using ratio data by awarding marks out of ten for each of the variables). (This follows the rule that there should be more subjects in the sample than there are variables.) Bryman and Cramer (1990: 255) suggest that there should be at least five subjects per variable and a total of no fewer than 100 subjects in the total sample.

First the researcher has to determine whether the data are, in fact, suitable for factor analysis (Tabachnick and Fidell, 2007: 613–15). This involves checking the sample size, which varies in the literature, from a minimum of 30 to a minimum of 300. Tabachnick and Fidell (2007: 613) suggest that a sample size of 50 is very poor, 100 is poor, 200 is fair, 300 is good, 500 is very good and 1,000 is excellent; they suggest that 300 should be regarded as a general minimum, and if the sample size is small then the factors loadings (discussed later) should be high. It also involves having neither too few nor too many variables: too few and the extraction of the factors may only extract one or two items per factor, and this gives very little 'added value', too many and the number of factors extracted could be so many as to be unhelpful in identifying underlying latent factors. The data must also be ratio or interval. The researcher also needs to consider the ratio of sample size to number of variables (different ratios are given in literature, from 5:1 to 30:1), and the strength of intercorrelations between the variables should be no less than 0.3 (below this and the data may not be suitable for finding latent, underlying factors, as the variables are not sufficiently closely related). Factor analysis assumes a normal distribution (measured by kurtosis and skewness), linearity of relationships between pairs of variables (rather than, for example, curvilinearity (see Chapter 34)) and the removal or reduction in the number of outliers.

Two specific statistics can also be computed to test for the suitability of the data for factorization:

- the Bartlett test of sphericity, which investigates the correlations between variables, and which should show statistical significance ($\rho < 0.05$) (but mainly to be used where the number of cases per variable is five or fewer);
- the Kaiser-Mayer-Olkin measure of sampling adequacy, which correlates pairs of variables and the magnitude of partial correlations amongst variables, and which requires many pairs of variables to be statistically significantly, and which should yield an overall measure of 0.6 or higher (maximum is one).

TABLE 37.4   INITIAL SPSS OUTPUT FOR PRINCIPAL COMPONENTS ANALYSIS (SPSS OUTPUT)

Total Variance Explained

Component	Initial Eigenvalues			Extraction Sums of Squared Loadings			Rotation Sums of Squared Loadings		
	Total	% of Variance	Cumulative %	Total	% of Variance	Cumulative %	Total	% of Variance	Cumulative %
1	9.343	38.930	38.930	9.343	38.930	38.930	4.037	16.820	16.820
2	1.424	5.931	44.862	1.424	5.931	44.862	2.810	11.706	28.527
3	1.339	5.580	50.442	1.339	5.580	50.442	2.779	11.578	40.105
4	1.220	5.085	55.526	1.220	5.085	55.526	2.733	11.386	51.491
5	1.085	4.520	60.047	1.085	4.520	60.047	2.053	8.556	60.047
6	.918	3.825	63.872						
7	.826	3.443	67.315						
8	.723	3.013	70.329						
9	.685	2.855	73.184						
10	.658	2.743	75.927						
11	.623	2.596	78.523						
12	.562	2.342	80.864						
13	.532	2.216	83.080						
14	.512	2.132	85.213						
15	.493	2.055	87.268						
16	.466	1.942	89.210						
17	.437	1.822	91.032						
18	.396	1.650	92.682						
19	.376	1.566	94.247						
20	.364	1.517	95.764						
21	.307	1.280	97.044						
22	.271	1.129	98.174						
23	.232	.965	99.138						
24	.207	.862	100.000						

Extraction Method: Principal Component Analysis.

If the data are suitable for factor analysis then the researcher can proceed. This analysis will assume that the data are suitable for factor analysis to proceed and is based on SPSS processing and output (Table 37.4).

Though Table 37.4 seems to contain a lot of complicated data, in fact most of this need not trouble us at all. SPSS has automatically found and reported five factors for us through sophisticated correlational analysis, and it presents data on these five factors (the first five rows of the chart, marked 'Component'). Table 37.4 takes the 24 variables (listed in order on the left-hand column (Component)) and then it provides three sets of readings: Eigenvalues, Extraction Sums of Squared Loadings, and Rotation Sums of Squared Loadings. Eigenvalues are measures of the variance between factors, and are the sum of the squared loadings for a factor, representing the amount of variance accounted for by that factor. We are only interested in those Eigenvalues that are greater than 1, since those that are smaller than 1 generally are not of interest to researchers as they account for less than the variation explained by a single variable. Indeed SPSS automatically filters out for us the Eigenvalues that are greater than 1, using the Kaiser criterion (in SPSS this is termed the Kaiser Normalization).

A scree plot can also be used at this stage, to identify and comment on factors (this is available at the click of a button in SPSS). A scree plot shows each factor on a chart, in descending order of magnitude. For researchers the scree plot becomes interesting where it flattens out (like the rubble that collects at the foot of a scree), as this indicates very clearly which factors account for a lot of the variance, and which account for little. In the scree plot here (Figure 37.1) one can see that the scree flattens out considerably after the first factor, then it levels out a little for the next four factors, tailing downwards all the time. This suggests that the first factor is the significant factor in explaining the greatest amount of variance.

Indeed, in using the scree plot one perhaps has to look for the 'bend in the elbow' of the data (after factor one), and then regard those factors above the bend in the elbow as being worthy of inclusion, and those below the bend in the elbow as being relatively unimportant (Pallant, 2001: 154). However, this is draconian, as it risks placing too much importance on those items above the bend in the elbow and too little importance on those below it. The scree plot in Figure 37.1 adds little to the variance table presented in Table 37.4, though it does enable one to see at a glance which are the significant and less significant factors, or, indeed, which factors to focus on (the ones before the scree levels off) and which to ignore.

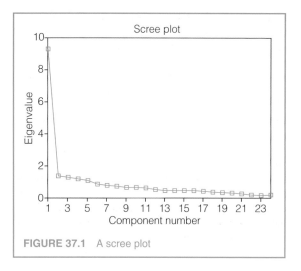

FIGURE 37.1 A scree plot

Next we turn to the columns in Table 37.4 labelled 'Extraction Sums of Squared Loadings'. The Extraction Sums of Squared Loadings contain two important pieces of information. First, in the column marked '% of variance' SPSS tells us how much variance is explained by each of the factors identified, in order from the greatest amount of variance to the least amount of variance. So, here the first factor accounts for 38.930% of the variance in the total scenario – a very large amount – whilst the second factor identified accounts for only 5.931% of the total variance, a much lower amount of explanatory power. Each factor is unrelated to the other, and so the amount of variance in each factor is unrelated to, or explained by, the other factors; they are independent of each other. By giving us how much variance in the total picture is explained by each factor we can see which factors possess the most and least explanatory power – the power to explain the total scenario of 24 factors. Second, SPSS keeps a score of the cumulative amount of explanatory power of the five factors identified. In the column 'Cumulative' it tells us that in total 60.047% of the total picture (of the 24 variables) is accounted for – explained – by the five factors identified. This is a moderate amount of explanatory power, and researchers would be happy with this.

However, the three columns under 'Extraction Sums of Squared Loadings' give us the initial, rather crude, unadjusted percentage of variance of the total picture explained by the five factors found. These are crude in the sense that the full potential of factor analysis has not been caught. What SPSS has done here is to plot the factors on a two-dimensional chart (which it does not present in the data output) to identify groupings of variables, the two dimensions being vertical and horizontal axes as in a conventional graph like a scattergraph. On such a two-dimensional chart some of the factors and variables could be plotted quite close to each other, such that discrimination between the factors would not be very clear. However, if we were to plot the factors and variables on a three-dimensional chart that includes not only horizontal and vertical axes but also *depth* by *rotating* the plotted points through 90 degrees, then the effect of this would be to bring closer together those variables that are similar to each other and to separate them more fully – in distance – from those variables that have no similarity to them, i.e. to render each group of variables (factors) more homogeneous and to separate more clearly one group of variables (factor) from another group of variables (factor). The process of rotation keeps together those variables that are closely interrelated and keeps them apart from those variables that are not closely related. This is represented in Figure 37.2.

This distinguishes more clearly one factor from another than that undertaken in the Extraction Sums of Squared Loadings.

Rotation can be conducted in many ways (Tabachnick and Fidell, 2007: 637–8), of which there are two main forms:

- Direct Oblimin: which is used if the researcher believes that there may be correlations between the factors (an oblique, correlated) rotation.
- Varimax rotation: which is used if the researcher believes that the factors may be uncorrelated (orthogonal).

Pallant (2007: 183) argues for the importance of researchers giving strong consideration to the Direct Oblimin rotation. Even though it is more difficult to interpret, it is often actually more faithful to the correlated nature of the data and factors. The default setting

in SPSS is the orthogonal, varimax rotation, and this may misrepresent the correlations between the factors, even though it is easier to analyse. Indeed Pallant (2007: 184) suggests starting with Direct Oblimin rotation.

Rotation in the example in Figure 37.2 is undertaken by *varimax rotation*. This maximizes the variance between factors and hence helps to distinguish them from each other. In SPSS the rotation is called *orthogonal* because the factors are unrelated to, and independent of, each other.

In the column 'Rotation Sums of Squared Loadings' of Table 37.4, the fuller power of factor analysis is tapped, in that the rotation of the variables from a two-dimensional to a three-dimensional chart has been undertaken, thereby identifying more clearly the groupings of variables into factors, and separating each factor from the other much more clearly. We advise researchers to use the Rotation Sums of Squared Loadings rather than the Extraction Sums of Squared Loadings. With the Rotation Sums of Squared Loadings the percentage of variance explained by each factor is altered, even though the total cumulative per cent (60.047%) remains the same. For example, one can see that the first factor in the rotated solution no longer accounts for 38.930% as in the Extraction Sums of Squared Loadings, but only 16.820% of the variance, and that factors 2, 3 and 4, which each only accounted for just over 5% of the variance in the Extraction Sums of Squared Loadings now each account for over 11% of the variance, and that factor 5, which accounted for 4.520% of the variance in the Extraction Sums of Squared Loadings now accounts for 8.556% of the variance in the Rotated Sums of Squared Loadings.

By this stage we hope that the reader has been able to see that:

1 factor analysis brings variables together into homogeneous and distinct groups, each of which is a factor and each of which has an Eigenvalue of greater than 1;
2 factor analysis in SPSS indicates the amount of variance in the total scenario explained by each individual factor and all the factors together (the cumulative per cent);
3 the Rotation Sums of Squared Loadings is preferable to the Extraction Sums of Squared Loadings.

We are ready to proceed to the second stage.

Stage 2

Stage 2 consists of presenting a matrix of all of the relevant data for the researcher to be able to identify which

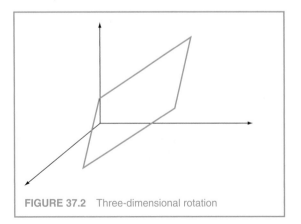

FIGURE 37.2 Three-dimensional rotation

variables belong to which factor (Table 37.5). SPSS presents what at first sight is a bewildering set of data, but the reader is advised to keep cool and to look at the data slowly, as, in fact, they are not complicated. SPSS often presents researchers with more data than they need, overwhelming the researcher with data. In fact the data in Table 37.5 are comparatively straightforward.

Across the top of the matrix in Table 37.5 we have a column for each of the five factors (1–5) that SPSS had found for us. The left-hand column prints the names of each of the 24 variables with which we are working. We can ignore those pieces of data which contain the letter 'E' (exponential), as these contain figures that are so small as to be able to be discarded. Look at the column

labelled '1' (factor 1). Here we have a range of numbers that range from 0.114 (for the variable 'Teamwork amongst school staff' to 0.758 (for the variable 'The drive and confidence of the leader'). The researcher now has to use her professional judgement, to decide what the 'cut off' points should be for inclusion in the factor. Not all 24 variables will appear in factor one, only those with high values (factor loadings – the amount that each variable contributes to the factor in question). The decision on which variables to include in factor one is not a statistical matter but a matter of professional judgement. Factor analysis is an art as well as a science. The researcher has to find those variables with the highest values (factor loadings) and include those in the factor. The variables

---

TABLE 37.5   THE ROTATED COMPONENTS MATRIX IN PRINCIPAL COMPONENTS ANALYSIS (SPSS OUTPUT)

Rotated Component Matrix[a]

	Component				
	1	2	3	4	5
The clarity of the direction that is set by the school leadership	.559	.133	7.552E-02	.248	.212
The ability of the leader to motivate and inspire the educators	.743	.142	.176	9.058E-02	.160
The drive and confidence of the leader	.758	2.151E-02	.122	2.796E-02	.222
The consultation abilities/activities of the leader	.548	.342	.208	.278	.160
The example set by the leader	.572	.239	.126	.319	.209
The commitment of the leader to the school	.513	.290	.252	.329	.137
The versatility of the leader's styles	.284	.332	.377	.285	5.668E-02
The ability of the leader to communicate clear, individualized expectations	.449	.246	.303	.351	.205
The respect in which the leader is held by staff	.184	7.988E-02	.154	.810	.240
The staff's confidence in the SMT	.180	.121	7.859E-02	.809	.279
The effectiveness of the teamwork of the SMT	.385	.445	.249	.443	8.104E-02
The extent to which the vision for the school impacts on practice	.413	.341	.305	.379	.113
Educators given opportunities to take on leadership roles	.247	.225	.494	.339	-2.66E-02
The creativity of the SMT	.212	7.188E-02	.822	-2.97E-03	.189
Problem-posing, problem-identifying and problem-solving capacity of SMT	.459	.351	.262	.361	-3.21E-02
The use of data to inform planning and school development	.690	.167	.188	5.158E-02	-3.79E-02
Valuing of professional development in the school	.187	.249	.551	.260	7.013E-02
Staff consulted about key decisions	.148	6.670E-02	.854	7.531E-02	.167
The encouragement and support for innovativeness and creativity	.143	5.187E-02	.189	.269	.661
Everybody is free to make suggestions to inform decision-making	.165	.150	.172	.264	.642
The school works in partnership with parents	.222	.804	8.173E-02	.143	.199
People take positive risks for the good of the school and its development	.206	.778	8.998E-02	.181	2.635E-02
Staff voluntarily taking on coordination roles	.195	.210	2.681E-02	3.660E-02	.779
Teamwork amongst school staff	.114	.642	.220	-3.41E-02	.277

Extraction Method: Principal Component Analysis.
Rotation Method: Varimax with Kaiser Normalization.
a. Rotation converged in 6 iterations.

---

chosen should not only have high values but also have values that are close to each other (homogeneous) and be some numerical distance away from the other variables. In the column labelled '1' we can see that there are seven such variables, and we set these out in the example below. Other variables from the list are some numerical distance away from the variables selected (see below) and also seems to be conceptually unrelated to the seven variables identified for inclusion in the factor. The variables selected are high, close to each other and distant from the other variables. The lowest of these seven values is 0.513; hence the researcher would report that seven variables had been selected for inclusion in factor one, and that the cut-off point was 0.51 (i.e. the lowest point, above which the variables have been selected). Having such a high cut-off point gives considerable power to the factor. Hence we have factor one, that contains seven variables.

Let us look at a second example, that of factor two (the column labelled '2'). Here we can identify four variables that have high values that are close to each other and yet some numerical distance away from the other variables (see example below). These four variables would constitute factor two, with a reported cut-off point of 0.445. At first glance it may seem that 0.445 is low; however, recalling that the data in the example were derived from 1,000 teachers, 0.445 is still highly statistically significant, statistical significance being a combination of the coefficient *and* the sample size.

We repeat this analysis for all five factors, deciding the cut-off point, looking for homogeneous high values and numerical distance from other variables in the list.

Stage 3

By this time we have identified five factors. However neither SPSS nor any other software package tells us what to name each factor. The researcher has to devise a name that describes the factor in question. This can be tricky, as it has to catch the issue that is addressed by all the variables that are included in the factor. We have undertaken this for all five factors, and we report this below, with the factor loadings for each variable reported in brackets.

Factor One: Leadership skills in school management
Cut-off point: 0.51
Variables included:

- The drive and confidence of the leader (factor loading 0.758).
- The ability of the leader to motivate and inspire the educators (factor loading 0.743);
- The use of data to inform planning and school development (factor loading 0.690);

- The example set by the leader (factor loading 0.572);
- The clarity of the direction set by the school leadership (factor loading 0.559);
- The consultation abilities/activities of the leader (factor loading 0.548);
- The commitment of the leader to the school (factor loading 0.513).

Factor Two: Parent and teacher partnerships in school development
Cut-off point: 0.44
Variables included:

- The school works in partnership with parents' (factor loading 0.804)
- People take positive risks for the good of the school and its development (factor loading 0.778)
- Teamwork amongst school staff (factor loading 0.642)
- The effectiveness of the teamwork of the SMT (factor loading 0.445).

Factor Three: Promoting staff development by creativity and consultation
Cut-off point: 0.55
Variables included:

- Staff consulted about key decisions (factor loading 0.854)
- The creativity of the SMT (senior management team) (factor loading 0.822)
- Valuing of professional development in the school (0.551).

Factor Four: Respect for, and confidence in, the senior management
Cut-off point: 0.44
Variables included:

- The respect in which the leader is held by staff (factor loading 0.810)
- The staff's confidence in the SMT (factor loading 0.809)
- The effectiveness of the teamwork of the SMT (factor loading 0.443).

Factor Five: Encouraging staff development through participation in decision making
Cut-off point 0.64
Variables included:

- Staff voluntarily taking on coordination roles (factor loading 0.779)
- The encouragement and support for innovativeness and creativity (factor loading 0.661)

■ Everybody is free to make suggestions to inform decision making (factor loading 0.642).

Each factor should usually contain a minimum of three variables, though this is a rule of thumb rather than a statistical necessity. Further, in the example here, though some of the variables included have considerably lower factor loadings than others in that factor (e.g. in factor two: the effectiveness of the teamwork of the SMT (0.445)), nevertheless the conceptual similarity to the other variables in that factor, coupled with the fact that, with 1,000 teachers in the study, 0.445 is still highly statistically significant, combine to suggest that this still merits inclusion. As we mentioned earlier, factor analysis is an art as well as a science.

If one wished to suggest a more stringent level of exactitude then a higher cut-off point could be taken. In the example above, factor one could have a cut-off point of 0.74, thereby including only two variables in the factor; factor two could have a cut-off point of 0.77, thereby including only two variables in the factor; factor three could have a cut-off point of 0.82, thereby including only two variables in the factor; factor four could have a cut-off point of 0.80, thereby including only two variables in the factor; and factor five could have a cut-off point of 0.77, thereby including only one variable in the factor. The decision on where to place the cut-off point is a matter of professional judgement when reviewing the data.

In reporting factor analysis the above data would all be included, together with a short commentary, for example:

In order to obtain conceptually similar and significant clusters of issues of the variables, principal components analysis with varimax rotation and Kaiser Normalization were conducted. Eigenvalues equal to or greater than 1.00 were extracted. With regard to the 24 variables used, orthogonal rotation of the variables yielded five factors, accounting for 16.820, 11.706, 11.578, 11.386 and 8.556 per cent of the total variance respectively, a total of 60.047 per cent of the total variance explained. The factor loadings are presented in table such-and-such. To enhance the interpretability of the factors, only variables with factor loadings as follows were selected for inclusion in their respective factors: >0.51 (factor one), >0.44 (factor two), >0.55 (factor three), >0.44 (factor four) and >0.64 (factor five). The factors are named, respectively: *Leadership skills in school management*; *Parent and teacher partnerships in school development*; *Promoting staff development by creativity and consultation*; *Respect for, and con-* *fidence in, the senior management*; and *Encouraging staff development through participation in decision making.*

Having presented the data for the factor analysis the researcher would then comment on what it showed, fitting the research that was being conducted.

The SPSS command sequence for factor analysis is thus, clicking on each of the following: Descriptives → Click on KMO and Bartlett's test of sphericity → Coefficients → Continue → Extraction → Principal components → Correlation matrix → Unrotated factor solution → Scree plot → Based on Eigenvalue → Continue → Rotation → Direct Oblimin or Varimax (depending on whether the rotation is oblique or orthogonal) → Continue → return to main screen and Click OK.

37.4 What to look for in factor analysis output

SPSS typically produces many sets of data in factor analysis. What follows is a set of pointers for what to look at in the different tables that SPSS typically produces. The example uses a Direct Oblimin rotation, using an example of research on factors that affect teacher stress. In some cases the SPSS tables are too large to reproduce in their entirety, so extracts are included that illustrate the main points being made. Imagine that we have given SPSS all the instructions indicated above, to run the SPSS analysis, and to check for the suitability of the data for factorization. In Table 37.6 the researcher checks that most of the correlation coefficients in the cells are greater than 0.3.

In Table 37.7 the researcher checks the suitability of the data for factor analysis by examining the output concerning the Kaiser-Meyer-Olkin (KMO) and the Bartlett test. Here the KMO measure is greater than 0.6 (0.845) and the Bartlett test is statistically significant (0.000), so the researcher is safe to continue, knowing that the data are suitable for factorization.

Table 37.8 indicates the amount of variance explained by each item (if it is lower than 0.3 then the item is a poor fit).

Table 37.9 indicates that two factors have been extracted (two components): factor one explains 45.985 per cent of the total variance; factor two explains 18.851 per cent of the total variance.

Table 37.10 provides the pattern matrix, from which the researcher can identify which variables load onto the factors. Here we have emboldened and circled the variables that load onto each factor, for ease of identification.

TABLE 37.6 CHECKING THE CORRELATION TABLE FOR SUITABILITY OF THE DATA FOR FACTORIZATION (SPSS OUTPUT)

		How much do you feel that working with colleagues all day is really a strain for you?	How much do you feel emotionally drained by your work?	How much do you worry that your job is hardening you emotionally?	How much frustration do you feel in your job?
Correlation	How much do you feel that working with colleagues all day is really a strain for you?	1.000	.554	.507	.461
	How much do you feel emotionally drained by your work?	.554	1.000	.580	.518
	How much do you worry that your job is hardening you emotionally?	.507	.580	1.000	.646
	How much frustration do you feel in your job?	.461	.518	.646	1.000

TABLE 37.7 CHECKING THE SUITABILITY OF THE DATA FOR FACTOR ANALYSIS (SPSS OUTPUT)

KMO and Bartlett's Test

Kaiser-Meyer-Olkin Measure of Sampling Adequacy.		.845
Bartlett's Test of Sphericity	Approx. Chi-Square	5460.475
	df	36
	Sig.	.000

TABLE 37.8   CHECKING THE VARIANCE EXPLAINED BY EACH ITEM (SPSS OUTPUT)

Communalities

	Initial	Extraction
How hard do you feel you are working in your job?	1.000	.779
How much do you feel exhausted by the end of the workday?	1.000	.818
How much do you feel that you cannot cope with your job any longer?	1.000	.578
How much do you feel that you treat colleagues as impersonal objects?	1.000	.578
How much do you feel that working with colleagues all day is really a strain for you?	1.000	.602
How much do you feel emotionally drained by your work?	1.000	.629
How tired do you feel in the morning, having to face another school day?	1.000	.595
How much do you worry that your job is hardening you emotionally?	1.000	.661
How much frustration do you feel in your job?	1.000	.595

Extraction Method: Principal Component Analysis.

Guidelines for which variables to select to include in each factor are:

- include the highest scoring variables;
- omit the low scoring variables;
- look for where there is a clear scoring distance between those included and those excluded;
- review your selection to check that no lower scoring variables have been excluded which are conceptually close to those included;

TABLE 37.9 EXTRACTION OF TWO FACTORS (SPSS OUTPUT)

Total Variance Explained

Component	Initial Eigenvalues			Extraction Sums of Squared Loadings			Rotation Sums of Squared Loadings[a]
	Total	% of Variance	Cumulative %	Total	% of Variance	Cumulative %	Total
1	4.139	45.985	45.985	4.139	45.985	45.985	4.028
2	1.697	18.851	64.836	1.697	18.851	64.836	1.991
3	.661	7.342	72.178				
4	.542	6.023	78.202				
5	.531	5.900	84.102				
6	.451	5.006	89.107				
7	.395	4.390	93.497				
8	.323	3.593	97.090				
9	.262	2.910	100.000				

Extraction Method: Principal Component Analysis.

a. When components are correlated, sums of squared loadings cannot be added to obtain a total variance.

TABLE 37.10 PATTERN MATRIX (SPSS OUTPUT WITH MARKINGS ADDED)

Pattern Matrix[a]

	Component	
	1	2
How hard do you feel you are working in your job?	.005	⟨882⟩
How much do you feel exhausted by the end of the workday?	.252	⟨834⟩
How much do you feel that you cannot cope with your job any longer?	⟨591⟩	.234
How much do you feel that you treat colleagues as impersonal objects?	⟨674⟩	-.459
How much do you feel that working with colleagues all day is really a strain for you?	⟨782⟩	-.158
How much do you feel emotionally drained by your work?	⟨774⟩	.096
How tired do you feel in the morning, having to face another school day?	⟨697⟩	.247
How much do you worry that your job is hardening you emotionally?	⟨814⟩	-.008
How much frustration do you feel in your job?	⟨752⟩	.097

Extraction Method: Principal Component Analysis.

Rotation Method: Oblimin with Kaiser Normalization.

a. Rotation converged in 6 iterations.

- review your selection to check whether some higher scoring variables should be excluded if they are not sufficiently conceptually close to the others that have been included;
- review your final selection to see that they are conceptually similar.

The researcher is advised that deciding on inclusions and exclusions is an art, not a science; there is no simple formula, so the researcher has to use his/her judgement.

In reporting the factor analysis the researcher should consider:

- Reporting the method of factor analysis used (Principal components; Direct Oblimin; KMO and Bartlett test of sphericity; Eigenvalues greater than 1; scree test; rotated solution).
- Reporting how many factors were extracted with Eigenvalues greater than 1.
- Reporting how many factors were included as a result of the scree test.
- Giving a name/title to each of the factors.
- Reporting how much of the total variance was explained by each factor.
- Reporting the cut-off point for the variables included in each factor.
- Reporting the factor loadings of each variable in the factor.
- Reporting what the results show.

For examples of research that uses factor analysis we refer the reader to Note 1.

37.5 Cluster analysis

Whereas factor analysis and elementary linkage analysis enable the researcher to group together factors and variables, cluster analysis enables the researcher to group together similar and homogeneous subsamples of *people*. This is best approached through software packages such as SPSS, and we illustrate this here. SPSS creates a dendrogram of results, grouping and regrouping groups until all the variables are embraced.

For example, Figure 37.3 is a simple cluster based on 20 cases (people). Imagine that their scores have been collected on an item concerning the variable 'the attention given to teaching and learning in the school'. One can see that at the most general level there are two clusters (cluster one=persons 19, 20, 2, 13, 15, 9, 11, 18, 14, 16, 1, 10, 12, 5, 17; cluster two=persons 7, 8, 4, 3, 6). If one wished to have smaller clusters then three grouping could be found: cluster one: persons 19, 20, 2, 13, 15, 9, 11, 18; cluster two: persons 14, 16, 1, 10, 12, 5, 17; cluster three: persons 7, 8, 4, 3, 6.

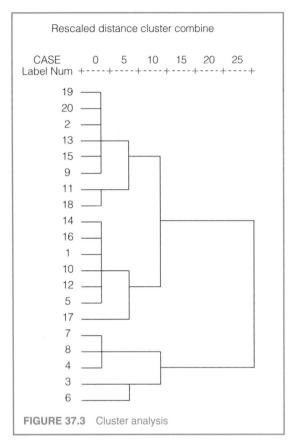

FIGURE 37.3 Cluster analysis

Using this analysis enables the researcher to identify important groupings of people in a *post hoc* analysis, i.e. not setting up the groupings and subgroupings at the stage of sample design, but *after* the data have been gathered. In the example of the two-group cluster here one could examine the characteristics of those participants who were clustered into groups one and two, and, for the three-group cluster, one could examine the characteristics of those participants who were clustered into groups one, two and three for the variable 'the attention given to teaching and learning in the school'.

37.6 Examples of studies using multidimensional scaling and cluster analysis

Forgas (1976) studied housewives' and students' perceptions of typical social episodes in their lives, the episodes having been elicited from the respective groups by means of a diary technique. Subjects were required to supply two adjectives to describe each of the social episodes they had recorded as having occurred during the previous 24 hours. From a pool of some 146 adjectives thus generated, ten (together with their antonyms) were selected on the basis of their salience, their diversity of usage and their independence of one another. Two more scales from speculative taxonomies were added to give 12 unidimensional scales purporting to describe the underlying episode structures. These scales were used in the second part of the study to rate 25 social episodes in each group, the episodes being chosen as follows. An 'index of relatedness' was computed on the basis of the number of times a pair of episodes was placed in the same category by respective housewife

and student judges. Data were aggregated over the total number of subjects in each of the two groups. The 25 'top' social episodes in each group were retained. Forgas's analysis is based upon the ratings of 26 housewives and 25 students of their respective 25 episodes on each of the 12 unidimensional scales. Figure 37.4 shows a three-dimensional configuration of 25 social episodes rated by the student group on three of the scales. For illustrative purposes some of the social episodes numbered in Figure 37.4 are identified by specific content.

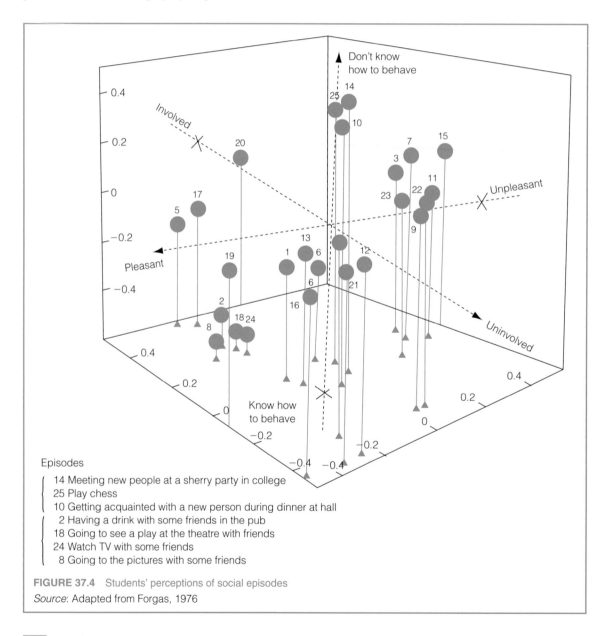

Episodes

⎰ 14 Meeting new people at a sherry party in college
⎱ 25 Play chess
  10 Getting acquainted with a new person during dinner at hall
⎰ 2 Having a drink with some friends in the pub
⎪ 18 Going to see a play at the theatre with friends
⎨ 24 Watch TV with some friends
⎩ 8 Going to the pictures with some friends

FIGURE 37.4 Students' perceptions of social episodes

Source: Adapted from Forgas, 1976

In another study, Forgas examined the social environment of a university department consisting of tutors, students and secretarial staff, all of whom had interacted both inside and outside the department for at least six months prior to the research and thought of themselves as an intensive and cohesive social unit. Forgas's interest was in the relationship between two aspects of the social environment of the department – the perceived structure of the group and the perceptions that were held of specific social episodes. Participants were required to rate the similarity between each possible pairing of group members on a scale ranging from '1=extremely similar' to '9=extremely dissimilar'. An individual differences multidimensional scaling procedure (INDSCAL) produced an optimal three-dimensional configuration of group structure accounting for 68 per cent of the variance, group members being differentiated along the dimensions of sociability, creativity and competence.

A semi-structured procedure requiring participants to list typical and characteristic interaction situations was used to identify a number of social episodes. These in turn were validated by participant observation of the ongoing activities of the department. The most commonly

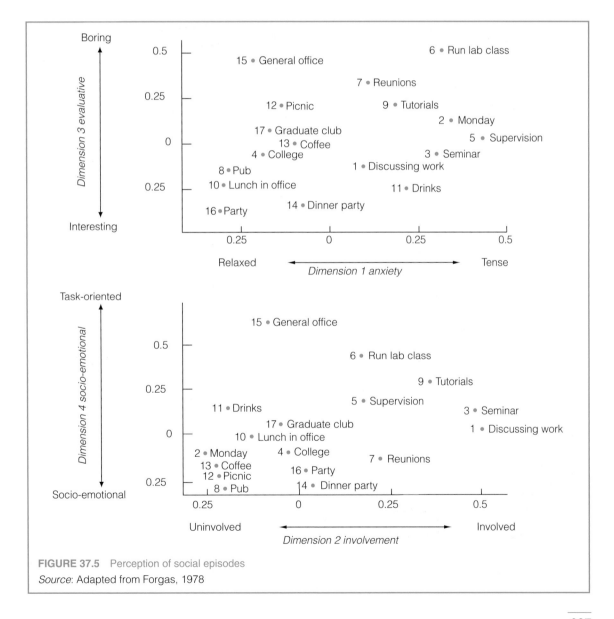

FIGURE 37.5 Perception of social episodes
Source: Adapted from Forgas, 1978

occurring social episodes (those mentioned by nine or more members) served as the stimuli in the second stage of the study. Bipolar scales similar to those reported by Forgas (1976) and elicited in like manner were used to obtain group members' judgements of social episodes.

An interesting finding reported by Forgas was that formal status differences exercised no significant effect upon the perception of the group by its members, the absence of differences being attributed to the strength of the department's cohesiveness and intimacy. In Forgas's analysis of the group's perceptions of social episodes, the INDSCAL scaling procedure produced an optimal four-dimensional solution accounting for 62 per cent of the variance, group members perceiving social episodes in terms of anxiety, involvement, evaluation and social-emotional versus task orientation. Figure 37.5 illustrates how an average group member would see the characteristics of various social episodes in terms of the dimensions by which the group commonly judged them.

Finally we outline a classificatory system that has been developed to process materials elicited in a rather structured form of account gathering. Peevers and Secord's (1973) study of developmental changes in children's use of descriptive concepts of persons, illustrates the application of quantitative techniques to the analysis of one form of account.

In individual interviews, children of varying ages were asked to describe three friends and one person whom they disliked, all four people being of the same sex as the interviewee. Interviews were tape-recorded and transcribed. A person-concept coding system was developed, the categories of which are illustrated in Table 37.11. Each person-description was divided into items, each item consisting of one discrete piece of information. Each item was then coded on each of four major dimensions. Detailed coding procedures are set out in Peevers and Secord (1973).

Tests of interjudge agreement on descriptiveness, personal involvement and evaluative consistency in which two judges worked independently on the interview transcripts of 21 boys and girls aged between five and 16 years resulted in interjudge agreement on those three

---

TABLE 37.11   PERSON-CONCEPT CODING SYSTEM

Dimension	Levels of descriptiveness
DESCRIPTIVENESS	1 *Undifferentiating* . . . (person not differentiated from his environment) 2 *Simple differentiating* . . . (person differentiated in simple global terms) 3 *Differentiating* . . . (person differentiated in specific characteristics) 4 *Dispositional* . . . (person differentiated in terms of traits)
PERSONAL INVOLVEMENT	*Degrees of involvement* 1 *Egocentric* . . . (other person described in self-oriented terms) 2 *Mutual* . . . (other person described in terms of his relationship to perceiver) 3 *Other oriented* . . . (no personal involvement expressed by perceiver)
EVALUATIVE CONSISTENCY	*Amount of consistency* 1 *Consistent* . . . (nothing favourable about 'disliked', nothing unfavourable about 'liked') 2 *Inconsistent* . . . (some mixture of favourableness and unfavourableness)
DEPTH	*Levels of depth* *Level 1* (includes all undifferentiated and simple differentiated descriptions) *Level 2* (includes differentiated and some dispositional descriptions) *Level 3* (includes explanation-type differentiated and dispositional descriptions)

Source: Adapted from Peevers and Secord, 1973

dimensions of 87 per cent, 79 per cent and 97 per cent respectively.

Peevers and Secord (1973) also obtained evidence of the degree to which the participants themselves were consistent from one session to another in their use of concepts to describe other people. Children were re-interviewed between one week and one month after the first session on the pretext of problems with the original recordings. Indices of test-retest reliability were computed for each of the major coding dimensions. Separate correlation coefficients (eta) were obtained for younger and older children in respect of their descriptive concepts of liked and disliked peers. Reliability coefficients are as set out in Table 37.12. Secord and Peevers (1973) conclude that their approach offers the possibility of an exciting line of enquiry into the depth of insight that individuals have into the personalities of their acquaintances. Their 'free commentary' method is a modification of the more structured interview, requiring the interviewer to probe for explanations of why a person behaves the way he or she does or why a person is the kind of person he or she is. Peevers and Secord found that older children in their sample readily volunteered this sort of information. Harré (1977b) observes that this approach could also be extended to elicit commentary upon children's friends and enemies and the ritual actions associated with the creation and maintenance of these categories.

For a further example of research using cluster analysis see Seifert (1997).

37.7 Multidimensional data: some words on notation

The hypothetical data in Table 37.13 refer to a survey of voting behaviour in a sample of men and women in Britain. The outline that follows draws closely on an exposition by Whiteley (1983):

the row variable (sex) is represented by i;
the column variable (voting preference) is represented by j;
the layer variable (social class) is represented by k.

The number in any one cell in Table 37.13 can be represented by the symbol n_{ijk} that is to say, the score in row category i, column category j, and layer category k, where:

$i = 1$ (men), 2 (women)
$j = 1$ (Conservative), 2 (Labour)
$k = 1$ (middle class), 2 (working class).

It follows therefore that the numbers in Table 37.13 can also be represented as in Table 37.14 Thus,

$n_{121} = 30$ (men, Labour, middle class)

and

$n_{212} = 40$ (women, Conservative, working-class)

TABLE 37.12 RELIABILITY COEFFICIENTS FOR PEER DESCRIPTIONS

Dimension	Liked peers		Disliked peers	
	Younger subjects	Older subjects	Younger subjects	Older subjects
Descriptiveness	0.83	0.91	0.80	0.84
Personal involvement	0.76	0.80	0.84	0.77
Depth	0.65	0.71	0.65	0.75
Evaluative consistency	0.69	0.92	0.76	0.69

Source: Peevers and Secord, 1973

TABLE 37.13 SEX, VOTING PREFERENCE AND SOCIAL CLASS: A THREE-WAY CLASSIFICATION TABLE

	Middle class		Working class	
	Conservative	Labour	Conservative	Labour
Men	80	30	40	130
Women	100	20	40	110

Source: Adapted from Whiteley, 1983

TABLE 37.14   SEX, VOTING PREFERENCE AND SOCIAL CLASS: A THREE-WAY NOTATIONAL CLASSIFICATION

	Middle class		Working class	
	Conservative	Labour	Conservative	Labour
Men	n_{111}	n_{121}	n_{112}	n_{122}
Women	n_{211}	n_{221}	n_{212}	n_{222}

Three types of marginals can be obtained from Table 37.14 by:

1   Summing over two variables to give the marginal totals for the third. Thus:
  n_{++k}=summing over sex and voting preference to give social class, for example:
  $n_{111}+n_{121}+n_{211}+n_{221}=230$ (middle class)
  $n_{112}+n_{122}+n_{212}+n_{222}=320$ (working class)
  n_{+j+}=summing over sex and social class to give voting preference
  n_{i++}=summing over voting preference and social class to give sex.
2   Summing over one variable to give the marginal totals for the second and third variables. Thus:
  $n_{+11}=180$ (middle-class Conservative)
  $n_{+21}=50$ (middle-class Labour)
  $n_{+12}=80$ (working-class Conservative)
  $n_{+22}=240$ (working-class Labour).
3   Summing over all three variables to give the grand total. Thus:
  $n_{+++}=550=N$

37.8 Using the chi-square test in a three-way classification table

Whiteley (1983) shows how easy it is to extend the 2 × 2 chi-square test to the three-way case. The probability that an individual taken from the sample at random in Table 37.14 will be a woman is:

$$p_{2++}=\frac{n_{2++}}{n_{+++}}=\frac{270}{550}=0.49$$

and the probability that a respondent's voting preference will be Labour is:

$$p_{+2+}=\frac{n_{+2+}}{n_{+++}}=\frac{290}{550}=0.53$$

and the probability that a respondent will be working class is:

$$p_{++2}=\frac{n_{++2}}{n_{+++}}=\frac{320}{550}=0.58$$

To determine the expected probability of an individual being a woman, Labour supporter and working class we assume that these variables are statistically independent (that is to say, there is no relationship between them) and simply apply the multiplication rule of probability theory:

$$p_{222}=(p_{2++})\,(p_{+2+})\,(p_{++2})=(0.49)\,(0.53)\,(0.58)=0.15$$

This can be expressed in terms of the expected frequency in cell n_{222} as:

$$N\,(p_{2++})\,(p_{+2+})\,(p_{++2})=550\,(0.49)\,(0.53)\,(0.58)=82.8$$

Similarly, the expected frequency in cell n_{112} is:

$$N(p_{1++})\,(p_{+1+})(p_{++2})\text{ where:}$$

$$p_{1++}=\frac{n_{1++}}{n_{+++}}=\frac{280}{550}=0.51$$

and

$$p_{+1+}=\frac{n_{+1+}}{n_{+++}}=\frac{260}{550}=0.47$$

and

$$p_{++2}=\frac{n_{++2}}{n_{+++}}=\frac{320}{550}=0.58$$

Thus $N\,(p_{1++})\,(p_{+1+})\,(p_{++2})=550\,(0.51)\,(0.47)\,(0.58)=77.0$

Table 37.15 gives the expected frequencies for the data shown in Table 37.14.

With the observed frequencies and the expected frequencies to hand, chi-square is calculated in the usual way:

$$\chi^2=\sum\frac{(O-E)^2}{E}=159.41$$

Whiteley (1983) observes that degrees of freedom in a three-way contingency table is more complex than in a 2 × 2 classification. Essentially, however, degrees of

---

TABLE 37.15   EXPECTED FREQUENCIES IN SEX, VOTING PREFERENCE AND SOCIAL CLASS

	Middle class		Working class	
	Conservative	Labour	Conservative	Labour
Men	55.4	61.7	77.0	85.9
Women	53.4	59.5	74.3	82.8

Source: Adapted from Whiteley, 1983

---

freedom refer to the freedom with which the researcher is able to assign values to the cells, given fixed marginal totals. This can be computed by first determining the degrees of freedom for the marginals.

Each of the variables in our example (sex, voting preference and social class) contains two categories. It follows therefore that we have $(2-1)$ degrees of freedom for each of them, given that the marginal for each variable is fixed. Since the grand total of all the marginals (i.e. the sample size) is also fixed, it follows that one more degree of freedom is also lost. We subtract these fixed numbers from the total number of cells in our contingency table. In general therefore:

degrees of freedom (df)=the number of cells in the table – 1 (for N) – the number of cells fixed by the hypothesis being tested.

Thus; where r=rows, c=columns and l=layers:

$df=rcl\,(r-1)-(c-1)-(l-1)-1 =$
$rcl-r-c-l+2$

that is to say $df=rcl-r-c-l+2$ when we are testing the hypothesis of the mutual independence of the three variables.

In our example:

$df=(2)\,(2)\,(2)-2-2-2+2=4$

From chi-square tables we see that the critical value of χ^2 with four degrees of freedom is 9.49 at $p=0.05$. Our obtained value greatly exceeds that number. We reject the null hypothesis and conclude that sex, voting preference and social class are significantly interrelated.

Having rejected the null hypothesis with respect to the mutual independence of the three variables, the researcher's task now is to identify which variables cause the null hypothesis to be rejected. We cannot simply assume that because our chi-square test has given a significant result, it therefore follows that there

are significant associations between all three variables. It may be the case, for example, that an association exists between two of the variables whilst the third is completely independent. What we need now is a test of 'partial independence'. Whiteley (1983) shows the following three such possible tests in respect of the data in Table 37.13. First, that sex is independent of social class and voting preference:

(1) $p_{ijk}=(p_i)\,(p_{jk})$

Second, that voting preference is independent of sex and social class:

(2) $p_{ijk}=(p_j)\,(p_{ik})$

And third, that social class is independent of sex and voting preference:

(3) $p_{ijk}=(p_k)\,(p_{ij})$

The following example shows how to construct the expected frequencies for the first hypothesis. We can determine the probability of an individual being, say, woman, Labour, and working class, assuming hypothesis (1), as follows:

$$p_{222}=(p_{2++})\,(p_{+22})=\frac{(n_{2++})}{(N)}\,\frac{(n_{+22})}{(N)}$$

$$p_{222}=\frac{(270)}{(550)}\,\frac{(240)}{(550)}=0.214$$

$$E_{222}=N(p_{2++})\,(p_{+22})=550\,\frac{(270)}{(550)}\,\frac{(240)}{(550)}=117.8$$

That is to say, assuming that sex is independent of social class and voting preference, the expected number of female, working-class Labour supporters is 117.8.

When we calculate the expected frequencies for each of the cells in our contingency table in respect of

> **TABLE 37.16   EXPECTED FREQUENCIES ASSUMING THAT SEX IS INDEPENDENT OF SOCIAL CLASS AND VOTING PREFERENCE**
>
> | | Middle class | | Working class | |
> | --- | --- | --- | --- | --- |
> | | Conservative | Labour | Conservative | Labour |
> | Men | 91.6 | 25.5 | 40.7 | 122.2 |
> | Women | 88.4 | 24.5 | 39.3 | 117.8 |
>
> *Source*: Adapted from Whiteley, 1983

our first hypothesis $(p_{ijk})=(p_i)(p_{jk})$, we obtain the results shown in Table 37.16.

$$\chi^2=\sum\frac{(O-E)^2}{E}=5.71$$

Degrees of freedom is given by:

$$df=rcl-(cl-1)-(r-1)-1=rcl-cl-r+1$$
$$=8-4-2+1=3$$

Whiteley observes:

> Note that we are assuming c and l are interrelated so that once, say, p_{+ii} is calculated, then p_{+12}, p_{+21} and p_{+22} are determined, so we have only 1 degree of freedom; that is to say, we lose $(cl-1)$ degrees of freedom in calculating that relationship.
>
> (Whiteley, 1983)

From chi-square tables we see that the critical value of χ^2 with three degrees of freedom is 7.81 at $p=0.05$. Our obtained value is less than this. We therefore accept the null hypothesis and conclude that *there is no relationship between sex on the one hand and voting preference and social class on the other*.

Suppose now that instead of casting our data into a three-way classification as shown in Table 37.13, we had simply used a 2×2 contingency table and that we had sought to test the null hypothesis that *there is no relationship between sex and voting preference*. The data are shown in Table 37.17.

When we compute chi-square from the above data our obtained value is $\chi^2=4.48$. Degrees of freedom are given by $(r-1)(c-1)=(2-1)(2-1)=1$.

From chi-square tables we see that the critical value of χ^2 with 1 degree of freedom is 3.84 at $p=0.05$. Our obtained value exceeds this. We reject the null hypothesis and conclude that *sex is significantly associated with voting preference*.

But how can we explain the differing conclusions that we have arrived at in respect of the data in Tables

> **TABLE 37.17   SEX AND VOTING PREFERENCE: A TWO-WAY CLASSIFICATION TABLE**
>
> | | Conservative | Labour |
> | --- | --- | --- |
> | Men | 120 | 160 |
> | Women | 140 | 130 |
>
> *Source*: Adapted from Whiteley, 1983

37.13 and 37.17? These examples illustrate an important and general point, as Whiteley observes. In the bivariate analysis (Table 37.17) we concluded that there was a significant relationship between sex and voting preference. In the multivariate analysis (Table 37.13) that relationship was found to be non-significant when we controlled for social class. The lesson is plain: use a multivariate approach to the analysis of contingency tables wherever the data allow.

37.9 A note on structural equation modelling

Though this book will not concern itself with structural equation modelling (SEM), nevertheless we will note it here, as a powerful tool in the armoury of statistics-based research using interval and ratio data. Structural equation modelling is the name given to a group of techniques that enable researchers to construct models of putative causal relations, and to test those models against data. It is designed to enable researchers to confirm, modify and test their models of causal relations between variables. It is based on multiple regression and factor analysis, but advances beyond these techniques to create and test models of relationships, often causal, to see how well the models fit the data. Though SPSS does not have a function to handle this, the Analysis of Moment Structures (AMOS) is a software package that enables the researcher to import and work with SPSS files.

As was mentioned earlier, factor analysis can be both exploratory and confirmatory. Whilst the earlier discussion concerned exploratory factor analysis, confirmatory factor analysis is a feature of the group of latent variable models (models of factors rather than observed variables) which includes factor analysis, path analysis and structural equation analysis. Confirmatory factor analysis seeks to verify (to confirm) the researcher's predictions about factors and their factor loadings in data and data structures. As was mentioned earlier, factors are latent, they cannot be observed as they underlie variables.

By contrast, path analysis – an extension of multiple regression – only works with observed variables, and it attempts to estimate and test the magnitude and significance of relationships, often putatively causal, between sets of observed variables.

Path analysis is a statistical method that enables a researcher to determine how well a multivariate set of data fits with a particular (causal) model that has been set up in advance by the researcher (i.e. an a priori model). It is a particular kind of multiple regression analysis that enables the researcher to see the relative weightings of observed independent variables on each other and on a dependent variable, to establish pathways of causation, and to determine the direct and indirect effects of independent variables on a dependent variable (Morrison, 2009: 96). The researcher constructs what she or he thinks will be a suitable model of the causal pathway between independent variables and between independent and dependent variables, often based on literature and theory, and then tests this to see how well it fits with the data.

In constructing path analysis computer software is virtually essential. Programs such as AMOS (in SPSS) and LISREL are two commonly used examples.

Morrison (2009: 96–8) gives an example of path analysis in degree classification, with three independent variables and their relationship to the dependent variable of degree classification:

- socio-economic status
- part-time working
- level of motivation for academic study.

These three variables are purported to have an effect on the class of degree that a student gains (the dependent variable), as shown in Figure 37.6 (which is constructed from the AMOS software).

The researcher believes that, in this non-recursive model (a model in which the direction of causality is not solely one-way – see the arrows joining 'part-time work' and 'level of motivation for academic study', which go to and from each other – in contrast to a recursive model, in which the direction of putative causality is one-way

only), socio-economic status determines part-time working, level of motivation for academic study and the dependent variable 'class of degree'. The variable 'socio-economic status' is deemed to be an exogenous variable (a variable caused by variables that are *not* included in the causal model), whilst the variables 'part-time working' and 'level of motivation for academic study' are deemed to be endogenous variables (those caused by variables that *are* included in the model) as well as being affected by exogenous variables.

In the model (Figure 37.6) the dependent variable is 'class of degree' and there are directional causal arrows leading both to this dependent variable and to and from the three independent variables. The model assumes that the variables 'part-time work' and 'level of motivation for academic study' influence each other and that socio-economic status precedes the other independent variables rather than being caused by them. In the model there are also three variables in circles, termed 'e1', 'e2' and 'e3'; these three additional variables are the error factors, i.e. additional extraneous/exogenous factors which may also be influencing the three variables in question, and AMOS adjusts the results for these factors. (AMOS enables the researcher to draw the model and manipulate its layout.)

AMOS then calculates the regression coefficient of each relationship and places each coefficient on the

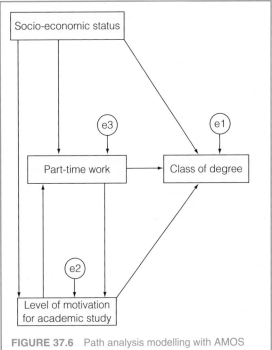

FIGURE 37.6 Path analysis modelling with AMOS (AMOS output)

model. An example of the model generated by AMOS is presented in Figure 37.7 (using the 'standardized estimates' in AMOS).

Here one can see that:

a   'Socio-economic' status exerts a direct powerful influence on class of degree (0.18), and that this is higher than the direct influence of either 'part-time work' (–0.01) or 'level of motivation for academic study' (0.04).

b   'Socio-economic status' exerts a powerful direct influence on 'level of motivation for academic study' (0.52), and this is higher than the influence of 'socio-economic status' on 'class of degree' (0.18).

c   'Socio-economic status' exerts a powerful direct and negative influence on 'part-time work' (–0.21), i.e. the higher the socio-economic status, the lesser is the amount of part-time work undertaken.

d   'Part-time work' exerts a powerful direct influence on 'level of motivation for academic study' (1.37), and this is higher than the influence of 'socio-economic status' on 'level of motivation for academic study' (0.52).

e   'Level of motivation for academic study' exerts a powerful negative direct influence on 'part-time work' (–1.45), i.e. the higher is the level of motiva-

tion for academic study, the lesser is the amount of part-time work undertaken.

f   'Level of motivation for academic study' exerts a slightly more powerful influence on 'class of degree' (0.04) than does 'part-time work' (–0.01).

g   'Part-time work' exerts a negative influence on the class of degree (–0.01), i.e. the more one works part-time, the lower is the class of degree obtained.

AMOS also yields a battery of statistics about the 'goodness of fit' of the model to the data, most of which is beyond the scope of this book; suffice it to say here that the chi-square statistic must *not* be statistically significant (i.e. $p > 0.05$), i.e. to indicate that the model does not differ statistically significantly from the data (i.e. the model is faithful to the data), and the goodness of fit index (the Normed Fit Index (NFI) and the Comparative Fit Index (CFI)) should be 0.9 or higher.

Path analysis assumes that the *direction* of causation in the variables can be identified, that the data are at the interval level, that the relations are linear, that the data meet the usual criteria for regression analysis and that the model's parsimony (inclusion of few variables) is fair. Morrison (2009: 98) argues that path analysis is only as good as the causal assumptions that underpin it, nor does it prove unequivocally that causation is present; rather it only tests a model based on *assumed* causal directions and influences. Nevertheless, its utility lies in its ability to test models of causal directions, to establish relative weightings of variables, to look at direct and indirect effects of independent variables and to handle several independent variables simultaneously.

Structural equation modelling combines the features of confirmatory factor analysis (i.e. it works with *latent* factors) and of path analysis (i.e. it works with *observed*, manifest variables). Here each factor is a latent construct comprising several variables. This is shown in Figure 37.8, in which each factor appears in the ovals and each observed variable appears in a rectangle. Here the factor 'socio-economic status' (S) has three variables (S1, S2, S3), the factor 'part-time work' (P) has two variables (P1, P2) and the factor 'level of motivation for academic study' (L) has three variables (L1, L2, L3). Each variable has its own error factor (the small circles with 'E' inside them).

Structural equation modelling requires the researcher to:

■   construct the model (the factors and the variables);
■   decide the direction of causality (recursive or non-recursive);
■   identify the number of parameters to be estimated (number of factor coefficients, covariances, observations);

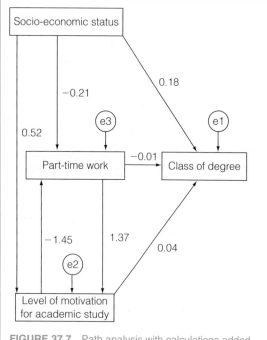

FIGURE 37.7   Path analysis with calculations added (AMOS output)

- run the AMOS analysis (or another piece of software) and check the goodness of fit of the model to the data;
- make any necessary modifications to the model.

This is a highly simplified overview of the process and nature of structural equation modelling, and the reader is strongly advised to read further, more detailed texts, e.g. Loehlin (2004), Schumacker and Lomax (2004), Kline (2005). Website introductions can be found at:

http://luna.cas.usf.edu/~mbrannic/files/regression/
   Pathan.html
http://faculty.chass.ncsu.edu/garson/PA765/path.htm
www.sgim.org/userfiles/file/AMHandouts/AM05/hand-
   outs/PA08.pdf
http://people.exeter.ac.uk/SEGLea/multvar2/pathanal.
   html

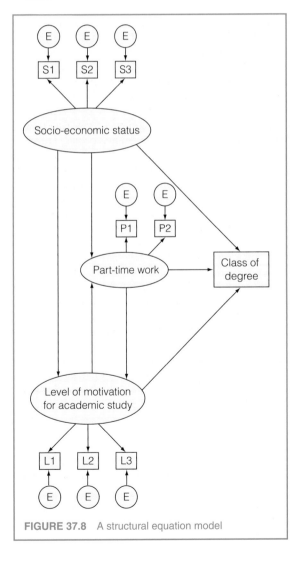

FIGURE 37.8 A structural equation model

http://userwww.sfsu.edu/~efc/classes/biol710/path/
   SEMwebpage.htm
http://ikki.bokee.com/inc/AMOS.pdf
http://core.ecu.edu/psyc/wuenschk/MV/SEM/Path-
   SPSS-AMOS.doc

37.10 A note on multilevel modelling

Multilevel modelling (also known as multilevel regression) is a statistical method that recognizes that it is uncommon to be able to assign students in schools randomly to control and experimental groups, or indeed to conduct an experiment that requires an intervention with one group whilst maintaining a control group (Keeves and Sellin, 1997: 394).

Typically in most schools, students are brought together in particular groupings for specified purposes and each group of students has its own different characteristics which renders it different from other groups. Multilevel modelling addresses the fact that, unless it can be shown that different groups of students are, in fact, alike, it is generally inappropriate to aggregate groups of students or data for the purposes of analysis. Multilevel models avoid the pitfalls of aggregation and the *ecological fallacy* (Plewis, 1997: 35), i.e. making inferences about individual students and behaviour from aggregated data.

Data and variables exist at individual and group levels, indeed Keeves and Sellin (1997) break down analysis further into three main levels: (a) between students over all groups; (b) between groups; and (c) between students within groups. One could extend the notion of levels, of course, to include individual, group, class, school, local, regional, national and international levels (Paterson and Goldstein, 1991). Data are 'nested' (Bickel, 2007), i.e. individual-level data are nested within group, class, school, regional and so on levels; a dependent variable is affected by independent variables at different levels (p. 3). In other words, data are hierarchical. Bickel gives the example of IQ (p. 8), which operates simultaneously at an individual level and at an aggregated group IQ level. If we are looking at, say, the effectiveness of a reading programme in a region, we have to recognize that student performance at the individual level is also affected by group and school level factors (e.g. differences within a school may be smaller than differences between schools). Individuals within families may be more similar than individuals between families. Using multilevel modelling researchers can ascertain, for example, how much of the variation in student attainment might be attributable to differences within students in a single school or to differences between schools (i.e. how much influence is exerted on student attainment by the school that the student attends). Another example might be the extent to which factors such as sex, ethnicity, type of school, locality of school and school size account for variation in student performance. Multilevel modelling enables the researcher to calculate the relative impact on a dependent variable of one or more independent variables at each level of the hierarchy, and, thereby, to identify factors at each level of the hierarchy that are associated with the impact of that level.

Multilevel modelling has been conducted using multilevel regression and hierarchical linear modelling (HLM). Multilevel models enable researchers to ask questions hitherto unanswered, e.g. about variability between and within schools, teachers and curricula (Plewis, 1997: 34–5), in short about the *processes* of teaching and learning.[2] Useful overviews of multilevel modelling can be found in Goldstein (1987), Fitz-Gibbon (1997) and Keeves and Sellin (1997).

Multilevel analysis avoids statistical treatments associated with experimental methods (e.g. analysis of variance and covariance); rather it uses regression analysis and, in particular, multilevel regression. Regression analysis, argues Plewis (1997: 28), assumes *homoscedasticity* (where the residuals demonstrate equal scatter), that the residuals are independent of each other and, finally, that the residuals are normally distributed.

Multilevel modelling is the basis of much research on the 'value-added' component of education and the comparison of schools in public 'league tables' of results (Fitz-Gibbon, 1991, 1997). However Fitz-Gibbon (1997: 42–4) provides important evidence to question the value of some forms of multilevel modelling. She demonstrates that residual gain analysis provides answers to questions about the value-added dimension of education which differ insubstantially from those answers that are given by multilevel modelling (the lowest correlation coefficient being 0.93 and 71.4 per cent of the correlations computed correlating between 0.98 and 1). The important point here is that residual gain analysis is a much more straightforward technique than multilevel modelling. Her work strikes at the heart of the need to use complex multilevel modelling to asses the 'value-added' component of education. In her

work (Fitz-Gibbon, 1997: 5) the value-added score – the difference between a statistically predicted performance and the actual performance – can be computed using residual gain analysis rather than multilevel modelling.

Similarly, Gorard (2007: 221) argues that multilevel modelling has 'an unclear theoretical and empirical basis', is unnecessarily complex, that it has not produced any important practical research results and that, due to the presence of alternatives, is largely unnecessary, with limited ease of readability possible by different audiences. Nonetheless, multilevel modelling now attracts worldwide interest.

Whereas ordinary regression models do not make allowances, for example, for different schools (Paterson and Goldstein, 1991), multilevel regression can include school differences and, indeed, other variables, for example: socio-economic status (Willms, 1992), single and co-educational schools (Daly, 1996; Daly and Shuttleworth, 1997), location (Garner and Raudenbush, 1991), size of school (Paterson, 1991) and teaching styles (Zuzovsky and Aitken, 1991). Indeed Plewis (1991) indicates how multilevel modelling can be used in longitudinal studies, linking educational progress with curriculum coverage.

The Bristol Centre for Multilevel Modelling (www. cmm.bristol.ac.uk/) produces online courses, introductory materials, workshops and downloads for multilevel modelling, software downloads for conducting multilevel modelling, and full sets of references and papers. Further materials and references can be found at Scientific Software International (www.ssicentral.com/ hlm/references.html#softwarew). See also

http://mlsc.lboro.ac.uk/resources/statistics/Multilevel_
    modelling.pdf
http://statcomp.ats.ucla.edu/mlm/default.htm
http://stat.gamma.rug.nl/multilevel.htm

Straightforward introductions to multilevel modelling are provided by Snijders and Bosker (1999), Bickel (2007), O'Connell and McCoach (2008) and the publications from the Bristol Centre for Multilevel Modelling.

 Companion Website

The companion website to the book includes PowerPoint slides for this chapter, which list the structure of the chapter and then provide a summary of the key points in each of its sections. This resource can be found online at **www.routledge.com/textbooks/cohen7e**.

Additionally readers are recommended to access the online resources for Chapter 36 as these contain materials that apply to the present chapter, such as the SPSS Manual which guides readers through the SPSS commands required to run statistics in SPSS, together with data files of different data sets.

Choosing a statistical test ◀ **CHAPTER 38**

Having set out a battery of statistical tests in the preceding chapters, this chapter provides guidance to the researcher on which tests to use with particular kinds of data and for specific purposes, i.e. to address fitness for purpose. The chapter proceeds thus, indicating different considerations which researchers must bear in mind when selecting the most appropriate tests:

■ how many samples?
■ the types of data used
■ choosing the right statistic
■ assumptions of tests

The chapter provides several tables to guide the researcher in making choices here.

38.1 Introduction

There are very many statistical tests available to the researcher. Which test one employs depends on several factors, for example:

■ the purpose of the analysis (e.g. to describe or explore data, to test a hypothesis, to seek correlations, to identify the effects of one or more independent variables on a dependent variable, to identify differences between two or more groups, to look for underlying groupings of data, to report effect sizes);
■ the kinds of data with which one is working (parametric and non-parametric);
■ the scales of data being used (nominal, ordinal, interval, ratio);
■ the number of groups in the sample;
■ the assumptions in the tests;
■ whether the samples are independent of each other or related to each other.

Researchers wishing to use statistics will need to ask questions such as:

What statistics do I need to answer my research questions?

Are the data parametric or non-parametric?
How many groups are there (e.g. two, three or more)?
Are the groups related or independent?
What kind of test do I need (e.g. a difference test, a correlation, factor analysis, regression)?

We have addressed several of these points in the preceding chapters; those not addressed in previous chapters are addressed here. In this chapter we draw together the threads of the discussion of statistical analysis and address what, for many researchers, can be a nightmare: deciding which statistical tests to use. In the interests of clarity we have decided to use tables and graphic means of presenting the issues in this chapter.

38.2 How many samples?

In addition to the scale of data being used (nominal, ordinal, interval, ratio), the *kind* of statistic that one calculates depends in part on first, whether the samples are related to, or independent of, each other; and second, the number of samples in the test. With regard to the first point, as we have seen in previous chapters, different statistics are sometimes used when groups are related to each other and when they are independent of each other. Groups will be independent when they have no relationship to each other, e.g. in conducting a test to see if there is any difference between the voting of males and females on a particular item, say mathematics performance. The tests that one could use here are, for example: the chi-square test (for nominal data), the Mann-Whitney U test and Kruskal-Wallis (for ordinal data), and the t-test and analysis of variance (ANOVA) for interval and ratio data.

However, there are times when the groups might be related. For example we may wish to measure the performance of the same group at two points in time – before and after a particular intervention – or we may wish to measure the voting of the same group on two different factors, say preference for mathematics and preference for music. Here it is not different groups that are being involved, but the same group on two occasions and the same two on two variables respectively.

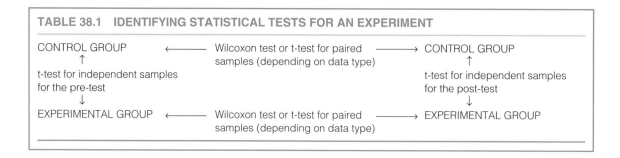

TABLE 38.1 IDENTIFYING STATISTICAL TESTS FOR AN EXPERIMENT

CONTROL GROUP ←—————— Wilcoxon test or t-test for paired —————→ CONTROL GROUP
↑   samples (depending on data type)   ↑
t-test for independent samples   t-test for independent samples
for the pre-test   for the post-test
↓   ↓
EXPERIMENTAL GROUP ←—————— Wilcoxon test or t-test for paired —————→ EXPERIMENTAL GROUP
                                                 samples (depending on data type)

In this case different statistics would have to be used, for example the Wilcoxon test, the Friedman test, the t-test for paired samples, and the sign test. Let us give a frequently used example of an experiment (Table 38.1).

In preceding chapters we have indicated which tests are to be used with independent samples and which are to be used with related samples. With regard to the number of samples in the test, there are statistical tests which are for single samples (one group only, e.g. a single class in school), for two samples (two groups, e.g. males and females in a school) and for more than two samples, e.g.

parents, teachers, students and administrative staff in a school. Tests which can be applied to a *single* group include the binomial test, the chi-square one-sample test and the Kolmogorov-Smirnov one-sample test; tests which can be applied to *two* groups include the chi-square test, Mann-Whitney U test, the t-test, the Spearman and Pearson tests of correlation; tests which can be applied to *three or more* samples include the chi-square test, analysis of variance and the Tukey test. We set out some of these tests in Table 38.2. It is essential to use the correct test for the correct number of groups.

TABLE 38.2 STATISTICAL TESTS TO BE USED WITH DIFFERENT NUMBERS OF GROUPS OF SAMPLES

Scale of data	One sample	Two samples		More than two samples	
		Independent	*Related*	*Independent*	*Related*
Nominal	Binomial	Fisher exact test	McNemar	Chi-square (χ^2) k-samples test	Cochran Q
	Chi-square (χ^2) one-sample test	Chi-square (χ^2) two-samples test			
Ordinal	Kolmogorov-Smirnov one-sample test	Mann-Whitney U test	Wilcoxon matched pairs test	Kruskal-Wallis test	Friedman test
		Kolmogorov-Smirnov test	Sign test	Ordinal regression analysis	
		Wald-Wolfowitz			
		Spearman rho			
		Ordinal regression analysis			
Interval and ratio	t-test	t-test	t-test for paired samples	One-way ANOVA	Repeated measures ANOVA
		Pearson product moment correlation		Two-way ANOVA	
				Tukey hsd test	
				Scheffé test	

38.3 The types of data used

The statistical tests to be used also depend on the scales of data being treated (nominal – ratio) and the tasks which the researcher wishes to perform – the purpose of the analysis (e.g. to discover differences between groups, to look for degrees of association, to measure the effect of one or more independent variables on a dependent variable, etc.). In preceding chapters we have described the different scales of data and the kinds of tests available for different purposes. In respect of these considerations, Table 38.3 summarizes some of the main tests here.

The type of tests used also varies according to whether one is working with parametric or non-parametric data.

38.4 Choosing the right statistic

Figure 38.1 and Table 38.4 draw together and present the kinds of statistical tests available, depending on whether one is using parametric and non-parametric data, together with the purpose of the analysis. Table 38.4 sets out the commonly used statistics for data types and purposes (Siegel, 1956; Cohen and Holliday, 1996; Hopkins *et al*., 1996).

38.5 Assumptions of tests

Statistical tests are based on certain assumptions. It is important to be aware of these assumptions and to operate fairly within them. Some of the more widely used tests have assumptions as illustrated in Table 38.5.

TABLE 38.3   TYPES OF STATISTICAL TESTS FOR FOUR SCALES OF DATA

	Nominal	*Ordinal*	*Interval and ratio*
Measures of association	Tetrachoric correlation	Spearman's rho	Pearson product-moment correlation
	Point biserial correlation	Kendall rank order correlation	
	Phi coefficient	Kendall partial rank correlation	
	Cramer's *V*		
Measures of difference	Chi-square	Mann-Whitney U test	t-test for two independent samples
	McNemar	Kruskal-Wallis	t-test for two related samples
	Cochran Q	Wilcoxon matched pairs	One-way ANOVA
	Binomial test	Friedman two-way analysis of variance	Two-way ANOVA for more
		Wald-Wolfowitz test	Tukey hsd test
		Kolmogorov-Smirnov test	Scheffé test
Measures of linear relationship between independent and dependent variables		Ordinal regression analysis	Linear regression
			Multiple regression
Identifying underlying factors, data reduction			Factor analysis
			Elementary linkage analysis

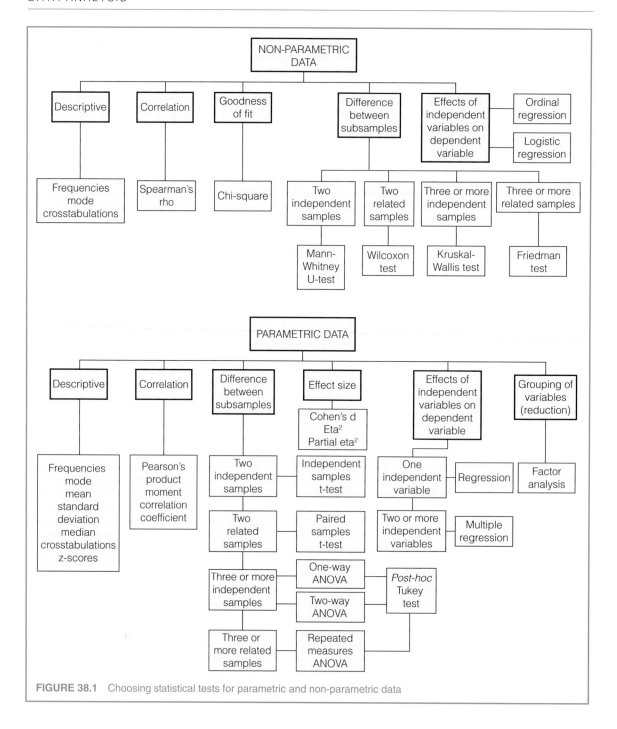

FIGURE 38.1 Choosing statistical tests for parametric and non-parametric data

TABLE 38.4   STATISTICS AVAILABLE FOR DIFFERENT TYPES OF DATA

Data type	Legitimate statistics	Points to observe/questions/examples
Nominal	i Mode (the score achieved by the greatest number of people)	Is there a clear 'front runner' that receives the highest score with low scoring on other categories, or is the modal score only narrowly leading the other categories? Are there two scores which are vying for the highest score – a bi-modal score?
	ii Frequencies	Which are the highest/lowest frequencies? Is the distribution even across categories?
	iii Chi-square (χ^2) (a statistic that charts the difference between statistically expected and actual scores)	Are differences between scores caused by chance/accident or are they statistically significant, i.e. not simply caused by chance?
Ordinal	i Mode	Which score on a rating scale is the most frequent?
	ii Median (the score gained by the middle person in a ranked group of people or, if there is an even number of cases, the score which is midway between the highest score obtained in the lower half of the cases and the lowest score obtained in the higher half of the cases).	What is the score of the middle person in a list of scores?
	iii Frequencies	Do responses tend to cluster around one or two categories of a rating scale? Are the responses skewed towards one end of a rating scale (e.g. 'strongly agree')? Do the responses pattern themselves consistently across the sample? Are the frequencies generally high or generally low (i.e. whether respondents tend to feel strongly about an issue)? Is there a clustering of responses around the central categories of a rating scale (the central tendency, respondents not wishing to appear to be too extreme)?
	iv Chi-square (χ^2)	Are the frequencies of one set of nominal variables (e.g. sex) significantly related to a set of ordinal variables?
	v Spearman rank order correlation (a statistic to measure the degree of association between two ordinal variables)	Do the results from one rating scale correlate with the results from another rating scale? Do the rank order positions for one variable correlate with the rank order positions for another variable?
	vi Mann-Whitney U-test (a statistic to measure any significant difference between two independent samples)	Is there a significant difference in the results of a rating scale for two independent samples (e.g. males and females)?
	vii Kruskal-Wallis analysis of variance (a statistic to measure any significant differences between three or more independent samples)	Is there a significant difference between three or more nominal variables (e.g. membership of political parties) and the results of a rating scale?

continued

Data type	Legitimate statistics		Points to observe/questions/examples
Interval and ratio	i	Mode	What is the average score for this group?
	ii	Mean	
	iii	Frequencies	
	iv	Median	
	v	Chi-square (χ^2)	
	vi	Standard deviation (a measure of the dispersal of scores)	Are the scores on a parametric test evenly distributed? Do scores cluster closely around the mean? Are scores widely spread around the mean? Are scores dispersed evenly? Are one or two extreme scores ('outliers') exerting a disproportionate influence on what are otherwise closely clustered scores?
	vii	z-scores (a statistic to convert scores from different scales, i.e. with different means and standard deviations, to a common scale, i.e. with the same mean and standard deviation, enabling different scores to be compared fairly)	How do the scores obtained by students on a test which was marked out of 20 compare to the scores by the same students on a test which was marked out of 50?
	viii	Pearson product moment correlation (a statistic to measure the degree of association between two interval or ratio variables)	Is there a correlation between one set of interval data (e.g. test scores for one examination) and another set of interval data (e.g. test scores on another examination)?
	ix	t-tests (a statistic to measure the difference between the means of one sample on two separate occasions or between two samples on one occasion)	Are the control and experimental groups matched in their mean scores on a parametric test? Is there a significant difference between the pre-test and post-test scores of a sample group?
	x	Analysis of variance (a statistic to ascertain whether two or more means differ significantly)	Are the differences in the means between test results of three groups statistically significant?
	xi	Regression	What are the predicted scores on one variable if we know the scores on another variable?
	xii	Multiple regression	What are the relative weightings of two or more independent variables on a dependent variable?
	xiii	Factor analysis	What are the underlying, latent factors into which variables can be grouped?
	xiv	Structural equation modelling	What is the causal model of relations between independent variables and factors on a dependent variable?

TABLE 38.5   ASSUMPTIONS OF STATISTICAL TESTS

Test	Assumptions
Mean	Data are normally distributed, with no outliers
Mode	There are few values, and few scores, occurring which have a similar frequency
Median	There are many ordinal values
Chi-square	Data are categorical (nominal); Randomly sampled population; Mutually independent categories; Data are discrete (i.e. no decimal places between data points); 80% of all the cells in a crosstabulation contain five or more cases
Kolmogorov-Smirnov	The underlying distribution is continuous; Data are nominal
t-test and Analysis of Variance	Population is normally distributed; Sample is selected randomly from the population; Each case is independent of the other; The groups to be compared are nominal, and the comparison is made using interval and ratio data; The sets of data to be compared are normally distributed (the bell-shaped Gaussian curve of distribution); The sets of scores have approximately equal variances, or the square of the standard deviation is known; The data are interval or ratio
Wilcoxon Test	The data are ordinal; The samples are related
Mann-Whitney and Kruskal-Wallis	The groups to be compared are nominal, and the comparison is made using ordinal data; The populations from which the samples are drawn have similar distributions; Samples are drawn randomly; Samples are independent of each other
Spearman rank order correlation	The data are ordinal;
Pearson correlation	The data are interval or ratio
Regression (simple and multiple)	The data derive from a random or probability sample; The data are interval or ratio (unless ordinal regression is used); Outliers are removed; There is a linear relationship between the independent and dependent variables; The dependent variable is normally distributed (the bell-shaped Gaussian curve of distribution); The residuals for the dependent variable (the differences between calculated and observed scores) are approximately normally distributed; Collinearity is removed (where one independent variable is an exact or very close correlate of another)
Factor analysis	The data are interval or ratio; The data are normally distributed; Outliers have been removed; The sample size should not be less than 100–150 persons; There should be at least five cases for each variable; The relationships between the variables should be linear; The data must be capable of being factored

The choice of which statistics to employ is not
arbitrary, but dependent on purpose.

 Companion Website

The companion website to the book includes PowerPoint slides for this chapter, which list the structure of the
chapter and then provide a summary of the key points in each of its sections. In addition there is further
information in the form of a short quiz for asking which statistics should be used for certain research questions, and a table of statistics that are permissible for different kinds of data. These resources can be found
online at **www.routledge.com/textbooks/cohen7e**.

Notes

1 The nature of enquiry – setting the field

1 We are not here recommending, nor would we wish to encourage, exclusive dependence on rationally derived and scientifically provable knowledge for the conduct of education – even if this were possible. There is a rich fund of traditional and cultural wisdom in teaching (as in other spheres of life) which we would ignore to our detriment. What we are suggesting, however, is that total dependence on the latter has tended in the past to lead to an impasse; and that for further development and greater understanding to be achieved education must needs resort to the methods of science and research.

2 A classic statement opposing this particular view of science is that of Kuhn, T. S. (1962) *The Structure of Scientific Revolutions*. Chicago, IL: University of Chicago Press. Kuhn's book, acknowledged as an intellectual tour de force, makes the point that science is not the systematic accumulation of knowledge as presented in textbooks; that it is a far less rational exercise than generally imagined. In effect, 'it is a series of peaceful interludes punctuated by intellectually violent revolutions … in each of which one conceptual world view is replaced by another.'

3 For a straightforward overview of the discussions here see Chalmers, A. F. (1999) *What Is this Thing Called Science?* (third edition). Milton Keynes: Open University Press.

4 The formulation of scientific method outlined earlier has come in for strong and sustained criticism. Mishler (1990), for example, describes it as a 'storybook image of science', out of tune with the actual practices of working scientists who turn out to resemble craftpersons rather than logicians. By craftpersons, Mishler is at pains to stress that competence depends upon 'apprenticeship training, continued practice and experienced-based, contextual knowledge of the specific methods applicable to a phenomenon of interest rather than an abstract "logic of discovery" and application of formal "rules"'. The knowledge base of scientific research, Mishler contends, is largely tacit and unexplicated; moreover, scientists learn it through a process of socialization into a 'particular form of life'. The discovery, testing and validation of findings is embedded in cultural and linguistic practices and experimental scientists proceed in pragmatic ways, learning from their errors and failures, adapting procedures to their local contexts, making decisions on the basis of their accumulated experiences. See, for example, Mishler, E. G. (1990) Validation in inquiry-guided research: the role of exemplars in narrative studies. *Harvard Educational Review*, 60 (4), 415–42.

5 See, for example, Rogers, C. R. (1969) *Freedom to Learn*. Columbus, OH: Merrill; and also Rogers, C. R. and Stevens, B. (1967) *Person to Person: The Problem of Being Human*. London: Souvenir Press.

6 Investigating social episodes involves analysing the accounts of what is happening from the points of view of the actors and the participant spectator(s)/investigator(s). This is said to yield three main kinds of interlocking material: images of the self and others, definitions of situations, and rules for the proper development of the action. See Harré, R. (1976) The constructive role of models, in L. Collins (ed.), *The Use of Models in the Social Sciences*. London: Tavistock Publications.

7 Hoyles, C., Küchemann, D., Healy, L. and Yang, M. (2005) Students' developing knowledge in a subject discipline: insights from combining quantitative and qualitative methods. *International Journal of Social Research Methodology*, 8 (3), 225–38. Blatchford, P. (2005) A multi-method approach to the study of school class size differences. *International Journal of Social Research Methodology*, 8 (3), 195–205. Plewis, I. and Mason, P. (2005) What works and why: combining quantitative and qualitative approaches in large-scale evaluations. *International Journal of Social Research Methodology*, 8 (3), 185–94. Suter, L. (2005) Multiple methods: research methods in education projects at NSF. *International Journal of Research and Method in Education*, 28 (2), 171–81. Ivankova *et al.* (2006) Using mixed-methods sequential explanatory design: from theory to practice. *Field Methods*, 18 (3), 3–13. Jang, E. E. *et al.* (2008) Integrative mixed methods data analytic strategies in research on school success in challenging circumstances. *Journal of Mixed Methods Research*, 2 (3), 221–47 (useful for concurrent mixed methods approaches). See also the Special Issues of *International Journal of Social Research Methodology*, 8 (5), 2005, and *Evaluation and Research in Education*, 19 (2), 2006.

3 Evaluation and the politics of educational research

1 Hammersley (2000) identifies several kinds of research, distinguished by whether they are scientific or practical research, theoretical or substantive, contract-based or autonomous, dedicated or democratic, and by their audience and mode of validation.

5 The ethics of educational and social research

1 For example, American Psychological Association (2000); American Sociological Association (1999); British Sociological Association (2002); Social Research Association (2003); the British Educational Research Association (2002); British Psychological Society (2005). Comparable developments may be found in other fields of endeavour.

For an examination of key ethical issues in medicine, business and journalism together with reviews of common ethical themes across these areas, see Serafini, A. (ed.) (1989) *Ethics and Social Concern*, New York: Paragon House. The book also contains an account of principal ethical theories from Socrates to R. M. Hare.

2 US Dept of Health, Education and Welfare, Public Health Service and National Institute of Health (1971) *The Institutional Guide to DHEW Policy on Protecting Human Subjects*. DHEW Publication (NIH): December 2, 72–102.

3 The word 'subjects' is ambiguous: contrasted with 'objects' it could be positive, according equal status and respect to the participants; on the other hand it could be negative in that participants are subjected to the wishes of the researchers ('subject' literally means 'thrown under' or 'thrown below').

4 As regards judging researchers' behaviour, perhaps the only area of educational research where the term ethical absolute can be unequivocally applied and where subsequent judgement is unquestionable is that concerning researchers' relationship with their data. Should they choose to abuse their data for whatever reason, the behaviour is categorically wrong; no place here for moral relativism. For once a clear dichotomy is relevant: if there is such a thing as clearly ethical behaviour, such abuse is clearly unethical. It can take the form of, first, falsifying data to support a preconceived, often favoured, hypothesis; second, manipulating data, often statistically, for the same reason (or manipulating techniques used – deliberately including leading questions, for example); third, using data selectively, that is, ignoring or excluding the bits that don't fit one's hypothesis; and fourth, going beyond the data, in other words, arriving at conclusions not warranted by them (or over-interpreting them). But even malpractice as serious as these examples cannot be controlled by fiat: ethical injunctions would hardly be appropriate in this context, let alone enforceable. The only answer (in the absence of professional monitoring) is for the researcher to have a moral code that is 'rationally derived and intelligently applied', to use the words of the philosopher, R. S. Peters, and to be guided by it consistently. Moral competence, like other competencies, can be learned. One way of acquiring it is to bring interrogative reflection to bear on one's own code and practice, e.g. did I provide suitable feedback, in the right amounts, to the right audiences, at the right time? In sum, ethical behaviour depends on the concurrence of ethical thinking which in turn is based on fundamentally thought-out principles. Readers wishing to take the subject of data abuse further should read Peter Medawar's (1991) elegant and amusing essay, 'Scientific fraud', in D. Pike (ed.) *The Threat and the Glory: Reflections on Science and Scientists*. Oxford: Oxford University Press; and also Broad, W. and Wade, N. (1983) *Betrayers of Truth: Fraud and Deceit in the Halls of Science*. New York: Century.

9 Sensitive educational research

1 See also Walford (2001: 38) in his discussion of gaining access to public schools in the UK, where an early question that was put to him was 'are you one of us?'.

2 Walford (2001: 69) comments on the very negative attitudes of teachers to research on independent schools in the UK, the teachers feeling that researchers had been dishonest and had tricked them, looking only for salacious, sensational and negative data on the school (e.g. on bullying, drinking, drugs, gambling and homosexuality).

13 Surveys, longitudinal, cross-sectional and trend studies

1 There are several examples of surveys, including: Borg, M. G. (1998) Secondary school teachers' perceptions of pupils' undesirable behaviours. *British Journal of Educational Psychology*, 68, 67–79; Boulton, M. J. (1997) Teachers' views on bullying: definitions, attitudes and abilities to cope. *British Journal of Educational Psychology*. 67 (2), 223–33; Cline, T. and Ertubney, C. (1997) The impact of gender on primary teachers' evaluations of children's difficulties in school. *British Journal of Educational Psychology*, 67, 447–56; Dosanjh, J. S. and Ghuman, P. A. S. (1997) Asian parents and English education – 20 years on: a study of two generations. *Educational Studies*, 23 (3), 459–72; Foskett, N. H. and Hesketh, A. J. (1997) Constructing choice in continuous and parallel markets: institutional and school leavers' responses to the new post-16 marketplace. *Oxford Review of Education*, 23 (3), 299–319; Gallagher, T., McEwen, A. and Knip, D. (1997) Science education policy: a survey of the participation of sixth-form pupils in science and the subjects over a 10-year period, 1985–95. *Research Papers in Education*, 12 (2), 121–42; Hall, K. and Nuttall, W. (1999) The *relative* importance of class size to infant teachers in England. *British Educational Research Journal*, 25 (2), 245–58; Jules, V. and Kutnick, P. (1997) Student perceptions of a good teacher: the gender perspective. *British Journal of Educational Psychology*, 67 (4), 497–511; Millan, R., Gallagher, M. and Ellis, R. (1993) Surveying adolescent worries: development of the 'Things I Worry About' scale. *Pastoral Care in Education*, 11 (1), 43–57; Papasolomoutos, C. and Christie, T. (1998) Using national surveys: a review of secondary analyses with special reference to schools. *Educational Research*, 40 (3), 295–310; Rigby, K. (1999) Peer victimisation at school and the health of secondary school students. *British Journal of Educational Psychology*, 69 (1), 95–104; Strand, S. (1999) Ethnic group, sex and economic disadvantage: associations with pupils' educational progress from Baseline to the end of Key Stage 1. *British Educational Research Journal*, 25 (2), 179–202; Tatar, M. (1998) Teachers as significant others: gender differences in secondary school pupils' perceptions. *British Journal of Educational Psychology*, 68 (2), 255–68; Terry, A. A. (1998) Teachers as targets of bullying by their pupils: a study to investigate incidence. *British Journal of Educational Psychology*, 68 (2), 255–68.

Examples of different kinds of survey studies are as follows: (a) Francis's (1992) 'true cohort' study of patterns of reading development, following a group of 54 young children for two years at six monthly intervals; (b) Blatchford's 1992 cohort/cross-sectional study of 133–75 children (two samples) and their attitudes to work at 11 years of age; (c) a large-scale/cross-sectional study by Munn, Johnstone and Holligan (1990) into pupils' perceptions of effective disciplinarians, with a sample size of 543; (d) a trend/prediction study of school building requirements by a government department (Department of Education and Science, 1977), identifying building and improvement needs based on estimated pupil populations from births during the decade 1976–86; (e) a survey study by Belson (1975) of 1,425 teenage boys' theft behaviour; (f) a survey by Hannan and Newby (1992) of 787 student teachers (with a 46 per cent response rate) and their views on government proposals to increase the amount of time spent in schools during the training period.

2 Examples of longitudinal and cross-sectional studies include: Busato, V. V., Prins, F. J., Elshant, J. J. and Hamaker, C. (1998) Learning styles: a cross-sectional and longitudinal study in higher education. *British Journal of Educational Psychology*, 68 (3), 427–41; Davenport, E. C. Jr., Davison, M. L., Kuang, H., Ding, S., Kin, S.-K. and Kwak, N. (1998) High school mathematics course-taking by gender and ethnicity. *American Educational Research Journal*, 35 (3), 497–514; Davies, J. and Brember, I. (1997) Monitoring reading standards in year 6: a 7-year cross-sectional study. *British Educational Research Journal*, 23 (5), 615–22; Davies, J. and Brember, I. (1998) Standards in reading at key stage 1 – a cross-sectional study. *Educational Research*, 40 (2), 153–60; Galton, M., Hargreaves, L., Comber, C., Wall, D. and Pell, T. (1999) Changes in patterns in teacher interaction in primary classrooms, 1976–1996. *British Educational Research Journal*, 25 (1), 23–37; Marsh, H. W. and Yeung, A. S. (1998) Longitudinal structural equation models of academic self-concept and achievement: gender differences in the development of math and English constructs. *American Educational Research Journal*, 35 (4), 705–38; Noack, P. (1998) School achievement and adolescents' interactions with the fathers, mothers, and friends. *European Journal of Psychology of Education*, 13 (4), 503–13; Preisler, G. M. and Ahström, M. (1997) Sign language for hard of hearing children – a hindrance or a benefit for their development? *European Journal of Psychology of Education*, 12 (4), 465–77.

14 Case studies

1 For further examples of case studies see: Bates, I. and Dutson, J. (1995) A Bermuda triangle? A case study of the disappearance of competence-based vocational training policy in the context of practice. *British Journal of Education and Work*, 8 (2), 41–59; Jacklin, A. and Lacey, C. (1997) Gender integration in the infant classroom: a case study. *British Educational Research Journal*, 23 (5), 623–40; Woods, P. (1993) Managing marginality: teacher development through grounded life history. *British Educational Research Journal*, 19 (5), 447–88.

16 Experiments, quasi-experiments, single-case research and internet-based experiments

1 Questions have been raised about the authenticity of both definitions and explanations of the Hawthorne effect. See Diaper, G. (1990) The Hawthorne Effect: a fresh examination. *Educational Studies*, 16 (3), 261–7.

2 Examples of experimental research can be seen in: Alfassi, M. (1998) Reading for meaning: the efficacy of reciprocal teaching in fostering reading comprehension in high school

students in remedial reading classes. *American Educational Research Journal*, 35 (2), 309–22; Bijstra, J. O. and Jackson, S. (1998) Social skills training with early adolescents: effects on social skills, well-being, self-esteem and coping. *European Journal of Psychology of Education*, 13 (4), 569–83; Bryant, P., Devine, M., Ledward, A. and Nunes, T. (1997) Spelling with apostrophes and understanding possession. *British Journal of Educational Psychology*, 67 (1), 91–110; Cline, T., Proto, A., Raval, P. D. and Paolo, T. (1998) The effects of brief exposure and of classroom teaching on attitudes children express towards facial disfigurement in peers. *Educational Research*, 40 (1), 55–68; Didierjean, A. and Cauzinille-Marmèche, E. (1998) Reasoning by analogy: is it schema-mediated or case-based? *European Journal of Psychology of Education*, 13 (3), 385–98; Dugard, P. and Todman, J. (1995) Analysis of pre-test and post-test control group designs in educational research. *Educational Psychology*, 15 (2), 181–98; Hall, E., Hall, C. and Abaci, R. (1997) The effects of human relations training on reported teacher stress, pupil control ideology and locus of control. *British Journal of Educational Psychology*, 67 (4), 483–96; Littleton, K., Ashman, H., Light, P., Artis, J., Roberts, T. and Oosterwegel, A. (1999) Gender, task contexts, and children's performance on a computer-based task. *European Journal of Psychology of Education*, 14 (1), 129–39; Marcinkiewicz, H. R. and Clariana, R. B. (1997) The performance effects of headings within multi-choice tests. *British Journal of Educational Psychology*, 67 (1), 111–17; Overett, S. and Donald, D. (1998) Paired reading: effects of a parental involvement programme in a disadvantaged community in South Africa. *British Journal of Educational Psychology*, 68 (3), 347–56; Sainsbury, M., Whetton, C., Mason, K. and Schagen, I. (1998) Fallback in attainment on transfer at age 11: evidence from the summer literacy schools evaluation. *Educational Research*, 40 (1), 73–81; Tones, K. (1997) Beyond the randomized controlled trial: a case for 'judicial review'. *Health Education Research*, 12 (2), i–iv; Brooks, G., Burton, M., Miles, J., Torgerson, C. and Torgerson, D. (2008) Randomised controlled trial of incentives to improve attendance at adult literacy classes. *Oxford Review of Education*, 34 (5), 493–504.

3 For a detailed discussion of the practical issues in educational experimentation, see Evans (1978, chapter 4), Riecken and Boruch (1974), and Bennett and Lumsdaine (1975).

17 Meta-analysis, research syntheses and systematic reviews

1 An example of meta-analysis in educational research can be seen in Severiens, S. and ten Dam, G. (1998) A multi-level meta-analysis of gender differences in learning orientations. *British Journal of Educational Psychology*, 68 (4), 595–618. The use of meta-analysis is widespread, indeed the Cochrane Collaboration is a pioneer in this field, focusing on meta-analyses of randomized controlled trials, see Maynard and Chalmers, 1997.

19 Virtual worlds in educational research

1 The term virtual world, as used here, presumes the presence of human users, although strictly speaking even when empty of participants such an environment may remain a

virtual world. Part of the reason for the ongoing debate about what is and what is not a virtual world and whether these things should be given a different name, is that the use of virtual world features is becoming more common in the technologies of the World Wide Web, in which one increasingly sees visually realistic three-dimensional virtual environments on websites, discussion forums, blogs, chatrooms and social network sites where user involvement is mediated by avatars.

2 For further information on complexity theory and simulations we suggest that readers visit websites such as: www.santafe.edu (the website of the Santa Fe Institute – a major institute for the study of complexity theory); www.brint.com/Systems.htm (a website that provides an index of material on complexity theory); www.complexity-society.com (The Complexity Society of the UK); http://emergence.org/ (website of the journal: *Emergence: Complexity and Organization*); http://journal-ci.csse.monash.edu.au// (the website of the journal: *Complexity International*); www.udel.edu/aeracc/sites.html (links to websites on complexity theory); www.answers.com/complex%20 systems%20theory (links to websites on complexity theory).

3 Agent-based models can be traced back to notions of a device able to reproduce itself proposed by the mathematicians von Neumann and Ulam. One of the earliest studies to use the word 'agent' within self-replicating systems appears in Artificial Adaptive Agents in Economic Theory (Holland and Miller, 1991). Kauffman's book *The Origins of Order: Self-Organization and Selection in Evolution* (1993) invokes automatic self-replication and agent-based models to propose that a complex biological system may emerge inevitably from self-organization.

4 For more on Reynolds's work and useful links to related sites see: www.red3d.com/cwr/boids/.

5 See note 3 above.

6 These features are often provided within the software. See http://wiki.secondlife.com/wiki/Video_Tutorial/Record_voice_chat_and_sounds for guidance on how to record sound or live talk in Second Life, or http://wiki.secondlife.com/wiki/Recording_Video for information on how to video activity. These links also provide advice on ethical and legal implications.

7 The Hawthorne effect: www.newworldencyclopedia.org/entry/Elton_Mayo.

8 Internal validity: the extent to which the treatment, programme or experiment made a difference, i.e. in our example, did their experiences within the virtual world make any difference to what young people think it should mean to be a citizen.

9 External validity: the extent to which the results from one study or experiment can be applied (generalized) to other people or settings.

10 Gapminder: www.gapminder.org/; Google docs: http://docs.google.com; Dropbox https://www.dropbox.com.

11 Virtual Worlds: Club Penguin: www.clubpenguin.com/; Everquest: http://everquest.station.sony.com/; Habbo Hotel: www.habbo.co.uk/; Lineage: www.lineage.com/; Runescape: www.runescape.com/a=135/; Second Life: http://secondlife.com/?v=1.1; Second Life Community Standards: http://secondlife.com/corporate/cs.php; Second

Life for educators: http://secondlifegrid.net/slfe/education-use-virtual-world; World of Warcraft: www.worldofwarcraft.com/index.xml.

12 Comparisons of technical affordances of several virtual worlds: www.meta-mole.com.

13 See: www.futurelab.org.uk/projects/harnessing-technology.

14 Methodologies: ethnographic research: www.geo.mtu.edu/rs4hazards/links/Social-KateG/Ethnographic%20Methodology.htm; methodologies (general): http://onlineqda.hud.ac.uk/methodologies.php; phenomenology: http://onlineqda.hud.ac.uk/resources.php#Phenomenology; qualitative research: (*Forum*) www.qualitative-research.net/index.php/fqs/issue/archive; ethical standards for online research: www.bera.ac.uk/files/guidelines/ethica1.pdf; technology-enhanced research: www.bera.ac.uk/technology-enhanced-research-educational-ict-systems-as-research-instruments/.

15 Data capture from virtual worlds: *TAMSAnalyzer* (transcription and coding of audio/video – Mac only): www.apple.com/downloads/macosx/productivity_tools/tamsanalyzer.html; *Transana* (transcription and coding of audio/video – Mac and PC): www.transana.org/; *FRAPS* screen capture (PC): www.fraps.com/l; *Capture Me* (screen capture – Mac): http://capture-me.en.softonic.com/mac; *Camtasia* (screen capture): www.techsmith.com/download/camtasiatrial.asp (PC); www.techsmith.com/camtasiamac/ (Mac); *Bristol Online Survey*: www.survey.bris.ac.uk/; *Survey Gizmo*: www.surveygizmo.com; *Survey Monkey*: www.surveymonkey.com; *Zoomerang*: www.zoomerang.com/. Useful sites for finding similar technologies include: *Centre for Learning and Performance Technologies*: www.c4lpt.co.uk/Directory/ and *Wild Apricot* (a blog listing useful online survey instruments): www.wildapricot.com/blogs/newsblog/archive/2007/09/06/looking-for-a-good-cheap-web-polling-service.aspx. A brief introduction to using such tools can be found at: www.greatbrook.com/online_survey_tools.htm and an extensive list of many of these with web links to their home sites is given at: www.greatbrook.com/survey_software_list.htm.

16 See note 10 above.

17 See Second Life's https://www.xstreets1.com for passive tracking systems for avatar activity, e.g. www.mayarealities.com/ or https://www.xstreetsl.com/modules.php?ItemID=120285andfile=itemandname=Marketplace as well as for links to real-world interviews, simulations, journals and experiments.

20 Questionnaires

1 This is the approach used in Belbin's (1981) celebrated work on the types of personalities in a management team.

21 Interviews

1 Examples of interviews in educational research include: Carroll, S. and Walford, G. (1997) Parents' responses to the school quasi-market. *Research Papers in Education*, 12 (1), 3–26; Cicognani, C. (1998) Parents' educational styles and adolescent autonomy. *European Journal of Psychology of Education*, 13 (4), 485–502; Cullen, K. (1997) Headteacher appraisal: a view from the inside. *Research Papers in Education*, 12 (2), 177–204; Ferris, J. and Gerber, R. (1996) Mature-age students' feelings of enjoying learning in a further education context. *European*

Journal of Psychology of Education, 11 (1), 79–96; Robinson, P. and Smithers, A. (1999) Should the sexes be separated for secondary education – comparisons of single-sex and co-educational schools? *Research Papers in Education*, 14 (1), 23–49; Van Etten, S., Pressley, M., Freebern, G. and Echevarria, M. (1998) An interview study of college freshmen's beliefs about their academic motivation. *European Journal of Psychology of Education*, 13 (1), 105–30.

22 Accounts

1 For an example of concept mapping in educational research see: Lawless, L., Smee, P. and O'Shea, T. (1998) Using concept sorting and concept mapping in business and public administration, and education: an overview. *Educational Research*, 40 (2), 219–35.

2 For further examples of discourse analysis see: Butzkamm, W. (1998) Code-switching in a bilingual history lesson: the mother tongue as a conversational lubricant. *Bilingual Education and Bilingualism*, 1 (2), 81–99; Mercer, N., Wegerif, R. and Dawes, L. (1999) Children's talk and the development of reasoning in the classroom. *British Educational Research Journal*, 25 (1), 95–111; Ramsden, C. and Reason, D. (1997) Conversation – discourse analysis in library and information services. *Education for Information*, 15 (4), 283–95.

3 Cohen, L. (1993) *Racism Awareness Materials in Initial Teacher Training*. Report to the Leverhulme Trust, 11–19, New Fetter Lane, London, EC4A 1NR. The video scenarios are part of an enquiry into pupils' perceptions of the behaviour of white teachers towards minority pupils in school. See Naylor, P. (1995) Adolescents' perceptions of teacher racism. Unpublished Ph.D. dissertation, Loughborough University of Technology.

23 Observation

1 For an example of time sampling see: Childs, G. (1997) A concurrent validity study of teachers' ratings for nominated 'problem' children. *British Journal of Educational Psychology*, 67, 457–74.

2 For an example of critical incidents see: Tripp, D. (1994) Teachers' lives, critical incidents and professional practice. *International Journal of Qualitative Studies in Education*, 7 (1), 65–72.

25 Personal constructs

1 For examples of repertory grid studies in education, see Cole, A. L. (1991) Personal theories of teaching: development in the formative years. *Alberta Journal of Educational Research*, 37 (2), 119–32; Corporal, A. H. (1991) Repertory grid research into cognitions of prospective primary school teachers. *Teaching and Teacher Education*, 36, 315–29; Lehrer, R. and Franke, M. L. (1992) Applying personal construct psychology to the study of teachers' knowledge of fractions. *Journal for Research in Mathematical Education*, 23 (3), 223–41; Shapiro, B. L. (1990) A collaborative approach to help novice science teachers reflect on changes in their construction of the role of the science teacher. *Alberta Journal of Educational Research*, 36 (3), 203–22; Shaw, E. L. (1992) The influence of methods instruction on the beliefs of preservice elementary and secondary science teachers: preliminary

comparative analyses. *School Science and Mathematics*, 92 (1), 14–22; Morris, P. (1983) Teachers' perceptions of their pupils: a Hong Kong case study. *Research in Education*, 29, 81–6; Derry, S. J. and Potts, M. K. (1998) How tutors model students: a study of personal constructs in adaptive tutoring. *American Educational Research Journal*, 35 (1), 65–99; McLoughlin, T. (2002) The use of repertory grid analysis in studying students' conceptual frameworks in science. Paper presented at the European Conference on Educational Research. University of Lisbon, 11–14 September.

36 Inferential statistics

1 Muijs (2004) indicates that, in SPSS, one can find multicollinearity by looking at 'collinearity diagnostics' in the 'Statistics' command box, and in the collinearity statistics one should look at the 'Tolerance' column on the output. He indicates that values will vary from 0 to 1, and the higher the value the less is the collinearity, whereas a value close to 0 indicates that nearly all the variance in the variable is explained by the other variables in the model.

37 Multidimensional measurement and factor analysis

1 Andrews, P. and Hatch, G. (1999) A new look at secondary teachers' conception of mathematics and its teaching. *British Educational Research Journal*, 25 (2), 203–23; McEneaney, J. E. and Sheridan, E. M. (1996) A survey-based component for programme assessment in undergraduate pre-service teacher education. *Research in Education*, 55, 49–61; Prosser, M. and Trigwell, K. (1997) Relations between perceptions of the teaching environment and approaches to teaching. *British Journal of Educational Psychology*, 67 (1), 25–35; Valadines, N. (1999) Formal reasoning performance of higher secondary school students: theoretical and educational implications. *European Journal of Psychology of Education*, 14 (1), 109–17; Vermunt, J. D. (1998) The regulation of constructive learning processes. *British Journal of Educational Psychology*, 68 (2), 149–71.

2 Examples of multilevel modelling in educational research can be seen in: Bell, J. F. (1996) Question choice in English literature examination. *Oxford Review of Education*, 23 (4), 447–58; Croxford, L. (1997) Participation in science subjects: the effect of the Scottish curriculum framework. *Research Papers in Education*, 12 (1), 69–89; Fitz-Gibbon, C. T. (1991) Multilevel modelling in an indicator system. In S. W. Raudenbush and J. D. Willms (eds) *Schools, Classrooms and Pupils. International Studies of Schooling from a Multilevel Perspective*. San Diego, CA: Academic Press; Hill, P. W. and Rowe, K. J. (1996) Multilevel modelling in school effectiveness research. *School Effectiveness and School Improvement*, 7 (1), 1–34; Kivulu, J. M. and Rogers, W. T. (1998) A multilevel analysis of cultural experience and gender influences on causal attributions to perceived performance in mathematics. *British Journal of Educational Psychology*, 68 (1), 25–37; McNiece, R. and Jolliffe, F. (1998) An investigation into regional differences in educational performance in the National Child Development Study. *Educational Research*, 40 (1), 13–30; Mooij, T. (1998) Pupil-class determinants of aggressive and victim behaviour in pupils.

Bibliography

AACU (Association of American Colleges and Universities) (2002) *Greater Expectations: A New Vision for Learning as a Nation Goes to College.* Washington, DC: Association of American Colleges and Universities.

Acker, S. (1989) *Teachers, Gender and Careers.* Lewes: Falmer.

Acker, S. (1990) Teachers' culture in an English primary school: continuity and change. *British Journal of Sociology of Education*, 11 (3), 257–73.

Acton, H. B. (1975) Positivism. In J. O. Urmson (ed.) *The Concise Encyclopedia of Western Philosophy.* London: Hutchinson, 253–6.

Adams-Webber, J. R. (1970) Elicited versus provided constructs in repertory grid technique: a review. *British Journal of Medical Psychology*, 43, 349–54.

Adelman, C., Kemmis, S. and Jenkins, D. (1980) Rethinking case study: notes from the Second Cambridge Conference. In H. Simons (ed.) *Towards a Science of the Singular.* Centre for Applied Research in Education, University of East Anglia, Norwich, UK, 45–61.

Adeyemi, M. B. (1992) The effects of a social studies course on the philosophical orientations of history and geography graduate students in Botswana. *Educational Studies*, 18 (2), 235–44.

Adler, P. A. and Adler, P. (1994) Observational techniques. In N. K. Denzin and Y. S. Lincoln (eds) *Handbook of Qualitative Research.* London: Sage, 377–92.

Agar, M. (1993) Speaking of ethnography. Cited in D. Silverman, *Interpreting Qualitative Data.* London: Sage, 520–30.

Aiken, L. R. (2003) *Psychological Testing and Assessment* (eleventh edition). Boston, MA: Pearson Education.

Airasian, P. W. (2001) *Classroom Assessment: Concepts and Applications* (fourth edition). New York: McGraw-Hill.

Aitkin, M., Bennett, N. and Hesketh, J. (1981) Teaching styles and pupil progress: a re-analysis. *British Journal Educational Psychology*, 51 (2), 170–86.

Alban-Metcalf, R. J. (1997) Repertory grid technique. In J. P. Keeves (ed.) *Educational Research, Methodology and Measurement: An International Handbook* (second edition). Oxford: Elsevier Science, 315–18.

Aldrich, R. (2003) The three duties of the historian of education. *History of Education*, 32 (2), 133–43.

Aldridge, A. and Levine, K. (2001) *Surveying the Social World: Principles and Practice in Survey Research.* Buckingham: Open University Press.

Aldridge, J. M. and Fraser, B. J. (2000) A cross-cultural study of classroom learning environments in Australia and Taiwan. *Learning Environments Research*, 3 (2), 101–34.

Aldridge, J. M., Fraser, B. J. and Huang, T.-C. I. (1999) Investigating classroom environments in Taiwan and Australia with multiple research methods. *Journal of Educational Research*, 93 (1), 48–62.

Alexander, P. C. and Neimeyer, G. J. (1989) Constructivism and family therapy. *International Journal of Personal Construct Psychology*, 2 (2), 111–21.

Alexander, R. J. (2000) *Culture and Pedagogy: International Comparisons in Primary Education.* Oxford: Basil Blackwell.

Alfassi, M. (1998) Reading for meaning: the efficacy of reciprocal teaching in fostering reading comprehension in high school students in remedial reading classes. *American Educational Research Journal*, 35 (2), 309–22.

Alkin, M. C., Daillak, R. and White, P. (1991) Does evaluation make a difference? In D. S. Anderson and B. J. Biddle (eds) *Knowledge for Policy: Improving Education Through Research.* London: Falmer, 268–75.

Allison, P. D. (1984) Event history analysis: regression for longitudinal event data. *Sage University Papers: Quantitative Applications in the Social Sciences.* No. 46. Beverly Hills: Sage.

Allison, P. D. (2001) *Missing Data.* Thousand Oaks, CA: Sage.

Altricher, H. and Gstettner, P. (1993) Action research: a closed chapter in the history of German social science? *Educational Action Research*, 1 (3), 329–60.

Åm, O. (1994) *Back to Basics. Introduction to Systems Theory and Complexity.* Retrieved 10 June 2000, from www.stud.his.no/~onar/Ess/Back-to-Basics.html.

American Educational Research Association (2000) *Ethical Standards of the American Educational Research Association 2000.* Washington, DC: American Educational Research Association. Retrieved 17 April 2010, from www.aera.net/uploadedFiles/About_AERA/Ethical_Standards/Ethical-Standards.pdf.

American Psychological Association (1973) *Ethical Principles in the Conduct of Research with Human Subjects.* Washington, DC: Ad hoc Committee on Ethical Standards in Psychological Research.

American Psychological Association (1994) *Publication Manual of the American Psychological Association* (fourth edition). Washington, DC: B. Thompson.

American Psychological Association (1999) *Standards for Educational and Psychological Testing.* Retrieved 15 May 2005, from www.apa.org/science/standards/html.

American Psychological Association (2002) *Ethical Principles and Code of Conduct.* Retrieved 15 May 2005, from www.apa.org/ethics/code2002.html.

American Sociological Association (1999) *Code of Ethics and*

Policies and Procedures of the ASA Committee on Professional Ethics. Retrieved 15 May 2005, from www.asanet. org/members/ecoderev.html.

Anderson, D. S. and Biddle, B. J. (eds) (1991) *Knowledge for Policy: Improving Education through Research*. London: Falmer.

Anderson, G. and Arsenault, N. (1998) *Fundamentals of Educational Research* (second edition). London: RoutledgeFalmer.

Andrew, A. (1985) In pursuit of the past: some problems in the collection, analysis and use of historical documentary evidence. In R. Burgess (ed.) *Strategies of Educational Research*. London: Falmer, 153–78.

Andrews, P. and Hatch, G. (1999) A new look at secondary teachers' conception of mathematics and its teaching. *British Educational Research Journal*, 25 (2), 203–23.

Anfara, V. A., Brown, K. M. and Mangione, T. L. (2002) Qualitative analysis on stage: making the research process more public. *Educational Researcher*, 31 (7), 28–38. Retrieved 29 October 2005, from http://35.8.171.42/aera/ pubs/er/pdf/vol. 31_07/AERA310706.pdf.

Angoff, W. H. (1971) Scales, norms, and equivalent scores. In R. L. Thorndike (ed.) *Educational Measurement* (second edition). Washington, DC: American Council on Education, 508–600.

Antonsen, E.A. (1988) Treatment of a boy of twelve: help with handwriting, play therapy and discussion of problems. *Journal of Education Therapy*, 2 (1), 2–32.

Apple, M. (1990) *Ideology and Curriculum* (second edition). London: Routledge and Kegan Paul.

Applebee, A. N. (1976) The development of children's responses to repertory grids. *British Journal of Social and Clinical Psychology*, 15, 101–2.

Arditti, J. A. (2002) Doing family research at the jail: reflections of a prison widow. *The Qualitative Report*, 7 (4). Retrieved 21 November 2003, from www.nova.edu/ssss/ QR/QR7–4/arditti.html.

Argyle, M. (1978) Discussion chapter: an appraisal of the new approach to the study of social behaviour. In M. Brenner, P. Marsh and M. Brenner (eds) *The Social Contexts of Method*. London: Croom Helm, 237–55.

Argyris, C. (1958) Review of supervisory and executive development. A manual for role playing. *Management Science*, 4 (3), 321–2.

Argyris, C. (1990) *Overcoming Organisational Defenses – Facilitating Organisational Learning*. Boston, MA: Allyn and Bacon.

Arksey, H. and Knight, P. (1999) *Interviewing for Social Scientists*. London: Sage.

Arnold, P. and Atkins, J. (1991) The social and emotional adjustment of hearing-impaired children integrated in primary schools. *Educational Researcher*, 33 (3), 223–8.

Arnold, R. (1998) The drama in research and articulating dynamics. In J. Saxton and C. Miller (eds) *The Research of Practice. The Practice of Research*. Victoria, BC: International Drama in Education Research Institute, 110–31.

Arnon, S. and Reichel, N. (2009) Closed and open questions tools in a telephone survey about 'the good teacher'. *Journal of Mixed Methods Research*, 3 (2), 172–96.

Aronowitz, S. and Giroux, H. (1986) *Education Under Siege*. London: Routledge and Kegan Paul.

Aronson, E. and Carlsmith, J. M. (1969) Experimentation in social psychology. In G. Lindzey and E. Aronson (eds) *The Handbook of Social Psychology, Volume 2*. Reading, MA: Addison-Wesley, 1–79.

Aronson, E., Ellsworth, P. C., Carlsmith, J. M. and Gonzalez, M. H. (1990) *Methods of Research in Social Psychology*. New York: McGraw-Hill.

Arsenault, N. and Anderson, G. (1998) Qualitative research. In G. Anderson and N. Arsenault, *Fundamentals of Educational Research* (second edition). London: Routledge-Falmer, 119–35.

Ary, D., Jacobs, L. C. and Razavieh, A. (1972) *Introduction to Research in Education*. New York: Holt, Rinehart and Winston.

Ary, D., Jacobs, L. C., Razavieh, A. and Sorensen, C. (2006) *Introduction to Research in Education* (seventh edition). Belmont, CA: Wadsworth.

Ary, D., Jacobs, L. C., Sorensen, C. and Razavieh, A. (2009) *Introduction to Research in Education* (eighth edition). Belmont, CA: Wadsworth.

Ashmore, M. (1989) *The Reflexive Thesis*. Chicago, IL: University of Chicago Press.

Atkinson, J. M. and Heritage, J. (1999) Transcript notation: structures of social action: studies in conversation analysis. *Aphasiology*, 13 (4), 243–9.

Atkinson, R. (1998) *The Life Interview*. London: Sage.

Aubusson, P., Fogwill, S., Barr, R. and Perkovic, L. (1997) What happens when students do simulation-role-play in science? *Research in Science Education*, 27 (4), 565–79.

Auerbach, C. F. and Silverstein, L. B. (2003). *Qualitative Data: An Introduction to Coding and Analysis*. New York: New York University Press.

Austin, J. L. (1962) *How to Do Things with Words*. Oxford: Oxford University Press.

Axelrod, R. (1997) *The Complexity of Co-operation: Agent-Based Models of Competition and Collaboration*. Princeton, NJ: Princeton University Press.

Axline, V. (1964) *Dibs in Search of Self*. New York: Ballantine.

Ayres, I. (2008) *Super Crunchers*. London: John Murray.

Babbie, E. R. (2010) *The Practice of Social Research* (eleventh edition). New York: Thompson.

Babha, H. (1994) *The Location of Culture*. London: Routledge.

Bailey, K. D. (1994) *Methods of Social Research* (fourth edition). New York: The Free Press.

Bailey, K. D. (2007) *Methods of Social Research* (fifth edition). New York: The Free Press.

Bak, P. (1996) *How Nature Works*. New York: Copernicus.

Baker, T. L. (1994) *Doing Social Research* (second edition). New York: McGraw-Hill.

Ball, S. J. (1990) *Politics and Policy Making in Education*. London: Routledge.

Ball, S. J. (1994a) *Education Reform: A Critical and Post-Structuralist Approach*. Buckingham: Open University Press.

Ball, S. J. (1994b) Political interviews and the politics of interviewing. In G. Walford (ed.) *Researching the Powerful in Education*. London: UCL Press, 96–115.

Bampton, R. and Cowton, C. J. (2002). The e-interview. *Forum Qualitative Sozialforschung/Forum: Qualitative*

Social Research, 3 (2), 1–12. Article 4. Retrieved 28 March 2010, from http://nbnresolving.de/urn:nbn:de:0114-fqs02 0295.

Banham, M. (ed.) (1995) *The Cambridge Guide to Theatre* (second edition). Cambridge: Cambridge University Press.

Banks, M. (1995) Visual research methods. *Social Research Update*, 11, 1–6. Retrieved 10 May 2010, from http://sru. soc.surrey.ac.uk/sru11/sru11.html.

Banks, M. (2007) *Using Visual Data in Qualitative Research*. London: Sage.

Bannister, D. (ed.) (1970) *Perspectives in Personal Construct Theory*. London: Academic Press.

Bannister, D. and Mair, J. M. M. (1968) *The Evaluation of Personal Constructs*. London: Academic Press.

Banuazizi, A. and Movahedi, A. (1975) Interpersonal dynamics in a simulated prison: a methodological analysis. *American Psychologist*, 30, 152–60.

Banville, D., Desrosiers, P. and Genet-Volet, Y. (2000) Translating questionnaires and inventories using a cross-cultural translation technique. *Journal of Teaching in Physical Education*, 19 (3), 374–97.

Barabási, A. L. (2002) *Linked: The New Science of Networks*. Cambridge, MA: Perseus Publishing.

Bargh, J. A., McKenna, K. Y. A. and Fitzsimons, G. M. (2002) Can you see the real me? Activation and expression of the 'true self' on the internet. *Journal of Social Issues*, 58 (1), 33–48.

Barker, C. D. and Johnson, G. (1998) Interview talk as professional practice. *Language and Education*, 12 (4), 229–42.

Barr Greenfield, T. (1975) Theory about organisations: a new perspective and its implications for schools. In M. G. Hughes (ed.) *Administering Education: International Challenge*. London: Athlone Press, 71–99.

Barratt, P. E. H. (1971) *Bases of Psychological Methods*. Sydney: J. Wiley and Sons Australasia.

Barron, K. (1999) Ethics in qualitative social research on marginalized groups. *Scandinavian Journal of Disability Research*, 1 (1), 38–49.

Barthes, R. (1972) *Critical Essays*. Evanston, IL: Northwestern University Press.

Bartlett, J. E II, Kotrlik, J. W. and Higgins, C. C. (2001) Organizational research: determining appropriate sample size in survey research. *Information Technology, Learning and Performance Journal*, 19 (1), 43–50.

Barton, A. (2002) Evaluation research as passive and apolitical? Some reflections from the field. *International Journal of Social Research Methodology*, 5 (4), 371–8.

Barton, E. S., Walton, T. and Rowe, D. (1976) Using grid technique with the mentally handicapped. In P. Slater (ed.) *The Measurement of Intrapersonal Space by Grid Technique, Vol 1. Explorations of Intrapersonal Space*. London: John Wiley, 47–68.

Bar-Yam, Y. (1997) *Dynamics of Complex Systems*. New York: Perseus Press.

Bassey, M. (1998) *Action Research for Improving Educational Practice*. In R. Halsall (ed.) *Teacher Research and School Improvement*. Buckingham: Open University Press. 167–78.

Bates, I. and Dutson, J. (1995) A Bermuda triangle? A case study of the disappearance of competence-based vocational training policy in the context of practice. *British Journal of Education and Work*, 8 (2), 41–59.

Batliwala, S. and Patel, S. (2005) Enumeration. In R. Tandon (ed.) *Participatory Research: Revisiting the Roots*. New Delhi: Mosaic Books, 295–312.

Batteson, C. and Ball, S. J. (1995) Autobiographies and interviews as means of 'access' to elite policy making in education. *British Journal of Educational Studies*, 43 (2), 201–16.

Bauman, R. (1986) *Story, Performance and Event*. Cambridge: Cambridge University Press.

Baumrind, D. (1964) Some thoughts on ethics of research. *American Psychologist*, 19 (6), 421–3.

Bazeley, P. (2006) The contribution of computer software to integrating qualitative and quantitative data and analysis. *Research in the Schools*, 13 (1), 64–74.

Beach, R. and Doerr-Stevens, C. (2009) Learning argument practices through online role-play: toward a rhetoric of significance and transformation. *Journal of Adolescent & Adult Literacy*, 52 (6), 460–8.

Beck, R. N. (1979) *Handbook in Social Philosophy*. New York: Macmillan.

Becker, H. (1968) Whose side are you on? *Social Problems*, 14 (3), 239–47.

Becker, H. (1970) *Sociological Work*. Chicago, IL: Aldane.

Becker, H. S. (1986) *Doing Things Together: Selected Papers*. Evanston, IL: Northwestern University Press.

Becker, H. S. and Geer, B. (1960) Participant observation: the analysis of qualitative field data. In R. Adams and J. Preiss (eds) *Human Organization Research: Field Relations and Techniques*. Homewood, IL: Dorsey, 267–89.

Beckett, C. and Clegg, S. (2007) Qualitative data from a postal questionnaire: questioning the presumption of the value of presence. *International Journal of Social Research Methodology*, 10 (4), 307–17.

Beer, M., Eisenstadt, R. A. and Spector, B. (1990) Why change programs don't produce change. *Harvard Business Review*, 68 (6), 158–66.

Belbin, R. M. (1981) *Management Teams: Why they Succeed or Fail*. London: Heinemann.

Bell, J. (1991) *Doing Your Research Project* (second edition). Milton Keynes: Open University Press.

Bell, J. F. (1996) Question choice in English literature examination. *Oxford Review of Education*, 23 (4), 447–58.

Bell, R. C. (2000) On testing the commonality of constructs in supplied grids. *Journal of Constructivist Psychology*, 13 (4), 303–11.

Bell, R. C. (2004a) Predictive relationships in repertory grid data: a new elaboration of Kelly's organization corollary. *Journal of Constructivist Psychology*, 17 (4), 281–95.

Bell, R. C. (2004b) A new approach to measuring conflict or inconsistency in grids. *Personal Construct Theory and Practice*, 1 (1), 53–9.

Bell, R. C., Vince, J. and Costigan, J. (2002) Which vary more in repertory grid data: constructs or elements? *Journal of Constructivist Psychology*, 15 (4), 305–14.

Belson, W. A. (1975) *Juvenile Theft: Causal Factors*. London: Harper and Row.

Belson, W. A. (1986) *Validity in Survey Research*. Aldershot: Gower.

Benn, T. (1990) *Against the Tide: Diaries 1973–76* (ed. R. Winstone). London: Arrow.

Bennett, A. (1969) *Forty Years On*. London: Faber and Faber.

Bennett, A. (2004) *The History Boys*. London: Faber and Faber.

Bennett, C. A. and Lumsdaine, A. A. (1975) *Evaluation and Experimentation*. New York: Academic Press.

Bennett, S. and Bowers, D. (1977) *An Introduction to Multivariate Techniques for Social and Behavioural Sciences*. London: Macmillan.

Bennett, S. N. (1976) *Teaching Styles and Pupil Progress*. Shepton Mallett: Open Books.

Bennett, S. N., Desforges, C. and Wilkinson, E. (1984) *The Quality of Pupil Learning Experience*. London: Lawrence Erlbaum.

Berg, J. (1957) Review of 'Supervisory and Executive Development. A Manual for Role Playing'. *Journal of Counseling Psychology*, 4 (4), 332–3.

Bergen, D. (2009) Play as the learning medium for future scientists, mathematicians, and engineers. *American Journal of Play*, 1 (4), 413–48.

Berger, J. (1972) *Ways of Seeing*. London: BBC and Harmondsworth: Penguin.

Berger, P. L. and Luckmann, T. (1967) *The Social Construction of Reality*. Harmondsworth: Penguin.

Bernard, H. R. (1994) *Research Methods in Anthropology: Qualitative and Quantitative Approaches* (second edition). Walnut Creek, CA: AltaMira Press.

Bernstein, B. (1970) Education cannot compensate for society. *New Society*, February, 387, 344–57.

Bernstein, B. (1971) On the classification and framing of educational knowledge. In M. F. D. Young (ed.) *Knowledge and Control*. Basingstoke: Collier-Macmillan, 47–69.

Bernstein, B. (1974) Sociology and the sociology of education: a brief account. In J. Rex (ed.) *Approaches to Sociology: An Introduction to Major Trends in British Sociology*. London: Routledge and Kegan Paul, 145–59.

Bernstein, B. (1975) Class and pedagogies: visible and invisible. In B. Bernstein, *Class, Codes and Control (Volume 3)*. London: Routledge and Kegan Paul.

Bernstein, R. J. (1983) *Beyond Objectivism and Relativism*. Oxford: Blackwell.

Best, D. (1992) *The Rationality of Feeling: Understanding the Arts in Education*. London: Falmer.

Best, J. W. (1970) *Research in Education*. Englewood Cliffs, NJ: Prentice-Hall.

Beynon, H. (1988) Regulating research: politics and decision making in industrial organizations. In A. Bryman (ed.) *Doing Research in Organizations*. London: Routledge, 21–33.

Bezzi, A. (1999) What is this thing called Geoscience? Epistemological dimensions elicited with the repertory grid and their implications for scientific literacy. *Science Education*, 83 (6), 675–700.

Bhadwal, S. C. and Panda, P. K. (1991) The effects of a package of some curricular strategies on the study habits of rural primary school students: a year long study. *Educational Studies*, 17 (3), 261–72.

Bickel, R. (2007) *Multilevel Analysis for Applied Research*. New York: Guilford Press.

Biddle, B. J. and Anderson, D. S. (1991) Social research and educational change. In D. S. Anderson and B. J. Biddle (eds) *Knowledge for Policy: Improving Education through Research*. London: Falmer, 1–20.

Bieri, J. (1955) Cognitive complexity-simplicity and predictive behavior. *Journal of Abnormal and Social Psychology*, 51 (2), 263–8.

Bijstra, J. O. and Jackson, S. (1998) Social skills training with early adolescents: effects on social skills, well-being, self-esteem and coping. *European Journal of Psychology of Education*, 13 (4), 569–83.

Billings, D. M. and Halstead, J. A. (2005) *Teaching in Nursing: A Guide for Faculty* (second edition). St. Louis, MO: Elsevier.

Bimrose, J. and Bayne, R. (1995) A multicultural framework in counsellor training: a preliminary evaluation. *British Journal of Guidance and Counselling*, 23 (2), 259–65.

Binet, A. (1905) Methode nouvelle pour le diagnostic de l'intelligence des anormaux. Cited in G. de Landsheere (1997) History of educational research. In J. P. Keeves (ed.) *Educational Research, Methodology, and Measurement: An International Handbook* (second edition). Oxford: Elsevier Science, 8–16.

Birnbaum, M. H. (2009) Designing online experiments. In H. Joinson, K. McKenna, T. Postmes and U.-D. Reips (eds) *The Oxford Handbook of Internet Psychology*. Oxford: Oxford University Press, 391–403.

Black, P. (1998) *Testing: Friend or Foe?* London: Falmer.

Black, T. R. (1999) *Doing Quantitative in the Social Sciences*. London: Sage.

Blalock, H. Jnr. (1979) *Social Statistics* (second edition). New York: McGraw-Hill.

Blalock, H. M. (1991) Dilemmas of social research. In D. S. Anderson and B. J. Biddle (eds) *Knowledge for Policy: Improving Education through Research*. London: Falmer, 60–9.

Blatchford, P. (1992) Children's attitudes to work at 11 years. *Educational Studies*, 18 (1), 107–18.

Blatchford, P. (2005) A multi-method approach to school class size differences. *International Journal of Social Research Methodology*, 8 (3), 195–205.

Blease, D. and Cohen, L. (1990) *Coping with Computers: An Ethnographic Study in Primary Classrooms*. London: Paul Chapman.

Bless, H., Bohner, G., Traudel, H. and Schwartz, N. (1992) Asking difficult questions: task complexity increases the impact of impact alternatives. *European Journal of Social Psychology*, 22, 309–12.

Bliss, J., Monk, M. and Ogborn, J. (1983) *Qualitative Data Analysis for Educational Research*. London: Croom Helm.

Blodgett, H. (1988) *Centuries of Female Days: Englishwomen's Private Diaries*. Brunswick, NJ: Rutgers University Press.

Bloom, B. (ed.) (1956) *Taxonomy of Educational Objectives: Handbook 1: Cognitive Domain*. London: Longman.

Bloor, M. (1978) On the analysis of observational data: a discussion of the worth and uses of induction techniques and respondent validation. *Sociology*, 12 (3), 545–52.

Blumenfeld-Jones, D. (1995) Fidelity as a criterion for practising and evaluating narrative inquiry. *International Journal of Qualitative Studies in Education*, 8 (1), 25–33.

Blumer, H. (1969) *Symbolic Interactionism: Perspective and Method*. Englewood Cliffs, NJ: Prentice-Hall.

Boal, A. (1979) *Theatre of the Oppressed*. London: Pluto Press.

Boal, A. (2002) *Games for Actors and Non-Actors*. London: Routledge.

Boas, F. (1943) Recent anthropology. *Science*, 98, 311–14.

Boellstorff, T. (2008) *Coming of Age in Second Life: An Anthropologist Explores the Virtually Human*. Oxford: Princeton University Press.

Bogdan, R. G. and Biklen, S. K. (1992) *Qualitative Research for Education* (second edition). Boston, MA: Allyn and Bacon.

Bolton, G. (1996) Drama as research. In P. Taylor (ed.) *Researching Drama and Arts Education. Paradigms and Possibilities*. London: Falmer, 187–94.

Bolton, G. M. and Heathcote, D. (1999) *So You Want to Use Role-Play? A New Approach in How to Plan*. Stoke on Trent, UK: Trentham Books.

Bonabeau, E. (2002) Agent-based modeling: methods and techniques for simulating human systems. *Proceedings of the National Academy of Sciences*, 99 (3): 7280–7.

Borg, M. G. (1998) Secondary school teachers' perceptions of pupils' undesirable behaviours. *British Journal of Educational Psychology*, 68, 67–79.

Borg, W. R. (1963) *Educational Research: An Introduction*. London: Longman.

Borg, W. R. (1981) *Applying Educational Research: A Practical Guide for Teachers*. New York: Longman.

Borg, W. R. and Gall, M. D. (1979) *Educational Research: An Introduction* (third edition). London: Longman.

Borg, W. R. and Gall, M. D. (1996) *Educational Research: An Introduction* (sixth edition). New York: Longman.

Borgatta, E. F. (1957) 'Supervisory and Executive Development. A Manual for Role-playing'. A review. *American Sociological Review*, 22 (4), 477.

Borkowsky, F. T. (1970) The relationship of work quality in undergraduate music curricula to effectiveness in instrumental music teaching in the public schools. *Journal of Experimental Education*, 39 (1), 14–19.

Borsboom, D., Mellenbergh, G. D. and van Heerden, J. (2004) The concept of validity. *Psychological Review*, 111 (4), 1061–71.

Boruch, R. F. (1997) *Randomized Experiments for Planning and Evaluation*. Applied Social Research Methods Series, vol. 44. Thousand Oaks, CA: Sage.

Boruch, R. F. and Cecil, J. S. (1979) *Assuring the Confidentiality of Social Research Data*. Philadelphia, PA: University of Pennsylvania Press.

Boston, M. D. (2008) Using classroom artifacts as evidence of quality instruction in mathematics. Paper presented at the Annual Conference of the Association of American Colleges of Teacher Education, New Orleans. Retrieved 20 May 2010, from www.allacademic.com/meta/p_mla_apa_research_citation/2/0/7/4/6/pages207464/p207464–2.php.

Boudon, R. (1973) *Education, Opportunity and Social Inequality*. New York: John Wiley.

Boulton, M. J. (1992) Participation in playground activities at middle school. *Education Research*, 34 (3), 167–82.

Boulton, M. J. (1997) Teachers' views on bullying: definitions, attitudes and abilities to cope. *British Journal of Educational Psychology*, 67 (2), 223–33.

Bourdieu, P. and Darbel, A. with Schnapper, D. (1991) *The Love of Art: European Art Museums and their Public*. Cambridge: Polity Press.

Bourne-Day, J. and Lee-Treweek, G. (2008) Interconnecting lives: Examining privacy as a shared concern for the researched and researchers. In B. Jegatheesan (ed.) *Access: A Zone of Comprehension, and Inclusion*. London: Emerald Group, 29–61.

Bowe, R., Ball, S. J. and Gold, A. (1992) *Reforming Education and Changing Schools*. London: Routledge.

Bowles, S. and Gintis, H. (1976) *Schooling in Capitalist America*. London: Routledge and Kegan Paul.

Bracht, G. H. and Glass, G. V. (1968) The external validity of experiments, *American Educational Research Journal*, 4 (5), 437–74.

Brackertz, S. (2007) Who is hard to reach and why? *ISR Working Paper*. Adelaide: Institute for Social Research Swinburne University of Technology. Retrieved 16 February 2010, from www.sisr.net/publications/0701brackertz.pdf.

Bradburn, N. M. and Berlew, D. E. (1961) *Economic Development and Cultural Change*. Chicago, IL: University of Chicago Press.

Bradburn, N. M. and Sudman, S. (1979) *Improving Interview Method and Questionnaire Design*. San Francisco, CA: Jossey-Bass.

Brannen, J. (2005) Mixing methods: the entry of qualitative and quantitative approaches into the research process. *International Journal of Social Research Methodology*, 8 (3), 173–84.

Breakwell, G. M. (1990) *Interviewing*. London: Routledge/ British Psychological Society.

Breakwell, G. M. (2000) Interviewing. In G. M. Breakwell, S. Hammond and C. Fife-Shaw (eds) *Research Methods in Psychology* (second edition). London: Sage, 239–50.

Breakwell, G. M., Hammond, S., Fife-Shaw, C. and Smith, J. A. (2006) *Research Methods in Psychology* (third edition). London: Sage.

Brenner, M., Brown, J. and Canter, D. (1985) *The Research Interview*. London: Academic Press.

Brenner, M. and Marsh, P. (eds) (1978) *The Social Contexts of Method*. London: Croom Helm.

Briggs, A. and Burke, P. (2002) *A Social History of the Media: From Gutenberg to the Internet*. Cambridge: Polity Press.

Brislin, R. W. (1970) Back-translation for cross-cultural research. *Journal of Cross-cultural Psychology*, 1 (3), 185–216.

British Educational Research Association (2000) *Ethical Guidelines*. Retrieved 14 June 2000, from www.bera.ac.uk.

British Educational Research Association (2004) *Revised Ethical Guidelines for Educational Research*. Southwell, Nottinghamshire, UK: British Educational Research Association. Retrieved 17 April 2010, from www.bera.ac.uk/files/guidelines/ethica1.pdf.

British Psychological Society (2005) *Code of Conduct, Ethical Principles and Guidelines*. Retrieved 20 May 2007, from www.bps.org.uk/document-download-area/document-download$.cfm?file_uuid=6D0645CC-7E96-C67F-D75E2648E5580115andext=pdf.

British Sociological Association (2002) *Statement of Ethical Practice for the British Sociological Association*. Durham, UK: British Sociological Association. Retrieved 17 April 2010, from www.britsoc.co.uk/NRrdonlyres/801B9A62–5

CD3–4BC2–93E1-FF470FF10256/0/StatementofEthical-Practice.pdf.

British Sociological Association (2006) *Statement of Ethical Practice for the British Sociological Association – Visual Sociology Group*. Durham, UK. Retrieved 17 April 2010, from http://www.visualsociology.org.uk/about/ethical_statement.php.

Broad, W. and Wade N. (1983) *Betrayers of Truth: Fraud and Deceit in the Halls of Science*. New York: Century.

Broadribb, S., Peachey, A., Carter, C. and Westrap, F. (2009) Using Second Life at the Open University: how the virtual world can facilitate learning for staff and students. In C. Wankel and J. Kingsley (eds) *Higher Education in Virtual Worlds: Teaching and Learning in Second Life*. Bingley: Emerald, 203–20.

Brock-Utne, B. (1996) Reliability and validity in qualitative research within education in Africa. *International Review of Education*, 42 (6), 605–21.

Brooks, G., Burton, M., Miles, J., Torgerson, C. and Torgerson, D. (2008) Randomised controlled trial of incentives to improve attendance at adult literacy classes. *Oxford Review of Education*, 34 (5), 493–504.

Brown, A. L. (1992) Design experiments: theoretical and methodological challenges in creating complex interventions in classroom settings. *Journal of the Learning Sciences*, 2 (2), 141–78.

Brown, J. and Sime, J. D. (1977) Accounts as general methodology. Paper presented to the British Psychological Society Conference. University of Exeter.

Brown, J. and Sime, J. D. (1981) A methodology of accounts. In M. Brenner (ed.) *Social Method and Social Life*. London: Academic Press.

Brown, L. D. (2005a) People-centred development and participatory research. In R. Tandon (ed.) *Participatory Research: Revisiting the Roots*. New Delhi: Mosaic Books, 90–9.

Brown, L. D. (2005b) Ambiguities in participatory research. In R. Tandon (ed.) *Participatory Research: Revisiting the Roots*. New Delhi: Mosaic Books, 197–202.

Brown, L. D. and Tandon, R. (2005) Ideology and political economy in inquiry: participatory research. In R. Tandon (ed.) *Participatory Research: Revisiting the Roots*. New Delhi: Mosaic Books, 54–66.

Brown, R. and Herrnstein, R. J. (1975) *Psychology*. London: Methuen.

Browne, K. (2005) Snowball sampling: using social networks to research non-heterosexual women. *International Journal of Social Research Methodology*, 8 (1), 47–60.

Bruner, J. (1986) *Actual Minds, Possible Worlds*. Cambridge, MA: Harvard University Press.

Bruner, J. S. (2004) Life as narrative. *Social Research*, 71 (3), 691–710.

Bryant, P., Devine, M., Ledward, A. and Nunes, T. (1997) Spelling with apostrophes and understanding possession. *British Journal of Educational Psychology*, 67 (1), 91–110.

Bryceson, D., Manicom, L. and Kassam, Y. (2005) The methodology of the participatory research approach. In R. Tandon (ed.) *Participatory Research: Revisiting the Roots*. New Delhi: Mosaic Books, 179–96.

Bryman, A. (2007a) Barriers to integrating quantitative and qualitative research. *Journal of Mixed Methods Research*, 1 (1), 8–22.

Bryman, A. (2007b) The research question in social research: what is its role? *International Journal of Social Research Methodology*, 19 (1), 5–20.

Bryman, A. and Cramer, D. (1990) *Quantitative Data Analysis for Social Scientists*. London: Routledge.

Buch, K. and Wetzel, D. K. (2001) Analyzing and realigning organizational culture. *Leadership and Organizational Development Journal*, 22 (1), 40–3.

Buchanan, M. (2003) *Nexus: Small Worlds and the Groundbreaking Theory of Networks*. New York: W. W. Norton.

Buckley, C. and Waring, M. (2009) The evolving nature of grounded theory: experiential reflections on the potential of the method for analysing children's attitudes towards physical activity. *International Journal of Social Research Methodology*, 12 (4), 317–34.

Buhler, C. and Allen, M. (1972) *Introduction to Humanistic Psychology*. Monterey, CA: Brooks/Cole.

Bulmer, M. (ed.) (1982) *Social Research Ethics*. London and Basingstoke: Macmillan.

Burgess, R. (ed.) (1985) *Strategies of Educational Research: Qualitative Methods*. London: Falmer.

Burgess, R. G. (ed.) (1989) *The Ethics of Educational Research*. Lewes: Falmer.

Burgess, R. G. (1993) Biting the hand that feeds you? Educational research for policy and practice. In R. G. Burgess (ed.) *Educational Research and Evaluation for Policy and Practice*. Lewes: Falmer, 1–18.

Burke, M., Noller, P. and Caird, D. (1992) Transition from probationer to educator: a repertory grid analysis. *International Journal of Personal Construct Psychology*, 5 (2), 159–82.

Burman, E. and Parker, I. (1993) *Discourse Analytical Research*. London: Routledge.

Burrell, G. and Morgan, G. (1979) *Sociological Paradigms and Organizational Analysis*. London: Heinemann Educational.

Burton, D. (ed.) (2000) *Research Training for Social Scientists: A Handbook for Postgraduate Researchers*. London: Sage.

Busato, V. V., Prins, F. J., Elshant, J. J. and Hamaker, C. (1998) Learning styles: a cross-sectional and longitudinal study in higher education. *British Journal of Educational Psychology*, 68 (3), 427–41.

Butt, T. (1995) What's wrong with laddering? *Changes*, 13, 81–7.

Butt, T. (2008) *George Kelly: The Psychology of Personal Constructs*. London: Palgrave Macmillan.

Button, E. (1994) Personal construct measurement of self esteem. *Journal of Constructivist Psychology*, 7 (1), 53–65.

Butzkamm, W. (1998) Code-switching in a bilingual history lesson: the mother tongue as a conversational lubricant. *Bilingual Education and Bilingualism*, 1 (2), 81–99.

Bynner, J. and Stribley, K. M (eds) (1979) *Social Research: Principles and Procedures*. London: Longman and Open University Press.

Byrne, D. (1997) Complexity theory and social research. *Social Research Update 18*. Retrieved 4 July 2005 from www.soc.surrey.ac.uk/sru/SRU18.html.

Cabral, R. J. (1987) Role playing as group intervention. *Small Group Research*, 18 (4), 470–82.

Calder, J. (1979) Introduction to applied sampling. *Research Methods in Education and the Social Sciences*. Block 3, Part 4, DE304. Milton Keynes: Open University Press.

Caldwell Cook, H. (1917) *The Play Way*. London: Heinemann.

Callawaert, S. (1999) Philosophy of Education, Frankfurt critical theory, and the sociology of Pierre Bourdieu. In. T. Popkewitz and L. Fendler (eds) *Critical Theories in Education: Changing Terrains of Knowledge and Politics*. London: Routledge, 117–44.

Campbell, D. T. (1975) Degrees of freedom and the case study. *Comparative Political Studies*, 8, 178–93. Cited in R. K. Yin (2009) *Case Study Research* (fourth edition). Thousand Oaks, CA: Sage, 5.

Campbell, D. T. and Fiske, D. W. (1959) Convergent and discriminant validation by the multitrait-multimethod matrix. *Psychological Bulletin*, 56 (2), 81–105.

Campbell, D., Sanderson, R. E. and Laverty, S. G. (1964) Characteristics of a conditioned response in human subjects during extinction trials following a single traumatic conditioning trial. *Journal of Abnormal and Social Psychology*, 68 (4), 627–39.

Campbell, D. T. and Stanley, J. (1963) *Experimental and Quasi-Experimental Designs for Research on Teaching*. Boston, MA: Houghton Mifflin.

Campbell, J. (2002) A critical appraisal of participatory methods in development research. *International Journal of Social Research Methodology*, 5 (1), 19–29.

Cannell, C. F. and Kahn, R. L. (1968) Interviewing. In G. Lindzey and A. Aronson (eds) *The Handbook of Social Psychology, Vol. 2: Research Methods*. New York: Addison Wesley, 526–95.

Caplan, A. (1982) On privacy and confidentiality in social science research. In T. Beauchamp, R. Faden, R. Wallace and L. Walters (eds) *Ethical Issues in Social Science Research*. Baltimore, MD: Johns Hopkins University Press, 315–28.

Caplan, N. (1991) The use of social research knowledge at the national level. In D. S. Anderson and B. J. Biddle (eds) *Knowledge for Policy: Improving Education through Research*. London: Falmer, 193–202.

Capra, F. (1996) *The Web of Life*. New York: Anchor Books.

Capraro, R. M. and Capraro, M. (2002) Treatments of effect sizes and statistical significance tests in textbooks. *Educational and Psychological Measurement*, 62 (5), 771–82.

Caracelli, V. and Greene, J. (1993) Data analysis strategies for mixed-method evaluation designs. *Educational Evaluation and Policy Analysis*, 15 (2), 195–207.

Cardinal, B. J., Tuominen, K. J. and Rintala, P. (2003) Psychometric assessment of Finnish versions of exercise-related measures of transtheoretical model constructs. *International Journal of Behavioral Medicine*, 19 (1), 31–43.

Carmines, E. G. and Zeller, R. A. (1979) *Reliability and Validity in Assessment*. Beverly Hills, CA: Sage.

Carotenuto, M. and Luongo, K. (2005) Navigating the Kenya National Archives: research and its role in Kenyan society. *History in Africa*, 32, 445–55.

Carr, W. and Kemmis, S. (1986) *Becoming Critical*. Lewes: Falmer.

Carroll, S. and Walford, G. (1997) Parents' responses to the school quasi-market. *Research Papers in Education*, 12 (1), 3–26.

Carspecken, P. F. (1996) *Critical Ethnography in Educational Research*. London: Routledge.

Carspecken, P. F. and Apple, M. (1992) Critical qualitative research: theory, methodology and practice. In M. LeCompte, W. L. Millroy and J. Preissle (eds) *The Handbook of Qualitative Research in Education*. London: Academic Press, 507–53.

Cartwright, D. (1991) Basic and applied social psychology. In D. S. Anderson and B. J. Biddle (eds) *Knowledge for Policy: Improving Education through Research*. London: Falmer, 23–31.

Carver, R. P. (1978) The case against significance testing. *Harvard Educational Review*, 48 (3), 378–99.

Cassell, J. (1993) The relationship of observer to observed when studying up. Cited in R. M. Lee, *Doing Research on Sensitive Topics*. London: Sage.

Castells, M. (2009) *The Rise of the Network Society: Information Age: Economy, Society, and Culture Volume 1 (Information Age Series)*. Oxford: WileyBlackwell.

Castronova, E. (2005) *Synthetic Worlds: The Business and Culture of Online Games*. London: University of Chicago Press.

Cavan, S. (1977) Review of J. D. Douglas's (1976) 'Investigative Social Review: Individual and Team Field Research'. *American Journal of Sociology*, 83, (3), 809–11.

Chalmers, A. F. (1999) *What Is this Thing Called Science?* (third edition). Milton Keynes: Open University Press.

Chambers, K. (2003) How often do you have sex: problem gambling as a sensitive issue. Paper presented at the Twelfth International Congress on Gambling and Risk Taking. Vancouver, BC.

Chang, H. (2008) *Autoethnography as Method*. Walnut Creek, CA: Left Coast Press.

Charmaz, K. (2006) *Constructing Grounded Theory: A Practical Guide through Qualitative Data Analysis*. London: Sage.

Chatterji, M. (2004) Evidence on 'what works': an argument for Extended-Term Mixed-Method (ET MM) Evaluation Designs. *Educational Researcher*, 33 (9), 3–13.

Chelinsky, E. and Mulhauser, F. (1993) Educational evaluations for the US Congress: some reflections on recent experience. In R. G. Burgess (ed.) *Educational Research and Evaluation for Policy and Practice*. London: Falmer, 44–60.

Childs, G. (1997) A concurrent validity study of teachers' ratings for nominated 'problem' children. *British Journal of Educational Psychology*, 67, 457–74.

Chomsky, N. (1959) Review of Skinner's *Verbal Behaviour*. *Language*, 35 (1), 26–58.

Christian, L. M., Parsons, N. L. and Dillman, D. A. (2009) Designing scalar questions for web surveys. *Sociological Methods and Research*, 37 (3), 393–425.

Cicognani, C. (1998) Parents' educational styles and adolescent autonomy. *European Journal of Psychology of Education*, 13 (4), 485–502.

Cicourel, A. V. (1964) *Method and Measurement in Sociology*. New York: The Free Press.

Clark, A. (2006) *Anonymising Research Data*. Working Paper 7/06 for ESRC National Centre for Research Methods. Manchester: ESRC National Centre for Research Methods.

Retrieved 19 May 2010, from http://eprints.ncrm.ac. uk/480/1/0706_anonymising_research_data.pdf.

Clark, P. (2009) 'Great chorus of protest': a case study of conflict over the 1909 Eaton's readers. *History of Education*, 38 (5), 681–703.

Clarke, A. and Dawson, R. (1999) *Evaluation Research*. London: Sage.

Clarke, F. (1940) *Education and Social Change: An English Interpretation*. London: Sheldon Press.

Clifton, J. (2006) A conversation analytical approach to business communication: the case of leadership. *Journal of Business Communication*, 43 (3), 202–19.

Cline, T. and Ertubney, C. (1997) The impact of gender on primary teachers' evaluations of children's difficulties in school. *British Journal of Educational Psychology*, 67, 447–56.

Cline, T., Proto, A., Raval, P. D. and Paolo T. (1998) The effects of brief exposure and of classroom teaching on attitudes children express towards facial disfigurement in peers. *Educational Research*, 40 (1), 55–68.

Clogg, C. C. and Haritou, A. (1997) The regression method of causal inference and a dilemma confronting this method. In V. R. McKim and S. P. Turner (eds) *Causality in Crisis? Statistical Methods and the Search for Causal Knowledge in the Social Sciences*, Notre Dame, IN: University of Notre Dame Press, 83–112.

Cobb, P., Confrey, J., diSessa A., Lehrer, R. and Schauble, L. (2003) Design experiments in educational research. *Educational Researcher*, 32 (1), 9–13.

Coch, D. (2007) Neuroimaging research with children: ethical issues and case scenarios. *Journal of Moral Education*, 36 (1), 1–18.

Cochrane, A. L. (1972) *Effectiveness and Efficiency: Random Reflections on Health Services*. London: Nuffield Provincial Hospitals Trust.

Codd, J. (1988) The construction and deconstruction of educational policy documents. *Journal of Education Policy*, 3 (3), 235–47.

Coe, R. (1999) A Manifesto for Evidence-Based Education. Durham, University of Durham Curriculum Evaluation and Management Centre. Retrieved 7 January 2005, from www. cemcentre.org/renderpage.asp?linkID=30317000.

Coe, R. (2000) What is an 'Effect Size'? CEM Centre, University of Durham. Retrieved 7 January 2005, from www. cemcentre.org/renderpage.asp?linkid=30325016.

Coe, R. (2002) It's the effect size, Stupid. Paper presented at the British Educational Research Association annual conference, Exeter, September. Retrieved 7 January 2005, from www.cemcentre.org/Documents/CEM%20ExtraEBE/ ESguide.pdf.

Coe, R., Fitz-Gibbon, C. T. and Tymms, P. (2000) Promoting Evidence-Based Education: The Role of Practitioners. Roundtable paper presented at the British Educational Research Association, University of Cardiff, UK, 7–10 September.

Coffey, A., Holbrook, B. and Atkinson, P. (1996) Qualitative data analysis: technologies and representations. *Sociological Research Online*. Retrieved 14 November 2000, from www.socresonline.org.uk/socresonline/1/1/4.html.

Cohen, A. and Wollack, J. A. (2010) *Handbook on Test Development: Helpful Tips for Creating Reliable and Valid Classroom Tests*. University of Wisconsin: Testing and Evaluation Services University of Wisconsin-Madison. Retrieved 25 April 2010, from http://testing.wisc.edu/ Handbook%20on%20Test%20Construction.pdf.

Cohen, D. K. and Garet, M. S. (1991) Reforming educational policy with applied social research. In D. S. Anderson and B. J. Biddle (eds) *Knowledge for Policy: Improving Education through Research*. London: Falmer, 123–40.

Cohen, J. (1988) *Statistical Power Analysis for the Behavioral Sciences*. Hillsdale, NJ: Erlbaum.

Cohen, J. and Stewart, I. (1995) *The Collapse of Chaos*. Harmondsworth: Penguin.

Cohen, L. (1977) *Educational Research in Classrooms and Schools: A Manual of Materials and Methods*. London: Harper and Row.

Cohen, L. (1993) *Racism Awareness Materials in Initial Teacher Training*. Report to the Leverhulme Trust, 11–19 New Fetter Lane, London, EC4A 1NR.

Cohen, L. and Holliday, M. (1979) *Statistics for Education and Physical Education*. London: Harper and Row.

Cohen, L. and Holliday, M. (1982) *Statistics for Social Scientists*. London: Harper and Row.

Cohen, L. and Holliday, M. (1996) *Practical Statistics for Students*. London: Paul Chapman.

Cohen, L. and Manion, L. (1994) *Research Methods in Education* (fourth edition). London: Routledge.

Cohen, L., Manion, L. and Morrison, K. R. B. (2004) *A Guide to Teaching Practice* (fifth edition). London: Routledge.

Cohen, L., Manion, L. and Morrison, K. (2007) *Research Methods in Education* (sixth edition). London: Routledge.

Cohen, M. R. and Nagel, E. (1961) *An Introduction to Logic and Scientific Method*. London: Routledge and Kegan Paul.

Cohen, S. (1999) *Challenging Orthodoxies: Toward a New Cultural History of Education*. New York: Peter Lang.

Colborn-Roxworthy, E. (2004) Role-play training at 'violent Disneyland': the FBI academy's performance paradigms. *The Drama Review*, 48 (4), 81–108.

Cole, A. L. (1991) Personal theories of teaching: development in the formative years, *Alberta Journal of Educational Research*, 37 (2), 119–32.

Coleman, J. S. (1991) Social policy research and societal decision making. In D. S. Anderson and B. J. Biddle (eds) *Knowledge for Policy: Improving Education through Research*. London: Falmer, 113–22.

Coleridge, S. T. (1817) *Biographia Literaria*. Retrieved 20 May 2010, from www.gutenberg.org/etext/6081.

Collins, J. S. and Duguid, P. (1989) Situated cognition and the culture of learning. *Educational Researcher* 18 (1), 32–42.

Collins, P. (1963) *Dickens and Education*. London: Macmillan.

Connell, R. W., Ashenden, D. J., Kessler, S. and Doswett, G. W. (1996) Making the difference: schools, families and social division. Cited in B. Limerick, T. Burgess-Limerick and M. Grace, The politics of interviewing: power relations and accepting the gift. *International Journal of Qualitative Studies in Education*, 9 (4), 449–60.

Connelly, F. M. and Clandinin, D. J. (1999) Narrative inquiry. In J. P. Keeves and G. Lakomski (eds) *Issues in Educational Research*. Oxford, Elsevier Science, 132–40.

Connolly, P. (2003) *Ethical Principles for Researching Vulnerable Groups*. Ulster: University of Ulster. Retrieved

17 February 2010, from www.ofmdfmni.gov.uk/ethical-principles.pdf.

Conover, N. J. (1971) *Practical Nonparametric Statistics*. New York: John Wiley.

Cook, T. D. (1991) Postpositivist criticisms, reform associations, and uncertainties about social research. In D. S. Anderson and B. J. Biddle (eds) *Knowledge for Policy: Improving Education through Research*. London: Falmer, 43–59.

Cook, T. D. and Campbell, D. T. (1979) *Quasi-experimentation: Design and Analysis Issues for Field Settings*. Boston, MA: Houghton Mifflin.

Cook, T. D., Cooper, H., Cordray, D. S., Hartmann, H., Hedges, L. V., Light, R. J., Louis, T. A. and Mosteller, F. (1992) *Meta-Analysis for Explanation*. New York: Russell Sage Foundation.

Cooke, R. A. and Lafferty, J. C. (1989) *The Organizational Culture Inventory*. Plymouth, MI: Human Synergistics International.

Cooley, C. H. (1902) *Human Nature and the Social Order*. New York: Charles Scribner.

Coomber, R. (1997) Using the internet for survey research. *Sociological Research Online*, 2 (2). Retrieved 14 November 2000, from www.socresonline.org.uk/socresonline/2/2/2.html.

Cooper, D. C. and Schindler, P. S. (2001) *Business Research Methods* (seventh edition). New York: McGraw-Hill.

Cooper, H. M. (2010) *Research Synthesis and Meta-evaluation: A Step-by-Step Approach*. Thousand Oaks, CA: Sage.

Cooper, H. M. and Hedges, L. V. (1994) *The Handbook of Research Synthesis*. New York: Russell Sage Foundation.

Cooper, H. M. and Rosenthal, R. (1980) Statistical versus traditional procedures for summarizing research findings. *Psychological Bulletin*, 87, 442–9.

Cooper, M. (1976) An exact probability test for use with Likert scales. *Educational and Psychological Measurement*, 36 (3), 647–55.

Corey, S. M. (1953) *Action Research to Improve School Practice*. New York: Teachers College, Columbia University.

Cormack, M. (1992) *Ideology*. London: Batsford.

Corporal, A. H. (1991) Repertory grid research into cognitions of prospective primary school teachers. *Teaching and Teacher Education*, 36, 315–29.

Coser, L. A. and Rosenberg, B. (1969) *Sociological Theory: A Book of Readings* (third edition). New York: Macmillan.

Cothran, D. J., Kulinna, P. H., Banville, D., Choi E., Amade-Escot, A., MacPhail, A., Macdonald, D., Richard, J.-F., Sarmento, P. and Kirk, D. (2005) A cross-cultural investigation of the use of teaching styles. *Research Quarterly for Exercise and Sport*, 76 (2), 193–201.

Coyle, A. (1995) Discourse analysis. In G. M. Breakwell, S. Hammond and C. Fife-Shaw (eds) *Research Methods in Psychology*. London: Sage, 243–58.

Cresswell, M. J. and Houston, J. G. (1991) Assessment of the national curriculum – some fundamental considerations. *Educational Review*, 43 (1), 63–78.

Creswell, J. W. (1994) *Research Design: Qualitative and Quantitative Approaches*. Thousand Oaks, CA: Sage.

Creswell, J. W. (1998) *Qualitative Inquiry and Research Design: Choosing among the Five Traditions*. Thousand Oaks, CA: Sage.

Creswell, J. W. (2002) *Educational Research: Planning, Conducting and Evaluating Quantitative and Qualitative Research*. Upper Saddle River, NJ: Merrill Prentice-Hall.

Creswell, J. W. (2009) Mapping the field of mixed methods research. *Journal of Mixed Methods Research*, 3 (2), 95–108.

Creswell, J. W. and Tashakkori, A. (2007) Differing perspectives on mixed methods research. *Journal of Mixed Methods Research*, 1 (4), 303–8.

Cronbach, L. J. (1949) *Essentials of Psychological Testing* (first edition). New York: Harper and Row.

Cronbach, L. J. (1970) *Essentials of Psychological Testing* (third edition). New York: Harper and Row.

Crook, D. (2000) Net gains? The internet as a research tool for historians of education. In D. Crook and R. Aldrich (eds) *History of Education for the Twenty-First Century*. London: University of London Institute of Education, 36–49.

Crow, G. M. (1992) The principalship as a career: in need of a theory. *Educational Management and Administration*, 21 (2), 80–7.

Crow, G., Wiles, R., Heath, S. and Charles, V. (2006) Research ethics and data quality: the implications of informed consent. *International Journal of Social Research Methodology*, 9 (2), 83–95.

Crowley, C., Harré, R. and Tagg, C. (2002) Qualitative research and computing: methodological issues and practices in using QSR NVivo and NUD*IST. *International Journal of Social Research Methodology*, 5 (3), 193–7.

Croxford, L. (1997) Participation in science subjects: the effect of the Scottish curriculum framework. *Research Papers in Education*, 12 (1), 69–89.

Crudge, S. E. and Johnson, F. C. (2007) Using the repertory grid and laddering technique to determine the user's evaluative model of search engines. *Journal of Documentation*, 63 (2), 259–80.

Cuban, L. (1986) *Teachers and Machines: Classroom Use of Technology Since 1920*. New York: Teachers College Press.

Cuban, L. (2003) *Oversold and Underused: Computers in the Classroom*. London: Harvard University Press.

Cuff, E. G. and Payne, G. C. F. (eds) (1979) *Perspectives in Sociology*. London: George Allen and Unwin.

Cullen, K. (1997) Headteacher appraisal: a view from the inside. *Research Papers in Education*, 12 (2), 177–204.

Cummings, L. (1985) Qualitative research in the infant classroom: a personal account. In R. Burgess (ed.) *Issues in Educational Research: Qualitative Methods*. Lewes: Falmer, 216–50.

Cunningham, G. K. (1998) *Assessment in the Classroom*. London: Falmer.

Cunningham, P. (1992) Teachers' professional image and the Press, 1950–1990. *History of Education*, 21 (1), 37–56.

Curr, D. (1994) Role play. *British Medical Journal*, 308 (6930), 725.

Curriculum Evaluation and Management Centre (2000) *A Culture of Evidence*. Retrieved 21 May 2000, from http://cem.dur.ac.uk/ebeuk/culture.htm.

Curtis, B. (1978) Introduction. In B. Curtis and W. Mays (eds) *Phenomenology and Education*. London: Methuen, ix–xxvi.

Cutler, C. and Hay. I. (2000) 'Club Dread': applying and

refining an issues-based role-play on environment, economy, and culture. *Journal of Geography in Higher Education*, 24 (2), 179–97.

Dale, A. (2006) Quality issues with survey research. *International Journal of Social Research Methodology*, 9 (2), 143–58.

Daly, P. (1996) The effects of single-sex and co-educational secondary schooling on girls' achievement. *Research Papers in Education*, 11 (3), 289–306.

Daly, P. and Shuttleworth, I. (1997) Determinants of public examination entry and attainment in mathematics: evidence of gender and gender-type of school from the 1980s and 1990s in Northern Ireland. *Evaluation and Research in Education*, 11 (2), 91–101.

Data Protection Act 1984. London: HMSO.

Data Protection Act 1998. London: HMSO.

Davenport, E. C. Jr., Davison, M. L., Kuang, H., Ding, S., Kin, S.-K. and Kwak, N. (1998) High school mathematics course-taking by gender and ethnicity. *American Educational Research Journal*, 35 (3), 497–514.

David, M. (2002) Problems of participation. *International Journal of Social Research Methodology*, 5 (1), 11–17.

Davidson, J. (1970) *Outdoor Recreation Surveys: The Design and Use of Questionnaires for Site Surveys*. London: Countryside Commission.

Davie, R. (1972) The longitudinal approach. *Trends in Education*, 28 (8), 8–13.

Davies, J. and Brember, I. (1997) Monitoring reading standards in year 6: a 7-year cross-sectional study. *British Educational Research Journal*, 23 (5), 615–22.

Davies, J. and Brember, I. (1998) Standards in reading at key stage 1 – a cross-sectional study. *Educational Research*, 40 (2), 153–60.

Davies, P. (1999) What is evidence-based education? *British Journal of Educational Studies*, 47 (2), 108–21.

Davies, P. (2000) The relevance of systematic reviews to educational policy and practice. *Oxford Review of Education*, 26 (3 and 4), 365–78.

Davis, B. and Sumara, D. (2005) Challenging images of knowing: complexity science and educational research. *International Journal of Qualitative Studies in Education*, 18 (3), 305–21.

Davis, D. (1995) Evidence-based education. *Canadian Association for Medical Education Newsletter*, 7 (1), 1–5. Retrieved 2 September 2001, from www.medicine.dal.ca/gorgs/came/clinic.htm.

Davis, D. and Lawrence, C. (1987) *Gavin Bolton: Selected Writings on Drama in Education*. London: Longman.

Day, C. and Sammons, P. (2008) Combining qualitative and quantitative methodologies in research on teachers' loves, work, and effectiveness: from integration to synergy. *Educational Researcher*, 37 (6), 330–42.

Day, K. J. (1985) Perspectives on privacy: a sociological analysis. Unpublished PhD thesis, University of Edinburgh. Quoted in R. M. Lee (1993) *Doing Research on Sensitive Topics*. London: Sage.

De Laine, M. (2000) *Fieldwork, Participation and Practice*. London: Sage.

Deem, R. (1994) Researching the locally powerful: a study of school governance. In G. Walford (ed.) *Researching the Powerful in Education*. London: UCL Press, 151–71.

Delamont, S. (1976) *Interaction in the Classroom*. London: Methuen.

Delamont, S. (1981) All too familiar? A decade of classroom research. *Educational Analysis*, 3 (1), 69–83.

Delamont, S. (1992) *Fieldwork in Educational Settings: Methods, Pitfalls and Perspectives*. London: Falmer.

DeMunck, V. C. and Sobo, E. (eds) (1998) *Using Methods in the Field: A Practical Introduction and Casebook*. Walnut Creek, CA: AltaMira Press.

DeNeve, K. and Heppner, M. (1997) Role play simulations: the assessment of an active learning technique and comparisons with traditional lectures. *Innovative Higher Education*, 21 (3), 231–46.

Dennett, D. C. (1978) *Brainstorms: Philosophical Essays on Mind and Psychology*. Brighton, UK: Harvester Press.

Denscombe, M. (1995) Explorations in group interviews: an evaluation of a reflexive and partisan approach. *British Educational Research Journal*, 21 (2), 131–48.

Denscombe, M. (2008) Communities of practice: a research paradigm for the mixed methods approach. *Journal of Mixed Methods Research*, 2 (3), 270–83.

Denscombe, M. (2009) Item non-response rates: a comparison of online and paper questionnaires. *International Journal of Social Research Methodology*, 12 (4), 281–91.

Denzin, N. K. (1970) *The Research Act in Sociology: A Theoretical Introduction to Sociological Methods*. London: Butterworths.

Denzin, N. K. (1989) *The Research Act: A Theoretical Introduction to Sociological Methods* (third edition). Englewood Cliffs, NJ: Prentice-Hall.

Denzin, N. K. (1990) On understanding emotion: the interpretive-cultural agenda. In T. D. Kemper (ed.) *Research Agendas in the Sociology of Emotions*. New York: State University of New York Press, 85–116.

Denzin, N. K. (1997) Triangulation in educational research. In J. P. Keeves (ed.) *Educational Research, Methodology and Measurement: An International Handbook* (second edition). Oxford: Elsevier Science, 318–22.

Denzin, N. K. (1999) Biographical research methods. In J. P. Keeves and G. Lakomski (eds) *Issues in Educational Research*. Oxford: Elsevier Science, 92–102.

Denzin, N. K. (2004) Reading film: using photos and video as social science material. In U. Flick, E. von Kardoff and I. Steinke (eds) *A Companion to Qualitative Research*. London: Sage, 234–47.

Denzin, N. K. (2008) The new paradigm dialog and qualitative inquiry. *International Journal of Qualitative Studies in Education*, 21 (4), 315–25.

Denzin, N. K. and Lincoln, Y. S. (eds) (1994) *Handbook of Qualitative Research*. Thousand Oaks, CA: Sage.

Department of Education and Science (1977) *A Study of School Buildings*. Annex 1. London: HMSO.

Derry, S. J. and Potts, M. K. (1998) How tutors model students: a study of personal constructs in adaptive tutoring. *American Educational Research Journal*, 35 (1), 65–99.

Design-Based Research Collective (2003) Design-based research: an emerging paradigm for educational inquiry. *Educational Researcher*, 32 (1), 5–8.

Deutskens, E., De Ruyter, K. and Wetzels, M. (2005) An assessment of measurement invariance between online and mail surveys. *Research Memoranda 3*. Maastricht:

University of Maastricht, Faculty of Economics and Business Administration.

Deyle, D. L., Hess, G. and LeCompte, M. L. (1992) Approaching ethical issues for qualitative researchers in education. In M. LeCompte, W. L. Millroy and J. Preissle (eds) *The Handbook of Qualitative Research in Education*. London: Academic Press, 597–642.

Diaper, G. (1990) The Hawthorne Effect: a fresh examination. *Educational Studies*, 16 (3), 261–7.

Diaz de Rada, V. (2005) Influence of questionnaire design on response to mail surveys. *International Journal of Social Research Methodology*, 8 (1), 61–78.

Dicker, R. and Gilbert, J. (1988) The role of the telephone in educational research. *British Educational Research Journal*, 14 (1), 65–72.

Dickson-Swift, V., James, E. L., Kippen, S. and Liamputtong, P. (2006) Blurring boundaries in qualitative health research on sensitive topics. *Qualitative Health Research*, 16 (6), 853–71.

Didierjean, A. and Cauzinille-Marmèche, E. (1998) Reasoning by analogy: is it schema-mediated or case-based? *European Journal of Psychology of Education*, 13 (3), 385–98.

Diener, E. and Crandall, R. (1978) *Ethics in Social and Behavioral Research*. Chicago, IL: University of Chicago Press.

Dietz, S. M. (1977) An analysis of programming DRL schedules in educational settings. *Behaviour Research and Therapy*, 15, 103–11.

Dillman, D. A. (2001) Navigating the rapids of change: some observations on survey methodology in the early 21st century. Presidential address at the American Association for Public Opinion Research, St. Petersburg, Florida.

Dillman, D. A. (2007) *Mail and Internet Surveys: The Tailored Design Method* (second edition). New York: John Wiley.

Dillman, D. A. and Bowker, D. K. (2000) The web questionnaire challenge to survey methodologists. In U.-D. Reips and M. Bosnjak (eds) *Dimensions of Internet Science*. Lengerich, Germany: Pabst Science Publishers. Retrieved 26 February 2005, from http://survey.sesrc.wsu.edu/dillman/zuma_paper_dillman_bowker.pdf.

Dillman, D. A., Carley-Baxter, L. and Jackson, A. (1999) Skip pattern compliance in three test forms: a theoretical and empirical evaluation. SESRC Technical Report #99–01. Social and Economic Sciences Research Center. Pullman: Washington State University.

Dillman, D. A., Smyth, J. D., Christian, L. M. and Stern, M. J. (2003) Multiple answer questions in self-administered surveys: the use of check-all-that-apply and forced-choice question formats. Paper presented at the American Statistical Association, San Francisco, CA.

Dillman, D. A., Tortora, R. D. and Bowker, D. (1998a) Influence of plain vs. fancy design in response rates for web surveys. Proceedings of Survey Methods Section, annual meeting of the American Statistical Association, Dallas, TX. Retrieved 8 February 2005, from http://survey.sesrc.wsu.edu/dillman.papers.htm.

Dillman, D. A., Tortora, R. D. and Bowker, D. (1998b) Principles for constructing web surveys. Retrieved 8 February 2005, from http://survey.sesrc.wsu.edu/dillman/papers/websurveyppr.pdf.

Dixon-Woods, M., Agarwal S., Jones D., Young B. and Sutton A. (2005) Synthesising qualitative and quantitative evidence: a review of possible methods. *Journal of Health Services Research and Policy*, 10 (1), 45–53.

Dixon-Woods, M., Fitzpatrick, R. and Roberts, K. (2001) Including qualitative research in systematic reviews: opportunities and problems. *Journal of Evaluation in Clinical Practice*, 7 (2), 125–33.

Dobbert, M. L. and Kurth-Schai, R. (1992) Systematic ethnography: toward an evolutionary science of education and culture. In M. LeCompte, W. L. Millroy and J. Preissle (eds) *The Handbook of Qualitative Research in Education*. London: Academic Press, 93–160.

Dobson, M. (2009) Letters. In M. Dobson and B. Ziemann (eds) *Reading Primary Sources: The Interpretation of Texts from Nineteenth- and Twentieth-Century History*. London: Routledge, 57–73.

Dobson, M. and Ziemann, B. (eds) (2009) *Reading Primary Sources: The Interpretation of Texts from Nineteenth- and Twentieth-Century History*. London: Routledge.

Dochartaigh, N. O. (2002) *The Internet Research Handbook*. London: Sage.

Docherty, S. and Sandelowski, M. (1999) Focus on qualitative methods: interviewing children. *Research in Nursing and Health*, 22 (2), 177–85.

Doll, W. E. (1993) *A Post-modern Perspective on Curriculum*. New York: Teachers College Press.

Donovan, O. M. (2009) Building personal and social competence through cancer-related issues. *Journal of School Health*, 79 (3), 138–43.

Dooley, D. (2001) *Social Research Methods* (fourth edition). Englewood Cliffs, NJ: Prentice-Hall.

Dosanjh, J. S. and Ghuman, P. A. S. (1997) Asian parents and English education – 20 years on: a study of two generations. *Educational Studies*, 23 (3), 459–72.

Douglas Home, C. (2007) Revealing insight into the parallel world of gangs. *Herald Scotland*, 4 September. Retrieved 2 June 2010, from http://www.heraldscotland.com/revealing-insight-into-the-parallel-world-of-gangs-1.864507.

Douglas, J. D. (1973) *Understanding Everyday Life*. London: Routledge and Kegan Paul.

Douglas, J. D. (1976) *Investigative Social Research*. Beverly Hills, CA: Sage.

Douglas, J. W. B. (1976) The use and abuse of national cohorts. In M. D. Shipman (ed.) *The Organization and Impact of Social Research*. London: Routledge and Kegan Paul, 3–21.

Dugard, P. and Todman, J. (1995) Analysis of pre-test and post-test control group designs in educational research. *Educational Psychology*, 15 (2), 181–98.

Duncan, M. G. (1968) *A Dictionary of Sociology*. London: Routledge and Kegan Paul.

Duncombe, J. and Jessop, J. (2002) 'Doing rapport' and the ethics of 'faking friendship'. In M. Mauthner, M. Birch, J. Jessop and T. Miller (eds) *Ethics in Qualitative Research*. London: Sage, 107–22.

Dunham, R. B. and Smith, F. J. (1979) *Organizational Surveys: An Internal Assessment of Organizational Health*. Glenview, IL: Scott, Foreman.

Dunning, G. (1993) Managing the small primary school: the problem role of the teaching head. *Educational Management and Administration*, 21 (2), 79–89.

Durkheim, E. (1956) *Education and Sociology*. Glencoe, IL: The Free Press.

Durkheim, E. (1982) *The Rules of Sociological Method*. Glencoe, IL: The Free Press.

Durrant, G. B. (2006) Missing data methods in official statistics in the United Kingdom: some recent developments. *Allgemeines Statistisches Archiv*, 90 (4), 577–93.

Durrant, G. B. (2009) Imputation methods for handling non-response in practice: methodological issues and recent debates. *International Journal of Social Research Methodology*, 12 (4), 293–304.

Dyer, C. (1995) *Beginning Research in Psychology*. Oxford: Blackwell.

Eagleton, T. (1991) *Ideology*. London: Verso.

Earle, R. (ed.) (1999) *Epistolary Selves: Letters and Letter-Writers, 1600–1945*. Aldershot, UK: Ashgate.

Ebbinghaus, H. (1897) Über eine neue methode zur Prüfung geistiger Fähigkeiten. Cited in G. de Landsheere (1997) History of educational research. In J. P. Keeves (ed.) *Educational Research, Methodology, and Measurement: An International Handbook* (second edition). Oxford: Elsevier Science, 8–16.

Ebbutt, D. (1985) Educational action research: some general concerns and specific quibbles. In R. Burgess (ed.) *Issues in Educational Research: Qualitative Methods*. Lewes: Falmer, 152–74.

Ebel, R. L. (1979) *Essentials of Educational Measurement* (third edition). Englewood Cliffs, NJ: Prentice-Hall.

Economic and Social Research Council (2008) *Visual Ethics: Ethical Issues in Visual Research*. NCRM/011.

Economic and Social Research Council (2009) *Research Ethics Framework*. Swindon, UK: Economic and Social Research. Retrieved 10 February 2010, from www.esrc.ac.uk/esrcinfo-centre/images/esrc_re_ethics_frame_tcm6–11291.pdf.

Eder, D. and Fingerson, L. (2003) Interviewing children and adolescents. In J. A. Holstein and J. F. Gubrium (eds) *Inside Interviewing: New Lenses, New Concerns*. Thousand Oaks, CA: Sage, 33–53.

Edwards, A. D. (1976) *Language in Culture and Class*. London: Heinemann.

Edwards, A. D. (1980) Patterns of power and authority in classroom talk. In P. Woods (ed.) *Teacher Strategies: Explorations in the Sociology of the School*. London: Croom Helm, 237–53.

Edwards, A. D. and Westgate, D. P. G. (1987) *Investigating Classroom Talk*. Lewes: Falmer.

Edwards, D. (1991) Discourse and the development of understanding in the classroom. In O. Boyd-Barrett and E. Scanlon (eds) *Computers and Learning*. Wokingham: Addison-Wesley, 186–204.

Edwards, D. (1993) Concepts, memory and the organisation of pedagogic discourse: a case study. *International Journal of Educational Research*, 19 (3), 205–25.

Edwards, D. and Mercer, N. M. (1987) *Common Knowledge: The Development of Understanding in the Classroom*. London: Routledge and Kegan Paul.

Edwards, D. and Potter, J. (1993) Language and causation: a discursive action model of description and attribution. *Psychological Review*, 100 (1), 23–41.

Edwards, R. and Mauthner, M. (2002) Ethics and feminist research: theory and practice. In M. Mauthner, M. Birch, J. Jessop and T. Miller (eds) *Ethics in Qualitative Research*. London: Sage, 14–31.

Eisenhart, M. (2001) Educational ethnography past, present, and future: ideas to think with. *Educational Researcher*, 30 (8), 16–27.

Eisenhart, M. A. and Howe, K. R. (1992) Validity in educational research. In M. D. LeCompte, W. L. Millroy and J. Preissle (eds) *The Handbook of Qualitative Studies in Education*. New York: Academic Press, 643–80.

Eisner, E. (1985) *The Art of Educational Evaluation*. Lewes: Falmer.

Eisner, E. (1991) *The Enlightened Eye: Qualitative Inquiry and the Enhancement of Educational Practice*. New York: Macmillan.

Eisner, E. (1997) The promise and perils of alternative forms of data representation. *Educational Researcher*, 26 (6), 4–10.

Ekehammar, B. and Magnusson, D. (1973) A method to study stressful situations. *Journal of Personality and Social Psychology*, 27 (2), 176–9.

Elliott, J. (1978) What is action-research in schools? *Journal of Curriculum Studies*, 10 (4), 355–7.

Elliott, J. (1991) *Action Research for Educational Change*. Buckingham: Open University Press.

Elliott, J. (2001) Making evidence-based practice educational. *British Educational Research Journal*, 27 (5), 555–74.

Ellis, C. (2004) *The Ethnographic I: A Methodological Novel about Autoethnography*. Walnut Creek, CA: AltaMira Press.

Ellsmore, S. (2005) *Carry On, Teachers! Representations of the Teaching Profession in Screen Culture*. Stoke on Trent, UK: Trentham Books.

English, H. B. and English, A. C. (1958) *A Comprehensive Dictionary of Psychological and Psychoanalytic Terms*. London: Longman.

Epstein, J. M. (1996) *Growing Artificial Societies: Social Science from the Bottom up (Complex Adaptive Systems)*. Cambridge, MA: MIT Press/Brookings Institution.

Epting, F. R., Suchman, D. I. and Nickeson, K. J. (1971) An evaluation of elicitation procedures for personal constructs. *British Journal of Psychology*, 62 (4), 513–17.

Ercikan, K. and Roth, W. M. (2006) What good is polarizing research into qualitative and quantitative? *Educational Researcher*, 35 (5), 14–23.

Erickson, F. (1973) What makes school ethnography 'ethnographic'? *Anthropology and Education Quarterly*, 4 (2), 10–19.

Erickson, F. E. (1992) Ethnographic microanalysis of interaction. In M. LeCompte, W. L. Millroy and J. Preissle (eds) *The Handbook of Qualitative Research in Education*. London: Academic Press, 201–26.

Erikson, K. T. (1967) A comment on disguised observation in sociology. *Social Problems*, 14 (4), 366–73.

Errington, E. (1997) *Role Play* (HERDSA Green Guide No. 21). Australia: Higher Education Research and Development Society of Australasia.

Ess, C. and the Association of Internet Researchers (2002) *Ethical Decision-making and Internet Research: Recommendations from the AoIR Ethics Working Committee*. Retrieved 14 February 2010, from www.aoir.org/reports/ethics.pdf.

Evans, J. and Benefield, P. (2001) Systematic reviews of educational research: does the medical model fit? *British Educational Research Journal*, 27 (5), 527–541.

Evans, J., Sharp, C. and Benefield, P. (2000) Systematic reviews of educational research: does the medical model fit? Paper presented at the British Educational Research Association Conference, University of Cardiff, UK, 7–10 September.

Evans, K. M. (1978) *Planning Small Scale Research*. Windsor: NFER Publishing.

Eysenck, H. (1978) An exercise in mega-silliness. *American Psychologist*, 33 (5), 517.

Ezzy, D. (2002) *Qualitative Analysis: Practice and Innovation*. London: Routledge.

Fairclough, N. (1995) *Critical Discourse Analysis: The Critical Study of Language*. London: Longman.

Farberow, N. L. (ed.) (1963) *Taboo Topics*. New York: Atherton Press.

Farquharson, K. (2005) A different kind of snowball: identifying key policymakers. *International Journal of Social Research Methodology*, 8 (4), 345–53.

Faugier, J. and Sargeant, M. (1997) Sampling hard to reach populations. *Journal of Advanced Nursing*, 26 (4), 790–7.

Fay, B. (1987) *Critical Social Science*. New York: Cornell University Press.

Feilzer, M. Y. (2010) Doing mixed methods research pragmatically: implications for the rediscovery of pragmatism as a research paradigm. *Journal of Mixed Methods Research*, 4 (1), 6–16.

Feldt, L. S. and Brennan, R. L. (1993) Reliability. In R. Linn (ed.) *Educational Measurement*. New York: Macmillan, 105–46.

Fendler, L. (1999) Making trouble: prediction, agency, critical intellectuals. In T. S. Popkewitz and L. Fendler (eds) *Critical Theories in Education: Changing Terrains of Knowledge and Politics*. London: Routledge, 169–88.

Ferrance, E. (2000) *Action Research*. Providence, RI: Northeast and Islands Regional Educational Laboratory at Brown University. Retrieved 16 April 2010, from www.alliance.brown.edu/pubs/themes_ed/act_research.pdf.

Ferris, J. and Gerber, R. (1996) Mature-age students' feelings of enjoying learning in a further education context. *European Journal of Psychology of Education*, 11 (1), 79–96.

Festinger, L. and Katz, D. (1966) *Research Methods in the Behavioral Sciences*. New York: Holt, Rinehart and Winston.

Fetscherin, M. and Lattemann, C. (2007) *User Acceptance of Virtual Worlds: An Explorative Study about Second Life*. Rollins College, FL/University of Potsdam, Germany.

Feyerabend, P. (1975) *Against Method: Outline of an Anarchistic Theory of Knowledge*. London: New Left Books.

Fiedler, J. (1978) *Field Research: A Manual for Logistics and Management of Scientific Studies in Natural Settings*. London: Jossey-Bass.

Field, P. A. and Morse, J. M. (1989) *Nursing Research: The Application of Qualitative Methods*. London: Chapman and Hall.

Fielding, N. G. and Fielding, J. L. (1986) *Linking Data*. Beverly Hills, CA: Sage.

Fielding, N. G. and Lee, R. M. (1998) *Computer Analysis and Qualitative Research*. London: Sage.

Fielding, N. G., Lee, R. M and Blank, G. (eds) (2008) *The Sage Handbook of Internet Online Research Methods*. London: Sage.

Figueroa, S. K. (2008) The grounded theory analysis of audiovisual texts. *International Journal of Social Research Methodology*, 11 (1), 1–12.

Finch, J. (1985) Social policy and education: problems and possibilities of using qualitative research. In R. G. Burgess (ed.) *Issues in Educational Research: Qualitative Methods*. Lewes: Falmer, 109–28.

Finch, J. (2004) Feminism and qualitative research. *International Journal of Social Research Methodology*, 7 (1), 61–4.

Fine, G. A. and Sandstrom, K. L. (1988) *Knowing Children: Participant Observation with Minors*. Qualitative Research Methods Series 15. Thousand Oaks, CA: Sage.

Fine, M. (2010) *A Brief History of the Participatory Action Research Collective*. Institute for Participatory Action Research and Design, City of New York Graduate Center. New York. Retrieved 18 April 2010, from http://web.gc.cuny.edu/che/start.htm.

Finlay-Johnson, H. (1912/2008) *The Dramatic Method of Teaching*. London: Kessinger Publishing.

Finn, C. E. (1991) What ails education research? In D. S. Anderson and B. J. Biddle (eds) *Knowledge for Policy: Improving Education through Research*. London: Falmer, 39–42.

Finnegan, R. (1996) Using documents. In R. Sapsford and V. Jupp (eds) *Data Collection and Analysis*. London: Sage and the Open University Press, 138–51.

Fisher, B., Russell, T. and McSweeney, P. (1991) Using personal constructs for course evaluation. *Journal of Further and Higher Education*, 15 (1), 44–57.

Fiske, J. (1995) Audiencing. In N. K. Denzin and Y. S. Lincoln (eds) *Handbook of Qualitative Methods*. London: Sage, 188–98.

Fiske, S. T. (1993) Controlling other people: the impact of power on stereotyping. *American Psychologist*, 48 (6), 621–8.

Fitz, J. and Halpin, D. (1994) Ministers and mandarins: educational research in elite settings. In G. Walford (ed.) *Researching the Powerful in Education*. London: UCL Press, 32–50.

Fitz-Gibbon, C. T. (1984) Meta-analysis: an explanation. *British Educational Research Journal*, 10 (2), 135–44.

Fitz-Gibbon, C. T. (1985) The implications of meta-analysis for educational research, *British Educational Research Journal*, 11 (1), 45–9.

Fitz-Gibbon, C. T. (1991) Multilevel modelling in an indicator system. In S. W. Raudenbush and J. D. Willms (eds) *Schools, Classrooms and Pupils. International Studies of Schooling from a Multilevel Perspective*. San Diego, CA: Academic Press, 67–83.

Fitz-Gibbon, C. T. (1996) *Monitoring Education: Indicators, Quality and Effectiveness*. London: Cassell.

Fitz-Gibbon, C. T. (1997) *The Value Added National Project. Final Report*. London: School Curriculum and Assessment Authority.

Fitz-Gibbon, C. T. (1999) Education: high potential not yet realized. *Public Money and Management*, 19 (1), 33–9.

Fitz-Gibbon, C. T. and Morris, L. L. (1987) *How to Design a Program Evaluation*. Newbury Park, CA: Sage.

Flanagan, J. (1949) Critical requirements: a new approach to employee evaluation. Cited in E. C. Wragg, *An Introduction to Classroom Observation*. London: Routledge.

Flanders, N. (1970) *Analyzing Teacher Behaviour*. Reading, MA: Addison-Wesley.

Flaugher, R. (1990) Item pools. In H. Wainer (ed.) *Computerized Adaptive Testing: A Primer*. Mahwah, NJ: Lawrence Erlbaum, 41–64.

Flick, U. (1998) *An Introduction to Qualitative Research*. London: Sage.

Flick, U. (2004a) *An Introduction to Qualitative Research* (fourth edition). London: Sage.

Flick, U. (2004b) Design and process in qualitative research. In U. Flick, E. von Kardoff and I. Steinke (eds) *A Companion to Qualitative Research*. London: Sage, 146–52.

Flick, U. (2009) *An Introduction to Qualitative Research* (fourth edition). London: Sage.

Flick, U., von Kardoff, E. and Steinke, I. (eds) (2004) *A Companion to Qualitative Research* (trans. B. Jenner). London: Sage.

Floud, R. (1979) *An Introduction to Quantitative Methods for Historians* (second edition). London: Methuen.

Fogelman, K. (2002) Surveys and sampling. In M. Coleman and A. R. J. Briggs (eds) *Research Methods in Educational Leadership*. London: Paul Chapman, 93–108.

Forgas, J. P. (1976) The perception of social episodes: categoric and dimensional representations in two different social milieux. *Journal of Personality and Social Psychology*, 34 (2), 199–209.

Forgas, J. P. (1978) Social episodes and social structure in an academic setting: the social environment of an intact group. *Journal of Experimental Social Psychology*, 14 (5), 434–8.

Foskett, N. H. and Hesketh, A. J. (1997) Constructing choice in continuous and parallel markets: institutional and school leavers' responses to the new post-16 marketplace. *Oxford Review of Education*, 23 (3), 299–319.

Foster, P. (1989) Change and adjustment in a Further Education college. In R. G. Burgess (ed.) *The Ethics of Educational Research*, Lewes: Falmer, 188–204.

Foster, S. (1999) The struggle for American identity: treatment of ethnic groups in United States history textbooks. *History of Education*, 28 (3), 251–78.

Fothergill, R. (1974) *Private Chronicles: A Study of English Diaries*. London: Oxford University Press.

Foucault, M. (1998) *The History of Sexuality: The Will to Knowledge*. London: Penguin.

Fournier, V. (1997) Graduates' construction systems and career development. *Human Relations*, 50, 363–91.

Fowler, F. J. Jr. (2009) *Survey Research Methods* (fourth edition). Thousand Oaks, CA: Sage.

Fowler, J., Cohen, L. and Jarvis, P. (2000) *Practical Statistics for Field Biology*. Chichester: John Wiley.

Fox, D. J. (1969) *The Research Process in Education*. New York: Holt, Rinehart and Winston.

Francis, B. (2010) Gender, toys and learning. *Oxford Review of Education*, 36 (3), 325–44.

Francis, H. (1992) Patterns of reading development in the first school. *British Journal of Educational Psychology*, 62, 225–32.

Frankfort-Nachmias, C. and Nachmias, D. (1992) *Research Methods in the Social Sciences*. London: Edward Arnold.

Fransella, F. (2003) *International Handbook of Personal Construct Psychology*. New York: John Wiley.

Fransella, F. and Bannister, D. (1977) *A Manual for Repertory Grid Technique*. London: Academic Press.

Fransella, F., Bell, R. and Bannister, D. (2004) *A Manual for the Repertory Grid Technique* (second edition). Chichester: Wiley.

Fraser, H. (2004) Doing narrative research: analysing personal stories line by line. *Qualitative Social Work*, 3 (2), 179–201.

Fredericksen, J. R. and Collins, A. (1989) A systems approach to educational testing. *Educational Researcher*, 189, 27–32.

Freeman, L. (2003) Simulation and role playing with LEGO ® Blocks. *Journal of Information Systems Education*, 14 (2), 137–44.

Freire, P. (1972) *Pedagogy of the Oppressed*. Harmondsworth: Penguin.

Frick, A., Bächtiger, M. T. and Reips, U.-D. (1999) Financial incentives, personal information and dropout rate in online studies. In U.-D. Reips and M. Bosnjak (eds) *Dimensions of Internet Science*. Lengerich, Germany: Pabst Science, 209–19.

Fricker, R. D. Jr. and Schonlau, M. (2002) *Advantages and Disadvantages of Internet-Surveys: Evidence from the Literature*. Washington: Rand Organization. Retrieved 26 January 2005, from www.schonlau.net/publication/ 02field-methods.pdf.

Friedman, H. H. and Amoo, T. (1999) Rating the rating scales. *Journal of Marketing Management*, 9 (3), 114–23.

Frisbie, D. (1981) The relative difficulty ratio – a test and item index. *Educational and Psychological Measurement*, 41 (2), 333–9.

Frost, J. L., Wortham, S. C. and Reifel, S. (2008) *Play and Child Development* (third edition). Upper Saddle River, NJ: Pearson.

Fullan, M. G. (1999) *Change Forces* (second edition). London: Falmer.

Fullan, M. G. (2007) *The New Meaning of Educational Change*. London: Routledge.

Furlong, J. and Oancea, A. (2005) *Assessing Quality in Applied and Practice-based Educational Research*. Oxford: Department of Educational Studies, University of Oxford. Retrieved 10 October 2008, from www.esrc.ac.uk/ESRCInfoCentre/Images/assessing_quality_shortreport_tcm6–8232.pdf.

Gadamer, H. G. (1975) *Truth and Method*. New York: Polity Press.

Gadd, D. (2004) Making sense of interviewee–interviewer dynamics in narratives about violence in intimate relationships. *International Journal of Social Research Methodology*, 7 (5), 383–401.

Gage, N. L. (1989) The paradigm wars and their aftermath. *Teachers College Record*, 91 (2), 135–50.

Gallagher, T., McEwen, A. and Knip, D. (1997) Science education policy: a survey of the participation of sixth-form pupils in science and the subjects over a 10-year period, 1985–95. *Research Papers in Education*, 12 (2), 121–42.

Galton, M., Hargreaves, L., Comber, C., Wall, D. and Pell, T. (1999) Changes in patterns in teacher interaction in primary classrooms, 1976–1996. *British Educational Research Journal*, 25 (1), 23–37.

Galton, M. and Simon, B. (1980) *Inside the Primary Classroom*. London: Routledge.

García-Horta, J. B. and Guerra-Ramos, M. T (2009) The use of CAQDAS in educational research: some advantages, limitations and potential risks. *International Journal of Research and Method in Education*, 32 (2), 151–65.

Gardner, G. (1978) *Social Surveys for Social Planners*. Milton Keynes: Open University Press.

Gardner, H. (1993) *Multiple Intelligences: The Theory in Practice*. New York: Basic Books.

Gardner, P. (2003) Oral history in education: teachers' memory and teachers' history. *History of Education*, 32 (2), 175–88.

Garfinkel, H. (1967) *Studies in Ethnomethodology*. Englewood Cliffs, NJ: Prentice-Hall.

Garner, C. and Raudenbush, S. W. (1991) Neighbourhood effects in educational attainment: a multilevel analysis. *Sociology of Education*, 64 (4), 251–62.

Garrahan, P. and Stewart, P. (1992) *The Nissan Enigma: Flexibility at Work in a Local Economy*. London: Mansell.

Gaskell, G. D., O'Muircheartaigh, C. A. and Wright, D. B. (1994). Survey questions about the frequency of vaguely defined events: the effects of response alternatives. *Public Opinion Quarterly*, 58 (2), 241–54.

Gaukroger, A. and Schwartz, L. (1997) A university and its region: student recruitment to Birmingham, 1945–75. *Oxford Review of Education*, 23 (2), 185–202.

Gee, J. P. (2004) *Situated Language in Learning: A Critique of Traditional Schooling*. New York: Routledge.

Geertz, C. (1973) *The Interpretation of Cultures*. New York: Basic Books.

Geertz, C. (1974) From the native's point of view: on the nature of anthropological understanding. *Bulletin of the American Academy of Arts and Sciences*, 28 (1), 26–45.

Geuss, R. (1981) *The Idea of a Critical Theory*. London: Cambridge University Press.

Gewirtz, S. and Ozga. J. (1993) Sex, lies and audiotape: interviewing the education policy elite. Paper presented to the Economic and Research Council, 1988 Education Reform Act Research seminar. University of Warwick.

Gewirtz, S. and Ozga, J. (1994) Interviewing the education policy elite. In G. Walford (ed.) *Researching the Powerful in Education*. London: UCL Press, 186–203.

Gibbs, G. (2007) *Analyzing Qualitative Data*. London: Sage.

Gibson, R. (1985) Critical times for action research. *Cambridge Journal of Education*, 15 (1), 59–64.

Giddens, A. (1975) *Positivism and Sociology*. London: Heinemann.

Giddens, A. (1976) *New Rules of Sociological Method: A Positive Critique of Interpretative Sociologies*. London: Hutchinson.

Giddens, A. (1979) *Central Problems in Social Theory*. London: Macmillan.

Giddens. A. (1984) *The Constitution of Society*. Cambridge: Polity Press.

Giddings, L. S. (2006) Mixed methods research: positivism dressed in drag? *Journal of Research in Nursing*, 11 (3), 195–203.

Gilbert, N. and Troitzsch, K. G. (2005) *Simulation for the Social Scientist* (second edition). Maidenhead: Open University Press.

Gillies, V. and Alldred, P. (2002) The ethics of intention: research as a political tool. In M. Mauthner, M. Birch, J. Jessop and T. Miller (eds) *Ethics in Qualitative Research*. London: Sage, 32–52.

Ginsberg, G. P. (1978) Role playing and role performance in social psychological research. In M. Brenner and P. Marsh (eds) *The Social Context of Method*. London: Croom Helm, 91–121.

Gipps, C. (1994) *Beyond Testing: Towards a Theory of Educational Assessment*. London: Falmer.

Giroux, H. A. (1983) *Theory and Resistance in Education*. London: Heinemann.

Giroux, H. A. (1989) *Schooling for Democracy*. London: Routledge.

Glaser, B. G. (1978) *Theoretical Sensitivity: Advances in the Methodology of Grounded Theory*. Mill Valley, CA: Sociology Press.

Glaser, B. G. (1996) Grounded theory: an interview with Barney Glaser. Video material for Program 8 of the course *Doing a Ph D in Business and Management*. University of Stirling and Heriot-Watt University.

Glaser, B. G. and Strauss, A. L. (1967) *The Discovery of Grounded Theory*. Chicago, IL: Aldane.

Glass, G. V. (1976) Primary, secondary and meta-analysis. *Educational Researcher*, 5 (10), 3–8.

Glass, G. V. (1977) Integrating findings: the meta-analysis of research. *Review of Research in Education*, 5, 351–79.

Glass, G. V. and Hopkins, K. D. (1996) *Statistical Methods in Education and Psychology* (third edition). Boston, MA: Allyn and Bacon.

Glass, G. V. and Smith, M.L. (1978) *Meta-Analysis of Research on the Relationship of Class-size and Achievement*. San Francisco, CA: Farwest Laboratory.

Glass, G. V. and Worthen, B. R. (1971) Evaluation and research: similarities and differences. *Curriculum Theory Network*, 3 (Fall), 149–65.

Glass, G. V., McGaw, B. and Smith, M. L. (1981) *Meta-Analysis in Social Research*. Beverly Hills, CA: Sage.

Gleick, J. (1987) *Chaos*. London: Abacus.

Glover, D. and Bush, T. (2005) The online or e-survey: a research approach for the ICT age. *International Journal of Research and Method in Education*, 28 (2), 135–46.

Gobo, G. and Diotti, A. (2008) Useful resources: ethnography through the internet. *International Journal of Social Research Methodology*, 11 (4), 357–82.

Goffman, E. (1968) *Asylums*. Harmondsworth: Penguin.

Goffman, E. (1969) *The Presentation of Self in Everyday Life*. Harmondsworth: Penguin.

Goffman, E. (1976) The presentation of self in everyday life. In J. E. Combs and M. W. Mansfield (eds) *Drama in Life: The Uses of Communication in Society*. New York: Hastings House Publishers, 62–72.

Golafshani, N. (2003) Understanding reliability and validity in qualitative research. *Qualitative Report*, 8 (4), 597–607. Retrieved 29 October 2005, from www.nova.edu/ssss/QR/QR8–4/golafshani.pdf.

Gold, R. L. (1958) Roles in sociological field observations. *Social Forces*, 36 (3), 217–23.

Goldstein, H. (1987) *Multilevel Modelling in Educational and Social Research*. London: Charles Griffin.

Goldstein, R. J. (ed.) (2009) *The Frightful Stage: Political Censorship of the Theater in Nineteenth-Century Europe*. Providence, RI: Berghahn Books.

Goldthorpe, J. H. (2007) *On Sociology. Volume Two: Illustration and Retrospect* (second edition). Stanford, CA: Stanford University Press.

Gomm, R. and Hammersley, M. (2001) Thick description and thin models of complexity. Paper presented at the annual conference of the British Educational Research Association. University of Leeds, September.

Gonzales, L., Brown, M. S., Slate, J. R. (2008) Teachers who left the teaching professions: a qualitative understanding. *Qualitative Report*, 13 (1), 1–11.

Good, C. V. (1963) *Introduction to Educational Research.* New York: Appleton-Century-Crofts.

Goodson, I. (1983) The use of life histories in the study of teaching. In M. Hammersley (ed.) *The Ethnography of Schooling.* Driffield: Nafferton Books, 129–54.

Goodson, I. (1988) *The Making of Curriculum: Collected Essays.* London: Falmer.

Goodwin, B. (2000) Out of control into participation. *Emergence*, 2 (4), 40–9.

Goossens, L., Marcoen, A., van Hees, S. and van de Woestljne, O. (1998) Attachment style and loneliness in adolescence. *European Journal of Psychology of Education*, 13 (4), 529–42.

Gorard, S. (2001a) A changing climate for educational research? The role of research capability-building. Paper presented at the British Educational Research Association annual conference, University of Leeds, September.

Gorard, S. (2001b) *Quantitative Methods in Educational Research: The Role of Numbers Made Easy.* London: Continuum.

Gorard, S. (2003) *Quantitative Methods in Social Science.* London: Continuum.

Gorard, S. (2007) The dubious benefits of multi-level modelling. *International Journal of Research and Method in Education*, 30 (2), 221–36.

Gorard, S., Roberts, K. and Taylor, C. (2004) What kind of creature is a design experiment? *British Educational Research Journal*, 30 (4), 575–88.

Gorard, S. and Smith, E. (2006) Editorial: combining numbers with narratives. *Evaluation and Research in Education*, 19 (2), 59–62.

Gorard, S. and Taylor, C. (2004) *Combining Methods in Educational and Social Research.* Buckingham, UK: Open University Press.

Gorard, S., Taylor, C. and Fitz, J. (2002) Markets in public policy: the case of the United Kingdom Education Reform Act. *International Studies in Sociology of Education*, 12 (1), 23–42.

Gordon, T. and Lahelma, E. (2003) From ethnography to life history: tracing transitions of school students. *International Journal of Social Research Methodology*, 6 (3), 245–54.

Gosden, P. (1981) Twentieth-century archives of education as sources for the study of education policy and administration, *Archives*, 66, 86–95.

Gottschalk, L. (1951) *Understanding History.* New York: Alfred A. Knopf.

Graue, M. E. and Walsh, D. J. (1998) *Studying Children in Context: Theories, Methods and Ethics.* London: Sage.

Greckhamer, T. and Koro-Ljungberg, M. (2005) The erosion of a method: examples from grounded theory. *International Journal of Qualitative Studies in Education*, 18 (6), 729–50.

Greene, J. C. (2005) The generative potential of mixed methods inquiry. *International Journal of Research and Method in Education*, 28 (2), 207–11.

Greene, J. C. (2008) Is mixed methods social inquiry a distinctive methodology? *Journal of Mixed Methods Research*, 2 (1), 7–22.

Greig, A. D. and Taylor, J. (1999) *Doing Research with Children.* London: Sage.

Gronlund, N. E. (1981) *Measurement and Evaluation in Teaching* (fourth edition). New York: Collier-Macmillan.

Gronlund, N. E. (1985) *Stating Objectives for Classroom Instruction* (third edition). New York: Macmillan.

Gronlund, N. E. and Linn, R. L. (1990) *Measurement and Evaluation in Teaching* (sixth edition). New York: Macmillan.

Grosvenor, I. (2007) From the 'eye of history' to a 'second gaze': the visual archive and the marginalized in the history of education. *History of Education*, 36 (4 and 5), 607–22.

Grumet, M. (1998) Research conversations: visible pedagogies/generous pedagogies. In J. Saxton and C. Miller (eds) *The Research of Practice. The Practice of Research.* Victoria, BC, International Drama in Education Research Institute, 7–11.

Grundy, S. (1987) *Curriculum: Product or Praxis.* Lewes: Falmer.

Grundy, S. (1996) Towards empowering leadership: the importance of imagining. In O. Zuber-Skerritt (ed.) *New Directions in Action Research.* London: Falmer, 106–20.

Grundy, S. and Kemmis, S. (1988) Educational action research in Australia: the state of the art (an overview). In S. Kemmis and R. McTaggart (eds) *The Action Research Reader* (second edition). Victoria: Deakin University Press, 83–97.

Guardian (2003) article: Online archive brings Britain's migration story to life, 30 July, p. 7.

Guardian (2007) supplement, The Archive, 3 November.

Guba, E. G and Lincoln, Y. S. (1989) *Fourth Generation Evaluation.* Beverly Hills, CA: Sage.

Guba, E. G. and Lincoln, Y. S. (1994) Competing paradigms in qualitative research. In N. K. Denzin and Y. S. Lincoln (eds) *Handbook of Qualitative Research.* Beverly Hills, CA: Sage, 105–117.

Guilford, J. P. and Fruchter, B. (1973) *Fundamental Statistics in Psychology and Education.* New York: McGraw-Hill.

Gwartney, P. A. (2007) *The Telephone Interviewer's Handbook.* San Francisco, CA: Jossey-Bass.

Habermas, J. (1970) Toward a theory of communicative competence. *Inquiry*, 13 (1–4), 360–75.

Habermas, J. (1972) *Knowledge and Human Interests* (trans. J. Shapiro). London: Heinemann.

Habermas, J. (1974) *Theory and Practice* (trans. J. Viertel). London: Heinemann.

Habermas, J. (1976) *Legitimation Crisis* (trans. T. McCarthy). London: Heinemann.

Habermas, J. (1979) *Communication and the Evolution of Society* (trans. T. McCarthy). London: Heinemann.

Habermas, J. (1982) A reply to my critics. In J. Thompson and D. Held (eds) *Habermas: Critical Debates.* London: Macmillan, 219–83.

Habermas, J. (1984) *The Theory of Communicative Action. Volume One: Reason and the Rationalization of Society* (trans. T. McCarthy). Boston, MA: Beacon Press.

Habermas, J. (1987) *The Philosophical Discourse of Modernity* (trans. F. Lawrence). Cambridge, MA: MIT.

Habermas, J. (1988) *On the Logic of the Social Sciences* (trans. S. Nicholsen and J. Stark). Oxford: Polity Press in association with Basil Blackwell.

Habermas, J. (1990) *Moral Consciousness and Communicative Action* (trans. C. Lenhardt and S. Nicholsen). Cambridge: Polity Press in association with Basil Blackwell.

Hage, J. and Meeker, B. F. (1988) *Social Causality*. London: Unwin Hyman.

Haig, B. D. (1997) Feminist research methodology. In J. P. Keeves (ed.) *Educational Research, Methodology, and Measurement: An International Handbook* (second edition). Oxford: Elsevier Science, 180–5.

Haig, B. D. (1999) Feminist research methodology. In J. P. Keeves and G. Lakomski (eds) *Issues in Educational Research*. Oxford: Elsevier Science, 222–31.

Hakim, C. (1982) *Secondary Analysis in Social Research: A Guide to Data Sources and Methods with Examples*. London: George Allen and Unwin.

Haladyna, T. M. (1997) *Writing Test Items to Evaluate Higher Order Thinking*. Needham Heights, MA: Allyn and Bacon.

Haladyna, T. M., Nolen, S. and Haas, N. (1991) Raising standardised achievement test scores and the origins of test score pollution. *Educational Researcher*, 20 (5), 2–7.

Hall, B. (2005) Breaking the monopoly of knowledge: research methods, participation and development. In R. Tandon (ed.) *Participatory Research: Revisiting the Roots*. New Delhi: Mosaic Books, 9–21.

Hall, E., Hall, C. and Abaci, R. (1997) The effects of human relations training on reported teacher stress, pupil control ideology and locus of control. *British Journal of Educational Psychology*, 67 (4), 483–96.

Hall, K. and Nuttall, W. (1999) The *relative* importance of class size to infant teachers in England. *British Educational Research Journal*, 25 (2), 245–58.

Hall, S. (1996) Reflexivity in emancipatory action research: illustrating the researcher's constitutiveness. In O. Zuber-Skerritt (ed.) *New Directions in Action Research*. London: Falmer, 26–48.

Halperin, D. M (1997) *Saint Foucault: Towards a Gay Hagiography*. New York: Oxford University Press.

Halsey, A. H. (ed.) (1972) *Educational Priority: Volume 1: E. P. A. Problems and Policies*. London: HMSO.

Halstead, M. (1988) *Education, Justice and Cultural Diversity: An Examination of the Honeyford Affair, 1984–85*. London: Falmer.

Hambleton, R. K. (1993) Principles and selected application of item response theory. In R. Linn (ed.) *Educational Measurement* (third edition). Phoenix: AZ American Council on Education and the Oryx Press, 147–200.

Hamilton, V. L. (1976) Role play and deception: a re-examination of the controversy. *Journal for the Theory of Social Behaviour*, 6 (2), 233–50.

Hammersley, M. (1992a) Deconstructing the qualitative-quantitative divide. In J. Brannen (ed.) *Mixing Methods: Qualitative and Quantitative Research*. Aldershot, UK: Avebury, 39–57.

Hammersley, M. (1992b) *What's Wrong with Ethnography?* London: Routledge.

Hammersley, M. (1993) *Social Research: Philosophy, Politics and Practice*. London: Sage with the Open University Press.

Hammersley, M. (2000) Varieties of social research: a typology. *International Journal of Social Research Methodology*, 3 (5), 221–9.

Hammersley, M. (2006) Ethnography: problems and prospects. *Ethnography and Education*, 1 (1), 3–14.

Hammersley, M. (2008) Paradigm war revived? On the diagnosis of resistance to randomized controlled trials and systematic review in education. *International Journal of Research and Method in Education*, 31 (1), 3–10.

Hammersley, M. (2009) Against the ethicists: on the evils of ethical regulation. *International Journal of Social Research Methodology*, 12 (3), 211–25.

Hammersley, M. and Atkinson, P. (1983) *Ethnography: Principles in Practice*. London: Routledge.

Hampden-Turner, C. (1970) *Radical Man*. Cambridge, MA: Schenkman.

Haney, C., Ranks, C. and Zimbardo, P. (1973) Interpersonal dynamics in a simulated prison. *International Journal of Criminology and Penology*, 1 (1), 69–97.

Haney, C. and Zimbardo, P. G. (1998) The past and future of U.S. prison policy: twenty-five years after the Stanford Prison Experiment. *American Psychologist*, 53 (7), 709–27.

Hanna, G. S. (1993) *Better Teaching through Better Measurement*. Fort Worth, TX: Harcourt Brace Jovanovich.

Hannan, A. and Newby, M. (1992) Student teacher and headteacher views on current provision and proposals for the future of Initial Teacher Education for primary schools (mimeo). Rolle Faculty of Education, University of Plymouth.

Hare, A. P. (1985) *Social Interactions as Drama: Applications from Conflict Resolution*. Beverly Hills, CA: Sage.

Haritos, A., Gindidis, A., Doan, C. and Bell, R. C. (2004) The effect of element role titles on construct structure and content. *Journal of Constructivist Psychology*, 17 (3), 221–36.

Harlen, W. (ed.) (1994) *Enhancing Quality in Assessment*. London: Paul Chapman.

Harper, D. (2000) Reimagining visual methods: Galileo to Neuromancer. In N. Denzin and Y. S. Lincoln (eds) *Handbook of Qualitative Research* (second edition). London: Sage, 717–32.

Harper, D. (2004) Photography as social science data. In U. Flick, E. von Kardoff and I. Steinke (eds) *A Companion to Qualitative Research*. London: Sage, 237–42.

Harré, R. (1972) *The Philosophies of Science*. Oxford: Oxford University Press.

Harré, R. (1974) Some remarks on 'rule' as a scientific concept. In T. Mischel (ed.) *On Understanding Persons*. Oxford: Basil Blackwell, 143–84.

Harré, R. (1976) The constructive role of models. In L. Collins, (ed.) *The Use of Models in the Social Sciences*. London: Tavistock Publications, 16–43.

Harré, R. (1977a) The ethogenic approach: theory and practice. In L. Berkowitz (ed.) *Advances in Experimental Social Psychology*, Vol. 10. New York: Academic Press, 284–314.

Harré, R. (1977b) Friendship as an accomplishment. In S. Duck (ed.) *Theory and Practice in Interpersonal Attraction*. London: Academic Press, 339–54.

Harré, R. (1978) Accounts, actions and meanings – the practice of participatory psychology. In M. Brenner, P. Marsh and M. Brenner (eds) *The Social Contexts of Method*. London: Croom Helm, 44–66.

Harré, R. and Secord, P. (1972) *The Explanation of Social Behaviour*. Oxford: Basil Blackwell.

Harris, N., Pearce, P. and Johnstone, S. (1992) *The Legal Context of Teaching*. London: Longman.

Harrison, R. and Stokes, H. (1992) *Diagnosing Organizational Culture*. San Francisco, CA: Jossey-Bass.

Hart, R. (1992) *Children's Participation: from Tokenism to Citizenship*. Paris: UNICEF.

Hartley, J. and Betts, L. R. (2010) Four layouts and a finding: the effects of changes in the order of the verbal labels and numerical values on Likert-type scales. *International Journal of Social Research Methodology*, 13 (1), 17–27.

Hartley, S., Gerhardt-Powals, J., Jones, D., McCormack, C., Medley, D., Price, B., Reek, M. and Summers, M. (1997) *Evaluating Educational Materials on the Web*. University of Washington. Retrieved 1 May 2003, from http://staff.washington.edu/rells/pod97/evaluate.htm.

Harvey, C. D. H. (1988) Telephone survey techniques. *Canadian Home Economics Journal*, 38 (1), 30–5.

Healy, K. (2001) Participatory action research and social work. *International Social Work*, 4 (1), 93–105.

Heath, C. and Hindmarsh, J. (2002) Analysing interaction: video, ethnography and situated conduct. In T. May (ed.) *Qualitative Research in Action*. London: Sage, 99–120.

Heath, D. (2009) *The Literature Review: A Few Tips On Conducting It*. Health Sciences Writing Center, University of Toronto. 2010 *Literature Reviews*. Retrieved 6 February 2009, from www.writing.utoronto.ca/advice/specific-types-of-writing/literature-review.

Heath, S. B. (1982) Questioning at home and at school: a comparative study, In G. Spindler (ed.) *Doing the Ethnography of Schooling*. New York: Holt, Rinehart and Winston, 102–31.

Heath, S. B. (1997) Child's play or finding the ephemera of home. In M. Hilton, M. Styles and V. Watson (eds) *Opening the Nursery Door: Reading, Writing and Childhood 1600–1900*. London: Routledge, 17–30.

Heathcote, D. (1980) Drama and education: subject or system? In N. Dodds and W. Hickson (eds) *Drama and Theatre in Education*. London: Heinemann Educational, 42–62.

Heathcote, D. (1991) *Collected Writings on Education and Drama* (edited by L. Johnson and C. O'Neill). Evanston, IL: Northwestern University Press.

Heckathorn, D. D. (1997) Respondent-driven sampling: a new approach to the study of hidden populations. *Social Problems*, 44 (2), 174–99.

Heckathorn, D. D. (2002) Respondent-driven sampling II: deriving population estimates from chain-referral samples of hidden populations. *Social Problems*, 49 (1), 11–34.

Hedges, A. (1985) Group interviewing. In R. Walker (ed.) *Applied Qualitative Research*. Aldershot: Gower, 71–91.

Hedges, L. (1981) Distribution theory for Glass's estimator of effect size and related estimators. *Journal of Educational Statistics*, 6 (2), 107–28.

Hedges, L. (1990) Directions for future methodology. In K. W. Wachter and M. L. Straf (eds.) *The Future of Meta-analysis*. New York: Russell Sage Foundation, cited in B. McGaw, Meta-analysis. In J. P. Keeves (ed.) *Educational Research,*

Methodology, and Measurement: an International Handbook (second edition). Oxford: Elsevier Science Ltd., 371–80

Hedges, L. and Olkin, I. (1980) Vote-counting methods in research synthesis. *Psychological Bulletin*, 88 (2), 359–69.

Hedges, L. and Olkin, I. (1985) *Statistical Methods for Meta-analysis*. New York: Academic Press.

Heerwegh, D., Vanhove, T., Matthijs, K. and Loosveldt, G. (2005) The effect of personalization on response rates and data quality in web surveys. *International Journal of Social Research Methodology*, 8 (2), 85–99.

Held, D. (1980) *Introduction to Critical Theory*. Los Angeles, CA: University of California Press.

Hemsley-Brown, J. and Sharp, C. (2003) The use of research to improve professional practice: a systematic review of the literature. *Oxford Review of Education*, 29 (4), 449–70.

Hesse, M. (1982) Science and objectivity. In J. Thompson and D. Held (eds) *Habermas: Critical Debates*. London: Macmillan, 98–115.

Heward, C. (1988) *Making a Man of Him: Parents and their Sons' Education at an English Public School, 1929–50*. London: Routledge.

Hewson, C., Yule, P., Laurent, D. and Vogel, C. (2003) *Internet Research Methods*. London: Sage.

Hickey, D. T. and Zuiker, S. J. (2005) Engaged participation: a socio-cultural model of motivation with implications for educational assessment. *Educational Assessment*, 10 (3), 277–305.

Higgins, J. M. and McAllaster, C. (2004) If you want strategic change, don't forget to change your cultural artifacts. *Journal of Change Management*, 4 (1), 63–73.

Higgs, G., Webster, C. J. and White, S. D. (1997) The use of geographical information systems in assessing spatial and socio-economic impacts of parental choice. *Research Papers in Education*, 12 (1), 27–48.

Hildenbrand, B. (2004) *Anselm Strauss*. In U. Flick, E. von Kardoff and I. Steinke (eds) *A Companion to Qualitative Research*. London: Sage, 17–23.

Hill, J. E. and Kerber, A. (1967) *Models, Methods and Analytical Procedures in Educational Research*. Detroit, MI: Wayne State University Press.

Hill, P. W. and Rowe, K. J. (1996) Multilevel modelling in school effectiveness research. *School Effectiveness and School Improvement*, 7 (1), 1–34.

Hilton, A. and Skrutkowski, M. (2002) Translating instruments into other languages: development and testing processes. *Cancer Nursing*, 25 (1), 1–7.

Hilton, J. (1934) *Goodbye, Mr. Chips*. London: Hodder and Stoughton.

Hinkle, D. N. (1965) The change of personal constructs from the viewpoint of a theory of implications. Unpublished PhD thesis. Ohio State University.

Hitchcock, C. (2002) Probabilistic causation. In *Stanford Encyclopedia of Philosophy*. Retrieved 31 December 2007, from http://plato.stanford.edu/entried/causation-probabilistic/.

Hitchcock, G. and Hughes, D. (1989) *Research and the Teacher*. London: Routledge.

Hitchcock, G. and Hughes, D. (1995) *Research and the Teacher* (second edition). London: Routledge.

Hobsbawm, E. (2002) *Interesting Times: A Twentieth-Century Life*. London: Allen Lane.

Hockett, H. C. (1955) *The Critical Method in Historical Research and Writing*. London: Macmillan.

Hodder, I. (1998) The interpretation of documents and material culture. In N. K. Denzin and Y. S. Lincoln (eds) *Collecting and Interpreting Qualitative Materials*. London: Sage, 110–29.

Hoffman, C. (2001) *Introduction to Sociometry*. Retrieved 10 November 2009, from www.hoopandtree.org/sociometry.htm.

Hofstede, G. H. (1980) *Culture's Consequences: International Differences in Work-related Values*. Beverly Hills, CA: Sage.

Hofstede, G. H. and Bond, M. H. (1984) Hofstede's Cultural dimensions: an independent validation using Rokeach's Value survey. *Journal of Cross-Cultural Psychology*, 15 (4), 417–33.

Hoinville, G. and Jowell, R. (1978) *Survey Research Practice*. London: Heinemann.

Holbrook, D. (1977) *Education, Nihilism and Survival*. London: Darton, Longman and Todd.

Holland, J. H. (1992). *Adaptation in Natural and Artificial Systems: An Introductory Analysis with Applications to Biology, Control, and Artificial Intelligence*. Cambridge, MA: MIT Press.

Holland, J. H. and Miller, J. H. (1991) Artificial adaptive agents in economic theory. *American Economic Review*, 81 (2), 356–71. Retrieved 20 May 2010, from http://ideas.repec.org/s/aea/aecrev17.html.

Holland, P. W. (1986) Statistics and causal inference. *Journal of the American Statistics Association*, 81, 945–70.

Holland, P. W. (2004) 'Evidence for *causal* influence in education research', paper presented at the annual conference of the American Educational Research Association, San Diego, CA. April, 2004.

Holly, P. (1984) *Action Research: A Cautionary Note*. Classroom Action Research Network, Bulletin No. 6. Cambridge Institute of Education.

Holly, P. and Whitehead, D. (1986) *Action Research in Schools: Getting It into Perspective*. Classroom Action Research Network. Cambridge Institute of Education.

Holmes, P. and Karp, M. (1991) *Psychodrama – Inspiration and Technique*. London: Routledge.

Holmes, R. M. (1998) *Fieldwork with Children*. London: Sage.

Holsti, O. R. (1968) Content analysis. In G. Lindzey and E. Aronson (eds) *The Handbook of Social Psychology. Volume 2: Research Methods*. Reading, MA: Addison-Wesley, 596–692.

Hopkins, D. (1985) *A Teacher's Guide to Classroom Research*. Milton Keynes: Open University Press.

Hopkins, K. D., Hopkins, B. R. and Glass, G. V. (1996) *Basic Statistics for the Behavioral Sciences* (third edition). Boston, MA: Allyn and Bacon.

Horkheimer, M. (1972) *Critical Theory: Selected Essays* (trans. M. Connell). New York: Herder and Herder.

Hornsby-Smith, M. (1993) Gaining access. In N. Gilbert (ed.) *Researching Social Life*. London: Sage, 52–67.

Horowitz, I. L. and Katz, J. E. (1991) Brown vs Board of Education. In D. S. Anderson and B. J. Biddle (eds) *Knowledge for Policy: Improving Education Through Research*. London: Falmer, 237–44.

Horwich, P. (1993) Lewis's programme. In E. Sosa and M.

Tooley (eds) *Causation*, Oxford: Oxford University Press, 208–16.

Houchin, J. H. (2003) *Censorship of the American Theatre in the Twentieth Century*. Cambridge: Cambridge University Press.

Houghton, D. (1991) Mr. Chong: a case study of a dependent learner of English for academic purposes. *System*, 19 (1 and 2), 75–90.

Houtkook-Steenstra, H. and van den Bergh, H. (2000) Effects of introductions in large-scale telephone interviews. *Sociological Methods and Research*, 28 (3), 281–300.

Howe, K. R. (1988) Against the quantitative-qualitative incompatibility thesis (or dogmas die hard). *Educational Researcher*, 17 (8), 42–61.

Howe, K. R. and Moses, M. S. (1999) Ethics in educational research. *Review of Research in Education*, 24 (1), 21–59.

Howell Major, C. and Savin-Baden, M. (2010) *An Introduction to Qualitative Research Syntheses: Managing the Information Explosion in Social Science Research*. London: Routledge.

Howitt, D. and Cramer, D. (2005) *Introduction to Research Methods in Psychology*. Harlow: Pearson Education.

Hoyle, E. (1986) *The Politics of School Management*. Sevenoaks: Hodder and Stoughton.

Hoyles, C., Küchemann, D., Healy, L. and Yang, M. (2005) Students' developing knowledge in a subject discipline: insights from combining quantitative and qualitative methods. *International Journal of Social Research Methodology*, 8 (5), 225–38.

Hudson, J. M. and Bruckman, A. (2005) Using empirical data to reason about Internet Research Ethics. In H. Gellersen, K. Schmidt, M. Beaudouin-Lafon and W. E. Mackay (eds) *Proceedings of the Ninth European Conference on Computer-Supported Cooperative Work*, Paris. Berlin: Springer, 287–306.

Hudson, P. and Miller, C. (1997) The treasure hunt: strategies for obtaining maximum response to a postal survey. *Evaluation and Research in Education*, 11 (2), 102–12.

Hughes, J. A. (1976) *Sociological Analysis: Methods of Discovery*. Sunbury-on-Thames: Nelson.

Huizinga, J. (1949) *Homo Ludens*. London: Routledge and Kegan Paul, subsequently published by Paladin.

Hult, M. and Lennung, S. (1980) Towards a definition of action-research: a note and bibliography. *Journal of Management Studies*, 17 (2), 241–50.

Hume, D. (1955) *An Inquiry Concerning Human Understanding*. New York: Liberal Arts Press.

Hume, D. (2000) *A Treatise on Human Nature*, ed. D. E. Norton and M. J. Norton. Oxford: Oxford University Press.

Humphreys, L. (1970) *Tearoom Trade: A Study of Homosexual Encounters in Public Places*. London: Gerald Duckworth.

Humphreys, L. (1975) *Tearoom Trade: Impersonal Sex in Public Places* (enlarged edition). New York: Aldine.

Humphries, S. (1981) *Hooligans or Rebels? An Oral History of Working Class Childhood and Youth*. Oxford: Blackwell.

Hunter, J. E., Schmidt, F. L. and Jackson, G. B. (1982) *Meta-analysis: Cumulating Research Findings across Studies*. Beverly Hills, CA: Sage.

Hurn, C. J. (1978) *The Limits and Possibilities of Schooling.* Boston, MA: Allyn and Bacon.

Hutchinson, B. and Whitehouse, P. (1986) Action research, professional competence and school organization. *British Educational Research Journal*, 12 (1), 85–94.

Hycner, R. H. (1985) Some guidelines for the phenomenological analysis of interview data, *Human Studies*, 8, 279–303.

Hydén, L. C. and Bülow, P. H. (2003) Who's talking: drawing conclusions from focus groups – some methodological considerations. *International Journal of Social Research Methodology*, 6 (5), 305–21.

Ijsselsteijn, W. A., de Ridder, H., Freeman, J. and Avons, S. E. (2000) Presence: concept, determinants and measurement, *Proceedings of the SPIE*, 3959, 520–9.

INCITE (2010) *Participatory Action Research.* Redmond, WA: INCITE. Retrieved 24 April 2010, from www.incite-national.org/media/docs/5614_toolkitrev-par.pdf.

Ions, E. (1977) *Against Behaviouralism: A Critique of Behavioural Science.* Oxford: Basil Blackwell.

Isenberg, J. P. and Jalongo, M. R. (2006) *Creative Expression and Play in Early Childhood* (fourth edition). Upper Saddle River, NJ: Prentice-Hall.

Ivankova, N. V., Creswell, J. W. and Stick, S. L. (2006) Using mixed-methods sequential explanatory design: from theory to practice. *Field Methods*, 18 (3), 3–20.

Jacklin, A. and Lacey, C. (1997) Gender integration in the infant classroom: a case study. *British Educational Research Journal*, 23 (5), 623–40.

Jackson, G. B. (1980) Methods for integrative reviews. *Review of Educational Research*, 50 (3), 438–60.

Jackson, P. W. (1968) *Life in Classrooms.* New York: Holt, Rinehart and Winston.

Jacob, E. (1987) Qualitative research traditions: a review. *Review of Educational Research*, 57 (1), 1–50.

James, M. (1993) Evaluation for policy: rationality and political reality: the paradigm case of PRAISE? In R. G. Burgess (ed.) *Educational Research and Evaluation for Policy and Practice.* London: Falmer, 119–38.

James, N. (2007) The use of email interviewing as a qualitative method of inquiry in educational research. *British Educational Research Journal*, 33 (6), 963–76.

James, N. and Busher, H. (2006) Credibility, authenticity and voice: dilemmas in online interviewing. *Qualitative Research*, 6 (3), 403–20.

James, N. and Busher, H. (2007) Ethical issues in online educational research: protecting privacy, establishing authenticity in email interviewing. *International Journal of Research and Method in Education*, 30 (1), 101–13.

Jameson, F. (1991) *Postmodernism, or the Cultural Logic of Late Capitalism.* London: Verso.

Jang, E. E., McDougall, D. E., Pollon, D., Herbert, M. and Russell, P. (2008) Integrative mixed methods data analytic strategies in research on school success in challenging circumstances. *Journal of Mixed Methods Research*, 2 (3), 221–47.

Jankowicz, D. (2003) *The Easy Guide to Repertory Grids.* Chichester: John Wiley.

Jarmon, L., Traphagan, T. W., Traphagan, J. W. and Eaton, L. J. (2009) Ageing, lifelong learning and the virtual world of Second Life. In C. Wankel and J. Kingsley (eds) *Higher Education in Virtual Worlds: Teaching and Learning in Second Life.* Bingley: Emerald, 221–42.

Jayaratne, T. E. (1993) The value of quantitative methodology for feminist research. In M. Hammersley (ed.) *Social Research: Philosophy, Politics and Practice.* London: Sage with the Open University Press, 109–23.

Jayaratne, T. E. and Stewart, A. (1991) Quantitative and qualitative methods in the social sciences: current feminist issues and practical strategies. In M. Fonow and J. Cook (eds) *Beyond Methodology: Feminist Scholarship as Lived Research.* Bloomington: Indiana University Press.

Johnson, A. and Sackett, R. (1998). Direct systematic observation of behavior. In H. R. Bernard (ed.) *Handbook of Methods in Cultural Anthropology.* Walnut Creek, CA: Altamira Press, 301–31.

Johnson, J. E. (1998) Play development from ages four to eight. In D. P. Fromberg and D. Bergen (eds) *Play from Birth to Twelve and Beyond: Contexts, Perspectives, and Meanings.* New York: Garland, 146–53.

Johnson, M. (2008) Assessing at the borderline: judging a vocationally related portfolio holistically. *Issues in Educational Research*, 18 (1), 26–43.

Johnson, R. B. and Onwuegbuzie, A. J. (2004) Mixed methods research: a research paradigm whose time has come. *Educational Researcher*, 33 (7), 14–26.

Johnson, R. B., Onwuegbuzie, A. J. and Turner, L. A. (2007) Toward a definition of mixed methods research. *Journal of Mixed Methods Research*, 1 (2), 112–33.

Joinson, A., McKenna, K., Postmes, T. and Reips, U.-D. (eds) (2009) *The Oxford Handbook of Internet Psychology.* Oxford: Oxford University Press.

Jones, J. (1990) The role of the headteacher in staff development. *Educational Management and Administration*, 18 (1), 27–36.

Jones, N. (1999) The changing management agenda for primary heads. *International Journal of Public Sector Management*, 12 (4), 324–37.

Jones, S. (1987) The analysis of depth interviews. In R. Murphy and H. Torrance (eds) *Evaluating Education: Issues and Methods.* London: Paul Chapman, 263–77.

Jones, S. (ed.) (1999) *Doing Internet Research.* Thousand Oaks, CA: Sage.

Joy, G. T. (2003) A brief description of culturally valid knowledge. Personal communication. Sophia Junior College, Hakone-machi, Kanagawa-ken, Japan.

Joyce, P. (1999) The politics of the liberal archive. *History of the Human Sciences*, 12 (2), 35–49.

Jules, V. and Kutnick, P. (1997) Student perceptions of a good teacher: the gender perspective. *British Journal of Educational Psychology*, 67 (4), 497–511.

Jupp, V. and Norris, C. (1993) Traditions in documentary analysis. In M. Hammersley (ed.) *Social Research: Philosophy, Politics and Practice*, London: Sage, 37–51.

Kalton, G. (1983) *Compensating for Missing Survey Data.* Ann Arbor, MI: Survey Research Centre, Institute for Social Research, University of Michigan.

Kamin, L. (1991) Some historical facts about IQ testing. In D. S. Anderson and B. J. Biddle (eds) *Knowledge for Policy: Improving Education through Research.* London: Falmer, 259–67.

Kapoor, D. and Jordan, S. (2009) *Education, Participatory Action Research, and Social Change.* New York: Palgrave Macmillan.

Kasper, G. and Roever, C. (2005) Pragmatics in second language learning. In E. Hinkel (ed.) *Handbook of Research in Second Language Teaching and Learning*. Mahwah, NJ: Lawrence Erlbaum, 317–34.

Kauffman, S. A. (1993) *The Origins of Order: Self-Organization and Selection in Evolution*. Oxford: Oxford University Press.

Kauffman, S. A. (1995) *At Home in the Universe: The Search for the Laws of Self-Organization and Complexity*. Harmondsworth: Penguin.

Kavanaugh, K., Moro, T., Savage, T. and Mehendale, R. (2006) Enacting a theory of caring to recruit and retain vulnerable participants for sensitive research. *Research in Nursing and Health*, 29 (3), 244–52.

Kawulich, B. B. (2005) Participant observation as a data collection method. *Forum Qualitative Sozialforschung/Forum: Qualitative Social Research*, 6 (2), Article 43. Retrieved 6 April 2010, from http://nbnresolving.de/urn:nbn:de:0114-fqs0502430.

Kazdin, A. E. (1982) *Single-case Research Designs*. New York: Oxford University Press.

Keat, R. (1981) *The Politics of Social Theory*. Oxford: Basil Blackwell.

Keet, H. M., Van Den Oord, E. J. C. G., Verhulst, F. C. and Boomsman, D. L. (1997) Behavioral and emotional problems in young preschoolers: cross-cultural testing of the validity of the Child Behavior Checklist/2–3. *Journal of Abnormal Child Psychology*, 25 (3), 183–96.

Keeves, J. P. (1997a) Longitudinal research methods. In J. P. Keeves (ed.) *Educational Research, Methodology and Measurement: An International Handbook* (second edition). Oxford: Elsevier Science, 138–49.

Keeves, J. P. (ed.) (1997b) *Educational Research, Methodology and Measurement: An International Handbook* (second edition). Oxford: Elsevier Science.

Keeves, J. P. and Sellin, N. (1997) Multilevel analysis. In J. P. Keeves (ed.) *Educational Research, Methodology and Measurement: An International Handbook* (second edition). Oxford: Elsevier Science, 394–403.

Kelle, U. (1995) (ed.) *Computer-Aided Qualitative Data Analysis*. London: Sage.

Kelle, U. (1997) Theory building in qualitative research and computer programmes for the management of textual data. *Sociological Research Online*, 2 (2). Retrieved 1 May 2010, from www.socresonline.org.uk/2/2/1.html.

Kelle, U. (2000) Computer assisted analysis: coding and indexing. In M. Bauer and G. Gaskell (eds) *Qualitative Researching with Text, Image, and Sound*. London: Sage, 282–98.

Kelle, U. (2004) Computer-assisted analysis of qualitative data. In U. Flick, E. von Kardoff and I. Steinke (eds) *A Companion to Qualitative Research* (trans. B. Jenner). London: Sage, 276–93.

Kelle, U. and Laurie, H. (1995) Computer use in qualitative research and issues of validity. In U. Kelle (ed.) *Computer-Aided Qualitative Data Analysis*. London: Sage, 19–28.

Kelly, A. (1978) Feminism and research. *Women's Studies International Quarterly*, 1 (3), 225–32.

Kelly, A. (1985) Action research: what is it and what can it do? In R. G. Burgess (ed.) *Issues in Educational Research: Qualitative Methods*. Lewes: Falmer, 129–51.

Kelly, A. (1986) The development of children's attitudes to science: a longitudinal study. *European Journal of Science Education*, 8 (4), 399–412.

Kelly, A. (1987) *Science for Girls?* Milton Keynes: Open University Press.

Kelly, A. (1989a) Education or indoctrination? The ethics of school-based action research. In R. G. Burgess (ed.) *The Ethics of Educational Research*. Lewes: Falmer, 100–13.

Kelly, A. (1989b) *Getting the GIST: A Qualitative Study of the Effects of the Girls Into Science and Technology Project*. Manchester Sociology Occasional Papers, no. 22. Manchester: University of Manchester.

Kelly, A. and Smail, B. (1986) Sex stereotypes and attitudes to science among eleven-year-old children. *British Journal of Educational Psychology*, 56 (2), 158–68.

Kelly, B. (2007) Methodological issues for qualitative research with learning disabled children. *International Journal of Social Research Methodology*, 10 (1), 21–35.

Kelly, G. A. (1955) *The Psychology of Personal Constructs*. New York: Norton.

Kelly, G. A. (1969) *Clinical Psychology and Personality: The Selected Papers of George Kelly* (ed. B. A. Maher). New York: John Wiley.

Kelly, S. and Allison, M. A. (1999) *The Complexity Advantage: How the Science of Complexity Can Help Your Business Achieve Peak Performance*. New York: McGraw-Hill.

Kelman, H. C. (1967) Human use of human subjects. *Psychological Bulletin*, 67 (1), 1–11.

Kemmis, S. (1982) Seven principles for programme evaluation in curriculum development and innovation. *Journal of Curriculum Studies*, 14 (3), 221–40.

Kemmis, S. (1997) Action research. In J. P. Keeves (ed.) *Educational Research, Methodology, and Measurement: An International Handbook* (second edition). Oxford: Elsevier Science, 173–9.

Kemmis, S. and McTaggart, R. (eds) (1981) *The Action Research Planner* (first edition). Geelong, Victoria: Deakin University Press.

Kemmis, S. and McTaggart, R. (eds) (1988) *The Action Research Planner* (second edition). Geelong, Victoria: Deakin University Press.

Kemmis, S. and McTaggart, R. (1992) *The Action Research Planner* (third edition). Geelong, Victoria: Deakin University Press.

Kenett, R. S. (2006) On the planning and design of sample surveys. *Journal of Applied Statistics*, 33 (4), 405–15.

Kerlinger, F. N. (1970) *Foundations of Behavioral Research*. New York: Holt, Rinehart and Winston.

Kerlinger, F. N. (1986) *Foundations of Behavioral Research* (third edition). New York: Holt, Rinehart and Winston.

Kerlinger, F. N. (1991) Science and behavioural research. In D. S. Anderson and B. J. Biddle (eds) *Knowledge for Policy: Improving Education through Research*. London: Falmer, 87–102.

Kerr, D., Troth, A. and Pickering, A. (2003) The use of role playing to help students understand information systems case studies. *Journal of Information Systems Education*, 14 (2), 167–71.

Kgaile, A. P. and Morrison, K. R. B. (2006) Measuring and targeting internal conditions for school effectiveness in the

Free State of South Africa. *Educational Management, Administration and Leadership*, 34 (1), 47–68.

Khot, S. (2005) Popular theatre. In R. Tandon (ed.) *Participatory Research: Revisiting the Roots*. New Delhi: Mosaic Books, 313–20.

Kierkegaard, S. (1974) *Concluding Unscientific Postscript*. Princeton, NJ: Princeton University Press.

Kimmel, A. J. (1988) *Ethics and Values in Applied Social Research*. Beverly Hills, CA: Sage.

Kincheloe, J. L. (1991) *Teachers as Researchers: Qualitative Inquiry as a Path to Empowerment*. London: Falmer.

Kincheloe, J. L. (2003) *Teachers as Researchers: Qualitative Inquiry as a Path to Empowerment* (second edition). London: RoutledgeFalmer.

Kincheloe, J. L. and McLaren, P. (1994) Rethinking critical theory and qualitative research. In N. K. Denzin and Y. S. Lincoln (eds) *Handbook of Qualitative Research*. Beverly Hills, CA: Sage, 105–17.

King, J. A., Morris, L. L. and Fitz-Gibbon, C. T. (1987) *How to Assess Program Implementation*. Beverly Hills, CA: Sage.

King, R. (1979) *All Things Bright and Beautiful?* Chichester: John Wiley.

Kirk, J. and Miller, M. L. (1986) *Reliability and Validity in Qualitative Research*. Qualitative Research Methods Series No. 1. Beverly Hills, CA: Sage.

Kirk, R. E. (1999) *Statistics: An Introduction*. London: Harcourt Brace.

Kitwood, T. M. (1977) Values in adolescent life: towards a critical description, Unpublished PhD dissertation, School of Education, University of Bradford.

Kivulu, J. M. and Rogers, W. T. (1998) A multilevel analysis of cultural experience and gender influences on causal attributions to perceived performance in mathematics. *British Journal of Educational Psychology*, 68 (1), 25–37.

Kleven, T. A (1995) Reliabilitet som pedagogisk problem (trans: Reliability as an educational problem). Mimeo for doctoral lecture, 17 February. Oslo: Institute for Educational Research. Quoted in B. Brock-Utne (1996) Reliability and validity in qualitative research within education in Africa. *International Review of Education*, 42 (6), 605–21.

Kline, P. (2000) *Handbook of Psychological Testing* (second edition). London: Routledge.

Kline, R. B. (2004) *Beyond Significance Testing: Reforming Data Analysis Methods in Behavioral Research*, Washington, DC: American Psychological Association.

Kline, R. B. (2005) *Principles and Practice of Structural Equation Modeling* (second edition). New York: Guilford Press.

Kline, T. J. B. (2005) Classical test theory. In T. J. B. Kline, *Psychological Testing: A Practical Approach to Design and Evaluation*, chapter five. Thousand Oaks, CA: Sage. Retrieved 25 April 2010, from www.sagepub.com/upm-data/4869_Kline_Chapter_5_Classical_Test_Theory.pdf.

Klockars, C. B. (1979) Dirty hands and deviant subjects. In C. B. Klockars and F. O'Connor (eds) *Deviance and Decency: The Ethics of Research with Human Subjects*. Beverly Hills, CA: Sage, 261–82.

Knoblauch, H., Schnettler, B., Raab, J. and Soeffner, H. G. (eds) (2006) *Video Analysis: Methodology and Methods*. Frankfurt: Peter Lang.

Knoke, D. and Yang, S. (2008) *Social Network Analysis* (second edition). Thousand Oaks, CA: Sage.

Knott, J. and Wildavsky, A. (1991) If dissemination is the solution, what is the problem? In D. S. Anderson and B. J. Biddle (eds) *Knowledge for Policy: Improving Education through Research*. London: Falmer, 214–24.

Kogan, M. and Atkin, J. M. (1991) Special commissions and educational policy in the U.S.A. and U.K. In D. S. Anderson and B. J. Biddle (eds) *Knowledge for Policy: Improving Education through Research*. London: Falmer, 245–58.

Kohn, A. (2000) *The Case against Standardized Testing: Raising the Scores, Ruining the Schools*. Portsmouth, NH: Heinemann.

Kolakowski, L. (1978) *Main Currents of Marxism, Volume Three: The Breakdown* (trans. P. S. Falla). Oxford: Clarendon Press.

Konecki, K. (2009) Teaching visual grounded theory. *Qualitative Sociology Review*, 5 (3), 64–92. Retrieved 18 May 2010, from www.qualitativesociologyreview.org/ENG/archive_eng.php.

Krejcie, R. V. and Morgan, D. W. (1970) Determining sample size for research activities. *Educational and Psychological Measurement*, 30 (3), 607–10.

Krippendorp, K. (2004) *Content Analysis: An Introduction to its Methodology*. Thousand Oaks, CA: Sage.

Krosnick, J. A. (1991) Response strategies for coping with the cognitive demands of attitude measurement in surveys. *Applied Cognitive Psychology*, 5 (3), 213–36.

Krosnick, J. A. (1999) Survey research. *Annual Review of Psychology*, 50 (1), 537–67.

Krosnick, J. A. and Alwin, D. F. (1987) An evaluation of a cognitive theory of response-order effects in survey measurement. *Public Opinion Quarterly*, 51 (2), 201–19.

Krueger, R. A. (1988) *Focus Groups: A Practical Guide for Applied Research*. Beverly Hills, CA: Sage.

Krueger, R. A. and Casey, M. A. (2000) *Focus Groups: A Practical Guide for Applied Research* (third edition). Thousand Oaks, CA: Sage.

Kuhn, L. (2007) Why utilize complexity principles in social inquiry? *World Futures*, 63 (3), 156–75.

Kuhn, T. S. (1962) *The Structure of Scientific Revolutions*. Chicago. IL: University of Chicago Press.

Kumar, S. R. and Narayanan, S. N. (2008) Role-playing lecturing: a method for teaching neuroscience to medical students. *Advances in Physiology Education*, 32 (4), 329–31.

Kvale, S. (1996) *Interviews*. London: Sage.

Labov, W. (1969) The logic of non-standard English. In N. Keddie (ed.) *Tinker, Tailor … the Myth of Cultural Deprivation*. Harmondsworth: Penguin, 21–66.

Labov, W. (1972) The transformation of experience in narrative syntax. In W. Labov (ed.) *Language in the Inner City: Studies in the Black English Vernacular*. Philadelphia, PA: University of Pennsylvania Press, 354–96.

Laing, R. D. (1967) *The Politics of Experience and the Bird of Paradise*. Harmondsworth: Penguin.

Lakatos, I. (1970) Falsification and the methodology of scientific research programmes. In I. Lakatos and A. Musgrave (eds) *Criticism and the Growth of Knowledge*. London: Cambridge University Press, 91–195.

Lakomski, G. (1999) Critical theory. In. J. P. Keeves and

G. Lakomski (eds) *Issues in Educational Research*. Oxford: Elsevier Science, 174–83.

Lamb, S., Bibby, P., Wood, D. and Leyden, G. (1997) Communication skills, educational achievement and biographic characteristics of children with moderate learning difficulties. *European Journal of Psychology of Education*, 12 (4), 401–14.

Landfield, A. W. (1971). *Personal Construct Systems in Psychotherapy*. Lincoln, NB: University of Nebraska Press.

Langton, C. G. (1984) Self-reproduction in cellular automata. In D. Farmer, T. Toffoli and S. Wolfram (eds) *Cellular Automata: Proceedings of an Interdisciplinary Workshop, Los Alamos March 7–11, 1983.* (Physica D, 10, 1–2). Amsterdam: North Holland.

Lansing, J. B., Ginsburg, G. P. and Braaten, K. (1961) *An Investigation of Response Error* (Studies in Consumer Savings, No. 2). Urbana, IL: University of Illinois Bureau of Economic and Business Research.

Larsson, S. (2009) A pluralist view of generalization in qualitative research. *International Journal of Research and Method in Education*, 32 (1), 25–38.

Lather, P. (1986) Research as praxis. *Harvard Educational Review*, 56 (3), 257–77.

Lather, P. (1991) *Getting Smart: Feminist Research and Pedagogy within the Post Modern*. New York: Routledge.

Laudan, L. (1990) *Science and Relativism*. Chicago, IL: University of Chicago Press.

Lave, J. and Kvale, S. (1995) What is anthropological research? An interview with Jean Lave by Steiner Kvale. *International Journal of Qualitative Studies in Education*, 8 (3), 219–28.

Lawless, L., Smee, P. and O'Shea, T. (1998) Using concept sorting and concept mapping in business and public administration, and education: an overview. *Educational Research*, 40 (2), 219–35.

Layder, D. (1994) *Understanding Social Theory*. London: Sage.

Lazarsfeld, P. P. and Barton, A. (1951) Qualitative measurement in the social sciences: classification, typologies and indices. In D. P. Lerner and H. D. Lasswell (eds) *The Policy Sciences*. Stanford, CA: Stanford University Press, 155–92.

LeCompte, M. and Preissle, J. (1993) *Ethnography and Qualitative Design in Educational Research* (second edition). London: Academic Press.

LeCompte, M., Millroy, W. L. and Preissle, J. (eds) (1992) *The Handbook of Qualitative Research in Education*. London: Academic Press.

Lee, R. M. (1993) *Doing Research on Sensitive Topics*. London: Sage.

Lee, R. M. and Renzetti, C. M. (1993) The problems of researching sensitive topics: an overview and introduction. In C. Renzetti and R. M. Lee (eds) *Researching Sensitive Topics*. London: Sage, 3–12.

Leech, N. L. and Onwuegbuzie, A. J. (2004) A proposed fourth measure of significance: the role of economic significance in educational research. *Evaluation and Research in Education*, 18 (3), 179–98.

Leech, N. L. and Onwuegbuzie, A. J. (2009) A typology of mixed methods research designs. *Quantity and Quality*, 43 (2), 265–75.

Lehrer, R. and Franke, M. L. (1992) Applying personal construct psychology to the study of teachers' knowledge of fractions. *Journal for Research in Mathematical Education*, 23 (3), 223–41.

Leistyna, P., Woodrum, A. and Sherblom, S. A. (1996) *Breaking Free*. Cambridge, MA: Harvard Educational Review.

Lemke, J. (2001) *Toward Systemic Educational Change: Questions from a Complex Systems Perspective*. Cambridge, MA: New England Complex Systems Institute. Retrieved, 10 November 2001, from www.necsi.org/events/cxedk16_3.html.

Lempert, L. B. (2007) Asking questions of the data: memo writing in the grounded theory tradition. In A. Bryant and K. Charmaz (eds) *The SAGE Handbook of Grounded Theory*. London: Sage, 245–65.

Leow, C. (2009) Conducting a rigorous quasi-experimental evaluation using a school district's existing student database. *International Journal of Research and Method in Education*, 32 (1), 69–88.

Levačić, R. and Glatter, R. (2000) Really good ideas: developing evidence-informed policy and practice in educational leadership and management. *Educational Management and Administration*, 29 (1), 5–25.

Levin, H. M. (1991) Why isn't educational research more useful? In D. S. Anderson and B. J. Biddle (eds) *Knowledge for Policy: Improving Education through Research*. London: Falmer, 70–8.

Levine, M. (1984) *Canonical Analysis and Factor Comparisons*. Beverly Hills, CA: Sage.

Lewin, K. (1946) Action research and minority problems. *Journal of Social Issues*, 2 (4), 34–46.

Lewin, K. (1948) *Resolving Social Conflicts*. New York: Harper.

Lewin, K. (1952) *Field Theory in Social Science*. London: Tavistock Publications.

Lewin, R. (1993) *Complexity: Life on the Edge of Chaos*. London: Phoenix.

Lewin, R. and Regine, B. (2000) *The Soul at Work: Listen, Respond, Let Go: Embracing Complexity Science for Business Success*. New York: Simon and Schuster.

Lewins, A. and Silver, C. (2004) *Choosing a CAQDAS Package: A Working Paper*. CAQDAS Networking Project: http://caqdas.soc.surrey.ac.uk/. Surrey: University of Surrey. Retrieved 1 May 2010, from http://cue.berkeley.edu/qdaarticle.pdf.

Lewins, A. and Silver, C. (2009) *Choosing a CAQDAS Package: A Working Paper* (sixth edition). CAQDAS Networking Project: http://caqdas.soc.surrey.ac.uk/. Surrey: University of Surrey. Retrieved 1 May 2010, from http://eprints.ncrm.ac.uk/791/1/2009ChoosingaCAQDASPackage. pdf.

Lewis, A. (1992) Group child interviews as a research tool. *British Educational Research Journal*, 18 (4), 413–21.

Lewis, D. (1974) *Assessment in Education*. London: University of London Press.

Lewis, J. (2006) Making order out of a contested disorder: the utilisation of online support groups in social science research. *Qualitative Researcher*, 3, 4–7.

Lewis, S. and Allan, B. (2005) *Virtual Learning Communities*. Maidenhead, UK: Open University Press.

Lewis-Beck, M. S. (ed.) (1993) *Experimental Design and Methods*. London: Toppan Co. with the cooperation of Sage.

Liebling, H. and Shah, S. (2001) Researching sensitive topics: investigations of the sexual abuse of women in Uganda and girls in Tanzania. *Law, Social Justice and Global Development.* Retrieved 20 May 2010, from http://www2.warwick.ac.uk/fac/soc/law/elj/lgd/2001_1/liebling/.

Lietz, P. and Keeves, J. P. (1997) Cross-sectional research methods. In J. P. Keeves (ed.) *Educational Research, Methodology and Measurement: An International Handbook* (second edition). Oxford: Elsevier Science, 138–49.

Light, R. J., Singer, J. and Willett, J. (1990) *By Design: Conducting Research on Higher Education.* Cambridge, MA: Harvard University Press.

Light, R. J. and Smith, P. V. (1971) Accumulating evidence: procedures for resolving contradictions among different research studies. *Harvard Educational Review,* 41 (4), 429–71.

Likert, R. (1932) *A Technique for the Measurement of Attitudes.* New York: Columbia University Press.

Limerick, B., Burgess-Limerick, T. and Grace, M. (1996) The politics of interviewing: power relations and accepting the gift. *International Journal of Qualitative Studies in Education,* 9 (4), 449–60.

Lin, N. (1976) *Foundations of Social Research.* New York: McGraw-Hill.

Lincoln, Y. S. (1990) Toward a categorical imperative for qualitative research. In E. Eisner and A. Peshkin (eds) *Qualitative Inquiry in Educational Research: The Continuing Debate.* New York: Teachers College Press, 277–95.

Lincoln, Y. S. and Guba, E. (1985) *Naturalistic Inquiry.* Beverly Hills, CA: Sage.

Lincoln, Y. S. and Guba, E. (1986) But is it rigorous? Trustworthiness and authenticity in naturalistic inquiry. In. D. D. Williams (ed.) *Naturalistic Evaluation.* San Francisco, CA: Jossey-Bass, 73–84.

Linn, R. L. (ed.) (1993) *Educational Measurement* (third edition). Phoenix, AZ: American Council on Education and the Oryx Press.

Lipsey, M. W. (1992) Juvenile delinquency treatment: a meta-analytic inquiry into the variability of effects. In T. D. Cook, H. Cooper, D. S. Cordray, H. Hartmann, L. V. Hedges, R. J. Light, T. A. Louis and F. Mosteller (eds) *Meta-Analysis for Explanation.* New York: Russell Sage Foundation, 83–127.

Little, R. J. A. and Rubin, D. B. (1989) The analysis of social science data with missing values. *Sociological Methods and Research,* 6 (3), 292–326.

Littleton, K., Ashman, H., Light, P., Artis, J., Roberts, T. and Oosterwegel, A. (1999) Gender, task contexts, and children's performance on a computer-based task. *European Journal of Psychology of Education,* 14 (1), 129–39.

Liu, H. J. C. (2002) Translation of instruments for cross-cultural research. *Journal of the Da-Yeh University,* 11 (2), 79–88.

Livingstone, D. and Bloomfield, P. R. (2010) Mixed-methods and mixed-worlds: engaging globally distributed user groups for extended evaluation and studies. In A. Peachey, J. Gillen, D. Livingstone and S. Smith-Robbins (eds) *Researching Learning in Virtual Worlds.* London: Springer, 159–76.

Livingstone, I. (1999) Role-playing planning public inquiries. *Journal of Geography in Higher Education,* 23 (1), 63–76.

Lobato, J. (2003) How design experiments can inform a rethinking of transfer and vice versa. *Educational Researcher,* 32 (1), 17–20.

Lodico, M. G., Spaulding, D. T. and Voegtle, K. H. (2010) *Methods in Educational Research.* San Francisco, CA: Jossey-Bass.

Loehlin, J. (2004) *Latent Variable Models* (fourth edition). Mahwah, NJ: Lawrence Erlbaum.

Loevinger, J. (1957) Objective tests as instruments of psychological theory. *Psychological Review,* 72, 143–55.

Loewenthal, K. M. (2001) *An Introduction to Psychological Tests and Scales.* Hove: Psychology Press.

Lofland, J. (1970) Interactionist imagery and analytic interrupts. In T. Shibutani (ed.) *Human Nature and Collective Behaviour: Papers in Honour of Herbert Blumer.* Englewood Cliffs, NJ: Prentice-Hall, 35–45.

Lofland, J. (1971) *Analyzing Social Settings.* Belmont, CA: Wadsworth.

Lonkila, M. (1995) Grounded theory as an emerging paradigm for computer-assisted qualitative data analysis. In U. Kelle (1995) (ed.) *Computer-Aided Qualitative Data Analysis.* London: Sage, 41–51.

Lord, H. G. (1973) *Ex Post Facto Studies as a Research Method.* Special Report no. 7320. New York: Syracuse City School District. Retrieved 10 April 2010, from www.eric.ed.gov/ERICDocs/data/ericdocs2sql/content_storage_01/0000019b/80/39/5f/df.pdf.

Lown, N., Davies, I., Cordingley, L., Bundy, C. and Braidman, I. (2009) Development of a method to investigate medical students' perceptions of their personal and professional development. *Advances in Health Science Education,* 14 (4), 475–86.

Lui, C. C. and Lee, J. H. (2005) Prompting conceptual understanding with computer-mediated peer discourse and knowledge acquisition techniques. *British Journal of Educational Technology,* 36 (5), 821–37.

Lutz, C. A. and Collins, J. L. (1993) *Reading National Geographic.* Chicago, IL: University of Chicago Press.

McAleese, R. and Hamilton, D. (eds) (1978) *Understanding Classroom Life.* Windsor: NFER.

McCandliss, B. D., Kalchman, M. and Bryant, P. (2003) Design experiments and laboratory approaches to learning: steps towards collaborative exchange. *Educational Researcher,* 32 (1), 14–16.

McCarthy, P. J. and Anderson, L. (2000) Active learning techniques versus traditional teaching styles: two experiments from history and political science. *Innovative Higher Education,* 24 (4), 279–94.

McCormick, J. and Solman, R. (1992) Teachers' attributions of responsibility for occupational stress and satisfaction: an organisational perspective, *Educational Studies,* 18 (92), 201–22

McCormick, R. and James, M. (1988) *Curriculum Evaluation in Schools* (second edition). London: Croom Helm.

McCulloch, G. (1986) 'Secondary education without selection'? School zoning policy in Auckland since 1945. *New Zealand Journal of Educational Studies,* 21 (2), 98–112.

McCulloch, G. (1989) *The Secondary Technical School: A Usable Past?* London: Falmer.

McCulloch, G. (2004) *Documentary Research in Education, History and the Social Sciences.* London: Routledge.

McCulloch, G. (ed.) (2005) *The RoutledgeFalmer Reader in the History of Education*. London: RoutledgeFalmer.

McCulloch, G. (2007) *Cyril Norwood and the Ideal of Secondary Education*. New York: Palgrave Macmillan.

McCulloch, G. (2008) Historical insider research in education. In P. Sikes and A. Potts (eds) *Researching Education from the Inside: Investigations from Within*. London: Routledge, 51–63.

McCulloch, G. (2009) The moral universe of Mr. Chips: veteran teachers in British literature and drama. *Teachers and Teaching*, 15 (4), 409–20.

McCulloch, G. (in press) *The Struggle for the History of Education*. London: Routledge.

McCulloch, G., Helsby, G. and Knight, P. (2000) *The Politics of Professionalism: Teachers and the Curriculum*. London: Continuum.

McCulloch, G. and Richardson, W. (2000) *Historical Research in Educational Settings*. Buckingham: Open University Press.

MacDonald, B. (1987) *Research and Action in the Context of Policing*. Paper commissioned by the Police Federation. Norwich: Centre for Applied Research in Education, University of East Anglia.

MacDonald, G. (1997) Social work: beyond control? In A. Maynard and I. Chalmers (eds) *Non-random Reflections on Health Service Research*. London: BMJ Publishing, 122–46.

McEneaney, J. E. and Sheridan, E. M. (1996) A survey-based component for programme assessment in undergraduate pre-service teacher education. *Research in Education*, 55, 49–61.

McGaw, B. (1997) Meta-analysis. In J. P. Keeves (ed.) *Educational Research, Methodology and Measurement: An International Handbook* (second edition). Oxford: Elsevier Science, 371–80.

McHugh, J. D. (1994) The Lords' will be done: interviewing the powerful in education. In G. Walford (ed.) *Researching the Powerful in Education*. London: UCL Press, 51–66.

McIntyre, D. and MacLeod, G. (1978) The characteristics and uses of systematic classroom observation. In R. McAleese and D. Hamilton (eds) *Understanding Classroom Life*. Windsor: NFER, 102–31.

McKeachie, W. J. and Svinicki, M. (2006) *McKeachie's Teaching Tips: Strategies, Research and Theory for College and University Teachers* (twelfth edition). Boston, MA: Houghton Mifflin.

McKernan, J. (1991) *Curriculum Action Research*. London: Kogan Page.

Mackie, J. L. (1993) Causes and conditions. In E. Sosa and M. Tooley (eds) *Causation*. Oxford: Oxford University Press, 33–55.

McLaren, P. (1995) *Critical Pedagogy and Predatory Culture*. London: Routledge.

McLoughlin, T. (2002) The use of repertory grid analysis in studying students' conceptual frameworks in science. Paper presented at the European Conference on Educational Research, University of Lisbon, 11–14 September.

McNiece, R. and Jolliffe, F. (1998) An investigation into regional differences in educational performance in the National Child Development Study. *Educational Research*, 40 (1), 13–30.

McNiff, J. (1988) *Action Research: Principles and Practice*. Basingstoke: Macmillan.

McNiff, J. (2002a) *Action Research for Professional Development: Concise Advice for New Action Researchers* (third edition). Retrieved 17 April 2010, from www.jeanmcniff.com/booklet1.html.

McNiff, J. (2002b) *Action Research: Principles and Practice (second edition)*. London: RoutledgeFalmer.

McNiff, J., Lomax, P. and Whitehead, J. (1996) *You and Your Action Research Project*. London: Routledge, with Hyde Publications, Bournemouth.

McNiff, J. with Whitehead, J. (2002) *Action Research: Principles and Practice* (second edition). London: RoutledgeFalmer.

McNiff, J. and Whitehead, J. (2009) *Doing and Writing Action Research*. London: Sage.

Macpherson, I., Brooker, R. and Ainsworth, P. (2000) Case study in the contemporary world of research: using notions of purpose, place, process and product to develop some principles for practice. *International Journal of Research Methodology*, 3 (1), 49–61.

McQuitty, L. L. (1957) Elementary linkage analysis for isolating orthogonal and oblique types and typal relevancies. *Educational and Psychological Measurement*, 17 (2), 207–29.

McTaggart, R. (1989) *16 Tenets of Participatory Action Research*. Retrieved 24 April 2010, from www.caledonia.org.uk/par.htm.

McTaggart, R. (1996) Issues for participatory action researchers. In O. Zuber-Skerritt (ed.) *New Directions in Action Research*. London: Falmer, 243–55.

Maddrell, A. (1994) A scheme for effective use of role plays for an emancipatory geography. *Journal of Geography in Higher Education*, 18 (2), 155–62.

Madge, J. (1963) *The Origin of Scientific Sociology*. London: Tavistock Publications.

Madge, J. (1965) *The Tools of Social Science*. London: Longman.

Madill, A. and Latchford, G. (2005) Identity change and the human dissection experience over the first year of medical training. *Social Science and Medicine*, 60 (7), 1637–47.

Madison, D. S. (2005) *Critical Ethnography: Methods, Ethics and Performance*. London: Sage.

Mager, R. F. (1962) *Preparing Instructional Objectives*. Belmont, CA: Fearon Publishers.

Magnusson, D. (1971) An analysis of situational dimensions. *Perceptual and Motor Skills*, 32 (3), 851–67.

Maguire, M. H. (2005) What if you talked to me? I could be interesting: ethical research considerations in engaging with bilingual/multicultural child participants in human inquiry. *Forum: Qualitative Sozialforschung/Forum: Qualitative Social Research*, 6 (1), 1–24. Article 4. Retrieved 28 March 2010, from www.qualitative-research.net/index.php/fqs/article/viewArticle/530/1148.

Maier, N. R. F., Solem, A. R. and Maier, A. A. (1957) *Supervisory and Executive Development: A Manual for Role-playing*. Oxford: John Wiley.

Malinowski, B. (1922) *Argonauts of the Western Pacific: an Account of Native Enterprise and Adventure in the Archipelagoes of Melanesian New Guinea*. New York: Dutton.

Mangan, J. A. (1986) *Athleticism in the Victorian and Edwardian Public School: The Emergence and Consolidation of an Educational Ideology*. London: Falmer.

Mannheim, K. (1936) *Ideology and Utopia*. London: Routledge and Kegan Paul.

Marcinkiewicz, H. R. and Clariana, R. B. (1997) The performance effects of headings within multi-choice tests. *British Journal of Educational Psychology*, 67 (1), 111–17.

Marion, R. (1999) *The Edge of Organization: Chaos and Complexity Theories of Formal Social Systems*. London: Sage.

Markham, A. N. and Baym, N. K. (eds) (2008) *Internet Inquiry: Conversations about Method*. London: Sage.

Markus, H. R. and Kitayama, S. (1991) Culture and the self: implications for cognition, emotion and motivation. *Psychological Review*, 98, 224–54.

Marris, P. and Rein, M. (1967) *Dilemmas of Social Reform: Poverty and Community Action in the United States*. London: Routledge and Kegan Paul.

Marsh, H. W. and Yeung, A. S. (1998) Longitudinal structural equation models of academic self-concept and achievement: gender differences in the development of math and English constructs. *American Educational Research Journal*, 35 (4), 705–38.

Marshall, C. and Rossman, G. B. (1995). *Designing Qualitative Research*. Newbury Park, CA: Sage.

Martin, S. (2010) Research affordances and opportunities in immersive virtual environments: citizenship identity formation in young adults. When I grow up, what will I be? (7th Pan-Hellenic Conference Proceedings. Korinthos, Greece.) Retrieved 20 May 2010, from http://web.me.com/stewartmartin2/Stewart_Martin/Publications.html.

Martin, S. and Vallance, M. (2008) The impact of synchronous inter-networked teacher training in information and communication technology integration. *Computers and Education*, 51 (1), 34–53.

Martin, S., Vallance, M., van Schaik, P. and Wiz, C. (2010) Learning spaces, tasks and metrics for effective communication in Second Life within the context of programming LEGO NXT Mindstorms™ robots: towards a framework for design and implementation. *Journal of Virtual Worlds Research*, 3 (1) (forthcoming).

Maslow, A. H. (1954) *Motivation and Personality*. New York: Harper and Row.

Mason, J. (2002) *Qualitative Researching* (second edition). London: Sage.

Mason, M., Mason, B. and Quayle, T. (1992) Illuminating English: how explicit language teaching improved public examination results in a comprehensive school. *Educational Studies*, 18 (3), 341–54.

Masschelein, J. (1991) The relevance of Habermas's communicative turn. *Studies in Philosophy and Education*, 11 (2), 95–111.

Matsumoto, D. and Yoo, S. H. (2006) Toward a new generation of cross-cultural research. *Perspectives on Psychological Science*, 1 (3), 234–50.

Mauthner, M., Birch, M., Jessop, J. and Miller, T. (2002) *Ethics in Qualitative Research*. London: Sage.

Maxwell, J. A. (1992) Understanding and validity in qualitative research, *Harvard Educational Review*, 62 (3), 279–300.

Maxwell, J. A. (2004) Causal explanation, qualitative research, and scientific inquiry in education. *Educational Researcher*, 33 (2), 3–11.

Maxwell, J. A. (2005) *Qualitative Research Design: An Interactive Approach* (second edition). Thousand Oaks, CA: Sage.

May, T. (ed.) (2002) *Qualitative Research in Action*. London: Sage.

Mayall, B. (1999) Children and childhood. In S. Hood, B. Mayall and S. Oliver (eds) *Critical Issues in Social Research: Power and Prejudice*. Philadelphia, PA: Open University Press, 10–24.

Maynard, A. and Chalmers, I. (eds) (1997) *Non-random Reflections on Health Service Research*. London: BMJ Publishing.

Maynard, M. (1993) Feminism and the possibilities of a postmodern research practice. *British Journal of Sociology of Education*, 14 (3), 327–31.

Mayring, P. (2004) Qualitative content analysis. In U. Flick, E. von Kardoff and I. Steinke (eds) *A Companion to Qualitative Research*. London: Sage.

Mead, G. H. (1934) *Mind, Self and Society* (ed. Charles Morris). Chicago, IL: University of Chicago Press.

Medawar, P. B. (1972) *The Hope of Progress*. London: Methuen.

Medawar, P. B. (1981) *Advice to a Young Scientist*. London: Pan Books.

Medawar, P. B. (1991) Scientific fraud. In D. Pike (ed.) *The Threat and the Glory: Reflections on Science and Scientists*. Oxford: Oxford University Press, 64–70.

Medd, W. (2002) Complexity and the social world. *International Journal of Social Research Methodology*, 5 (1), 71–81.

Mee, J. F. (1957) 'Supervisory and Executive Development. A Manual for Role-playing'. A review. *Industrial and Labor Relations Review*, 11 (1), 135.

Megarry, J. (1978) Retrospect and prospect. In R. McAleese (ed.) *Perspectives on Academic Gaming and Simulation 3: Training and Professional Education*. London: Kogan Page, 187–207.

Mehrens, W. and Kaminski, J. (1989) Methods for improving standardised test scores: fruitful, fruitless or fraudulent? *Educational Measurement: Issues and Practice*, Spring, 14–22.

Meinefeld, W. (2004) Hypotheses and prior knowledge in qualitative research. In U. Flick, E. von Kardoff and I. Steinke (eds) *A Companion to Qualitative Research*. London: Sage, 153–8.

Mellor, D. H. (1995) *The Facts of Causation*. Abingdon, UK: Routledge.

Melrose, M. J. (1996) Got a philosophical match? Does it matter? In O. Zuber-Skerritt (ed.) *New Directions in Action Research*. London: Falmer, 49–65.

Menzel, H. (1978) Meaning – who needs it? In M. Brenner, P. Marsh and M. Brenner (eds) *The Social Contexts of Method*. London: Croom Helm, 140–71.

Mercer, N., Wegerif, R. and Dawes, L. (1999) Children's talk and the development of reasoning in the classroom. *British Educational Research Journal*, 25 (1), 95–111.

Merriam, S. B. (1998) *Qualitative Research and Case Study Applications in Education*. Dev. Ed) San Francisco, CA: Jossey-Bass Publishers.

Mertens, D. M. (2007) Transformative paradigm: mixed methods and social justice. *Journal of Mixed Methods Research*, 1 (3), 212–25.

Merton, R. K. (1949) *Social Theory and Social Structure*. New York: The Free Press.

Merton, R. K. (1967) *On Theoretical Sociology*. New York: The Free Press.

Merton, R. K., Fiske, M. and Kendall, P. L. (1956) *The Focused Interview*. Glencoe, IL: The Free Press.

Merton, R. K. and Kendall, P. L. (1946) The focused interview. *American Journal of Sociology*, 51, 541–57.

Messick, S. (1993) Validity. In R. Linn (ed.) *Educational Measurement* (third edition). Phoenix, AZ: American Council on Education and the Oryx Press, 13–103.

Mickelson, R. A. (1994) A feminist approach to researching the powerful in education. In G. Walford (ed.) *Researching the Powerful in Education*. London: UCL Press, 132–50.

Miedama, S. and Wardekker, W. L. (1999) Emergent identity versus consistent identity: possibilities for a postmodern repoliticization of critical pedagogy. In T. Popkewitz and L. Fendler (eds) *Critical Theories in Education: Changing Terrains of Knowledge and Politics*. London: Routledge, 67–83.

Mies, M. (1993) Towards a methodology for feminist research. In M. Hammersley (ed.) *Social Research: Philosophy, Politics and Practice*. London: Sage with the Open University Press, 64–82.

Miles, M. and Huberman, A. M. (1984) *Qualitative Data Analysis*. Beverly Hills, CA: Sage.

Miles, M. and Huberman, A. M. (1994) *Qualitative Data Analysis* (second edition). Beverly Hills, CA: Sage.

Milgram, S. (1963) Behavioral study of obedience. *Journal of Abnormal and Social Psychology*, 67 (4), 371–8.

Milgram, S. (1974) *Obedience to Authority*. New York: Harper and Row.

Millan, R., Gallagher, M. and Ellis, R. (1993) Surveying adolescent worries: development of the 'Things I Worry About' scale. *Pastoral Care in Education*, 11 (1), 43–57.

Miller, C. (1995) In-depth interviewing by telephone: some practical considerations. *Evaluation and Research in Education*, 9 (1), 29–38.

Miller, G. and Dingwall, R. (1997) *Context and Method in Qualitative Research*. London: Sage.

Miller, P. V. and Cannell, C. F. (1997) Interviewing for social research. In J. P. Keeves (ed.) *Educational Research, Methodology and Measurement: An International Handbook* (second edition). Oxford: Elsevier Science, 361–70.

Miller, T. and Bell, L. (2002) Consenting to what? Issues of access, gatekeeping and 'informed consent'. In M. Mauthner, M. Birch, J. Jessop and T. Miller (eds) *Ethics in Qualitative Research*. London: Sage, 53–69.

Millmann, J. and Greene, J. (1993) The specification and development of tests of achievement and ability. In R. Linn (ed.) *Educational Measurement* (third edition). Phoenix, AZ: American Council on Education and the Oryx Press, 147–200.

Miltiades, H. B. (2008) Interview as a social event: cultural influences experienced while interviewing older adults in India. *International Journal of Social Research Methodology*, 11 (4), 277–91.

Milwain, C. (1998) *Assembling, Maintaining and Disseminating a Social and Educational Controlled Trials Register (SPECTR): A Collaborative Endeavour*. Oxford: UK Cochrane Centre.

Milwain, C., Chalmers, I., Macdonald, S. and Smith, P. (1999) *Cochrane Collaboration Methods Group Newsletter, June, 1999*. Retrieved 2 September 2001, from www.cochrane-collaboration.com/newslett/MGNews_1999.pdf.

Mishler, E. G. (1986) *Research Interviewing: Context and Narrative*. Cambridge, MA: Harvard University Press.

Mishler, E. G. (1990) Validation in inquiry-guided research: the role of exemplars in narrative studies. *Harvard Educational Review*, 60 (4), 415–42.

Mishler, E. G. (1991) Representing discourse: the rhetoric of transcription. *Journal of Narrative and Life History*, 1 (4), 255–80.

Mitchell, M. and Jolley, J. (1988) *Research Design Explained*. New York: Holt, Rinehart and Winston.

Mitchell, R. G. (1993) *Secrecy in Fieldwork*. London: Sage.

Mitchell, W. and Sloper, T. (2008) *Evaluation of the Pilot Programme of the Integrated Children's System: The Disability Study*. York: University of York Social Policy Research Unit. Retrieved 2 April 2010, from www.york.ac.uk/inst/spru/pubs/pdf/ics.pdf.

Mitri, M. and Cole, C. (2007) A systems analysis role play case: We Sell Stuff, Inc. *Journal of Information Systems Education*, 18 (2), 163–8.

Mixon, D. (1974) If you won't deceive, what can you do? In N. Armistead (ed.) *Reconstructing Social Psychology*. Harmondsworth: Penguin, 72–85.

Moghaddam, A. (2006) Coding issues in grounded theory. *Issues in Educational Research*, 16 (1), 52–66. Retrieved 28 July 2006, from www.iier.org.au/iier16/moghaddam.html.

Monge, D. and Contractor, N. (2003) *Theories of Communication Networks*. Oxford: Oxford University Press.

Montgomery, K., Brown, S. and Deery, C. (1997) Simulations: using experiential learning to add relevancy and meaning to introductory courses. *Innovative Higher Education*, 21 (3), 217–29.

Mooij, T. (1998) Pupil-class determinants of aggressive and victim behaviour in pupils. *British Journal of Educational Psychology*, 68 (3), 373–85.

Moreno, J. L. (1934) *Who Shall Survive?* Beacon, NY: Beacon House.

Moreno, J. L. (1939) Psychodramatic shock therapy: a sociometric approach to the problem of mental disorders. *Sociometry*, 2 (1), 1–30.

Moreno, J. L. (1960). *The Sociometry Reader*. Glencoe, IL: The Free Press.

Morgan, C. (1999) Personal communication with one of the authors. University of Bath, Department of Education.

Morgan, C. (2005). Cultural validity. Personal communication. University of Bath, Department of Education.

Morgan, D. L. (1988) *Focus Groups as Qualitative Research*. Beverly Hills, CA: Sage.

Morgan, D. L. (1996) Focus groups. *Annual Review of Sociology*, 22 (1), 129–52.

Morison, M., Moir, J. and Kwansa, T. (2000) Interviewing children for the purposes of primary health care. *Primary Health Care Research and Development*, 1 (2), 113–30.

Morris, L. L., Fitz-Gibbon, C. T. and Lindheim, E. (1987) *How to Measure Performance and Use Tests*. Beverly Hills, CA: Sage.

Morris, P. (1983) Teachers' perceptions of their pupils: a Hong Kong case study. *Research in Education*, 29, 81–6.

737

Morrison, K. R. B. (1993) *Planning and Accomplishing School-Centred Evaluation*. Norfolk: Peter Francis Publishers.

Morrison, K. R. B. (1995a) Habermas and the School Curriculum. Unpublished PhD thesis, School of Education, University of Durham.

Morrison, K. R. B. (1995b) Dewey, Habermas and reflective practice. *Curriculum*, 16 (2), 82–94.

Morrison, K. R. B. (1996a) Developing reflective practice in higher degree students through a learning journal. *Studies in Higher Education*, 21 (3), 317–32.

Morrison, K. R. B. (1996b) Why present school inspections are unethical. *Forum*, 38 (3), 79–80.

Morrison, K. R. B. (1997) Researching the need for multicultural perspectives in counsellor training: a critique of Bimrose and Bayne, *British Journal of Guidance and Counselling*, 25 (1), 135–42.

Morrison, K. R. B. (1998) *Management Theories for Educational Change*. London: Paul Chapman.

Morrison, K. R. B. (2001) Randomised controlled trials for evidence-based education: some problems in judging 'what works'. *Evaluation and Research in Education*, 15 (2), 69–83.

Morrison, K. R. B. (2002a) *School Leadership and Complexity Theory*. London: RoutledgeFalmer.

Morrison, K. R. B. (2002b) Education for the open, democratic society in Macau. Paper presented to the Catholic Teachers' Association, Macau, April.

Morrison, K. R. B. (2003) Complexity theory and curriculum reforms in Hong Kong. *Pedagogy, Culture and Society*, 22 (2), 279–302.

Morrison, K. R. B. (2005) Improving teaching and learning in higher education: metaphors and models for partnership consultancy. *Evaluation and Research in Education*, 17 (1), 31–44.

Morrison, K. R. B. (2006) Sensitive educational research in small states and territories: the case of Macau. *Compare*, 36 (2), 249–64.

Morrison, K. R. B. (2008) Educational philosophy and the challenge of complexity theory. In M. M. Mason (ed.) *Complexity Theory and the Philosophy of Education*. Chichester, UK: John Wiley, 16–31.

Morrison, K. R. B. (2009) *Causation in Educational Research*. London: Routledge.

Morrison, K. R. B. and Tam, O. I. (2005) Undergraduate students in part-time employment in China. *Educational Studies*, 31 (2), 169–80.

Morrison, K. R. B and Tang, F. H. (2002) Testing to destruction: a problem in a small state. *Assessment in Education: Principles, Policy and Practice*, 9 (3), 289–317.

Morse, J. M. (1994) Design in funded qualitative research. In N. K. Denzin and Y. S. Lincoln (eds) *Handbook of Qualitative Research*. Thousand Oaks, CA: Sage, 220–35.

Morse, J. M., Barrett, M., Mayan, M., Olson, K. and Spiers, J. (2002) Verification strategies for establishing reliability and validity in qualitative research. *International Journal of Qualitative Methods*, 1 (2), 1–19.

Mortimore, P., Sammons, P., Stoll, L., Lewis, D. and Ecob, R. (1988) *School Matters: The Junior Years*. London: Open Books.

Moschini, E. (2010) The Second Life Researcher Toolkit: an exploration of inworld tools, methods and approaches for researching educational projects in Second Life. In A. Peachey, J. Gillen, D. Livingstone and S. Smith-Robbins (eds) *Researching Learning in Virtual Worlds*. London: Springer, 31–52.

Moser, C. and Kalton, G. (1971) *Survey Methods in Social Investigation*. London: Heinemann.

Moser, C. and Kalton, G. (1977) *Survey Methods in Social Investigation* (second edition). London: Heinemann.

Mouly, G. J. (1978) *Educational Research: The Art and Science of Investigation*. Boston, MA: Allyn and Bacon.

Moyles, J. (2002) Observation as a research tool. In M. Coleman, and A. J. Briggs (eds) *Research Methods in Educational Leadership*. London: Paul Chapman, 172–91.

Muijs, D. (2004) *Doing Quantitative Research in Education with SPSS*. London: Sage.

Mukerji, P. and Albon, D. (2010) *Research Methods in Early Childhood: An Introductory Guide*. London: Sage.

Munn, P., Johnstone, M. and Holligan, C. (1990) Pupils' perceptions of effective disciplinarians. *British Educational Research Journal*, 16 (2), 191–8.

Munro, A., Holly, L., Rainbird, H. and Leisten, R. (2004) Power at work: reflections on the research process. *International Journal of Social Research Methodology*, 7 (4), 289–304.

Murphy, J., John, M. and Brown, H. (eds) (1984) *Dialogues and Debates in Social Psychology*. London: Lawrence Erlbaum.

Murphy, L. L., Geisinger, K. F., Carlson, J. F. and Spies, R. A. (eds) (2010) *Tests in Print VII*. Lincoln, NB: University of Nebraska Press.

Murthy, N. N., Challagalla, G. N., Vincent, L. H. and Shervani, T. A. (2008) The impact of simulation training on call center agent performance: a field-based investigation. *Management Science*, 54 (2), 384–99.

Musch, J. and Bröder, A. (1999) Test anxiety versus academic skills: a comparison of two alternative models for predicting performance in a statistics exam. *British Journal of Educational Psychology*, 69 (1), 105–16.

National Education Association of the United States: Association for Supervision and Curriculum Development (1959) *Learning about Learning from Action Research*. Washington, DC: National Education Association of the United States.

Naylor, P. (1995) Adolescents' perceptions of teacher racism. Unpublished PhD dissertation, Loughborough University of Technology.

Neal, S. (1995) Researching powerful people from a feminist and anti-racist perspective: a note on gender, collusion and marginality. *British Educational Research Journal*, 21 (4), 517–31.

Nedelsky, L. (1954) Absolute grading standards for objective tests. *Educational and Psychological Measurement*, 14 (1), 3–19.

Neelands, J. and Goode, T. (2000) *Structuring Drama Work*. Cambridge: Cambridge University Press.

Neimeyer, G. J. and Hagans, C. L. (2002) More madness in our method? The effects of repertory grid variations on construct differentiation. *Journal of Constructivist Psychology*, 15 (2), 139–60.

Nesfield-Cookson, B. (1987) *William Blake: Prophet of Universal Brotherhood*. London: Crucible.

Newby, P. (2010) *Research Methods for Education*. Harlow, UK: Pearson Education.

Nias, J. (1991) Primary teachers talking: a reflexive account of longitudinal research. In G. Walford (ed.) *Doing Educational Research*. London: Routledge, 147–65.

Nicholson, W. (1906) *The Struggle for a Free Stage in London*. London: Archibald Constable.

Nisbet, J. and Watt, J. (1984) Case study. In J. Bell, T. Bush, A. Fox, J. Goodey and S. Goulding (eds) *Conducting Small-Scale Investigations in Educational Management*. London: Harper and Row, 79–92.

Nisbett, R. E. (2005) *The Geography of Thought*. London: Nicholas Brealey Publishers.

Nixon, J. (ed.) (1981) *A Teacher's Guide to Action Research*. London: Grant McIntyre.

Noack, P. (1998) School achievement and adolescents' interactions with their fathers, mothers, and friends. *European Journal of Psychology of Education*, 13 (4), 503–13.

Noffke, S. E. and Zeichner, K. M. (1987) Action research and teacher thinking. Paper presented at the annual meeting of the American Educational Research Association, Washington, DC.

Nolen, A. L. and Vander Putten, J. (2007) Action research in education: addressing gaps in ethical principles and practices. *Educational Researcher*, 36 (7), 401–7. Retrieved 24 April 2010, from www.aera.net/uploadedFiles/Publications/Journals/Educational_Researcher/3607/10EDR07_401–407.pdf.

Norris, N. (1990) *Understanding Educational Evaluation*. London: Kogan Page.

Norton, D. F. and Norton, M. J. (eds) (2000) *David Hume: A Treatise of Human Nature*. Oxford: Oxford University Press.

Noy, C. (2008) Sampling knowledge: the hermeneutics of snowball sampling in qualitative research. *International Journal of Social Research Methodology*, 11 (4), 327–44.

Nuttall, D. (1987) The validity of assessments. *European Journal of Psychology of Education*, 11 (2), 109–18.

O'Connell, A. A. and McCoach, D. B. (eds) (2008) *Multilevel Modeling of Educational Data*. Charlotte, NC: Information Age Publishing.

O'Donoghue, D. (2010) Classrooms as installations: a conceptual framework for analyzing classroom photographs from the past. *History of Education*, 39 (3), 401–15.

O'Neill, B. and McMahon, H. (1990) *Opening New Windows and Bubble Dialogue*. Coleraine, Northern Ireland: Language Development and Hypermedia Research Group, Faculty of Education, University of Ulster at Coleraine.

O'Neill, C. (1995) *Drama Worlds: A Framework for Process Drama*. Portsmouth, NH: Heinemann.

O'Sullivan, C. (2005) Drama as an educational intervention. Keynote address at the International conference on Asperger Syndrome, University College Dublin, Ireland.

O'Sullivan, C. and Heeran-Flynn, L. (2010) 'Breaking the Code' – an investigation of the use of drama in education in the development of pupils' oral language skills. Unpublished PhD thesis, Trinity College Dublin, Ireland.

O'Sullivan, C., McKernan, D., O'Halloran, S. and Rowland, J. (2009) *Asperger Syndrome: A Practical Guide for Parents, Teachers, Young People and Other Professionals*. [DVD] Dublin: Specialist AV Ltd.

O'Sullivan, C., McNulty, U., Conroy, L., Walsh, A. and McKernan, D. (2010) Asperger Syndrome and social skills education through creative drama. In D. Lyons (ed.) *Creative Studies for the Caring Professions*. Dublin: Gill and McMillan, 178–89.

O'Sullivan, C. and Murphy, A. (2006) Drama as a framework for integrating teaching and learning in the early years. Unpublished Master's thesis, Trinity College Dublin, Ireland.

O'Toole, J. and Haseman, B. (1992) *Dramawise. An Introduction to GCSE Drama*. Oxford: Heinemann Educational.

Oakley, A. (1981) Interviewing women: a contradiction in terms. In H. Roberts (ed.) *Doing Feminist Research*. London: Routledge and Kegan Paul, 30–61.

Oakley, A. (1998) Gender, methodology and people's ways of knowing. *Sociology* 34 (4), 707–31.

Oakley, A. (1999) Paradigm wars: some thoughts on a personal and public trajectory. *International Journal of Social Research Methodology*, 2 (3), 247–54.

Oberle, A. P. (2004) Understanding public land management through role-playing. *Journal of Geography*, 103 (5), 199–210.

Oja, S. N. and Smulyan, L. (1989) *Collaborative Action Research: A Developmental Approach*. Lewes: Falmer.

Oldroyd, D. (1986) *The Arch of Knowledge: An Introductory Study of the History of the Philosophy and Methodology of Science*. New York: Methuen.

Olejnik, S. and Algina J. (2000) Measures of effect size for comparative studies: applications, interpretations, and limitations. *Contemporary Educational Psychology*, 25 (3), 241–86.

Oliver, P. (2003) *The Student's Guide to Research Ethics*. Maidenhead: Open University Press.

Onwuegbuzie, A. J. and Johnson, R. B. (2006) The validity issue in mixed research. *Research in the Schools*, 13 (1), 48–63.

Onwuegbuzie, A. J. and Leech, N. L. (2005a) On becoming a pragmatic researcher: the importance of combining quantitative and qualitative research methodologies. *International Journal of Social Research Methodology*, 8 (5), 375–87.

Onwuegbuzie, A. J. and Leech, N. L. (2005b) Taking the 'Q' out of research: teaching research methodology courses without the divide between quantitative and qualitative paradigms. *Quantity and Quality: International Journal of Methodology*, 39 (3), 267–96.

Onwuegbuzie, A. J. and Leech, N. L. (2006a) Linking research methods to mixed methods data analysis procedures. *Qualitative Report*, 11 (3), 474–98.

Onwuegbuzie, A. J. and Leech, N. L. (2006b) Validity and qualitative research: an oxymoron? *Quality and Quantity*, 41 (2), 233–49.

Onwuegbuzie, A. J. and Leech, N. L. (2007) Sampling designs in qualitative research: making the sampling process more public. *Qualitative Report*, 12 (2), 238–54.

Oppenheim, A. N. (1966) *Questionnaire Design and Attitude Measurement*. London: Heinemann.

Oppenheim, A. N. (1992) *Questionnaire Design, Interviewing and Attitude Measurement*. London: Pinter.

Osgood, C. E., Suci, G. S. and Tannenbaum, P. H. (1957) *The Measurement of Meaning*. Urbana, IL: University of Illinois.

Ovadia, S. (2004) Ratings and rankings: reconsidering the structure of values and their measurement. *International Journal of Social Research Methodology*, 7 (5), 403–14.

Overett, S. and Donald, D. (1998) Paired reading: effects of a parental involvement programme in a disadvantaged community in South Africa. *British Journal of Educational Psychology*, 68 (3), 347–56.

Pallant, J. (2001) *SPSS Survival Manual*. Maidenhead: Open University Press and McGraw-Hill Education.

Pallant, J. (2007) *SPSS Survival Manual* (third edition). Maidenhead: Open University Press.

Palys, T. S. (1978) Simulation methods and social psychology. *Journal for the Theory of Social Behaviour*, 8 (3), 341–68.

Papasolomoutos, C. and Christie, T. (1998) Using national surveys: a review of secondary analyses with special reference to schools. *Educational Research*, 40 (3), 295–310.

Parker, H. J. (1974) *View from the Boys*. Newton Abbot: David and Charles.

Parker, I. (1992) *Discourse Dynamics: Critical Analysis for Social and Individual Psychology*. London: Routledge.

Parker, L. and Lynn, M. (2002) What's race got to do with it? Critical race theory's conflicts with and connections to qualitative research methodology and epistemology. *Qualitative Inquiry*, 8 (1), 7–22.

Parlett, M. and Hamilton, D. (1976) Evaluation as illumination. In D. Tawney (ed.) *Curriculum Evaluation Today: Trends and Implications*. London: Macmillan, 84–101.

Parsons, M. and Lyons, G. (1979) An alternative approach to enquiry in educational management. *Educational Management and Administration*, 8 (1), 75–84.

Paterson, L. (1991) An introduction to multilevel modelling. In S. W. Raudenbush and J. Willms (eds) *Schools, Classrooms and Pupils: International Studies of Schooling from a Multilevel Perspective*. San Diego, CA: Academic Press, 13–24.

Paterson, L. and Goldstein, H. (1991) New statistical methods for analysing social structures: an introduction of multilevel models. *British Educational Research Journal*, 17 (4), 387–93.

Patrick, J. (1973) *A Glasgow Gang Observed*. London: Methuen.

Patton, M. Q. (1980) *Qualitative Evaluation Methods*. Beverly Hills, CA: Sage.

Patton, M. Q. (1990) *Qualitative Evaluation and Research Methods* (second edition). London: Sage.

Payne, G., Dingwall, R., Payne, J. and Carter, M. (1980) *Sociology and Social Research*. London: Routledge and Kegan Paul.

Peak, D. and Frame, M. (1994) *Chaos under Control: The Art and Science of Complexity*. New York: W. H. Freeman.

Pearl, J. (2009) *Causality* (second edition). New York: Cambridge University Press.

Pearson, G. (2009) The researcher as hooligan: where 'participant' observation means breaking the law. *International Journal of Social Research Methodology*, 12 (3), 243–55.

Peevers, B. H. and Secord, P. F. (1973) Developmental changes in attribution of descriptive concepts to persons. *Journal of Personality and Social Psychology*, 27 (1), 120–8.

Penny, K. (2008) HIV/AIDS role-play activity. *Journal of Nursing Education*, 47 (9), 435–6.

Phelps, R. and Graham, A. (2010) Exploring the complementarities between complexity and action research: the story of *Technology Together*. *Cambridge Journal of Education*, 40 (2), 183–97.

Phillips, R. (1998) Some methodological and ethical dilemmas in élite-based research. *British Educational Research Journal*, 24 (1), 5–20.

Piaget, J. (1932) *The Moral Judgement of the Child*. London: Routledge and Kegan Paul.

Pike, D. (ed.) (1991) *The Threat and the Glory: Reflections on Science and Scientists*, Oxford: Oxford University Press.

Pilliner, A. (1973) *Experiment in Educational Research*. E 341. Milton Keynes: Open University Press.

Pimlott, B. (2002) Dear diary…, *The Guardian*, 18 October, G2, 2–3.

Pink, S. (2007) *Doing Visual Ethnography* (second edition). London: Sage.

Pinney, C. (2004) *'Photos of the Gods': The Printed Image and Political Struggle in India*. London: Reaktion Books.

Pinto, M. (2000) *Doing Research with People*. New Delhi: Participatory Research in Asia.

Pitman, M. A. and Maxwell, J. A. (1992) Qualitative approaches to evaluation: models and methods. In M. LeCompte, W. L. Millroy and J. Preissle (eds) *The Handbook of Qualitative Research in Education*. London: Academic Press, 729–70.

Platt, J. (1981) Evidence and proof in documentary research: some specific problems of documentary research. *Sociological Review*, 29 (1), 31–52.

Plewis, I. (1985) *Analysing Change: Measurement and Explanation Using Longitudinal Data*. Chichester: John Wiley.

Plewis, I. (1991) Using multilevel models to link educational progress with curriculum coverage. In S. W. Raudenbush and J. Willms (eds) *Schools, Classrooms and Pupils: International Studies of Schooling from a Multilevel Perspective*. San Diego, CA: Academic Press, 53–65.

Plewis, I. (1997) *Statistics in Education*. London: Arnold.

Plewis, I. and Mason, P. (2005) What works and why: combining quantitative and qualitative approaches in large-scale evaluations. *International Journal of Social Research Methodology*, 8 (3), 185–94.

Plummer, K. (1983) *Documents of Life: An Introduction to the Problems and Literature of a Humanistic Method*. London: Allen and Unwin.

Plummer, K. (1995) *Telling Sexual Stories: Power, Change and Social Worlds*. London: Routledge.

Plummer, K. (2001) *Documents of Life 2: An Invitation to a Critical Humanism*. London: Sage.

Pollard, A. (1985) *The Social World of the Primary School*. Eastbourne: Holt, Rinehart and Winston.

Pope, M. L. and Keen, T. R. (1981) *Personal Construct Psychology and Education*. London: Academic Press.

Popper, K. (1968) *The Logic of Scientific Discovery* (second edition). London: Hutchinson.

Popper, K. (1980) *Conjectures and Refutations* (third edition). London: Routledge and Kegan Paul.

Potter, J. and Wetherell, M. (1987) *Discourse and Social Psychology: Beyond Attitudes and Behaviour*. London: Sage.

Potter, J. and Wetherell, M. (1994) Analyzing discourse. In A. Brymer and R. G. Burgess (eds) *Analyzing Qualitative Data*. London: Routledge, 46–66.

Prein, G., Kelle, U. and Bird, K. (1995) An overview of software. In U. Kelle (ed.) *Computer-Aided Qualitative Data Analysis*. London: Sage, 199–210.

Preisler, G. M. and Ahström, M. (1997) Sign language for hard of hearing children – a hindrance or a benefit for their development? *European Journal of Psychology of Education*, 12 (4), 465–77.

Preissle, J. (2006) Envisioning qualitative inquiry: a view across four decades. *International Journal of Qualitative Studies in Education*, 19 (6), 685–95.

Prigogine, I. and Stengers, I. (1985) *Order out of Chaos*. London: Flamingo.

Pring, R. (1984) The problems of confidentiality. In. M. Skilbeck (ed.) *Evaluating the Curriculum in the Eighties*. Sevenoaks: Hodder and Stoughton, 38–44.

Prosser, J. (ed.) (1998) *Image-Based Research: A Sourcebook for Qualitative Researchers*. London: Falmer.

Prosser, J., Clark, A. and Wiles, R. (2008) *Visual Research Ethics at the Crossroads*. Working Paper No. 10. Manchester: ESRC National Centre for Research Methods. Retrieved 17 May 2010, from www.socialsciences.manchester.ac.uk/realities/publications/workingpapers/10–2008–11-realities-prosseretal.pdf.

Prosser, J. and Loxley, A. (2008) *Introducing Visual Methods*. NCRM Methodological Review. Manchester: ESRC National Centre for Research Methods. Retrieved 17 May 2010, from www.ncrm.ac.uk/research/outputs/publications/.

Prosser, M. and Trigwell, K. (1997) Relations between perceptions of the teaching environment and approaches to teaching. *British Journal of Educational Psychology*, 67 (1), 25–35.

Punch, K. F. (2003) *Survey Research: The Basics*. London: Sage.

Purvis, J. (1985) Reflections upon doing historical documentary research from a feminist perspective. In R. Burgess (ed.) *Strategies of Educational Research*. London: Falmer, 179–205.

Quantz, R. A. (1992) On critical ethnography (with some postmodern considerations). In M. LeCompte, W. L. Millroy and J. Preissle (eds) *The Handbook of Qualitative Research in Education*. London: Academic Press, 447–506.

Radford, M. (2006) Researching classrooms: complexity and chaos. *British Educational Research Journal*, 32 (2), 177–90.

Radford, M. (2007) Action research and the challenge of complexity. *Cambridge Journal of Education*, 37 (2), 263–78.

Radford, M. (2008) Prediction, control and the challenge of complexity. *Oxford Review of Education*, 34 (5), 505–20.

Raento, M., Oulasvirta, A. and Eagle, N. (2009) Smartphones. *Sociological Methods and Research*, 37 (3), 426–54.

Raffe, D., Bundell, I. and Bibby, J. (1989) Ethics and tactics: issues arising from an educational survey. In R. G. Burgess (ed.) *The Ethics of Educational Research*. Lewes: Falmer, 13–30.

Ramsden, C. and Reason, D. (1997) Conversation – discourse analysis in library and information services. *Education for Information*, 15 (4), 283–95.

Rapoport, R. N. (1970) Three dilemmas in action research. *Human Relations*, 23 (6), 499–513.

Rasmussen, D. M. (1990) *Reading Habermas*. Oxford: Basil Blackwell.

Ravenscroft, A. and McAllister, S. (2006) Digital games, learning in cyberspace: a dialogical approach. *E-Learning*, 3 (1), 38–51.

Reams, P. and Twale, D. (2008) The promise of mixed methods: discovering conflicting realities in the data. *International Journal of Research and Method in Education*, 31 (2), 133–42.

Redline, C. D., Dillman, D. A., Carley-Baxter, L. and Creecy, R. (2002) Factors that influence reading and comprehension in self-administered questionnaires. Paper presented at the Workshop on Item-Nonresponse and Data Quality, Basel, Switzerland, 10 October.

Reed-Danahay, D. (1997) *Auto/Ethnography: Rewriting the Self and the Social*. Oxford: Berg.

Reed-Danahay, D. (2002) Being real: moving inward towards social change. *International Journal of Qualitative Studies in Education*, 15 (4), 399–406.

Reese, W. J. and Rury, J. L. (eds) (2008) *Rethinking the History of American Education*. New York: Palgrave Macmillan.

Reichardt, C. S. and Rallis, S. F. (1994) Qualitative and quantitative inquiries are not incompatible: a call for a new partnership. In C. S. Reichardt and S. F. Rallis (eds) *The Qualitative-Quantitative Debate: NewPerspectives*. San Francisco, CA: Jossey-Bass, 85–92.

Reichenbach, H. (1956) *The Direction of Time*. Berkeley and Los Angeles, CA: University of California Press.

Reid, J. (2009) Novels. In M. Dobson and B. Ziemann (eds) *Reading Primary Sources: The Interpretation of Texts from Nineteenth- and Twentieth-Century History*. London: Routledge, 159–74.

Reid, W. A. and Holley, B. J. (1972) An application of repertory grid techniques to the study of choice of university. *British Journal of Educational Psychology*, 42 (1), 52–9.

Reinfandt, C. (2009) Reading texts after the linguistic turn: approaches from literary studies and their implications. In M. Dobson and B. Ziemann (eds) *Reading Primary Sources: The Interpretation of Texts from Nineteenth- and Twentieth-Century History*. London: Routledge, 37–54.

Reips, U.-D. (2002a) Internet-based psychological experimenting: five dos and don'ts. *Social Science Computer Review*, 20 (3), 241–9.

Reips, U.-D. (2002b) Standards for internet-based experimenting. *Experimental Psychology*, 49 (4), 243–56.

Reips, U.-D. (2009) The methodology of internet-based experiments. In H. Joinson, K. McKenna, T. Postmes and U.-D. Reips (eds) *The Oxford Handbook of Internet Psychology*. Oxford: Oxford University Press, 373–90.

Renkema, J. (2004) *Introduction to Discourse Studies*. Amsterdam: John Benjamins Publishing.

Renzetti, C. M. and Lee, R. M. (1993) *Researching Sensitive Topics*. London: Sage.

REPGRID 2 (1993) *RepGrid Manual, Version 2.1b Release*. Calgary, Alberta: Centre for Person-Computer Studies.

Rex, J. (ed.) (1974) *Approaches to Sociology: An Introduction to Major Trends in British Sociology*. London: Routledge and Kegan Paul.

Reynolds, C. R. and Kamphaus, R. W. (eds) (2003) *Handbook of Psychological and Educational Assessment of Children: Intelligence, Aptitude and Achievement* (second edition). New York: Guildford Press.

Reynolds, C. W. (1987) Flocks, herds, and schools: a distributed behavioral model, *Computer Graphics*, 21 (4), 25–34. (SIGGRAPH '87 Conference Proceedings).

Reynolds, P. D. (1979) *Ethical Dilemmas and Social Science Research*. San Francisco, CA: Jossey-Bass.

Reynolds, T. J. and Gutman, J. (1988) Laddering theory, method, analysis, and interpretation. *Journal of Advertising Research*, 28 (1), 11–31.

Ribbens, J. and Edwards, R. (1997) *Feminist Dilemmas in Qualitative Research: Public Knowledge and Private Lives*. London: Sage.

Rice, J. M. (1897) The futility of the spelling grind. Cited in G. de Landsheere (1997) History of educational research. In J. P. Keeves (ed.) *Educational Research, Methodology, and Measurement: An International Handbook* (second edition). Oxford: Elsevier Science, 8–16.

Richards, L. (2002) Qualitative computing: a methods revolution? *International Journal of Social Research Methodology*, 5 (3), 263–76.

Richardson, J. T. E. (1996) Measures of effect size. *Behavior Research Methods Instruments and Computers*, 28 (1), 12–22.

Ridley, D. (2008) *The Literature Review: A Step-by-Step Guide for Students*. London: Sage.

Riecken, H. W. and Boruch, R. F. (1974) *Social Explanation: A Method for Planning and Evaluating Social Intervention*. New York: Academic Press.

Riessman, C. K. (1993) *Narrative Analysis*. Newbury Park, CA: Sage.

Rigby, K. (1999) Peer victimisation at school and the health of secondary school students. *British Journal of Educational Psychology*, 69 (1), 95–104.

Riley, M. W. (1963) *Sociological Research 1: A Case Approach*. New York: Harcourt, Brace and World.

Ringer, F. (1997) *Max Weber's Methodology*. Cambridge, MA: Harvard University Press.

Riordan, C. M. and Vandenburg, R. J. (1994) A central question in cross-cultural research: do employees of different cultures interpret work-related measures in an equivalent manner? *Journal of Management*, 20 (3), 643–71.

Riva, G., Lorerti, P., Lunghi, M., Vatalaro, F. and Davide, F. (2003) Presence 2010: The emergence of ambient intelligence. In G. Riva, F. Davide and W. A. Ijsselsteijn (eds) *Being There: Concepts, Effects and Measurements of User Presence in Synthetic Environments*. Amsterdam: International Operations Press.

Roberts, S. (1991) Exploring alternative paradigms in higher education. Paper presented at the Annual Meeting of the Association for the Study of Higher Education, Boston, MA. ERIC Document Reproduction Service No. ED 339 327.

Robinson, B. (1982) *Tutoring by Telephone: A Handbook*. Milton Keynes: Open University Press.

Robinson, L. A. and Kelley, B. (2007) Developing reflective thought in pre-service educators: utilizing role-plays and digital video. *Journal of Special Education Technology*, 22 (2), 31–43.

Robinson, P. and Smithers, A. (1999) Should the sexes be separated for secondary education – comparisons of single-sex and co-educational schools? *Research Papers in Education*, 14 (1), 23–49.

Robson, C. (1993) *Real World Research*. Oxford: Blackwell.

Robson, C. (2002) *Real World Research* (second edition). Oxford: Blackwell.

Roderick, R. (1986) *Habermas and the Foundations of Critical Theory*. Basingstoke: Macmillan.

Rodrigues, D. and Rodriques, R. (2000) *The Research Paper and the World Wide Web*. Englewood Cliffs, NJ: Prentice-Hall.

Rohner, R., and Katz, L. (1970) Testing for validity and reliability in cross-cultural research. *American Anthropologist*, 1068–73.

Rogers, C. R. (1942) *Counselling and Psychotherapy*. Boston, MA: Houghton Mifflin.

Rogers, C. R. (1945) The non-directive method as a technique for social research. *American Journal of Sociology*, 50, 279–83.

Rogers, C. R. (1969) *Freedom to Learn*. Columbus, OH: Merrill.

Rogers, C. R. and Stevens, B. (1967) *Person to Person: The Problem of Being Human*. London: Souvenir Press.

Roman, L. G. and Apple, M. (1990) Is Naturalism a move away from positivism? Materialist and feminist approaches to subjectivity in ethnographic research. In E. Eisner and A. Peshkin (eds) *Qualitative Inquiry in Education: The Continuing Debate*. New York: Teachers College Press, 38–73.

Rose, D. and Sullivan, O. (1993) *Introducing Data Analysis for Social Scientists*. Buckingham: Open University Press.

Rose, G. (2007) *Visual Methodologies* (second edition). London: Sage.

Rose, J. (2001) *The Intellectual Life of the British Working Classes*. London: Yale University Press.

Rose, J. (2007) The history of education as the history of reading. *History of Education*, 36 (4/5), 595–606.

Rosenthal, R. (1991) *Meta-analysis Procedures for Social Research*. Beverly Hills, CA: Sage.

Rosier, M. J. (1997) Survey research methods. In J. P. Keeves (ed.) *Educational Research, Methodology and Measurement: An International Handbook* (second edition). Oxford: Elsevier Science, 154–62.

Ross, K. N. and Rust, K. (1997) Sampling in survey research. In J.P. Keeves (ed.) *Educational Research, Methodology, and Measurement: An International Handbook* (second edition). Oxford: Elsevier Science, 427–38.

Ross, K. N. and Wilson, M. (1997) Sampling error in survey research. In. J. P. Keeves (ed.) *Educational Research, Methodology and Measurement: An International Handbook* (second edition). Oxford: Elsevier Science, 663–70.

Rossi, P. H. and Freeman, H. E. (1993) *Evaluation: A Systematic Approach*. Beverly Hills, CA: Sage.

Roszak, T. (1970) *The Making of a Counter Culture*. London: Faber and Faber.

Roszak, T. (1972) *Where the Wasteland Ends*. London: Faber and Faber.

Roth, W. D. and Mehta, J. D. (2002) The Rashomon effect. *Sociological Methods and Research*, 31 (2), 131–73.

Rozeboom, W. W. (1997) Good science is abductive, not hypothetico-deductive. In L. L. Harlow, S. A. Muliak and J. H. Steiger (eds) *What if There Were No Significance Tests?* Mahwah, NJ: Erlbaum, 335–92.

Roztocki, N. and Lahri, N. A. (2002) Is the applicability of web-based surveys for academic research limited to the field of information technology? Proceedings of the 36th Hawaii International Conference on System Sciences. Retrieved 26 February 2005, from http://csdl.computer.org/comp/proceedings/hicss/2003/1874/08/187480262a.pdf.

Ruane, J. M. (2005) *Essentials of Research Methods: A Guide to Social Science Research*. Oxford: Blackwell.

Rubin, D. B. (1987) *Multiple Imputation for Nonresponse in Surveys*. New York: John Wiley.

Ruddock, J. (1981) *Evaluation: A Consideration of Principles and Methods*. Manchester Monographs 10: University of Manchester.

Ruspini, E. (2002) *Introduction to Longitudinal Research*. London: Routledge.

Rybas, N. and Gajjala, R. (2007) Developing cyberethnographic research methods for understanding digitally mediated identities. *Forum: Qualitative Social Research*, 8(3). Retrieved 20 April 2010, from www.qualitative-research.net/index.php/fqs/article/view/282/620.

Sacks, H. (1984) On doing 'being ordinary'. In J. Atkinson and J. Heritage (eds) *Structures of Social Action: Studies in Conversation Analysis*. Cambridge: Cambridge University Press, 413–29.

Sacks, H. (1992) *Lectures on Conversation* (ed. G. Jefferson). Oxford: Basil Blackwell.

Sadowski, W. J. and Stanney, K. M. (2002) Presence in virtual environments. In K.M. Stanney (ed.) *Handbook of Virtual Environments Technology*. Mahwah, NJ: Lawrence Erlbaum, 791–806.

Sagor, R. (2005) *The Action Research Guidebook: A Four-Step Process for Educators and Teams*. Thousand Oaks, CA: Corwin Press.

Said, E. (1978) *Orientalism*. London: Routledge and Kegan Paul.

Sainsbury, M., Whetton, C., Mason, K. and Schagen, I. (1998) Fallback in attainment on transfer at age 11: evidence from the summer literacy schools evaluation. *Educational Research*, 40 (1), 73–81.

Saklofske, D. H., Andrews, J. J. W., Janzen, H. L. and Phye, G. D. (2001) *Handbook of Psychoeducational Assessment: A Practical Handbook*. New York: Academic Press.

Salmon, P. (1969) Differential conforming of the developmental process. *British Journal of Social and Clinical Psychology*, 8 (1), 22–31.

Salmon, P. (1976) Grid measures with child subjects. In P. Slater (ed.) *The Measurement of Intrapersonal Space by Grid Technique*, Vol. 1. London: Wiley, 15–46.

Salmon, W. C. (1998) *Causality and Explanation*. Oxford: Oxford University Press.

Sanday, A. (1993) The relationship between educational research and evaluation and the role of the local education authorities. In R. G. Burgess (ed.) *Educational Research and Evaluation for Policy and Practice*. London: Falmer, 32–43.

Sandelowski, M., Voils, C. I. and Knafl, G. (2009) On quantitizing. *Journal of Mixed Methods Research*, 3 (3), 208–22.

Santonus, M. (1998) *Simple, Yet Complex*. Retrieved 10 November 2000, from www.cio.com/archive/enterprise/041598_qanda_content.html.

Sapsford, R. (1999) *Survey Research*. London: Sage.

Saran, R. (1985) The use of archives and interviews in research on education policy. In R. Burgess (ed.) *Strategies of Educational Research*. London: Falmer, 207–41.

Sartre, J. P. (1964) *Words*. (Trans I. Clepane). Harmondsworth: Penguin.

Sartre, J. P. (1976) *Sartre on Theatre*. New York: Random House.

Schagen. I. and Sainsbury, M. (1996) Multilevel analysis of the key stage 1 national curriculum data in 1995. *Oxford Review of Education*, 22 (3), 265–72.

Schama, S. (1999) People's history, *Guardian*, 13 November, p. 24.

Schatzman, L. and Strauss, A. L. (1973) *Field Research: Strategies for a Natural Sociology*. Englewood Cliffs, NJ: Prentice-Hall.

Schein, E (1992) *Organizational Culture and Leadership* (second edition). San Francisco, CA: Jossey-Bass.

Schellenberg, E. G. (2004) Music lessons enhance IQ. *Psychological Science*, 15 (8), 511–54.

Schensul, S. L., Schensul, J. J. and LeCompte, M. D. (1999). *Essential Ethnographic Methods: Observations, Interviews and Questionnaires*. Walnut Creek, CA: AltaMira Press.

Scheper-Hughes, N. (1979) *Saints, Scholars and Schizophrenic Mental Illness in Rural Ireland*. Mahwah, NJ: Lawrence Erlbaum.

Scheurich, J. J. (1995) A postmodernist critique of research interviewing. *Qualitative Studies in Education*, 8 (3), 239–52.

Scheurich, J. J. (1996) The masks of validity: a deconstructive investigation. *International Journal of Qualitative Studies in Education*, 9 (1), 49–60.

Schneider, B., Carnoy, M., Kilpatrick, J., Schmidt, W. H. and Shavelson, R. J. (2007) *Estimating Causal Effects Using Experimental and Observational Designs*. Washington, DC: American Educational Research Association.

Schofield, J. W. (1990) Generalizability in qualitative research. In E. Eisner and A. Peshkin (eds.) *Qualitative Inquiry in Education*. New York: Teachers College Press, 201–32.

Schofield, W. (1996) Survey sampling. In R. Sapsford and V. Jupp (eds) *Data Collection and Analysis*. London: Sage and the Open University Press, 25–55.

Schön, D. (1983) *The Reflective Practitioner: How Professionals Think in Action*. London: Temple Smith.

Schön, D. (1987) *Educating the Reflective Practitioner*. San Francisco, CA: Jossey-Bass.

Schonlau, M., Van Soest, A., Kapteyn, A. and Couper, M. (2009) Selection bias in web surveys and the use of propensity scores. *Sociological Methods and Research*, 37 (3), 291–318.

Schuemie, M. J., Van der Straaten, P., Krijn, M. and Van der Mast, C. A. (2001) Research on presence in virtual reality: a survey. *Cyberpsychology and Behaviour*, 4, 183–201.

Schumacker, R. E. and Lomax, R. G. (2004) *A Beginner's Guide to Structural Equation Modeling* (second edition). Mahwah, NJ: Lawrence Erlbaum.

Schutz, A. (1962) *Collected Papers*. The Hague: Nijhoff.

Schwandt, T. A. (2000) Three epistemological stances for qualitative inquiry. In N. K. Denzin and Y. S. Lincoln (eds) *Handbook of Qualitative Research* (second edition). Thousand Oaks, CA: Sage, 189–213.

Schwartz, N. and Bienias, J. (1990). What mediates the impact of response alternatives on frequency reports of mundane behaviors? *Applied Cognitive Psychology*, 4 (1), 61–72.

Schwartz, N., Grayson, C. A. and Knauper, B. (1998) Formal meaning of rating scales and the interpretation of questions. *International Journal of Public Opinion Research*, 10 (2) 177–83.

Schwartz, N., Knauper, B., Rippler, H. J., Noelle-Neumann, E. and Clark, F. (1991) Rating scales: numeric values may change the meaning of scale labels. *Public Opinion Quarterly*, 55 (4), 570–82.

Schwarz, S. and Reips, U.-D. (2001) CGI versus Javascript: a web experiment on the reversed hindsight bias. In U.-D. Reips and M. Bosnjak (eds) *Dimensions of Internet Science*. Lengerich, Germany: Pabst Science, 75–90.

Scott, D. (2000) *Reading Educational Research and Policy*. London: RoutledgeFalmer.

Scott, J. (1990) *A Matter of Record: Documentary Sources in Social Research*. Cambridge: Polity Press.

Scott, S. (1985) Feminist research and qualitative methods: a discussion of some of the issues. In R. G. Burgess (ed.) *Issues in Educational Research: Qualitative Methods*. Lewes: Falmer, 67–85.

Searle, J. (1969) *Speech Acts*. London: Cambridge University Press.

Sears, R. R., Maccoby, E. and Levin, H. (1957) *Patterns of Child Rearing*. Paulo Alto, CA: Stanford University Press.

Sears, R. R., Rau, L. and Alpert, R. (1965) *Identification and Child Rearing*. Stanford, CA: Stanford University Press.

Sebba, J. (1999) Developing evidence-informed policy and practice in education. Paper presented at the British Educational Research Association conference, University of Sussex. Brighton, 2–5 September.

Sechrest, L. and Sidana, S. (1995) Quantitative and qualitative methods: is there an alternative? *Evaluation and Program Planning*, 18 (1), 77–87.

Secord, J. A. (2000) *Victorian Sensation: The Extraordinary Publication, Reception, and Secret Authorship of Vestiges of the Natural History of Creation*. Chicago, IL: University of Chicago Press.

Secord, P. F. and Peevers, B. H. (1974) The development and attribution of person concepts. In T. Mischel (ed.) *On Understanding Persons*. Oxford: Basil Blackwell.

Seedhouse, D. (1998a) *Ethics: The Heart of Healthcare*. Chichester: Wiley.

Seedhouse, D. (1998b) *Ethical Grid*. Retrieved 10 February 2010, from www.priory.com/images/ethicgrid.jpg.

Seidel, J. and Kelle, U. (1995) Different functions of coding in the analysis of textual data. In U. Kelle (ed.) *Computer-aided Qualitative Data Analysis: Theory, Methods and Practice*. London: Sage, 52–61.

Seidman, I. E. (1998) *Interviewing as Qualitative Research* (second edition). New York: Teachers College Press.

Seifert, T. L. (1997) Academic goals and emotions results of a structural equation model and a cluster analysis. *British Journal of Educational Psychology*, 67 (3), 323–38.

Selleck, R. W. J. (1991) The Manchester Statistical Society and the foundation of social science research. In D. S. Anderson and B. J. Biddle (eds) *Knowledge for Policy: Improving Education through Research*. London: Falmer, 291–304.

Sellers, S. C. (2002) Testing theory through teaching theatrics. *Journal of Nursing Education*, 41 (11), 498–500.

Sellitz, C., Wrightsman, L. S. and Cook, S. W. (1976) *Research Methods in Social Relations*. New York: Holt, Rinehart and Winston.

Sequeira, G. M., Howroid, S., MacPherson, S. and Lo, O.Y. (1996) *The Poverty Research Project*. Hong Kong: City University of Hong Kong.

Serafini, A. (ed.) (1989) *Ethics and Social Concern*. New York: Paragon House.

Severiens, S. and ten Dam, G. (1998) A multilevel meta-analysis of gender differences in learning orientations. *British Journal of Educational Psychology*, 68 (4), 595–618.

Shaffer, D. W. (2006) *How Computer Games Help Children Learn*. New York: Macmillan.

Shapiro, B. L. (1990) A collaborative approach to help novice science teachers reflect on changes in their construction of the role of the science teacher. *Alberta Journal of Educational Research*, 36 (3), 203–22.

Shaughnessy, J. J., Zechmeister, E. B. and Zechmeister, J. S. (2003) *Research Methods in Psychology* (sixth edition). New York: McGraw-Hill.

Shavelson, R. J. and Berliner, D. C. (1991) Erosion of the education research infrastructure: a reply to Finn. In D. S. Anderson and B. J. Biddle (eds) *Knowledge for Policy: Improving Education through Research*. London: Falmer, 79–84.

Shavelson, R. J., Phillips, D. C., Towne, L. and Feuer, M. J. (2003) On the science of education design studies. *Educational Researcher*, 32 (1), 25–8.

Shaw, E. L. (1992) The influence of methods instruction on the beliefs of preservice elementary and secondary science teachers: preliminary comparative analyses. *School Science and Mathematics*, 92 (1), 14–22.

Shaw, M. L. G. and Thomas, L. F. (1978) FOCUS on education – an interactive computer system for the development and analysis of repertory grids. *International Journal of Man-Machine Studies*, (10), 139–73.

Sheehy, K. (2010) Virtual environments: issues and opportunities for researching inclusive educational practices. In A. Peachey, J. Gillen, D. Livingstone and S. Smith-Robbins (eds) *Researching Learning in Virtual Worlds*. London: Springer, 1–16.

Sheldon, T. and Chalmers, I. (1994) The UK Cochrane Centre and the NHS Centre for Reviews and Dissemination: respective roles within the Information Systems Strategy of the NHS R&D Programme, coordination and principles underlying collaboration. *Health Economics*, 3, 201–3.

Sheppard, J. (1980) Vive la difference?!: An outsider's view of French archives. *Archives*, 14, 151–62.

Sheridan, T. B. (1992) Musings on telepresence and virtual presence. *Presence: Teleoperators and Virtual Environments*, 1 (1), 120–5.

Shropshire, K. O., Hawdon, J. E. and Witte, J. C. (2009) Web survey design: balancing measurement, response, and topical interest. *Sociological Methods and Research*, 37 (3), 344–70.

Shuy, R. W. (2003) In-person versus telephone interviewing. In J. A. Holstein and J. F. Gubrium (eds) *Inside Interviewing: New Lenses, New Concerns*. Thousand Oaks, CA: Sage, 175–95.

Sieber, J. E. (1992) *Planning Ethically Responsible Research: A Guide for Students and Internal Review Boards*. Beverly Hills, CA: Sage.

Sieber, J. E. and Stanley, B. (1988) Ethical and professional dimensions of socially sensitive research. *American Psychologist*, 43 (1), 49–55.

Siegel, H. (1987) *Relativism Refuted*. Dordrecht, Netherlands: D. Reidel Publishing.

Siegel, S. (1956) *Nonparametric Statistics for the Behavioral Sciences*. New York: McGraw-Hill.

Sikes, P. (2006) On dodgy ground? Problematics and ethics in educational research. *International Journal of Research and Method in Education*, 29 (1), 105–17.

Sikes, P., Measor, L. and Woods, P. (1985) *Teacher Careers*. Lewes: Falmer.

Sikes, P. and Troyna, B. (1991) True stories: a case study in the use of life histories in teacher education. *Educational Review*, 43 (1), 3–16.

Silverman, D. (1985) *Qualitative Methodology and Sociology: Describing the Social World*. Brookfield, VT: Gower.

Silverman, D. (1993) *Interpreting Qualitative Data*. London: Sage.

Silverman, D. (2001) *Interpreting Qualitative Data: Methods for Analysing Talk, Text and Interaction* (second edition). London: Sage.

Simon, H. A. (1996) *The Sciences of the Artificial* (third edition). Cambridge, MA: The MIT Press.

Simon, J. L. (1978) *Basic Research Methods in Social Science*. New York: Random House.

Simons, H. (1982) Conversation piece: the practice of interviewing in case study research. In R. McCormick (ed.) *Calling Education to Account*. London: Heinemann, 239–46.

Simons, H. (1989) *Getting to Know School in a Democracy*. London: Falmer.

Simons, H. (1996) The paradox of case study. *Cambridge Journal of Education*, 26 (2), 225–40.

Simons, H. (2000) Damned if you do, damned if you don't: ethical and political dilemmas in education. In H. Simons and R. Usher (eds) *Situated Ethics in Educational Research*. London: RoutledgeFalmer, 39–55.

Simons, H. and Usher, R. (eds) (2000) *Situated Ethics in Educational Research*. London: RoutledgeFalmer.

Simpson, M. and Tuson, J. (2003) *Using Observations in Small-Scale Research: A Beginner's Guide* (revised edition). Glasgow: University of Glasgow, the SCRE Centre.

Skåreus, E. (2009) Pictorial analysis in research on education: methods and concepts. *International Journal of Research and Method in Education*, 32 (2), 167–83.

Skelton, C., Francis, B. and Smulyan, L. (2006) *The Sage Handbook of Gender and Education*. London: Sage.

Slater, M. and Steed, A. (2000) A virtual presence counter. *Presence Teleoperators and Virtual Environments* 9, 413–34.

Slater, P. (1964) *The Principal Components of a Repertory Grid*. London: Vincent Andrews.

Slavin, R. E. (1984a) Meta-analysis in education: how has it been used? *Educational Researcher*, 13 (8), 6–15.

Slavin, R. E. (1984b) A rejoinder to Carlberg *et al. Educational Researcher*, 13 (8), 24–7.

Slavin, R. E. (1986) Best-evidence synthesis: an alternative to meta-analytic and traditional reviews. *Educational Researcher*, 15 (9), 5–11.

Slavin, R. E. (1995) Best evidence synthesis: an intelligent alternative to meta-analysis. *Journal of Clinical Epidemiology*, 48 (1), 9–18.

Slavin, R. (2007) *Educational Research in an Age of Accountability*. Boston, MA: Pearson Education Inc.

Slee, P. (1986) *Learning and a Liberal Education: The Study of Modern History in the Universities of Oxford, Cambridge and Manchester, 1800–1914*. Manchester: Manchester University Press.

Sloane, F. C. and Gorard, S. (2003) Exploring modeling aspects of design experiments. *Educational Researcher*, 32 (1), 29–31.

Small, R. (2001) Codes are not enough: what philosophy can contribute to the ethics of educational research. *Journal of Philosophy of Education*, 35 (3), 387–405.

Smith, H. W. (1975) *Strategies of Social Research: The Methodological Imagination*. London: Prentice-Hall.

Smith, H. W. (1991) *Strategies of Social Research* (third edition). Orlando, FL: Holt, Rinehart and Winston.

Smith, J. T. (1998) *Punch* and elementary education, 1860–1900. *History of Education*, 27 (2), 125–40.

Smith, L. M. (1987) *Kensington Revisited*. Lewes: Falmer.

Smith, M. A. and Leigh, B. (1997) Virtual subjects: using the internet as an alternative source of subjects and research environment. *Behavior Research Methods, Instruments and Computers*, 29 (4), 496–505.

Smith, M. L. and Glass, G. V. (1977) Meta-analysis of psychotherapy outcome studies. *American Psychologist*, 32 (9), 752–60.

Smith, M. L. and Glass, G. V. (1987) *Research and Evaluation in Education and the Social Sciences*. Englewood Cliffs, NJ: Prentice-Hall.

Smithson, J. (2000) Using and analyzing focus groups: limitations and possibilities. *International Journal of Social Research Methodology*, 3 (2), 103–19.

Smyth, J. (1989) Developing and sustaining critical reflection in teacher education. *Journal of Teacher Education*, 40 (2), 2–9.

Smyth, J. D., Dillman, D. A., Christian, L. M. and Stern, M. J. (2004) How visual grouping influences answers to internet surveys. Paper presented at the American Association for Public Opinion Research, Phoenix, AZ.

Snijders, T. A. B. and Bosker, R. (1999) *Multilevel Analysis*. London: Sage.

Social and Community Planning Research (1972) *Questionnaire Design Manual No. 5*. London: 16 Duncan Terrace, NI 8BZ.

Social Research Association (2003) *Ethical Guidelines*. Retrieved 15 May 2005, from www.the-sra.org.uk/ethics03.pdf.

Social Sciences and Humanities Research Council of Canada (1981) *Ethical Guidelines for the Institutional Review Committee for Research with Human Subjects*. Ottawa: Ministry of Supply and Services.

Soffer, R. (1994) *Discipline and Power: The University, History, and the Making of an English Elite, 1870–1930*. Stanford, CA: Stanford University Press.

Solomon, D. J. (2001) Conducting web-based surveys. ERIC Digest. ED458291 ERIC Clearinghouse on Assessment and Evaluation. College Park, MD. Retrieved 14 April 2004, from www.ericdigests.org/2002–2/surveys.htm.

Somekh, B. (1995) The contribution of action research to development in social endeavours: a position paper on action research methodology. *British Educational Research Journal*, 21 (3), 339–55.

Southgate, V., Arnold, H. and Johnson, S. (1981) *Extending Beginning Reading*. London: Heinemann Educational for the Schools Council.

Sova, D. B. (2004) *Banned Plays: Censorship Histories of 125 Stage Dramas*. New York: Facts on File.

Spector, P. E. (1993) Research designs. In M. L. Lewis-Beck (ed.) *Experimental Design and Methods. International Handbook of Quantitative Applications in the Social Sciences, Vol. 3*. London: Sage, 1–74.

Spencer, J. R. and Flin, R. (1990) *The Evidence of Children*. London: Blackstone.

Spies, R. A., Carlson, J. F. and Geisinger, K. F. (eds) (2010) *The Eighteenth Mental Measurements Yearbook*. Lincoln, NB: University of Nebraska-Lincoln. Buros Institute of Mental Measurements.

Spindler, G. (ed.) (1982) *Doing the Ethnography of Schooling*. New York: Holt, Rinehart and Winston.

Spindler, G. and Spindler, L. (1992) Cultural process and ethnography: an anthropological perspective. In M. LeCompte, W. L. Millroy and J. Preissle (eds) *The Handbook of Qualitative Research in Education*. London: Academic Press, 53–92.

Spradley, J. P. (1979) *The Ethnographic Interview*. New York: Holt, Rinehart and Winston.

Spradley, J. P. (1980) *Participant Observation*. New York: Holt, Rinehart and Winston.

Stables, A. (1990) Differences between pupils from mixed and single-sex schools in their enjoyment of school subjects and in their attitude to Science in school. *Educational Review*, 42 (3), 221–30.

Stacey, J. (1988) Can there be a feminist ethnography? *Women's Studies International Forum*, 11 (1), 21–7.

Stacey, R. D. (1992) *Managing the Unknowable*. San Francisco, CA: Jossey-Bass.

Stacey, R. D. (2000) *Strategic Management and Organisational Dynamics* (third edition). Harlow: Pearson Education.

Stake, R. E. (1978) The case study method in social inquiry. *Educational Researcher*, 7 (2), 5–8.

Stake, R. E. (1994) Case studies. In N. K. Denzin and Y. S. Lincoln (eds) *Handbook of Qualitative Research*. London: Sage, 236–47.

Stake, R. E. (1995) *The Art of Case Study Research*. Thousand Oaks, CA: Sage.

Steedman, C. (2001) *Dust*. Manchester: Manchester University Press.

Stenbacka, C. (2001) Qualitative research requires quality concepts of its own. *Management Decision*, 39 (7), 551–5.

Stenhouse, L. (1975) *An Introduction to Curriculum Research and Development*. London: Heinemann.

Stenhouse, L. (1979) What is Action Research? (mimeo). Norwich: Classroom Action Research Network.

Stenhouse, L. (1985) Case study methods. In T. Husen and T. N. Postlethwaite (eds) *International Encyclopaedia of Education* (first edition). Oxford: Pergamon, 640–6.

Stewart, I. (1997) *Does God Play Dice? The New Mathematics of Chaos*. Harmondsworth: Penguin.

Stewart, J. and Yalonis, C. (2001) *Internet-Based Surveys and Sampling Issues*. Communique Partners. Retrieved 26 January 2005, from www.communiquepartners.com/white_papers/sampling_issues_and_the_internet_briefing_paper.pdf.

Stewart, M. (2001) *The Co-Evolving Organization*. Rutland, UK: Decomplexity Associates. Retrieved 14 November 2001 from www.decomplexity.com/Coevolving%20Organization%20VU.pdf.

Stewart, V. (1990) *The David Solution: How to Reclaim Power and Liberate Your Organization*. London: Gower.

Stiggins, R. J. (2001) *Student-Involved Classroom Assessment* (third edition). Upper Saddle River, NJ: Merrill Prentice-Hall.

Stillar, G. F. (1998) *Analysing Everyday Texts: Discourses, Rhetoric and Social Perspectives*. London: Sage.

Strand, S. (1999) Ethnic group, sex and economic disadvantage: associations with pupils' educational progress from Baseline to the end of Key Stage 1. *British Educational Research Journal*, 25 (2), 179–202.

Strange, V., Forest, S., Oakley, A. and the Ripple Study Team (2003) Using research questionnaires with young people in schools: the influence of social context. *International Journal of Social Research Methodology*, 6 (4), 337–46.

Strauss, A. L. (1987) *Qualitative Analysis for Social Scientists*. Cambridge: Cambridge University Press.

Strauss, A. L. and Corbin, J. (1990) *Basics of Qualitative Research*. Newbury Park, CA: Sage.

Strauss, A. L. and Corbin, J. (1994) Grounded theory methodology: an overview. In N. K. Denzin and Y. Lincoln (eds) *Handbook of Qualitative Research*. Thousand Oaks, CA: Sage, 273–85.

Stray, C. (1994) Paradigms regained: towards a historical sociology of the textbook. *Journal of Curriculum Studies*, 26 (1), 1–29.

Strike, K. A. (1990) The ethics of educational evaluation. In J. Millman and L. Darling-Hammond (eds) *A New Handbook of Teacher Evaluation*. Newbury Park, CA: Corwin Press, 356–73.

Stronach, I. and Morris, B. (1994) Polemical notes on educational evaluation in an age of 'policy hysteria'. *Evaluation and Research in Education*, 8 (1 and 2), 5–19.

Stubbs, M. and Delamont, S. (eds) (1976) *Explorations in Classroom Observation*. Chichester: John Wiley.

Sturman, A. (1997) Case study methods. In J. P. Keeves (ed.) *Educational Research, Methodology and Measurement: An International Handbook* (second edition). Oxford: Elsevier Science, 61–6.

Sturman, A. (1999) Case study methods. In J. P. Keeves and G. Lakomski (eds) *Issues in Educational Research*. Oxford: Elsevier Science, 103–12.

Stutchbury, K. and Fox, A. (2009) Ethics in educational research: introducing a methodological tool for effective ethical analysis. *Cambridge Journal of Education*, 39 (4), 489–504.

Stylianou, S. (2008) Interview control questions. *International Journal of Social Research Methodology*, 11 (3), 239–56.

Sudman, S. and Bradburn, N. M. (1982) *Asking Questions: A Practical Guide to Questionnaire Design*. San Francisco, CA: Jossey-Bass.

Sumathipala, A. and Murray, J. (2006) New approach to translating instruments for cross-cultural research: a combined qualitative and quantitative approach for translation and consensus generation. *International Journal of Methods in Psychiatric Research*, 9 (2), 87–95.

Sun, R. (2008) *Cognition and Multi-Agent Interaction*. Cambridge: Cambridge University Press.

Suter, L. E. (2005) Multiple methods: research methods in education projects at NSF. *International Journal of Research and Method in Education*, 28 (2) 171–81.

Suto, W. M. and Nádas, R. (2009) Why are some GCSE examination questions harder to mark accurately than others? Using Kelly's Repertory Grid technique to identify relevant question features. *Research Papers in Education*, 24 (3), 335–77.

Swain, J. (2006) An ethnographic approach to researching children in junior school. *International Journal of Social Research Methodology*, 9 (3), 199–213.

Swain, J., Heyman, B. and Gillman, M. (1998) Public research, private concerns: ethical issues in the use of open-ended interviews with people who have learning difficulties. *Disability and Society*, 13 (1), 21–36.

Swantz, M. (1996) A personal position paper on participatory research: personal quest for living knowledge. *Qualitative Inquiry*, 2 (1), 120–36.

Sykes, W. and Hoinville, G. (1985) *Telephone Interviewing on a Survey of Social Attitudes*. London: Social and Community Planning Research.

Tabachnick, B. G. and Fidell, L. S. (2007) *Using Multivariate Statistics* (fifth edition). Boston, MA: Pearson Education.

Tandon, R. (2005a) Introduction: revisiting the roots. In R. Tandon (ed.) *Participatory Research: Revisiting the Roots*. New Delhi: Mosaic Books, vii–xiii.

Tandon, R. (2005b) A critique of monopolistic research. In R. Tandon (ed.) *Participatory Research: Revisiting the Roots*. New Delhi: Mosaic Books, 3–8.

Tandon, R. (2005c) Participatory research: main concepts and issues. In R. Tandon (ed.) *Participatory Research: Revisiting the Roots*. New Delhi: Mosaic Books, 22–39.

Tandon, R. (2005d) Knowledge as power. In R. Tandon (ed.) *Participatory Research: Revisiting the Roots*. New Delhi: Mosaic Books, 40–53.

Tandon, R. (2005e) Dialogue. In R. Tandon (ed.) *Participatory Research: Revisiting the Roots*. New Delhi: Mosaic Books, 275–94.

Tashakkori, A. and Creswell, J. W. (2007) Exploring the nature of research questions in mixed methods research. *Journal of Mixed Methods Research*, 1 (3), 207–11.

Tashakkori, A. and Teddlie, C. (eds) (2003) *Handbook of Mixed Methods Research*. Thousand Oaks, CA: Sage.

Task Group on Assessment and Testing (1988) *National Curriculum: Testing and Assessment: A Report*. London: HMSO.

Tatar, M. (1998) Teachers as significant others: gender differences in secondary school pupils' perceptions. *British Journal of Educational Psychology*, 68 (2), 255–68.

Taylor, P. (ed.) (1996) *Researching Drama and Arts Education. Paradigms and Possibilities*. London: Falmer.

Teddlie, C. and Tashakkori, A. (2003) Preface. In A. Tashakkori and C. Teddlie (eds) *Handbook of Mixed Methods in Social and Behavioral Research*. Thousand Oaks, CA: Sage, vi–viii.

Teddlie, C. and Tashakkori, A. (2006) A general typology of research designs featuring mixed methods. *Research in the Schools*, 13 (1), 12–28.

Teddlie, C. and Tashakkori, A. (2009) *Foundations of Mixed Methods Research*. Thousand Oaks, CA: Sage.

Teddlie, C. and Yu, F. (2007) Mixed methods sampling: a typology with examples. *Journal of Mixed Methods Research*, 1 (1), 77–100.

Terry, A. A. (1998) Teachers as targets of bullying by their pupils: a study to investigate incidence. *British Journal of Educational Psychology*, 68 (2), 217–77.

Tesch, R. (1990) *Qualitative Research: Analysis Types and Software*. London: Falmer.

Thapar-Björkert, S. and Henry, M. (2004) Reassessing the research relationship: location, position and power in fieldwork accounts. *International Journal of Social Research Methodology*, 7 (5), 363–81.

Thissen, D. (1990) Reliability and measurement precision. In H. Wainer (ed.) *Computer Adaptive Testing: A Primer*. Hillsdale, NJ: Lawrence Erlbaum, 161–86.

Thody, A. (1997) Lies, damned lies – and storytelling. *Educational Management and Administration*, 25 (3), 325–38.

Thomas, G. and Pring, R. (2004) *Evidence-Based Practice in Education*. Maidenhead: Open University Press.

Thomas, J. (1993) *Doing Critical Ethnography*. Newbury Park, CA: Sage.

Thomas, P. (1991) Research models: insiders, gadflies, limestone. In D. S. Anderson and B. J. Biddle (eds) *Knowledge for Policy: Improving Education through Research*. London: Falmer, 225–33.

Thomas, S., Sammons, P., Mortimore, P. and Smees, R. (1997) Differential secondary school effectiveness: comparing the performance of different pupil groups. *British Educational Research Journal*, 23 (4), 351–69.

Thomas, W. I. (1923) *The Unadjusted Girl*. Boston, MA: Little, Brown.

Thomas, W. I. (1928) *The Child in America*. New York: Knopf.

Thompson, B. (1994) Guidelines for authors. *Educational and Psychological Measurement*, 54 (4), 837–47.

Thompson, B. (1996) AERA editorial policies regarding statistical significance testing: three suggested reforms. *Educational Researcher*, 25 (2), 26–30.

Thompson, B. (1998) In praise of brilliance: where that praise really belongs. *American Psychologist*, 53 (7), 799–800.

Thompson, B. (2001) Significance, effect sizes, stepwise methods, and other issues: strong arguments move the field. *Journal of Experimental Education* 70 (1), 80–93.

Thompson, B. (2002) What future quantitative social science research could look like: confidence intervals for effect sizes. *Educational Researcher*, 31 (3), 25–32.

Thompson, B. and Snyder, P. A. (1997) Statistical significance testing practices in the Journal of Experimental Education. *Journal of Experimental Education*, 66, 75–83.

Thomson, R. and Holland, J. (2003) Hindsight, foresight and insight: the challenges of longitudinal qualitative research. *International Journal of Social Research Methodology*, 6 (3), 233–44.

Thorne, B. (1994) *Gender Play: Girls and Boys in School*. New Brunswick, NJ: Rutgers University Press.

Thurstone, L. L. and Chave, E. J. (1929) *The Measurement of Attitudes*. Chicago, IL: University of Chicago Press.

Ticehurst, G. W. and Veal, A. J. (2000) *Business Research Methods*. Frechs Forest, New South Wales: Pearson.

Tierney, W. (2002) Get real: representing reality. *International Journal of Qualitative Studies in Education*, 15 (4), 385–98.

Tillman, L. C. (2002) Culturally sensitive research

approaches: an African-American perspective. *Educational Researcher*, 31 (9), 3–12.

Timutimu, N., Simon, J. and Matthews, K. (1998) Historical research as a bicultural project: seeking new perspectives on the New Zealand Native Schools system. *History of Education*, 27 (2), 109–24.

Toepoel, V., Vis, C., Das, M. and Van Soest, A. (2009) Design of web questionnaires. *Sociological Methods and Research*, 37 (3), 371–92.

Tombari, M. and Borich, G. (1999) *Authentic Assessment in the Classroom*. Englewood Cliffs, NJ: Prentice-Hall.

Tones, K. (1997) Beyond the randomized controlled trial: a case for 'judicial review'. *Health Education Research*, 12 (2), i–iv.

Torgerson, C. J. and Torgerson, D. J. (2003a) The design and conduct of randomized controlled trials in education: Lessons from health care. *Oxford Review of Education*, 29 (1), 67–80.

Torgerson, D. J. and Torgerson, C. J. (2003b) Avoiding bias in randomized controlled trials in educational research. *British Journal of Educational Studies*, 51 (1), 36–45.

Torres, C. A. (1992) Participatory action research and popular education in Latin America. *International Journal of Qualitative Studies in Education*, 5 (1), 51–62.

Tosh, J. (2002) *The Pursuit of History: Aims, Methods and New Directions in the Study of Modern History* (revised third edition). London: Longman.

Travers, J. and Milgram, S. (1969) An experimental study of the small world problem. *Sociometry*, 32 (4), 425–43.

Triandis, H. C. (1994) *Culture and Social Behaviour*. New York: McGraw-Hill.

Trifonas, P. P. (2009) Deconstructing research: paradigms lost. *International Journal of Research and Method in Education*, 32 (3), 297–308.

Tripp, D. H. (1985) Case study generalisation: an agenda for action. *British Educational Research Journal*, 11 (1), 33–43.

Tripp, D. H. (1993) *Critical Incidents in Teaching*. London: Routledge.

Tripp, D. H. (1994) Teachers' lives, critical incidents and professional practice. *International Journal of Qualitative Studies in Education*, 7 (1), 65–72.

Tripp, D. H. (2003) Action Inquiry. *Action Research e-Reports*. Retrieved 16 April 2010, from http://www2.fhs.usyd.edu.au/arow/arer/017.htm#Distinguishing%20action%20research.

Tuckman, B. W. (1972) *Conducting Educational Research*. New York: Harcourt Brace Jovanovich.

Tukey, J. (1962) The future of data analysis. *Annals of Mathematical Statistics*, 33 (1), 1–67.

Turkle, S. (2000) Cyborg babies and cy-dough-plasm: ideas about self and life in the culture of simulation. In D. Bell and B. M. Kennedy (eds) *The Cybercultures Reader*. London: Routledge, 547–56.

Turnbull, C. M. (1972) *The Mountain People*. New York: Simon and Schuster.

Tweddle, S., Avis, P., Wright, J. and Waller, T. (1998) Towards evaluating web sites. *British Journal of Educational Technology*, 29 (3), 267–70.

Tyacke, S. (2001) Archives in a wider world: the culture and politics of archives. *Archivaria*, 52 (Fall), 1–25.

Tyler, R. (1949) *Basic Principles of Curriculum and Instruction*. Chicago, IL: University of Chicago Press.

Tymms, P. (1996) Theories, models and simulations: school effectiveness at an impasse. In J. Gray, D. Reynolds, C.T. Fitz-Gibbon and D. Jesson (eds) *Merging Traditions: The Future of Research on School Effectiveness and School Improvement*. London: Cassell, 121–35.

Tymms, P. B. (1999) *Baseline Assessment and Monitoring in the Primary Schools*. London: David Fulton Publishers.

Ulam, S. M. (1992) *Adventures of a Mathematician*. Berkeley, University of California Press.

UNESCO (1996) *Learning: the Treasure Within*. Paris: UNESCO.

University of Berkeley (2002) Types of research questions. *Thinkertools*. Retrieved 30 January 2010, from http://faculty.plattsburgh.edu/carla.hendrix/LIB102/QuestionType.htm.

University of California at Santa Cruz (2010) *Choose a Research Topic*. Retrieved 30 January 2010, from http://library.ucsc.edu/help/howto/choose-a-research-topic.

University of Loughborough (2009) *Doing a Literature Review*. Retrieved 6 February 2010, from http://info.lboro.ac.uk/library/skills/Advice/Litreview.pdf.

University of North Carolina (2007) *Literature Reviews*. Retrieved 6 February 2010, from www.unc.edu/depts/wcweb/handouts/literature_review.html.

US Dept of Health, Education and Welfare, Public Health Service and National Institute of Health (1971) *The Institutional Guide to DHEW Policy on Protecting Human Subjects*, DHEW Publication (NIH), December 2, 72–102.

Usher, P. (1996) Feminist approaches to research. In D. Scott and R. Usher (eds) *Understanding Educational Research*. London: Routledge, 120–42.

Usher, R. and Scott, D. (1996) Afterword: the politics of educational research. In D. Scott and R. Usher (eds) *Understanding Educational Research*. London: Routledge, 175–80.

Valadines, N. (1999) Formal reasoning performance of higher secondary school students: theoretical and educational implications. *European Journal of Psychology of Education*, 14 (1), 109–17.

Vallance, M. and Wiz, C. (2008) The realities of working in virtual worlds. *Proceedings of World Conference on Educational Multimedia, Hypermedia and Telecommunications 2008*. Chesapeake, VA: AACE, 3085–90.

Vallerand, R. J. (1989) Vers une méthodologie de validation trans-culturelle de questionnaires psychologiques. (Toward a methodology of cross-cultural validation of psychological questionnaires). *Psychologie Canadienne*, 30 (4), 662–80.

Vallerand, R. J., Pelletier, L. G., Blais, M. R., Brière, N. M. Senécal, C. and Vallières, E. F. (1992) The academic motivation scale: a measure of intrinsic, extrinsic and amotivation in education. *Educational and Psychological Measurement*, 52 (4), 1003–17.

Van Etten, S., Pressley, M., Freebern, G. and Echevarria, M. (1998) An interview study of college freshmen's beliefs about their academic motivation. *European Journal of Psychology of Education*, 13 (1), 105–30.

Van Meter, K. M. (2000) Sensitive topics – sensitive questions: overview of the sociological research literature. *Bulletin de Methodologie Sociologique*, 68 (1), 59–79.

van Rekom, J. and Wierenga, B. (2007) On the hierarchical

nature of means-end relationships in laddering data. *Journal of Business Research*, 60 (4), 401–10.

Vasta, R. (1979) *Studying Children: An Introduction to Research Methods*. San Francisco, CA: W. H. Freeman.

Vella, S. (2009) Newspapers. In M. Dobson and B. Ziemann (eds) *Reading Primary Sources: The Interpretation of Texts from Nineteenth- and Twentieth-Century History*. London: Routledge, 192–208.

Verma, G. K. and Mallick, K. (1999) *Researching Education: Perspectives and Techniques*. London: Falmer.

Vermunt, J. D. (1998) The regulation of constructive learning processes. *British Journal of Educational Psychology*, 68 (2), 149–71.

Verschuren, P. J. M. (2003) Case study as a research strategy: Some ambiguities and opportunities. *International Journal of Research Methodology*, 6 (2), 121–39.

Vincent, D. (1981) *Bread, Knowledge and Freedom: A Study of Nineteenth-Century Working Class Autobiography*. London: Methuen.

Virtual Surveys Limited (2003) *How to Do Online Research*. Virtual Surveys Limited. Retrieved 6 January 2003, from www.virtualsurveys.com/papers/paper_3.asp.

Voss, R., Thorsten, G. and Szmigin, I. (2007) Service quality in higher education: the role of student expectations. *Journal of Business Research*, 60 (9), 949–59.

Vulliamy, G. (1990) The potential of qualitative educational research in developing countries. In G. Vulliamy, K. Lewin and D. Stephens, *Doing Educational Research in Developing Countries: Qualitative Strategies*. London: Falmer, 7–25.

Vulliamy, G., Lewin, K. and Stephens, D. (1990) *Doing Educational Research in Developing Countries: Qualitative Strategies*. London: Falmer.

Wadsworth, Y. (1998) What is participatory action research? *Action Research International*, Paper 2. Retrieved 20 April 2010, from www.scu.edu.au/schools/gcm/ar/ari/p-ywadsworth98.html.

Wagner, B. J. (1998) Drama as a way of knowing. In J. Saxton and C. Miller (eds) *The Research of Practice. The Practice of Research*. Victoria, BC: International Drama in Education Research Institute, 55–72.

Wainer, H. (ed.) (1990) *Computerized Adaptive Testing: A Primer*. Mahwah, NJ: Lawrence Erlbaum.

Wainer, H. and Dorans, N. J. (2000) *Computerized Adaptive Testing: A Primer* (second edition). Mahwah, NJ: Lawrence Erlbaum.

Wainer, H. and Mislevy, R. J. (1990) Item response theory, item calibration and proficiency estimation. In H. Wainer (ed.) *Computerized Adaptive Testing: A Primer*. Mahwah, NJ: Lawrence Erlbaum, 65–102.

Waldrop, M. M. (1992) *Complexity: The Emerging Science at the Edge of Order and Chaos*. Harmondsworth: Penguin.

Walford, G. (ed.) (1994) *Researching the Powerful in Education*. London, UCL Press.

Walford, G. (1994a) A new focus on the powerful. In G. Walford (ed.) *Researching the Powerful in Education*. London: UCL Press, 2–11.

Walford, G. (1994b) Ethics and power in a study of pressure group politics. In G. Walford (ed.) *Researching the Powerful in Education*. London: UCL Press, 81–93.

Walford, G. (1994c) Reflections on researching the powerful. In G. Walford (ed.) *Researching the Powerful in Education*. London: UCL Press, 222–31.

Walford, G. (2001) *Doing Qualitative Educational Research: A Personal Guide to the Research Process*. London: Continuum.

Walford, G. (2005) Research ethical guidelines and anonymity. *International Journal of Research and Method in Education*, 28 (1), 83–93.

Walker, R. (1980) Making sense and losing meaning: problems of selection in doing case study. In H. Simons (ed.) *Towards a Science of the Singular*. University of East Anglia: Centre for Applied Research in Education, 222–35.

Waller, D., Hunt, E. and Knapp, D. (1998) The transfer of spatial knowledge in virtual environment training. *Presence: Teleoperators and Virtual Environments*, 7 (2), 129–43.

Waltz, M. (2007) The relationship of ethics to quality: a particular case of research in autism. *International Journal of Research and Method in Education*, 30 (3), 353–61.

Wang, J. (2008) Effect size and practical importance: a non-monotonic match. *International Journal of Research and Method in Education*, 31 (2), 125–32.

Warburton, T. and Saunders, M. (1996) Representing teachers' professional culture through cartoons. *British Journal of Educational Studies*, 44 (3), 307–25.

Wardekker, W. L. and Miedama, S. (1997) Critical pedagogy: an evaluation and a direction for reformulation. *Curriculum Inquiry*, 27 (1), 45–61.

Warnock, M. (1970) *Existentialism*. London: Oxford University Press.

Waterman, A. H., Blades, M. and Spencer, C. (2001) Interviewing children and adults: the effect of question format on the tendency to speculate. *Applied Cognitive Psychology*, 15 (5), 521–31.

Watkins, D. A. (2007) Comparing ways of learning. In M. Bray, R. Adamson and M. Mason (eds) *Comparative Education Research: Approach and Methods*. Hong Kong: Comparative Education Research Centre, University of Hong Kong, 299–313.

Watt, J. H. (1997) Using the internet for quantitative survey research. *Quirk's Marketing Research Review*, July. Retrieved 6 January 2003, from www.swiftinteractive.com.white1.asp.

Watts, D. J. (2003) *Six Degrees: The Science of a Connected Age*. New York: W. W. Norton.

Watts, M. and Ebbutt, D. (1987) More than the sum of the parts: research methods in group interviewing, *British Educational Research Journal*, 13 (1), 25–34.

Wax, M. (1982) Research reciprocity rather than informed consent in fieldwork. In J. Sieber (ed.) *The Ethics of Social Research: Fieldwork, Regulation and Publication*. New York: Springer-Verlag, 33–48.

Webb, G. (1996) Becoming critical of action research for development. In O. Zuber-Skerritt (ed.) *New Directions in Action Research*. London: Falmer, 137–61.

Webb, L. M., Walker, K. L. and Bollis, T. S. (2004) Feminist pedagogy in the teaching of social research methods. *International Journal of Social Research Methodology*, 7 (5), 415–28.

Weber, R. P. (1990) *Basic Content Analysis* (second edition). Thousand Oaks, CA: Sage.

Weber, S. and Mitchell, C. (1995) *'That's Funny, You Don't Look Like a Teacher': Interrogating Images and Identity in Popular Culture*. London: RoutledgeFalmer.

Wedeen, P., Winter, J. and Broadfoot, P. (2002) *Assessment: What's in it for Schools?* London: RoutledgeFalmer.

Weems, G. H., Onwuegbuzie, A. J. and Lustig, D. (2003) Profiles of respondents who respond inconsistently to positively- and negatively-worded items on rating scales. *Evaluation and Research in Education*, 17 (1), 45–60.

Weisberg, H. F., Krosnick, J. A. and Bowen, B. D. (1996) *An Introduction to Survey Research, Polling, and Data Analysis* (third edition). Thousand Oaks, CA: Sage.

Weiskopf, R. and Laske, S. (1996) Emancipatory action research: a critical alternative to personnel development or a new way of patronising people? In O. Zuber-Skerritt (ed.) *New Directions in Action Research*. London: Falmer, 121–36.

Weiss, C. (1991a) The many meanings of research utilization. In D. S. Anderson and B. J. Biddle (eds) *Knowledge for Policy: Improving Education through Research*. London: Falmer, 173–82.

Weiss, C. (1991b) Knowledge creep and decision accretion. In D. S. Anderson and B. J. Biddle (eds) *Knowledge for Policy: Improving Education through Research*. London: Falmer, 183–92.

Wetherell, M., Taylor, S. and Yates, S. (2001) *Discourse as Data*. London: Sage.

Wheatley, M. (1999) *Leadership and the New Science: Discovering Order in a Chaotic World* (second edition). San Francisco, CA: Berrett-Koehler Publishers.

Whitehead, J. (1985) An analysis of an individual's educational development: the basis for personally oriented action research. In M. Shipman (ed.) *Educational Research: Principles, Policies and Practices*. Lewes: Falmer, 97–108.

Whiteley, P. (1983) The analysis of contingency tables. In D. McKay, N. Schofield and P. Whiteley (eds) *Data Analysis and the Social Sciences*. London: Frances Pinter, 72–119.

Whitty, G. and Edwards, A. D. (1994) Researching Thatcherite policy. In G. Walford (ed.) *Researching the Powerful in Education*. London: UCL Press, 14–31.

Whyte, J. (1986) *Girls into Science and Technology: The Story of a Project*. London: Routledge and Kegan Paul.

Whyte, W. F. (1955) *Street Corner Society: The Social Structure of an Italian Slum* (second edition). Chicago, IL: University of Chicago Press.

Whyte, W. F. (1982) Interviewing in field research. In R. Burgess (ed.) *Field Research: A Sourcebook and Field Manual*. London: Allen and Unwin, 111–22.

Whyte, W. F. (1993) *Street Corner Society: The Social Structure of an Italian Slum* (fourth edition and fourth revised edition). Chicago, IL: University of Chicago Press.

Wickens, P. (1987) *The Road to Nissan: Flexibility, Quality, Teamwork*. Basingstoke: Macmillan.

Wiggins, G. (1998) *Educative Assessment*. San Francisco, CA: Jossey-Bass.

Wilcox, R. R. (1997) Simulation as a research technique. In J. P. Keeves (ed.) *Educational Research, Methodology and Measurement: An International Handbook* (second edition). Oxford: Elsevier Science, 150–4.

Wild, P., Scivier, J. E. and Richardson, S. J. (1992) Evaluating information technology-supported local management of schools: the user acceptability audit. *Educational Management and Administration*, 20 (1), 40–8.

Wiles, J. and Bondi, J. C. (1984) *Curriculum Development: A Guide to Practice* (second edition). Columbus, OH: Charles E. Merrill Publishing.

Wiles, R., Crow, G., Heath, S. and Charles, V. (2008) The management of confidentiality and anonymity in social research. *International Journal of Social Research Methodology*, 11 (5), 417–28.

Wiles, R., Prosser, J., Bagnoli, A., Clark, A., Davies, K., Holland, S. and Renold, E. (2008) *Visual Ethics: Ethical Issues in Visual Research*. Working Paper NCRM/011 for ESRC National Centre for Research Methods. Manchester: ESRC National Centre for Research Methods. Retrieved 18 May 2010, from http://eprints.ncrm.ac.uk/421/1/Methods-ReviewPaperNCRM-011.pdf.

Wiliam, D. (1996) Standards in examinations: a matter of trust. *Curriculum Journal*, 7 (3), 293–306.

Wilkins, L. T. (1969) *Evaluation of Penal Measures*. New York: Random House.

Wilkinson, J. (2000) Direct observation. In G. M. Breakwell, S. Hammond and C. Fife-Shaw (eds) *Research Methods in Psychology* (second edition). London: Sage, 224–38.

Wilkinson, L. and the Task Force on Statistical Inference, APA Board of Scientific Affairs (1999) Statistical methods in psychology journals: guidelines and explanations. *American Psychologist*, 54 (8), 594–604.

Willis, P. E. (1977) *Learning to Labour*. Farnborough: Saxon House.

Willms, J. D. (1992) Pride or prejudice? Opportunity structure and the effects of Catholic schools in Scotland. In A. Yogev (ed.) *International Perspectives on Education and Society: A Research and Policy Annual (Vol. 2)*. Greenwich, CT: JAI Press, 189–213.

Wilson, C. and Powell, M. (2001) *A Guide to Interviewing Children: Essential Skills for Counsellors, Social Workers, Police, Lawyers*. London: Routledge.

Wilson, I., Huttly, S. R. A. and Fenn, B. (2006) A case study of sample design for longitudinal research: Young Lives. *International Journal of Social Research Methodology*, 9 (5), 351–65.

Wilson, M. (1996) Asking questions. In R. Sapsford and V. Jupp (eds) *Data Collection and Analysis*. London: Sage and the Open University Press, 94–120.

Wilson, N. and McLean, S. (1994) *Questionnaire Design: A Practical Introduction*. Newtown Abbey, Co. Antrim: University of Ulster Press.

Wineburg, S. S. (1991) The self-fulfilment of the self-fulfilling prophecy. In D. S. Anderson and B. J. Biddle (eds) *Knowledge for Policy: Improving Education through Research*. London: Falmer, 276–90.

Winter, D. A., Bell, R. C. and Watson, S. B. (2010) Midpoint ratings on personal constructs: constriction or the middle way? *Journal of Constructivist Psychology*, 23: 337–56.

Winter, G. (2000) A comparative discussion of the notion of 'validity' in qualitative and quantitative research. *Qualitative Report*, 4 (3 and4), March. Retrieved 29 October 2005, from www.nova.edu/sss/QR/QR4–3/winter.html.

Winter, R. (1982) Dilemma analysis: a contribution to

methodology for action research. *Cambridge Journal of Education*, 12 (3), 161–74.

Winter, R. (1996) Some principles and procedures for the conduct of action research. In O. Zuber-Skerritt (ed.) *New Directions in Action Research*. London: Falmer, 13–27.

Witkin, R. (1974) *The Intelligence of Feeling*. London: Heinemann.

Witmer, D. F., Colman, R. W. and Katzman, S. L. (1999) From paper-and-pencil to screen-and-keyboard: toward a methodology for survey research on the internet. In S. Jones (ed.) *Doing Internet Research*. Thousand Oaks, CA: Sage, 145–61.

Witte, J. C., Amoroso, L. M. and Howard, P. E. N. (1999) Method and representation in internet-based survey tools: mobility, community, and cultural identity in Survey2000. Department of Sociology, Northwestern University.

Wittgenstein, L. (1974) *Tractatus Logico-Philosophicus* (trans. D. Pears and B. McGuiness). London: Routledge and Kegan Paul.

Witzel, A. (2000) The problem-centered interview. *Forum Qualitative Sozialforschung/Forum: Qualitative Social Research [Online Journal]*, 1 (1), 1–9. Article 22. Retrieved 6 March 2003, from www.qualitative-research. net/index.php/fqs/article/view/1132/2522.

Wolcott, H. F. (1973) *The Man in the Principal's Office*. New York: Holt, Rinehart and Winston.

Wolcott, H. F. (1990) On seeking – and rejecting – validity in qualitative research. In E. W. Eisner and A. Peshkin (eds) *Qualitative Inquiry in Education: The Continuing Debate*. New York: Teachers College Press, 121–52.

Wolcott, H. F. (1992) Posturing in qualitative research. In M. LeCompte, W. L. Millroy and J. Preissle (eds) *The Handbook of Qualitative Research in Education*. London: Academic Press, 3–52.

Wolcott, H. F. (1994) *Transforming Qualitative Data: Description, Analysis and Interpretation*. Thousand Oaks, CA: Sage.

Wolf, F. M. (1986) *Meta-Analysis: Quantitative Methods for Research Synthesis*. Newbury Park, CA: Sage.

Wolf, R. M. (1994) The validity and reliability of outcome measure. In A. C. Tuijnman and T. N. Postlethwaite (eds) *Monitoring the Standards of Education*. Oxford: Pergamon, 121–32.

Wolff, S. (2004) Ways into the field and their variants. In U. Flick, E. von Kardoff and I. Steinke (eds) *A Companion to Qualitative Research*. London: Sage, 195–202.

Wood, P. (1995) Meta-analysis. In G. M. Breakwell, S. Hammond and C. Fife-Shaw (eds) *Research Methods in Psychology*. London: Sage, 396–9.

Wood, S. (1980) Reactions to redundancy. Unpublished PhD thesis, University of Manchester. Quoted in R. M. Lee (ed.) (1993) *Doing Research on Sensitive Topics*. London: Sage.

Woods, D. (2010) Transana Keyboard Shortcuts and Transcript Notation (originally by R. Henne and subsequently modified by D. Woods). Retrieved 1 May 2010, from www.transana.org/images/TransanaShortcuts.pdf.

Woods, P. (1979) *The Divided School*. London: Routledge and Kegan Paul.

Woods, P. (1983) *Sociology and the School*. London: Routledge and Kegan Paul.

Woods, P. (1986) *Inside Schools: Ethnography in Educational Research*. London: Routledge and Kegan Paul.

Woods, P. (1989) *Working for Teacher Development*. Dereham, Norfolk: Peter Francis Publishers.

Woods, P. (1992) Symbolic interactionism: theory and method. In M. LeCompte, W. L. Millroy and J. Preissle (eds) *The Handbook of Qualitative Research in Education*. London: Academic Press, 337–404.

Woods, P. (1993) Managing marginality: teacher development through grounded life history. *British Educational Research Journal*, 19 (5), 447–88.

Wooffitt, R. (1993) Analysing accounts. In N. Gilbert (ed.) *Researching Social Life*. London: Sage, 287–305.

Worch, E. A., Scheuermann, A. M. and Haney, J. J. (2009) Methods and strategies: role-play in the science classroom. *Science and Children*, 47 (1), 54–9.

Worrall, D. (2006) *Theatric Revolution: Drama, Censorship and Romantic Period Subcultures, 1773–1832*. New York: Oxford University Press.

Worrall, L. (ed.) (1990) *Geographic Information Systems: Developments and Applications*. London: Belhaven Press.

Wragg, E. C. (1994) *An Introduction to Classroom Observation*. London: Routledge.

Wragg, E. C. (2002) Interviewing. In M. Coleman and A. R. J. Briggs (eds) *Research Methods in Educational Leadership*. London: Paul Chapman, 143–58.

Wright, D. B. (2003) Making friends with your data: improving how statistics are conducted and reported. *British Journal of Educational Psychology*, 73 (1), 123–36.

Wright, R. and Powell, M. B. (2006) Investigative interviewers' perceptions of their difficulty in adhering to open-ended questions with child witnesses. *International Journal of Police Science and Management*, 8 (4), 316–25.

Wright, R. P. and Lam, S. S. K. (2002) Comparing apples with apples: the importance of element wording in grid applications. *Journal of Constructivist Psychology*, 15 (2), 109–19.

Yeung, K. W. and Watkins, D. (2000) Hong Kong student teachers' personal construction of teaching efficacy. *Educational Psychology*, 20 (2), 213–35.

Yin, R. K. (1984) *Case Study Research: Design and Methods*. Beverly Hills, CA: Sage.

Yin, R. K. (2006) Mixed methods research: are the methods genuinely integrated or merely parallel? *Research in Schools*, 13 (1), 41–7.

Yin, R. K. (2009) *Case Study Research: Design and Methods* (fourth edition). Thousand Oaks, CA: Sage.

Yorke, D. M (1978) Repertory grids in educational research: some methodological considerations. *British Educational Research Journal*, 4 (2), 63–74.

Young, J. (1971) *The Drugtakers*. London: Paladin.

Youngblood, M. (1997) *Life at the Edge of Chaos*. Dallas, TX: Perceval Publishing.

Youngman, M. B. (1984) Designing questionnaires. In J. Bell, T. Bush, A. Fox, J. Goodey and S. Goulding (eds) *Conducting Small-Scale Investigations in Educational Management*. London: Harper and Row, 156–76.

Zechmeister, E. B. and Shaughnessy, J. J. (1992) *A Practical Introduction to Research Methods in Psychology*. New York: McGraw-Hill.

Zhao, S. (2003) 'Being there' and the role of presence technology. In G. Riva, F. Davide and W. A. Ijsselsteijn (eds) *Being There: Concepts, Effects and Measurements of User*

Presence in Synthetic Environments. Amsterdam: International Operations Press, 137–46.

Zimbardo, P. C. (1984) On the ethics of intervention in human psychological research with specific reference to the 'Stanford Prison Experiment'. In J. Murphy, M. John. and H. Brown (eds) *Dialogues and Debates in Social Psychology*. London: Lawrence Erlbaum with the Open University Press.

Zimbardo, P. G. (2007a) *The Lucifer Effect: Understanding How Good People Turn Evil*. New York: Random House.

Zimbardo, P. G. (2007b) Revisiting the Stanford Prison Experiment: a lesson in the power of situation. *Chronicle of Higher Education*, 30 March.

Zimbardo, P. G. (2008) From the Bronx to Stanford to Abu Ghraib. In R. V. Levine, A. Rodrigues and L. Zelezny (eds) *Journeys in Social Psychology: Looking Back to Inspire the Future*. New York: Taylor and Francis, 85–104.

Zimbardo, P. G., Maslach, C. and Haney, C. (2000) Reflections on the Stanford Prison Experiment: genesis, transformations, consequences. In T. Blass (ed.) *Obedience to Authority: Current Perspectives on the Milgram Paradigm*. Mahwah, NJ: Lawrence Erlbaum, 193–237.

Znaniecki, F. (1934) *The Method of Sociology*. New York: Farrar and Rinehart.

Zuber-Skerritt, O. (1996a) Introduction. In O. Zuber-Skerritt (ed.) *New Directions in Action Research*. London: Falmer, 3–9.

Zuber-Skerritt, O. (1996b) Emancipatory action research for organisational change and management development. In O. Zuber-Skerritt (ed.) *New Directions in Action Research*. London: Falmer, 83–105.

Zuzovsky, R. and Aitkin, M. (1991) Curriculum change and science achievement in Israel elementary schools. In S. W. Raudenbush and J. Willms (eds) *Schools, Classrooms and Pupils: International Studies of Schooling from a Multilevel Perspective*. San Diego, CA: Academic Press, 25–36.

Index